Roger Ebert's Movie Home Companion
1989 Edition

Other Books by Roger Ebert

An Illini Century
A Kiss Is Still a Kiss
The Perfect London Walk (with Daniel Curley)
Two Weeks in the Midday Sun: A Cannes Notebook

ROGER EBERT'S MOVIE HOME COMPANION 1989 EDITION

by Roger Ebert

Andrews and McMeel
A Universal Press Syndicate Company
Kansas City • New York

For information write Andrews and McMeel,
a Universal Press Syndicate Company, 4900 Main Street, Kansas City, Missouri 64112.

Library of Congress Cataloging-in-Publication Data

Ebert, Roger.
Roger Ebert's movie home companion.

"Reviews in this book originally appeared in the Chicago sun-times."—T.p. verso.
Includes index.
1. Moving-pictures—Reviews. 2. Video recordings—Reviews. I. Title. II. Title: Movie home companion.
PN1995.E318 1987 791.43'75 87-17497
ISBN 0-8362-6239-5 (pbk.)

All the reviews in this book originally appeared in the *Chicago Sun-Times*.

Cover photographs taken at
Video Schmideo, Chicago.

This book is dedicated to
Robert Zonka, 1928–1985,
God love ya.

Acknowledgments

Donna Martin, editor and friend, was instrumental in the conception of this book. The design is by Cameron Poulter and the cover photographs by Jack Lane, fellow Chicagoans. Patty Dingus typed the reviews and she and Dorothy O'Brien prepared the manuscript. I have been blessed with the unfailingly expert and discriminating copy-editing of Lon Grahnke, Lynn Roberts, Laura Emerick, Joe Pixler, Jeff Johnson, and Jennifer Steinbeck at the *Chicago Sun-Times,* and Sue Grieser at Universal Press Syndicate.

ROGER EBERT

Contents

Key to Symbols, viii
Introduction, ix
Reviews, 1
Film Clips, 739
- Albert Brooks *(Broadcast News)*, 739
- Woody Allen *(September)*, 741
- Dennis Quaid *(Suspect)*, 744
- Albert Finney *(Orphans)*, 745
- Cher *(Suspect)*, 747
- Martin Short *(Cross My Heart)*, 749
- *Fatal Attraction*'s Fatal Flaw, 752
- Lee Marvin (In Memoriam), 754
- John Huston (In Memoriam), 756
- Michael J. Fox *(Bright Lights, Big City)*, 758
- Kelly McGillis *(The House on Carroll Street)*, 761
- Spike Lee *(School Daze)*, 763
- Demi Moore *(The Seventh Sign)*, 765
- Tom Selleck *(Three Men and a Baby)*, 767
- Sean Penn *(Colors)*, 769
- Barbara Hershey *(Shy People)*, 772
- Melanie Griffith *(Stormy Monday)*, 775
- James Belushi *(Red Heat)*, 777
- Peter Weller *(RoboCop)*, 779
- Kim Basinger *(Nadine)*, 781
- Richard Dreyfuss *(Stakeout)*, 784
- Trevor Howard (In Memoriam), 787
- *Barfly*, 790

Judging the Classics, 797
My Ten Great Films, and Why, 803
High-Definition Television, 809
The Basic Video Library, 813
Glossary of Movie Terms, 817
List of Reviews That Appeared in Previous Editions, 823
Index, 825

Key to Symbols

★ ★ ★ ★ A great film
★ ★ ★ A good film
★ ★ Fair
★ Poor

G, PG, PG-13, R Ratings of the Motion Picture Association of America

- **G** indicates that the movie is suitable for general audiences
- **PG** suitable for general audiences but parental guidance is suggested
- **PG-13** recommended for viewers 13 years or above; may contain material inappropriate for younger children
- **R** recommended for viewers 17 or older

141 m. Running time

1983 Year of theatrical release

✓ Indicates movie for which videocassette was not yet available at time of publication

Introduction to the 1989 Edition

Faithful readers will know that I began as an opponent of the home video revolution, an unreconstructed traditionalist who once seriously argued that if people wanted movies at home, they should buy their own 16-millimeter projectors. As a film lover who grew up in the darkness of real movie theaters, I was adamant in my belief that there was one good way to see a movie, and that was on a big screen, in a darkened room, surrounded by strangers. I still believe that to be the case, in the best of worlds. But during the years since I purchased my first VCR, and then my first LaserVision player, I have come not only to accept home video but even to love it.

What I like most about it is access to the films of my choice. I would love to live down the street from a repertory theater that showed sparkling 35-millimeter prints of great movies twenty-four hours a day (a house, in fact, much like the late and lamented Clark Theater in Chicago, where I did much of my homework on the classics). But in most cities such theaters no longer exist, if they ever did, and even in movie capitals like New York and Los Angeles the revival house is threatened—not, ironically, by a lack of customers, but by the disinterest of the major studios in maintaining access to 35-millimeter prints of old movies. The alternative can be found in a good video store or mail-order catalog; at present there are some 12,000 tapes and 4,000 LaserDiscs available, with more to come.

I also find that there are certain kinds of movies that possibly improve on being seen at home, in a quiet situation. It is obvious that thrillers, comedies, and musicals are best seen on a big screen with a big crowd, but certain kinds of movies—quiet art films, brooding melodramas—sometimes seem to benefit from increased intimacy. Recently I watched Antonioni's *The Passenger* on home video, and found that its meditative revelations actually seemed to play better in the more intimate format.

When you bring your tape or disc home and play it on television, of course, you are not getting the same video and audio experience you could expect in a movie theater. But the situation is improving, especially since LaserVision got its second wind. In the early days of home video, consumers were amazed by the simple fact that they could actually show movies on their own television screens. The situation was parallel to the early days of phonograph records. But now mere access is no longer enough; viewers are beginning to demand a higher quality experience, in a parallel to the hi-fi and stereo movement. Quality in home video, at this moment, means LaserVision or Super VHS. Within a decade it will mean High-Definition Television.

When I wrote an introduction to this *Companion* a year ago, Super VHS seemed poised to enter the marketplace in a big way. But now twelve months have passed and there is still only a handful of public domain feature films available on SuperVHS, and no company which has announced plans to supply new releases. At present, SuperVHS seems to exist primarily as a format for camcorders.

LaserVision, on the other hand, has gained increasing acceptance as a superior way to watch movies at home. A full-page rave in *Time* magazine ("The next best thing to owning your own theater") attracted a lot of attention, and so did the introduction of CD-V, the audio/video music singles and albums. In the showdown between VHS and LaserVision, the numbers tell the story. The average prerecorded VHS cassette contains about 240 horizontal lines of information. LaserVision players made before 1988 deliver 380 to 400 lines to the screen, and the new Laser players claim 450 lines. The difference in quality is dramatic, especially on a large-screen TV. My 45-inch rear-projection TV shows me a LaserDisc picture as sharp as my 21-inch TV with VHS tapes. In the area of sound, of course, there is no comparison; Laser sound is based on CD technology, has imperceptible noise, and delivers true surround stereo. I've lined my basement viewing room with industrial carpeting, and like to turn the sound up nice and loud.

I mentioned High-Def TV. I have seen it, and it is amazingly good. It will provide a modified wide screen image, about five to three as opposed to the current four to three standard TV ratio. It will also provide picture quality so good that you will be able to pull down a screen in your living room and use a projection version of High-Def TV to deliver a large-size, nearly theatrical-quality image. Screens will be measured in feet, not inches.

The High-Def revolution will require the retooling of the entire television industry as we know it, and right now the networks and over-the-air stations are terrified that cable and home video will beat them to the marketplace with High Def. How long before High Def hits the marketplace? All of the technology exists and has been perfected. High-priced equipment, which would use prerecorded discs, could be sold today. But the manufacturers are holding back until an international accord is reached on standards and procedures. (The world currently has two standards for television signals, and the one thing everybody agrees on is that, next time, there should only be one.)

To return to the present day, there are several interesting developments on the home video scene:

• ***Price Breakthroughs.*** Within the past year, a conviction has been growing in the movie industry that the future of home video is in "sell-through." There have been major price reductions for many movies on cassettes, all the way down to the $9.95 tag on some RKO classics, and the $14.95 prices for many Republic, Nostalgia Merchant, and RKO films. *E. T.* goes into the marketplace on October 27 at $24.95. Within the coming year, many more cassettes will be dropped to between $29.95 and $19.95, and an increasing number of top-quality, studio-originated cassettes will be in the $14.95 bracket. There will also be major prices breaks in LaserDiscs, with one major studio preparing a line of $19.95 "evergreen" classics. Since discs are cheaper to produce than tapes, LaserDiscs of all but current hit movies may level off around $24.95.

The reason why many tapes were priced as high as $99.95 was transparently simple: Seeing home video as essentially a rental market, the studios wanted to soak the video rental stores for as much money as possible. A typical major film would go into the marketplace at $79.95 or more, hold that price level until the rental demand wore off, and then be reduced by stages to below $30. The problem, as the studios discovered, was that as the rental demand wore off, so did the sales demand. Market studies have shown that a studio can make more money by initially launching a popular movie at a low sell-through price, as Disney did with *Lady and the Tramp.* The most dramatic recent illustration of different pricing strategies came with the long-delayed introduction of *Platoon* to the marketplace. The movie sold for $99.95 on tape, but only $39.95 on LaserDisc, because discs are more commonly purchased than rented.

These lower prices are good news for consumers, and good news for video store owners, too, since they'll be able to buy the average new hit tape for much less. The studios are not happy to help video rentals, but the overall rewards of immediate low-priced "sell-through" are too great to be ignored.

• ***Hit-Driven Rentals.*** In the best of worlds, lower tape and disc prices will help reverse one of the most unfortunate trends of the last year, the tilting of video stories toward a hit-driven mentality. Instead of stocking a wide variety of tapes, many stores have invested their capital in large buys of new hits. They'll buy twenty, thirty, forty, or more copies of *Beverly Hills Cop II*, but no copies of more marginal films. "It's not my fault," one video store owner complained. "A lot of people come into the store and ask me what's new, instead of what's good." The major video distributors encourage this trend by offering bonus tapes—buy five and get the sixth one free. The store might otherwise have bought four tapes; the purchase of the fifth represents a lost sale for a more marginal movie. At least with lower unit prices, stores will have more capital to invest in a wider range of titles.

• ***Letterboxing.*** Also known by such names as "videoscope," this is the process that allows viewers to see the entire frame of a wide-screen movie. The entire width of the movie is shown, and then there are black bands at the top and bottom of the screen. In the case of foreign films, the black band at the bottom makes an ideal backdrop for the subtitles. At first there was some consumer resistance to "letterboxing," as pioneered by Woody Allen in his home video version of *Manhattan.* Consumers didn't know if they liked those black bands. There was the hilarious example of one nationally televised film critic complaining in a video magazine that he felt shortchanged by the borders—he wanted his whole screen covered with a picture! The problem, of course, is one of simple euclidean geometry. If you show a four-by-three section of a six-by-three image, you lose much of the original picture.

"Planning and scanning" is sometimes used, to move back and forth to either side of a too-wide image. This is a desperate compromise, and can become so annoying that a movie becomes unwatchable. Every single camera movement means something, in a well-directed film, and the addition of manic pans-and-scans horrifies fastidious directors (and film lovers). On the "Siskel & Ebert" program, we toggled back and forth between the letterboxed and "full screen" version of *The Graduate* and *Blade Runner,* and the contrast was dramatic. In the full-screen *Graduate,* for example, you do *not even see* Mrs. Robinson during her famous bedroom argument with Benjamin. There is no question: Letterboxing is always preferable for wide-screen movies, and I am happy to see it gaining acceptance. The Criterion Collection has "videoscope" versions of *The Seven Samurai, Hidden Fortress, Blade Runner,* and others. MGM has recently started bringing out such films as *Fellini Satyricon* in letterbox format, and for *Sweet Charity* Universal reached an interesting compromise. They went "full screen" for the dramatic scenes but used letterboxing to preserve Bob Fosse's choreography during the dance numbers.

• ***Colorization.*** The battle continues. Colorized videos have found little acceptance in the sell-through market, and their prices have been slashed while the stocks of the colorizing companies continue to fall. But on television, especially on Ted Turner's TBS, colorized movies continue to assault the taste and intelligence of the viewing public. I have had the greatest admiration for what Turner has achieved with CNN and Headline News, and am mystified by his support of colorization. It is his fatal blind spot. The beauty of black and white is an art form in and of itself. Black and white does not *lack* something, but *adds* something. The real world, after all, is in color. Color is the most realistic of mediums. Black and white has intrigue and mystery. Look at Fred Astaire dancing in black and white, where shape, timing, and movement are everything, and then look at him dancing in color—where the purity of line and form are muddled by the unwanted emotional disinformation of the colors.

The issue is so clear, and the opposition so dense. Recently I was sent a clipping in which Charlie Powell, one of the top colorization executives, was asked if he would colorize *Citizen Kane.* "I'd love to," he replied. "It's one of my favorite films." Aaaargh! Some people defend colorization because (a) you can always turn off the color on your set, and (b) the movies wouldn't get seen otherwise, and (c) young people won't watch black and white. My answers are (a) colorizing can subtly affect the tones of the gray areas even after you turn off the color, (b) you can only see a movie for the first time once, and if you see it in color you will not have had an authentic first viewing of it, and (c) I have never yet met one single one of the mythical young people who will not watch black and white, and indeed on MTV and other youth-oriented cable channels there is a real vogue for black and white.

* * *

For this fourth annual edition of the *Companion,* we have added some 150 new reviews, and removed some of the less-interesting reviews from the previous edition. In particular, I have added another 50 or so movies made before 1980. I have also continued the "Film Clips," which are interviews with directors and actors involved with some of the major films of 1987–88. These articles were scattered thoughout the 1988 edition, but for 1989 I am collecting them all in the back of the book. As before, there is a built-in bias toward better films; as the winnowing process takes place, I am more inclined to include good films than bad ones, and so it may appear that I am too generous with my star ratings. Perhaps I am. Or perhaps someday there should be a companion to the *Companion,* collecting only reviews of bad movies.

* * *

Many of you have written complaining that you cannot find some of the movies listed in this book. The hit-driven mentality of many local video stores means that this problem will only get worse. There are several mail-order organizations that sell and rent through the mail. As before, I'm recommending Home Film Festival (1-800-258-3456, or, in Pennsylvania, 1-800-633-3456), Facets Multimedia (1-800-331-6197, or, in Illinois, 1-312-281-9075), and Movies Unlimited (1-800-523-0823). All three organizations produce large, informative catalogs, for which there is a charge. There are also several more specialized video firms working through the mails and you can find their advertisements in the back pages of *Video Review, Video,* and *V* magazines.

Many readers have written with suggestions, corrections, and counterattacks, which are always gratefully received and read, and sometimes even replied to. I cannot, however, help you locate individual videos. There are several comprehensive guides to films available on video, including Leonard Maltin's excellent book, and this year saw the publication of an especially useful reference on discs, *The Laser Video Disc Companion,* by Douglas Pratt.

Several people have asked that I include a "basic library" of books of movie criticism. I can do no better than to recommend the collected works of Pauline Kael, Stanley Kauffmann, Dwight Macdonald, Manny Farber, and James Agee. For information on screenwriting, I recommend *The Screenwriter Looks at the Screenwriter,* by William Froug. Another valuable reference resource can be found on LaserDisc, in the parallel sound tracks containing expert analysis of such films as *Citizen Kane, The Magnificent Ambersons, King Kong,* and *Swing Time.*

ROGER EBERT

A

About Last Night . . . ★ ★ ★ ★
R, 116 m., 1986

Rob Lowe (Danny), Demi Moore (Debbie), James Belushi (Bernie), Elizabeth Perkins (Joan), George DiCenzo (Mr. Favio), Michael Alldredge (Mother Malone), Robin Thomas (Steve), Joe Greco (Gus). Directed by Edward Zwick and produced by Jason Brett and Stuart Oken. Screenplay by Tim Kazurinsky and Denise DeClue.

If one of the pleasures of moviegoing is seeing strange new things on the screen, another pleasure, and probably a deeper one, is experiencing moments of recognition—times when we can say, yes, that's exactly right, that's exactly the way it would have happened. *About Last Night . . .* is a movie filled with moments like that. It has an eye and an ear for the way we live now, and it has a heart, too, and a sense of humor.

It is a love story. A young man and a young woman meet, and fall in love, and over the course of a year they try to work out what that means to them. It sounds like a simple story, and yet *About Last Night . . .* is one of the rarest of recent American movies, because it deals fearlessly with real people, instead of with special effects.

If there's anyone more afraid of a serious relationship than your average customer in a singles bar, it's a Hollywood producer. American movies will cheerfully spend millions of dollars on explosions and chases to avoid those moments when people are talking seriously and honestly to one another. After all, writing good dialogue takes some intelligence.

And intelligence is what sparkles all through *About Last Night . . .*—intelligence and a good, bawdy comic sensibility. The movie stars Rob Lowe as a salesman for a Chicago grocery wholesaler, and Demi Moore as an art director for a Michigan Avenue advertising agency. They meet at a softball game in Grant Park. Their romance blossoms in the singles bars of Rush Street, with a kindly bartender as father figure. At first they are attracted mostly by biological reasons (they belong to a generation that believes it's kind of embarrassing to sleep with someone for the first time after you know them too well). Then they get to like each other. Then it is maybe even love, although everyone tap-dances around that word. Commitment, in their world, is the moment when Lowe offers Moore the use of a drawer in his apartment. Her response to that offer is one of the movie's high points.

Meanwhile, there is counterpoint, too. Lowe's best friend is his partner at work, played by James Belushi. Moore's best friend is Elizabeth Perkins, her roommate and fellow warrior on the singles scene. While Lowe and Moore start getting really serious about each other, Belushi and Perkins grow possessive—and also develop a spontaneous dislike for one another.

The story is kind of predictable in *About Last Night . . .*, if you have ever been young and kept your eyes open. There are only a limited number of basic romantic scenarios for young people in the city, and this movie sees through all of them. What's important is the way the characters look and sound, the way they talk, the way they reveal themselves, the way they grow by taking chances. Time after time, there are shocks of recognition, as the movie shows how well it understands what's going on.

Lowe and Moore, members of Hollywood's "Brat Pack," are survivors of 1985's awful movie about yuppie singles, *St. Elmo's Fire*. This is the movie *St. Elmo's Fire* should have been. The 1985 movie made them look stupid and shallow. *About Last Night . . .* gives them the best acting opportunities either one has ever had, and they make the most of them. Moore is especially impressive. There isn't a romantic note she isn't required to play in this movie, and she plays them all flawlessly.

Belushi and Perkins are good, too, making us realize how often the movies pretend that lovers live in a vacuum. When a big new relationship comes into your life, it requires an adjustment of all the other relationships, and a certain amount of discomfort and pain. Belushi and Perkins provide those levels for the story, and a lot of its loudest laughs, too.

The movie is based on *Sexual Perversity in Chicago*, a play by David Mamet. The screenplay by Tim Kazurinsky and Denise DeClue smooths out Mamet's more episodic structure, and adds three-dimensional realism. It's a wonderful writing job, and Edward Zwick, directing a feature for the first time, shows a sure touch. His narrative spans an entire year, and the interest never lags.

Why is it that love stories are so rare from Hollywood these days? Have we lost faith in romance? Is love possible only with robots and cute little furry things from the special-effects department? Have people stopped talking? *Top Gun* was so afraid of a real relationship that its real love affair was with airplanes. *About Last Night . . .* is a warm-hearted and intelligent love story, and one of 1986's best movies.

Above the Law ★ ★ ★
R, 97 m., 1988

Steven Seagal (Nico Toscani), Henry Silva (Zagon), Pam Grier (Delores Jackson), Sharon Stone (Sara Toscani), Joe Grego (Father Gennaro), Jack Wallace (Uncle Branca), Daniel Faraldo (Salvano), Ronnie Barron (Bartender), Ron Dean (Lukich), Joseph Kosala (Strozah), Chelcie Ross (Fox), John Drummond (TV Reporter). Directed by Andrew Davis and produced by Steven Seagal and Davis. Screenplay by Steven Pressfield, Ronald Shusett, and Davis, from a story by Davis and Seagal.

Some people in Hollywood think Steven Seagal is the hot new action star—heir to Eastwood and Bronson, contemporary of Stallone, Norris, and Schwarzenegger. The influential Calendar section of the *Los Angeles Times* carried a cover story in early 1988, outlining the campaign to establish Seagal in the box office big leagues. His stats: He's 6-foot-4, with a sixth degree black belt in aikido, and he ran his own martial arts school in Japan before returning to Los Angeles, where he worked as an aikido instructor and bodyguard (it says in his bio) for stars and heads of state. He's married to actress Kelly LeBrock, the one with the great lips. A studio executive was quoted as saying Seagal has "extraordinary" screen magnetism.

With a buildup like that, doesn't Seagal's first movie almost have to be anticlimactic? And yet the curious thing is, Seagal more or less deserves the buildup. He does have a strong and particular screen presence. It is obvious that he is doing a lot of his own stunts, and some of the fight sequences are impressive and apparently unfaked. He isn't just a hunk, either. He can play tender and he can play smart, two notes often missing on the Bronson and Stallone accordions. His aquiline face and slicked-back, slightly receding hairline accentuate the macho exterior. He moves around too much in close-ups, but then he moves around a lot anyway, seeming restless on screen, sometimes swaggering instead of walking.

His first movie is *Above the Law*, and it is nothing if not ambitious; it contains fifty percent more plot than it needs, but that allows it room to grow in areas not ordinarily covered in action thrillers. When was the last time you saw Norris or Schwarzenegger in a film where they ran cars through walls and killed people with their bare hands *and* went to Mass, stood up at baptisms, meditated, hugged their wives, kidded their partners, and made speeches about the need for a free and open society? If this film is an audition, it demonstrates that Seagal is willing to try anything.

The movie costars Pam Grier, who plays Seagal's partner but not his squeeze (he's a happily married father). She was one of the most intriguing action stars of the 1970s, before the collapse of the black film market took her down with it. Seagal and Grier play plainclothes Chicago police detectives who engineer a major drug bust, only to find that their arrests have been quashed by the FBI and they've been ordered to stay away from a cocaine kingpin. Why should this guy be immune?

In a less ambitious picture, we'd find out about a payoff, blackmail, or extortion. *Above the Law* does not lack ambition. We get flashbacks to the hero's service in the CIA in Vietnam, where he first stumbled across evidence that a CIA official (Henry Silva, venomous and sleek) was using the agency as a cover for drug smuggling. Now there's another element involved: Central American political refugees have taken sanctuary in the basement of Seagal's church, and their priest has information about Silva's plan to assassinate a senator.

The movie was cowritten and directed by Andrew Davis, whose *Code of Silence* remains the best movie Chuck Norris has ever made, and contains the best use of Chicago locations I've seen. *Above the Law* also exploits great locations, from the unexpected (a vast old Catholic church) to the bizarre (there's a struggle to the death on the roof of the Executive House). Davis also seems concerned to create a community around the Seagal character, and so we spend time in well-written scenes with his wife (Sharon Stone), his priest (Joe Greco), his uncle (Jack Wallace), and a tough cop (Joseph Kosala, a real Chicago cop). As in his previous film, Davis gets mileage out of supporting players who do not look or sound like professional actors, and so add a level of realism to the action.

Seagal doesn't look or sound like a professional actor, either, but he's effective in his film debut. His voice has a certain quality to it, like Richard Gere's, that suggests he would sometimes rather keep talking after he barks out typical action dialogue. He is physical enough to create a believable menace in the violent scenes, and yet we can believe that sensitivity coexists with brutality in his makeup. Is he indeed Hollywood's hottest new action star? Who knows. But he has the stuff.

Absence of Malice ★ ★ ★

PG, 116 m., 1981

Paul Newman (Michael Gallagher), Sally Field (Megan Carter), Bob Balaban (Rosen), Melinda Dillon (Teresa), Wilford Brimley (D.A.), John Harkins (Libel Lawyer). Directed and produced by Sydney Pollack. Screenplay by Kurt Luedtke.

There are at least two ways to approach *Absence of Malice,* and I propose to take the second. The first approach, no doubt, would be to criticize this film's portrait of an investigative newspaper reporter—to say that no respectable journalist would ever do the things that Sally Field does about, to, and with Paul Newman in this movie. She is a disgrace to her profession. What journalistic sins does she commit in this film? She allows the facts of a secret investigation to be leaked to her. She prints an unattributed story about the investigation. Then she becomes "personally involved with the subject of the investigation," as they say. In other words, she falls in love with Paul Newman. Then she prints another story she should never have printed, and as a result an innocent bystander commits suicide. Then . . .

But you get the idea. Would real investigative reporters actually commit Field's mistakes, improprieties, misjudgments, indiscretions, and ethical lapses? Generally speaking, no, they wouldn't. And if they did, they shouldn't have. And furthermore, their editors would never let them get away with it. (The unbelievable laxity of the editors in *Absence of Malice* creates the movie's greatest credibility gap.) But let's face it: Sometimes reporters *do* commit acts such as Sally Field allows herself in this movie. Sometimes news of an investigation is printed without official attribution. And so on.

One of my colleagues cornered me at the water fountain to say indignantly that, whatever else you might think about this movie, you'd have to admit that no reporter would *ever* sleep with a news source.

"Oh yeah?" asked a woman who was standing by. "Who was the news source?"

"Paul Newman," I said.

"I'd sleep with that news source in a second," she said.

And that leads us out of the first, or socially responsible, approach to *Absence of Malice*, and into the second, or romantic, approach. I not only liked this movie despite its factual and ethical problems—I'm not even so sure they matter so much to most viewers. In the newspaper business we're quick to spot the errors of movies about newspaper reporters, but where were we when the archaeologists squirmed over Harrison Ford's barbaric conduct in *Raiders of the Lost Ark?* The fact is, this movie is *really* about a woman's spunk and a common man's sneaky revenge. And on that level it's absorbing and entertaining. Sally Field's newspaper reporter is created through a quietly original performance that is *not* Norma Rae with a pencil behind her ear, but is an earnest, nervous, likable young woman who makes mistakes when she listens too closely to her heart, her ambition, or her editor (which of us cannot admit the same?).

Paul Newman's character is a liquor distributor who is (presumably) totally innocent of the murder for which he is being investigated. But because his father was a Mafioso, he finds his name being dragged through the press, and he achieves a vengeance that is smart, wicked, appropriate, and completely satisfying to the audience. Besides these two performances, there are some other good ones, most notably one by Wilford Brimley, as a district attorney who takes brusque command of an informal hearing and reduces everyone but Newman to quivering surrender, and another by John Harkins, as a newspaper libel lawyer who is able to make the restraints (and freedoms) of libel law clear not only to Sally Field but even to us.

There's a story about a legendary Chicago editor who was presented with a major scoop obtained by dubious means. First he convinced himself the story was factually sound. Then he issued the classic instruction: "Print it tonight, and call the lawyers in the morning." Now there's an editor who might have enjoyed *Absence of Malice.* He would not have approved of what Sally Field does in this movie. But he would have understood it.

After Hours ★ ★ ★ ★

R, 96 m., 1985

Griffin Dunne (Paul Hackett), Rosanna Arquette (Marcy), Linda Fiorentino (Kiki), Verna Bloom (June), Thomas Chong (Pepe), Teri Garr (Julie), John Heard (Bartender), Catherine O'Hara (Gail). Directed by Martin Scorsese and produced by Amy Robinson, Griffin Dunne, and Robert F. Colesberry. Screenplay by Joseph Minion.

Martin Scorsese's *After Hours* is a comedy, according to the strict definition of that word: It ends happily, and there are indications along the way that we're not supposed to take it seriously. It is, however, the tensest comedy I can remember, building its nightmare situation step by insidious step until our laughter is hollow, or defensive. This is the work of a master filmmaker who controls his effects so skillfully that I was drained by this film—so emotionally depleted that there was a moment, two-thirds of the way through, when I wondered if maybe I should pause and gather my thoughts and come back later for the rest of the "comedy."

The movie tells the story of a night in the life of Paul Hackett (Griffin Dunne), a midtown Manhattan word processing specialist who hates his job and his lonely private life. One night in a restaurant he strikes up a conversation with a winsome young woman (Rosanna Arquette). They seem to share some of the same interests. He gets her telephone number. He calls her, she suggests he come downtown to her apartment in Soho, and that is the beginning of his Kafkaesque adventure.

The streets of Soho are dark and deserted. Clouds of steam escape from the pavement, as they did in Scorsese's *Taxi Driver,* suggesting that Hades lurks just below the field of vision. The young woman is staying for a few days in the apartment of a friend (Linda Fiorentino), who makes bizarre sculptures, has kinky sexual tastes, and talks in a strange, veiled way about being burned. In Arquette's bedroom, Dunne makes the usual small talk of a first date, and she gushes that she's sure they'll have a great time, but then everything begins to fall apart.

At first, we think perhaps Dunne is the victim of random bad luck, as he is confronted with nightmares both tragic and trivial: Ominous strangers, escalating subway fares, a shocking suicide, sadomasochistic sexual practices, a punk nightclub where he almost has his head shaved, a street mob that thinks he is a thief. Only later, much later, on this seemingly endless night, do we find how everything is connected—and even then, it doesn't make any logical sense. For Paul Hackett, as for the Job of the Old Testament, the plague of bad luck seems generated by some unexplained divine wrath.

And yet Scorsese does not simply make a horror movie, or some kind of allegory of doom. Each of his characters is drawn sharply, given quirky dialogue, allowed to be offbeat and funny. Teri Garr has a scene as a waitress who has tried to make sense of New York for so long that it has driven her around the bend. Fiorentino has a dry, sardonic angle on things. Arquette speaks wonderingly of a lover who was so obsessed by *The Wizard of Oz* that he always called her Dorothy in bed. John Heard is a bartender who has seen everything walk in through the doors of his all-night saloon and has lost the capacity for astonishment.

After Hours is another chapter in Scorsese's continuing examination of Manhattan as a state of mind; if he hadn't already used the title *New York, New York,* he could have used it this time. The movie earns its place on the list with his great films *Mean Streets, Taxi Driver,* and *Raging Bull.* For New Yorkers, parts of the film will no doubt play as a documentary. In what other city is everyday life such an unremitting challenge?

After Hours is a brilliant film, one of the year's best. It is also a most curious film. It comes after Scorsese's *The King of Comedy,* a film I thought was fascinating but unsuccessful, and continues Scorsese's attempt to combine comedy and satire with unrelenting pressure and a sense of all-pervading paranoia. This time he succeeds. The result is a film that is so original, so particular, that we are uncertain from moment to moment exactly how to respond to it. The style of the film creates, in us, the same feeling that the events in the film create in the hero. Interesting.

After the Rehearsal ★ ★ ★ ★

R, 72 m., 1984

Erland Josephson (Henrik Vogler), Ingrid Thulin (Rakel), Lena Olin (Anna Egerman), Nadja Palmstjerna-Weiss (Anna at Twelve). Directed by Ingmar Bergman and produced by Jorn Donner. Screenplay by Bergman.

Ingmar Bergman's *After the Rehearsal* seems to be as simple and direct as a tape recording of actual conversations, and yet look at the thickets of interpretation it has inspired in its critics. After seeing it, I thought I understood the film entirely. Now I am not so sure. Like so many of Bergman's films, and especially the spare "chamber films" it joins *(Winter Light, Persona),* it consists of unadorned surfaces concealing fathomless depths.

It is safest to begin with the surfaces. All of the action takes place on a stage prepared for a production of Strindberg's *A Dream Play.* An aging director sits among the props, and every chair and table reminds him of an earlier production. The rehearsal has ended some time ago, and now the director simply sits, as if the stage were his room. A young actress returns to the stage for a missing bracelet. But of course the bracelet is an excuse, and she wants to talk to the great man, and perhaps to begin a relationship with him (as, perhaps, she has heard that many other actresses have done over the years). The old director was once the lover of the girl's mother. It is even possible that this girl is his daughter. They talk. Then an older actress enters. She has a few lines in the play, and wants to know—frankly, brutally—if her career as a leading actress is really over because she is known as a drunk. She cries, she rants, she bares her breasts to show the old man that her body is still sound, if sodden. The director is tempted: He was once this woman's lover, and perhaps her daughter is his.

The young girl stays on stage during the extraordinary display of the older actress. When the older woman leaves, the director and ingenue talk again, and this time the old man, who has been through the turmoil of love too many times, talks her through their probable future: We could make love, we could have an affair, we would call it part of our art, you would be the student, I would be the teacher, I would grow tired, you would feel trapped, all our idealism would turn into ashes. Since the relationship is foredoomed, why bother with it?

Just in terms of these spare passages of dialogue and passion, *After the Rehearsal* is an important and painful confessional, for the old director, of course, bears many points of resemblance to Bergman, whose lovers have included his actresses Harriet Andersson, Bibi Anderson, and Liv Ullmann, among others, and whose daughter by Ullmann appeared in *Face to Face.* But the film is not a scandalous revelation: It is actually more of a sacramental confession, as if Bergman, the son of a Lutheran bishop, now sees the stage as his confessional and is asking the audience to bless and forgive him. (His gravest sin, as I read the film, is not lust or adultery, but the sin of taking advantage of others—of manipulating them with his power and intellect.)

If that were the extent of *After the Rehearsal,* it would be deep enough. But Bergman has surrounded the bare bones of his story with mystifying problems of interpretation. Just as in *Persona* he included scenes in which his characters exchanged personalities and engaged in scenes that might have or might not have been fantasies and dreams, so here, too, he gives us things to puzzle over. Reading the earlier reviews of the film, I discover that one critic realized only belatedly that the younger actress, Anna, was onstage the whole time the older actress, Rakel, poured out her heart. Strange, and yet another critic thought the whole scene with Rakel was the director's own dream. Yet another suggested that Anna represents not only herself but also Rakel's absent daughter. And another theory is that Anna is the daughter of the director and Rakel, and is brought into being by the residual love between them, as a sort of theatrical Holy Spirit. The age of Anna has been variously reported as ranging from twelve to twenty, with one critic reporting that both ages of the character are represented.

Which is the correct interpretation? They are all correct. Each and every one is equally correct; otherwise what is the use of a dream play? The point is not to find the literal meaning, anyway, but to touch the soul of the director, and find out what still hurts him after all these years. After all the sex and all the promises, all the lies and truths and messy affairs, there is still one critical area where he is filled with guilt and passion. It is revealed when Anna tells him she is pregnant. He is enraged. How could she, a young actress given the role of a lifetime, jeopardize her career and his play by getting pregnant? Then she tells him she has had an abortion, for the sake of the play. And then he really is torn in two, for he does not believe, after all, that a play—not even his play—is worth the sacrifice of a life. What we are left with at the end of *After the Rehearsal,* however, is the very strong sense of an artist who has sacrificed many lives for the sake of his art, and now wonders if perhaps one of those lives was his own.

Against All Odds ★ ★ ★

R, 128 m., 1984

Rachel Ward (Jessie Wyler), Jeff Bridges (Terry Brogan), James Woods (Jake Wise), Alex Karras (Hank Sully), Jane Greer (Mrs. Wyler), Richard Widmark (Ben Caxton). Directed by Taylor Hackford and produced by Hackford and William S. Gilmore. Screenplay by Eric Hughes.

There have been too many sweet girls in thrillers. What we need are more no-good, double-dealing broads who can cross their legs and break your heart. *Against All Odds* has a woman like that, and it makes for one of the most intriguing movie relationships in a long time; in thirty-five years, to be exact, which is when they told this story for the first time. You may remember the original movie. It was called *Out of the Past.* It starred Robert Mitchum and Kirk Douglas, and it was the greatest cigarette-smoking movie of all time. Mitchum and Douglas smoked all the way through every scene, and they were always blowing sinister, aggressive clouds of smoke at each other. The movie was shot so there was always a lot of light on the place in midair where their smoke was aimed. The only drawback to the fact that smoking is no longer fashionable in movies is that we don't get any great smoking scenes anymore. Anyway, if you remember that movie, you remember that Kirk Douglas was a hoodlum and Robert Mitchum was a guy who would take a job for a buck, and Douglas hired Mitchum to track down his missing girlfriend, who was played by Jane Greer. After Mitchum found Greer, they had a big love affair—or so Mitchum thought. But Greer, that no-good, two-timing, double-crossing broad, liked security more than passion.

Against All Odds is not really a remake of *Out of the Past.* The only similarity between the two movies is in the cynical love triangle. And it was a real inspiration to tell that story again, since it makes for an intriguing, complicated, interesting romance. This time, the bad guy is a gambler, played by James Woods. His girlfriend (Rachel Ward) is the daughter of the owner of a pro-football team (played by Jane Greer, of all people). And the guy who tracks her down (Jeff Bridges), is a team player who's just been fired after a knee injury.

There is a lot of plot in this movie—probably too much. The best thing to do is to accept the plot, and then disregard it, and pay attention to the scenes of passion. They really work. Bridges and Ward have an interesting sexual tension in *Against All Odds,* since their relationship is not simply sweetness and light, but depends upon suspicion, dislike, and foul betrayal. That's ever so much more interesting than just falling in love. And the situation liberates Ward from the trap she'd been in; the trap of playing attractive, sexy, strong heroines. This time, as a complicated schemer, she's fascinating.

The movie has a lot of muted social criticism in it, involving professional sports and ecology. The Jane Greer character has a plan to destroy several beautiful canyons to build houses. The Bridges character is a victim of unfair labor practices. And so on. Sometimes we get the idea we're watching a clone of *Chinatown*—but not with that jealous triangle. Woods is the villain, so he does smoke, of course. But Bridges and Ward are so consumed with passion, they don't even need to.

Agnes of God ★

PG-13, 99 m., 1985

Jane Fonda (Dr. Livingston), Anne Bancroft (Mother Miriam), Meg Tilly (Sister Agnes), Anne Pitoniak (Dr. Livingston's Mother), Winston Rekert (Detective Langevin), Gratien Gelinas (Father Martineau). Directed by Norman Jewison and produced by Patrick Palmer and Jewison. Screenplay by John Pielmeier.

It might have been impossible to convert *Agnes of God* from a play into a movie under any circumstances, since the intrinsic reality of film throws the play's conceits and contrivances into sharp relief. Speeches that seemed stylishly theatrical onstage seem, in screen close-ups, to be . . . merely theatrical. But that's just the beginning of this film's problems. It considers, or pretends to consider, some of the most basic questions of human morality and treats them on the level of *Nancy Drew and the Secret of the Old Convent.*

The story: A dead baby is found in a lonely convent, where the nuns lead a sequestered life and there are no men who could possibly have been the father—unless you count poor old Father Martineau, the nuns' spiritual adviser, who has a drinking problem.

The police investigation indicates that the baby's mother, and possibly its murderer, was Sister Agnes (Meg Tilly), a young, simple-minded girl of total naiveté. It is never made quite clear what specific problem Sister Agnes suffers from, but she clearly has parts on order.

A psychiatrist (Jane Fonda) is assigned to the case, and it quickly becomes clear that she will learn little from Sister Agnes, who has total amnesia regarding the entire incident. The convent's mother superior (Anne Bancroft) at first seems more helpful—she is a "modern" woman who was married before she entered the convent and who shares a forbidden cigarette with Fonda—but she turns hostile as the investigation continues.

I will be giving away no essential secrets if I reveal that the precise details of the conception, birth, and murder of the child are never cleared up to anybody's satisfaction. More to the point: The solution to the crime hardly seems to be the point of the movie. It reaches for a far loftier philosophical subject, which is, I think, the possibility of miracles.

Although the movie deals in the basic materials of a criminal investigation (cynical cops, forensic details, courtroom testimony), it has a seriously clouded agenda. The mechanism of the crime story whirls busily and goes nowhere, and meanwhile, we learn that Fonda has a personal hatred of the Catholic church, that Mother Miriam seems overly concerned with protecting Sister Agnes, that Sister Agnes herself has made the sort of ecstatic world-vision usually reserved for saints, and that we should not overlook the possibility that the baby, in fact, had no father. In other words, Sister Agnes had a virgin birth. Or, in case the point still seems obscure, the murdered infant was a child of God.

There is a certain amount of pressure on the Fonda character, an agnostic, to accept the possibility that a miracle has occurred. She resists it, quite sensibly, since the implications of the miracle are horrifying: If

God indeed conceived the child in Sister Agnes's womb, then why did he in his omnipotence allow her to kill it? But of course (you argue), God also gave Sister Agnes free will, so she was free to kill the child no matter what the details of its conception. True, and yet then, we must ask, why did God create a baby to be killed?

Here we enter, of course, into the still larger question of why God has created all of us and placed us in this life where we will most assuredly all die. Religion centers on the answers to that question. The infuriating thing about *Agnes of God* is that it tells a story that makes such questions essential and then ignores them.

This is a very badly confused movie. It takes the form of a murder investigation and then uses hints of the supernatural to avoid all the hard-edged questions raised by the murder. Then—just when it seems to be edging close to the fundamental supernatural questions it contains—it's back to the courtroom. The movie uses each half of its story to avoid dealing with the other.

Under the circumstances, the performances are as good as can be expected. Given dialogue that sounds as if it were written to be read, given characters who consistently avoid asking the obvious questions, given a story that refuses to declare what it is about, Bancroft, Fonda, and Tilly use their craft to give the illusion that they know where they stand. It is service in a lost cause.

Airplane! ★ ★ ★
PG, 88 m., 1980

Lloyd Bridges (McCroskey), Peter Graves (Captain Oveur), Kareem Abdul-Jabbar (Murdock), Julie Hagerty (Elaine), Robert Hays (Ted Striker), Leslie Nielsen (Dr. Rumack), Howard Jarvis (Man in Taxi), Ethel Merman (Lieutenant Hurwitz). Directed and written by Jim Abrahams, David Zucker, and Jerry Zucker and produced by Howard W. Koch.

Airplane! is a comedy in the great tradition of high school skits, the Sid Caesar TV show, *Mad* magazine, and the dog-eared screenplays people's nephews write in lieu of earning their college diplomas. It is sophomoric, obvious, predictable, corny, and quite often very funny. And the reason it's funny is frequently *because* it's sophomoric, predictable, corny, etc. Example:

Airplane Captain (Peter Graves): Surely you can't be serious!

Doctor (Leslie Nielsen): Of course I am! And stop calling me Shirley!

This sort of humor went out with Milton Berle, Jerry Lewis, and knock-knock jokes. That's why it's so funny. Movie comedies these days are so hung up on being contemporary, radical, outspoken, and cynically satirical that they sometimes forget to be funny. And they've lost the nerve to be as corny as *Airplane!*—to actually invite loud groans from the audience. The flop *Wholly Moses*, for example, is no doubt an infinitely more intelligent comedy—but the problem was, we didn't laugh.

Airplane! has a couple of sources for its inspiration. One of them is obviously *Airport* (1970) and all of its sequels and rip-offs. The other might not come immediately to mind unless you're a fan of the late show. It's *Zero Hour!* (1957), which starred the quintessential 1950s B-movie cast of Dana Andrews, Linda Darnell, and Sterling Hayden. *Airplane!* comes from the same studio (Paramount) and therefore is able to cheerfully borrow the same plot (airliner is imperiled after the crew and most of the passengers are stricken with food poisoning). The *Zero Hour!* crisis situation (how to get the airplane down) was also borrowed for the terrible *Airport 1975*, in which Karen Black played a stewardess who tried to follow instructions radioed from the ground.

Airplane! has two desperate people in the cockpit: Julie Hagerty, as the stewardess, and Robert Hays, as a former Air Force pilot whose traumatic war experiences have made him terrified of flying. (The cockpit also contains a very kinky automatic pilot . . . but never mind.)

The movie exploits the previous films for all they're worth. The passenger list includes a little old lady (like Helen Hayes in *Airport*), a guitar-playing nun (like Helen Reddy in *Airport 1975*), and even a critically ill little girl who's being flown to an emergency operation (Linda Blair played the role in *Airport 1975*). Predictable results occur, as when the nun's guitar knocks loose the little girl's intravenous tubes, and she nearly dies while all the passengers sing along inspirationally.

The movie's funniest scene, however, occurs in a flashback explaining how the stewardess and the Air Force pilot first met and fell in love years ago. The scene takes place in an exotic Casablanca-style bar, which is miraculously transformed when somebody's hurled at the jukebox and it starts playing "Stayin' Alive" by the Bee Gees. The scene becomes a hilarious send-up of the disco scenes in *Saturday Night Fever*, with the young pilot defying gravity to impress the girl.

Airplane! is practically a satirical anthology of classic movie clichés. Lloyd Bridges, as the ground-control officer, seems to be satirizing half of his straight roles. The opening titles get an enormous laugh with an unexpected reference to *Jaws*. The neurotic young pilot is talked back into the cockpit in a scene from *Knute Rockne, All American*. And the romantic scenes are played as a soap opera. None of this really adds up to great comic artistry, but *Airplane!* compensates for its lack of original comic invention by its utter willingness to steal, beg, borrow, and rewrite from anywhere.

Airport ★ ★
G, 137 m., 1970

Burt Lancaster (Mel Bakersfield), Dean Martin (Vernon Demerest), Jean Seberg (Tanya), Jacqueline Bisset (Gwen Meighen), George Kennedy (Patroni), Helen Hayes (Ada Quonsett), Van Heflin (D.O. Guerrero). Directed by George Seaton and produced by Ross Hunter. Screenplay by Seaton.

On some dumb fundamental level, *Airport* kept me interested for a couple of hours. I can't quite remember why. The plot has few surprises (you know and I know that no airplane piloted by Dean Martin ever crashed). The gags are painfully simpleminded (a priest, pretending to cross himself, whacks a wise guy across the face). And the characters talk in regulation B-movie clichés like no B-movie you've seen in ten years. Example: A bomb blows a hole in the airplane and weakens the tail structure. Martin's co-pilot says: "Listen, Vern, I want you to know that if there's anything I can do. . . ." What's he talking about? Martin's girl.

The movie has a lot of expensive stars, but only two (Helen Hayes and Van Heflin) have wit enough to abandon all pretense of seriousness. Even Martin, who can be charming in a movie when he relaxes, plays a straight hero-type this time. Burt Lancaster is even straighter and more heroic, as needs be, since he has to run the airport, supervise George Kennedy in pulling out a stuck Boeing 707, and decide to divorce his wife, all at the same time.

But Miss Hayes and Heflin apparently realized early on that *Airport* was going to be a deadly dull affair, and they went about salvaging their own roles, at least. Miss Hayes milks her role of a little-old-lady stowaway for all it's conceivably worth, and I have a suspicion she wrote some of her own dialogue. It's warmer and more humorous than the stiff lines everyone else has to recite, and she won an Oscar for the role.

Heflin, as the guy with the bomb in his briefcase, is perhaps the only person in the cast to realize how metaphysically absurd *Airport* basically is. The airplane already has a priest, two nuns, three doctors, a stowaway, a customs officer's niece, a pregnant stewardess, two black GIs, a loudmouthed kid, a henpecked husband, and Dean Martin aboard, right? So obviously the bomber has to be typecast, too. Heflin sweats, shakes, peers around nervously, clutches his briefcase to his chest, refuses to talk to anybody, and swallows a lot. The customs officer sees him going on the plane and notices "something in his eyes." Also in his ears, nose, and throat. What Heflin does is undermine the structure of the whole movie with a sort of subversive overacting. Once the bomber becomes ridiculous, the movie does, too. That's good, because it never had a chance at being anything else.

Airport 1975 ★ ★ 1/2
PG, 106 m., 1974

Charlton Heston (Murdock), Karen Black (Nancy), George Kennedy (Patroni), Efrem Zimbalist, Jr. (Stacy), Susan Clark (Mrs. Patroni), Helen Reddy (Sister Ruth). Directed by Jack Smight and produced by William Frye. Screenplay by Don Ingalls.

The original *Airport* was never one of my favorite movies, but I had to admire the slick, competent way it worked us over for two hours. Its clichés were ancient and its typecasting was relentless, but it didn't bore us. *Airport 1975*, a reworking of the same good old ingredients happens, by some happy chance, to be better than the original.

The story is familiar to anyone. A private plane crashes into the flight deck of a 747, killing or disabling its crew. A stewardess pilots the plane by following radioed instructions, and then a rescue pilot (Charlton Heston, inevitably) is lowered from an Air Force helicopter into the gaping hole in the plane. Meanwhile, a young kidney patient grows weaker, a drunk accosts the pilot, and Gloria Swanson dictates the finishing touches on her autobiography ("I never did want the damn thing published while I was alive, anyway").

What makes this work so well is that the screenplay and direction concentrate on the action, instead of getting bogged down in so many subplots, as *Airport* did. It can't be helped, I suppose, that Heston and the brave stewardess (Karen Black) have been having an affair for six years, or that the airline vice president (George Kennedy, promoted from his operations command in *Airport*) has a wife and daughter on the crippled plane, or that we have the usual ecumenical mixture of stereotypes, racial groups, ages, sexes, and occupants on board. That's all part of the formula.

But at least *Airport 1975* introduces its characters quickly and without fuss, and then gets on with the business at hand. And after the midair collision (which has been telegraphed for at least twenty minutes), the movie's excellent special effects become really gripping. With *Airport*, you never quite felt those people were on a real plane. The exterior shots looked faked. *Airport 1975* has a much more plausible look and a lot of effective aerial photography.

It also gives us a compelling performance by Karen Black, the stewardess. She's probably too good an actress for a role like this, but she makes it real. (And who could ever quite believe Dean Martin as the pilot in *Airport?*) The only quarrel I have with the role is that it falls into the trap of assuming she's incompetent because she's a woman. Her lip quivers, her eyes well up with tears, she's indecisive at key moments. The men on the ground decide they have to get a real pilot on board. My notion is that a real stewardess, faced with such an unlikely situation, would respond professionally and coolly.

No matter. While the wind rips into the plane and the passengers bundle up with blankets and the mountains loom up ahead and the first rescue pilot falls to his death and Gloria Swanson remembers her first flight ("It was in 1917, Cecil B. DeMille was the pilot, and we flew nonstop from Los Angeles to Pasadena"). *Airport 1975* is good, exciting, corny escapism and the kind of movie you would *not* want to watch as an in-flight film.

Alex in Wonderland ★ ★ ★ ★

R, 109 m., 1971

Donald Sutherland (Alex), Ellen Burstyn (Beth), Meg Mazursky (Amy), Glenna Sergent (Nancy), Viola Spolin (Mother), Paul Mazursky (Hal Stern). Directed by Paul Mazursky and produced by Larry Tucker. Screenplay by Mazursky and Tucker.

"Who are you," said the Caterpillar.

This was not an encouraging opening for a conversation. Alice replied rather shyly. "I—hardly know, Sir, just at present—at least I know who I was when I got up this morning, but I think I must have changed several times since then."

That was exactly the case in Hollywood in the early seventies. Works of genius were showered on us by bright, radical, young, etc., filmmakers who announced their intention to overturn the Hollywood establishment. Occasionally one of their films did make it very big, as *Easy Rider* did. Within weeks, the Hollywood hills were jammed with other would-be geniuses, shooting nihilistic cycle flicks with pseudo-Dylan lyrics. Meanwhile, the original boy wonders . . . Have got to make themselves another film. That was the situation for Paul Mazursky and Larry Tucker, who wrote, produced, and directed *Bob & Carol & Ted & Alice.* That movie was an artistic and financial success. It was chosen to open the New York Film Festival. It was argued about in all the best publications. Elliott Gould became a star. Natalie Wood made her comeback. Tucker and Mazursky got rich. The whole enchilada, baby.

Alex in Wonderland was their response to that situation; it's a movie about a director whose first movie is a success and who's at a loss for another project. In this sense, it's autobiographical; not in the details of life, but in the crises. Mazursky himself even appears, as Hal Stern, the doggedly mod movie producer who hopes to interest Donald Sutherland in *Don Quixote* as a Western? Or maybe . . .?

If the director's dilemma sounds familiar, perhaps you're reminded of Fellini's *8½*. Mazursky and Tucker were. The blocked director's daughter even asks why he doesn't do a movie about not knowing what to do next, and he says, no, Fellini already did that. *Alex in Wonderland* is a deliberately Felliniesque movie, all the same, and all the more fun for that. Fellini himself appears briefly, to no special purpose, and Fellini trademarks like parades, circuses, and clowns keep turning up in the hero's daydreams.

If *Alex* had been left just on this level, however, it would have been of little interest. What makes it so good is the gift Mazursky, Tucker, and their actors have of fleshing out the small scenes of human contact that give the movie its almost frightening resonance.

Sutherland, as the director, has trouble handling his success. His uncertainty about what to do next spills over into aloofness, even cruelty, toward his wife (Ellen Burstyn) and mother (Viola Spolin). A short scene in a car with his mother, and a long scene in a kitchen with his wife, actually make the rest of the movie work, because they give the character a depth that sticks even through the superficial dream sequences.

And beyond these intimate scenes, there are icily observant portraits of the "new Hollywood." Of aimless "idealistic" arguments on the beach, of luncheon meetings, of idle people trying somehow to be idly committed. These scenes are the 1970 equivalent of Fitzgerald's *The Last Tycoon* or Nathanael West's *The Day of the Locust*: Unforgivingly accurate studies of the distance between America and the filmmakers who would be "relevant" about it.

The Fellini elements are laid onto the film and don't quite sink in (although buffs will enjoy them just as parody). But the human story does work, remarkably well, and if the movie doesn't hold together we're not disposed to hold that against it. Half an enchilada is better than none.

Alice Doesn't Live Here Anymore

★ ★ ★ ★

PG, 113 m., 1975

Ellen Burstyn (Alice Hyatt), Kris Kristofferson (David), Billy Green Bush (Donald), Diane Ladd (Flo), Alfred Lutter (Tommy), Harvey Keitel (Ben). Directed by Martin Scorsese and produced by David Susskind and Audrey Maas. Screenplay by Robert Getchell.

Martin Scorsese's *Alice Doesn't Live Here Anymore* opens with a parody of the Hollywood dream world little girls were expected to carry around in their intellectual baggage a generation ago. The screen is awash with a fake sunset, and a sweet little thing comes strolling along home past sets that seem rescued from *The Wizard of Oz*. But her dreams and dialogue are decidedly not made of sugar, spice, or anything nice: This little girl is going to do things her way.

That was her defiant childhood notion, anyway. But by the time she's thirty-five, Alice Hyatt has more or less fallen into society's rhythms. She's married to an incommunicative truck driver, she has a precocious twelve-year-old son, she kills time chatting with the neighbors. And then her husband is unexpectedly killed in a traffic accident and she's left widowed and—almost worse than that—independent. After all those years of having someone there, can she cope by herself?

She can, she says. When she was a little girl, she idolized Alice Faye and determined to be a singer when she grew up. Well, she's thirty-five, and that's grown-up. She has a garage sale, sells the house, and sets off on an odyssey through the Southwest with her son and her dreams. What happens to her along the way provides one of the most perceptive, funny, occasionally painful portraits of an American woman I've seen.

The movie has been both attacked and defended on feminist grounds, but I think it belongs somewhere outside ideology, maybe in the area of contemporary myth and romance. There are scenes in which we take Alice and her journey perfectly seriously, there are scenes of harrowing reality and then there are other scenes (including some hilarious passages in a restaurant where she waits on tables) where Scorsese edges into slight, cheerful exaggeration. There are times, indeed, when the movie seems less about Alice than it does about the speculations and daydreams of a lot of women about her age, who identify with the liberation of other women, but are unsure on the subject of themselves.

A movie like this depends as much on performances as on direction, and there's a fine performance by Ellen Burstyn (who won an Oscar for this role) as Alice. She looks more real this time than she did as Cybill Shepherd's available mother in *The Last Picture Show* or as Linda Blair's tormented mother in *The Exorcist.* It's the kind of role she can relax in, be honest with, allow to develop naturally (although those are often the hardest roles of all). She's determined to find work as a singer, to "resume" a career that was mostly dreams to begin with, and she's pretty enough (although not good enough) to almost pull it off. She meets some generally good people along the way, and they help her when they can. But she also meets some creeps, especially a deceptively nice guy named Ben (played by Harvey Keitel, the autobiographical hero of Scorsese's two films set in Little Italy). The singing jobs don't materialize much, and it's while she's waitressing that she runs into a divorced young farmer (Kris Kristofferson).

They fall warily in love, and there's an interesting relationship between Kristofferson and Alfred Lutter, who does a very good job of playing a certain kind of twelve-year-old kid. Most women in Alice's position probably wouldn't run into a convenient, understanding, and eligible young farmer, but then a lot of the things in the film don't work as pure logic. There's a little myth to them, while Scorsese sneaks up on his main theme.

The movie's filled with brilliantly done individual scenes. Alice, for example, has a run-in with a fellow waitress with an inspired vocabulary (Diane Ladd, an Oscar nominee for this role). They fall into a friendship and have a frank and honest conversation one day while sunbathing. The scene works perfectly. There's also the specific way her first employer backs into offering her a singing job, and the way Alice takes leave from her old neighbors, and the way her son persists in explaining a joke that could only be understood by a twelve-year-old. These are great moments in a film that gives us Alice Hyatt: female, thirty-five, undefeated.

Aliens ★ ★ ★ 1/2

R, 135 m., 1986

Sigourney Weaver (Ripley), Carrie Henn (Newt), Michael Biehn (Corporal Hicks), Paul Reiser (Burke), Lance Henriksen (Bishop), Jenette Goldstein (Private Vasquez). Directed by James Cameron and produced by Gale Anne Hurd. Screenplay by Cameron.

This movie is so intense that it creates a problem for me as a reviewer: Do I praise its craftsmanship, or do I tell you it left me feeling wrung out and unhappy? When I walked out of the theater, there were knots in my stomach from the film's roller-coaster ride of violence. This is not the kind of movie where it means anything to say you "enjoyed" it.

Aliens is a sequel to the very effective 1979 film, *Alien,* but it tells a self-contained story that begins fifty-seven years after the previous story ended. The first time around, you may recall, Sigourney Weaver and a shipload of her fellow space voyagers were exploring a newly discovered planet when they found an abandoned spaceship. Surviving in the ship was an alien life-form that seemed to consist primarily of teeth. The aliens were pure malevolence; their only function was to attack and eat anything that was warm and moved. And they incubated their young inside the bodies of their victims.

Weaver was the only survivor of that first expedition, and after saving her ship by expelling an alien through the air lock into deep space, she put herself into hibernation. She is found fifty-seven years later by a salvage ship, and when she awakes she is still tormented by nightmares. (The script does not provide her, however, with even a single line of regret after she learns that fifty-seven years have passed and everyone she knew is dead.)

A new expedition is sent back to the mystery planet. Weaver is on board. She knows what the aliens are like and thinks the only sane solution is to nuke them from outer space. But in the meantime, she learns to her horror that a human colony has been established on the planet and billions of dollars have been invested in it. Now Earth has lost contact with the colony. Has it been attacked by aliens? Are there stars in the sky?

The crew is made up of an interesting mixed bag of technicians and military personnel. My favorites were Lance Henriksen as a loyal android, Jenette Goldstein as a muscular marine private, and Michael Biehn as the uncertain Corporal Hicks. Also on board is the slimy Burke (Paul Reiser), who represents the owners of the planet's expensive colony and dreams of making millions by using the aliens as a secret weapon.

The movie gives us just enough set-up to establish the characters and explain the situation. Then the action starts. The colony has, of course, been overrun by the aliens, all except for one plucky little girl (Carrie Henn) who has somehow survived by hiding in the air ducts. The marines explore the base on foot, which seems a little silly in view of the great speed with which the aliens attack. Nobody seems very interested in listening to Weaver's warnings. After all, she's only the one person who has seen an alien, so what does she know? And then the movie escalates into a nonstop war between human and alien.

It's here that my nerves started to fail. *Aliens* is absolutely, painfully, and unremittingly intense for at least its last hour. Weaver goes into battle to save her colleagues, herself, and the little girl, and the aliens drop from the ceiling, pop up out of the floor, and crawl out of the ventilation shafts. (In one of the movie's less plausible moments, one alien even seems to know how to work the elevator buttons.) I have never seen a movie that maintains such a pitch of intensity for so long; it's like being on some kind of hair-raising carnival ride that never stops.

I don't know how else to describe this: The movie made me feel bad. It filled me with feelings of unease and disquiet and anxiety. I didn't want to talk to anyone. I was drained. I'm not sure *Aliens* is what we mean by entertainment. Yet I have to be accurate about this movie: It is a superb example of filmmaking craft.

The director, James *(The Terminator)* Cameron, has been assigned to make an intense and horrifying thriller, and he has delivered. Weaver, who is onscreen almost all the time, comes through with a very strong, sympathetic performance: She's the thread that holds everything together.

The supporting players are sharply drawn. The special effects are professional. I'm giving the movie a high rating for its skill and professionalism and because it does the job it says it will do. I am also advising you not to eat before you see it.

All of Me ★ ★ ★ ½

PG, 93 m., 1984

Steve Martin (Roger Cobb), Lily Tomlin (Edwina Cutwater), Victoria Tennant (Terry Hoskins), Madolyn Smith (Peggy), Richard Libertini (Prahka Lasa), Jason Bernard (Tyrone Wattel). Directed by Carl Reiner. Screenplay by Phil Alden Robinson.

All of Me shares with a lot of great screwball comedies a very simple approach: Use absolute logic in dealing with the absurd. Begin with a nutty situation, establish the rules, and follow them. The laughs happen when ordinary human nature comes into conflict with ridiculous developments.

We can identify with almost all of the motives of the characters in *All of Me*. There is, for example, the millionaire spinster Edwina Cutwater (Lily Tomlin), who wants to live forever and thinks she has found a way to do that. There is the unhappy lawyer Roger Cobb (Steve Martin), who is desperately unhappy with his work and will do anything to get a promotion—even cater to nutcase clients like Edwina. There is the evil Terry Hoskins (Victoria Tennant), who plans to cruelly deceive Edwina, and there is the beatific Prahka Lasa (Richard Libertini), who hopes to transfer Edwina's soul into a brass pot, and then insert it in Miss Hoskins's body. There is, however, a terrible psychic miscalculation, and when Edwina dies, she transmigrates instead into Cobb's body. When I heard *All of Me* described, I couldn't think of any way this plot could possibly work. To begin with, why put one of my favorite comedians, Tomlin, inside Martin, a man whose movies I have not admired? And yet it does work. The moment it starts to work is the first time Martin has to deal with this alien female entity inside his brain. He retains control of the left side of his body. She controls the right. They are trying to cross the sidewalk together, each in their own way, and this sets up a manic tug-of-war that is one of the funniest scenes I've seen in a long time.

There are other great scenes, some of them probably obligatory, as when Martin has to go to the bathroom. The movie doesn't just go for obvious physical jokes, however; it scores a lot of points by speculating on the ways in which a man and a woman could learn to coexist in such close quarters. Against all the odds, a certain tenderness and sweetness develops by the end of the film. Although it is Tomlin who disappears into Martin's body, she does not disappear from the movie. For one thing, her reflection can be seen in mirrors, and there is some exquisite timing involved in the way they play scenes with each other's mirror images. For another thing (and this is really curious), there is a real sense of her presence even when Martin is alone on the screen: The film's premise, which seems so unlikely, begins to work.

The movie is filled with good supporting performances. My favorites are Richard Libertini, as the guru of transmigration, who speaks incomprehensible words in a tone of complete agreement, and Jason Bernard, as a black musician who is Martin's friend and partner during several tricky scenes of body-snatching and brain-grabbing. *All of Me* is in a class with *Ghostbusters,* and for some of the same reasons.

All the President's Men ★ ★ ★ ½
PG, 135 m., 1976

Robert Redford (Bob Woodward), Dustin Hoffman (Carl Bernstein), Jack Warden (Harry Rosenfeld), Martin Balsam (Howard Simons), Hal Holbrook (Deep Throat), Jason Robards (Ben Bradlee), Jane Alexander (Bookkeeper), Stephen Collins (Hugh Sloan), Robert Walden (Donald Segretti), Frank Wills (Frank Wills). Directed by Alan J. Pakula and produced by Walter Coblenz. Screenplay by William Goldman.

All the President's Men is truer to the craft of journalism than to the art of storytelling, and that's its problem. The movie is as accurate about the processes used by investigative reporters as we have any right to expect, and yet process finally overwhelms narrative—we're adrift in a sea of names, dates, telephone numbers, coincidences, lucky breaks, false leads, dogged footwork, denials, evasions, and sometimes even the truth. Just such thousands of details led up to Watergate and the Nixon resignation, yes, but the movie's more about the details than about their results. That's not to say the movie isn't good at accomplishing what it sets out to do. It provides the most observant study of working journalists we're ever likely to see in a feature film (Bob Woodward and Carl Bernstein may at last, merciful God, replace Hildy Johnson and Walter Burns as career models). And it succeeds brilliantly in suggesting the mixture of exhilaration, paranoia, self-doubt, and courage that permeated the *Washington Post* as its two young reporters went after a presidency.

Newspaper movies always used to play up the excitement and ignore the boredom and the waiting. This one is all about the boredom and the waiting and the tireless digging; it depends on what we already know about Watergate to provide a level of excitement. And yet, given the fact that William Goldman's screenplay is almost all dialogue, almost exclusively a series of scenes of people talking (or not talking) to each other, director Alan J. Pakula has done a remarkable job of keeping the pace taut. Who'd have thought you could build tension with scenes where Bernstein walks over to Woodward's desk and listens in on the extension phone? But you can. And the movie's so well paced, acted, and edited that it develops the illusion of momentum even in the scenes where Woodward and Bernstein are getting doors slammed in their faces.

When Robert Redford announced that he'd bought the rights to *All the President's Men,* the joke in the newsroom was about reporters becoming movie stars. What in fact has happened is that the stars, Redford as Woodward and Dustin Hoffman as Bernstein, became reporters: They sink into their characters and become wholly credible. There's not a false or "Hollywood" note in the whole movie, and that's commendable—but how much authenticity will viewers settle for? To what secret and sneaky degree do they really want Redford and Hoffman to come on like stars?

There must have been a temptation to flesh out the Woodward and Bernstein characters, to change the pace with subplots about their private lives, but the film sticks resolutely to its subject. This is the story of a story: of two reporters starting with an apparently minor break-in and following it, almost incredulously at times, as it finally leads all the way to the White House. At times the momentum of Watergate seems to propel Woodward and Bernstein, instead of the other way around. It must have occasionally been like that at the time, and it's to the movie's credit that it doesn't force its characters into the center of every scene.

All the President's Men doesn't dwell on the private lives of its characters, but it does have a nice touch with their professional lives, and especially with their relationships with editors. The Watergate story started as a local story, not a national one, and it was a continuing thorn in the side of the *Post*'s prestigious national staff as Woodward and Bernstein kept it as their own. We meet the *Post* metro editor, Harry Rosenfeld (Jack Warden), defending and badgering "Woodstein" as the team came to be known. Martin Balsam plays Howard Simons, the managing editor, and Jason Robards is Benjamin Bradlee, the executive editor. All three are well cast; they may never have been in a newspaper office before, but they've learned the correct tone, they carry on a news conference as if they've held one before, and they even exhibit typical shadings of office fashion—the closer in time you are to having once covered a daily beat, the more you're permitted to loosen your tie and have baggy pants.

The movie has dozens of smaller character roles, for all the people who talked to Woodstein, or who refused to, and there's one cameo from real life: Frank Wills, the Watergate guard who found the fateful tape on the lock, plays himself. Some of the other roles tend to blend into one faceless Source, but Robert Walden makes a memorable Donald Segretti, playing the "dirty tricks" expert with bravado shading into despair. And two of the key informants are portrayed in interestingly different ways. Jane Alexander is a bookkeeper who gives the team some of their best leads, and is plain, honest, and scared; Hal Holbrook, as the mysterious "Deep Throat," the source inside the administration, is disturbingly detached, almost as if he's observing the events with a hollow laugh.

All of these elements in *All the President's Men* are to be praised, and yet they don't quite add up to a satisfying movie experience. Once we've seen one cycle of investigative reporting, once Woodward and Bernstein have cracked the first wall separating the break-in from the White House, we understand the movie's method. We don't need to see the reporting cycle repeated several more times just because the story grows longer and the sources more important. For all of its technical skill, the movie essentially shows us the same journalistic process several times as it leads closer and closer to an end we already know. The film is long, and would be dull if it weren't for the wizardry of Pakula, his actors, and technicians. What saves it isn't the power of narrative, but the success of technique. Still, considering the compromises that could have been made, considering the phony "newspaper movie" this could have been, maybe that's almost enough.

All the Right Moves ★ ★ ★

R, 91 m., 1983

Tom Cruise (Stef), Craig T. Nelson (Nickerson), Lea Thompson (Lisa). Directed by Michael Chapman and produced by Stephen Deutsch. Screenplay by Michael Kane.

I started on newspapers as a sportswriter, covering local high school teams. That was a long time ago, and I had almost forgotten, until I saw *All the Right Moves*, how desperately important every game seemed at the time. When the team members and the fans are all teen-agers, and when a school victory reflects in a significant way upon your own feelings of worth, when "We won!" means that we won, a football game can take on aspects of Greek tragedy.

All the Right Moves remembers the strength of those feelings, but does not sentimentalize them. The movie stars Tom Cruise (from *Risky Business*) as a high school football player in a small Pennsylvania mill town where unemployment is a way of life. His ticket out of town is a football scholarship to a good engineering school. The high school football coach (Craig T. Nelson) also is looking for a ticket, to an assistant coaching job in a college. On the night of the big game, these two people get into a position where each one seems to have destroyed the hopes of the other.

The movie plays this conflict against an interesting background. This isn't another high school movie with pompom girls and funny principals and weirdo chem teachers. The movie gets into the dynamics of the high school student body and into the tender, complicated relationship between the Cruise character and his girlfriend (Lea Thompson).

After all the junk high school movies in which kids chop each other up, seduce the French teacher, and visit whorehouses in Mexico, it is so wonderful to see a movie that remembers that most teen-agers are vulnerable, unsure, sincere, and fundamentally decent. The kid, his girlfriend, and all of their friends have feelings we can recognize as real. The plot feels real, too, because it centers around those kinds of horrible misunderstandings and mistakes that we all remember from high school. A lot of teenagers walk around all day feeling guilty, even if they're totally innocent. Get them into a situation that gives them the appearance of guilt and they're in trouble. And it is so easy to get into trouble when you are old enough to do wrong but too young to move independently to avoid it. A lot of kids who say they were only along for the ride are telling the simple truth.

The movie frames the Cruise character in a situation like that, one we can identify with. And then it does an interesting thing. Instead of solving the problem with a plot twist, it solves it through the exercise of genuine human honesty: Two people finally tell each other the truth. This is, of course, an astonishing breakthrough in movies about teen-agers, and *All the Right Moves* deserves credit for that achievement.

Allegro non Tropo ★ ★ ★ ½

NO MPAA RATING, 75 m., 1977

An animated feature by Bruno Bozzetto.

Classical music illustrated with animated fantasies! What an inspiration! The impresario in the vast old Italian opera house can hardly contain himself. He bustles about the stage, confiding his plans: He'll have an animator as his chief soloist. A full orchestra of little old ladies. A selection from the greatest symphonic works of all time . . .

The telephone rings. It's Hollywood calling. The impresario can't believe his ears. It's been done already! Somebody had the same idea years ago—somebody named, ah, Prisney. Something like that. No matter. He'll do it anyway! His little old ladies arrive in a horse-drawn wagon guided by the impresario himself. Did that Prisney, or whatever his name is, give you stuff like this?

And so Bruno Bozzetto introduces his *Allegro non Tropo,* a tribute to Walt Disney's *Fantasia* and at the same time a delightfully original animated feature itself. The two movies show how limitless the possibilities are: Animation, which has few boundaries, reveals none here.

Bozzetto's animated fantasies are funny and sad, erotic and the opposite, pessimistic and visionary. He selects such familiar symphonic works as Stravinsky's *Firebird,* Sibelius's *Valse Triste,* Vivaldi's *Concerto in C,* Debussy's *Prelude to the Afternoon of a Faun,* and Ravel's *Bolero,* and then he finds ways of illustrating them that are inspired, and amusing, and somehow just right.

Take *Bolero,* for example, that majestic progression to larger and larger statements. How would you visualize it? Bozzetto begins with an empty Coke bottle, tossed from a spaceship visiting a barren planet. The bottle comes to rest just as the spaceship departs. There's a little Coke left in the bottom of it. And as Ravel's music relentlessly builds, the stuff in the bottle ferments. Simple forms of life become more complex. Weird and wonderful shapes form, and try to crawl up the side of the bottle, and fail. And then finally one succeeds. And Bozzetto marches through the stages of a strange evolution, as bizarre monsters struggle across the barren landscape, learning very suddenly to fly, and swim, and do the other things to keep from becoming meals.

The Sibelius is illustrated with an affecting idea: A scrawny house cat wanders forlorn through the streets of a city destroyed by war. No people live there anymore, but some ancient racial cat memory inhabits the ruins with dream-images of people: with quiet domestic scenes that evaporate, one after another, leaving the cat alone, lonely and afraid. An idea like this is in Loren Eiseley's biography, *All the Strange Hours.* He wonders if the dogs and cats that cast their lot with us so many tens of thousands of years ago will remember us uneasily for a few generations after we've annihilated ourselves; Bozzetto illustrates the idea beautifully.

And then there's his version of Stravinsky's *Firebird,* in which the serpent in the Garden of Eden eats the apple himself and has a very hard time of it as a result. And the aging, self-deluded rake in *Prelude to the Afternoon of a Faun,* trying to make himself look younger in his doomed pursuit of a nymph. And the busy little bee in Vivaldi's *Concerto in C,* who sets her table at one promising flower after another, only to be disturbed by two vulgar, gigantic humans who insist on making love in her meadow.

Bozzetto, one of the best animators now at work, has been making shorts for years. *Allegro non Tropo,* his first feature, is a treasure. It deserves its place beside *Fantasia,* is as delightful and inspired, and will no doubt be around as long. Even what's-his-name, Prisney, would agree.

Alligator ★
R, 92 m., 1980

Robert Forster (Madison), Robin Riker (Herpetologist), Michael Gazza (Chief), Jack Carter (Reporter), Dean Jagger (Hunter). Directed by Lewis Teague and produced by Brandon Chase. Screenplay by John Sayles.

This movie was probably inevitable. What's amazing is that they took so long to make it. *Alligator* is inspired by one of the most persistent Urban Legends of recent years: That countless pet alligators, given as gifts when they were babies, were flushed down toilets when they grew too large . . . and that down there in the sewers of our major cities, they're growing to unimaginable size.

My own fantasies about sewers go all the way back to the old "Honeymooners" TV skits, with Ed Norton breathlessly telling Ralph Cramden about the beasts he encountered on his daily patrols beneath the city streets. But Norton never met anything like the alligator in this movie. In the tradition of *Jaws,* this creature is gigantic, voracious, and insatiable. It will eat anything (as you might imagine, considering where it lives).

The story opens as it's gobbling down dead dogs from a laboratory that's experimenting with new growth hormones. You got it: The alligator reacts to the hormones and grows to a length of thirty or forty feet. People start disappearing down in the sewers. A New York cop (Robert Forster) goes down with his buddy to see what's happening. The alligator eats the buddy. But Forster can't get anyone to believe his story.

These early scenes in the movie are probably the best, because they work on the dumb fundamental level where we're all afraid of being eaten by an alligator in a sewer. (Show me a man who is not afraid of being eaten by an alligator in a sewer, and I'll show you a fool.) Forster splashes along with his flashlight, and the alligator slinks around just out of view.

Come to think of it, the alligator does a lot of slinking in this movie—maybe because it was too difficult to show the whole alligator. There are a couple of fairly phony special effects shots, as when the alligator bursts up through the sidewalk, but for the most part we just see parts of the alligator: His mean little eyes, his big tail, and his teeth. Especially his teeth.

The plot is absolutely standard; this story has been filmed dozens of times. You have, of course, the small-minded mayor who is concerned only with re-election. The police chief, a folksy character who fires Forster for not catching the alligator, but later rehires him. The girl scientist, who falls in love with the hero and helps hunt for the alligator. The villain, an out-of-town big game hunter brought in to replace Forster. All of these people do incredibly stupid things, like walking into dark alleys after the alligator, or putting a dynamite charge on a time-delay fuse while they're still trapped in a sewer with the alligator and the dynamite.

The alligator, on the other hand, is smart enough to travel all over the city without being seen: in one shot, he's in a suburban swimming pool, and seconds later, he's midtown. You would not think it would be that easy for a forty-foot alligator to sneak around incognito, but then, New Yorkers are awfully blasé. Meanwhile, I suggest a plan: Why not try flushing this movie down the toilet to see if it also grows into something big and fearsome?

Altered States ★ ★ ★ ½
R, 103 m., 1980

William Hurt (Eddie Jessup), Blair Brown (Emily Jessup), Bob Balaban (Arthur Rosenberg), Charles Haid (Mason Parrish), Thaao Penghlis (Eccheverria), Miguel Godreau (Primal Man). Directed by Ken

Russell and produced by Howard Gottfried. Screenplay by Sidney Aaron.

Altered States is one hell of a movie—literally. It hurls its characters headlong back through billions of years to the moment of creation and finds nothing there except an anguished scream of "No!" as the life force protests its moment of birth. And then, through the power of the human ego to insist on its own will even in the face of the implacable indifference of the universe, it turns "No!" into "Yes!" and ends with the basic scene in all drama, the man and the woman falling into each other's arms.

But hold on just a second here: I'm beginning to sound like the movie's characters, a band of overwrought pseudo-intellectuals who talk like a cross between Werner Erhard, Freud, and Tarzan. Some of the movie's best dialogue passages are deliberately staged with everybody talking at once: It doesn't matter what they're saying, only that they're incredibly serious about it. I can tell myself intellectually that this movie is a fiendishly constructed visual and verbal roller coaster, a movie deliberately intended to overwhelm its audiences with sensual excess. I know all that, and yet I *was* overwhelmed, I *was* caught up in its headlong energy.

Is that a worthy accomplishment for a movie? Yes, I suppose it is, if the movie earns it by working as hard as *Altered States* does. This is, at last, the movie that Ken Russell was born to direct—the same Ken Russell whose wretched excesses in the past include *The Music Lovers, The Devils,* and *Lisztomania.* The formula is now clear. Take Russell's flair for visual pyrotechnics and apocalyptic sexuality, and channel it through just enough scientific mumbo jumbo to give it form. The result may be totally meaningless, but while you're watching it you are not concerned.

The movie is based on a Paddy Chayevsky novel, which was, in turn, inspired by the experiments of Dr. John Lilly, the man who placed his human subjects in total immersion tanks—floating them in total darkness so that their minds, cut off from all external reality, could play along the frontiers of sanity. In *Altered States,* William Hurt plays a Harvard scientist named Jessup who takes such an experiment one step further, by ingesting a drug made from the sacred hallucinatory mushrooms of a primitive tribe. The strange thing about these mushrooms, Hurt observes in an easily missed line of dialogue in the movie, is that they give everyone who takes them the same hallucinatory vision. Perhaps it is our cellular memory of creation: There is chaos, and then a ball of light, and then the light turns into a crack, and the crack opens onto Nothing, and that is all there was and all there will be, except for life, which has its only existence in the mind.

Got that? It hardly matters. It is a breathtaking concept, but *Altered States* hardly slows down for it. This is the damnedest movie to categorize. Just when it begins to sound like a 1960s psychedelic fantasy, a head trip—it turns into a farce. The scientist immerses himself in his tank for too long, he regresses to a simian state, physically turns into some kind of ape, attacks the campus security guards, is chased by a pack of wild dogs into the local zoo, and kills and eats a sheep for his supper before turning *back* into the kindly Professor Jessup, the Intellectual Hulk.

The movie splits up into three basic ingredients: The science, the special effects, and the love relationship between the professor and his wife. The science is handled deliciously well. We learn as much as we need to (that is, next to nothing) about total immersion, genetics, and the racial memory. Then come the special effects, in four long passages and a few short bursts. They're good. They may remind you at times of the sound-and-light extravaganza toward the end of 2001, but they are also supposed to evoke the birth of the universe in a pulsating celestial ovum. In the center of this vision is Dr. Jessup, his body pulsing in and out of an ape-shape, his mouth pulled into an anguished "O" as he protests the hell of being born. These scenes are reinforced by the music and are obviously intended to fuel the chemically altered consciousness of the next generation of movie cultists.

But then there is the matter of the love relationship between the professor and his wife (Blair Brown), and it is here that we discover how powerful the attraction of love really is. During the professor's last experiment, when he is disappearing into a violent whirlpool of light and screams on the laboratory floor, it is his wife who wades into the celestial mists, gets up to her knees in eternity, reaches in, and pulls him out. And this is despite the fact that he has filed for divorce. The last scene is a killer, with the professor turning into the protoplasm of life itself, and his wife turning into a glowing shell of rock-like flesh, with her inner fires glowing through the crevices (the effect is something like an overheated Spiderman). They're going through the unspeakable hell of reliving the First Moment, and yet as the professor, as Man, bangs on the walls and crawls toward her, and she reaches out, and the universe rocks, the Man within him bursts out of the ape-protoplasm, and the Woman within her explodes back into flesh, and they collapse into each other's arms, and all the scene really needs at that point is for him to ask, "Was it as good for you as it was for me?"

Altered States is a superbly silly movie, a magnificent entertainment, and a clever and brilliant machine for making us feel awe, fear, and humor. That is enough. It's pure movie and very little meaning. Did I like it? Yeah, I guess I did, but I wouldn't advise trying to think about it very deeply.

Amadeus ★ ★ ★ ★

PG, 158 m., 1984

F. Murray Abraham (Salieri), Tom Hulce (Mozart), Elizabeth Berridge (Constanze), Simon Callow (Emanuel Schikaneder), Roy Dotrice (Leopold Mozart), Christine Ebersole (Katerina Cavalieri), Jeffrey Jones (Joseph II). Directed by Milos Forman and produced by Saul Zaentz. Screenplay by Peter Shaffer.

Milos Forman's *Amadeus* is one of the riskiest gambles a filmmaker has taken in a long time—a lavish movie about Mozart that dares to be anarchic and saucy, and yet still earns the importance of tragedy. This movie is nothing like the dreary educational portraits we're used to seeing about the Great Composers, who come across as cobwebbed profundities weighed down with the burden of genius. This is Mozart as an eighteenth-century Bruce Springsteen, and yet (here is the genius of the movie) there is nothing cheap or unworthy about the approach. *Amadeus* is not only about as much fun as you're likely to have with a movie, it also is disturbingly true. The truth enters in the character of Salieri, who tells the story. He is not a great composer, but he is a good enough composer to know greatness when he hears it, and that is why the music of Mozart breaks his heart. He knows how good it is, he sees how easily Mozart seems to compose it, and he knows that his own work looks pale and silly beside it.

The movie begins with the suggestion that Salieri might have murdered Mozart. The movie examines the ways in which this possibility might be true, and by the end of the film we feel a certain kinship with the weak and jealous Salieri—for few of us can identify with divine genius, but many of us probably have had dark moments of urgent self-contempt in the face of those whose effortless existence illustrates our own inadequacies. Salieri, played with burning intensity by F. Murray Abraham, sits hunched in a madhouse confessing to a priest. The movie flashes back to his memories of Wolfgang Amadeus Mozart, the child genius who composed melodies of startling originality and who grew up to become a prolific, driven artist.

One of the movie's wisest decisions is to cast Mozart not as a charismatic demigod, not as a tortured superman, but as a goofy, immature, likable kid with a ridiculous laugh. The character is played by Tom Hulce, and if you saw *Animal House*, you may remember him as the fraternity brother who tried to seduce the mayor's daughter, while an angel and a devil whispered in his ears. Hulce would seem all wrong for Mozart, but he is absolutely right, as an unaffected young man filled with delight at his own gifts, unaware of how easily he wounds Salieri and others, tortured only by the guilt of having offended his religious and domineering father.

The film is constructed in wonderfully well-written and acted scenes—scenes so carefully constructed, unfolding with such delight, that they play as perfect compositions of words. Most of them will be unfamiliar to those who have seen Peter Shaffer's brooding play, on which this film is based; Shaffer and Forman have brought light, life, and laughter to the material, and it plays with grace and ease. It's more human than the play; the characters are people, not throbbing packages of meaning. It centers on the relationships in Mozart's life: with his father, his wife, and Salieri. The father never can be pleased, and that creates an undercurrent affecting all of Mozart's success. The wife, played by delightful, buxom Elizabeth Berridge, contains in one person the qualities of a jolly wench and a loving partner: She likes to loll in bed all day, but also gives Mozart good, sound advice and is a forceful person in her own right. The patrons, especially Joseph II, the Austro-Hungarian emperor, are connoisseurs and dilettantes, slow to take to Mozart's new music but enchanted by the audacity with which he defends it. And then there is Salieri (F. Murray Abraham), the gaunt court composer whose special torture is to understand better than anybody else how inadequate he is, and how great Mozart is.

The movie was shot on location in Forman's native Czechoslovakia, and it looks exactly right; it fits its period comfortably, perhaps because Prague still contains so many streets and squares and buildings that could be directly from the Vienna of Mozart's day. Perhaps his confidence in his locations gave Forman the freedom to make Mozart slightly *out* of period. Forman directed the film version of *Hair*, and Mozart in this movie seems to share a spirit with some of the characters from *Hair*. Mozart's wigs do not look like everybody else's. They have just the slightest suggestion of punk, just the smallest shading of pink. Mozart seems more a child of the 1960's than of any other age, and this interpretation of his personality—he was an irreverent proto-hippie who trusted, if you will, his own vibes—sounds risky, but works.

I have not mentioned the music. There's probably no need to. The music provides the understructure of the film, strong, confident, above all, *clear* in a way that Salieri's simple muddles only serve to illustrate. There are times when Mozart speaks the words of a child, but then the music says the same things in the language of the gods, and all is clear.

Amadeus is a magnificent film, full and tender and funny and charming—and, at the end, sad and angry, too, because in the character of Salieri it has given us a way to understand not only greatness, but our own lack of it. This movie's fundamental question, I think, is whether we can learn to be grateful for the happiness of others, and that, of course, is a test for sainthood. How many movies ask such questions and succeed in being fun, as well?

Amarcord ★ ★ ★ ★

R, 127 m., 1974

Magali Noel (Gradisca), Bruno Zamin (Titta), Pupella Maggio (His Mother), Armando Drancia (His Father), Giuseppe Lanigro (His Grandfather), Nando Orfei (Pataca), Chiccio Ingrassia (Uncle Teo), Luigi Rossi (Lawyer). Directed by Federico Fellini and produced by Iranco Cristaldi. Screenplay by Fellini.

Federico Fellini's *Amarcord* takes us back to the small Italian town of his birth and young manhood, and gives us a joyful, bawdy, virtuoso portrait of the people he remembers there. He includes a character undoubtedly meant to be young Federico—earnest, awkward, yearning with all the poignancy of adolescent lust after the town beauties. But the movie's not an autobiography of a character. It's the story of the town itself.

We see it first when the dandelion seeds blow in from the fields, signaling the arrival of spring. The townspeople gather in the piazza to build a ceremonial bonfire and burn the witch of winter, and as they dance around the flames in one of Fellini's beloved processions, we get to know them.

They're of all sizes, sexes, and ages, but they're bound together by their transparent simplicity and a strain of cheerful vulgarity. Fellini likes their weaknesses as much as their virtues, and gives us the pompous lawyer, the egotistical theater owner (who cultivates a resemblance to Ronald Coleman), the buxom beautician Gradisca flaunting her delightful derriere and especially the lustful adolescents and their tormenting fantasies.

Fellini also gives us, in a much more subtle way, some notion of the way fascist Italy of the early 1930s helped to shape these people. In an authoritarian system, the individual has fewer choices to make, and there's a temptation to surrender the responsibilities of freedom. The townspeople are almost children in their behavior, taking delight in the simple joys of eating and making love and parading around the square and gossiping about each other and about the hypnotic Gradisca. Fellini implies that this simple behavior is nourished by a system that encourages a mindless going along—but

Amarcord isn't a political movie. It is a memory, fond but merciless, of how it was in Italy at a certain time.

It's also absolutely breathtaking filmmaking. Fellini has ranked for a long time among the five or six greatest directors in the world, and of them all, he's the natural. Bergman achieves his greatness through thought and soul-searching, Hitchcock built with meticulous craftsmanship, and Bunuel used his fetishes and fantasies to construct barbed jokes about humanity. But Fellini . . . well, moviemaking for him seems almost effortless, like breathing, and he can orchestrate the most complicated scenes with purity and ease. He's the Willie Mays of movies.

He did hit upon hard critical times, though. After the towering success of *La Dolce Vita* and *8½*, and such 1950s landmarks as *La Strada* and *I Vitelloni*, he began to indulge himself (his critics said). *Juliet of the Spirits* was too fantastical and structureless, and *Satyricon* was an exercise in excess, and *The Clowns* was really only a TV show, and *Fellini Roma* was episodic—a great director spinning out sequences that contained brilliance, yes, but no purpose or direction.

I couldn't agree with those criticisms. I find Fellini's magic spellbinding even when he's only marking time, as he was to some extent in *Roma*. But now, with *Amarcord*, Fellini returns to the very top of his form. And he has the last laugh on the critics of his "structureless" films. Because *Amarcord* seems at first to be a series of self-contained episodes and then reveals a structure so organic and yet so effortless that at its end, we can only marvel at this triumph over ordinary movie forms.

And we can marvel, too, at how universal *Amarcord* is. This is a movie for everybody, even those who hardly ever see foreign or "art" films. Fellini's greatest achievement, in my opinion, was *8½*. But that was a difficult film that revealed its meaning only after a good deal of thought and repeated viewings.

Amarcord, on the other hand, is a totally accessible film. It deals directly, hilariously, and sometimes poignantly with the good people of this small town (actually Fellini's birthplace, Rimini). It's no more complicated than they are, it understands them inside-out, and the audiences I've seen it with (three times) have been moved to horselaughs, stilled by moments of beauty, and then brought back almost to tears. It's not only a great movie, it's a great joy to see.

Someone once remarked that Fellini's movies are filled with symbols, but they're all obvious symbols. At the beginning of *La Dolce Vita*, for example, he wanted to symbolize the gulf between modern, decadent Rome and its history as the center of the Church, so he gave a statue of Christ being helicoptered by pilots who wave and whistle at girls sunning themselves in bikinis. The scene says everything it needs to say, openly and with great economy.

Amarcord is obvious in that way, with a showman's flair for the right effect. There is a night, for example, when all the people of the town get into their boats and sail out to wait for the great new Italian liner to pass by. And when it comes, it towers hundreds of feet above the waves and has thousands of portholes—and is, of course, only a prop built by the special-effects men. It drifts away into invisibility like a candle dying out. The image is of Italy itself in the 1930s: all grandeur and pomp and nationalism, but with an insubstantial soul.

The movie is filled with moments like that, and they're just right. But then there are moments of inexplicable, almost mystical beauty, as when the dandelion seeds drift in on the wind, or when an old lady sweeps up the ashes of the bonfire, or when a peacock spreads its tail feathers in the snow. At moments like that we're almost blinded with delight. Hitchcock once said he wanted to play his audiences like a piano. Fellini requires the entire orchestra.

American Flyers ★ ★ ½
PG-13, 113 m., 1985

Kevin Costner (Marcus), David Grant (David), Rae Dawn Chong (Sarah), Alexandra Paul (Becky), Janice Rule (Mrs. Sommers), John Amos (Dr. Conrad), Doi Johnson (Randolph), Luca Bercovici (Muzzin). Directed by John Badham and produced by Gareth Wigan and Paula Weinstein. Screenplay by Steve Tesich.

American Flyers tells the story of a grueling bicycle race named "The Hell of the West" and of the grueling relationships within a sick family. That is apparently too much for the movie to deal with, and so we get a bike race surrounded by giant unanswered questions. This is one of those stories timed so that all of the personal crises come to a climax at the finish line, and maybe the approach would work if there weren't so many enormous inconsistencies and loose ends and puzzlements.

The movie stars David Grant as an eighteen-year-old in St. Louis who trains on his bicycle every day, hoping someday to be as good a racer as his older brother. Kevin Costner is the big brother, a doctor in Madison, and Janice Rule is their mother. A painful dinner scene at the beginning of the movie sets up the conflict in the family, caused because the father died painfully and the mother apparently did nothing during his last two weeks on earth to make his passing less painful. The movie never spells out what she didn't do, but that's only the first of many mysteries.

The father died of a stroke from a weakened blood vessel in the brain. Now Costner fears that Grant may have the same condition. He takes him to Madison and runs him through a series of tests, which do indeed indicate the family condition. Then he decides not to tell him, and the two brothers set out by van to compete in the Hell of the West race, in Colorado. Meanwhile, we meet Costner's girlfriend (Rae Dawn Chong), and along the way they pick up a hitchhiker (Alexandra Paul) who pairs off with Grant.

The race then becomes several showdowns. The brothers must compete against the other racers, and also against the shadow of death. Their main competition comes from a mean SOB named Muzzin (Luca Bercovici), who used to be married to Rae Dawn Chong. The race is run in three stages, and in the second stage, the older brother begins to bleed from the nose and lose his orientation. So then it's up to the kid brother to win the race.

That leaves us with certain problems.

1. Does the older brother have the family condition, or only a nosebleed? I ask because after the frightening scene where he loses control and almost dies, he is taken, not to a hospital, but to his hotel room.

2. Is Muzzin as mean as he seems? I ask because he is cruel to Chong prior to the race and threatens to make her boyfriend "bleed." Then, after Costner's illness, he is tender toward Chong and she is sweet toward him. Then he tries to kill Grant.

3. What's with the mother? Since we never know what she did, or didn't, do during her husband's last weeks, we don't know how to read her. But she turns up for the finish of the race, and there is a reconciliation which is happy or not, depending on issues we don't understand.

Against these large and troubling matters, which probably indicate that many key scenes were cut from the movie, there are several good things to consider. The bicycle race is brilliantly photographed, and very exciting, despite the fact that we can easily guess who will win. The performances are all interesting, especially Rae Dawn Chong's sweet patience as the girlfriend. There are some great supporting characters, including John Amos as Grant's trainer and Doi Johnson as his chubby teen-age son who hates to exercise and dreams of being the first black bowling star. But the movie is shaky at the core, because it tries to tap-dance around its own central issues.

American Gigolo ★ ★ ★ ½

R, 117 m., 1980

Richard Gere (Julian), Lauren Hutton (Michelle), Hector Elizondo (Sunday), Nina Van Pallandt (Anne), Bill Duke (Leon Jaimes), Brian Davies (Stratton). Directed by Paul Schrader and produced by Jerry Bruckheimer. Screenplay by Schrader.

The bare outline of its plot makes *American Gigolo* sound like a fairly sleazy package: A Hollywood male prostitute is framed in a kinky murder case, tracks down the pimp who's responsible for the framing, watches in horror as the pimp himself is killed, and then finds himself faced with prison unless the wife of a senator provides him with an alibi. This is strong stuff—almost sensational enough for daytime soap opera.

But the film *American Gigolo* is a stylish and surprisingly poignant handling of this material. The experiences in the film may be alien to us, but the emotions of the characters are not: Julian Kay, the gigolo of the title, is played by Richard Gere as tender, vulnerable, and a little dumb. We care about him. His business—making love to rich women of a certain age—allows him to buy the baubles by which Beverly Hills measures success, and he has his Mercedes, his expensive wardrobe, his antique vases, his entrée to country clubs.

But he says he's in business for reasons other than money, and we believe him, if only because he hardly seems to value his possessions as anything other than props. He feels a sense of satisfaction when he makes a middle-aged woman happy, he says. He seems to see himself as a cross between a sexual surrogate and a therapist, and the movie does, too: Why, he's hardly a whore at all, not even counting his heart of gold.

The movie sentimentalizes on this point, setting up the character of Julian Kay as so sympathetic that we forgive him his profession. That's a tactic that *American Gigolo*'s writer and director, Paul Schrader, is borrowing from one of his own heroes, the French director Robert Bresson, whose *Pickpocket* makes a criminal into an antihero. Schrader is setting the stage for the key relationship in the film, between Julian and the senator's wife (Lauren Hutton).

He tries to pick her up in an exclusive restaurant, but breaks off their conversation when he decides she's not a likely client. But she is all *too* likely, and tracks him down to his apartment. They fall in love, at about the time he's being framed for the murder of a Palm Springs socialite, and the movie wants us to believe in the power of love to redeem both characters: Julian learns to love unselfishly, without money, and the woman learns to love honestly, without regard for her husband's position.

This business of redemption would work better if *American Gigolo* had at least a few more scenes developing the relationship between Gere and Hutton: Her character, so central to the movie's upbeat conclusion, isn't seen clearly enough. We aren't shown the steps by which she moves from sex to love with him (unless she's simply been won over by the old earth-shaking orgasm ploy). We aren't given enough detail about their feelings.

That's a weakness, but not a fatal one, because when Schrader cuts away from their relationship, it's to develop a very involving story about the murder, the framing, and the police investigation. The movie has an especially effective performance by Hector Elizondo as a cigar-chomping vice detective who cheerfully admits he thinks Gere is guilty as sin.

Gere tries to find out who's framing him by descending into the Los Angeles sexual underground. Schrader explored this same universe in his previous film, *Hardcore*, but this time he seems more restrained: The sexual netherlands seem less lurid, more commonplace and sad.

The whole movie has a winning sadness about it; take away the story's sensational aspects and what you have is a study in loneliness. Richard Gere's performance is central to that effect, and some of his scenes—reading the morning paper, rearranging some paintings, selecting a wardrobe—underline the emptiness of his life. We leave *American Gigolo* with the curious feeling that if women weren't paying this man to sleep with them, he'd be paying them: He needs the human connection and he has a certain shyness, a loner quality, that makes it easier for him when love seems to be just another deal.

American Graffiti ★ ★ ★ ★

PG, 112 m., 1973

Ron Howard (Steve), Cindy Williams (Laurie), Richard Dreyfuss (Curt), Paul Le Mat (John), Mackenzie Phillips (Carol), Charles Martin Smith (Terry), Candy Clark (Debbie), Wolfman Jack (Disc Jockey). Directed by George Lucas and produced by Francis Ford Coppola. Screenplay by Lucas, Gloria Katz, and Willard Huyck.

My first car was a '54 Ford and I bought it for $435. It wasn't scooped, channeled, shaved, decked, pinstriped, or chopped, and it didn't have duals, but its hubcaps were a wonder to behold.

On weekends my friends and I drove around downtown Urbana—past the Princess Theater, past the courthouse—sometimes stopping for a dance at the youth center or a hamburger at the Steak 'n' Shake ("In Sight, It Must Be Right"). And always we listened to Dick Biondi on WLS. Only two years earlier, WLS had been the Prairie Farmer Station; now it was the voice of rock all over the Midwest.

When I went to see George Lucas's *American Graffiti* that whole world—a world that now seems incomparably distant and innocent—was brought back with a rush of feeling that wasn't so much nostalgia as culture shock. Remembering my high school generation, I can only wonder at how unprepared we were for the loss of innocence that took place in America with the series of hammer blows beginning with the assassination of President Kennedy.

The great divide was November 22, 1963, and nothing was ever the same again. The teen-agers in *American Graffiti* are, in a sense, like that cartoon character in the magazine ads: the one who gives the name of his insurance company, unaware that an avalanche is about to land on him. The options seemed so simple then: to go to college, or to stay home and look for a job and cruise Main Street and make the scene.

The options were simple, and so was the music that formed so much of the way we saw ourselves. *American Graffiti*'s sound track is papered from one end to the other with Wolfman Jack's nonstop disc jockey show, that's crucial and absolutely right. The radio was on every waking moment. A character in the movie only realizes his car, parked nearby, has been stolen when he hears the music stop: He didn't hear the car being driven away.

The music was as innocent as the time. Songs like "Sixteen Candles" and "Gonna Find Her" and "The Book of Love" sound touchingly naive today; nothing prepared us for the decadence and the aggression of rock only a handful of years later. The Rolling Stones of 1972 would have blown WLS off the air in 1962.

American Graffiti acts almost as a milestone to show us how far (and in many cases how tragically) we have come. Stanley Kauffmann, who liked it, complained in the *New Republic* that Lucas had made a film more fascinating to the generation now between thirty and forty than it could be for other generations, older or younger.

But it isn't the age of the characters that matters; it's the time they inhabited. Whole cultures and societies have passed since 1962. *American Graffiti* is not only a great movie but a brilliant work of historical fiction; no sociological treatise could duplicate the movie's success in remembering exactly how it was to be alive at that cultural instant.

On the surface, Lucas has made a film that seems almost artless; his teen-agers cruise Main Street and stop at Mel's Drive-In and listen to Wolfman Jack on the radio and neck and lay rubber and almost convince themselves their moment will last forever. But the film's buried structure shows an innocence in the process of being lost, and as its symbol Lucas provides the elusive blond in the white Thunderbird—the vision of beauty always glimpsed at the next intersection, the end of the next street.

Who is she? And did she really whisper "I love you" at the last traffic signal? In *8½*, Fellini used Claudia Cardinale as his mysterious angel in white, and the image remains one of his best; but George Lucas knows that for one brief afternoon of American history angels drove Thunderbirds and could possibly be found at Mel's Drive-In tonight . . . or maybe tomorrow night, or the night after.

An American Werewolf in London ★ ★

R, 95 m., 1981

David Naughton (David), Griffin Dunne (Jack), Jenny Agutter (Alex), John Woodvine (Dr. Hirsch). Directed by John Landis and produced by George Folsey, Jr. Screenplay by Landis.

An American Werewolf in London seems curiously unfinished, as if director John Landis spent all his energy on spectacular set-pieces and then didn't want to bother with things like transitions, character development, or an ending. The movie has sequences that are spellbinding, and then long stretches when nobody seem sure what's going on. There are times when the special effects almost wipe the characters off the screen. It's weird. It's not a very good film, and it falls well below Landis's work in the anarchic *National Lampoon's Animal House* and the rambunctious *Blues Brothers*. Landis never seems very sure whether he's making a comedy or a horror film, so he winds up with genuinely funny moments acting as counterpoint to the gruesome undead. Combining horror and comedy is an old tradition (my favorite example is *The Bride of Frankenstein*), but the laughs and the blood co-exist very uneasily in this film.

One of the offscreen stars of the film is Rick Baker, the young makeup genius who created the movie's wounds, gore, and werewolves. His work is impressive, yes, but unless you're single-mindedly interested in special effects, *American Werewolf* is a disappointment. And even the special effects, good as they are, come as an anticlimax if you're a *really* dedicated horror fan, because if you are, you've already seen this movie's high point before: the onscreen transformation of a man into a werewolf was anticipated in *The Howling*, in which the special effects were done by a Baker protegé named Rob Bottin.

The movie's plot involves two young American students (David Naughton and Griffin Dunne), who are backpacking across the English moors. They stumble into a country pub where everyone is ominously silent, and then one guy warns them to beware the full moon and stick to the road. They don't, and are attacked by werewolves. Dunne is killed, Naughton is severely wounded, and a few days later in the hospital Naughton is visited by the decaying cadaver of Dunne—who warns him that he'll turn into a werewolf at the full moon. Naughton ignores the warning, falls in love with his nurse (Jenny Agutter), and moves in with her when he's discharged from the hospital. Then follows a series of increasingly gruesome walk-ons by Dunne, who begs Naughton to kill himself before the full moon. Naughton doesn't, turns into a werewolf, and runs amok through London. That gives director Landis his chance to stage a spectacular multi-car traffic accident in Piccadilly Circus; crashes have been his specialty since the homecoming parade in *Animal House* and the nonstop carnage in *Blues Brothers*.

The best moments in *American Werewolf* probably belong to Dunne, who may be a decaying cadaver but keeps right on talking like a college student: "Believe me," he says at Naughton's bedside, "this isn't a whole lot of fun." The scene in which Naughton turns into a werewolf is well done, with his hands elongating and growing claws, and his face twisting into a snout and fangs. But it's as if John Landis thought the technology would be enough. We never get a real feeling for the characters, we never really believe the places (especially that awkwardly phony pub and its stagy customers), and we are particularly disappointed by the ending. I won't reveal the ending, such as it is, except to say it's so sudden, arbitrary, and anticlimactic that, although we are willing for the movie to be over, we still can't quite believe it.

Angel Heart ★ ★ ★ ½

R, 113 m., 1987

Mickey Rourke (Harry Angel), Robert De Niro (Louis Cyphre), Lisa Bonet (Epiphany Proudfoot), Charlotte Rampling (Margaret Krusemark), Brownie McGhee (Toots Sweet), Stocker Fontelieu (Ethan Krusemark). Directed by Alan Parker and produced by Alan Marshall and Elliott Kastner. Screenplay by Parker.

After everything is all over and the dust has settled and the blood has dried, it is possible to unsort the plot of *Angel Heart* and see that it's really fairly simple. But it doesn't feel that way at the time. It has the unsettled logic of a nightmare, in which nothing fits and everything seems inevitable and there are a lot of arrows in the air and they are all flying straight at you.

The movie stars Mickey Rourke as Harry Angel, an unwashed private eye who works out of an office that looks like Sam Spade gave it to the Goodwill. He gets a call to visit some kind of devil-worship cult in Harlem, where a strange man wants to talk to him. The man's name is Louis Cyphre (Robert De Niro), and he wants Angel to track down a missing person for him. Angel takes the case for five grand and follows a trail that is littered with stale leads and fresh corpses.

This sounds like a million other private eye movies, and, in a way, it is. A few things make it different: a sly sense of humor, good acting and directing, and a sudden descent into the supernatural as Harry Angel discovers the horrifying true nature of his investigation.

The movie is by Alan Parker, a director who has vowed to work in every genre before he dies. After *Angel Heart*, he can cross two off his list: private eye movies and supernatural horror films. Parker's films are always made with great gusto, as if he were in up to his elbows and taking no hostages.

He enjoys what timid folks might call stylistic excess, and that's what got him in trouble with the MPAA ratings board over a scene involving Rourke and Lisa Bonet, who plays a young Louisiana woman who holds the secrets of the past. They meet in a leaky hotel room during a rainstorm, and while they make love the raindrops from the ceiling turn to blood. In the context of the movie, the blood makes perfect sense, although the scene had to be trimmed to qualify the movie for an R rating.

The scene is consistent with the whole film, which is sensuous and depraved. The De Niro character sets the tone, with his sharp, pointed fingernails and his elegant black suits. De Niro must have had fun preparing for the character: He uses a neatly trimmed black beard, slicked-back hair, and tricks of lighting and makeup to make himself look uncannily like Martin Scorsese, his favorite director. Given what we eventually discover about the character, it's a wicked homage.

Rourke occupies the center of the film like a violent unmade bed. No other actor, with the possible exception of France's Gerard Depardieu, has made such a career out of being a slob. He looks unshaven, unwashed, hungover, and desperate, and that's at the beginning of the film, before things start to go wrong. By the end, he is a man whose nerves are screaming for help.

His odyssey in *Angel Heart* takes him from New York to Algiers, Louisiana, a town across from New Orleans that makes the fleshpots of Bourbon Street look like Disneyland. He is advised to go back home by a crusty old blues player (played by the fast-talking Brownie McGhee in a performance that proves Dexter Gordon isn't the only old musician who can act). But he doesn't listen and gets drawn deeper into bayou country, where he spies on the forbidden rituals of a voodoo cult.

Bonet is the priestess of the cult and plays the role with an abandoned sexuality that you wouldn't have expected after watching her on the "Cosby Show." She was probably right to take this controversial role as her movie debut; it's such a stretch from the Cosby character that it establishes her as a plausible movie actress.

The movie's final revelations make a weird sense, once we figure them out. This is one of those movies where you rerun the plot in your head, re-interpreting the early scenes in terms of the final shocking revelations. *Angel Heart* is a thriller and a horror movie, but most of all it's an exuberant exercise in style, in which Parker and his actors have fun taking it to the limit.

Angelo My Love ★ ★ ★ ½

R, 91 m., 1983

Angelo Evans, Michael Evans, Steve Tsigonoff, Millie Tsigonoff. Written and directed by Robert Duvall. Associate producer, Gail Youngs.

The late Italian director Vittoria De Sica once said that anyone can play at least one role—himself—better than anybody else possibly could. De Sica illustrated that belief in his late-1940s neo-realist films like *Bicycle Thief,* and now the American actor Robert Duvall proves it again, in a wonderful and unique movie he has written and directed, named *Angelo My Love.* Here is a movie that could not exist without the people who are in it—and of how many movies is that true? The film is about the lives, feuds, rivalries, and dreams of a group of New York Gypsies, and Duvall has recruited real Gypsies to play themselves. His inspiration for the movie came when he saw a young Gypsy boy named Angelo Evans conning a much older woman during an argument on a Manhattan sidewalk.

Duvall thought Angelo belonged in the movies. Having seen the movie, I agree. Here is a street-smart, inventive kid of about eleven or twelve who has some of the moves and some of the cynicism of an experienced con man. ("He's got his tiny macho moves down so pat," David Anson wrote in *Newsweek,* "he's like a child impersonator.") Angelo is the product of a culture that has taught him that the world owes him a living, and he cheerfully agrees. What we sometimes almost forget is that Angelo is also a child, vulnerable and easily wounded, and that a lot of his act is a veneer.

Duvall weaves his story around Angelo. We meet his mother, father, sister, and girlfriend, and a couple of villainous Gypsies who steal a ring that Angelo had intended to present to his future bride. All of these people play themselves, more or less. Angelo's family really is his family; the villains are played by a brother and sister, Steve and Millie Tsigonoff, whom Duvall met in Los Angeles. Although the movie's plot is basically a device for letting us watch the lives of the characters, it's the kind of plot, I suspect, that Gypsies might be able to identify with—involving theft, pride, thwarted justice, and revenge. After the Tsigonoffs steal the ring, there's an ill-advised chase to Canada to get it back (and a wonderful set-piece in a Gypsy camp supposedly under attack by ghosts). Then there's a trial scene in the backroom of an Irish-American bar in Brooklyn. It's all done with great energy and seriousness, even though by the movie's end the ring hardly seems to matter.

Angelo also stars in several fairly self-contained scenes that abundantly illustrate why Duvall found him so fascinating. He makes a defiant mess of his one day in school. He attempts to pick up a pretty country singer who is at least ten years older than he is. He and his sister engage in a long, ingratiating conversation with an old lady in a cafeteria; they want to inveigle her into their mother's fortune-telling parlor, but the lady is a New Yorker and wasn't born yesterday.

All of these scenes have a special magic because we sense that they're real, that they come out of people's lives. *Angelo My Love* is technically a fictional film, but Duvall has worked so close to his sources that it has the conviction of a documentary. Maybe because he's such a good actor, Duvall has been able to listen to his characters, to really see *them* rather than his own notion of how they should move and behave. There are moments in this movie when the camera lingers for an extra moment, and scenes that do not quite dovetail into everything else, and we sense that Duvall left them in because they revealed something about his Gypsies that he had observed and wanted to share.

At the end of the movie we ask ourselves a question the movie does not attempt to answer: What will become of Angelo in the years to come? It's one thing to be a cute, street-wise kid. It's another thing to try to carry that role on through life with you. Angelo might be able to pull it off, but the movie doesn't try to sell us that romanticized hope. Instead, Duvall seems to be suggesting that Angelo is more than a colorful Gypsy kid; that he has real potential as a person, if he can grow out of the trd his glib mannerisms and is not too badly scarred by his upside-down childhood. Who knows? One day ten years from now, there might be a movie named *Angelo My Friend.*

Annie ★ ★ ★

PG, 128 m., 1982

Aileen Quinn (Annie), Albert Finney (Daddy Warbucks), Carol Burnett (Miss Hannigan), Bernadette Peters (Lily), Ann Reinking (Grace Farrell), Tim Curry (Rooster), Geoffrey Holder (Punjab), Edward Herrmann (F.D.R.). Directed by John Huston and produced by Ray Stark. Screenplay by Carol Sobieski.

In the abstract, *Annie* is fun. It has lots of movement and color, dance and music, sound and fury. In the particular, it has all sorts of problems, and I guess the only way to really enjoy the movie is to just ignore the particulars. I will nevertheless mention a few particulars. One is the story itself, about how Little Orphan Annie is rescued from a cruel orphanage by a billionaire who wants a Rent-An-Orphan for Christmas. This is said to be a universal story. Critics have written that you just can't help cheering for Annie as she faces the cold world with pluck and courage. I didn't find myself cheering much, though, since Annie didn't seem to need the encouragement; as played by the feisty young Aileen Quinn, she is the sort of child who makes adults run for the hills.

The adventures she gets herself into are likewise questionable. I've never thought of *Oliver!* as a particularly realistic musical, but at least when its little hero said "Please, sir, more food?" there was a hint of truth. *Annie* has been plunged into pure fantasy, into the mindless sort of musical boosterism that plays big for Broadway theater parties but almost always translates to the movie screen as sheer contrivance. *Annie* is not *about* anything. It *contains* lots of subjects (such as cruel orphanages, the Great Depression, scheming conmen, heartless billionaires, and President Franklin Delano Roosevelt) but it isn't *about* them. It's not even really about whether Annie will survive her encounters with them, since the book of this musical is so rigorously machine-made, so relentlessly formula, it's one of those movies where you can amaze your friends by leaving the auditorium, standing blindfolded in the lobby and correctly predicting the outcome.

And yet I sort of enjoyed the movie. I enjoyed the energy that was visible on the screen, and the sumptuousness of the production numbers, and the good humor of several of the performances—especially those by Albert Finney, as Daddy Warbucks, and Carol Burnett, as the wicked orphanage supervisor, Miss Hannigan. Aileen Quinn sort of grew on me, too. She cannot be said to really play a child—at least not the sort of plausible flesh-and-blood child that Henry Thomas creates in *E.T.* But Quinn is talented, can dance well and sing passably, and does not seem to be an overtrained puppet like, say, Ricky Schroeder. She seems more like the kind of kid who will get this acting out of her system and go on to be student body president.

If there is a center to the film, it belongs to Albert Finney. He has a thankless task: He must portray Daddy Warbucks as a self-centered, smug rich man who has everything in the world, except love, and who learns to love through the example of a little girl. This is the sort of role actors kill over—to avoid playing. Albert Finney has the true grit. He's gone through this personality transformation twice; he starred in *Scrooge* in 1970. This time, he even pulls it off, by underplaying. He isn't too aloof at the beginning, and he's not too softhearted at the end. He has a certain detachment. Annie may win his heart, but she'll still have to phone for an appointment.

Will kids like the movie? I honestly don't know. When I was a kid, I didn't much like movies about other kids, maybe because I was jealous (why does *that* kid get to ride a horse in the Derby?). The movie was promoted as a family entertainment, but was it really a family musical, even on the stage? I dunno. I think it was more of a product, a clever concoction of nostalgia, hard-sell sentiment, small children, and cute dogs. The movie is the same mixture as before. It's like some kind of dumb toy that doesn't do anything or go anywhere, but it is fun to watch as it spins mindlessly around and around.

Annie Hall ★ ★ ★ ½

PG, 95 m., 1977

Woody Allen (Alvy Singer), Diane Keaton (Annie Hall), Tony Roberts (Rob), Carol Kane (Allison), Paul Simon (Tony Lacey), Shelley Duvall (Pam), Janet Margolin (Robin), Colleen Dewhurst (Mom Hall). Directed by Woody Allen and produced by Charles H. Joffe. Screenplay by Allen and Marshall Brickman.

Woody Allen's *Annie Hall* explores new dimensions of the persona Allen has constructed in movies, on the stage, and even in a comic strip. We're all familiar by now with "Woody," the overanxious, underachieving intellectual with the inept social life. We've watched him develop from bits in a stand-up comedy routine to a fully developed comic character in the tradition of Chaplin's tramp or Fields's drunk. We know how "Woody" will act in so many situations that we're already laughing before the punch line. Maybe nobody since Jack Benny has been so hilariously predictable.

And yet there's always the realization that "Woody" is a projection of a real Woody Allen. That beneath the comic character is a certain amount of painful truth. That just as W.C. Fields really *was* a drunk, so Woody Allen perhaps really is insecure about his height, shy around girls, routinely incompetent in the daily joust with life.

It's not that the "real" Woody Allen is as hapless as his fictional creation, but that the character draws from life by exaggerating it. *Annie Hall* is the closest Allen has come to dealing with that real material. It's not an autobiography, but we get the notion at times that scenes in the movie have been played before, slightly differently, for real.

Allen plays Alvy Singer, stand-up comic and incurable combination of neurotic and romantic. He's self-consciously a New Yorker, a liberal, a Jew, an intellectual, a seeker after the unattainable, and an expert at *making* it unattainable. One of Alvy Singer's problems is that he understands this all so well. He's not a victim of forces beyond his control, but their author.

And one of the problems he keeps providing for himself is the problem of love. He falls in love too easily, to girls who are right for him in all the little ways and incompatible in all the big ones. His girls tend to reflect the stages he's going through. When he's an Adlai Stevenson liberal in the late 1950s, he marries another one. When he's a romantic ten or fifteen years later, he finds another one, a kookier one. His only trouble is that women are people, not stages.

The movie dares to go into this material a little more seriously and cohesively than is usually the case in an Allen film. *Annie Hall* is a comedy, yes, and there are moments in it as funny as anything Woody has done, but the movie represents a growth on Allen's part. From a filmmaker who would do anything for a laugh, whose primary mission seemed to be to get through the next five minutes, Allen has developed in *Sleeper, Love and Death,* and this film into a much more thoughtful and (is it possible?) more mature director.

Maybe that's why *Annie Hall* is called a "nervous romance": because Allen himself is a little nervous about this frankly nostalgic, romantic, and sentimental material. He throws in a few gags (like the hilarious walk-on by Marshall McLuhan) almost to reassure his old fans that all's well at the laugh works. But he wants to do a lot more this time than just keep us laughing. By looking into some of his own relationships, some of his own patterns, he wants to examine how a personality works.

And so there are two Woody Allens here: Our old pal the original Woody, who's given to making asides directly into the camera, and a new Allen who creates Alvy Singer in his own image and then allows him to behave consistently, even sometimes at the cost of laughs. It's this new Woody who has the nervous romance, the complicated relationship with the would-be nightclub singer Annie Hall (played by Diane Keaton with an interesting mixture of maternal care, genuine love, and absolute craziness).

At the end of the affair, we've learned only two things for certain: That enduring relationships are very likely impossible in this time and place (i.e., New York City during Woody Allen's lifetime), and that life without the search for relationships is unthinkable. In the movie, Woody quotes Groucho Marx's statement that he'd never belong to any club that would accept someone like him as a member. Then Allen muses that maybe he should never get into a relationship in which one of the partners is himself. Tricky, isn't it? And in *Annie Hall* he makes it very funny, and sad, and tricky indeed.

Apocalypse Now ★ ★ ★ ★
R, 139 m., 1979

Marlon Brando (Colonel Kurtz), Robert Duvall (Lieutenant Colonel Kilgore), Martin Sheen (Captain Willard), Frederic Forrest (Chef), Albert Hall (Chief), Sam Bottoms (Lance), Larry Fishburne (Clean), Dennis Hopper (Photographer). Directed and produced by Francis Ford Coppola. Screenplay by John Milius and Coppola.

In his book *The Films of My Life,* the French director François Truffaut makes a curious statement. He used to believe, he says, that a successful film had to simultaneously express "an idea of the world and an idea of cinema." But now, he writes: "I demand that a film express either the joy of making cinema or the agony of making cinema. I am not at all interested in anything in between; I am not interested in all those films that do not pulse."

It may seem strange to begin a review of Francis Coppola's *Apocalypse Now* with those words, but consider them for a moment and they apply perfectly to this sprawling film. The critics who have rejected Coppola's film have mostly done so on Truffaut's earlier grounds: They have arguments with the ideas about the world and the war in *Apocalypse Now,* or they disagree with the very idea of a film that cost $31 million to make and was then carted all over the world by a filmmaker *still* uncertain whether he had the right ending.

That "other" film on the screen—the one we debate because of its ideas, not its images—is the one that caused so much controversy about *Apocalypse Now.* We have all read that Coppola took as his inspiration the Joseph Conrad novel *Heart of Darkness,* and that he turned Conrad's journey up the Congo into a metaphor for another journey up a jungle river, into the heart of the Vietnam War. We've all read Coppola's grandiose statements (the most memorable: "This isn't a film about Vietnam. This film *is* Vietnam."). We've heard that Marlon Brando was paid $1 million for his closing scenes, and that Coppola gambled his personal fortune to finish the film, and, heaven help us, we've even read a journal by the director's wife in which she discloses her husband's ravings and infidelities.

But all such considerations are far from the reasons why *Apocalypse Now* is a good and important film—a masterpiece, I believe. Now, when Coppola's budget and his problems have long been forgotten, *Apocalypse* stands, I think, as a grand and grave and insanely inspired gesture of filmmaking—of moments that are operatic in their style and scope, and of other moments so silent we can almost hear the director thinking to himself.

I should at this moment make a confession: I am not particularly interested in the "ideas" in Coppola's film. Critics of *Apocalypse* have said that Coppola was foolish to translate *Heart of Darkness,* that Conrad's vision had nothing to do with Vietnam, and that Coppola was simply borrowing Conrad's cultural respectability to give a gloss to his own disorganized ideas. The same objection was made to the hiring of Brando: Coppola was hoping, according to this version, that the presence of Brando as an icon would distract us from the emptiness of what he's given to say.

Such criticisms are made by people who indeed are plumbing *Apocalypse Now* for its ideas, and who are as misguided as the veteran Vietnam correspondents who breathlessly reported that *The Deer Hunter* was not "accurate." What idea or philosophy could we expect to find in *Apocalypse Now*—and what good would it really do, at this point after the Vietnam tragedy, if Brando's closing speeches *did* have the "answers"? Like all great works of art about war, *Apocalypse Now* essentially contains only one idea or message, the not-especially-enlightening observation that war is hell. We do not see Coppola's movie for that insight—something Coppola, but not some of his critics, knows well.

Coppola also well knows (and demonstrated in the *Godfather* films) that movies aren't especially good at dealing with abstract ideas—for those you'd be better off turning to the written word—but they *are* superb for presenting moods and feelings, the look of a battle, the expression on a face, the mood of a country. *Apocalypse Now* achieves greatness not by analyzing our "experience in Vietnam," but by re-creating, in characters and images, something of that experience.

An example: The scene in which Robert Duvall, as a crazed lieutenant colonel, leads his troops in a helicopter assault on a village is, quite simply, the best movie battle scene ever filmed. It's simultaneously numbing, depressing, and exhilarating: As the rockets jar from the helicopters and spring through the air, we're elated like kids for a half-second, until the reality of the consequences sinks in. Another wrenching scene—in which the crew of Martin Sheen's U.S. Army gunboat massacres the Vietnamese peasants in a small boat—happens with such sudden, fierce, senseless violence that it forces us to understand for the first time how such things could happen.

Coppola's *Apocalypse Now* is filled with moments like that, and the narrative device of the journey upriver is as convenient for him as it was for Conrad. That's really why he uses it, and not because of literary cross-references for graduate students to catalog. He takes the journey, strings episodes along it, leads us at last to Brando's awesome, stinking hideaway . . . and then finds, so we've all heard, that he doesn't have an ending. Well, Coppola *doesn't* have an ending, if we or he expected the closing scenes to pull everything together and make sense of it. Nobody should have been surprised. *Apocalypse Now* doesn't tell any kind of a conventional story, doesn't have a thought-out message for us about Vietnam, has no answers, and thus needs no ending. The way the film ends now, with Brando's fuzzy, brooding monologues and the final violence, feels much more satisfactory than any conventional ending possibly could.

What's great in the film, and what will make it live for many years and speak to many audiences, is what Coppola achieves on the levels Truffaut was discussing: the moments of agony and joy in making cinema. Some of those moments come at the same time; remember again the helicopter assault and its unsettlng juxtaposition of horror and exhilaration. Remember the weird beauty of the massed helicopters lifting over the trees in the long shot, and the insane power of Wagner's music, played loudly during the attack, and you feel what Coppola was getting at: Those moments as common in life as art, when the whole huge grand mystery of the world, so terrible, so beautiful, seems to hang in the balance.

The Apprenticeship of Duddy Kravitz

★ ★ ★

PG, 121 m., 1974

Richard Dreyfuss (Duddy), Micheline Lanctot (Yvette), Jack Warden (Max), Randy Quaid (Virgil), Joseph Wiseman (Uncle Benjy), Denholm Elliott (Friar), Henry Ramar (Dingleman), Joe Silver (Farber). Directed by

Ted Kotcheff and produced by John Kemeny. Screenplay by Mordecai Richler.

Duddy Kravitz has grown up hearing about the Boy Wonder. The Wonder, real name Dingleman, started out in life picking up bus transfers from the street and selling them for three cents. When he had a quarter, he got into a gin game and ran it up to ten dollars. With that as a nest egg, the Wonder parlayed a string of poker games and fly-by-night investments into a fortune, and returned home (according to legend) in a chauffeured limousine and with his own string of racehorses. And all from a handful of lousy three-cent bus transfers!

Duddy thinks he can do better than that. When we meet him, he's a sixteen-year-old Jewish kid from Montreal whose mother is dead and whose father drives a cab and does a little part-time pimping to send the older son through medical school. The Boy Wonder was a boyhood friend of Duddy's father; the story, whether true or not, has been told so many times that Duddy naturally assumes he will be a millionaire, or something, by the time he's twenty. And he's right. By the time he's twenty, he's something.

The Apprenticeship of Duddy Kravitz is a movie that somehow manages to be breakneck and curiously touching at the same time. It's a story of ambition and greed, with a hero that will stop at almost nothing (by the movie's end, Duddy has succeeded in alienating the girl who loves him, has lost all his friends, has brought his grandfather to despair, and has paralyzed his most loyal employee). And yet we like Duddy, with a kind of exasperation, because we get some notion of the hungers that drive him, and because nobody suffers at his hands more than he does himself.

The movie's a sort of Canadian *What Makes Sammy Run?* Duddy Kravitz even gets into the movie business, as Budd Schulberg's hero did. But Duddy doesn't exactly get to Hollywood. He runs across a blacklisted, alcoholic American director, in exile from Hollywood during the dark days of McCarthyism (the film is set somewhere in the late 1940s and early 1950s).

Duddy forms a movie production company (Dudley Kane Productions, inevitably), hires the director, and produces films of bar mitzvahs. Their first production, shown in its entirety, is a lunatic montage of off-the-wall images that have no perceptible relevance to the bar mitzvah itself; the director arguably got himself drunk and spliced together stock footage (after the opening temple scenes played over Beethoven's Fifth). But Duddy's client is (somewhat dazedly) pleased by the film, and Duddy is off and running.

His ambition is to own land. "A man without land is a nobody," his grandfather has told him. During a summer spent as a waiter at a resort, he finds a beautiful, half-hidden lake. He determines to buy it and develop it, and his dream is shared by a plain-pretty French Canadian girl who is a maid at the resort. They fall into love. Or, more precisely, she loves him and Duddy loves a prospect of his future life which includes her, slightly to one side of center. The ways in which he finally succeeds in driving her away, the ways in which he makes himself miserable before he is even twenty-one, are played against his own series of get-rich-fast schemes (during which he not only succeeds in meeting the real Boy Wonder but even unknowingly smuggles heroin over the border for him).

The movie is based on a Mordecai Richler novel and was the most popular film to have come out of Canada through the early seventies (that country which, in cinema as in other things, remains more foreign for many Americans than any place in Europe). It was filmed on location with a great sense of life and energy and with details seen as Duddy sees them. It's populated with an incredible gallery of character roles (I've only suggested a few of them). It's a little too sloppy, and occasionally too obvious, to qualify as a great film, but it's a good and entertaining one, and it leaves us thinking that Duddy Kravitz might amount to something after all, should he ever grow up.

Arthur ★ ★ ★ ½
PG, 97 m., 1981

Dudley Moore (Arthur Bach), Liza Minelli (Linda Marolla), John Gielgud (Hobson), Geraldine Fitzgerald (Martha Bach), Jill Eikenberry (Susan), Stephen Elliott (Burt), Tod Ross (Bitterman), Barney Martin (Linda's Father). Directed and written by Steve Gordon. Produced by Robert Greenhut.

Only someone with a heart of stone could fail to love a drunk like Arthur Bach, who spends his wasted days in a poignant search for someone who will love him, will care for him, will inflame his passions, and soothe his pain, and who, most of all, will laugh at his one-liners. Arthur is such a servant of humanity that he even dedicates himself to thinking up new one-liners and holding them in reserve, lest he be unprepared if someone walks into his life and needs a laugh, quick.

Arthur, played by Dudley Moore, is the alcoholic hero of *Arthur,* a comedy about a man who is worth $750 million and who would never think of trying to buy anyone's love with his money. Arthur is like the woman in the poem by Yeats, who spent her days in innocent good will, and her nights in argument, till her voice grew shrill. Arthur, God love him, is a drunk. He slips into his bath of a morning, and his butler brings him a martini. After he completes his bath, Arthur sets about the day's business, which consists of staying drunk, and being driven about Manhattan in a limousine in his endless quest for love.

Now the problems with searching for love while you are drunk are many. They include (a) no one will want to love you while you are drunk, (b) you are not at your best while you are drunk, so they won't know what they're missing, (c) you may be too drunk to notice it if someone does finally fall in love with you, and (d) if you survive all of these pitfalls, you will nevertheless wake up hung over, and scientific studies prove that hangovers dissolve love. All of these things having been said, Arthur, against all odds, does find love. He finds it in the person of Linda (Liza Minelli), a smart cookie who doesn't care about his money but is overwhelmed by the dimensions of his needs. Arthur would like to marry Linda. But his billionaire father insists that he marry a perfectly boring WASP (Jill Eikenberry) whose idea of a good holiday is probably the January white sales.

Arthur turns for help to his loyal butler, Hobson, who is played by John Gielgud with an understated elegance and a naughty tongue. Hobson is dying. But Hobson wishes to see Arthur prevail, for once, against Arthur's father, a sadistic puppetmaster. So Hobson subtly manipulates the situation so that the lovers are thrown together at the party announcing Arthur's engagement to the WASP. That inspires a rupture within the family, and a very drunken odyssey by Arthur, who wants to press $100,000 upon Linda, and visits her at home. When Linda turns him down, her father (Barney Martin) becomes a grown man who sheds tears, creating perhaps the funniest moment in the movie.

Dudley Moore became a star, of course, with *10*, playing a man who became obsessed with Bo Derek, and who could blame him? In *Arthur,* he makes his bid for world-class status as a comic character actor. He brings a wonderful intensity to scenes like the one near the beginning of the film where he has invited a hooker to dinner at the Plaza and then forgotten who she is, and what she is, or why he is with her. It is marvelous to see him try to focus his attention, which he seems to believe is all concentrated in his eyebrow muscles.

Apart from Moore, the treasure of *Arthur* is in its many supporting performances, especially Gielgud's, although everyone in this movie has great moments. You might be tempted to think that *Arthur* would be a bore, because it is about a drunk who is always trying to tell you stories. You would be right if *Arthur* were a party and you were attending it. But *Arthur* is a movie. And so its drunk, unlike real drunks, is more entertaining, more witty, more human, and more poignant than you are. He embodies, in fact, all the wonderful human qualities that drunks fondly, mistakenly believe the booze brings out in them.

The Assault ★ ★ ★

NO MPAA RATING, 149 m., 1987

Derek de Lint (Anton Steenwijk), Marc van Uchelen (Anton as a Boy), Monique van de VenCor (Truus Coster), John Kraaykamp (Takes). Directed and produced by Fons Rademakers. Screenplay by Gerard Soeteman.

The Assault, which won the 1987 Academy Award as best foreign film, begins in Nazi-occupied Holland in the bitter late days of World War II. On a quiet suburban street, a Dutch collaborator is shot to death by partisans. From behind their curtains, the fearful residents peek out into the night, certain that the Nazis will perform dreadful reprisals. Shadowy figures dart out and drag the body to the front of the house next door, and then the movie is the story of the rest of the life of Anton Steenwijk, the young boy who lived in that house.

His family is taken away by the Nazis. All of them disappear, apparently liquidated, except for Anton, who is spared through a combination of bureaucratic oversights and lucky chances. After the war, Anton goes to college, marries, and becomes successful in his profession. Always his life is haunted by the aftermath of that terrible night.

But there are two other families also scarred by the assault. One is the family of the murdered Nazi collaborator. Anton runs across the collaborator's son a few years later and finds that he has become a bitter young right-winger, a youth whose father's political choice made him into an outsider and menial laborer who was scorned after the war.

Even later, in a 1960s ban-the-bomb parade, Anton meets the woman who lived next door on that night and learns why her father dragged the dead body to the front of his house, assuring that another family would be punished by the Nazis. He had his reasons. Perhaps they were good. Of course, from the point of view of a man who lost his entire family because of those reasons, they were not good enough.

The Assault is like a fictional footnote to *Shoah*, the great documentary that also asked difficult, perhaps unanswerable, questions about guilt and blame in the Holocaust. It also is a little like *Rashomon*, the Japanese film that looked at the same crime from many different viewpoints and discovered many different versions of the truth.

A terrible thing happened on that night. Lives were destroyed. For those who survived, each one had to deal with the guilt in a different way. Even Anton had guilt, because he was spared when all of his family was murdered. The truest and most painful moment in the film takes place at a time about twenty years after the night of the assault. Anton—happily married, a father, successful, content—is suddenly visited by a great devastation. To call it a depression would be too mild. He is overcome with a crushing awareness of the fact that utter injustice exists in our world, that evil is real, that death is irrevocable. In a way, this movie is about how he is able to continue his life in the face of that realization.

Although *The Assault* is a film that asks important questions and examines them fearlessly, it is not as effective as it could be. The film covers nearly forty years, and that is a weakness as well as a strength. The power of the film is that it shows how one night of tragedy has echoed down the decades, affecting many lives for years afterward. Multiply this assault by the millions of others, and you have some measure of the devastation caused by the war.

Yet at the same time, by covering so many lives for so many years, the film loses something in energy and focus. The canvas is too large. The moments I will remember best are the small ones, one in particular: On the night of the assault, Anton is comforted in a jail cell by the young woman partisan who committed the murder that led to his family's death. Years later, through a coincidence, he is able to meet her partner and tell the man, now old and ill, something he never knew: that she loved him.

Asylum ★ ★

PG, 100 m., 1972

Barbara Perkins (Bonnie), Peter Cushing (Smith), Britt Ekland (Lucy), Patrick Magee (Dr. Rutherford), Richard Todd (Walter), Charlotte Rampling (Barbara). Directed by Roy Ward Baker and produced by Max J. Rosenberg and Milton Subotsky. Screenplay by Robert Bloch.

Asylum is a British anthology of short horror stories from the same good old folks who gave us *Torture Garden* and *Tales from the Crypt*. I had the opportunity to interview one of the producers, Max J. Rosenberg, when he visited Chicago, and the thing I remember about him is his great devotion to coleslaw. He kept ordering more and more plates of coleslaw, until he had put away about a gallon. With a taste like that, he should live upstairs from a delicatessen.

Anyway, I didn't think much about Rosenberg or the coleslaw until *Asylum* opened. Now I'm wondering. This is a movie about people with obsessions. There's a man who's obsessed with murdering his wife. A tailor who's obsessed with collecting his bills. A girl obsessed with her alter ego. A guy who makes little voodoo dolls.

These people aren't crazy, you see. They're obsessed. They aren't crazy because all the unbelievable things in the movie really happen to them. The man who kills his wife puts her in the deep-freeze, for example, after first carving her up and neatly packaging each limb in brown paper with string around it. But the arms and legs and head (and even the torso, a little awkwardly) climb out of the freezer and go after the guy and his mistress. An arm without a body that is capable of strangling people is indeed an arm obsessed.

Anyway, I got to thinking about these people, especially the guy who devotes his life to making little dolls until he *becomes* his own little doll. And I began to wonder what it was with Max J. Rosenberg and the coleslaw. Is he, in fact, a cabbage? Does he want to turn into one? Has his soul been occupied by a rabbit? Is he the victim of a delicatessen owner's curse?

This movie was written by Robert Bloch, who lives in Wisconsin and has also found inspiration from the sere northern landscape to write *Psycho*, *Torture Garden*, and assorted other tales of unearthly goings-on. I wonder if he has ever had dinner with Rosenberg and, if so, if he wondered about the coleslaw. Of course, the coleslaw Rosenberg was eating was at the Cape Cod Room, which has some of the best coleslaw in the world, but a man with Rosenberg's obsession probably keeps in practice wherever he goes. If nothing else, he can eat bad coleslaw just to remind himself of what's he's missing.

I think Bloch and Rosenberg should get organized and take on the cabbage. If nothing else, a horror movie about cabbages could help Rosenberg work through his obsession and save a lot of analyst's fees. I see a horror movie about a man who turns into coleslaw . . . no, wait. A movie about a cabbage that gets horribly shredded when . . . hold on, I've got it. A cabbage that is, against its will, stuffed with a tomato and some rice, and gruesomely baked in an oven for hours.

At Close Range ★ ★ ★ 1/2

R, 115 m., 1986

Sean Penn (Brad, Jr.), Christopher Walken (Brad, Sr.), Mary Stuart Masterson (Terry), Christopher Penn (Tommy), Millie Perkins (Julie), Eileen Ryan (Grandma). Directed by James Foley and produced by Elliott Lewitt and Don Guest. Screenplay by Nicholas Kazan.

Here is a spare, violent, unforgiving story of a boy's need for a father who does not love him and who would, if necessary, murder him. It is also a story with passages of love and adventure and cheerfulness, as a teenager grows up in the hills of rural Pennsylvania. The way that the two sides of the story grow together creates a tragedy that reminds me of myth, of the ancient stories of children betrayed by their parents, and yet *At Close Range* is based on a true story. It happened in 1978.

The movie stars Sean Penn, probably the best of the younger actors, as Bradford Whitewood, Jr. He lives with his divorced mother and grandmother and half-brother in a setting of shabby poverty, nonstop TV watching, and boredom. Once in a while, his father, Brad Senior, appears out of nowhere and throws money on the table. Then Brad Senior drives away in a fast car with a pretty girl. The kid would like a taste of his father's life. It looks a lot better than what he has.

The father is played by Christopher Walken, in one of the great hateful performances of recent years. Walken is a strange actor, hard to pin down, but when he is given the right role (as he is here, and in *Dead Zone* and *The Deer Hunter*), there is nobody to touch him for his chilling ability to move between easy charm and vile evil. In the movie, he's the leader of a gang of professional thieves who have recently been specializing in stealing tractors. He likes to play the big shot, and in a way he enjoys the fact that his young son has started to idolize him.

Penn, as Brad Junior, isn't really criminal material, but he's a misfit and an outcast and absolutely nothing is happening for him in his own life. He drifts into the orbit of his father, looking for love but also looking for action. He's the leader of a young gang of his own, and his father assigns the kids to a couple of easy jobs—getting them ready for the big time. But when the big time turns dangerous, and it looks as if the gang might be busted, the Walken character is absolutely prepared to save his own skin, even at the cost of betraying his own child.

At Close Range is not a pleasant movie. Few recent films have painted such a bleak picture of human nature. The Walken character is pure evil, wrapped in easy charm, and most of the other characters in the film are weak, or deprived, or lacking in the ability to see beyond their own immediate situation. That's especially true of Brad Junior's mother (Millie Perkins) and grandmother (Eileen Ryan), who sit endlessly around the house, their eyes straying away from every conversation, toward the TV set. Only Brad Junior and his local girlfriend (Mary Stuart Masterson) have a chance of breaking free, and their love affair is on a collision course with Brad Senior.

Because this film is violent and cruel and very sad, why would you want to see it? For a couple of reasons, perhaps. One might be to watch two great actors, Penn and Walken, at the top of their forms, in roles that give them a lot to work with. Another might be to witness some of the dynamics of a criminal society, some of the forces that push criminals farther than they intend to go. It's the same dynamic you could see in the great crime film *In Cold Blood* (1967)—seemingly ordinary people whose moral sense is missing, and who drift into actions so evil that perhaps even they are appalled.

Au Revoir les Enfants ★ ★ ★ ★

PG, 103 m., 1988

Gaspard Manesse (Julien Quentin), Raphael Fejto (Jean Bonnet), Francine Racette (Madame Quentin), Stanislas Carre de Malberg (Francois Quentin), Philippe Morier-Genoud (Father Jean), Francois Berleand (Father Michel), Francois Negret (Joseph), Peter Fitz (Muller). Directed, written, and produced by Louis Malle.

Which of us cannot remember a moment when we did or said precisely the wrong thing, irretrievably, irreparably? The instant the action was completed or the words were spoken, we burned with shame and regret, but what we had done could never be repaired. Such moments are rare, and they occur most often in childhood, before we have been trained to think before we act. *Au Revoir les Enfants* is a film about such a moment, about a quick, unthinking glance that may have cost four people their lives.

The film was written and directed by Louis Malle, who based it on a childhood memory. Judging by the tears I saw streaming down his face on the night the film was shown at the Telluride Film Festival, the memory has caused him pain for many years. His story takes place in 1944, in a Catholic boarding school in Nazi-occupied France. At the start of a new semester, three new students are enrolled, and we realize immediately that they are Jews, disguised with new names and identities in an attempt to hide them from the Nazis.

To Julien Quentin (Gaspard Manesse), however, this is not at all obvious. Julien, who is intended as Malle's autobiographical double, does not quite understand all of the distinctions involving Jews and gentiles in a country run by Nazis. All he knows is that he likes one of the new boys, Jean Bonnet (Raphael Fejto), and they become friends. Bonnet is not popular with the other students, who follow the age-old schoolboy practice of closing ranks against newcomers, but then Julien is not very popular either; the two boys are a little dreamy and thoughtful—absorbed in themselves and their imaginations, as bright adolescents should be. Malle's film is not filled with a lot of dramatic incidents. Unlike such roughly comparable Hollywood films as *The Lords of Discipline*, it feels no need for strong plotting and lots of dramatic incidents leading up to the big finale. Instead, we enter the daily lives of these boys. We see the classroom routine, the air raid drills, the way each teacher has his own way of dealing with problems of discipline. More than anything else, we get a feeling for the rhythm of the school. Malle has said that when, years later, he visited the actual site of the boarding school he attended, he found that the building had disappeared and the school was forgotten. But to a student enrolled in such a school, the rules and rituals seem timeless, handed down by innumerable generations and destined to survive forever. A schoolboy cannot be expected to understand how swiftly violence and evil can strike out and change everything.

Julien and Jean play together, study together, look at dirty postcards together. One day, one of those cold early spring days when the shadows seem ominous and there is an unsettling wind in the trees, they go exploring in a nearby forest, and darkness falls. They get lost, or almost lost, and they weather this adventure and become even closer friends. One day, Julien accidentally discovers that "Jean Bonnet" is not his friend's real name. A few days later, when Julien's mother comes to visit, he invites Jean to join them at lunch in a local restaurant, and they witness an anti-Semitic incident as a longtime local customer is singled out because he is Jewish.

That is about all the input that Julien receives, and it is hard to say exactly what he knows, or suspects, about Jean. But when Nazis visit the school, Julien performs in one tragic second an action that will haunt him for the rest of his days. Malle has said that the incident in *Au Revoir les Enfants* does not exactly parallel whatever happened in real life, but the point must be the same: In an unthinking moment, action is taken that can never be retrieved.

Is the film only about guilt? Not at all. It is constructed very subtly to show that Julien only half-realized the nature of the situation, anyway. It isn't as if Julien knew absolutely that Jean was Jewish. It's more as if Julien possessed a lot of information that he had never quite put together, and when the Nazis came looking for hidden Jews, Julien suddenly realized what his information meant. The moment in which he makes his tragic mistake is also, perhaps, the moment when he comprehends for the first time the shocking fact of racism.

Autumn Sonata ★ ★ ★ ★

PG, 97 m., 1978

Ingrid Bergman (Charlotte), Liv Ullmann (Eva), Lena Nyman (Helena), Halvor Bjork (Viktor), Georg Lokkeberg (Leonardo), Knut Wigert (The Professor). Directed by Ingmar Bergman. Screenplay by Bergman.

Ingrid Bergman was certainly one of the most beautiful women to ever appear in a film, but that is not the source of her mysterious appeal. There is something there, in that voice and those eyes and in the way her mouth thinks words before she says them, that is, quite simply, unduplicated in the movies. It took Ingmar Bergman thirty-five years to finally cast her in one of his films, and then, in her fortieth year as an actress, Ingrid Bergman called *Autumn Sonata* her last film. Sweden's two most important film artists finally worked together.

The movie is a historic event, taking us back to so many different areas of our memories. We remember Ingrid Bergman from some of the basic cinematic artifacts of all time, movies like *Casablanca* and *Notorious*. But we've never seen her really pushed, really tested, by a director whose commitment to honesty is nothing short of merciless.

Ingmar Bergman didn't cast her for reasons of nostalgia, or sentiment: He cast her because he had an idea for a role she could brilliantly contain and that would contain her, and in *Autumn Sonata* she gives nothing less than the performance of her lifetime. We can only be quietly grateful that she performs opposite Liv Ullmann, who is herself good enough to meet her on the same very high level.

They play mother and daughter. The mother is an internationally famous pianist (and we remember Ingrid Bergman's first great success, as the pianist in *Intermezzo*). She has not seen her daughter for seven years. She's too busy and always traveling and booked up almost every night of the week . . . and, not incidentally, terrified of confronting her daughter.

There are, in fact, two daughters: The one played by Ullmann, who is serious and introspective and filled with guilt and blame and love, and then the other daughter (Lena Nyman), who lives with her, and who suffers from a degenerative nerve disease. The mother's solution to this daughter's illness was to place her in a "home;" Ullmann has taken her out of the institution and brought her home to live with her.

On the morning when the mother arrives for her long-delayed visit, she has no idea that the sick daughter will be there. Her response, on learning that her other daughter is upstairs, is dismay. She's never been able to deal with the illness—but, then, she's never been able to deal at all with the fact of being a mother. She doesn't merely reject the responsibility; she flees from it.

Autumn Sonata then gives us a sort of long day's journey into night in which the pleasantries of the opening hours give way to deeper and deeper terrors and guilts, accusations and renunciations, cries and whispers. And Ingmar Bergman, standing apart from this material and regarding it with clarity and detachment, refuses to find any solutions. There are none, I suppose. A lesser filmmaker would have resolved everything at the end in some sort of neat Freudian bookkeeping, but Bergman finds in his story only two people, each demanding love from the other, each doomed by the past to fall just short of the ability to love.

This is excruciatingly difficult material. Ingrid Bergman and Liv Ullmann confront it with a courage and skill that is astonishing. We've always known that Liv Ullmann was a great actress (that is one of the givens of film in the past two decades), and we've known, too, that Ingrid Bergman was a great movie star. But how important that in her sixties, acting in her native language for the first time in four decades, working with one of the supreme film directors, Bergman was able to use not only her star qualities but also every last measure of her artistry and her humanity. It is not just that *Autumn Sonata* was Ingrid Bergman's last film. It's that she knew she had to make it before she died.

B

Baby Boom ★ ★ ★
PG, 110 m., 1987

Diane Keaton (J.C. Wiatt), Sam Shepard (Dr. Jeff Cooper), Harold Ramis (Steven Buchner), Sam Wanamaker (Fritz Curtis), James Spader (Ken Arrenberg), Pat Hingle (Hughes Larrabee), Kristina and Michelle Kennedy (Baby Elizabeth). Directed by Charles Shyer and produced by Nancy Meyers. Screenplay by Shyer and Meyers.

Baby Boom tells the story of a yuppie who receives the ultimate toy, a cute little baby daughter. At first she doesn't want to play with it, but eventually it grows on her, and even provides the inspiration for her to acquire other toys, such as a farm in Vermont, a baby food company, and a handsome veterinarian.

This story could have been told as a satire, but the filmmakers aren't quite sure. They see a lot of humor in the yuppie's lifestyle, but they love the baby so much that the movie finally turns into a sweet romance. I guess that's all right. It sure is a cute baby.

The yuppie is played by Diane Keaton, whose Annie Hall more or less created the category. As the film opens, she is a hard-driving Manhattan business executive who works hard and takes no hostages. The opening narration by Linda Ellerbee supplies some details: She has a salary in six figures, a corner apartment in the right part of town, and a live-in lover (Harold Ramis) who is her perfect match because he, too, is a workaholic.

Then two of Keaton's long-lost relatives die in a traffic accident in Britain, and she inherits their pride and joy, a baby girl named Elizabeth (played by twins, Kristina and Michelle Kennedy). There is, of course, no question of her raising the baby herself. After all, she's just had a partnership dangled in front of her. She copes with the kid as best she can for a few days, feeding it gourmet pasta and checking it in a restaurant cloakroom during a power lunch. Then she takes it to be adopted, but finds she just can't part with this sweet little girl.

Right then is when the movie changes tone. Up until Keaton's decision to keep the child, *Baby Boom* has been a hard-edged satire (the dialogue between Keaton and the hat-check attendant is an example, as Keaton thrusts the squawling infant across the counter and promises "a big, big tip"). But after the film's turning point, it turns from a satire into an escapist fantasy, a harmless one, in one of those worlds where everything turns out more or less right, because folks are more or less nice.

The film is careful never to confront the Keaton character with any of the real messiness of the world, such as poverty, illness, and catastrophe. After she quits her job, she has enough money in the bank to buy a sixty-two-acre home in Vermont for herself and baby Elizabeth. And when the money runs low, she starts a gourmet baby-food company that is worth millions within a few months. She also discovers companionship up there in the woods, from Sam Shepard, the local vet and only person under sixty in the immediate surrounding area.

All of this is too good to be true, of course, but that's why I enjoyed it. *Baby Boom* makes no effort to show us real life. It is a fantasy about mothers and babies and sweetness and love, with just enough wicked comedy to give it an edge. The screenplay by Nancy Meyers and Charles Shyer has some of the same literate charm as their previous film, *Irreconcilable Differences,* and some of the same sly observation of a generation that wages an interior war between selfishness and good nature.

The flaw in *Baby Boom* is that the Keaton character ends up not having sacrificed a single thing by leaving the business world to become a mom. In fact, she becomes a millionaire as a direct result of keeping the baby. It doesn't often happen that way, but, of course, it should. Like a Frank Capra film, *Baby Boom* shows us a little of the darkness and a lot of the dawn.

Baby, It's You ★ ★ ★
R, 105 m., 1983 ✓

Rosanna Arquette (Jill), Vincent Spano (Sheik), Joanna Merlin (Mrs. Rosen), Jack Davidson (Dr. Rosen). Directed by John Sayles and produced by Griffin Dunne and Amy Robinson. Screenplay by Sayles.

Rosanna Arquette has a way about her. She's a natural actress, and by that I don't mean she was born talented (although perhaps she was), but that she is able to appear onscreen with such an unaffected natural quality that I feel as if I'm looking past the script and direction and actually experiencing the life of her character. That's the feeling I got during *Baby, It's You,* a sometimes very good, sometimes disappointingly uneven movie that she carries from beginning to end. Even when her scenes aren't working, her character is, and we're getting to know this young woman she plays, this Jill Rosen, who turns from an uncommonly engaging high school student to a scared-stiff college freshman.

The movie is by John Sayles, who has built a career for himself out of the carefully observed events that make up ordinary lives. His first film was *Return of the Secaucus Seven,* about some thirty-fiveish survivors of the 1960s. Then he made *Lianna,* about a thirty-fiveish faculty wife who discovers, with fear and some anticipation, that she is a lesbian. Now here is Jill Rosen, a high school student from the 1960s who could, we suspect, easily grow up to be any of the women in Sayles's first two films.

Jill is smart and pretty, especially when she smiles. Her brains and her smile are only the half of it. She's also got a personal style. She has this way of letting you know she's listening, even when she seems to be ignoring you. A way of caring for you, even when she's mad at you. You get the feeling this is a woman whose love would be a very important thing for you to count on. And that's certainly the opinion of the Sheik (Vincent Spano), a semi-greaser who is consumed by his desire to be exactly like Frank Sinatra. The Sheik and (actually) a lot of this movie seem to belong more to the fifties than the sixties—but never mind. Here is a kid who's a sharp dresser, has a lot of apparent self-confidence, and doesn't mind that he stands out like a sore thumb with his brazen ways and his Sinatra wardrobe. He's a rebel with ambitions. Jill loves him, but when she leaves Trenton, New Jersey, and enters the uncertain world of Sarah Lawrence College, the Sheik doesn't fit in.

Baby, It's You does two things with this material. First, it remembers it accurately, right down to the irritating mannerisms of preppy college boys with too much unearned self-confidence. Then, it uses it as a meditation on growing up—which means learning to listen to your heart as well as to your ambitions. The movie works best in its high school segments, and the opening hour is wonderful. Then the infuriating stuff begins, when this movie that has been so sure-footed loses its way in the college scenes, and allows us to wonder at times what we're supposed to be thinking. Rosanna Arquette is equally good, however, in the good parts and the disappointing ones.

Bachelor Party ★ ★ ★
R, 100 m., 1984

Tom Hanks (Rick), Tawny Kitaen (Debbie), Adrian Zmed (Jay), George Grizzard (Mr. Thompson), Robert Prescott (Cole). Directed by Neal Israel and produced by Ron Moler and Bob Israel. Screenplay by Neal Israel and Pat Proft.

Bachelor Party is 1984's version of the Annual Summer Food Fight Movie. With a movie like this, it doesn't really matter whether anyone actually throws mashed potatoes across the room; what matters is whether the movie is faithful to the spirit of Blotto Bluto in *Animal House* when he yelled "Food fight!" and the madness began. The story this time is about this guy who decides to get married, and his friends decide to throw him a bachelor party. That's about it. The first half of the movie sets up the party and the second half of the movie is the party. Both halves of the movie are raunchy, chaotic, and quite shameless in aiming at the lowest possible level of taste, of course.

The bachelor in the movie is played by Tom Hanks. He was the guy from *Splash* who the mermaid fell in love with. I didn't think he was all that terrific in *Splash*—I thought he was miscast, and they should have gone for somebody who was less of a conventional leading man—but in *Bachelor Party* he's a lot more funny and I enjoyed the performance. He plays the kind of guy who goes over to his fiancée's house for dinner and drops table scraps onto the floor in *case* they have a dog. He has a great one-liner when he has to introduce himself to his fiancée's nerdy ex-boyfriend: "The name is Bond. James Bond." During the chaos of the party itself, one of his primary roles is simply to direct traffic.

The idea during the party, I think, is to approximate the spirit of one of those Jack Davis drawings in *Mad* magazine, where dozens of people are running around like crazy, and down in the corners you can see strange little figures doing inexplicable things. Most of the gags depend on varieties of public embarrassment and some of them are pretty funny, especially when the women decide to have their revenge by visiting a male go-go bar.

Is *Bachelor Party* a great movie? No. Why do I give it three stars? Because it honors the tradition of a reliable movie genre, because it tries hard, and because when it is funny, it is very funny. It is relatively easy to make a comedy that is totally devoid of humor, but not all that easy to make a movie containing some genuine laughs. *Bachelor Party* has some great moments and qualifies as a raunchy, scummy, grungy Blotto Bluto memorial.

Back to School ★ ★ ★
PG-13, 94 m., 1986

Rodney Dangerfield (Thornton Melon), Sally Kellerman (Diane), Burt Young (Lou), Keith Gordon (Jason Melon), Robert Downey, Jr. (Derek), Paxton Whitehead (Philip Barbay), M. Emmet Walsh (Coach Turnbull), Ned Beatty (Dean Martin). Directed by Alan Metter and produced by Chuck Russell. Screenplay by Steven Kampmann, Will Porter, Peter Torokvei, and Harold Ramis.

Rodney Dangerfield has been giving interviews lately on the subject of his loneliness. Why, he asks, should a guy like him, who is able to fill up giant concert halls and pull down millions of dollars a year, be condemned to go through life without the love of a woman? This is not the sort of thing you want to hear from a comedian. You want him to be zany and madcap, to stand astride the problems of the mundane world and laugh at them.

Yet in Dangerfield, there has always been something else in addition to the comedian. This is a man who has failed at everything, even comedy. Rodney Dangerfield is his third name in show business; he flopped under two earlier names as well as his real name. Who is really at home inside that red, sweating face and that knowing leer?

The most interesting thing about *Back to School,* which is otherwise a pleasant but routine comedy, is the puzzle of Rodney Dangerfield. Here is a man who reminds us of some of the great comedians of the early days of the talkies—of Groucho Marx and W.C. Fields—because, like them, he projects a certain mystery. Marx and Fields were never just being funny. There was the sense that they were getting even for hurts so deep that all they could do was laugh about them. It's the same with Dangerfield.

He plays Thornton Melon, a millionaire clothing manufacturer who owns a chain of Tall & Fat Shops. His father was a penniless Italian immigrant who took him into the family business as a child. He never had the opportunity to get an education. Now he is rich, his second wife is an obnoxious bauble, and all he cares about is his son, Jason, who is a college student.

Dangerfield fondly believes Jason is a fraternity member and a star of the diving team. But actually Jason is the campus wimp, the team's towel boy, and, naturally, he gets no respect. When Dangerfield discovers the truth, he decides to enroll in the university as a freshman so he can teach his son the ropes. Of course, there's resistance to this plan, but not after Dangerfield endows the Melon School of Business Administration.

The campus characters are predictable, but well-cast. Sally Kellerman is the sexy English teacher, Paxton Whitehead is the Anglophile business teacher, and Ned Beatty is the venal administrator, always referred to as Dean Martin. Dangerfield takes the "drinks for everybody" approach, throwing his money around and hiring expensive coaches to help him pass his classes. Kurt Vonnegut, Jr., turns up as a paid expert on his own work. Meanwhile, young Jason learns how to be a big man on campus.

This is exactly the sort of plot Marx or Fields could have appeared in. Dangerfield brings it something they might also have brought along: a certain pathos. Beneath his loud manner, under his studied obnoxiousness, there is a real need. He laughs that he may not cry.

Dangerfield has been looking for a movie style for a couple of years now. The problem with his last movie, *Easy Money,* was that he wanted to seem like a basically nice guy. He isn't a nice guy. Or at least, when he is nice, there is nothing simple about his niceness. The interesting achievement of *Back to School* is its ability to make contradictions part of the character.

Back to the Beach ★ ★ ★ ½
PG, 94 m., 1987

Frankie Avalon (The Big Kahuna), Annette Funicello (Annette), Lori Loughlin (Sandi), Tommy Hinkley (Michael), Demian Slade (Bobby), Connie Stevens (Connie). Directed by Lyndall Hobbs and produced by Frank Mancuso, Jr. Screenplay by Peter Krikes, Steve Meerson, and Christopher Thompson.

This movie absolutely blind-sided me. I don't know what I was expecting from *Back to the Beach,* but it certainly wasn't the funniest, quirkiest musical comedy since *Little Shop of Horrors.* Who would have thought Frankie Avalon and Annette Funicello would make their best beach party movie twenty-five years after the others?

For those who have never seen them, a description is probably better than the actual experience: The beach party movies were a series of chaste comedies in which Frankie and Annette and the gang hung out on the beach, rode the big waves, necked a little, and tried to defend their lifestyle against the old fogeys who were always trying to ban rock & roll. The movies were a tie between harmless and brainless.

Now comes *Back to the Beach,* a wicked satire that pokes fun at Frankie, Annette, and the whole genre, but does it with a lot of good humor and with the full cooperation of the victims. Avalon and Funicello do a better job of satirizing themselves than anyone else possibly could.

The story: Frankie and Annette have gotten married and moved to Ohio, where Frankie sells cars on television, riding a phony surfboard in his sharkskin suit, while Annette prepares endless meals of peanut butter sandwiches. They have two children: a daughter who has moved to Malibu and a young teen-age son who is a punk, wears leather, flicks his switchblade, and mercilessly attacks the inane banality of his parents.

The kid (Demian Slade) almost steals the opening scenes of the movie. He has spray-painted graffiti on the fireplace in the living room, he practices karate moves on the family dog, and when Frankie and Annette exchange empty-headed clichés, he's ironic: "This is the sort of conversation you'd hear at the Kissingers.' "

The three of them head to Hawaii on vacation but get sidetracked to Malibu, where Frankie is horrified to learn that his daughter has shacked up with a beach bum (in the beach party movies, the sexes always were strictly segregated at bedtime). Meanwhile, he and Annette discover that some of the old gang still is hanging out at the beach, including Connie Stevens, Miss Lip Gloss of 1962, who still looks luscious.

Frankie flirts with Connie. Annette pouts. There is a confrontation between the clean-cut surfers and the punk surfers. There's a surfing competition, and Frankie comes out of retirement to win it. Annette sings a reggae song. Frankie sings a few rock songs. So does Connie Stevens. And at one point, Pee-Wee Herman jets in from nowhere, does a virtuoso version of "Surfin' Bird," and disappears.

All of this sounds, I suppose, like the kind of movie you could afford to miss, because a plot summary only suggests the elements of the movie, not the style. Director Lyndall Hobbs, an Australian making her feature debut, has a good eye and a good ear, and the movie is filled with satirical angles from beginning to end.

No one was more surprised than I was. I walked in with a sinking heart, because the studio, Paramount, had so little confidence in the picture they enforced various embargos on review deadlines. I guess the studio missed the point. This is a quirky little gem filled with good music, a lot of laughs, and proof that Annette still knows how to make a polka-dot dress seem ageless.

Back to the Future ★ ★ ★ ½
PG, 116 m., 1985

Michael J. Fox (Marty McFly), Christopher Lloyd (Dr. Brown), Lea Thompson (Lorraine Baines), Crispin Glover (George McFly), Thomas F. Wilson (Biff Tannen), Claudia Wells (Jennifer Parker). Directed by Robert Zemeckis and produced by Bob Gale and Neil Canton. Screenplay by Zemeckis and Gale.

One of the things all teen-agers believe is that their parents were never teen-agers. Their parents were, perhaps, children once. They are undeniably adults now. But how could they have ever been teen-agers, and yet not understand their own children? This view is actually rather optimistic, since it assumes that you can learn something about teen-agers by being one. But *Back to the Future* is even more hopeful: It argues that you can travel back in time to the years when your parents were teen-agers and straighten them out right at the moment when they need help the most.

The movie begins in the present, with a teen-ager named Marty (Michael J. Fox). His parents (let's face it) are hopeless nerds. Dad tells corny jokes and Mom guzzles vodka in the kitchen and the evening meal is like feeding time at the fun house. All that keeps Marty sane is his friendship with the nutty Dr. Brown (Christopher Lloyd), an inventor with glowing eyes and hair like a fright wig.

Brown believes he has discovered the secret of time travel, and one night in the deserted parking lot of the local shopping mall, he demonstrates his invention. In the long history of time travel movies, there has never been a time machine quite like Brown's, which resembles nothing so much as a customized DeLorean.

The gadget works, and then, after a series of surprises, Marty finds himself transported back thirty years in time, to the days when the shopping mall was a farmer's field (there's a nice gag when the farmer thinks the DeLorean, with its gull-wing doors, is a flying saucer). Marty wanders into town, still wearing his 1985 clothing, and the townsfolk look at his goose down jacket and ask him why he's wearing a life preserver.

One of the running gags in *Back to the Future* is the way the town has changed in thirty years (for example, the porno house of 1985 was playing a Ronald Reagan movie in 1955). But a lot of the differences run more deeply than that, as Marty discovers when he sits down at a lunch counter next to his dad—who is, of course, a teen-ager himself. Because the movie has so much fun with the paradoxes and predicaments of a kid meeting his own parents, I won't discuss the plot in any detail. I won't even get into the horrifying moment when Marty discovers his mother "has the hots" for him. The movie's surprises are one of its great pleasures.

Back to the Future was directed by Robert (*Romancing the Stone*) Zemeckis, who shows not only a fine comic touch but also some of the lighthearted humanism of a Frank Capra. The movie, in fact, resembles Capra's *It's a Wonderful Life* more than other, conventional time-travel movies. It's about a character who begins with one view of his life and reality, and is allowed, through magical intervention, to discover another. Steven Spielberg was the executive producer, and the movie's world view (smart kid in Yuppie suburb redefines reality for his parents) is part of the basic Spielberg approach. This time it comes with charm, brains, and a lot of laughter.

Bad Boys ★ ★ ★ ½
R, 123 m., 1983

Sean Penn (Mick O'Brien), Reni Santoni (Ramon Herrera), Esai Morales (Paco Moreno), Jim Moody (Gene Daniels), Eric Gurry (Horowitz), Clancy Brown (Viking Lofgren). Directed by Richard Rosenthal and produced by Robert Solo. Screenplay by Richard Di Lello.

Bad Boys tells the story of some tough Chicago street-gang kids who get in a lot of trouble, get sent to a juvenile correctional institution, and get in a lot more trouble once they're inside. Following the tradition governing such movies, the story eventually comes to a moral crossroad at which a bad boy has to decide whether to become a good man—and that's too bad, because until the movie turns predictable it is very, very good. The acting, the direction, and the sense of place in *Bad Boys* is so strong that the movie deserves more than an obligatory fight scene for its conclusion.

The movie stars Sean Penn as Mick O'Brien, a teen-age Irish-American hood and Esai Morales as Paco, a Latino hood. They are both tough, mean, anti-social kids; this movie doesn't sentimentalize street gangs. Their paths cross in connection with a drug deal that Paco is doing with a black gang. There's a misunderstanding, a sudden, shocking exchange of gunfire, and Paco's kid brother is dead. Mick killed him. Mick is sent to prison, and then Paco has his revenge by raping Mick's girlfriend (Ally Sheedy). Paco is caught and sent to the same prison where Mick is being held. Mick already has learned the ropes, and Paco learns them quickly: The prison guards preside sincerely but ineffectually over a reign of terror enforced by the toughest kids in the prison. Violence and sexual crimes are commonplace. The strongest survive. This situation is complicated, of course, by the fact that everyone in the prison immediately knows that Mick and Paco will have to fight to the death over the feud of honor.

And it's at precisely that moment, when the two kids are being set up for an eventual showdown, that *Bad Boys* begins to unwind. The first hour of this movie is so good it's scary; Penn and Morales and the supporting actors are completely convincing, and *Bad Boys* is the first movie I've seen in which the street gangs are not glamorized *(West Side Story),* stylized *(The Warriors),* or romanticized *(The Wanderers).* We believe, watching *Bad Boys,* that we are observing an approximation of the real thing. The direction, by Richard Rosenthal, is sure-footed, confident, and fluid; we are in the hands of a fine director, even if he *did* make *Halloween II.* Sean Penn is mean and defiant in a real star performance, and the other kids in the prison include such inimitable characters as Horowitz (Eric Gurry), a bright kid who invents things and talks casually of his arson conviction; Viking (Clancy Brown), the hard but vulnerable boss of the prisoners; and Tweety (Robert Lee Rush), who rules at Viking's side.

These performances are good. That's why it's such a disappointment when the movie allows itself to become just another prison picture. Although the second half of the movie continues its close, convincing observations of everyday life in the youth prison, the story structure begins to feel programmed: We know we're heading for a big fight, we think we know who'll win—and what is this, anyway? They've *already* made *Rocky* three times. *Bad Boys* misses its chance at greatness, but it's saying something that this movie *had* a chance. It stands as one of those benchmark movies that we'll look back at for the talent it introduced. On the basis of their work here, Penn, Morales, and Rosenthal prove they have important careers ahead of them, and some of the supporting actors do, too. This movie's not a complete success, but it's a damned good try.

Bad Dreams ½★
R, 85 m., 1988 ✓

Jennifer Rubin (Cynthia), Bruce Abbott (Dr. Karmen), Richard Lynch (Harris), Dean Cameron (Ralph), Harris Yulin (Dr. Berrisford), Susan Barnes (Connie), John Scott Clough (Victor). Directed by Andrew Fleming and produced by Gale Anne Hurd. Screenplay by Fleming and Steven E. deSouza.

Bad Dreams opens with a scene in which a demented guru pours gasoline over his teenage followers and then sets them all afire. Miraculously, a young girl escapes instant death, but is hospitalized in a coma for thirteen years. When she reawakens, she is placed in a psychiatric hospital for treatment, only to become the victim of another twisted fiend, a psychiatrist who deliberately gives her medication that will make her suicidal.

Why do they make movies like this? The hypocrisy begins with the gruesome imagery and violence, which earn the film an R rating even though the primary audience for *Bad Dreams* is under seventeen. This is another of those foul teen-age vomitoriums in which the only message is that the world is evil and brutal. In this world, adults, with a few exceptions, want to kill teen-agers. The healing professions contain, of course, the sickest people of all.

The film has been given top-level production values by a successful Hollywood team. The producer, Gale Anne Hurd, has made two films I admired (*Terminator* and *Aliens*). The director, Andrew Fleming, is described as a brilliant recent graduate of the NYU film school, making his feature debut. The cast includes solid performances by Jennifer Rubin as the tortured girl, Bruce Abbott as the good doctor, Richard Lynch as the cult leader, and Harris Yulin as the demented shrink. The climactic scene is a cleverly crafted screamer.

I praise the production only to suggest that these people should be better employed in worthier projects. It is not surprising to see a violent teen-age film exploiting the lowest common denominator and preaching a message of nihilism and despair. It is not surprising to see the latest special effects technology supplying lingering close-ups of burnt flesh and other horrors. What is surprising, I suppose, is that nice people would want to wade in this sewer.

Maybe I'm naive. Maybe I don't completely understand the power of money to justify all ends. The *Nightmare on Elm Street* movies (of which *Bad Dreams* is an obvious clone) have made a lot of money at the box office. Perhaps *Bad Dreams* will, too. If it is a big enough hit, it may derail Andrew Fleming's career for years. Like Sean Cunningham, a nice man who devised the *Friday the 13th* series, he'll be typecast by Hollywood as a specialist in shock, blood, and nausea, and never get the chance to make anything worthwhile. He'll be trapped in his professional nightmare longer than his characters are trapped in theirs.

What was said at the story conferences for this movie? Were any doubts expressed, or did everyone pitch in with new ideas—like the scene where the girl is hanging from the rooftop by one hand and the psychiatrist is stabbing that hand with a needle containing deadly drugs? Did anyone wonder if maybe there were some creative, cheerful, and life-affirming screenplays floating around? Did the filmmakers even recognize that their work was a commercial for death? Do they know any teen-agers, especially younger, troubled ones, like the ones in their movie and in their potential audience? Are they aware of the national epidemic of teen-age suicides? Do they even think about such things, or was this movie simply a mindless exercise in technology?

I ask such questions because I watched the movie with a tide of unease rising within me. There is hardly a shred of hope anywhere in this film. It sinks to such depths that even the heroine's group therapy session turns into a grisly lottery of death, with first one and then another member killing himself.

I am aware that teen-agers go to these films and "like" them. I have seen many similar films with teen-age audiences—and you can forget about the R rating, because this is a movie aimed at high school and junior high school students, as any honest person in the movie industry will admit. Almost all teen-agers have a vein of low self-esteem, self-doubt, and despair. Most of them learn to deal with it, and to grow in confidence and maturity. *Bad Dreams* is poison for that process. Like the doctor in the film, whose care makes people sick or dead, the makers of this film are supplying "entertainment" that celebrates doom.

Badlands ★ ★ ★ ★

PG, 94 m., 1974

Martin Sheen (Kit), Sissy Spacek (Holly), Warren Oates (Holly's Father), Ramon Bieri (Cato), Ramon Vint (Deputy). Directed, produced, and written by Terence Malick.

They meet for the first time when she is in her front yard practicing baton-twirling. He has just walked off his job on a garbage truck. She thinks he is the handsomest man she's ever seen—he looks just like James Dean. He likes her because he never knew a fifteen-year-old who knowed so much: "She could talk like a grown-up woman, without a lot of giggles." Within a few weeks, they will be the targets of a manhunt after he has shot down half a dozen victims.

Terence Malick's *Badlands* calls them Kit and Holly, but his characters are inspired, of course, by Charles Starkweather and Caril Ann Fugate. They went on a wild ride in 1958 that ended with eleven people shot dead. The press named him the Mad Dog Killer, and Sunday supplement psychoanalysts said he killed because the kids at school kidded him about his bowlegs. Starkweather got the electric chair on June 25, 1959. From time to time a story appears about Caril Fugate's appeals to her parole board. She was sentenced to life.

She claimed she was kidnapped and forced to go along with Starkweather. When they first were captured, he asked the deputies to leave her alone: "She didn't do nothing." Later, at his trial, he claimed she was the most trigger-happy person he ever knew, and was responsible for some of the killings. It is a case that is still not closed, although *Badlands* sees her as a child of vast simplicity who went along at first because she was flattered that he liked her: "I wasn't popular at school on account of having no personality and not being pretty."

The film is tied together with her narration, written like an account of summer vacation crossed with the breathless prose style of a movie magazine. Some of the dialogue is loosely inspired by a book written by James Reinhardt, a criminologist who interviewed Starkweather on death row. Starkweather was offended by his death sentence. He viewed his crimes with total uninvolvement and asked how it was fair for him to die before he'd even been to a big city, or eaten in a fine restaurant, or seen a major-league game. That's what the movie captures, too: The detachment with which Kit views his killings, as Holly eventually draws away from him. He gets no pleasure from killing. He sees it only as necessary. He offers explanations which satisfy her for a while: "I killed them because they was bounty hunters who wanted the reward money. If they was policemen, just being paid for doing their job, that would have been different."

The movie makes no attempt to psychoanalyze its Kit Carruthers, and there are no symbols to note or lessons to learn. What comes through more than anything is the enormous loneliness of the lives these two characters lived, together and apart. He is ten years older than she is, but they're both caught up in the same adolescent love fantasy at first, as if Nat King Cole would always be there to sing "A Blossom Fell" on the portable radio while they held their sweaty embrace. He would not. To discourage his daughter from seeing "the kind of a man who collects garbage," her father punishes her by shooting her dog. She is "greatly distressed."

Kit is played by Martin Sheen, in one of the great modern film performances. He looks like James Dean, does not have bowlegs, and plays the killer as a plain and simple soul who has somehow been terribly damaged by life (the real Starkweather, his father explained at the time, was never quite right after being hit between the eyes with a two-by-four). Holly is played by the freckle-faced redhead Sissy Spacek. She takes her schoolbooks along on the murder spree so as not to get behind. She is in love with Kit at first, but there is a stubborn logic in her makeup and she eventually realizes that Kit means trouble. "I made a resolution never again to take up with any hell-bent types," she confides.

After the first murder and their flight, they never have any extended conversations about anything, nor are they seen to make love, nor is their journey given any symbolic meaning. They hope to reach refuge in the "Far North," where Kit might find employment as a mounted policeman. They follow their case in the newspapers, become aware of themselves as celebrities, and, in a brilliant scene at the end, the captured Kit hands out his comb, his lighter, and his ball-point pen as souvenirs to the National Guardsmen who had been chasing him.

The movie is very reserved in its attitude toward the characters. It observes them, most of the time, dispassionately. They are strange people, as were their real-life models; they had no rationalizations like Dillinger's regard for the poor or Bonnie and Clyde's ability to idealize themselves romantically. They were just two dumb kids who got into a thing and didn't have the sense to stop. They're something like the kids in Robert Altman's *Thieves Like Us* and the married couple in *The Sugarland Express.* They are in over their heads, incapable of understanding murder as a crime rather than a convenience, inhabitants of lives so empty that even their sins cannot fill them.

Bang the Drum Slowly ★ ★ ★ ★
PG, 98 m., 1973

Michael Moriarty (Henry Wiggen), Robert De Niro (Bruce Pearson), Vincent Gardenia (Dutch Schnell), Phil Foster (Joe), Ann Wedgeworth (Katie), Patrick McVey (Mr. Pearson). Directed by John Hancock and produced by Maurice and Lois Rosenfield. Screenplay by Mark Harris.

Bang the Drum Slowly is the ultimate baseball movie—and, despite what a plot summary might suggest, I think it's more about baseball than death. It takes place during the last season on this Earth of one Bruce Pearson, an earnest but dumb catcher from Georgia who learns, in the movie's first scene, that he is suffering from an incurable disease. The movie is about that season and about his friendship with Henry Wiggen, a pitcher, who undertakes to see that Bruce at least lives his last months with some dignity, some joy, and a few good games.

On the surface, then, the movie seems a little like *Brian's Song*. But it's not: It's mostly about baseball and the daily life of a major league club on the road. The fact of Bruce's approaching death adds a poignancy to the season, but *Bang the Drum Slowly* doesn't brood about death and it isn't morbid. In its mixture of fatalism, roughness, tenderness, and bleak humor, indeed, it seems to know more about the ways we handle death than a movie like *Love Story* ever guessed. The movie begins at the Mayo Clinic, follows the team through spring training, and then carries it through a season that feels remarkably like a Chicago Cubs year: a strong start, problems during the hot weather, dissension on the team, and then a pennant drive that (in the movie, anyway) is successful. There isn't a lot of play-by-play action, only enough to establish the games and make the character points. So when the team manager and the pitcher conspire to let Bruce finish his last game, despite his illness, the action footage is relevant and moving.

Bang the Drum Slowly was adapted for the screen by Mark Harris, from his observant 1955 novel. He seems to understand baseball players, or at least he can create convincing ones; if real baseball players aren't like the ones in this movie, somehow they should be. The director, John Hancock, is good with his actors and very good at establishing a lot of supporting characters without making a point of it (in this area he reminds me of Robert Altman's shorthand typecasting in *M*A*S*H* and *McCabe and Mrs. Miller).* Some of the best scenes are in the clubhouse, an arena of hope, despair, anger, practical jokes, and impassioned speeches by the manager.

He's played by Vincent Gardenia as a crafty, tough tactician with a heart of gold he tries to conceal. ("When I die," he says during one pre-game pep talk, "in the newspapers they'll write that the sons of bitches of this world have lost their leader.") He knows Bruce and Henry are concealing something, but he doesn't know what, and his efforts to find out are hilariously frustrated. At various times, the midwinter visit to the Mayo Clinic is explained as a fishing trip, a hunting trip, a wenching trip, and a secret mission to rid Bruce of the clap.

Gardenia, as the manager, is the third angle of a triangle that includes very good acting by Michael Moriarty, as Henry, and Robert De Niro, as Bruce. Henry is the All Star with the $70,000 contract and Bruce is a mediocre catcher who is constantly being ragged by his teammates. Henry's his only friend, until somehow when the team comes together for the pennant stretch, Bruce starts playing the best ball in his life, and the club (somewhat predictably) accepts him.

Hancock and Harris avoid any temptation to structure *Bang the Drum Slowly* as a typical sports movie. Although the team does win the pennant, not much of a point is made of that. There are no telegraphed big moments on the field, when everything depends on a strikeout or a home run or something. Even Bruce's last big hit in his last time at bat is limited, tactfully, to a triple.

Instead of going for a lot of high points, the movie paints characters in their everyday personalities. We get some feeling of life on the road as Henry talks with a hotel telephone operator who's a baseball fanatic, and Bruce moons over the prostitute he's in love with. Phil Foster has a great cameo role as a first-base coach with a genius for luring suckers into card games with remarkably elastic rules. Occupying the background in a lot of shots is the team's Cuban third baseman, who has it written into his contract that he be provided with a translator. And then, as the movie's shape begins to be visible, we realize it's not so much a sports movie as a movie about those elusive subjects, male bonding and work in America. That the males play baseball and that sport is their work is what makes this the ultimate baseball movie; never before has a movie considered the game from the inside out.

Barfly ★ ★ ★ ★

R, 110 m., 1987

(See related Film Clip, p. 790.)

Mickey Rourke (Henry), Faye Dunaway (Wanda Wilcox), Alice Krige (Tully), Jack Nance (Detective), J.C. Quinn (Jim), Frank Stallone (Eddie), Gloria LeRoy (Grandma Moses). Directed by Barbet Schroeder and produced by Schroeder, Fred Roos, and Tom Luddy. Screenplay by Charles Bukowski.

Louis Armstrong was trying to explain jazz one day, and he finally gave up and said, "There are some folks that, if they don't know, you can't tell 'em." The world of Charles Bukowski could be addressed in the same way. Bukowski is the poet of Skid Row, the Los Angeles drifter who spent his life, until age fifty, in an endless round of saloons and women, all of them cheap, expensive, bad, or good in various degrees. *Barfly*, based on his original screenplay, is a grimy comedy about what it might be like to spend a couple of days in his skin—a couple of the better and funnier days, although they aren't exactly a lark.

The movie takes place in a gutbucket bar down on the bad side of town, where the same regulars take up the same positions on the same bar stools every day. Your private life is nobody's business, but everybody in the joint knows all about it. To this bar, day after day, comes Henry (Mickey Rourke), a drunk who is sometimes also a poet. The day bartender hates him, probably for the same reason all bartenders in gutter saloons hate their customers: It's bad enough that they have to serve these losers, without taking a lot of lip from them, too.

Henry and the bartender head for the back alley to have a fight. Henry is beaten to a pulp. Hawking up spit and blood, he tosses down another drink and heads off for the hovel he calls his room. Another day, another adventure. One day he looks up from his drink and sees, sitting at the other end of the bar, a woman named Wanda (Faye Dunaway). She looks like she belongs in the place, and she doesn't look like she belongs in the place, you know? She looks like a drunk, all right, but she's still kind of classy. Henry and Wanda strike up a conversation, and, seeing that Henry is broke, Wanda invites him home.

The dialogue scenes between Rourke and Dunaway in this movie are never less than a pleasure, but their exchanges on that first night are poetry. She explains that if a guy comes along with a fifth, she is likely to leave with that guy, since when she drinks she always makes bad decisions. He nods. What other kinds of decisions are there when you're drunk? They drink, they talk, they flirt, they coexist. Another day, another adventure.

One day a beautiful rich girl with long hair (Alice Krige) comes to the bar looking for Henry. She publishes a literary magazine and has purchased some of Henry's stuff. He likes this development. They go to her house and drink, talk, flirt and coexist. The next time she turns up in the bar, Wanda is already there. The rich girl and Wanda do not coexist.

That's basically what the movie is about. *Barfly* is not heavy on plot, which is correct, since in the disordered world of the drinker, one thing rarely leads to another through any visible pattern. Each day is a window that opens briefly after the hangover and before the blackout, and you can never tell what you'll see through that window.

Barfly was directed by Barbet Schroeder, who commissioned the original screenplay by Bukowski and then spent eight years trying to get it made. (At one point, he threatened to cut off his fingers if Cannon Group president Menahem Golan did not finance it; the outcome of the story can be deduced by the fact that this is a Cannon release.) Rourke and Dunaway take their characters as opportunities to stretch as actors, to take chances and do extreme things. Schroeder never tries to impose too much artificial order on the events; indeed, he committed to filming Bukowski's screenplay exactly as written, in all its rambling but romantic detail.

The result is a truly original American movie, a film like no other, a period of time spent in the company of the kinds of characters Saroyan and O'Neill would have understood, the kinds of people we try not to see, and yet might enjoy more than some of our more visible friends. *Barfly* was one of 1987's best films.

Beetlejuice ★ ★
PG, 105 m., 1988

Alec Baldwin (Adam), Geena Davis (Barbara), Michael Keaton (Betelgeuse), Jeffrey Jones (Charles), Catherine O'Hara (Delia), Winona Ryder (Lydia), Sylvia Sidney (Juno). Directed by Tim Burton and produced by Michael Bender, Larry Wilson, and Richard Hashimoto. Screenplay by Michael McDowell and Warren Skaaren.

Beetlejuice gets off to a start that's so charming it never lives it down. The movie is all anticlimax once we realize it's going to be about gimmicks, not characters. During the enchanted opening minutes of the film, we meet a young married couple who have just moved into a strange new house, and we're introduced to some of the local townspeople. All of these characters have an offhand, unforced innocence, and no wonder: The movie was directed by Tim Burton, who created a similar feeling in *Pee Wee's Big Adventure.*

It's hard to describe what makes the opening scenes so special. Alec Baldwin and Geena Davis, as the young couple, seem so giddy, so heedlessly in love, that they project an infectious good cheer. The local folks are so gosh-darn down-home they must have been sired by L.L. Bean out of the *Prairie Home Companion.* The movie is bathed in a foolish charm. And, fool that I am, I expected that note to be carried all the way through the film. But it was not to be.

The young couple die in a silly accident. But they still live in the same house. The only problem is, there's nothing outside the door except for a strange science-fiction landscape that looks borrowed from Paul Schrader's *Cat People.* It takes them a while to figure out they're dead, and even longer to realize what has happened: Their fate is to remain in their former home as ghosts, while it is sold to a New York family (Jeffrey Jones and Catherine O'Hara, and Winona Ryder as their daughter) who have big plans for remodeling it.

This is all, I guess, a fairly clever idea. And the movie is well-played, especially by Davis (the girlfriend in *The Fly*) and Jones (the emperor in *Amadeus,* the teacher in *Ferris Bueller's Day Off*). But the story, which seemed so original, turns into a sitcom fueled by lots of special effects and weird sets and props, and the inspiration is gone.

To be sure, there has never before been a movie afterworld quite like this one. Heaven, or whatever it is, seems a lot like a cruise ship with a cranky crew. The "newlydeads" find a manual that instructs them on how to live as ghosts, and they also find an advertisement from a character named Betelgeuse (Michael Keaton), who specializes in "exorcisms of the living." They enlist him to try to scare the New Yorkers out of the house, but he turns out to be a cantankerous demon, and a lot more trouble than he's worth.

The best thing about the movie, apart from the opening, is the set design by Bo Welch. Both he and Burton seem inspired by the spirit of "Pee Wee's Playhouse" and *Pee Wee's Big Adventure,* in which objects can have lives of their own, and architectural details have an unsettling way of rearranging themselves. The look of the film might be described as cartoon surrealistic. But the film's dramatic method isn't nearly as original.

One of the problems is Keaton, as the exorcist. Nearly unrecognizable behind pounds of makeup, he prances around playing Betelgeuse as a mischievous and vindictive prankster, but his scenes don't seem to fit with the other action, and his appearances are mostly a nuisance. It's also a shame that Baldwin and Davis, as the ghosts, have to spend most of their time playing tricks on Jones and O'Hara and winning the sympathy of their daughter; I would have been more interested if the screenplay had preserved their sweet romanticism and cut back on the slapstick.

Being There ★ ★ ★ ★
PG, 130 m., 1980

Peter Sellers (Chance), Shirley MacLaine (Eve Rand), Melvyn Douglas (Ben Rand), Jack Warden (President), Richard Dysart (Dr. Allenby), Richard Basehart (Skrapinov). Directed by Hal Ashby and produced by Andrew Braunsberg. Screenplay by Jerzy Kosinski.

There's an exhilaration in seeing artists at the very top of their form: It almost doesn't matter what the form is, if they're pushing their limits and going for broke and it's working.

We can sense their joy of achievement—and even more so if the project in question is a risky, off-the-wall idea that could just as easily have ended disastrously.

Hal Ashby's *Being There* is a movie that inspires those feelings. It begins with a cockamamie notion, it's basically one joke told for two hours, and it requires Peter Sellers to maintain an excruciatingly narrow tone of behavior in a role that has him onscreen almost constantly. It's a movie based on an idea, and all the conventional wisdom agrees that emotions, not ideas, are the best to make movies from. But *Being There* pulls off its long shot and is a confoundingly provocative movie.

Sellers plays a mentally retarded gardener who has lived and worked all of his life inside the walls of an elegant Washington town house. The house and its garden are in a decaying inner-city neighborhood, but what goes on outside is of no concern to Sellers: He tends his garden, he watches television, he is fed on schedule by the domestic staff, he is content.

Then one day the master of the house dies. The household is disbanded. Sellers, impeccably dressed in his employer's privately tailored wardrobe, wanders out into the city. He takes along the one possession he'll probably need: His remote-control TV channel switcher. He uses it almost immediately; surrounded by hostile street kids, he imperturbably tries to switch channels to make them go away. He hasn't figured out that, outside his garden, life isn't television.

And that is the movie's basic premise, lifted intact from a Jerzy Kosinski novel. The Sellers character knows almost nothing about real life, but he has watched countless hours of television and he can be pleasant, smile, shake hands, and comport himself; he learned from watching all those guests on talk shows. He knows nothing about *anything*, indeed, except gardening. But when he stumbles into Washington's political and social upper crust, his simple truisms from the garden ("Spring is a time for planting") are taken as audaciously simple metaphors. This guy's a Thoreau! In no time at all, he's the closest confidant of a dying billionaire industrialist (Melvyn Douglas)—and the industrialist is the closest confidant of the president.

This is, you can see, a one-joke premise. It has to be if the Sellers performance is to work. The whole movie has to be tailored to the narrow range within which Sellers's gardener can think, behave, speak, and make choices. The ways in which this movie could have gone out of control, could have been relentlessly boring on the one hand, or manic with its own audacity on the other, are endless. But the tone holds. That's one of the most exhilarating aspects of the joy you can sense, as Ashby pulls this off: Every scene needs the confidence to play the idea completely straight.

There are wonderful comic moments, but they're never pushed so far that they strain the story's premise. Some of them involve: a battle between the CIA and the FBI as to which agency destroyed the gardener's files; Shirley MacLaine unsuccessfully attempts to introduce Sellers to the concept of romance; Sellers as a talk-show guest himself (at last!), and Sellers as the hit of a Washington cocktail party. The movie also has an audacious closing shot that moves the film's whole metaphor into a brand-new philosophical arena.

What is *Being There* about? I've read reviews calling it an indictment of television. But that doesn't fit; Sellers wasn't warped by television, he was retarded to begin with, and has TV to thank for what abilities he *has* to move in society. Is it an indictment of society, for being so dumb as to accept the Sellers character as a great philosophical sage? Maybe, but that's not so fascinating either. I'm not really inclined to plumb this movie for its message, although I'm sure that'll be a favorite audience sport. I just admire it for having the guts to take this weird conceit and push it to its ultimate comic conclusion.

Best Boy ★ ★ ★ ★

NO MPAA RATING, 111 m., 1980

A documentary produced, directed, and edited by Ira Wohl.

Sometimes there are movies that absorb you so completely that you forget you're watching them: They're simply happening to you. Ira Wohl's *Best Boy* is a movie like that. To see it is to participate in the lives of other people and to learn just a little more about being human. *Best Boy*, which won the 1980 Academy Award as best documentary, is the story of an only son named Philly, whose parents have always been too protective of him. But as the movie opens, it is time for Philly to go out a little more on his own—to go down to the corner for an ice cream cone, for example, or to look forward to his first day of school. Philly is fifty-two years old. He is mentally retarded, but otherwise, as a psychiatrist explains in the film, "quite normal." He is also warm and lovable, and when Wordsworth wrote that heaven was all about us when we were children, did he guess that would also be true for someone like Philly, who will never really leave childhood?

Best Boy deals intelligently with real people and their problems. It is not simply a documentary; it contains the surprises of true drama, and it is put together so thoughtfully that it takes what could have been a case study and turns it into a cliff-hanger. That is largely due to the complete access that the filmmaker, Ira Wohl, had to his subject. Philly is Wohl's cousin, and Philly's parents are Wohl's aunt and uncle. All the time he was growing up, Ira knew Philly—he played with him, presumably, when he was four or five and Philly seemed to be about the same age. Philly stayed four or five. As Wohl grew older, he realized that sooner or later Philly's parents would die, and that Philly's total dependence on them would leave him defenseless.

Philly had been at home almost all his life. The movie begins as his parents make the first reluctant, tentative steps to allow him a little more independence—to set him free. *Best Boy* moves very delicately around this subject, and with good reason: As we watch it, we realize that the parents have come to depend on Philly, too. He provided them with a rationale for their own lives and choices. He is their crutch as well as their burden. And there is yet another drama that unfolds within the film—unfolds so subtly we barely realize it is there, and yet concludes so inevitably that it casts a light back on all the scenes that went before. Philly's father is dying. There is a time in the film when the father clearly knows that and no one else in the film does, but we, strangers, share his secret with him.

You see what I mean when I say *Best Boy* isn't a case study. It's not about what should be done with Philly, and it has little to do with the "problem" of mental retardation. It is so specifically about Philly and his family and their daily choices in life that we almost feel adopted into the family. And we get to like Philly so much! He is sweet and cheerful, patient and good-humored, with a child's logic that cuts right through so much of the confusion adults surround him with. There is a wonderful scene with a psychiatrist, who is trying to administer a series of questions Philly obviously feels are silly. There is a visit to the theater, where Philly is allowed backstage to meet Zero Mostel, and they sing "If I Were a Rich Man" together. Why is it, the movie asks but never answers, that Philly can remember songs better than speech?

Best Boy suffers, I suppose, from being labeled a documentary: Some small-minded people make it a policy never to watch one. But at the Toronto Festival of Festivals, where the patrons are asked to vote for their favorite film, it astonished everyone by defeating all the features in the festival and placing first. It's a wonderfully positive experience.

The Best Little Whorehouse in Texas ★ ★

R, 114 m., 1982

Burt Reynolds (Ed Earl), Dolly Parton (Miss Mona), Charles Durning (Governor), Dom DeLuise (Melvin Thorpe), Jim Nabors (Deputy), Lois Nettleton (Dulcie Mae), Theresa Merritt (Jewel). Directed by Colin Higgins and produced by Thomas L. Miller, Edward K. Milkis, and Robert L. Boyett. Screenplay by Larry L. King, Peter Masterson, and Higgins.

If I were asked what image dominates *The Best Little Whorehouse in Texas,* the honest answer would have to be: Dolly Parton's plunging neckline. I am not trying to be cute. The awesome swell of her wondrous bosom dominates every scene Dolly appears in, and that includes just about every scene in the movie. W.C. Fields, the old scene-stealer, rebelled against appearing on screen with an animal, a child, or a plunging neckline, on the not unreasonable grounds that audiences would not be looking at him. Fields could have appeared incognito in *Whorehouse,* as, indeed, Burt Reynolds occasionally does.

The puzzling thing about the Parton décolletage is that so little is made of so much. You'd think there would be sizzling chemistry between Parton and Reynolds, who are two of my favorite movie sex symbols simply because they always seem so full of good cheer. But that isn't the case here. They're great looking, they smile a lot, they've been provided with good dialogue, but somehow they seem a little bored with each other, as if their affair has been going on a little too long; they're a happy old cheatin' couple. There is some passion in the movie, but it's concentrated in two scenes where Dolly is absent. In both of them, Reynolds lets loose with a non-stop cussing barrage, chewing out a foppish TV interviewer (Dom DeLuise) and a slippery governor (Charles Durning). Dolly never *really* gets to let go, and the limitless exuberance she displayed in *9 to 5* seems as tightly corseted here as her costumes are.

What's the problem? I think maybe the movie's story got misplaced somewhere in the middle of the movie's legend. The best little whorehouse of the movie's title was a legendary Texas brothel named the Chicken Ranch, which was immortalized first by generations of young Texans and later in a Broadway play by Larry King and Peter Masterson. Whorehouses, Texas ones included, are not exactly very nice places, but the whorehouse in this movie almost seems like a refuge for wayward girls. The story has been cleaned up so carefully to showcase Parton and Reynolds that the scandal has been lost; the movie has been turned into a defense of free enterprise and a hymn to romance.

That's too bad. I kept waiting for Dolly Parton to be sexy in this movie, and she never was. She was cheerful, spunky, energetic, angry, sad, and loyal, but she was never sexy—not even in bed. Her feelings for Reynolds seemed to be largely therapeutic, and I believe there were even times when they discussed the nature of their relationship. Since just the mere word "relationship" is profoundly subversive to eroticism and sexuality, we're a little baffled to see the madam and the sheriff turned into the sort of couple that discusses itself in first-person articles for *Cosmo*. This is carried so far that Parton's only reference to her bosom (indeed, the only moment in the movie when anyone deigns to even *notice* it) is about her problems "luggin' these around." It's all so matter-of-fact, it's asexual.

Parton and Reynolds are pleasant enough in *Whorehouse*, and we expect that from two such likable actors. Dom DeLuise is wildly improbable and distractingly bizarre as the TV investigative reporter who wants to shut down the Chicken Ranch. Charles Durning has a lot of fun with a sly song-and-dance routine. Lois Nettleton has a thankless role as Reynold's "other" mistress (we never do know what to make of *their* relationship, which must have been mangled in the editing). There are a few funny jokes, some raunchy one-liners, some mostly forgettable songs set to completely forgettable choreography, and then there is Dolly Parton. If they ever give Dolly her freedom and stop packaging her so antiseptically, she could be terrific. But Dolly and Burt and *Whorehouse* never get beyond the concept stage in this movie.

Betrayal ★ ★ ★ ★

R, 95 m., 1983

Jeremy Irons (Jerry), Ben Kingsley (Robert), Patricia Hodge (Emma). Directed by David Jones and produced by Sam Spiegel. Screenplay by Harold Pinter.

Love stories have beginnings, but affairs . . . affairs have endings, too. Even sad love stories begin in gladness, when the world is young and the future reaches out cheerfully forever. Then, of course, eventually you get Romeo and Juliet dead in the tomb, but that's the price you have to pay. Life isn't a free ride. Think how much *more* tragic a sad love story would be, however, if you could see into the future, so that even *this* moment, *this* kiss, is in the shadow of eventual despair.

The absolutely brilliant thing about *Betrayal* is that it is a love story told backward. There is a lot in this movie that is wonderful—the performances, the screenplay by Harold Pinter—but what makes it all work is the structure. When Pinter's stage version of *Betrayal* first appeared, back in the late 1970s, there was a tendency to dismiss his reverse chronology as a gimmick. Not so. It is the very heart and soul of this story. It means that we in the audience know more about the unhappy romantic fortunes of Jerry and Robert and Emma at *every moment* than they know about themselves. Even their joy is painful to see.

Jerry is a youngish London literary agent, clever, good-looking, confused about his feelings. Robert, his best friend, is a publisher. Robert is older, stronger, smarter, and more bitter. Emma is Robert's wife and becomes Jerry's lover. But that is telling the story chronologically. And the story begins at the end, with Robert and Emma fighting, and with Robert slapping her, and with Emma and Jerry meeting in a pub for a painful reunion two years after their affair is over. Each additional scene takes place further back in time, and the sections have uncanny titles: Two years earlier. Three years earlier. We aren't used to this. At a public preview of the film, some people in the audience actually *resisted* the backward timeframe, as if the purpose of the playwright was just to get on with the story, damn it all, and stop this confounded fooling around.

The *Betrayal* structure strips away all artifice. It shows, heartlessly, that the very capacity for love itself is sometimes based on betraying not only other loved ones, but even ourselves. The movie is told mostly in encounters between two of the characters; all three are not often on screen together, and we never meet Jerry's wife. These people are smart and they talk a lot—too much, maybe, because there is a peculiarly British reserve about them that sometimes prevents them from quite saying what they mean. They lie and they half-lie. There are universes left unspoken in their unfinished sentences. They are all a little embarrassed that the messy urges of sex are pumping away down there beneath their civilized deceptions.

The performances are perfectly matched. Ben Kingsley (of *Gandhi*) plays Robert, the publisher, with such painfully controlled fury that there are times when he actually is frightening. Jeremy Irons, as Jerry, creates a man whose desires are stronger than his convictions, even though he spends a lot of time talking about his convictions, and almost none acknowledging his desires. Patricia Hodge, as Emma, loves them both and hates them both and would have led a much happier life if they had not been her two choices. But how could she know that when, in life, you're required by the rules to start at the beginning?

Beverly Hills Cop ★ ★ ½

R, 105 m., 1984

Eddie Murphy (Axel Foley), Judge Reinhold (Detective Billy Rosewood), John Ashton (Sergeant Taggart), Lisa Eilbacher (Jenny), Ronny Cox (Lieutenant Bogomil). Directed by Martin Brest and produced by Don Simpson and Jerry Bruckheimer. Screenplay by Daniel Petrie.

Eddie Murphy looks like the latest victim of the Star Magic Syndrome, in which it is assumed that a movie will be a hit simply because it stars an enormously talented person. Thus it is not necessary to give much thought to what he does or says, or to the story he finds himself occupying. *Beverly Hills Cop* is a movie with an enormously appealing idea—a tough black detective from Detroit goes to Beverly Hills to avenge the murder of a friend—but the filmmakers apparently expected Murphy to carry this idea entirely by himself.

Murphy plays a street-wise rebel who is always getting in trouble with his commanding officer because he does things his own way. The movie opens with an example of that: Murphy is single-handedly running a sting operation when the cops arrive unexpectedly, setting off a wild car-truck chase through the city streets. Even while we're watching the thrilling chase, however, stirrings of unease are beginning to be felt: Any movie that *begins* with a chase is not going to be heavy on originality and inspiration. Then Murphy's old friend comes to town, fresh from a prison term and six months of soaking up the rays in California. The friend has some negotiable bonds with him, and then some friends of the guy who owns the bonds turn up and murder Murphy's friend. That makes Eddie mad, and he drives his ancient beater out to Beverly Hills, where it sort of stands out among the Porsches and Mercedes. He also meets a childhood friend (Lisa Eilbacher) who now works for an art dealer.

At this point, the movie can go in one of two directions. It can become a perceptive and pointed satire about American attitudes, showing how the ultrachic denizens of Beverly Hills react to this black cop from Detroit. Or it can go for broad, cheap laughs, and plug into a standard plot borrowed from countless TV crime shows. *Bev-*

erly Hills Cop doesn't pause a moment before taking the low road. We figure that out right away, when Murphy tries to register in a hotel and is told there isn't any room. He loudly pulls both ranks and race, claiming to be a correspondent from *Rolling Stone* and accusing the desk clerk of racism. This is (a) not funny, and (b) not convincing, because Beverly Hills desk clerks were not born yesterday. If the people who made this movie had been willing to listen to the ways that real people really talk, they could have made the scene into a jewel instead of an embarrassment.

Meanwhile, the plot thickens. It turns out that the killers of Eddie's friend were employees of the evil Victor Maitland (Steven Berkoff), a Beverly Hills criminal whose art gallery—where Eilbacher works—is a front for cocaine smuggling. When Murphy tries to move against Maitland, he comes up against the Beverly Hills Cops, including an Abbott and Costello team that supplies unnecessary pratfalls, successfully undermining the credibility of any police scene that threatens to work. But wait a minute. What's this movie about, anyway? Is it a comedy or an action picture? Audiences may expect a comedy, but the closing shootout seems inspired by the machine gun massacre at the end of Brian De Palma's *Scarface*, and the whole business with the cocaine is so very, very tired that when we see the boss and his henchmen in the warehouse, we feel like we've switched to another movie—maybe a dozen other movies. Murphy is one of the smartest and quickest young comic actors in the movies. But he is not an action hero, despite his success in *48 HRS*, and by plugging him into an action movie, the producers of *Beverly Hills Cop* reveal a lack of confidence in their original story inspiration. It's like they had a story conference that boiled down to: "Hey gang! Here's a great idea! Let's turn it into a standard idea and fill it with clichés, and take out the satire and put in a lot of machine guns!"

Beverly Hills Cop II ★
R, 105 m., 1987

Eddie Murphy (Axel Foley), Judge Reinhold (Detective Rosewood), Brigitte Nielsen (Karla Fry), Dean Stockwell (Chip Cain), John Ashton (Sergeant Taggart). Directed by Tony Scott produced by Don Simpson and Jerry Bruckheimer. Screenplay by Larry Ferguson and Warren Skaaren.

Something has gone terribly wrong here. They've made the wrong sequel. The original *Beverly Hills Cop* was a screenplay written for Sylvester Stallone, but filmed by Eddie Murphy. After it was such a big hit, the theory was that *Beverly Hills Cop II* would be a *real* Eddie Murphy movie, with more comedy and fewer guns and chases.

Alas, Part Two seems even more like a Stallone vehicle than the first movie. I'm not even sure it's intended as a comedy. It's filled wall-to-wall with the kind of routine action and violence that Hollywood extrudes by the yard and shrink-wraps to order. But it makes no particular effort to be funny, and actually seems to take its ridiculous crime plot seriously—as if we cared.

There's another problem, too. A big one. Eddie Murphy is not likable in this movie. He comes across as a loud, arrogant boor; a little of him goes a long way. Somehow they've lost track of their original appealing idea, which was that a smart, funny street cop from Detroit would waltz into Beverly Hills and deflate the Porsche and sunglasses set.

Doesn't work that way this time. Murphy's idea of a comic scene in this movie is to shout endlessly at people in a shrill, angry voice. There's a scene where he visits the Playboy mansion and shouts at the receptionist, and you want to crawl under your seat in embarrassment. Murphy comes across as the problem rather than the solution.

What is comedy? That's a pretty basic question, I know, but *Cop II* never thought to ask it. Doesn't comedy usually center around a series of surprises based on insights into human nature? Let's assume that everyone in Beverly Hills is obsessed with money, power, possessions, and social status. Let's further assume that a black cop from Detroit rides into town and doesn't give a damn for their effete values and conspicuous consumption, and cuts through the crap like a knife through butter. That would be funny. It is, however, an idea which this series has been unable to fully exploit after two tries. Instead, Murphy and his associates make the fatal error of assuming that the way you deal with jerks is to be a bigger jerk.

For what they probably paid for the screenplay for this movie, they should have been able to buy a new one. The plot of *Cop II* is recycled right out of every other brainless, routine modern high-tech crime picture. It's not really even a plot; it's a series of standard sequences, involving the Chase, the Powerful Men of Evil, the Sexy Bitch-Goddess, the Hit Men, and the Shoot-Out. (The chase involves a cement truck, and proves definitely that cement trucks do not work very well in chases.)

I'm an Eddie Murphy fan. I think that on a good day he is capable of being funnier than anybody else in the movies right now. I was one of the admirers of *The Golden Child*, which plugged him into a cheerfully ridiculous plot, and made him a lovable character who was doggedly trying to endure a series of exotic dangers. I also like Murphy when he's street-smart and capable, as in *48 HRS*.

What I don't like is the unstated assumption, in *Cop II*, that he is funny by definition, and that anybody who gets in his way is a fool. Maybe Murphy should study some of those old "I Love Lucy" episodes where Lucy gets into situations she can't handle—she's up against a snooty headwaiter in a stuck-up restaurant, let's say. What does she do? Scream at the guy? No, she always finds a way to deflate the guy simply by remaining true to her own character and insisting on being treated as a human being. That's what's missing in *Cop II*.

We don't object to the way the jerks in Beverly Hills want to treat Murphy, because, frankly, he's a bigger jerk. Because he's the star, of course, no one else in the plot is allowed to lay a glove on him. But here's an interesting possibility. Given the character he plays in *Cop II*, the movie might have been funnier if they'd reversed every situation and made him the butt of the jokes.

Beyond the Limit ★ ★ ½
R, 103 m., 1983

Michael Caine (Charlie Fortnum), Richard Gere (Eduardo Plan), Bob Hoskins (Colonel Perez), Joaquim De Alameia (Leon), Elpidia Carrilo (Clara). Directed by John Mackenzie and produced by Norma Heyman. Screenplay by Christopher Hampton.

There are times when this movie is a mess. There are other times when it becomes quietly moving. *Beyond the Limit* has one of the best endings I can remember in a mediocre film, an ending that goes a long way toward redeeming some of the sloppiness that went before. And all through the film, there is a remarkable performance by Michael Caine, who has been around for so long, in so many movies, that it's easy to forget what a fine actor he is.

The film is based on *The Honorary Consul*, Graham Greene's novel about a bungled South American terrorist kidnapping. The movie tells most of the same story, involving the alcoholic British honorary consul (Caine), the young half-British doctor (Richard Gere), the priest turned revolutionary (Joaquim De Alameia), and the beautiful Indian prostitute (Elpidia Carrilo) who becomes Caine's wife and Gere's lover. The film is also fairly faithful to Greene's ending, a study in conflicting morality, where the priest kidnaps the worthless British consul under the impression he is the American ambassador—and then the doctor's loyalties are torn between his friend the consul, his lover the consul's wife, and his old friend the priest.

What is not faithful to the novel is the casting of Gere as the doctor. Gere is so wrong for the role that he undermines every scene he's in, distracting attention from Caine's understated, quietly poignant performance. Halfway through the movie, as I was witnessing the obligatory Gere sex scene, I began to grow angry. Not at Gere, who can be effective in the right role, but at the producers, who chose his popular appeal over the obvious demands of the material. The doctor in the Greene novel is not a swaggering bodybuilder with a smoldering sexuality, but a troubled, worried, overworked young man with a conscience. The amoral way in which Gere possesses his friend's wife is totally false to the spirit of the book.

What is true, though, is the Michael Caine performance. The character he plays is Charlie Fortnum, a pathetic drunk holding onto the honorary consulship as a last vestige of dignity, investing all of his higher feelings into love for his wife. Caine gives a great performance, sweaty, exhausted, red-eyed, filled with false bonhomie, always with his eye on the level in the whiskey bottle. There is a kind of nobility in the way he accepts his fate, after the terrorists kidnap him and nobody, frankly, cares enough to ransom him. There is also a real person here, in a performance that suggests Fortnum's life up until this point, his history of failure, his essential good nature. The movie's final scene, between Caine and Carrillo, is one of the best scenes Caine has ever played.

Unhappily, it comes in a movie that never comes together, and that lingers too long on a Richard Gere who seems to have wandered in from another movie, would-be British accent and all. The casting is one of the movie's mysteries; another one is the change to a meaningless and forgettable title; a third is how Michael Caine succeeded in delivering an intact performance right there in the middle of all the lost dreams.

Big ★ ★ ★
PG, 102 m., 1988 ✓

Tom Hanks (Josh Baskin), Elizabeth Perkins (Susan Lawrence), Robert Loggia (MacMillan), Jared Rushton (Billy Kopeche). Directed by Penny Marshall and produced by James L. Brooks and Robert Greenhut. Screenplay by Anne Spielberg and Gary Ross.

Sooner or later, they're going to get this right. *Big* is no less than the fourth almost simultaneous variation on the same theme—a kid trapped in an adult body. How did four Hollywood studios simultaneously find themselves making essentially the same story? I guess each one thought its was the best, and refused to back down. And so we got *Like Father, Like Son* and *Vice Versa* and *18 Again* and now *Big*, which is a streamlined edition.

Instead of having a father and son exchange bodies, this one does away with the second character and simply gives us a thirteen-year-old who wishes he was big, and gets his wish. That's a useful inspiration, because it spares the filmmakers from the task of cutting back and forth between two different stories (dad in kid's body goes out with teen-age girl while kid in dad's body dates sexpot). Instead, we follow one character on his journey across the generation gap, and because there's more time to develop his dilemma, the movie is more persuasive.

Big describes the adventures of Josh Baskin, who, in a brief opening sequence, is a normal, pint-sized adolescent. He has a crush on one of the girls in his class—a girl who stands a head taller than he does. I had forgotten (or repressed) my memories of those strange days in the seventh grade when all the girls suddenly become amazons, but they all came crashing back during the movie's most poignant scene. In a carnival, Josh manages to stand in line next to the girl of his dreams, and it looks like he'll be able to sit next to her on the ride—but when they get to the front of the line, the carnival guy tells him he's not tall enough to go on the ride.

This is a species of humiliation beyond the limits of human endurance. As the girl gets on the ride with a taller boy, Josh wanders off forlorn and lonely, to a remote corner of the midway where he finds a strange fortune-telling machine. He puts in a quarter, wishes he were big, and wakes up the next morning as Tom Hanks.

Hanks carries most of the movie, and does it well; as a thirteen-year-old in a thirty-year-old body, he is able to suggest such subtle things as a short attention span, a disregard for social niceties, and an ability to hop, skip, and jump through an office lobby. Through a stroke of good luck, he gets hired by a toy company, where his childlike innocence soon gets him a promotion to vice president in charge of product development. He and the company president (Robert Loggia) are the only two guys in the place who really like to play with toys, and there is a brilliant comic sequence where the two of them play "Chopsticks" by dancing on a giant computerized piano keyboard.

The movie is never quite able to deal successfully with the fact that the kid's mother thinks he has been kidnapped—it's cruel the way that plot thread is left dangling. But as Hanks slowly adjusts to his incredible good fortune, he attracts the attention of Elizabeth Perkins, a company executive who falls genuinely in love with his childlike innocence, little realizing it is real.

Big is a tender, soft-hearted, and cheerful movie, well-directed by Penny Marshall and with a script by Anne Spielberg and Gary Ross that has a lot of fun with simple verbal misunderstandings. (When the kid says, "What's a market research report?" Loggia nods and barks, "Exactly!") Hanks, who had a tendency to push too hard, I thought, in *Nothing in Common*, this time finds a vulnerability and sweetness for his character that's quite appealing.

In the sweepstakes of generation-gap movies, *Big* is not as funny as *Vice Versa*, and Hanks does not have as much fun with physical humor as Judge Reinhold did in that movie. But both films are way ahead of the other two contenders, and this one may be the only one of the four that could really be identified with by a thirteen-year-old kid.

Big Business ★ ★

PG, 94 m., 1988 ✓

Bette Midler (Sadie Shelton/Ratliff), Lily Tomlin (Rose Shelton/Ratliff), Fred Ward (Roone Dimmick), Edward Herrmann (Graham Sherbourne), Michele Placido (Fabio Alberici), Daniel Gerroll (Chuck), Barry Primus (Michael). Directed by Jim Abrahams and produced by Steve Tisch and Michael Peyser. Screenplay by Dori Pierson and Marc Rubel.

Big Business opens with a scene in which two sets of twins are mixed up, so that in later life each set will contain one Bette Midler and one Lily Tomlin. This ought to have inspired a funny movie, but instead, what it inspires is an endless and dreary series of scenes in which the various twins just barely miss running into each other in the Plaza Hotel. You can picture the scenes. The elevator doors close on one Bette Midler just as the other Bette Midler comes running down the hallway.

This is not funny. It is never funny, in this movie or any other movie. People running into each other can be funny, but when they just miss, what are we supposed to do? Slap our knees and say, "Lord a-mighty, they dern near ran into each other and wouldn't *that* have been funny!" Early in the production history of this movie, somebody should have made the following observation: Scenes of people barely missing one another in hotels are not amusing.

In its presentation of the two sets of non-twins, the movie backs genetics rather than environment as the prime formative factor in human development. Both Bette Midlers are conniving and materialistic, and both Lily Tomlins are flutter-brained and well-meaning. But the Midler/Tomlin team from down South in Jupiter Hollow is a little nicer. They work in the local factory, which has manufactured porch swings from time immemorial.

Meanwhile, the New York Midler wants to sell out the factory and the town to a shifty Italian investor who wants to strip-mine the whole county right off the map. The impending sale inspires the Jupiter Hollow women to travel up north to New York for the annual stockholders' meeting of the company controlled by the Manhattan women. Both sets of women check into the Plaza Hotel at the same time, inspiring numerous flat and tedious scenes that are structured as if they were intended to be slapstick.

The life all seems to have escaped from this movie. Midler and Tomlin can be funny actors, but here they both seem muted and toned down in all of the characters they play. The most promising character is probably Sadie Shelton, Midler's New York company executive, who has the potential to be a bitch on wheels but never realizes it. The Jupiter Hollow Midler seems unfocused, and both Tomlins seem to be the same rather vague woman who has trouble with her shoulder pads.

The fundamental problems of the movie can all be traced, I suspect, back to the screenplay. After the babies have been switched and the premise has been set up, far too much time is spent with the futile manipulation of the four characters in the Plaza Hotel. One begins a breakfast and the other finishes it. One doesn't recognize the Italian, but the other one does. In the least amusing of several would-be running gags, a bum outside the hotel does double takes when he thinks he's seeing double. All of these scenes are givens—and should have been given away, to make room for laughs that could come from character, dialogue, and conflict.

In a movie of disappointments, the major disappointment is a shocker. What have we been waiting for through the whole movie? For the moment when the four women all meet in the same place at the same time, right? So what happens when they do? After the first shocked moment of mutual recognition—*nothing* happens! The movie cuts to the next scene. There is *no* scene in which the women reconstruct what must have happened, and deal with their new reality. No scene in which the two nice Tomlins gang up on the two bitchy Midlers. If there's anything worse than a long, slow, boring buildup to a payoff, it's the buildup without the payoff. This movie doesn't feel finished.

The Big Chill ★ ★ ½

R, 108 m., 1983

Tom Berenger (Sam), Glenn Close (Sarah), William Hurt (Nick), Jeff Goldblum (Michael), Meg Tilly (Chloe), Kevin Kline (Harold), Mary Kay Place (Meg), JoBeth Williams (Karen). Directed by Lawrence Kasdan. Screenplay by Kasdan and Barbara Benedek.

I was going through some old papers the other night, from cardboard boxes that were packed at the end of college and have followed me around ever since. To open them up was like walking into a time capsule. There they were, the little campus literary magazines and the yellowing issues of the University of Illinois' *Daily Illini*, and a photo of a political demonstration on the steps of the student union.

On the other hand, I was going through my mail today and I got a letter from a teen-ager who wanted to know why they were making so many movies about the 1960s. "These are the 1980s," he informed me. "Who cares what happened in the olden days?" I think "olden days" was an attempt at humor.

In any event, I wrote back that the 1960s were big in the movies right now because the people who make the movies were students in the 1960s, and that the teen-agers of 2001 would no doubt be sick and tired of the olden days of the 1980s. And then I thought about *The Big Chill*, a movie in which survivors of the 1960s ask themselves how they could possibly be in their thirties. This is the second movie on almost exactly the same theme—a weekend reunion among college friends from the sixties, during which they relive the past, fear the present, and regret the interim. They could have called it *Son of the Return of the Secaucus Seven.*

It's a good movie. It's well acted, the dialogue is accurately heard, and the camera is extremely attentive to details of body language. It observes wonderfully well how its veterans of the 1960s have grown up into adulthood, consumerhood, parenthood, drunkenhood, adulteryhood, and regrethood. These people could all be wearing warm-up jackets with *poignancy* stenciled on the backs.

The movie begins at a funeral. One of the old college friends has killed himself, for reasons that never become clear. The others gather for his funeral and stay for a weekend in a big old summer house. We get to meet them: the intellectual, the failed writer, the confused TV star, the woman who wants to have a baby and can't tear her eyes away from the biological clock. They eat, they drink, they pair up in various combinations, and they ask themselves questions like, Who were we? Who are we now? What happened to us? What will happen to us?

Because they are all graduates of the University of Michigan at Ann Arbor, they phrase these questions with style, of course. The dialogue sounds like a series of bittersweet captions from *New Yorker* cartoons. And at the end, of course, nothing is really discovered, nothing is really settled, and they go back into holding patterns until the next funeral.

The Big Chill is a splendid technical exercise. It has all the right moves. It knows all the right words. Its characters have all the right clothes, expressions, fears, lusts, and ambitions. But there's no payoff and it doesn't lead anywhere. I thought at first that was a weakness of the movie. There also is the possibility that it's the movie's message.

The Big Easy ★ ★ ★ ★

R, 106 m., 1987

Dennis Quaid (Remy McSwain), Ellen Barkin (Anne Osborne), Ned Beatty (Jack Kellom), John Goodman (Andre De Soto), Lisa Jane Persky (McCabe), Ebbe Roe Smith (Ed Dodge), Tom O'Brien (Bobby McSwain), Charles Ludlam (Lamar Parmentel). Directed by Jim McBride and produced by Stephen Friedman. Screenplay by Daniel Petrie, Jr.

The Big Easy is one of the richest American films of 1987. It also happens to be a great thriller. I say "happens," because I believe the plot of this movie is only an excuse for its real strength: the creation of a group of characters so interesting, so complicated, and so original that they make a lot of other movie people look like paint-by-number characters.

The movie takes place in New Orleans, that most mysterious of American cities, a city where you have the feeling you will never really know what goes on down those shadowy passages into those green and humid courtyards so guarded from the street. The heroes of the film are two law enforcement officials: Remy (Dennis Quaid), a vice cop, and Anne (Ellen Barkin), a special prosecutor for the D.A. They meet over the dead body of a Mafia functionary, and of course they are immediately attracted to each other.

So far, no surprises. But when they go out to dinner and the restaurant owner won't think of accepting their money, Anne accuses Remy of being on the take and he accuses her of not understanding how the system operates. Later we learn more about the system in New Orleans and come to understand more about Remy. He is an honest cop in the ways that really count and a dishonest cop in small ways he has been able to rationalize. He doesn't have a problem, for example, with the department's illegal "widows and orphans fund," because he's using the money to send his kid brother through college.

There are more killings. There also is, between Anne and Remy, one of the most erotic love scenes I have ever seen in a movie—all the more erotic because the two lovers do not perform like champions in the sexual Olympics, but come to bed with all the insecurity of people who are almost afraid to believe it could, this time, be for real.

The background of their story is populated with characters so well-drawn and with character actors so finely chosen that the movie is fascinating from moment to moment, even when nothing much seems to be happening.

My favorite supporting performance in the movie is by Charles Ludlam, as a defense attorney, impeccable in his Panama hat and summer suit, talking a mile a minute in a shrill Cajun shriek, like a cross between Truman Capote and F. Lee Bailey. Another slick Southerner is created by Ned Beatty, in his finest performance in years, as the police chief who sincerely wants to do the right thing and sincerely cannot.

All of these characters inhabit the most convincing portrait of New Orleans I've ever seen. The authentic local Cajun music on the sound track and the instinctive feel for the streets and alleys, the lives and the ways of doing business, the accents and the evasions, make the city itself into a participant in what happens.

In the middle of this riotous gumbo of colorful life, Quaid and Barkin construct a relationship that, by itself, would be enough for a whole movie. They love each other. They are disillusioned. They face each other as enemies in court. They reconcile at a wonderful scene at a fish boil and Cajun hootenanny thrown by Quaid's friends.

The movie indeed ends with the obligatory scene of climactic violence that is required in all thrillers, but it's well-handled and the actions at least do seem to be consistent with the characters.

The movie was directed by Jim McBride, whose previous film was *Breathless*, with Richard Gere, a high-style pastiche of 1940s crime movies and 1980s art direction. *The Big Easy* seems to be by a different man, a director not only in full mastery of his materials but in full sympathy with his characters. Forget it's a thriller. See it because you want to meet these people.

Big Foot ½★

PG, 76 m., 1971

John Carradine (Trader), Joi Lansing (Girl Pilot), Chris Mitchum (Second Cyclist), Ken Maynard (Shopkeeper), Lindsay Crosby (Motorcyclist). Directed by Robert F. Slater and produced by Tony Cardoza. Screenplay by Slater and James Gordon White.

Why, you are asking, did I decide to see *Big Foot*? Why am I taking your time—time you could spend trimming your toenails and talking to your indoor plants, telling them what nice plants they are—to review *Big Foot*? What strange light in the sky, what weird whistling in my ear, what blood-soaked note tied to a rock and thrown through my window, sent me to see *Big Foot*? These are good questions. The cast alone convinced me. Let me put it as simply as I can. If you have ever wanted to see a movie starring John Carradine, Joi Lansing, Lindsay Crosby, Chris Mitchum, and Ken Maynard, then *Big Foot* is almost certainly going to be your only chance. Not since Joan Crawford starred in *Trog* has there been such an opportunity.

Joi Lansing began her career as a model in a provocative magazine. Lansing is still startling, especially with a jumpsuit. She parachutes in it. It conceals a minidress slit to the waist, and a top that is slashed to the belt, and she runs away from Big Foot for about five minutes in this costume, bouncing through the woods but not (for some mysterious reason) from her blouse.

No matter. There is always John Carradine. He plays a backwoods trader with a line of goods packed into the rear of his 1958 Ford station wagon. He stops at a general store run by Ken Maynard (yes, Ken Maynard) and Ken makes a phone call while standing in front of a poster from one of his old movies (*Texas Gunfighter,* if I remember correctly) wearing the same ten-gallon hat that's on the poster. "There have been a lot of strange things going on up in those hills," he informs the sheriff, after Chris Mitchum's girlfriend has been carried away by a half-human, half-animal creature with big feet. But the sheriff refuses to go up on the mountain after dark, and so Chris enlists his buddies in a motorcycle gang led by Lindsay Crosby (yes, Lindsay Crosby).

This is no ordinary motorcycle gang. All of its members ride identical brand-new medium-sized Yamahas, which are credited in the titles to a Hollywood Yamaha agency. The gang members also wear bright-colored nylon Windbreakers with pull-strings at the bottom, and they wear new knit shirts and dress loafers. The girls wear bikinis. The gang's hairstyle is set by Lindsay Crosby's receding ducktail.

Meanwhile, Lansing and another girl are tied to trees (saplings would be a better word) by the creatures, and then Lansing is carried off and given to Big Foot. Big Foot is usually shot from a camera angle between his toes, making him loom over the camera like King Kong, but when we see him straight-on he looks about five feet ten inches or eleven inches tall. He wears a shaggy costume stitched together out of old, dirty brown shag rugs.

Anyway, there is an exciting chase through the woods, which is only slowed down a little bit by the fact that the movie has nine unidentified extras who have to file past the camera. Then Big Foot runs into a cave. This has us hoping that Joan Crawford will appear and explain that the creature has been misunderstood (in *Trog,* she went into the cave with a twenty-nine-cent bunch of carrots, calling "Here, Trog?").

But, no, a motorcyclist pulls a bundle of dynamite from his belt and throws it into the cave. No fuse, just the dynamite. Then we cut to footage apparently taken from another film, showing towers of flame. The mountain shakes. Yards below, an old Indian woman cocks her head and nods wisely at the sky. Mountain speak with big voice. Then we cut to a sound stage set decorated with trees, bushes, and a steaming pile of rocks in one corner—the remains of the cave and the mountain, too, for that matter. "Do you . . . think it's dead?" Joi Lansing asks. "Nothing could live through that," Lindsay Crosby assures her. I certainly hope he is right.

The Big Red One ★ ★ ★

PG, 113 m., 1980

Lee Marvin (Sergeant), Mark Hamill (Griff), Robert Carradine (Zab), Bobby Di Cicco (Vinci), Kelly Ward (Johnson), Siegfried Rauch (Schroeder), Stephanie Audran (Walloon). Directed and written by Samuel Fuller and produced by Gene Corman.

Sam Fuller's *The Big Red One* is a lot of war stories strung together in a row, almost as if the director filmed it for the thirty-fifth reunion of his old Army outfit, and didn't want to leave anybody out. That's one of the most interesting things about it—the feeling that the movie's events are included, not because they help the plot or make a point, but just because they happened.

Some of them happened to Fuller himself, he tells us, and there's a kid in the movie who's obviously supposed to be young Sam. Other scenes are based on things Fuller heard about. Some of them are brutal and painful, some of them are romantic, a lot of them are corny. The movie takes no position on any of them: This movie is resolutely nonpolitical, is neither pro- nor anti-war, is deliberately just a record of five dogfaces who found themselves in the middle of the action.

The movie's title refers to the U.S. Army's First Infantry Division, and the action follows one rifle squad through the entire war. The squad leader is a hard-bitten sergeant, played by Lee Marvin with the kind of gravel-voiced, squint-eyed authority he had more than a decade before in *The Dirty*

Dozen. His four squad members are kids in their teens, and his job is to whip them into shape. He does. The squad is so efficient, or competent, or just plain lucky, that it survives to see action in half the major theaters of the war in Europe. At a rough count, they fight in North Africa, Tunis, Sicily, Normandy, Omaha Beach, rural France, Belgium, Czechoslovakia, and Germany. Halfway through this litany, we begin to suspect that *The Big Red One* is supposed to be something more than plausible.

The squad fights in so many places, stays together in one piece for so long, experiences so many of the key events of World War II (from the invasion of Europe to the liberation of the Nazi death camps) that of course these characters are meant to be symbols of all the infantrymen in all the battles. But Fuller, who fought in the First Division, seems determined to keep his symbols from illustrating a message. They fight. They are frightened. Men kill, other men are killed. What matters is if you're still alive. "I don't cry because that guy over there got hit," Fuller said in an interview, "I cry because I'm gonna get hit next."

This leads to a deliberately anecdotal structure for the film. One battle ends, another begins. A little orphan kid appears out of the smoke, is befriended, braids flowers into the netting of a helmet, is forgotten for the rest of the film. What we have is a series of experiences so overwhelming that the characters can't find sense or pattern in them, and so simply try to survive them through craft and experience.

Is this all Fuller got out of the war? He seems to believe it's all anybody really gets, that the vast patterns of war's meaning are really just the creations of novelists, filmmakers, generals, and politicians, and that for the guy under fire there is no pattern, just the desperately sincere desire to get out in one piece.

The Big Red One is Sam Fuller's first film in more than a decade, and by far the most expensive and ambitious film he's ever made. It's like a dream come true, the capstone of a long career. Fuller began as a newspaperman in New York, he fought in the war, he went to Hollywood and he directed a lot of B-action pictures that are considered by connoisseurs to be pulp landmarks: *I Shot Jesse James, Pickup on South Street, Hell and High Water, Shock Corridor.* His previous film, hardly seen in this country, was a 1972 West German production with the marvelous title *Dead Pigeon on Beethoven Street.*

While this is an expensive epic, he hasn't fallen to the temptations of the epic form. He doesn't give us a lot of phony meaning, as if to justify the scope of the production. There aren't a lot of deep, significant speeches. In the ways that count, *The Big Red One* is still a B-movie—hard-boiled, filled with action, held together by male camaraderie, directed with a lean economy of action. It's one of the most expensive B-pictures ever made, and I think that helps it fit the subject. "A" war movies are about War, but "B" war movies are about soldiers.

The Big Town ★ ★ ★ ½
R, 110 m., 1987

Matt Dillon (J.C. Cullen), Diane Lane (Lorry Dane), Tommy Lee Jones (George Cole), Bruce Dern (Mr. Edwards), Lee Grant (Ferguson Edwards), Tom Skeritt (Phil Carpenter), Suzy Amis (Maggie Donaldson), Del Close (Deacon Daniels). Directed by Ben Bolt and produced by Martin Ransohoff. Screenplay by Robert Roy Pool.

This story has been told a hundred times, and yet, when it is told well, it is always fun to watch it being told again. The kid comes from the small town to the big city. He has a gift. He signs up as a professional, working for some pretty tough people. He meets a good girl. He meets a bad girl. He meets a villain. He wants more independence than his employers will give him. At the end of the story, we don't have to be movie producers to know that he will reject the bad girl, embrace the good girl, defeat the villain, triumph in his big test, and win his independence.

This story could be about baseball, jazz, open-heart surgery, computer programming, tap-dancing, or mind-reading. In *The Big Town,* it's about gambling. Matt Dillon plays the farm boy from Iowa who keeps winning at the crap tables because he knows the odds cold, and also because he has amazing good luck. Suzy Amis is the good girl, a waitress supporting her small son. Diane Lane plays the bad girl, a stripper who is married to Tommy Lee Jones, who is the villain. The employers are Lee Grant and

Bruce Dern, a married couple who are professional gamblers with a string of dice-players, or "arms," under contract.

Add a few character touches and you've got it. For example, Dern was blinded by acid years ago, and is looking for the man who did it—a man with a heart tattooed on the inside of his wrist. Lane married Jones because she thought she'd get control of half of his business, but she was wrong. And Lee Grant used to be in love with the Iowa gambler who sent Matt Dillon to the big city to work for her.

Why am I persisting in describing so much of the plot? So you can see that the story has little to do with the brilliance of this film. *The Big Town* is compulsively watchable not because of its plot, which is predictable down to the smallest detail, but because of its acting, its direction, and its style. This is a great-looking movie that never steps wrong, and Matt Dillon uses it to demonstrate once again that he is a master of unforced, natural acting. In a 1950s period film that's wall-to-wall with clichés, he never seems less than absolutely at home.

Dillon has some kind of spontaneous rapport with the camera. He never seems aware of it, never seems aware that he's playing a character; his acting is graceful and fluid, and his scenes always seem to start before the first shot, so that we see him in the middle of a motion. *The Big Town* requires Dillon to spend a lot of time shooting craps, and you wouldn't think it would be possible to bring anything new to the sight of a man throwing dice onto a table, but Dillon does it. He has little moves, subtle small touches of body language, that make every throw important. (That's a neat trick, since he hardly ever loses.)

The actors around him also are good, especially Tommy Lee Jones as the evil vice boss, who has his best moments when he simply stands and looks at Dillon with eyes filled with hate. Suzy Amis, a newcomer, is fresh and appealing as the waitress who loves this small-town boy, and Diane Lane is able to seem sincere to Dillon while letting us know she's calculating every move.

The look of the movie is effective in its studied artificiality. It's set in Chicago's South Loop, under the el tracks, in a series of exteriors and sets that are supposed to represent both sides of only a block or two—this is the 1950s backlot look, brought to a location. The photography and the wall-to-wall period music on the sound track (Ivory Joe Hunter, Big Joe Turner, Little Willie John, Ray Charles, Red Sovine) get the right balance between the wickedness of the big city and the dreams of the small-town kid. The story is predictable, but the style had me on the edge of my seat.

Billy Jack ★ ★ ½

PG, 112 m., 1971

Tom Laughlin (Billy Jack), Delores Taylor (Jean), Clark Howat (Sheriff), Julie Webb (Barbara). Directed and produced by T.C. Frank (Tom Laughlin). Screenplay by Frank and Teresa Christina.

Billy Jack was not only the first film by Tom Laughlin and Delores Taylor since *Born Losers* (1967), but in many respects the same film, with the same hero and the same theme. Both films were directed by Laughlin himself, using the pseudonym of T.C. Frank, and they represent a passionate obsession with the role of violence in society. Laughlin and Taylor surface so rarely because their movies are personal ventures, financed in unorthodox ways and employing the kind of communal chance-taking that Hollywood finds terrifying. The chances they take sometimes create flaws in their films, but flaws that suggest they were trying to do too much, never too little.

What I find interesting is that they decided, in effect, to remake their earlier film: not to copy it, but to grapple again with the same identities and ideas. Both films are about a character named Billy Jack (Laughlin), who is a returned Vietnam hero, half-Indian, a master of karate, who takes the law into his own hands because he believes that's the only way to obtain justice.

In *Born Losers* an outlaw motorcycle gang terrorizes a community and its sheriff's office. When they brutally beat a teen-ager, Billy Jack steps in and shoots one of them. He gets ninety days. The gang members get a slap on the wrist for assault. But when he gets out of jail he finds the police powerless and the community terrified. So, because he feels he must, he fights them again, using karate, gasoline, Indian tricks, and his rifle.

In *Billy Jack*, the same character has become more mythic and supernatural. "We don't know how to contact Billy Jack," one of his friends says. "We communicate with him Indian-style; when we need him, somehow he's there." And indeed he is, riding his horse or motorcycle out of the woods, an almost supernatural presence. This time the town is terrorized, not by a bike gang, but by a brutal local businessman and his half-crazy sadomasochistic son. With the exception of the sheriff himself, who has good intentions but is ineffectual, the local law officers are on the side of evil against good.

"Good" is represented by a freedom school run by Delores Taylor, "where children can come when they have no place else to go." The townspeople (who are conveniently represented as hateful, violent, and prejudiced) resent the "hippie school," but it's on an Indian reservation and thus accountable only to federal law.

The daughter of a deputy sheriff runs away after a beating and is hidden at the school, and this provides the food for the plot: The deputy and the other bad guys go after Billy Jack, who single-handedly cuts them down with karate blows, etc. The kids and staff at the school are all pacifists, but Billy Jack can't buy that. His morality is a simple Old Testament one, an eye for an eye.

There are a lot of things in *Billy Jack* that are seriously conceived and very well-handled. Some of the scenes at the school, for example, with real kids experimenting with psychodrama, are interesting. Some of the action scenes are first-rate. There's a lot of dialogue, mostly involving putdown of the older generation.

But the movie has as many causes in it as a year's run of the *New Republic*. There's not a single contemporary issue, from ecology to gun control, that's not covered, and toward the movie's end you're wondering how these characters—who are just ordinary folks in a small Southwestern town—managed to confront every single ethical hurdle in a few weeks of living. It's possible, I guess, but it would keep you awfully busy, and then there are always the Jews in the Soviet Union to think about, and the Pakistan refugees.

I'm also somewhat disturbed by the central theme of the movie. *Billy Jack* seems to be saying the same thing as *Born Losers*, that a gun is better than a constitution in the enforcement of justice. Is democracy totally obsolete, then? Is our only hope that the good fascists defeat the bad fascists? Laughlin and Taylor are still asking themselves these questions, and *Billy Jack* arrives at a conclusion that is only slightly more encouraging.

Birdy ★ ★ ★ ★

R, 120 m., 1985

Nicolas Cage (Al), Matthew Modine (Birdy). Directed by Alan Parker and produced by Alan Marshall. Screenplay by Sandy Kroopf and Jack Behr.

The strangest thing about *Birdy*, which is a very strange and beautiful movie indeed, is that it seems to work best at its looniest level, and is least at ease with the things it takes most seriously. You will not discover anything new about war in this movie, but you will find out a whole lot about how it feels to be in love with a canary.

The movie is about two friends from South Philadelphia. One of them, Al, played by Nicolas Cage, is a slick romeo with a lot of self-confidence and a way with the women. The other, nicknamed Birdy (Matthew Modine), is goofy, withdrawn, and absolutely fascinated with birds. As kids, they are inseparable friends. In high school, they begin to grow apart, separated by their individual quests for two different kinds of birds. But they still share adventures, as Birdy hangs upside-down from elevated tracks to capture pigeons, or constructs homemade wings that he hopes will let him fly. Then the war comes. Both boys serve in Vietnam and both are wounded. Cage's face is disfigured, and he wears a bandage to cover the scars. Modine's wounds are internal: He withdraws entirely into himself and stops talking. He spends long, uneventful days perched in his room at a mental hospital, head cocked to one side, looking up longingly at a window, like nothing so much as a caged bird.

Because *Birdy* is not told in chronological order, the story takes a time to sort itself out. We begin with an agonizing visit by Cage to his friend Birdy. He hopes to draw him out of his shell. But Birdy makes no sign of recognition. Then, in flashbacks, we see the two lives that led up to this moment. We see the adventures they shared, the secrets, the dreams. Most importantly, we go inside Birdy's life and begin to glimpse the depth of his obsession with birds. His room turns into a birdcage. His special pets—including a cocky little yellow canary—take on individual characteristics for us. We can begin to understand that his love for birds is sensual, romantic, passionate. There is a wonderful scene where he brushes his fingers against a feather, showing how marvelously it is constructed, and how beautifully.

Most descriptions of *Birdy* tend to dwell on what seems to be the central plot, the story of the two buddies who go to Vietnam and are wounded, and about how one tries to help the other return to the real world. I felt that the war footage in the movie was fairly routine, and that the challenge of dragging Birdy back to reality was a good deal less interesting than the story of how he arrived at the strange, secret place in his mind. I have seen other, better, movies about war, but I have never before seen a character quite like Birdy.

As you may have already guessed, *Birdy* doesn't sound like a commercial blockbuster. More important are the love and care for detail that have gone into it from all hands, especially from Cage and Modine. They have two immensely difficult roles, and both are handicapped in the later scenes by being denied access to some of an actor's usual tools; for Cage, his face; for Modine, his whole human persona. They overcome those limitations to give us characters even more touching than the ones they started with.

The movie was directed by Alan Parker. Consider this list of his earlier films: *Bugsy Malone*, *Fame*, *Midnight Express*, *Shoot the Moon*, *Pink Floyd: The Wall*. Each one coming out of an unexpected place, and avoiding conventional movie genres. He was the man to direct *Birdy*, which tells a story so unlikely that perhaps even my description of it has discouraged you—and yet a story so interesting it is impossible to put this movie out of my mind.

The Black Marble ★ ★ ★ 1/2

PG, 110 m., 1980

Robert Foxworth (Sergeant Valnikov), Paula Prentiss (Sergeant Zimmerman), Harry Dean Stanton (Philo Skinner), Barbara Babcock (Madeline Whitfield), John Hancock (Clarence Cromwell), Raleigh Bond (Captain Hooker), Judy Landers (Pattie Mae), Pat Corley (Itchy Mitch). Directed by Harold Becker and produced by Frank Capra, Jr. Screenplay by Joseph Wambaugh.

The Black Marble is a delightfully twisted comedy, backing into itself, starting out in one direction, ending up somewhere else, constantly surprising us with its offbeat characters. It's so many things at once it's a juggling act: It's a police movie with lots of authentic details; it's a bizarre comedy about a kidnapped prize dog; it's a shaggy romance; it's got the most excruciating chase sequence I can remember; it's goofy, but it moves us.

The movie centers around several days in the life of a Los Angeles police sergeant named Valnikov (Robert Foxworth), an incurably romantic Russian who has been drinking too much since his partner's suicide. He gets a new partner, Sgt. Natalie Zimmerman, played by Paula Prentiss as a combination of Sally Kellerman and Lucille Ball. His new partner thinks Valnikov is insane. Maybe she's right.

The case they begin working on together involves a prize bitch that has been kidnapped and is being held for $85,000 ransom. Valnikov goes to interview the kidnapped dog's grieving owner, an attractive woman of a certain age. And, in a delightful scene that illustrates the movie's gift of being able to slide ever so lightly from drama into cheerful comedy, he winds up on the sofa with the woman, drying her tears and vowing, "Don't worry; I promise I'll get your doggie back."

The dry tone Foxworth brings to the pronunciation of such lines is one of the movie's charms. He is mustachioed, mournful-eyed, usually hung over, and filled with ancient Russian dreams and curses. It is inevitable, of course, that he and the sexy Zimmerman fall in love, and they have a wonderful seduction scene in his apartment. He puts sweepingly romantic Russian folk music on his stereo. They dance. "Translate the lyrics for me!" she whispers into his ear. He does. It does not bother either of them that there *are* no lyrics since the song is instrumental.

Meanwhile, a parallel plot involves the evil dog kidnapper, played by that uniquely malevolent character actor Harry Dean Stanton, who looks and talks like Robert

Mitchum's mean kid brother. Stanton is a veterinarian who has never hurt a dog in his life. But he needs the ransom to pay a gambling debt before he is killed. Coughing, wheezing, and spitting through an endless chain of cigarettes, he makes telephone threats to the dog's owner, who counters with descriptions of her own financial plight, unpaid bills, and tax problems.

When Valnikov and the kidnapper finally meet face to face, they get into what is undoubtedly the most painful chase sequence I can remember, a chase that requires them to climb mesh fences separating a series of savage and terrified dogs that snap maniacally at their legs. The chase is another scene illustrating the curious way in which *The Black Marble* succeeds in being funny, painful, and romantic, sometimes simultaneously. The movie's not altogether a comedy, although we laugh; it's a love story that kids itself and ends up seriously; it contains violence but is not really violent. What it always does is keep us off balance. Because we can't anticipate what's going to happen next, the movie has a persistent interior life; there's never the sense that a scene is included because it's expected.

The performances go to show you that a good actor in a bad film can have a very hard time appearing to be any good. Foxworth's previous screen credits include *The Omen, Part II* and *Prophecy.* Neither film gave me the slightest reason to look forward to him in *The Black Marble,* but he's wonderful here. He gives his character weariness and craziness and then covers them both with warmth. He and Prentiss have so much fun with the long seduction scene that we can sense the joy of acting craftsmanship going into it.

The movie's the second production by Joseph Wambaugh, the L.A. cop who became a best-selling novelist only to see Hollywood doing terrible things to his novels. Wambaugh vowed to produce his own books. The industry had its doubts, especially when Wambaugh hired a little-known British director, Harold Becker, to direct his first project, *The Onion Field.* But that was a strong, edgy, effective movie, and now Wambaugh and Becker are back with this unusual and distinctive comedy. Because it is uneven and moves so easily among its various tones and moods, it's possible, I suppose, to fault it on form: This isn't a seamless piece of work, but it's infectious and charming.

The Black Stallion ★ ★ ★ ★

G, 120 m., 1980

Kelly Reno (Alec Ramsey), Mickey Rooney (Henry Dailey), Teri Garr (Alec's Mother), Clarence Muse (Snoe), Hoyt Axton (Alec's Father), Michael Higgins (Neville). The black stallion is portrayed by Cass-ole, owned by San Antonio Arabians. Directed by Carroll Ballard and produced by Francis Ford Coppola, Fred Roos, and Tom Sternberg. Screenplay by Melissa Mathison, Jeanne Rosenberg and William D. Wittliff.

The first half of *The Black Stallion* is so gloriously breathtaking that the second half, the half with all the conventional excitement, seems merely routine. We've seen the second half before—the story of the kid, the horse, the veteran trainer, and the big race. But the first hour of this movie belongs among the great filmgoing experiences. It is described as an epic, and earns the description.

The film opens at sea, somewhere in the Mediterranean, forty or so years ago, on board a ship inhabited by passengers who seem foreign and fearsome to a small boy. They drink, they gamble, they speak in foreign tongues, they wear caftans and beards and glare ferociously at anyone who comes close to their prize possession, a magnificent black stallion.

The boy and his father are on board this ship for reasons never explained. The father gambles with the foreigners and the boy roams the ship and establishes a shy rapport with the black stallion, and then a great storm sweeps over the ocean and the ship catches fire and is lost. The boy and the stallion are thrown free, into the boiling sea. The horse somehow saves the boy, and in the calm of the next morning they both find themselves thrown onto a deserted island.

This sequence—the storm, the ship's sinking, the ordeal at sea—is a triumphant use of special effects, miniature models, back projection, editing, and all the tricks of craft that go into the filming of a fantasy. The director, Carroll Ballard, used the big water tank at Cinecitta Studios in Rome for the storm sequences; a model ship, looking totally real, burns and sinks headfirst, its propellers churning slowly in the air, while the horse and boy struggle in the foreground.

The horse in this film (its name is Cassole) is required to perform as few movie horses ever have. But its finest scene is the quietest one, and takes place on the island a few days after the shipwreck. Ballard and his cinematographer, Caleb Deschanel, have already established the mood of the place, with gigantic, quiet, natural panoramas. The boy spears a fish. The horse roams restlessly from the beaches to the cliffs. And then, in a single shot that is held for a long time, Ballard shows us the boy inviting the horse to eat out of his hand.

It is crucial here that this action be seen in a *single* shot; lots of short cuts, edited together, would simply be the filmmakers at work. But the one uninterrupted shot, with the horse at one edge of the screen and the boy at the other, and the boy's slow approach, and the horse's skittish advances and retreats, shows us a rapport between the human and the animal that's strangely moving.

All these scenes of the boy and horse on the island are to be treasured, especially a montage photographed underwater and showing the legs of the two as they splash in the surf. There are also wonderfully scary sequences, such as one in which the boy awakens to find a poisonous snake a few feet away from him on the sand. This scene exploits the hatred and fear horses have for snakes, and is cut together into a terrifically exciting climax.

But then, as all good things must, the idyll on the island comes to an end. The boy and the horse are rescued. And it's here that the film, while still keeping our interest, becomes more routine. The earlier passages of the film were amazing to look at (they were shot, with great difficulty and beauty, on Sardinia). Now we're back to earth again, with scenes shot around an old racetrack in Toronto.

And we've seen the melodramatic materials of the movie's second half many times before. The boy is reunited with his mother, the horse returns home with him, and the boy meets a wise old horse trainer who admits that, yes, that Arabian *can* run like the wind—but the fool thing doesn't have any papers. The presence of Mickey Rooney, who plays the trainer, is welcome but perhaps too familiar. Rooney has played this sort of role so often before (most unforgettably in *National Velvet*) that he almost seems to be visiting from another movie. His Academy Award nomination for the performance is probably a recognition of that.

Still, the melodrama is effective. Everything depends on the outcome of the big race at the film's end. The young boy, of course, is the jockey (the Elizabeth Taylor role, so to speak). Ballard and Deschanel are still gifted at finding a special, epic look for the movie; one especially good scene has the stallion racing against time, in the dark before dawn, in the rain.

The Black Stallion is a wonderful experience at the movies. The possibility remains, though, that in these cynical times it may be avoided by some viewers because it has a G rating—and G movies are sometimes dismissed as being too innocuous. That's sure not the case with this film, which is rated G simply because it has no nudity, profanity, or violence—but it does have terrific energy, beauty, and excitement. It's not a children's movie; it's for adults *and* for kids.

Black Widow ★ ★ ½

R, 100 m., 1987

Debra Winger (Alex), Theresa Russell (Catherine), Sami Frey (Paul), Nicol Williamson (Macauley), Dennis Hopper (Ben), Diane Ladd (Etta), James Hong (Shin), Terry O'Quinn (Bruce). Directed by Bob Rafelson and produced by Laurence Mark and Harold Schneider. Screenplay by Ron Base.

Black Widow is an interesting movie struggling to escape from a fatal overload of commercial considerations. When the film is over, there's the strange feeling that an opportunity was lost here. First I'll describe the movie that was made, then I'll speculate on the better movie trapped inside.

The film stars Debra Winger as a plucky federal investigator, although the opening scenes are so fuzzy that at first I thought she was a newspaper reporter. Using her computer, she stumbles over a series of apparently unrelated deaths in which millionaires are victims of a rare syndrome causing them to die in their sleep. Winger, who is either psychic or has read the script, intuits that the deaths are related and develops a theory that the same woman has killed all of the men to inherit their fortunes.

She is absolutely right. We know she is right because the movie makes no effort to keep us in suspense; the opening scene shows the "black widow" (Theresa Russell) learning of the death of her latest victim. After Winger announces her suspicions to her boss, much time is wasted on unnecessary scenes in which she plays poker, flirts with a colleague, and has conversations about her lonely life.

Then she figures out who Russell will kill next: a wealthy Seattle art collector (Nicol Williamson). She flies to Seattle, acts too late to prevent the death, and then tracks Russell to her next victim, a hotel tycoon who lives in Hawaii. The two women become friends, Russell offers to share her boyfriend with Winger, Winger falls in love with the tycoon, Russell tries to kill him, and there's a surprise ending.

Well, at least it's supposed to be a surprise ending. It didn't come as a surprise to me, however, because I am of adequate intelligence and have seen more than three movies. Therefore, like any reasonably capable viewer, I knew approximately what was going to happen, and I was right.

Is there some kind of law governing Hollywood movies that says audiences don't like surprises? I don't mean predictable would-be surprises, but real surprises, such as when a story ends on a nihilistic note. *Black Widow* has an ending that is so false to the emotional truth of the movie that it looks tacked on by the censors of the 1930s.

Here's why: From the moment Winger and Russell meet, there's a strong undercurrent of eroticism between the two women. We feel it, they feel it, and the movie allows it one brief expression—when Russell roughly reaches out and kisses Winger. But Ron Base, who wrote the screenplay, and Bob Rafelson, who directed, don't follow that magnetism. They create the unconvincing love affair between Winger and the tycoon to set up a happy ending that left me feeling cheated.

What would have been more intriguing? Why not follow a more cynical, truly diabolical course—something inspired by the soul of *film noir*? Why not have Winger fall completely under the spell of the black widow and stand by while the tycoon is murdered so the two women can live happily ever after? And then end on an eerie note as Winger begins to wonder if Russell can trust her with the secret?

That kind of psychological double-reverse would give the actresses something to work with. The story of *Black Widow*, as told, is the kind of shallow, one-dimensional plotting we expect on television, where there are no unpleasant surprises to upset the audience. There are just enough subtle hints in *Black Widow* to suggest that certain more sinister possibilities occurred to Rafelson and Base. But I guess they manfully resisted them and did the safe thing.

Too bad. The acting in this movie is good throughout, especially in the chemistry between Winger and Russell. I also liked Williamson as the lonely, isolated art collector, and James Hong as the jittery Hawaiian private eye. Sami Frey is such an odd and unmagnetic actor, however, that he's miscast as the hotel tycoon. As a general rule, in order to believe that two women can fall in love with the same man, we have to be able to believe that one woman could fall in love with him.

Blade Runner ★ ★ ★

R, 114 m., 1982

Harrison Ford (Deckard), Rutger Hauer (Batty), Sean Young (Rachel), Edward James Olmos (Gaff), M. Emmet Walsh (Bryant), Daryl Hannah (Pris). Directed by Ridley Scott and produced by Michael Deeley. Screenplay by Hampton Fancher and David Peoples.

The strangest thing about the future is that *this* is now the future that was once foretold. Twenty years ago, we thought of "now" as "the year 1987," and we wondered what life would be like. Little could we have guessed that there would be no world government, that the cars would look like boxes instead of rocket ships, and that there would still be rock 'n' roll on the radio. *Blade Runner* asks us to imagine its own future, in "the year 2020." The movie takes place in a Los Angeles that looks like a futuristic Tokyo, with gigantic billboards showing smiling Japanese girls drinking Coca-Cola. I would have predicted L.A. would be Hispanic, but never mind, it looks sensational. The city is dominated by almost inconceivably huge skyscrapers. People get around in compact vehicles that fly, hover, climb, and swoop. (In a lot of fictional futures, people seem to zip around the city in private aircraft; can you imagine the traffic problems?) At ground level, however, the L.A. of the future is an urban jungle.

The movie stars Harrison Ford as a cop who moves confidently through the city's mean streets. He is laconic, cynical, competent. He has a difficult assignment. A group of "replicants," artificial people who seem amazingly human, have escaped from "off-world," and are trying to inflict themselves on Earth. Ford's job is to track them down and eliminate them. Anyone who has read this far can predict what happens next: He falls in love with one of the replicants. She may not be quite human, but, oh, you kid.

This basic story comes from a Philip K. Dick novel with the intriguing title, *Do Androids Dream of Electric Sheep?* The book examined the differences between humans and thinking machines, and circled warily around the question of memory: Does it make an android's personal memories less valid if they are inspired by someone else's experiences—especially if the android does not know that? Ford says he originally signed on for *Blade Runner* because he found such questions intriguing. For director Ridley Scott, however, the greater challenge seemed to be creating that future world. Scott is a master of production design, of imagining other worlds of the future *(Alien)* and the past *(The Duellists)*. He seems more concerned with creating his film worlds than populating them with plausible characters, and that's the trouble this time. *Blade Runner* is a stunningly interesting visual achievement, but a failure as a story.

The special effects were supervised by Douglas Trumbull, whose credits include *2001* and *Silent Running*, and who is about as good as anyone in the world at using miniatures, animation, drawings, optical effects, and other ways of tricking the eye. The visual environments he creates for this film are wonderful to behold, and there's a sense of detail, too; we don't just get the skyways and the monolithic skyscrapers and the sky-taxis, we also get notions about how restaurants, clothes, and home furnishings will look in 2020 (not too different). *Blade Runner* is worth seeing just to witness this artistry. The movie's weakness, however, is that it allows the special effects technology to overwhelm its story. Ford is tough and low-key in the central role, and Rutger Hauer and Sean Young are effective as two of the replicants, but the movie isn't really interested in these people—or creatures. The obligatory love affair is pro forma, the villains are standard issue, and the climax is yet one more of those cliffhangers, with Ford dangling over an abyss by his fingertips. The movie has the opposite trouble as the replicants: Instead of flesh and blood, its dreams are of mechanical men.

Blood Simple ★ ★ ★ ★

R, 96 m., 1985

John Getz (Ray), Frances McDormand (Abby), Dan Hedaya (Julian Marty), M. Emmet Walsh (Detective), Samm-Art Williams (Meurice). Directed by Joel Coen and produced by Ethan Coen. Screenplay by Coen and Coen.

A lot has been written about the visual style of *Blood Simple*, but I think the appeal of the movie is more elementary. It keys into three common nightmares: (1) You clean and clean, but there's still blood all over the place; (2) You know you have committed a murder, but you are not sure quite how or why; (3) You know you have forgotten a small detail that will eventually get you into a lot of trouble. *Blood Simple* mixes those fears and guilts into an incredibly complicated plot, with amazingly gory consequences. It tells a story in which every individual detail seems to make sense, and every individual choice seems logical, but the choices and details form a bewildering labyrinth in which there are times when even the murderers themselves don't know who they are.

Because following the plot is one of this movie's most basic pleasures, I will not reveal too much. The movie begins with a sleazy backwoods bar owner's attempt to hire a scummy private detective to murder his wife. The private eye takes the money and then pulls a neat double-cross, hoping to keep the money and eliminate the only witness who could implicate him. Neat. And then it *really* gets complicated.

The movie has been shot with a lot of style, some of it self-conscious, but deliberately so. One of the pleasures in a movie like this is enjoying the low-angle and tilt shots that draw attention to themselves, that declare themselves as being part of a movie. The movie does something interesting with its timing, too. It begins to feel inexorable. Characters think they know what has happened; they turn out to be wrong; they pay the consequences, and it all happens while the movie is marching from scene to scene like an implacable professor of logic, demonstrating one fatal error after another.

Blood Simple was directed by Joel Coen, produced by his brother, Ethan, and written by the two of them. It's their first film, and has the high energy and intensity we associate with young filmmakers who are determined to make an impression. Some of the scenes are virtuoso, including a sequence in which a dead body becomes extraordinarily hard to dispose of, and another one in which two people in adjacent rooms are trapped in the same violent showdown. The central performance in the movie is by the veteran character actor M. Emmet Walsh, who plays the private eye like a man for whom idealism is a dirty word. The other actors in the movie are all effective, but they are obscured, in a way, by what happens to them: This movie weaves such a bloody web that the characters are upstaged by their dilemmas.

Is the movie fun? Well, that depends on you. It is violent, unrelenting, absurd, and fiendishly clever. There is a cliché I never use: "Not for the squeamish." But let me put it this way. *Blood Simple* may make you squeam.

Blow Out ★ ★ ★ ★

R, 107 m., 1981

John Travolta (Jack), Nancy Allen (Sally), John Lithgow (Burke), Dennis Franz (Manny Karp), Peter Boydon (Sam), Curt May (Donohue). Directed by Brian De Palma and produced by George Litto. Screenplay by De Palma.

There are times when *Blow Out* resembles recent American history trapped in the "Twilight Zone." Episodes are hauntingly familiar, and yet seem slightly askew. What if the "grassy knoll" recordings from the police radio in Dallas had been crossed with Chappaquiddick and linked to Watergate? What if Jack Ruby had been a private eye specializing in divorce cases? What if Abraham Zapruder—the man who took the home movies of President John F. Kennedy's death—had been a sound effects man? And what if Judith Exner—remember her?—had been working with Ruby? These are some of the inspirations out of which Brian De Palma constructs *Blow Out,* a movie which continues his practice of making cross-references to other movies, other directors, and actual historical events, and which nevertheless is his best and most original work.

The title itself, of course, reminds us of *Blow Up,* the 1966 film by Michelangelo Antonioni in which a photographer saw, or thought he saw, a murder—and went mad while obsessively analyzing his photographs of the "crime." *Was* there a dead body to be found on that fuzzy negative? Was there even such a thing as reality? In *Blow Out,* John Travolta plays the character who confronts these questions. He's a sound man for a sleazy Philadelphia B-movie factory. He works on cheap, cynical exploitation films. Late one night, while he's standing on a bridge recording owls and other night sounds, he becomes a witness to an accident. A car has a blow out, swerves off a bridge, and plunges into a river. Travolta plunges in after it, rescues a girl inside (Nancy Allen), and later discovers that the car's drowned driver was a potential presidential candidate. Still later, reviewing his sound recording of the event, Travolta becomes convinced that he can hear a gunshot just before the blow out. Was the accident actually murder? He traces down Nancy Allen, discovers that she was part of a blackmail plot against the candidate, and then comes across the trail of a slimy private eye (Dennis Franz) who wanted to cause a blow out, all right, but didn't figure on anybody getting killed.

The plot thickens beautifully. De Palma doesn't have just a handful of ideas to spin out to feature length. He has an abundance. We meet a gallery of violent characters, including Burke (John Lithgow), a dirty-tricks specialist who seems inspired by G. Gordon Liddy. The original crime is complicated by a series of other murders, designed to lay a false trail and throw the police off the scent of political conspiracy.

Meanwhile, the Travolta character digs deeper. For him, it's a matter of competence, of personal pride. Arguing with a cop about his tapes, Travolta denies that he's just imagining things: "I'm a *sound* man!" He stumbles across a series of photos of the fatal accident. In a brilliantly crafted sequence, we follow every step as he assembles the film and his recording into a movie of the event, doggedly extracting what seem to be facts from what looks like chaos.

De Palma's visual images in *Blow Out* invite comparison to many Alfred Hitchcock films, and indeed De Palma invited such comparisons when the posters for *Dressed to Kill,* described him as "Master of the Macabre." In *Blow Out* there are such Hitchcock hallmarks as a shower scene (played this time for laughs rather than for the chills of *Dressed to Kill*), several grisly murders in unexpected surroundings, violence in public places, and a chase through Philadelphia on the anniversary of the ringing of the Liberty Bell. This last extended chase sequence reminds us of two Hitchcock strategies: His juxtaposition of patriotic images and espionage, as in *North by Northwest* and *Saboteur,* and his desperate chases through uncaring crowds, reminders of *Foreign Correspondent* and *Strangers on a Train.*

But *Blow Out* stands by itself. It reminds us of the violence of *Dressed to Kill,* the startling images of *The Fury,* the clouded identities of *Sisters,* the uncertainty of historical "facts" from *Obsession,* and it ends with the bleak nihilism of *Carrie.* But it moves beyond those films, because this time De Palma is more successful than ever before at populating his plot with three-dimensional characters. We believe in the reality of the people played by John Travolta, Nancy Allen, John Lithgow, and Dennis Franz. They have all the little tics and eccentricities of life. And although they're caught in the mesh of a labyrinthine conspiracy, they behave as people probably would behave in such circumstances—they're not pawns of the plot.

Best of all, this movie is inhabited by a real cinematic intelligence. The audience isn't condescended to. In sequences like the one in which Travolta reconstructs a film and sound record of the accident, we're challenged and stimulated: We share the excitement of figuring out how things develop and unfold, when so often the movies only need us as passive witnesses.

Blue Collar ★ ★ ★ ★

R, 114 m., 1978

Richard Pryor (Zeke), Harvey Keitel (Jerry), Yaphet Kotto (Smokey), Ed Begley, Jr. (Bobby Joe), Harry Bellaver (Eddie Johnson), George Memmoli (Jenkins). Directed by Paul Schrader and produced by Don Guest. Screenplay by Paul and Leonard Schrader.

Detroit. Dawn. The next shift arrives for work. On the sound track, music of pounding urgency, suggesting the power of the machines that stamp out car doors from sheets of sheel. The camera takes us into the insides of an automobile factory, takes us close enough to almost smell the sweat and shield our eyes against the sparks thrown off by welding torches.

Blue Collar is about life on the Detroit assembly lines, and about how it wears men down and chains them to a lifetime installment plan. It is an angry, radical movie about the vise that traps workers between big industry and big labor. It's also an enormously entertaining movie; it earns its comparison with *On the Waterfront.* And it's an extraordinary directing debut for Paul Schrader, whose credits include *Taxi Driver* and *Rolling Thunder.*

Schrader tells the story of three workers, buddies on and off the job, who are all more or less in the same boat. They work, they drink after work in the bar across the street, they go home to mortgages or bills or kids who need braces on their teeth. One day they get fed up enough to decide to rob the safe in the office of their own union. What they find there is only a few hundred bucks—and a ledger that seems to contain the details of illegal loans of union funds.

The three guys are played by Richard Pryor, Harvey Keitel, and Yaphet Kotto, and they're all three at the top of their forms. Pryor, in particular, is a revelation: He's been good in a lot of movies, but almost always as himself, fast-talking, wise-cracking, running comic variations on the themes suggested by his dialogue. This time, held in rein by Schrader, he provides a tight, convincing performance as a family man.

Yaphet Kotto plays his opposite, an ex-con who likes to throw all-night parties with lots of sex, booze, and grass. And Harvey Keitel is their white friend, always behind on his loan company payments, who comes home one day to discover that his daughter has tried to bend paper clips over her teeth to convince her friends at school that she's got the braces she should have.

Schrader goes for a nice, raunchy humor in the scenes involving the three guys: The movie is relaxed and comfortable with itself, and we get the precise textures and tones of the society they live in. We understand their friendship, too, because it defies one of the things the movie passionately charges: That unions and management tacitly collaborate on trying to set the rich against the poor, the black against the white, the old against the young, to divide and conquer.

The burglary caper begins innocently enough with Pryor's demand, at a union meeting, that the company repair his locker: He's cut his hand trying to get the damn thing open. But the union representatives seem indifferent to Pryor and just about everyone else, and so Pryor marches into the office of the shaggy, white-maned union leader who was a radical himself, once, back in the 1930s. And while the great statesman is feeding him several varieties of lies, Pryor sees the office safe and gets his idea.

The burglary itself finds the right line between humor and suspense, and then the movie's anger begins to burn. Because when the three men discover that the ledger may be more important than any money in the safe, they're torn between using it for blackmail, or using it to expose the corruption of their own union. Schrader gradually reveals his total vision in the film's second hour: A friendship that was sound and healthy suddenly goes sour. The system drives a wedge between them, as Pryor is offered a union job, Keitel becomes an FBI informer, and Kotto is killed in a scene of great and gruesome power.

It took a measure of courage to make *Blue Collar,* and especially to follow its events through to their inevitable conclusion. The movie could have copped out in its last thirty minutes, and given us a nice, safe Hollywood ending. Instead, it makes criticisms of mass production that social critics like Harvey Swados and Paul Goodman might have agreed with. This isn't a liberal movie but a radical one, and one I suspect a lot of assembly-line workers might see with a shock of recognition.

It took courage to make the movie that honest. But it also took a special filmmaking gift to make it burst with humor, humanity, and suspense as well. Like *On the Waterfront,* it's both an indictment and an entertainment, working just as well on its human levels as with its theoretical concerns. Paul Schrader has been a Hollywood wonder kid ever since negotiating a $450,000 deal for his first screenplay, *The Yakuza.* After *Taxi Driver* and *Obsession,* he was able to demand that he direct his own work, and *Blue Collar* is a stunning debut, taking chances and winning at them.

The Blue Lagoon ½★

R, 102 m., 1980

Brooke Shields (Emmeline), Christopher Atkins (Richard), Leo McKern (Paddy Button), William Daniels (Arthur Lestrange). Directed and produced by Randal Kleiser. Screenplay by Douglas Day Stewart.

This movie made me itch. It's about a young girl and a young boy who are shipwrecked on a beautiful Pacific island. It shows how they grow up, mostly at sunset. It follows their progress as they discover sex and smile sweetly at each other, in that order. It concludes with a series of scenes designed to inspire the question: If these two young people had grown up in civilized surroundings, wouldn't they have had to repeat the fourth grade?

The Blue Lagoon was the dumbest movie of the year. It could conceivably have been made interesting, if any serious attempt had been made to explore what might really happen if two seven-year-old kids were shipwrecked on an island. But this movie isn't a realistic movie. It's a wildly idealized romance, in which the kids live in a hut that looks like a Club Med honeymoon cottage, while restless natives commit human sacrifice on the other side of the island. (It is a measure of the filmmakers' desperation that the kids and natives never meet one another and the kids leave the island without even one obligatory scene of being tied to a stake.)

Why was this movie made? Presumably because Randal Kleiser, the director and producer, read the 1903 novel it's based on and vowed that this story had to be brought to the screen. It had been filmed previously, as Jean Simmons's 1949 movie debut, but no matter. Kleiser had another go.

It's intriguing to try to guess, on the basis of the film he made, what he thought the original story had to tell us. This movie could have been made as a tale of wilderness survival: *The Swiss Family Robinson Meets Lord of the Flies.* But Kleiser's details about daily life are wildly unconvincing. This movie could have been made as an adventure epic, but, as I've already mentioned, the threat of the natives on the other side of the island is introduced only to be dropped. This movie could have been made as a soft-core sex film, but it's too restrained: There are so many palms carefully arranged in front of genital areas, and Brooke Shields's long hair is so carefully draped to conceal her breasts, that there must have been a whole squad of costumers and set decorations on permanent Erogenous Zone Alert.

Let's face it. Going to this film knowing what we've heard about it, we're anticipating the scenes in which the two kids discover the joys of sex. This is a prurient motive on our part, and we're maybe a little ashamed of it, but our shame turns to impatience as Kleiser intercuts countless shots of the birds and the bees (every third shot in this movie seems to be showing a parrot's reaction to something). And there is no way to quite describe my feelings about the scene that takes place the morning after the young couple have finally made love. They go swimming, see two gigantic *turtles* copulating, and smile sweetly at each other. Based on the available evidence in the movie, they know more at this point about the sex lives of turtles than about their own.

But wait, these kids aren't finished. They have a baby, after long, puzzled months of trying to figure out those stirring feelings in the girl's stomach. "Why did you have a baby?" the boy asks. "I don't know," the girl says. They try to feed the kid fresh fruit, and then they look on in wonder as the baby demonstrates the theory and practice of breast-feeding (so *that's* what they're for!).

The movie's ending is enraging. It turns out the boy's father has been sailing the South Seas for years, looking for the castaways, who meanwhile manage to set themselves adrift at open sea again (they lose their oars . . . but never mind). Despairing of being rescued, the kids have just eaten berries that are supposed to put them permanently asleep. Then their unconscious bodies are rescued. Will they live? Die? What were those berries, anyway? The movie cops out: The burden of contriving an ending was apparently too much for such a feeble movie to support.

The Blues Brothers ★ ★ ★

R, 133 m., 1980

John Belushi (Jake Blues), Dan Aykroyd (Elwood Blues), Ray Charles (Ray), Aretha Franklin (Waitress), James Brown (Rev. James), Cab Calloway (Curtis), Charles Napier (Good Ol' Boy), Henry Gibson (Nazi), John Candy (Burton Mercer), Murphy Dunne (Piano Player), Carrie Fisher (Mystery Lady). Directed by John Landis and produced by Robert K. Weiss. Screenplay by Dan Aykroyd and Landis.

The Blues Brothers is the Sherman tank of musicals. When it was being filmed in Chicago in 1979—with dozens of cars piling up in intersections, caroming down Lake Shore Drive and crashing through the Daley Center—it seemed less like a film than a war. The movie feels the same way. It's a big, raucous powerhouse that proves against all the odds that if you're loud enough, vulgar enough, and have enough raw energy, you can make a steamroller into a musical, and vise versa.

This is some weird movie. There's never been anything that looked quite like it; was it dreamed up in a junkyard? It stars John Belushi and Dan Aykroyd as the Blues Brothers, Jake and Elwood, characters who were created on "Saturday Night Live" and took on a fearsome life of their own. The movie tells us something of their backgrounds: They were reared in a sadistic West Side orphanage, learned the blues by osmosis, and, as the movie opens, have teamed up again after Jake's release from the Joliet pen.

The movie's plot is a simple one, to put it mildly. The brothers visit their old orphanage, learn that its future is in jeopardy because of five thousand dollars due in back taxes, and determine to raise the money by getting their old band together and putting on a show. Their odyssey takes them to several sleazy Chicago locations, including a Van Buren flophouse, Maxwell Street, and lower Wacker Drive. They find their old friends in unlikely places, like a restaurant run by Aretha Franklin, a music shop run by

Ray Charles, and a gospel church run by James Brown.

Their adventures include run-ins with suburban cops, good ol' boys, and Nazis who are trying to stage a demonstration. One of the intriguing things about this movie is the way it borrows so freely and literally from news events. The plot develops into a sort of musical *Mad Mad Mad Mad World*, with the Blues Brothers being pursued at the same time by avenging cops, Nazis, and an enraged country and western band led by Charles Napier, that character actor with the smile like Jaws. The chase is interrupted from time to time for musical numbers, which are mostly very good and filled with high-powered energy.

Aretha Franklin occupies one of the movie's best scenes, in her South Side soul food restaurant. Cab Calloway, as a sort of road manager for the Blues Brothers, struts through a wonderful old-style production of *Minnie the Moocher.* The Brothers themselves star in several improbable numbers; the funniest has the band playing in a country and western bar where wire mesh has been installed to protect the band from beer bottles thrown by the customers.

I was saying the musical numbers interrupt the chases. The fact is, the whole movie is a chase, with Jake and Elwood piloting a used police car that seems, as it hurdles across suspension bridges from one side to the other, to have a life of its own. There can rarely have been a movie that made so free with its locations as this one. There are incredible, sensational chase sequences under the elevated train tracks, on overpasses, in subway tunnels under the Loop, and literally through Daley Center. One crash in particular, a pileup involving maybe a dozen police cars, has to be seen to be believed: I've never seen stunt coordination like this before.

What's a little startling about this movie is that all of this works. *The Blues Brothers* cost untold millions of dollars and kept threatening to grow completely out of control. But director John Landis (of *Animal House*) has somehow pulled it together, with a good deal of help from the strongly defined personalities of the title characters. Belushi and Aykroyd come over as hard-boiled city guys, total cynics with a world-view of sublime simplicity, and that all fits perfectly with the movie's other parts. There's even room, in the midst of the carnage and mayhem, for a surprising amount of grace, humor, and whimsy.

Blue Velvet ★

R, 120 m., 1986

Kyle MacLachlan (Jeffrey Beaumont), Isabella Rossellini (Dorothy Valiens), Dennis Hopper (Frank Booth), Laura Dern (Sandy Williams), Hope Lange (Mrs. Williams), Dean Stockwell (Gar), George Dickerson (Detective Williams). Directed by David Lynch and produced by Richard Roth. Screenplay by Lynch.

Blue Velvet contains scenes of such raw emotional energy that it's easy to understand why some critics have hailed it as a masterpiece. A film this painful and wounding has to be given special consideration. And yet those very scenes of stark sexual despair are the tip-off to what's wrong with the movie. They're so strong that they deserve to be in a movie that is sincere, honest, and true. But *Blue Velvet* surrounds them with a story that's marred by sophomoric satire and cheap shots. The director is either denying the strength of his material or trying to defuse it by pretending it's all part of a campy in-joke.

The movie has two levels of reality. On one level, we're in Lumberton, a simple-minded small town where people talk in television clichés and seem to be clones of 1950s sitcom characters. On another level, we're told a story of sexual bondage, of how Isabella Rossellini's husband and son have been kidnapped by Dennis Hopper, who makes her his sexual slave. The twist is that the kidnapping taps into the woman's deepest feelings. She finds that she is a masochist who responds with great sexual passion to this situation.

Everyday town life is depicted with a deadpan irony; characters use lines with corny double meanings and solemnly recite platitudes. Meanwhile, the darker story of sexual bondage is told absolutely on the level in cold-blooded realism.

The movie begins with a much-praised sequence in which picket fences and flower beds establish a small-town idyll. Then a man collapses while watering the lawn, and a dog comes to drink from the hose that is still held in his unconscious grip. The great imagery continues as the camera burrows into the green lawn and finds hungry insects beneath—a metaphor for the surface and buried lives of the town.

The man's son, a college student (Kyle MacLachlan), comes home to visit his dad's bedside and resumes a romance with the daughter (Laura Dern) of the local police detective. MacLachlan finds a severed human ear in a field, and he and Dern get involved in trying to solve the mystery of the ear. The trail leads to a nightclub singer (Rossellini) who lives alone in a starkly furnished flat.

In a sequence that Hitchcock would have been proud of, MacLachlan hides himself in Rossellini's closet and watches, shocked, as she has a sadomasochistic sexual encounter with Hopper, a drug-sniffing pervert. Hopper leaves. Rossellini discovers MacLachlan in the closet and, to his astonishment, pulls a knife on him and forces him to submit to her seduction. He is appalled but fascinated; she wants him to be a "bad boy" and hit her.

These sequences have great power. They make *9 ½ Weeks* look rather timid by comparison, because they do seem genuinely born from the darkest and most despairing side of human nature. If *Blue Velvet* had continued to develop its story in a straight line, if it had followed more deeply into the implications of the first shocking encounter between Rossellini and MacLachlan, it might have made some real emotional discoveries.

Instead, director David Lynch chose to interrupt the almost hypnotic pull of that relationship in order to pull back to his jokey, small-town satire. Is he afraid that movie audiences might not be ready for stark S&M unless they're assured it's all really a joke?

I was absorbed and convinced by the relationship between Rossellini and MacLachlan, and annoyed because the director kept placing himself between me and the material. After five or ten minutes in which the screen reality was overwhelming, I didn't need the director prancing on with a top hat and cane, whispering that it was all in fun.

Indeed, the movie is pulled so violently in opposite directions that it pulls itself apart. If the sexual scenes are real, then why do we need the send-up of the "Donna Reed Show"? What are we being told? That beneath the surface of Small Town, U.S.A., passions run dark and dangerous? Don't stop the presses.

The sexual material in *Blue Velvet* is so disturbing, and the performance by Rossellini is so convincing and courageous, that it demands a movie that deserves it. American movies have been using satire for years to take the edge off sex and violence. Occasionally, perhaps sex and violence should be treated with the seriousness they deserve. Given the power of the darker scenes in this movie, we're all the more frustrated that the director is unwilling to follow through to the consequences of his insights. *Blue Velvet* is like the guy who drives you nuts by hinting at horrifying news and then saying, "Never mind."

There's another thing. Rossellini is asked to do things in this film that require real nerve. In one scene, she's publicly embarrassed by being dumped naked on the lawn of the police detective. In others, she is asked to portray emotions that I imagine most actresses would rather not touch. She is degraded, slapped around, humiliated, and undressed in front of the camera. And when you ask an actress to endure those experiences, you should keep your side of the bargain by putting her in an important film.

That's what Bernardo Bartolucci delivered when he put Marlon Brando and Maria Schneider through the ordeal of *Last Tango in Paris*. In *Blue Velvet*, Rossellini goes the whole distance, but Lynch distances himself from her ordeal with his clever asides and witty little in-jokes. In a way, his behavior is more sadistic than the Hopper character.

What's worse? Slapping somebody around, or standing back and finding the whole thing funny?

Blume in Love ★ ★ ★ ★

R, 116 m., 1973

George Segal (Blume), Susan Anspach (Nina), Kris Kristofferson (Elmo), Marsha Mason (Arlene), Shelley Winters (Mrs. Cramer), Donald F. Muhich (Analyst), Paul Mazursky (Hellman). Directed, produced, and written by Paul Mazursky.

Paul Mazursky's *Blume in Love* begins with a busted-up Southern California marriage.

The marriage belonged to Blume, divorce lawyer, and his wife Nina, a social worker. It busted up all of a sudden one weekday afternoon when Nina came home with a cold and found Blume in bed with his secretary. Why, you may ask (Blume certainly does), could his wife not forgive this indiscretion—especially as Blume is madly in love with Nina and must have her back or die? ("And I don't want to die," he reasons, "so I have to get her back.")

Well, maybe Nina was sort of halfway ready for the marriage to end. She's into her own brand of self-improvement and women's lib, and isn't sure she approves of marriage anymore. She takes up with an out-of-work (for twelve years) musician who lives in a VW truck with his dreams. She gets into yoga and learns to play the guitar and to rely on herself instead of men.

Little good that does Blume, whose love for her becomes a consuming passion. It is complicated by the fact that he gets to like the musician, too: thinks, in fact, that the bearded Elmo is the nicest man he has ever met. Blume even goes so far as to start a beard himself. But nothing will work for him, because of the fact he refuses to accept: Nina simply does not love him anymore. Does not. Period. Blume is driven into a frenzy of love, desire, frustration.

This material, so far, doesn't exactly sound like the stuff of a great film. It sounds more like the brainy, funny dissections of California dreamin' that Mazursky carried out in three previous films, *I Love You, Alice B. Toklas*, *Bob & Carol & Ted & Alice*, and *Alex in Wonderland*. Those were all fine films—Mazursky is one of the best directors of comedy in Hollywood—but they were all more concerned with the laugh than with reality.

With *Blume in Love*, however, he seems to have pulled off what everybody is always hoping for from Neil Simon: a comedy that transcends its funny moments, that realizes we laugh so we may not cry, and that finally is about real people with real desperations. He's done that in a number of scenes, and yet somehow even during the movie's gloomiest moments he keeps some sort of hope alive. That's probably because Blume is played by the charming George Segal, who seems intrinsically optimistic. No matter what Nina says, he cannot quite give up on her, because he knows she must eventually love him again—because he loves her.

He carries this hope with him on a trip to Venice, which is where the film opens; she's asked him to go away somewhere for a couple of weeks, while she thinks. They had their first and second honeymoons in Venice, but now Blume wanders through Piazza San Marco in the autumn, stranded with a few other lonely tourists looking for love. The story is told in flashbacks from Venice, and it ends there. It ends with a note so unashamedly romantic that Mazursky gets away with "Tristan and Isolde" as his sound track music. He's right. The ending would not be believable at all, except as hyperbole.

Nina—thin, earnest, determined to do the right thing and no longer be mastered by mere emotion—is played with a very complex charm by Susan Anspach. We have to like her even though she doesn't like Blume, whom we're cheering for. We do, and we like her boyfriend as much as Blume does. The itinerant musician is played by Kris Kristofferson, who gives evidence once again that he has a real acting talent—particularly in the scene where he hits Segal and then bursts into tears, and in the scene where he tells Segal he's hitting the road again.

Blume in Love has a quality that's hard to analyze but impossible to miss: It sets up an intimate rapport with its audiences.

Body Double ★ ★ ★ ½

R, 110 m., 1984

Craig Wasson (Jake), Melanie Griffith (Holly), Gregg Henry (Sam), Deborah Shelton (Gloria). Directed and produced by Brian De Palma. Screenplay by Robert H. Averch and De Palma.

Body Double is an exhilarating exercise in pure filmmaking, a thriller in the Hitchcock tradition in which there's no particular point except that the hero is flawed, weak, and in terrible danger—and we identify with him completely. The movie is so cleverly constructed, with the emphasis on visual storytelling rather than dialogue, that we are neither faster nor slower than the hero as he gradually figures out the scheme that has entrapped him. And the casting of a Hitchcockian average guy also helps.

The movie stars Craig Wasson, an open-faced actor with an engaging smile, as its hero, an unemployed actor named Jake. He isn't smart, he isn't dumb, he isn't perfect, he isn't bad. He is an ideal choice to set up as a witness to a murder. Jake needs a place to stay, and another actor (Gregg Henry) offers him a job house-sitting in a weird, modernistic home on stilts up in the hills above Los Angeles. The other actor also points out all the sights—including a shapely neighbor who does a nightly striptease dance in front of her open window. Jake is only human. For two nights, he uses a telescope to watch the striptease. He also begins to suspect that the woman may be in danger. In sequences inspired by *Rear Window*, he begins to follow the woman (Deborah Shelton), but he keeps his distance because he's caught in the same dilemma as Jimmy Stewart was in the Hitchcock picture: He is, after all, technically a Peeping Tom, and he wouldn't know the woman was in danger if he hadn't been breaking the law.

Since the plot is so important in *Body Double*, and because the movie contains so many nice surprises, I won't reveal very much more of the story. Let me describe in a carefully vague way, however, some of the pleasures of the movie. After a murder does indeed seem to have been committed, Jake's path leads him into the world of pornographic filmmaking. He wants to meet and hire a porno superstar (Melanie Griffith) who he thinks can help him figure out the mystery. His attempts lead to a series of very funny conversations, as the blonde porno actress talks to him with a Runyonesque mixture of jaded sophistication and startling ignorance. The speech in which she explains exactly what she will, and will not, do in a movie is shocking, sad, and curiously moving. *Body Double*'s excursion into the world of pornography (we see some fairly mild porno scenes, shot by De Palma himself) is part of a veritable anthology of styles in this movie. The film opens with a satire on vampire movies, includes a Hitchcockian cat-and-mouse sequence, and even borrows some of the clichés of 1940s thrillers, including a detailed recapitulation at the end, complete with flashbacks. There is also a sharp 1940s look to the cinematography, which uses dramatic lighting, tilted cameras, and carefully constructed shots to make the style part of the story.

But the movie is not just an exercise in style. It is also a genuinely terrifying thriller, in which an almost clockwork plot brings the hero and the killer together without a single logical glitch. De Palma is at home in this genre. Although his *Scarface* was more of a serious social commentary, thrilling suspense movies are his specialty, and his credits include *Carrie*, *Obsession*, and *Dressed to Kill*. With *Body Double*, he has his most airtight plot. He also has, once again, his almost unique courage to go over the top—to push scenes beyond the edge of common sense and into cheerfully heightened and impassioned overkill. The graveyard sequence next to the Hollywood reservoir, for example, or the photography in the tunnel during one of the Jake's attacks of claustrophobia, are so uninhibited that they skirt the dangerous edge of being ridiculous. But because the story's so strong, they're not. They work.

Bolero ½★

NO MPAA RATING, 105 m., 1984

Bo Derek, George Kennedy, Andrea Occhipinti. Directed by John Derek.

Bolero is a film starring Bo Derek as a woman who believes that the cure for a man's impotence is for his woman to train as a bullfighter. "Bolero" is also the name of the composition by Ravel which Dudley Moore played in *10* while making love with Derek. So much we already know. Also, let's see here, paging through the old dictionary . . . a bolero is a Spanish dance, characterized by sharp turns and revolutions of the body and stamping of the feet, and it also is a jacket of waist-length or shorter, usually worn open. So *that* explains the jacket of waist-length or shorter, usually worn open, which is Bo Derek's only item of clothing during one scene in the movie! It also explains the sharp turns and revolutions of her body during the same scene, although there is no stamping of the feet, except by the viewer.

But I am still a little confused by the relationship between Derek and the bullfighter who is her lover. If you have not seen the movie, let me explain. Derek has graduated from a fancy women's boarding school, and after mooning her professors she departs in search of a tall, dark, and handsome lover. First she meets a sheik, but he turns out to be a dud, maybe because he spends too much time inhaling the magic fumes of his hookah.

So Bo goes to Spain, where she meets this all-around guy who herds cattle on a mountaintop, owns a winery, and is a bullfighter. If he also was an investment banker whose last book read was *The Prophet,* he could be a Dewar's Profile. Bo and the guy make love at sunrise. Unfortunately, the sun rises directly into the camera at crucial moments. Then her lover goes into the ring to fight with the bull, and is gored in that portion of his anatomy he could least afford to spare in any continuing relationship with Derek. He is brave. While doctors fight to save his life, his only thought is for his dog. He asks Bo to be sure that the dog gets home safely.

Before long, Bo is observing that her lover is acting depressed and distant. Could this possibly be because of his horrible injuries? You would think so, and I would think so, but Bo tells him it doesn't matter, and then she vows that he will live to fight again another day, so to speak. Then she starts taking bullfighting lessons. Oh, but I almost forgot. The Arab sheik tears himself away from his hookah long enough to fly to Spain and kidnap her. She is tied up in his open biplane, but manages to untie herself and jump over the edge. Then Bo is immediately back in her lover's hacienda again. How did she get to the ground? For anyone with Bo's faith, all is possible, and I think this is a real good omen for the lover. If she can get down in one piece, think what he might be able to do.

Let's face it. Nobody is going to *Bolero* for the plot anyway. They're going for the Good Parts. There are two Good Parts, not counting her naked ride on horseback, which was the only scene in the movie that had me wondering how she did it. The real future of Bolero is in home cassette rentals, where your fast forward and instant replay controls will supply the editing job the movie so desperately needs.

The Bostonians ★ ★ ★

PG, 120 m., 1984

Christopher Reeve (Basil Ransom), Vanessa Redgrave (Olive Chancellor), Madeleine Potter (Verena Tarrant), Jessica Tandy (Miss Birdseye), Nancy Marchand (Mrs. Burrage). Directed and produced by Ismail Merchant, James Ivory, and Ruth Prawer Jhabvala. Screenplay by Merchant, Ivory, and Jhabvala.

One of the qualities I like best in the novels of Henry James is the way his characters talk and talk about matters of passion and the heart, and never quite seem to act. One of his favorite words, in many of his books, is "intercourse," by which, significantly, he seems to mean conversation, although you can never quite be sure. James's novels run long and deep, and because he was writing for a 19th century that was not always open to the kinds of passions felt by his characters, he beat a lot, if you will, around the bush, so to speak, with lots of commas and asides and subtle hints of unspeakable practices.

The Bostonians is a novel with a lot of asides, and hundreds of pages of hints. We can summarize it boldly: It is about a sweet and somewhat inconsequential young woman who has inspired crushes in two of her admirers. One of her would-be lovers is a straight-spoken lawyer from the South, who wants to sweep her off her feet and make her his wife. The other is a woman, who does not seem quite in touch with the true nature of her feelings; today she would know she was a lesbian, but in the world of James it is necessary for her to displace her feelings—to convince herself that she is in love with the young woman's politics. Those politics are mostly secondhand, made up of things the young woman has been told by others. The story is set at the birth of the suffragette movement, and women meet in each others homes to talk about the right to vote and, by extension, the right to lead full lives. *The Bostonians* shows us several of those women, including the veteran leader Mrs. Birdseye (wonderfully played by Jessica Tandy) and the younger firebrand Olive Chancellor (Vanessa Redgrave).

Chancellor is in love with Verena Tarrant (Madeleine Potter). That is clear to us, but not as clear to Chancellor. She promotes the young woman as a lecturer and campaigner, filled with visions of her role in social reform—a role that will necessarily require her to become Chancellor's associate, and have little to do with men. Then the tall Southern lawyer (Christopher Reeve) arrives on the scene, and the movie turns into a tug-of-war in which nobody is quite frank about the real nature of the battle.

The Bostonians is by the veteran producer-director-writer team of Ismail Merchant, James Ivory and Ruth Prawer Jhabvala, who collaborated on a 1979 film version of Henry James's *The Europeans*. This is a much better film, intelligent and subtle and open to the underlying tragedy of a woman who does not know what she wants, a man who does not care what he wants, and a girl who does not need what she wants.

The Bounty ★ ★ ★ ★

PG, 130 m., 1984

Anthony Hopkins (Lieutenant William Bligh), Mel Gibson (Fletcher Christian), Tevaite Vernette (Mauatua), Laurence Olivier (Admiral Hood), Edward Fox (Captain Greetham), Daniel Day-Lewis (Fryer). Directed by Roger Donaldson and produced by Bernard Williams. Screenplay by Robert Bolt.

The relationship between Fletcher Christian and Captain William Bligh is one of the most familiar in the movies: We've seen it acted between Clark Gable and Charles Laughton, and between Marlon Brando and Trevor Howard, but it's never before been quite as intriguing as in *The Bounty*, the third movie based on the most famous mutiny in the history of the sea. The movie suggests that Bligh and Christian were friends, of all things, and that Bligh—far from being the histrionic martinet of earlier movies—was an intelligent, contemplative man of great complications. The story is well-known, and simple: *HMS Bounty* sets sail for the South seas, has a difficult voyage that frays everyone's tempers, and then anchors at a Polynesian island. During the trip, the original first mate has been replaced by the young Fletcher Christian, whom Bligh decides to trust. But Christian tires of the voyage and of the dangers and probable death that lie ahead. He falls in love with a native girl and leads a mutiny of sailors who choose to stay on their island paradise.Bligh is played by Anthony Hopkins in one of the most interesting performances of 1984: He is unyielding, but not mindlessly rigid; certain he is right, but not egotistical; able to be realistic about his fate and his chances, and yet completely loyal to his ideas of a British naval officer's proper duties. When Fletcher Christian leads a mutiny against his command, it is not seen simply as a revolt against cruel authority (as in the earlier movies) but as a choice between a freer life-style, and Bligh's placing of duty above ordinary human nature.

Every *Bounty* movie seems to shape its Fletcher Christian somewhat to reflect the actor who plays him. Gable's Christian was a man of action, filled with physical strength and high spirits. Brando's was introverted and tortured. Mel Gibson's is maybe the hardest to figure of the three. He is a man of very few words (the screenplay gives him little to say, and almost no philosophizing), quiet, observant, an enigma. Only in the arms of the woman he comes to love, the Tahitian girl Mauatua, does he find the utter simplicity that perhaps he was looking for when he went to sea. It is a decision of some daring to give Gibson so noticeably little dialogue in this movie, but it works.

This *Bounty* is not only a wonderful movie, high-spirited and intelligent, but something of a production triumph as well. Although this third *Bounty* film was originally conceived as a big-budget, two-part epic to be directed by David *(Dr. Zhivago)* Lean, the current version was prepared and directed after only a few months' notice by a talented young New Zealander named Roger Donaldson, whose previous credits included the brilliant *Smash Palace*, a critical hit and commercial failure. What's interesting is that Donaldson's film doesn't feel like a secondhand treatment; he directs with flair and wit, and the spectacular scenes (like a stormy crossing of the Cape) never allow the special effects to steal the film away from the actors.

The sea voyage is done with the sort of macho confidence that a good sea movie needs, and the land portions to do an interesting job of contrasting the proper, civilized British (represented by Laurence Olivier, as an admiral) with the cheerful absolute freedom of Polynesia. The romance between Gibson and the beautiful Tevaite Vernette, as his island lover, is given time to develop instead of just being thrown in as a plot point. And the Polynesians, for once, are all allowed to go topless all the time (the movie nevertheless gets the PG rating, qualifying under the *National Geographic* loophole in which nudity doesn't count south of the equator). *The Bounty* is a great adventure, a lush romance, and a good movie.

The Boy Who Could Fly ★ ★ ★

PG, 114 m., 1986

Lucy Deakins (Milly), Jay Underwood (Eric), Bonnie Bedelia (Charlene), Fred Savage (Louis), Colleen Dewhurst (Mrs. Sherman), Fred Gwynne (Uncle Hugo), Louise Fletcher (Psychiatrist). Directed by Nick Castle and produced by Gary Adelson. Screenplay by Castle.

Here is a sweet and innocent parable about a boy who could fly—and about a girl who could fly, too, when the boy held her hand. The lesson the girl learns in this film is that anything is possible, if only you have faith. The movie could have been directed fifty years ago by Frank Capra, except that in the Capra version, the boy wouldn't have been autistic and the girl wouldn't have been grieving because of the recent suicide of her father, who was dying of cancer. Parables have harder edges these days.

The movie takes place in a small town with picket fences, shade trees, and mean boys who won't let little kids ride their tricycles around the block. Into a run-down house on one of these streets, a small family moves: a mother, teen-age daughter, and little brother. The girl looks out her bedroom window to the house next door, and there she sees, poised on the roof, a teen-age boy with his arms outstretched, poised to fly.

She learns his story. When he was five, his parents died in an airplane crash. At the exact moment of the crash, he started to try to fly, as if he could have saved them. But can he really fly? The boy lives with an alcoholic uncle, who swears he has seen the kid fly. But the uncle sees a lot of things, not all of them real.

The Boy Who Could Fly surrounds this situation with small stories of everyday life. The mother (Bonnie Bedelia) goes back to her old job in the insurance industry and discovers she has to learn to use a computer. Her daughter (Lucy Deakins) goes to high school and makes friends with an understanding teacher (Colleen Dewhurst). The little brother (a small, fierce tyke named Fred Savage) plots to overcome the bullies who live around the corner. And next door, the strange boy (Jay Underwood) lives in his world of dreams and silence.

Can anything break through to him? Yes, as it turns out, one power on Earth is strong enough to penetrate his autism, and that power is adolescent love.

He gets a crush on his new neighbor. She cares for him. One day, he saves her life. She believes he can really fly, but nobody else does, and then the kid is taken away from his drunken uncle and placed in an institution, which could crush his spirit.

The movie develops along lines that we can more or less anticipate, and it ends on a note of high sentimentality. What's good about it are the performances, especially by Deakins, a warm and empathetic teen-ager, Savage, a plucky little kid who could play Dennis the Menace, and Bedelia, a widow still mourning her husband.

Movies like this can be insufferable if they lay it on too thick. *The Boy Who Could Fly* finds just about the right balance between its sunny message and the heartbreak that's always threatening to prevail.

Brazil ★ ★

R, 130 m., 1985

Jonathan Pryce (Sam Lowry), Robert De Niro (Tuttle), Katherine Helmond (Ida Lowry), Ian Holm (Kurtzmann), Bob Hoskins (Spoor), Michael Palin (Jack Lint). Directed by Terry Gilliam and produced by Arnon Milchan. Screenplay by Tom Stoppard, Charles McKeown, and Gilliam.

Just as Orwell's *1984* is an alternative vision of our times, so *Brazil* is an alternative to Orwell. The movie happens in a time and place that seem vaguely like our own, but with different graphics, hardware, and politics. Society is controlled by a monolithic organization, and citizens lead lives of paranoia and control. Thought police are likely to come crashing through the ceiling and start bashing at dissenters. Life is mean and grim.

The hero of *Brazil* is Sam Lowry (Jonathan Pryce), a meek, desperate little man who works at a computer terminal all day. Occasionally he cheats; when the boss isn't looking, he and his fellows switch the screens of their computers to reruns of exciting old TV programs. Sam knows his life is drab and lockstep, but he sees no way out of it, and his only escape is into his fantasies—into glorious dreams of flying high above all the petty cares of the world, urged on by the vision of a beautiful woman.

His everyday life offers no such possibilities. Even the basic mechanisms of life support seem to be failing, and one scene early in the movie has Robert De Niro, in a walk-on, as an illegal free-lance repairman who defies the state by fixing things. De Niro makes his escapes by sliding down long cables to freedom, like Spider-Man. For Sam, there seems to be no escape.

But then he gets involved in an intrigue that involves the girl of his dreams, the chief executive of the state, and a shadowy band of dissenters. All of this is strangely familiar; the outlines of *Brazil* are much the same as those of *1984*, but the approach is different. While Orwell's lean prose was translated, last year, into an equally lean and dour film, *Brazil* seems almost like a throwback to the psychedelic 1960s, to an anarchic vision in which the best way to improve things is to blow them up.

The other difference between the two worlds—Orwell's, and the one created here by director and co-writer Terry Gilliam—is that Gilliam has apparently had no financial restraints. Although *Brazil* has had a checkered history since it was made (for a long time, Universal Pictures seemed unwilling to release it), there was a lot of money available to make it, and the movie is awash in elaborate special effects, sensational sets, apocalyptic scenes of destruction, and a general lack of discipline. It's as if Gilliam sat down and wrote out all of his fantasies, heedless of production difficulties, and then they were filmed—this time, heedless of sense.

The movie is very hard to follow. I have seen it twice, and am still not sure exactly who all the characters are, or how they fit. Perhaps I am not supposed to be clear; perhaps the movie's air of confusion is part of its paranoid vision. There are individual moments that create sharp images (shock troops drilling through a ceiling, De Niro wrestling with the almost obscene wiring and tubing inside a wall, the movie's obsession with bizarre ductwork), but there seems to be no sure hand at the controls.

The best scene in the movie is one of the simplest, as Sam moves into half an office and finds himself engaged in a tug-of-war over his desk with the man through the wall. I was reminded of a Chaplin film like *Modern Times*, and reminded, too, that in Chaplin economy and simplicity were virtues, not the enemy.

The Breakfast Club ★ ★ ★

R, 95 m., 1985

Emilio Estevez (Andrew Clark), Anthony Michael Hall (Brian Johnson), Judd Nelson (John Bender), Molly Ringwald (Claire Standish), Ally Sheedy (Allison Reynolds), Paul Gleason (Teacher), John Kapelos (Janitor). Directed by John Hughes and produced by Ned Tanen and Hughes. Screenplay by Hughes.

The Breakfast Club begins with an old dramatic standby. You isolate a group of people in a room, you have them talk, and eventually they exchange truths about themselves and come to new understandings. William Saroyan and Eugene O'Neill have been here before, but they used saloons and drunks. *The Breakfast Club* uses a high school library and five teen-age kids.

The movie takes place on a Saturday. The five kids have all violated high school rules in one way or another, and they've qualified for a special version of detention, all day long, from eight to four, in the school library. They arrive at the school one at a time. There's the arrogant, swaggering tough guy (Judd Nelson). The insecure neurotic (Ally Sheedy) who hides behind her hair and her clothes. The jock from the wrestling team (Emilio Estevez). The prom queen (Molly Ringwald). And the class brain (Anthony Michael Hall). These kids have nothing in common, and they have an aggressive desire *not* to have anything in common. In ways peculiar to teen-agers, who sometimes have a studious disinterest in anything that contradicts their self-image, these kids aren't even curious about each other. Not at first, anyway. But then the day grows longer and the library grows more oppressive, and finally the tough kid can't resist picking on the prom queen, and then there is a series of exchanges.

Nothing that happens in *The Breakfast Club* is all that surprising. The truths that are exchanged are more or less predictable, and the kids have fairly standard hang-ups.

It comes as no surprise, for example, to learn that the jock's father is a perfectionist, or that the prom queen's parents give her material rewards but withhold their love. But *The Breakfast Club* doesn't need earthshaking revelations; it's about kids who grow willing to talk to one another, and it has a surprisingly good ear for the way they speak. (Ever notice the way lots of teen-age girls, repeating a conversation, say "she goes . . ." rather than "she says . . ."?)

The movie was written and directed by John Hughes, who also made 1984's *Sixteen Candles.* Two of the stars of that movie (Ringwald and Hall) are back again, and there's another similarity: Both movies make an honest attempt to create teen-agers who might seem plausible to other teen-agers. Most Hollywood teen-age movies give us underage nymphos or nostalgia-drenched memories of the 1950s. The performances are wonderful, but then this is an all-star cast, as younger actors go; in addition to Hall and Ringwald from *Sixteen Candles,* there's Sheedy from *WarGames* and Estevez from *Repo Man.* Judd Nelson is not yet as well known, but his character creates the strong center of the film; his aggression is what breaks the silence and knocks over the walls. The only weaknesses in Hughes's writing are in the adult characters: The teacher is one-dimensional and one-note, and the janitor is brought onstage with a potted philosophical talk that isn't really necessary. Typically, the kids don't pay much attention.

Note: The "R" rating on this film refers to language; I think a PG-13 rating would have been more reasonable. The film is certainly appropriate for thoughtful teen-agers.

Breakin' 2—Electric Boogaloo ★ ★ ★

PG, 94 m., 1984

Adolfo "Shabba-Doo" Quinones (Ozone), Michael "Boogaloo Shrimp" Chambers (Turbo), Lucinda Dickey (Kelly). Directed by Sam Firstenberg and produced by Menachem Golan and Yoram Globus. Written by Jan Ventura and Julie Reichert.

Movie musicals used to be allowed to be goofy and lightweight, but in recent years they've turned into ponderous, over-budgeted artifacts that take themselves so seriously you feel guilty if you're having a good time. Remember all the self-importance of *Annie?* That's why a modest, cheerful little movie like *Breakin' 2—Electric Boogaloo* is so refreshing. Here is a movie that wants nothing more than to allow some high-spirited kids to sing and dance their way through a silly plot just long enough to make us grin.

The movie is a sequel to 1983's very successful *Breakin'.* I guess that explains the ungainly title. It involves the same actors, including a team of street-dance artists named Shabba-Doo Quinones and Boogaloo Shrimp Chambers, who more or less seem to be playing themselves. The plot is so familiar that if you're a fan of Mickey Rooney musicals or even the Beach Party movies, you may start rubbing your eyes. But the movie is a lot of fun.

Familiar? Try this plot out on your nearest trivia expert. A bunch of kids get together to turn a run-down old theater into a community center. The center is run by a nice old guy (who is not, for some reason, called "Pops"), and the ringleaders are Shabba-Doo and Boogaloo. In the last movie, they formed a dance team with a rich girl (Lucinda Dickey), and as this movie opens she visits their center and decides to stay and pitch in, despite the opposition of her WASP parents, who want her to enroll in an Ivy League university. Then the plot thickens, when an evil real estate developer wants to tear down the center and put up a big retail development. With just a few minor modifications, this story could be about Mickey and Judy, or Frankie and Annette. But what does it matter, when the whole point of the enterprise is to provide an excuse for song and dance? Quinones, Chambers, and Dickey can indeed dance, very well, and there are a lot of other street dancers in the movie, but what's interesting is the way the traditions of street dancing are combined in this movie with the older traditions of stage dancing and chorus lines. The big extravaganza at the end (a benefit to save the center, needless to say) is a unique hybrid of old and new dance styles.

Electric Boogaloo is not a great movie, but it's inexhaustible, entertaining, and may turn out to be influential. It could inspire a boomlet of low-priced movie musicals—movies not saddled with multimillion dollar budgets, Broadway connections, and stars who are not necessarily able to sing and dance. And at a time when movie musicals (as opposed to movie sound tracks) are seriously out of touch with the music that is really being played and listened to by teenagers, that could be a revolutionary development.

Breaking Away ★ ★ ★ ★
PG, 100 m., 1979

Dennis Christopher (Dave), Dennis Quaid (Mike), Daniel Stern (Cyril), Jackie Earle Haley (Moocher), Paul Dooley (Dad), Barbara Barrie (Mom), Robyn Douglass (Katherine). Directed and produced by Peter Yates. Screenplay by Steve Tesich.

Here's a sunny, goofy, intelligent little film about coming of age in Bloomington, Indiana. It's about four local kids, just out of high school, who mess around for one final summer before facing the inexorable choices of jobs or college or the Army. One of the kids, Dave (Dennis Christopher), has it in his head that he wants to be a champion Italian bicycle racer, and he drives his father crazy with opera records and ersatz Italian.

His friends have more reasonable ambitions: One (Dennis Quaid) was a high school football star who pretends he doesn't want to play college ball, but he does; another (Jackie Earle Haley) is a short kid who pretends he doesn't want to be taller, but he does; and another (Daniel Stern) is one of those kids like we all knew, who learned how to talk by crossing Eric Sevareid with Woody Allen.

There's the usual town-and-gown tension in Bloomington, between the jocks and the townies (who are known, in Bloomington, as "cutters"—so called after the workers in the area's limestone quarries). There's also a poignant kind of tension between local guys and college girls: Will a sorority girl be seen with a cutter? Dave finds out by falling hopelessly in love with a college girl named Kathy (Robyn Douglass), and somehow, insanely, convincing her he's actually an Italian exchange student.

The whole business of Dave's Italomania provides the movie's funniest running joke: Dave's father (Paul Dooley) rants and raves that he didn't raise his boy to be an Eye-talian, and that he's sick and tired of all the eenees in the house: linguini, fettucini . . . even Jake, the dog, which Dave has renamed Fellini. The performances by Dooley and Barbara Barrie as Dave's parents are so loving and funny at the same time that we remember, almost with a shock, that *every* movie doesn't have to have parents and kids who don't get along.

The movie was directed as a work of love by Peter Yates, whose big commercial hits have included *Bullitt* and *The Deep*. The Oscar-winning original screenplay was written by Steve Tesich, who was born in Yugoslavia, was moved to Bloomington at the age of thirteen, won the Little 500 bicycle race there in 1962, and uses it for the film's climax. Yates has gone for the human elements in *Breaking Away*, but he hasn't forgotten how to direct action, and there's a bravura sequence in which Dave, on a racing bicycle, engages in a high-speed highway duel with a semitrailer truck.

In this scene, and in scenes involving swimming in an abandoned quarry, Yates does a tricky and intriguing thing: He suggests the constant possibility of sudden tragedy. We wait for a terrible accident to happen, and none does, but the hints of one make the characters seem curiously vulnerable, and their lives more precious.

The whole movie, indeed, is a delicate balancing act of its various tones: This movie could have been impossible to direct, but Yates has us on his side almost immediately. Some scenes edge into fantasy, others are straightforward character development, some (like the high school quarterback's monologue about his probable future) are heartbreakingly true. But the movie always returns to light comedy, to romance, to a wonderfully evocative instant nostalgia.

Breaking Away is a movie to embrace. It's about people who are complicated but decent, who are optimists but see things realistically, who are fundamentally comic characters but have three full dimensions. It's about a Middle America we rarely see in the movies, yes, but it's not corny and it doesn't condescend. Movies like this are hardly ever made at all; when they're made this well, they're precious cinematic miracles.

Breathless ★ ★ ½
R, 100 m., 1983

Richard Gere (Jesse Lujack), Valerie Kaprisky (Monica Poiccard). Directed by Jim McBride and produced by Martin Erlichman. Screenplay by McBride and L.M. (Kit) Carson.

There are several levels of cinematic incest at work in *Breathless*, an American film inspired by a 1959 French film that was itself inspired by countless even earlier Hollywood crime films, including *Gun Crazy*—a movie that turns up in this movie. This is the kind of movie for which you need your *Filmgoer's Companion*. Or maybe not; for its announced purpose, as a lurid melodrama about sex and death, it works well enough even without the cross-references. The movie stars Richard Gere, Hollywood's ranking male sex symbol, and Valerie Kaprisky, an unknown French actress, in a story of doom and obsession adapted from Jean-Luc Godard's *Breathless*.

The 1959 *Breathless* starred Jean-Paul Belmondo as a loutish young Frenchman who modeled his behavior on Bogart and Cagney, and bluffed his way into a fatal confrontation with the cops. Jean Seberg played a young American girl who came to Paris to study, met Belmondo, and found herself sharing his bed and his fate. Godard's *Breathless* superimposed Hollywood images on French life-styles. Jim McBride's 1983 *Breathless*, from a script by L.M. (Kit) Carson, does a reverse on the same theme. This time the student (Kaprisky) is French; she's studying in Los Angeles. The lout (Gere) is an American hustler who has to get out of Las Vegas in a hurry, is chased by a highway patrolman, and kills him in a confrontation that is deliberately ambiguous: Did he mean to shoot him or not?

On the run, Gere moves in with Kaprisky, whom he knows only from a weekend fling in Vegas. They make passionate love. The girl gradually becomes aware that her lover is the subject of a statewide manhunt, and the chase leads from punk discos to the Hollywood hills. McBride and Carson position their film somewhere between plausibility (in scenes on a campus, in a grocery store, and in a Mexican restaurant) and stylized fantasy (in the garish red tones of the opening scenes and in Gere's deliberate overacting).

Although movie buffs will probably enjoy this movie's cross-references, this *Breathless* is going to depend on its appeal to ordinary audiences. I imagine they'll be attracted by the notion of Gere as an erotic outlaw on the run, but how will they like him in this role? I thought Gere was deliberately repugnant, but in an interesting way. He plays a character so conceited, so self-absorbed and, I'm afraid, so dim-witted, that there's no opportunity to ever really care for or about him. Kaprisky, as the young French student, is an unknown in a role too large and complex for her, and there are times when she seems lost in a scene, looking to Gere for guidance. The result is a stylistic exercise without any genuine human concerns we can identify with—and yet, an exercise that does have a command of its style, is good looking, fun to watch, and develops a certain morbid humor.

Bright Lights, Big City ★ ★ ★ ½
R, 107 m., 1988 ✓
(See related Film Clip, p. 758.)

Michael J. Fox (Jamie), Kiefer Sutherland (Tad), Phoebe Cates (Amanda), Swoosie Kurtz (Megan), Frances Sternhagen (Clara), Tracy Pollan (Vicky), John Houseman (Mr. Vogel), Charlie Schlatter (Michael), Jason Robards (Alex Hardy), Dianne Wiest (Mother). Directed by James Bridges and produced by Mark Rosenberg and Sydney Pollack. Screenplay by Jay McInerney.

What does cocaine make you feel like? It makes you feel like having some more cocaine.
—George Carlin

And that is what Jamie Conway feels like, all day, every day. The chasm between his professional existence and his private life is laughable, and it's growing impossible to keep up the charade that he even cares about the things he's supposed to be doing. He works for a high-powered New York magazine, and the only two things that keep him on the job are guilt and the need for money. He needs the money because he puts it into his nose. He needs the guilt because it's his only link to his ambitions.

Bright Lights, Big City is the record of Jamie's search for the bottom. It takes place over the course of a week or so, a chaotic week in which people, events, and even whole days drift in and out of focus. He is completely out of control. The irony is that he still looks halfway okay, if you don't look too hard. He's together enough to sit in a club and drink double vodkas and engage in absentminded conversation with transparent people. He drinks prodigious amounts of booze, punctuated by cocaine.

It's hard to classify a guy like this. Is he (a) an alcoholic, using the coke so he can stay awake and drink more? Or (b) a cokehead, using the booze to level off? Those are the two choices on Jamie's multiple-part exam. There are no other parts of his life worth serious discussion. His "life" consists, in fact, of the brief window that opens every day between his hangover and oblivion.

Jamie is played by Michael J. Fox, red-eyed and puffy-faced, and trembling with fear every morning when the telephone rings. He once lived in Kansas City and dreamed of becoming a writer, and it was there he met and married Amanda (Phoebe Cates), his pretty young wife. They met in a bar. The movie deliberately never makes clear what, if anything, they truly had to share. In New York, she finds overnight success as a model, and drifts away from him. That's no surprise; the movie makes it pretty clear that Jamie is the kind of port where the tide is always going out.

Now Jamie hauls himself, filled with nausea and self-loathing, into the magazine office every day. He works as a fact-checker. He could care less. He had dreams once. He can barely focus on them. One day he's cornered at the water cooler by the pathetic old drunk Alex Hardy (Jason Robards), who once wrote good fiction and knew Faulkner, and now exists as the magazine's gin-soaked fiction editor.

Alex drags Jamie out to a martini lunch, where the conversation is the typical alcoholic mixture of resentment against those who have made it, and self-hatred for drinking it all away. Jason Robards has always been a great actor, but there is a fleeting moment in this scene that is as good as anything he has ever done. It is a totally blank look. A moment when we can look into the face and eyes of his character and see that nobody, literally nobody, is at home. It's as if his mind has stalled. By supplementing booze with cocaine, Jamie is going to be able to reach Alex's state of numbed incomprehension decades more quickly.

There is one glimmer of hope in Alex's life. He has dinner one night with a bright college student (Tracy Pollan) who is the cousin of his drinking buddy (Kiefer Sutherland). At a restaurant, he goes into the toilet and then decides not to use cocaine: "Let's see if I can get through one evening without chemicals," he muses. He likes her. She is intelligent and kind. Several days later, at the end of a lost weekend of confusion and despair, he looks at himself in a mirror and says, "I need help." He telephones her in the middle of the night. His conversation is disconnected and confused, but what he is really doing is calling for help.

Maybe she can help him, maybe not. The movie ends with Jamie staggering out into the bright dawn of a new day and, in a scene a little too contrived for my taste, trading his dark glasses for a loaf of bread. *Bright Lights, Big City* is a *Lost Weekend* for the 1980s, a chronicle of wasted days and misplaced nights. It was directed by James Bridges, whose *Urban Cowboy* was in many ways an earlier version of the same story. Fox is very good in the central role (he has a long drunken monologue that is the best thing he has ever done in a movie). To his credit, he never seems to be having fun as he journeys through clubland. Few do, for long. If you know someone like Jamie, show him this movie, and don't let him go to the john.

Brighton Beach Memoirs ★ ★

PG-13, 115 m., 1986

Jonathan Silverman (Eugene), Blythe Danner (Kate), Bob Dishy (Jack), Brian Drillinger (Stanley), Stacey Glick (Laurie), Judith Ivey (Blanche). Directed by Gene Saks and produced by Ray Stark. Screenplay by Neil Simon.

Neil Simon's *Brighton Beach Memoirs* leaves little doubt why he grew up to be a successful playwright: Everyone in his family talked in dialogue. The movie feels so plotted, so constructed, so written, that I found myself thinking maybe they shouldn't have filmed the final draft of the screenplay. Maybe there was an earlier draft that was a little disorganized and unpolished, but still had the jumble of life in it.

The stage version of *Brighton Beach Memoirs* seemed much more alive than this film. Some of the difference is in the casting of the hero—Jonathan Silverman does not wear as well and is not as infectiously likable as Matthew Broderick, who had the role on stage—but most of the difference, I think, is in the direction.

The movie was directed by Gene Saks, who directs many of Simon's plays on both the stage and the screen, and whose gift is for the theater. His plays have the breath of life; his movies feel like the official authorized version. Everything is by the numbers. After we learn that the hero's family always pronounces diseases with a whisper, we know with total certainty that at least one whispered disease will be "diarrhea," and that the joke will be carried on for one disease too long.

The movie is the first in an autobiographical triology by Simon, who here remembers his early adolescence; still ahead were the uncertain war years of *Biloxi Blues*, and the family wars and heartbreaks of *Broadway Bound*, his subsequent stage successes. Simon tells his story through the eyes of Eugene (Silverman), a kid who seems more like a future golfer than a future playwright, and whose life is consumed by a great and solemn desire to see at least one naked girl.

Eugene lives in a home filled with relatives; not only his parents and an important older brother, but also an aunt and a cousin. In the stage version, I could feel the crowding, the way the overlapping lives within the house raised the family's collective temperature. In the movie, there's no sense of other lives being lived through the walls, and the characters seem to walk on for their assigned material and then evaporate.

Nor does the Brighton Beach neighborhood really come to life, despite untold effort spent to dress the street where Jonathan lives. When he leaves home, it's usually to go to Greenblatt's grocery, where his mother sends him several times a day (another standing joke). On his way there and back, he never seems to encounter anyone except characters specifically involved with the plot; this isn't a Brooklyn teeming with life and excitement, it's a backdrop for schtick.

Sometimes the family feels like a backdrop, too. Jonathan's mother is intended to be one of the great towering figures of his life, but Blythe Danner doesn't bring much force to the character. She proved in *The Great Santini* that she can bring great passion to the role of the mother of a troubled family, but here there seems to be an invisible line she's not allowed to cross, a certain level above which she must not raise her voice. There's that feeling all through the movie—the feeling that a safe middle ground has been established, and that nothing will grow too fearsome, too passionate, or too angry.

Not long ago I went to a memorial service for Sydney J. Harris, the columnist, and I heard Saul Bellow remember the adolescence of his best friend. They walked back and forth between their homes, talking late into the night. They argued about ideas and everything else. Harris wrote a novel and Bellow wrote the introduction, and they decided it should be taken to a New York publisher, so Harris stuck out his thumb on Division Street and hitched all the way to New York, and Bellow kept his secret—even when his older brother and Harris's mother marched him in for questioning at the Missing Person's Bureau.

Bellow spoke in direct, affectionate sentences that captured the passion of that time of their lives, the seriousness of their convictions. He created mental pictures of kids who took risks and put themselves on the line, and as I listened to him speak, I reflected on how pale everyone seemed in *Brighton Beach Memoirs*, by comparison—even though the milieus are so similar. It's all too even, too smooth, too easy. Simon and Saks should have taken some chances and cut closer to the bone.

Bring Me the Head of Alfredo Garcia

★ ★ ★ ★
R, 112 m., 1974

Warren Oates (Bennie), Isela Vega (Elita), Kris Kristofferson (Paco), Gig Young (Killer). Directed by Sam Peckinpah and produced by Martin Baum. Screenplay by Gordon T. Dawson and Peckinpah.

Sam Peckinpah's *Bring Me the Head of Alfredo Garcia* is a weird, horrifying film that somehow transcends its unlikely material. It's the story of a drunken and violent odyssey across Mexico by a dropout bartender who, if he returns Alfredo Garcia's head, stands to be paid a million dollars. The head accompanies him in a burlap bag, tossed into the front seat of a beat-up old

Ford convertible, and it gathers flies and symbolic meaning at about the same pace.

The movie is some kind of bizarre masterpiece. It's probably not a movie that most people would like, but violence, with Peckinpah, sometimes becomes a psychic ballet. His characters don't look for it, they don't like it, and they negotiate it with weariness and resignation. They're too beat up by life to get any kind of exhilaration from a fight. They've been in far too many fights already, and lost most of them, and the violence they encounter is just another cross to bear.

That's the case with Bennie, the antihero of *Bring Me the Head of Alfredo Garcia.* He's played by Warren Oates, one of that breed of movie actors who attract us, somehow, through their negative qualities. He's like some of the characters played by Jack Nicholson or Bruce Dern; we like him because he's suffered so much more than we ever will (we hope) that no matter what horrors he goes through, or inflicts, we still care about him.

Bennie is a bartender and plays a little piano, and he hears about the head of Alfredo Garcia from a couple of bounty hunters who pass through his saloon. They're played, by the way, by the unlikely team of Gig Young and Robert Webber, who between them define dissipation. Garcia's head is worth a million bucks because Garcia, it turns out, has impregnated the daughter of a rich Mexican industrialist. The millionaire is almost a caricature of macho compulsiveness; he simultaneously puts a price on the head of the culprit, and looks forward with pride to the birth of a grandson.

Bennie sees the million dollars as his ticket out of hell, and on the way to finding it he runs across Alfredo Garcia's former lover, Elita (Isela Vega, looking as moistly erotic as anyone since young Anna Magnani). They fall in love, or something; their relationship is complicated by Bennie's crude shyness and her own custom of being abused by men. The most perversely interesting relationship in the movie, however, is the friendship that grows between Bennie and Alfredo's head, once Bennie has gotten possession of it. That's made somewhat easier by the fact that Alfredo, it turns out, is already dead. But there is a gruesome struggle over his grave, and once Bennie finally gets the head he has to kill to protect his prize. His drive across Mexico is fueled by blood and tequila, and about halfway through it we realize why Peckinpah set his movie in the present, instead of in the past; this same material wouldn't have worked as a historical Western. The conventions of the genre would have insulted us from the impact of what happens. There would have been horses and watering holes and clichés. Instead, we get unforgettable scenes of Warren Oates with that grisly burlap bag and the bottle next to him in the front seat, and the nakedness of his greed is inescapable.

Somewhere along the way Oates, as Bennie, makes a compact with the prize he begins to call "Al." They both loved the same woman, they are both being destroyed by the same member of an upper class, they're both poor bastards who never asked for their grief in life. And slowly, out of the haze of the booze and the depths of his suffering, Bennie allies himself with Al and against the slob with the money. *Bring Me the Head of Alfredo Garcia* is Sam Peckinpah making movies flat out, giving us a desperate character he clearly loves, and asking us to somehow see past the horror and the blood to the sad poem he's trying to write about the human condition.

Broadcast News ★ ★ ★ ★

R, 125 m., 1987

(See related Film Clip, p. 739.)

William Hurt (Tom Grunick), Albert Brooks (Aaron Altman), Holly Hunter (Jane Craig), Lois Chiles (Jennifer Mack), Joan Cusack (Blair Litton), Robert Prosky (Bureau Chief). Directed, produced, and written by James L. Brooks.

Broadcast News is as knowledgeable about the TV news-gathering process as any movie ever made, but it also has insights into the more personal matter of how people use high-pressure jobs as a way of avoiding time alone with themselves. The movie was described as being about a romantic triangle, but that's only partly true. It is about three people who toy with the idea of love, but are obsessed by the idea of making television.

Deadline pressure attracts people like that. The newspapers are filled with them, and also ad agencies, brokerages, emergency rooms, show business, sales departments, and police and fire stations. There's a certain adrenaline charge in delivering on a commitment at the last moment, in rushing out to be an instant hero or an instant failure. There's a kind of person who calls you up to shout into the phone, "I can't talk to you now—I'm busy!" This kind of person is always busy, because the lifestyle involves arranging things so you're always behind. Given plenty of time to complete a job, you wait until the last moment to start—guaranteeing a deadline rush.

I know all about that kind of obsession (you don't think I finished this review early, do you?). *Broadcast News* understands it from the inside out, and perhaps the most interesting sequence in the whole movie is a scene where a network news producer sweats it out with a videotape editor to finish a report that is scheduled to appear on the evening news in fifty-two seconds. In an atmosphere like that, theoretical questions get lost. The operational reality, day after day, is to get the job done and beat the deadline and make things look as good as possible. Positive feedback goes to people who deliver. Yesterday's job is forgotten. What have you got for me today?

Right at the center of *Broadcast News* is a character named Jane Craig (Holly Hunter), who is a newswriter-producer for the Washington bureau of one of the networks. She is smart and fast and cherishes certain beliefs about TV news—one of them being that a story should be covered by the person best-qualified to cover it. One of her best friends is Aaron Altman (Albert Brooks), a bright, aggressive reporter. He's one of the best in the business, but he's not especially good on camera. During a trip south she meets Tom Grunick (William Hurt), a sportscaster who cheerfully admits he has little education, is not a good reader, and doesn't know much about current events. But he has been hired for the Washington bureau because he looks good and has a natural relationship with the camera.

The Hunter character is only human. She is repelled by this guy's credentials, but she likes his body. After he comes to Washington, he quickly gains the attention of the network brass, while the Brooks character goes into eclipse. Hunter is torn between the two men: Brooks, who says he loves her and is the better reporter, and Hurt, who says he wants to learn, and who is sexier.

The tricky thing about *Broadcast News*—the quality in James L. Brooks's screenplay that makes it so special—is that all three characters have a tendency to grow emotionally absentminded when it's a choice between romance and work. Frankly, they'd rather work. After Hunter whispers into Hurt's earpiece to talk him through a crucial live report on a Middle East crisis, he kneels at her feet and says it was like sex, having her voice inside his head. He never gets that excited about sex. Neither does she.

Much of the plot of *Broadcast News* centers around a piece that Hurt reports about "date rape." Listening to one woman's story, he is so moved that a tear trickles down his cheek. It means a great deal to Hunter whether that tear is real or faked. Experienced TV people will question why Hunter, a veteran producer, didn't immediately notice the detail that bothers her so much later on. But in a way, *Broadcast News* is not about details, but about the larger question of whether TV news is becoming show business.

Jack Nicholson has an unbilled supporting role in the movie as the network's senior anchorman, an irascible man who has high standards himself, but is not above seeing his ratings assisted by coverage that may be questionable. The implication is that the next anchor will be a William Hurt-type, great on camera, but incapable of discerning authenticity from fakery. Meanwhile, the Albert Brooks types will end up doing superior journalism in smaller "markets" (the TV word for "cities"), and the Holly Hunter types will keep on fighting all the old deadlines, plus a new one, the biological clock.

Broadcast News has a lot of interesting things to say about television. But the thing it does best is look into a certain kind of personality and a certain kind of relationship. Like *Terms of Endearment*, the previous film by James Brooks, it does not see relationships as a matter of meeting someone you like and falling in love. Brooks, almost alone among major Hollywood filmmakers, knows that some people have higher priorities than love, and deeper fears.

Broadway Danny Rose ★ ★ ★ ½
PG, 86 m., 1984

Woody Allen (Danny Rose), Mia Farrow (Tina Vitale), Nick Apollo Forte (Lou Canova). Directed by Woody Allen and produced by Robert Greenhut and Charles H. Joffe. Screenplay by Allen.

The first time we see him, he's talking fast, and his arms are working like a guy doing an imitation of an air traffic controller. His hands keep coming in for landings. This is Broadway Danny Rose, the most legendary talent agent in New York, the guy who will represent you after you've been laughed off every stage in the Catskills. He represents blind xylophonists, piano-playing birds, and has-been crooners with drinking problems. He's the kind of guy that comics sitting around on their day off tell stories about. He also is Woody Allen, but he is less like Woody Allen than some of the other characters Allen has played. After the autobiography of *Stardust Memories,* after the whimsy of *A Midsummer Night's Sex Comedy,* and the antiseptic experimentation of *Zelig,* this movie has Allen creating a character and following him all the way through a crazy story. After a period when Allen seemed stuck in self-doubt and introspection, he loosens up and has a good time.

Broadway Danny Rose, like all of Allen's best movies, is a New York movie. It starts at the Carnegie Deli, with comedians sitting around a table trading Danny Rose stories, and then it flashes back to the best Danny Rose story of them all, about how Danny signed up this has-been alcoholic tenor and carefully nurtured his career back to the brink of stardom. Riding the nostalgia boom, Danny takes the guy and books him into Top Forty concerts, until finally he gets him a date at the Waldorf—and Milton Berle is in the audience, looking for guests for his TV special. Except the crooner has a complicated love life. He has a wife, and he also has a girlfriend. He wants Danny Rose to be the "beard" and take the girlfriend to the concert. Otherwise he won't feel right. But then the crooner and the girl have a fight, and the girl goes back to her Mafioso boyfriend, and Danny Rose winds up at a mob wedding with a gun in his face.

All of this is accomplished with wonderfully off-the-wall characterizations. Allen makes Danny Rose into a caricature, and then, working from that base, turns him back into a human being: By the end of the film, we see the person beneath the mannerisms. Nick Apollo Forte, an actor I've never seen before, plays the has-been crooner with a soft touch: he's childish, he's a bear, he's loyal, he has a monstrous ego. The real treasure among the performances, however, is Mia Farrow's work as Tina Vitale, the crooner's girlfriend. You would think that Mia Farrow would be one of the most instantly recognizable actresses in the movies with those finely chiseled features and that little-girl voice. But here she is a chain-smoking, brassy blonde with her hair piled up on top of her head, and a pair of fashionable sunglasses, and dresses that look like they came from the boutique in a Mafia resort hotel.

Broadway Danny Rose uses all of the basic ingredients of Damon Runyon's Broadway: the pathetic acts looking for a job, the guys who get a break and forget their old friends, the agents with hearts of gold, the beautiful showgirls who fall for Woody Allen types, the dumb gangsters, big shots at the ringside tables (Howard Cosell plays himself). It all works.

The Brother from Another Planet
★ ★ ★ ½
PG, 110 m., 1984

Joe Morton (The Brother), Maggie Renzi (Noreen), Fisher Stevens (Card Trickster), John Sayles (Man in Black). Directed by John Sayles and produced by Sayles and Maggie Renzi. Screenplay by Sayles.

When the movies started to talk, they began to lose the open-eyed simplicity with which they saw the world. *The Brother from Another Planet* tells the story of a man who cannot talk, but who can read minds, listen carefully, look deep into eyes, and provide a sort of mirror for our society. That makes it sound serious, but like all the most serious movies, it's a comedy.

The film stars Joe Morton as a visitor from outer space, who looks like a black human being, unless you look carefully at the three funny toes on his feet. He arrives on Earth in a spaceship that looks borrowed from the cheapest B space operas from the 1950s, swims ashore, and finds himself on Manhattan Island. At first he is completely baffled. Before long, everyone he meets is just as baffled. It is strange to deal with people who confound all your expectations: It might even force you to reevaluate yourself.

The brother is not looking for trouble, is not controversial, wants only to make sense of this weird new world. Because his instinctive response to most situations is a sort of blank reserve, people project their own feelings and expectations upon him. They tell him what he must be thinking, and behave as if they are right. He goes along.

The movie finds countless opportunities for humorous scenes, most of them with a quiet little bite, a way of causing us to look at our society. The brother runs into hookers and connivers, tourists from Indiana, immigrant shopkeepers, and a New York weirdo who, in one of the movie's best scenes, shows him a baffling card trick, and then demonstrates another trick that contains a cynical grain of big-city truth. The brother walks through this menagerie with a sometimes bemused, sometimes puzzled look on his face. People seem to have a lot of problems on this planet. He is glad to help out when he can; for example, curing video games by a laying on of hands. His right hand contains the power to heal machines, and it is amazing how quickly people accept that, if it is useful to them.

The Brother from Another Planet was written and directed by John Sayles, who is a one-man industry in the world of the American independent film. His credits include *Return of the Secaucus Seven*, *Lianna*, and *Baby, It's You*, and in this film—by using a central character who cannot talk—he is sometimes able to explore the kinds of scenes that haven't been possible since the death of silent film. There are individual moments here worthy of a Keaton, and there are times when Joe Morton's unblinking passivity in the midst of chaos really does remind us of Buster.

There is also a curious way in which the film functions as more subtle social satire than might seem possible in a low-budget, good-natured comedy. Because the hero, the brother, has literally dropped out of the skies, he doesn't have an opinion on anything. He only gradually begins to realize that on this world he is "black," and that his color makes a difference in some situations. He tries to accept that. When he is hurt or wronged, his reaction is not so much anger as surprise: It seems to him so unnecessary that people behave unkindly toward one another. He is a little surprised they would go to such an effort. His surprise, in its own sweet and uncomplicated way, is one of the most effective elements in the whole movie.

Brubaker ★ ★ ½

R, 131 m., 1980

Robert Redford (Brubaker), Yaphet Kotto (Dickie Coombes), Jane Alexander (Lillian), Murray Hamilton (Deach), David Keith (Larry Lee Bullen), Morgan Freeman (Walter), M. Emmet Walsh (C.P. Woodward), Matt Clark (Purcell), Richard Ward (Abraham). Directed by Stuart Rosenberg and produced by Ron Silverman. Screenplay by W.D. Richter.

Brubaker is a grim and depressing drama about prison outrages—a movie that should, given its absolutely realistic vision, have kept us involved from beginning to end. That it doesn't is the result, I think, of a deliberate but unwise decision to focus on the issues involved in the story, instead of on the characters.

All the people in this movie have roles that represent something; there's the Idealistic Reformer, the Pragmatic Politician, the Corrupt Administrator, the Noble Prisoner, the Tough Guard. The problem is that once they're assigned an ideological niche at the beginning of the movie, they behave with absolute consistency. There's no room for the spontaneity of real human personalities caught in real situations.

That's especially annoying with the character of Brubaker himself, played well but within a frustratingly narrow range by Robert Redford. Brubaker is the reform warden assigned to clean up the violence and corruption of Wakefield Prison Farm, a hellhole of sadism where no guards are needed because the prisoner trusties are armed and get time off their sentences for shooting escapees. The movie's first twenty or thirty minutes, which are sickeningly effective, document conditions in the prison, where the commonplaces include beatings, bribery, rape, and slum living conditions.

Brubaker finds out about these outrages firsthand. He has himself been brought into the prison anonymously, as a prisoner. This is supposed to provide the movie's biggest surprise, when he finally steps forward and identifies himself, but the ads for the movie spoiled the surprise by identifying Redford as the warden. What seems a little unlikely in these opening scenes is that Redford, as a new prisoner, would emerge unscathed: He observes, he listens, and he's mostly left alone by the other prisoners, even though his fellow new recruits are being raped, beaten, and forced into the prison's system of corruption.

After Redford takes charge, the movie disintegrates into predictability. He takes a position in favor of progressive reforms, and the state board of corrections takes a position in favor of corrupt business as usual. Some interesting characters are introduced, especially Yaphet Kotto as a hard-boiled trusty who can't make up his mind about the warden, and Jane Alexander, as a pragmatic aide to the state governor. Murray Hamilton, as a corrupt member of the state prison board, does his usual venal capitalist and does it well, but he has played this role so frequently (in the first two *Jaws* movies, for example), that he must know it by heart.

In the meantime, we're growing a little restless because of the movie's refusal to permit its characters more human dimensions. We want to know these people better, but the screenplay throws up a wall; they act according to the ideological positions assigned to them in the screenplay, and that's that. Half of Redford's speeches could have come out of newspaper editorials, but we never find out much about him. What's his background? Was he ever married? Is this his first prison job? What's his relationship with the Jane Alexander character, who seems to have gotten him this job? (Alexander has one almost subliminal moment when she fans her neck and looks at Redford and seems to be thinking unpolitical thoughts, but the movie hurries on.) *Brubaker* is a well-crafted film that does a harrowingly effective job of portraying the details of its prison, but it populates it with positions rather than people.

The Buddy Holly Story ★ ★ ★ 1/2

PG, 113 m., 1978

Bill Jordan (Riley Randolph), Maria Richwine (Maria Elena Holly), Conrad Janis (Ross Turner), Dick O'Neil (Sol Zuckerman), Gary Busey (Buddy Holly), Don Stroud (Jesse), Charles Martin Smith (Ray Bob). Directed by Steve Rash and produced by Fred Bauer. Screenplay by Robert Gittler.

On February 3, 1959, a small plane crashed outside Mason City, Iowa, killing Buddy Holly, Richie Valens, and J.P. (The Big Bopper) Richardson. Don McLean sang about that day in "American Pie." He called it the day the music died.

Walking out of *The Buddy Holly Story*, you wonder if maybe he wasn't right. It's no use trying to guess how things might have turned out if Holly hadn't been on that flight. He might have continued to develop as the most original rock and roll artist of his generation. He might, on the other hand, have gradually become a Paul Anka or a Barry Manilow, a polished performer of comfortably mainstream pop. The movie makes a pretty good case for the first possibility.

It also involves us as show biz biographies rarely do. This is one rock and roll movie with a chance of being remembered, one with something to say and the style and energy to say it well. That's partly because it had good material to start with; Holly's life provides a microcosm of rock and roll's transformation into the dominant music of the last decades. But it's also because of Gary Busey's remarkable performance as Buddy Holly. If you're a fan of Holly and his music, you'll be quietly amazed at how completely Busey gets into the character. His performance isn't an imitation, a series of "impressions." It's a distillation of how Holly *seemed*, and how he sounded. That's all the more impressive because the movie doesn't use dubbing from the original records: Busey himself sings Holly's arrangements. And the movie's many concert scenes don't use post-dubbing, which almost always result in a flat and unconvincing sound. Busey did the material live.

That's crucial, in a way, because if *The Buddy Holly Story* doesn't convince (or remind) us that Holly's music was good, and important, the movie itself fails. Busey and the filmmakers do convince us, without even seeming to try. Walking out of the theater, I overheard a teen-age couple expressing surprise that Holly had composed "It's So Easy to Fall in Love." They thought it was a Linda Ronstadt original.

More performers than Ronstadt learned from Holly. All the important rockers of the last thirty years, and particularly the Beatles, benefited from Holly's fusion of basic rock and roll, deeper musical sophistication, and lyrics that came with a sincere intensity ("I *was* Buddy Holly," John Lennon once said.) Most albums cut in 1958 or 1959 sound dated today, even the good ones. Holly's old albums still sound fresh.

The movie follows the events of Holly's life, more or less, from his beginnings in Lubbock, Texas, through his early hit records, his quick national fame, his performances on "The Ed Sullivan Show," his marriage, his death. Rock historians have pointed out the ways in which the screenplay alters the facts (Holly's parents were not opposed to his musical career; his romance with his wife, Maria, was whirlwind, not the stubborn courtship in the movie; the decision to take a plane that last night was made, not because the bus broke down, but because Holly and the others wanted to get their laundry done).

Details like that don't matter much. The movie gets the feel right, and there's real energy in the concert scenes, especially the tricky debut of Buddy Holly and the Crickets as the first white act in Harlem's famous Apollo Theater. And the supporting performances are convincing; they're not walk-ons, as they tend to be in show biz movies. Don Stroud and Charles Martin Smith are just right as the down-home Crickets. Maria Richwine brings a sweetness, an understanding to the role of Holly's wife, and Gloria Irricari, as her aunt, steals a wonderful scene. And Dick O'Neil, as the white booker who thought Holly was black when he booked him into the Apollo, does an inspired double-take.

When all of this has been said, there are still the songs to be considered. "That'll Be the Day." "Peggy Sue." "Oh, Boy!" "Words of Love." "True Love Ways." "It's So Easy." "It Doesn't Matter Anymore." Gary Busey sings them with a style that does Holly justice. And that's saying something. They live, and the movie's concert sequences have the immediacy and energy of documentary footage—which is essentially what they are.

Bugsy Malone ★ ★ ★ ½

G, 94 m., 1976

Jodie Foster (Nightclub Singer), Scott Baio (Bugsy Malone), John Cassisi (Boss), Paul Murphy (Hit Man). Directed by Alan Parker and produced by Alan Marshall. Screenplay by Parker.

At first the notion seems alarming: a gangster movie cast entirely with kids. Especially when we learn that *Bugsy Malone* isn't intended as a kid's movie so much as a cheerful comment on the childlike values and behavior in classic Hollywood crime films. What are kids doing in something like this? But then we see the movie and we relax. *Bugsy Malone* is like nothing else. It's an original, a charming one, and it has yet another special performance by Jodie Foster, who at thirteen was already getting the roles that grown-up actresses complained weren't being written for women anymore. She plays a hard-bitten nightclub singer and vamps her way through a torch song by Paul Williams with approximately as much style as Rita Hayworth brought to *Gilda.* She starts on stage, drifts down into the audience, arches her eyebrows at the fat cats (all about junior high school age), and, in general, earns herself an Oscar nomination. And her performance seems just right in the film; *Bugsy Malone* depends almost totally on tone, put kids in these situations and direct them just a little wrongly and the movie would be offensive. But it's not, and it's especially right with Foster.

It tells a gangster story we know almost by heart, about the tough new gang that wants to take over the territory. Da Boss (a kid named John Cassisi who looks like he was born wearing a carnation in the lapel of his pinstripe) recruits hired guns to help protect his turf. Bugsy Malone (Scott Baio in training for John Garfield) is the guy he's gotta have. But maybe even Bugsy can't help, because the other gang has a dreaded new weapon. In Al Capone's day, it was machine guns. In Bugsy's movie, it's marshmallow guns. They open up on you with one of these, and you got more than egg on your face. Old-fashioned weapons like custard pies are useless in a one-on-one situation.

Halfway through *Bugsy Malone,* I started wondering how anyone ever came up with this idea for a movie. Alan Parker, who wrote and directed it, claims his inspiration came while he was watching *The Godfather.* I dunno, I think the movie has more insights into kids than into gangsters.

When kids play, it's real. That's one of the things we lose when we grow up: the ability to turn the backyard into the OK Corral. The kids in *Bugsy Malone* don't behave as if the material is camp or a put-on. For them, it's real—especially the indignity of catching a marshmallow in your ear. And so in an uncanny way the movie works as a gangster movie and we remember that the old Bogart and Cagney classics had a childlike innocence, too. The world was simpler then. Now it's so complicated maybe only a kid can still understand the Bogart role.

Bull Durham ★ ★ ★ ½

R, 108 m., 1988 ✓

Kevin Costner (Crash Davis), Susan Sarandon (Annie Savoy), Tim Robbins ("Nuke" LaLoosh), Trey Wilson (Skip), Robert Wuhl (Larry), William O'Leary (Jimmy). Directed by Ron Shelton and produced by Thom Mount and Mark Burg. Screenplay by Shelton.

"Some days, you win. Some days, you lose. And some days, it rains."—Baseball proverb

Bull Durham is a baseball version of *Wall Street,* in which everybody's takeover bid is for someone else's heart. The movie was promoted as a romantic comedy, but Susan Sarandon has a great scene right at the outset where she corrects that notion. She holds a little meeting between two of the new members of the local minor league ball club and explains that every year she chooses one player to spend the season with, and they are the two current finalists. The rest of the movie involves, in one way or another, a three-way contest to see (a) who really loves whom, (b) who really can trust whom, and (c) whether the answers to (a) and (b) involve the same two persons.

A lot of baseball is played along the way. *Bull Durham* was written and directed by Ron Shelton, who spent some time in the minor leagues, and this is a sports movie that knows what it is talking about. There are quiet little scenes that have the ring of absolute accuracy, as when a player is called into the office and told his contract is not being picked up, and the blow is softened by careful mention of a "possibility of a coaching job in the organization next season . . ." And there probably isn't a coaching job and nobody wants it anyway, but by such lies can sad truths be told.

The movie stars Kevin Costner as Crash Davis, an aging catcher and minor league veteran who knows the ropes, and Tim Robbins as "Nuke" LaLoosh, a hot young pitcher who has one hell of a fastball but no control and no maturity. Costner has been brought to the club to provide some seasoning for the rookie, and so inevitably they get into a fight before they've even been introduced. Costner has observed that Robbins has great control—unless he thinks about what he's doing. One moment of thought, and the ball gets pitched into the stands. So Costner stands outside a bar and taunts Robbins to hit him in the chest with his best fastball—something, of course, that once he starts thinking about it, Robbins is absolutely unable to do.

That kind of baseball philosophy provides a sound background for the movie, which has its foreground in Susan Sarandon's bedroom. I don't know who else they could have hired to play Annie Savoy, the Sarandon character who pledges her heart and her body to one player a season, but I doubt if the character would have worked without Sarandon's wonderful performance. Annie could have been portrayed as a lot of things—as a tramp, maybe, or a pathetic case study—but Sarandon portrays her as a woman who, quite simply, loves baseball and baseball players and wants to do her thing for the home team. Why does she limit her love affairs to one season? Anyone who has ever been a minor league baseball fan knows the answer to that one: Anybody who's any good goes up to the big leagues after a year, and Annie, of course, is only interested in the best players.

The romantic triangle unfolds during a season in which it never seems to matter very much how well the Durham Bulls are doing. They lose, they win, they spend a lot of time on buses and in hotel rooms, and meanwhile, Sarandon and Costner begin to realize that she is more than a groupie and he is more than a catcher. They find each other dropping the names of writers and making references to things they should not necessarily know, and finally one day Costner explodes in frustration: "Who *are* you, anyway?" Perhaps he suspects that if he finds the answer to that question, she will steal his heart away.

The kid pitcher is a lot less subtle about all of this. He enjoys being Annie's lover, for a time, but when he gets to a winning streak, he starts believing all those old stories about conserving your precious bodily fluids, and he becomes chaste as a monk. Costner, of course, is feeding him the stories. Meanwhile, we're getting to know some of the other members of the team and management, in a low-key, Altman-style directorial approach that fills up the background with a lot of atmosphere and action.

Bull Durham is a treasure of a movie because it knows so much about baseball and so little about love. The movie is a completely unrealistic romantic fantasy, and in the real world the delicate little balancing act of these three people would crash into pieces—but this is a movie, and so we want to believe in love, and we want to believe that once in a while lovers can get a break from fate. That's why the movie's ending is so perfect. Not because it seems just right, but because it seems wildly impossible and we want to believe it anyway.

Burden of Dreams ★ ★ ★ ★

NO MPAA RATING, 94 m., 1982

Featuring Werner Herzog, Klaus Kinski, Claudia Cardinale, Jason Robards, Jr., and Mick Jagger. Directed and produced by Les Blank, with Maureen Gosling.

Les Blank's *Burden of Dreams* is one of the most remarkable documentaries ever made about the making of a movie. There are at least two reasons for that. One is that the movie being made, Werner Herzog's *Fitzcarraldo,* involved some of the most torturous and dangerous on-location shooting experiences in film history. The other is that the documentary is by Les Blank, himself a brilliant filmmaker, who is unafraid to ask difficult questions and portray Herzog, warts and all.

The story of Herzog's *Fitzcarraldo* is already the stuff of movie legend. The movie was shot on location deep within the rain forests of South America, one thousand miles from civilization. When the first version of the film was half-finished, its star, Jason Robards, was rushed back to New York with amoebic dysentery and forbidden by his doctors to return to the location. Herzog replaced Robards with Klaus Kinski (star of his *Aguirre, the Wrath of God*), but meanwhile, co-star Mick Jagger left the production because of a commitment to a concert tour. Then the Kinski version of *Fitzcarraldo* was caught in the middle of a border war between tribes of Indians. The whole production was moved twelve hundred miles, to a new location where the mishaps included plane crashes, disease, and attacks by unfriendly Indians. And all of those hardships were on top of the incredible task Herzog set himself to film: He wanted to show his obsessed hero using teams of Indians to pull an entire steamship up a hillside using only block and tackle!

Blank and his associate, Maureen Gosling, visited both locations of Herzog's film. Their documentary includes the only available record of some of the earlier scenes with Robards and Jagger. It also includes scenes in which Herzog seems to be going slowly mad, blaming the evil of the jungle and the depth of his own compulsions. In *Fitzcarraldo,* you can see the incredible strain as men try to pull a steamship up a sharp incline, using only muscle power and a few elementary principles of mechanics. In *Burden of Dreams,* Blank's camera moves back one more step, to show the actual mechanisms by which Herzog hoped to move his ship. A giant bulldozer is used to augment the block-and-pulley, but it proves barely equal to the task, and at one point the Brazilian engineer in charge of the project walks off, warning that lives will be lost.

What drives Herzog to make films that test his sanity and risk his life and those of his associates? Stanley Kauffmann, in the *New Republic,* argued that, for Herzog, the purpose of film is to risk death, and each of his films is in some way a challenge hurled at the odds. Herzog has made films on the slopes of active volcanoes, has filmed in the jungle and in the middle of the Sahara, and has made films about characters who live at the edges of human achievement. *Burden of Dreams* gives us an extraordinary portrait of Herzog trapped in the middle of one of his wildest dreams.

Burglar ★
R, 98 m., 1987

Whoopi Goldberg (Bernice Rhodenbarr), Bob Goldthwait (Carl Hefler), G.W. Bailey (Ray Kirschman), Lesley Ann Warren (Dr. Sheldrake), James Handy (Carson Verrill). Directed by Hugh Wilson and produced by Kevin McCormick and Michael Hirsh. Screenplay by Joseph Loeb III, Matthew Weisman, and Wilson.

Does Hollywood think Whoopi Goldberg recently arrived here from another planet? Do they think she has one of those invisible protective shields around her, like in the old toothpaste commercials? Do they respond at all to her warmth, her energy, her charisma? Sure, she looks a little funny, but why isn't she allowed to have normal relationships in the movies? Why is she always packaged as the weirdo from Planet X?

The occasion for these questions is *Burglar*, a witless, hapless exercise in the wrong way to package Goldberg. This is a woman who is original. Who is talented. Who has a special relationship with the motion picture screen. It is criminal to put her into brain-damaged, assembly-line thrillers.

Can't Goldberg or anyone in her entourage tell the difference between a movie and a deal? Can't they read a script and see that it is simply recycled elements from hundreds of other movies? Films like *Burglar* and *Jumpin' Jack Flash*, her previous effort, will continue to be made as long as there are writers with nothing to say, agents with nothing to deal, and directors who don't care what their films are about. But let them feed off each other. Don't throw Goldberg to those sharks.

Seen simply as a project, *Burglar* is relentlessly conventional. A colorful character (in this case, a burglar played by Goldberg) is implicated in a murder. The police are convinced she's guilty. She has to prove she is innocent. That involves her with several bizarre characters. The movie ends in a chase scene. Watching these parboiled elements on the screen, I felt a real sense of anger that Goldberg was being forced to march through such clichés.

Let's face it. Hollywood knows Goldberg is talented, but nobody knows how to handle her in the movies. She is a woman. She is black. She looks goofy. So, they take the path of no resistance. They ignore all of those realities about her. It is one thing to argue that casting directors should be color-blind, but another thing altogether to cast Whoopi Goldberg in a role so impersonal that it could be filled by Robert Redford, Seka, or Rin-Tin-Tin—all without a rewrite.

Nothing in *Burglar* depends on or grows out of Goldberg's sex. With a few costume changes, her role could be played by a man. Nothing depends on her race. As nearly as I could tell, this movie thinks she is the only black person in the world and nobody knows it. Nothing depends on her personality, because she has no meaningful or comprehensible relationships with anybody except for a weirdo played by Bob Goldthwait. His role is almost an insult: What are we to make of the fact that Goldberg's only close friend is insane?

Is there anything worth seeing in this movie? Maybe the motorcycle chase up and down the hills of San Francisco, but that could have been in any movie. Does Goldberg show her talent? She does in the quiet way she makes observations, in the sweet way she tries to angle around frontal assaults, in the way she tries to talk herself out of tight corners. In an intelligent movie, those qualities would have contributed to the effect, instead of existing apart from it.

Here is what is happening: Goldberg's career is being destroyed. She came out of nowhere, she had some success on the stage, she was brilliant in *The Color Purple* and now, with one cynical deal after another, she is being shoehorned into formula movies that don't even have a chance of being good. Soon she will be "unbankable," and that will be that. The system will have chewed up and spit out another talent who suffers from the terrible quality of being unique.

Buster and Billie ★ ★ ★
R, 100 m., 1974

Jan-Michael Vincent (Buster), Joan Goodfellow (Billie), Pamela Sue Martin (First Girlfriend). Directed by Dan Petrie and produced by Ron Silverman. Screenplay by Ron Turbeville.

The problem with a lot of nostalgia is that it captures the surface sound and style of a decade with an appreciation that works only with hindsight. People didn't spend all their time listening to Elvis, lowering their Chevys, and scuffing their white bucks in the fifties. Adolescence then, as now, was a time of uncertainty and confusion, and the surface stuff often only concealed the kids inside. *The Lords of Flatbush* did a good job of seeing past its black leather jackets and into the hearts of the essentially immature and unsure people who wore them, as does *Buster and Billie* with a memory of what it might have been like to go to high school in the South, circa 1948.

The movie's no masterpiece, but it's an affecting story well told, it observes its teenage characters with a fine insight, and it almost earns its tragic ending. Happy endings used to be Hollywood clichés; now, if we ever got one, it would almost feel original.

The story gives us some ordinary high school kids growing up in a pleasant semirural section of Georgia. They drive around in cars and pickup trucks, they go to dances, they study, and when the guys hang around with the guys and the girls hang around with the girls, the subject of conversation is, always and eternally, the mysteries of the opposite sex. Nobody knows much about sex, period, much less the opposite one, but there's a lot of big talk and an insatiable curiosity.

Curiosity is satisfied, however, for some of the guys through the friendliness of Billie, a shy, pretty girl who lives with subliterate parents and who is so lacking in self-confidence that she seeks to find acceptance by, as the fine old phrase has it, putting out. Several guys in the school have been with Billie, or say they have, or mean to, or in any event may.

But not Buster, who is your typical high school jock and a little something more. He knows his own mind, is independent, is admired, and has a much larger measure of compassion than his friends. He's engaged to marry an insipid girl, the kind who wins the Homecoming Queen title and believes the momentum will carry her straight through life. But Buster becomes intrigued with Billie. He senses something about her that has value; he seems to instinctively understand why she behaves as she does, and (more importantly) why she doesn't have to.

Most of the movie is about the love that slowly grows up between them as Buster wins Billie's trust and helps her to develop self-confidence. The fact that Buster would be seen publicly with Billie (would, indeed, take her to Sunday church) causes indignation within the cliquish high school crowd he runs with, and especially among Billie's numerous former boyfriends.

What's good about the movie—what you'll remember—are the tender and rather lovely scenes between Buster and Billie, and the strength with which Buster faces down the disapproval of his friends. What doesn't work, for me, anyway, is the violent and tragic ending. It's not that the ending isn't plausible; indeed, as it's presented, it seems inevitable enough. It's just that somehow the human values in the film should have been developed more fully, so that at the end we could have some sort of resolution based on changes in the characters, rather than on their violent acts.

Much of the movie's affecting quality comes from fine performances by Jan-Michael Vincent and Joan Goodfellow, as the young lovers. There's a scene showing their first date, with the girl too shy, almost, to talk, and it's so quiet and warm we can really understand how these two kids feel. There's a scene where Buster defends Billie to his parents, and another one in a pool room where he faces his friends. This kind of movie, honestly examining the bonds of both friendship and cruelty that hold together adolescent peer groups, is a lot more accurate about the old days than any number of golden-oldie sound tracks and gee-whiz sock hops.

Bye Bye Brazil ★ ★ ★ ★

NO MPAA RATING, 100 m., 1979

Jose Wilker (Lord Gypsy), Betty Faria (Salome), Fabio Junior (Cico), Zaira Zambelli (Desdo), Principe Nabor (Swallow). Directed by Carlos Diegues and produced by L.C. Barreto. Screenplay by Diegues.

It's rare to come across truly great movie images, and we share them like treasured souvenirs—images like Jack Nicholson in the football helmet in *Easy Rider,* the bone turning into a spaceship in *2001,* the peacock spreading its feathers in the snow in *Amarcord,* and the helicopter assault in *Apocalypse Now.*

To the short list of great images, a film named *Bye Bye Brazil* adds one more. A small, raggedy troupe of traveling entertainers is putting on a show in a provincial Brazilian town. The townspeople sit packed together in a sweaty, smoky room, while the magician creates for brief moments the illusion that both he and his audience are more sophisticated than they are. It is time for the climax of his act, and he springs a completely unexpected image on his audience, and on us: Bing Crosby sings "White Christmas" while it snows on his amazed patrons.

That moment provides more than an image. It provides a neatly summarized little statement about *Bye Bye Brazil*, a film which exists exactly on the fault line between Brazil's modern civilization and the simple backwaters of its provinces. The film sees Brazil as a nation where half-assimilated Western culture (in the form of Bing Crosby, public address systems, and politicians) coexists with poverty, superstition, simple good nature, and the permanent fact of the rain forest.

The movie is about the small troupe of entertainers, who travel the backroads in a truck that contains living quarters, a generator, and the props for their nightly shows. The troupe is led by Lord Gypsy, a young man who is half-hippie, half-nineteenth-century medicine show huckster. At his side is Salome, a damply sultry beauty who is his assistant but also has a tendency to do business on her own. Swallow, a strongman, doubles as crew and supporting act.

These three pick up two hitchhikers, a young accordion player and his pregnant wife. And then *Bye Bye Brazil* tells the story of the changing relationships among the five people, and their checkered success with roadshow vaudeville.

Having said that, I've conveyed almost no notion of this movie's special charms. It shows us a society that most American audiences never have seen in the movies, the world of very old, very small Brazilian towns perched precariously along the roads that link them to far-away, half-understood cities.

Television has not come to most of these towns. Electricity is uncertain. The traveling entertainers provide more than music and magic; they provide a link with style that is more fascinating to the audiences than the magician's tricks. People do not pay to see the show, so much as to wonder at these strange performers who speak the same language but could be from another planet.

C

Cabaret ★ ★ ★ ½
PG, 119 m., 1972

Liza Minnelli (Sally Bowles), Michael York (Brian Roberts), Joel Grey (Master of Ceremonies), Helmut Griem (Fritz Wendel), Fritz Wepper (Fraulein Schneider). Directed by Bob Fosse and produced by Cy Feuer. Screenplay by Jay Allen.

Cabaret explores some of the same kinky territory celebrated in Visconti's *The Damned.* Both movies share the general idea that the rise of the Nazi party in Germany was accompanied by a rise in bisexuality, homosexuality, sadomasochism, and assorted other activities. Taken as a generalization about a national movement, this is certainly extreme oversimplification. But taken as one approach to the darker recesses of Nazism, it may come pretty close to the mark. The Nazi gimmicks like boots and leather and muscles and racial superiority and outdoor rallies and Aryan comradeship offered an array of machismo-for-rent that had (and has) a special appeal to some kinds of impotent people.

Cabaret is about people like that, and it takes place largely in a specific Berlin cabaret, circa 1930, in which decadence and sexual ambiguity were just part of the ambience (like the women mud-wrestlers who appeared between acts). This is no ordinary musical. Part of its success comes because it doesn't fall for the old cliché that musicals have to make you happy. Instead of cheapening the movie version by lightening its load of despair, director Bob Fosse has gone right to the bleak heart of the material and stayed there well enough to win an Academy Award for Best Director.

The story concerns one of the more famous literary inventions of the century, Sally Bowles, who first came to life in the late Christopher Isherwood's *Berlin Stories,* and then appeared in the play and movie *I Am a Camera* before returning to the stage in this musical, and then making it into the movies a second time—a modern record, I'd say.

Sally is brought magnificently to the screen in an Oscar-winning performance by Liza Minnelli, who plays her as a girl who's bought what the cabaret is selling. To her, the point is to laugh and sing and live forever in the moment; to refuse to take things seriously—even Nazism—and to relate with people only up to a certain point. She is capable of warmth and emotion, but a lot of it is theatrical, and when the chips are down she's as decadent as the "daringly decadent" dark fingernail polish she flaunts.

Liza Minnelli plays Sally Bowles so well and fully that it doesn't matter how well she sings and dances, if you see what I mean. In several musical numbers (including the stunning finale *Cabaret* number), Liza demonstrates unmistakably that she's one of the great musical performers of our time. But the heartlessness and nihilism of the character is still there, all the time, even while we're being supremely entertained.

Sally gets involved in a triangular relationship with a young English language teacher (Michael York) and a young baron (Helmut Griem), and if this particular triangle didn't exist in the stage version, that doesn't matter. It helps define the movie's whole feel of moral anarchy, and it is underlined by the sheer desperation in the cabaret itself.

Here the festivities are overseen by a master of ceremonies (Joel Grey, whose performance received an Oscar for best supporting actor) whose determination to keep the merriment going, at whatever psychic cost, has a poignant compulsiveness. When the song *Cabaret* comes at the end, you realize for the first time that it isn't a song of happiness, but of desperation. The context makes the difference. In the same way, the context of Germany on the eve of the Nazi ascent to power makes the entire musical into an unforgettable cry of despair.

Cactus ★ ★ ★

NO MPAA RATING, 95 m., 1987

Isabelle Huppert (Colo), Robert Menzies (Robert), Norman Kaye (Tom), Monica Maughan (Bea), Banduk Marika (Banduk), Sheila Florance (Martha). Directed by Paul Cox and produced by Jane Ballantyne and Cox. Screenplay by Cox, Norman Kaye, and Bob Ellis.

One of the first shots in *Cactus* is a long, unbroken take in which the camera pans from a veranda across a lush landscape, all green and semi-tropical, while on the sound track we hear the loud cry of an exotic bird. The sound seems too loud, somehow, but what is being set up here is the condition of blindness, in which sounds take on an extraordinary importance.

The heroine of the film is a young French woman (Isabelle Huppert), who has come out to Australia on holiday. There is the suggestion that she has left an unhappy marriage behind in France. She has an accident, loses the sight of one eye, and is threatened with the loss of the other. The doctors offer her a choice. If she has the bad eye removed, the remaining eye may retain its function. Otherwise, "sympathetic blindness" may occur, and she will be totally blind.

No matter how this sounds, *Cactus* is not a docudrama, not a movie about medical problems. It is a movie about how we see, and what we choose to see. While she is trying to decide what to do, Huppert meets a young man who is blind. They talk, they understand each other, they fall in love. She seriously considers the option of choosing blindness, so that she will be able to share the world of her lover.

These episodes take place within the arms of a large, sheltering family. The woman's friends are middle-aged, literate, political. There are moments that have little to do with the movie's central problem; moments when friends gather to drink, talk, and listen to music. During those scenes, *Cactus* has an interesting, subtle technique. The visuals are always alive and inviting—rooms filled with unusual objects, landscapes jammed with life. And the sound track is filled, too, with words and music. Both senses, sight and sound, are calling out to be recognized.

Cactus was directed by Paul Cox, who is not one of the best-known of the new generation of Australian filmmakers, but in many ways is the most inventive, the most individual. His films are always about people who are cut off from normal relationships, and who try to improvise substitutes.

Lonely Hearts (1981) was about two people who met through a singles group, and found out why each was single. *Man of Flowers* (1983) was about a lonely, reclusive millionaire who paid a young woman to pose for him, so that he could fill his empty room with company. *My First Wife* (1984) was about a woman who decided that she could scarcely be lonelier outside marriage than inside it.

Cactus is not as satisfying as those three films, perhaps because its themes are not as clear. I was so distracted by the reality of the woman's choice—sight or blindness—that I found it hard to pull back to the larger question of how she should choose to communicate with the man she loved. In a way, the woman's choice is one we all have to make. Because there is such a gulf between all people, to bridge it we have to take on some of the blindness of others, and they have to share ours; two people who see things exclusively their own way may never be able to share the world. That is the issue in *Cactus*; the blindness is simply the way Cox chooses to dramatize it.

Although the movie is less than completely satisfying, it is worth seeing, as everything by Cox is worth seeing, because there is always the sense in his films of an active intelligence at work. He doesn't make routine genre pictures; he begins with complicated people and watches them as they live. Sometimes he seems as mystified by the results as we are.

Caddyshack ★ ★ ½
R, 99 m., 1980

Chevy Chase (Ty Webb), Rodney Dangerfield (Al Czervik), Ted Knight (Judge Smails), Michael O'Keefe (Danny), Bill Murray (Carl), Sarah Holcomb (Maggie). Directed by Harold Ramis and produced by Douglas Kenney. Screenplay by Brian Doyle-Murray, Ramis, and Kenney.

Caddyshack never finds a consistent comic note of its own, but it plays host to all sorts of approaches from its stars, who sometimes hardly seem to be occupying the same movie. There's Bill Murray's self-absorbed craziness, Chevy Chase's laid-back bemusement, and Ted Knight's apoplectic overplaying. And then there is Rodney Dangerfield, who wades into the movie and cleans up.

To the degree that this is anybody's movie, it's Dangerfield's—and he mostly seems to be using his own material. He plays a loud, vulgar, twitching condo developer who is thinking of buying a country club and using the land for housing. The country club is one of those exclusive WASP enclaves, a haven for such types as the judge who founded it (Knight), the ne'er-do-well club champion (Chase), and the manic assistant grounds keeper (Murray).

The movie never really develops a plot, but maybe it doesn't want to. Director Harold Ramis brings on his cast of characters and lets them loose at one another. There's a vague subplot about a college scholarship for the caddies, and another one about the judge's nubile niece, and continuing warfare waged by Murray against the gophers who are devastating the club. But Ramis is cheerfully prepared to interrupt everything for moments of comic inspiration, and there are three especially good ones: The caddies in the swimming pool doing a Busby Berkeley number, another pool scene that's a scatalogical satire of *Jaws*, and a sequence in which Dangerfield's gigantic speedboat devastates a yacht club.

Dangerfield is funniest, though, when the movie just lets him talk. He's a Henny Youngman clone, filled with one-liners and insults, and he's great at the country club's dinner dance, abusing everyone and making rude noises. Surveying the crowd from the bar, he uses lines that he has, in fact, stolen directly from his nightclub routine ("This steak still has the mark of the jockey's whip on it"). With his bizarre wardrobe and trick golf bag, he's a throwback to the Groucho Marx and W.C. Fields school of insult comedy; he has a vitality that the movie's younger comedians can't match, and they suffer in comparison.

Chevy Chase, for example, has some wonderful moments in this movie, as a studiously absent-minded hedonist who doesn't even bother to keep score when he plays golf. He's good, but somehow he's in the wrong movie: His whimsy doesn't fit with Dangerfield's blatant scenery-chewing or with the Bill Murray character. Murray, as a slob who goes after gophers with explosives and entertains sexual fantasies about the women golfers, could be a refugee from *Animal House*.

Maybe one of the movie's problems is that the central characters are never really involved in the same action. Murray's off on his own, fighting gophers. Dangerfield arrives, devastates, exits. Knight is busy impressing the caddies, making vague promises about scholarships, and launching boats. If they were somehow all drawn together into the same story, maybe we'd be carried along more confidently. But *Caddyshack* feels more like a movie that was written rather loosely, so that when shooting began there was freedom—too much freedom—for it to wander off in all directions in search of comic inspiration.

California Split ★ ★ ★ ★
R, 109 m., 1974

George Segal (Bill Denny), Elliott Gould (Charlie Waters), Ann Prentiss (Barbara Miller), Gwen Welles (Susan Peters), Edward Walsh (Lew), Joseph Walsh (Sparkle), Bert Remsen ("Helen Brown"). Directed by Robert Altman and produced by Altman and Joseph Walsh, based on a screenplay by Walsh.

They meet in a California poker parlor. One wins, despite a heated discussion with a loser over whether or not a dealt card hit the floor. They drink. They become friends after they are jointly mugged in the parking lot by the sore loser.

They did not know each other before, and they don't know much about each other now, but they know all they need to know:

They're both compulsive gamblers, and the dimensions of the world of gambling equal the dimensions of the world they care anything about. It is a small world and a flat one, like one of those maps of the world before Columbus, and they are constantly threatened with falling over the edge.

They're the heroes (or at least the subjects) of *California Split,* the magnificently funny, cynical film by Robert Altman. Their names are Bill and Charlie, and they're played by George Segal and Elliott Gould with a combination of unaffected naturalism and sheer raw nervous exhaustion. We don't need to know anything about gambling to understand the odyssey they undertake to the tracks, to the private poker parties, to the bars, to Vegas, to the edge of defeat, and to the scene of victory. Their compulsion is so strong that it carries us along. The movie will be compared with *M*A*S*H,* the first big hit by Altman (who is possibly our best and certainly our most diverting American director). It deserves that comparison, because it resembles *M*A*S*H* in several big ways: It's funny, it's hard-boiled, it gives us a bond between two frazzled heroes trying to win the rules in a game where the rules require defeat. But it's a better movie than *M*A*S*H* because here Altman gets it all together. Ever since *M*A*S*H,* he's been trying to make a kind of movie that would function like a comedy but allow its laughs to dig us deeper and deeper into the despair underneath.

Bill and Charlie are driven. We laugh at their hangovers, their bruises (treated with hot shaving cream), the kooky part-time prostitutes who serve them breakfasts of Froot Loops and beer. We move easily through the underworld of their friends, casually introduced through Altman's gift of overlapping dialogue and understated visual introductions, so that we're not so much shown a new character as encouraged to assume we knew him all along. And because Joseph Walsh's screenplay is funny and Segal and Gould are naturally engaging, we have a good time.

But then there are moments that take on bleaker meanings. At one point, for example, at the ragged edge of sleep, boozed out, defeated, Bill and Charlie cling desperately to a bar and very seriously bet with each other on the names of the Seven Dwarfs (There was Droopy . . . Sleepy . . . Dumbo?). And at another time, cornered with their winnings in still another parking lot by still another mugger, this one armed, they hand over half their winnings and bet him that's all they have.

He takes it and runs; they win; they could have been killed but their gambler's instinct forced them to make the try. At the end of *California Split* we realize that Altman has made a lot more than a comedy about gambling; he's taken us into an American nightmare, and all the people we met along the way felt genuine and looked real. This movie has a taste in its mouth like stale air-conditioning, and no matter what time it seems to be, it's always five in the morning in a second-rate casino.

As always, Altman fills his movie with quirky supporting roles—people who have somehow become caricatures of themselves. At the private poker game, Segal stands at the bar, surveys the table, and quietly describes every player. He's right about them, although he (and we) have never seen them before. We know he's right because these people wear their styles and destinies on their faces.

So do the hookers (played with a kind of tart-next-door wholesomeness by Ann Prentiss and Gwenn Welles). So does "Helen Brown," one of their customers who's a middle-aged man who likes drag as much as he's terrified of the cops (inspiring a scene of true tragicomedy). Altman's movies always seem full, somehow; we don't have the feeling of an empty screen into which carefully drawn characters are introduced, but of a camera plunging into a boiling sea of frenzied human activity.

What Altman comes up with is sometimes almost a documentary feel; at the end of *California Split* we know something about organized gambling in this country we didn't know before. His movies always seem perfectly at home wherever they are, but this time there's an almost palpable sense of place. And Altman has never been more firmly in control of his style. He has one of the few really individual visual styles among contemporary American directors; we can always see it's an Altman film. He bases his visual strategies on an incredibly attentive sound track, using background noises with particular care so that our ears tell us we're moving through these people—instead of that they're lined up talking to us. *California Split* is a great movie and it's a great experience, too; we've been there with Bill and Charlie.

Caligula no stars
NO MPAA RATING, 143 m., 1980

Malcolm McDowell (Caligula), Teresa Ann Savoy (Drusilla), John Gielgud (Nerva), Peter O'Toole (Tiberius). Produced by Bob Guccione and Franco Rossellini.

Caligula is sickening, utterly worthless, shameful trash. If it is not the worst film I have ever seen, that makes it all the more shameful: People with talent allowed themselves to participate in this travesty. Disgusted and unspeakably depressed, I walked out of the film after two hours. This film is not only garbage on an artistic level, but it is also garbage on the crude and base level where it no doubt hopes to find its audience. *Caligula* is not good art, it is not good cinema, and it is not good porn.

I've never had anything against eroticism in movies. There are X-rated films I've enjoyed, from the sensuous fantasies of *Emmanuelle* to the pop-comic absurdities of Russ Meyer. All I can say is that the makers of *Caligula* have long since lost touch with any possible common erotic denominator, and that they suggest by the contents of this film that they are jaded, perverse, and cruel human beings. There are no scenes of joy, natural pleasure, or good sensual cheer. There is, instead, a nauseating excursion into base and sad fantasies.

This is a violent film. There are scenes depicting a man whose urinary tract is closed, and who has gallons of wine poured down his throat. His bursting stomach is punctured with a sword. There is a scene in which a man is emasculated, and his genitals thrown to dogs, who eagerly eat them on the screen. There are scenes of decapitation, evisceration, rape, bestiality, sadomasochism, necrophilia.

These scenes—indeed, the movie itself—reflect a curiously distanced sensibility. Nobody in this film really seems to be there. Not the famous actors like Malcolm McDowell and (very briefly) Peter O'Toole and John Gielgud, whose scenes have been augmented by additional porn shot later with other people inserted to spice things up. Not the director (who removed his credit from the film). Not the writer (what can it mean that this movie is "*Adapted* from an Original Screenplay by Gore Vidal"?). Not even the sound track. The actors never quite seem to be speaking their own words, which are so badly dubbed that the dialogue never seems to be emerging from the drama itself.

The film even fails to involve itself in the action. *Caligula* has been photographed and directed with such clumsiness and inelegance that pieces of action do not seem to flow together, the plot is incomprehensible, the events are frequently framed as if the camera was not sure where it was, and everything is shot in muddy, ugly, underlit dungeon tones. The music is also execrable.

So what are we left with? A movie, I am afraid, that may be invulnerable to a review like this one. There are no doubt people who believe that if this movie is as bad as I say it is, it must be worth seeing. People who simply cannot believe any film could be this vile. But people learn fast. "This movie," said the lady in front of me at the drinking fountain, "is the worst piece of shit I have ever seen."

The Cannonball Run ½★
PG, 95 m., 1981

Burt Reynolds (J.J. McClure), Roger Moore (Seymour), Farrah Fawcett (Pamela), Dom DeLuise (Victor), Dean Martin (Jamie Blake), Sammy Davis, Jr. (Fenderbaum). Directed by Hal Needham and produced by Albert S. Ruddy. Screenplay by Brock Yates.

The Cannonball Run is an abdication of artistic responsibility at the lowest possible level of ambition. In other words, they didn't even care enough to make a good lousy movie. *Cannonball* was probably always intended as junk, as an easy exploitation picture. But it's possible to bring some sense of style and humor even to grade-zilch material. This movie doesn't even seem to be trying.

Burt Reynolds sleepwalks through a role he's played several times before, but never so indifferently. He's a hotshot driver in a big, illegal cross-country road race; first one to California wins. That means Reynolds gets to drink a lot of beer, talk like a good ol' boy, and get in the middle of a lot of crashes and other stunts. The movie was directed by Hal Needham, a onetime stuntman who graduated to directing with *Smokey and the Bandit* (1977), the first and still the best of the Burt Reynolds car-chase movies. After that, each Needham movie has been worse than the one preceding it. His downward spiral has included *Hooper, The Villain,* and *Smokey and the Bandit II.* Movie buffs will note that three of Needham's four movies have starred Burt Reynolds, one of the most important properties in Hollywood. Reynolds is so popular he can make money in almost anything—a maxim that *Cannonball Run* puts to the extreme test. Reynolds and Needham are friends, and indeed the whole cast of *Cannonball* seems to consider the movie a reunion. The film ends with outtakes—spoiled shots during which somebody breaks up or says the wrong line or otherwise goofs. It's supposed to show us how much fun everybody had. Alas, the outtakes don't look much more goofy than the takes they intended to put in the movie; *Cannonball* assembles a giant cast around an absolutely minimal amount of screenplay, and allows them to kill time expensively. There's not much plot and no suspense. The filmmakers' excuse, no doubt, is that they were really making a comedy, not a road-race picture. That would work if there were any laughs in the movie.

But just look at the cast. It's like a cattle call. It's like an Actor's Guild picket line. It's like Hollywood Squares on Wheels. Some of the actors are talented, some are not, but they look equally awful in this movie. At one time or another during this unspeakable experience, you can share it with not only Burt Reynolds but also Roger Moore, Farrah Fawcett, Dom DeLuise, Dean Martin (looking as if a big-a pizza pie hit him straight in the eye), Sammy Davis, Jr. (looking like a severe case of vitamin deficiency), Jack Elam, Adrienne Barbeau (whose role consists of unzipping her jump suit), Terry Bradshaw, Jackie Chan, Bert Convy, Jamie Farr, Peter Fonda (as an aging Hells Angel), Michael Hui, Bianca Jagger, Molly Picon, Jimmy "the Greek" Snyder, and Mel Tillis. This isn't a cast, it's the answer to a double acrostic.

Car Wash ★ ★ ★ 1/2
PG, 97 m., 1976

Franklin Ajaye (T.C.), Sully Boyer (Mrs. B.), Richard Brestoff (Irwin), George Carlin (Taxi Driver), Prof. Irwin Corey (Mad Bomber), Ivan Dixon (Lonnie), Richard Pryor (Daddy Rich). Directed by Michael Schultz and produced by Art Linson and Gary Stromberg. Screenplay by Joel Schumacher.

The boss is named Mr. B. and he walks around with a dead cigar stuck in his face, pleading "Wash the cars! Wash the cars!" But that's the last thing they get around to in *Car Wash*, a sunny, lively comedy. The movie covers a day in the life of the DeLuxe Car Wash, down from the Strip in Los Angeles, and by actual count only three totally sane people stop by all day. We meet the rest in a dizzying, nonstop kaleidoscope of cars, soul music, characters, crises, crazy kids on skateboards, hookers, television preachers, and lots of suds and hot wax—not to mention the Mad Pop Bottle Bomber, whose bottle turns out to be a cruel disappointment. The movie's put together with a manic energy, we never even quite get introduced to half the people in the cast, but by the movie's end we know them, and what they're up to, and we like them.

We meet the employees of the car wash in the locker room, as they're putting on their work clothes. Floyd and Lloyd enter doing their James Brown imitation. T.C. is convinced he'll be the lucky caller to win the free concert tickets in a radio station giveaway. Lindy, probably the first drag queen employed full-time by a car wash, corrects his makeup. Lonnie, the straw boss, provides an element of sanity, but he's outnumbered.

Sooner or later during the day, everyone seems to come through the car wash. While Floyd and Lloyd, as the steam men, practice their stage act on astonished customers, we watch the parade go by. George Carlin plays a bewildered taxi driver. Professor Irwin Corey is briefly mistaken for the Mad Pop Bottle Bomber. A limousine a yard long wheels up and discharges Richard Pryor, as Daddy Rich, the famous television evangelist. He has his backup singers with him: the Pointer Sisters, who do a number right in front of the gas pumps.

The movie looks like joyful chaos on the surface, but there are several stories running through it. One involves Bill Duke as a young Black Muslim with fierce resentments. Another—delicately handled—

involves a young black hooker who changes clothes in the rest room and then hangs around the corner all day lonely and lost. Another is the relationship between Mr. B. and Lonnie—Mr. B. tense and worried, Lonnie filled with ideas he can't get an audience for.

The car wash seems almost a natural gathering place. The kid on the skateboard whizzes past on a regular schedule. Wives and girlfriends of the workers stop by for brief sessions of fighting and making up. A guy named Kenny, who looks like he stepped out of the fashion ads, stops in and gets a date with the office girl. A man in a head-to-toe cast goes through the wash, considerably shaken. So does a little boy who first throws up on his mother's Mercedes and, when it's been washed, throws up on her.

All of this is held together by the music, which is nearly wall-to-wall, and by the picture's tremendous sense of life. It's one thing to have an idea like this—a zany, sometimes serious day in the life of a car wash—and another thing to make it work. But the screenplay and the direction juggle the characters so adroitly, this is almost a wash-and-wax *M*A*S*H.*

Carmen ★ ★ ★ ★

R, 95 m., 1983

Antonio Gades (Antonio), Laura Del Sol (Carmen), Paco De Lucia (Paco), Cristina Hoyos (Cristina). Sung by Regina Resnik and Maria Del Monaco. Directed by Carlos Saura and produced by Emiliano Piedra. Screenplay by Saura and Antonio Gades.

Carlos Saura's *Carmen* is an erotic roller coaster of a movie, incorporating dance into its story more effectively than any other movie I can remember. It isn't a "ballet movie," and it's not like one of those musicals where everybody is occasionally taken with the need to dance. It's a story of passion and jealousy—the story of Bizet's *Carmen*—with dance as part and parcel of its flesh and blood. The movie is based on the opera by Bizet, keeping the music and the broad outlines of the story of a poor girl whose fierce romantic independence maddens the men who become obsessed with her. Everything else is new. Saura, the greatest living Spanish film director, has collaborated with Antonio Gades, the Spanish dancer and choreographer, to make this *Carmen* into a muscular, contemporary story. Their strategy is to make a story within a story. The film begins with Gades as a dance teacher who is looking for the "perfect" Carmen. He finds one in a flamenco dancing school, and as he attempts to mold her into Carmen, their relationship begins to resemble the story of the opera.

Given this approach, *Carmen* could easily have turned into an academic exercise, one of those clever movies in which all the pieces fit but none of them matter. That doesn't happen, and one of the reasons it doesn't is the casting of a young woman named Laura Del Sol as Carmen. She is a twenty-one-year-old dancer who combines convincing technique with a healthy, athletic sexiness, and her dance duets (and duels) with Gades are bold, erotic, and uninhibited. What's fascinating is the way Saura is able to blend the dance, the opera, and the "modern" story. For example, Del Sol and Gades use dance to create a scene that begins as an argument, develops into fierce declarations of independence, and then climaxes in passionate romance. In another scene, a routine day in a dance studio becomes charged by the unexpected appearance of Carmen's other lover, an ex-convict.

I have an ambivalence about dance on film. I begin with the assumption that the ideal way to see dance is live, on a stage. Everything in dance begins with the fact that the dancers are physically present and are using their bodies to turn movement into art. Movies, with their complete freedom over time and space, break that contract between real time and the dancer. Dances can be constructed out of many different shots and even out of the work of more than one dancer (see *Flashdance*). If I can't see dancing on a stage, then, my preference is for classical movie dancing, by which I mean frankly artificial constructions of the Astaire and Rogers variety. Serious dance on film usually feels like a documentary. The great achievement of *Carmen* is that it takes serious dance and music, combines them with a plausible story, suspends our disbelief, and gives us a mesmerizing, electric experience.

Carmen ★ ★ ★ ★
PG, 152 m., 1984

Julia Migenes-Johnson (Carmen), Placido Domingo (Don Jose), Ruggero Raimondi (Escamillo), Faith Esham (Micaela), Jean-Philippe Lafont (Dancairo). Directed by Francesco Rosi and produced by Patrice Ledoux.

Bizet's *Carmen* is what movies are all about. It's one of the few modern movies that requires one of those legendary Hollywood advertising men who'd cook up copy like, for example . . .

Cheer! As Bizet's towering masterpiece blazes across the screen! Cry bravo! To passion, romance, adventure! From the bullrings of Spain to the innermost recesses of her gypsy heart, Carmen drives men mad and immortalizes herself as a romantic legend! Thrill! To the golden voice of Placido Domingo, and the tempestuous screen debut of the smouldering Julia Migenes-Johnson!

The temptation, of course, is to approach, a film like this with hushed voice and bended knee, uttering reverent phrases about art and music. But to hell with it: This movie is the *Indiana Jones* of opera films, and we might as well not beat around the bush. *Carmen* is a Latin soap opera if ever there was one, and the sheer passionate joy of Bizet's music is as vulgar as it is sublime, as popular as it is classical. *Carmen* is one of those operas ideally suited to the movies, and this version by Francesco Rosi is exciting, involving, and entertaining.

You are doubtless already familiar with the music. The sound track was recorded in Paris with Lorin Maazel conducting the National Orchestra of France. Placido Domingo is in great voice, and a relatively unknown American soprano named Julia Migenes-Johnson not only can sing the title role but, perhaps just as importantly, can look it and act it. There is chemistry here, and without the chemistry—without the audience's belief that the scornful gypsy Carmen could enslave the soldier Don Jose—there would only be an illustrated sound track. After the recording was completed, the movie was shot on locations in Spain by Francesco Rosi, the Italian director of *Three Brothers* and *Christ Stopped at Eboli.* He has discovered lush, sun-drenched villages on hillsides, and a bullring of such stark Spanish simplicity that the ballet within the ring for once seems as elegant as the emotions it is reflecting. He also has found moonlight, rich firelight, deep reds and yellows—colors so glowing that the characters seem to warm themselves at his palette.

Opera films are traditionally not successful. They play in festivals, they find a small audience of music lovers, maybe they make some money in Italy. Domingo broke that pattern with his *La Traviata* (1983), directed by Franco Zeffirelli. It had good long runs around the United States, and even broke through to audiences beyond the core of opera lovers. But we Americans are so wary of "culture." Opera for many of us still consists of the fat lady on "The Ed Sullivan Show." And for many of the rest, it is something that inhabits a cultural shrine and must be approached with reverence. Maybe it takes the movies, that most popular of art forms, to break that pattern. Rosi, Domingo, and Migenes-Johnson have filmed a labor of love.

Carrie ★ ★ ★ ½
R, 98 m., 1976

Sissy Spacek (Carrie), William Katt (Her Prom Date), Piper Laurie (Her Mother). Directed by Brian De Palma and produced by Paul Monash. Screenplay by Lawrence D. Cohen.

Brian De Palma's *Carrie* is an absolutely spellbinding horror movie, with a shock at the end that's the best thing along those lines since the shark leaped aboard in *Jaws.* It's also (and this is what makes it so good) an observant human portrait. This girl Carrie isn't another stereotyped product of the horror production line; she's a shy, pretty, and complicated high school senior who's a lot like kids we once knew. There is a difference, though. She has telekenesis, the ability to manipulate things without touching them. It's a power that came upon her gradually, and was released in response to the shrill religious fanaticism of her mother. It manifests itself in small ways. She looks in a mirror, and it breaks. Then it mends itself. Her mother tries to touch her and is hurled back against a couch. But then, on prom night . . .

Well, what makes the movie's last twenty minutes so riveting is that they grow so relentlessly, so inevitably, out of what's gone before. This isn't a science-fiction movie with a tacked-on crisis, but the study of a character we know and understand. When she fully uses (or is used by) her strange power, we know why. This sort of narrative development hasn't exactly been De Palma's strong point, but here he exhibits a gift for painting personalities; we didn't know De Palma, ordinarily so flashy on the surface, could go so deep. Part of his success is a result of the very good performances by Sissy Spacek, as Carrie, and by Piper Laurie, as Carrie's mother. They form a closed-off, claustrophobic household, the mother has translated her own psychotic fear of sexuality into a twisted personal religion. She punishes the girl constantly, locks her in closets with statues of a horribly bleeding Christ, and refuses to let her develop normal friendships.

At school, then, it's no wonder Carrie is so quiet. She has long blonde hair but wears it straight and uses it mostly to hide her face. She sits in the back of the room, doesn't speak up much, and is the easy butt of jokes by her classmates. Meanwhile, the most popular girl in the class devises a truly cruel trick to play on Carrie. It depends on Carrie being asked to the senior prom by the popular girl's equally popular boyfriend—he's one of your average Adonises with letters in every sport. He's not in on the joke, though, and asks Carrie in all seriousness.

And then De Palma gives us a marvelously realized scene at the prom—where Carrie does, indeed, turn out to be beautiful. There's a little something wrong, though, and De Palma has an effective way to convey it: As Carrie and her date dance, the camera moves around them, romantically at first, but then too fast, as if they're spinning out of control.

I wouldn't want to spoil the movie's climax for you by even hinting at what happens next. Just let me say that *Carrie* is a true horror story. Not a manufactured one, made up of spare parts from old Vincent Price classics, but a real one, in which the horror grows out of the characters themselves. The scariest horror stories—the ones by M.R. James, Edgar Allan Poe, and Oliver Onions—are like this. They develop their horrors out of the people they observe. That happens here, too. Does it ever.

Cat People ★ ★ ★ ½
R, 118 m., 1982

Nastassja Kinski (Irena Gallier), Malcolm McDowell (Paul Gallier), John Heard (Oliver Yates), Annette O'Toole (Alice Perrin), Ruby Dee (Female), Ed Begley, Jr. (Joe Creigh). Directed by Paul Schrader and produced by Charles Fries. Screenplay by Alan Ormsby.

It is a preposterous idea. Untold centuries ago, when all the world was a desert of wind-whipped, blood-orange sand, and leopards lounged lazily in barren trees and arrogantly ruled all they could see, a few members of the puny race of human beings made their own accommodation with the fearsome beasts. They sacrificed their women to them. And the leopards did not kill the women, but mated with them. From those mists of prehistory, the race they created lives even today: The Cat People.

These people have had a hard time of it. They have the physical appearance of ordinary humans, except for something feline around the eyes and a certain spring in their step. They have all the mortal appetites, too, but there are complications when they make love, because in the heat of orgasm they are transformed into savage black leopards and kill their human lovers. They should mate only with their own kind. But as our story opens, there are only two Cat People—and, like their parents before them, are brother and sister.

This is the stuff of audacious myth, combining the perverse, the glorious, and the ridiculous. The movies were invented to tell such stories. Paul Schrader's *Cat People* moves boldly between a slice-of-life in present-day New Orleans and the wind-swept deserts where the Cat People were engendered, and his movie creates a mood of doom, predestination, forbidden passion, and, to be sure, a certain silliness. It's fun in the way horror movies should be fun; it's totally unbelievable in between the times it's scaring the popcorn out of you.

Nastassja Kinski stars as the young sister, Irena. She is an orphan, reunited in New Orleans with her long-lost brother, Paul (Malcolm McDowell). She also is a virgin, afraid of sex and liquor because they might unleash the animal inside of her. (Little does she suspect that is literally what would happen.) She is tall, with a sensual mouth, wide-set green eyes, and a catlike walk. She catches the attention of the curator at the New Orleans zoo (John Heard). He senses danger in her. He also senses that this is the creature he has been waiting for all his life—waiting for her as the leopards in their cells wait, expecting nothing, ready for anything.

We have here, then, a most complex love triangle. Kinski fears her brother because she fears incest. She fears the curator but loves him. To love him is, eventually, to kill him. The curator is in love with the idea of her threat, but does not realize she *really* will turn into a leopard and rend his flesh. There are some supporting characters: Annette O'Toole is the sensible friend who senses danger, and Ed Begley, Jr. is the lackadaisical custodian whose arm is ripped from its socket. You shouldn't mess with leopards.

Schrader tells his story in two parallel narratives. One involves the deepening relationships among the sister, the brother, and the curator. The other, stunningly photographed, takes place in an unearthly terrain straight from Frank Herbert's Dune books. The designer, Ferdinando Scarfiotti, and the veteran special effects artist, Albert Whitlock, have created a world that looks completely artificial, with its drifting red sands and its ritualistic tableau of humans and leopards—and yet looks realistic in its fantasy. In other words, you know this world is made up, but you can't see the seams; it's like the snow planet in *The Empire Strikes Back*.

Cat People moves back and forth between its mythic and realistic levels, held together primarily by the strength of Kinski's performance and John Heard's obsession. Kinski is something. She never overacts in this movie, never steps wrong, never seems ridiculous; she just steps onscreen and convincingly underplays a leopard. Heard also is good. He never seems in the grip of an ordinary sexual passion, but possesses one of those obsessions men are willing (and often are called upon) to die for. *Cat People* is a good movie in an old tradition, a fantasy-horror film that takes itself just seriously enough to work, has just enough fun to be entertaining, contains elements of intrinsic fascination in its magnificent black leopards, and ends in one way just when we were afraid it was going to end in another.

Chapter Two ★ ★

PG, 124 m., 1980

James Caan (George), Marsha Mason (Jennie), Joseph Bologna (Leo), Valerie Harper (Faye), Alan Fudge (Lee), Judy Farrell (Gwen). Directed by Robert Moore and produced by Ray Stark. Screenplay by Neil Simon.

After the early loss of his first wife, playwright Neil Simon married again soon afterwards. Six months after the death, he fell in love at first sight with actress Marsha Mason, and they were married after a romance of only twenty-two days. Simon transformed those events of 1973 into an autobiographical play that opened in 1977, and now this film stars Mason in a role that is based, we guess, more or less upon herself.

Simon says the story isn't an actual record of what happened, but was just loosely inspired by his remarriage. There is no way for us to know. What we can say, on the basis of *Chapter Two*, is that if the key dialogue between husband and new wife wasn't taken from life, it is possibly taken from that wonderful category of what they *should* have said. And there is a great deal that they should have said. Simon is usually the most quick-footed and -witted of dialogue writers, but this time he gives us more than two hours of discussions, arguments, debates, reconciliations, and accusations that quickly become tedious.

The conversations in his screenplay are too long and too literal to begin with, but they suffer from two additional handicaps: (a) They do not take place between two characters whose motives have been well established, and (b) they have the misfortune to involve James Caan, who is so tense, uptight, and verbally constipated that it's a trial to wait out his speeches.

Caan plays the Simon-like character, a writer and new widower who is inconsolable in his grief until Mason happens along. Caan has previously survived a series of blind dates with the usual assortment of hopeless choices, and so Mason enchants him: She's outspoken, direct, spunky. Their first "trial date" lasts five minutes (one of those standard Hollywood "meet cutes"), and in no time at all they're in Bermuda on their honeymoon.

So far, not so bad. This is all the stuff of

dependable romantic comedy, and we know where we stand. But we are about to find ourselves at sea for the rest of the movie, because the Caan character suddenly has agonizing second thoughts . . . his new bride gets on his nerves . . . he doesn't know what's bugging him . . . he's hurtful . . . he splits. The movie never really bothers itself with *why* he behaves this way, unless we're supposed to supply our own instant Freudian analysis. Caan is awkward all through this movie (he never seems happy playing this part), but he's never more lost than when he undergoes this dramatic character transformation. And you can't really blame him: Simon just hasn't given him the words or actions to make himself clear.

After the split, the rest of the movie is devoted to attempts by first one and then the other of the newlyweds to figure out what went wrong. Their scenes are so tediously top-heavy with dialogue that we can barely stand to listen. And then there's the added distraction of a parallel plot involving an affair between their best friends (Valerie Harper and Joe Bologna).

There is absolutely no rational reason why this subplot is in the movie. Maybe it made sense in the mechanics of the stage play, but it doesn't belong here. And it's all the more distracting because, whatdaya know, Bologna and Harper are much better than Caan and Mason at conjuring up the romantic and comic juices of a love affair. Their scenes are meaningless and unnecessary, but at least they're alive, and just when they get their emotional rhythm flowing, the movie cuts back to the nonstop marriage counseling session that occupies the main plot.

Chapter Two is called a comedy, maybe because that's what we expect from Neil Simon. It's not, although it has that comic subplot. It's a middlebrow, painfully earnest, overwritten exercise in pop sociology. I'm not exactly happy describing Neil Simon's semi-real-life in those terms, but then those are the terms in which he's chosen to present it. My notion is that Simon would have been wiser to imagine himself writing about another couple, and writing for another actress than his own wife; that way maybe he wouldn't have felt it so necessary to let both sides have the last word.

Chariots of Fire ★ ★ ★ ★

PG, 123 m., 1981

Ben Cross (Harold Abrahams), Ian Charleson (Eric Liddell), Nigel Havers (Lord Andrew Lindsay), Ian Holm (Coach Mussabini), Sir John Gielgud (Master of Trinity), Lindsay Anderson (Master of Caius), David Yelland (Prince of Wales), Nicholas Farrell (Aubrey Montague). Directed by Hugh Hudson and produced by David Puttnam. Screenplay by Colin Welland.

This is strange. I have no interest in running and am not a partisan in the British class system. Then why should I have been so deeply moved by *Chariots of Fire*, a British film that has running and class as its subjects? I've toyed with that question since I first saw this remarkable film in May 1981 at the Cannes Film Festival, and I believe the answer is rather simple: Like many great films, *Chariots of Fire* takes its nominal subjects as occasions for much larger statements about human nature.

This is a movie that has a great many running scenes. It is also a movie about British class distinctions in the years after World War I, years in which the establishment was trying to piece itself back together after the carnage in France. It is about two outsiders—a Scot who is the son of missionaries in China, and a Jew whose father is an immigrant from Lithuania. And it is about how both of them use running as a means of asserting their dignity. But it is about more than them, and a lot of this film's greatness is hard to put into words. *Chariots of Fire* creates deep feelings among many members of its audiences, and it does that not so much with its story or even its characters as with particular moments that are very sharply seen and heard.

Seen, in photography that pays grave attention to the precise look of a human face during stress, pain, defeat, victory, and joy. Heard, in one of the most remarkable sound tracks of any film in a long time, with music by the Greek composer Vangelis Papathanassiou. His compositions for *Chariots of Fire* are as evocative, and as suited to the material, as the different but also perfectly matched scores of such films as *The Third Man* and *Zorba the Greek*. The music establishes the tone for the movie, which is one of nostalgia for a time when two young and naturally gifted British athletes ran fast enough to bring home medals from the 1924 Paris Olympics.

The nostalgia is an important aspect of the film, which opens with a 1979 memorial service for one of the men, Harold Abrahams, and then flashes back sixty years to his first day at Cambridge University. We are soon introduced to the film's other central character, the Scotsman Eric Liddell. The film's underlying point of view is a poignant one: These men were once young and fast and strong, and they won glory on the sports field, but now they are dead and we see them as figures from long ago.

The film is unabashedly and patriotically British in its regard for these two characters, but it also contains sharp jabs at the British class system, which made the Jewish Abrahams feel like an outsider who could sometimes feel the lack of sincerity in a handshake, and placed the Protestant Liddell in the position of having to explain to the peeved Prince of Wales why he could not, in conscience, run on the Sabbath. Both men are essentially proving themselves, their worth, their beliefs, on the track. But *Chariots of Fire* takes an unexpected approach to many of its running scenes. It does not, until near the film's end, stage them as contests to wring cheers from the audience. Instead, it sees them as *efforts,* as endeavors by individual runners—it tries to capture the exhilaration of running as a celebration of the spirit.

Two of the best moments in the movie: A moment in which Liddell defeats Abrahams, who agonizingly replays the defeat over and over in his memory. And a moment in which Abrahams' old Italian-Arabic track coach, banned from the Olympic stadium, learns who won his man's race. First he bangs his fist through his straw boater, then he sits on his bed and whispers, "My son!"

All of the contributions to the film are distinguished. Neither Ben Cross, as Abrahams, nor Ian Charleson, as Liddell, are accomplished runners but they are accomplished actors, and they *act* the running scenes convincingly. Ian Holm, as Abrahams' coach, quietly dominates every scene he is in. There are perfectly observed cameos by John Gielgud and Lindsay Anderson, as masters of Cambridge colleges, and by David Yelland, as a foppish, foolish young Prince of Wales. These parts and others make up a greater whole.

Chariots of Fire is one of the best films of recent years, a memory of a time when men still believed you could win a race if only you wanted to badly enough.

The China Syndrome ★ ★ ★ ★

PG, 122 m., 1979

Jane Fonda (Kimberly Wells), Jack Lemmon (Jack Godell), Michael Douglas (Richard Adams), Scott Brady (Herman DeYoung), James Hampton (Bill Gibson), Peter Donat (Don Jacovich), Wilford Brimley (Ted Spindler). Directed by James Bridges and produced by Michael Douglas. Screenplay by Mike Gray, T.S. Cook, and Bridges.

The China Syndrome is a terrific thriller that incidentally raises the most unsettling questions about how safe nuclear power plants really are. It was received in some quarters as a political film, and the people connected with it make no secret of their doubts about nuclear power. But the movie is, above all, entertainment: well-acted, well-crafted, scary as hell.

The events leading up to the "accident" in *The China Syndrome* are indeed based on actual occurrences at nuclear plants. Even the most unlikely mishap (a stuck needle on a graph causing engineers to misread a crucial water level) really happened at the Dresden plant outside Chicago. And yet the movie works so well not because of its factual basis, but because of its human content. The performances are so good, so consistently, that *The China Syndrome* becomes a thriller dealing in personal values. The suspense is generated not only by our fears about what might happen, but by our curiosity about how, in the final showdown, the characters will react.

The key character is Godell (Jack Lemmon), a shift supervisor at a big nuclear power plant in Southern California. He lives alone, quietly, and can say without any self-consciousness that the plant is his life. He believes in nuclear power. But when an earthquake shakes his plant, he becomes convinced that he felt an aftershock—caused not by an earthquake but by rumblings deep within the plant.

The quake itself leads to the first "accident." Because a two-bit needle gets stuck on a roll of graph paper, the engineers think they need to lower the level of the water shield over the nuclear pile. Actually, the level is already dangerously low. And if the pile were ever uncovered, the result could be the "China syndrome," so named because the superheated nuclear materials would melt directly through the floor of the plant and, theoretically, keep on going until they hit China. In practice, there'd be an explosion and a release of radioactive materials sufficient to poison an enormous area.

The accident takes place while a TV news team is filming a routine feature about the plant. The cameraman (Michael Douglas) secretly films events in the panicked control room. And the reporter (Jane Fonda) tries to get the story on the air. Her superiors refuse, influenced by the power industry's smoothly efficient public relations people. But the more Fonda and Douglas dig into the accident, the less they like it.

Meanwhile, obsessed by that second tremor, Lemmon has been conducting his own investigation. He discovers that the X-rays used to check key welds at the plant have been falsified. And then the movie takes off in classic thriller style: The director, James Bridges, uses an exquisite sense of timing and character development to bring us to the cliffhanger conclusion.

The performances are crucial to the movie's success, and they're all the more interesting because the characters aren't painted as anti-nuclear crusaders, but as people who get trapped in a situation while just trying to do their jobs. Fonda is simply superb as the TV reporter; the range and excellence of her performance are a wonder. Douglas is exactly right as the bearded, casually anti-establishment cameraman. And Jack Lemmon, reluctant to rock the boat, compelled to follow his conscience, creates a character as complex as his Oscar-winning businessman in *Save the Tiger.*

Chinatown ★ ★ ★ ★

R, 131 m., 1974

Jack Nicholson (J.J. Gittes), Faye Dunaway (Evelyn Mulwray), John Huston (Noah Cross), Perry Lopez (Escobar), John Hillerman (Yelburton), Darrell Zwerling (Hollis Mulwray), Diane Ladd (Ida Sessions), Roman Polanski (Man with Knife). Directed by Roman Polanski and produced by Robert Evans. Screenplay by Robert Towne.

Roman Polanski's *Chinatown* is not only a great entertainment, but something more, something I would have thought almost impossible: It's a 1930s private-eye movie that doesn't depend on nostalgia or camp for its effect, but works because of the enduring strength of the genre itself. In some respects, this movie actually could have been made forty-five years ago. It accepts its conventions and categories at face value and doesn't make them the object of satire or filter them through a modern sensibility, as Robert Altman did with *The Long Goodbye.* Here's a private-eye movie in which all the traditions, romantic as they may seem, are left intact.

At its center, of course, is the eye himself: J.J. Gittes, moderately prosperous as a result of adultery investigations. He isn't the perenially broke loner like Philip Marlowe, inhabiting a shabby office and buying himself a drink out of the office bottle. He's a successful investigator with a two-man staff, and he dresses well and is civilized and intelligent. He does, however, possess the two indispensable qualities necessary for any traditional private eye. He is deeply cynical about human nature, and he has a personal code and sticks to it.

There is also, of course, the woman, who comes to the private eye for help but does not quite reveal to him the full dimensions of her trouble. And there are the other inevitable ingredients of the well-crafted private-eye plot, as perfected by Raymond Chandler and Dashiell Hammett and practiced by Ross Macdonald. There's the woman's father, and the skeletons in their family closet, and the way that a crime taking place now has a way of leading back to a crime in the past.

These plots work best when they start out seeming impossibly complicated and then end up with watertight logic, and Robert Towne's screenplay for *Chinatown* does that with consummate skill. But the whole movie is a tour de force; it's a period movie, with all the right cars and clothes and props, but we forget that after the first ten minutes. We've become involved in the movie's web of mystery, as we always were with the best private-eye stories, whether written or filmed. We care about these people and want to see what happens to them.

And yet, at the same time, Polanski is so sensitive to the ways in which 1930s' movies in this genre were made that we're almost watching a critical essay. Godard once said that the only way to review a movie is to make another movie, and maybe that's what Polanski has done here. He's made a perceptive, loving comment on a kind of movie and a time in the nation's history that are both long past. *Chinatown* is almost a lesson on how to experience this kind of movie.

It's also a triumph of acting, particularly by Jack Nicholson, who is one of the most interesting actors now working and who contributes one of his best performances. He inhabits the character of J. J. Gittes like a second skin; the possession is so total that there are scenes in the movie where we almost have telepathy; we *know* what he's thinking, so he doesn't have to tell us. His loyalty is to the woman, but on several occasions, evidence turns up that seems to incriminate her. And then he must pull back, because his code will not admit clients who lie to him. Why he's this way (indeed, even the fact that he's this way) is communicated by Nicholson almost solely in the way he plays the character; dialogue isn't necessary to make the point.

The woman is Faye Dunaway, looking pale and neurotic and beautiful, and justifying for us (if not always for him) J. J.'s trust in her. And then there are all the other characters, who revolve around a complicated scheme to float a bond issue and build a dam to steal water from Los Angeles, in a time of drought. Because the film depends so much on the exquisite unraveling of its plot, it would be unfair to describe much more; one of its delights is in the way that dropped remarks and chance clues gradually build up the portrait of a crime.

And always at the center, there's the Nicholson performance, given an eerie edge by the bandage he wears on his nose after it's slit by a particularly slimy character played by Polanski himself. The bandage looks incongruous, we don't often see a bandaged nose on a movie private eye, but it's the kind of incongruity that's creepy and not funny. The film works similar ground: Drifting within sight of parody every so often, it saves itself by the seriousness of its character.

Choose Me ★ ★ ★ 1/2

R, 106 m., 1984

Genevieve Bujold (Dr. Love), Keith Carradine (Mickey), Lesley Ann Warren (Eve), Patrick Bauchau (Zack), Rae Dawn Chong (Pearl). Directed by Alan Rudolph and produced by Carolyn Pfeiffer and David Blocker. Screenplay by Rudolph.

Apart from its other qualities, which are many, Alan Rudolph's *Choose Me* is an audaciously intriguing movie. Its main purpose, indeed, may be to intrigue us—as other films aim to thrill or arouse or mystify. There is hardly a moment in the whole film when I knew for sure what was going to happen next, yet I didn't feel manipulated; I felt as if the movie were giving itself the freedom to be completely spontaneous.

The movie begins with strangers talking to each other. One of the strangers is a radio talk show host. Her name is Dr. Love, and she gives advice to the lovelorn over the radio (most of her advice seems to be variations on "That's not my problem"). One of her regular callers, we learn, is a woman named Eve who owns a bar. One day a mental patient named Mickey, a guy whose past seems filled with mysterious connections to the CIA, the space program, and the Russians, walks out of a closed ward and into the bar and meets Eve. A few days later, Dr. Love, hoping to do some research into the ways that we ordinary folk live, adopts an assumed name and goes looking for a roommate. She finds Eve and moves in with her, and neither woman knows who the other woman really is. They also don't make the connection that Eve is a regular caller to the radio program (highly unlikely, since she speaks with an accent). None of this is really as hard to follow as it sounds. And since one of the pleasures of this movie is the leisurely and logical way it explores the implications of mistaken identity, I'm not going to write another word about the confusions the characters get involved in.

Choose Me is a deliberate throwback to the *film noir* of the 1940s—to those movies made up of dark streets and wet pavements, hookers under streetlamps, pimps in shiny postwar Studebakers, and people who smoke a lot. It's also about lonely people, but it's not one of those half-witted TV movies about singles bars and single women. It's about smart, complicated people who are trying to clear a space for themselves and using romance as an excavating tool. The performances are key to this strategy. The best thing in the movie is Genevieve Bujold's performance as Dr. Love. She is interesting, if detached, as the radio personality, but when love finally does touch her life, she is so unabashedly open and confessional and red-faced and sincere that we want to hug her. Bujold just gets better and better; coming so soon after her good work in *Tightrope*, this is a reminder of how many different kinds of roles she can play so well.

Keith Carradine is the drifter with the dangerous past. We are never quite sure how seriously to take him, and that's the idea behind his performance, I think: He is able to quite sincerely tell two different women he loves them and wants to marry them, and the funny thing is, we believe him, both times. Eve, the former hooker who owns a bar, is played by Lesley Ann Warren. It's another good performance, nervous and on-edge; she's the kind of woman who seeks a different man every night as a protection against winding up with the same guy for a whole lifetime in a row. There are other intriguing characters in this story, most notably Rae Dawn Chong as a cute young alcoholic with a weird marriage, a naive way of trusting strangers, and dreamy plans of becoming a poet someday. Her husband (Patrick Bauchau) begins to get real tired of seeing the Carradine character, who through a series of misunderstandings seems to specialize in robbing him of poker pots, dates, and the attentions of his wife.

All of these people interact throughout the whole movie without *Choose Me* ever settling into familiar patterns. It's as if Rudolph wanted to tell a story as it might actually have happened, with coincidental meetings, dumb misunderstandings, random chance, and the endless surprises of human nature. At the end of the movie we haven't learned anything in particular, but we have met these people and their loneliness and punch-drunk optimism, and we have followed them a little time through the night.

A Chorus Line ★ ★ ★ ½
PG-13, 117 m., 1985

Michael Blevins (Mark), Yamil Borges (Morales), Sharon Brown (Kim), Gregg Burge (Richie), Michael Douglas (Zach), Cameron English (Paul), Tony Fields (Al), Nicole Fosse (Kristine), Vicki Frederick (Sheila), Jan Gan Boyd (Connie), Michelle Johnston (Bebe), Janet Jones (Judy), Pam Klinger (Maggie), Audrey Landers (Val), Terrence Mann (Larry), Charles McGowan (Mike), Alyson Reed (Cassie), Justin Ross (Greg), Blane Savage (Don), Matt West (Bobby). Directed by Richard Attenborough and produced by Cy Feuer and Ernest Martin. Screenplay by Arnold Schulman.

Show business is the only business that reminds us there is no business like it. And it never tires of that message. If there were as many books about books as there are musicals about musicals, there wouldn't be room on the shelf for books about anything else. *A Chorus Line* is the quintessential backstage musical, a celebration of the lives and hard times of the gypsy dancers who turn up by the hundreds to audition for a handful of jobs on Broadway. It takes years of brutal hard work to become a good enough dancer to dare go to an audition, and then the reward is usually a brusque "thank you" and a sweaty ride home on the subway. In order to succeed as a Broadway dancer, applicants need a limitless capacity to absorb rejection, and *A Chorus Line* celebrates that masochism in song and dance.

A Chorus Line has spent more than a decade on stages all over the world; its story is by now well known. A choreographer is casting eight dancers for a new musical he hopes to stage, and during one long and truthful day he auditions dozens of dancers before he makes his final selection. Richard Attenborough's film treatment of this story sticks to the outlines of the stage version, by and large, although he leaves the stage to fill in the details of the choreographer's old romance, and he leaves out some of the original songs to make room for some new ones.

The result may not please purists who want a film record of what they saw on stage, but this is one of the most intelligent and compelling movie musicals in a long time—and the most grown-up, since it isn't limited, as so many contemporary musicals are, to the celebration of the survival qualities of geriatric actresses.

Most of the scenes take place inside a theater. Zack (Michael Douglas), the choreographer, sits behind a writing platform somewhere out there in the darkness. Occasionally he lights a cigarette, and the ash glows as he takes the measure of the dancers on the stage. He can see them. They can't see him. He communicates by microphone. They step hesitantly to the edge of the stage, blinded by the spotlight, and talk into the void. Well, if that isn't the life they wanted, why did they volunteer for it?

Platoons of dancers are brought on stage, winnowed, dismissed. Finally there are sixteen left, and Zack asks each one of them to talk on a personal level—talk about when they were born, and where, and what their lives have been like, and what their dreams are. Many of the dancers have the most extraordinary difficulties in doing this, and one of them is frank: "Give me the lines, and I can play anybody. Just don't ask me to talk about myself."

Meanwhile, backstage drama is taking shape. An unexpected dancer has appeared for the auditions—Cassie (Alyson Reed), Zack's former girlfriend. They met in the theater, courted in the theater, broke up because Zack's job left no time for a personal life. Cassie was a star, but now she simply needs a job.

The movie opens up the play by going offstage for flashbacks to their affair, but the flashbacks are notable mostly for the way they focus on the theatrical lives of this couple—the way their private lives seem valid only to the degree that they reflect acceptance from the audience. The underlying tension in the movie circles around Zack's eventual decision: Will his heart or his profession make the eventual decision about Cassie? Douglas plays Zack on a staccato, harsh note; this is a workaholic who walks around with a lot of anger. That makes it all the more effective when he occasionally relents and gives one of the dancers a break; softening momentarily before putting his mask on again.

I thought Zack's most revealing moment came when he made the cut from sixteen dancers to eight, reading out eight names and then, when the eight were assembled downstage with smiles on their faces, thanking them and dismissing them; he had chosen the eight he did not name. Was this a misguided attempt to tell the rejected eight that they were also winners? Or was it simply cruelty? We are left to answer for ourselves.

Such questions are intercut with song and dance, with virtuoso solo numbers (my favorite was Charles McGowan's "I Can Do That!") and ensemble production numbers, leading up to a big and splashy finale, in which all of the dancers who originally auditioned are back on stage, together once again.

That leads to my one major difference with Attenborough's approach. Since *A Chorus Line* is a musical about itself, and since the whole hard, bitter, romantic truth of the story is that many are called but few are chosen, the roll call at the end strikes a false note of triumph. Better, perhaps, to have eight dancers on stage, and then cut to the others putting on their street clothes, waiting at bus stops, explaining to friends how they didn't get the job, or going to their dance classes yet again. I think the message of the play is that you don't get called back for a grand finale; you simply go to another audition.

Christiane F. ★ ★ ★ 1/2

R, 130 m., 1981

Natja Brunkhorst (Christiane), Thomas Haustein (Detlev), Jens Kuphal (Axel), Reiner Wolk (Leiche). Directed by Ulrich Edel and produced by Bernd Eichinger and Hans Weth.

This is one of the most horrifying movies I have ever seen. The fact that it's based on actual events makes it heartbreaking. *Christiane F.* is the portrait of a young girl who between her thirteenth and fifteenth years went from a fairly average childhood into the horrors of drug addiction, prostitution, and life on the brink of death.

The movie has become notorious in Europe, where both the film and book versions of Christiane's adventures have been bestsellers. The real Christiane first came to light as a witness in the trial of a man accused of having sex with minors. A reporter at the trial was intrigued by her appearance on the witness stand and tracked her down. His tape-recorded interviews with her became the basis for a twelve-part series in *Stern,* the German news magazine, which inspired the movie.

It is one of the most unremittingly grim

portraits of drug addiction ever filmed. The only American equivalent that comes to mind is Shirley Clarke's *The Connection* (1961), but in that film the hell of heroin addiction was tempered by the story construction of the film, which evolved as a well-told play. *Christiane F.* simply evolves as one lower plateau of suffering after another, until Christiane hits a low bottom.

The movie opens with Christiane as an unexceptional young teen-ager, given to such minor vices as playing rock records too loud and staying out too late. She lives in an apartment with her mother and resents the regular presence of her mother's boyfriend. With friends, she experiments with alcohol and pot, and them, after a rock concert (David Bowie, playing himself), she sniffs some heroin, "just out of curiosity." She likes the feeling it gives her. She tries to get it again. She has young friends who are already junkies, but she disregards their warnings that she'll get hooked. She mindlessly repeats the addict's ageless claim: "I can't get hooked if I just use a little, only once in a while. I can control my using." She cannot. Before long, she's shooting heroin, and not much longer after that she is selling her body to buy it.

This is a common story in the big cities of the world. It is relatively unusual among girls as young as Christiane (I hope), but even more unusual is the fact that she finds her own way into the heroin-and-hooker underground, without being enslaved by a pimp. The movie is relentless in depicting the drug culture of West Berlin. We see unspeakable sights: a junkie leaping over a toilet stall to yank the needle from Christiane's arm and plunge it into his own, stealing her fix; Christiane and her boyfriend trying to withdraw cold turkey and vomiting all over one another; the discovery of dead overdose victims, and, unforgettably, the pale, sad faces of the junkies lined up in a subway station, all hope gone from their once-young eyes.

Christiane F. made lots of the "best ten" lists of European critics in 1982, but I found it hard to judge its artistic quality because of the shockingly bad dubbing job. The film has been dubbed into mid-Atlantic British, by voices that are often clearly too old and in slang that is ten to fifteen years out of date. New World should ask for its money back from the dubbers. And yet—the movie still works. After a time we forget the bad dubbing, because the images are so powerful, the horrors so strong and the performances (by a cast of young unknowns) so utterly, bleakly, realistic. This is a movie of hell.

Christine ★ ★ ★

R, 110 m., 1983

Keith Gordon (Arnie), John Stockwell (Dennis), Alexandra Paul (Leigh), Robert Prosky (Garage owner), Harry Dean Stanton (Junkins). Directed by John Carpenter and produced by Richard Kobritz. Screenplay by Bill Phillips.

I've seen a lot of movies where the teen-age guy parks in a car with the girl he loves. This is the first one where he parks with a girl in the car he loves. I knew guys like this in high school. They spent their lives customizing their cars. Their girlfriends were accessories who ranked higher, say, than foam-rubber dice, but lower than dual carbs.

The car is named *Christine.* It's a bright red 1958 Plymouth Fury, one of those cars that used to sponsor the "Lawrence Welk Show," with tail fins that were ripped off for the *Jaws* ad campaign. This car should have been recalled, all right—to hell. It kills one guy and maims another before it's off the assembly line. Its original owner comes to a sad end in the front seat. And later, when Christine is twenty-one years old and rusting away, Arnie buys her. Arnie is a wimp. He's the kind of guy you'd play jokes on during lunch period, telling him the class slut wanted to talk to him, and then hiding his lunch tray while she was telling him to get lost. The kind of guy who was always whining, "Come on, guys—the joke's over!" But after Arnie buys Christine, he undergoes a strange metamorphosis. He becomes cool. He starts looking better. He stops with the greasy kid stuff. He starts going out with the prettiest girl in the school. That's where he makes his mistake. Christine gets jealous.

The entire movie depends on our willingness to believe that a car can have a mind of its own. I have believed in stranger things in the movies. Christine can drive around without a driver, play appropriate 1950s rock songs, lock people inside, and repair its own crushed fenders. The car is another inspiration from Stephen King, the horror novelist who specializes in thrillers about everyday objects. We saw his *Cujo*, about a rabid St. Bernard, and any day now I expect him to announce *Amityville IV: The Garage Door-Opener.*

Christine is, of course, utterly ridiculous. But I enjoyed it anyway. The movies have a love affair with cars, and at some dumb elemental level we enjoy seeing chases and crashes. In fact, under the right circumstances there is nothing quite so exhilarating as seeing a car crushed, and one of the best scenes in *Christine* is the one where the car forces itself into an alley that's too narrow for it.

Christine was directed by John Carpenter, who made *Halloween*, and his method is to take the story more or less seriously. One grin and the mood would be broken. But by the end of the movie, Christine has developed such a formidable personality that we are actually taking sides during its duel with a bulldozer. This is the kind of movie where you walk out with a silly grin, get in your car, and lay rubber halfway down the freeway.

A Christmas Story ★ ★ ★

PG, 94 m., 1983

Melinda Dillon (Mrs. Parker), Darren McGavin (The Old Man), Peter Billingsley (Ralphie). Directed by Bob Clark and produced by Rene Dupont and Clark. Screenplay by Jean Shepherd, Leigh Brown, and Clark.

Of course. That's what I kept saying during *A Christmas Story*, every time the movie came up with another one of its memories about growing up in the 1940s. Of course, any nine-year-old kid in the '40s would passionately want, for Christmas, a Daisy Brand Red Ryder repeating BB carbine with a compass mounted in the stock. Of course. And of course, his mother would say, "You'll shoot your eye out." That's what mothers always said about BB-guns. I grew up in downstate Illinois. The hero of this film, Ralphie, grew up in Gary, Ind. Looking back over a distance of more than thirty years, the two places seem almost identical—Middle American outposts where you weren't trying to keep up with the neighbors, you were trying to keep up with Norman Rockwell.

The movie is based on a nostalgic comic novel named *In God We Trust, All Others Pay Cash*, by Jean Shepherd, the radio humorist, who also narrates it. He remembers the obvious things, like fights with the bullies at school, and getting into impenetrable discussions with younger kids who do not quite know what all the words mean. He remembers legendary schoolteachers and hiding in the cupboard under the sink and having fantasies of defending the family home with a BB-gun.

But he also remembers, warmly and with love, the foibles of parents. The Old Man in *A Christmas Story* is played by Darren McGavin as an enthusiast. Not an enthusiast of anything, just simply an enthusiast. When he wins a prize in a contest, and it turns out to be a table lamp in the shape of a female leg in a garter, he puts it in the window, because it is the most amazing lamp he has ever seen. Of course. I can understand that feeling. I can also understand the feeling of the mother (Melinda Dillon), who is mortified beyond words.

The movie's high point comes at Christmastime, when Ralphie (Peter Billingsley) goes to visit Santa Claus. Visits to Santa Claus are more or less standard in works of this genre, but this movie has the best visit to Santa I've ever seen. Santa is a workaholic, processing kids relentlessly. He has one helper to spin the kid and deposit him on Santa's lap, and another one to grab the kid when the visit is over, and hurl him down a chute to his parents below. If the kid doesn't want to go, he gets Santa's boot in his face. Of course.

Chuck Berry Hail! Hail! Rock 'n' Roll ★ ★ ★ ★

PG, 120 m., 1987

Featuring Chuck Berry, Keith Richards, Eric Clapton, Robert Cray, Etta James, Johnnie Johnson, Julian Lennon, and Linda Ronstadt. Directed by Taylor Hackford and produced by Stephanie Bennett. Music produced by Keith Richards.

I expected *Chuck Berry Hail! Hail! Rock 'n' Roll!* to be a great concert film, and it is. What I did not expect was that it would also be a tantalizing mystery, a study of Chuck Berry that makes him seem as shrouded and enigmatic as Charles Foster Kane. Here is a sixty-year-old man singing *Sweet Little Sixteen*, and he sings it with total conviction, and we have no idea what he means, or ever meant, by it.

The argument of this film is that Chuck Berry was a crucial figure in the development of rock 'n' roll, that fusion of black gospel and rhythm and blues with mainstream pop and teen-age trauma. A good case is made, especially when Eric Clapton and Keith Richards explain precisely which chords and guitar strategies Berry used, and how you can still hear them today. There is a moment in the film when Berry and Richards are rehearsing, and Berry makes Richards do the same passage over and over again until he duplicates an effect that was first heard on records thirty years ago. It still sounds exactly right.

The film is a documentary about the sixtieth birthday concert that Berry performed in his hometown of St. Louis in 1987. The concert was the inspiration of Richards, lead guitarist for The Rolling Stones, who says he wanted to repay Berry for all the things the Stones and other rock groups have stolen from him. The way he wanted to do that was by producing a concert in which Berry would be backed by Richards and—for once—a first-rate, well-rehearsed band.

We quickly learn that this is not the way Berry has been operating in recent years. In testimony from Bruce Springsteen (who once opened for Berry) and in documentary footage of Berry himself, we learn that Berry has reduced his public appearances to an absolute routine. He travels alone, arrives backstage minutes before showtime, requires a local back-up band that knows his hit songs, walks onstage, does his thing, collects his money, and gets out of town.

Money seems to be very important to Berry. He discusses his original decision to become a full-time musician entirely in terms of money; he describes his guitar as "tax-deductible," and he shows off some vintage Cadillacs that he refuses to sell until he gets his price. He never discusses his music with a tenth of the interest he has for his bank account.

And yet the man is a terrific musician, and his songs retain an elemental, driving power that defines rock 'n' roll. There is a lot of concert footage in the film, and the audience I saw it with was rocking in their seats. Although Berry is a tough customer during the rehearsals (at one point, he shouts at Richards, "I been doin' it my way for sixty years"), the concert is a magnificent celebration of Berry's work as a composer and performer.

Berry is all over the stage, doing his famous duck walk, assaulting the microphone, nailing the beat, exuding the kind of forbidden anarchic sexuality that startled the bland teen-agers of the 1950s. He sings, he says, about the things that mattered to kids: school, romance, and cars.

Berry is backed up onstage by a band including Johnnie Johnson, the piano player who led the original trio where Berry got his start. There is some speculation that Johnson may have helped originate Berry's style, but he seems happier in the background, pounding out the beat. Richards oversees the band and plays lead guitar to Berry's rough rhythm, and there are several guest artists including Clapton, Julian Lennon, Robert Cray, Linda Ronstadt, and, stealing the show, Etta James.

It's one hell of a concert, a joyous celebration of the music, yet always lurking just offstage is the sense of Berry's obsessive privacy about his personal life. One of the movie's quietest moments is unforgettable. We see Berry's wife on camera. She introduces herself. She is asked a question. We hear Berry's voice from off camera: "OK, that's enough." The screen goes black, and we never see her again. Behind the man who helped create a music that let it all hang out, there is an other man who plays it all very close to the vest.

Cinderella ★ ★ ★

G, 74 m., 1950 ✓

Voices by Ilene Woods, Eleanor Audley, Verna Felton, Claire Dubrey, Helene Stanley, Luis Van Rooten, Don Barclay, Rhoda Williams, and James MacDonald. Directed by Wilfred Jackson, Hamilton Luske, and Clyde Geronimi. Directing animators: Eric Larson, Milt Kahl, Frank Thomas, John Lounsbery, Wolfgang Reitherman, Ward Kimball, Ollie Johnston, Marc Davis, Les Clark, and Norm Ferguson.

Walt Disney's *Cinderella* is considered by the studio to be a perennial that blooms every seven years or so, just in time for a new generation of kids. It has been several generations since I saw it as a kid, although when I saw it again recently, it was clear that it hadn't changed that much in thirty-eight years, and neither, in certain ways, had I.

This time around I was more aware of the power of the full-animation techniques, and I appreciated Disney's policy of using unfamiliar voices for the dubbing, instead of the studio's guess-that-voice derbies of recent years. But in other ways the movie still worked for me just as it had the first time. When those little mice bust a gut trying to drag that key up hundreds of stairs in order to free Cinderella, I don't care how many Kubrick pictures you've seen, it's still exciting.

You doubtless remember the original story. You may not—as I did not—remember how much the Disney studio expanded and supplemented it. Disney's most valuable and original contribution to the *Cinderella* tale was the addition of dozens of animals to the story. The screen fairly bursts with little birds helping Cinderella to dress, little mice helping her to plot, a dog to leap to the rescue, and an evil cat named Lucifer to chase the birds, pounce on the mice, spit at the dog, and do its best to come between Cinderella and Prince Charming.

These animals serve much the same function as the Seven Dwarfs (and assorted birds and forest animals) did in *Snow White.* They provide a chorus, moral support, additional characters to flesh out a thin story, and a kaleidoscope of movement on the screen. When one of the little birds creeps under Cinderella's pillow to awaken her in the morning, it doesn't matter that I was aware of the shameless manipulation of the animators; I grinned anyway.

Using the traditional techniques of full animation, the Disney artists provided each animal with a unique flavor and personality. What they also did (as Richard Shickel observed in *The Disney Version*) was shamelessly wag the buttocks of all of the animals as a way of making them seem even livelier; a Disney quadruped has its center of gravity somewhere below its navel and its pivot point right beneath the wallet. With all that action going on, no wonder they never wore pants.

If there is an obvious difference between *Cinderella* and such predecessors as *Pinocchio* and *Snow White,* it's in the general smoothing-out of the central characters' appearances. Snow White herself looked fairly bland, but the other characters in the first decade of Disney animation had a lot of personality in their faces. They were allowed to look odd. *Cinderella* seems to come right out of its time, the bland post-war 1950s. Cinderella looks like the Draw Me girl, Prince Charming has all of the charm of a department store dummy, and even the wicked stepsisters seem petulant rather than evil. Only the old king, his aide, and a few of the mice look bright enough to split a ticket.

Yet the movie works. There are dozens of little dramas played out for a minute or two by the mice, who must outsmart the cat and alert the dog. There are touching moments involving the king, who wants an heir more than anything, and looks on glumly as his son rejects all the women in the kingdom—except for one. And then there is that thrilling montage at the end, while the stepsisters desperately try to get the glass slipper to fit, while the mice sneak the key to Cinderella. You've got to hand it to her: The kid still has life. Another seven years, anyway.

City Heat ½★

PG, 94 m., 1984

Clint Eastwood (Lieutenant Speer), Burt Reynolds (Mike Murphy), Jane Alexander (Addy), Madeline Kahn (Caroline Howley), Rip Torn (Prime Pitt), Irene Cara (Ginny Lee). Directed by Richard Benjamin and produced by Fritz Maners. Screenplay by Sam O. Brown and Joseph C. Stinson.

Sometimes you get the idea that the deal behind a movie was so complicated and exhausting that they just didn't have the strength left to make the movie itself. *City Heat,* for example, stars two of the top box-office attractions in the recent history of Hollywood: Clint Eastwood and Burt Reynolds. It was originally going to be directed by Blake Edwards, but he was fired after "creative differences" with the two stars, and then several other directors were approached before Richard Benjamin agreed to pick up the reins. The depth of Edwards's feelings about the whole episode can be guessed from the *nom de plume* he used for his original screenplay credit, "Sam O. Brown." Check the initials.

We will never know what Edwards might have made of *City Heat.* That's bad enough. What's worse is that we can barely tell what Benjamin made of it. This movie is a confusing mess with a plot so pointless that there's a fight scene every ten minutes, just to distract us. The movie's so bewildered it doesn't even seem sure about the relationship between Eastwood and Reynolds: Are they really enemies, or just friends who talk tough to one another, or are they former friends who became enemies and are now becoming friends again? And does it matter?

The movie's a period gangster picture, with lots of antique cars and mustaches and snap-brim fedora hats. Eastwood plays a police detective who is mild-mannered, and somebody crosses him, and then he turns into a ferocious fighting machine. Reynolds is a former cop who is now a private eye. Early in the film, he goes to his office for consultations with Richard Roundtree and Jane Alexander, and it is a measure of the film's confusion that when he mentions his partner, we are not quite sure which one he means. There are other loose ends. For example, Reynolds kisses Alexander tenderly, but then she goes on a date with Eastwood. The guys go to a boxing match that has no logical purpose other than to serve as a setup for a meeting *after* the match. A criminal gang, headed by Rip Torn, will kill to get its hands on a box that contains . . . what? Ledger records, I think. Of illegal gambling debts, I think. You know a movie is desperately in trouble when the audience isn't even sure what the bad guys are after.

There are a lot of talented people in this movie, including Irene Cara in a throwaway role as a nightclub singer, and Madeline Kahn in her basic performance as a Dietrich-esque vamp. There are also incessant fight scenes and shoot-outs, in which the bad guys are consistently unable to hit the side of a barn, and Eastwood is incapable of missing. All of this is maybe supposed to be an ironic commentary on Eastwood's Dirty Harry character, but so what? Almost every scene in the movie seems to have been a separate inspiration, thrown in with no thought for the movie as a whole.

How do travesties like this get made? I have a feeling the problem starts at the level of negotiations, in which everybody protects his own turf, and the movie suffers. There are moments here when you want to squirm, especially when Clint Eastwood allows his incomparable screen persona to be parodied. The Dirty Harry movies themselves border on parody—that's part of their charm—but they know what they're doing. *City Heat* is a movie in which people almost obviously don't have a clue.

City of Women ★ ★ 1/2

R, 140 m., 1981

Marcello Mastroianni (Snaporaz), Ettor Manni (Dr. Zberkock), Anna Prucnal (Elena), Bernice Stegers (Woman on Train), Donatella Damiani (Feminist on Skates). Directed by Federico Fellini. Screenplay by Fellini and Bernardino Zapponi.

If there is one central image in the work of Federico Fellini, it's of Fellini's autobiographical hero being smothered by women. They come in all shapes and ages, from old crones to young innocents, from heavy-breasted mother figures to seductive nymphs. One of Fellini's favorite strategies is to gather all the women into one fantasy and place his hero at the center of it. That's what he did in the celebrated harem sequence in *8½*, and that's what he does throughout *City of Women.*

There is, however, an additional twist this time. Since the basic Fellini universe was created in *La Strada, La Dolce Vita, 8½,* and *Juliet of the Spirits,* beliefs about the role of women have undergone a revolution, even in Italy. It is no longer enough that Fellini deal with the ways women tantalize, dominate, and possess his male heroes. Now he must also deal with the women themselves. For Fellini, this is probably not nearly so much fun. His idea of a liberated woman is fairly clear from the wife-character in *8½* (1963). She is severe, wears tailored suits and horn-rim glasses, and wants to spoil all the fun. Fellini's hero, in that film and in *City of Women,* is named Guido, is played by Marcello Mastroianni, and wants to escape from the horn-rim types and lose himself in the capacious bosom of a thoroughly undemanding sex object.

At the beginning of *City of Women,* however, Guido finds himself riding on a train across from a severe-looking woman in a tailored suit. He tries to seduce her. She sentences him to an imaginary odyssey through a series of sexual fantasies, most of them devoted to the unpleasant fates of men who do not have the correct attitude about women. Most of these fantasies, and indeed many of the specific images, are familiar to anyone who has seen several Fellini films. There is a long circus chute for Mastroianni to tumble down *(Juliet)*, and a group of circus scenes (from half his other films), and a wall covered with portraits (remember *Fellini Roma?*), and an insatiable satyr, and, of course, the full-lipped, full-bosomed, smiling and inexhaustible temptress who turns up, in one manifestation or another, throughout Fellini.

City of Women does nothing original or very challenging with this material. Although it pretends to be Fellini's film about feminism, it reveals no great understanding of the subject; Fellini basically sees feminists as shrill harems of whip-wielding harridans, forever dangling the carrot of sex just out of reach of his suffering hero. Fellini has rarely been able to discover human beings hidden inside his female characters, and it's a little late for him to start blaming that on the women's liberation movement.

Is *City of Women* worth seeing? Yes, probably, even though it is not a successful movie and certainly not up to Fellini's best work. It's worth seeing because it's a bedazzling collection of images, because at times it's a graceful and fluid celebration of pure film-making skill, and because Fellini can certainly make a bad film but cannot quite make a boring one.

Claire's Knee ★ ★ ★ ★

PG, 103 m., 1971

Jean-Claude Brialy (Jerome), Aurora Cornu (Aurora), Beatrice Romand (Laura), Laurence de Monaghan (Claire). Directed by Eric Rohmer and produced by Pierre Cottrell. Screenplay by Eric Rohmer.

Now if I were to say, for example, that *Claire's Knee* is about Jerome's desire to caress the knee of Claire, you would be about a million miles from the heart of this extraordinary film. And yet, in a way, *Claire's Knee* is indeed about Jerome's feelings for Claire's knee, which is a splendid knee.

Jerome encounters Claire and the other characters in the film during a month's holiday he takes on a lake between France and Switzerland. He has gone there to rest and reflect before he marries Lucinda, a woman he has loved for five years. And who should he run into but Aurora, a novelist who he's also been a little in love with for a long time.

Aurora is staying with a summer family that has two daughters: Laura, who is sixteen and very wise and falls in love with Jerome, and Claire, who is beautiful and blonde and full of figure and spirit. Jerome and Aurora enter into a teasing intellectual game, which requires Jerome to describe to Aurora whatever happens to him during his holiday. When they all become aware that Laura has fallen in love with the older man, Jerome encourages her in a friendly, platonic way. They have talks about love and the nature of life, and they grow very fond of each other, although of course the man does not take advantage of the young girl.

But then Claire joins the group, and one day while they are picking cherries, Jerome turns his head and finds that Claire has climbed a ladder and he is looking directly at her knee. Claire herself, observed playing volleyball or running, hand-in-hand, with her boyfriend, is a sleek animal, and Jerome finds himself stirring with desire.

He doesn't want to run away with Claire, or seduce her, or anything like that; he plans to marry Lucinda. But he tells his friend Aurora that he has become fascinated by Claire's knee; that it might be the point through which she could be approached, just as another girl might respond to a caress on the neck, or the cheek, or the arm. He becomes obsessed with desire to test this theory, and one day has an opportunity to touch the knee at last.

As with all the films of Eric Rohmer, *Claire's Knee* exists at levels far removed from plot (as you might have guessed while I was describing the plot). What is really happening in this movie happens on the level of character, of thought, of the way people approach each other and then shy away. In some movies, people murder each other and the contact is casual; in a work by Eric Rohmer, small attitudes and gestures can summon up a university of humanity.

Rohmer has an uncanny ability to make his actors seem as if they were going through the experiences they portray. The acting of Beatrice Romand, as sixteen-year-old Laura, is especially good in this respect; she isn't as pretty as her sister, but we feel somehow she'll find more enjoyment in life because she is a . . . well, a better person underneath. Jean-Claude Brialy is excellent in a difficult role. He has to relate with three women in the movie, and yet remain implicitly faithful to the unseen Lucinda. He does, and since the sexuality in his performance is suppressed, it is, of course, all the more sensuous. *Claire's Knee* is a movie for people who still read good novels, care about good films, and think occasionally.

Clan of the Cave Bear ★ 1/2
R, 120 m., 1985

Darryl Hannah (Ayla), Pamela Reed (Iza), James Remar (Creb), Thomas G. Waites (Broud), John Doolittle (Brun), Curtis Armstrong (Goov). Directed by Michael Chapman and produced by Gerald I. Isenberg. Screenplay by John Sayles.

What was it like, back there at the dawn of time? What was it like to be a human being, and yet have none of the things we take for granted, like houses, feminism, and shoes? How did we take that first great leap, out of the caves and into the Iron Age? Or, if you really want to get idealistic about it, that leap out of the rain and into the caves?

Clan of the Cave Bear attempts to answer those questions by making a great leap backward in the imagination, to that precise moment when the first Cro-Magnons were moving in and the last Neanderthals were becoming obsolete. Unfortunately, the movie never really does reconcile itself to the prehistoric past. It approaches those times with a modern sensibility. It shows us a woman winning respect from a patriarchal tribe, when in reality the men would have just banged her over the head real good. It isn't grim enough about what things were probably like back then.

It tells a nice little modern parable about a distant past that is hardly less idealistic than the Garden of Eden. Instead of people who are scarred, wind-burned, thin, and toothless, it gives us graduates of the Los Angeles health club scene, and a heroine who looks as if she just walked over from make-up.

It also packs a lot of things into a short span of that long-ago time. Although whole eons were available to it, the movie covers just a few short seasons, as a wandering tribe of primitive Neanderthals encounters an amazing sight: A Cro-Magnon woman (Daryl Hannah), tall and blonde and smarter than they are.

The girl is adopted into the tribe, and right away she causes trouble. She can't understand why the men get to have all the fun, and use all of the weapons, and make all of the decisions. One day she sneaks out and practices on the slingshot. On another day, she challenges the tribe's attitude about sex, seniority, and even about self-defense. In her spare time, she invents arithmetic and becomes chief adviser to the medicine man. This isn't the first Cro-Magnon, it's the first Rhodes scholar.

The movie dresses its actors in furs and skins, and has them walk around barefoot and talk in monosyllables. But it never quite makes them seem frightened and ignorant and vulnerable and bewildered. To capture the sense of wonder of those days when the human race reached its turning point, *Clan of the Cave Bear* needs great images, not tidy little dramatic scenes with predictable conclusions. It needs sights like the opening of *2001,* when the bone went flying into the air. Or it needs the muddy, exhausted desperation of the characters in *Quest for Fire,* a movie that *did* feel as if it took place in prehistory. *Clan of the Cave Bear* is about the first generation of designer cavemen.

The performances are doomed from the start, because the actors are asked to play characters who are modern in everything but dress and language. Every one of these people has motives that are instantly recognizable and predictable. There is no sense of the alien and the unknown, no sense that these people have ideas and feelings that would be strange to us. Even their quasi-religion is familiar: They believe each person has an animal spirit which is its partner or symbol, and that if a person's spirit is strong, it gives them strength. This is pseudo-anthropology crossed with Indian folklore and the Boy Scouts.

The ending of *Clan of the Cave Bear* betrays its bankruptcy, because there isn't really an ending, just a conclusion—a romantic shot of the woman continuing on her lonely quest. The great failure of the movie is a failure of imagination. The filmmakers made no effort to empathize with their prehistoric characters, to imagine what it might really have been like back then. They are content to assemble the usual narrative clichés and standard storylines, and apply them to some actors in costume. If modern men came from beginnings like this, why did they even bother to develop civilization, since they already possess its most wretched excesses?

Clash of the Titans ★ ★ ★ ½
PG, 118 m., 1981

Harry Hamlin (Perseus), Judi Bowker (Andromeda), Burgess Meredith (Ammen), Laurence Olivier (Zeus), Maggie Smith (Thetis), Neil McCarthy (Calibos). Directed by Desmond Davis and produced by Charles H. Schneer and Ray Harryhausen, with special effects created by Harryhausen.

Clash of the Titans is a grand and glorious romantic adventure, filled with grave heroes, beautiful heroines, fearsome monsters, and awe-inspiring duels to the death. It is a lot of fun. It was quite possibly intended as a sort of Greek mythological retread of *Star Wars* (it has a wise little mechanical owl in it who's a third cousin of R2-D2), but it's also part of an older Hollywood tradition of special-effects fantasies, and its visual wonderments are astonishing.

The story, on the other hand, is robust and straightforward. Perseus (Harry Hamlin) is locked into a coffin with his mother and cast into the sea, after she has angered the gods. But Zeus (Laurence Olivier) takes pity and sees that the coffin washes ashore on a deserted island, where Perseus grows to manhood and learns of his mission in life. The mission, in a nutshell, is to return to Joppa and rescue Andromeda (Judi Bowker) from a fate worse than death: marriage to the hideously ugly Calibos, who was promised her hand in marriage before he was turned into a monster by the wrath of the gods. Calibos lives in a swamp and dispatches a gigantic, scrawny bird every night to fetch him the spirit of the sleeping Andromeda in a gilded cage. If Perseus is to marry Andromeda, he must defeat Calibos in combat and also answer a riddle posed by Cassiopeia, Andromeda's mother. Those who answer the riddle incorrectly are condemned to die. Love was more complicated in the old days.

There are, of course, other tests. To follow the bird back to the lair of Calibos, the resourceful Perseus must capture and tame Pegasus, the last of the great winged horses. He must also enter the lair of Medusa, who turns men to stone with one glance, and behead her so that he can use her dead eyes to petrify the gargantuan monster Kraken, who is unchained from his cage on the ocean floor so that he can ravish Joppa in general and Andromeda in particular.

All of this is gloriously silly. But because the movie respects its material, it even succeeds in halfway selling us this story; movies that look like *Clash of the Titans* have a tendency to seem ridiculous, but this film has the courage of its convictions. It is also blessed with a cast that somehow finds its way past all the monsters and through all the heroic dialogue and gets us involved in the characters. Harry Hamlin is a completely satisfactory Perseus, handsome and solemn and charged with his own mission. Judi Bowker is a beautiful princess and a great screamer, especially in the scene where she's chained to the rock and Kraken is slobbering all over her. Burgess Meredith has a nice little supporting role as Ammon, an old playwright who thinks he may be able to turn all of this into a quick epic. And Laurence Olivier is just as I have always imagined Zeus: petulant, but a pushover for a pretty face.

The real star of the movie, however, is Ray Harryhausen, who has worked more than forty years as a creator of special effects. He uses combinations of animation, miniatures, optical tricks, and multiple images to put humans into the same movie frames as the most fantastical creatures of legend, and more often than not, they look pretty convincing: when Perseus tames Pegasus, it sure looks like he's dealing with a real horse (except for the wings, of course).

Harryhausen's credits include *Mighty Joe Young*, *Jason and the Argonauts*, and *The Golden Voyage of Sinbad*, but *Clash of the Titans* is his masterwork. Among his inspired set-pieces: the battle in the Medusa's lair, with her hair writhing with snakes; the flying horse scenes; the gigantic prehistoric bird; the two-headed wolf-dog, Dioskilos; the Stygian witches; and, of course, Kraken, who rears up from the sea and causes tidal waves that do a lot of very convincing damage to a Greek city that exists only in Harryhausen's art. The most lovable special-effects creation in the movie is little Bubo, a golden owl sent by the gods to help

Perseus in his trials. Bubo whistles and rotates his head something like R2-D2 in *Star Wars,* and he has a similar personality, too, especially at the hilarious moment when he enters the film for the first time.

Clash of the Titans is a family film (there's nothing in it that would disturb any but the most impressionable children), and yet it's not by any means innocuous: It's got blood and thunder and lots of gory details, all presented with enormous gusto and style. It has faith in a story-telling tradition that sometimes seems almost forgotten, a tradition depending upon legends and myths, magical swords, enchanted shields, invisibility helmets, and the overwhelming power of a kiss.

The Class of 1984 ★ ★ ★ ½

R, 93 m., 1982

Perry King (Andy Norris), Timothy Van Patten (Stegman), Roddy McDowell (Terry Corrigan). Directed by Mark Lester and produced by Lester and Merrie Lynn Ross. Screenplay by Lester, John Saxton, and Tom Holland.

Movies like this either grab you, or they don't. *The Class of 1984* grabbed me. I saw it for the first time at the 1982 Cannes Film Festival, where I wandered into the theater expecting to find the dog of the week and wandered out two hours later, a little dazed and sort of overwhelmed. *The Class of 1984* is not a great movie but it works with quiet, strong efficiency to achieve more or less what we expect from a movie with such a title. It is violent, funny, scary, contains boldly outlined characters, and gets us involved. It also has a lot of style. One of the reasons for the film's style may be that it was made by people who knew what they were doing. The whole Dead Teen-ager genre has been seriously weakened in the last several years by wave upon wave of cheap, idiotic tax shelter films from Canada and elsewhere: films in which a Mad Slasher and a lot of screaming adolescents have been substituted for talent, skill, and craft—movies such as *Prom Night* and *Terror Train* and *The Burning.*

Mark Lester's *The Class of 1984* stands head and shoulders above movies like that. It tells a strong, simple story. It is acted well. It is not afraid to be comic at times and, even better, it's not afraid at the end to pull out all the stops and give us the sort of Grand Guignol conclusion that the slasher movies always botch. You may or may not think it's any good, but you'll have to admit that it works.

The movie stars Perry King, a skilled actor who has survived a lot of junk, as a music teacher who takes a job at a big city high school. The first day he walks into class, he faces trouble, and trouble is personified by Stegman (Timothy Van Patten), the brilliant but crazed leader of the high school gang. Stegman dresses as a cross between a punk rocker and a Hell's Angel. He terrorizes half the school with his violence and mesmerizes the other half with his charisma. He also happens to be a brilliant musician. King tries to deal with him, reason with him, outthink him, and even outmuscle him, but the kid is strong, smart, and mean. The other teachers and the school officials have mostly surrendered to the reign of terror. A few put up a fight, most memorably the biology teacher, played by Roddy McDowell. He has one of the great scenes in the movie as he pulls a gun on his class and invites them to share with him the joys of education, or else.

The movie builds toward one of those nightmarish conclusions where everything's happening at once. While the teacher prepares to lead his school orchestra in a concert, the thugs terrorize his helpless wife at home. The teacher turns the baton over to his best student, a shy young girl, and goes off to do battle with the punks. After a great deal of blood has been shed, the teacher and the gang leader are finally face to face, high in the wings over the high school auditorium stage, and the climax is a cross between *The Hunchback of Notre Dame* and *Beyond the Valley of the Dolls.*

The Class of 1984 has received some really savage criticism. Newsweek called it "*The Class of 1982* with herpes." What does that mean? I dunno. I guess it means the critic found the movie so hateful that it wasn't worth anything more than cheap wisecracks. But unless we can accept talent wherever we find it in the movies, and especially in smaller genre movies without big stars, we're going to be left with nothing but overpriced lead balloons and delicate little exercises in sensibility. *The Class of 1984* is raw, offensive, vulgar, and violent, but it contains the sparks of talent and wit, and it is acted and directed by people who cared to make it special.

Close Encounters of the Third Kind: The Special Edition ★ ★ ★ ★
PG, 152 m., 1980

Richard Dreyfuss (Roy Neary), Francois Truffaut (Claude Lacombe), Teri Garr (Ronnie Neary), Melinda Dillon (Jillian Guiler). Directed and written by Steven Spielberg and produced by Julia Phillips and Michael Phillips.

Close Encounters of the Third Kind: The Special Edition is the movie Steven Spielberg wanted to make in the first place. The changes Spielberg has made in his original 1978 film are basic and extensive, adding up to essentially a new moviegoing experience. Spielberg's changes fall into four categories:

• He's provided an entirely new conclusion, taking us inside the alien spaceship that visits at the end of the film.

• He's provided more motivation for the strange behavior of the Richard Dreyfuss character—who is compelled by "psychic implanting" to visit the Nevada mountain where the spaceship plans to land.

• He's added additional manifestations of UFO intervention in earthly affairs—including an ocean-going freighter deposited in the middle of the Gobi Desert.

• In addition to the sensational ending, he's added more special effects throughout the film. One shot seems like a light-hearted quote from Spielberg's own *Jaws*. In that film, a high-angle shot showed the shadow of the giant shark passing under a boat. In this one, a high-angle shot shows the shadow of a giant UFO passing over a pickup truck.

Spielberg's decision to revise the original version of *Close Encounters* is all but unprecedented. Some directors have remade their earlier films (Hitchcock did British and American versions of *The Man Who Knew Too Much*), and others have thought out loud about changes they'd like to make (Robert Altman wanted to edit a nine-hour version of *Nashville* for TV). And countless directors, of course, have given us sequels—"part two" of their original hits.

Spielberg's *Special Edition* is sort of a *Close Encounters: Part 1½*. It is also a very good film. I thought the original film was an astonishing achievement, capturing the feeling of awe and wonder we have when considering the likelihood of life beyond the Earth. I gave that first version a four-star rating. This new version gets another four stars: It is, quite simply, a better film—so much better that it might inspire the uncharitable question, "Why didn't Spielberg make it this good the *first* time?"

His changes fall into three categories. He has (1) thrown away scenes that didn't work, like the silly sequence in which Dreyfuss dug up half of his yard in an attempt to build a model of the mountain in his vision; (2) put in scenes he shot three years ago but did not use, such as the Gobi sequence and Dreyfuss flipping out over the strange compulsion that has overtaken him, and (3) shot some entirely new scenes.

The most spectacular of these is the new ending, which shows us what Dreyfuss sees when he enters the spacecraft. He sees a sort of extraterrestrial cathedral, a limitless interior space filled with columns of light, countless sources of brilliance, and the machinery of an unimaginable alien technology. (The new special effects were designed by the underground artist R. Cobb, I understand; no credit is given.) This new conclusion gives the movie the kind of overwhelming final emotional impact it needed; it adds another dimension to the already impressive ending of the first version.

The movie gains impact in another way. Spielberg has tightened up the whole film. Dead ends and pointless scenes have been dropped. New scenes do a better job of establishing the characters—not only of Dreyfuss, but also of Francois Truffaut, as the French scientist. The new editing moves the film along at a faster, more absorbing pace to the mind-stretching conclusion. *Close Encounters*, which was already a wonderful film, now transcends itself; it's one of the great moviegoing experiences. If you've seen it before, I'm afraid that now you'll have to see it again.

Coal Miner's Daughter ★ ★ ★
PG, 125 m., 1980

Sissy Spacek (Loretta Lynn), Tommy Lee Jones (Mooney Lynn), Beverly D'Angelo (Patsy Cline), Levon Helm (Ted Webb), Phyllis Boyens (Clara Webb). Directed by

Michael Arted and produced by Bernard Schwarts. Screenplay by Tom Rickman.

What improbable lives so many Americans lead, compared to the more orderly and predictable careers of the Swedes, say, or the French. It's not just that we're the most upwardly mobile society in history, we're the most mobile, period: We go to ruin as swiftly and and dramatically as we hit the jackpot. No wonder one of our favorite myths involves a rags to riches story in which success then destroys the hero.

Look at country music star Loretta Lynn. If we can believe *Coal Miner's Daughter* (and I gather that, by and large, we can), here's a life which began in the poverty of the coalfields of Kentucky and led almost overnight to show-business stardom. And what's astonishing is that it wasn't even really planned that way: Loretta learned to play on a pawnshop guitar, her husband thought she could sing, and one day she just sorta found herself on stage. The movie's about Loretta Lynn's childhood, her very early marriage, her quick four kids, her husband's move to Washington State looking for a job, her humble start in show business, her apparently quick rise to stardom, and then the usual Catch-22 of self-destructivenss.

We're not surprised, somehow, that right after the scenes where she becomes a superstar, there are scenes where she starts using pills, getting headaches, and complaining that everybody's on her case all the time. We fiercely want to believe in success in this country, but for some reason we also want to believe that it takes a terrible human toll. Sometimes it does—and that always makes for a better story. Straightforward success sagas, in which the heroes just keep on getting richer, are boring. We want our heroes to suffer. We like to identify—it makes stars more human, somehow, if they get screwed by Valium, too.

What's refreshing about *Coal Miner's Daughter* is that it takes the basic material (rags to riches, overnight success, the onstage breakdown, and, of course, the big comeback) and relates them in wonderfully human terms. It's fresh and immediate. That is due most of all to the performance by Sissy Spacek as Loretta Lynn. With the same sort of magical chemistry she's shown before, when she played the high school kid in *Carrie,* Spacek at twenty-nine has the ability to appear to be almost any age onscreen. Here she ages from about fourteen to somewhere in her thirties, always looks the age, and never seems to be wearing makeup. I wonder if she does it with her posture; early in the film, as a poor coal miner's kid, she slouches and slinks around, and then later she puts on dignity with the flashy dresses she wears onstage.

The movie is mostly about Lynn's relationships with her husband, Mooney (played by Tommy Lee Jones), and her first close show-business friend and mentor, Patsy Cline (Beverly D'Angelo). Both of these relationships are developed in direct, understated, intelligent ways; we are spared, for example, a routine portrait of Mooney Lynn as Official Show Biz Husband, and given instead a portrait of a recognizable human being who is aggressive, confident, loving, and fallable. The fact that this movie felt free to portray Mooney as hard-nosed is one of the most interesting things about it: Loretta Lynn, who had a certain amount of control over the project, obviously still has her feet on the ground and didn't insist that this movie be some kind of idealized fantasy.

We are left to speculate, of course, on whether Lynn's rise to stardom was really as picaresque as *Coal Miner's Daughter* suggests. She seems to get on the Grand Ole Opry mighty fast, and Patsy Cline seems to adopt her almost before she knows her. But then the amazing thing about Loretta Lynn's life seems to be how fast everything happened, and how wide open the avenues to success are in this country—if you're talented and, of course, lucky.

The most entertaining scenes in the movie are in the middle, after the coal mines and before the Top 40, when Loretta and Mooney are tooling around the back roads trying to convince country disc jockeys to play her records. The scene with Mooney taking a publicity photo of Loretta is a little gem illustrating the press agent that resides within us all.

So, anyway . . . how good *is* this movie? I think it's one of those films people like so much while they're watching it that they're inclined to think it's better than it is. It's warm, entertaining, funny, and centered around that great Sissy Spacek performance, but it's essentially pretty familiar material (not that Loretta Lynn can be blamed that Horatio Alger wrote her life before she lived it). The movie isn't great art, but it has been made with great taste and style; it's more intelligent and observant than movie biographies of singing stars used to be. That makes it a treasure to watch, even if we sometimes have the feeling we've seen it before.

Cocoon ★ ★ ★
PG-13. 115 m., 1985

Wilford Brimley (Ben), Steve Guttenberg (Jack), Brian Dennehy (Walter), Hume Cronyn (Joe), Don Ameche (Art), Maureen Stapleton (Mary), Jessica Tandy (Alma), Jack Gilford (Bernie), Tahnee Welch (Kitty). Directed by Ron Howard and produced by Richard D. Zanuck, David Brown, and Lili Fini Zanuck. Screenplay by Tom Benedek.

Cocoon is one of the sweetest, gentlest science-fiction movies I've seen, a hymn to the notion that aliens might come from outer space and yet still be almost as corny and impulsive as we are. It is also the first film since *On Golden Pond* to deal at length with old people, and you can tell by their performances that these older actors have been waiting a long time to get something nice and meaty and silly to sink their choppers into.

The movie opens with the suggestion that aliens have landed on Earth. Then we see apparently normal human beings renting a boat and a beachfront estate. Meanwhile, in a nearby retirement home, three of the old guys have started sneaking onto the estate to take illegal swims in a big enclosed pool. One day, they discover some large, mossy rocks on the bottom of the pool. That doesn't stop them. They dive in, and before long they feel terrific—and curiously youthful.

The rocks are actually cocoons collected from the bottom of the sea by aliens, who left them behind 10,000 years ago when they were forced to evacuate Atlantis in a hurry. The pool has been charged with a life force to reawaken the cocoons, and the force works on elderly humans, too. When the leader of the aliens (Brian Dennehy) finds the old guys in the pool, he doesn't zap them with extraterrestrial weaponry. He smiles and tells them to go ahead and keep using the pool—but not to tell anyone else.

That's impossible. The old guys can't keep a secret long in a retirement home, and before long this literal fountain of youth has totally changed the lifestyles of the senior citizens. The old guys are played by three wonderful actors: Hume Cronyn, Don Ameche, and, best of all, Wilford Brimley, who has a way of investing each word with such simple truth that his dialogue seems more weighted, more real, than the other dialogue in the movie.

Brimley is sort of a ringleader. He is also a homespun philosopher, who goes fishing with his grandson and talks about the meaning of life and death. Others in the retirement home are not so serene, especially the stubborn Jack Gilford, who does not want to feel young and does not want to go swimming and thinks we should all be satisfied with the time allotted us on this planet. The introduction of the mysterious pool and its life force tests Gilford's friendships with the others, and it also puts strains on the marriage between Cronyn and Jessica Tandy. The scenes involving these characters are the best scenes in the movie.

But I also liked the treatment of the aliens, especially the Dennehy character, who observes that every 10,000 years he's entitled to do something silly. Dennehy eventuallly offers the old folks eternal life, under certain rather difficult conditions, and the way they consider his offer is rather thought-provoking—especially in the scenes between Brimley and his grandson. That's really the payoff of the movie, right there, but the ending is too drawn-out. We could also do without the romance between the boat's human captain (Steve Guttenberg) and the beautiful alien (Tahnee Welch). But the good parts in *Cocoon* are warm and sort of tender.

Code of Silence ★ ★ ★ 1/2
R, 102 m., 1985

Chuck Norris (Eddie Cusack), Henry Silva (Luis Comacho), Bert Remsen (Commander Kates), Mike Genovese (Tony Luna), Molly Hagan (Diana Luna), Nathan Davis (Felix Scalese), Ralph Roody (Cragie). Directed by Andy Davis and produced by Raymond Wagner. Screenplay by Michael Butler, Dennis Shryack, and Mike Gray.

Chuck Norris is still identified with a series of grade-zilch karate epics, but *Code of Silence* is a heavy-duty thriller—a slick, energetic movie with good performances and a lot of genuine human interest. It grabs you right at the start with a complicated triple-cross, and then it develops into a stylish urban action picture with sensational stunts. How sensational? How about an unfaked fight on top of a speeding elevated train, ending when both fighters dive off the train into the Chicago River? The stunts are great, but not surprising; Chuck Norris is famous for the stunts he features in all of his movies. What is surprising is the number of interesting characters in *Code of Silence.* The screenplay doesn't give us the usual cardboard clichés; there's a lot of human life here, in a series of carefully crafted performances. For once, here's a thriller that realizes we have to care about the characters before we care about their adventures.

Norris stars as a veteran Chicago vice cop named Cusack. He's a straight arrow, an honest cop that his partners call a "one-man army." As the film opens, he's setting up a drug bust, but a Latino gang beats him to it, stealing the money and the drugs and leaving a roomful of dead gangsters. That sets off a Chicago mob war between the Italian and Latino factions, and as bodies pile up in the streets, Cusack begins to worry about the daughter of a Mafia chieftain—a young artist named Diana (Molly Hagan) who wants nothing to do with her father's business, but finds she can't be a bystander. After an elaborate cat-and-mouse chase through the Loop, she's kidnapped and Cusack wants to save her.

Meanwhile, the movie has an interesting subplot about a tired veteran cop (Ralph Roody) who has mistakenly shot and killed a Latino kid while chasing some mobsters through a tenement. The veteran's young partner (Joseph Guzaldo) watches him plant a gun on the dead kid and claim that the shooting was in self-defense. It's up to the rookie, backed up by Cusack, to decide what he'll say at the departmental hearing.

The movie has a knack for taking obligatory scenes and making them more than routine. Among the small acting gems in the movie is the performance of Chicago actor Nathan Davis as Felix Scalese, a wrinkled, wise old Mafia godfather who sits on his yacht and counsels against a mob war—to no avail. Mike Genovese plays the mob chief whose daughter is kidnapped, and his first scene, as he wishes his wife a happy birthday while hurrying out the door to do battle, is wonderfully timed. Roody has some nice scenes as the tired old cop, hanging around a bar talking big and looking scared.

Holding all of the performances together is Norris's work as Cusack. Bearded, dressed in jeans for undercover street duty, and driving a battered old beater, Norris seems convincing as a cop—with, of course, the degree of heroic exaggeration you need in a role like this. By the end of the film, when he is reduced to functioning as a one-man army, we can't really believe the armored robot tank that he brings into action, but, what the hell, we accept it. Norris resembles Clint Eastwood in his insistence on the barest minimum of dialogue; there's a scene where he quietly, awkwardly tries to comfort the mobster's daughter, and it rings completely true. He also seems to be doing a lot of his own stunts, and although the credits list a lot of stuntmen and they were all obviously kept busy, it looks to me like that's really Norris on top of that elevated train.

The movie was directed by Andy Davis, who was a cinematographer on Haskell Wexler's 1968 Chicago film *Medium Cool,* and returned to some of the same locations to film this picture. Davis's directorial debut was the low-budget *Stony Island* (1977), which had moments of truth and insight but nothing like the assurance he shows this time; *Code of Silence* is a thriller so professional that it has the confidence to go for drama and humor as well as thrills. It may be the movie that moves Norris out of the ranks of dependable action heroes and makes him a major star.

The Color of Money ★ ★ ½

R, 119 m., 1986

Paul Newman (Eddie), Tom Cruise (Vincent), Mary Elizabeth Mastrantonio (Carmen), Helen Shaver (Janelle), John Turturro (Julian), Bill Cobbs (Orvis). Directed by Martin Scorsese and produced by Irving Axelrad and Barbara De Fina. Screenplay by Richard Price.

If this movie had been directed by someone else, I might have thought differently about it because I might not have expected so much. But *The Color of Money* is directed by Martin Scorsese, the most exciting American director now working, and it is not an exciting film. It doesn't have the electricity, the wound-up tension of his best work, and as a result I was too aware of the story marching by.

Scorsese may have thought of this film as a deliberately mainstream work, a conventional film with big names and a popular subject matter; perhaps he did it for that reason. But I believe he has the stubborn soul of an artist, and cannot put his heart where his heart will not go. And his heart, I believe, inclines toward creating new and completely personal stories about characters who have come to life in his imagination—not in finishing someone else's story, begun twenty-five years ago.

The Color of Money is not a sequel, exactly, but it didn't start with someone's fresh inspiration. It continues the story of "Fast Eddie" Felson, the character played by Paul Newman in Robert Rossen's *The Hustler* (1961). Now twenty-five years have passed. Eddie still plays pool, but not for money and not with the high-stakes, dangerous kinds of players who drove him from the game. He is a liquor salesman, a successful one, judging by the long, white Cadillac he takes so much pride in. One night, he sees a kid playing pool, and the kid is so good that Eddie's memories are stirred.

This kid is not simply good, however. He is also, Eddie observes, a "flake," and that gives him an idea: With Eddie as his coach, this kid could be steered into the world of big-money pool, where his flakiness would throw off the other players. They wouldn't be inclined to think he was for real. The challenge, obviously, is to train the kid so he can turn his flakiness on and off at will—so he can put the making of money above every other consideration, every other lure and temptation, in the pool hall.

The kid is named Vincent (Tom Cruise), and Eddie approaches him through Vincent's girlfriend, Carmen (Mary Elizabeth Mastrantonio). She is a few years older than Vince and a lot tougher. She likes the excitement of being around Vince and around pool hustling, but Eddie sees she's getting bored. He figures he can make a deal with the girl; together, they'll control Vince and steer him in the direction of money.

A lot of the early scenes setting up this situation are very well handled, especially the moments when Eddie uses Carmen to make Vince jealous and undermine his self-confidence. But of course these scenes work well, because they are the part of the story that is closest to Scorsese's own sensibility. In all of his best movies, we can see this same ambiguity about the role of women, who are viewed as objects of comfort and fear, creatures that his heroes desire and despise themselves for desiring. Think of the heroes of *Mean Streets*, *Taxi Driver*, and *Raging Bull* and their relationships with women, and you sense where the energy is coming from that makes Vincent love Carmen, and distrust her.

The movie seems less at home with the Newman character, perhaps because this character is largely complete when the movie begins. "Fast Eddie" Felson knows who he is, what he thinks, what his values are. There will be some moments of crisis in the story, as when he allows himself, to his shame, to be hustled at pool. But he is not going to change much during the story, and maybe he's not even free to change much, since his experiences are largely dictated by the requirements of the plot.

Here we come to the big weakness of *The Color of Money*: It exists in a couple of time-worn genres, and its story is generated out of standard Hollywood situations. First we have the basic story of the old pro and the talented youngster. Then we have the story of the kid who wants to knock the master off the throne. Many of the scenes in this movie are almost formula, despite the energy of Scorsese's direction and the good performances. They come in the same places we would expect them to come in a movie by anybody else, and they contain the same events.

Eventually, everything points to the ending of the film, which we know will have to be a showdown between Eddie and Vince, between Newman and Cruise. The fact that the movie does not provide that payoff scene is a disappointment. Perhaps Scorsese thought the movie was "really" about the personalities of his two heroes, and that it was unnecessary to show who would win in a showdown. Perhaps, but then why plot the whole story with genre formulas and only bail out at the end? If you bring a gun onstage in the first act, you've gotta shoot somebody by the third.

The side stories are where the movie really lives. There is a warm, bittersweet relationship between Newman and his long-time girlfriend, a bartender wonderfully played by Helen Shaver. And the greatest energy in the story is generated between Cruise and Mastrantonio—who, with her hard edge and her inbred cynicism, keeps the kid from ever feeling really sure of her. It's a shame that even the tension of their relationship is allowed to evaporate in the closing scenes, where Cruise and the girl stand side by side and seem to speak from the same mind, as if she were a standard movie girlfriend and not a real original.

Watching Newman is always interesting in this movie. He has been a true star for many years, but sometimes that star quality has been thrown away. Scorsese has always been the kind of director who lets his camera stay on an actor's face, who looks deeply into them and tries to find the shadings that reveal their originality. In many of Newman's close-ups in this movie, he shows an enormous power, a concentration and focus of his essence as an actor.

Newman, of course, had veto power over who would make this movie (because how could they make it without him?), and his instincts were sound in choosing Scorsese. Maybe the problems started with the story, when Newman or somebody decided that there had to be a young man in the picture; the introduction of the Cruise character opens the door for all of the preordained teacher-pupil clichés, when perhaps they should have just stayed with Newman, and let him be at the center of the story. Then Newman's character would have been free (as the Robert De Niro characters have been free in other Scorsese films) to follow his passions, hungers, fears, and desires wherever they led him—instead of simply following the story down a well-traveled path.

The Color Purple ★ ★ ★ ★
PG-13, 155 m., 1985

Danny Glover (Mister), Whoopi Goldberg (Celie), Margaret Avery (Shug Avery), Oprah Winfrey (Sofia), Willard Pugh (Harpo), Akosua Busia (Nettie), Adolph Caesar (Old Mister), Rae Dawn Chong (Squeak), Dana Ivey (Miss Millie). Directed by Steven Spielberg and produced by Kathleen Kennedy, Frank Marshall, Quincy Jones, and Spielberg. Screenplay by Menno Meyjes.

There is a moment in Steven Spielberg's *The Color Purple* when a woman named Celie smiles and smiles and smiles. That was the moment when I knew this movie was going to be as good as it seemed, was going to keep the promise it made by daring to tell Celie's story. It is not a story that would seem easily suited to the movies.

Celie is a black woman who grows up in the rural South in the early decades of this century, in a world that surrounds her with cruelty. When we first see her, she is a child, running through fields of purple flowers with her sister. But then she comes into clear view, and we see that she is pregnant, and we learn that her father has made her pregnant, and will give away the child as he has done with a previous baby.

By the time Celie is married—to a cruel, distant charmer she calls only "Mister"—she will have lost both her children and the ability to bear children, will have been separated from the sister who is the only person on Earth who loves her, and will be living in servitude to a man who flaunts his love for another woman.

And yet this woman will endure, and in the end she will prevail. *The Color Purple* is not the story of her suffering but of her victory, and by the end of her story this film had moved me and lifted me up as few films have. It is a great, warm, hard, unforgiving, triumphant movie, and there is not a scene that does not shine with the love of the people who made it.

The film is based on the novel by Alice Walker, who told Celie's story through a series of letters, some never sent, many never received, most addressed to God. The letters are her way of maintaining sanity in a world where few others ever cared to listen to her. The turning point in the book, and in the movie, comes after Celie's husband brings home the fancy woman he has been crazy about for years—a pathetic, alcoholic juke-joint singer named Shug Avery, who has been ravaged by life yet still has an indestructible beauty.

Shug's first words to Celie are: "You are as ugly as sin." But as Shug moves into the house, and Celie obediently caters to her husband's lover, Shug begins to see the beauty in Celie, and there is a scene where they kiss, and Celie learns for the first time that sex can include tenderness, that she can dare to love herself. A little later, Celie looks in Shug's eyes and allows herself to smile, and we know that Celie didn't think she had a pretty smile until Shug told her so. That is the central moment in the movie.

The relationship between Shug and Celie is a good deal toned down from the book, which deals in greater detail with sexual matters. Steven Spielberg, who made the movie, is more concerned with the whole world of Celie's life than he is with her erotic education. We meet many members of the rural black community that surrounds Celie. We meet a few of the local whites, too, but they are bit players in this drama.

Much more important are people like Sofia (Oprah Winfrey), an indomitable force of nature who is determined to marry Harpo, Mister's son by a first marriage. When we first see Sofia, hurrying down the road with everyone trying to keep up, she looks like someone who could never be stopped. But she is stopped, after she tells the local white mayor to go to hell, and the saddest story in the movie is the way her spirit is forever dampened by the beating and jailing she receives. Sofia is counterpoint to Celie: She is wounded by life, Celie is healed.

Shug Avery is another fascinating character, played by Margaret Avery as a sweet-faced, weary woman who sings a little bit like Billie Holiday and has long since lost all of her illusions about men and everything else. Her contact with Celie redeems her; by giving her somebody to be nice to, it allows her to get in touch with what is still nice inside herself.

Mister, whose real name is Albert, is played by Danny Glover, who was the field hand in *Places in the Heart*. He is an evil man, his evil tempered to some extent by his ignorance; perhaps he does not fully understand how cruel he is to Celie. Certainly he seems outwardly pleasant. He smiles and jokes and sings, and then hurts Celie to the quick—not so much with his physical blows as when he refuses to let her see the letters she hopes are coming from her long-lost sister.

And then, at the center of the movie, Celie is played by Whoopi Goldberg in one of the most amazing debut performances in movie history. Goldberg has a fearsomely difficult job to do, enlisting our sympathy for a woman who is rarely allowed to speak, to dream, to interact with the lives around her. Spielberg breaks down the wall of silence around her, however, by giving her narrative monologues in which she talks about her life and reads the words in the letters she composes.

The wonderful performances in this movie are contained in a screenplay that may take some of the smoking edges off Walker's novel, but keeps all the depth and dimension. The world of Celie and the others is created so forcibly in this movie that their corner of the South becomes one of those movie places—like Oz, like Tara, like Casablanca—that lay claim to their own geography in our imaginations. The affirmation at the end of the film is so joyous that this is one of the few movies in a long time that inspires tears of happiness, and earns them.

Colors ★ ★ ★

R, 120 m., 1988 ✓

(See related Film Clip, p. 769.)

Sean Penn (Danny McGavin), Robert Duvall (Bob Hodges), Maria Conchita Alonso (Louisa Gomez), Randy Brooks (Ron Delaney), Grand Bush (Larry Sylvester), Don Cheadle (Rocket). Directed by Dennis Hopper and produced by Robert H. Solo. Screenplay by Michael Schiffer.

There are many good moments in *Colors*, but the one I will remember the longest is in the scene where a group of Los Angeles gang members is trying to explain why the gang is so important to them. Talking to a couple of cops, they describe the feeling of belonging—of feeling for the first time in their lives that they were part of a "family" that cared for them and was ready to die for them.

The product of their family is, of course, tragic. Their gang deals in drugs, defends its turf, and uses murder to enforce its authority. Sometimes innocent bystanders are shot dead in the middle of a party, or while standing on their own lawns. Because the gangs represent a good deal of what little authority and structure survives in their neighborhoods, they help to set the tone for a segment of society—a tone of desperation, despair, and reckless, doomed grandiose gestures. Because there are so many gangs, so well-entrenched, the police are all but helpless to bring about any fundamental change in the situation.

That helplessness of the police is the central subject of Dennis Hopper's *Colors,* which stars Sean Penn and Robert Duvall as two cops, one newly assigned to the gang unit, one a veteran. But what makes *Colors* special is not the portraits of the cops, but the movie's willingness to look inside the gangs. Almost without exception, American movies about gangs have either romanticized them in fantasies (*West Side Story, Warriors*) or viewed them from outside, as a monolithic, dangerous unit. This movie tries to understand a little of the tragic gang dynamic, to explain why in some devastated inner-city neighborhoods they seem to offer the only way for young men to find power and status.

The story of the two cops, on the other hand, is not exactly new. We have the street-smart veteran (Duvall), who has a realistic assessment of the situation and knows that he sometimes has to bend the rules to get results. And then we have the hotheaded younger cop (Penn), who has a simplistic us-against-them mentality, and wants to bust heads and make arrests. That leads into scenes where the cops come dangerously close to losing their street authority because they're fighting with each other instead of presenting a unified front to the gangs.

If the situation is not new, it is redeemed by the performances. Robert Duvall and Sean Penn are two of the best actors in America, bringing a flavor and authority to their roles that make them specific. A lot of their acting in this movie is purely physical, as when Penn disarms, frisks, and handcuffs a suspect, seeming sure and confident at every moment. Other moments, when the two actors are talking to each other, contain that electricity that makes you think these words are being said for the first time.

The plot involves the attempts of the two cops to come to terms with a gang that is involved, we discover, in dealing drugs. During the course of the film they follow the brief life of the younger brother of one of the gang members, who seems for a time to have a chance to escape gang society. And there is a brief, doomed romance between Penn and Maria Conchita Alonso, as a Chicano who loves him but cannot reconcile his status as a cop and her perception of how cops like Penn treat her people.

The movie has some flaws. The story is needlessly complicated, and at times we're not sure who is who on the gang side. And some of the action seems repetitious; Hopper, trying to show the routine, makes it feel routine. But *Colors* is a special movie: Not just a police thriller, but a movie that has researched gangs and given some thought to what it wants to say about them.

Coma ★ ★ ★

PG, 113 m., 1978

Genevieve Bujold (Dr. Susan Wheeler), Michael Douglas (Dr. Mark Bellows), Elizabeth Ashley (Mrs. Emerson), Rip Torn (Dr. George), Richard Widmark (Dr. Harris), Lois Chiles (Nancy Greenly). Directed by Michael Crichton and produced by Martin Erlichman. Screenplay by Crichton.

They're always writing about the great movie kisses, and the great movie chase scenes, and the great movie saloon brawls. But what about the great movie surgical incisions? Just about every movie even remotely involved with medicine has at least one moment when the surgeon says "Scalpel, please," and chicken-hearts like me close our eyes.

A lot of movie fans, though, seem to live for the moment of incision. *Coma* must be a godsend for them; it has more hypodermic needles than your average junkie movie, and more kidneys and livers than your local meat counter. In the midst of the gruesome and the gory, though, there's a pretty good thriller here. *Coma* was written by Robin Moore, a doctor, and directed by Michael Crichton, who graduated from Harvard Medical School, and it takes place almost entirely within a hospital. The feeling of reality is inescapable, as when a veteran anesthetist lectures two students on what can go wrong during an operation, and we get the creepiest feeling that those very things are about to go wrong.

There seems to be a lot wrong with the surgical procedures, in fact, at "Boston Memorial," the (thank God) fictional hospital where *Coma* is set. Just in the last year, twelve perfectly healthy young people have gone into irreversible comas during minor operations. When the best friend of a spunky young resident doctor (Genevieve Bujold) goes into a coma, that's one too many. Bujold tries to find a pattern in the deaths, which involve many different doctors, anesthetists, and operations . . . but always the same operating room.

Everybody thinks she's crazy. Michael Douglas does. He's her boyfriend, but if he can't keep her in line he'll lose his shot at becoming chief resident. Richard Widmark does. He's the chief-of-staff, constantly on the phone to senators and presidents. The hospital's resident shrink does. And so does the guy hired to kill Bujold (she outsmarts him in an especially creepy scene in the anatomy department's cold room, burying him under corpses).

Movies like this have a way of turning silly, of producing a lot of unintentional laughs. But *Coma* really works pretty well, partly because Crichton is a competent technician who knows his subject matter first hand, but mostly because of Genevieve Bujold. She's a fine craftsman of an actress, playing her big scenes straight and seriously, selling us the material by getting so involved in it herself.

Thirty years ago, the Bujold role might have been played by a man. Now we seem to have entered an era of big female roles, and so the doctor's a woman. That gives the movie an opportunity to add one more interesting level to the ready-made thriller material: No one will quite take her seriously. The psychiatrist says she's hysterical because of the death of her friend. "She's a little paranoid," Douglas offhandedly explains to Widmark. Women have a tendency to get all emotional, y'know.

When she comes up with absolute proof that Operating Room No. 8 is about as safe as an airplane crash, all Douglas does is call the hospital, presumably so the fellows with the butterfly nets can hurry over. Such oversights have their advantages, though, giving us that terrific final sequence with Bujold, drugged and helpless, being rolled into the fatal operating room—desperately trying to get Douglas to believe her *now*, anyway . . . while Widmark pronounces those magic words, "Nurse? Scalpel, please . . ."

Come Back to the 5 & Dime, Jimmy Dean, Jimmy Dean ★ ★ ★

PG, 109 m., 1982

Sandy Dennis (Mona), Cher (Sissy), Karen Black (Joanne), Sudie Bond (Juanita), Kathy Bates (Stella Mae), Marta Heflin (Edna). Directed by Robert Altman and produced by Scott Bushnell. Screenplay by Ed Graczyk.

If Robert Altman hadn't directed this movie, the reviews would have described it as Altmanesque. It's a mixture of the bizarre and the banal, a slice of lives that could never have been led, a richly textured mixture of confessions, obsessions, and surprises.

The movie takes place in a worn-out Woolworth's in a small Texas town not far from the locations where James Dean shot *Giant* in 1955. The story begins twenty years later, at a reunion of the local James Dean fan club; the members swore a solemn vow to get together after two decades, and they drift in one by one, greeted by the tired waitress who's still on duty. There's Sandy Dennis, the flaky, visionary local woman who's convinced that she bore a son by James Dean. Then Cher walks in—looking not like the glamorous Cher of television, but like a small-town sexpot unsure of her appeal. The last arrival is Karen Black, who drove in all the way from California, and is not surprised when nobody recognizes her at first.

The fan club members and a few local good ol' girls join in a long afternoon of memories, nostalgia, self-analysis, accusation, shocking revelations, and anger, while heat-lightning flickers offscreen. And their memories trigger flashbacks to the time twenty years earlier when the proximity of James Dean served as a catalyst in all of their lives, giving some the courage to realize their dreams and others, the timid ones, the courage at least to dream them.

Jimmy Dean was a Broadway play before it was a movie, and Altman, who directed it first on stage, stays pretty close here to Ed Graczyk's script. He works just as closely with David Gropman's extraordinary stage set, on which the movie was shot. Gropman has actually created two dime stores, one a mirror-image of the other. They're separated by a two-way mirror, so that at times we're looking at the reflection of the "front" store, and at other times, the glass is transparent and we see the second store. Altman uses the front as the present and the back as the past, and there are times when a foreground image will dissolve into a background flashback. In an age of sophisticated optical effects, this sort of dissolve looks routine—until you learn that Altman isn't using opticals, he's actually shooting through the two-way mirror. His visual effects sometimes require fancy offscreen footwork for his actors to be in two places during the same shot.

Jimmy Dean's script also requires some fancy footwork, as we reel beneath a series of predictable revelations in the last twenty minutes. This is not a great drama, but two things make the movie worth seeing: Altman's visual inventiveness and the interesting performances given by everyone in the cast. Although Sandy Dennis and Karen Black in many ways have more difficult roles, Cher is the one I watched the most because her performance here is a revelation. After years and years of giving us "Cher," she gives us a new character here, in a fine performance that creates sympathy for a sexpot who doubts her own sensuality.

Coming Home ★ ★ ★ ★
R, 127 m., 1978

Jane Fonda (Sally Hyde), Jon Voight (Luke Martin), Bruce Dern (Bob Hyde), Robert Carradine (Bill Munson), Penelope Milford (Vi Munson), Robert Ginty (Sergeant Mobley). Directed by Hal Ashby and produced by Jerome Hellman. Screenplay by Waldo Salt and Robert C. Jones.

Sally Hyde makes an ideal wife for a Marine: She is faithful, friendly, sexy in a quiet way, and totally in agreement with her husband's loyalties. Since his basic loyalty is to the Marine Corps, that presents difficulties at times. ("You know what they tell them," a girl friend says. "'If the Marine Corps had wanted you to have a wife, they would have issued you one.'") Still, she's reasonably happy in the spring of 1968, as her husband prepares to ship out for a tour of duty in Vietnam. There's every chance he'll get a promotion over there. And the war, of course, is for a just cause, isn't it? It has to be, or we wouldn't be fighting it.

That is the Sally Hyde at the beginning of Hal Ashby's *Coming Home*, an extraordinarily moving film. The Sally Hyde at the end of the film—about a year later—is a different person, confused in her loyalties, not sure of her beliefs, awakened to new feelings within her. She hasn't turned into a political activist or a hippie or any of those other radical creatures of the late 1960s. But she is no longer going to be able to accept anything simply because her husband, or anybody else, says it's true.

Coming Home considers a great many subjects, but its heart lies with that fundamental change within Sally Hyde. She is played by Jane Fonda as the kind of character you somehow wouldn't expect the outspoken, intelligent Fonda to play. She's reserved, maybe a little shy, of average intelligence and tastes. She was, almost inevitably, a cheerleader in high school. She doesn't seem to have a lot of ideas or opinions. Perhaps she even doubts that it's necessary for her to have opinions—her husband can have them for her.

When her husband (Bruce Dern) goes off to fight the war, though, she finds herself on her own for the first time in her life. There's no home, no high school, no marriage, no Officers' Club to monitor her behavior. And she finds herself stepping outside the role of a wife and doing . . . well, not strange things, but things that are a little unusual for her. Like buying a used sports car. Like renting a house at the beach. Like volunteering to work in the local Veterans' Administration hospital. That's where she meets Luke (Jon Voight), so filled with his pain, anger, and frustration. She knew him vaguely before; he was the captain of the football team at her high school. He went off to fight the war, came home paralyzed from the waist down, and now, strapped on his stomach to a table with wheels, uses canes to propel himself furiously down hospital corridors. In time, he will graduate to a wheelchair. He has ideas about Vietnam that are a little different from her husband's.

Coming Home is uncompromising in its treatment of Luke and his fellow paraplegics, and if that weren't so the opening sequences of the film wouldn't affect us so deeply. Luke literally runs into Sally on their first meeting, and his urine bag spills on the floor between them. That's the sort of embarrassment he has to learn to live with—and she too, if she is serious about being a volunteer.

She is, she finds. Luke in the early days is

a raging troublemaker, and the hospital staff often finds it simpler just to tranquilize him with medication. Zombies are hardly any bother at all. Sally tries to talk to Luke, gets to know him, invites him for dinner. He begins to focus his anger away from himself and toward the war; he grows calmer, regains maturity. One day, softly, he tells her: "You know there's not an hour goes by that I don't think of making love with you."

They do eventually make love, confronting his handicap in a scene of great tenderness, beauty, and tact. It is the first time Sally has been unfaithful. But it isn't really an affair; she remains loyal to her husband, and both she and Luke know their relationship will have to end when her husband returns home. He does, too soon, having accidentally wounded himself, and discovers from Army Intelligence what his wife has been up to. The closing scenes show the film at its most uncertain, as if Ashby and his writers weren't sure in their minds how the Dern character should react. And so Dern is forced into scenes of unfocused, confused anger before the film's not very satisfying ending. It's too bad the last twenty minutes don't really work, though, because for most of its length *Coming Home* is great filmmaking and great acting.

And it is also greatly daring, since it confronts the relationship between Fonda and Voight with unusual frankness—and with emotional tenderness and subtlety that is, if anything, even harder to portray.

Consider. The film has three difficulties to confront in this relationship, and it handles all three honestly. The first is Voight's paralysis: "You aren't one of these women that gets turned on by gimps?" he asks. She is not. The second is the sexual and emotional nature of their affair, an area of enormous dramatic danger, which the movie handles in such a straightforward way, and with such an obvious display of affection between the characters, that we accept and understand.

The third is the nature of the *friendship* between Voight and Fonda, and here *Coming Home* works on a level that doesn't depend on such plot elements as the war, the husband, the paralysis, the time and place, or anything else. Thinking about the movie, we realize that men and women have been so polarized in so many films, have been made into so many varieties of sexual antagonists or lovers or rivals or other couples, that the mutual human friendship of these two characters comes as something of a revelation.

The Competition ★ ★ ★

PG, 125 m., 1981

Richard Dreyfuss (Paul Dietrich), Amy Irving (Heidi Schoonover), Lee Remick (Greta Vandemann), Sam Wanamaker (Erskine). Directed and written by Joel Oliansky and produced by William Sackheim.

The Competition is a cornball, romantic, old-fashioned, utterly predictable movie—and enormously entertaining. It's the kind of movie where you speculate on what's going to happen next, and usually you're right. When you're wrong, somehow *that's* predictable, too, as in the big international piano competition that ends the movie. We think we know who's going to win, but the surprise ending is a built-in convention of this kind of movie.

The movie's about a big international competition in San Francisco among six world-class pianists who are fighting for a $20,000 first prize and a two-year concert contract. The movie has two counterpoints to its main theme. One involves a love affair between two of the finalists, Richard Dreyfuss and Amy Irving. The other one, ridiculous but forgivable, involves a Russian piano teacher who defects to the United States, creating an international incident that causes the competition to be postponed a week.

Both of these story lines are somehow time-honored, once we realize that *The Competition* is not intended as a deadly serious treatise on big-league pianists, but as an offbeat love story. Dreyfuss and Amy Irving have a real charm and rapport as the two lovers, especially in the scenes where they argue that love has absolutely no place in a piano competition—not if it's being used as a psychological weapon to undermine one of the competitors. That's exactly what Amy Irving's piano coach (Lee Remick) thinks the dastardly Dreyfuss is trying to do.

There are three areas that the movie gets into, superficially but earnestly. One has to do with the competition itself—with the idea of artists competing with one another. Another has to do with relationships between men and women: Will the love affair between Amy and Richard be destroyed if she should win? How will his fragile male ego be able to take that? The third has to do with the idea of the artist's career, and here Remick has several good scenes and intelligently written speeches, as she tries to explain the realities of a concert career to Irving.

There is, of course, a lot of music in this movie, in addition to all the scenes of romance, backstage butterflies, international intrigue, and self-examination. And *The Competition* does an extraordinary job of persuading us that the actors are really playing their own pianos. They're not. Stay for the credits if you want the names of the real pianists on the sound track. But Dreyfuss, Irving, and the rest really *look* as if they're playing, and it took them four months of daily rehearsal to learn to fake it so well.

The Competition isn't a great movie, but it's a warm, entertaining one. It has the nerve to tell a story about serious, interesting, complicated people, who are full of surprises, because Joel Oliansky, the writer-director, has thought about them and cared enough about them to let their personalities lead him down unexpected avenues. There's only one major lapse: the inclusion, after two hours of great piano compositions, of Lalo Schifrin's dreadful song, "People Alone," sung by Randy Crawford over the end titles as if none of those great composers should be allowed to rest in peace.

Conan the Barbarian ★ ★ ★
R, 129 m., 1982

Arnold Schwarzenegger (Conan), James Earl Jones (Thulsa Doom), Max von Sydow (King Osric), Sandahl Bergman (Valeria), Ben Davidson (Rexor). Directed by John Milius and produced by Buzz Feitshans and Rafaella de Laurentiis. Screenplay by Milius and Oliver Stone.

Not since Bambi's mother was killed has there been a cannier movie for kids than *Conan the Barbarian.* It's not supposed to be just a kids' movie, of course, and I imagine a lot of other moviegoers will like it—I liked a lot of it myself, and with me, a few broadswords and leather jerkins go a long way. But *Conan* is a perfect fantasy for the alienated preadolescent. Consider: Conan's parents are brutally murdered by the evil Thulsa Doom, which gets *them* neatly out of the way. The child is chained to the Wheel of Pain, where he goes around in circles for years, a metaphor for grade school. The kid builds muscles so terrific he could be a pro football player. One day he is set free. He teams up with Subotai the Mongol, who is an example of the classic literary type—the Best Pal—and with Valeria, Queen of Thieves, who is a *real* best pal.

Valeria is everything you could ever hope for in a woman, if you are a muscle-bound preadolescent, of course. She is lanky and muscular and a great sport, and she can ride, throw, stab, fence, and climb ropes as good as a boy. Sometimes she engages in sloppy talk about love, but you can tell she's only kidding, and she quickly recovers herself with coverup talk about loyalty and betrayal—emotions more central to Conan's experience and maturity.

With the Mongol and the Queen at his side, Conan ventures forth to seek the evil Thulsa Doom and gain revenge for the death of his parents. This requires him to journey to the mysterious East, where he learns a little quick kung-fu, and then to the mountainside where Doom rules his slave-priests from the top of his Mountain of Power. There are a lot of battles and a few interesting nights at crude wayside inns and, in general, nothing to tax the unsophisticated. *Conan the Barbarian* is, in fact, a very nearly perfect visualization of the Conan legend, of Robert E. Howard's tale of a superman who lived beyond the mists of time, when people were so pure, straightforward, and simple that a 1930s pulp magazine writer could write about them at one cent a word and not have to pause to puzzle out their motivations.

The movie's casting is ideal. Arnold Schwarzenegger is inevitably cast as Conan, and Sandahl Bergman as Valeria. Physically, they look like artist's conceptions of themselves. What's nice is that they also create entertaining versions of their characters; they, and the movie, are not without humor and a certain quiet slyness that is never allowed to get out of hand. Schwarzenegger's slight Teutonic accent is actually even an advantage, since Conan lived, of course, in the eons before American accents.

The movie is a triumph of production design, set decoration, special effects and makeup. At a time when most of the big box-office winners display state-of-the-art technology, *Conan* ranks right up there with the best. Ron Cobb, the sometime underground cartoonist who did the production design on this film (and on *Alien*) supervises an effort in which the individual frames actually do look like blowups of panels from the Marvel Comics "Conan" books. Since this Conan could have so easily looked ridiculous, that's an accomplishment.

But there is one aspect of the film I'm disturbed by. It involves the handling of Thulsa Doom, the villain. He is played here by the fine black actor James Earl Jones, who brings power and conviction to a role that seems inspired in equal parts by Hitler, Jim Jones, and Goldfinger. But when Conan and Doom meet at the top of the Mountain of Power, it was, for me, a rather unsettling image to see this Nordic superman confronting a black, and when Doom's head was sliced off and contemptuously thrown down the flight of stairs by the muscular blonde Conan, I found myself thinking that Leni Reifenstahl could have directed the scene, and that Goebbels might have applauded it.

Am I being too sensitive? Perhaps. But when Conan appeared in the pulps of the 1930s, the character suggested in certain unstated ways the same sort of Nordic superrace myths that were being peddled in Germany. These days we are more innocent again, and Conan is seen as a pure fantasy, like his British cousin, Tarzan, or his contemporary, Flash Gordon. My only reflection is that, at a time when there are *no* roles for blacks in Hollywood if they are not named Richard Pryor, it is a little unsettling to see a great black actor assigned to a role in which he is beheaded by a proto-Nordic avenger.

That complaint aside, I enjoyed *Conan.* Faithful readers will know I'm not a fan of Sword & Sorcery movies, despite such adornments as Sandahl Bergman—having discovered some time ago that heaving bosoms may be great, but a woman with a lively intelligence and a sly wit is even greater.

The problem with *Conan* is the problem with all S & S movies. After the initial premise (which usually involves revenge) is established, we suspect there's little to look forward to *except* the sets, special effects, costumes, makeup, locations, action, and surprise entrances. Almost by definition, these movies exclude the possibility of interesting, complex characters. I'd love to see them set loose an intelligent, questing, humorous hero in one of these prehistoric sword-swingers. Someone at least as smart as, say, Alley Oop.

Conan the Destroyer ★ ★ ★

PG, 103 m., 1984

Arnold Schwarzenegger (Conan), Grace Jones (Zula), Wilt Chamberlain (Bombaata), Mako (The Wizard), Tracey Walter (Malak), Sarah Douglas (Queen). Directed by Richard Fleischer and produced by Raffaella de Laurentiis. Screenplay by Stanley Mann.

What you can see in *Conan the Destroyer,* if you look closely, is the beginning of a movie dynasty. This is the film that points the way to an indefinite series of Conan adventures—one that could even replace Tarzan in supplying our need for a noble savage in the movies. Tarzan was more or less stuck in Africa; Conan can venture wherever his sword and sorcery can take him. The first Conan movie, *Conan the Barbarian,* was a dark and gloomy fantasy about the shadows of prehistory. This second film is sillier, funnier, and more entertaining. It doesn't take place before the dawn of time, but instead in that shadowy period of movie history occupied by queens and monsters, swords and castles, warriors and fools. There's more Prince Valiant and King Arthur than *Quest for Fire.*

And Conan is defined a little differently, too. He doesn't take himself as seriously. He's not just a muscle-bound superman, but a superstitious half-savage who gets very nervous in the presence of magic. Arnold Schwarzenegger, who plays Conan again, does an interesting job of defining his pop hero: Like James Bond, Conan now stands a little aside from the incessant action around him, and observes it with a bit of relish. The story this time involves the usual nonsense. Conan is recruited by an imperious queen (Sarah Douglas, looking vampirish) to take a virgin princess (Olivia D'Abo) on a mission to an enchanted crystal palace guarded by a monster, etc. He will be joined on his quest by the head of the queen's palace guard (Wilt Chamberlain). And along the way he rescues a savage woman warrior (Grace Jones) and earns her undying gratitude.

Let's face it. The Conan series does not require extraordinary acting ability, although Schwarzenegger provides a sound professional center to the story, and the film would be impossible if he couldn't carry off Conan. The characters around him, however, are basically atmosphere, and that frees the filmmakers to abandon the usual overexposed Hollywood character actors and go for really interesting types like Chamberlain and Jones. And Grace Jones is really sensational. She has all the flash and fire of a great rock stage star, and it fits perfectly into her role as Zula, the fierce fighter. Sarah Douglas provides the necessary haughty iciness as the queen, Chamberlain gives a good try at the thankless role of the turncoat guard, and only D'Abo is a disappointment: Her princess seems to have drifted in from a teen-age sitcom.

Conan the Destroyer is more entertaining than the first Conan movie, more cheerful, and it probably has more sustained action, including a good sequence in the glass palace. Compared to the first Conan movie, which was rated R for some pretty gruesome violence, this one is milder. That's part of the idea, I think: They're repackaging Conan as your friendly family barbarian.

Continental Divide ★ ★ ★

PG, 103 m., 1981

John Belushi (Souchak), Blair Brown (Nell), Allen Goorwitz (Howard), Carlin Glynn (Sylvia), Tony Ganios (Possum), Val Avery (Yablonowitz). Directed by Michael Apted and produced by Bob Larson. Written by Lawrence Kasdan.

Here is a movie that is supposed to be about a newspaperman—a columnist for the *Chicago Sun-Times,* in fact—who is like no newspaperman I know, but exactly like every newspaperman would like to be. In my opinion, that makes it accurate. *Continental Divide* stars John Belushi as the journalist, obviously inspired by Mike Royko. He likes to walk along the lakeshore with the towers of the city outlined behind him against the lonely sky at dusk, a notebook stuck in his pocket and a cigarette stuck in his mug, on his way to rendezvous with stoolie aldermen and beautiful women.

The movie takes this character, played by Belushi with a surprising tenderness and charm, and engages him in an absolute minimum of newspaper work before spiriting him off to the Rocky Mountains for what the movie is *really* about, a romance with an eagle expert. The movie opens as if it's going to be a tough Chicago slice-of-life, with Belushi getting tips from an insider about city graft and payola, but then the columnist is beaten up by a couple of cops on an alderman's payroll. The managing editor suggests this might be a good time for Belushi to spend a few weeks out of town, and so the columnist heads for the Rockies to get an interview with a mysterious and beautiful woman (Blair Brown) who has generated worldwide curiosity by becoming a hermit to spy on the habits of bald eagles.

The whole center section of the movie takes place in the mountains, and if nothing very original happens there, we are at least reminded of several beloved movie clichés that seemed, until this film, to belong exclusively in the comedies that Katharine Hepburn and Spencer Tracy used to make together. After the city slicker Belushi crawls wearily up a mountainside (losing his booze and cigarette supply in the process), he meets the beautiful birdwatcher and falls instantly in love. She's having none of it. She's one of those independent women who marches from crag to aerie in her L.L. Bean boots and designer wardrobe.

Because Belushi's grizzled mountain guide already has disappeared down the mountain, the two of them are destined to spend the next two weeks together in a cabin. This sets up a classic situation in which the girl talks tough but starts to fall for the big lunkhead. And there are the obligatory switches on male-female roles as Brown climbs mountains and Belushi stays home and makes goulash. Occasionally, a mountain lion attacks.

This all sounds predictable, of course, and yet this movie's predictability is one of its charms. It's rare these days to find a film that is basically content to be about a colorful man and an eccentric woman who are opposites and yet fall madly in love. It is even rarer to find a movie cast with performers who are offbeat and appealing and do not have obvious matinee-idol appeal. Belushi's character in this movie is quite unlike his self-destructive slob in *National Lampoon's Animal House;* it shows the gentleness and vulnerability that made him so appealing in some of Second City's quieter skits. Brown is also a revelation. She has been in several other movies without attracting a great deal of attention, but here she is unmistakably and wonderfully a star, a tousled-haired, big-eyed warm person who does not project sex appeal so much as warmth and humor. In other words, she has terrific sex appeal.

One of Belushi's special qualities was always an underlying innocence. Maybe he created his Blues Brothers persona in reaction to it. He's an innocent in this movie, an idealist who's a little kid at heart and who wins the love of Brown not by seducing her but by appealing to her protective qualities. That's the secret of the character's appeal. We're cheering for the romance because Belushi makes us protective, too, and we want him to have a woman who'd be good for him.

What about the movie's view of journalism? It's really just a romanticized backdrop, *The Front Page* crossed with "Lou Grant" and modernized with a computerized newsroom. The newspaper scenes in the movie were shot on location in the *Sun-Times* features department, and one of the quietly amusing things about *Continental Divide*'s view of newspaper life is that in the movie it's more sedate and disciplined than the real thing. In the "real" *Sun-Times* features department, there's a lot of informality and chaos and good-natured confusion and people shouting at one another and eating lunch at their desks. In the movie, the extras (recruited from the *Sun-Times* staff) forget about real life and sit dutifully at their video display terminals, grinding out the news.

The newspaper's managing editor is played by Allen Goorwitz, a gifted character actor who usually plays manic overcompensators, but who this time is reasonable, calm, civilized, compassionate, and understanding, just like my boss. The movie's city of Chicago is populated by colorful old newsstand operators, muggers who apologize before taking your watch, and city council bosses who make sure their shady deals don't get into the official transcript. The newsies and muggers are fiction. The movie itself is fun: goofy, softhearted, fussy, sometimes funny, and with the sort of happy ending that columnists like to find for their stories and hardly ever find themselves.

The Conversation ★ ★ ★ ★

PG, 113 m., 1974

Gene Hackman (Harry Caul), John Cazale (Stan), Allen Garfield (Bernie Moran), Frederic Forrest (Mark), Cindy Williams (Ann), Michael Higgins (Paul). Directed by Francis Ford Coppola and produced by Fred Roos. Screenplay by Coppola.

As he is played by Gene Hackman in *The Conversation*, an expert wiretapper named Harry Caul is one of the most affecting and tragic characters in the movies; he ranks with someone like Willy Loman in *Death of a Salesman* or the pathetic captives of the middle class in John Cassavetes's *Faces*. Hackman is such a fine actor in so many different roles, from his action roles like *The French Connection* to this introverted, frightened, paranoid who is "the best bugger on the West Coast." He is, indeed, maybe the best wiretapper in the country, but he hasn't gone back to the East Coast since a bugging assignment there led to the deaths of three people. He tries to force himself not to care. He goes to confession and begs forgiveness for not paying for some newspapers, but not for bringing about a murder—because the murder, you see, was none of his business. He is only a professional. He does his job and asks no questions: doesn't *want* to know the answers.

His latest job has been a tactical masterpiece. The assignment: Bug a noon-hour conversation between two young people as they walk in a crowded plaza. He does it by tailing them with a guy who's wired for sound, and also by aiming parabolic microphones at them from buildings overlooking the plaza. This gives him three imperfect recordings of their conversation, which he can electronically marry into one fairly good tape. He is a good craftsman, and, although the film doesn't belabor his techniques, it does show us enough of how bugging is done to give us a cynical education.

It's a movie not so much about bugging as about the man who does it, and Gene Hackman's performance is a great one. He does not want to get involved (whenever he says anything like that, it sounds in italics)—but he does. After he has recorded the conversation, he plays it again and again and becomes convinced that a death may result from it, if he turns the tape in. The ways in which he interprets the tape, and the different nuances of meaning it seems to contain at different moments, remind us of Antonioni's *Blow Up*. Both movies are about the unreality of what seems real: We have here in our hands a document that is maddeningly concrete and yet refuses to reveal its meaning. And the meaning seems to be a matter of life and death.

The movie is a thriller with a shocking twist at the end, but it is also a character study. Hackman plays a craftsman who has perfected his skill at the expense of all other human qualities; he lives in paranoia in a triple-locked apartment, and is terrified when it turns out his landlady has a key. She explains she might have to get in in case of some emergency—his furniture might burn up or something. He explains that none of his possessions is important to him—except his keys.

He has no friends, but he does have acquaintances in the bugging industry, and they're in town for a convention. One of them (played by Allen Garfield) is a truly frightening character. He's the one who talks about the three murders, and he's the one whose hateful envy reveals to us how good Harry Caul really is. A boozy scene in Harry's workshop, with some colleagues and their random dates, provides a perfect illustration of the ways in which even Harry's pathetically constrained social life is expressed through his work.

The Conversation is about paranoia, invasion of privacy, bugging—and also about the bothersome problem of conscience. The Watergate crew seems, for the most part, to have had no notion that what they were doing was objectively wrong. Harry wants to have no notion. But he does, and it destroys him.

Cop ★ ★ ★

R, 110 m., 1988

James Woods (Lloyd Hopkins), Lesley Ann Warren (Kathleen McCarthy), Charles Durning (Dutch), Charles Haid (Whitey Haines), Raymond J. Barry (Gaffney), Randi Brooks (Joanie), Steven Lambert (Bobby Franco), Christopher Wynne (Jack Gibbs), Jan McGill Jen Hopkins), Vicki Wauchope (Penny Hopkins). Directed by James B. Harris and produced by Harris and James Wood. Screenplay by Harris.

Anyone without a history of watching James Woods in the movies might easily misread *Cop*. They might think this was simply a violent, sick, contrived exploitation picture—and that would certainly be an accurate description of its surfaces. But Woods operates in this movie almost as if he were writing his own footnotes. He uses his personality, his voice, and his quirky sense of humor to undermine the material and comment on it, until *Cop* becomes an essay on this whole genre of movie. And then, with the movie's startling last shot, Woods slams shut the book.

The film stars Woods, who is the most engaging and unconventional of leading men, as a brilliant but twisted cop. He's a lone ranger, and he likes to shoot first and ask questions later. In the movie's unsettling opening scene, he kills a man who is possibly innocent, and then lets his partner clean up the mess while he tries to pick up the dead man's date. No wonder Woods is considered a danger to public safety, even by his own superiors. He makes Dirty Harry look cool and reflective.

Before long a plot begins to emerge. A dead body is discovered, and Woods, working backward from the date of the crime and piecing together apparently unrelated clues, becomes convinced that the dead woman is the latest of a long string of murders by the same serial killer. His superiors don't want to hear about it. The last thing Los Angeles needs is another mass murderer.

But Woods persists. He interviews a kinky cop, and cross-examines a feminist bookstore owner (Lesley Ann Warren), whose high school yearbook may contain the clue to the mystery. Can it be that events twenty years ago in high school have triggered a series of killings which have continued ever since? It can in Woods's mind, and he stays on the case even after the department has stripped him of his badge and gun because of . . . well, because basically he represents a danger to the community.

The screenplay of *Cop* was based by the director, James B. Harris, on a thriller by James Ellroy. It contains echoes of the great *film noir* stories of the 1940s, where the supporting cast is filled with various sleazebags and weirdos who are ticked off, one by one, by the hero. The difference this time is that Woods is as sleazy and weird as any of them, and not above breaking and entering and stealing evidence and making love to potential witnesses in order to get information (or, for that matter, simply in order to get laid). He wants to solve this case, but not so much because he wants to punish evildoing as because he is one stubborn S.O.B. and he doesn't like to be told not to do something.

James Woods was born to play this role. He uses a curious and effective technique to get laughs, of which the movie has plenty. Instead of saying funny things, he knows how to throw in a pause, just along enough for the audience to figure out what he's really thinking, so that when he says a straight line, it's funny. The result is creepy; he invites us into his mind, and makes us share his obsession.

Cop is a very violent movie, all the more so because it is so casual about the violence most of the time. It sees its events through the mind of a man who should never have been a cop, and who has been a cop much too long. Yet the Woods character is not stupid and not brutal, just several degrees off from normal.

As we follow him through his "case of the yearbook murders," we can figure out the clues and sometimes arrive at conclusions before he does, but we can never quite figure out what is driving him on this case. There are strange psychological clues, as in the unforgettable scene where he tells his little daughter a bedtime story that's based on straight police procedure, but by the end, the character still remains an enigma. It's as if Woods and Harris watched a Dirty Harry movie one night and decided to see what would happen if Harry were *really* dirty.

The Cotton Club ★ ★ ★ ★

R, 121 m., 1984

Richard Gere (Dixie Dwyer), Gregory Hines (Sandman Williams), Diane Lane (Vera Cicero), Lonette McKee (Lila Rose Oliver), Bob Hoskins (Owney Madden), James Remar (Dutch Schultz), Fred Gwynne (Frenchy). Directed by Francis Ford Coppola and produced by Robert Evans. Screenplay by William Kennedy and Coppola.

After all the rumors, all the negative publicity, all the stories of fights on the set and backstage intrigue and imminent bankruptcy, Francis Ford Coppola's *The Cotton Club* is, quite simply, a wonderful movie. It has the confidence and momentum of a movie where every shot was premeditated—and even if we know that wasn't the case, and this was one of the most troubled productions in recent movie history, what difference does that make when the result is so entertaining?

The movie takes place in New York in the 1920s and 1930s, where Irish and Jewish gangsters battled the Italians for the rackets. Most of their intrigues were played out in public, in flashy settings like the Cotton Club, a Harlem nightclub that featured the nation's most talented black entertainers on stage—playing before an all-white audience. By telling us two love stories, Coppola shows us both sides of that racial divide. He begins by introducing Dixie Dwyer (Richard Gere), a good-looking young musician who saves the life of a gangster and is immediately recruited into the hood's inner circle. There he meets the gangster's teen-age girlfriend (Diane Lane), and they immediatley fall in love—but secretly, because they'll live longer that way. Then we meet Sandman Williams (Gregory Hines), a black tap dancer who dreams of appearing at the Cotton Club, and falls in love with a member of the chorus line (Lonette McKee), a mulatto who talks about her secret life among people who think she is white.

The two love stories are developed against a background of a lot of very good jazz, some great dancing, sharply etched character studies of the gang bosses, and a couple of unexpected bursts of violence that remind us, in their sudden explosion, of moments in Coppola's *Godfather* films. Indeed, there's a lot of *The Godfather* in *The Cotton Club*, especially in the movie's almost elegiac sadness: We get the feeling of time passing, and personal histories being written, and some people breaking free and other people dying or surrendering to hopelessness.

There's another reminder of *The Godfather* movies, and that's in the brilliant, in-depth casting. There's not an uninteresting face or a boring performance in this movie, but two supporting characters really stand out: Bob Hoskins, as a crooked club owner named Madden, and Fred Gwynne, as a towering hulk named Frenchy. They are friends. They also are criminal associates. Hoskins is a bantamweight filled with hostility; Gwynne is a giant with a deep voice and glowering eyes. After Gwynne is kidnapped and Hoskins pays the ransom, the scene between the two of them begins as a routine confrontation and unfolds into something surprisingly funny and touching.

Coppola has a way, in this film, of telling all the different stories without giving us the impression he's jumping around a lot. Maybe the music helps. It gives the movie a continuity and an underlying rhythm that makes all of the characters' lives into steps in a sad ballet. We like some of the characters, but we don't have much respect for them, and the movie doesn't bother with clear distinctions between good and evil. *The Cotton Club* is a somewhat cynical movie about a very cynical time, and along with the music and the romance there is racism, cruelty, betrayal, and stunning violence. Romance with a cutting edge.

The performances are well-suited to the material. Richard Gere is especially good as Dixie Dwyer, maybe because the camera has a way of seeing him off-balance, so that he doesn't dominate the center of each shot like a handsome icon; Coppola stirs him into the action. Diane Lane, herself still a teen-ager, is astonishing as the party girl who wants to own her own club. Gregory Hines and his brother, Maurice, create a wonderful moment of reconciliation when they begin to tap dance and end by forgiving each other for a lifetime's hurts. And Hoskins, the British actor who played the unforgettable mob chief in *The Long Good Friday*, is so wound-up and fierce and funny as the mobster that he takes a cliché and turns it into an original.

The Cotton Club took months to shoot, and they claim they have another 200,000 feet of footage as good as this movie. I doubt it. Whatever it took to do it, Coppola has extracted a very special film out of the checkered history of this project.

Country ★ ★ ★ 1/2

PG, 108 m., 1984

Jessica Lange (Jewell Ivy), Sam Shepard (Gil Ivy), Wilford Brimley (Otis Stewart), Matt Clark (Tom McMullen), Therese Graham (Marlene Ivy), Levi L. Knebel (Carlisle Ivy). Directed by Richard Pearce and produced by William D. Wittliff and Jessica Lange. Screenplay by Wittliff.

The opening moments of *Country* show a woman frying hamburgers and wrapping them up and sending them out to her men, working in the fields. The movie is using visuals to announce its intentions: It wants to observe the lives of its characters at the level of daily detail and routine, and to avoid pulling back into "Big Country" cliché shots. It succeeds. This movie observes ordinary American lives carefully, and passionately. The family lives on a farm in Iowa. Times are hard, and times are now. This isn't a movie about symbolic farmers living in some colorful American past. It is about the farm policies of the Carter and Reagan administrations, and how the movie believes that those policies are resulting in the destruction of family farms. It has been so long since I've seen a Hollywood film with specific political beliefs that a funny thing happened: The movie's anger moved me as much as its story.

The story is pretty moving, too. We meet the members of the Ivy family: Jewell Ivy (Jessica Lange), the farm wife; her husband, Gil (Sam Shepard); her father, Otis (Wilford Brimley), and the three children, especially Carlisle (Levi L. Knebel), the son who knows enough about farming to know when his father has given up. The movie begins at the time of last year's harvest. Some nasty weather has destroyed part of the yield. The Ivys are behind on their FHA loan. Ordinarily, that would be no tragedy; farming is cyclical and there are good years and bad years, and eventually they'll catch up with the loan. But this year is different. An FHA regional administrator, acting on orders from Washington, instructs his people to enforce all loans strictly, and to foreclose when necessary. He uses red ink to write his recommendation on the Ivy's loan file: *Move toward voluntary liquidation.* Since there is no way the loan can be paid off, the Ivys will lose the land that Jewell's family has farmed for one hundred years. The farm agent helpfully supplies the name of an auctioneer.

All of this sounds just a little like the dire opening chapters of a story by Horatio Alger, but the movie never feels dogmatic or forced because *Country* is so clearly the particular story of these people and the way they respond. Old Otis is angry at his son-in-law for losing the farm. Jewell defends her husband, but he goes into town to drink away his impotent rage. There are loud fights far into the night in a house that had been peaceful. The boy asks, "Would somebody mind telling me what's going on around here?"

The movie's strongest passages deal with Jewell's attempts to enlist her neighbors in a stand against the government. The most touching scenes, though, are the ones showing how abstract economic policies cause specific human suffering, cause lives to be interrupted, and families to be torn apart, all in the name of the balance sheet. *Country* is as political, as unforgiving, as *The Grapes of Wrath.*

The movie has, unfortunately, one important area of weakness, in the way it handles the character of Gil (Shepard). At the beginning we have no reason to doubt that he is a good farmer. Later, the movie raises questions about that assumption, and never clearly answers them. Gil starts drinking heavily, and lays a hand on his son, and leaves the farm altogether for several days. The local farm agent tells him, point blank, that he's a drunk and a bad farmer. Well, is he? In an affecting scene where Gil returns and asks for the understanding of his family, his drinking is not mentioned. It's good that the movie tries to make the character more complex and interesting—not such a noble hero—but if he really is a drunk and a bad farmer, then maybe that's why he's behind on the loan. The movie shouldn't raise the possibility without dealing with it.

In a movie with the power of *Country,* I can live with a problem like that because there are so many other good things. The performances are so true you feel this really is a family; we expect the quality of the acting by Lange, Shepard, and gruff old Brimley, but the surprise is Levi L. Knebel, as the son. He is so stubborn and so vulnerable, so filled with his sense of right when he tells his father what's being done wrong, that he brings the movie an almost documentary quality; this isn't acting, we feel, but eavesdropping.

The Cowboys ★ ★ ½

PG, 128 m., 1972

John Wayne (Wil Anderson), Roscoe Lee Browne (Jebediah Nightlinger), Bruce Dern (Long Hair), Colleen Dewhurst (Madam), Slim Pickens (Anse), Lonny Chapman (Preacher). Directed and produced by Mark Rydell. Screenplay by Irving Ravetch, Harriet Frank, Jr., and William Dale Jennings.

It isn't just that John Wayne gets killed. He was killed before in the movies—although not very often, and certainly not after he assumed the mantle of legend. No, it isn't that; he had to catch it sometime. And give him credit. He can absorb lead like nobody since The Thing. He gets shot in the leg. Then in the arm. Then in the other arm. Then in the back. And he still lives until morning, and has a noble speech or two left inside him.

The thing is, when John Wayne finally dies, it is because *The Cowboys* has violated a Western convention. It is a sacred belief of the genre that good guys never miss, and bad guys never hit. The bad guys can pour a rain of lead into a besieged position and hit nothing more than a lantern or a whisky bottle, even by accident. But then all a good guy has to do is pop up and squeeze the trigger, and a villain bites the dust at 200 yards.

The Cowboys tries to get around the convention by depriving Wayne of a chance to shoot at all, and disarming his dozen or so teen-aged sidekicks. He's killed while he's unarmed (and after having already beaten the daylights out of a man thirty-five years his junior). But then . . .

Well, the kids break open a packing crate and get their rifles and pistols back. These are kids without a lot of heavy shooting behind them, you understand. Two of them are fifteen. The others are younger. One stands about as high as the Duke's gunbelt. But, by golly, they ambush ten bad guys! Lure three of them off into the woods on ruses. Take advantage of the fact that all bad guys and movie Nazis are deaf, never look behind themselves, and never realize their partners have been replaced by the enemy.

This is all in preparation for the final shootout, during which every one of the range-wise, hardened, experienced, jailbird gunmen is killed—and not a single kid gets nicked, even. Let me tell you, it takes a lot of heroic music to paper over this ending. Lots of wide eyes and grave grins and a tear or two over Duke's grave. But doesn't it seem to you that John Wayne shouldn't have been killed in a movie where not a single bad guy can hit a single greenhorn kid?

It's the ending, really, that spoils *The Cow-*

boys. Otherwise, it's a good-to-fine Western, with a nice, sly performance by Roscoe Lee Browne as the trail cook, and the usual solid Wayne performance. The scenes along the way of the kids learning to be cowboys are good, warm fun, and it's a shame they had to go for the unlikely, violent, and totally contrived last thirty minutes.

Creepshow ★ ★ ★
R, 129 m., 1982

Hal Holbrook (Henry Northrup), Adrienne Barbeau (Wilma Northrup), Fritz Weaver (Dexter Stanley), Leslie Nielsen (Richard Vickers), Carrie Nye (Sylvia Graham), E.G. Marshall (Upson Pratt), Viveca Lindfors (Aunt Bedelia). Directed by George A. Romero and produced by Richard P. Rubinstein. Screenplay by Stephen King.

Creepshow plays like an anthology of human phobias. What could be more horrifying that sticking your hand into a long-forgotten packing crate and suddenly feeling teeth sink into you? Unless it would be finding yourself buried up to the neck on the beach, with the tide coming in? Or trapped in an old grave, with the tombstone toppling down on top of you? Or having green stuff grow all over you? Or how about being smothered by cockroaches?

The horrors in *Creepshow* are universal enough, and so is the approach. These stories have been inspired, right down to the very camera angles, by the classic EC Comics of the early 1950s—titles like "Tales from the Crypt," which curdled the blood of Eisenhower-era kids raised on such innocent stuff as Captain Marvel, and appalled their elders. (EC Comics almost single-handedly inspired the creation of the Comics Code Authority.) The filmmakers of *Creepshow* say they were raised on those old comics, and it would appear that their subsequent careers were guided by the Ol' Crypt-Keeper's bag of tales. The movie's director is George A. Romero, whose most famous credit is *Night of the Living Dead*, and the original screenplay is by Stephen King, who wrote *Carrie* and *The Shining*. What they've done here is to recapture not only the look and the storylines of old horror comics, but also the peculiar feeling of poetic justice that permeated their pages. In an EC horror story, unspeakable things happened to people—but, for the most part, they deserved them.

The five stories told in this film often center around a fatal flaw. Upson Pratt, for example, the hero of the fifth story, is a compulsively neat and tidy man who lives in a hermetically sealed command center, much like Howard Hughes. What could be more suitable than an invasion of his stronghold by cockroaches? The professors in the story about the thing in the box have spent their lives collecting old facts: how perfect that one long-collected piece of evidence should still bite back!

Romero and King have approached this movie with humor and affection, as well as with an appreciation of the macabre. They create visual links to comic books by beginning each segment with several panels of a comic artist's version of the story, and then dissolving from the final drawn panel to a reality that exactly mirrors it. The acting also finds the right note. Such veterans of horror as Hal Holbrook, E.G. Marshall, and Adrienne Barbeau know how to paint their personalities broadly, edging up to caricature. Nobody in this movie is a three-dimensional person, or is meant to be. They are all types. And their lives are all object lessons.

The original full name of EC Comics was "Educational Comics," and you got an education, all right. You learned it was unwise to stick your hand into a box labeled "Danger—Do Not Open." It was unwise to speak ill of the dead. And it was quite unwise to assume that cockroaches would never decide to gang up and fight back.

Cries and Whispers ★ ★ ★ ★
R, 106 m., 1973

Harriet Andersson (Agnes), Kari Sylwan (Anna), Ingrid Thulin (Karin), Liv Ullmann (Maria), Erland Josephson (Lakaren), Henning Moritzen (Joakim). Directed, produced, and written by Ingmar Bergman.

Cries and Whispers is like few movies we'll ever see. It is hypnotic, disturbing, frightening. It envelops us in a red membrane of passion and fear, and in some way that I do not fully understand, it employs taboos and ancient superstitions to make its effect. We slip lower in our seats, feeling claustrophobia and sexual disquiet, realizing that we have been surrounded by the vision of a filmmaker who has absolute mastery of his art. *Cries and Whispers* is about dying, love, sexual passion, hatred, and death—in that order.

The film inhabits a manor house set on a vast country estate. The rooms of the house open out from each other like passages in the human body; with the exception of one moment when Agnes, the dying woman, opens her window and looks at the dawn, the house offers no views. It looks in upon itself.

Three woman stay in the house with Agnes (Harriet Andersson), waiting for her to die. She is in the final stages of cancer and in great pain. The women are Karin and Maria, her sisters, and Anna, the stout, round-cheeked servant. In elliptical flashbacks (intended to give us emotional information, not to tell a story), we learn that the three sisters have made little of their lives. Karin (Ingrid Thulin) is married to a diplomat she despises. Maria (Liv Ullmann) is married to a cuckold, and so she cuckolds him (what is one to do?). Agnes, who never married, gave birth to a few third-rate watercolors. Now, in dying, she discovers at last some of the sweetness of life.

The sisters remember that they were close in childhood, but somehow in growing up they lost the ability to love, to touch. Only Anna, the servant, remembers how. When Agnes cries out in the night, in fear and agony, it is Anna who cradles her to her bosom, whispering soft endearments.The others cannot stand to be touched. In a moment of conjured nostalgia, Maria and Karin remember their closeness as children. Now, faced with the fact of their sister's death, they deliberately try to synthesize feeling and love. Quickly, almost frantically, they touch and caress each other's faces, but their touching is a parody and by the next day they have closed themselves off again.

These two scenes—of Anna embracing Agnes, and of Karin and Maria touching like frightened kittens—are two of the greatest Bergman has ever created. The feeling in these scenes—I should say, the way they force us to feel—constitutes the meaning of this film. It has no abstract message; it communicates with us on a level of human feeling so deep that we are afraid to invent words for the things found there.

The camera is as uneasy as we are. It stays at rest mostly, but when it moves it doesn't always follow smooth, symmetrical progressions. It darts, it falls back, is stunned. It lingers on close-ups of faces with the impassivity of God. It continues to look when we want to turn away; it is not moved. Agnes lies thrown on her deathbed, her body shuddered by horrible, deep gasping breaths, as she fights for air, for life. The sisters turn away, and we want to, too. We know things are this bad—but we don't want to know. Bergman's camera stays and watches.

The movie is drenched in red. Bergman has written in his screenplay what he thinks of the inside of the human soul as a membranous red. Color can be so important; in *Two English Girls*, a movie about the absence of passion, Francois Truffaut kept red out of his compositions until the movie's one moment of unfeigned feeling, and then he filled his screen with red.

All of *Cries and Whispers* is occupied with passion—but the passion is inside, the characters can't get it out of themselves. None of them can, except Anna (Kari Sylwan). The film descends into a netherworld of the supernatural; the dead woman speaks (or is it only that they think they hear her?). She reaches out and grasps for Karin (or does Karin move the dead arms?—Bergman's camera doesn't let us see).

The movie, like all supernatural myths, like all legends and fables (and like all jokes—which are talismans to take the pain from truth) ends in a series of threes. The dead woman asks the living women to stay with her, to comfort her while she pauses within her dead body before moving into the great terrifying void. Karin will not. Maria will not. But Anna will, and makes pillows of her breasts for Agnes. Anna is the only one of them who remembers how to touch and love. And she is the only one who believes in God.

We saw her in the morning, praying. We learned that she had lost her little daughter, but is resigned to God's will. Is there a God in Bergman's film, or is there only Anna's faith? The film ends with a scene of astonishing, jarring affirmation: We see the four women some months earlier, drenched with the golden sun, and we hear Anna reading from Agnes's diary: "I feel a great gratitude to my life, which gives me so much." And takes it away.

Crimes of Passion ★ ½
R, 107 m., 1984

Kathleen Turner (Joanna/China Blue), Anthony Perkins (Shayne), John Laughlin (Grady), Annie Potts (Amy). Directed by Ken Russell and produced by Barry Sandler. Screenplay by Sandler.

I like what George Burns said about his sex life: "I got more laughs in bed than I ever got in vaudeville." Sex is an activity of great and serious importance to its participants, but as a spectator sport it has a strange way of turning into comedy. Look, for example, at Ken Russell's overwrought film *Crimes of Passion*, in which good performances and an interesting idea are metamorphosed into one of the silliest movies in a long time.

Part of the fault for that lies with Russell. A great deal of the fault no doubt lies with the movie rating system, which required massive cuts in the movie before it could qualify for an R rating, and with New World Pictures, which was too chicken to release the movie with an X.* But some of the fault also lies with the subject of sex itself, because there is nothing quite so ridiculous as someone else's sexual fantasies, and nothing as fascinating as our own.

The movie stars Kathleen Turner in a performance which must have taken a great deal of nerve and curiosity. She plays a woman with a dual identity: by day, she's a sophisticated fashion designer named Joanne, and by night she's a kinky hooker named China Blue. The psychological reasons behind this double existence are dished up out of the usual Freudian stew. Turner's day work is photographed in a matter-of-fact way. The nighttime street scene is seen by Russell, however, as a lurid *film noir* world of flashing red neon signs, garter belts, squirming sadomasochists, and perverts like the one played by Anthony Perkins, who proves in this movie that there is probably no role he would turn down because it would be bad for his image. Perkins plays a demented street preacher who sniffs uppers, hangs out in peep shows, and brandishes a murder weapon that looks like *Jaws* crossed with the latest electronic sex toy.

Perkins is just one of the clients who enlivens Turner's evenings. Others are more poignant as when Turner is hired by the wife of a dying man, who wants her husband to feel like a man for one last time. She enters the man's room, and as they begin to talk, a touchingly authentic atmosphere is established.

The purpose of *Crimes of Passion* was apparently to explore the further shores of sexual behavior. Because of the double standard of the movie ratings system, which prizes violence more highly than sex, a great deal of the behavior is missing from the movie, and what is left is a steamy, bloody thriller. I'm not sure that's what Russell had in mind. Anthony Perkins distorts most of the scenes he's in, with overacting so blatant that the plausibility of the whole movie is undermined. Turner tries. So does John Laughlin, as a square young husband who learns a lot from her about sex and love. but when *Crimes of Passion* is over, what's left? Not much. You know you're in trouble in a sex movie when you spend more time thinking about the parts they left out than the parts they put in.

*The videocassette version restores some of the excised footage.

Critters ★ ★ ★
PG-13, 97 m., 1986

Dee Wallace Stone (Helen), M. Emmet Walsh (Harv), Billy Green Bush (Jay Brown), Scott Grimes (Brad Brown), Nadine Van Der Velde (April Brown), Don Opper (Charlie McFadden), Terrence Mann (Johnny Steele). Directed by Stephen Herek and produced by Rupert Harvey. Screenplay by Herek and Domonic Muir.

If perfect fools can hold drivers' licenses, why can't creatures from outer space be just as dumb? And if they *are* bounty hunters, why shouldn't they be trigger-happy—firing at everything that moves, like a television set, for example? We always assume that visitors from other worlds will be far more intelligent than we are, but maybe they'll just turn out to have faster means of intergalactic travel.

In the opening scenes of *Critters*, a spaceship is approaching a barren asteroid which has been converted into a prison. It carries on board several of the dreaded Cripes, who are furry little bowling balls with dozens of rows of sharp teeth. The Cripes escape, take over the ship, and land on earth. And bounty hunters follow them here, while the nasty little critters are terrorizing the countryside.

What this gives us is a truly ambitious rip-off of not one but four recent science-fiction movies: *Gremlins, E.T., The Terminator,* and *Starman.* We get the critters from the first and the hunters from the second, and from *Starman* the notion that an alien can assume the outward appearance of a human being. (That is a particularly attractive quality for an alien to have, especially in a low-budget picture, because then you can hire an actor and claim he is inhabited by an alien, and you can save a lot of money on special effects.) From *E.T.,* there is Dee Wallace Stone, who played Henry Thomas's mother in that film and is now the equally dubious and harried mother of young Scott Grimes, a plucky kid who goes into battle against the invaders.

The movie takes place in a small town and the surrounding countryside, where the vicious little furballs start attacking everything that moves. They have a lot of tricks at their command: They can eat you like a piranha, shoot darts at you from their foreheads, and curl up into a ball and roll away. That leads up to the big scene in the bowling alley, where we expect that someone's going to reach down and pick up a critter instead of a ball, but as it turns out, that scene contains other surprises.

We meet the folks in the area. There's the friendly farmer (Billy Green Bush), his wife (Stone), son (Grimes), and daughter (Nadine Van Der Veldt). They live on a farm that gives the critters their first haven, and there's the obligatory scary scene where the father goes down in the basement with his flashlight to see what's making the noise.

Meanwhile, the local lawman (that dependably slimy character actor M. Emmet Walsh) notices that strange things are happening in his territory. Two strangers from out of town have turned up and started to blast everybody away, and dang if one of them doesn't look exactly like the local minister! The other one soon assumes the outward appearance of the village idiot.

All of these plot threads move inexorably toward the final showdown, but what's interesting is the way the movie refuses to be just a thriller. The director, Stephen Herek, likes to break the mood occasionally with a one-liner out of left field, and he gives the critters some of the funniest lines. What makes *Critters* more than a rip-off are its humor and its sense of style. This is a movie made by people who must have had fun making it.

Crocodile Dundee ★ ★

PG-13, 98 m., 1986

Paul Hogan (Mike Dundee), Linda Koslowski (Sue Charlton), John Meillon (Wally), Michael Lombard (Sam Charlton), Mark Blum (Richard). Directed by Peter Faiman and produced by John Cornell. Screenplay by Hogan, Ken Shadie, and Cornell.

They made this kind of movie better in the 1930s, when audiences were more accustomed to the reliable old story line: Aggressive female newspaper reporter from New York tracks down legendary wilderness guide in Outback, is saved from crocodiles, falls in love, asks living legend to return with her to New York, there to meet her millionaire daddy and her fiancé, a wimp. Clark Gable and Carole Lombard could have made this movie. Maybe they did.

Crocodile Dundee knows the words to this story, but not the music. All of the clichés are in the right places, and most of the gags pay off, and there are moments of real amusement as the Australian cowboy wanders around Manhattan as a naive sightseer. The problem is, there's not one moment of chemistry between the two stars—Paul Hogan as "Crocodile" Dundee and Linda Kozlowski as the clever little rich girl. The movie feels curiously machine-made, as if they had all the right ingredients and simply forgot to add the animal magnetism.

The movie got a lot of attention because of Paul Hogan, a former truck driver who has become one of Australia's top TV stars, and is known over here for those Australian tourism commercials where he reminds us about who won the 1986 America's Cup. He's a lean, tanned, weathered man with a perpetual squint, and he looks right at home when he's stabbing crocodiles and strangling snakes. His co-star is not as well cast; Linda Kozlowski always looks a little too made up, a little too formal, to be able to really unwind and accept this sweaty folk hero. When she smiles at him, it's politely, not passionately. Maybe she's downwind.

The story begins with a New York newspaper sending her on assignment to interview Dundee, who allegedly lost a leg to a crocodile and then crawled for hundreds of miles through the Outback. She spends more money on this story than most newspapers earmark for a gubernatorial election. She hires a helicopter, pays a $2,500 fee to Dundee's partner, and later—after she brings the Croc back to New York—puts him in a $900-a-day suite at the Plaza. What she doesn't do is get the story.

The Manhattan scenes are the best, as Dundee scares off muggers, unmasks transvestites, hitches rides with mounted policemen, and sleeps on the floor of his hotel room. Many of the best scenes have the same whimsical quality as *The Gods Must Be Crazy*, in which a character with a truly direct and open mind is able to see right through the strange conventions of civilization.

What doesn't work is the love story. If we don't believe in the chemistry between Crocodile and the woman reporter, we certainly don't believe her fiancé, a simpering and supercilious jerk who tries to pull the old foreign language menu trick on the guy from the sticks. The ending of the movie (which I would not dream of revealing) involves a love scene on a subway platform. If these were two lovers we really cared about, the scene, as written, could have had the impact of that moment in *An Officer and a Gentleman* where Richard Gere carries Debra Winger off the factory floor. As it's acted in this movie, alas, the scene is so unconvincing that the lovers are upstaged by the other people on the train platform.

Cross My Heart ★ ★ ½

R, 96 m., 1987

(See related Film Clip, p. 749.)

Martin Short (David), Annette O'Toole (Cathy), Paul Reiser (Bruce), Joanna Kerns (Nancy), Lee Arenberg (Parking Lot Attendant), Jessica Puscas (Jessica). Directed by Armyan Bernstein and produced by Lawrence Kasdan. Screenplay by Bernstein and Gail Parent.

Cross My Heart begins with Martin Short and Annette O'Toole preparing themselves for going out together on a third date, an experience they both apparently equate with being locked in a small room with hungry rats. It's not that they don't like each other. On the contrary, they both feel they may actually be falling in love, and that the other person may be Right for them. That's the problem: Both Short and O'Toole have told so many lies on the first two dates that they don't see how they can start telling the truth now.

Short has claimed he is about to be appointed regional sales manager of his firm, which sells sunglasses. In fact, he has just been fired. O'Toole has neglected to reveal that she smokes, and has a seven-year-old daughter. Desperate to impress, Short picks up O'Toole in a car that is not his own, and tries to lure her back to a garishly stylish apartment, also not his own. The entire evening is a fragile construction of lies that threaten to come crashing down at any moment.

What director Armyan Bernstein does with this premise is courageous and ambitious, but only fitfully successful. Bernstein, who coauthored the script with Gail Parent, commits the long central passage of his film to an extended duet in the borrowed apartment, where Short inveigles O'Toole into bed, not exactly against her will, and the two of them earn a footnote in cinematic history by becoming the first characters in a major movie to discuss and use condoms. They are refreshingly frank about their choice of brands, but otherwise maintain their lies to orgasm and beyond ("It was a great little climax," O'Toole unhelpfully reassures Short).

These are the sorts of roles actors will kill for. Short and O'Toole are on screen for almost the whole movie, and are called upon to bare their souls and bodies, engage in meaningful conversation, laugh, cry, and star in slapstick and action sequences. It is always a pleasure to watch them, especially since Bernstein is giving both actors an opportunity to sound notes that have usually been denied to them.

Short, who is so much more than the Ed Grimly character he made famous on "Saturday Night Live," comes across as an engaging, intelligent, and actually sexy leading man, in the Dudley Moore mold. O'Toole, one of Hollywood's most unfairly overlooked actresses ever since *One on One*, is engaging, intelligent, and astonishingly sexy. And both of them can play comedy, especially with each other.

So where's the flaw in the movie? I think

it's in all the apparatus the screenplay erects around their lies. Although it is plausible that strangers would lie to one another, and inevitable that a moment of truth would have to come, Bernstein and Parent belabor the lies their characters tell until they become counterproductive. Up to a point, we are able to believe that O'Toole believes Short really lives in the vulgar apartment they visit. But eventually the evidence against this particular lie becomes so inescapable that the screenplay can maintain the deception only by descending to the level of the Idiot Plot—the story device by which secrets are kept only because all of the characters are idiots.

There is another flaw, I think, at a point after most of O'Toole's lies have been exposed but Short still has a few left. Because the two characters like each other very much, I thought the logical flow of the movie called for Short to confess his deceptions. Instead, he lashes out in anger at O'Toole, while still trying to keep his own secrets. The behavior is too hypocritical for a comedy.

The result is that *Cross My Heart* does the one thing that no romantic comedy should ever do: It causes us to lose confidence in one of the characters, and sympathy with the other one, fairly late in the story. All that spinning of the wheels of the plot also denies us the payoff we expect in a movie like this, which is the *real* love scene, in which the characters are allowed to be warm and forgiving after all the loose ends have been tidied up.

Crossover Dreams ★ ★ ★
PG-13, 85 m., 1985

Ruben Blades (Rudy Veloz), Shawn Elliott (Orlando), Tom Signorelli (Lou Rose), Elizabeth Pena (Liz Garcia), Frank Robles (Ray Solo), Joel Diamond (Neil Silver). Directed by Leon Ichaso and produced by Manuel Arce. Screenplay by Ichaso and Manuel Arce.

Crossover Dreams does not begin with an original idea. It shows the rise and fall of a musician whose talent takes him to the top, and whose ego and weaknesses pull him back to the bottom again. The first time I saw this story, it was about Gene Kruppa, and in his big comeback concert in Carnegie Hall, he dropped his drumsticks and had to find the courage to start again. I've seen the same story countless times again, translated into the idioms of jazz, country, rock, and classical, and now here is the salsa version, starring Ruben Blades.

The story isn't new, but it sure does wear well. Maybe that's because Blades is such an engaging performer, playing a character who is earnest and sincere when he needs to be, but who always maintains a veil over his deepest secrets. The story is formula, but the film's treatment of it is fresh and perceptive, and there's an exhilarating energy level. The opening shots, in fact, reminded me of the extraordinary opening of Martin Scorsese's first film, *Who's That Knocking at My Door?* Music pounds on the sound track, as young men race around the streets of New York, filled with their own life and importance.

The movie takes place largely in Spanish Harlem, where the Blades character, Rudy Veloz, makes the rounds of Latino nightclubs, working with a band of old friends and mentors. He dreams of "crossing over," of breaking out of the Latino circuit and making it downtown, to the world of national TV, music videos, and record contracts. And for a moment it looks as if he might.

He meets a shabby Broadway talent agent, who fails to impress him (but who gives him some of the most realistic advice he'll receive in this movie). Then he's "discovered" by a record producer, who picks him up out of his life, briefly shines the spotlight on him, and then throws him back into obscurity again. The movie's most convincing and painful scenes come after Veloz's brief moment of fame, when he has to return to his friends and try to conceal the extent of his failure.

Against this serious undertone, the movie hurls a lot of good music. Blades, the Panamanian salsa star who has crossed over, is not only a good singer but a surprisingly versatile actor who never seems to be straining for an effect, never seems to stray outside his character, and will probably get some more serious acting jobs after this debut.

Crossroads ★ ★ ★ ½
R, 98 m., 1985

Ralph Macchio (Eugene Martone), Joe Seneca (Willie Brown), Jami Gertz (Frances), Joe Morton (Scratch's Assistant), Robert

Judd (Scratch), Harry Carey, Jr. (Bartender). Directed by Walter Hill and produced by Mark Carliner. Screenplay by John Fusco.

Crossroads borrows so freely and is a reminder of so many other movies that it's a little startling, at the end, to realize how effective the movie is and how original it manages to feel despite all the plunderings. The movie stars Ralph Macchio as a bright teen-ager who studied classical guitar at Juilliard and worships as his heroes the great old blues musicians of the 1930s and 1940s. One day he tracks down a survivor of that era, a harmonica player named Willie Brown (Joe Seneca) in a nursing home. Macchio helps him escape, and they hit the road, hoboing their way down South to a crossroads where Seneca once made a deal with the devil.

With the devil? You bet. *Crossroads* is a cheerful cross between a slice of life and a supernatural fable. And at the end, it's up to the kid to pick up his guitar and outplay the devil's man, to save Seneca's soul. This story is a combination of no less than two reliable genres. It borrows, obviously, from Macchio's 1984 *The Karate Kid,* which was also the story of a young man's apprenticeship with an older master. It also borrows from the countless movies in which everything depends on who wins the big fight, match, game, or duel in the last scene. The notion of the showdown with the devil may have been suggested by the country song "Devil Went Down to Georgia."

And yet the remarkable thing is how fresh all this material seems, and how entertaining it is. Just when I'm ready to despair of a movie coming up with a fresh plot, a movie like *Crossroads* comes along to remind me that acting, writing, and direction can redeem any plot, and make any story new. The foundation for *Crossroads* is the relationship between the boy and the old man, and here we have two performances that are well suited to one another. Macchio, once again, as in *The Karate Kid,* has an unstudied, natural charm. A lot of young actors seem to take themselves seriously, but not many have Macchio's gift of seeming to take other things seriously. We really believe, in this movie, that he is a fanatic about the blues, and has read all the books and listened to all the records.

Seneca does a terrific job as a rock-solid, conniving, no-nonsense old man who doesn't take this kid seriously at first, and uses him as a way to get out of the nursing home and back down South to the crossroads, where he has a longstanding rendezvous. The kid knows that Willie was a partner of the legendary blues musician Robert Johnson and he makes a deal with the old man. He'll help him return to that crossroads if the old man will teach him a lost Johnson song.

Along the way, the two men pick up a third partner, a tough young runaway named Frances (Jami Gertz), and there is a brief, sweet romance between the two young people before she leaves one morning, perhaps because it is better for the old man and the young one to move on toward their mutual destiny.

Gertz is a newcomer: this was her second major movie in 1985, after a somewhat thankless role in *Quicksilver,* in which she worked for a bicycle messenger service. She's just right for this movie, with the toughness required by the character, and yet with the tenderness and the romantic notes that remind us that this is really a myth. Another good performance in the movie is by Joe Morton, who played *The Brother from Another Planet* and this time is the devil's assistant, sinister and ingratiating.

The film was directed by Walter Hill, who specializes in myths, in movie characters who seem to represent something greater than themselves. Detailed character studies are not his strong point; he makes movies like *The Warriors, 48 HRS,* and *Streets of Fire,* in which the characters seem made out of the stuff of legend. In *48 HRS,* though, he also found the human qualities in the Nick Nolte and Eddie Murphy characters, and he does that again this time, making Seneca and Macchio so individual, so particular, that we aren't always thinking that this movie is really about an old man and a boy and the devil.

A word about the music. Ry Cooder did most of the sound track, drawing from many blues scores, and the movie is wonderful to listen to: confident and sly and not all tricked up for Hollywood. The closing scene, the dueling guitars, presents a challenge that perhaps no film composer could quite solve (what's the right approach to music as a weapon?), but somehow Cooder actually does pull off the final showdown.

Cry Freedom ★ ★ ½
PG, 154 m., 1987

Kevin Kline (Donald Woods), Penelope Wilton (Wendy Woods), Denzel Washington (Steve Biko), John Thaw (Kruger), Sophie Mgcina (Evalina), Joseph Marcell (Moses). Directed and produced by Richard Attenborough. Screenplay by John Briley.

Cry Freedom begins with the story of a friendship between a white liberal South African editor and an idealistic young black leader who later dies at the hands of the South African police. But the black leader is dead and buried by the movie's halfway point, and the rest of the story centers on the editor's desire to escape South Africa and publish a book.

You know there is something wrong with the premise of this movie when you see that the actress who plays the editor's wife is billed above the actor who plays Biko. This movie promises to be an honest account of the turmoil in South Africa, but turns into a routine cliff-hanger about the editor's flight across the border. It's sort of a liberal yuppie version of that Disney movie where the brave East German family builds a hot-air balloon and floats to freedom. The problem with this movie is similar to the dilemma in South Africa: Whites occupy the foreground and establish the terms of the discussion while the eighty percent non-white majority remains a shadowy, half-seen presence in the background.

Yet *Cry Freedom* is a sincere and valuable movie, and despite my fundamental reservations about it, I think it probably should be seen. Although everybody has heard about apartheid, and South Africa remains a favorite subject of campus protest, few people have an accurate mental picture of what the country actually looks like and feels like. It is a place, not an issue, and *Cry Freedom* helps to visualize it. The movie was mostly shot across the border in Zimbabwe, the former nation of Southern Rhodesia, which serves as an adequate stand-in; we see the manicured lawns of the whites, who seem to live in country club suburbs, and the jerry-built "townships" of the blacks, and we sense the institutional racism of a system where black maids call their employers "master," and even white liberals accept that without a blink.

The film begins with the story of Donald Woods, editor of the *East London* (South Africa) *Daily Dispatch*, and Steve Biko, a young black leader who has founded a school and a clinic for his people, and continues to hold out hope that blacks and whites can work together to change South Africa. In the more naive days of the 1960s and 1970s, Biko's politics are seen as "black supremacy," and Woods writes sanctimonious editorials describing Biko as a black racist. Through an emissary, Biko arranges to meet Woods, and eventually the two men become friends and Woods sees black life in South Africa at first hand (something few white South Africans have done.)

Although Biko is played with quiet power by Academy Award-nominee Denzel Washington, he is seen primarily through the eyes of Woods (Kevin Kline). There aren't many scenes in which we see Biko without Woods, and fewer still in which his friendship with Woods isn't the underlying subject of the scene. No real attempt is made to show daily life in Biko's world; although we move into the Woods home, meet his wife, children, maid, and dog, and share his daily routine, there is no similar attempt to portray Biko's daily reality.

There is a reason for that. *Cry Freedom* is not about Steve Biko. It is Donald Woods's story from beginning to end, describing how he met Biko, how his thinking was changed by the man, how he actually witnessed black life at first hand (by patronizing a black speakeasy in a township and having a few drinks), and how, after he was placed under house arrest by the South African government, he engineered the escape from South Africa. The story has a happy ending: Donald Woods and his family made it safely to England, where he was able to publish two books about his experience. (The bad news is that Steve Biko was killed.)

For the first half of this movie, I was able to suspend judgment. Interesting things were happening, the performances were good, and it is always absorbing to see how other people live. Most of the second half of the movie, alas, is taken up with routine cloak-and-dagger stuff, including Woods's masquerade as a Catholic priest, his phony passport, and his attempt to fool South African border officials. These scenes could have been recycled out of any thriller from any country in any time, right down to the ominous long shots of the men patroling the border bridge, and the tense moment when the guard's eyes flick up and down from the passport photo.

Cry Freedom is not really a story of today's South Africa, and it is not really the story of a black leader who tried to change it. Like *All the President's Men,* it's essentially the story of heroic, glamorous journalism. Remember, *Ace in the Hole,* that Kirk Douglas movie where the man was trapped in the cave, and Douglas played the ambitious reporter who prolonged the man's imprisonment so he could make his reputation by covering the story? I'm not saying the Donald Woods story is a parallel. But somehow the comparison did arise in my mind.

D

Dark Eyes ★ ★ ★ ½

NO MPAA RATING, 118 m., 1987

Marcello Mastroianni (Romano), Silvana Mangano (Elisa), Marthe Keller (Tina), Elena Sofonova (Anna), Pina Cei (Elisa's Mother), Vsevolod Larionov (Pavel). Directed by Nikita Mikhalkov and produced by Silvia D'Amico Bendico and Carlo Cucchi. Screenplay by Alexander Adabachian and Mikhalkov.

Some stories need to be told after they are over. We need to know that all the events are past and gone in order to feel the same nostalgia as the storyteller. When a story is happening "now," there is always the possibility of surprise and happiness. But when a story happened "then," and it is a love story, then even the happy moments feel bittersweet, and, of course, that is the whole point of the story.

Dark Eyes is a story told by a man who sits at a table in the lounge of an ocean liner, the bottle in front of him, the glass in his hand, his voice steady as if he has rehearsed these same facts many times before. He is a middle-aged man with sad eyes and a weary face. His listener is about the same age, but not so sad and not so weary. Neither one seems to much care about the ship's destination.

The man telling the story is Marcello Mastroianni, the most complete of movie actors, his face never seeming composed for the screen but acting simply as a window for his words. He tells the stranger that once he was married, comfortably if not ecstatically, to a rich wife (Silvana Mangano). They were not in love, but they were content with one another. Then he went on a visit to a spa, and there he saw a young lady, and danced with her, and fell in love with her, and had one of those holiday romances that fade like postcards in the memory. After all, nothing could come of it; they were both married.

The problem with this romance, Mastroianni tells his listener, is that it did not fade. Back home again, he found he was still in love with the woman (Elena Sofonova). She grew stronger in his memory. He could not forget her. She was a Russian, and eventually he went to Russia in search of her, and found her, and they shared perfect love and vowed to divorce their spouses to marry each other. She went to tell her husband, and he returned to Italy to tell his wife, but at home he found his wife had lost all of her money, and his sense of loyalty was such that he could not leave her under those circumstances, and so . . .

Mastroianni continues with his story, but I will stop here, before all the twists and turns, the ironies and the final heartbreak. *Dark Eyes* tells one of those stories where you think you know everything, but you do not, and at the end of the story you know that everyone is very unhappy, but you cannot see precisely what they should have done differently. The movie is based on stories by Chekhov, and has been directed by a Russian, Nikita Mikhalkov, who is not afraid of large romantic gestures and tragic coincidences. You realize after a while that it doesn't matter that Mastroianni can do nothing, that his tragedy is in the past; the telling of the story is the whole point, and he travels the world with his sad tale, telling it probably again and again, for the whole importance of his life has been reduced to his great loss.

This is a beautiful film, lavishly shot on location at Italian and Russian spas and in great houses. The nineteenth-century period is important, not simply because it recalls a time before telephones (which could have solved the whole tragedy), but because it recalls a state of mind before telephones, a time when people did not much believe in easy solutions. The movie is intriguing because of its moral complexity. After it's over, you find yourself asking hard questions about who did right and who did wrong, and you're confronted with the ironic possibility that maybe it didn't matter, that maybe everyone was doomed from the start.

The ending of this film is a real stunner. If you see *Dark Eyes*, ask yourself this question afterward: How would it have felt if the movie had provided the encounter we anticipate will be the last scene, but isn't? Would it have been simply corny? Or too heartbreaking to be endured?

D.A.R.Y.L. ★ ★ ★

PG, 99 m., 1985

Barret Oliver (Daryl), Mary Beth Hurt (Joyce Richardson), Michael McKean (Andy Robinson), Daniel Bryan Corkill (Turtle), Josef Sommer (Dr. Stewart), Kathryn Walker (Ellen Lamb). Directed by Simon Wincer and produced by John Heyman and Burtt Harris. Screenplay by David Ambrose.

They know there is something odd about the kid when he starts doing his own laundry. That's not natural for a grade-schooler. Daryl has some other strange attributes. He is unfailingly polite, obsessively honest, and bats 1.000 in Little League. Finally his friend, Turtle, pulls him aside and explains that adults don't like it when a kid is too perfect. It makes them nervous. They need to connect with him so they can relax around him. Daryl nods gravely, and his next time at bat, he strikes out.

Daryl's history is strange. He was discovered by the side of the road, a neatly dressed little boy with amnesia. He didn't know who his parents were, or what his last name was, or where he lived. He is placed with a foster family, and by halfway through the movie *D.A.R.Y.L.* he is beginning to develop into a more typical kid, with real human emotions. That is against the game plan, unfortunately, because Daryl is both more and less than human. He is a prototype of a secret government attempt to combine a computer brain with a genetically cloned body, creating a humanoid who can use his five senses as input for his silicon mind.

D.A.R.Y.L. is sort of *Charly* in reverse. Instead of a retarded man who is allowed, through science, to have a brief glimpse of what it would be like to be normal, what we have here is a super-intelligent thinking machine who gets a taste of being a real little boy. It's an intriguing premise, and the movie handles it with skill. The boy is played by Barret Oliver with an earnest, touching solemnity. The people around him (including his foster parents, Mary Beth Hurt and Michael McKean) are out of a Norman Rockwell drawing: loving, generous, loyal. His best friend Turtle (Daniel Bryan Corkill) is tactful in trying to get this odd kid to act normal.

Tacked onto this small-town story, the details of the intrigue seem almost unnecessary. The movie contains the usual hard-nosed military men, visionary scientists, and officious cops. They've lost track of their expensive *D.A.R.Y.L.*, and want to find him and deprogram him. Daryl fights back by borrowing a supersecret fighter plane (as the movie is borrowing its ending from Clint Eastwood's *Firefox*), and the ending is really sort of neat; it's high-tech and heartwarming at the same time.

D.A.R.Y.L. is a good movie that could have been better. Maybe they should have screened *Charly* before making it. That would have reminded them that the scientific parts of their story are more or less predictable, and that the human elements are what keep us involved.

Dance With a Stranger ★ ★ ★ ★

R, 102 m., 1985

Miranda Richardson (Ruth Ellis), Rupert Everett (David Blakely), Ian Holm (Desmond Cussen), Matthew Carroll (Andy), Tom Chadbon (Anthony Findlater), Jane Bertish (Carole Findlater). Directed by Mike Newell and produced by Roger Randall Cutler. Screenplay by Shelagh Delaney.

Ruth Ellis and David Blakely were a tragedy waiting to happen. She was a B-girl, pouring drinks and massaging men's egos in a sleazy little 1950s London nightclub. He was a rich young brat, whose life centered around his career as a race driver. They met one boozy night in the club, and there was an instant spark of lust between them—Ruth, whose profession was to keep her distance from men, and David, who had never felt love in his life.

Dance With a Stranger is the story of their affair, which led to one of the most famous British murder trials of the decade. After Ellis shot Blakely dead in the street outside a pub, she was brought to trial, convicted, and executed with heartless speed; her trial began on June 20, 1955, and she was hanged on July 19—the last woman to receive the death penalty in England.

In the thirty years since Blakely and Ellis died, the case has fascinated the British, perhaps because it combines sexuality and the class system, two of their greatest interests. Blakely was upper-class, polished, affected, superior. Ellis was a working-class girl who made herself up to look like Marilyn Monroe and used the business of bar hostess as a way to support her young son and maintain her independence from men. Ironically, she was finally undone by her emotional dependence on Blakely, who gave and then withdrew his affection in a way that pushed her over the edge.

Their story is told by Mike Newell in a film of astonishing performances and moody, atmospheric visuals. Ruth Ellis is the emotional center of the film, and she is played by a newcomer, Miranda Richardson, as a woman who prides herself on not allowing men to hurt her, and who almost to the end cannot believe that the one man she loves would hurt her the most.

We see her first in the nightclub, where her blonde Monroe looks supply the only style in the whole shabby room. We meet her regular "friends," including Desmond Cussen (Ian Holm), a quiet, loyal bachelor who adores her in an unpossessive way. Then Blakely (played by Rupert Everett) walks into her life, and in an instant there is erotically charged tension between them; the way they both flaunt their indifference is a clue. Their relationship falls into a pattern: lust, sex, tears, quarrels, absences, and then lust and sex again. Newell tells the story only in terms of the events and characters themselves. There are no detours into shallow psychology; just the patterns of attraction and repulsion.

For Ruth Ellis, a woman living at a time when women's options were cruelly limited, the obsession with Blakely becomes totally destructive. She loses her job. She grows more dependent as he grows more cold and unpredictable, and everything is complicated by their mutual alcoholism. Cussen, the inoffensive, long-suffering admirer, takes her in, and she makes an effort to shape up, but Blakely sounds chords in her that she cannot ignore.

By the end of the movie, Blakely has done things to her that she cannot forgive. And they are not the big, melodramatic things like the violence that breaks out between them. They are little unforgivable things, as when he raises her hopes and then disappoints her. By the end, he is hardly even hurting her intentionally. He drinks in the company of fawning friends, he ignores responsibilities, he disappears into his own drunken absent-mindedness, and forgets her. And then one night outside a pub, she reminds him, once and for all.

The Dark Crystal ★ ★ 1/2

PG, 94 m., 1982

Performed by Jim Henson, Kathryn Mullen, Frank Oz, Dave Goelz, Brian Muehl, Jean Pierre Amiel, Kiran Shah. Directed by Jim Henson and Frank Oz and produced by Henson and Gary Kurtz.

You've got to hand it to Jim Henson and Frank Oz. First they enchanted a generation of kids with the Muppets. Now they're ready to scare the pants off them with the Skeksis, the Mystics and, not least, the Garthim. Those are three new races of ugly beasties invented by the Muppeteers for *The Dark Crystal*, an otherworldly fantasy. There are others. Watching this movie, I wondered at times whether Henson and Oz, who are longtime partners in the Muppet saga, made it in violent reaction to the charm of Miss Piggy, Kermit, and the other Muppets. There is nothing charming about most of the characters in this movie. They are hairy, smelly, cadaverous, loathsome, evil, cannibalistic, vindictive, slimy, mean-spirited, dripping, scaling, unkempt, and hateful, but charming they're not.

The movie *does* have a couple of heroes, who belong to the race of Gelflings, and who look related to those solemn children with gigantic, tearful eyes that you find on paintings in re-sale shops. There are two Gelf lings, a boy and a girl, and they follow in a time-hallowed tradition of monster fantasies, which says that the villains can be interesting, but the good guys have to be squeaky-voiced and innocuous.

The story takes place on a faraway planet that circles three suns. A thousand years ago, so the legend goes, the planet was prosperous and peaceful. But then there was a struggle over the Dark Crystal, a shard of it was lost and the ruling race on the planet split into two kinds of creatures: the Skeksis, who are reprehensible, and the Mystics, who are merely reptilian. (The Garthim are sort of a combination of crabs and armored beetles, and do the Skeksis's dirty work.) As the movie opens, the three suns are about to get back together again, and a little Gelfling gets a mission: Find the missing shard and repair the damage of the past millennium. *The Dark Crystal* is the story of his quest. And it *is* quite a quest, since the quest was designed and executed by some of the best special-effects people in the business, led by producer Gary *(Star Wars)* Kurtz, George Lucas's Industrial Light and Magic Co., and, of course, the Muppeteers themselves.

There are all sorts of amazing sights in this movie. An otherworldly rain forest is populated with weird plants that have lives of their own. A cliffside is the home of a race of beings who look like sponge-rubber sink scrubbers. The high point in animation is probably reached during a banquet scene—a slurpfest at which the slovenly Skeksis smear food all over their faces before bringing in the dessert, which is alive, and looks like what you fear may be lurking at the bottom of Love Canal.

The Dark Crystal is a labor of love, and on that basis, I salute it. A great deal of creativity and ingenious thinking went into the creation of these strange beings and their planet. But as a work of fiction, and more specifically as entertainment, I think it has two problems: (1) Many of the scenes last too long, because the special effects are lingered over, and (2) any kid younger than ten is probably going to lose some sleep after seeing the horrendous creatures in this movie. Sure, the Gelflings are cute, but the Garthim are unforgettable.

Date With an Angel ★

PG, 105 m., 1987

Michael E. Knight (Jim Sanders), Phoebe Cates (Patty Winston), Emmanuelle Beart (Angel), David Dukes (Ed Winston), Phil Brock (George), Albert Macklin (Don), Pete Kowanko (Rex), Vinny Argiro (Ben Sanders). Directed by Tom McLoughlin and produced by Martha Schumacher. Screenplay by McLoughlin.

If there is a heaven, I imagine it is an absolutely indescribable and overwhelmingly amazing place, but when it turns up in the movies, it always seems more like a place where you might want to go fly-fishing.

Why can't the movies really extend themselves and give us something more than clouds, nightgowns, and recycled plots about how dumb everyone is on earth? In late 1987 we got one vision of heaven, in *Made in Heaven,* and two visitors from heaven, Shelley Long in *Hello Again* and Emmanuelle Beart in *Date With an Angel.* Taken together, these three movies convinced me I would rather spend the afterlife on my own.

Made in Heaven made the best try, and its scenes in heaven were intriguing, even though the characters, given carte blanche to create any environment they fancied, showed an appalling lack of imagination. The other two movies had the same problem, a puzzling inability to make some kind of glorious metaphysical leap into the wonders that could be.

Take Shelley Long. Her character returned to earth after an entire year spent in the beyond. What did she experience there? What did she remember? Who did she bring greetings from? What message did she have for us? Nothing. Zero. Zip. Get this: She couldn't remember what happened. For the audience, this pay-off was roughly comparable to Stan Freberg's trained rat, which spent a lifetime learning to negotiate a maze, and was rewarded with a lousy chlorophyll gumball.

In *Date With an Angel,* the angel at least remembers heaven. She recognizes pictures of angels, anyway, in old art books, and starts cooing with pleasure. Her problem is, she doesn't speak any known language, and spends so much of her time making goo-goo eyes at the hero that even he finally gets tired of it. The angel is played by Emmanuelle

Beart, also seen in *Manon of the Spring,* and there is no doubt she is one beautiful woman—a dreamy adolescent version of Catherine Deneuve. In the movie, she crash-lands in a swimming pool during a mission to earth and injures herself. She is nursed back to health by Michael E. Knight, as a young yuppie who is engaged to marry Phoebe Cates.

Given this premise, the movie immediately tries to discover how many dumb things it can do with it, how many no-brainer plot twists it can discover, and how best to make both Beart and Cates into inanimate objects. The entire plot revolves around such stock figures as an angry father-in-law, a jealous girlfriend, and madcap buddies. It does not even spare us the obligatory press conference scene, which is mangled here almost as badly as it was in *Hello Again.* The angel finally speaks in a human tongue, all right, but in the last scene of the play. Just when she was ready to maybe say something interesting, the movie was over.

This movie ought to be shot. It wastes not only the idea of the angel, but also the human presence of Phoebe Cates, who is a bright and quick actress, but here is required to play a simpering bimbo. How come the filmmakers didn't have the wit to allow Cates to join her boyfriend in getting to know the angel, instead of making her into an idiotic shrew? Imagine the girl-talk she could have had with somebody her own age from heaven.

I fear this film will have a sequel. The last shot has Knight and Beart submerged in a passionate kiss, and Beart has traded in her wings for a nurse's uniform. Her first words are that she has been granted a "leave of absence," which is kind of a theological breakthrough, since angels have no bodies and exist outside of time, making it easy for them to handle the absence part, but almost impossible for them to leave—or arrive, for that matter. No doubt the sequel will be titled *Second Date With an Angel.* Stranger things happened in the year that gave us *Teen Wolf Too.*

Dawn of the Dead ★ ★ ★ ★
R, 126 m., 1979

With David Emge, Ken Foree, Scott H. Reiniger, and Gaylen Ross. Directed by George A. Romero and produced by Richard P. Rubenstein. Screenplay by Romero.

Dawn of the Dead is one of the best horror films ever made—and, as an inescapable result, one of the most horrifying. It is gruesome, sickening, disgusting, violent, brutal, and appalling. It is also (excuse me for a second while I find my other list) brilliantly crafted, funny, droll, and savagely merciless in its satiric view of the American consumer society. Nobody ever said art had to be in good taste.

It's about a mysterious plague that sweeps the nation, causing the recently dead to rise from their graves and roam the land, driven by an insatiable hunger for living flesh. No explanation is offered for this behavior—indeed, what explanation would suffice?—but there is a moment at which a survivor solemnly intones: "When there is no more room in hell, the dead will walk the Earth."

Who's that a quotation from? From George A. Romero, who wrote and directed *Dawn of the Dead* as a sequel to his *Night of the Living Dead,* which came out in 1968 and now qualifies as a cult classic. If you have seen *Night,* you will recall it as a terrifying horror film punctuated by such shocking images as zombies tearing human flesh from limbs. *Dawn* includes many more scenes like that, more graphic, more shocking, and in color. I am being rather blunt about this because there are many people who will *not* want to see this film. You know who you are. Why are you still reading?

Well . . . maybe because there's a little of the ghoulish voyeur in all of us. We like to be frightened. We like a good creepy thrill. It's just, we say, that we don't want a movie to go *too* far. What's too far? *The Exorcist? The Omen?* George Romero deliberately intends to go too far in *Dawn of the Dead.* He's dealing very consciously with the ways in which images can affect us, and if we sit through the film (many people cannot) we make some curious discoveries.

One is that the fates of the zombies, who are destroyed wholesale in all sorts of terrible ways, don't affect us so much after awhile. They aren't being killed, after all: They're already dead. They're even a little comic, lurching about a shopping center and trying to plod up the down escalator. Romero teases us with these passages of humor. We relax, we laugh, we see the satire in it all, and then—*pow!* Another disembowelment, just when we were off guard.

His story opens in a chaotic television studio, where idiotic broadcasters are desperately transmitting inaccurate information (one hopes the Emergency Broadcast System will do a whole lot better). National Guard troops storm public housing, where zombies have been reported. There are ten minutes of unrelieved violence, and then the story settles down into the saga of four survivors who hijack a helicopter, land on the roof of a suburban shopping center, and barricade themselves inside against the zombies.

Their eventual fates are not as interesting as their behavior in the meantime; there is nothing quite like a plague of zombies to wonderfully focus your attention on what really matters to you. Romero has his own ideas, too, and the shopping center becomes a brilliant setting for a series of comic and satiric situations: Some low humor, some exquisitely sly.

But, even so, you may be asking, how can I defend this depraved trash? I do not defend it. I praise it. And it is not depraved, although some reviews have seen it that way. It is *about* depravity. If you can see beyond the immediate impact of Romero's imagery, if you can experience the film as being more than just its violent extremes, a most unsettling thought may occur to you: The zombies in *Dawn of the Dead* are not the ones who are depraved. They are only acting according to their natures, and, gore dripping from their jaws, are blameless.

The depravity is in the behavior of the healthy survivors, and the true immorality comes as two bands of human survivors fight each other for the shopping center: *Now* look who's fighting over the bones! But *Dawn* is even more complicated than that, because the survivors have courage, too, and a certain nobility at times, and a sense of humor, and loneliness and dread, and are not altogether unlike ourselves. A-ha.

The Day After Trinity ★ ★ ★ ★

NO MPAA RATING, 88 m., 1980

A documentary produced and directed by Jon Else. Written by David Peoples, Janet Peoples, and Else.

There is a scene in *The Day After Trinity* showing the world's first atomic device being hoisted atop a steel frame tower that looks barely adequate to hold a windmill. The scene is not shot gracefully. The bomb looks like a giant steel basketball with some tubes and wires stuck onto it. In the background, the sky is a washed-out blue. In the next shot, the bomb is back on the ground again and a man is posing next to it, somewhat self-consciously. In 1945, the Russians would have killed for this footage.

On the sound track, the narrator reads sections of a personal diary kept by one of the scientists at Los Alamos, New Mexico, where the government ran its top-secret project to develop the atom bomb: *Gadget is in place . . . should we have the chaplain here?* It is all somewhat banal until, on reflection, it becomes emotionally shattering. The greatest achievement of *The Day After Trinity* is that it counts down those final days before nuclear weapons became a fact of our lives.

This is a documentary that develops more suspense than most of the thrillers I have seen. It includes photographs and film footage from the Los Alamos labaoratory, and it begins and ends with the story of J. Robert Oppenheimer, the brilliant scientist who was the "father of the atomic bomb" and then, a few years later, was branded as a security risk by Senator Joseph McCarthy. It includes newsreel footage of World War II, including the devastation of Hiroshima and Nagasaki, and more footage of Oppenheimer after the war and testifying before the McCarthy committee. And there are present-day interviews with some of the scientists who worked at Los Alamos.

All of this is gripping, especially the second thoughts of Oppenheimer and others about the wisdom of dropping the bomb. Of the wisdom of *developing* the bomb there seems to have been no doubt: The bomb was theoretically possible, it was technologically feasible, if we did not build it, the Russians would, and so we built it first, hurrah! Oppenheimer's brother, Frank, remembers that Robert's initial reaction to the first nuclear explosion (the "Trinity" blast) was, "it worked!" It wasn't until after Hiroshima, he says, that it occurred to him that it killed people.

The most riveting sections of the film deal with the establishment of Los Alamos and the weeks and days leading up to the Trinity test. The New Mexico base was a jerry-built collection of temporary housing, muddy streets, 6,000 people, and paranoid secrecy. But it seems to have been a glorious time for the people who were there: It was like a summer camp for Ph.D.s, with Glenn Miller records playing on the jukebox and bright young nuclear whiz kids given the full resources of the government.

Those who were there on the day of Trinity remember that nobody really knew what would happen. One scientist took side bets that New Mexico would be incinerated. In the event, it was just a very big bang. A woman who was driving through the desert with her sister remembers that her sister saw the blast from hundreds of miles away; her sister was blind. Today, physicist Robert Wilson asks himself why he—why *they*—didn't just all walk away from the bomb after they saw what it could do. But of course they did not.

Day for Night ★ ★ ★ ★
PG, 116 m., 1974

Francois Truffaut (Ferrand), Jean-Pierre Aumont (Alexandre), Jacqueline Bisset (Julie), Jean-Pierre Leaud (Alphonse), Valentina Cortese (Séverine). Directed by Francois Truffaut and produced by Marcel Bébert. Screenplay by Truffaut, Jean-Louis Richard, and Suzanne Shiffman.

Movies about movies usually don't quite get things right. The film business comes out looking more romantic and glamorous (or more corrupt and decadent) than it really is, and none of the human feeling of a movie set is communicated. That is not the case with Francois Truffaut's funny and touching film, *Day for Night*, which is not only the best movie ever made about the movies but is also a great entertainment.

A movie company, especially if it's away from home on a location somewhere, is a family that's been thrown into close and sometimes desperate contact; strangers become friends and even intimates in a few weeks, and in a few more weeks they're scattered to the winds. The family is complicated by the insecurities and egos of the actors, and by the moviemaking process itself: We see the result, but we don't see the hours and days spent on special effects, on stunts, on making it snow or making it rain or making an allegedly trained cat walk from A to B. *Day for Night* is about all of these aspects of moviemaking; about the technical problems, the boredom between takes (a movie set is one of the most boring places on earth most of the time), and about the romances and intrigues. It's real; this is how a movie set really looks, feels, and smells. Truffaut's story involves a movie company on location in Nice. They're making a melodrama called *Meet Pamela*, of which we see enough to know it's doomed at the box office. But good or bad, the movie must be made; Truffaut, who plays the director in his own film, says at one point: "When I begin a film, I want to make a great film. Halfway through, I just hope to finish the film."

His cast includes a beautiful American actress (Jacqueline Bisset); an aging matinee idol (Jean-Pierre Aumont), and his former mistress, also past her prime (Valentina Cortese); the young, lovestruck male lead (Jean-Pierre Leaud), and the entire crew of script girls, camera operators, stunt men, and a henpecked production manager. (And if you have ever wondered what the key grip does in a movie, here's your chance to find out.) Truffaut sets half a dozen stories in motion, and follows them all so effortlessly it's almost as if we're gossiping with him about his colleagues. The movie set is a microcosm: there is a pregnancy and a death; a love affair ended, another begun, and a third almost but not quite destroyed; and new careers to be nourished and old careers to be preserved.

Truffaut was always a master of quiet comedy, and there are fine touches like the aging actress fortifying herself with booze and blaming her lack of memory on her makeup girl. Then there's the young male lead's ill-fated love for Jacqueline Bisset; she is happily married to a doctor, but unwisely extends her sympathy to the youth, who repays her by very nearly destroying her marriage as well as himself. And all the time there is the movie to be made: Truffaut gives us a hilarious session with the "trained" cat, and shows us without making a point of it how snow is produced on a set, how stunt drivers survive car crashes, and how third-floor balconies can exist without buildings below them.

What we see on the screen is nothing at all

like what happens on the set—a truth the movie's title reflects. ("Day for night" is the technical term for "night" scenes shot in daylight with a special filter. The movie's original French title, *La Nuit Americaine*, is the French term for the same process—acknowledging their debt to Hollywood.)

The movie is just plain fun. Movie buffs will enjoy it like *Singin' in the Rain* (that perfect musical about the birth of talkies), but you don't have to be a movie buff to like it. Truffaut knows and loves the movies so much he's infectious; one of *Day for Night*'s best scenes is a dream in which the adult director remembers himself, as a little boy, slinking down a darkened street to steal a still from *Citizen Kane* from in front of a theater. We know who the little boy grew up to be, and that explains everything to us about how he feels now.

Day of the Dead ★ ½

R, 91 m., 1985

Lori Cardille (Sarah), Terry Alexander (John, the Pilot), Joseph Pilato (Rhodes), Richard Liberty (Dr. Logan), Howard Sherman (Bub, the Zombie). Directed by George A. Romero and produced by Richard P. Rubinstein. Screenplay by Romero.

The ghouls in *Day of the Dead* are marvels of special effects, with festoons of rotting flesh hanging from their purple limbs as they slouch toward the camera, moaning their sad songs. Truth to tell, they look a lot better than the ghouls in *Night of the Living Dead*, which was director George Romero's original ghoul film. His technology is improving; perhaps the recent emphasis on well-developed bodies (in *Perfect, Rambo*, etc.) has inspired a parallel improvement in dead bodies.

But the ghouls have another problem in *Day of the Living Dead:* They're upstaged by the characters who are supposed to be real human beings. You might assume that it would be impossible to steal a scene from a ghoul, especially one with blood dripping from his orifices, but you haven't seen the overacting in this movie. The characters shout their lines from beginning to end, their temples pound with anger, and they use distracting Jamaican and Irish accents, until we are so busy listening to their endless dialogue that we lose interest in the movie they occupy.

Maybe there's a reason for that. Maybe Romero, whose original movie was a genuine inspiration, hasn't figured out anything new to do with his ghouls. In his second ghoul film, the brilliant *Dawn of the Dead* (1980), he had them shuffling and moaning their way through a modern shopping mall, as Muzak droned in the background and terrified survivors took refuge in the Sears store. The effect was both frightening and satirical. The everyday location made the ghouls seem all the more horrible, and the shopping mall provided lots of comic props (as when several ghouls tried to crawl up the down escalator).

This time, though, Romero has centered the action in a visually dreary location—an underground storage cavern, one of those abandoned salt mines where they store financial records and the master prints of old movies. The ghouls have more or less overrun the surface of America, we gather, and down in the darkness a small team of scientists and military men are conducting experiments on a few captive ghoul guinea-pigs.

It's an interesting idea, especially if they had kept the semiseriousness of the earlier films. Instead, the chief researcher is a demented butcher with blood-stained clothes, whose idea of science is to teach a ghoul named Bub to operate a Sony Walkman. Meanwhile, the head of the military contingent (Joseph Pilato) turns into a violent little dictator who establishes martial law and threatens to end the experiments. His opponent is a spunky woman scientist (Lori Cardille), and as they shout angry accusations at each other, the real drama in the film gets lost.

In the earlier films, we really identified with the small cadre of surviving humans. They were seen as positive characters and we cared about them. This time, the humans are mostly unpleasant, violent, insane, or so noble that we can predict with utter certainty that they will survive. According to the mad scientist in *Day of the Dead*, the ghouls keep moving because of primitive impulses buried deep within their spinal columns—impulses that create the appearance of life long after consciousness and intelligence have departed. I hope the same fate doesn't befall

Romero's ghoul movies. He should quit while he's ahead.

The Day of the Jackal ★ ★ ★ ★
PG, 150 m., 1973

Edward Fox (The Jackal), Terence Alexander (Lloyd), Michel Auclair (Colonel Rolland), Alan Badel (The Minister), Tony Britton (Inspector Thomas), Denis Carey (Casson), Olga Georges-Picot (Denise), Cyril Cusack (The Gunsmith). Directed by Fred Zinnemann and produced by John Woolf. Screenplay by Kenneth Ross.

Fred Zinnemann's *The Day of the Jackal* is one hell of an exciting movie. I wasn't prepared for how good it really is: it's not just a suspense classic, but a beautifully executed example of filmmaking. It's put together like a fine watch. The screenplay meticulously assembles an incredible array of material, and then Zinnemann choreographs it so that the story—complicated as it is—unfolds in almost documentary starkness.

The "jackal" of the title is the code name for a man who may (or may not) be a British citizen specializing in professional assassinations. He allegedly killed Trujillo of the Dominican Republic in 1961 and, now, two years later, he has been hired by a group of Frenchmen who want de Gaulle assassinated. His price is $500,000; he says, "and considering that I'm handing you France, I wouldn't call that expensive."

Zinnemann, working from Frederick Forsyth's bestseller, tells both sides of the story that unfolds during the summer of 1963. The jackal prepares two disguises and three identities, gets a legal passport by applying in the name of a child who died in 1931, and calls on European experts for his materials. An old gunsmith hand-makes a weird-looking lightweight rifle with silencer, sniper scope, and explosive bullets. A forger provides French identity papers and a driver's license (and comes to an unexpected end). And then the jackal enters France.

Meanwhile, the government has received information that an attempt will be made on de Gaulle's life. The general absolutely insists that he will make no changes in his public schedule, and that any attempt to prevent an assassination must be made in secret. The French police cooperate "unofficially" with the top police forces of other nations in attempting an apprehension. But they don't even know who the jackal is.

How can they stop him? The movie provides a fascinating record of police investigative work, which combines exhaustive checking with intuition. But the jackal is clever, too, particularly when he's cornered. Some of the movie's finest moments come after the jackal's false identity is discovered and his license plates and description are distributed. He keeps running—and always convincingly; this isn't a movie about a killer with luck, but about one of uncommon intelligence and nerve.

Playing the jackal, Edward Fox is excellent. The movie doesn't provide much chance for a deep characterization, but he projects a most convincing persona. He's boyishly charming, impeccably groomed, possessed of an easy laugh, and casually ruthless. He will kill if there's the slightest need to. Fox's performance is crucial to the film, of course, and the way he carries it off is impressive.

The others on the case are uniformly excellent, especially Tony Britton as a harried police inspector and Cyril Cusack, in a nicely crafted little vignette, as the gunsmith. The movie's technical values (as is always the case with a Zinnemann film) are impeccable. The movie was filmed at great cost all over Europe, mostly on location, and it looks it. A production of this scope needs to appear absolutely convincing, and Zinnemann has mastered every detail—including the casting of a perfect de Gaulle look-alike.

The Day of the Jackal is two and a half hours long and seems over in about fifteen minutes. There are some words you hesitate to use in a review, because they sound so much like advertising copy, but in this case I can truthfully say that the movie is spellbinding.

Days of Heaven ★ ★ ★ ★
PG, 95 m., 1978

Richard Gere (Bill), Brooke Adams (Abby), Sam Shepard (The Farmer), Linda Manz (Linda), Robert Wilke (Foreman), Jackie Shultis (Linda's Friend), Stuart Margolin (Mill Foreman). Directed by Terence Malick and produced by Bert and Harold Schneider. Screenplay by Malick.

Can any description of Terence Malick's

Days of Heaven quite evoke the sense of wonder this film inspires? It's about a handful of people who find themselves shipwrecked in the middle of the Texas Panhandle—grain country—sometime before World War I. They involve themselves in a tragic love triangle, but their secrets seem insignificant, almost pathetic, seen against the awesome size of their world. Our wonder is that they endure at all in the face of the implacable land.

The land is farmed by a sick young man (Sam Shepard) who is widely believed to be on the edge of death. In the autumn, he and his foreman hire crews of itinerant laborers who ride out from the big cities on the tops of boxcars: swaggering, anonymous men who will follow the harvest north from Texas to Canada. Others pass through to entertain them and live off their brief periods of wage earning: aerial barnstormers, circus troupes, all specks on the great landscape.

We meet three people who set out together from the grime of Chicago, looking for harvest work: A strong young man (Richard Gere), his kid sister (Linda Manz), and the woman he lives with and also claims, for convenience, as his sister (Brooke Adams). They arrive at the farm of the sick young man, who falls in love with the older "sister."

Because they are so poor, because the farmer has a house, land, and money, the three keep quiet about his mistake and eventually the farmer and the "sister" marry. Her "brother"—her man—works on the farm and observes the marriage from a resentful, festering distance. The younger girl also observes, and the film's narration comes from her comments, deeply cynical, pathetically understated.

So goes the story of *Days of Heaven*, except that Malick's film doesn't really tell a story at all. It is an evocation of emptiness, loneliness, desolation, the slow accumulation of despair in a land too large for its inhabitants and blind to their dreams. Willa Cather wrote novels about such feelings—*The Lost Lady, Death Comes for the Archbishop*, the middle section of *The Professor's House*—and now Malick joins her company. This is a huge land we occupy. The first people to settle it must have wondered if they could ever really possess it.

Malick's vision of the land, indeed, is so sweeping that an ordinary, human-scale "story" in the foreground would be a distraction. We get a series of scenes, like tableaux, as the characters involve themselves in their mutual tragedy. The visual compositions often place them against vast backdrops (this is one of the most beautifully photographed films ever made), but Malick finds terror, too, in extreme close-ups of grasshoppers, of a germinating seed, of the little secrets with which nature ultimately builds her infinite secret.

When it develops that the girl has really fallen in love with her new husband, that she is not a con artist but just another victim, we might expect, in another movie, all sorts of blame and analysis. A director not sure of this material could have talked it away. But Malick brings a solemnity to his revelations, as the farmer gradually discovers the deception, as the laborer discovers his loss, as the little sister loses what little childhood she had.

Days of Heaven is a unique achievement—I can't think of another film anything like it. It's serious, yes, very solemn, but not depressing. More than anything else, it wants to re-create its time and place, as if Malick believes the decisions of his characters (and maybe his very characters themselves) come out of the time and place, and are caused by them.

So many movies are jammed with people talking to each other all the time, people obsessed with the conviction they're saying something. The people of *Days of Heaven* are so overwhelmed by the sheer force of nature, by the weight of the land, the bounty of the harvest, the casual distraction of fire and plague, the sharp, involuntary impulses of their passions, that they hardly know what to say. When you look at it that way, who does?

The Dead ★ ★ ★

PG, 83 m., 1987 ✓

(See related Film Clip, p. 756.)

Anjelica Huston (Gretta), Donal McCann (Gabriel), Rachel Dowling (Lily), Dan O'Herlihy (Mr. Browne), Donal Donnelly (Freddy), Cathleen Delany (Aunt Julia), Helena Carroll (Aunt Kate), Ingrid Craigie (Mary Jane), Frank Patterson (Bartell D'Arcy). Directed by John Huston and produced by Wieland Schulz-Keil and Chris Sievernich. Screenplay by Tony Huston.

Better pass boldly into that other world, in the full glory of some passion, than fade and wither dismally with age. The words are from James Joyce's *The Dead,* sometimes called the greatest short story ever written in English. The thoughts belong to a middle-aged man, Gabriel Conroy, and when he thinks them he is lying next to his sleeping wife in a Dublin hotel room, and the snow is falling all over Ireland. He has spent a musical evening at the home of his aunts, Julia and Kate, in the company of the same old friends who gather every Christmas to sing the same songs and tell the old stories and cluck over the fact that poor Freddy Malins has turned up drunk again, to the embarrassment of his mother.

Most of the story is devoted to the party—who is there, and what happens, and what they say. But Joyce is somehow able to use words to suggest some great silence beneath the chatter, deeper feelings that go unexpressed in all the holiday cheer. The story ends as Gabriel and his wife, Gretta, ride across Dublin to their hotel, and she confesses to him that one of the songs reminded her of a boy who loved her when she was seventeen, a boy named Michael Furey, who was ill. When she made plans to go up to Dublin to convent school, he begged her not to go, and came and stood outside her window in the winter rain. A week later he was dead.

After Gretta tells the story, Gabriel realizes that there is a large part of his wife's life that he did not even suspect existed. She goes to sleep, and he lies beside her in the dark. Joyce writes: "Generous tears filled Gabriel's eyes. He had never felt like that himself toward any woman, but he knew that such a feeling must be love." He can see through the window that it is snowing, and he knows it is snowing all over Ireland, even on the grave where Michael Furey lies.

I have described so much of the Joyce story because I want to illustrate what a hard challenge John Huston set for himself when he decided to make a film of *The Dead.* It is easy enough to film all the details of the party, all the comings and goings, the toasts and the songs. But all of those scenes are there for only one reason: to establish the surface of a commonplace, satisfactory life, so that the closing moments of the story can shock us by showing what hidden depths of loneliness and passion can exist secretly in the hearts of people we think we know.

The key emotional moment in *The Dead* does not belong to Gretta, who still mourns for her dead young lover. It belongs to Gabriel, who weeps for the man his wife once loved, a man he never met or even heard of before tonight. To cry for a stranger is to shed tears for the human condition, to weep because in giving us consciousness, God also gave us the ability to know loss and to mourn it.

There is no way in the world that any filmmaker can reproduce the thoughts inside Gabriel's head at the end of *The Dead.* And that must have been something Huston knew when he decided to make this film. Then why did he make it anyway? I think I know the answer. He made it because he came of Irish blood and lived for many years in Ireland. He made it because the film would be written by his son, Tony, and would star his daughter, Anjelica. And he made it because he knew he was dying, and it would be his last film.

And there was one last reason, which can be glimpsed in the words I began with: "Better pass boldly into that other world, in the full glory of some passion, than fade and wither dismally with age." Huston was an old man when he died, but he had not withered dismally with age because he still had the courage and the imagination to attempt to make an impossible film of the greatest story that he had ever read. Look at Huston's *The Dead* and you will not see a successful film, but you will see a grand gesture, and you will see the best film that Huston could possibly have made. And now the snow falls upon every part of the lonely churchyard on the hill where John Huston lies buried.

Dead of Winter ★ ★ 1/2

PG-13, 100 m., 1987

Mary Steenburgen (Katie McGovern), Roddy McDowall (Mr. Murray), Jan Rubes (Dr. Lewis), William Russ (Rob Sweeney), Ken Pogue (Officer Mullavy), Mark Malone (Roland). Directed by Arthur Penn and produced by John Bloomgarden and Marc Shmuger. Screenplay by Shmuger and Mark Malone.

Dead of Winter is one of those movies where you shout advice at the screen. The plot involves a young woman in mortal danger, and we can see how she can save herself, even if she can't.

It's easy to pick holes in movies like this, to find the inconsistencies and the oversights, and say the movie's no good because we're smarter than it is. But maybe that's exactly the point. Maybe the actual pleasure comes from the fun of being frustrated and full of free advice while the character marches to her doom.

The movie stars Mary Steenburgen as an out-of-work actress who is pleased to pass an audition and be summoned to an isolated country mansion for a screen test. She arrives in the middle of a howling blizzard, to meet her host, a meticulously polite old gentleman in a wheelchair, and his assistant, an obsequious, but sinister, Roddy McDowall.

What we know and she doesn't is that the two men need her because she's an exact double for a kidnap victim they've killed. They tell her she's needed as the double for an actress in a movie they're making, and she unknowingly studies the appearance and voice patterns of the dead woman, until she's good enough to read a script into a video camera. Of course, then they plan to kill her.

The plot is not really the point in a movie like this. Thriller plots are born to be manipulated and then forgotten. What counts is the architecture of the house, the exact locations of the one-way mirrors and the hidden staircases, the existence of a working telephone in the attic, the alarming moments when the heroine discovers that all is not as it seems. The plot is simply a device to get us from one heart-stopping moment to the next.

I must tread carefully, or I will give away important secrets. Let it be said that Miss Steenburgen functions in the time-honored tradition of damsels in distress, and does her share of screaming, running up and down stairs, and clawing her way up an icy hillside in a blizzard.

The evil doctor and his assistant are also well within movie tradition, but Jan Rubes and McDowall make the relationship more complex than usual; the older man seems to have some sort of subtle hold over the younger. McDowall is good in these blood-soaked roles, as he proved as the vampire-killer in *Fright Night*. He demonstrates the principle that a friendly villain is almost always more frightening than a threatening one.

For Steenburgen, there's a nice passage near the end where she tries to play a dual role; I won't say more. The movie itself is finally just an exercise in silliness—great effort to little avail—but the actors have fun with it, and the sets work, and there are one or two moments with perfect surprises.

And then, for the rest, there are the loopholes, such as (a) how many gas stations do you know that give away free goldfish in the winter—or give away anything at any time? Or (b) why couldn't Steenburgen look at the shoulder patches of the visiting cops to discover the name of the nearby town? Or (c) why can't the cops ever seem to put two and two together? And so on. Maybe they're not important. Maybe they come with the territory.

The Dead Zone ★ ★ ★ ½

R, 103 m., 1983

Christopher Walken (Johnny), Brooke Adams (Sarah), Herbert Lom (Dr. Weizak), Tom Skeritt (Sheriff), Martin Sheen (Candidate). Directed by David Cronenberg and produced by Debra Hill. Screenplay by Jeffrey Boam.

The Dead Zone does what only a good supernatural thriller can do: It makes us forget it is supernatural. Like *Rosemary's Baby* and *The Exorcist*, it tells its story so strongly through the lives of sympathetic, believable people that we not only forgive the gimmicks, we accept them. There is pathos in what happens to the Christopher Walken character in this movie and that pathos would never be felt if we didn't buy the movie's premise.

Walken plays a high school teacher whose life is happy (he's in love with Brooke Adams), until the night an accident puts him into a coma for five years. When he "returns," he has an extrasensory gift. He can touch people's hands and "know" what will happen to them. His first discovery is that he can foresee the future. His second is that he can change it. By seeing what "will" happen and trying to prevent it, he can bring about a different future. Of course, then he's left with the problem of explaining how he knew something "would have" happened, to people who can clearly see that it did not. Instead of ignoring that problem as a lesser movie might have, *The Dead Zone* builds its whole premise on it.

The movie is based on a novel by Stephen King and was directed by David Cronenberg, the Canadian who started with low-budget shockers *(The Brood, It Came From Within)* and worked up to big budgets *(Scanners).* It's a happy collaboration. No other King novel has been better filmed (certainly not the dreadful *Cujo*), and Cronenberg, who knows how to handle terror, also knows how to create three-dimensional, fascinating characters.

In that he gets a lot of help from Walken, whose performance in this movie in a semi-reputable genre is the equal of his work in *The Deer Hunter.* Walken does such a good job of portraying Johnny Smith, the man with the strange gift, that we forget this is science fiction or fantasy or whatever, and just accept it as this guy's story.

The movie is filled with good performances: Adams, as the woman who marries someone else during Johnny's coma, but has a clear-eyed, unsentimental love for him at a crucial moment; Tom Skeritt, as the local sheriff who wants to enlist this psychic to solve a chain of murders; Herbert Lom as a sympathetic doctor; and Martin Sheen as a conniving populist politician. They all work together to make a movie that could have been just another scary thriller, and turn it into a believable thriller—which, of course, is even scarier.

Death in Venice ★ ★ ½

PG, 127 m., 1971

Dirk Bogarde (Aschenbach), Bjorn Andresen (Tadzio), Silvana Mangano (The Mother), Romolo Valli (Hotel Manager). Directed and produced by Luchino Visconti. Screenplay by Visconti and Nicola Badalucco.

I think the thing that disappoints me most about Luchino Visconti's *Death in Venice* is its lack of ambiguity. Visconti has chosen to abandon the subtleties of the Thomas Mann novel and present us with a straightforward story of homosexual love, and although that's his privilege, I think he has missed the greatness of Mann's work somewhere along the way. In the novel, Count Aschenbach goes to Venice at a certain season in his life, driven by a compulsion he does not fully understand and confronted by strange presences who somehow seem to be mocking or tempting him. Once settled in his grand hotel on the Lido, he becomes aware of a beautiful boy who is also visiting there with his family from Poland. His feelings toward this boy are terribly complicated, and to interpret them as a simple homosexual attraction is vulgar and simplistic. The boy represents, above all, an ideal of perfect physical beauty apart from sexuality; the irony is that this beauty stirs emotions in a man who (in the novel) has insisted on occupying the world of the intellect. The boy's youth and naturalness become a reproach to the older man's vanity and creative sterility.

Visconti undermines this contrast between beauty and the intellect by changing the Aschenbach character from a writer to a composer. He made the change, reportedly, because he decided that Mann had "really" based his character on Gustav Mahler, but so what? There are flashbacks where Aschenbach argues that beauty resides in the intellect, and a friend declares that beauty is a quality naturally possessed by beautiful things. Aschenbach's position could be held by a philosopher and scholar, but not (I imagine) by the composer of the romantic Mahler symphonies that are constantly present on the sound track.

Visconti also misses, or avoids, the subtlety of the novel's development of the relationship between the two characters. In the Mann version, the man can never really know what the boy thinks of him; they do not speak, and if the boy favors him sometimes with a look or a smile, he favors many others as well, because that is his nature. It is entirely possible, the way Mann tells the story, that the boy is totally unaware of any homosexual implication—and the man, indeed, may also be in love with an ideal rather than a person. No such possibility exists in the heavy-handed Visconti retelling. The boy's function in the film, which he performs at least two dozen times, is to self-consciously pose in front of the man, turn slowly, smile sweetly, and turn languorously away. This is almost literally the only physical characteristic the boy has in the movie; and Visconti lays on the turns, looks, and smiles with such a heavy hand that the boy could almost be accused of hustling.

By choosing to limit his story to this level, Visconti loses the philosophical content of the Thomas Mann work, and no amount of heavy-handed flashbacks can restore it. We see Aschenbach in discussions with colleagues, with his wife and child, and then at the child's funeral; we see him seemingly impotent in a bordello, and, unforgivably, Visconti even throws in a concert at which Aschenbach is booed, then comforted by his wife. Scenes in which the genius is assured that (someday!) his genius will be recognized went out, I thought, with *The Eddy Duchin Story.*

Visconti fails, then, to develop characters and relationships that matter. The failure is fatal to the movie's success; but the physical beauty of the film itself is overwhelming. The world of the Lido of sixty years ago has been re-created in painstaking detail. The fashions, the entertainments, the table settings reveal Visconti's compulsion for accuracy. The photography is almost the first I have seen that is fully worthy of the beauty of Venice; the pink-and-gray city rises from waters of a glasslike smoothness, so that the water and the quality of light itself seem to suggest the presence of the plague-bearing sirocco wind. The wind brings both plague and beauty, which is its function in the Mann novel, and Visconti's mastery of visual style almost succeeds in creating the very ideas and feelings that his heavy-handed narrative entirely misses.

Death Wish ★ ★ ★

R, 94 m., 1974

Charles Bronson (Paul Kersey), Hope Lange (Joanna Kersey), Vincent Gardenia (Frank Ochoa), Steve Keats (Jack Toby), William Redfield (Sam Kreutzer), Stuart Margolin (Ames), Jack Wallace (Policeman). Directed by Michael Winner and produced by Dino de Laurentiis. Screenplay by Wendell Mayes.

Death Wish is a quasifascist advertisement for urban vigilantes, done up as a slick and exciting action movie; we like it even while we're turned off by the message. It gives us Charles Bronson in a role that starts out by being somewhat out of character: He plays a liberal, an architect, a former conscientious objector. But he turns into the familiar Bronson man of action after his wife is murdered and his daughter reduced to catatonia by muggers.

His immediate reaction is one of simple grief. But then, seeking a change of scenery, he visits his firm's Arizona office. And there he meets an architect with two deep convictions: a love for the land and a love of guns. He takes Bronson to his gun club, watches him squeeze off a few perfect practice rounds and slips a present into his suitcase when he heads back to New York. It's a .32-caliber revolver.

Alone in his apartment, Bronson examines snapshots from his recent Hawaiian vacation with his wife. Then he examines the gun. He goes out into the night, is attacked by a mugger and shoots him dead. Then he goes home and throws up. But the taste for vengeance, once acquired, has a fascination of its own. And the last half of *Death Wish* is essentially a series of cat-and-mouse games, in which Bronson poses as a middle-aged citizen with a bag of groceries and then murders his attackers.

They are, by the way, everywhere. Director Michael Winner gives us a New York in the grip of a reign of terror; this doesn't look like 1974, but like one of those bloody future cities in science fiction novels about anarchy in the twenty-first century. Literally every shadow holds a mugger; every subway train harbors a killer; the park is a breeding ground for crime. Urban paranoia is one thing, but *Death Wish* is another. If there were really that many muggers in New York, Bronson could hardly have survived long enough to father a daughter, let alone grieve her.

The movie has an eerie kind of fascination, even though its message is scary. Bronson and Winner have worked together on several films, and they've perfected the Bronson persona. He's a steely instrument of violence, with few words and fewer emotions. In *Death Wish* we get just about the definitive Bronson; rarely has a leading role contained fewer words or more violence.

And Winner directs with a cool precision. He's one of the most efficient directors of action and violence. His muggings and their surprise endings have a sort of inevitable rhythm to them; we're set up for each one almost like the gunfights in Westerns. There's never any question of injustice, because the crimes are attempted right there before our eyes. And then Bronson becomes judge and jury—and executioner.

That's what's scary about the film. It's propaganda for private gun ownership and a call to vigilante justice. Even the cops seem to see it that way; Bronson becomes a folk hero as the New York Vigilante, and the mugging rate drops fifty percent. So the police want to catch Bronson, not to prosecute him for murder, but to offer him a deal: Get out of town, stay out of town, and we'll forget this. Bronson accepts the deal, and in the movie's last scene we see him taking an imaginary bead on a couple of goons in Chicago.

Death Wish II no stars
R, 89 m., 1982

Charles Bronson (Paul Kersey), Jill Ireland (Geri Nichols), Vincent Gardenia (Frank Ochoa), Anthony Frannciosa (Commissioner), Robert F. Lyons (Fred). Directed by Michael Winner and produced by Menahem Golan and Yoram Globus. Screenplay by David Engleback.

You will have noticed that I've given a "no stars" rating for *Death Wish II,* starring Charles Bronson as an urban vigilante. A word of explanation. In my movie rating system, the most a movie can get is four stars *(My Dinner With André)* and the least is ordinarily half a star (even *The Beast Within* got a whole star). I award "no stars" only to movies that are artistically inept and morally repugnant. So *Death Wish II* joins such unsavory company as *Penitentiary II* and *I Spit on Your Grave.* And that, in a way, is a shame. I have a certain admiration for the screen presence of Charles Bronson. In his good roles, he can be lean, quiet, and efficient. He often co-stars with his wife, Jill Ireland, as he does in this movie, and she is a pleasant and capable actress. They were charming together in a little-seen movie named *From Noon to Three.*

This time, however, Bronson and Ireland and everyone else involved with *Death Wish II* create a great disappointment. Although the original *Death Wish* (1974) had its detractors, it was an effective movie that spoke directly to the law-and-order mentality of the Nixon-Ford era. It was directed with a nice slick polish by Michael Winner, and, on its own terms, it worked. *Death Wish II* is a disaster by comparison. It has the same director, Winner, but he directs the dialogue scenes as if the actors' shoes were nailed to the floor. It has two of the same stars—Bronson and New York cop Vincent Gardenia—but they seem shell-shocked by weariness in this film. It has the same plot (Bronson's loved ones are attacked, and he goes out into the streets to murder muggers). But while the first film convinced me of Bronson's need for vengeance, this one is just a series of dumb killings.

You will remember that *Death Wish* opened with home invaders killing Bronson's wife and raping his daughter. After Bronson used himself as bait to trap and kill nine New York City muggers, he became a folk hero. Gardenia, the cop, found out who he was, but decided not to arrest him. Bronson left town, and in this film, he's in Los Angeles. The film opens with his daughter being killed, and then Bronson hits the streets again. Ireland plays the woman he loves, and who suspects his guilty secret.

What's most shocking about *Death Wish II* is the lack of artistry and skill in the filmmaking. The movie is underwritten and desperately underplotted, so that its witless action scenes alternate with lobotomized dialogue passages. The movie doesn't contain an ounce of life. It slinks onto the screen and squirms for a while, and is over.

Death Wish 3 ★
R, 100 m., 1985

Charles Bronson (Paul Kersey), Ed Lauter (Captain Striker), Gavan O'Herlihy (Fraker), Martin Balsam (Bennett), Kirk Taylor (Giggler), Deborah Raffin (Kathryn). Directed by Michael Winner and produced by Menahem Golan and Yoram Globus. Screenplay by Michael Edmonds.

Death Wish 3 is a marginally better movie than the second part of this series; enough better to earn a one-star rating, instead of none. The action, direction, and special effects are all better than the last time around, which isn't saying much, since *Death Wish II* was so ineptly directed and edited that it was an insult even to audiences that were *looking* for a bad movie.

The plot is as before. Charles Bronson plays Paul Kersey, who was an architect in the original 1974 film, but has now apparently moved into a new career, as a professional vigilante. After knocking off several muggers in Kansas City and a few thieves in Chicago, he is back in New York at the beginning of this film, just in time to find an old friend dying after a vicious beating.

Kersey is arrested for the crime, but allowed back on the streets by the police captain (Ed Lauter), who offers a deal: Kersey can murder all the creeps he wants, if he keeps the cops informed. Kersey does not agree to this deal, but Lauter does not seem to notice. Indeed, by the end of the film, the two of them are stalking the mean streets side-by-side, like killers in the old West.

Bronson moves into a tenement building which seems to be in the middle of a vast burned-out wasteland, but which is still occupied by terrified old people. Among the tenants are an old watch repairman (Martin Balsam), who keeps a couple of machine guns in his closet, and an elderly Jewish couple who live on the first floor and make stuffed cabbage rolls while the creeps jump in through the window and toss their TV set outside. It is a little amazing that they still have a TV set when this movie opens, since the neighborhood has been under siege for weeks.

The neighborhood is ruled by a gang headed by Fraker (Gavan O'Herlihy), who wears a reverse Mohawk: He keeps his hair on the sides, but shaves down the middle, to make room for a gang symbol in warpaint. O'Herlihy looks a little like Richard Widmark, and is quite satisfactory as a snarling, sadistic creep. He is also, of course, white. One of the hypocrisies practiced by the *Death Wish* movies is that they pretend to ignore racial tension in big cities. In their horrible new world, all of the gangs are integrated, so that the movies can't be called racist. I guess it's supposed to be heartwarming to see whites, blacks, and Latinos working side-by-side to rape, pillage, and murder.

Not quite so much equality applies to the victims, however. All of the good speaking roles go to white victims (especially Balsam). Two Latinos get to be minor supporting players (the wife is raped and murdered, the husband gets to sob and pound his fist on the table). The black victims are represented by an old lady who gets her purse snatched.

If it seems strange for me to be making a racial head-count like this, reflect that the filmmakers no doubt assigned races to their characters with equal cynicism. Since there is not a single character in this movie who *has* to belong to any particular race, *Death Wish 3* could have had Bronson protecting black citizens against black gang violence. That would reflect the reality of most big cities, but it would not, of course, have been as commercial as the integrated violence we get instead.

My only other observation has to be about Bronson himself. He looks very tired in this movie. In interviews, he has expressed his unhappiness with it. Despite the fact that he's the central character, he doesn't seem eager to leap in and take charge. And he probably says fewer words in *Death Wish 3* than any other major leading character since the introduction of sound. My guess is that he utters less than one hundred words in the whole movie. My hunch is he would have liked that number to be closer to zero.

Deathtrap ★ ★ ★

R, 116 m., 1982

Michael Caine (Sidney Bruhl), Christopher Reeve (Clifford Anderson), Dyan Cannon (Myra Bruhl), Irene Worth (Psychic). Directed by Sidney Lumet, produced by Burtt Harrisand. Screenplay by Jay Presson Allen.

Deathtrap is a wonderful windup fiction machine with a few modest ambitions: It wants to mislead us at every turn, confound all our expectations, and provide at least one moment when we levitate from our seats and come down screaming. It succeeds, more or less. It's a thriller that depends on all sorts of surprises for its effects, and you may continue reading in the confidence that I'll reveal none of them.

That doesn't leave me much to write about, however. Let's see. I can tell you something about how the movie begins. Michael Caine plays a very successful Broadway playwright whose latest mystery is a total flop. We see him at the outset, standing at the back of the house, a gloomy witness to a disastrous opening night. (It's a Broadway in-joke that the play he's watching is being performed on the stage set of *Deathtrap*.) Caine gets drunk and goes home to his farmhouse in Connecticut and sinks into despair. There is perhaps, however, some small shred of hope. In the mail the next day Caine receives a manuscript from a former student (Christopher Reeve). It is a new thriller, and Caine sees at once that it's a masterpiece. It could run for years and earn millions of dollars. As he talks with his wife (Dyan Cannon) about it, he slowly develops the idea that he could *steal* the play, kill Reeve, and produce the hit himself.

A plausible plan? Perhaps. Caine and Cannon invite Reeve to come for a visit to the country. They grill him, subtly, and discover that absolutely no one else knows he has written the play. The stage is set for murder, betrayal, and at least an hour and a half of surprises. The tables are turned so many times in this movie that you would think they were on wheels.

Anyway, that's all I'll say about the plot. It is fair to observe, however, that *Deathtrap* is a comic study of ancient and honorable human defects, including greed, envy, lust, pride, avarice, sloth, and falsehood. Interest in the movie depends on its surprises, but its delight grows basically out of the human characteristics of its performers. They do a very good job. Thrillers like this don't always bother to pay attention to the human nature of their characters (for example, the Agatha Christie omnibus whodunits, with their cardboard suspects). *Deathtrap*, however, provides a fascinating, quirky character in Sydney Bruhl, played by Caine, and two strong supporting performances in his goofy, screaming wife (Cannon, looking great) and his talented, devious student (Reeve, who has a light, handsome comic touch not a million miles removed from Cary Grant's). The dialogue is witty without being Neil Simonized. The sets are so good they're almost distracting (a windmill appears to operate in close association with the Bruhls' bed). The only distraction is a strange character played by Irene Worth—a next-door neighbor who's a busybody, snooping psychic who sniffs down false leads. We don't know why she's even in the play, until it's much too late.

Deathtrap is not a great film and will not live forever, but if you're an aficionado of whodunits and haven't seen this one, it'll be a treat. It's more fiendishly complicated than, for example, Caine's similar outing in *Sleuth*. It plays absolutely fair, more or less, and yet fools us every time, more or less. And perhaps its greatest gift is the sight of three lighthearted comic actors having a good time chewing on the dialogue, the scenery, and each other.

The Deer Hunter ★ ★ ★ ★

R, 183 m., 1979

Robert De Niro (Michael), John Cazale (Stan), John Savage (Steven), Christopher Walken (Nick), Meryl Streep (Linda), George Dzundza (John), Chuck Aspegren (Axel). Directed by Michael Cimino and produced by Barry Spikings, Michael Deeley, Cimino, and John Peverall. Screenplay by Deric Washburn.

Michael Cimino's *The Deer Hunter* is a three-hour movie in three major movements. It is a progression from a wedding to a funeral. It is the story of a group of friends. It is the record of how the war in Vietnam entered several lives and altered them terribly forever. It is not an anti-war film. It is not a pro-war film. It is one of the most emotionally shattering films ever made.

It begins with men at work, at the furnaces of the steel mills in a town somewhere in Ohio or Pennsylvania. The klaxon sounds, the shift is over, the men go down the road to a saloon for a beer. They sing "I Love You *Bay*-bee" along with the jukebox. It is still morning on the last day of their lives that will belong to them before Vietnam.

The movie takes its time with these opening scenes, with the steel mill and the saloon and especially with the wedding and the party in the American Legion Hall. It's important not simply that we come to know the characters, but that we feel absorbed into their lives, that the wedding rituals and rhythms feel like more than just ethnic details. They do.

The opening moment is lingered over; it's like the wedding celebration in *The Godfather*, but celebrated by hard-working people who have come to eat, dance, and drink a lot and wish luck to the newlyweds and to say good-bye to the three young men who have enlisted in the army. The party goes on long enough for everyone to get drunk who is ever going to, and then the newlyweds drive off and the rest of the friends go up into the mountains to shoot some deer. There is some Hemingwayesque talk about what it means to shoot deer: We are still at a point where shooting something is supposed to mean something.

Then Vietnam occupies the screen, suddenly, with a wall of noise, and the second movement of the film is about the experiences that three of the friends (Robert De Niro, John Savage, and Christopher Walken) have there. At the film's center comes one of the most horrifying sequences ever created in fiction, as the three are taken prisoner and forced to play Russian roulette while their captors gamble on who will, or will not, blow out his brains.

The game of Russian roulette becomes the organizing symbol of the film: Anything you can believe about the game, about its deliberately random violence, about how it touches the sanity of men forced to play it, will apply to the war as a whole. It is a brilliant symbol because, in the context of this story, it makes any ideological statement about the war superfluous.

The De Niro character is the one who somehow finds the strength to keep going and to keep Savage and Walken going. He survives the prison camp and helps the others. Then, finally home from Vietnam, he is surrounded by a silence we can never quite penetrate. He is touched vaguely by desire for the girl that more than one of them left behind, but does not act decisively. He is a "hero," greeted shyly, awkwardly, by the hometown people.

He delays for a long time going to the VA hospital to visit Savage, who has lost his legs. While he is there he learns that Walken is still in Vietnam. He had promised Walken—on a drunken moonlit night under a basketball hoop on a playlot, the night of the wedding—that he would never leave him in Vietnam. They were both thinking, romantically and naively, of the deaths of heroes, but now De Niro goes back in an altogether different context to retrieve the living Walken. The promise was adolescent stuff, but there is no adolescence left when De Niro finds Walken still in Saigon, playing Russian roulette professionally.

At about this point in a review it is customary to praise or criticize those parts of a film that seem deserving: the actors, the photography, the director's handling of the material. It should be said, I suppose, that *The Deer Hunter* is far from flawless, that there are moments when its characters do not behave convincingly, such as implausible details involving Walken's stay and fate in Vietnam, and unnecessary ambiguities in the De Niro character. It can also be said that the film contains greatly moving performances, and that it is the most impressing blending of "box office" and "art" in American movies since *Bonnie and Clyde, The Godfather,* and *Nashville.* All of those kinds of observations will become irrelevant as you experience the film: It gathers you up, it takes you along, it doesn't let up.

The Deer Hunter is said to be about many subjects: About male bonding, about mindless patriotism, about the dehumanizing effects of war, about Nixon's "silent majority." It is about any of those things that you choose, if you choose, but more than anything else it is a heartbreakingly effective fictional machine that evokes the agony of the Vietnam time.

If it is not overtly "anti-war," why should it be? What *The Deer Hunter* insists is that we not *forget* the war. It ends on a curious note: The singing of "God Bless America." I won't tell you how it arrives at that particular moment (the unfolding of the final passages should occur to you as events in life) but I do want to observe that the lyrics of "God Bless America" have never before seemed to me to contain such an infinity of possible meanings, some tragic, some unspeakably sad, some few still defiantly hopeful.

Defence of the Realm ★ ★ ★
PG, 94 m., 1987

Gabriel Byrne (Nick Mullen), Greta Scacchi (Nina Beckman), Denholm Elliott (Vernon Bayliss), Ian Bannen (Dennis Markham), Fulton Mackay (Victor Kingsbrook), Bill Paterson (Jack Macleod). Directed by David Drury and produced by Robin Douet and Lynda Myles. Screenplay by Martin Stellman.

Defence of the Realm is a newspaper thriller about a touchy investigation into British security matters. The story ends the way many newspaper stories end—inconclusively—but the movie ends with a shocking event that suggests the British and their U.S. allies would do anything to defend the American nuclear presence in the U.K.

The movie stars Gabriel Byrne as a young, ambitious newspaper reporter who covers a scandal involving an MP who has the bad judgment to patronize the same call girl used by a KGB agent. Is he a security risk, or does he only seem to be one? Byrne's paper doesn't ask too many questions before putting the story on page one and forcing the politician's resignation.

But there's an older, more experienced hand at the newspaper—a veteran political reporter played by Denholm Elliott, that most dependable and believable of British character actors. He believes the MP may have been framed by people who wanted to silence his embarrassing questions in Parliament. Byrne half-listens to him, and halfway wants to go with the story just because it's so spicy. Upstairs on the executive floor, the proprietor of the paper likes the scandal because it increases circulation.

The film moves quickly and confidently into a net of intrigue, and the director, David Drury, does a good job of keeping us oriented even though the facts in the case remain deliberately confusing. In one especially effective scene, he shows Byrne pretending to be a policeman in order to get quotes from the wife of the disgraced MP; her simple, quiet dignity when she discovers the deception is a rebuke to him.

So is the dogged professionalism of the veteran reporter, who has an anonymous source who insists the MP is innocent. But then the old-timer dies suspiciously, and it's up to Byrne to decide whether there's a deeper story involved, or only a coincidence.

Defence of the Realm reminded me sometimes of *All the President's Men*, but this is a bleaker, more pessimistic movie, which assumes that a conspiracy can be covered up, and that the truth will not necessarily ever be found. The real target of the movie is the American nuclear presence in Britain, and the exciting framework of the newspaper story is an effective way to make a movie against nuclear arms without ever really addressing the point directly.

The acting is strong throughout, but Elliott is especially effective. What is it about this actor, who has been in so many different kinds of movies and seems to make each role special? You may remember him as the Thoreau-quoting father in *A Room With a View*, or as Ben Gazzara's lonely friend in *Saint Jack*. Here he is needed to suggest integrity and scruples, and does it almost simply by the way he looks.

Gabriel Byrne, a relative newcomer, is quietly effective as the reporter, and Greta Scacchi, as a woman who gets involved on both sides of the case, shows again that she can project the quality of knowing more than she reveals. *Defence of the Realm* ends on a bleak and cynical note—unless you count the somewhat contrived epilogue—and gets there with intelligence and a sharp, bitter edge.

The Delta Force ★ ★ ★

R, 129 m., 1985

Chuck Norris (Major McCoy), Lee Marvin (Colonel Alexander), Robert Forster (Abdul), Martin Balsam (Ben Kaplan), Joey Bishop (Harry Goldman), Lainie Kazan (Sylvia Goldman), George Kennedy (Father O'Malley), Hanna Schygulla (Ingrid), Bo Svenson (Captain). Directed by Menahem Golan and produced by Golan and Yoram Globus. Screenplay by James Bruner and Golan.

Some of the opening moments of *The Delta Force* had me ready to laugh. Here was a movie about an airplane hijacking, and who was on the passenger list? Why, George Kennedy, of course—fresh from four *Airport* movies and *Earthquake*—and Shelley Winters, going on her first vacation since the *Poseidon* sank. I thought this was going to be another hilarious disaster movie, but I was wrong. *The Delta Force* settles down into a well-made action film that tantalizes us with its parallels to real life.

The movie was inspired by the June 1985 hijacking of the TWA airplane and the hostage crisis after the passengers were held captive in Beirut. (In the movie, the airline is renamed ATW—real subtle.) Many of the moments in the film are drawn directly from life, as when an American serviceman is beaten to death by terrorists, and his body is dumped on the runway, or when a terrorist holds a gun to the head of the pilot during a press conference.

The docudrama approach gives an eerie conviction to the movie, although later, after Chuck Norris and Lee Marvin arrive on the scene, there's not much we would mistake for reality. The movie caters directly to our national revenge fantasies; in *The Delta Force*, the hijacking ends the way we might have wanted it to.

The story establishes the plane and its passengers, and then intercuts the hijacking with the movements of the Delta Force, a crack U.S. commando unit that specializes in antiterrorist missions. Delta is led by grizzled old Lee Marvin, and its best fighter is a hot dog played by Chuck Norris, who once again this time is depicted as a man who yearns only for retirement, but cannot resist the call to action, and arrives at the last moment in his trusty pickup truck. (If I were Chuck Norris's agent, I'd insist that his next movie include a new way of introducing him into the plot.)

There are a couple of hazards here that the movie has to face. The action inside the airplane has a tendency to degenerate into a retread of the old *Airport* movies, but director Menahem Golan wisely has his cast keep their acting fairly low-key. And the action involving Norris has a tendency to resemble his activities in *Missing in Action* and *Invasion USA*. Golan does nothing to fight this tendency—indeed, he relishes it, in scenes like the one where Norris drives his rocket-firing motorcycle right through the window of a terrorist hideout, and socks the bad guy on the jaw. This is the second movie in a row where Norris has possessed X-ray vision; in *Invasion USA* he drove his pickup into a department store to stop a terrorist attack. How does he know what's on the other side of the barriers he crashes through?

It's a funny thing about action movies. When they don't work, we have a lot of fun picking holes in them, like the fallacy of the hero's X-ray vision. When they do work, though, we forgive them their inconsistencies. *The Delta Force* works. It is taut and exciting and well-tuned to the personalities of Marvin and Norris, who work together here like a couple of laconic veterans of lots of tough jobs.

The movie also has the one other attribute that any good thriller needs: A first-rate performance by the actor playing the villain. As Abdul, the chief terrorist, an American actor named Robert Forster gives a frightening, good performance, intense and uncompromising. He makes the threat real, and keeps *The Delta Force* from becoming just an action comic book.

Desperately Seeking Susan ★ ★ ★
PG-13, 103 m., 1985

Rosanna Arquette (Roberta), Madonna (Susan), Aidan Quinn (Dez), Mark Blum (Gary), Robert Joy (Jim), Laurie Metcalf (Leslie). Directed by Susan Seidelman and produced by Sarah Pillsbury and Midge Sanford. Screenplay by Leora Barish.

Desperately Seeking Susan is a movie that begins with those three words, in a classified ad. A time and place are suggested where Susan can rendezvous with the person who is desperately seeking her. A bored housewife (Rosanna Arquette) sees the ad and becomes consumed with curiosity. Who is Susan and who is seeking her, and why? So Arquette turns up at the rendezvous, sees Susan (Madonna), and inadvertently becomes so involved in her world that for a while she even *becomes* Susan.

This sounds complicated, but, believe me, it's nothing compared to the complexities of this movie. *Desperately Seeking Susan* is a screwball comedy based on several cases of mistaken identity. Susan, for example, is a punk drifter who is in a hotel room with a mobster the first time we see her. Shortly after, the mobster is killed and the mob hit man comes back looking for Susan, who may have been a witness. But meanwhile, Susan has sold the jacket that is her trademark, and the housewife has bought it, and then the housewife has banged her head and become a temporary amnesia victim, and there are people who see her jacket and think she's Susan.

But enough of the plot. I wouldn't even dream of trying to explain how Arquette ends up being sawed in half by a nightclub magician. The plot isn't the point, anyway; once you realize the movie is going to be a series of double-reverses, you relax and let them happen. The plot is so unpredictable that, in a way, it's predictable; that makes it the weakest part of the movie.

What I liked in *Desperately Seeking Susan* was the cheerful way it hopped around New York, introducing us to unforgettable characters, played by good actors. For example, Aidan Quinn plays a guy who thinks Arquette is Susan, his best friend's girl. He lets her spend the night, and inadvertently feeds her amnesia by suggesting that she *is* Susan. Laurie Metcalf plays Arquette's yuppie sister-in-law. Robert Joy plays Susan's desperately seeking lover. Peter Maloney is the broken-down magician. New York underground characters such as Richard Hell, Anne Carlisle, and Rockets Red Glare also surface briefly. The director is Susan Seidelman, whose previous film, *Smithereens,* was a similar excursion through the uncharted depths of New York.

Desperately Seeking Susan does not move with the self-confidence that its complicated plot requires. But it has its moments, and many of them involve the different kinds of special appeal that Arquette and Madonna are able to generate. They are very particular individuals, and in a dizzying plot they somehow succeed in creating specific, interesting characters.

Diamonds Are Forever ★ ★ ★

PG, 119 m., 1971

Sean Connery (James Bond), Jill St. John (Tiffany Case), Charles Gray (Blofeld), Lana Wood (Plenty O'Toole), Jimmy Dean (Willard Whyte), Bruce Cabot (Saxby), Bernard Lee (M), Desmond Llewelyn (Q). Directed by Guy Hamilton and produced by Albert R. Broccoli and Harry Saltzman.

The cultists like the early James Bond movies best, but I dunno. They may have been more tightly directed films, but they didn't understand the Bond mythos as fully as *Goldfinger* and *Diamonds Are Forever.* We see different movies for different reasons, and *Diamonds Are Forever* is great at doing the things we see a James Bond movie for.

Not the least of these is the presence of Sean Connery, who was born to the role: dry, unflappable (even while trapped in a coffin at a crematorium), with a mouth that does as many kinds of sly grins as there are lascivious possibilities in the universe. There's something about his detachment from danger that props up the whole Bond apparatus, insulating it from the total ridiculousness only an inch away.

In *Diamonds Are Forever,* for example, Bond finds himself driving a moon buggy (antennae wildly revolving and robot arms flapping) while being chased across a desert—never mind why. The buggy looks comical, but Connery does not; he is completely at home, as we know by now, with every form of transportation. Later, after outsmarting five Las Vegas squad cars in a lovely chase scene, he nonchalantly flips his Mustang up on two wheels to elude the sixth. But not a sign of a smile. There is an exhiliration in the way he does it, even more than in the stunt itself.

The plot of *Diamonds Are Forever* is as complicated as possible. That's necessary in order to have somebody left after nine dozen bad guys have been killed. It has been claimed that the plot is too complicated to describe, but I think I could if I wanted to. I can't imagine why anyone would want to, though. The point in a Bond adventure is the moment, the surface, what's happening now. The less time wasted on plot, the better.

Diary of a Mad Housewife ★ ★ ★

R, 95 m., 1970

Carrie Snodgress (Tina Balser), Richard Benjamin (Jonathan Balser), Frank Langella (George). Directed and produced by Frank Perry. Screenplay by Eleanor Perry.

Frank Perry's *Diary of a Mad Housewife* is about a long-suffering young woman who has somehow gotten herself married to the most supercilious dope in Manhattan. He's egotistical, cruel, insecure, immature, and bitchy. He sides with "his" children against his wife. He considers her a household drudge, good for housework during the day, and, maybe, a "little roll in de hay" at night. He humiliates her in public, and humiliates himself, too, by his shameless social-climbing. Does she hate him? Not exactly.

She's a masochistic type who sees her husband as, somehow, her fate in life. She enjoys martyrdom, I guess; I can't imagine any other reason why she'd put up with this monster she's married to. And that's at the base of our initial irritation with the film; she stays with this guy we can't stand, and so we have trouble admiring her. We even begin to doubt her sanity, until she falls into a love affair with a writer. And then *he* turns out to be such an egotistical, selfish, cruel type that we just about give up on her. She has what's known, I believe, as self-destructive tendencies. Not that she'd ever try suicide; that'd be too easy, and end the delight of suffering. What makes the movie work, however, is that it's played entirely from the housewife's point of view, and that the housewife is played brilliantly by Carrie Snodgress. We're irritated by the things the character puts up with, but Miss Snodgress is beautifully good at putting up with them.

Still, when you've finished watching this

movie you start getting mad at Richard Benjamin. He overplays his character so much that he nearly destroys the role; nobody, but nobody, is that supercilious. Near the beginning of the movie there's a scene when the whole family is in an elevator, and Benjamin gives instructions to his wife about packing a suitcase. He describes everything in highly specific brand names, and with such precision that the dialogue passes beyond reality and becomes satire. You can see it as a caption under a *New Yorker* cartoon.

But then, then . . . you start thinking about the title and the point of view of the movie, and you realize this is indeed a diary; that we're getting the housewife's version of the story. So of course she seems noble and long-suffering, and of course he's a witless bastard—because that's the way she sees it. And of course his dialogue is extreme and hers isn't, because in her version of the story, she's sane, and he's not.

Dim Sum ★ ★ ★

PG, 88 m., 1985 ✓

Laureen Chew (Geraldine Tam), Kim Chew (Mrs. Tam), Victor Wong (Uncle Tam), Ida F.O. Chung (Auntie Mary), Cora Miao (Julia), John Nishio (Richard). Directed by Wayne Wang and produced by Tom Sternberg, Wang, and Danny Yung. Screenplay by Terrel Seltzer.

Director Wayne Wang says his favorite image in *Dim Sum* is the sight of the shoes left outside the living room door in the Tam household in San Francisco's Chinatown. They are Western shoes, taken off as the characters enter a home that is still run according to Chinese values by old Mrs. Tam, a sweet widow with a strong but quietly concealed will. After the success of *Chan Is Missing*, his first slice-of-life about Chinese-Americans, Wang was looking for another story, and when he saw some shoes left outside a Chinese home, he knew he had his viewpoint, and only had to create his characters.

He has created some unforgettable ones, including Mrs. Tam (Kim Chew), a sixtyish woman whose husband is dead and whose children have left home, all except for the youngest daughter; Geraldine Tam (Laureen Chew), the daughter, who says she wants to get married but feels she should stay with her mother, and Uncle Tam (Victor Wong), a jolly, worldly bartender who would marry Mrs. Tam if Geraldine would only get out of the way.

These three characters dance a subtle little emotional ballet during the film, as we gradually become aware of their true motives. Mrs. Tam is given to sadly shaking her head and bemoaning the fact that her daughter is thirty and still single, but there are clues that she enjoys the fact that Geraldine has stayed at home with her. That way, she will not have to deal with Uncle Tam, who, for that matter, may only be paying lip service to his desire to marry her. Meanwhile, Geraldine has a boyfriend in Los Angeles who has been waiting patiently to marry her, and perhaps Geraldine uses her mother as an excuse to avoid the idea of marriage.

What is remarkable is the way Wang deals with this complex set of emotions, in a movie that is essentially a comedy. Some of the scenes in *Dim Sum* are as quietly funny as anything I've seen, especially Mrs. Tam's birthday party, a long conversation she has over the back fence with a neighbor, and the way Uncle Tam effortlessly mixes his Chinese wisdom with the lessons he has learned as a bartender.

The movie is not heavily plotted, and that's good; a heavy hand would spoil this fragile material. Wang's camera enters quietly and observes as his characters lead their lives, trying to find a compromise between too much loneliness and too much risk. At the end, everyone is more or less happy, and more or less sad, and in this movie that is satisfactory.

Note: Although this is no doubt not what Wang had in mind, I couldn't help thinking, as I watched Dim Sum, *that the movie's characters and situations could be effortlessly spun off into a wonderful TV sitcom.*

Diner ★ ★ ★ ½

R, 110 m., 1982

Steve Guttenberg (Eddie), Daniel Stern (Shrevie), Mickey Rourke (Boogie), Kevin Bacon (Fenwick), Timothy Daly (Billy), Ellen Barkin (Beth). Directed by Barry Levinson and produced by Jerry Weintraub. Screenplay by Levinson.

Women are not strange, not threatening, not mysterious, unless you happen to be a man. Young men in particular seem to regard women with a combination of admiration, desire, and dread that is quite out of their control. This was especially true in the late 1950s, a decade during which the Playmate of the Month was more alien than E.T. is today. Women were such a puzzling phenomenon to 1950s young men that, after a date, the best way for males to restore their equilibrium was to regroup with the guys for the therapeutic consumption of cheeseburgers, greasy fries, black coffee, chocolate malteds, Lucky Strikes, and loud arguments about football teams and pop singers. *Diner* is a story about several such young men, who live in Baltimore. They share one awkward problem: They are growing up, painfully and awkwardly, at an age when they are supposed to have already grown up. Adolescence lasts longer for some people than society quite imagines. These guys are best friends for this summer, although in the fall they will go separate ways, to schools and jobs and even marriage, and it's possible they will never be this close again. They cling to one another for security, because out there in the real world, responsibility lurks, and responsibility is spelled *woman.* They have plans, but their plans are not as real as their dreams.

Diner is structured a lot like *American Graffiti* and Fellini's *I Vitelloni.* It's episodic, as the young men venture out for romantic and sexual adventures, practical jokes, drunken Friday evenings, and long mornings of hangovers and doubt. Some of the movie's situations seem quite implausible, but they all fit within the overall theme of fear of women. One bizarre sequence, for example, involves a young man who insists that his fiancée pass a tough quiz about pro football before he'll agree to marry her. He's serious: If she flunks, the wedding is off. This situation doesn't seem possible to me, but it's right symbolically, since what the man is really looking for in a wife is one of the guys—a woman who will agree to become an imitation man.

Another character, already married, is much more realistic. He has absolutely no communication with his wife and no way to develop any, since he sees her only as a "wife" and not as a friend, a companion, or even a fellow human being. Her great failure is an inability to regard his life with the proper reverence; when she gets his record collection out of alphabetical order, it's grounds for a fight. He's flabbergasted that she hasn't memorized the flip sides of all the Top 40 hits of 1958, but he never even suspects that he doesn't know what's inside her mind.

Diner is often a very funny movie, although I laughed most freely not at the sexual pranks but at the movie's accurate ear, as it reproduced dialogue with great comic accuracy. If the movie has a weakness, however, it's that it limits itself to the faithful reproduction of the speech, clothing, cars, and mores of the late 1950s, and never quite stretches to include the humanity of the characters. For all that I recognized and sympathized with these young men and their martyred wives, girlfriends, and sex symbols, I never quite believed that they were three-dimensional. It is, of course, a disturbing possibly that, to the degree these young men denied full personhood to women, they didn't *have* three-dimensional personalities.

Dirty Dancing ★
PG-13, 100 m., 1987

Jennifer Grey (Baby Houseman), Patrick Swayze (Johnny Castle), Jerry Orbach (Jake Houseman), Cynthia Rhodes (Penny Johnson), Jack Weston (Max Kellerman), Jane Brucker (Lisa Houseman), Kelly Bishop (Marjorie Houseman). Directed by Emile Ardolino and produced by Linda Gottlieb. Screenplay by Eleanor Bergstein.

Well, you gotta hand it to *Dirty Dancing* for one thing at least: It's got a great title. The title seemed to promise a guided tour into the anarchic practices of untrammeled teen-age lust, but the movie turns out to be a tired and relentlessly predictable story of love between kids from different backgrounds.

The movie takes place at a resort hotel that I guess is supposed to be in the Catskills. The hotel is run by Jack Weston, who wants to play matchmaker for his obnoxious nephew. When the Houseman family checks in, he immediately introduces this brat to Baby Houseman (Jennifer Grey), the daughter of Dr. Houseman, if you get the point. Baby doesn't like the brat, and she finds herself bored by the old people at the hotel. But from the cabins out back she hears the insistent beat of rock & roll, and when she sneaks a peek inside she finds the hotel staff engaged in an orgiastic dance sequence.

I use the word "sequence" advisedly. The actors playing the staff in this movie are such good dancers, and their dancing is so over-choreographed, that there's no question that these are just ordinary kids who can dance pretty well. Nope. It's pretty clear they're in a movie.

Baby falls in love with the best-looking dancer, a handsome jock named Johnny Castle (Patrick Swayze), who dances professionally in the hotel's show. At first, he doesn't pay her much attention, but then he kinda starts to like the kid, like in millions of other movies. Meanwhile, a waiter impregnates Swayze's partner, and when there's an emergency, Baby asks her father to help out. Her father (Jerry Orbach) assumes that Swayze was the father of the child, and so he is violently opposed to any romance between his Baby and this greasy jerk.

Of course, Swayze is not the father. There is no reason for Orbach to think so, except for the requirements of the movie's Idiot Plot, which obligates everyone to say exactly the wrong thing at the wrong time in order to protect the idiocy of his mistake. Meanwhile, the sick girl cannot dance in a big show at a nearby hotel, so Grey volunteers to take her place. And after some doubt, Swayze becomes her dance coach.

Can you figure out the rest of the plot? What's your best guess? Does Grey turn out to be a great dancer? Does Swayze fall in love with her? Do they dance together in front of everybody, while her father fumes and her mother keeps a cool head, and then does Orbach finally realize his mistake and accept the kid as his daughter's boyfriend? Are there stars in the sky?

The movie makes some kind of half-hearted attempt to rip off *West Side Story* by making the girl Jewish and the boy Italian—or Irish, I forget. It doesn't much matter, since the movie itself never, ever uses the word "Jewish" or says out loud what obviously is the main point of the plot: the family's opposition to a gentile boyfriend of low social status. I guess people who care about such things are supposed to be able to read between the lines, and the great unwashed masses of American moviegoers are condemned to think the old man doesn't like Swayze's dirty dancing.

This might have been a decent movie if it had allowed itself to be about anything. The performances are good. Swayze is a great dancer, and Grey, who is appealing, is also a great dancer. But the filmmakers rely so heavily on clichés, on stock characters in old situations, that it's as if they never really had any confidence in their performers.

This movie could have been about the subjects it pussyfoots around so coyly. It could have found a big scene a little more original than the heroine stepping in for the injured star. It could have made the obnoxious owner's nephew less of a one-dimensional S.O.B. But the movie plays like one long, sad compromise; it places packaging ahead of ambition. Where did I get that idea? I dunno. Maybe from the title.

Dirty Harry ★ ★ ★

R, 103 m., 1971

Clint Eastwood (Harry), Harry Guardino (Bressler), Reni Santoni (Chico), Andy Robinson (Killer), John Vernon (Mayor). Directed and produced by Don Siegel. Screenplay by Harry Julian Fink.

There is a book named *From Caligari to Hitler* that tries to penetrate the German national subconscious by analyzing German films between 1919 and the rise of the Nazis. I have my doubts about the critical approach (it gets cause and effect backwards), but if anybody is writing a book about the rise of fascism in America, they ought to have a look at *Dirty Harry.* The film is directed by Don Siegel, and like *Coogan's Bluff* it considers the role of a cop in society with lots of dynamite action and enough wry cynicism to keep the blood from getting too thick. It is photographed all over San Francisco, and is filled with good character actors.

The presence of Eastwood in an action role is enough to explain the movie's popularity, but when you see it you discover that the movie has a message with a vengeance. It is loosely based on 1970's headlines, and makes Eastwood a cop who is assigned to find a mysterious killer named Scorpio. The killer has kidnapped and killed various girls, he has tried to extract $200,000 ransom from the city, and in the film's climax he hijacks a school bus. The gimmick is that Eastwood is so filled with hatred for Scorpio that he violates the poor fiend's civil rights. While attempting to find out where a kidnapped girl is, for example, Eastwood gets no less than four amendments wrong. And so the city has to set Scorpio free—even though they have a murder weapon and a confession.

Eastwood doesn't care; he says to hell with the Bill of Rights and stalks out of the district attorney's office. But when Scorpio hijacks the school bus, it is Eastwood again, who is asked to be bag man and carry the ransom. This time he refuses. He wants Scorpio on his own. We've already seen him twisting Scorpio's broken arm ("I have a right to a lawyer!" Scorpio shouts), and soon we will see him kill Scorpio in cold blood. Then, in a thoughtful final scene, Eastwood takes his police badge and throws it into a gravel pit.

It is possible to see the movie as just another extension of Eastwood's basic screen character: He is always the quiet one with the painfully bottled-up capacity for violence, the savage forced to follow the rules of society. This time, by breaking loose, he did what he was always about to do in his earlier films. If that is all, then *Dirty Harry* is a very good example of the cops-and-killers genre, and Siegel proves once again that he understands the Eastwood mystique.

But wait a minute. The movie clearly and unmistakably gives us a character who understands the Bill of Rights, understands his legal responsibility as a police officer, and nevertheless takes retribution into his own hands. Sure, Scorpio is portrayed as the most vicious, perverted, warped monster we can imagine—but that's part of the same stacked deck. The movie's moral position is fascist. No doubt about it.

I think films are more often a mirror of society than an agent of change, and that when we blame the movies for the evils around us we are getting things backward. *Dirty Harry* is very effective at the level of a thriller. At another level, it uses the most potent star presence in American movies—Clint Eastwood—to lay things on the line. If there aren't mentalities like Dirty Harry's at loose in the land, then the movie is irrelevant. If there are, we should not blame the bearer of the bad news.

The Discreet Charm of the Bourgeoisie ★ ★ ★ ★

PG, 100 m., 1972

Fernando Rey (Ambassador), Stephane Audran (Mrs. Scnechal), Delphine Seyrig (Mrs. Thevenot), Bulle Ogier (Florence), Jean-Pierre Cassel (Senechal), Michel Piccoli (Secretary of State). Directed by Luis Bunuel and produced by Serge Silberman. Screenplay by Bunuel and Jean-Claude Carriere.

"The best explanation of this film is that, from the standpoint of pure reason, there is no explanation."—Bunüel's preface to *The Exterminating Angel*

There is never quite an explanation in the universe of Luis Bunuel. His characters slip in and out of each other's fantasies, driven by compulsions that are perhaps not even their own. Bunuel doesn't like characters who have free will; if they inhabit his films, they will do what he tells them. And his fancies are as unpredictable as they are likely to be embarrassing.

His theme is almost always entrapment. His characters cannot get loose. He places them in either literal or psychological bondage, and forces them to watch with horror as he demonstrates the underlying evil of the universe. Bunuel is the most pessimistic of filmmakers, the most negative, certainly the most cynical. He is also the most obsessive, returning again and again to the same situations and predicaments; it's as if filmmaking, for him, is a grand tour of his favorite fetishes.

The Discreet Charm of the Bourgeoisie (which won the Oscar as 1972's best foreign film) has nothing new in it; but Bunuel admirers don't want anything new. They want the same old stuff in a different way, and Bunuel doesn't—perhaps cannot—disappoint them. The most interesting thing about *Discreet Charm* is the way he neatly reverses the situation in his *The Exterminating Angel* (1962).

In that film, one of my favorites, a group of dinner guests find themselves in an embarrassing predicament: After dinner, no one can leave the drawing room. There is nothing to prevent them; the door stands wide open. But, somehow, they simply . . . can't leave. They camp out on the floor for several days of gradually increasing barbarism, black magic, death, suicide, and visits from a bear and two sheep (which they capture and barbecue).

The film, as Bunuel noted in his opening title, makes no sense. Not that it needs to; it gives us an eerie feeling, and we look at his trapped characters with a mixture of pity and the notion that they got what was coming to them. In *The Discreet Charm of the Bourgeoisie,* Bunuel reverses the mirror; this time, his characters are forever sitting down to dinner—but they never eat.

The consummation of their feast is prevented by a series of disasters—some real, some dreams, some obviously contrived to feed some secret itch of Bunuel's. At first there is a simple misunderstanding; the guests have arrived on the wrong night. Later, at an inn, their appetites are spoiled when it develops that the owner has died and is laid out in the next room. Still later, there are interruptions from the army, the police . . . and the guests' own dreams. All of the fantasies of public embarrassment are here, including a scene in which the guests sit down to eat and suddenly find themselves on a stage in front of an audience.

The movie isn't about anything in particular, I suppose, although devoted symbol-mongers will be able to make something of the ambassador who is a cocaine smuggler and the bishop who gets off by hiring himself out as a gardener. Bunuel seems to have finally done away with plot and dedicated himself to filmmaking on the level of pure personal fantasy.

Since the form of a movie is so much more important than the content anyway, this decision gives Bunuel's immediately preceding films (*Tristana, Belle de Jour*) a feeling almost of relief. We are all so accustomed to following the narrative threads in a movie that we want to *make* a movie make "sense," even if it doesn't. But the greatest directors can carry us along breathlessly on the wings of their own imaginations, so that we don't ask questions; we simply have an experience. Ingmar Bergman's *Cries and Whispers* did that; now here comes old Bunuel to show that he can, too.

Diva ★ ★ ★ ★
R, 123 m., 1981

Wilhelmenia Wiggins Fernandez (Cynthia,) Frédéric Andrei (Jules), Richard Bohringer (Gordorish), Thay An Luu (Alba), Jacques Fabbri (Saporta), Chantal Deruaz (Nadia). Directed by Jean-Jacques Beineix and produced by Irene Silberman. Screenplay by Beineix and Jean Van Hamme.

The opening shots inform us with authority that *Diva* is the work of a director with an enormous gift for creating visual images. We meet a young Parisian mailman. His job is to deliver special delivery letters on his motor scooter. His passion is opera, and, as *Diva* opens, he is secretly tape-recording a live performance by an American soprano. The camera sees this action in two ways. First, with camera movements that seem as lyrical as the operatic performance. Second, with almost surreptitious observations of the electronic eavesdropper at work. His face shows the intensity of a fanatic: He does not simply admire this woman, he adores her. There is a tear in his eye. The operatic performance takes on a greatness, in this scene, that is absolutely necessary if we're to share his passion. We do. And, doing so, we start to like this kid.

His name is Frédéric Andrei, an actor I do not remember having seen before. But he could be Antoine Doinel, the subject of *The 400 Blows* and several other autobiographical films by Francois Truffaut. He has the same loony idealism, coexisting with a certain hard-headed realism about Paris. He lives and works there, he knows the streets, and yet he never quite believes he could get into trouble. *Diva* is the story of the trouble he gets into. It is one of the best thrillers of recent years but, more than that, it is a brilliant film, a visual extravaganza that announces the considerable gifts of its young director, Jean-Jacques Beineix. He has made a film that is about many things, but I think the real subject of *Diva* is the director's joy in making it. The movie is filled with so many small character touches, so many perfectly observed intimacies, so many visual inventions—from the sly to the grand—that the thriller plot is just a bonus. In a way, it doesn't really matter what this movie is about; Pauline Kael has compared Beineix to Orson Welles and, as Welles so often did, he has made a movie that is a feast to look at, regardless of its subject.

But to give the plot its due: *Diva* really gets under way when the young postman slips his tape into the saddlebag of his motor scooter. Two tape pirates from Hong Kong know that the tape is in his possession, and, since the American soprano has refused to ever allow any of her performances to be recorded, they want to steal the tape and use it to make a bootleg record. Meanwhile, in a totally unrelated development, a young prostitute tape-records accusations that the Paris chief of police is involved in an international white-slavery ring. The two cassette tapes get exchanged, and *Diva* is off to the races.

One of the movie's delights is the cast of characters it introduces. Andrei, who plays the hero, is a serious, plucky kid who's made his own accommodation with Paris. The diva herself, played by Wilhelmenia Wiggins Fernandez, comes into the postman's life after a most unexpected event (which I deliberately will not reveal, because the way in which it happens, and *what* happens, are enormously surprising). We meet others: A young Vietnamese girl who seems so blasé in the face of Paris that we wonder if anything truly excites her; a wealthy man-about-town who specializes in manipulating people for his own amusement; and a grab bag of criminals.

Most thrillers have a chase scene, and mostly they're predictable and boring. *Diva's* chase scene deserves ranking with the all-time classics, *Raiders of the Lost Ark*, *The French Connection*, and *Bullitt*. The kid rides his motorcycle down into the Paris Metro system, and the chase leads on and off trains and up and down escalators. It's pure exhilaration, and Beineix almost seems to be doing it just to show he knows how. A lot of the movie strikes that note: Here is a director taking audacious chances, doing wild and unpredictable things with his camera and actors, just to celebrate moviemaking.

There is a story behind his ecstasy. Jean-Jacques Beineix has been an assistant director for ten years. He has worked for directors ranging from Claude Berri to Jerry Lewis. But the job of an assistant director is not always romantic and challenging. Many days, he's a glorified traffic cop, shouting through a bullhorn for quiet on the set, and knocking on dressing room doors to tell the actors they're wanted. Day after day, year after year, the assistant director helps set up situations before the director takes control of them. The director gives the instructions, the assistant passes them on. Perhaps some assistants are always thinking of how *they* would do the shot. Here's one who finally got his chance.

Divine Madness ★ ★ ★ ½

R, 94 m., 1980

Bette Midler, with the Harlettes (Jocelyn Brown, Ula Hedwig, Diva Gray) and Irving Sudrow as the Head Usher. Directed and produced by Michael Ritchie. Written by Jerry Blatt, Bette Midler, and Bruce Vilanch.

Think of a concert film and you think of a camera bolted to the floor in front of the stage and shooting straight up into the singer's nostrils, which are half-concealed by the microphone. Those films are all right as recordings of song performances, but as cinema they stink. Some directors have broken out of the mold by making documentaries about the event of a concert; the best of those films is still Michael Wadleigh's *Woodstock* (1970).

Here Michael Ritchie, whose background is almost entirely in dramatic features *(Downhill Racer, The Candidate, The Bad News Bears)*, tries a new approach. There are times in Ritchie's *Divine Madness* when he seems to be trying to turn a live Bette Midler stage concert into a Hollywood genre musical. He opens as if *Divine Madness* is going to be a traditional concert film—Bette charges on stage, the audience cheers, there's an electric performance feel. But from that beginning, Ritchie subtly moves into the material until there are times when we almost forget we're watching an actual concert performance.

Ritchie's first decision was to declare an absolute ban on visible cameras. At no moment during *Divine Madness* do we see any cameras or any members of Ritchie's crew onstage, even though twenty cameras were used to shoot the performance. Ritchie and Midler used a week of rehearsal to choreograph the camera moves and time them to Midler's own abundant energy. So instead of looking beyond the performer and being distracted by cinematographers carrying handheld cameras and sneaking around in their Adidas, we see only the stage, Midler, and her backup singers, the Harlettes. Ritchie also uses camera techniques that are rarely seen in concert films. There are, for example, crane shots in this movie—shots where the camera swoops up to look down on Midler or to circle down and toward her. That's especially effective during the Magic Lady sequence, in which Bette portrays a sort of dreamy bag lady on a park bench. This sequence comes closest to capturing the feel of a studio musical. That's not to say that *Divine Madness* loses the impact of a live concert performance. This movie is amazingly alive and involving, and Midler, who has become one of the great live performers, has an energy that steamrollers through an incredible variety of material.

When you think about *Divine Madness* after it's over, you realize what a wide range of material Midler covers. She does rock 'n' roll, she sings blues, she does a hilarious stand-up comedy routine, she plays characters (including a tacky show-lounge performer who enters in a motorized wheelchair outfitted with a palm tree), she stars in bizarre pageantry, and she wears costumes that Busby Berkeley would have found excessive. That's one reason *Divine Madness* doesn't drag: Midler changes pace so often that there's never too much of the same thing.

Is there a weakness in the film? I think there's one—a curious one. I don't think Ritchie intercuts enough close-up shots of the audience. That may seem like a curious objection, since I've already praised *Divine Madness* for sometimes feeling more like a movie musical than a concert documentary. But you can use people in an audience as characters. Richard Lester did in the original Beatles film, *A Hard Day's Night* (and who can ever forget that blonde girl weeping and screaming?).

With a Midler concert, the audience is part of the show. Intercutting selected audience shots with the stage material could have set up a nice byplay in some of the numbers. But Ritchie keeps the audience mostly in long shot; it looks like a vast, amorphous mass out there in the dark. Since the film was actually edited together from three different concert performances, maybe he was concerned about matching audiences. But close-ups would have eliminated that problem.

No matter, though, really. Bette Midler is a wonderful performer with a high and infectious energy level and a split-second timing instinct that allows her to play with raunchy material instead of getting mired in it. She sings well, but she performs even better than she sings: She's giving a dramatic performance in music, and *Divine Madness* does a good job of communicating that performance without obscuring it in the distractions of most concert documentaries.

D.O.A. ★ ★ ★

R, 100 m., 1988

Dennis Quaid (Dexter Cornell), Meg Ryan (Sydney Fuller), Charlotte Rampling (Mrs. Fitzwaring), Daniel Stern (Hal Petersham), Jane Kaczmarek (Gail Cornell), Christopher Neame (Bernard), Robin Johnson (Cookie Fitzwaring), Rob Knepper (Nicholas Lang). Directed by Rocky Morton and Annabel Jankel and produced by Ian Sander and Laura Ziskin. Screenplay by Charles Edward Pogue.

Are we in the middle of something new here? Are thrillers abandoning supermen and embracing everyman? For a decade or more we've had the spectacle of the violent man of action, smashing everything that stands in his way. The only question was how long it would take him to kill everyone he didn't like. But lately, there's been a return of a quieter, more intriguing kind of thriller—in which ordinary people get caught up against their will in mysteries they don't understand.

D.O.A. is a movie like that, in which a college professor learns he has been poisoned, and has twenty-four hours to live—twenty-four hours to find his killer. Look at some other movies that came out at about the same time. In *Masquerade*, Meg Tilly plays a la-de-dah rich girl who falls blissfully in love, unaware that she is surrounded by a pack of vipers. *Frantic* stars Harrison Ford as an American doctor whose wife is kidnapped from their Paris hotel, all because of a baggage mix-up at the airport. In *The House on Carroll Street*, Kelly McGillis overhears a conversation and is plunged into the midst of Nazi schemes.

What all of these movies have in common is that the hero is passive, and wants only to be left alone. But other people have other plans, and the hero is swept along by the tide. This is, of course, the classic definition of *film noir*, those 1940s thrillers in which ordinary people discovered the evil that lurked beneath the surface of society, and

D.O.A. itself is inspired by a 1949 thriller starring Edmond O'Brien.

The plot is irresistible from the first frame onward. A man staggers into a police station to report a murder. A cop asks him who was murdered. "I was," he says. The man is a college English professor (Dennis Quaid), who has been told that his body contains a radioactive substance that will give him only twenty-four hours to live. During that time he must discover the identity of his killer, a problem made more complicated because he is being sought by the police on framed-up murder charges.

His search leads him into more bizarre corners than you would expect to find at the University of Texas at Austin, where the movie is set during the Christmas season. There are all sorts of suspects. The bright young student, for example, who commits suicide after Quaid delays in reading his novel. The jealous assistant professor who is enraged because Quaid has tenure and he does not. The mysterious mother of the dead student. Quaid's own ex-wife. And so on.

Although the plot follows the broad outlines of a 1940s whodunit, Charles Edward Pogue's screenplay adds a lot of campus atmosphere and academic intrigue. The Quaid character once published a brilliant first novel, we learn, and for a time was a promising writer, but he has produced nothing for four years. "They didn't kill me; I was dead already," he says at one point, equating, as only a writer could, death and writer's block. The whole story plays sly variations on the theme of "publish or perish."

It is required, of course, that the hero of a story like this fall in love along the way, in order to have company on his quest. Quaid's companion is a bright young student (Meg Ryan) who first flirts with him, then is frightened of him, and finally believes in him. Together, they travel a bloody road that leads from ancient family secrets to a deadly tar pit. The family with the secrets is headed by a mysterious widow (Charlotte Rampling), who may have poisoned Quaid in revenge for her son's suicide. Then again, maybe not. Everything is settled in an ending that seems contrived and is the movie's weakest link.

D.O.A. is a witty and literate thriller, with a lot of irony to cut the violence. Quaid is convincing as the chain-smoking English professor, Meg Ryan is true-blue as the stalwart co-ed, and Rampling looks capable of keeping her victims alive just to toy with them. The film was directed by Rocky Morton and Annabel Jankel, who created Max Headroom. This is their first feature, showing an almost sensuous love for the shadows and secrets of *film noir.*

Dog Day Afternoon ★ ★ ★ ½

R, 120 m., 1975

Al Pacino (Sonny), Charles Durning (Moretti), James Broderick (FBI Man), John Cazale (Sal), Chris Sarandon (Leon), Judith Malina (Sonny's Mother). Directed by Sidney Lumet and produced by Martin Bregman and Martin Elfand. Screenplay by Frank Pierson.

There's a point midway in *Dog Day Afternoon* when a bank's head teller, held hostage by two very nervous stick-up men, is out in the street with a chance to escape. The cops tell her to run. But, no, she goes back inside the bank with the other tellers, proudly explaining, "My place is with my girls." What she means is that her place is at the center of live TV coverage inspired by the robbery. She's enjoying it.

Criminals become celebrities because their crimes provide fodder for the media. Many of the fashionable new crimes—hijacking, taking hostages—are committed primarily as publicity stunts. And a complex relationship grows up among the criminals, their victims, the police, and the press. Knowing they're on TV, hostages comb their hair and killers say the things they've learned on the evening news. That's the subject, in a way, of Sidney Lumet's pointed film. It's based on an actual bank robbery that took place in New York in the 1970s. And it seems to borrow, too, from that curious episode in Stockholm when hostages, barricaded in a bank vault with would-be robbers, began to identify with their captors. The presence of reporters and live TV cameras changed the nature of those events, helped to dictate them, made them into happenings with their own internal logic.

But Lumet's film is also a study of a fascinating character: Sonny, the bank robber who takes charge, played by Al Pacino as a compulsive and most complex man. He's street-smart, he fought in Vietnam, he's running the stick-up in order to get money for his homosexual lover to have a sex-change operation. He's also married to a chubby and shrill woman with three kids, and he has a terrifically possessive mother (the Freudianism gets a little thick at times). Sonny isn't explained or analyzed—just presented. He becomes one of the most interesting modern movie characters, ranking with Gene Hackman's eavesdropper in *The Conversation* and Jack Nicholson's Bobby Dupre in *Five Easy Pieces*.

Sonny and his zombie-like partner, Sal, hit the bank at closing time (a third confederate gets cold feet and leaves early). The stick-up is discovered, the bank is surrounded, the live TV mini-cams line up across the street, and Sonny is in the position, inadvertently, of having taken hostages. Sal (John Cazale) is very willing to shoot them, a factor in all that follows.

There are moments when *Dog Day Afternoon* comes dangerously close to the clichés of old Pat O'Brien gangster movies and the great Lenny Bruce routine inspired by them (the Irish cop shouts into his bullhorn "Come on out, Sonny, and nobody's gonna get hurt," and Sonny's mother pleads with him from the middle of the street). But Lumet is exploring the clichés, not just using them. And he has a good feel for the big-city crowd that's quickly drawn to the action. At first, Sonny is their hero, and he does a defiant dance in front of the bank, looking like a rock star playing to his fans. When it becomes known that Sonny's bisexual, the crowd turns against him. But within a short time (New York being New York), gay libbers turn up to cheer him on.

The movie has an irreverent, quirky sense of humor, and we get some notion of the times we live in when the bank starts getting obscene phone calls—and the giggling tellers breathe heavily into the receiver. There's also, in a film that's probably about fifteen minutes too long, an attempt to take a documentary look at the ways police and banks try to handle situations like this. And through it all there's that tantalizing attraction of instant celebrityhood, caught for an instant when a pizza deliveryman waves at the cameras and shouts, "Hey, I'm a star!"

Dominick and Eugene ★ ★ ★ ½

PG-13, 111 m., 1988 ✓

Tom Hulce (Dominick), Ray Liotta (Eugene), Jamie Lee Curtis (Jennifer), Robert Levine (Dr. Levinson), Todd Graff (Larry Higgins), Bill Cobbs (Jesse Johnson), Tommy Snelfire (Mickey), David Strathairn (Mickey's Father). Directed by Robert M. Young and produced by Marvin Minoff and Mike Farrell. Screenplay by Alvin Sargent and Corey Blechman.

Dominick was dropped on his head when he was young, and now he is a little "slow," but not so slow that he can't hold down a good job as a garbageman, and use his salary to send his brother through medical school. Eugene, the brother, is an overworked intern who is on duty long hours at a stretch, and hardly has time for a girlfriend, but does have time to love and care for Dominick. Their parents are dead, and the two brothers live upstairs over a deli in Philadelphia, where Dominick dreams of the day he'll be able to see Hulk Hogan in person.

This might possibly sound like one of those tearjerker plots that inspire you to start giggling halfway through (there is nothing quite so funny as melodramatic pathos). But *Dominick and Eugene* is a special movie, a movie that somehow negotiates its plot without becoming corny or ridiculous, and leaves us feeling surprisingly moved.

The film stars Tom Hulce in the crucial role of Dominick, a friendly, outgoing young man whose retardation has left him well able to function, but not always able to understand other people's motives. He is completely trusting, likes everyone, and expects everyone to like him, but it doesn't work that way with one of the stops on his garbage route. There's a young boy there named Mickey (Tommy Snelfire) who shares his love of comic books, and they trade back issues until Mickey's drunken father (David Strathairn) tells Dominick, "Stop hanging around my kid!"

Dominick's feelings are hurt. And there are other complications in his life. His brother, Eugene (Ray Liotta), turns up one day with a date (Jamie Lee Curtis), and Dominick fears that Eugene will run away and leave him. Larry (Todd Graff), the guy who works with him on the garbage truck, fills his head with bad ideas all the time, including the suggestion that Eugene may run away to Atlantic City and gamble away all of their money.

The director, Robert M. Young, regards this situation with an evenhanded point of view. We see Dominick's world through his own eyes, and then we see the world of Eugene at the hospital. Attention is paid to Eugene's relationship with Jamie Lee Curtis; they're both so busy, so ambitious, and so overworked as medical students that they seem to realize there is no place in their plans for each other. Sometimes Eugene grows frustrated with Dominick, and sometimes his temper explodes, but they have a loving relationship.

Then one day Dominick sees something. Little Mickey's drunken father mistreats him, and throws him down the basement steps, and as Dominick accidentally witnesses this act there is a long, painful closeup on his face and we realize he is remembering something. The way in which Tom Hulce projects his thoughts, in this scene and others, is surprisingly effective. His performance is a courageous one, completely uninhibited and without any fear of looking silly. Many actors protect themselves, refuse to go "too far," worry about their image; Hulce dedicates himself absolutely to this character.

I was also impressed by Ray Liotta's work as Dominick's brother. You may remember Liotta from *Something Wild*, where he was the mysterious, violent husband who turned up unexpectedly two-thirds of the way through. Liotta's ability to suggest an undercurrent of danger is present in this role, too, but channeled in a different direction. What comes out more strongly is his tenderness, his willingness to meet Tom Hulce's lack of inhibition and go with it. Jamie Lee Curtis has a fairly thankless role as an intelligent observer admitted into the family circle, but she is right for it, and projects a kind of fierce careerism that doesn't quite mask her emotions.

Dominick and Eugene is a message movie with several different messages, but it never feels like a messenger. In the way it shows the two brothers caring for each other, it captures a tenderness and intimacy that few love stories ever reach. It reminded me sometimes of *Midnight Cowboy*, another movie in which two men learned to take care of one another and make allowances for each other's weaknesses. The danger is that any description of the plot will make it sound so melodramatic that its genuine human qualities get overlooked. It's quite an experience.

Down and Out in Beverly Hills

★ ★ ★ ★

R, 103 m., 1986

Nick Nolte (Jerry Baskin), Richard Dreyfuss (Dave Whiteman), Bette Midler (Barbara Whiteman), Little Richard (Orvis Goodnight), Tracy Nelson (Jenny Whiteman), Elizabeth Pena (Carmen). Directed and produced by Paul Marzursky. Screenplay by Marzursky and Leon Capetanos.

Buddy Hackett once said that the problem with Beverly Hills is, you go to sleep beside your pool one day and when you wake up you're seventy-five years old. *Down and Out in Beverly Hills* understands that statement inside-out.

It tells the story of a rich family that lives in the timeless comfort of a Beverly Hills mansion—in the kind of house where they use *Architectural Digest* for pornography. One day a bum wanders down the alley and into their backyard and tries to drown himself in their swimming pool. After he is saved, he changes their lives forever.

In its broad outlines, this story is borrowed from Jean Renoir's classic film *Boudo Saved from Drowning*. But this isn't just a remake. The director, Paul Mazursky, makes his whole film depend on the very close observation of his characters. Mazursky knows Beverly Hills (he lives there, on the quiet cloistered flatlands below Sunset Boulevard), and he knows the deceptions and compromises of upper-middle-class life (his credits include *An Unmarried Woman* and *Bob & Carol & Ted & Alice*). With great attention and affection, he shows us the lives that are disrupted by the arrival of the derelict—this seedy failure whose whole life is an affront to the consumer society.

The film's heroes are the Whitemans, Dave and Barbara (Richard Dreyfuss and Bette Midler), and the bum, Jerry Baskin. He is played by Nick Nolte as the kind of guy who didn't set out in life to be a failure, but just sort of drifted from one plateau down to the next one, until finally he was spending most of his time talking to his dog.

It is, indeed, the dog's disappearance that inspires Nolte's suicide attempt, and it will be the Whitemans' own amazing dog, named Matisse, that gets some of the loudest laughs in the movie. Maybe Mazursky is trying to tell us something about the quality of human relationships in Beverly Hills.

The Dreyfuss character is a coat-hanger manufacturer. He didn't set out in life to be rich (one of his favorite conversational gambits involves his own good luck and assurances that it could have happened to you as easily as to him—nice if you are him, but not if you are you). Here he is, living in a manicured mansion, exploiting wetback labor, sleeping with the Mexican maid, driving a Rolls convertible, selling 900 million coat hangers to the Chinese, and yet, somehow, something is missing. And almost from the first moment he sets eyes on the Nolte character, he realizes what it is: the authenticity of poverty.

The movie has a quiet, offhand way of introducing us to the the rich man's milieu. We meet his wife, whose life involves long sessions with masseurs, yogis, and shrinks (even her dog has a doggie psychiatrist). We meet his daughter (Tracy Nelson), a sunny-faced, milk-fed child of prosperity. We meet the Whitemans' neighbor, played by Little Richard with an incongruous mixture of anger and affluence (he complains that he doesn't get full service from the police; when he reports prowlers, they don't send helicopters and attack dogs).

We meet Carmen (Elizabeth Pena), the maid, who greets her employer lustily in her servant's quarters, but who grows, during the movie, from a soap opera addict into a political radical. We also meet the extended family and friends of the Whitemans, each one a perfectly written vignette, right down to the dog's analyst.

Down and Out in Beverly Hills revolves around the fascination that Dreyfuss feels for Nolte's life of dissipation and idleness. He is drawn to the shiftless sloth like a moth to a flame. A bum's life seems to have more authenticity than his own pampered existence. And, indeed, perhaps the last unreachable frontier of the very rich, the one thing they cannot buy, is poverty. Dreyfuss spends a night down on the beach with Nolte and his bum friends, and there is a breathtaking moment at sundown when Nolte (who claims to be a failed actor) recites Shakespeare's lines beginning "What a piece of work is a man!"

Certain predictable things happen. Nolte not only becomes Dreyfuss's good buddy, but is enlisted by all of the women in the household—the wife, the daughter, and the maid—as a sex therapist. Dreyfuss will put up with almost anything, because he really likes this guy, and Nolte's best hold on them is the threat to leave. Mazursky makes the most of that paradox, and gradually we see the buried theme of the movie emerging, and it is the power of friendship. What these people all really lacked, rich and poor, sane and crazy alike, was the power to really like other people.

The movie should get some kind of award for its casting. Dreyfuss, who has been so good in the past as a hyperactive overachiever, succeeds here in slightly deflecting that energy. He has the success, but is bedazzled by it, as if not quite trusting why great wealth should come to him for doing so little. He channels his energy, not into work, but into enthusiasms—and Nolte becomes his greatest enthusiasm.

For Bette Midler, Barbara Whiteman is the perfect character, all filled with the distractions of living up to her level of consumption. Nolte in some ways has the subtlest role to play, although when we first see it, it seems the broadest. His shiftless drifter has to metamorphose into a man who understands his hosts so deeply that he can play them like a piano.

The supporting roles are so well filled, one after another, that we almost feel we recognize the characters before they're introduced. And Mike, the dog, should get an honorary walk-on at the Oscars.

Perhaps I have made the movie sound too serious. Mazursky has a way of making comedies that are more intelligent and relevant than most of the serious films around; his last credit, for example, was the challenging *Moscow on the Hudson*. So let me just say that *Down and Out in Beverly Hills* made me laugh longer and louder than any film I've seen in a long time.

Down by Law ★ ★ ★

R, 95 m., 1986

Tom Waits (Jack), John Lurie (Roberto), Roberto Benigni (Nicoletta), Braschi (Laurette), Ellen Barkin (Bobbie). Directed by Jim Jarmusch. Screenplay by Jarmusch.

It's a sad and beautiful world.
—Line of dialogue

Down by Law is a movie about cheap whiskey and black coffee, all-night drunks and lost jobs, and the bad times you can have with good-time girls. It tells the story of a pimp, an unemployed disc jockey, and a bewildered Italian tourist, and how they escape from jail together and wind up slogging through the Louisiana bayous looking for a decent place to have breakfast. It's like a collage made out of objects from old gangster movies, old blues songs, and old jailhouse stories. At the end, it's like that line of dialogue. It's a sad and beautiful world, someone says, and someone else should say, yeah, but so what?

The movie was directed by Jim Jarmusch. You may remember his *Stranger than Paradise* (1984), a deadpan black-and-white comedy in which three strangely assorted friends decided it was too cold in Cleveland in the winter, and went to Florida and lost all their money at the dog races. *Down by Law* has the same sort of feeling; it's about two people who choose to be losers and a third who has bought the American Dream.

The movie stars Tom Waits, whose sandpaper voice sounds like he's pushing his words through three layers of hangovers. The other two guys are played by John Lurie, who was the Hungarian-American poker player in *Stranger than Paradise*, and Roberto Benigni, a previously unknown Italian actor who resembles a cross between Father Guido Sarducci and Woody Allen. They meet in the same Louisiana jail cell through a series of misadventures in which two of the guys are framed and the third is severely misunderstood.

No cell is large enough to hold these three. Lurie and Waits hate each other, but hate is nothing compared to the emotions they feel for the Italian, who commits the unpardonable sin of being cheerful and constantly pleased with himself. Eventually the three prisoners escape, and the movie follows them through the swamps as they slog through every cliché Jarmusch can remember.

In notes accompanying the film, Jarmusch is at pains to explain that he never saw the Louisiana bayou country before he went to shoot a movie there. What he has seen are lots of movies, and *Down by Law* is an anthology of pulp images from the world of *film noir*. On the surface, it's grim and relentless, but there's a thread of humor running through everything, and that takes the curse off. We are never quite sure that Jarmusch intends us to take anything seriously, and there are times when the actors seem to be smiling to themselves as they growl through their lines.

Lurie is known from the previous film, and from his work as a musician. Tom Waits is a star playing himself. The discovery in the picture is the redoubtable Roberto Benigni, who has an irrepressible, infectious manner, and is absolutely delighted to be himself. I don't know where he came from and I can't imagine what he's going to do next, but he could have a long comic career ahead of himself; he's like a show-off kid who gets you laughing and then starts laughing at himself, he's so funny, and then tries to top himself no matter what.

Down by Law is a true original that kind of grows on you. Maybe it goes on a little too long, and maybe it depends too much on its original inspiration—these three misfits and the oddballs they meet along the way—instead of trying to be about something. It doesn't have the inspired perfection of *Stranger than Paradise*, in which every shot seemed inevitable, but it's a good movie, and the more you know about movies the more you're likely to like it.

Dragnet ★ ★ ★

PG-13, 100 m., 1987

Dan Aykroyd (Friday), Tom Hanks (Pep Streebek), Christopher Plummer (Whirley), Harry Morgan (Bill Gannon), Alexandra Paul (Connie Swail), Jack O'Halloran (Emil Muzz), Elizabeth Ashley (Jane Kirkpatrick), Dabney Coleman (Jerry Caesar). Directed by Tom Mankiewicz and produced by David Permut and Robert K. Weiss. Screenplay by Aykroyd, Alan Zweibel, and Mankiewicz.

From the loud, confident opening chords of the famous "Dragnet" theme music, I was filled with confidence that this 1987 *Dragnet* knew what it was doing. My confidence lasted several seconds. Then the original music segued into some kind of dreadful disco rap unmusic, and my heart sank. How could they? How could they possibly make a movie called *Dragnet* and think that *anything* had to be done to the music?

They make the same mistake at the end, over the closing titles. I guess it's some kind of a business deal, and they want to make a lot of money with the music video or something. Hollywood is so greedy these days. God forbid that whoever wrote the original "Dragnet" theme should make a dime, when it can be cloned and corrupted for profit.

In between, the movie's pretty good. To be more precise, it is great for an hour, good for about twenty-five munutes, and then heads doggedly for the Standard 1980s High Tech Hollywood Ending, which means an expensive chase scene and a shoot-out. God, I'm tired of chases and shoot-outs.

The movie takes the basic ingredients of the *Dragnet* TV shows, kids them, and plugs them into a bizarre plot about a cult of Los Angeles pagans who hold weird satanic rites. Dan Aykroyd stars as Joe Friday, nephew of the original, and he was born to play this role, with his off-the-rack brown suit, his felt fedora, and his square jaw with the Chesterfield pasted into it. Tom Hanks is his partner, the nonconforming Detective Streebeck, game for anything but puzzled by Aykroyd's straight-arrow squareness.

There's a series of "pagan murders" in L.A. and the two cops get on the trail, which leads to a phony TV preacher, some highly placed creeps, and an absolutely hilarious pagan rite scene, in which oddly assorted would-be pagans stomp around in thighhigh sheepskins, while the Virgin Connie Swail (Alexandra Paul) is prepared for a sacrifice.

That's what she's always called, the Virgin Connie Swail. Friday falls in love with her, and his heart beats so hard that he stays on the case even after Chief Gannon (the legendary Harry Morgan) lifts his badge. Among other familiar faces involved in the case is Jack O'Halloran, as Emil Muzz, the big killer (you may remember him as Moose Malloy in the Mitchum version of *Farewell, My Lovely*).

Aykroyd's performance is the centerpiece of the film. He must have practiced for hours, even days, to perfect the rapid-fire delivery he uses to rattle off polysyllabic utterances of impenetrable but kaleidoscopic complexity. Listening to him talk in this movie is a joy.

It's an open question, I think, how much they really wanted to kid the old "Dragnet" shows. Jack Webb's visual style was built around a series of deadpan close-ups and clipped one-liners, and there's a little of that in this movie, but they never make a real point of it or have a lot of fun with it. The visuals are a lot looser than Webb would have enjoyed. And the color photography, of course, is all wrong; this is a movie that begs to be in black-and-white.

Still, it's fun, a lot of the time. Several individual shots are hilarious, including a long shot in pantomime of the two partners tring to show Harry Morgan how the pagans did their dance. Hanks and Aykroyd have an easy, unforced chemistry, growing out of their laconic delivery and opposite personalities, and the movie is filled with nice supporting turns, especially from Elizabeth Ashley and Dabney Coleman, as crooked city officials.

This would have been a great movie if they'd bothered to think of an ending for it. And used the original "Dragnet" theme. The end of the film cries out—*cries* out, mind you—for the simple, stark, authority of *dum-de-dum-dum*. I wanted to hear it so badly I walked out of the screening singing the notes out loud, to drown out the disco Drano from the screen.

Dragonslayer ★ ★ ★

PG, 108 m., 1981

Peter MacNicol (Galen), Caitlin Clarke (Valerian), Ralph Richardson (Ulrich), John Haliam (Tyrian), Peter Eyre (Casidorus Rex), Albert Saimi (Grell). Directed by Matthew Robbins and produced by Hal Barwood. Screenplay by Barwood and Robbins.

I'd like to think the Dark Ages looked something like *Dragonslayer*, all fearsome and muddy and overcast most of the time, and that their inhabitants walked around in a constant state of fear that something unspeakably evil was just about to eat off their ear. *Dragonslayer*'s vision is more convincing than the Dark Ages created by John Boor-mann in *Excalibur,* with everybody riding around in suits of armor that wouldn't be invented for another seven hundred years.

The real Dark Ages must have been a time of ignorance, tyranny, and superstition. And its heroes must have been something like the two young heroes of *Dragonslayer,* Peter MacNicol and Caitlin Clarke, both looking about fifteen years old. In a time of disease, plague, and epidemic, fifteen was old.

Here is a movie with the courage to be grungy. Dragons live in smelly lairs deep beneath crumbling mountains, and to reach them you have to cross lakes of fire and somehow avoid being eaten alive by little baby dragons. The mission in this movie is a simple one, as all fairy-tale missions must be: Galen, a young sorcerer's apprentice (MacNicol) must travel to a faraway kingdom and kill a fearsome dragon who holds the countryside under its fiery scorn. The ruler of the kingdom has meanwhile instituted some stopgap measures. He holds a lottery every year involving all the virgins in his kingdom, and the unlucky virgin who loses the lottery is sacrificed to the dragon. Galen, the dragonslayer, vows to save the virgins by killing the dragon. (There are easier ways of saving a girl from being sacrificed as a virgin, but they didn't call these the Dark Ages for nothing.) Before he leaves on his mission, Galen is inspired by the grave words and magical death of his teacher, Ulrich the Sorcerer (Ralph Richardson, in an absolutely wonderful performance). On his way to the far-off kingdom, he meets a youth named Valerian (Caitlin Clarke), who turns out to be a girl disguised as a boy so that she can avoid being drafted in the lottery.

The scenes involving the dragon are first-rate. The beast is one of the meanest, ugliest, most reprehensible creatures I've ever seen in a film, and when it breathes flames it looks like it's *really* breathing flames. Its lair, its flaming lake, and its monstrous attacks on the population are also well handled. The real star of the movie, indeed, is the production designer, Elliott Scott, who created the look of this world. (The special effects were produced at Industrial Light and Magic Inc., which is George Lucas's shop in Marin County, Calif.)

If the movie has a flaw, it is in MacNicol's performance, which is so feckless, cheerfully adolescent, and untextured that he could almost be a surfer caught in a time warp. MacNicol isn't bad in the role, mind you—just awfully cheeky. But then maybe dragonslaying is a young man's trade, and when you grow old and wise and have a long beard and are the sorcerer, you've learned enough to send your apprentice to kill the dragon.

The Draughtsman's Contract

★ ★ ★ ★

R, 103 m., 1983

Anthony Higgins (Mr. Neville), Janet Suzman (Mrs. Herbert), Anne Louise Lambert (Mrs. Talmann). Directed by Peter Greenaway and produced by David Payne.

What we have here is a tantalizing puzzle, wrapped in eroticism and presented with the utmost elegance. I have never seen a film quite like it. *The Draughtsman's Contract* seems to be telling us a very simple story in a very straightforward way, but after it's over you may need hours of discussion with your friends before you can be sure (if even then) exactly what happened.

The film takes place in 1694, in the English countryside. A rich lady (Janet Suzman) hires an itinerant artist to make twelve detailed drawings of her house. The artist (Anthony Higgins) strikes a hard bargain. In addition to his modest payment, he demands "the unrestricted freedom of her most intimate hospitality." Since the gentleman of the house is away on business, the lady agrees, and thus begins a pleasant regime divided between the easel and the boudoir.

All of this is told in the most precise way. All of the characters speak in complete, elegant, literary sentences. All of the camera strategies are formal and mannered. The movie advances with the grace and precision of a well-behaved novel. There is even a moment, perhaps, when we grow restless at the film's deliberate pace. But then, if we are sharp, we begin to realize that strange things are happening under our very noses.

The draughtsman demands perfection. There must be no change, from day to day, in the view he paints. He aims for complete realism. But little changes do creep in. A window is left open. A ladder is found standing against a wall. There are things on the lawn that should not be on the lawn. The lady's daughter calls on the artist and suggests that a plot may be under way and that her father, the lord of the manor, may have been murdered. Furthermore, the artist may be about to be framed for the crime. As a payment for her friendship, the daughter demands the same payment in "intimate hospitality" as her mother. Now the artist is not only draughtsman but lover to mother and daughter *and* the possible object of a plot to frame him with murder.

There is more. There is a lot more, all allowed to unfold at the same deliberate pace. There is a mysterious statue in the garden. An eavesdropper. Misbehaved sheep. The raw materials of this story could have been fashioned into a bawdy romp like *Tom Jones*. But the director, Peter Greenaway, has made a canny choice. Instead of showing us everything, and explaining everything, he gives us the clues and allows us to draw our own conclusions. His movie is like a crossword puzzle for the senses.

Dreamchild ★ ★ ★
PG, 94 m., 1985

Coral Browne (Mrs. Hargreaves), Ian Holm (Reverend Dodgson), Peter Gallagher (Jack Dolan), Caris Cofman (Sally Mackeson), Nicola Cowper (Lucy), Jane Asher (Mrs. Liddell). Directed by Gavin Miller and produced by Rick McCallum and Kenith Trodd. Screenplay by Dennis Potter.

It probably comes as no surprise that the man who wrote *Alice's Adventures in Wonderland* was not an absolute paragon of normality. His biographers have recently revealed that the Rev. Charles Dodgson (who wrote under the pen name Lewis Carroll) had an obsession with young girls, which he satisfied through hundreds of photographic studies and through lots of chummy friendships and correspondence. *Dreamchild* deals with his obsession as a problem that he tried to resolve in basically healthy ways, but it does argue that the writing of *Alice* created lifelong problems for the girl who inspired it.

According to this movie, which is fiction inspired by fact, the original Alice was a girl named Alice Liddell. She suffered Dodgson's attentions for a time and allowed herself to be rowed up and down a river by him one sunny afternoon, but she was more interested in playing with her friends than in having the original manuscript of *Alice* read to her. "But I wrote this just for you!" protests the anguished clergyman (played with a nice quiet intensity by Ian Holm).

Dreamchild is not, in any event, a psychological case study. It's too much fun for that. The movie begins some seventy years after the book was published. The young girl, now eighty years old, is known as Mrs. Alice Hargreaves (Coral Browne) and is sailing for America to receive an honorary degree on the centennial of Dodgson's birth. She is accompanied by a young traveling companion named Lucy (Nicola Cowper), and on arrival in New York in 1932 she is surrounded by a mob of aggressive newspaper reporters. One of them (Peter Gallagher) succeeds in pushing his way into Mrs. Hargreaves's life and Lucy's heart.

What happens next is sort of sweet. As the reporter and Lucy gradually fall in love, Hargreaves at first is violently opposed to their relationship. She is, indeed, a rather unpleasant old lady—inflexible and dogmatic, with definite ideas about the proper conduct of young people.

But she is much more complex than we think, as we learn by sharing her private nightmares and fantasies. In her mind, the world of Alice's Wonderland still has a scary reality, and we see the original fantasy figures (the king and queen, the Cheshire cat, and so on) as grotesque caricatures designed not to delight a little girl, but to frighten her.

The movie uses these fantasy sequences as counterpoint for more realistic flashbacks in which we meet Dodgson, see Alice as a young girl, and begin to sense some of the pathetic extremes to which Dodgson went to satisfy his passion for her, which was platonic but nonetheless bothering. We begin to realize, as old Mrs. Hargreaves herself begins to realize, that her whole life has been shaped by things that happened seventy years before.

Dreamchild is a remarkable film in many ways, not least because it gives itself such freedom of style and subject matter. For example, all the creatures in Alice's fantasies appear as muppetlike creations done by Jim Henson and his Creature Shop, but they are not Muppets. The movie has some subtle points to make with them.

At the same time, *Dreamchild* is not unremittingly grim, and it is not just a case study. The newspaper world of New York in the

1930s is re-created with style and humor, and the love story between the two young people is handled with a lot of cheerful energy. *Dreamchild* is an ambitious movie that tries to do a lot of things, and does most of them surprisingly well.

Dreamscape ★ ★ ★
PG-13, 99 m., 1984

Dennis Quaid (Alex), Max von Sydow (Dr. Novotny), Kate Capshaw (Jane DeVries), Christopher Plummer (Bob Blair), Eddie Albert (President), David Patrick Kelly (Tommy Ray). Directed by Joseph Ruben and produced by Bruce Cohn Curtis. Screenplay by David Loughery, Chuck Russell, and Ruben.

Dreamscape is three different movies, all fighting to get inside one another. It's a political conspiracy thriller, a science fiction adventure, and sort of a love story. Most movies that try to crowd so much into an hour and a half end up looking like a shopping list, but *Dreamscape* works, maybe because it has a sense of humor.

The movie stars Dennis Quaid, that open-faced specialist in crafty sincerity, as the possessor of rare psychic powers. Once, years before, he had been the best ESP subject in the laboratory of a kindly old parapsychologist (Max von Sydow), but then he disappeared. Now he is wanted again. The government is sponsoring explosive secret research in a brand new field: It believes there is a way for people to enter other people's dreams. The possibilities are limitless. For example, a therapist could enter the nightmares of his clients and become an eyewitness to buried phobias. Jungians could rub shoulders with subconscious archetypes. Lovers could visit each other's erotic dreams. And, of course, evil dreamers could drive their victims mad, or kill them with fright.

Quaid reluctantly agrees to become a subject for dream research, and almost immediately falls in love with von Sydow's assistant, the healthy and cheerful Kate Capshaw, of *Indiana Jones*. Then the plot thickens. Christopher Plummer turns up as the head of U.S. "covert intelligence." He is best friends with the president (Eddie Albert), who is, needless to say, having trouble sleeping these days. Albert has nightmares about starting World War III, and Plummer has nightmares that Albert will turn into a pacifist. He wants to use the dreamscape program to control the presidency. All of this plot stuff alternates with visits to people's dreams, and it's here that the movie gets interesting; movie dreams are usually clichés, and *Dreamscape* remains within the tradition, but comes up with some nice touches, including a crazy staircase that zigzags into darkness and looks precarious and surreal. There is also a funny sequence in which Quaid discovers Capshaw taking a nap, and impudently enters her dream with lust on his mind.

The whole business about the plot against the president is recycled from countless other thrillers. Two things redeem it: The gimmick of the dream invasions and the quality of the acting. Science fiction movies routinely run the risk of seeming ridiculous, and with bad performances they can inspire unwanted laughs. *Dreamscape* places its characters in a fantastical situation, and then lets them behave naturally, and with a certain wit. Dennis Quaid is especially good at that; his face lends itself to a grin, and he is a hero without ever being self-consciously heroic.

As for the dreams themselves, as I watched the movie I found myself trying to remember some of my own dreams. The movie's dreams include rooms with lots of windows and doors at crazy angles, railway coaches that are twice as wide as train tracks, and other visual distortions. I usually have more realistic dreams. Rooms and spaces have realistic proportions, and the distortions of reality come, not in the set decorating, but in the editing; flashbacks and intercutting points of view are not uncommon in my dreams, maybe because I see so many films. But movies can't use flashbacks and viewpoint tricks to manufacture dreams—because then the movie would look like a movie and not like a dream. So the movies have created a conventional dream language. What *Dreamscape* does is enlarge it with brief, sometimes funny little asides that do feel like dreams, as when Quaid is inside the nightmare of a little boy, and they're running from a Snake Man, and they see an adult seated at the end of a long table, and the kid says, "That's my dad. He won't be any help."

Dressed to Kill ★ ★ ★
R, 105 m., 1980

Michael Caine (Dr. Elliott), Angie Dickinson (Kate Miller), Nancy Allen (Liz Blake), Keith Gordon (Peter Miller), Dennis Franz (Detective Marino), David Margulies (Dr. Levy). Directed by Brian De Palma and produced by George Litto. Screenplay by De Palma.

When Alfred Hitchcock died, the obituaries puzzled over the fact that Hitchcock had created the most distinctive and easily recognizable visual style of his generation—but hadn't had a great influence on younger filmmakers. The obvious exception is Brian De Palma, who deliberately set out to work in the Hitchcock tradition, and directed this Hitchcockian thriller that's stylish, intriguing, and very violent.

The ads for De Palma's *Dressed to Kill* describe him as "the master of the macabre," which is no more immodest, I suppose, than the ads that described Hitchcock as "the master of suspense." De Palma is not yet an artist of Hitchcock's stature, but he does earn the right to a comparison, especially after his deliberately Hitchcockian films *Sisters* and *Obsession.* He places his emphasis on the same things that obsessed Hitchcock: precise camera movements, meticulously selected visual details, characters seen as types rather than personalities, and violence as a sudden interruption of the most mundane situations.

He also has Hitchcock's delight in bizarre and unexpected plot twists, and the chief delight of the first and best hour of *Dressed to Kill* comes from the series of surprises he springs on us. Although other key characters are introduced, the central character in these early scenes is Kate Miller (Angie Dickinson), an attractive forty-fiveish Manhattan woman who has a severe case of unsatiated lust. De Palma opens with a deliberately shocking shower scene (homage to Hitch), and then follows the woman as her sexual fantasies become unexpectedly real during a lunchtime trip to the museum.

The museum sequence is absolutely brilliant, tracking Dickinson as she notices a tall, dark, and handsome stranger. She makes eye contact, breaks it, tries to attract the stranger's attention by dropping her glove, and then is tracked *by* the stranger. To her, and our, astonishment, this virtuoso scene (played entirely without dialogue) ends in a passionate sexual encounter in the back of a taxicab.

Later, she wakes up in the stranger's apartment, and De Palma shamelessly manipulates her, and us, by springing a series of plot surprises involving embarrassment and guilt: What would *you* do if you were a cheating wife and had just forgotten your wedding ring in a stranger's apartment? The plot now takes several totally unanticipated turns, and I, of course, would not dream of revealing them. Indeed, I'll be vague about the plot from now on, because De Palma's surprises are crucial to his effect.

The movie's other characters include Michael Caine, who's the psychiatrist of two of the characters in the film. Then there's Nancy Allen, who's wonderfully off-beat as a sweet Manhattan hooker who discovers a body and gets trapped in the investigation. And there's Keith Gordon: He's one of those teen-age scientific geniuses, and he invents brilliant gimmicks to investigate the crime.

Some people are going to object to certain plot details in *Dressed to Kill,* particularly the cavalier way it explains a homocidal maniac's behavior by lumping together transsexuality and schizophrenia. But I doubt that De Palma wants us to take his explanations very seriously; the pseudoscientific jargon used to "explain" the case reminds me of that terrible psychiatric explanation at the end of *Psycho*—a movie De Palma has been quoting from all along.

Dressed to Kill is an exercise in style, not narrative; it would rather look and feel like a thriller than make sense. Its plot has moments of ludicrous implausibility, it nearly bogs down at one point near the end and it cheats on us with the old "it was only a dream!" gimmick. But De Palma has so much fun with the conventions of the thriller that we forgive him and go along. And there are really nice touches in the performances: Dickinson's guilt-laden lust, Caine's analytical detachment, Allen's street-wise cool in life and death situations, Gordon's wise-guy kid. De Palma earns the title of master, all right . . . but Hitch remains the grand master.

The Dresser ★ ★ ★ ★
PG, 118 m., 1984

Albert Finney (Sir), Tom Courtenay (Norman), Edward Fox (Oxenby), Zena Walker (Her Ladyship). Directed and produced by Peter Yates. Screenplay by Ronald Harwood.

Much of mankind is divided into two categories, the enablers and the enabled. Both groups accept the same mythology, in which the enablers are self-sacrificing martyrs and the enabled are egomaniacs. But the roles are sometimes reversed; the stars are shaken by insecurities that are subtly encouraged by enablers who, in their heart of hearts, see themselves as the real stars. It's human nature. Ever hear the one about the guy who played the gravedigger in *Hamlet*? He was asked what the play was about, and he answered, "It's about this gravedigger. . . ."

The Dresser is about a guy like that, named Norman. He has devoted the best years of his life to the service of an egomaniacal actor, who is called Sir even though there is some doubt he has ever been knighted. Sir is an actor-manager who runs his own traveling theatrical troupe, touring the provinces to offer a season of Shakespeare. One night he plays King Lear. The next night, Othello. The next, Richard III. Most nights he has to ask his dresser what role he is playing. Dressers in the British theater do a great deal more than dress their employers. In *The Dresser,* Norman is also Sir's confidant, morale booster, masseur, alter ego, and physician, nursing him through hangovers with medicinal amounts of brandy. Norman has been doing this job for years, and Sir is at the center of his life. Sir, however, takes Norman very much for granted, and it is this difference between them that provides the emotional tension.

The Dresser is a backstage movie, based on a backstage play, but the movie leaves the theater for a few wonderful additions to the play, as when Sir commands a train to stop, and the train does. Mostly, though, the action is in a little provincial theater, where tonight's play is *King Lear,* and Sir looks as if he had spent the last week rehearsing the storm scene. It is Norman's job to whip him into shape. Sir is seriously disoriented. He is so hung over, shaky, and confused that he can't even remember how the play begins—indeed, he starts putting on the makeup for *Othello.* There are other problems for Norman to handle, such as Sir's relationships with his wife, his adoring stage manageress, and a young actress he is considering for Cordelia (she is slim, and would be easier to carry onstage). There are also an angry supporting player and a quaking old trouper who is being pressed into service as the Fool.

The minor characters are all well-drawn, but *The Dresser* is essentially the story of two people, and the movie has been well-cast to make the most of both of them; no wonder both actors won Oscar nominations. Norman is played by Tom Courtenay, who had the role on stage in London and New York and will also be remembered from all those British Angry Young Men films like *Billy Liar* and *Loneliness of the Long Distance Runner.* He is perfect for playing proud, resentful, self-doubting outsiders. Sir is played by Albert Finney, who manages to look far older than his forty-seven years and yet to create a physical bravura that's ideal for the role. When he shouts "Stop . . . that . . . train!" we are not too surprised when the train stops.

On the surface, the movie is a wonderful collection of theatrical lore, detail, and superstition (such as the belief that it is bad luck to say the name "Macbeth" aloud—safer to refer always to "the Scottish tragedy"). The physical details of makeup and costuming are dwelled on, and there is a great backstage moment when the primitive thunder machine is rattled to make a storm. Beneath those details, though, a human relationship arrives at a crisis point and is resolved, in a way. Sir and Norman come to the end of their long road together, and, as is the way with enablers and enabled, Norman finally understands the real nature of their relationship, while Sir, of course, can hardly be bothered. This is the best sort of drama, fascinating us on the surface with color and humor and esoteric detail, and then revealing the truth underneath.

Drive, He Said ★ ★ ★
R, 90 m., 1971

William Tepper (Hector), Karen Black (Olive), Michael Margotta (Gabriel), Bruce Dern (Coach Builion), Robert Towne (Richard),

Harry Jaglom (Conrad). Directed by Jack Nicholson and produced by Steve Blauner and Nicholson. Screenplay by Jeremy Larner and Nicholson.

Jack Nicholson's *Drive, He Said* is a disorganized but occasionally brilliant movie about two college students and the world they, and we, inhabit. Their campus is a microcosm of the least reassuring aspects of contemporary America; the two overwhelming mental states are paranoia and compulsive competitiveness. Sufferers from both conditions are obsessed by the fear that something might be gaining on them. In *Drive, He Said,* the paranoic student is afraid of the draft, the System, and They, whoever They are. The other student is a star basketball player, or, as his friends tell him, "You stay after school to run around in your underwear." His fears are more general and vague and, therefore, more frightening.

The movie has a sort of jumpy, nervous rhythm, as if it were on speed, and sometimes that works but it's finally just distracting. The problem is that the stories of the two main characters don't mesh. They're roommates, to be sure, but that's a tenuous connection. And when the paranoid (Michael Margotta) has his three big adventures—freaking out at the draft physical, attacking a faculty wife, and freeing all the animals in a biology lab—the scenes feel like set-pieces, unrelated to the movie.

The movie that surrounds them involves Hector (played with laconic charm by William Tepper), who plays basketball not because he's a jock but because he enjoys the self-testing that the game involves. By the time we meet him, he has become a star and a prime choice for the pro draft, but, well, somehow the whole thing is falling apart on him.

One of his problems is the faculty wife, played by Karen Black. He has been having an affair with her, but she breaks it off just as he discovers, uncomfortably, that he might be in love. And then it turns out she's pregnant. This is a real-life experience of the most unsettling sort, and makes it difficult for him to take basketball as seriously as his coach thinks he should.

The coach is an intense competitor who positively believes in all the values, moral and physical, that have been preached by all coaches since the dawn of time-outs. Bruce Dern's performance as the coach, by the way, is a small masterpiece of accurate observation.

The performances, indeed, are the best thing in the movie. Nicholson himself is a tremendously interesting screen actor, and he directs his actors to achieve a kind of intimacy and intensity that is genuinely rare. But if Nicholson is good on the nuances, he's weak on the overall direction of his film. It doesn't hang together for us as a unified piece of work.

I have a notion he may have been trying for an effect similar to that in his three previous films as an actor (*Easy Rider, Five Easy Pieces*, and *Carnal Knowledge*), which were deliberately episodic and depended on the cumulative effect of the episodes for a structure that occurred to us only gradually. But the episodes refuse to come together in *Drive, He Said*, and what we're left with are some very good scenes in search of a home.

E

E.T.—The Extra-Terrestrial ★ ★ ★ ★

PG, 115 m., 1982*

Henry Thomas (Elliott), Dee Wallace (Mary), Peter Coyote (Keys), Robert MacNaughton (Michael), Drew Barrymore (Gertie). Directed by Steven Spielberg and produced by Spielberg and Kathleen Kennedy. Screenplay by Melissa Mathison.

This movie made my heart glad. It is filled with innocence, hope, and good cheer. It is also wickedly funny and exciting as hell. *E.T.—The Extra-Terrestrial* is a movie like *The Wizard of Oz,* that you can grow up with and grow old with, and it won't let you down. It tells a story about friendship and love. Some people are a little baffled when they hear it described: It's about a relationship between a little boy and a creature from outer space that becomes his best friend. That makes it sound like a cross between *The Thing* and *National Velvet.* It works as science fiction, it's sometimes as scary as a monster movie, and at the end, when the lights go up, there's not a dry eye in the house.

E.T. is a movie of surprises, and I will not spoil any of them for you. But I can suggest some of the film's wonders. The movie takes place in and around a big American suburban development. The split-level houses march up and down the curved drives, carved out of hills that turn into forest a few blocks beyond the backyard. In this forest one night, a spaceship lands, and queer-looking little creatures hobble out of it and go snuffling through the night, looking for plant specimens, I guess. Humans arrive—authorities with flashlights and big stomping boots. They close in on the spaceship, and it is forced to take off and abandon one of its crew members. This forlorn little creature, the *E.T.* of the title, is left behind on Earth—abandoned to a horrendous world of dogs, raccoons, automobile exhausts, and curious little boys.

The movie's hero is one particular little boy named Elliott. He is played by Henry Thomas in what has to be the best little boy performance I've ever seen in an American film. He doesn't come across as an over-coached professional kid; he's natural, defiant, easily touched, conniving, brave, and childlike. He just *knows* there's something living out there in the backyard, and he sits up all night with his flashlight, trying to coax the creature out of hiding with a nearly irresistible bait: Reese's Pieces. The creature, which looks a little like Snoopy but is very, very wise, approaches the boy. They become friends. The E.T. moves into the house, and the center section of the film is an endless invention on the theme of an extra-terrestrial's introduction to bedrooms, televisions, telephones, refrigerators, and six-packs of beer. The creature has the powers of telepathy and telekinesis, and one of the ways it communicates is to share its emotions with Elliott. That's how Elliott knows that the E.T. wants to go home.

And from here on out, I'd better not describe what happens. Let me just say that the movie has moments of sheer ingenuity, moments of high comedy, some scary moments, and a very sad sequence that has everybody blowing their noses.

What is especially wonderful about all of those moments is that Steven Spielberg, who made this film, creates them out of legitimate and fascinating plot developments. At every moment from its beginning to its end, *E.T.* is really *about* something. The story is quite a narrative accomplishment. It reveals facts about the E.T.'s nature; it develops the personalities of Elliott, his mother, brother, and sister; it involves the federal space agencies; it touches on extra-terrestrial medicine, biology, and communication, and *still* it inspires genuine laughter and tears.

A lot of those achievements rest on the very peculiar shoulders of the E.T. itself. With its odd little walk, its high-pitched squeals of surprise, its tentative imitations of human speech, and its catlike but definitely alien purring, E.T. becomes one of the most intriguing fictional creatures I've ever seen on a screen. The E.T. is a triumph of special effects, certainly; the craftsmen who made this little being have extended the boundaries of their art. But it's also a triumph of imagination, because the filmmakers had to imagine E.T., had to see through its eyes, hear with its ears, and experience this world of ours through its utterly alien experience in order to make a creature so absolutely convincing. The word for what they exercised is empathy. *E.T.—The Extra-Terrestrial* is a reminder of what movies are for. Most movies are not for any one thing, of course. Some are to make us think, some to make us feel, some to take us away from our problems, some to help us examine them. What is enchanting about *E.T.* is that, in some measure, it does all of those things.

Easy Money ★ ★ ½

R, 95 m., 1983

Rodney Dangerfield (Monty Capuletti), Joe Pesci (Nicky Cerone), Geraldine Fitzgerald (Mrs. Monahan), Candy Azzara (Rose), Taylor Negron (Julio), Jennifer Jason Leigh (Allison). Directed by James Signorelli and produced by John Nicoletta. Screenplay by Dangerfield, Michael Enderl, P.J. O'Rourke, and Dennis Blair.

Easy Money is an off-balance and disjointed movie, but that's sort of okay, since it's about an off-balance and disjointed kinda guy. The credits call him Monty Capuletti, but he is clearly Rodney Dangerfield, gloriously playing himself as the nearest thing we are likely to get to W.C. Fields in this lifetime.

The movie's plot is simply a line to hang gags on. It stars Rodney as a baby photographer whose rich mother-in-law leaves him an inheritance of a $10 million department store. He can collect—but only if he stops drinking, gambling, smoking dope, running around late, and betting on the horses. This is a very tall order, but Rodney tries to fill it. The movie surrounds Dangerfield with a lot of good New York character actors, who populate the endless poker games and saloon scenes his life revolves around. There's also a very funny sequence involving his daughter's wedding to a Puerto Rican, an alliance that inspires a great backyard wedding party scene.

Because Rodney is Rodney, I laughed a lot during this movie. But I left it feeling curiously unsatisfied. I think maybe that was for two reasons: Because the movie introduces too many subplots that it never really deals with, and because Rodney isn't allowed to be hateful enough. First, the plot. I have the strangest feeling that *Easy Money* once had a much longer script than it has now. There are big scenes (like one where the Puerto Rican groom is sneaking into the bathroom) that end abruptly without a payoff or follow-through. There are whole sequences (like the department store's fashion show, based on Rodney's wardrobe) that seem to coexist uneasily with the rest of the movie. And the movie doesn't get enough comic mileage out of Rodney's attempt to quit drinking, smoking, and gambling (think of the fun you could have with Dangerfield attending an A.A. meeting).

Second, Rodney. I like him best when he's cynical and hard-edged. The Dangerfield of his concerts and records has been smoothed out for this movie, into a slightly more lovable guy. It looks like a masterstroke to make Rodney a baby photographer (think of W.C. Fields in that role), but not enough is done with it. He occasionally loses his temper at the little monsters, but he never seems to detest and despise them enough to be really funny. That's a problem. If you are a Rodney Dangerfield fan, it will not be insurmountable. If you are not a Dangerfield fan, of course, probably nothing on earth could induce you to go to this movie. The great Dangerfield movie, however, has still to be made. This one doesn't get quite enough respect.

Eating Raoul ★ ★

R, 87 m., 1983

Paul Bartel (Paul Bland), Mary Woronov (Mary Bland), Robert Beltran (Raoul). Directed by Paul Bartel. Screenplay by Bartel and Richard Blackburn.

Eating Raoul is one of the more deadpan black comedies I've seen: It tries to position itself somewhere between the bizarre and the banal, and most of the time, it succeeds. This has got to be the first low-key, laid-back comedy about murder, swingers' ads, and dominating women. Problem is, it's so laid-back it eventually gets monotonous. If the style and pacing had been as outrageous as the subject matter, we might have had something really amazing here.

The movie's about a happily married couple, Paul and Mary Bland, who are victims of bad times. Paul gets fired from his job in the liquor store, and there's just not much work around for a dilettante with no skills. He's spent his last rent money when providence suggests a way for the Blands to support themselves. A lecherous swinger from the upstairs apartment tries to assault Mary, and Paul bops him over the head with the frying pan. The swinger dies, and the Blands overcome their horror long enough to check out his wallet. He's loaded.

What the movie does next is to present the most outrageous events in the most matter-of-fact manner. The Blands hit upon a scheme to take ads in swingers' tabloids, lure victims to their apartment, tap them over the head with the trusty skillet, and rob them. The only problem is disposing of their victims' bodies. That's where Raoul comes in. He's a locksmith who discovers the Blands' dirty little secret and offers to sell the bodies to a dog-food factory. All's well until Raoul becomes smitten with Mary. Then Paul grows jealous, especially when he discovers that Raoul has been stealing from them. The next step is perhaps suggested by the title of the movie, or perhaps not—I wouldn't want to give anything away.

The plot of *Eating Raoul* reminds me a little of *Motel Hell,* that truly ghastly movie about a farmer who kidnapped his motel customers, buried them in the garden up to their necks, force-fed them until they were plump, and then turned them into sausages. (His motto: "It takes lots of critters to make Farmer Vincent's fritters.") I liked *Motel Hell* more than *Eating Raoul,* however, because it had the courage of its execrable taste. *Eating Raoul,* on the other hand, wants to be an almost whimsical black comedy. It's got its tongue so firmly in cheek there's no room for Raoul. The movie's got some really funny stuff in it, and I liked a lot of it, and I wouldn't exactly advise not seeing it, but it doesn't quite go that last mile. It doesn't reach for the truly unacceptable excesses, the transcendent breaches of taste, that might have made it inspired instead of merely clever.

Educating Rita ★ ★

PG, 110 m., 1983

Michael Caine (Dr. Frank Bryant), Julie Walters (Rita). Directed and produced by Lewis Gilbert. Screenplay by Willy Russell.

If only I'd been able to believe they were actually reading the books, then everything else would have fallen into place. But I didn't believe it. And so *Educating Rita,* which might have been a charming human comedy, disintegrated into a forced march through a formula relationship. The movie stars Michael Caine as a British professor of literature and Julie Walters as the simple cockney girl who comes to him for night-school lessons. She has problems: She is a working-class punk with an unimaginative husband. He has problems: He is a drunk whose only friends are cheating on him with each other. They have problems: Walters begins to idealize Caine, who then falls in love with her.

Perhaps it would be more accurate to say they both fall into love with the remake job they'd like to do on each other. Caine sees Walters as a fresh, honest, unspoiled intelligence. She sees him as a man who ought to sober up and return to his first love, writing poems. The idea of the curmudgeon and the cockney was not new when Bernard Shaw wrote *Pygmalion,* and it is not any newer in *Educating Rita.* But it could have been entertaining, if only I'd believed they were reading those books. They pass the books back and forth a lot. They sometimes read a line or two. There is a lot of talk about Blake this and Wordsworth that. But it's all magic. The books are like incantations that, used properly, will exorcise cockney accents and alcoholism. But the movie doesn't really believe that, so it departs from the stage play to bring in a lot of phony distractions.

The original *Educating Rita,* a long-running London stage hit by Willy Russell, had only the two characters. They were on the stage together for a long time, and by the end of the play we had shared in their developing relationship. Russell's movie rewrite has added mistresses, colleagues, husbands, in-laws, students, and a faculty committee, all unnecessary.

To the degree that *Educating Rita* does work, the credit goes to Michael Caine, who plays a man weary and kind, funny and self-hating. There is a real character there, just as there was in Caine's boozy diplomat in *Beyond the Limit.* In both movies, though, the characters are not well-served by the story. They're made to deliver speeches, take positions, and make decisions that are required by the plot, not by their own inner promptings. When Caine's professor, at the end of this movie, flies off to Australia to maybe sober up and maybe make a fresh start, it's a total cop-out—not by him, but by the screenplay. Maybe that's what happens when you start with an idealistic, challenging idea, and then cynically try to broaden its appeal.

The Effect of Gamma Rays on Man-in-the-Moon Marigolds ★ ★ ★

PG, 100 m., 1973

Joanne Woodward (Beatrice), Nell Potts (Matilda), Roberta Wallach (Ruth), Judith Lowry (Granny), Richard Venture (Floyd). Directed and produced by Paul Newman. Screenplay by Alvin Sargent.

The Effect of Gamma Rays on Man-in-the-Moon Marigolds is about a beautiful mutation: a shy, quiet, intelligent girl who somehow finds the strength to survive inside a terribly disturbed family. At first, we think the movie is about the girl's mother, a frumpy alcoholic played with great energy by Joanne Woodward. But no, the character of the mother is meant mostly to establish the environment within which the sixteen-year-old grows and learns.

The movie, which is hard-edged enough to be less depressing than it sounds, takes place in a lower-middle-class neighborhood of a rundown city. The mother lives in a world largely without men; her husband had the bad taste to not only abandon his family, but to die in a Holiday Inn. There are two daughters: Matilda, the idealist, and Ruth, a baton-twirling, boy-crazy, ordinary sort.

Not very much happens in the course of the movie. The family takes in a boarder, a senile old woman they name Fanny Annie; a pet rabbit is murdered; and the mother, Beatrice, spends a drunken night with a lecherous antique dealer, then has a run-in the next morning with a local cop who used to be in her high school home room.

Meanwhile, Matilda is preparing her exhibit for the finals of the high school science fair. Her big competition is a horrid girl who has assembled the skeleton of a cat after boiling off its skin. "No matter what anyone says," the little sadist explains, "the cat was dead when I got it from the animal shelter." Matilda's project has to do, as the title suggests, with an experiment to determine how small amounts of radium affect marigolds. Sometimes the flowers die, alas; but sometimes the radiation causes strange and beautiful mutations, totally unlike the original plants.

That is what has happened, of course, to Matilda. Living in a grim world, she has somehow remained uncorrupted. Faced with the problem of an alcoholic mother who sometimes embarrasses her in public, she responds with a quiet understanding of the situation that is heroic.

And, most of all, she understands—all three of them understand—that they are a family. That they share a love and a determination to survive that runs deeper than the problems in their lives. It is this sense of pluckiness that makes the film bearable. Without it, the cataloging of Beatrice's offenses against social conventions would be pointless.

Joanne Woodward's performance is not like anything she'd ever done before; coming after *Rachel, Rachel,* it served notice that she was capable of experimenting with roles that are against type and making them work. Paul Newman's direction is unobtrusive; he directs as we expect an actor might, looking for the dramatic content of a scene rather than its visual style. This means that the material has to carry the movie—for Newman, story comes before form—but he has found a story strong enough to do that. And the performance by Nell Potts (Newman and

Woodward's daughter) is extraordinary. She glows.

84 Charing Cross Road ★ ★
PG, 99 m., 1987

Anne Bancroft (Helene Hanff), Anthony Hopkins (Frank Doel), Judi Dench (Nora Doel), Jean De Baer (Maxine Bellamy), Maurice Denham (George Martin). Directed by David Jones and produced by Geoffrey Helman. Screenplay by Hugh Whitemore.

Miss Fiske would have loved this movie. And I would have loved seeing it with her, through her eyes. I almost even loved it myself, because *84 Charing Cross Road* is a movie made for people who love London and books. The only problem is that the heroine doesn't get to London until it's too late, and nobody ever seems to read in this movie.

The film is based on a hit London and New York play, which was based on a best-selling book. Given the thin and unlikely subject matter, that's already a series of miracles. And yet there are people who are pushovers for this material. I should know. I read the book and I saw the play and now I am reviewing the movie, and I still don't think the basic idea is sound.

The story begins in the years right after World War II, when London was still gripped by food rationing and pocked by bomb craters. A New York woman (Anne Bancroft), who loves books but cannot afford expensive ones, sees an ad in *Saturday Review* for a London bookstore. She sends them her want list and is soon delighted to receive a package of used books—good readable editions, cheap. She begins a correspondence with the bookseller (Anthony Hopkins), and thus commences a relationship that lasts for years without the two people ever meeting each other.

There is not a lot of drama in this story. Most of the action takes place in the post office. The director, David Jones, does what he can. His previous film was Harold Pinter's *Betrayal*, which was a love story told backward, beginning with the unhappy conclusion and ending with the lovers' first kiss. Now he has a love story in which the lovers do not meet. What can he look forward to next: autoeroticism?

Bancroft sends care packages of ham to postwar England. Hopkins sends precious editions of Boswell, Chesterton, and Cardinal Newman ("Dear John Henry," Bancroft calls him). Bancroft leads a lonely life in a New York apartment. Hopkins occupies a silent marriage in a London bedroom suburb. After many years, Hopkins dies and then Bancroft finally goes to London and visits the now-empty bookstore.

Sigh. Miss Fiske, who you may remember from the first paragraph of this review, was the librarian at the Urbana Free Library when I was growing up. She instilled such a love of books in me that I still search used bookstores for the adventures of the Melody Family by Elizabeth Enricht; those were the first "real books" I read. Miss Fiske ran the book club and the Saturday morning puppet shows and the book fairs and the story readings. She never had to talk to me about the love of books because she simply exuded it and I absorbed it.

She would have loved this movie. Sitting next to her, I suspect, I would have loved it, too. But Miss Fiske is gone now, and I found it pretty slow going on my own. And for that matter, Miss Fiske had a sharp critical intelligence, and I suspect that after seeing this movie she would have nodded and said she enjoyed it, but then she might have added, "Why didn't that silly woman get on the boat and go to London ten years sooner and save herself all that postage?"

El Norte ★ ★ ★ ★
R, 141 m., 1983

Zaide Sylvia Gutierrez (Rosa), David Villalpando (Enrique), Ernesto Gomez Cruz (Father), Alicia del Lago (Mother), Trinidad Silva (Monty). Directed by Gregory Nava and produced by Anna Thomas. Screenplay by Nava and Thomas.

From the very first moments of *El Norte*, we know that we are in the hands of a great movie. It tells a simple story in such a romantic and poetic way that we are touched, deeply and honestly, and we know we will remember the film for a long time. The movie tells the story of two young Guatemalans, a brother and sister named Rosa and Enrique, and of their long trek up through Mexico to *el Norte*—the United States. Their journey begins in a small village and ends in Los Angeles, and their dream is the American Dream.

But *El Norte* takes place in the present, when we who are already Americans are not so eager for others to share our dream. Enrique and Rosa are not brave immigrants who could have been our forefathers, but two young people alive now, who look through the tattered pages of an old *Good Housekeeping* for their images of America. One of the most interesting things about the film is the way it acknowledges all of the political realities of Latin America and yet resists being a "political" film. It tells its story through the eyes of its heroes, and it is one of the rare films that grants Latin Americans full humanity. They are not condescended to, they are not made to symbolize something, they are not glorified, they are simply themselves.

The movie begins in the fields where Arturo, their father, is a *bracero*—a pair of arms. He goes to a meeting to protest working conditions and is killed. Their mother disappears. Enrique and Rosa, who are in their late teens, decide to leave their village and go to America. The first part of the film shows their life in Guatemala with some of the same beauty and magical imagery of Gabriel Garcia Marquez's *One Hundred Years of Solitude*. The middle section shows them going by bus and foot up through Mexico, which is as harsh on immigrants from the South as America is. At the border they try to hire a "coyote" to guide them across, and they finally end up crawling to the promised land through a rat-infested drainage tunnel.

The final section of the film takes place in Los Angeles, which they first see as a glittering carpet of lights, but which quickly becomes a cheap motel for day laborers, and a series of jobs in the illegal, shadow job market. Enrique becomes a waiter. Rosa becomes a maid. Because they are attractive, intelligent, and have a certain naive nerve, they succeed for a time, before the film's sad, poetic ending.

El Norte is a great film, one of 1983's best, for two different kinds of reasons. One is its stunning visual and musical power; the approach of the film is not quasidocumentary, but poetic, with fantastical images that show us the joyous hearts of these two people.

The second reason is that this is the first film to approach the subject of "undocumented workers" solely through *their* eyes. This is not one of those docudramas where we half-expect a test at the end, but a film like *The Grapes of Wrath* that gets inside the hearts of its characters and lives with them.

The movie was directed by Gregory Nava and produced by Anna Thomas, who wrote it together. It's been described by *Variety* as the "first American independent epic," and it is indeed an epic film made entirely outside the studio system by two gifted filmmakers (their credits include *The Confessions of Amans*, which won a Gold Hugo at the Chicago Film Festival, and *The Haunting of M*, one of my favorite films from 1979). This time, with a larger budget and a first-rate cast, they have made their breakthrough into the first ranks of young directors.

Electric Dreams ★ ★ ★ ½

PG, 96 m., 1984

Lenny Von Dohlen (Miles), Virginia Madsen (Madeline), Maxwell Caulfield (Bill), Bud Cort (Computer). Directed by Steve Barron and produced by Rusty Lemorande and Larry DeWaay. Screenplay by Lemorande.

In a way, it's one of the oldest stories in the movies. You start with a sweet guy who's kind of a wimp. You have him rent an apartment downstairs from a good-looking blonde girl who's really classy—maybe she even plays cello in a symphony orchestra. Then you supply the wimp with a know-it-all roommate who can do anything. Then the wimp has the roommate compose a love song for the girl upstairs. The girl falls for it, there's love at first sight, but then the wimp feels that he is living a lie. He must tell the girl the truth or he will not truly deserve her. (This begs the question, of course, of whether he should make an ethical investment in a girl who can be swayed by a single love song.)

In *Electric Dreams*, they've made one slight change in this age-old scenario, to bring it up to date. The roommate is a computer. In the old movies, there was usually a touchy moment or two when it looked like the roommate was going to fall for the girl upstairs. They even have a version of that here: The computer gets wildly jealous and possessive about its owner, and begins to inquire winsomely about the meanings of all those nice words in the love songs: How, exactly, *does* one touch? The guy in the movie is one of those cases of chronic disorganization: He's right on time but this is yesterday's training session. Somebody tells him he ought to get a computer to help him keep track of things. He buys a computer and, predictably, drops it while he is taking it out of the box. Apparently that was just what the computer needed to upgrade itself to a level of sophistication far above anything ever dreamed of by the folks at the computer store.

If *Electric Dreams* were only about this ancient old plot, it would have been a fairly routine movie. Several things make it more than that, and, in order of importance, they are: (1) the ingenious way the movie creates a personality for the computer, with the help of Bud Cort as the computer's voice; (2) the perfect casting of Lenny Von Dohlen as the wimp, and Virginia Madsen, an engaging newcomer, as the girl upstairs; (3) the graphics, and particularly the way the movie pictures the computer's wilder flights of fancy, and (4) the music by Giorgio Moroder, who seems to compose the scores for half the films in Hollywood these days, but who has certainly found the right tone for this one.

One of the nicest things about the movie is the way it maintains its note of slightly bewildered innocence. When Van Dohlen unpacks his computer and starts to assemble it, he reminds us a little of somebody like Harold Lloyd, determined to lick this thing. It's not often that a modern movie has the courage to give us a hero who doesn't seem to be a cross between a disco god and an aerobics instructor, but the Von Dohlen character is a nice change. He's likable, incompetent, and slightly dense. Virginia Madsen makes it clear right from the start that she loves her cello more than almost anything else in the world, and the movie's best single scene is the one where the computer, eavesdropping through a ventilation duct as she rehearses, joins in and plays a duet with her.

That scene, and a lot of other virtuoso moments in the movie, are photographed by Alex Thompson with a kind of fluid, poetic visual abandon that makes the movie a lot of fun to watch. The camera sweeps low over a keyboard, taking a flight that's almost as exhilarating as one of those swoops in *Star Wars*. During the songs, the screen fills with a kind of orgasmic computer screen display. They didn't stop after they figured out the story of this movie; it's obvious that the director, Steve Barron, spent a lot of time with his collaborators talking about how they could elevate their simple little story into something approaching a romantic flight of fancy. They were successful.

The Electric Horseman ★ ★ ★

PG, 120 m., 1979

Robert Redford (Sonny), Jane Fonda (Hallie), Valerie Perrine (Charlotta), Willie Nelson (Wendell), John Saxon (Hunt Sears), Nicholas Coster (Fitzgerald). Directed by Sydney Pollack and produced by Ray Stark. Screenplay by Robert Garland.

The Electric Horseman is the kind of movie they used to make. It's an oddball love story about a guy and a girl and a prize racehorse, and it has a chase scene and some smooching and a happy ending. It could have starred Tracy and Hepburn, or Gable and Colbert, but it doesn't need to because this time it stars Robert Redford and Jane Fonda.

The movie almost willfully wants to be old-fashioned. It's got bad guys from a big corporation, and big kisses seen in silhouette in the sunset, and it works Fonda and Redford for all the star quality they've got. But *Electric Horseman* doesn't try to be completely guileless. It has a bunch of contemporary themes and causes to dress up its basic situation—which is, let's face it, Girl meets Boy (and Horse). And although we are never for a moment in doubt about the happy ending, there *is* a certain basic suspense as Redford and Fonda head for the hills and the evil corporation follows by helicopter.

The movie begins with Redford in the process of downfall. He plays a former five-time national champion rodeo cowboy named Sonny, who has retired from competition and signed on as the spokesman for a cereal named "Ranch Breakfast." This is some cereal. It is fortified, we gather, not only with vitamins, minerals, and bran, but also with leather, nails, and sagebrush. Redford makes personal appearances on behalf of the cereal, wearing a garish electrified cowboy suit that plugs into the saddle of his horse. The cowboy outfit isn't the only thing that's lit up: Redford's drunk most of the time, and ignominiously falls off his horse during a half-time show.

Things come to a climax during a big Las Vegas convention sponsored by the conglomerate that owns Ranch Breakfast. Redford's supposed to ride onstage on a multimillion-dollar champion racehorse. But he has a run-in with the president of the conglomerate, discovers that the horse is drugged and on steroids, and decides to make his own personal gesture of defiance. He rides onstage, all right—and right offstage, too, and down the Vegas strip, and out into the desert.

Jane Fonda plays a TV newswoman who's covering the convention, and she does some clever detective work to figure out where Redford might be headed. And then the movie's more or less predictable: Fonda finds Redford, grows to share his indignation at how the horse has been treated, and trades her loyalty for exclusive rights to the story. It turns out to be a really big story, of course, as the conglomerate tries to track down its racehorse and the TV networks get in a race to find Redford.

If you spend much time scrutinizing the late show on television, some of this material might not sound dazzlingly original. The device of the famous runaway with a journalist in hot pursuit, for example, is straight out of *It Happened One Night*—and as Fonda calls her office from remote pay phones, we're reminded of Clark Gable in exactly the same situations. The notion of the last of the cowboys heading for the hills and being tracked by helicopters is also familiar; it's from *Lonely Are the Brave*, with Kirk Douglas, and some of the shots look hauntingly familiar.

The relationship between Fonda and Redford is also pretty basic stuff, in which the gruff outdoorsman and the perfect lady grow to respect each other while sharing the rigors of life on the run. Bogart and Hepburn made that relationship a classic in *The African Queen*, but Redford and Fonda have much the same chemistry. Remember that scene on the boat with Hepburn putting her chin in her hand and giving Bogart the old once-over? Fonda does that to Redford, and it's about as erotic as six of your average love scenes.

Both Redford and Fonda have identified themselves with a lot of the issues in this movie (which are—I have a list right here—the evils of corporate conglomeratism, the preservation of our wild lands, respect for animals, the phoniness of commercialism, the pack instinct of TV journalism, and nutritious breakfasts). But although this is a movie filled with messages, it's not a message movie. The characters and plot seem to tap-dance past the serious stuff and concentrate on the human relationships.

If *Electric Horseman* has a flaw, it's that the movie's so warm and cozy it can hardly be electrifying. The director, Sydney Pollack, gives us solid entertainment, but he doesn't take chances and he probably didn't intend to. He's an ideal choice for orchestrating Redford and Fonda; he directed Fonda in *They Shoot Horses, Don't They?* and has made a subsidiary career out of directing Redford (in *This Property is Condemned*, *Jeremiah Johnson*, *The Way We Were*, and *Three Days of the Condor*). He has grown up with them, he respects the solidity of their screen personas, and he seems to understand (as the directors of Bogart, Hepburn, Gable, et al., did in the forties) that if you have the right Boy and the right Girl and the right story, about all you have to do is stay out of the way of the Horse.

The Elephant Man ★ ★

PG, 123 m., 1980

Anthony Hopkins (Frederick Treves), John Hurt (John Merrick), Anne Bancroft (Mrs. Kendal), John Gielgud (Carr Gomm). Directed by David Lynch and produced by Jonathan Sanger. Screenplay by Christopher DeVore, Eric Bergren, and David Lynch.

The film of *The Elephant Man* is not based on the successful stage play of the same name, but they both draw their sources from the life of John Merrick, the original "elephant man," whose rare disease imprisoned him in a cruelly misformed body. Both the play and the movie adopt essentially the same point of view, that we are to honor Merrick because of the courage with which he faced his existence.

The Elephant Man forces me to question this position on two grounds: first, on the meaning of Merrick's life, and second, on the ways in which the film employs it. It is conventional to say that Merrick, so hideously misformed that he was exhibited as a sideshow attraction, was courageous. No doubt he was. But there is a distinction here that needs to be drawn, between the courage of a man who chooses to face hardship for a good purpose, and the courage of a man who is simply doing the best he can, under the circumstances.

Wilfrid Sheed, an American novelist who is crippled by polio, once discussed this distinction in a *Newsweek* essay. He is sick and tired, he wrote, of being praised for his "courage," when he did not choose to contract polio and has little choice but to deal with his handicaps as well as he can. True courage, he suggests, requires a degree of choice. Yet the whole structure of *The Elephant Man* is based on a life that is said to be courageous, not because of his hero's achievements, but simply because of the bad trick played on him by fate. In the film and the play (which are similar in many details), John Merrick learns to move in society, to have ladies in to tea, to attend the theater, and to build a scale model of a cathedral. Merrick may have had greater achievements in real life, but the film glosses them over. How, for example, did he learn to speak so well and eloquently? History tells us that the real Merrick's jaw was so misshapen that an operation was necessary just to allow him to talk. In the film, however, after a few snuffles to warm up, he quotes the Twenty-Third Psalm and *Romeo and Juliet*. This is pure sentimentalism.

The film could have chosen to develop the relationship between Merrick and his medical sponsor, Dr. Frederick Treves, along the lines of the bond between doctor and child in Truffaut's *The Wild Child*. It could have bluntly dealt with the degree of Merrick's inability to relate to ordinary society, as in Werner Herzog's *Kaspar Hauser*. Instead, it makes him noble and celebrates his nobility.

I kept asking myself what the film was *really* trying to say about the human condition as reflected by John Merrick, and I kept drawing blanks. The film's philosophy is this shallow: (1) Wow, the Elephant Man sure looked hideous, and (2) gosh, isn't it wonderful how he kept on in spite of everything? This last is in spite of a real possibility that John Merrick's death at twenty-seven might have been suicide.

The film's technical credits are adequate. John Hurt is very good as Merrick, somehow projecting a humanity past the disfiguring makeup, and Anthony Hopkins is correctly aloof and yet venal as the doctor. The direction, by David *(Eraserhead)* Lynch, is competent, although he gives us an inexcusable opening scene in which Merrick's mother is trampled or scared by elephants or raped—who knows?—and an equally idiotic closing scene in which Merrick becomes the Star Child from *2001*, or something.

Emmanuelle ★ ★ ★

x, 92 m., 1975

Sylvia Kristel (Emmanuelle), Alain Cuny (Mario), Marika Green (Bee), Daniel Sarky (Jean), Jeanne Colletin (Ariane), Christine Boisson (Marie-Ange). Directed by Just Jaeckin and produced by Yves Rousset-Rouard. Screenplay by Jean-Louis Richard.

Emmanuelle is a silly, classy, enjoyable erotic film that became an all-time box office success in France. It's not remotely significant enough to deserve that honor, but in terms of its genre (soft-core skin flick) it's very well done: lushly photographed on location in Thailand, filled with attractive and intriguing people, and scored with brittle, teasing music. Now that hard-core porno has become passé, it's a relief to see a movie that drops the gynecology and returns to a certain amount of sexy sophistication.

There have been movies influenced by other movies, and directors influenced by other directors, but *Emmanuelle* may be the first movie influenced by magazine centerfolds. Its style of color photography seems directly ripped off from the centerfolds in *Penthouse*, including even the props and decor. Its characters (French diplomats and—especially—their women in Thailand) inhabit a world of wicker furniture, soft pastels, vaguely Victorian lingerie, backlighting, forests of potted plants, and lots of diaphanous draperies shifting in the breeze. It's a world totally devoid of any real content, of course, and Emmanuelle is right at home in it. She's the young, virginal wife of a diplomat, and has just flown out from Paris to rejoin him. Her husband refuses to be possessive, and indeed almost propels her into a dizzying series of sexual encounters that range from the merely kinky to the truly bizarre. In the midst of this erotic maelstrom, Emmanuelle somehow retains her innocence.

The director, Just Jaeckin, correctly understands that gymnastics and heavy breathing do not an erotic movie make, nor does excessive attention to gynecological detail. Carefully deployed clothing can, indeed, be more erotic than plain nudity, and the decor in *Emmanuelle* also tends to get into the act. Jaeckin is a master of establishing situations; the seduction of Emmanuelle on the airplane, for example, is all the more effective because of its forbidden nature. And the encounter after the boxing match (Emmanuelle is the prize for the winning fighter and tenderly licks the sweat from his eyebrow) is given a rather startling voyeuristic touch (the spectators don't leave after the fight).

The movie's first hour or so is largely given over to lesbian situations, but then Emmanuelle comes under the influence of the wise old Mario (played by Alain Cuny, the French actor immortalized as Steiner, the intellectual who committed suicide in Fellini's *La Dolce Vita*). She is turned off at first by his age, but with age, she is assured, comes experience, and does it ever. Mario delivers himself of several profoundly meaningless generalizations about finding oneself through others and attaining true freedom, and then he introduces her to a series of photogenic situations. Mario's philosophy is frankly foolish, but Cuny delivers it with such solemn, obsessed conviction that the scenes become a parody, and *Emmanuelle*'s comic undertones are preserved.

What also makes the film work is the performance of Sylvia Kristel as Emmanuelle. She's a slender actress who isn't even the prettiest woman in the film, but she projects a certain vulnerability that makes several of the scenes work. The performers in most skin flicks seem so impervious to ordinary mortal failings, so blasé in the face of the most outrageous sexual invention, that finally they just become cartoon characters. Kristel actually seems to be present in the film, and as absorbed in its revelations as we are. It's a relief, during a time of cynicism in which sex is supposed to sell anything, to find a skin flick that's a lot better than it probably had to be.

Empire of the Sun ★ ★ ½

PG, 152 m., 1987

Christian Bale (Jim Graham), John Malkovich (Basie), Nigel Havers (Dr. Rawlins). Directed by Steven Spielberg and produced by Spielberg, Kathleen Kennedy, and Frank Marshall. Screenplay by Tom Stoppard.

Day and night, the boy dreams of flying. He knows the names of all the airplanes, and can spot them by their silhouettes. When planes fly overhead in Shanghai in the last days before the war breaks out, they may be an ominous omen for his parents, but for him they are wondrous great machines, free of gravity, free to soar.

The boy's parents are wealthy British citizens who enjoy a life of great luxury in Shanghai, a life in which limousines hurry them through the crowded streets to business meetings and masquerade balls, and you hardly need notice the ordinary people in those streets. Sometimes the Chinese press too close to the car, sometimes they hold up traffic, but mostly they are simply invisible—until war breaks out, and the boy's whole world is shattered.

The most agonizing moment in Steven Spielberg's *Empire of the Sun* comes near the beginning, as the streets of Shanghai are filled with a panic-stricken mob, and the boy is separated from his parents as they flee to sanctuary. One moment his mother has him by the hand, and the next moment he has dropped his toy airplane and stooped to pick it up, and they are separated by five thousand frightened people, never to see each other again until the war is over.

The boy is lost, left behind, and finally placed in a Japanese prisoner of war camp. His story is based on the autobiographical novel by J.G. Ballard, who actually lived through a similar experience as an adolescent, but if Ballard had not written his novel, Spielberg might have been forced to, because the story is so close to his heart. Not only do we have the familiar Spielberg theme of a child searching for his parents, but we also have the motif of the magic above reality—the escape mechanism into a more perfect world, a world that may be represented by visitors from another planet, or time travel, or hidden treasure. This time, it is the world of the air, and airplanes.

Life on earth is not so enjoyable for the boy, whose name is Jim, and who is played by Christian Bale with a kind of grim poetry that suggests a young Tom Courtenay. There are no free passes for kids in the prison camp, and Jim soon finds a protector of sorts in Basie, an American prisoner played by John Malkovich with a laconic cynicism. Basie is a merchant seaman and born hustler, and his corner of the prison camp is a miraculous source for Hershey bars and other contraband (in his resourcefulness and capitalistic zeal, he's a reminder of the William Holden character in *Stalag 17*). Basie doesn't exactly play father to the kid; he permits him to exist in his sphere, and to survive.

Jim is a quick learner. Short, fast, and somewhat invisible because of his youth, he has the run of the camp. He knows all the shortcuts and all the scams, and steals to survive. He also dreams of airplanes, although as the months go by, he dreams less frequently of his parents and finally cannot quite even remember their faces. Spielberg portrays the prison camp as another of those typically Hollywood enclosures where the jailors embody cruel authority while somehow permitting the heroes to raise hell and have a relatively good time; like the adolescent in John Boorman's *Hope and Glory*, Jim in *Empire of the Sun* finds that young boys can even enjoy war, up to a point.

The movie is always interesting from a narrative point of view—Spielberg is a good storyteller with a good tale to tell. But it never really adds up to anything. What statement does Spielberg want to make about Jim, if any? That dreams are important? That survival is a virtue? The movie falls into the trap of so many war stories, and turns horror into nostalgia. The process is a familiar one. War experiences are brutal, painful, and tragic, but sometimes they call up the best in human beings, and after the war is over, the survivors eventually begin to yearn for that time when they surpassed themselves, when during better and worse they lived at their peak.

The movie is wonderfully staged and shot, and the prison camp looks and feels like a real place. But Spielberg allows the airplanes, the sun, and the magical yearning to get in his way. Jim has a relationship, at a distance, with a young Asian boy who lives outside the prison fence, and this friendship ends in a scene that is painfully calculated and manipulative. There is another moment, at about the same time in the film, where Jim creeps outside the camp by hiding in a drainage canal, and escapes capture and instant death not because of his wits, but because Spielberg forces a camera angle. And there is the inevitable moment when the boy is associated with a huge telephoto image of the sun, and we respond not to the shot, but to the memory that Spielberg loves huge celestial orbs so passionately that Jim isn't having a spontaneous moment, he's paying homage to the sun of *The Color Purple* and the moon of *E. T.*

The movie's general lack of direction leads to what seems like a series of possible endings; having little clear idea of where he was going, Spielberg isn't sure if he's arrived there. The movie's weakness is a lack of a strong narrative pull from beginning to end. The whole central section is basically just episodic daily prison life and the dreams of the boy. *Empire of the Sun* adds up to a promising idea, a well-seen production, and some interesting performances. But despite the emotional potential in the story, it didn't much move me. Maybe, like the kid, I decided that no world where you can play with airplanes can be all that bad.

Endless Love ★ ★

R, 115 m., 1981

Brooke Shields (Jade), Martin Hewitt (David), Shirley Knight (Anne), Don Murray (Hugh), Richard Kiley (Arthur), Beatrice Straight (Rose), Penelope Milford (Ingrid). Directed by Franco Zeffirelli and produced by Dyson Lovell. Screenplay by Judith Rascoe.

The novel *Endless Love* is about a teen-age boy who remembers, with full ferocity and grief and yearning, the great love of his life, after it has been ended by fate and the adult world. The movie *Endless Love* is about a teen-age boy and girl who are in love, until fate and adults end their relationship. There is all the difference in the world between these two story sequences, and although there are a great many things wrong with the movie, this blunder on the narrative level is the worst.

Didn't the makers of this movie understand the poignancy at the very heart of the novel? The book begins with its hero, David, committing an act that will end all of his happiness for years. Forbidden to see his girl, Jade, for thirty days, he sets a fire of newspapers on the porch of her house—hoping to win a reprieve by being the hero who "discovers" the fire. The house burns down, and David is sent into a long exile in a mental institution. The novel's point of view is of a boy who has lost everything he values and remembers it with undying passion. But the movie rearranges the events of the book into chronological order. That means that the love affair between Jade and David, instead of being remembered as a painful loss, is seen in the "now" as . . . well, as a teen-age romance. Its additional level of meaning is lost.

A story that began as a poem to the fierce pride of adolescent passion gets transmuted into a sociological case study. This movie contains some of the same characters and events as Scott Spencer's wonderful novel (indeed, at times it is unnecessarily faithful to situations and dialogue from the book), but it does not contain the book's reason for being. It is about events and it should be about passion.

There are many other problems in the film. One crucial mistake is in casting: Martin Hewitt, as David, the seventeen-year-old boy, is a capable actor but is too handsome, too heavily bearded, too old in appearance to suggest an adolescent bundle of vulnerability and sensitivity. Another mistake is in narrative: The sequence of events involving David's release from the institution, his trip to New York, and exactly what happens there, is so badly jumbled that some audience members will not know how and why he went to New York, and hardly anyone will be able to follow the circumstances that reunite him with Jade.

A third mistake is in this movie's ending, or rather, its lack of one: The final three minutes in this movie are enraging to anyone who has made an emotional investment in it, because they are a cop-out, a refusal to deal with the material and bring it to a conclusion. The fourth mistake is the one that made me most angry, because it deals with the central act of the narrative, with the disaster around which the story revolves. In the book, David sets fire to the newspaper as an act of passion, confusion, and grief—sure it's dumb, but he's confused and in turmoil. The movie, with offensive heavy-handedness, has another youth *suggest* the fire to David as a strategy. Apparently the filmmakers thought the fire had to be "explained." The result is to take a reckless act and turn it into a stupid one, diminishing both David's intelligence and the power of his passion.

The movie's central relationship, between Jade (Brooke Shields) and David, comes out as a disappointment, because their scenes are not allowed to develop human resonances. We never really feel and understand the bond between these two people. That's partly because of Hewitt's inability to project uncertainty and adolescent awkwardness; he comes on so strong and self-confident that David seems like a young man making a bold bid for a good-looking girl, rather than as one-half of a pair of star-crossed adolescent lovers.

Is there anything good in the movie? Yes. Brooke Shields is good. She is a great natural beauty, and she demonstrates, in a scene of tenderness and concern for Jewitt and in a scene of rage with her father, that she has a strong, unaffected screen acting manner. But the movie as a whole does not understand the particular strengths of the novel that inspired it, does not convince us it understands adolescent love, does not seem to know its characters very well, and is a narrative and logical mess.

Evil Dead 2: Dead by Dawn ★ ★ ★

NO MPAA RATING, 96 m., 1987

Bruce Campbell (Ash), Sarah Berry (Annie), Dan Hicks (Jake), Kassie Wesley (Bobby Joe), Theodore Raimi (Henrietta). Directed by Sam Raimi and produced by Robert G. Tapert. Screenplay by Raimi and Scott Spiegel.

Evil Dead 2: Dead by Dawn is a comedy disguised as a blood-soaked shock-a-rama. It looks superficially like a routine horror movie, a vomitorium designed to separate callow teen-agers from their lunch. But look a little closer and you'll realize that the movie is a fairly sophisticated satire. Level One viewers will say it's in bad taste. Level Two folks like ourselves will perceive that it is about bad taste.

The plot: Visitors to a cottage in the Michigan woods discover a rare copy of the *Book of the Dead* and accidentally invoke evil spirits. The spirits run amok, disemboweling and vivisecting their victims. The hero battles manfully with the dread supernatural forces, but he is no match for the unspeakably vile creatures in the basement, in the woods, and behind every door.

This story is told with wall-to-wall special effects. Skeletons dance in the moonlight. Heads spin on top of bodies. Hands go berserk and start attacking their owners. After they are chopped off, they have a life of their own. Heads are clamped into vises and squashed. Blood sprays all over everything. Guts spill. Slime spews. If nauseating images of horrific gore are not, as they say, your cup of tea, the odds are good you will not have a great time during this movie.

On the other hand, if you know it's all special effects, and if you've seen a lot of other movies and have a sense of humor, you might even have a great time seeing *Evil Dead 2.* I did—up to a point. The movie devours ideas at such a prodigious rate that it begins to repeat itself toward the end, but the first forty-five minutes have a kind of manic, inspired genius to them.

Consider, for example, the scene where the hero severs his hand from his body and the hand takes on a life of its own, attacking him. Leave out the blood and the gore and a few of the details, and this entire sequence builds like a tribute to the Three Stooges. Consider the scene where the hero attaches a chainsaw to what's left of his amputated arm. Disgusting, right? But the director, Sam Raimi, approaches it as a sly jab at *Taxi Driver.*

I'm not suggesting that *Evil Dead 2* is fun merely because you can spot the references to other movies. It is fun because (a) the violence and gore are carried to such an extreme that they stop being disgusting and become surrealistic; (b) the movie's timing aims for comedy, not shocks; and (c) the grubby, low-budget intensity of the film gives it a lovable quality that high-tech movies wouldn't have.

There is one shot in the film that is some kind of masterpiece. There is a force out there in the woods. We never see it, but we see things from its point of view. In one long and very complex unbroken point-of-view shot, this force roars through the woods, flattens everything, crashes through the cabin door, and roars through room after room with invincible savagery, chasing the hero until . . . but I wouldn't dream of giving away the joke.

Evil Under the Sun ★ ★ ★

PG, 102 m., 1982

Peter Ustinov (Hercule Poirot), Colin Blakely (Sir Horace Blatt), Jane Birkin (Christine Redfern), Nicholas Clay (Patrick Redfern), Maggie Smith (Daphne Castle), Roddy McDowall (Rex Brewster), Sylvia Miles (Myra Gardener), James Mason (Odell Gardener). Directed by Guy Hamilton and produced by John Brabourne and Richard Goodwin. Screenplay by Anthony Shaffer.

The delicious moments in an Agatha Christie film are supposed to come at the end, when the detective (in this case, the redoubtable Hercule Poirot) gathers everyone in the sitting room and toys with their guilt complexes before finally fingering the murderer. Well, there are delicious moments in the final fifteen minutes of *Evil Under the Sun,* but what I especially liked about this Christie were the opening scenes—the setup. They had a style and irreverence that reminded me curiously of *Beat the Devil,* with Bogart and Robert Morley chewing up the scenery. *Evil Under the Sun* is not, alas, as good as *Beat the Devil,* but it is the best of the recent group of Christie retreads (which include *Murder on the Orient Express, Death on the Nile,* and *The Mirror Crack'd*).

It begins in the usual way, with a corpse. It continues in obligatory fashion with the gathering of a large number of colorful and eccentric suspects in an out-of-the-way spot, which just happens to also be the destination of Hercule Poirot. It continues with the discovery of another corpse, with the liberal distribution of gigantic clues and with Poirot's lip-smacking summary of the evidence. It's the cast that makes *Evil* more fun than the previous manifestations of this identical plot. As Poirot, Peter Ustinov creates a wonderful mixture of the mentally polished and physically maladroit. He has a bit of business involving a dip in the sea that is so perfectly timed and acted it tells us everything we ever wanted to know about Poirot's appetite for exercise. He is so expansive, so beaming, so superior, in the opening scenes that he remains spiritually present throughout the film, even when he's not on screen.

All of the rest of the cast are suspects. They include Maggie Smith, a former actress who now runs an elegant spa in the Adriatic Sea; Diana Rigg, as her jealous contemporary; Sylvia Miles and James Mason, as a rich couple who produce shows on Broadway; Jane Birkin and Nicholas Clay as a young couple constantly arguing over his roving eye; Colin Blakely as a rich knight who's been taken by a gold digger; Emily Hone as the young new wife, and Roddy McDowell as a bitchy gossip columnist who knows the dirt about everybody. The newly discovered corpse belongs to one of the above. The murderer is one (or more) of the above. Nothing else I could say about the crime would be fair.

I can observe, however, that one of the delights of the movies made from Agatha Christie novels is their almost complete lack of passion: They substitute wit and style. Nobody really cares who gets bumped off, and nobody really misses the departed. What's important is that all the right clues be distributed, so that Poirot and the audience can pick them up, mull them over, and discover the culprit. Perhaps, then, one of the reasons I liked *Evil Under the Sun* was that this time, when Ustinov paused in his summation (after verbally convicting everyone in the room), and it was clear he was about to finger the real killer, I guessed the killer's identity, and I was right. Well, half right. That's better than I usually do.

The Exorcist ★ ★ ★ ★

R, 121 m., 1973

Ellen Burstyn (Chris), Linda Blair (Regan), Jason Miller (Father Karras), Max von Sydow (Father Merrin), Kitty Winn (Sharon), Lee J. Cobb (Kinderman). Directed by William Friedkin and produced by William Peter Blatty. Screenplay by Blatty.

1973 began and ended with cries of pain. It began with Ingmar Bergman's *Cries and Whispers*, and it closed with William Friedkin's *The Exorcist*. Both films are about the weather of the human soul, and no two films could be more different. Yet each in its own way forces us to look inside, to experience horror, to confront the reality of human suffering. The Bergman film is a humanist classic. The Friedkin film is an exploitation of the most fearsome resources of the cinema. That does not make it evil, but it does not make it noble, either.

The difference, maybe, is between great art and great craftsmanship. Bergman's exploration of the lines of love and conflict within the family of a woman dying of cancer was a film that asked important questions about faith and death, and was not afraid to admit there might not be any answers. Friedkin's film is about a twelve-year-old girl who either is suffering from a severe neurological disorder or—perhaps has been possessed by an evil spirit. Friedkin has the answers; the problem is that we doubt he believes them.

We don't necessarily believe them ourselves, but that hardly matters during the film's two hours. If movies are, among other things, opportunities for escapism, then *The Exorcist* is one of the most powerful ever made. Our objections, our questions, occur in an intellectual context after the movie has ended. During the movie there are no reservations, but only experiences. We feel shock, horror, nausea, fear, and some small measure of dogged hope.

Rarely do movies affect us so deeply. The first time I saw *Cries and Whispers*, I found myself shrinking down in my seat, somehow trying to escape from the implications of Bergman's story. *The Exorcist* also has that effect—but we're not escaping from Friedkin's implications, we're shrinking back from the direct emotional experience he's attacking us with. This movie doesn't rest on the screen; it's a frontal assault.

The story is well-known; it's adapted, more or less faithfully, by William Peter Blatty from his own bestseller. Many of the technical and theological details in his book are accurate. Most accurate of all is the reluctance of his Jesuit hero, Father Karras, to encourage the ritual of exorcism: "To do that," he says, "I'd have to send the girl back to the sixteenth century." Modern medicine has replaced devils with paranoia and schizophrenia, he explains. Medicine may have, but the movie hasn't. The last chapter of the novel never totally explained in detail the final events in the tortured girl's bedroom, but the movie's special effects in the closing scenes leave little doubt that an actual evil spirit was in that room, and that it transferred bodies. Is this fair? I guess so; in fiction the artist has poetic license.

It may be that the times we live in have prepared us for this movie. And Friedkin has admittedly given us a good one. I've always preferred a generic approach to film criticism; I ask myself how good a movie is of its type. *The Exorcist* is one of the best movies of its type ever made; it not only transcends the genre of terror, horror, and the supernatural, but it transcends such serious, ambitious efforts in the same direction as Roman Polanski's *Rosemary's Baby.* Carl Dreyer's *The Passion of Joan of Arc* is a greater film—but, of course, not nearly so willing to exploit the ways film can manipulate feeling.

The Exorcist does that with a vengeance. The film is a triumph of special effects. Never for a moment—not when the little girl is possessed by the most disgusting of spirits, not when the bed is banging and the furniture flying and the vomit is welling out—are we less than convinced. The film contains brutal shocks, almost indescribable obscenities. That it received an R rating and not the X is stupefying.

The performances are in every way appropriate to this movie made this way. Ellen Burstyn, as the possessed girl's mother, rings especially true; we feel her frustration when doctors and psychiatrists talk about lesions on the brain and she *knows* there's something deeper, more terrible, going on. Linda Blair, as the little girl, has obviously been put through an ordeal in this role, and puts us through one. Jason Miller, as the young Jesuit, is tortured, doubting, intelligent.

And the casting of Max von Sydow as the older Jesuit exorcist was inevitable; he has been through so many religious and metaphysical crises in Bergman's films that he almost seems to belong on a theological battlefield the way John Wayne belonged on a horse. There's a striking image early in the film that has the craggy von Sydow facing an ancient, evil statue; the image doesn't so much borrow from Bergman's famous chess game between von Sydow and Death (in *The Seventh Seal)* as extend the conflict and raise the odds.

I am not sure exactly what reasons people will have for seeing this movie; surely enjoyment won't be one, because what we get here aren't the delicious chills of a Vincent Price thriller, but raw and painful experience. Are people so numb they need movies of this intensity in order to feel anything at all? It's hard to say.

Even in the extremes of Friedkin's vision there is still a feeling that this is, after all, cinematic escapism and not a confrontation with real life. There is a fine line to be drawn there, and *The Exorcist* finds it and stays a millimeter on this side.

Experience Preferred . . . But Not Essential ★ ★ ★

PG, 77 m., 1983

Elizabeth Edmonds (Annie), Sue Wallace (Mavis), Geraldine Griffith (Doreen), Karen Meagher (Paula), Ron Bain (Mike), Alun Lewis (Hywel). Directed by Peter Duffell and produced by David Puttnam and Chris Griffin. Screenplay by June Roberts.

This movie is so slight and charming you're almost afraid to breathe during it, for fear of disturbing the spell. It's about ordinary people in an ordinary setting, but because the setting is a small resort hotel in Wales, and the time is the summer of 1962, there's also the strange feeling that we've entered another time and place, where some of the same rules apply, but by no means all of them.

The movie tells the story of a young woman named Annie (Elizabeth Edmonds) who comes to work for the summer in a hotel, and finds that she's entered a cozy little backstairs world with its own sets of loyalties and jealousies. All of the other waitresses at the hotel have their own stories, some funny, some sad, and Annie feels a little left out. "I'm the only one here without a past," she complains, but of course one of the reasons for spending your summer working in a hotel is to accumulate a past. The other women are suspicious of her because she's a student, but as the waitresses cram into the servants' quarters, three to a room and sometimes two to a bed, a sort of democracy sets in, and Annie is accepted.

The movie uses a wonderfully offhand style for filling us in on the characters. There's the gallant cook, who immediately takes a liking to Annie. And the redheaded bartender, who makes it a nightly habit to sleepwalk in the nude. And the conceited young waiter whose idea of a courtship is to belt his girl in the eye every once in a while. And the pretty hostess of the dining room, who owes her position and her private boudoir to the favors she supplies the hotel's owner. ("How did you get such a nice room?" Annie asks her, innocently.)

There's not much of a plot. Things just

sort of happen. Young men and women work from dawn to dusk and then collapse into each other's arms, almost but not quite too exhausted for sex. And the sexual customs of the pre-Pill era take on a certain quaintness, and a certain desperation, as couples grimly try to walk the line between lust and prudence. *Experience Preferred* is charming precisely because of its inconsequential air. It's funny because it goes for whimsical little insights into human nature rather than for big, obvious jokes. It's charming because it doesn't force the charm.

Exposed ★ ★ ★ ½

R, 100 m., 1983

Nastassja Kinski (Elizabeth), Rudolph Nureyev (Daniel), Harvey Keitel (Rivas), Ian McShane (Miller), Bibi Andersson (Margaret), Pierre Clementi (Vic). Directed and produced by James Toback. Screenplay by Toback.

This movie contains moments so exhilarating they reawakened me to the infinite possibilities of movies. Yet this movie loses itself in its closing sequences and meanders through the details of a routine terrorist plot. Somewhere between its greatness and its wandering there must be a compromise, and I would strike it this way: *Exposed* contains the most exciting evidence I have seen so far that Nastassja Kinski is the next great female superstar. I do not say that she is a great actress; not yet, and perhaps not ever. I do not compare her with Meryl Streep or Kate Nelligan, Jill Clayburgh or Jessica Lange. I am not talking in those terms of professional accomplishment. I am talking about the mysterious, innate quality that some performers have to cast a special spell, to develop a relationship with the camera that you can call stardom or voodoo or magic, because its name doesn't really matter.

Kinski has it. There are moments in this film (two virtuoso scenes, in particular, and then many other small moments and parts of scenes) when she affects me in the same way that Marilyn Monroe must have affected her first viewers, in movies like *The Asphalt Jungle* or *All About Eve*. She was not yet a star and audiences did not even know her name, but there was a quality about her that could not be dismissed. Kinski has that quality. She has exhibited it before in better films, such as *Tess*, and in ambitious, imperfect films such as *Cat People* and *One from the Heart*. Now here is *Exposed*, written and directed by James Toback, who in screenplays such as *The Gambler* and his brilliant, little-seen directing debut *Fingers*, has specialized in characters who live on the edge.

There are two sequences in *Exposed* where he pulls out all the stops. In one of them, Kinski (who plays a college dropout, lonely and sexually frustrated) dances all by herself in a nearly empty apartment. In another one, she meets a violinist (Rudolph Nureyev), they fall instantly into a consuming passion, and after he has tantalized her with a violin bow they make sudden, passionate love. The sheer quality of Kinski's abandon in these two scenes made me realize how many barriers can sometimes exist between a performance and an audience: Here there are none.

The movie is wonderful for its first hour or more. It follows Kinski through a brief, unhappy love affair with her professor (played by Toback), shows her moving to New York, has her discovered by a photographer and becoming a world-famous model (because she is Kinski, this is believable), and brings her up through the love affair with Nureyev. At this moment, *Exposed* seems poised on the brink of declaring itself one of the most riveting character portraits ever made.

And that is the moment where it falters, and loses itself in the details of a plot involving Harvey Keitel, as the leader of an underground terrorist cell in Paris. It's as if Toback didn't trust the strength of this character he had created (or, more likely, didn't know when he wrote his thriller that Kinski would bring the character so completely to life). The rest of the movie is okay, I suppose, in a somewhat familiar way. But its special quality is lost in plot details. Too bad. But if a movie can electrify me the way this one did, not once but twice and then some, I'm prepared to forgive it almost anything.

The Exterminator no stars

R, 101 m., 1980

Christopher George (Detective Dalton), Samantha Eggar (Dr. Stewart), Robert Ginty (John Eastland), Steve James (Michael Jefferson). Directed and written by James Glickenhaus and produced by Mark Buntzman.

The Exterminator is a sick example of the almost unbelievable descent into gruesome savagery in American movies. It's a direct rip-off of *Death Wish,* a 1974 Charles Bronson hit about a man who kills muggers to avenge the death of his wife. *Death Wish* was violent, yes, but it remained within certain boundaries. It established a three-dimensional character, it gave him reasons for his actions, it allowed us to sympathize with those reasons and yet still disapprove of the murders he was committing. *The Exterminator* does none of those things. It is essentially just a sadistic exercise in moronic violence, supported by a laughable plot. The "exterminator" of the movie's title (Robert Ginty) has his life saved in Vietnam by a black man (Steve James), who becomes his closest friend. Back home in Brooklyn, they break up a gang in the process of stealing beer from a loading dock. The gang gets revenge by attacking and permanently paralyzing the black man. The hero vows revenge.

So far, so good. What's profoundly disturbing about the film is that it uses this "justification" in the plot as an excuse for revenge scenes of the sickest possible perversion. The motive is obviously to shock or titillate the audience, not to show plausible actions by the character. For example: Ginty gets one gang member to talk by tying him to a wall and threatening him with an acetylene torch. Then he machine-guns the men who attacked his buddy.

They get off easy. Determined to get money to support the family of his paralyzed friend, Ginty kidnaps a Mafia boss. He hangs him by chains over a huge meat grinder, goes to rob his house and then lowers the man into the grinder, converting him to ground meat. He justifies this crime in a letter to anchorman Roger Grimsby (who plays himself—to his horror, no doubt, when he saw this film). And then he goes on a one-man vigilante campaign to clean up New York.

To help him in his campaign, the movie shows the audience evil situations and then lets the "exterminator" remedy them. For example, a hooker is lured to a house of male prostitution, where a sadistic client disfigures her with a soldering iron. Some weeks later, the "exterminator" picks up the hooker, sees the burn scars when she undresses and decides to avenge her. He goes to the male brothel, sets the owner on fire and shoots a customer dead.

There's more, involving an insipid policeman (Christopher George) and his girlfriend (Samantha Eggar), who turns out to be the paralyzed man's doctor. This is the kind of movie that establishes their relationship by sending them to a concert and then focusing on the concert because they have no dialogue. The CIA also gets involved, but who cares? *The Exterminator* exists primarily to show burnings, shootings, gougings, grindings, and beheadings. It is a small, unclean exercise in shame.

Extreme Prejudice ★ ★ ★

R, 104 m., 1987

Nick Nolte (Jack Benteen), Powers Boothe (Cash Bailey), Michael Ironside (Major Hackett), Maria Conchita Alonso (Sarita Cisneros), Rip Torn (Sheriff Pearson), Clancy Brown (Sergeant McRose). Directed by Walter Hill and produced by Buzz Feitshans. Screenplay by Deric Washburn.

The story elements in *Extreme Prejudice* are so ancient they sound like ad copy: Two strong men, one good, one evil, battle each other for justice—and for the heart of the woman they both love. Walter Hill is the right director for this material. He specializes in male action movies where the characters are all a little taller, leaner, meaner, and more obscene than in real life.

Hill doesn't really try to avoid the clichés in a story like this. He simply turns up the juice. Like his *Southern Comfort*, *48 HRS*, and *The Warriors*, this is a movie that depends on style, not surprises. He doesn't want to make a different kind of movie; he wants to make a familiar story look better than we've seen it look recently. And yet there is a big surprise in *Extreme Prejudice* in the appearance and character of Nick Nolte.

When last seen, Nolte had successfully overcome his early pretty-boy image and turned into one of the shabbier ruins on the landscape of American leading men. His performance in *Teachers* needed a diagnosis, not a review. But then, about halfway through *Down and Out in Beverly Hills*, he underwent some kind of metamorphosis. He shaved off the beard and emerged as a weathered, older, more attractive actor; for the first time, I realized that he had the materials to become a big-league star like Cooper or Gable.

In *Extreme Prejudice*, he is working in the Cooper tradition. He is leaner than before, his face chiseled like some Western artifact, and he wears his Texas Ranger hat down on his forehead, so his eyes are always in shadow. He works the border, trying to control the drug trade, and at night he comes home exhausted to the bed of his girl (Maria Conchita Alonso).

She is restless with this arrangement. Her previous lover was Cash Bailey (Powers Boothe), once Nolte's best friend, now a drug baron who controls the flow across the border. Cash moves with immunity back and forth in a fleet of helicopters and offers Alonso more than a Ranger's salary can buy. One day, she packs up and goes to live with him. Meanwhile, Nolte's territory is invaded by an unofficial, top-secret cadre of American combat veterans who apparently are working for the CIA. Their mission remains murky (they screw up a mysterious bank heist), but they seem to be after Cash, too. That leads to the shoot-out at Cash's Mexican fortress, not to mention a lot of last-minute switching of sides and loyalties.

The specifics of the plot you can do without. You've seen this movie before, right down to the dozing guards who permit the enemy gunmen to walk right into the stronghold.

What makes the film good are Hill's style and the acting. Everything is cranked up about ten degrees. Nolte is quiet and tough, Boothe gives a great performance as a slimy drug merchant with some residual charm, and Alonso was born for her role as the passionate senorita trapped between two men who will kill for her.

The love triangle is sort of a broad, bloody version of *The Third Man*, where Orson Welles and Joseph Cotten were childhood friends who ended up on opposite sides of the law and in love with Alida Valli. The conflict in these triangles is always the same: The woman knows the bad guy is a slimy snake, but she loves him, anyway. That breaks the good guy's heart and leaves him free to kill his childhood buddy. Then you get the poignant ending.

Hill has made a lot of movies in the last fifteen years, and I guess it's too late to hope that he'll develop a real interest in his female characters. They're the pawns of his male buddies, and everything else boils down to the way the characters walk, the way they look at each other, the personal tics they develop, and the new ways the stunt men find for people to die. *Extreme Prejudice* offers a lot of technique, some strong acting, and the absolute confidence of a good director who knows what he wants to do and doesn't care if that limits him.

Extremities ★

R, 89 m., 1986

Farrah Fawcett (Marjorie Easton), James Russo (Joe), Diana Scarwid (Terry), Alfre Woodard (Patricia). Directed by Robert M. Young and produced by Burt Sugarman. Screenplay by William Mastrosimone.

Extremities is a film in which a male psychopath tortures a female psychopath for an hour, and then they trade places. I know that isn't what the filmmakers believe the film is about, but I can only go by what's on the screen.

Farrah Fawcett plays a woman who is attacked by a would-be rapist. After she escapes, she discovers that she can expect precious little help from the police. A few days later, when the rapist corners her at home, she endures his sadistic treatment until she sees her chance, and then she blinds him with insecticide, bangs him over the head, ties him up, and imprisons him in the fireplace. Then she goes out into the backyard to dig a grave, so that she can bury him alive.

I assume this movie is supposed to be a statement about rape. It is so confused in its writing and direction, however, that the only scenes with any dramatic force are the ones that exploit sex and violence. Although the stage version of *Extremities* received a lot of praise when Fawcett appeared in it off-Broadway, the film belongs on the same shelf with trash like *I Spit on Your Grave*. The director, Robert M. Young, is known for sincere, socially responsible films like *The Ballad of Gregorio Cortez*. This one really gets away from him.

We learn next to nothing about the characters. Fawcett is a woman who does not seem to have a job or a past; she shares a house with two other women, and plays racketball, and fools around with her roommate's boyfriend, and those are the only details we learn about her that do not apply directly to her violent experiences. Her attacker (James Russo) is married and has a kid. What that has to do with his behavior is never explained.

The roommates consist of an airhead (Diana Scarwid), whose purpose is to turn up late in the film and get hysterical, and a sensible social worker (Alfre Woodard), who turns up a little later and acts as the voice of responsibility. She believes Fawcett should call the cops instead of burying the guy in the tomato patch.

The movie seems to argue, however, that it's Fawcett's word against Russo's, and that since justice will never be done, Fawcett should take the law into her own hands. Argument and logic are not really the movie's purpose, however. The opening passages are mostly dramatic scenes of Fawcett's degradation, as Russo forces her to strip, crawl around on the floor, and cook him breakfast, while he pulls her hair and slaps her around. After Fawcett gets the upper hand, she blinds him, jabs him in the groin, ties him up, and threatens to kill him with a shovel and a hammer, not to mention burying him alive.

The movie never really works even on a debased level. Fawcett's performance is hard to follow; she doesn't seem frightened enough when Russo first appears at her home, and after he begins to mistreat her she uses lots of sobs and sniffles instead of letting us see her character's mind at work. After she gets the upper hand, she goes through the motions of using violence against him, but there's never any true electricity, any feeling that her character is truly consumed by violence. Her behavior, indeed, seems inspired more by petulance than revenge.

After the roommates turn up and begin to debate the villain's fate, the movie becomes completely ridiculous, a series of half-baked philosophical arguments, soap opera revelations, and lines of dialogue good only for unintentional laughs. By the film's last shot, a long close-up of Fawcett's face, we are so confused that we don't know what she's supposed to be thinking, or what she may have learned, or even, for that matter, if there's anyone at home.

Eye of the Needle ★ ★ ★

R, 118 m., 1981

Donald Sutherland (Faber), Kate Nelligan (Lucy), Christopher Cazenova (David), Ian Bannon (Canter). Directed by Richard Marquand and produced by Stephen Friedman. Screenplay by Stanley Mann.

Eye of the Needle resembles nothing so much as one of those downbeat, plodding, quietly horrifying, and sometimes grimly funny war movies that used to be made by the British film industry, back when there was a British film industry. They used to star Stanley Baker or Trevor Howard. This one stars Donald Sutherland, as the kind of introverted psychopath who should inhabit only black-and-white movies, although the color here is sometimes gloomy enough to suffice. I admired the movie. It is made with quiet competence, and will remind some viewers of the Alfred Hitchcock who made *The 39 Steps* and *Foreign Correspondent.* It is about a German spy, the "Needle," who dropped out of sight in Germany in 1938 and now inhabits a series of drab bed-sitting-rooms in England while he spies on the British war effort. He is known as the Needle because of his trademarked way of killing people by jabbing a stiletto into their rib cages. He kills with a singular lack of passion; this is Jack the Ripper crossed with J. Alfred Prufrock. As played by Sutherland, the Needle is a very lonely man. We are given hints to explain his isolation: He was raised by parents who did not love him, he was shipped off to boarding schools, he spent parts of his childhood in America, where he learned English. None of these experiences fully explains his ruthlessness, but then perhaps it is just a spy's job to be ruthless.

The plot is part espionage, part cliffhanger. The Needle discovers phony plywood "airplanes" intended to look, from the air, like Patton's invasion force—a ruse to throw off the Germans. His assignment is to personally deliver news of the actual Allied invasion plans to Hitler. This he intends to do with every fiber of his being, and yet we never get the feeling that the this man is a patriotic Nazi. He is more of a dogged functionary. In his attempts to rendezvous with a Nazi submarine, he's shipwrecked on an isolated island occupied only by a lighthousekeeper and by a young married couple—a woman (Kate Nelligan), her legless husband (Christopher Cazenove), and their son. The last third of the movie turns into a bloody melodrama, as the Needle kills the husband and the lighthouse-keeper and threatens the woman, first in a psychological way and then with violence. But before the final standoff, he pretends to be merely a lost sailor. And the woman, frustrated by her husband's drunkenness and refusal to love, becomes attracted to the stranger. They make love. She grows fond of him. Does he grow fond of her? We can never be sure, but he tells her things he has told to no one else.

Some people will find the movie slow going. I preferred to think of it as deliberate. It is effective, I think, to develop a plot like this at a deliberate pace, instead of rushing headlong through it. That gives us time to meditate on the character of the Needle, and to ponder his very few, enigmatic references to his own behavior. We learn things about him that he may not even know about himself, and that is why the film's final scene is so much more complex than it seems. "The war has come down to the two of us," Sutherland tells Nelligan, and in the final exchange of desperate looks between the man and the woman there is a whole universe left unspoken. The movie ends with Nelligan regarding a man who is either a treacherous spy or an unloved child, take your choice.

Eyewitness ★ ★ ★

R, 102 m., 1981

William Hurt (Daryll Deever), Sigourney Weaver (Tony Sokolow), Christopher Plummer (Joseph), James Woods (Aldo), Irene Worth (Mrs. Sokolow), Pamela Reed (Linda). Directed and produced by Peter Yates. Screenplay by Steve Tesich.

Somebody was explaining the difference between European and American movies to me the other day: European movies are about people, but American movies are about stories. It's an interesting idea, especially when it's applied to a thriller like *Eyewitness*, which is good precisely because it pays more attention to its people than its story. Does that make it European? Well, it was directed by Peter Yates, who is British but has directed some of the most "American" movies of the past decade, from *Bullitt* to *Breaking Away*. It is definitely set in America—from the bowels of a Manhattan boiler room to the newsroom of a TV station. But it's about such interesting, complicated, quirky, and sometimes funny people that it must at the least be mid-Atlantic.

The movie stars William Hurt as a janitor who stumbles across evidence that could lead to the solution of a murder investigation. But he doesn't go to the police with it because he's too complicated, too introspective, too distrustful of his own discovery . . . and, mostly, he's too much in love from afar with a TV news reporter (Sigourney Weaver). Maybe he can win her attention by giving her the scoop?

There are other complications. Sigourney Weaver is engaged to an Israeli agent (Christopher Plummer) who is involved in secret international negotiations to smuggle Jews out of the Soviet Union. His plan involves clandestine payments to a Vietnamese agent who got rich on the black market in Saigon and has now moved to Manhattan. The other characters include James Woods, as Hurt's eccentric and unpredictable fellow janitor, and Steven Hill and Morgan Freeman as a couple of cops who wearily track down leads in the case (their best line: "When Aldo was a little boy, he must have wanted to grow up to be a suspect").

The development and solution of the murder mystery are handled with professional dispatch by Yates and his writer, Steve Tesich (who also wrote *Breaking Away*). A final shoot-out in a midtown riding stable has a touch of Hitchcock to it; the old master always loved to mix violence with absolutely inappropriate settings. But what makes this movie so entertaining is the way Yates and Tesich and their characters play against our expectations.

Examples. Weaver is not only a TV newswoman, but also a part-time serious pianist and the unhappy daughter of her domineering parents. Hurt is not only a janitor but also a sensitive soul who can talk his way into Weaver's heart. Woods is not only a creepy janitor but also the enthusiastic promoter of a marriage between his sister and Hurt. Hurt and the sister (Pamela Reed) carry on the courtship because they are both too embarrassed to tell the other one they're not in love. Plummer is the most complicated character of all, and it's a very good question whether he's a villain. It all depends on how you view his own personal morality.

I've seen so many thrillers that, frankly, I don't always care how they turn out—unless they're really well-crafted. What I like about *Eyewitness* is that, although it *does* care how it turns out, it cares even more about the texture of the scenes leading to the denouement. There's not a scene in this movie that exists only to provide us with plot information. Every scene develops characters. And they're developed in such offbeat fidelity to the way people do behave that we get all the more involved in the mystery, just because, for once, we halfway believe it could really be happening.

F

F/X ★ ★ ★ ½
R, 108 m., 1985

Bryan Brown (Rollie Tyler), Cliff DeYoung (Lipton), Brian Dennehy (Lieutenant Leo McCarthy), Trey Wilson (Lieutenant Murdoch), Mason Adams (Mason), Martha Gehman (Andy), Diane Venora (Ellen), Jerry Orbach (DeFranco), Tim Gallin (Adams). Directed by Robert Mandel and produced by Dodi Fayed and Jack Wiener. Screenplay by Robert T. Megginson and Gregory Fleeman.

F/X is Hollywood shorthand for "effects," or special effects, the art form that creates bullet holes and gaping wounds, fake shotgun blasts, and severed limbs.

In the movie, Bryan Brown plays a special effects man whose customized truck is a mobile effects lab. He can create his illusions almost anywhere, and is in big demand from the Hollywood studios. Then one day he gets an unusual request from the federal government. As part of their witness relocation and protection program, they want to fake the murder of an organized crime leader. Their reasoning: If everybody thinks DeFranco is dead, nobody will try to kill him, and he will survive and be able to testify in court.

This premise is only the beginning of the movie's ingenuity. Like *Jagged Edge,* this is one of those tightly constructed plots in which the hero is almost the last person to find out anything. Who can he trust? Who is really on his side, who is lying to him, who is trying to kill him? One of the pleasures of *Jagged Edge* was that we could watch the central character, the lawyer played by Glenn Close, use all of her intelligence and intuition and still walk right into danger, because she could not believe that people could be such deceptive swine.

The same thing happens in *F/X,* and I will have to tread carefully to avoid giving away too much of the plot. Briefly, there are large, basic questions about who wants DeFranco, the underworld leader, killed, and who wants him alive. There are other fundamental questions about whether special effects have indeed been used, or whether he actually was killed. And there are great ominous possibilities that the special effects man himself might be next on the hit list.

The movie moves quickly through a large gallery of players. At the center of everything is Rollie Tyler, the effects man, given a nice, laconic professionalism by Bryan Brown, whose Australian accent reminds us that he was not brought up to automatically trust the U.S. government in all matters.

The Broadway veteran Jerry Orbach plays DeFranco as an expensively barbered creep. Halfway through the movie, the dependable character actor Brian Dennehy turns up as a city cop not in on the scam. Cliff DeYoung is the slippery Lipton, mastermind of the federal scheme. Martha Gehman is Andy, the loyal assistant of the effects man, and Diane Venora is his doomed girlfriend.

I mention so many of these actors because, more than most thrillers that depend on tightly constructed plots, *F/X* also depends on good, well-observed performances. This movie takes a lot of delight in being more psychologically complex than it has to be. It contains fights and shoot-outs and big chase scenes, but they're all firmly centered on who the characters are and what they mean to one another. And by the end of the film when everything comes down to the events in a large, scary, and isolated mansion, the movie is able to use the personalities of the characters as part of the payoff.

Every year should bring a few good thrillers, to balance out all the failed and shallow attempts. The irony of *F/X*, which is a very good thriller indeed, is that it avoids the pitfall of so many thrillers; it doesn't degenerate into a mindless display of special effects. The effects in this film just happen to be the ways the hero has of expressing himself.

Fade to Black ★ ★ ½
R, 100 m., 1980

Dennis Christopher (Eric Binford), Tim Thomerson (Dr. Moriarty), Gwynne Gilford (Anne), Linda Kerridge (Marilyn), Morgan Paull (Gary Bially), Eve Brent Ashe (Aunt Stella). Directed by Vernon Zimmerman. Produced by George G. Braunstein and Ron Hamady. Screenplay by Zimmerman.

It will probably help to be a movie buff if you find yourself watching *Fade to Black*. This is a weird, uneven, generally intriguing thriller about a young man whose fantasy life is totally controlled by images from movies. He works in a Los Angeles film exchange, checking and shipping movie prints, and at night he comes home to his museumlike room in the home of his aunt—a shrill harridan who would feel less secure in her wheelchair if she had ever seen *Kiss of Death*.

The young man is played with a kind of creepy power by Dennis Christopher, in a role completely opposite from his performance as the hero of *Breaking Away*. He is lonely, socially isolated, hostile. He has memorized every movie ever made, although when he bets money on a trivia question, it's one with a ridiculously easy answer: He wants to know Humphrey Bogart's full name in *Casablanca*. Everybody knows that one.

Things start going wrong in the kid's life. His boss gets on his case at work. His aunt is impossible. He makes a date with a young girl (Linda Kerridge) who looks just like Marilyn Monroe, and then he thinks she stood him up. This is too much all at once, and the kid goes berserk.

In a scene we know is inevitable, he mimics Richard Widmark in *Kiss of Death* and pushes his aunt down the stairs. Then he begins masquerading as his other movie heroes—Hopalong Cassidy, James Cagney, the Mummy—and wiping out the rest of his opposition. These scenes are handled by director Vernon Zimmerman with a mixture of reality and stylized fantasy. For example, when Hoppy gets in a shoot-out, the scene is staged and lit like a movie, which heightens the effect. But it's not lit like a Hopalong Cassidy movie; it's lit to backlight and isolate the hero, and that, no doubt, is the kid's own fantasy.

I don't want to give away too many of the movie's surprises, although if you're a movie buff you'll anticipate a lot of them. The climax, though, is a bravura piece of stylistic overkill, with Christopher creeping around of the roof of Hollywood's Chinese Theater, looking like a cross between the Phantom of the Opera and Cary Grant in *To Catch a Thief*.

What's the point of all this? Just pure escapist silliness, I suppose. But I was rather moved by the Christopher character's loneliness in the earlier scenes (later, he's frankly just a caricature manipulated by the plot). I also liked the way that some of the minor roles, including Kerridge's were handled to develop the humanity of the characters rather than just the stereotypes.

The Falcon and the Snowman
★ ★ ★ ★
R, 131 m., 1985

Timothy Hutton (Christopher Boyce), Sean Penn (Daulton Lee), Pat Hingle (Mr. Boyce), Joyce Van Patten (Mrs. Boyce), David Suchet (Alex), Boris Leskin (Mikhail). Directed by John Schlesinger and produced by Gabriel Katska and Schlesinger. Screenplay by Steven Saillian.

A few years ago there were stories in the papers about a couple of California kids who were caught selling government secrets to the Russians. The stories had an air of unreality about them. Here were a couple of middle-class young men from suburban backgrounds, who were prosecuted as spies and traitors and who hardly seemed to have it quite clear in their own minds how they had gotten into the spy business. One of the many strengths of *The Falcon and the Snowman* is that it succeeds, in an admirably matter-of-fact way, in showing us exactly how these two young men got in way over their heads. This is a movie about spies, but it is not a thriller in any routine sense of the word; it's just the meticulously observant record of how naiveté, inexperience, misplaced idealism, and greed led to one of the most peculiar cases of treason in American history.

The movie stars Timothy Hutton as Christopher Boyce, a seminarian who has a crisis of conscience, drops out of school, and ends up working almost by accident for a message-routing center of the CIA. Sean Penn is his best friend, Daulton Lee. Years ago, they were altar boys together, but in recent times their paths have diverged; while Boyce was studying for the priesthood, Lee was setting himself up as a drug dealer. By the time we meet them, Boyce is earnest and clean-cut, just the kind of young man the CIA might be looking for (it doesn't hurt that his father is a former FBI man). And Lee, with a mustache that makes him look like a failed creep, is a jumpy, paranoid drug dealer who is one step ahead of the law.

The whole caper begins so simply. Boyce, reading the messages he is paid to receive and forward, learns that the CIA is engaged in dirty tricks designed to influence elections in Australia. He is deeply offended to learn that his government would be interfering in the affairs of another state, and the more he thinks about it, the more he wants to do something. For example, supply the messages to the Russians. He doesn't want to be a Russian *spy*, you understand, just to bring this injustice to light. Lee has some contacts in Mexico, where he buys drugs. One day, in a deceptively casual conversation by the side of a backyard swimming pool, the two friends decide to go into partnership to sell the information to the Soviet Embassy in Mexico City. Lee takes the documents south and launches them both on an adventure that is a lark at first, and then a challenge, and finally just a very, very bad dream.

These two young men have one basic problem. They are amateurs. The Russians don't necessarily like that any better than the Americans would; indeed, even though the Russians are happy to have the secrets that are for sale, there is a definite sense in some scenes that the key Russian contact agent, played by David Suchet, is almost offended by the sloppy way Penn deals in espionage. The only thing Penn seems really serious about is the money.

The Falcon and the Snowman never steps wrong, but it is best when it deals with the relationship between the two young American spies. The movie was directed by John Schlesinger, an Englishman whose understanding of American characters was most unforgettably demonstrated in *Midnight Cowboy*, and I was reminded of Joe Buck and Ratso Rizzo from that movie as I watched this one. There is even a quiet, understated quote to link Ratso with the Penn character: a moment in a parking garage when Penn defies a car to pull in front of him, and we're reminded of Ratso crossing a Manhattan street and hurling the line "I'm *walking* here!" at a taxi that dares to cut him off. Instead of relying on traditional methods for creating the suspense in spy movies, this one uses the energy generated between the two very different characters, as the all-American Boyce gradually begins to understand that his partner is out of control. *The Falcon and the Snowman*, like most good movies, is not really about its plot but about its characters. These two young men could just as easily be selling stolen IBM programs to Apple, instead of CIA messages to the Russians; the point is that they begin with one set of motives and then the implacable real world supplies them with another, harder, more unforgiving set of realities.

Just as with *Midnight Cowboy*, it's hard to say who gives the better performance this time: Sean Penn, with his twitching intensity as he angles for respect from the Russians, or Timothy Hutton, the straight man, earnestly telling his girlfriend that she should remember he really loves her—"no matter what you may hear about me in a few days from now."

Fame ★ ★ ★ ½
R, 133 m., 1980

Eddie Barth (Angelo), Irene Cara (Coco), Lee Curreri (Bruno), Laura Dean (Lisa), Antonia Franceschi (Hilary), Boyd Gaines (Michael), Albert Hague (Shorofsky), Tresa Hughes (Mrs. Finsecker). Directed and produced by David De Silva and Alan Marshall. Screenplay by Christopher Gore.

Mrs. Seward, the draconian rhetoric teacher who drilled literacy into generations of Urbana (Ill.) High School students, used to tell us we were having the best four years of our lives. We groaned. *Fame* is a movie that she might have enjoyed. It's about a dozen or so talented kids who enter New York's High

School of the Performing Arts as freshmen and emerge four years later as future Freddie Prinzes and Benny Goodmans, Leonard Bernsteins and Mrs. Sewards.

Fame is a genuine treasure, moving and entertaining, a movie that understands being a teen-ager as well as *Breaking Away* did, but studies its characters in a completely different milieu. It's the other side of the coin: A big-city, aggressive, cranked-up movie to play against the quieter traditions of *Breaking Away*'s small Indiana college town. *Fame* is all New York City. It's populated by rich kids, ghetto kids, kids with real talent, and kids with mothers who think they have real talent. They all go into the hopper, into a high school of kids who are worked harder because they're "special"—even if they're secretly not so sure they're so special.

The movie has the kind of sensitivity to the real lives of real people that we don't get much in Hollywood productions anymore. Anyone who ever went to high school will recognize some of *Fame*'s characters: the quiet little girl who blossoms, the class genius who locks himself up in the basement with his electronic equipment, the kid who can't read but is a naturally gifted performer, the wiseass, the self-destructive type, the sexpot, the rich kid, and on and on. The cast has been recruited from New York's most talented young performers, some of them almost playing themselves. The teachers are familiar too: self-sacrificing, perfectionist, cranky, love-hate objects.

If the character types seem familiar, the movie's way of telling their stories is not. This isn't a movie that locks its characters into a conventional plot. Instead, it fragments the experiences of four years into dozens of vignettes, loosely organized into sections titled "The Auditions," "Freshman Year," and so on. We get to know the characters and their personalities gradually, as we see them in various situations. The effect is a little like high school itself; you come in as a total stranger and by the time you leave, the school has become your world.

If the kids in *Fame* are like high school kids anywhere, they're also different because they *are* talented, and the movie's at its best when it examines the special pressures on young people who are more talented than they are mature, experienced, or sure of themselves. The ghost that hovers over everyone in this school is a former graduate, Freddie Prinze, who had the talent but never figured out how to handle it.

The movie's director, Alan Parker, seems to have a knack for isolating just those moments in the lives of his characters when growth, challenge, and talent are all on the line at once. Where did he find his insights into talented young people? Probably while he was directing his first film, the wonderful *Bugsy Malone* (1976), which was a gangster musical with an all-kid cast. *Fame* is a perfect title for this movie; it establishes an ironic distance between where these kids are now and where they'd like to be someday, and then there's also the haunting suggestion that some of the ones who find fame will be able to handle it, and some will not.

Fanny and Alexander ★ ★ ★ ★

R, 197 m., 1983

Pernilla Allwin (Fanny Ekdahl), Bertil Guve (Alexander Ekdahl), Jan Malmsjo (Bishop Vergerus), Erland Josephson (Isak Jacobi), Kabi Laretei (Aunt Emma), Gunn Wallgren (Helena Ekdahl), Ewa Froling (Emilie Ekdahl), Gunnar Bjornstrand (Filip Landahl). Directed by Ingmar Bergman and produced by Jorn Donner. Screenplay by Bergman.

There was a time when Ingmar Bergman wanted to make films reflecting the whole of human experience. He asked the big questions about death, sex, and God, and he wasn't afraid of the big, dramatic image, either. Who else (except Woody Allen) has had the temerity to show a man playing chess with Death? Bergman was swinging for the fences in those deliberately big, important films. But he has discovered that a better way to encompass all human experience is to be specific about a small part of it and let the audience draw its own conclusions. In *The Seventh Seal* (1956), he portrayed Death as a symbolic grim reaper. But in *Cries and Whispers* (1973), by showing one particular woman dying painfully while her sisters and her maid stood by helplessly, he said infinitely more about death.

His film *Fanny and Alexander* is one of the most detailed and specific he's ever made, and therefore one of the most universal. It comes directly out of his experiences as a Swede in his mid-sixties who was born into a world of rigid religious belief, grew up in a world of war and turmoil, and is now old enough, wise enough, and resigned enough to develop a sort of philosophical mysticism about life. In its chronology, the film covers only a handful of years. But in its buried implications about life, I believe, it traces the development of Bergman's thought from his school days until the day before yesterday.

Fanny and Alexander is a long film that contains many characters and many events. Very simply: In a Swedish provincial town in the early years of this century, two children are growing up within the bosom of a large, jolly extended family. Their father dies and their mother remarries. Their new stepfather is a stern, authoritarian clergyman who means well but is absolutely incapable of understanding the feelings of others. Escape from his household leads them, by an indirect path, into the life of an old Jewish antique dealer whose life still has room for the mysticism and magic of an earlier time. Not everything is explained by the end of the film, but everything is reconciled.

Bergman has confessed that a great deal of the movie is autobiographical—if not literally, then in terms of its feelings. He had, for example, a father who was a strict clergyman. But it's too easy to assume the bishop in the movie represents only Bergman's father: Can he not also represent Bergman himself, who is seen within the circle of his collaborators as an authoritarian figure with a tendency to know what is right for everyone else? Bergman has hinted that there's a little of himself, indeed, in *all* the male characters in his movie. Looking for Bergman's autobiography in his characters is one thing. I think we also can see *Fanny and Alexander* as the autobiography of his career. The warm humanism of the early scenes reflects his own beginnings in naturalism. The stern aestheticism of the middle scenes reflects his own middle period, with its obsession with both philosophical and stylistic black-and-white. The last third of the film, like the last third of his career, admits that there are more things in heaven and on Earth than dreamed of in his philosophy.

Fanny and Alexander is a big, exciting, ambitious film—more of a beginning than, as Bergman claims, the summary of his career. If you've followed him on his long trek of discovery, this will feel like a film of resolution. If you're coming fresh to Bergman, it may, paradoxically, seem to burst with the sort of invention we associate with young first-time directors. It's a film for all seasons.

Farewell, My Lovely ★ ★ ★ ★

R, 95 m., 1975

Robert Mitchum (Philip Marlowe), Charlotte Rampling (Velma), John Ireland (Lieutenant Nulty), Sylvia Miles (Mrs. Nulty), Jack O'Halloran (Moose Malloy), Anthony Zerbe (Brunette), Harry Dean Stanton (Billy Rolfe), Walter McGinn (Tommy Ray). Directed by Dick Richards and produced by George Pappas and Jerry Bruckheimer. Screenplay by David Zelag Goodman.

Los Angeles, 1941. A run-down street of seedy shop fronts and blinking neon signs. Music from a lonely horn. The camera pans up to a second-story window of a flophouse. In the window, his hat pushed back, his tie undone, Philip Marlowe lights another cigarette and waits for the cops to arrive. He is ready to tell his story.

These opening shots are so evocative of Raymond Chandler's immortal Marlowe, archetypical private eye, haunting the underbelly of Los Angeles, that if we're Chandler fans we hold our breath. Is the ambience going to be maintained, or will this be another campy ripoff? Half an hour into the movie, we relax. *Farewell, My Lovely* never steps wrong. It is, indeed, the most evocative of all the private detective movies we have had in the last few years. It is not as great as Roman Polanski's *Chinatown*, which was concerned with larger subjects, but in the genre itself there hasn't been anything this good since Hollywood was doing Philip Marlowe the first time around. One reason is that Dick Richards, the director, takes his material and character absolutely seriously. He is not uneasy with it, as Robert Altman was when he had Elliott Gould flirt with seriousness in *The Long Goodbye*. Richards doesn't hedge his bet.

And neither does Robert Mitchum, in what becomes his definitive performance. Mitchum is one of the great screen presences. He was born to play the weary, cynical, doggedly romantic Marlowe. His voice and his face and the way he lights his cigarette are all exactly right, and seem totally effortless. That's his trademark. In a good Mitchum performance, we are never aware he is acting. And it is only when we measure the distances between his characters that we can see what he is doing. Mitchum is at home on the kinds of streets Philip Marlowe worked: streets of one-room furnished flats and pink stucco hotels, out-of-town newsstands and seedy bars, and always the drowsy commonness of the flat lands leading up to the baroque mansions in the hills and canyons.

Farewell, My Lovely, gets all of this just right—Angelo Graham's art direction is a triumph—and then places Mitchum's Marlowe in the center of it and leads him through one of Chandler's tortuous plots. Although everything does finally tie together in this one (as it never did in Chandler's labyrinthine *The Big Sleep*), it doesn't matter that much. What's important is the gallery of characters Marlowe encounters, each grotesque and beautiful in his own way. The most touching is Moose Malloy, played by an ex-prizefighter named Jack O'Halloran. Moose towers over everyone in the film, both in stature and in the immensity of his need. Seven years ago he fell in love with a hooker named Velma and they were going to be married, but something went wrong during a bank job, and Moose took the rap. When he gets out of prison, he hires Marlowe to find his Velma.

Marlowe's quest for Velma, a faded memory from a hopeless love affair, leads him, as we might have known, into a case a lot larger and more important than he could have suspected. There is an odyssey through a lurid whorehouse and a killing in a ghetto bar, and a midnight rendezvous that ends in another death, and always there is Lieutenant Nulty, of the Los Angeles Police Department, trying to figure out why Marlowe winds up attached to so many dead bodies. Richards's approach, with screenplay by David Zelag Goodman, is to start the story at the end with Marlowe trying to explain things to Nulty and then flash back to the beginning and let Marlowe elaborate on the story voice-over. It is a strategy that is often distracting in movies. But not this time, because it borrows from Chandler's own first-person narrative. And it provides great one-liners, as when the elusive Velma (Charlotte Rampling) sizes Marlowe up and down and he says, "She threw me a look I caught in my hip pocket."

Farewell, My Lovely is a great entertainment and a celebration of Robert Mitchum's absolute originality. The day after you view it, you might find yourself quoting lines to friends, which is always the test in these cases, because most of the time private-eye stories have no meaning at all unless it is in the way their heroes behave in the face of the most unsettling revelations about human nature. This time Philip Marlowe behaves very well.

Fast Times at Ridgemont High ★

R, 92 m., 1982

Sean Penn (Jeff Spicoli), Jennifer Jason Leigh (Stacy Hamilton), Judge Reinhold (Brad Hamilton), Robert Romanus (Mike Damone), Brian Backer (Rat Ratner), Phoebe Cates (Linda Barrett). Directed by Amy Heckerling and produced by Art Linson and Irving Azoff. Screenplay by Cameron Crowe.

How could they do this to Jennifer Jason Leigh? How could they put such a fresh and cheerful person into such a scuz-pit of a movie? Don't they know they have a star on their hands? I didn't even know who Leigh was when I walked into *Fast Times at Ridgemont High,* and yet I was completely won over by her. She contained so much life and light that she was a joy to behold. And then she and everybody else in this so-called comedy is invited to plunge into offensive vulgarity. Let me make myself clear. I am not against vulgarity as a subject for a movie comedy. Sometimes I treasure it, when it's used with inspiration, as in *The Producers* or *National Lampoon's Animal House.* But vulgarity is a very tricky thing to handle in a comedy; tone is everything, and the makers of *Fast Times at Ridgemont High* have an absolute gift for taking potentially funny situations and turning them into general embarrassment. They're tone-deaf.

The movie's another one of those adolescent sex romps, such as *Porky's* and *Animal House,* in which part of the humor comes from raunchy situations and dialogue. This movie is *so* raunchy, however, that the audience can't quite believe it. I went to a sneak preview thrown by a rock radio station, and the audience had come for a good time. But during a scene involving some extremely frank talk about certain popular methods of sexual behavior, even the rock fans were grossed out. There's a difference between raunchiness and gynecological detail.

The movie's cast struggles valiantly through all this dreck. Rarely have I seen so many attractive young performers invited to appear in so many unattractive scenes. Leigh, for example, plays a virginal young student at Ridgemont High. She's curious about sex, so the script immediately turns her into a promiscuous sex machine who will go to bed with anybody. And then her sexual experiences all turn out to have an unnecessary element of realism, so that we have to see her humiliated, disappointed, and embarrassed. Whatever happened to upbeat sex? Whatever happened to love and lust and romance, and scenes where good-looking kids had a little joy and excitement in life, instead of all this grungy downbeat humiliation? Why does someone as pretty as Leigh have to have her nudity exploited in shots where the only point is to show her ill-at-ease?

If this movie had been directed by a man, I'd call it sexist. It was directed by a woman, Amy Heckerling—and it's sexist all the same. It clunks to a halt now and then for some heartfelt, badly handled material about pregnancy and abortion. I suppose that's Heckerling paying dues to some misconception of the women's movement. But for the most part this movie just exploits its performers by trying to walk a tightrope between comedy and sexploitation.

In addition to Leigh's work, however, there are some other good performances. Sean Penn is perfect as the pot-smoking space cadet who has been stoned since the third grade. Phoebe Cates is breathtaking as the more experienced girl who gives Leigh those distasteful lessons in love. Judge Reinhold has fun as a perennial fast-food cook who rebels against the silly uniforms he's supposed to wear. Ray Walston is suitably hateful as the dictatorial history teacher, Mr. Hand. But this movie could have been a *lot* more fun if it hadn't chosen to confuse embarrassment with humor. The unnecessary detail about sexual functions isn't funny, it's distasteful. Leigh looks so young, fresh, cheerful, and innocent that we don't laugh when she gets into unhappy scenes with men—we wince. The whole movie is a failure of taste, tone, and nerve—the waste of a good cast on erratic, offensive material that hasn't been thought through, or maybe even thought about.

Fatal Attraction ★ ★ ½

R, 120 m., 1987

(See related Film Clip, p. 752.)

Michael Douglas (Dan Gallagher), Glenn Close (Alex Forrest), Anne Archer (Beth Gallagher), Ellen Hamilton Latzen (Ellen), Stuart Pankin (Jimmy), Ellen Foley (Hildy), Fred Gwynne (Arthur). Directed by Adrian Lyne and produced by Stanley R. Jaffe and Sherry Lansing. Screenplay by James Dearden.

Fatal Attraction is a spellbinding psychological thriller, and could have been a great movie if the filmmakers had not thrown character and plausibility to the winds in the last act to give us their version of a grown-up *Friday the 13th*.

Because the good things in the movie, including the performances, are so very good, it's a shame that the film's potential for greatness was so blatantly compromised. The movie is so right for so long that you can almost feel the moment when the script goes "click" and sells out.

The story stars Michael Douglas as a lawyer who has been happily married for nine years, has a six-year-old daughter, loves his wife, and has no particular problems on the day when he meets an intriguing blonde (Glenn Close) at a business party. She makes it her business to get to know him, and one weekend when Douglas's wife and daughter are out of town visiting his in-laws, he invites the blonde out to dinner.

She finds him willing to be seduced, and they have wild, passionate sex. Their couplings take place in a freight elevator, on the kitchen sink, and, I think, in bed; the film was directed by Adrian *(9½ Weeks)* Lyne, whose ideas of love and genital acrobatics seem more or less equivalent.

Douglas has made it clear that he's a happily married man and that he sees their meeting as a one-night stand ("Two adults who saw an opportunity and took advantage of it"), but Close doesn't see it that way. The moment sex is over for her, capture begins, and she starts a series of demands on Douglas's time and attention.

He tells her to get lost. She grows pathological. She visits him at the office, calls him at home in the middle of the night, throws acid on his car, visits his wife under the pretext of buying their apartment. Desperate to keep his secret and preserve his happy marriage, Douglas tries to reason with her, threaten her, and even hide from her, but she is implacable. (And you should read no further if you plan to view the movie—or perhaps, come to think of it, you should.)

The early and middle passages of the movie are handled with convincing psychological realism; James Dearden's dialogue sounds absolutely right, especially the way he allows the Close character to bait her hook with honeyed come-ons and then set it with jealousy, possessiveness, and finally guilt (after she says, inevitably, that she is pregnant). With the exception of the silly sex scenes, *Fatal Attraction* never steps wrong until its third act—and then it steps very wrong.

First, let me suggest how I hoped the movie would continue. Having created a believable and interesting marriage between Michael Douglas and Anne Archer (who is wonderful as his wife), and having drawn Glenn Close as a terrifying and yet always plausible other woman, I hoped the film would continue to follow its psychological exploration through to the end.

I wanted, for example, to hear a good talk between Douglas and Archer, in which truth was told and the strength of the marriage was tested. I wanted to see more of the inner workings of Close's mind. I wanted to know more about how Douglas really felt about the situation; although he grows to hate Close, is he really completely indifferent to the knowledge that she carries his child?

The movie does not explore any of those avenues, although the filmmakers clearly have the intelligence to do so. Instead, the last third of the movie collapses into pathetic melodrama. The big scene of truth between Douglas and Archer is short-changed and feels unfinished. There is a pathetic sequence in which Close captures their daughter and scares her with a roller-coaster ride, while a frantic Archer gets in a car crash and breaks her arm. Give me a break.

And then there is the horror movie conclusion, complete with the unforgivable *Friday the 13th* cliché that the villain is never *really* dead. The conclusion, by the way, operates on the premise that Douglas cares absolutely nothing for his unborn child.

Fatal Attraction was produced by Stanley R. Jaffe and Sherry Lansing, and it seems to repeat a pattern for them. In 1984 they made *Firstborn,* with Teri Garr as a divorced mother who falls in love with Peter Weller as a man who is very wrong for her family. The first two-thirds of that film are also psychologically sound and dramatically fascinating, and then it degenerates into a canned formula of violence and an idotic chase scene. Now they throw away the ending of *Fatal Attraction.* What's the matter here? Do they lack the courage to follow their convictions through to the end? They seem to have a knack for finding thoughtful, sensitive screenplays about interesting adults, and then adding gruesome Hollywood horror formulas to them. *Fatal Attraction* clearly had the potential to be a great movie. I walked out feeling cheated and betrayed.

Fellini's Roma ★ ★ ★ ★

R, 128 m., 1973

Featuring Peter Gonzales, Stefano Majore, Britta Barnes, Pia de Doses, Fiona Florence, Marno Maitland, Giovannoli Renato, Anna Magnani, Gore Vidal, and Federico Fellini. Directed by Federico Fellini. Screenplay by Bernardino Zapponi and Fellini.

Federico Fellini first included his name in the title of one of his movies with *Fellini Satyricon* (1969), and then for legal reasons: A quickie Italian version of the Satyricon was being palmed off in international film markets as the real thing. Once having savored the notion, however, Fellini found it a good one, and so we have *Fellini's Roma,* which was followed by *Fellini Casanova*.

The name in the title doesn't seem conceited or affected, as it might from another director (*Peckinpah's Albuquerque*?). This *is* Fellini's Rome and nobody else's, just as all of his films since *La Dolce Vita* have been autobiographical musings and confessions from the most personal—and the best—director of his time. Any connection with a real city on the map of Italy is libelous. Fellini's Rome gets its suburbs trimmed when he goes for a haircut.

The movie isn't a documentary, although sometimes he lets it look like one. It's a rambling essay, meant to feel like free association. There's a very slight narrative thread, about a young man named Fellini who leaves the little town of Rimini and comes to the great city and is overwhelmed by its pleasures of body and spirit. He moves into a mad boarding house that would make a movie all by itself; he dines with his neighbors in great outdoor feasts when the summer heat drives everyone into the piazzas; he attends a raucous vaudeville show and he visits his first whorehouse . . . and then his second.

This material, filmed with loving attention to period detail, exists by itself in the movie; there's no effort to link the naive young Fellini with the confident genius who appears elsewhere in the movie. It's as if Fellini, the consummate inventor of fantasies, didn't grow out of his young manhood—he created it from scratch.

The autobiographical material is worked in between pseudo-documentary scenes that contain some of the most brilliant images Fellini has ever devised. The movie opens with a monumental Roman traffic jam that, typically, becomes important because Fellini has deigned to photograph it. He swoops above it on a crane, directing his camera, his movie, and the traffic. A blinding rainstorm turns everything into a hellish apparition, and then there's a final shot, held just long enough to make its point, of the autos jammed around the Colosseum.

The image is both perfect and natural; as someone commented about Fellini's *8½*, his movies are filled with images, and they're all obvious. If Bergman is the great introvert of the movies, forever probing more and more deeply, Fellini is the joyous exponent of surfaces and excess, of letting more hang out than there is.

The obviousness of his images gives his movies a curious kind of clarity; he isn't reaching for things to say, but finding ways to say the same things more memorably. The decadence of Rome has been one of his favorite subjects throughout his career, and who could forget Anita Ekberg in the fountain, or the Mass procession at dawn, in *La Dolce Vita*?

But in *Roma,* he is even more direct, more stark: An expedition to inspect progress on the Rome subway system suddenly becomes transcendent when workmen break through to an underground crypt from pre-Christian times. The frescoes on the walls are so clear they might have been painted yesterday—until the air of the modern city touches them.

Rome, the eternal city, has historically been as carnal as it has been sacred. Fellini won't settle for one or the other; he uses scenes of carnality to symbolize a blessed state, and vice versa. Nothing could be more eternal, more patient, and more resigned than Fellini's use of a weary prostitute standing beside a highway outside Rome. She is tall, huge-bosomed, garishly made up, and her feet are tired. She stands among the broken stones of the Roman Empire, expecting nothing, hoping for nothing.

The prostitute, so often used as a symbol of fleeting moments and insubstantial experiences, becomes eternal; and the Church, always the symbol of the unchanging, the rock, becomes temporal. In his most audacious sequence, Fellini gives us an "ecclesiastical fashion show," with roller-skating priests, and nuns whose habits are made of blinking neon lights. What is unreal, and where is the real? Fellini doesn't know, and he seems to believe that Rome has never known. Rome has simply endured, waiting in the hope of someday finding out.

Fellini's Roma was attacked in some circles as an example of Fellini coasting on his genius. I find this point of view completely incomprehensible. Critics who would force Fellini back into traditional narrative films are missing the point; Fellini isn't just giving us a lot of flashy scenes, he's building a narrative that has a city for its protagonist instead of a single character.

The only sly thing is that the city isn't Rome—it's Fellini, disguised in bricks, mortar, and ruins. Fellini, who cannot find his way between the flesh and the spirit, who cannot find the connection between his youth and his greatness, and whose gift is to make movies where everything is obvious and nothing is simple. That was the dilemma that the Fellini character faced in *8½*, when he couldn't make sense of his life, and it's the dilemma we all face every day, isn't it?

Ferris Bueller's Day Off ★ ★ ★
PG-13, 103 m., 1986

Matthew Broderick (Ferris), Alan Ruck (Cameron Frye), Mia Sara (Sloane), Jeffrey Jones (Ed Rooney), Cindy Pickett (Mrs. Bueller), Jennifer Grey (Katie Bueller), Lyman Ward (Mr. Bueller), Edie McClurg (Secretary), Charlie Sheen (Young Punk). Directed by John Hughes and produced by Hughes and Tom Jacobson. Screenplay by Hughes.

Here is one of the most innocent movies in a long time, a sweet, warmhearted comedy about a kid who skips school so he can help his best friend win some self-respect. The therapy he has in mind includes a day's visit to Chicago, and after we've seen the Sears Tower and a parade down Dearborn Street, the Art Institute and the Board of Trade, architectural landmarks and lunch on Rush Street, and a game at Wrigley Field, we've got to concede that the city and state film offices have done their job. If *Ferris Bueller's Day Off* fails on every other level, at least it works as a travelogue.

It does, however, work on at least a few other levels. The movie stars Matthew Broderick as Ferris, a bright kid from the North Shore who fakes an illness so he can spend a day in town with his best friend, Cameron (Alan Ruck). At first, it seems as if skipping school is all he has in mind—especially after he talks Cameron into borrowing his dad's antique red Ferrari, a car the father loves more than Cameron himself.

The body of the movie is a lighthearted excursion through the Loop, including a German-American Day parade in which Ferris leaps aboard a float, grabs a microphone, and starts singing "Twist and Shout" while the polka band backs him up. The kids fake their way into a fancy restaurant for lunch, spend some time gawking at the masterpieces in the Art Institute, and then go out to Wrigley Field, where, of course, they are late and have to take left-field seats (the movie gets that detail right; it would be too much to hope that the kids could arrive in the third inning and find seats in the bleachers).

There is one great, dizzying moment when the kids visit the top of the Sears Tower and lean forward and press their foreheads against the glass, and look straight down at the tiny cars and little specks of life far below, and begin to talk about their lives. And that introduces, subtly, the buried theme of the movie, which is that Ferris wants to help Cameron gain self-respect in the face of his father's materialism.

Ferris is, in fact, a bit of a preacher. "Life goes by so fast," he says, "that if you don't stop and look around, you might miss it." He's sensitive to the hurt inside his friend's heart, as Cameron explains how his dad has cherished and restored the red Ferrari and given it a place of honor in the house—a place denied to Cameron.

Ferris Bueller was directed by John Hughes, the philosopher of adolescence, whose credits include *Sixteen Candles*, *The Breakfast Club*, and *Pretty in Pink*. In all of his films, adults are strange, distant creatures, who love their teen-agers, but fail completely to understand them. That's the case here, all right: All of the adults, including a bumbling high school dean (Jeffrey Jones) are dim-witted and one-dimensional. And the movie's solutions to Cameron's problems are pretty simplistic. But the film's heart is in the right place, and *Ferris Bueller* is slight, whimsical, and sweet.

52 Pickup ★ ★ ★ ½
R, 111 m., 1986

Roy Scheider (Harry Mitchell), Ann-Margret (Barbara Mitchell), Vanity (Doreen), John Glover (Alan Raimy), Clarence Williams III (Bobby Shy), Lonny Chapman (Jim O'Boyle), Kelly Preston (Cini), Doug McClure (Mark Averson). Directed by John Frankenheimer and produced by Menahem Golan and Yorum Globus. Screenplay by Elmore Leonard and John Steppling.

The old golden-age Warner Brothers crime dramas knew something that most modern movies have forgotten: Heroes are great, but a movie is only as good as its villain. John Frankenheimer's *52 Pickup* provides us with the best, most reprehensible villain of 1986, and uses his vile charm as the starting point for a surprisingly good film.

The villain's name is Raimy, and he is played by John Glover as a charming blackmailer with the looks of an aging British juvenile and a conscience with parts on order. He tries to pull a slick job on a rich businessman named Harry (Roy Scheider). He shows him videotapes of an affair Harry is having with a topless dancer. He wants $110,000.

Harry thinks it over, decides not to pay, and confesses everything to his wife, Barbara (Ann-Margret). She is very hurt, and in a scene of powerful understatement she says she had guessed the truth for a long time, but she just doesn't know why he had to tell her. Then Raimy turns up with another videotape. This one shows the topless dancer being murdered with Harry's gun.

This plot is not startlingly original (although there are some unexpected developments later in the film). What makes it special is the level at which it is told. The screenplay is based on an Elmore Leonard novel, and retains Leonard's gift for terse, colorful dialogue. It also isolates the key ingredient in Leonard's best novels, which is the sight of a marginal character being pushed far beyond his capacity to cope. In *52 Pickup*, there are actually three such characters, and by the end of the movie they are all desperately confused and frightened.

One is Raimy, a well-dressed sleazebag who makes porno movies and is capable of cold-blooded murder but caves in completely at the thought of his own destruction. One is Harry, an ordinary amoral businessman who rises to the challenge and figures out a way to outsmart his blackmailers by using their own character defects against them. The third is a sweaty little guy named Leo (Robert Trebor), who works for Raimy and went along with the crime but, holy God, never figured anyone was actually going to get hurt.

The problem with so many action adventures is that nobody in the movies ever seems scared enough. People are getting killed in every other scene, and they stay cool. If the movies were like real life and this kind of torture and murder were going on, everybody would be throwing up every five minutes—like they do in John D. MacDonald's novels. *52 Pickup* creates that sense of hopelessness and desperation, and it does it with those three performances—three guys who are in way over their heads, and know it all too well.

There are three other good performances in the movie, by Ann-Margret, Vanity, and Clarence Williams III (as a black pimp who is a lot more experienced about violence and death than his cheerful white partners). Is it still necessary to be surprised when Ann-Margret is good in a role, as if she were still making *Viva Las Vegas*? She has grown into a dependable serious actress, and here she does a delicate job of finding the line between anger at what her husband has done and pride in how he is trying to fix it. Vanity has a smaller role, as a prostitute with crucial information, and she does what all good character actors can do—she gives us the sense that she's fresh from intriguing off-screen action.

The story of *52 Pickup* is basically revenge melodrama. No thriller fan is going to be very astonished by what happens. What matters is the energy level, and the density of detail in the performances. This is a well-crafted movie by a man who knows how to hook the audience with his story—it's John Frankenheimer's best work in years. And if we can sometimes predict what the characters will do, there's the fascination of seeing them behave like unique and often very weird individuals; they aren't clones. I have gotten to the point where the one thing I know about most thrillers is that I will not be thrilled. *52 Pickup* blind-sided me.

Firefox ★ ★ ★ 1/2
PG, 136 m., 1982

Clint Eastwood (Mitchell Gant), Freddie Jones (Kenneth Aubrey), David Huffman (Buckholz), Warren Clarke (Pavel Upenskoy), Ronald Lacey (Semelovsky), Kenneth Colley (Colonel Kontarsky), Stefan Schnabel (First Secretary). Directed and produced by Clint Eastwood. Screenplay by Alex Lasker and Wendell Wellman.

Clint Eastwood's *Firefox* is a slick, muscular thriller that combines espionage with science fiction. The movie works like a well-crafted machine, and it's *about* a well-crafted machine. The *Firefox* of the title is a top-secret Russian warplane capable of flying six times the speed of sound while remaining invisible on radar. Eastwood's mission, if he chooses to accept it: Infiltrate the Soviet Union disguised as a Las Vegas drug smuggler, and then steal the Firefox by flying it to the West.

This is one of those basic movie plots that can generate a lot of entertainment if it's handled properly. *Firefox* knows the territory. It complicates things slightly by making Eastwood a Vietnam veteran who is sometimes overcome by the hallucination that he's still in combat. The movie calls it Post-Combat Stress Syndrome. But the CIA man who recruits him explains that the government isn't much worried, because you don't have the syndrome while you're *in* combat, you see, but only afterward. Somebody ought to compile a textbook of psychology as practiced in movies.

Anyway, Eastwood trains for the mission, is disguised with a mustache and horn-rim glasses, and survives some uncomfortable moments at Moscow customs before he makes it into Russia. Then he makes contact with a confederation of spies and double agents who lead him to a Jewish dissident who is such a brilliant scientist that he is still being allowed to work on Firefox. Why does the dissident *want* to work on it? Because he knows how Eastwood could steal the plane. All of these scenes include obligatory shots, which are kind of fun to anticipate, if you're a fan of the Alistair Maclean–James Bond–"Mission: Impossible"–*Guns of Navarone* genre. The one indispensable scene is probably the Introduction of the MacGuffin. A MacGuffin, you will remember, was what Alfred Hitchcock called that element of the plot that everybody thinks is important. In this case, it's the Firefox, a long, sleek, cruel-looking machine that looks like a cross between a guided missle and a DeLorean. Eastwood and the camera circle it lovingly; this is the sexiest shot in a movie without a romantic subplot. The movie's climax involves Eastwood's attempt to fly this plane north to the Arctic Circle, make a refueling rendezvous, and then take it on home. His flight is intercut with comic opera scenes involving members of the Russian high command, who argue and bicker while looming over an illuminated map that casts an eerie underlight on their faces, making them look like ghouls from old E.C. comics.

Does Eastwood make it out in one piece? Does he bring along the plane? I wouldn't dream of giving away the plot. But I will say that the movie's climax is a sensational high-altitude dogfight between two different Firefoxes, and that as Eastwood occupies the Firefox cockpit, surrounded by video screens and computer displays of flight patterns and missile trajectories, it looks as if Dirty Harry has died and gone to Atari heaven. The special effects are really pretty good in this movie. The planes looked surprisingly real to me, and the choreography of the dogfight was not only realistic but understandable. There's one sensational chase sequence that's an homage to *Star Wars.* Remember the *Star Wars* scene where the two ships chased each other between the towering walls of the city in space? Eastwood and his Russian pursuer rocket through a crevice between two ice cliffs, and it looks great even while we're realizing it's logically impossible. I guess that goes for the whole movie.

First Blood ★ ★ ★

R, 94 m., 1982

Sylvester Stallone (Rambo), Richard Crenna (Trautman), Brian Dennehy (Teasle), David Caruso (Mitch). Directed by Ted Kotchoff and produced by Buzz Feitshans. Screenplay by Michael Kozoll, William Sackheim, and Q. Moonblood.

Sylvester Stallone is one of the great physical actors in the movies, with a gift for throwing himself so fearlessly into an action scene that we can't understand why somebody doesn't *really* get hurt. When he explodes near the beginning of *First Blood,* hurling cops aside and breaking out of a jail with his fists and speed, it's such a convincing demonstration of physical strength and agility that we never question the scene's implausibility. In fact, although almost all of *First Blood* is implausible, because it's Stallone on the screen, we'll buy it.

What we can't buy in this movie is the message. It's handled in too heavy-handed a way. Stallone plays a returned Vietnam veteran, a Green Beret skilled in the art of jungle survival and fighting, and after a small-town police force sadistically mishandles him, he declares war on the cops. All of this is set up in scenes of great physical power and strength—and the central sections of the movie, with Stallone and the cops stalking each other through the forests of the Pacific Northwest, have a lot of authority. But then the movie comes down to a face-off between Stallone and his old Green Beret commander (Richard Crenna), and the screenplay gives Stallone a long, impassioned speech to deliver, a speech in which he cries out against the injustices done to him and against the hippies who demonstrated at the airport when he returned from the war, etc. This is all old, familiar material from a dozen other films—clichés recycled as formula. Bruce Dern did it in *Coming Home* and William Devane in *Rolling Thunder.* Stallone is made to say things that would have much better been implied; Robert De Niro, in *Taxi Driver,* also plays a violent character who was obviously scarred by Vietnam, but the movie wisely never makes him talk about what happened to him. Some things are scarier and more emotionally moving when they're left unsaid.

So the ending doesn't work in *First Blood.* It doesn't necessarily work as action, either. By the end of the film, Stallone has taken on a whole town and has become a one-man army, laying siege to the police station and the hardware store and exploding the pumps at the gas station. This sort of spectacular conclusion has become so commonplace in action movies that I kind of wonder, sometimes, what it would be like to see one end with a whimper rather than a bang.

Until the last twenty or thirty minutes, however, *First Blood* is a very good movie, well-paced, and well-acted not only by Stallone (who invests an unlikely character with great authority) but also by Crenna and Brian Dennehy, as the police chief. The best scenes come as Stallone's on the run in the forest, using a hunting knife with a compass in the handle, and living off the land. At one point he's trapped on a cliffside by a police helicopter, and we really feel for this character who has been hunted down through no real fault of his own. We feel more deeply for him then, in fact, than we do later when he puts his grievances into words. Stallone creates the character and sells the situation with his presence itself. The screenplay should have stopped while it was ahead.

Fitzcarraldo ★ ★ ★ ★

PG, 157 m., 1982

Klaus Kinski (Fitzcarraldo), Claudia Cardinale (Molly), Jose Lewgoy (Don Aquilino), Miguel Angel Fuentes (Cholo). Directed by Werner Herzog. Screenplay by Herzog.

Werner Herzog's *Fitzcarraldo* is a movie in the great tradition of grandiose cinematic visions. Like Coppola's *Apocalypse Now* or Kubrick's *2001,* it is a quest film in which the hero's quest is scarcely more mad than the filmmaker's. Movies like this exist on a plane apart from ordinary films. There is a sense in which *Fitzcarraldo* is not altogether successful—it is too long, we could say, or too meandering—but it is still a film that I would not have missed for the world. The movie is the story of a dreamer named Brian Sweeney Fitzgerald, whose name has been simplified to "Fitzcarraldo" by the Indians and Spanish who inhabit his godforsaken corner of South America. He loves opera. He spends his days making a little money from an ice factory and his nights dreaming up new schemes. One of them, a plan to build a railroad across the continent, has already failed. Now he is ready with another: He seriously intends to build an opera house in the rain jungle, twelve hundred miles upstream from the civilized coast, and to bring Enrico Caruso there to sing an opera.

If his plan is mad, his method for carrying it out is madness of another dimension. Looking at the map, he becomes obsessed with the fact that a nearby river system offers access to hundreds of thousands of square miles of potential trading customers—if only a modern steamship could be introduced into that system. There is a point, he notices, where the other river is separated only by a thin finger of land from a river that already is navigated by boats. His inspiration: Drag a steamship across land to the other river, float it, set up a thriving trade, and use the profits to build the opera house—and then bring in Caruso! This scheme is so unlikely that perhaps we should not be surprised that Herzog's story is based on the case of a real Irish entrepreneur who tried to do exactly that.

The historical Irishman was at least wise enough to disassemble his boat before carting it across land. In Herzog's movie, however, Fitzcarraldo determines to drag the boat up one hill and down the other side in one piece. He enlists engineers to devise a system of blocks-and-pulleys that will do the trick, and he hires the local Indians to work the levers with their own muscle power. And it is here that we arrive at the thing about *Fitzcarraldo* that transcends all understanding: Werner Herzog determined to literally drag a real steamship up a real hill, using real tackle and hiring the local Indians! To produce the movie, he decided to do personally what even the original Fitzgerald never attempted.

Herzog finally settled on the right actor to play Fitzcarraldo, author of this plan: Klaus Kinski, the shock-haired German who starred in Herzog's *Aguirre, the Wrath of God* and *Nosferatu,* is back again to mastermind the effort. Kinski is perfectly cast. Herzog's original choice for the role was Jason Robards, who is also gifted at conveying a consuming passion, but Kinski, wild-eyed and ferocious, consumes the screen. There are other characters important to the story, especially Claudia Cardinale as the madam who loves Fitzcarraldo and helps finance his attempt, but without Kinski at the core it's doubtful this story would work.

The story of Herzog's own production is itself well-known, and has been told in Les Blank's *Burden of Dreams,* a brilliant documentary about the filming. It's possible that every moment of *Fitzcarraldo* is colored by our knowledge that Herzog was "really" doing the things we see Fitzcarraldo do. (The movie uses no special effects, no models, no opticals, no miniatures.) Perhaps we're even tempted to give the movie extra points because of Herzog's ordeal in the jungle. But *Fitzcarraldo* is not all sweat and madness. It contains great poetic images of the sort Herzog is famous for: An old phonograph playing a Caruso record on the desk of a boat spinning out of control into a rapids; Fitzcarraldo frantically oaring a little rowboat down a jungle river to be in time to hear an opera; and of course the immensely impressive sight of that actual steamship, resting halfway up a hillside.

Fitzcarraldo is not a perfect movie, and it never comes together into a unified statement. It *is* meandering, and it is slow and formless at times. Perhaps the conception was just too large for Herzog to shape. The movie does not approach perfection as *Aguirre* did. But as a document of a quest and a dream, and as the record of man's audacity and foolish, visionary heroism, there has never been another movie like it.

Five Easy Pieces ★ ★ ★ ★

R, 98 m., 1970

Jack Nicholson (Robert Dupea), Karen Black (Rayette), Susan Anspach (Catherine), Billy Green Bush (Elton), Helena Kallianiotes (Hitchhiker), Ralph Waite (Carl Dupea), William Challee (Nicholas Dupea), John Ryan (Spicer). Directed by Bob Rafelson and produced by Richard Wechsler and Rafelson. Screenplay by Adrien Joyce.

The title of *Five Easy Pieces* refers not to the women its hero makes along the road, for there are only three, but to a book of piano exercises he owned as a child. The film, one of the best American films, is about the distance between that boy, practicing to become a concert pianist, and the need he feels twenty years later to disguise himself as an oil field rigger. When we sense the boy, tormented and insecure, trapped inside the adult man, *Five Easy Pieces* becomes a masterpiece of heartbreaking intensity.

At the outset, we meet only the man—played by Jack Nicholson with the same miraculous offhandedness that brought *Easy Rider* to life. He's an irresponsible roustabout, making his way through the oil fields, sleeping with a waitress (Karen Black) whose every daydreaming moment is filled with admiration for Miss Tammy Wynette. The man's name is Robert Eroica Dupea. He was named after Beethoven's Third Symphony and he spends his evenings bowling and his nights wearily agreeing that, yes, his girl sings "Stand By Your Man" just like Tammy.

In these first marvelous scenes, director Bob Rafelson calls our attention to the grimy life textures and the shabby hopes of these decent middle Americans. They live in a landscape of motels, highways, TV dinners, dust, and jealousy, and so do we all, but they seem to have nothing else. Dupea's friends are arrested at the mental and emotional level of about age seventeen; he isn't, but thinks or hopes he is.

Dupea discovers his girl is pregnant (his friend Elton breaks the news out in the field, suggesting maybe it would be good to marry her and settle down). He walks out on her in a rage, has a meaningless little affair with a slut from the bowling alley, and then discovers more or less by accident that his father is dying. His father, we discover, is a musical genius who moved his family to an island and tried to raise them as Socrates might have. Dupea feels himself to be the only failure.

The movie bares its heart in the scenes on

the island, where Dupea makes an awkward effort to communicate with his dying father. The island is peopled with eccentrics, mostly Dupea's own family, but including a few strays. Among their number is a beautiful young girl who's come to the island to study piano with Dupea's supercilious brother. Dupea seduces this girl, who apparently suggests the early life he has abandoned. He does it by playing the piano; but when she says she's moved, he says he isn't—that he played better as a child and that the piece was easy anyway.

This is possibly the moment when his nerve fails and he condemns himself, consciously, to a life of self-defined failure. The movie ends, after several more scenes, on a note of ambiguity; he is either freeing himself from the waitress or, on the other hand, he is setting off on a journey even deeper into anonymity. It's impossible to say, and it doesn't matter much. What matters is the character during the time covered by the film: a time when Dupea tentatively reapproaches his past and then rejects it, not out of pride, but out of fear.

The movie is joyously alive to the road life of its hero. We follow him through bars and bowling alleys, motels and mobile homes, and we find him rebelling against lower-middle-class values even as he embraces them. In one magical scene, he leaps from his car in a traffic jam and starts playing the piano on the truck in front of him; the scene sounds forced, described this way, but Rafelson and Nicholson never force anything, and never have to. Robert Eroica Dupea is one of the most unforgettable characters in American movies.

The Flamingo Kid ★ ★ ★ ½
PG-13, 100 m., 1984

Matt Dillon (Jeffrey Willis), Hector Elizondo (Arthur Willis), Molly McCarthy (Ruth Willis), Martha Gehman (Nikki Willis), Richard Crenna (Phil Brody), Jessica Walter (Phyllis Brody), Carole R. Davis (Joyce Brody). Directed by Garry Marshall and produced by Michael Phillips. Screenplay by Neal and Garry Marshall.

"When I was eighteen, my father was ignorant on a great many subjects," Mark Twain once said, "but by the time I was twenty-five, it was amazing the things the old man had learned." Here is a movie that condenses that process into one summer. The summer begins with a kid from a poor Brooklyn neighborhood taking a job as a cabana boy at a posh beach club out on Long Island. That's against the advice of his father, a plumber, who wants his son to get a job where he can learn about hard work. By the middle of the summer, the kid has started to idolize a flashy car dealer who's the champion of the gin rummy tables. By Labor Day, he has found out more about the car dealer than he wanted to know. And he has come to love and understand his father in a new way.

The Flamingo Kid stars Matt Dillon as the teen-ager, Hector Elizondo as his father, and Richard Crenna as the car dealer. There are other characters—in particular, a bikinied goddess who helps sell Matt on life at the beach—but these are the three characters who stand at the heart of the story. Elizondo is a hard-working man who still remembers how to dream, but knows that life has few openings for dreamers. In some of the movie's most poetic passages, he reveals a lifelong obsession with ships, and the ways of harbor pilots. Crenna, on the other hand, is a man who firmly believes "You are what you wear," and values his status as the club's gin rummy champion as if it really meant something.

Dillon is a revelation in this movie. Perhaps because of his name, Matt Dillon has risked being confused with your average teen-age idol, the kind the pimple magazines put on their covers. Yet he has been an extraordinarily sensitive actor ever since his first appearance, in the unsung 1977 movie about alienated teen-agers, *Over the Edge.* In two movies based on novels by S.E. Hinton, *Tex* and *Rumble Fish,* he had the kind of clarity, the uncluttered relationship with the camera, that you see in only a handful of actors: He was a natural. He is here, too. His role in *The Flamingo Kid* could easily have been turned into an anthology of twitches and psychic anguish as he wrestles with the meaning of life. But Dillon has the kind of acting intelligence that allows him to play each scene for no more than that particular scene is really about; he's not trying to summarize the message in every speech. That gives him an ease, an ability to play the teen-age hero as if every day were a whole summer long.

We fall into the rhythm of the beach club. Into the sunny days where all the members have lots of time to know and envy each other, and time is so plentiful that it can take hours for a nasty rumor to sweep through the cabanas. Dillon hurries from one member to another with drinks, towels, club sandwiches, messages. He feels acutely that he does not belong at this level of society—and when Richard Crenna takes notice of him, and even more when Crenna's daughter invites him home for dinner, Dillon feels that he's cutting loose from the boring life back in Brooklyn. But this will be a summer of learning, and by autumn he will have learned how wise and loving his own father is, and how easy it is to be deceived by surfaces. Along the way to that lesson, *The Flamingo Kid* has a lot of fun (I hope I haven't made this social comedy sound dreary), and at the end it has a surprisingly emotional impact.

Flashdance ★ ½

R, 96 m., 1983

Jennifer Beals (Alex), Michael Nouri (Nicky), Belinda Bauer (Katie Hurley), Lilia Skala (Hanna Long). Directed by Adrian Lyne and produced by Don Simpson and Jerry Bruckheimer. Screenplay by Tom Hedley and Joe Eszterhas.

I have a friend who has a simple test for a movie: Is this movie as interesting as the same things would be, happening in real life? A lot of movies aren't, and *Flashdance* sure isn't. If this movie had spent just a little more effort getting to know the heroine of its story, and a little less time trying to rip off *Saturday Night Fever,* it might have been a much better film.

My friend's simple test applies to this movie in another way: The movie is *not* as interesting as the real-life story of Jennifer Beals, the young actress who stars in it. Beals launched a career as a model (covers on *Town & Country* and *Vogue*) at the age of 15, after being discovered by Chicago photographer Victor Skrebneski. She enrolled in Yale, took some acting classes in New York, went to an audition, and won this role. The irony is that her story, simply and directly told, might have been a lot more interesting than the story of *Flashdance,* which is so loaded down with artificial screenplay contrivances and flashy production numbers that it's waterlogged. This is one of those movies that goes for a slice of life and ends up with three pies.

Jennifer Beals plays Alex, an eighteen-year-old who is a welder by day, *and* a go-go dancer by night, *and* dreams of being a ballet star, *and* falls in love with the Porsche-driving boss of the construction company. These are a lot of "character details" even if she *didn't* also have a saintly old woman as a mentor, a big slobbering dog as a friend, a bicycle she rides all over Pittsburgh, a loft the size of a sweatshop, a sister who ice skates, a grumpy old pop, *and* the ability to take off her bra without removing her sweatshirt. This poor kid is so busy performing the pieces of business supplied to her by the manic screenwriters that she never gets a chance to develop a character.

Meanwhile, the movie has a disconcerting way of getting sidetracked with big dance scenes. The heroine works in the most improbable working-class bar ever put on film, a joint named Mawby's that has a clientele out of Miller's Beer TV ads, stage lighting reminiscent of Vegas, go-go dancers who change their expensive costumes every night, *and* put on punk rock extravaganzas, *and* never take off all their clothes, *and* never get shouted at by the customers for not doing so.

Flashdance is like a movie that won a free ninety-minute shopping spree in the Hollywood supermarket. The director (Adrian Lyne, of the much better *Foxes*) and his collaborators race crazily down the aisles, grabbing a piece of *Saturday Night Fever,* a slice of *Urban Cowboy,* a quart of *Marty,* and a two-pound box of "Archie Bunker's Place." The result is great sound and flashdance, signifying nothing. But Jennifer Beals shouldn't feel bad. She is a natural talent, she is fresh and engaging here, and only needs to find an agent with a natural talent for turning down scripts.

Fletch ★ ★ ½

PG, 110 m., 1985

Chevy Chase (I.M. Fletcher), Joe Don Baker (Chief Karlin), Dana Wheeler-Nicholson (Gail Stanwyk), Richard Libertini (Walker), Tim Matheson (Alan Stanwyck), M. Emmet Walsh (Dr. Dolan). Directed by Michael Ritchie and produced by Alan Greisman and

Peter Douglas. Screenplay by Andrew Bergman.

Why did Chevy Chase want to play I.M. Fletcher, the laconic hero of Gregory McDonald's best sellers? Was it because Chase saw a way to bring Fletch to life? Or was it because Chase thought Fletch was very much like himself? The problem with *Fletch* is that the central performance is an anthology of Chevy Chase mannerisms in search of a character. Other elements in the movie are pretty good: the supporting characters, the ingenious plot, the unexpected locations. But whenever the movie threatens to work, there's Chevy Chase with his monotone, deadpan cynicism, distancing himself from the material.

Fletch is not the first movie that Chase has undercut with his mannerisms, but it is the best one—since *Foul Play*, anyway. His problem as an actor is that he perfected a personal style on "Saturday Night Live" all those many years ago, and has never been able to work outside of it. The basic Chevy Chase personality functions well at the length of a TV sketch, when there's no time to create a new character, but in a movie it grows deadening. *Fletch* is filled with a series of extraordinary situations, and Chase seems to react to all of them with the same wry dubiousness. His character this time is an investigative reporter for a Los Angeles newspaper. Deep into an investigation of drug traffic on the city's beaches, Fletch is approached by a young man (Tim Matheson) with a simple proposition: He wants to be killed. The story is that Matheson is dying of cancer and wants to die violently so his family can qualify for enlarged insurance benefits, but Fletch doesn't buy it. Something's fishy, and Fletch pretends to take the job, while conducting his own investigation.

The case leads him to an extraordinary series of interesting characters; the film's director, Michael Ritchie is good at sketching human originals, and we meet an aging farm couple in Utah, a manic editor, a no-nonsense police chief, a mysterious drug dealer, a slimy doctor, a beautiful wife, and a lot of mean dogs. Every one of the characters is played well, with the little details that Ritchie loves: The scene on a farmhouse porch in Utah is filled with such sly, quiet social satire that it could stand by itself. The movie's physical comedy is good, too. A scene where Fletch breaks into a realtor's office—scaling a fence and outsmarting vicious attack dogs—is constructed so carefully out of comedy and violence that it's a little masterpiece of editing.

The problem is, Chase's performance tends to reduce all the scenes to the same level, at least as far as he's concerned. He projects such an inflexible mask of cool detachment, of ironic running commentary, that we're prevented from identifying with him. If he thinks this is all just a little too silly for words, what are we to think? If we're more involved in the action than he is, does that make us chumps? *Fletch* needed an actor more interested in playing the character than in playing himself.

Fool for Love ★ ★ ★
R, 107 m., 1985

Sam Shepard (Eddie), Kim Basinger (May), Harry Dean Stanton (Old Man), Randy Quaid (Martin). Directed by Robert Altman and produced by Menahem Golan and Yoram Globus. Screenplay by Sam Shepard.

At the center of Sam Shepard's *Fool for Love* are two people whose hurts are so deep, whose angers are so real, that they can barely talk about what they really feel. That does not stop them from talking, on and on into the hurtful night, and eventually we can put together their stories, using what they have said, and especially what they have not said.

One of the characters is a blonde slattern named May, whose natural beauty has been rearranged into a parody of the classic movie baby doll—Brigitte Bardot, say. The other character is named Eddie, and he is a cowboy who drives through the empty Texas reaches in the obligatory pickup truck with the obligatory rifle rack behind his head and the obligatory horse trailer behind. One night May is working behind the counter of a restaurant in a crumbling motel, and she sees Eddie's pickup coming down the road. She runs and hides. Standing in the shadows of the rundown motel is an older man (Harry Dean Stanton) who simply waits and watches.

Shepard's method is direct. He allows his characters to talk around what they're really thinking, and occasionally the talk escalates into brief, incisive bursts of action—even violence. Eventually we learn that the older man is the father of both Eddie and May, that they had different mothers, that the old man commuted between two families, and that Eddie and May eventually met under circumstances that were later determined to be incestuous.

These developments would provide the ingredients for a basic story of redneck passion, and there are times when *Fool for Love* wants to strike those very notes. We feel we might be looking at the characters in a story by William Faulkner or Erskine Caldwell, and the visual compositions look inspired by the lurid covers of 1940s paperback novels. The deliberately trashy surface, however, conceals deeper levels of feeling, and by the end of *Fool for Love* we have witnessed some sort of classic tragedy, set there in the Texas backlands.

Robert Altman's movie version of Shepard's play stars Shepard himself, in a strong performance as Eddie. But he doesn't dominate the story as much as you might think. The central performance in the movie is really Kim Basinger's, as May. Although she has played sexpots before—has indeed specialized in them—nothing prepared me for the dimensions she was able to find in this one. What's astonishing is that *Fool for Love* is essentially a male drama, told from a male point of view, and yet Basinger is able to suggest so much with her performance that she steals the center of the stage right away from the man who wrote the lines and is playing opposite her.

Part of her impact is probably because the director is Altman. Few other major directors are more interested in women, and in his films like *Thieves Like Us*, *Three Women*, and *Come Back to the 5 & Dime, Jimmy Dean, Jimmy Dean*, he has shown women in settings very similar to this one: unfulfilled women, conscious of the waste of their lives, living in backwaters where their primary pastime is to await the decisions of men.

Altman does a brilliant job of visualizing this particular backwater. From the opening aerial shots of the godforsaken motel, he creates a tangibly real, dusty, forlorn world. Some of his shots are so beautiful it's hard to figure how he obtained them: That ominous dark sky lowering over the motel, for example, looks almost like a painting. Altman is also up to some of the same visual tricks he used in *Jimmy Dean*, including the use of windows and mirrors to give us two planes of action at the same time. And he has a wonderfully subtle way of showing us the Harry Dean Stanton character in both the past and the present.

This is Altman's fourth movie in a row based on a play. It comes after *Jimmy Dean*, *Streamers*, and the extraordinary *Secret Honor*, about Richard Nixon (he has filmed three other plays for cable television). After a career as one of the most free-swinging of all modern movie directors *(M*A*S*H, McCabe and Mrs. Miller, Nashville)* it is interesting to see him embracing the discipline of a play script. Having made movies that were all over the map, he now inhabits interiors—of rooms, and of people's minds. With *Fool for Love*, he has succeeded on two levels that seem opposed to each other. He has made a melodrama, almost a soap opera, in which the characters achieve a kind of nobility.

Footloose ★ 1/2

PG, 106 m., 1984

Kevin Bacon (Ren), Lori Singer (Ariel), John Lithgow (Reverend Moore). Directed by Herbert Ross and produced by Lewis J. Rachmil and Craig Zadan. Screenplay by Dean Pitchford.

Footloose is a seriously confused movie that tries to do three things, and does all of them badly. It wants to tell the story of a conflict in a town, it wants to introduce some flashy teen-age characters, and part of the time it wants to be a music video. It's possible that no movie with this many agendas *can* be good; maybe somebody should have decided, early on, exactly what the movie was supposed to be about. The film tells the story of a Chicago kid named Ren (Kevin Bacon), who has a fashionable haircut and likes to dance. He moves with his mother to a small town named Bomont, which is somewhere in the Midwest, although I seriously doubt a town like this exists anywhere outside of standard movie clichés. The old fuddies in Bomont have imposed a total ban on rock 'n' roll and dancing. The ban is led by an uptight preacher named Shaw Moore (John Lithgow), who is still grieving because he lost a child in a car wreck five years ago. To the Reverend Moore, dancing and rock lead to booze and drugs.

Ren falls in love with the preacher's daughter (Lori Singer). He also has the usual standard showdowns with the locals, including the high school bully. Ren decides what this town needs is a dance. His assignment, should he choose to accept it, is to (1) win the approval of the preacher and the town council to allow dancing, (2) beat up the bully, and (3) star in at least three segments of the movie that can be used as TV music videos. The basic conflict in this movie was not new when the *Beach Party* gang discovered it. Remember Annette and Frankie trying to persuade the old folks to let them hold a dance on the beach? If the movie had only relaxed and allowed itself to admit how silly the situation is, it could have been more fun. Instead, it gets bogged down in the peculiar personality of the preacher, who is played by Lithgow as a man of agonizing complexity.

Footloose makes one huge, inexplicable error with the Lithgow character. It sets him up as an unyielding reactionary, and then lets him change his mind 180 degrees without a word of explanation. In one scene, the preacher's daughter confronts her dad in church and announces she isn't a virgin (the movie never remembers to tell us whether she really is or not). The preacher turns livid, starts to scream, and then is interrupted by news that they're burning books down at the library. In the *very next scene*, the preacher is arguing against the book burners—and before long, without any meaningful transitional scenes, he has caved in to the idea of the dance. It's cheating to set up Lithgow as the enemy and then turn him into a friend without a word of explanation.

I mentioned the flashy teen-age characters. The one who gave me the most trouble was that preacher's daughter. She enjoys suicidal games of chicken, like balancing with her legs on the doors of a speeding car and a speeding truck while a speeding semi bears down on her. This trick is, of course, impossible to do in real life, and so it simultaneously makes her into an idiot and a stuntwoman. As for the music video scenes: On three different occasions, the movie switches gears and goes into prepackaged MTV-type production numbers, with the fancy photography and the flashy quick cuts. These scenes may play well on TV, but they break what little reality the story has, and expose *Footloose* as a collection of unrelated ingredients that someone thought would be exploitable.

For Keeps ★ ★ ★

PG-13, 98 m., 1988

Molly Ringwald (Darcy), Randall Batinkoff (Stan), Kenneth Mars (Mr. Bobrucz), Miriam Flynn (Mrs. Elliot), Conchata Ferrell (Mrs. Bobrucz), Sharon Brown (Lila), Jack Ong (Reverend Kim), Sean Frye (Wee Willy), Allison Roth (Ambrosia), Trevor Edmond (Ace). Directed by John G. Avildsen and produced by Jerry Belson and Walter Coblenz. Screenplay by Tim Kazurinsky and Denise DeClue.

The movies of Molly Ringwald have been responsible for a revolution in the way Hollywood regards teen-agers. Before Ringwald (and her mentor, John Hughes) there were horny teen-agers, dead teen-agers, teen-age vampires, and psychotic crack-ups. Now teen-age movies are gradually working their way through some of the aspects of the normal lives of American teen-agers, and in *For Keeps*, Ringwald plays a popular high school senior who gets pregnant and gets married.

Because she is Ringwald, and because this is a movie, her experience of these adventures is probably a good deal more pleasant than the average American teen-age girl could look forward to. There is a line in the movie that could apply to the movie itself, when a high school teacher asks the very pregnant Ringwald to drop out of school and take night classes, because she's so popular that other girls might want to imitate her and get pregnant themselves.

If the movie lacks something, it is a sense of the real pain, shame, and suffering that someone like this high school senior might undergo with a pregnancy. She seems too sound, too well-adjusted, too resilient. And yet there is a certain bottom line of honesty in this movie, and if it is about the joy of young love, it is also about the pressures of young responsibility (I hope impressionable teen-age viewers will devote careful attention to the scenes where Molly is stuck at home in her walk-up apartment while her young husband is out having a beer with his buddies).

In the film, Ringwald and her boyfriend, played by Randall Batinkoff, begin to sleep together and almost immediately have to face the pregnancy. In a plot that centers around national holidays, she blurts out the news at Thanksgiving, and they decide to get married at Christmas. Both of these decisions are met with varying degrees of horror by their parents—by Miriam Flynn, as Ringwald's divorced and bitter mother, and by Kenneth Mars and Conchata Ferrell, as Batinkoff's loving, conventional parents.

The movie is perhaps a bit too willing to play Batinkoff's parents for laughs, and I could have done without a scene of a toppling Christmas tree. But the moments between Ringwald and Batinkoff are well-written and played with a quiet, touching sensitivity; we recognize elements of real life in their relationship.

The movie was written by Tim Kazurinsky and Denise DeClue, whose last collaboration was the wonderful *About Last Night* . . . . That movie, based very loosely on a play by David Mamet, was about swinging singles in their twenties and thirties. This one, an original, has the same feel for plausible dialogue and the same knack for finding scenes that reveal personalities, instead of simply advancing the plot. Consider, for example, the sequence after the birth, when Ringwald suffers from post-partum depression; this is the sort of touching realism you wouldn't expect from a "teen-age movie," and yet it lends weight and importance to the sequences that follow.

I also liked the way in which her husband was shown as unready to accept the responsibilities of marriage and fatherhood, and then the way the movie subtly suggests that Ringwald isn't ready, either—but as the woman, she's the one who gets stuck at home with the kid. All of this is made more dramatic because of a subplot about the husband's full-ride college scholarship, Ringwald's own college potential, and the lack of campus facilities for married freshmen.

The ending of the movie is too contrived, as all of the threads come together—marriage, parenthood, scholarships, family acceptance, college plans. And yet *For Keeps* is an intriguing movie that succeeds in creating believable characters, keeping them alive, and steering them more or less safely past the clichés that are inevitable with this kind of material. It's a movie with heart, and that compensates for a lot of the predictability. The one thing it lacks, perhaps, is a notice at the end advising teen-agers that for every young couple like this one, there are a thousand broken hearts.

For Your Eyes Only ★ ★

PG, 127 m., 1981

Roger Moore (James Bond), Carole Bouquet (Melina), Topol (Columbo), Julian Glover (Kristatos), Cassandra Harris (Lisl), Janet Brown (Prime Minister). Directed by John Glen and produced by Albert R. Broccoli. Screenplay by Richard Malbaum and Michael Wilson.

For Your Eyes Only is a competent James Bond thriller, well-crafted, a respectable product from the 007 production line. But it's no more than that. It doesn't have the special sly humor of the Sean Connery Bonds, of course, but also doesn't have the visual splendor of such Roger Moore Bonds as *The Spy Who Loved Me*, or special effects to equal *Moonraker*. And in this era of jolting, inspired visual effects from George Lucas and Steven Spielberg, it's just not quite in the same league. That will no doubt come as a shock to Producer Albert (Cubby) Broccoli, who has made the James Bond series his life's work.

Broccoli and his late partner, Harry Saltzman, all but invented the genre that Hollywood calls "event films" or "special effects films." The ingredients, which Bond popularized and others imitated, always included supervillains, sensational stunts, sex, absurd plots to destroy or rule the world and, of course, a hero. The 007 epics held the patent on that formula in the late '60s and early '70s, but they are growing dated. *For Your Eyes Only* doesn't have any surprises. We've seen all the big scenes before, and when the villains turn out to be headquartered in an impregnable mountaintop fortress, we yawn. After *Where Eagles Dare* and *The Guns of Navarone* and the hollow Japanese volcano that Bond himself once infiltrated, let's face it: When you've seen one impregnable mountaintop fortress, you've seen 'em all.

The movie opens with James Bond trapped inside a remote-controlled helicopter being guided by a bald sadist in a wheelchair. After Bond triumphs, the incident is never referred to again. *This* movie involves the loss of the secret British code controlling submarine-based missiles. The Russians would like to have it. Bond's mission: Retrieve the control console from a ship sunk in the Aegean. The movie breaks down into a series of set-pieces. Bond and his latest Bondgirl (long-haired, undemonstrative Carole Bouquet) dive in a mini-sub, engage in a complicated chase through the back roads of Greece, crawl through the sunken wreck in wet suits, are nearly drowned and blown up, etc. For variety, Bond and Bouquet are dragged behind a powerboat as shark bait, and then Bond scales the fortress mountain. A fortress guard spots Bond dangling from a rope thousands of feet in the air. What does he do? Does he just cut the rope? No, sir, the guard descends part way to tantalize Bond by letting him drop a little at a time. The rest is predictable.

In a movie of respectable craftsmanship and moderate pleasures, there's one obvious disappointment. The relationship between Roger Moore and Carole Bouquet is never worked out in an interesting way. Since the days when he was played by Sean Connery, agent 007 has always had a dry, quiet, humorous way with women. Roger Moore has risen to the same challenge, notably opposite Barbara Bach in *The Spy Who Loved Me.* But Moore and Bouquet have no real chemistry in *For Your Eyes Only.* There's none of that kidding byplay. It's too routine. The whole movie is too routine.

48 HRS ★ ★ ★ ½

R, 100 m., 1982

Nick Nolte (Cates), Eddie Murphy (Reggie), James Remar (Ganz), Sonny Landham (Billy Bear), Annette O'Toole (Elaine). Directed by Walter Hill and produced by Lawrence Gordon and Joel Silver. Screenplay by Roger Spottiswoode, Hill, Larry Gross, and Steven E. de Souza.

Sometimes an actor becomes a star in just one scene. Jack Nicholson did it in *Easy Rider,* wearing the football helmet on the back of the motorcycle. It happened to Faye Dunaway when she looked sleepily out of a screen window at Warren Beatty in *Bonnie and Clyde.* And in *48 HRS,* it happens to Eddie Murphy. His unforgettable scene comes about halfway through *48 HRS.* He plays a convict who has done thirty months for theft and will do six more unless he helps out Nick Nolte, a hungover hot dog of a detective who's on the trail of some cop killers. Nolte has sprung Murphy from jail for forty-eight hours, with the promise of freedom if they get the killers. Murphy thinks there's a bartender who may have some information. The thing is, the bar is a redneck country joint, the kind where urban cowboys drink out of longneck bottles and salute the Confederate flag on the wall. Murphy has been jiving Nolte about how he can handle any situation. Nolte gives him a chance. And Murphy, impersonating a police officer, walks into that bar, takes command, totally intimidates everybody, and gets his information. It's a great scene—the mirror image of that scene in *The French Connection* where Gene Hackman, as Popeye Doyle, intimidated the black regulars in a Harlem bar.

Murphy has other good moments in this movie, and so does Nolte, who gives a wonderful performance as a cynical, irresponsible, and immature cop who's always telling lies to his girlfriend and sneaking a jolt of whiskey out of his personal flask. The two men start out suspicious of each other in this movie and work up to a warm dislike. But eventually, grudgingly, a kind of respect starts to grow.

The movie's story is nothing to write home about. It's pretty routine. What makes the movie special is how it's made. Nolte and Murphy are good, and their dialogue is good, too—quirky and funny. Character actor James Remar makes a really slimy killer, genuinely evil. Annette O'Toole gets third billing as Nolte's lover, but it's another one of those thankless women's roles. Not only could O'Toole have phoned it in—she does, spending most of her scenes on the telephone calling Nolte a no-good bum. The direction is by Walter Hill, who has never been any good at scenes involving women and doesn't improve this time. What he is good at is action, male camaraderie and atmosphere. His movies almost always feature at least one beautifully choreographed, unbelievably violent fight scene (remember Charles Bronson's bare-knuckle fight in *Hard Times?*), and the fight scene this time is exhausting.

Where Hill grows in this movie is in his ability to create characters. In a lot of his earlier movies *(The Warriors, The Driver, Long Riders, Southern Comfort)* he preferred men who were symbols, who represented things and so didn't have to be human. In *48 HRS,*

Nolte and Murphy are human, vulnerable, and touching. Also mean, violent, and chauvinistic. It's that kind of movie.

Four Friends ★ ★ ★ ★
R, 114 m., 1981

Craig Wasson (Danilo Prozor), Jodi Thelen (Georgia Miles), Jim Metzler (Tom Donaldson), Michael Huddleston (David Levine), Reed Birney (Louie Carnahan), Julie Murray (Adrienne Carnahan), Miklos Simon (Mr. Prozor). Directed by Arthur Penn and produced by Penn and Gene Lasko. Screenplay by Steven Tesich.

Somewhere in the middle of *My Dinner with André,* Andre Gregory wonders aloud if it's not possible that the 1960s were the last decade when we were all truly alive—that since then we've sunk into a bemused state of self-hypnosis, placated by consumer goods and given the illusion of excitement by television. Walking out of *Four Friends,* I had some of the same thoughts. This movie brings the almost unbelievable contradictions of that decade into sharp relief, not as nostalgia or as a re-creation of times past, but as a reliving of all of the agony and freedom of the weirdest ten years any of us is likely to witness.

The movie is told in the form of a loose-knit autobiography, somewhat inspired by the experiences of Steve Tesich, the son of Yugoslavian parents who moved to this country as a boy and lived in the neighborhoods of East Chicago, Indiana, that provide the film's locations. If the film is his emotional autobiography, it is also perhaps the intellectual autobiography of Arthur Penn, the film's director, whose *Bonnie and Clyde* was the best American film of the 1960s and whose *Alice's Restaurant* (1970) was an earlier examination of that wonderful and haunted time.

Their movie tells the stories of four friends. When we meet them, they're entering their senior year of high school. It is 1961. That is so long ago that nobody has yet heard of the Beatles. One of the friends is a young woman (Jodi Thelen), who imagines she is the reincarnation of Isadora Duncan, and who strikes attitudes and poses in an attempt to appear altogether too much of an artistic genius for East Chicago to contain. The other three friends are male classmates. They all love the girl in one way or another, or perhaps it's just that they've never seen anyone like her before. In the ten years to follow, these four people will have lives that were not imaginable in 1961. They will have the opportunity to break out of the sedate conservatism of the Eisenhower era and into the decade of "alternative life-styles."

The movie is ambitious. It wants to take us on a tour of some of the things that happened in the 1960s, and some of the ways four midwestern kids might have responded to them. It also wants to be a meditation on love, and on how love changes during the course of a decade. When Thelen turns up at the bedroom window of her "real" true love (Craig Wasson) early in the movie and cheerfully offers to sleep with him, Wasson refuses, not only because he's a high school kid who's a little afraid of her—but also because he's too much in love with his idea of her to want to make it real. By the time they finally do come back together, years later, they've both been through bad scenes, through madness, drug abuse, and the trauma of the war in Vietnam. They have also grown up, some. The wonder is not that *Four Friends* covers so much ground, but that it makes many of its scenes so memorable that we learn more even about the supporting characters than we expect to.

There are individual scenes in this movie that are just right. One of them involves a crowd of kids walking home in the dusk after school. Another happens between Wasson and Miklos Simon, who plays his gruff, defensive Yugoslavian father, and who finally, painfully, breaks down and smiles after a poker-faced lifetime. A relationship between Wasson and a dying college classmate (Reed Birney) is well drawn, to remind us of undergraduate friendships based on idealism and mutual discovery. And the scene where Wasson and Thelen see each other after many years is handled tenderly and with just the right notes of irony.

Four Friends is a very good movie. Like *Breaking Away,* the story of growing up in Bloomington, Indiana (for which Tesich also wrote the original screenplay), this is a movie that remembers times past with such clarity that there are times it seems to be making it all up. Did we really say those things? Make those assumptions? Live on the edge of what seemed to be a society gone both free and mad at once? Some critics have said the people and events in this movie are not plausible. I don't know if they're denying the movie's truth, or arguing that from a 1980s point of view the '60s were just a bad dream. Or a good one.

The Fourth Protocol ★ ★ ★ 1/2
R, 119 m., 1987

Michael Caine (John Preston), Pierce Brosnan (Petrofsky), Ned Beatty (Borisov), Joanna Cassidy (Vassilieva), Julian Glover (Brian Harcourt-Smith), Michael Gough (Sir Bernard Hemmings), Ray McAnally (General Karpov), Ian Richardson (Sir Nigel Irvine). Directed by John Mackenzie and produced by Timothy Burrill. Screenplay by Frederick Forsyth.

August 1987. I am writing this review in the Scottish Highlands, where the peace is broken only by the occasional low-level flyby of a jet fighter plane. I was walking yesterday along the banks of Loch Tummell, and I came to a lively waterfall that was tumbling through the woods. The birds were singing and the sun was doing its best to penetrate the mist, and then the sky was shattered by the arrogant roar of a warplane, swooping low over the hills, then gone in an instant.

The flights are part of a joint defense exercise by the United States and Royal Air Forces, and they fly on nearly every clear day. Folks up here don't like them much. It's like being subjected to a daily version of one of those moronic displays where the Blue Angels demonstrate how much noise they can make.

The low-level training missions are no doubt important for security, but they have contributed to a good deal of grumbling among the citizens who live in their path. That grumbling, in a way, is what *The Fourth Protocol* is about. There are a lot of U.S. military bases on British soil, including the famous one at Greenham Common where anti-nuclear protesters have been camping out for years. If there were a nuclear accident at one of those bases, it would seriously undermine our welcome over here.

The Fourth Protocol involves a Soviet plan to smuggle the elements for a nuclear device into Britain, assemble it, and detonate it right next to a U.S. base. The explosion would be so huge that its precise location would be obliterated, and it would look exactly like an American accident. Result: pressure for the Yankees to go home and a strategic victory for the Russians.

The key Russian operative is played by Pierce Brosnan, in what certainly is the best performance he has ever given, as a dark, brooding man with an outwardly cheerful disposition and a perfect British accent. The only person who seems capable of anticipating his plan, and stopping it, is Michael Caine as a British intelligence officer who is in political trouble with his bosses because he's too independent.

This is essentially the same character Caine played in the second movie role of his career, *The Ipcress File* (1965). This time, though, he's older, less cocksure, and more wily in getting his way. After his superiors take him off the case, he simply works on it in a different way. Eventually he puts the pieces together and realizes what the Soviets are up to, and then the movie becomes a race against time.

The Fourth Protocol is based on a novel by Frederick Forsyth, whose *Day of the Jackal* also made a terrific thriller. The stories have similar structures: The villain is as strongly drawn as the heroes, and there is a sympathetic woman character who loves the villain—unwisely, as it turns out. The woman in *The Fourth Protocol* is a Russian intelligence agent played by Joanna Cassidy, who does not work often enough in the movies but always is a strong, sure center for every scene. (Remember her in *Under Fire,* as the foreign correspondent caught between Nick Nolte and Gene Hackman?) This time she arrives with the key element Brosnan needs for his bomb, and if his treatment of her is unkind, consider what will happen to everyone within a forty-mile radius.

The Fourth Protocol is first-rate because it not only is a thriller, but it also pays attention to its characters and shows how their actions grow out of their personalities. Like Michael Caine's other 1987 British spy film, *The Whistle Blower,* it is effective not simply because it's a thriller but also because for long stretches it simply is a very absorbing drama.

The Fox and the Hound ★ ★ ★
G, 83 m., 1981

With the voices of Pearl Bailey (Big Mama), Kurt Russell (Copper), Mickey Rooney (Tod), Sandy Duncan (Vixey), Pat Buttram (Chief),

Jack Albertson (Slade). Directed by Art Stevens, Ted Berman, and Richard Rich and produced by Wolfgang Reitherman and Stevens. Screenplay by Larry Clemmons and others.

In all the old familiar ways, *The Fox and the Hound* looks like a traditional production from Walt Disney animators. In has cute little animals and wise old owls. It has a villain in the shape of a mountainous grizzly bear, and comic relief in a long-standing feud between a woodpecker and a caterpillar. And it has songs that contain such uncontroversial wishes as, "If only the world wouldn't get in the way . . . If only the world would let us play." And yet, for all of its familiar qualities, this movie marks something of a departure for the Disney studio, and its movement is in an interesting direction. *The Fox and the Hound* is one of those relatively rare Disney animated features that contains a useful lesson for its younger audiences. It's not just cute animals and frightening adventures and a happy ending; it's also a rather thoughtful meditation on how society determines our behavior.

The movie is a fable about a small puppy named Tod and an orphaned fox named Copper. At the outset we sense something unusual—after the camera traces a gloomy path through the shadows of the forest, a mother fox and her baby come running terrified out of the woods, chased by hunters and hounds. Will the mother and child escape? They almost do. But then the mother hides her baby and sacrifices her life to draw attention away from him. This is the cruel world, without any magical cartoon escapes.

The little fox is taken under the wing, so to speak, by wise old Big Mama Owl, who arranges for the baby to be adopted by a kindly farm woman. It's at this point that the puppy comes into the plot. Puppy and fox become great friends in their childhoods and pledge to be loyal to each other forevermore. But then the quickly growing hound is taken away to be trained as a hunter, and the next time the two friends meet, the hound is savagely trying to chase down the fox. After they are almost killed by the bear, there is a reconciliation of sorts. They realize (and perhaps the kids in the audience will realize, too) how quickly our better impulses can be drowned out by the noise of society. The message is not heavy-handed, nor does it need to be, because the lessons in the movie are so firmly illustrated by the lives of the animals.

Although *The Fox and the Hound* is the first Disney animated feature to have been made mostly by a newer generation of artists at the studio, the film's look still is in the tradition of *The Rescuers* (1977) and other Disney work in the 1970s. That means we don't get the painstaking, frame-by-frame animation of individual leaves and flowers and birds that made *Snow White* magical back when animator man-hours were cheaper. But we do get a lot of life and energy on the screen.

The star of the movie's sound track is Pearl Bailey as Big Mama Owl. She sings three songs, dispenses advice with a free hand, and struts around in the forest as a sort of feathered Ann Landers. The animators have done a wonderful job of giving their cartoon owl some of Pearlie Mae's personality traits, but the two leading characters (with Mickey Rooney as the fox and Kurt Russell as the hound) are more straightforward.

The bottom line, I suppose, is: Will kids like this movie? And the answer is, sure, I think so. It's a fast-moving, colorful story, and as I watched the animated images on the screen, I was suddenly reminded of a curious belief I held when I was a kid. I believed that cartoons looked more real than "live" features, because everything on the screen had sharper edges. I outgrew my notion, but I'm not sure that represents progress.

Foxes ★ ★ ★

R, 106 m., 1980

Jodie Foster (Jeanie), Scott Baio (Brad), Sally Kellerman (Mary), Randy Quaid (Jay), Lois Smith (Mrs. Axman), Adam Faith (Bryan), Cherie Currie (Annie), Marilyn Kagan (Madge), Kandice Stroh (Dierdre). Directed by Adrian Lyne and produced by David Puttnam and Gerald Ayres. Screenplay by Ayres.

God help us if many American teen-agers are like the ones in this movie—but God love *them*, for that matter, for surviving in the teen-age subculture of Los Angeles. *Foxes* is a movie about four teen-age girls who live in the San Fernando Valley, who come from broken or unhappy homes, who are surrounded by a teen-age subculture of sex, dope, booze, and rock and roll . . . and who aren't bad kids, not really.

They run in a pack, sleeping over at each other's homes, going to school together, hanging out together, forming a substitute family because home doesn't provide a traditional one. They form the fierce loyalties that all teen-agers depend upon—loyalties of friendship that run deeper than the instant romances and sudden crushes that are a dime a dozen. They live in a world where sixteen-year-old kids are somehow expected to live in adult society, make decisions about adult vices, and yet not be adult. That's what's scariest about *Foxes:* Our knowledge that alcohol, pot, and pills *are* available to teen-agers unwise enough to go looking for them, and that they can provide emotional overloads far beyond the ability of the kids to cope.

One of the kids in the movie does cope fairly well, though. She's Jeanie, played by Jodie Foster as a sort of teen-age mother hen, a young girl who's got problems of her own but is intelligent, balanced, and enough of a survivor to clearly see the mistakes the others are making. That doesn't mean she rejects her friends. She runs with the pack and she takes her chances, but she's not clearly doomed. And some of the others are.

The movie follows its four foxes through several days and several adventures. It's a loosely structured film, deliberately episodic to suggest the shapeless form of these teen-agers' typical days and nights. Things happen on impulse. Stuff comes up. Kids stay out all night, or run away, or get drunk, or get involved in what's supposed to be a civilized dinner party until it's crashed by a mob of greasers.

The subject of the movie is the way these events are seen so very differently by the kids and their parents. And at the heart of the movie is one particular, wonderful, and complicated parent-child relationship, between Jodie Foster and Sally Kellerman. They only have a few extended scenes together, but the material is written and acted with such sensitivity that we really understand the relationship. And we understand Kellerman, as an attractive woman in her thirties, divorced from a rock promoter, who is trying to raise a sixteen-year-old, attend college, and still have a love life of her own. Kellerman has a line that evokes whole lives, when she talks about "all those desperately lonely, divorced UCLA undergraduates."

The parallels here are obvious. The Kellerman character, we suspect, got swept up in the rock and drug subculture, got married too young, got pregnant immediately, and now, the mother of a sixteen-year-old, is *still* in the process of growing up herself. She doesn't want her kid to go through what she went through. But kids grow up so fast these days that, oddly enough, these two women are almost in the same boat.

Foxes is an ambitious movie, not an exploitation picture. It's a lot more serious, for example, than the hit *Little Darlings*. It contains the sounds and rhythms of real teen-age lives; it was written and directed after a lot of research, and is acted by kids who are to one degree or another playing themselves. The movie's a rare attempt to provide a portrait of the way teen-agers really do live today in some suburban cultures.

Frances ★ ★ ★ ½

R, 139 m., 1983

Jessica Lange (Frances Farmer), Sam Shepard (Harry York), Bart Burns (Farmer). Directed by Graeme Clifford and produced by Jonathan Sanger. Screenplay by Eric Bergren, Christopher Devore, and Nicholas Kazan.

Graeme Clifford's *Frances* tells the story of a small-town girl who tasted the glory of Hollywood and the exhilaration of Broadway and then went on to lead a life during which everything went wrong. It is a tragedy without a villain, a sad story with no moral except that there, but for the grace of God, go we. The movie is about Frances Farmer, a beautiful and talented movie star from the 1930s and 1940s who had a streak of independence and a compulsion toward self-destruction, and who went about as high and about as low as it is possible to go in one lifetime. She came out of Seattle as a high school essay-contest winner and budding intellectual. She was talented and pretty enough to make her way fairly easily into show business, where she immediately gravitated to the left-wing precincts of the Group Theater and such landmark productions as Clifford Odets's *Waiting for Lefty.* She also became a movie star, and there was a time when her star shone so brightly that it seemed it would last forever.

It did not. She was a stubborn, opinionated star who fought with the studio system, defied the bosses, drank too much, took too many pills, and got into too much trouble. Her strong-willed mother stepped in to help her, and that's when Frances's troubles really began. The mother orchestrated a series of hospitalizations in bizarre mental institutions, where Frances Farmer was brutally mistreated and finally, horrifyingly, lobotomized. She ended her days as a vague, pleasant middle-age woman who did a talk show in Indianapolis and finally died of alcoholism.

Jessica Lange plays Frances Farmer in a performance that is so driven, that contains so many different facets of a complex personality, that we feel she has an intuitive understanding of this tragic woman. She is just as good when she portrays Farmer as an uncertain, appealing teen-ager from the Northwest as she is when she plays her much later, snarling at a hairdresser and screaming at her mother. All of those contradictions were inside Farmer, and if she had learned to hide or deal with some of them she might have lived a happier life.

The story of Frances Farmer makes a fascinating movie, if only because it's such a contrast to standard show-business biographies. They usually come in two speeds: rags to riches, or rags to riches to victim. *Frances* never really lays blame for the tragedy of Farmer's life. It presents a number of causes for Farmer's destruction. (A short list might include her combative personality, her shrewish mother, the studio system, betrayal by her lovers, alcoholism, drug abuse, psychiatric malpractice, and the predations of a mad lobotomist.) But the movie never comes right out and says what it believes "caused" Farmer's tragedy. That is good, I think, because no simple explanation will do for Farmer's life. The movie is told from her point of view, and from where she stood, she was surrounded. On one day she had one enemy, and on another day, another enemy. Always, of course, her worst enemy was herself. The movie doesn't let us off the hook by giving us someone to blame. Instead, it insists on being a bleak tragedy, and it argues that sometimes it is quite possible for everything to go wrong. Since most movies are at least optimistic enough to provide a *cause* for human tragedy, this one is sort of daring.

It is also well made by Clifford, whose credits as a film editor include such virtuoso work as *McCabe and Mrs. Miller* and *Don't Look Now.* In his debut as a director Clifford has made a period picture that wears its period so easily that we're not distracted by it, a movie that is bleak without being unwatchable.

There are a few problems with his structure, most of them centering around an incompletely explained friend of Farmer's, played by Sam Shepard as a guy who seems to drift into her life whenever the plot requires him. Kim Stanley plays Farmer's mother on a rather thankless note of shrillness, and the lobotomist in the picture seems to have wandered over from a nearby horror film. (He apparently gave the same impression in real life.) But Lange provides a strong emotional center for the film, and when it is over we're left with the feeling that Farmer never really got a chance to be who she should have been, or to do what she should have done. She had every gift she needed in life except for luck, useful friends, and an instinct for survival. She could have been one of the greatest movie stars of her time. As it is, when I was asked to name a few of Frances Farmer's best films, I had to admit that, offhand, I couldn't think of one.

Frantic ★ ★ ★

R, 115 m., 1988

Harrison Ford (Richard Walker), Emmanuelle Seigner (Michelle), Betty Buckley (Sondra Walker), John Mahoney (Embassy Official), Jimmie Ray Weeks (Embassy Security). Directed by Roman Polanski and produced by Thom Mount and Tim Hampton. Screenplay by Polanski and Gerard Brach.

The first thing I noticed were the tones of the voices, low, flat, and weary. Just like people should sound after the twelve-hour flight from San Francisco to Paris. They are happy to be in Paris, but would be happier to be in bed. This was where they spent their honeymoon, twenty years ago, and now Dr. Richard Walker and his wife, Sondra, have returned for a medical convention.

There is some confusion with the luggage; apparently she picked up the wrong bag at the airport. But everything else seems to be going perfectly when Walker steps into his hotel shower. The phone rings, his wife answers it and says something, but he can't hear her when the water is running. By the time he steps out of the shower, she has disappeared.

That's the set-up for *Frantic*, Roman Polanski's thriller and a professional comeback for the director of *Rosemary's Baby* and *Chinatown*, who was recently reduced to serving as gun-for-hire on the dreary *Pirates*. Every scene of this film feels like a project from Polanski's heart—a film to prove he is still capable of generating the kind of suspense he became famous for. And every scene, on its own, seems to work. It is only the total of the scenes that is wrong; the movie goes on too long, adds too many elaborations, tacks on too many complications, until the lean and economical construction of the first hour begins to drift into self-parody.

The movie stars Harrison Ford as the visiting American doctor, who is unable to convince the hotel, police, and American Embassy officials that his wife (Betty Buckley) is truly missing. He tries to track her down on his own, with only a few clues. After finding a drunk who saw his wife being forced into a car, he opens the "wrong" suitcase she picked up at the airport and finds a phone number that may be a lead.

The movie then develops into a cat-and-mouse game played out in Paris nightclubs, airports, and parking garages. Along the way, Ford teams up with the young woman (Emmanuelle Seigner) who brought the suitcase into the country. She's a mercenary courier, who was hired to carry the suitcase, doesn't know what was in it, but wants the 10,000 francs she was promised.

I will not reveal any additional plot details. I will say, however, that the nature of the mystery becomes clear to the audience some time before it becomes clear to Ford, and that the movie begins to lose its tightly wound tension about the time the Seigner character enters the plot. Until then, it develops with chilling logic, one step at a time. After the doctor and the girl become partners, it falls into more conventional patterns. And the series of endings—one false climax after another—is too contrived to be exciting.

Still, to watch the opening sequences of *Frantic* is to be reminded of Polanski's talent. Here is one of the few modern masters of the thriller and the *film noir*, whose career in exile has drifted aimlessly. *Frantic* would have benefited from the coldhearted cutting of some scenes and the trimming of others (such as a dance sequence in a nightclub that continues until it is inexplicable). But perhaps Polanski was so happy to be back where he belonged, making a big-budget thriller with a big star, that he lost his objectivity. It's understandable. And even with its excesses, *Frantic* is a reminder of how absorbing a good thriller can be.

Fraternity Vacation ★
R, 95 m., 1985

Stephen Geofferys (Wendell Tvedt), Sherre J. Wilson (Ashley Taylor), Cameron Dye (Joe Gillespie), Leigh McCloskey (Chas). Directed by James Frawley and produced by Robert C. Peters. Screenplay by Lindsay Harrison.

No women are hacked to pieces in *Fraternity Vacation*, but they are the victims of violence all the same—the kind of violence that denies them the opportunity to be as interesting, as aggressive, and as free to choose as all the guys in this brain-damaged film. Their basic role here is to be the prizes in a male sexual competition. Since the guys in this movie are shallow, narcissistic, self-obsessed dummies, to be the prize is to lose the game, but in a movie like this, those are the rules.

The film takes place in Palm Springs, during spring break, when a bunch of fraternity boys from Iowa descend on the town. Why Palm Springs and not Fort Lauderdale? Because Palm Springs is closer to Hollywood, and therefore a cheaper place to make a movie, that's why. So the movie glosses over the fact that Palm Springs is the most boring town in America for anyone who does not play golf and/or know Bob Hope or Betty Ford. In the movie, the college students cruise up and down the main drag in their convertibles, checking out the action, and we meet the main players. On one side there are three fraternity brothers—two jocks and a nerd. On the other side, two jocks from a rival fraternity. Everybody is out to get laid, of course, and that leads to the movie's painfully offensive opening sex scene.

You've got to see this episode to believe

what pathological attitudes the movie has about women. Let me set the scene. The guys from the rival fraternity—let's call them the bad guys—have brought along a couple of girlfriends, and convince them to stage a practical joke to make the good guys think they're going to get lucky. So the women go up to the good guys' room, make out for a while, completely strip, and then play the "joke" by pretending they have herpes. What a ton of fun. Consider: What's essentially happening, in this jocular, happy-go-lucky scene, is that the girlfriends are asked to behave like hookers, and they agree. You think that's bad? Get this: After that scene, the two women *are never seen again in this movie!* They are simply dropped as characters—and as girlfriends, too, I guess. How would you feel if you were an actress auditioning for a part, and the good news was you were the girlfriend of the star, and the bad news was that after you stripped and made a herpes joke, you disappeared from the movie?

Meanwhile, the arena of sexual competition changes. There's a beautiful, mysterious blonde (Sherre J. Wilson) at poolside, and all the guys lust after her. So, they make a $1,000 bet about who will be the first to get her in the sack. The rest of the movie consists of the idiotic things all five guys do to impress the blonde. At the end of the film, of course, it's not the jocks but the nerd who wins out. Who said this movie doesn't have a conscience?

Don't get me wrong. I have nothing against dumb sex comedies. All I object to is the fact that *Fraternity Vacation* is playing with half a deck—the male half. The men are the characters and the women are the objects. That's probably because the movie was made by men who lacked the imagination to get outside their own fat heads and imagine what it might be like to be a woman—not a woman in real life, mind you, but even a woman in their trashy little movie. Think how much more interesting it could have been if the women, as well as the men, were allowed to lust, to scheme, to make bets, to have competitions, and to do all sorts of fun things, instead of just tanning themselves by the side of the pool. Of course, that would be another movie. Maybe even another universe.

The French Lieutenant's Woman

★ ★ ★ ½

R, 124 m., 1981

Meryl Streep (Sarah and Anna), Jeremy Irons (Charles and Mike), Hilton McRae (Sam), Emily Morgan (Mary), Charlotte Mitchell (Mrs. Tranter), Lynsey Baxter (Ernestina). Directed by Karol Reisz and produced by Leon Clore. Screenplay by Harold Pinter.

Reading the last one hundred pages of John Fowles's *The French Lieutenant's Woman* is like being caught in a fictional labyrinth. We think we know where we stand in the story, and who the characters are and what possibilities are open to them, and then Fowles begins an astonishing series of surprises. He turns his story inside out, suggesting first one ending, then another, always in a way that forces us to rethink everything that has gone before. That complex structure was long thought to make Fowles's novel unfilmable. How could his fictional surprises, depending on the relationship between reader and omniscient narrator, be translated into the more literal nature of film? One of the directors who tried to lick *The French Lieutenant's Woman* was John Frankenheimer, who complained: "There is no way you can film the book. You can tell the same story in a movie, of course, but not in the same way. And how Fowles tells his story is what makes the book so good." That seemed to be the final verdict, until the British playwright Harold Pinter tackled the project.

Pinter's previous screenplays, such as *The Accident* and *The Go-Between*, are known for a mastery of ambiguity, for a willingness to approach the audience on more than one level of reality, and what he and director Karel Reisz have done with their film, *The French Lieutenant's Woman*, is both simple and brilliant. They have frankly discarded the multi-layered fictional devices of John Fowles, and tried to create a new cinematic approach that will achieve the same ambiguity. Fowles made us stand at a distance from his two doomed lovers, Sarah and Charles. He told their story, of a passion that was forbidden by the full weight of Victorian convention, and then he invited us to stand back and view that passion in terms of facts and statistics about . . . well, Victorian passions in general. Pinter and Reisz create a similar distance in their movie by telling us two parallel stories. In one of them, Sarah Woodruff (Meryl Streep) still keeps her forlorn vigil for the French lieutenant who loved and abandoned her, and she still plays her intriguing cat-and-mouse game with the obsessed young man (Jeremy Irons) who must possess her.

In the other story, set in the present, two actors named Anna and Mike are playing Sarah and Charles. And Anna and Mike are also having a forbidden affair, albeit a more conventional one. For the length of the movie's shooting schedule, they are lovers offscreen as well as on. But eventually Mike will return to his family and Anna to her lover.

This is a device that works, I think. Frankenheimer was right in arguing that just *telling* the Victorian love story would leave you with . . . just a Victorian love story. The modern framing story places the Victorian lovers in ironic relief. Everything they say and do has another level of meaning, because we know the "real" relationship between the actors themselves. Reisz opens his film with a shot that boldly states his approach: We see Streep in costume for her role as Sarah, attended by a movie makeup woman. A clapboard marks the scene, and *then* Streep walks into the movie's re-creation of the British coastal village of Lyme Regis.

"It's only a movie," this shot informs us. But, of course, it's *all* only a movie, including the story about the modern actors. And this confusion of fact and fiction interlocks perfectly with the psychological games played in the Victorian story by Sarah Woodruff herself.

The French lieutenant's woman is one of the most intriguing characters in recent fiction. She is not only apparently the victim of Victorian sexism, but also (as Charles discovers) its manipulator and master. She cleverly uses the conventions that would limit her, as a means of obtaining personal freedom and power over men. At least that is one way to look at what she does. Readers of the novel will know there are others.

The French Lieutenant's Woman is a beautiful film to look at, and remarkably well-acted. Streep was showered with praise for her remarkable double performance, and she deserved it. She is offhandedly contemporary one moment, and then gloriously, theatrically Victorian the next. Opposite her, Jeremy Irons is authoritative and convincingly bedeviled as the man who is frustrated by both of Streep's characters. The movie's a challenge to our intelligence, takes delight in playing with our expectations, and has one other considerable achievement as well: It entertains admirers of Fowles's novel, but does not reveal the book's secrets. If you see the movie, the book will still surprise you, and that's as it should be.

Frenzy ★ ★ ★ ★
R, 116 m., 1972

Jon Finch (Richard Blaney), Barry Foster (Rusk), Barbara Leigh-Hunt (Brenda Blaney), Anna Massey (Babs Mulligan), Alec McGowen (Chief Inspector Oxford), Vivien Merchant (Mrs. Oxford). Directed by Alfred Hitchcock. Associate producer William Hill. Screenplay by Anthony Schaffer.

Alfred Hitchcock's *Frenzy* is a return to old forms by the master of suspense, whose newer forms have pleased movie critics but not his public. This is the kind of thriller Hitchcock was making in the 1940s, filled with macabre details, incongruous humor, and the desperation of a man convicted of a crime he didn't commit.

The only 1970s details are the violence and the nudity (both approached with a certain grisly abandon that has us imagining *Psycho* without the shower curtain). It's almost as if Hitchcock, at seventy-three, was consciously attempting to do once again what he did better than anyone else. His films since *Psycho* struck out into unfamiliar territory and even got him involved in the Cold War *(Torn Curtain)* and the fringes of fantasy *(The Birds).* Here he's back at his old stand.

Frenzy, which allegedly has a loose connection with a real criminal case, involves us in the exploits of a murderer known as The Necktie Killer (Barry Foster). And involvement is the sensation we feel, I think, since we know his identity from the beginning and sometimes cannot help identifying with him. There is a scene, for example, in which he inadvertently gets himself trapped in the back of a potato truck with a sack containing the body of his latest victim. We know he is a slimy bastard, but somehow we're sweating along with him as he crawls through the potatoes trying to regain a bit of incriminating evidence. He is the killer but, as is frequently the case with Hitchcock, another man seems much more guilty. This is Richard Blaney (Jon Finch), an ex-RAF hero who is down on his luck and has just lost his job. Through a series of unhappy coincidences which I'd better not give away, he's caught red-handed with the evidence while the killer walks away.

Hitchcock sets his action in the crowded back alleys of Covent Garden, where fruit and vegetable vendors rub shoulders with prostitutes, third-rate gangsters, bookies, and barmaids. A lot of the action takes place in a pub, and somehow Hitchcock gets more feeling for the location into his films than he usually does. With a lot of Hitchcock, you have the impression every frame has been meticulously prepared. This time, the smell and tide of humanity slops over. (There is even one tide in the movie which does a little slopping over humanity itself—but never mind.)

It's delicious to watch Hitchcock using the camera. Not a shot is wasted, and there is one elaborate sequence in which the killer goes upstairs with his victim. The camera precedes them up the stairs, watches them go in a door, and then backs down the stairs, alone, and across the street to look at the outside of the house. This shot is not for a moment a gimmick; the melancholy of the withdrawing camera movement is one of the most touching effects in the film, despite the fact that no people inhabit it.

There's a lot of humor, too, including two hilarious gourmet meals served to the Chief Inspector (Alec McGowen) by his wife (Vivien Merchant). There is suspense, and local color ("It's been too long since the Christie murders; a good colorful crime spree is good for tourism") and, always, Hitchcock smacking his lips and rubbing his hands and delighting in his naughtiness.

Friday the 13th, Part II ½★
R, 87 m., 1981*

Amy Steel (Ginny), John Furey (Paul), Adrienne King (Alice), Kirsten Baker (Terry). Directed and produced by Steve Miner. Screenplay by Ron Kurz.

I saw *Friday the 13th Part II* at the Virginia Theater, a former vaudeville house in my hometown of Champaign-Urbana, Illinois. The late show was half-filled with high school and college students, and as the lights went down I experienced a brief wave of nostalgia. In this very theater, on countless Friday nights, I'd gone with a date to the movies. My nostalgia lasted for the first two minutes of the movie.

The pretitle sequence showed one of the heroines of the original *Friday the 13th*, alone at home. She has nightmares, wakes up, undresses, is stalked by the camera, hears a noise in the kitchen. She tiptoes into the kitchen. Through the open window, a cat springs into the room. The audience screamed loudly and happily: It's fun to be scared. Then an unidentified man sunk an ice pick into the girl's brain, and, for me, the fun stopped.

The audience, however, carried on. It is a tradition to be loud during these movies, I guess. After a batch of young counselors turns up for training at a summer camp, a girl goes out walking alone at night. Everybody in the audience imitated hoot-owls and hyenas. Another girl went to her room and started to undress. Five guys sitting together started a chant: "We want boobs!"

The plot: In the original movie, a summer camp staff was wiped out by a demented woman whose son had been allowed to drown by incompetent camp counselors. At the end of that film, the mother was decapitated by the young woman who is killed with an ice pick at the beginning of *Part II.* The legend grows that the son, Jason, did *not* really drown, but survived, and lurks in the woods waiting to take his vengeance against the killer of his mother . . . and against camp couselors in general, I guess.

That sets up the film. The counselors are introduced, very briefly, and then some of them go into town for a beer and the rest stay at the camp to make out with each other. A mystery assailant prowls around the main cabin. We see only his shadow and his shoes. One by one, he picks off the kids. He sinks a machete into the brain of a kid in a wheelchair. He surprises a boy and a girl making love, and nails them to a bunk with a spear through both their bodies. When the other kids return to the camp, it's their turn. After almost everyone has been killed in a disgusting and violent way, one girl chews up the assailant with a chain saw, *after* which we discover the mummies in his cabin in the woods, *after* which he jumps through a window at the girl, etc.

This movie is a cross between the Mad Slasher and Dead Teen-ager genres; about two dozen movies a year feature a mad killer going berserk, and they're all about as bad as this one. Some have a little more plot, some have a little less. It doesn't matter.

Sinking into my seat in this movie theater from my childhood, I remembered the movie fantasies when I was a kid. They involved teen-agers who fell in love, made out with each other, customized their cars, listened to rock and roll, and were rebels without causes. Neither the kids in those movies nor the kids watching them would have understood a world view in which the primary function of teen-agers is to be hacked to death.

*This review will suffice for the *Friday the 13th* film of your choice.

The Friends of Eddie Coyle ★ ★ ★ ★
R, 102 m., 1973

Robert Mitchum (Eddie Coyle), Peter Boyle (Dillon), Richard Jordan (Dave Foley), Steven Keats (Jackie), Alex Rocco (Scalise), Joe Santos (Artie Van). Directed by Peter Yates and produced and written by Paul Monash.

Someone remarks of Eddie, about halfway through *The Friends of Eddie Coyle,* that for a two-bit hood, he has fingers in a lot of pies. Too many, as it turns out. Without ever rising to the top, Eddie has been employed in organized crime for most of his life. He's kind of a utility infielder, ready to trade in some hot guns, drive a hijacked truck, or generally make himself useful.

Eddie got the nickname "Fingers" some years ago after a gun deal. The buyers he supplied got caught. Their friends slammed Eddie's fingers in a drawer. He understood. There is a certain code without which it would be simply impossible to go on doing business.

But as the movie opens, Eddie is in trouble, and it looks like he'll have to break the code. He's facing a two-year stretch in New Hampshire, and he wants out of it. He doesn't want to leave his wife and kids and see them go on welfare. He is, at heart, just a small businessman; he deals in crime but is profoundly middle class. He thinks maybe he can make a deal with the state's attorney and have a few good words put in for him up in New Hampshire.

The movie is as simple as that. It's not a high-strung gangster film, it doesn't have a lot of overt excitement in it, and it doesn't go in for much violence. He gives us a man, invites our sympathy for him, and then watches almost sadly as his time runs out. And *The Friends of Eddie Coyle* works so well because Eddie is played by Robert Mitchum, and Mitchum has perhaps never been better.

He has always been one of our best screen actors: sardonic, masculine, quick-witted, but slow to reveal himself. He has never been in an absolutely great film; he doesn't have masterpieces behind him like Brando or Cary Grant. More than half his films have been conventional action melodramas, and it is a rare summer without at least one movie in which Mitchum wears a sombrero and lights bombs with his cigar. But give him a character and the room to develop it, and what he does is wonderful. Eddie Coyle is made for him: a weary middle-aged man, but tough and proud; a man who has been hurt too often in life not to respect pain; a man who will take chances to protect his own territory.

The movie is drawn from a knowledgeable novel by George V. Higgins, himself a state's attorney, and has been directed by one of the masters of this sort of thing, Peter Yates (*Robbery, Bullitt*). Paul Monash's screenplay stays close to the real-life Massachusetts texture of the novel, and the dialogue sounds right. The story isn't developed in the usual movie way, with lots of importance being given to intricacies of plot; instead, Eddie's dilemma occurs to him as it occurs to us, and we watch him struggle with it.

If the movie has a flaw, it's that we don't really care that much about the bank robberies that are counterpointed with Eddie's situation. We're interested in him. We can get the bank robberies in any summer's caper picture. It's strange that a movie's interest should fall off during its action scenes. But this is Eddie Coyle's picture, and Mitchum's.

Fright Night ★ ★ ★
R, 106 m., 1985

Roddy McDowall (Peter Vincent), Chris Sarandon (Jerry, the Vampire), William Ragsdale (Charley), Amanda Bearse (Amy), Stephen Geoffreys (Evil Ed). Directed by Tom Holland and produced by Herb Jaffe. Screenplay by Holland.

The best line in *Fright Night* belongs to Roddy McDowall, who plays a broken-down old hambone actor who used to star in vampire movies. "The kids today," he complains, "don't have the patience for vampires. They want to see some mad slasher running around and chopping off heads." He's right. Vampires, who are doomed to live forever, have outlived their fashion. They've been replaced by guys in ski masks who hack their way through Dead Teen-ager Movies.

Fright Night is an attempt to correct that situation. It stars William Ragsdale as an impressionable teen-ager who becomes convinced that vampires have moved in next door. It doesn't take a detective to figure that out. The vampires almost flaunt their unholy natures, performing weird rites in front of open windows and disposing of the bodies of their victims in plastic garbage bags. They are safe in the knowledge that nobody believes in vampires anymore.

The kid calls the cops. The vampires have a plausible explanation for their activities. The kid claims there has to be a coffin somewhere down in the basement. The cops warn him to stop wasting their time. And then, when the vampires start getting really threatening, the kid has no place to turn—except to old Peter Vincent (McDowall), the former B-movie actor who has just been fired from his TV job as host of the local Creature Features.

McDowall knows all about vampires: How to detect them, how to repel them, how to kill them. He also knows all about being behind on the rent, being evicted, and being out of work. For 500 bucks, he agrees to have a go at the vampires, and that sets up the second half of *Fright Night.*

The first part of the movie is basically funny. The second half unleashes lots of spectacular special effects devised by Richard Edlund, the same man who created the effects for *Ghostbusters.* Since part of the fun with vampire movies is how bad the special effects usually are, Edlund has to walk a narrow line, and he does. He gives us satisfactory scenes of transformations and decompositions, and seems to know his way around vampires, but he doesn't overwhelm the action.

The center of the movie, however, is the Roddy McDowall character, whose name, Peter Vincent, is obviously supposed to remind us of Peter Cushing and Vincent Price. Throw in Christopher Lee, and you'd have a quorum. McDowall's performance is wickedly funny, and he must have enjoyed it, chewing the scenery on his horror movie TV program and then chewing real scenery down in the vampire's basement. *Fright Night* is not a distinguished movie, but it has a lot of fun being undistinguished.

The Fringe Dwellers ★ ★ ★ ½
PG-13, 98 m., 1987

Kristine Nehm (Trilby), Justine Saunders (Mollie), Bob Maza (Joe), Kylie Belling (Noonah), Denis Walker (Bartie), Ernie Dingo (Phil). Directed by Bruce Beresford and produced by Sue Milliken. Screenplay by Bruce and Rhoisin Beresford.

There always seem to be too many people in Trilby's home. She is a teen-age girl who lives in an aborigine shantytown in Australia, and who sometimes goes downtown to peer into the window of the travel agency and dream of Paris, London, and New York. At home, there are parents and brothers and sisters and uncles and aunts and cousins in a riotous, disorganized, and loving extended family. They all love Trilby, but she is a quiet child, proud and stubborn, determined that she will make something of her life.

Trilby's determination is the central story in *The Fringe Dwellers*, a gentle and powerful movie by Bruce Beresford, who made it between *Tender Mercies* and *Crimes of the Heart.* In all three films, he shows a strong instinct for people living on the outside of society, on their own terms, drawing strength when they can from the people who love them.

The Fringe Dwellers is probably the most interesting of the three, because it shows us a world we know little about: Aborigines in an uncertain relationship with white society in Australia. Trilby and her younger brother are both doing well in school. An older sister has a gift for nursing, and is well-regarded at the local hospital. But Trilby's parents belong to an earlier generation—their lives are still sometimes ordered by myths that go back to the traditional aborigine culture—and they are not, truth to tell, all that eager to embrace white society.

Trilby feels trapped by the communal life in the shantytown. She convinces her parents to buy a new home in a white housing development, even though they can hardly afford it. But all of the uncles and aunts and cousins and neighbors follow them there (her parents can't resist inviting them to move in), and she still doesn't have a room of her own.

The film unfolds in a series of brief episodes. Trilby and three other aborigines go into a soda shop and have to sit through rude stares and half-audible racist jokes from the white kids, which is bad, but then a white man assures everyone they have "a perfect right" to be there, and that's worse. "I don't want anyone speaking up for me," Trilby says.

In school, she slaps a white girl and is reprimanded. If she had been white, she tells her boyfriend, she would have been expelled: "They're going easy because they feel sorry for me." Through many small glimpses like this, we begin to know her as a young woman who wants to be judged entirely on her own.

The Fringe Dwellers is a movie filled with life and laughter, as well as hurtful silences. There is a remarkable scene between the mother and daughter in which some of the mother's heritage and wisdom is expressed. There are perhaps a dozen fringe characters, including an old cousin who feels his time has come to return to the Outback lands of his ancestors. And then there are the modern problems, as when Trilby gets pregnant.

Will the baby lock her into repeating the lifetime cycle of poverty? Here Beresford provides a mysterious, unexplained scene (which I will not reveal), which seems to answer that question with a much larger question. The scene, like a couple of others in the movie, seems to imply that aborigines really do have inherited psychic powers. This is a common theme in Australian films; stories may begin with racial prejudice as their subjects, but they tend to skew off into mystical speculations about the ancient traditions and metaphysical gifts of aborigines. These traditions and gifts may, for all I know, be real, but the function they play in the movies is the Australian equivalent of American truisms about how blacks have natural rhythm.

In *The Fringe Dwellers*, Trilby's life is touched by the supernatural—an old crone foretells the future in a disturbing scene—but it is controlled much more by Trilby's own determination. She is played by Kristine Nehm, in an extraordinary screen debut; this young actress is not only beautiful and graceful, but is able to express a great deal more than she says—which is the point. She is surrounded by wonderful performances, especially by Justine Saunders as her mother. And at the end of the movie, I found myself truly interested in what eventually would happen to her, and whether she would realize her dream. There aren't many movie characters I can really care about, but here is one.

Full Metal Jacket ★ ★ 1/2

R, 121 m., 1987

Matthew Modine (Private Joker), Arliss Howard (Cowboy), Vince D'Onofrio ("Gomer" Pyle), Dorian Harewood (Eightball), Lee Ermey (Sergeant Hartman), Adam Baldwin (Animal Mother), Kevyn Major Howard (Rafterman), Ed O'Ross (Lieutenant Touchdown). Directed and produced by Stanley Kubrick. Screenplay by Kubrick, Michael Herr, and Gustav Hasford.

Stanley Kubrick's *Full Metal Jacket* is more like a book of short stories than a novel. Many of the passages seem self-contained, and some of them are masterful, and others look like they came out of the bottom drawer. This is a stangely shapeless film from the man whose work usually imposes a ferociously consistent vision on his material.

The movie is about Vietnam, and was shot on stages and outdoor sets in England. To say it's one of the best-looking war movies ever made on sets and stages is not quite enough praise, after the awesome reality of *Platoon*, *Apocalypse Now*, and *The Deer Hunter*. The crucial last passages of the film too often look and feel like World War II films from Hollywood studios. We see the same sets from so many different angles that after the movie we could find our own way around Kubrick's Vietnam.

That would not be a problem if his material made the sets irrelevant. It does not, especially toward the end of the film. You can only watch so much footage of a man crouched behind a barrier, pinned down by sniper fire, before the situation turns into a cinematic cliché. We've been here before, in other war movies, and we keep waiting for Kubrick to spring a surprise, and he never does.

The opening passages of *Full Metal Jacket* promise much more than the film is finally able to deliver. They tell the story of a group of Marine grunts undergoing basic training on Paris Island, and the experience comes down to a confrontation between the Gunnery Sergeant (Lee Ermey) and a tubby misfit (Vince D'Onofrio) who is nicknamed Gomer Pyle. These are the two best performances in the movie, which never recovers after they leave the scene.

Ermey plays a character in the great tradition of movie drill instructors, but with great brio and amazingly creative obscenity. All situations in the Marines and in war seem to suggest sexual parallels for him, and one of the film's best moments has the recruits going to bed with their rifles and reciting a poem of love to them.

In scene after scene, the war/sex connection is reinforced, and it parallels the personal battle between Ermey and D'Onofrio, who at first fails all of the tasks in basic training, and then finds he has one skill; he is an expert marksman. It is likely that in a real boot camp D'Onofrio would have been thrown out after a week, but Kubrick's story requires him to stay, and so he does, until the final showdown between the two men.

In that showdown, and at several other times in the film, Kubrick indulges his favorite close-up, a shot of a man glowering up at the camera from beneath lowered brows. This was the trademark visual in *A Clockwork Orange*, and Jack Nicholson practiced it in *The Shining*. What does it mean? That Kubrick thinks it's an interesting angle from which to shoot the face, I think. In *Full Metal Jacket*, it promises exactly what finally happens, and spoils some of the suspense.

There is a surprise to come, however: The complete abandonment of the sexual metaphor once the troops are in Vietnam. The movie disintegrates into a series of self-contained set-pieces, none of them quite satisfying. The scene in the press room, for example with the lecture on propaganda, seems to reflect some of the same spirit as *Dr. Strangelove*. But how does it connect with the curious scene of the Vietnamese prostitute—a scene with a riveting beginning but no middle or end? And how do either lead to the final shoot-out with a sniper?

Time and again in the film, we get great shots with no payoffs. In one elaborate setup, for example, Kubrick shows us a cameraman and a soundman being led by their shirttails as they pan down a line of exhausted Marines. At first the shot has power. Then the outcome is that several soldiers deliver neat oneliners, all in a row, all in their turns, all perfectly timed, and the effect is so contrived that the idea of actual battle is completely lost.

Kubrick seems to want to tell us the story of individual characters, to show how the war affected them, but it has been so long since he allowed spontaneous human nature into his films that he no longer knows how. After the departure of his two most memorable characters, the sergeant and the tubby kid, he is left with no characters (or actors) that we really care much about, and in a key scene at the end, when a Marine feels joy after finally killing someone, the payoff is diminished because we don't give a damn about the character.

The movie has great moments. Ermey's speech to his men about the great Marine marksmen of the past (Charles Whitman and Lee Harvey Oswald among them) is a masterpiece. The footage on the Paris Island obstacle course is powerful. But *Full Metal Jacket* is uncertain where to go, and the movie's climax, which Kubrick obviously intends to be a mighty moral revelation, seems phoned in from earlier war pictures. After what has already been said about "Vietnam" in the movies, *Full Metal Jacket* is too little and too late.

Funny Farm ★ ★ ★ ½

PG, 98 m., 1988 ✓

Chevy Chase (Andy), Madolyn Smith (Elizabeth), Kevin O'Morrison (Sheriff Ledbetter), Joseph Maher (Michael Sinclair), Jack Gilpin (Bud Culbertson), Caris Corfman

(Betsy Culbertson), William Severs (Newspaper Editor), Mike Starr (Crocker). Directed by George Roy Hill and produced by Robert L. Crawford. Screenplay by Jeffrey Boam.

Funny Farm is one of those small miracles that start out like a lot of other movies and then somehow find their own way, step after step, to an original comic vision. *Funny Farm* is funny, all right, but it's more than funny, it's likable. It enlists our sympathies with the characters even while cheerfully exploiting their faults. And at the end, I had a goofy grin on my face because the movie had won me over so completely I was even willing to accept the final gag about the two ducks.

The movie stars Chevy Chase and Madolyn Smith as a married couple who decide to move to a small New England town so he can write his novel and they can breathe the fresh country air and mow their own lawn. Chase has been a sportswriter for years, but now he figures that with the typewriter placed just exactly right next to the big open window on the second floor overlooking the lawn, conditions will be perfect for the creation of a bestseller.

Conditions are not perfect. The birds sing too loudly. The mailman speeds by in a cloud of dust hurling letters from the window of his pickup. There are snakes in the lake and a corpse buried in the garden and it costs twenty cents to make a call from the pay phone in the kitchen. And the townspeople, they discover, are drawn more from Stephen King than Norman Rockwell. By wintertime, Chase is withdrawn and bitter, drinking heavily, and sleeping past noon, while his wife has sold a children's novel about a city squirrel who moves to the country and has the same name as her husband.

None of this, I imagine, sounds as good as it plays. *Funny Farm* has a good screenplay by Jeffrey Boam, and yet in other hands it might have yielded only a routine movie. George Roy Hill, the director, makes it better than that because he finds the right tone and sticks to it—a sort of bemused wonder at the insanity of it all, in a movie that doesn't underline its gags or force its punch lines but just lets everything develop naturally. Notice, for example, the timing in the sequence where the sheriff first comes to chat about the corpse in the garden.

Chevy Chase is not exactly playing a fresh kind of role here—his hero is a variation of the harassed husband he's been playing for years—but he has never been better in a movie. He has everything just right this time, and he plays the character without his usual repertory of witty asides and laconic one-liners. It's a performance, not an appearance. Madolyn Smith makes a good foil for him, although she isn't given enough to do in scenes of her own, and one scene in particular—a visit to an antique shop—felt suspiciously truncated.

The gallery of townspeople has to be seen to be believed. They are almost all mean-spirited, crafty, suspicious, and greedy, and happy to be just exactly who they are. The sheriff travels by taxi because he flunked his driving test, the lady who runs the antique shop seems to be selling nothing except her own precious and irreplaceable family heirlooms, and down at the local cafe, there's a competition to see who can eat the most stir-fried lamb testicles.

Funny Farm is kind of a loony, off-center comedy version of Hill's *The World According to Garp*, another movie about strange people in bizarre situations. *Garp* made too much of its significance, however, while the comedy in this film is light as a feather. The final sequence, in which the townspeople are bribed to act "normal," while Chase hands out Norman Rockwell covers from the *Saturday Evening Post* for them to admire, has a kind of inspired lunacy that is so fragile you almost don't want to laugh for fear of breaking the mood.

G

The Gambler ★ ★ ★ ★
R, 111 m., 1974

James Caan (Axel), Paul Sorvino (Hips), Lauren Hutton (Billie), Morris Carnovsky (A.R. Lowenthal), Jacqueline Brooks (Naomi), Burt Young (Carmine). Directed by Karel Reisz and produced by Irwin Winkler and Robert Chartoff. Screenplay by James Toback.

"Jeez, Axel, I never seen such bad cards," Axel Freed's friend tells him consolingly. They're standing in the kitchen of a New York apartment, and gray dawn is seeping through the smoke. Axel has never seen such bad cards either. His disbelief that anyone could draw so many lousy poker hands in a row has led him finally $44,000 into debt. He doesn't have the money, but it's been a bigtime game, and he has to find it somewhere or be in heavy trouble.

And that's how Karel Reisz's *The Gambler* begins: with a problem. The way Axel solves his problem is only fairly difficult. He borrows the money from his mother, who is a doctor. But then we discover that his problem is greater than his debt, because there is some final compulsion within him that won't let him pay back the money. He needs to lose, to feel risk, to place himself in danger. He needs to gamble away the forty-four grand on even more hopeless bets because in a way it isn't gambling that's his obsession—it's danger itself.

"I play in order to lose," he tells his bookie at one point. "That's what gets my juice going. If I only bet on the games I know, I could at least break even." But he doesn't want that. At one point, he's driven to bet money he doesn't really have on college basketball games picked almost at random out of the sports pages.

And yet Axel Freed is not simply a gambler, but a very complicated man in his midthirties who earns his living as a university literature teacher. He teaches Dostoyevsky, William Carlos Williams, Thoreau. But he doesn't seem to teach their works so much as what he finds in them to justify his own obsessions. One of the students in his class has Axel figured out so completely that she always has the right answer, when he asks what Thoreau is saying, or what Dostoyevsky is saying. They're saying, as Axel reads them, to take risks, to put the self on the line.

"Buffalo Bill's defunct," he says, quoting the e e cummings poem, and the death of the nineteenth century age of heroes obsesses him. In that earlier age, he could have tested himself more directly. His grandfather came to America flat broke, fought and killed to establish himself, and still is a man of enormous vitality at the age of eighty. The old man is respectable now (he owns a chain of furniture stores), but the legend of his youth fascinates Axel, who recites it poetically at the eightieth-birthday party.

Axel finds nothing in 1974 to test himself against, however. He has to find his own dangers, to court and seduce them. And the ultimate risk in his life as a gambler is that behind his friendly bookies and betting cronies is the implacable presence of the Mafia, the guys who take his bets like him, but if he doesn't pay, there's nothing they can do. "It's out of my hands," his pal Hips explains. "A bad gambling debt has got to be taken care of." And that adds an additional dimension to *The Gambler,* which begins as a portrait of Axel Freed's personality, develops into the story of his world, and then pays off as a thriller. We become so absolutely contained by Axel's problems and dangers that they seem like our own. There's a scene where he soaks in the bathtub and listens to the last minutes of a basketball game, and another scene where he sits in the stands and watches a basketball game he has tried to fix (while a couple of hit men watch him), and these scenes have a quality of tension almost impossible to sustain.

But Reisz sustains them, and makes them all the more real because he doesn't populate the rest of his movie with stock characters.

Axel Freed, as played by James Caan, is himself a totally convincing personality, and original. He doesn't derive from other gambling movies or even from other roles he's played.

And the people around him also are specific, original creations. His mother Naomi (Jacqueline Brooks) is a competent, independent person who gives him the money because she fears for his life, and yet understands that his problem is deeper than gambling. His grandfather, marvelously played by Morris Carnovsky, is able to imply by his behavior why he fascinates Axel so. The various bookies and collectors he comes across aren't Mafia stereotypes. They enforce more in sorrow than in anger. Only his girlfriend (Lauren Hutton) fails to seem very real. Here's still another demonstration of the inability of contemporary movies to give us three-dimensional women under thirty.

There's a scene in *The Gambler* that has James Caan on screen all by himself for two minutes, locked in a basement room, waiting to meet a Mafia boss who will arguably instruct that his legs be broken. In another movie, the scene could have seemed too long, too eventless.

But Reisz, Caan, and screenwriter James Toback have constructed the character and the movie so convincingly that the scene not only works, but works two ways: first as suspense, and then as character revelation. Because as we look into Axel Freed's caged eyes we see a person who is scared to death and yet stubbornly ready for this moment he has brought down upon himself.

Gandhi ★ ★ ★ ★

PG, 188 m., 1983

Ben Kingsley (Mahatma Gandhi), Candice Bergen (Margaret Bourke-White), Edward Fox (General Dyer), John Gielgud (Lord Irwin), Trevor Howard (Judge Broomfield), John Mills (The Viceroy) Martin Sheen (Walker), Rohini Hattangady (Kasturba Ghandi), Ian Charleson (Charlie Andrews), Athol Fugard (General Smuts). Directed and produced by Richard Attenborough. Screenplay by John Briley.

In the middle of this epic film there is a quiet, small scene that helps explain why *Gandhi* is such a remarkable experience. Mahatma Gandhi, at the height of his power and his fame, stands by the side of a lake with his wife of many years. Together, for the benefit of a visitor from the West, they reenact their marriage vows. They do it with solemnity, quiet warmth, and perhaps just a touch of shyness; they are simultaneously demonstrating an aspect of Indian culture and touching on something very personal to them both. At the end of the ceremony, Gandhi says, "We were thirteen at the time." He shrugs. The marriage had been arranged. Gandhi and his wife had not been in love, had not been old enough for love, and yet love had grown between them. But that is not really the point of the scene. The point, I think, comes in the quiet smile with which Gandhi says the words. At that moment we believe that he is fully and truly human, and at that moment, a turning point in the film, *Gandhi* declares that it is not only a historical record but a breathing, living document.

This is the sort of rare epic film that spans the decades, that uses the proverbial cast of thousands, and yet follows a human thread from beginning to end: *Gandhi* is no more overwhelmed by the scope of its production than was Gandhi overwhelmed by all the glory of the British Empire. The movie earns comparison with two classic works by David Lean, *Lawrence of Arabia* and *Dr. Zhivago,* in its ability to paint a strong human story on a very large canvas.

The movie is a labor of love by Sir Richard Attenborough, who struggled for years to get financing for his huge but "non-commercial" project. Various actors were considered over the years for the all-important title role, but the actor who was finally chosen, Ben

Kingsley, makes the role so completely his own that there is a genuine feeling that the spirit of Gandhi is on the screen. Kingsley's performance is powerful without being loud or histrionic; he is almost always quiet, observant, and soft-spoken on the screen, and yet his performance comes across with such might that we realize, afterward, that the sheer moral force of Gandhi must have been behind the words. Apart from all its other qualities, what makes this movie special is that it was obviously made by people who believed in it.

The movie begins in the early years of the century, in South Africa, where Gandhi was born and spent the first decades of his life. He was trained as a lawyer and received his degree, but, degree or not, he was a target of South Africa's system of racial segregation, in which Indians (even though they are Caucasian, and thus should "qualify") are denied full citizenship and manhood. Gandhi's reaction to the system is, at first, almost naive; an early scene on a train doesn't quite work only because we can't believe the adult Gandhi would still be so ill-informed about the racial code of South Africa. But Gandhi's response sets the tone of the film. He is nonviolent but firm. He is sure where the right lies in every situation, and he will uphold it in total disregard for the possible consequences to himself.

Before long Gandhi is in India, a nation of hundreds of millions, ruled by a relative handful of British. They rule almost by divine right, shouldering the "white man's burden" even though they have not quite been requested to do so by the Indians. Gandhi realizes that Indians have been made into second-class citizens in their own country, and he begins a program of civil disobedience that is at first ignored by the British, then scorned, and finally, reluctantly, dealt with, sometimes by subterfuge, sometimes by brutality. Scenes in this central passage of the movie make it clear that nonviolent protests could contain a great deal of violence. There is a shattering scene in which wave after wave of Gandhi's followers march forward to be beaten to the ground by British clubs. Through it all, Gandhi maintains a certain detachment; he is convinced he is right, convinced that violence is not an answer, convinced that sheer moral example can free his nation—as it did. "You have been guests in our home long enough," he tells the British, "Now we would like for you to leave."

The movie is populated with many familiar faces, surrounding the newcomer Kingsley. Where would the British cinema be without its dependable, sturdy, absolutely authoritative generation of great character actors like Trevor Howard (as a British judge), John Mills (the British viceroy), John Gielgud, and Michael Hordern? There are also such younger actors as Ian Bannen, Edward Fox, Ian Charleson, and, from America, Martin Sheen as a reporter and Candice Bergen as the photographer Margaret Bourke-White.

Gandhi stands at the quiet center. And Ben Kingsley's performance finds the right note and stays with it. There are complexities here; *Gandhi* is not simply a moral story with a happy ending, and the tragedy of the bloodshed between the Hindu and Buddhist populations of liberated India is addressed, as is the partition of India and Pakistan, which we can almost literally feel breaking Gandhi's heart.

I imagine that for many Americans, Mahatma Gandhi remains a dimly understood historical figure. I suspect a lot of us know he was a great Indian leader without quite knowing why and—such is our ignorance of Eastern history and culture—we may not fully realize that his movement did indeed liberate India, in one of the greatest political and economic victories of all time, achieved through nonviolent principles. What is important about this film is not that it serves as a history lesson (although it does) but that, at a time when the threat of nuclear holocaust hangs ominously in the air, it reminds us that we are, after all, human, and thus capable of the most extraordinary and wonderful achievements, simply through the use of our imagination, our will, and our sense of right.

The Garden of the Finzi-Continis

★ ★ ★ ★

R, 90 m., 1971

Dominique Sanda (Micol), Lino Capolicchio (Giorgio), Helmut Berger (Alberto), Fabrio Tesel (Malnate), Romolo Valli (Giorgio's Father). Directed by Vittorio de Sica and produced by Gianni Hecht Lucari. Screenplay by Ugo Pirro and Vittorio Bonicelli.

The Garden of the Finzi-Continis, as nearly as I can tell, is not an enclosed space but an enclosed state of mind. Eager for an afternoon of tennis, the young people ride into it on their bicycles one sunny Sunday afternoon. The Fascist government of Mussolini has declared the ordinary tennis clubs off limits for Italian Jews—but what does that matter, here behind these tall stone walls that have faithfully guarded the Finzi-Contini family for generations?

Micol, the daughter, welcomes her guests and gives some of them a little tour: That tree over there is said to be 500 years old and might even have been planted by the Borgias. If it has stood for all those years in this garden, she seems to believe, what is there to worry about in the world outside?

She is a tall blonde girl with a musical laugh and a way of turning away from a man just as he reveals himself to her. Giorgio, who has been helplessly in love with her since they were both children, deceives himself that she loves him. But she cannot quite love anyone, although she carries on an affair with a tall, athletic young man who is about to be drafted into the army. Giorgio's father says of the Finzi-Continis: "They're different. They don't even seem to be Jewish."

They're different because wealth and privilege and generations of intellectual and social position have bred them into a family as proud as it is vulnerable. The other Jews in the town react to Mussolini's edicts in various ways: Giorgio is enraged; his father is philosophical. But the Finzi-Continis hardly seem to know, or care, what is happening. They are above mere edicts; they chose to live behind their walls long before the Fascists said they must.

This is the situation as Vittorio de Sica sketches it for us at the outset of *The Garden of the Finzi-Continis,* which was a true surprise from a director who had seemed to lose his early genius. De Sica's previous two or three films (especially the disastrous *A Place for Lovers*) were embarrassments from the director of *Bicycle Thief* and *Shoeshine.*

But here he returned with a film that seems to owe little to his previous work. It is not neorealism; it is not a comic mixture of bawdiness and sophistication; it is most of all not the dreamy banality of his previous few films. In telling of the disintegration of the Jewish community in one smallish Italian town, de Sica merges his symbols with his story so that they evoke the meaning of the time.

It was a time in which many people had no idea what was really going on. Giorgio's younger brother, sent to France to study, finds out to his horror about the German concentration camps. There has been no word of them in Italy, of course. Italy in those final prewar years is painted by de Sica as a perpetual wait for something no one admitted would come: war and the persecution of the Jews.

The walled garden of the Finzi-Continis is his symbol for this waiting period. It seems to promise that nothing will change, and even the Jews who live in the village seem to cling to the apparent strength of the Finzi-Continis as assurance of their own power to survive.

In presenting the garden to us, de Sica uses an interesting visual strategy; he never completely orients us visually, and so we don't know its overall size and shape. Therefore, visually, we can't count on it: We don't know when it will give out. It's an uneasy feeling to be inside an undefined space, especially if you may need to hide or run, and that's exactly the feeling de Sica gets.

The ambiguity of the garden's space is matched by an understated sexual ambiguity. Nothing happens overtly, but de Sica uses looks and body language to suggest the complex varieties of sexual attractions among his characters. When Giorgio discovers Micol with her sleeping lover, she does a most interesting thing. She covers him, not herself, and stares at him until he goes away.

The thing is, you can't count on anything. And nothing permanent can be permitted to take place during this period of waiting. De Sica's film creates a feeling of nostalgia for a lost time and place, but it isn't the nostalgia of looking back. It's the nostalgia of the time itself, when people still inhabiting their world could sense it slipping away, and already missed what they had not yet lost.

Gardens of Stone ★ ★ ½

R, 112 m., 1987

James Caan (Clell Hazard), D.B. Sweeney (Jackie Willow), Anjelica Huston (Samantha Davis), James Earl Jones ("Goody" Nelson),

Dean Stockwell (Homer Thomas), Mary Stuart Masterson (Rachel Feld). Directed by Francis Coppola and produced by Michael I. Levy and Coppola. Screenplay by Ronald Bass.

The garden of stone is Arlington National Cemetery, its flowers the tombstones marking the graves of the nation's heroes. The garden is tended by the Old Guard, an elite Army unit led by decorated veterans—each and every one of whom would rather be on active duty. "We're toy soldiers," one of the professional soldiers says scornfully, as the daily schedule of burial details continues to grow. It is the time of the Vietnam war, and a young man has been assigned to the Old Guard. His father was a hero in the Korean war. His new sergeants knew his father, and loved him. Now they make things tough for the kid, but they love him, too.

Francis Coppola's *Gardens of Stone* tells the stories of several relationships at this outpost far behind the front lines. The film introduces the kid (D.B. Sweeney), his immediate superior (James Caan), and the sergeant above him (James Earl Jones). And then there is the girl the kid would like to marry (Mary Stuart Masterson), and there is Caan's new girlfriend (Anjelica Huston), who works for the *Washington Post* and considers the Vietnam War to be genocide.

Many of the movie's best scenes take place in Caan's civilian apartment, with long dinners with candlelight and wine and passionate conversations about what is right and what is wrong.

The kid wants to go to OCS, and then he wants to be assigned to the front. He wants to see combat. The two older soldiers see things a little differently. They would rather be fighting, too, and they hate the cemetery detail and their ceremonial duties, but they believe the war in Vietnam is stupid because the politicians are hamstringing the professionals, preventing them from fighting to win.

The movie's purpose is to re-create a specific time and place. The network news brings the reality of Vietnam home every night, and peace demonstrators march on the Pentagon, and at a cocktail party Caan is insulted by a long-haired liberal. But the kid seems to exist outside this time and place; he's an Army brat, brought up to be patriotic, a good soldier. He doesn't much seem to care about the political issues involved. He just wants to see action. His enthusiasm is the despair of the older soldiers who care for him.

The movie creates its characters with realism, love, and detail. The romance between Caan and Huston is one of the great adult love stories in recent movies, and the fact that they are such different people makes it even more emotionally involving. The kid is complicated, too, and we find that out when he runs into his college sweetheart (Masterson) and finds that she is still in love with him—that she would have married him if he'd had the guts to stand up to her father, a senior officer who didn't want his daughter marrying "beneath" herself in the ranks.

Everything seems to come together—the war, the love stories, the military careers—and everything leads to the day when the kid finally gets his wish and is shipped out to Vietnam.

There is no way to fault any particular moment in *Gardens of Stone*. The dialogue always sounds right. The emotions are always justified. The performances are wonderful (Caan and Huston have a very special chemistry). Even the jokes work.

But the movie finally doesn't add up in the way we feel it should. We think, at the beginning, that we can see where the film is headed—and at the end it turns out we were right. There is no narrative spring to uncoil, no jolt or surprise or discovery. The story is just what it seems to be, and somehow we want it to be more than that.

Coppola's *Apocalypse Now* (1979) remains the best movie ever made about Vietnam, because it was able to rise above the level of simple reality and make a great and wrenching parable out of the war. It took its material and shaped it into a point of view.

Gardens of Stone is content to be a slice of life, a story that says some of our best young people went to Vietnam and died there, and those who knew them missed them. We knew that already. Perhaps there is nothing else to be said, but this movie seems to give promise of seeing more deeply, and then it doesn't. Every moment is right, and yet the film as a whole is incomplete.

Gates of Heaven ★ ★ ★ ★

NO MPAA RATING, 85 m, 1978

A documentary produced, directed, and written by Errol Morris.

There are many invitations to laughter during this remarkable documentary, but what *Gates of Heaven* finally made me feel was an aching poignancy about its subjects. They say you can make a great documentary about almost anything, if only you see it well enough and truly, and this film proves it. *Gates of Heaven,* which has no connection with the unfortunate *Heaven's Gate,* is a documentary about pet cemeteries and their owners. It was filmed in Southern California, so of course we immediately anticipate a sardonic look at peculiarities of the Moonbeam State. But then *Gates of Heaven* grows ever so much more complicated and frightening, until at the end it is about such large issues as love, immortality, failure, and the dogged elusiveness of the American Dream.

The film was made by a California filmmaker named Errol Morris, and it has been the subject of notoriety because Werner Herzog, the West German director, promised to eat his shoe if Morris ever finished it. Morris did finish it, and at the film's premiere in Berkeley, Herzog indeed boiled and ate his shoe.

Gates of Heaven is so rich and thought-provoking, it achieves so much while seeming to strain so little, that it stays in your mind for tantalizing days. It opens with a monologue by a kind-looking, somewhat heavyset paraplegic, with a slight lisp that makes him sound like a kid. His name is Floyd McClure. Ever since his pet dog was run over years ago by a Model A Ford, he has dreamed of establishing a pet cemetery. The movie develops and follows his dream, showing the forlorn, bare patch of land where he founded his cemetery at the intersection of two superhighways. Then, with cunning drama, it gradually reveals that the cemetery went bankrupt and the remains of 450 animals had to be dug up. Various people contribute to the story: One of McClure's investors, a partner, two of the women whose pets were buried in his cemetery, and an unforgettable old woman named Florence Rasmussen, who starts on the subject of pets, and switches, with considerable fire, to her no-account son. Then the action shifts north to the Napa Valley, where a go-getter named Cal Harberts has absorbed what remained of McClure's dream (and the 450 dead pets) into his own pet cemetery, the Bubbling Well Pet Memorial Park. It is here that the movie grows heartbreaking, painting a portrait of a life-style that looks chillingly forlorn, and of the people who live it with relentless faith in positive thinking.

Harberts, a patriarch, runs his pet cemetery with two sons, Phil and Dan. Phil, the older one, has returned home after a period spent selling insurance in Salt Lake City. He speaks of having been overworked. Morris lets the camera stay on Phil as he solemnly explains his motivational techniques, and his method of impressing a new client by filling his office with salesmanship trophies. He has read all of Clement Stone's books on "Positive Mental Attitude," and has a framed picture of Stone on his wall. Phil looks neat, presentable, capable. He talks reassuringly of his positive approach to things, "mentally wise." Then we meet the younger brother, Dan, who composes songs and plays them on his guitar. In the late afternoon, when no one is at the pet cemetery, he hooks up his 100-watt speakers and blasts his songs all over the valley. He has a wispy mustache and looks like a hippie. The family hierarchy is clear. Cal, in the words of Phil, is "El Presidento." Then Dan comes next, because he has worked at the cemetery longer. Phil, the golden boy, the positive thinker, is maintaining his P.M.A. in the face of having had to leave an insurance business in Salt Lake City to return home as third in command at a pet cemetery.

The cemetery itself is bleak and barren, its markers informing us, "God is love; dog is god backwards." An American flag flies over the little graves. Floyd McClure tells us at the beginning of the film that pets are put on Earth for two reasons: to love and to be loved. At the end of this mysterious and great movie, we observe the people who guard and maintain their graves, and who themselves seem unloved and very lonely. One of the last images is of old Cal, the patriarch, wheeling past on his forklift, a collie-sized coffin in its grasp.

The Gauntlet ★ ★ ★
R, 111 m., 1977

Clint Eastwood (Ben Shockley), Sondra Locke (Gus Mally), Pat Hingle (Josephson), William Prince (Blakelock), Bill McKinney (Constable), Michael Cavanaugh (Feyderspiel). Directed by Clint Eastwood and produced by Robert Daley. Screenplay by Michael Butler and Dennis Shryack.

The Gauntlet is classic Clint Eastwood: fast, furious, and funny. It tells a cheerfully preposterous story with great energy and a lot of style, and nobody seems more at home in this sort of action movie than Eastwood. He plays a cop again this time, but not a supercop like Dirty Harry Callahan. He's a detective from Phoenix, and no hero: He drives up in front of police headquarters, opens his car door, and a whisky bottle crashes to the street.

Eastwood hasn't compiled the most stellar record in the department, but somehow the police commissioner thinks he's the right man for the next assignment: Fly to Las Vegas, take custody of a hooker there, and bring her back to Phoenix to be a witness in an important court case. It sounds routine to Eastwood, until he flies to Vegas, takes custody, and discovers that the Mafia is quoting sixty-to-one odds against his witness leaving Nevada alive. Maybe, he begins to suspect, this isn't a totally typical witness . . . .

The witness (played by Sondra Locke) isn't a totally typical hooker, either. She's a college graduate, spunky, pleasant. She tells Eastwood he'd be wise to catch the next flight home, because there's a contract out on her. Eastwood's too stubborn. He's taken the assignment and he'll carry it out through hell and high water (which turn out to be just about the only two things he doesn't have to survive on this mission).

The return trip gets off to a slightly shaky start when they survive an auto bomb. Then, after Eastwood commandeers an ambulance, they're involved in a high-speed chase with three gunmen. They take refuge in Locke's house, which is promptly surrounded by dozens of police marksmen, who open fire, achieving overkill so completely that (in one of the movie's many mixtures of humor and violence), the house simply topples over. Still ahead of them are nights in the desert, an encounter with Hell's Angels, a fight on a moving freight train, a chase in which their motorcycle is pursued by a rifle marksman in a helicopter . . . and then the grand finale, in which Eastwood hijacks a passenger bus, armor-plates it, and drives himself and his witness through downtown Phoenix against a hail of machine-gun fire. You see what I mean about the plot's being cheerfully preposterous.

Eastwood directed himself again this time, and he's a good action craftsman (as *The Outlaw Josey Wales* demonstrated). He's also good at developing relationships; despite the movie's barrage of violence, there's a nice pacing as his cop and hooker slog through their ordeals and begin to like and respect one another. As in most Eastwood movies, by the way, the woman's role is a good one: Eastwood has such a macho image that maybe people haven't noticed that his female sidekicks (like Tyne Daly, Dirty Harry's partner in *The Enforcer*) have minds of their own and are never intended to be merely decorative.

The Gauntlet will no doubt be attacked in various quarters because of its violence, but it's a harmless, pop-art type of violence, often with a comic quality. The wall of gunfire during the final bus ride up the steps of the Hall of Justice, for example, is an extravaganza of sound and action during which, incredibly, no one is killed. Eastwood himself fires his pistol only twice: once at a door, and once at a gas tank.

George Stevens: A Filmmaker's Journey ★ ★ ★ ½
PG, 113 m., 1985

A documentary written, produced, and directed by George Stevens, Jr. Edited by Catherine Shields. Music by Carl Davis.

The last shot of *Citizen Kane* showed the dead tycoon's storerooms, vast spaces filled with the jumble of a lifetime. One of the early shots in this documentary about George Stevens has something of the same quality. We see the memorabilia of his long career: cowboy hats, leather-bound scripts, cans of film, albums of photographs, Oscars, diaries, belt buckles—everything with a story, and half the stories already forgotten.

The voice on the sound track is the filmmaker's son, telling us about his famous father. One of the things the father told him, one day when they were driving past the warehouse where all of these memories were stored, was, "That'll all be yours when I'm gone." As he rummaged through the souvenirs of his father's lifetime, he made some extraordinary discoveries: Not only the prints and scripts of such classics as *Giant, A Place in the Sun,* and *Alice Adams,* but also documentary footage of Stevens on the set of his movies, and rare color footage Stevens shot for himself while he was leading a newsreel unit during World War II.

More than most men, Stevens seems to have been concerned to leave behind a record of his career. He began in movies almost at the beginning, as an assistant on the early silent films, and his first work as a director was on the Laurel and Hardy films. We see some of his earliest footage, and then we begin to hear the voices of the people who knew him then, and worked with him: Old directors like Rouben Mamoulian and John Huston, stars like Katharine Hepburn and Warren Beatty, writers like Irwin Shaw. Hepburn gave Stevens his real start, rescuing him from grade B features and second-unit work because she was impressed by his enthusiasm for *Alice Adams.* It became his first prestigious production, but then there was a flood of others: the definitive Astaire-Rogers musical *Swing Time,* the audacious *Gunga Din,* and *Woman of the Year,* and Stevens began to build a reputation as a man who saw his own way through the standard scripts he was handed, freeing his actors so that *Gunga Din,* for example, became a high-spirited comic masterpiece instead of just another swashbuckler.

The film contains a lot of home movies and private documentary footage; Stevens shot the only color footage of the landing at Normandy, and we also see moments of Stevens at work, always quietly professional, thoughtful, not the flamboyant self-promoter so many other directors of his generation became. Stevens, more than anyone else, fashioned the image of James Dean. He directed some of Elizabeth Taylor's most memorable scenes. And he pressed on in the face of daunting odds to direct such movies as *The Greatest Story Ever Told.* Shooting in Utah, he was faced with the first snowstorms in a generation, and when he asked the cast and crew to pitch in and shovel snow, they respected him enough that they did it.

A Filmmaker's Journey is a film biography of a movie director, and it inevitably shares some of the conventions of the genre. We see the clips of great scenes, we hear the memories of old colleagues. Two things distinguish the film: The quiet professionalism with which the materials have been edited together, and the feeling that George Stevens, Jr., really is engaging in a rediscovery of his father through the making of this film. By the end of the film, we are less aware of George Stevens as a filmmaker than as a good and gifted man who happened to use movies as a means of expressing his gifts.

Ghost Story ★ ★ ★

R, 110 m., 1981

Fred Astaire (Ricky Hawthorne), Melvyn Douglas (John Jeffrey), Douglas Fairbanks, Jr. (Edward Wanderly), John Houseman (Sears James), Craig Wasson (Don/David), Alice Krige (Alma/Eva), Patricia Neal (Stella). Directed by John Irvin and produced by Burt Weissbourd. Screenplay by Lawrence D. Cohen.

Ghost stories should always begin as this one does, in shadows so deep that the flickering light of the dying fire barely illuminates the apprehensive faces of the listeners. They should be told in an old man's voice, dry as dust. They should be listened to by other men who are so old and so rich that we can only guess at the horrors they have seen. And, of course, ghost stories should be about things that happened long ago to young, passionate lovers who committed unspeakable crimes and have had to live forever after with the knowledge of them. If at all possible, some of the characters should be living in this life, filled with guilt, while others should be living the half-lives of the Undead, filled with hatred and revenge.

Peter Straub's best-selling novel *Ghost Story* contained all of those elements, and so I plugged away at it for what must have been hundreds of pages before his unspeakable prose finally got to me. At least, he knows how to make a good story, if not how to tell it, and that is one way in which the book and the movie of *Ghost Story* differ. The movie is told with style. It goes without saying that style is the most important single element in every ghost story, since without it even the most ominous events disintegrate into silliness. And *Ghost Story*, perhaps aware that if characters talk too much they disperse the tension, adopts a very economical story-telling approach. Dialogue comes in short, straightforward sentences. Background is provided without being allowed to distract from the main event. The characters are established with quick, subtle strokes. This is a good movie.

The story involves four very old men, who have formed a club to tell each other ghost stories. The casting is crucial here, and the movie's glory is in the performances and presences of Fred Astaire, the late Melvyn Douglas, Douglas Fairbanks, Jr., and John Houseman. What a crowd.

There is also a young protagonist (Craig Wasson), who has a dual role as Fairbanks's twin sons. When one comes to a dreadful end, the other begins to suspect that a mysterious woman may have something to do with it. And indeed she may. I would not dream of even hinting at exactly what connection this young woman (played with creepy charm by Alice Krige) might have with the four old men, but of course there is a connection. The movie flashes back fifty or sixty years to establish the connection, but its scariest scenes are in the present. They involve a wonderful haunted house, a long-drowned auto, a series of horrendous accidents, a group of ghostly manifestations, and a truly horrible vengeance wreaked upon the living by the not-exactly-dead.

If you like ghost stories, you will appreciate that they cannot be told with all sorts of ridiculous skeletons leaping out of closets, as in Abbott and Costello. They must be told largely in terms of fearful and nostalgic memory, since (by definition) a ghost is a ghost because of something that once happened that shouldn't have happened. *Ghost Story* understands that, and restrains its performers so that the horror of the ghost is hardly more transparent than they are.

Ghostbusters ★ ★ ★ ½

PG, 107 m., 1984

Bill Murray (Venkman), Dan Aykroyd (Stantz), Harold Ramis (Spengler), Sigourney Weaver (Dana), Ernie Hudson (Winston), Rick Moranis (Louis). Directed and produced by Ivan Reitman. Screenplay by Dan Aykroyd and Harold Ramis.

Ghostbusters is a head-on collision between two comic approaches that have rarely worked together very successfully. This time, they do. It's (1) a special effects blockbuster, and (2) a sly dialogue movie, in which everybody talks to each other like smart graduate students who are in on the joke. In the movie's climactic scenes, an apocalyptic psychic mindquake is rocking Manhattan, and the experts talk like Bob and Ray.

This movie is an exception to the general rule that big special effects can wreck a comedy. Special effects require painstaking detail work. Comedy requires spontaneity and improvisation—or at least that's what it should feel like, no matter how much work has gone into it. In movies like Steven Spielberg's *1941*, the awesome scale of the special effects dominated everything else; we couldn't laugh because we were holding our breath. Not this time. *Ghostbusters* has a lot of neat effects, some of them mind-boggling, others just quick little throwaways, as when a transparent green slime monster gobbles up a mouthful of hot dogs. No matter what effects are being used, they're placed at the service of the actors; instead of feeling as if the characters have been carefully posed in front of special effects, we feel they're winging this adventure as they go along.

The movie stars Bill Murray, Dan Aykroyd, and Harold Ramis, three graduates of the Second City/*National Lampoon*/"Saturday Night Live" tradition. They're funny, but they're not afraid to reveal that they're also quick-witted and intelligent; their dialogue puts nice little spins on American clichés, and it uses understatement, irony, in-jokes, vast cynicism, and cheerful goofiness. Rarely has a movie this expensive provided so many quotable lines.

The plot, such as it is, involves an epidemic of psychic nuisance reports in Manhattan. Murray, Ramis, and Aykroyd, defrocked parapsychologists whose university experiments have been exposed as pure boondoggle, create a company named Ghostbusters and offer to speed to the rescue like a supernatural version of the Orkin man. Business is bad until Sigourney Weaver notices that the eggs in her kitchen are frying themselves. Her next-door neighbor, Rick Moranis, notices horrifying monsters in the apartment hallways. They both apparently live in a building that serves as a conduit to the next world. The ghostbusters ride to the rescue, armed with nuclear-powered backpacks. There is a lot of talk about arcane details of psychic lore (most of which the ghostbusters are inventing on the spot), and then an earthshaking showdown between good and evil, during which Manhattan is menaced by a monster that is twenty stories high, and about which I cannot say one more word without spoiling the movie's best visual moment.

Ghostbusters is one of those rare movies where the original, fragile comic vision has survived a multimillion-dollar production. It is not a complete vindication for big-budget comedies, since it's still true, as a general rule, that the more you spend, the fewer laughs you get. But it uses its money wisely, and when that, ahem, monster marches down a Manhattan avenue and climbs the side of a skyscraper . . . we're glad they spent the money for the special effects because it gets one of the biggest laughs in a long time.

Gloria ★ ★ ★

PG, 123 m., 1980

Gena Rowlands (Gloria Swenson), John Adames (Phil), Buck Henry (Jack), Julie Carmen (Jeri Dawn). Directed by John Cassavetes and produced by Sam Shaw. Screenplay by Cassavetes.

Well, it's a cute idea for a movie, and maybe that's why they've had this particular idea so often. You start with tough-talking, streetwise gangster types, you hook them up with a little kid, you put them in fear of their lives, and then you milk the situation for poignancy, pathos, excitement, comedy, and anything else that turns up. It's the basic situation of *Little Miss Marker*, the Damon Runyon story that has been filmed three times. And now John Cassavetes tells it again in *Gloria*. The twists this time: The tough-talking gangster type is a woman, and the kid is Puerto Rican. Cassavetes has cast his wife, Gena Rowlands, in the title role, and it's an infectious performance—if infectious is the word to describe a chain-smoking dame who charges around town in her high heels, dragging a kid behind her.

The kid is also well cast. He's a youngster named John Adames who has dark hair and big eyes and a way of delivering his dialogue as if daring you to change one single word. Precisely because the material of this movie is so familiar, almost everything depends on the performances. And that's where Cassavetes saves the material and redeems the corniness of his story. Rowlands propels the action with such appealing nervous energy that we don't have the heart to stop and think how silly everything is.

The movie begins with a two-bit hoodlum (Buck Henry, an inexplicable casting choice) barricaded in an apartment with his Puerto Rican wife (Julie Carmen) and their kids. Men are going to come through the door at any moment with guns blazing. There's a knock on the door. It's Rowlands, as the neighbor, with the somehow inevitable name of Gloria Swenson. She wants to borrow sugar. She winds up with the kid. She doesn't want the kid. She doesn't like kids, she tells Henry: "Especially your kids." But the kid tags along. There's a shoot-out, the kid's family is dead, and things get even more complicated when it turns out that Henry gave his kid a notebook that has information in it the mob will kill to retrieve. That's the premise for the rest of the movie, which is a cat-and-mouse chase through the sleazier districts of New York and New Jersey.

Cassavetes has a nice eye for locale. There's a crummy flophouse where the clerk tells Rowlands, "Just pick a room. They're all open." There's a garishly decorated love nest that Rowlands occasionally occupies with a mobster. There are bus stations, back alleys, dimly lit hallways, and the kinds of bars that open at dawn and do most of their business by 9 A.M. (That provides one of the movie's best scenes. Gloria and the kid argue, Gloria tells the kid to split if that's the way he feels, and then she marches into the bar, orders a beer, lights a cigarette and says to the bartender: "Listen. There are reasons why I can't turn around and look . . . but is there a little kid heading in here?").

Cassavetes remains one of the most consistently interesting Hollywood mavericks. He makes money by acting, and immediately spends it producing his own films. Most of them are passionately indulgent of the actors, who sometimes repay his indulgence with inspired performances. Rowlands won an Oscar nomination for Cassavetes's *A Woman Under the Influence*. His next picture starred Ben Gazzara in *The Murder of a Chinese Bookie* (1978), which has become an unseen, lost film—better, if the truth be known, than *Gloria*, which is fun and engaging but slight. What saves this movie is Cassavetes's reliance on a tried-and-true plot construction. For once, his characters aren't all over the map in nonstop dialogue, as they were in *Husbands*, the talkathon he made in 1970 with Peter Falk, Gazzara, and himself. *Gloria* is tough, sweet, and goofy.

The Go-Between ★ ★ ★ ½

PG, 116 m., 1971

Julie Christie (Marian), Alan Bates (Ted Burgess), Dominic Guard (Leo, as a Boy), Margaret Leighton (Leo, as a Man), Michael Gough (Mr. Maudsley). Directed by Joseph Losey and produced by John Heyman. Screenplay by Harold Pinter.

There was a time, fairly recent, when the British upper classes thought it was a shade embarrassing to have to work for a living. Boys from middle-class families might attend the same school as upper-class boys, but they were tarnished, somehow, by their parents' direct contact with money. Money was something that needed to pass through a few sets of intervening hands, to let the sweat dry, before it could be spent by the aristocracy.

In a famous essay about English boarding schools, George Orwell delineated this delicate, cruel class distinction. He came from a white-collar family that made less than many blue-collar families, and yet had to present certain "standards" to the world. One of these was the necessity to send its children away to schools which, although they were shabby by Eton standards, were at least private. The children were the ones who suffered directly at the hands of class snobbism, of course, and sometimes their personalities were marked for life.

Joseph Losey's *The Go-Between* is about class distinction and its warping effect upon the life of one small boy. The story is set in the days before World War I, privileged days that seemed to stretch endlessly before the British upper class. The boy, Leo, comes to spend a summer holiday at the home of a rich friend. And he falls in hopeless schoolboy love with the friend's older sister (Julie Christie).

The sister is engaged to marry well, but she is in love with a roughshod tenant farmer (Alan Bates), and she enlists the boy to carry messages back and forth between them. The boy has only a shadowy notion at first about the significance of the messages, but during the summer he is sharply disillusioned about love, fidelity, and his own place in the great scheme of things.

Losey and his screenwriter, Harold Pinter, are terribly observant about small nuances of class. In the family's matriarch (Margaret Leighton) they give us a woman who seems to support the British class system all by herself, simply through her belief in it. They show a father and a fiancé who are aware of the girl's affair with the farmer, but do nothing about it. They are confident she will do the "right thing" in the end, and she does. "Why don't you marry Ted," the boy asks the young woman. "Because I can't," she replies. "Then why are you marrying Trimmington?" "Because I must."

She understands, and she is tough enough to endure. Indeed, at the end of the film she turns up years later as an old lady very much in the image of her mother. The victim is the boy, who is scarred sexually and emotionally by his summer experience. When we see him at the film's end, he is a sort of bloodless eunuch, called in to perform one last errand for the woman.

Losey's production is elegantly costumed and mounted and has the same eye for details of character that distinguished his two previous films with Pinter (*The Servant* and *Accident*). One visual device is distracting, however, he keeps giving us short flash-forwards to the end of the film. On the one hand, this eventually gives the ending away. On the other, it imposes a ponderous significance on the events that go before, diluting their freshness.

If the film had been told in straight chronology followed by an epilogue, it would have been more effective. In fact, the epilogue could have been lost altogether with no trouble; everything that will become of this boy in his adult life is already there, by implication, at the end of his summer holiday.

The Godfather ★ ★ ★ ★
R, 171 m., 1972

Marlon Brando (Don Vito Corleone), Al Pacino (Michael Corleone), James Caan (Sonny Corleone), Robert Duvall (Tom Hagen), Richard Castellano (Clemenza). Directed by Francis Ford Coppola and produced by Albert S. Ruddy. Screenplay by Mario Puzo.

We know from Gay Talese's book *Honor Thy Father* that being a professional mobster isn't all sunshine and roses. More often, it's the boredom of stuffy rooms and a bad diet of carry-out food, punctuated by brief, terrible bursts of violence. This is exactly the feel of *The Godfather*, which brushes aside the flashy glamour of the traditional gangster picture and gives us what's left: fierce tribal loyalties, deadly little neighborhood quarrels in Brooklyn, and a form of vengeance to match every affront.

The remarkable thing about Mario Puzo's novel was the way it seemed to be told from the inside out; he didn't give us a world of international intrigue, but a private club as constricted as the seventh grade. Everybody knew everybody else and had a pretty shrewd hunch what they were up to.

The movie (based on a script labored over for some time by Puzo and then finally given form, I suspect, by director Francis Ford Coppola) gets the same feel. We tend to identify with Don Corleone's family not because we dig gang wars, but because we have been with them from the beginning, watching them wait for battle while sitting at the kitchen table and eating chow mein out of paper cartons.

The Godfather himself is not even the central character in the drama. That position goes to the youngest, brightest son, Michael, who understands the nature of his father's position while revising his old-fashioned ways. The Godfather's role in the family enterprise is described by his name; he stands outside the next generation which will carry on and, hopefully, angle the family into legitimate enterprises.

Those who have read the novel may be surprised to find Michael at the center of the movie, instead of Don Corleone. In fact, this is simply an economical way for Coppola to get at the heart of the Puzo story, which dealt with the transfer of power within the family. Marlon Brando, who plays the Godfather as a shrewd, unbreakable old man, actually has the character lead in the movie; Al Pacino, with a brilliantly developed performance as Michael, is the lead.

But Brando's performance is a skillful throwaway, even though it earned him an Academy Award for best actor. His voice is wheezy and whispery, and his physical movements deliberately lack precision; the effect is of a man so accustomed to power that he no longer needs to remind others. Brando does look the part of old Don Corleone, mostly because of acting and partly because of the makeup, although he seems to have stuffed a little too much cotton into his jowls, making his lower face immobile.

The best of the actors supply one example after another of inspired casting. Although *The Godfather* is a long, minutely detailed movie of some three hours, there naturally isn't time to go into the backgrounds and identities of such characters as Clemenza, the family lieutenant; Jack Woltz, the movie czar; Luca Brasi, the loyal professional killer; McCluskey, the crooked cop, and the rest. Coppola and producer Al Ruddy skirt this problem with understated typecasting. As the Irish cop, for example, they simply slide in Sterling Hayden and let the character go about his business. Richard Castellano is an unshakable Clemenza. John Marley makes a perfectly hateful Hollywood mogul (and, yes, he still wakes up to find he'll have to cancel his day at the races).

The success of *The Godfather* as a novel was largely due to a series of unforgettable scenes. Puzo is a good storyteller, but no great shakes as a writer. The movie gives almost everything in the novel except the gynecological repair job. It doesn't miss a single killing; it opens with the wedding of Don Corleone's daughter (and attendant upstairs activity); and there are the right number of auto bombs, double crosses, and garretings.

Coppola has found a style and a visual look for all this material so *The Godfather* becomes something of a rarity: a really good movie squeezed from a bestseller. The decision to shoot everything in period decor (the middle and late 1940s) was crucial; if they'd tried to save money as they originally planned, by bringing everything up-to-date, the movie simply wouldn't have worked. But it's uncannily successful as a period piece, filled with sleek, bulging limousines and postwar fedoras. Coppola and his cinematographer, Gordon Willis, also do some interesting things with the color photography. The earlier scenes have a reddish-brown tint, slightly overexposed and feeling like nothing so much as a 1946 newspaper rotogravure supplement.

Although the movie is three hours long, it absorbs us so effectively it never has to hurry. There is something in the measured passage of time as Don Corleone hands over his reins of power that would have made a shorter, faster moving film unseemly. Even at this length, there are characters in relationships you can't quite understand unless you've read the novel. Or perhaps you can, just by the way the characters look at each other.

The Godfather, Part II ★ ★ ★
R, 200 m., 1974

Al Pacino (Michael), Robert Duvall (Tom Hagen), Diane Keaton (Kay), Robert De Niro (Don Vito Corleone), John Cazale (Fredo), Lee Strasberg (Hyman Roth), G.D. Spradlin (Senator Geary). Directed by Francis Ford Coppola and produced by Gray Frederickson and Fred Ross. Screenplay by Coppola and Mario Puzo.

Moving through the deep shadows and heavy glooms of his vast estate, Michael Corleone presides over the destruction of his own spirit in *The Godfather, Part II*. The character we recall from *The Godfather* as the best and brightest of Don Vito's sons, the one who went to college and enlisted in the Marines, grows into a cold and ruthless man, obsessed with power. The film's closing scenes give us first a memory of a long-ago family dinner, and then Michael at mid-life, cruel, closed, and lonely. He's clearly intended as a tragic figure.

The Corleone saga, as painted by Francis Ford Coppola and Mario Puzo in two films totaling nearly seven hours, has been a sort of success story in reverse. In a crazy way, *The Godfather* and its sequel belong in the same category with those other epics of immigrant achievement in America, *The Emigrants* and *The New Land*. The Corleone family worked hard, was ambitious, remembered friends, never forgave disloyalty, and started from humble beginnings to become the most powerful Mafia organization in the country. If it were not that the family business was crime, these films could be an inspiration for us all.

Coppola seems to hold a certain ambivalence toward his material. Don Vito Corleone as portrayed by Marlon Brando in *The Godfather* was a man of honor and dignity, and it was difficult not to sympathize with him, playing with his grandchild in the garden, at peace after a long lifetime of murder, extortion, and the rackets. What exactly were we supposed to think about him? How did Coppola feel toward the Godfather?

The Godfather, Part II moves both forward and backward in time from the events in *The Godfather*, in an attempt to resolve our feelings about the Corleones. In doing so, it provides for itself a structural weakness from which the film never recovers, but it does something even more disappointing: It reveals a certain simplicity in Coppola's notions of motivation and characterization that wasn't there in the elegant masterpiece of his earlier film.

He gives us, first of all, the opening chapters in Don Vito's life. His family is killed by a Mafia don in Sicily, he comes to America at the age of nine, he grows up (to be played by Robert De Niro), and edges into a career of crime, first as a penny-ante crook and then as a neighborhood arranger and power broker: a man, as the movie never tires of reminding us, of respect.

This story, of Don Vito's younger days, occupies perhaps a fourth of the film's 200 minutes. Coppola devotes the rest to Michael Corleone, who has taken over the family's business after his father's death, has pulled out of New York, and consolidated operations in Nevada, and has ambitions to expand in Florida and Cuba. Michael is played, again and brilliantly, by Al Pacino, and among the other familiar faces are Robert Duvall as Tom Hagen, the family's lawyer; Diane Keaton as Michael's increasingly despairing wife Kay; and John Cazale as the weak older brother Fredo.

Coppola handles a lot of this material very well. As in the earlier film, he reveals himself as a master of mood, atmosphere, and period. And his exposition is inventive and subtle. The film requires the intelligent participation of the viewer; as Michael attempts to discover who betrayed him and attempted his assassination, he tells different stories to different people, keeping his own counsel, and we have to think as he does so we can tell the truth from the lies.

Pacino is very good at suggesting the furies and passions that lie just beneath his character's controlled exterior. He gives us a Michael who took over the family with the intention of making it "legitimate" in five years, but who is drawn more and more deeply into a byzantine web of deceit and betrayal, all papered over with code words like respect, honor, and gratitude. By the film's end he has been abandoned by almost everyone except those who work for him and fear him, and he is a very lonely man.

But what was his sin? It was not, as we might have imagined or hoped, that he presided over a bloody enterprise of murder and destruction. No, Michael's fault seems to be pride. He has lost the common touch, the dignity he should have inherited from his father. And because he has misplaced his humanity he must suffer.

Coppola suggests this by contrast. His scenes about Don Vito's early life could almost be taken as a campaign biography, and in the most unfortunate flashbacks we're given the young Vito intervening on behalf of a poor widow who is being evicted from her apartment. The don seems more like a precinct captain than a gangster, and we're left with the unsettling impression that Coppola thinks things would have turned out all right for Michael if he'd had the old man's touch.

The flashbacks give Coppola the greatest difficulty in maintaining his pace and narrative force. The story of Michael, told chronologically and without the other material, would have had really substantial impact, but Coppola prevents our complete involvement by breaking the tension. The flashbacks to New York in the early 1900s have a different, a nostalgic tone, and the audience has to keep shifting gears. Coppola was reportedly advised by friends to forget the Don Vito material and stick with Michael, and that was good advice.

There's also some evidence in the film that Coppola never completely mastered the chaotic mass of material in his screenplay. Some scenes seem oddly pointless (why do we get almost no sense of Michael's actual dealings in Cuba, but lots of expensive footage about the night of Castro's takeover?), and others seem not completely explained (I am still not quite sure who really did order that attempted garroting in the Brooklyn saloon).

What we're left with, then, are a lot of good scenes and good performances set in the midst of a mass of undisciplined material and handicapped by plot construction that prevents the story from ever really building.

There is, for example, the brilliant audacity of the first communion party for Michael's son, which Coppola directs as counterpoint to the wedding scene that opened *The Godfather*. There is Lee Strasberg's two-edged performance as Hyman Roth, the boss of the Florida and Cuban operations; Strasberg gives us a soft-spoken, almost kindly old man, and then reveals his steel-hard interior. There is Coppola's use of sudden, brutal bursts of violence to punctuate the film's brooding progress. There is Pacino, suggesting everything, telling nothing.

But Coppola is unable to draw all this together and make it work on the level of simple, absorbing narrative. The stunning text of *The Godfather* is replaced in *Part II* with prologues, epilogues, footnotes, and good intentions.

The Gods Must Be Crazy ★ ★ ★

PG, 109 m., 1984

N!xau (Xi), Marius Weyers (Andrew Steyn), Sandra Prinsloo (Kate Thompson), Louw Verwey (Sam Boga), James Uys (The Reverend). Directed and produced by Jamie Uys. Screenplay by Uys.

Here's a movie that begins with a Coke bottle falling from the heavens, and ends with a Jeep up in a tree. *The Gods Must Be Crazy* is a South African movie that arrived in Europe with little fanfare in 1982, broke box office records in Japan and South America and all over Europe, and even became a cult hit here in North America, where there has not been much of a demand for comedies from South Africa.

The film begins in the Kalahari Desert. A pilot in a private plane throws his empty Coke bottle out of the window. It lands near a Bushman who is on a hunting expedition. He has never seen anything like it before. He takes it back to his tribe, where it is put to dozens of uses: It becomes a musical instrument, a patternmaker, a fire starter, a cooking utensil, and, most of all, an object of bitter controversy. Everybody in the tribe ends up fighting over the bottle, and so the Bushman, played by the Xhosa actor N!xau (the exclamathoint represents a click), decides there is only one thing to do: He must return the bottle to the gods. This decision sends him on a long odyssey toward more settled lands on the edges of the desert, where the movie develops into a somewhat more conventional comedy.

We meetPtr some of the new characters: A would-be schoolteacher, a goofy biologist, and an insurgent leader. They are all intent on their own lives and plans, but in one way or another, the Xhosa and his Coke bottle bring them together into unexpected combinations. And the director, Jamie Uys, has the patience to develop some really elaborate sight gags, which require a lot of preparation but pay off with big laughs—particularly the sequence with an indecisive, back-and-forth Jeep.

The star of the movie is N!xau, who is so forthright and cheerful and sensible that his very presence makes some of the gags pay off. In any slapstick comedy, the gags must rest on a solid basis of logic: It's not funny to watch people being ridiculous, but it is funny to watch people doing the next logical thing, and turning out to be ridiculous. N!xau, because he approaches Western society without preconceptions, and bases all of his actions on logical conclusions, brings into relief a lot of the little tics and assumptions of everyday life. I think that reveals the thought that went into this movie: It might be easy to make a farce about screwball happenings in the desert, but it's a lot harder to create a funny interaction between nature and human nature. This movie's a nice little treasure.

Godspell ★ ★ ★ ★

G, 102 m., 1973 ✓

Victor Garber (Jesus), David Haskell (John, Judas), Jerry Sroka (Jerry), Lynne Thigpen (Lynne), Katie Hanley (Katie), Robin Lamont (Robin), Gilmer McCormick (Gilmer), Joanne Jonas (Joanne), Merrell Jackson (Merrell), Jeffrey Mylett (Jeffrey). Directed by David Greene.

The thing about *Godspell* that caught my heart was its simplicity, its refusal to pretend to be anything more than it is. It's not a message for our times, or a movie to cash in on the Jesus movement, or even quite a youth movie. It's a series of stories and songs, like the Bible is, and it's told with the directness that simple stories need: with no tricks, no intellectual gadgets, and a lot of openness.

This was the quality that attracted me to the stage version. I had to be almost dragged to the play, because its subject matter sounded so depressingly contemporary. But after I finally got into the theatre and sat down and let *Godspell* relax me, I found myself simply letting it happen. For a musical based on the Gospel according to St. Matthew, *Godspell* is strangly irreverent, wacky, and endearing.

The stage version has been opened up into a movie by taking the whole of New York as a set. Except for the scenes at the beginning and end—which show the city as a temple of mammon and a rat nest—the movie is populated only by its cast; we don't see anybody else, and the ten kids dance, sing, and act out parables in such unlikely places as the World Trade Center and a tugboat. This is a new use for New York, which looks unusually clean; even its tacky skyscrapers edge toward grandeur when the vast long shots engulf them.

Against this wilderness of steel and concrete, the characters come on like kids at a junior high reunion, clothed in comic book colors and bright tattered rags. Only two have names: Jesus, and a character who plays both John (who ushered Jesus into the Bible) and Judas (who hastened him out). The other eight characters, who seem to represent an on-the-spot gathering of disciples, are just themselves.

What's nice about the casting—which gives us all new faces—is that the characters don't look like professional stage youths. Remember *West Side Story*, where all the allegedly teen-age dancers looked like hardened theatrical professionals in greaser wigs? *Godspell*'s cast is not only young but is allowed to look like a collection of individuals. These could conceivably be real people, and their freshness helps put the material over even when it seems pretty obvious. For some blessed reason the director, David Greene, has resisted any temptation to make the movie visually fancy. With material of this sort, there must have been an impulse to go for TV-commercial trendiness, but Greene's style is unforced, and goes well with the movie's freshness and basic colors.

The movie characters, like the stage characters, are given little watercolor designs on their faces by Jesus. A girl gets a little yellow flower, a boy gets a tiny red star, and so on. It was necessary in the stage version to exaggerate this makeup to make it visible, but the movie underplays it and it was gentle and nice. It occurred to me, about an hour into the film, that maybe young people will pick up on this. Tattoos were big in the 70s—little butterflies and stars—so why not face-paint zigzags and pinwheels and flowers? Anything to brighten up this miserable world: Which is what *Godspell* is saying, anyway.

The Golden Child ★ ★ ★
PG-13 94 m., 1986

Eddie Murphy (Chandler), Charlotte Lewis (Kee Nang), Charles Dance (Sardo), Victor Wong (Old Man), J.L. Reate (Golden Child), "Tex" Cobb (Til Randall), James Hong (Dr. Wong). Directed by Michael Ritchie and produced by Edward S. Feldman and Robert D. Wachs. Screenplay by Dennis Feldman.

There are a lot of moments to remember in *The Golden Child*, but the one I will treasure the longest happens when Eddie Murphy gets behind the wheel of a beat-up station wagon and is led by a sacred parrot to the lair of the devil.

Maybe you had to be there. The parrot, which has already made the round-trip between Tibet and Los Angeles twice, chirps merrily and flies off down a dusty road. Murphy leans down to look up at it through his windshield, and the way he looks at it is what started me laughing. There is just something about the tilt of his head that seems entirely appropriate for a man who is following a sacred parrot. Murphy is exactly right in that moment, but then he is exactly right all through this movie, which is utterly ridiculous and jolly good fun.

The advance rumors about *The Golden Child* were not encouraging. I heard Paramount feared it had a bomb on its hands, but what were they worried about? The preview audience laughed all through the movie. No wonder, because this film—insignificant and lightweight and monumentally silly—is entertaining from beginning to end. Although it contains the usual scatological language, the sex and violence are mild.

Murphy plays the hero, a professional searcher for lost children. After agents from hell kidnap a holy child from Tibet, Murphy is recruited to recover the child, find a magic dagger, defeat Satan's henchmen, beat up some Hell's Angels, pass several death-defying trials by fire, follow the sacred parrot, and fall in love with the beautiful heroine who must first be brought back from the dead. You know, the usual stuff.

The movie's opening shots should have had a subtitle flashing "Raiders Rip-off!" Hollywood must have a whole industry supplying temples and gongs to the spawn of Indiana Jones. But from the moment Murphy appears on the screen, he makes the movie all his own; the special effects are basically just comic props. Murphy slides through the picture with easy wisecracks and unflappable cool, like a hip Bob Hope.

A lot of the time, he seems to improvise his wise-ass one-liners—I haven't seen the script, and so I can't say for sure. What's amazing is that his dialogue always seems to fit. A lot of stand-up comedians throw off the pacing in a movie by going for improv at the wrong moments (Robin Williams is sometimes an example). Murphy usually seems to have the perfect reaction, even when he's shocked to catch a wise old seer picking his nose. Maybe the director, Michael Ritchie, deserves some of the credit for that; he let Williams wreck his *The Survivors* with inappropriate one-liners, but this time everything flows.

The movie's plot is an anthology of clichés from every Oriental swashbuckler in history; just off the top of my head I can remember a bottomless cavern, a 300-year-old woman with a dragon's tail, a child whose touch turns bad men into good ones, an evil spirit that turns into a serpent, several dozen temple guards, countless karate fights, secret rooms beneath the stores in Chinatown, and, of course, the preternaturally beautiful heroine.

Her name is Kee Nang, and she is played by Charlotte Lewis, the London schoolgirl who starred in Roman Polanski's *Pirates*. That movie won her an audience of dozens; this one will likely do a lot better. She is very beautiful, and since that is her role in this movie, she fulfills it flawlessly. She also does a good job of keeping a straight face while Murphy uses her as the subject of speculation, rejection, romance, and betrayal and while she uses her effortless mastery of kung fu to protect him.

No silly swashbuckler is any better than its villain, and the leader of the evil forces is played by Charles Dance, last seen as Meryl Streep's coldly intellectual husband in *Plenty*. He, too, has to keep a straight face through this movie, in scenes such as the one where Murphy outsmarts him at airport customs and the scene where he turns into a rat. There's also good work from Victor Wong, who plays a wise old man in several different costumes and accents.

The Golden Child may not be the Eddie Murphy movie we were waiting for, but it will do. It is funnier, more assured and more tailored to Murphy than *Beverly Hills Cop* and it shows a side of his comic persona that I don't think has been much appreciated: his essential underlying sweetness. Murphy's comedy is not based here on hurt and aggression, but on affection and an understanding that comes from seeing right through the other characters. His famous laugh is not aimed as a weapon at anybody, but is truly amused. He is perfectly suited to survive this cheerfully ridiculous movie, and even lend it a little charm.

The Goodbye Girl ★ ★ ★

PG, 110 m., 1977

Richard Dreyfuss (Elliott Garfield), Marsha Mason (Paula McFadden), Quinn Cummings (Lucy McFadden), Paul Benedict (Mark), Barbara Rhoades (Donna), Theresa Merritt (Mrs. Crosby). Directed by Herbert Ross and produced by Ray Stark. Screenplay by Neil Simon.

Neil Simon's *The Goodbye Girl* is a funny movie with its heart finally in the right place, but all sorts of unacknowledged complications lurk just beneath its polished surface. The surface is pure Simon, which means that it's a funny-sad-tough-warm story about basically nice people who are given just three snappy one-liners too many to be totally human. But this time Simon has slipped in some subtleties we might miss the first time around.

The story's about three people we can instantly identify with. There's the former actress (Marsha Mason) and her cute ten-year-old daughter (Quinn Cummings), and the would-be actor from Chicago (Richard Dreyfuss). Until the moment before the movie opens, Miss Mason has been living with another actor in an apartment on New York's Upper East Side, where apartments are harder to find than cabs, which are harder to find than plumbers who make house calls on Sunday (which is a Simon kind of progression).

Miss Mason and her daughter come home to find that her roommate, that rat, has jumped the boat. He leaves a note explaining that he's got a great role in the new Bertolucci picture in Europe—and lotsa luck, kid. That's bad enough. Worse is when she finds out that the apartment has been sublet to this actor from Chicago, who's paid three months' rent and, reasonably enough, expects to move in, especially since at the moment he's standing in the rain.

After the two of them shout at each other for a sufficient period of time, she does allow him to move in (he gets the smaller bedroom). And then we know the basic plot structure: Total warfare in the apartment will de-escalate into a guarded truce, followed by alternating forays of warmth and decency, until the kid acts as a catalyst and they fall in love.

Wonderful. Not so wonderful is the way the Marsha Mason character is written and acted. She's hardly ever sympathetic. Sure, she's been burned by a lot of guys—but she's so hard-edged you wonder how she met them in the first place. She sees the situation strictly in economic terms, consistently behaves as a bitch, and gives Dreyfuss no reason for getting to like her.

Dreyfuss, on the other hand, is great. Eccentric, yes, since Simon always gives his characters off-the-wall touches to make them human (he meditates, plays his guitar in the middle of the night, sleeps in the nude, eats health food, etc.). But he's a nice guy. He's trapped in this weird off-off-off-Broadway production of Shakespeare's *Richard III*, and the director is convinced Richard should be played as a gay (the scenes involving the production, performance, and reception of the play are the funniest in a movie since Mel Brooks staged *Springtime for Hitler*). He fears, rightly, that the play could be the end of his New York career, and his fears are played against the unsympathetic Mason character and her basically lovable daughter.

He finally wins the mother through her child ("Listen, I can't stand you, but you got a ten-year-old in there I'm nuts about . . ."). But why does he want to? Simon short-circuits the first scene in which Mason says a decent and warm word by having Dreyfuss fall asleep so he doesn't hear it. He never really provides the dialogue and situations we need to *like* the female character—and so, in a funny way, we *aren't* rooting for them to get together. When they do, though, the movie works best. The first hour is awkward at times and never quite involving, but some of the later scenes, especially a dinner on a rooftop and the way Dreyfuss receives the disastrous reviews of his play, are really fine. It's strange: We leave the movie having enjoyed its conclusion so much that we almost forgot our earlier reservations. But they were there, and they were real.

Good Morning, Vietnam ★ ★ ★ ★

R, 119 m., 1988

Robin Williams (Adrian Cronauer), Forest Whitaker (Edward Garlick), Tung Thanh Tran (Tuan), Chintara Sukapatana (Trinh), Bruno Kirby (Lieutenant Hauk), Robert Wuhl (Marty Lee Dreiwitz), J.T. Walsh (Sergeant Dickerson), Noble Willingham (General Taylor). Directed by Barry Levinson and produced by Mark Johnson and Larry Brezner. Screenplay by Mitch Markowitz.

Like most of the great stand-up comedians, Robin Williams has always kept a certain wall between himself and his audience. If you watch his concert videos, you see him trying on a bewildering series of accents and characters; he's a gifted chameleon who turns into whatever makes the audience laugh. But who is inside?

With George Carlin, Richard Pryor, Steve Martin, Billy Crystal, Eddie Murphy, we have an idea—or think we do. A lot of their humor depends on confessional autobiography. With Robin Williams, the wall remains impenetrable. Like Groucho Marx, he uses comedy as a strategy for personal concealment.

Williams's best movies (*Popeye, The World According to Garp, Moscow on the Hudson*) are the ones where he is given a well-written character to play, and held to the character by a strong director. In his other movies, you can see him trying to do his stand-up act on the screen, trying to use comedy to conceal not only himself from the audience—but even his character. The one-liners and ad-libs distance him from the material and from his fellow actors. Hey, he's only a visitor here.

What is inspired about *Good Morning, Vietnam,* which contains far and away the best work Williams has ever done in a movie, is that his own tactics are turned against him. The director, Barry Levinson, has created a character who *is* a stand-up comic—he's a fast-talking disc jockey on Armed Forces Radio during the Vietnam War, directing a non-stop monologue at the microphone. There is absolutely no biographical information about this character. We don't know where he comes from, what he did before the war, whether he's ever been married, what his dreams are, what he's afraid of. Everything in his world is reduced to material for his program.

Levinson used Mitch Markowitz's script as a starting point for a lot of Williams's monologues, and then let the comedian improvise. Then he put together the best parts of many different takes to create sequences that are undeniably dazzling and funny. Williams is a virtuoso.

But while he's assaulting the microphone, Levinson is doing something fairly subtle in the movie around him. He has populated *Good Morning, Vietnam* with a lot of character actors who are fairly complicated types, recognizably human, and with the aid of the script, they set a trap for Williams. His character is edged into a corner where he *must* have human emotions, or die.

The character (his name is Adrian Cronauer) resists. At one point his Jeep breaks down in the middle of the jungle in Viet Cong territory, and he starts using one-liners on the trees. He meets a Vietnamese girl he likes, and uses one-liners on her, too, in a genuine exercise in cynicism since she doesn't understand any of his humor. He runs afoul of top Army brass that doesn't approve of his anti-establishment tone on the radio, and he wisecracks at them, too, trying to insist that he's always on stage, that nothing is real, that the whole war is basically just material.

And then things happen. To impress the girl and her brother, he starts teaching an English-language class for the Vietnamese. He finds that he likes them. He witnesses (and barely survives) a particularly gruesome terrorist attack. He gets thrown off the radio. He meets some kids who are going into battle, and who admire him, and in their eyes he sees something that makes him start to take himself a little more seriously. By the end of the movie, Cronauer has turned into a better, deeper, wiser man than he was at the beginning; the movie is the story of his education.

I know there are other ways to read this material. *Good Morning, Vietnam* works as straight comedy, and it works as a Vietnam-era *M*A*S*H,* and even the movie's love story has its own bittersweet integrity. But they used to tell us in writing class that if we wanted to know what a story was really about, we should look for what changed between the beginning and the end. In this movie, Cronauer changes. War wipes the grin off of his face. His humor becomes a humanitarian tool, not simply a way to keep him talking and us listening.

In a strange, subtle way, *Good Morning, Vietnam* is not so much about war as it is about stand-up comedy, about the need that compels people to get up in front of the room and try to make us laugh—to control us.

Why do comics do that? Because they need to have their power proven and vindicated. Why do they need that? Because they are the most insecure of earth's people (just listen to their language—they're gonna kill us, unless they die out there). How do you treat low self-esteem? By doing estimable things and then saying, hey, I did that! What happens to Cronauer in this movie? Exactly that. By the end of the film he doesn't wisecrack all the time because he doesn't need to. He no longer thinks he's the worthless (although bright, fast and funny) sack of crap that got off the plane. In the early scenes of the movie, the character's eyes are opaque. By the end, you can see what he's thinking.

The Goonies ★ ★ ★

PG, 114 m., 1985

Sean Astin (Mikey), Josh Brolin (Brand), Jeff Cohen (Chunk), Corey Feldman (Mouth), Kerri Green (Andy), Martha Plimpton (Stef), and Ke Huy Quan (Data). Directed by Richard Donner and produced by Donner and Harvey Bernhard. Executive producer, Steven Spielberg. Screenplay by Chris Columbus.

The Goonies is a smooth mixture of the usual ingredients from Steven Spielberg action movies, made special because of the high-energy performances of the kids who have the adventures. It's a fantastical story of buried pirate treasure, told with a slice-of-life approach that lets these kids use words Bogart didn't know in *Casablanca.* There used to be children's movies and adult movies. Now Spielberg has found an in-between niche, for young teen-agers who have fairly sophisticated tastes in horror. He supervises the formula and oversees the production, assigning the direction to stylish action veterans (this time, it's Richard Donner, of *Superman* and *Ladyhawke*).

Goonies, like *Gremlins,* walks a thin line between the cheerful and the gruesome, and the very scenes the adults might object to are the ones the kids will like the best: Spielberg is congratulating them on their ability to take the heavy-duty stuff. The movie begins with an assortment of engaging boys, including a smart kid, a kid with braces, a fat kid, an older brother, and an Asian kid whose clothing conceals numerous inventions. Along the way they pick up a couple of girls, whose function is to swap spit and get bats in their hair. The kids find an old treasure map and blunder into the hideout of a desperate gang of criminals—two brothers, led by a Ma Barker type. There is a third brother, a Quasimodish freak, who is kept chained down in the cellar, where he watches TV. The tunnels to the treasure begin under the hideout. The kids find the tunnels while fleeing from the bad guys, and then go looking for the treasure with the crooks on their tails. There are lots of special effects and among the set pieces are the same kinds of booby traps that Indiana Jones survived in *Raiders* (falling boulders, sharp spikes), and a toboggan ride on a water chute that will remind you of the runaway train in *The Temple of Doom.*

If the ingredients are familiar from Spielberg's high-powered action movies, the kids are inspired by *E.T.* The single most important line of dialogue in any Spielberg movie is probably the line in *E.T.* when one kid calls another kid "penis-breath." The dialogue hears and acknowledges the precocious way that kids incorporate vulgarity into their conversations, especially with each other; the line in *E.T.* created such a shock of recognition that the laughs swept away any objections.

This time, his kids say "shit" a lot, and it is a measure of Spielberg's insight that the word draws only a PG rating for the movie; Spielberg no doubt argues that most kids talk like that half the time, and he is right. His technique is to take his 13- and 14-year-olds and let them act a little older than their age. It's more refreshing than the old Disney technique, which was to take characters of all ages and have them behave as if they were 12.

Another Spielberg trademark, faithfully achieved by Donner, is a breakneck narrative speed. More things happen in this movie than in six ordinary action films. There's not just a thrill a minute; there's a thrill, a laugh, a shock, and a special effect. The screenplay has all the kids talking all at once, all the time, and there were times, especially in the first reel, when I couldn't understand much of what they were saying. The movie needs to be played loud, and with extra treble.

During *Goonies,* I was often exhilarated by what was happening. Afterwards, I was less enthusiastic. The movie is totally manipulative, which would be okay, except it doesn't have the lift of a film like *E.T.* It has the high energy without the sweetness. It uses what it knows about kids to churn them up, while *E.T.* gave them things to think about, the values to enjoy. *Goonies,* like *Gremlins,* shows that Spielberg and his directors are absolute masters of how to excite and involve an audience. *E.T.* was more like *Close Encounters;* it didn't simply want us to feel, but also to wonder, and to dream.

Gorky Park ★ ★ ★ ½

R, 128 m., 1983

William Hurt (Arkady Renko), Lee Marvin (Jack Osborne), Joanna Pakula (Irina), Brian Dennehy (Kirwell), Ian Bannen (Iamskoy). Directed by Michael Apted and produced by Gene Kirkwood and Howard W. Koch, Jr. Screenplay by Dennis Potter.

Mystery fans talk about the "police procedural," a crime novel that follows police work, step by meticulous step, from the opening of a case to its eventual resolution. The crimes aren't always solved, but then the solution isn't really the point. Instead, "procedurals" are a way to study human nature under stress, to see how a society works from the inside out and the bottom up. There are procedurals set all over the world, from Ed McBain's 87th Precinct on the East coast to the Martin Beck thrillers in Stockholm, but Martin Cruz Smith's *Gorky Park* was the first good police procedural set in Russia. It used the procedural approach to show us an honest cop under pressure, a system that functioned only through corruption, and a conflict between socialism and Russia's homegrown capitalism.

This is the movie of that book, and it has all of the same strengths. It begins with a shocking murder (three corpses found frozen in the snow with their faces and fingerprints removed). There are no clues. A police inspector named Renko (William Hurt) is assigned to the case, and makes it his personal crusade. He recruits a physical anthropologist to try to re-create the missing faces on the bodies. He prowls the black market, where deals are made in Western currency. He meets a beautiful young woman and a mysterious American businessman. And he learns about the obsessive power of sable fur coats.

The investigation of the crime has a fascination of its own, but what makes *Gorky Park* really interesting is its views of Soviet cops, criminals, bureaucrats, and ordinary citizens. As Renko gets closer and closer to a solution to the case, his investigation leads him to powerful circles in the Soviet Union. And his heart, of course, leads him closer to the girl, who may have all of the necessary information but has been so warped by paranoia that she refuses to betray those she thinks are her friends.

The movie is directed with efficiency by Michael *(Coal Miner's Daughter)* Apted, who knows that pacing is indispensable to a procedural. Too long a pause for anything—

romance, detail, speculation, explanation—and the spell is broken. He uses actors who are able to bring fully realized characters to the screen, so we don't have to stand around waiting for introductions. That involves a certain amount of typecasting. Lee Marvin, gravel-voiced, white-haired, expensively dressed, is perfect for the businessman. Joanna Pakula, a young Polish actress in her first Western role, is beautiful, vulnerable, wide-eyed, and fresh—and as an exile stranded in Paris when her Warsaw theater was closed by Poland's martial law, she doesn't have to fake her paranoia about the Soviet state.

William Hurt, as Renko, is probably the key to the picture. He makes this cop into a particular kind of person, cold, at times willfully blinded by duty, sublimating his feelings in his profession, until this case breaks him wide open. By the end of *Gorky Park*, we realize that it's not the solution that matters, but what the case itself forces the people to discover about themselves.

The Great Gatsby ★ ★ 1/2

PG, 146 m., 1974

Robert Redford (Gatsby), Mia Farrow (Daisy Buchanan), Bruce Dern (Tom Buchanan), Karen Black (Myrtle Wilson), Scott Wilson (George Wilson), Sam Waterston (Nick Carraway), Lois Chiles (Jordan Baker), Howard Da Silva (Meyer Wolfsheim), Robert Blossom (Mr. Gatz), Edward Hermann (Klipspringer). Directed by Jack Clayton and produced by David Merrick. Screenplay by Francis Ford Coppola.

The Great Gatsby is a superficially beautiful hunk of a movie with nothing much in common with the spirit of F. Scott Fitzgerald's novel. I wonder what Fitzgerald, whose prose was so graceful, so elegantly controlled, would have made of it: of the willingness to spend so much time and energy on exterior effect while never penetrating to the souls of the characters. It would take about the same time to read Fitzgerald's novel as to view this movie—and that's what I'd recommend.

The movie is "faithful" to the novel with a vengeance—to what happens in the novel, that is, and not to the feel, mood, and spirit of it. Yet I've never thought the events in *The Great Gatsby* were that important to the novel's success; Fitzgerald, who came out of St. Paul to personify the romance of an age, was writing in a way about himself when he created Gatsby. The mundane Midwestern origins had been replaced by a new persona, by a flash and charisma that sometimes only concealed the despair underneath. For Fitzgerald, there was always something unattainable; and for Gatsby, it was Daisy Buchanan, the lost love of his youth, forever symbolized by that winking green beacon at the end of her dock.

The beacon and the other Fitzgerald symbols are in this movie version, but they communicate about as much as the great stone heads on Easter Island. They're memorials to a novel in which they had meaning. The art director and set decorator seem to have ripped whole pages out of Fitzgerald and gone to work to improve on his descriptions. Daisy and her husband, the ruthless millionaire Tom Buchanan, live almost drowning in whites, yellows, and ennui. Tom's mistress Myrtle and her husband, the shabby filling station owner George, live in a wasteland of ashes in Fitzgerald's novel; in the movie, they seem to have landed on the moon.

All of this unfeeling physical excess might have been overcome by performances. But the director, Jack Clayton, having assembled a promising cast, fails to exploit them very well. When the casting of Robert Redford as Jay Gatsby was announced, I objected because he didn't fit my notion of Gatsby: He was too substantial, too assured, even too handsome. I saw him as Tom Buchanan, and somebody else as Gatsby (Jack Nicholson, maybe, or Bruce Dern—who plays Tom). Having seen the movie, I think maybe I was wrong: Redford could have played Gatsby. I'm not even sure it's his fault he doesn't. The first time Clayton shows us Gatsby, it's a low angle shot of a massive figure seen against the night sky and framed by marble: This isn't the romantic Gatsby on his doomed quest, it's Charles Foster Kane. A scene where Gatsby reaches out as if to snatch the green beacon in his hand is true to the book, but the movie's literal showing of it looks silly.

These hints of things to come lead up to two essential scenes in which Clayton fails to give us a Gatsby we care about. The first is the initial meeting between Gatsby and Nick

(Gatsby wants Nick, his neighbor and Daisy's cousin, to invite her to tea so they can meet again). Redford is so inarticulate and formal in this scene with Nick that we laugh; it's the first time we hear him talk, and he's so mannered that the acting upstages the content of the scene. Doesn't that have to be Clayton's fault? We know Redford has range enough to have played the scene in several better ways. And then the actul reunion between Gatsby and Daisy—the moment on which the rest of the movie is going to depend—gives us Gatsby's toothpaste grin and Daisy's stunned reaction and holds both for so long that any tension reduces itself to the ridiculous. It doesn't even feel as if Gatsby's happy to see Daisy—more that he assumes she's overjoyed to see him.

The message of the novel, if I read it correctly, is that Gatsby, despite his dealings with gamblers and bootleggers, is a romantic, naive, and heroic product of the Midwest—and that his idealism is doomed in any confrontation with the reckless wealth of the Buchanans. This doesn't come through in the movie. When Nick, at his last meeting with Gatsby, tells him how much he admires him ("You're worth the whole crowd of them"), we frankly don't know why unless we've read the book. Oh, we're *told*, to be sure: The sound track contains narration by Nick that is based pretty closely on his narration in the novel. But we don't feel. We've been distanced by the movie's overproduction. Even the actors seem somewhat cowed by the occasion; an exception is Bruce Dern, who just goes ahead and gives us a convincing Tom Buchanan. We don't have to be told the ways in which Tom is indifferent to human feeling, because we can sense them.

But we can't penetrate the mystery of Gatsby. Nor, to be honest, can we quite understand what's so special about Daisy Buchanan. Not as she's played by Mia Farrow, all squeaks and narcissism and empty sophistication. In the novel, Gatsby never understands that he is too good for Daisy. In the movie, we never understand why he thought she was good enough for him. And that's what's missing.

That, and one other small item: How could a screenplay that plundered Fitzgerald's novel so literally, that quoted so much of the narration and dialogue, have ended with a rinky-dink version of "Ain't We Got Fun" instead of the most famous last sentence of any novel of the century? Maybe because the movie doesn't ever come close to understanding it: "And so we beat on, boats against the current, borne back ceaselessly into the past."

The Great Mouse Detective ★ ★ ★
G, 102 m., 1986

Featuring the voices of Vincent Price, Barrie Ingham, Val Bettin, Susanne Pollatschek, Candy Candido, Diana Chesney, Evan Brenner, Alan Young, and Melissa Manchester. Directed by John Musker, Ron Clements, Dave Michener, and Bunny Mattison.

Philosophers have the notion of parallel universes—whole worlds that are right next to our own, but in a different dimension, so that we can't see them, even while our actions are mirrored with infinite variations. Movie animators have a similar notion, which is that human lives are mirrored on a smaller scale by the parallel lives of the little cartoon characters who live down there closer to the floor.

Near the beginning of *The Great Mouse Detective*, the camera moves through London, passing many of the familiar landmarks, before finally tilting down and moving in toward a little doorway down near to the ground. Inside there's a busy little mouse, a craftsman, hard at work. Like so many domesticated cartoon animals, he is the very soul of bourgeois respectability (I always liked it in the "Tom & Jerry" cartoons when they showed the floor lamps and chintz-covered sofas inside the mouse holes).

Before long, however, a mysterious figure appears who disrupts this image of comfortable domesticity. And then *The Great Mouse Detective* launches its story, which depends on the conceit that London in those days housed not only a great human detective (Sherlock Holmes), but also a mouse who was every bit as good a detective.

The Sherlock Holmes legend is such a durable story that all sorts of filmmakers have adapted it to their own ends, styles, and genres. Just in recent years, we've seen Billy Wilder's *The Private Life of Sherlock Holmes*, Gene Wilder's *Sherlock Holmes' Younger Brother*, Nicholas Meyer's *The Seven Per-*

cent Solution, and Steven Spielberg's *Young Sherlock Holmes*—which told the story of the schooldays of Sherlock and young Watson, surrounded by props and special effects borrowed from other Spielberg extravaganzas.

Here is the Disney version, told on a mouse scale in cartoon form, with a freedom and creativity of animation that reminded me of the earlier Disney feature-length cartoons. In recent decades, Disney and the other animators had started to cut corners; the old-style full animation of such classics as *Pinocchio* was simply too expensive to duplicate any more, with its endless man-hours of drawing. So we began to get backgrounds that didn't move, and actions that seemed recycled out of other actions. Now, however, computer animation has taken most of the drudgery and much of the expense out of animation, and the result is a movie like this, that looks more fully animated than anything in some thirty years.

The movie's story is the usual silliness about evil villains and abducted geniuses. Although the detective in the movie is not called Sherlock Holmes (or Sherlock Mouse, for that matter), he is obviously cut from the same cloth, right down to his ever-present pipe. And there is a Doctor Watson character, who befriends a bewildered waif in the street, and takes it to the great detective, who scents one of his greatest cases.

What's fun is the carefree way the animators swing through their story, using the freedom of the cartoon form to blend nineteenth-century realism with images that seem borrowed from more recent special effects pictures. For a long time, I was down on the full-length animated efforts of Disney and others, because they didn't seem to reflect the same sense of magic and wonderment that the original animated classics always had. Who, for example, could ever equate *101 Dalmations* with *Snow White*? But now, maybe thanks to computers, animated movies are beginning to sparkle again.

The Great Muppet Caper ★ ★

G, 95 m., 1981

Charles Grodin (Nicky), Diana Rigg (Lady Holiday). With the Muppets and their performers: Jim Henson, Frank Oz, Dave Goetz, Jerry Holson, and Richard Hunt. Cameo appearances by Robert Morley, Peter Ustinov, and Jack Warden. Directed by Jim Henson and produced by Frank Oz. Screenplay by Tom Patchett, Jay Tarses, Jerry Juhl, and Jack Rose.

The Muppets are a wonderful creation, but they lose their special quality in *The Great Muppet Caper.* They behave like clones of other popular kiddie superstars—like the basic cartoon heroes they once seemed destined to replace. Jim Henson's original inspiration with the Muppets was to invest them with very real human qualities: Miss Piggy's vanity and insecurity, Kermit's insouciant inquisitiveness, Fozzie's fuzzy desire to be loved, and so on. Then he involved them in situations that revolved around their personalities, so that the kids who watched them could perhaps learn something about human nature. A lot of suspense during a Muppet story depended on how a particular Muppet would *feel* about something.

That was the approach of many of the Muppet TV episodes and of the original *Muppet Movie* (1979). This time, though, Henson and his associates haven't developed a screenplay that pays attention to the Muppet personalities. Instead, they ship them to England and dump them into a basic caper plot, treating them every bit as much like a formula as James Bond. This won't do. We don't care about some dumb diamond the size of a baseball, and as Muppet fans we're probably also indifferent to Henson's ambition to satirize old movie genres.

When he gives us a Busby Berkeley-like water ballet starring Miss Piggy, our reaction is complex. We think (a) that kids in the audience won't know what is being satirized and (b) that Miss Piggy's fantasies have become less fun as they reveal less vulnerability. And as for Miss Piggy herself . . . I really hate to say this, but she's not nearly as appealing in *The Great Muppet Caper* as she's always been before. She is also alarmingly thinner. Are we witnessing the Hollywoodization of Miss Piggy? Is she perhaps beginning to believe her own publicity? She's less vulnerable this time, less touching, with fewer instantly recognizable human frailties.

The movie involves a Muppet expedition to London, a near-affair between Charles Grodin and Miss Piggy, and some missing jewels. It also features some cameo appearances by familiar stars, but Henson seems content that the stars are merely in his movie; he doesn't use them with comic imagination. Example: When the Muppets crash-land in the middle of a British pond, they're greeted by British Airways' TV spokesman Robert Morley. But Morley plays the scene absolutely straight. Here was a great chance to have fun with Morley's TV ads: He could have brusquely informed the Muppets that hotels were $400 a night, there were no theater tickets available, not a single rental car was to be had for miles around, and that, frankly, the British wished their American cousins would stay at home.

The lack of a cutting edge hurts this movie. It's too nice, too routine, too predictable, and too safe.

The Great Santini ★ ★ ★ ★

PG, 118 m., 1980

Robert Duvall (Bull Meechum), Blythe Danner (Lillian Meechum), Michael O'Keefe (Ben Meechum), Lisa Jane Persky (Mary Anne Meechum), Stan Shaw (Toomer Smalls), Theresa Merritt (Arrabelle Smalls). Directed by Lewis John Carlino and produced by Charles A. Pratt. Screenplay by Carlino.

Like almost all of my favorite films, *The Great Santini* is about people more than it's about a story. It's a study of several characters, most unforgettably the Great Santini himself—played by Robert Duvall. Despite his name, he is not a magician or an acrobat but a lieutenant colonel in the Marines with the real name of Bull Meechum. He sees himself as the Great Santini, an ace pilot, great Marine, heroic husband and father and, in general, a sterling man among men. His family is expected to go along with this—and to go along with him, as he's transferred to a duty camp in South Carolina in the early 1960s.

There are five other members of the Meechum family. His wife (Blythe Danner) is a sweet Southern girl who calls her kids "sugar" and understands her maverick husband with a love that is deep but unforgiving. His oldest son (Michael O'Keefe) is just turning eighteen and learning to stand up to a father who issues "direct orders," calls everyone "sports fan," and expects to be called "sir." There are two more daughters and a son, but the movie's main relationship is between the father and the oldest boy.

Santini, you understand, is one hell of a guy. All he understands is competition. He's a royal pain in the ass to his Marine superiors, because he's always pulling damn fool stunts and making a spectacle out of himself. But he's a great pilot and he's said to be a good leader (even though his first briefing session for the men under him in South Carolina leaves them totally bewildered). Santini wants to win at everything, even backyard basketball with his son.

But the son is learning to be his own man. And there's a subplot involving a friendship between O'Keefe and the intense actor Stan Shaw, who plays the son of the family's black maid. Marine kids grow up nowhere and everywhere, we learn, and in South Carolina these two kids go shrimping together, trade lore together, become friends. It's a nice relationship, although a little tangential to the main thrust of the movie.

It's Robert Duvall who really makes the movie live—Duvall and Blythe Danner in a stunning performance that nothing she's done before (in *1776*, *Hearts of the West*, etc.) prepares us for. Although *The Great Santini* is set about ten years before *Apocalypse Now*, Duvall is playing essentially the same character in both films—we remember his great scene in *Apocalypse*, shouting that napalm smells to him like victory, as he gives his gung-ho speeches in this movie.

Duvall and O'Keefe go hard at each other, in the father-son confrontation, and there's an especially painful scene where the father bounces a basketball off his son's head, egging him on. But this movie is essentially a comedy—a serious, tender one, like *Breaking Away*, which is also about a son getting to know his father.

There are wonderful little moments in the dialogue (as when the Great Santini's daughter wonders aloud if females are allowed full Meechum family status, or are only sort of one-celled Meechums). There are moments straight out of left field, as when Duvall and the family's new maid (the formidable Theresa Merritt) get into an impromptu shoulder-punching contest. There are moments so unpredictable and yet so natural they feel just like the spontaneity of life itself. And the movie's conclusion is the same way:

sentimental without being corny, a tear-jerker with dignity.

The Great Santini is a movie to seek out and to treasure.

The Green Room ★ ★ ★
PG, 90 m., 1978

Francois Truffaut (Julien), Nathalie Baye (Cecelia). Directed by Francois Truffaut. Screenplay by Truffaut and Jean Gruault.

The films of Francois Truffaut seem divided into two categories, which I admire for completely different reasons. On one side are the films affirming life, films like *Small Change*, *Day for Night*, and *Stolen Kisses*. On the other side are the films involving his obsession with death, films like *The Bride Wore Black*, *Two English Girls*, and *The Story of Adele H.*.

Truffaut's *The Green Room* most definitely belongs in the second category, and is in fact the closest he has come to suggesting that his own interest in death may be a morbid preoccupation. The film is based on one of the most death-obsessed stories in the English language, *The Altar of the Dead*, in which Henry James told the story of a man who worshiped the memory of his dead wife to the point of madness.

In the James story, and in the Truffaut film, the character arrives at a crisis when he falls in love with a woman who is undeniably still alive. How can the new love be reconciled with the adoration of the departed wife? The solution is appropriately macabre. The living woman is invited to join the man in worship at the altar of the dead—to become a fellow mourner.

That is the basic situation in James's version. What fascinates Truffaut about the story is where it leads from there, for the woman is obsessed with the dead, too, and has her own departed ones to worship. The man builds an altar, a shrine, photographs, and candles on every wall and in every corner, and he offers to admit the woman's dead to the shrine. But then he discovers that one of her dead is one of his old enemies—a man whose memory would desecrate his own dead. Thus his grief is betrayed as monstrously selfish.

Truffaut tells this story with necrophilic relish, and plays the leading role himself. Nathalie Baye, a young French actress who is usually unforced and natural, plays the woman, an equally obsessed person—but one who eventually wants to break away from the lure of the dead and admit love into her life again. To the man, of course, that is too much of a challenge. A perfect love can exist only with the dead, because it is always on the terms set down by the living.

The Green Room is, as you have intuited by now, a very somber and depressed film. But it is not depressing, because its characters are such grotesques, such caricatures, that we marvel at them instead of sympathizing. They carry their death obsessions so far that they almost exorcise them. Unlike the heroine of *Adele H.*, whose urge toward self-destruction was conceited, narcissistic, and a device to dramatize her own plight, the characters in *The Green Room* are so simple they are comic in a Dickensian sense; they exaggerate one attribute so absurdly that they lose all other human dimensions.

The Green Room should be seen by: admirers of Henry James, admirers of Truffaut, and admirers of crumbling old cemeteries where the tombs gape openly at passersby. As an admirer of all three of these subjects, no doubt I admired the film more than others might. I especially enjoyed the scene where the gates are bolted shut and Truffaut is locked among the graves overnight.

Gregory's Girl ★ ★ ★
PG, 93 m., 1982

Gordon John Sinclair (Gregory), Dee Hepburn (Dorothy), Chic Murray (Headmaster), Jake D'Arcy (Phil), Alex Norton (Alec), John Bott (Alistair). Directed by Bill Forsyth and produced by Clive Parsons and Davina Boling. Screenplay by Forsyth.

There was a little item in the paper not long ago that should have been front page news. It was about a survey reporting that physically handsome men were less successful in business, made less money, married younger, and had less "desirable" spouses than men of average or below-average looks. The sociologists who announced these conclusions speculated that the handsome guys tended to get sidetracked in high school, spending more time on social life and less time on studies; they tended to depend on their golden boy charm instead of plowing ahead through college; and they tended, because they were more sexually active at younger ages, to marry sooner and therefore to marry women who were looking for marriage rather than careers. On the average, therefore, the weird kid with acne who's president of Chem Club will do better in the long run than the prom king.

Bill Forsyth's *Gregory's Girl* is a charming, innocent, very funny little movie about the weird kid. It is set in Scotland, where the teen-agers are quieter, more civilized and more naive than, let's say, those in *The Class of 1984*. And it is about Gregory (Gordon John Sinclair), a gangling adolescent who has started to shoot up all of a sudden and finds he is hopelessly uncoordinated on the soccer field. Gregory looks sort of like an immensely likable stork. He loses his place on the soccer team to another student who is a good deal faster and more coordinated. The other student happens to be a girl. Her name is Dorothy (Dee Hepburn), and Gregory instantly falls deeply in love with her. Nothing like this has ever hit him before, and romance becomes for him almost a physical illness. Dorothy is sweet to him, but distant, because she not only suspects Gregory's feelings but is way ahead of him in her analysis of the whole situation.

The movie takes place mostly in a pleasant suburb of Glasgow, where the kids hang about and trade endless speculation on the impossibility of being sixteen and happy at the same time. Gregory turns for romantic advice to his younger sister, who is much more interested in ice cream. His sister, in fact, is oblivious to boys, although one pays her an earnest compliment: "She's only ten, but she has the body of a woman of thirteen." Meanwhile, Gregory consoles his best friend, who is fifteen and a half and has never known love.

This movie is a reminder that we tend to forget a lot of things about adolescence. For example: That it is no use telling a teen-ager what his faults are, because he is painfully aware of every possible fault in the minutest detail; that boys are absolutely helpless in the throes of teen-age romance, whereas girls tend to retain at least some perspective; that it is an unwritten law of the universe that no sixteen-year-old ever falls instantly in love with the right person at the right time.

The movie has a lot of gentle, civilized fun with insights like that. And along the way, Gregory the stork is led on a wild goose chase with a swan at the end. The movie contains so much wisdom about being alive and teen-aged and vulnerable that maybe it would even be painful for a teen-ager to see it; it's not much help, when you're suffering from those feelings of low self-esteem and an absolutely hopeless crush, to realize that not only are you in pain and suffering an emotional turmoil, but you're not even unique. Maybe only grown-ups should see this movie. You know, people who have gotten over the pains of unrequited love (hollow laugh).

Gremlins ★ ★ ★
PG, 111 m., 1984

Hoyt Axton (Rand Peltzer), Zach Galligan (Billy), Phoebe Cates (Kate), Scott Brady (Sheriff Frank), Polly Holliday (Mrs. Deagle). Directed by Joe Dante and produced by Michael Finnell. Executive producer Steven Spielberg. Screenplay by Chris Columbus.

Gremlins is a confrontation between Norman Rockwell's vision of Christmas and Hollywood's vision of the blood-sucking monkeys of voodoo island. It's fun. On the one hand, you have an idyllic American small town, with Burger Kings and Sears stores clustered merrily around the village square, and on the other hand you have a plague of reprehensible little beasties who behave like a rodent road company of Marlon Brando's motorcycle gang in *The Wild One*.

The whole movie is a sly series of send-ups, inspired by movie scenes so basic they reside permanently in our subconscious. The opening scene, for example, involves a visit to your basic Mysterious Little Shop in Chinatown, where, as we all know, the ordinary rules of the visible universe cease to operate and magic is a reality. Later on, after a kid's father buys him a cute little gremlin in Chinatown, we have a new version of your basic Puppy for Christmas Scene. Then there are such basic movie characters as the Zany Inventor, the Blustering Sheriff, the Clean-Cut Kid, the Cute Girlfriend, and, of course, the Old Bag.

The first half of the movie is the best. That's when we meet the little gremlins, which are unbearably cute and look like a cross between a Pekingese, Yoda from *Empire*, the Ewoks from *Jedi*, and kittens.

They have impossibly big eyes, they're cuddly and friendly, and they would make ideal pets except for the fact that they hate bright lights, should not be allowed to get wet, and must never be fed after midnight. Well, of course, it's *always* after midnight; that's the tip-off that this isn't a retread of *E.T.* but comes from an older tradition, the fairy tale or magic story. And in the second half of the movie, after the gremlins have gotten wet, been fed after midnight, etc., they turn into truly hateful creatures that look like the monster in *Alien*.

The movie exploits every trick in the monster-movie book. We have scenes where monsters pop up in the foreground, and others where they stalk us in the background, and others when they drop into the frame and scare the Shinola out of everybody. And the movie itself turns nasty, especially in a scene involving a monster that gets slammed in a microwave oven, and another one where a wide-eyed teen-age girl (Phoebe Cates) explains why she hates Christmas. Her story is in the great tradition of 1950s sick jokes, and as for the microwave scene, I had a queasy feeling that before long we'd be reading newspaper stories about kids who went home and tried the same thing with the family cat.

Gremlins was hailed as another *E.T.* It's not. It's in a different tradition. At the level of Serious Film Criticism, it's a meditation on the myths in our movies: Christmas, families, monsters, retail stores, movies, boogeymen. At the level of Pop Moviegoing, it's a sophisticated, witty B movie, in which the monsters are devouring not only the defenseless town, but decades of defenseless clichés. But don't go if you still believe in Santa Claus.

The Grey Fox ★ ★ ★ ½
PG, 92 m., 1983

Richard Farnsworth (Bill Miner), Jackie Burroughs (Kate Flynn), Wayne Robson (Shorty), Ken Pogue (Jack Budd). Directed by Phillip Borsos and produced by Peter O'Brian. Screenplay by John Hunter.

Here's a lovely adventure: a movie about a stubborn, indomitable character who robs people because that's what he knows best. A man should work at his craft, shouldn't he? *The Grey Fox* tells the story of Bill Miner, a man who was thrown into prison in the heyday of the Old West, was kept behind bars for thirty-three years, and who finally emerged, confused but interested, into the twentieth century, where the movie begins in 1901. Bill Miner robbed stagecoaches. What's he supposed to do with a train? He's a whiskery old man, stubborn as a mule, and his pride hasn't grown any smaller during those years in jail. He heads for his sister's place to look for work and a roof over his head, but he doesn't get along with his brother-in-law and he also doesn't much like picking oysters for a living. He leaves. He hits the road, drifting aimlessly, a man without a mission—until the night in 1903 when he sees Edwin S. Porter's *The Great Train Robbery*. That famous movie is only eleven minutes long, but long enough to make everything absolutely clear to Miner, who realizes he has a new calling in life, as a train robber.

All of this could, of course, be an innocuous Disney movie, but it's well-written and directed, and what gives it zest and joy is the performance by Richard Farnsworth, who plays Miner. Maybe you'll recognize Farnsworth when you see him on the screen. Maybe not. His life has been one of those careers that makes you realize Hollywood is a company town, where you can make a living for years and never be a star. Farnsworth has been in more than 300 movies. He was a stuntman for thirty years. He's had speaking roles in movies ranging from *The Cowboys* to *Resurrection*. He was even in "Roots" on TV. And yet there is absolutely no mention of his name in Leslie Halliwell's *Filmgoer's Companion*. Farnsworth is one of those unstudied, graceful, absolutely natural actors who has spent a lifetime behaving exactly as he feels. I think he is incapable of a false or a dishonest moment. He makes Miner so proud, so vulnerable, such a noble rascal, that the whole movie becomes just a little more complex because he's in it.

There's one scene where you can really see Farnsworth's gift for conviction. It's a love scene with a feminist lady photographer named Kate Flynn (Jackie Burroughs), who is touring the West to document its changing times. Bill and Kate are instantly attracted to one another. And their love scene together is a warm, amusing masterpiece of quiet affection. Miner doesn't deny his age; he triumphs with it. He's not handsome but he's damned attractive, and knows it. Kate Flynn can see that this man has six times the worth of an ordinary man, and adores him. The scene is a treasure, even when you don't know whether to laugh or cry.

The director, Phillip Borsos, is able to make this a human story and still keep it exciting as an action picture. And he gives it a certain documentary feel; *The Grey Fox* is apparently based, to some degree, on truth. That doesn't matter half as much as that Farnsworth bases his performance on how he sees the truth of Bill Miner.

Greystoke ★ ★ ★

PG, 129 m., 1984

Christopher Lambert (Tarzan), Ralph Richardson (Earl of Greystoke), Ian Holm (Captain D'Arnot), Andie MacDowell (Jane Porter). Directed by Hugh Hudson and produced by Hudson and Stanley S. Canter. Screenplay by P.H. Vazak and Michael Austin.

One of the most unforgettable mothers in the history of literature is named Kala, and she is an ape. Some people will immediately know that Kala is the great ape who adopted a shipwrecked orphan and raised him as her own, until he became Tarzan, Lord of the Apes. Other people will not know that, and for them, the movie *Greystoke* may be missing a certain resonance. I think it helps, in seeing this movie, to draw on a background of rainy Saturday afternoons when you were ten and had your nose buried in *Tarzan* books.

Greystoke, the Legend of Tarzan, Lord of the Apes is the most faithful film adaptation of the Tarzan legend ever made. That isn't saying much, because most of the forty or so Tarzan movies were laughable quickies with Tarzan trying not to be upstaged by cute chimps. *Greystoke* takes the legend seriously, and it's worthy of being taken seriously, I think, because the story of Tarzan has become one of the most durable of all the myths of the twentieth century. The obvious challenge for this movie is to convince an audience that it is actually looking at a little human baby being nurtured by wild animals. *Greystoke* passes that test. The movie combines footage of real animals with footage of human actors disguised by the special effects makeup of Rick Baker, and I was hard-pressed to tell the difference. The movie has an extended opening sequence that takes place entirely in the jungle, without spoken dialogue, and that captures the central mystery of the Tarzan legend as well as anything I've ever seen.

Unfortunately, there's one other aspect of Tarzan that *Greystoke* doesn't capture as well. The Tarzan adventures were all inspired by the imagination of a pulp writer named Edgar Rice Burroughs, who was not a stylist or a philosopher but was certainly a great plotter and knew how to entangle Tarzan in cliff-hanging melodrama. *Greystoke* isn't melodrama and doesn't try to be, and I missed that. After the great early jungle scenes, it has the grown-up Tarzan (Christopher Lambert) being discovered by a Belgian explorer (Ian Holm) who returns him to his ancestral Scottish home, Greystoke Manor, where he meets his grandfather (Ralph Richardson) and also a young lady named Jane (Andie MacDowell). The movie has fun showing Tarzan's introduction to civilization; there's a spine-tingling moment when he growls into Jane's ear. The characters also are well-drawn, especially Ralph Richardson's Earl of Greystoke, who childishly slides down a staircase on a silver tray, and who has a touching death scene that was acted not long before Richardson himself died.

But where's the action? Shouldn't there be some sort of pulp subplot about the ant men, or the jewels of Opar, or a wild elephant on a rampage? *Greystoke* is the story of the legend of Tarzan, but it doesn't contain an adventure *involving* Tarzan. Who would have guessed there'd ever be a respectable Tarzan movie?

H

Hair ★ ★ ★ ★
R, 118 m., 1979

John Savage (Claude), Beverly D'Angelo (Sheila), Dorsey Wright (Hud), Cheryl Barnes (Hud's Fiancee), Treat Williams (Berger), Annie Golden (Jeannie), Don Dacus (Woof). Directed by Milos Forman and produced by Lester Persky and Michael Butler. Screenplay by Michael Weller.

I walked into *Hair* with the gravest doubts that this artifact of 1960s social shock would transfer to our current, sleepier times. In the 1960s we went to angry musicals; now we line up for *La Cage aux Folles.* My doubts disappeared with the surge and bold authority of the first musical statement: *This is the dawning of the Age of Aquarius!*

So maybe it isn't, really, and maybe the sun set on that particular age back around the time they pinched the Watergate burglars. But Milos Forman's *Hair* opens with such confidence and joy, moves so swiftly and sustains itself so well that I wonder why I had any doubts. *Hair* is, amazingly, not a period piece but a freshly conceived and staged memory of the tribulations of the mid-sixties.

It is also a terrific musical. The songs, of course, were good to begin with: The glory of "Hair" and "Let the Sun Shine In" and "Age of Aquarius" and the sly, silly warmth of "Black Boys/White Boys." But to the original music, the film version adds a story that works well with it, airy and open photography, and glorious choreography by Twyla Tharp.

I said I lost my doubts about *Hair* during "Age of Aquarius." To be more precise, they disappeared during Tharp's opening scene in Central Park, when the dancers were joined by the horses of mounted policemen. Anyone who can sit through that opening dance sequence and not be thrilled should give up musicals.

The original play, you may recall, didn't exactly have what you could call much of a plot. The screenplay, by Michael Weller, remedies that, but not too much. Weller provides a framework structured around the experiences of a young Midwestern farmboy (John Savage) who takes the bus to Manhattan to be inducted into the army and makes instant friends with a family of hippies living in Central Park.

Savage is just right as the shy, introspective kid who feels suspicious of the hippies—and, indeed, of any alternative lifestyle. But he knows nobody else in New York, so he hangs around with these kids and suddenly a vision enters his life: a beautiful girl on horseback (Beverly D'Angelo), a debutante passing through Central Park and probably out of his life.

She comes from an incredibly wealthy family, he learns. They have nothing in common. But she's drawn, sort of, to the easy freedom of the hippies. And the leader of the hippies (Treat Williams, of *Jesus Christ Superstar*) leads them all in a high-spirited invasion of the girl's debutante party. It's one of the movie's best scenes, somehow finding a fresh way to handle the old cliché of the uninvited street people at a millionaire's party.

The movie also evokes the stylistic artifacts of the flower power time. The love beads and vests and headbands and fringed jackets and all the other styles that were only yesterday, already look more dated than costumes from the 1940s. And it remembers the conflicts in lifestyles, mostly strikingly in scenes between the young black man (Dorsey Wright) who has joined the hippies, and the mother of his child (Cheryl Barnes), whom he left behind.

The movie's final sequences center on Savage's induction, leading to the hilarious "Black Boys/White Boys" number, an omnisexual showstopper. Twyla Tharp's choreography here is wonderfully happy and grin-inducing, as enlisted men rub legs under the table.

This number, like a lot of the movie, is loosely structured around the political attitudes of the Vietnam era, but the politics isn't heavy-handed. The movie's ideas are handled with grace and style. And it's interesting how it recalls *Hair*'s myths of the 1960s—especially the image of the youth culture as a repository, simultaneously, of ancient American values and the new values aborning in the Age of Aquarius.

That this time and spirit could be evoked so well and so naturally is a tribute to the director, Forman. His accomplishment is all the more remarkable when you reflect that when *Hair* first occupied a stage, the Russians were in the process of occupying Forman's native Czechoslovakia, and he was in the process of becoming a filmmaker without a country.

He has since, however, shown an uncanny feeling for the textures of American life, in his *Taking Off*, with its runaway children; in his *One Flew Over the Cuckoo's Nest*, and now in *Hair*. Maybe it's just as well that this version had to wait a decade to be filmed so Forman could be hired to do it. He brings life to the musical form in the same way that *West Side Story* did, the last time everyone was saying the movie musical was dead.

Hairspray ★ ★ ★

PG, 89 m., 1988

Ricki Lake (Tracy Turnblad), Shawn Thompson (Corny Collins), Sonny Bono (Franklin Von Tussle), Colleen Fitzpatrick (Amber Von Tussle), Debbie Harry (Velma Von Tussle), Divine (Edna and Arvin), Ruth Brown (Maybell), Michael St. Gerard (Link Larkin), Leslie Ann Powers (Penny), Jerry Stiller (Wilbur Turnblad), Pia Zadora (Beatnik Girl). Directed by John Waters and produced by Rachel Talalay. Screenplay by Waters.

"If you remember the sixties, you weren't there."—Dennis Hopper

Yeah, but those were the *late* sixties. Everybody remembers the early sixties, that season of innocence when a man could be named Chubby Checker and still be a star. The early sixties were before the Beatles, LSD, Vietnam, and hippies. They were, in fact, a lot like the late fifties, except that the cars were not as stylish and people were joining the Peace Corps, and in every town large enough to support a TV station there was a version of "The Hop."

"The Hop" was the name of the show on Channel 3 in Champaign-Urbana, Illinois, where I grew up. It had other names in other towns, but it always had the same format: A studio full of pimply-faced teen-agers in ducktails and ponytails, pumping away to mainstream rock music under the benevolent supervision of the local clone of Dick Clark.

Everybody I knew watched "The Hop." Nobody I knew ever appeared on it. Where did they get these kids? Did they hire professional teen-agers from other towns? Nobody I knew dressed as cool or danced as well as the kids on "The Hop," and there was a sinking feeling, on those long-ago afternoons in front of the TV, that the parade had passed me by.

John Waters's *Hairspray* is a movie about that time and those kids and the sinking feeling. It takes place in 1962 in Baltimore, where a program known as "The Corny Collins Show" is at the center of many local teen-age fantasies. The kids on Corny's show are great dancers, with hair piled in grotesque mounds atop their unformed little faces. They are "popular." They are on the "Council," a quasi-democratic board of teen-agers who advise Corny on matters of music, and supervise auditions for kids who want to be on the show.

One kid who hungers to be on the show is Tracy (Ricki Lake), who is fat, but who can dance better than Amber (Colleen Fitzpatrick), who is not. Tracy dances in front of her TV set and knows all the right moves, and is tolerated in her fantasies by her parents, who are played by Jerry Stiller and Divine.

The plot of the movie loosely involves Ricki's attempts to win a talent show and win a place on the Council, and the attempts that are made to stop her by Amber and her ambitious parents (Sonny Bono and Debbie Harry). It is some kind of commentary on the decivilizing eighties that Stiller and Divine and Bono and Harry, who would have qualified as sideshow exhibits in the real sixties, look, in the context of this movie, like plausible parents. The supporting cast includes various local weirdos, including Pia Zadora as a "beatnik chick" (I quote from the credits). If nothing else is worth the price of renting this movie, perhaps you will be persuaded by the prospect of Pia Zadora reading from Allen Ginsberg's "Howl."

The movie carries a social message as sort of a sideline: "The Corny Collins Show" is racially segregated, and Ricki and her black friends help to change that situation, gate-crashing a Corny Collins night at the local amusement park. But basically the movie is a bubble-headed series of teen-age crises and crushes, alternating with historically accurate choreography of such forgotten dances as the Madison and the Roach.

The movie probably has the most to say to people who were teen-agers in the early sixties—but they are, I suppose, the last people likely to see this movie. It will also appeal to today's teen-agers, who will find that every generation has its own version of Corny Collins, and its own version of the Council, designed to make you feel like a worthless reject on the trash heap of teen-age history. If there is a message in the movie, it is that John Waters, who could never in a million years have made the Council, did, after all, survive to make the movie.

Half Moon Street ★ ★ ★

R, 90 m., 1986

Sigourney Weaver (Lauren Slaughter), Michael Caine (Lord Bulbeck), Ram John Holder (Lindsay Walker), Niall O'Brien (Captain Twilley), Patrick Kavanagh (General Newhouse), Nadim Sawalha (Karim Hatami), Michael Elwyn (Tom Haldane). Directed by Bob Swaim and produced by Geoffrey Reeve. Screenplay by Swaim and Edward Behr.

I was reflecting, as the lights went down before *Half Moon Street*, that I could not recall a single bad performance by either of the stars, Michael Caine and Sigourney Weaver. Caine's record is all the more remarkable because he has emerged untouched from some of the worst movies of the last twenty years with his unshakable self-confidence and quiet good humor. In a certain sense, it didn't even matter what *Half Moon Street* was about, or whether it was much good, because I was so curious to see what Caine and Weaver would be like together.

The movie stars Weaver as the wonderfully named Dr. Lauren Slaughter, an American academic who specializes in China and works for a cold-war think tank in London. She is tall, smart, calculating, and concerned with her own advantage. When she writes an article for the potty general who runs her organization and it turns up in the *Spectator* under his name, she doesn't go along with the program: She lets him know he's a spineless pig. And when she reflects that she is doing the work of her inferiors for starvation wages, she takes action.

It happens this way: She meets a man at a party, and he sends her a videotape documentary about a high-priced call-girl agency. She looks at the tape, considers the possibilities, and goes to interview for a job. She is completely open about the whole thing. She entertains clients using her real name, and when she is asked at an academic gathering what she does with her evenings, she replies that she has dinner with rich men.

One night she recognizes one of her clients. He tries to introduce himself as Sam Weller, but she has read her Dickens, smiles at that, and calls him by his name—Lord Bulbeck. He is a government spokesman on defense in the House of Lords and a lonely man who lives alone in a large house and says he doesn't have the time to find sex and companionship through ordinary channels.

That's fine with her. They make love, start talking, begin to like one another, and, before long, they have crossed over that great divide between asking each other what they like in bed and asking each other how they like their omelets. There is a certain instant compatibility between them. They are both friendly and outgoing people with something cold at their cores, and the device of the escort agency rather suits them: It provides a reason why they are in bed that does not involve such compiicated issues as love and affection.

Dr. Slaughter meets other clients, including rich Middle Easterners who set her up in an expensive flat in Mayfair. She continues to work at the think tank, where she doesn't much mind that certain people know about her moonlighting. Bulbeck gets involved in tricky negotiations involving a Middle East peace settlement, and of course the Special Branch monitors all of his activities. It checks out Dr. Slaughter and eavesdrops on his private moments with her, and that is as it should be.

What makes *Half Moon Street* so intriguing up to this point is the literal and almost offhand honesty that grows between the Weaver and Caine characters. Their feelings are clear, their motives are clear, and with their eyes wide open they're falling in love.

This whole aspect of the movie is essentially the contribution of the director, Bob Swaim, and his co-writer, Edward Behr. In Paul Theroux's original novel, *Doctor Slaughter*, Lord Bulbeck was older and less amusing, and Dr. Slaughter was very alone in the world she had made for herself. The love that grows between the bright young woman and the gentle middle-aged man provides a subject that wasn't there in the Theroux version, and so it's sort of a shock when the plot reintroduces itself.

The plot has to do with Middle Eastern intrigues, spy rings, terrorists, and plans to sabotage Lord Bulbeck's peace initiative. And it leads to the movie's closing sequence, in which we lose the particular charms of the growing romance and find ourselves back in those familiar movie clichés where everything is settled with violence. God, it's boring to have to wait through an obligatory series of scenes until all of the right people have been killed and the movie can be over.

The last scene in *Half Moon Street* is particularly unconvincing, because for a long time this movie seemed so unorthodox that I expected a tough and realistic ending in which at least one of the wrong people would get killed. No such luck. And so I was right: The movie is interesting primarily because of the interaction between Weaver and Caine. Swaim deserves credit for the intelligence and wit of the first eighty or ninety minutes, but must also take the blame for the ending, which is a complete surrender to generic conventions.

Halloween ★ ★ ★ ★

R, 93 m., 1978

With Donald Pleasence, Jamie Lee Curtis, P.J. Soles, and Nancy Loomis. Directed by John Carpenter and produced by Irving Yablans. Screenplay by Carpenter and Debra Hill.

"I enjoy playing the audience like a piano."
—Alfred Hitchcock

So does John Carpenter. *Halloween* is an absolutely merciless thriller, a movie so violent and scary that, yes, I *would* compare it to *Psycho.* It's a terrifying and creepy film about what one of the characters calls Evil Personified. Right. And that leads us to the one small piece of plot I'm going to describe. There's this six-year-old kid who commits a murder right at the beginning of the movie, and is sent away, and is described by his psychiatrist as someone he spent eight years trying to help, and then the next seven years trying to keep locked up. But the guy escapes. And he returns on Halloween to the same town and the same street where he committed his first murder. And while the local babysitters telephone their boyfriends and watch *The Thing* on television, he goes back into action.

Period: That's all I'm going to describe, because *Halloween* is a visceral experience—we aren't seeing the movie, we're having it happen to us. It's frightening. Maybe you don't like movies that are *really* scary: Then don't see this one. Seeing it, I was reminded of the favorable review I gave a few years ago to *The Last House on the Left,* another really terrifying thriller. Readers wrote to ask how I could possibly support such a movie. But it wasn't that I was supporting it so much as that I was describing it: You don't want to be scared? Don't see it. Credit must be paid to filmmakers who make the effort to really frighten us, to make a good thriller when quite possibly a bad one might have made as much money. Hitchcock is acknowledged as a master of suspense; it's hypocrisy to disapprove of other directors in the same genre who want to scare us too.

It's easy to create violence on the screen, but it's hard to do it well. Carpenter is uncannily skilled, for example, at the use of foregrounds in his compositions, and everyone who likes thrillers knows that foregrounds are crucial: The camera establishes the situation, and then it pans to one side, and something unexpectedly looms up in the foreground. Usually it's a tree or a door or a bush. Not always. And it's interesting how he paints his victims. They're all ordinary, everyday people—nobody's supposed to be the star and have a big scene and win an Academy Award. The performances are all the more absorbing because of that; the movie's a slice of life that is carefully painted (in drab daylights and impenetrable nighttimes) before its human monster enters the scene.

We see movies for a lot of reasons. Sometimes we want to be amused. Sometimes we want to escape. Sometimes we want to laugh, or cry, or see sunsets. And sometimes we want to be scared. I'd like to be clear about this. If you don't want to have a really terrifying experience, don't see *Halloween.*

Halloween II ★ ★

R, 92 m., 1981

Jamie Lee Curtis (Laurie), Donald Pleasence (Sam Loomis), Charles Cyphers (Leigh Brackett), Dick Warlock (The Shape). Directed by Rich Rosenthal and produced by Debra Hill and John Carpenter. Written by Hill and Carpenter.

It's a little sad to witness a fall from greatness, and that's what we get in *Halloween II.* John Carpenter's original 1978 *Halloween* was one of the most effective horror films ever made, a scarifying fable of a mad-dog killer's progress through a small Illinois town on Halloween. That movie inspired countless imitations, each one worse than the last, until the sight of a woman's throat being slashed became ten times more common in the movies than the sight of a kiss.

Mad Slasher Movies, they were called, and they became a genre of their own, even inspiring a book of pseudoscholarship, *Splatter Movies,* by John McCarty. His definition of a Splatter Film is concise and disheartening, and bears quoting: "[They] aim not to scare their audiences, necessarily, nor to drive them to the edge of their seats in suspense, but to *mortify* them with scenes of explicit gore. In splatter movies, mutilation is indeed the message—many times the only one."

Halloween II fits this description precisely. It is not a horror film but a geek show. It is technically a sequel, but it doesn't even attempt to do justice to the original. Instead, it tries to outdo all the other violent *Halloween* rip-offs of the last several years. The movie does not have the artistry or the imagination of the original, but it does have new technology: For those like McCarty who keep records of such things, this movie has the first close-up I can remember of a hypodermic needle being inserted into an eyeball. We see that twice. It mortifies the viewer nicely, just as scenes in Splatter Movies are supposed to do. There are a few other moments of passable originality, as when the killer disfigures the face of a beautiful woman by plunging her repeatedly into the scalding water of a whirlpool bath. But for the most part, *Halloween II* is a retread of *Halloween* without that movie's craft, exquisite timing, and thorough understanding of horror.

The movie begins just where the last one left off—with some of the same footage, indeed. The mysterious, invincible killer (who escaped from an institution earlier that Halloween day) has just tried to kill Jamie Lee Curtis. But Donald Pleasence, a psychiatrist who has decided the killer is literally inhuman, fires six bullets at close range. The killer is down, but not out. As the first movie ended, his body had disappeared. As this one opens, he's on the prowl again, still shuffling after screaming women at the same maddening slow pace.

The plot of *Halloween II* absolutely depends, of course, on our old friend the Idiot Plot which requires that everyone in the movie behave at all times like an idiot. That's necessary because if anyone were to use common sense, the problem would be solved and the movie would be over. So Jamie Lee Curtis and other young women consistently run into traps where the killer can corner them. In the first film, Jamie Lee locked herself in an upstairs closet. This time, it's a basement boiler room. The movie's other idiotic masterstroke comes when Curtis and a young kid are hiding in a car parked outside, and the kid slumps forward and honks the horn, revealing his hiding place. Inspired. The killer keeps coming. He's relentless. So is the movie. It uses the standard horror formula: Cause a false alarm, get a laugh, and then spring violence on the audience. You know how it works.

The heroine opens a creaking door into a dark room and peers inside. A hand claps her on the shoulder. The audience screams. But whaddya know, it's only the friendly teen-age intern. Laughter. *Then* the killer strikes.

This can get monotonous. But since most of this movie takes place in a hospital, the killer has lots of props to work with. I've already mentioned the whirlpool bath and the needles. Another particularly nasty gimmick is the intravenous tube. The killer uses it to drain the blood from one of his victims. That's gruesome, but give the filmmakers credit. They use that gimmick to deliver the one scene I've been impatiently expecting for years and years in gore films: Finally, one of the characters kills himself by slipping on the wet blood and hitting his head on the floor. Sooner or later, it had to happen.

Halloween III ★ ½

R, 98 m., 1982

Tom Atkins (Dr. Challis), Stacey Nelkin (Ellie Grimbridge), Dan O'Herlihy (Conal Cochran), Ralph Strait (Buddy). Directed by Tommy Lee Wallace and produced by Debra Hill and John Carpenter. Screenplay by Wallace.

There are a lot of problems with *Halloween III*, but the most basic one is that I could never figure out what the villain wanted to accomplish if he got his way. His scheme is easy enough to figure: He wants to sell millions of Halloween masks to the nation's kiddies and then brainwash them to put them on at the same time, whereupon laser beams at the base of the neck will fry the tykes. Meanwhile, he runs a factory that turns out lifelike robots. What's his plan? Kill the kids and replace them with robots? Why?

A half-baked scheme like that feels right at home in *Halloween III*, which is a low-rent thriller from the first frame. This is one of those Identikit movies, assembled out of familiar parts from other, better movies. It begins at the end of *Halloween II*, when the monster was burned up in the hospital parking lot, but it's not still another retread of the invincible monster. In fact, the monster is forgotten, except for a lab technician who spends the whole movie sifting through his ashes. Instead, the plot follows the young daughter (Stacey Nelkin) of one of the victims, who ran a toy shop. She enlists the aid of a local doctor (Tom Atkins), and they retrace her father's steps back to an ominous toy factory run by Dan O'Herlihy. The factory has the whole town bugged and under surveillance, and the factory's guards are androids who crush their victims' heads with their hands.

Like a lot of horror movies in this age of self-conscious filmmaking, *Halloween III* is filled with references to other movies. The friendly motel owner in the company town, for example, is dressed as a dead ringer for Henry Fonda in *On Golden Pond*. The scene where the bugs and snakes crawl out of the crushed skull is a cross-reference, sort of, to *The Thing*—the last movie by John Carpenter, whose original *Halloween* was incomparably better than Parts II and III. But the funniest reference comes when the hero and heroine break into O'Herlihy's factory and are captured. Then the demented toymaker takes them on a tour of his facility, while explaining his diabolical scheme. He's got an obligatory underground mad scientist laboratory, and we know the approach by heart from all the James Bond movies: White-coated technicians scurry around with clipboards, while the boss arranges a demonstration of the weird method of killing that will soon be tried on our heroes. The funny part is that the underground lab is so cheesy. It consists of a few TV monitors on high-tech bookshelves and a papier-mâché mock-up of one of the stones from Stonehenge. (If you can figure out what Stonehenge has to do with this movie, you're smarter than anyone in it.) Next, there are lots of shots of the guy and girl running from O'Herlihy's henchmen. These are all obligatory shots where the man grabs the woman's hand and yanks her along, she of course being too dumb to run from danger on her own.(Cf. "Me-Push-Pull-You," in the Glossary.)

The one saving grace in *Halloween III* is Stacey Nelkin, who plays the heroine. She has one of those rich voices that makes you wish she had more to say and in a better role. But watch her, too, in the reaction shots: When she's not talking, she's listening. She has a kind of rapt, yet humorous, attention that I thought was really fetching. Too bad she plays her last scene without a head.

Hannah and Her Sisters ★ ★ ★ ★

PG-13, 107 m., 1985

Woody Allen (Mickey), Michael Caine (Elliot), Mia Farrow (Hannah), Carrie Fisher (April), Barbara Hershey (Lee), Lloyd Nolan (Hannah's Father), Maureen O'Sullivan (Hannah's Mother), Daniel Stern (Dusty), Max von Sydow (Frederick), Dianne Wiest (Holly). Directed by Woody Allen and produced by Robert Greenhut. Screenplay by Allen.

Woody Allen's *Hannah and Her Sisters,* the best movie he has ever made, is organized like an episodic novel, with acute self-contained vignettes adding up to the big picture.

Each section begins with a title or quotation on the screen, white against black, making the movie feel like a stately progression through the lives of its characters. Then the structure is exploded, time and again, by the energy and the passion of those characters: an accountant in love with his wife's sister, a TV executive who fears he is going to die, a woman whose cocaine habit has made her life a tightrope of fear, an artist who pretends to be strong but depends pitifully on his girlfriend.

By the end of the movie, the section titles and quotations have made an ironic point: We try to organize our lives according to what we have read and learned and believed in, but our plans are lost in a tumult of emotion.

The movie spans two years in the lives of its large cast of characters—New Yorkers who labor in Manhattan's two sexiest industries, art and money. It begins and ends at family Thanksgiving dinners, with the dinner in the middle of the film acting as a turning point for several lives.

It is hard to say who the most important characters are, but my memory keeps returning to Elliot, the accountant played by Michael Caine, and Lee, the artist's girlfriend, played by Barbara Hershey. Elliot is married to Hannah (Mia Farrow), but has been blind-sided with a sudden passion for Lee. She lives in a loft with the tortured artist Frederick (Max von Sydow), who treats her like his child or his student. He is so isolated from ordinary human contact that she is actually his last remaining link with reality.

Lee and Hannah have a third sister, Holly (Dianne Wiest). They form parts of a whole. Hannah is the competent, nurturing one. Lee is the emotional, sensuous earth mother. Holly is a bundle of tics and insecurities. When they meet for lunch and the camera circles them curiously, we sense that in some ways the movie knows them better than they will ever know themselves. And to talk about the movie that way is to suggest the presence of the most important two characters in the movie, whom I will describe as Woody Allen and Mickey.

Mickey is the character played by Allen; he is a neurotic TV executive who lives in constant fear of death or disease. He was married to Hannah at one time. Even after Hannah's marriage to Elliot, Mickey remains a member of the family, circling its security with a winsome yearning to belong.

The family itself centers on the three women's parents, played by Maureen O'Sullivan and Lloyd Nolan as an aging show-business couple who have spent decades in loving warfare over his cheating and her drinking and their mutual career decisions.

If Mickey is the character played by Woody Allen in the movie, Allen also provides another, second character in a more subtle way. The entire movie is told through his eyes and his sensibility; not Mickey's, but Allen's. From his earlier movies, especially *Annie Hall* and *Manhattan,* we have learned to recognize the tone of voice, the style of approach.

Allen approaches his material as a very bright, ironic, fussy, fearful outsider; his constant complaint is that it's all very well for these people to engage in their lives and plans and adulteries because they do not share his problem, which is that he sees through everything, and what he sees on the other side of everything is certain death and disappointment.

Allen's writing and directing style is so strong and assured in this film that the actual filmmaking itself becomes a narrative voice, just as we sense Henry James behind all of his novels, or William Faulkner and Iris Murdoch, behind theirs.

The movie is not a comedy, but it contains big laughs, and it is not a tragedy, although it could be if we thought about it long enough. It suggests that modern big-city lives are so busy, so distracted, so filled with ambition and complication that there isn't time to stop and absorb the meaning of things. Neither tragedy nor comedy can find a place to stand; there are too many other guests at the party.

And yet, on reflection, there is a tragedy buried in *Hannah and Her Sisters,* and that is the fact of Mickey's status as the perennial outsider. The others get on with their lives, but Mickey is stuck with his complaints. Not only is he certain there is no afterlife, he is very afraid that this life might also be a sham. How he ever married Hannah in the first place is a mystery; it must have been an intermediate step on his journey to his true role in life, as the ex-husband and hanger-on.

There is a scene in the movie where Michael Caine confronts Barbara Hershey and tells her that he loves her. She is stunned, does not know what to say, but does not categorically deny that she has feelings for him. After she leaves him, he stands alone on the street, ecstatic, his face glowing, saying "I've got my answer! I've got my answer!"

Underlying all of *Hannah and Her Sisters* is the envy of Mickey (and Woody) that anyone could actually be happy enough and lucky enough to make such a statement. And yet, by the end of the movie, in his own way, Mickey has his answer, too.

Hard Choices ★ ★ ★ ½

NO MPAA RATING, 90 m., 1986

Margaret Klenck (Laura), Gary McCleery (Bobby), John Seitz (Sheriff Johnson), John Sayles (Don), John Snyder (Ben), Martin Donovan (Josh). Directed by Rick King and produced by Robert Mickelson and Earle Mack. Screenplay by King.

Many movies start out strong and end in confusion and compromise. *Hard Choices* starts out like a predictable action picture, and grows and grows until at the end it astonishes us. It gives its characters a freedom very few movies are willing to relinquish—the freedom to surprise us by moving in unexpected directions. The movie develops in ways we anticipate, and then there is a startling turning point, a moment when one of the characters makes a radical decision and acts on it, and from that moment on, *Hard Choices* never lets go.

Any review of this film has to be a tightwire act. This isn't a case of "not giving away the ending," it's a case of preserving a crucial surprise so that it can strike you with the same impact it struck me with. The people who released this film cared so little about their surprise that they actually revealed it in film clips supplied to television reviewers. I'm not going to repeat that mistake, because at a time when a reasonably intelligent moviegoer can predict eighty percent of what's going to happen in a movie, *Hard Choices* is a treasure.

The movie takes place in the backwoods of Tennessee, where Bobby (Gary McCleery), the hero, is a fifteen-year-old kid with good prospects for making something out of his life. His older brothers are into drugs and robberies. When they can't get the drugs they need, their insides fill up with a desperate vacuum, and they decide to rob a drugstore. They take their kid brother along. Everything goes wrong and a cop is killed and the three of them are caught and arrested, and the decision is made to try Bobby as an adult, for murder. There goes his life.

In jail, Bobby is not treated with the brutality that has become a cliché in movies like this. The local sheriff even has a sort of grudging sympathy for the kid. Meanwhile, a woman who works with juvenile offenders hears about his case; she travels to the small town and gets to know Bobby and becomes convinced that he did not want to go along on the robbery, did not pull the trigger, and was, in fact, an innocent bystander. The woman decides to do what she can to help Bobby.

This woman, played by Margaret Klenck, provides the central turning point in the movie. Until she appears, the story has developed along fairly routine lines. After she appears, there's nothing we can really count on. I don't want to say anything more about what actually happens in the movie, or what Klenck does. But look at her performance and you will see great screen action.

I've never seen Klenck before; I gather from the publicity material that she appeared for six years as Edwina Lewis on the TV soap opera "One Life to Live." What she does here is so deeply absorbing and yet so quiet that at first we don't even realize what's happening. She appears on screen wrapped in a cloak of conventionality. Everything is "normal" about her; how she looks, how she talks, how she behaves. And then, gradually, we realize that this woman is a true outsider, a person who works in the system but is not of the system, a person with an outlaw soul.

There are several other good performances in the movie, one by John Seitz, who turns the thankless role of the sheriff into a three-dimensional middle-aged guy with feelings; another by McCleery, as the kid, who has to survive a lot of tense and anguished scenes in the beginning before he can establish the interior rhythms of his character. One role is especially well-written: An intellectual, philosophical drug dealer, played by John Sayles, who does not remind us of any drug dealer we've ever seen in a movie before.

Hard Choices is a sleeper. That means it doesn't have any stars and was made on a small budget and got haphazard distribution around the country and will never be heard of by most people. No wonder it has a low profile; it's intelligent, surprising, powerful, and true to itself, and that sure puts it outside the mainstream. It's a classic example of a movie waiting to be discovered on video.

Hardcore ★ ★ ★ ★
R, 106 m., 1979

George C. Scott (Jake VanDorn), Peter Boyle (Andy Mast), Season Hubley (Niki), Dick Sargent (Wes DeJong), Leonard Gaines (Ramada), David Nichols (Kurt), Gary Rand Graham (Tod), Larry Block (Burrows). Directed by Paul Schrader and produced by Buzz Feitshans. Screenplay by Schrader.

Hardcore is said to be the story of a father's search for a daughter who has disappeared into the underworld of pornography and prostitution. That does indeed describe its beginning and ending. But there are moments in between when it becomes something much more interesting: The story of a tentative, trusting human relationship between the father and the young prostitute he enlists in his search.

The man is played by George C. Scott, the girl by Season Hubley. They have moments in the movie when they talk, really talk, about what's important to them—and we're reminded of how much movie dialogue just repeats itself, movie after movie, year after year. There's a scene in *Hardcore* where the man (who is a strict Calvinist) and the prostitute (who began selling herself in her early teens) talk about sex, religion, and morality, and we're almost startled by the belief and simple poetry in their words.

This relationship, between two people with nothing in common, who meet at an intersection in a society where many have nothing in common, is at the heart of the movie, and makes it important. It is preceded and followed by another of those story ideas that Paul Schrader seems to generate so easily. His movies are about people with values, in conflict with society. He wrote *Taxi Driver* and *Rolling Thunder* and wrote and directed *Blue Collar.* All three are about people prepared to defend (with violence, if necessary) their steadfast beliefs.

The Scott character is a fundamentalist from Grand Rapids, Michigan—Schrader's own hometown. The opening scenes establish the family setting, at Christmas, with a fairly thick theological debate going on around the dinner table. (The small boy listening so solemnly, Schrader has said, can be taken for himself.) A few days later, Scott's daughter leaves home for a church rally in California. She never returns. Scott hires a private detective (Peter Boyle) to try to find her, and Boyle does find her—in an 8-millimeter porno movie. Can it be traced? Boyle says not: "Nobody made it. Nobody sold it. Nobody *sees* it. It doesn't exist."

But Scott vows to follow his daughter into the sexual underworld and bring her back. His efforts to trace her, through San Francisco and Los Angeles and San Diego, make *Hardcore* into a sneakily fascinating guided tour through massage parlors, whorehouses, and the world of porno movies. Schrader sometimes seems to be having it both ways, here: Scott is repelled by the sex scenes he explores, but is the movie?

That doesn't matter so much after he meets Niki (Season Hubley), who might know some people who might know where his daughter is. She is in many ways like all the other lost young girls who drift to California and disappear. But she has intelligence and a certain insight into why she does what she does, and so their talks together become occasions for mutual analysis.

She has a deep psychological need for a father figure, a need she thinks Scott can meet. She also has insights into Scott's own character, insights his life hasn't previously made clear to him. There's a scene near the waterfront in San Diego that perfectly illuminates both of their personalities, and we realize how rare it is for the movies to show us people who are speaking in real words about real things.

The movie's ending is a mess, a combination of cheap thrills, a chase, and a shootout, as if Schrader wasn't quite sure how to escape from the depths he found. The film's last ten minutes, in fact, are mostly action, the automatic resolution of the plot; the relationship between Scott and Hubley ends without being resolved, and in bringing his story to a "satisfactory" conclusion, Schrader doesn't speak to the deeper and more human themes he's introduced. Too bad. But *Hardcore*, flawed and uneven, contains moments of pure revelation.

Harlan County, U.S.A. ★ ★ ★ ★

PG, 103 m., 1976

A documentary directed and produced by Barbara Kopple.

One moment among many in *Harlan County, U.S.A.*: The striking miners are holding an all-day rally and picnic. A big tent has been pitched, and it's filled with people—some of them familiar to us by now, others new. There are speeches and songs and union battle cries, and then an old woman takes the microphone. The words she sings are familiar: *They say in Harlan County, there are no neutrals there. You'll either be a union man or a thug for Sheriff Blair.* And then the whole tent-full joins in the chorus: *Which side are you on?*

The woman who is leading the singing wrote the song fifty years ago, during an earlier strike in the county the miners call "Bloody Harlan." And here it is 1973, in a county where the right of workers to organize has presumably long since been won, and the song is not being sung out of nostalgia. It is being sung by striking coal miners in Harlan County, where it still applies.

That's the most uncomfortable lesson we learn in Barbara Kopple's magnificent documentary: That there are still jobs for scabs and strike breakers, that union organizers still get shot at and sometimes get killed, and that in Harlan County, Kentucky, it still matters very much which side you're on. And so a song we know best from old Pete Seeger records suddenly proves itself still frighteningly relevant.

The movie, which won the 1976 Academy Award for best feature-length documentary, was shot over a period of eighteen months in eastern Kentucky, after the miners at the Brookside mine voted to join the United Mine Workers. The Duke Power Company refused to sign the UMW contract, fought the strike, and was fought in turn by the miners and—most particularly—their wives.

Barbara Kopple and her crew stayed in Harlan County during that entire time, living in the miners' homes and recording the day-by-day progress of the strike. It was a tumultuous period, especially since the mine workers' union itself was deep in the midst of the Tony Boyle-Jock Yablonsky affair. But what emerges from the film is not just a document of a strike, but an affecting, unforgettable portrait of a community.

The cameras go down into the mines to show us the work, which is backbreaking, dirty, and brutal. We get to meet many of the miners, and to notice a curious thing about the older ones: They tend to talk little, as if their attentions are turned inward to the source of the determination that takes them back down the mine every day. Their wives, on the other hand, seem born to lead strikes. The film shows them setting up committees, organizing picket lines, facing (and sometimes reciprocating) violence, and becoming eloquent orators.

Ms. Kopple is a feminist, and her work includes *Year of the Women.* In *Harlan County,* though, she doesn't seem to have gone looking for examples of capable, competent, strong women: They were simply inescapable. There are talents, energies, and intelligences revealed in this film that could, if we would tap them, transform legislatures and bring wholesale quantities of common sense to public life. There are tacticians, strategists, and philosophers in *Harlan County, U.S.A.* who make the UMW theoreticians look tame—and the company spokesmen look callow and inane.

The movie is a great American document, but it's also entertaining; Kopple structures her material to provide tension, brief but vivid characterizations, and dramatic confrontations (including one incredibly charged moment when the sheriff attempts to lead a caravan of scabs past the picket line). There are gunshots in the film, and a death, and also many moments of simple warmth and laughter. The many union songs on the sound track provide a historical context, and also help Kopple achieve a fluid editing rhythm. And most of all there are the people in the film, those amazing people, so proud and self-reliant and brave.

Harold and Maude ★ 1/2
PG, 92 m., 1971

Ruth Gordon (Maude), Bud Cort (Harold), Vivian Pickles (Mrs. Chasen), Cyril Cusack (Glaucus), Charles Tyner (Uncle Victor), Ellen Geer (Sunshine Dare). Directed by Hal Ashby and produced by Colin Higgins and Charles Mulverhill. Screenplay by Higgins.

Death can be as funny as most things in life, I suppose, but not the way Harold and Maude go about it. They meet because they're both funeral freaks, and one day their eyes lock over a grave. They fall into conversation after Maude steals Harold's hearse and offers him a ride. Harold drives a hearse, by the way, because he is fascinated by death, particularly his own. So fascinated that maybe the only reason he doesn't kill himself is that suicide would put an end to his suicide fantasies. You can see that Harold is a young man with a problem.

Now Maude, on the other hand, is seventy-nine years young, and has what is known in the trade as a lust for life. She lives in a railroad car, spends her afternoons uprooting city trees and returning them to the forest, and in general is an all-round booster of the life force. She goes to funerals because there is a time to live and a time to die, and she wants to be on time.

The word has gotten out that *Harold and Maude* is the story of a love affair between these two people. It is not, so necrophiliacs please stay cool. It is about how Harold annoys (yes, annoys would be the word) his mother by staging a staggering variety of suicide attempts. Let's see. There's immolation, hanging, whacking off his arm with a meat cleaver, driving his car over a cliff, drowning, and if I missed one, never mind. But his mother is merely annoyed. She takes a morning dip in the swimming pool, for example, and when she comes upon Harold's body floating face down, she merely swims another lap. Talk about exercise freaks.

Harold's mother figures maybe what Harold needs is a little female companionship. She signs him up with a computer dating service, but the girls are sort of put off when he sets himself afire on their date, and things like that. Maude, on the other hand, doesn't seem to mind. As played by Ruth Gordon, she is the same wise-cracking operator out of the side of the mouth that we met in *Rosemary's Baby.* When a traffic cop stops her for being in possession of a stolen truck, a stolen car, and a stolen shovel, she apologizes and then drives away. When he catches up with her again, she steals his motorcycle. You see what an indomitable sort she is.

Harold is played by Bud Cort, the round-eyed and solemn-mouthed announcer over the PA system in *M*A*S*H.* He is even rounder and more solemn this time, having perfected a funereal droop of the lower lip. It is hard to get very much animation into a character who is obsessed with his own oblivion, but Cort doesn't even try.

And so what we get, finally, is a movie of attitudes. Harold is death, Maude life, and they manage to make the two seem so similar that life's hardly worth the extra bother. The visual style makes everyone look fresh from the Wax Museum, and all the movie lacks is a lot of day-old gardenias and lilies and roses in the lobby, filling the place with a cloying sweet smell. Nothing more to report today. Harold doesn't even make pallbearer.

Harry and the Hendersons ★ ★
PG, 113 m,, 1987

John Lithgow (George), Melinda Dillon (Nancy), Margaret Langrick (Sarah), Joshua Rudoy (Ernie), Kevin Peter Hall (Harry), David Suchet (Jacques Lefleur), Lainie Kazan (Irene), Don Ameche (Dr. Wrightwood), M. Emmet Walsh (George, Sr.). Directed by William Dear and produced by Richard Vane and Dear. Screenplay by Dear, William E. Martin, and Ezra D. Rappaport.

Harry and the Hendersons doubtless will inspire a lot of comparisons to *E.T.*, if only because the story lines are similar: Typical American family takes a strange and exotic creature into its home and learns to love it, despite the havoc it wreaks. *Harry* contains a lot of the same elements as *E.T.*, and I enjoyed them, but it lacks one crucial element: awe.

No matter how lovable *E. T.* was, the little creature still possessed a certain mystery and majesty. To look into those wide-set eyes was to perceive a being that had seen a lot more than we had. The movie contained comedy, melodrama, and schmaltz, but it also was possessed of a rare spirit; there was an aura about *E. T.* that inspired a genuine sense of wonder.

Harry, the hero of *Harry and the Hendersons,* is a lovable creature, but he inspires condescension, not awe. He is a Bigfoot, a tall, shambling, hairy creature that the Henderson family adopts after they run him down with their family station wagon. At first he's a little scary, but before long it's clear all he wants is acceptance. And as he has been designed by Rick Baker, he doesn't look menacing for more than a moment. He looks more like a big, friendly stuffed toy.

I have a friend who likes to introduce himself at parties with this line, which he claims he memorized off of a card stuck into a baked potato: "I've been tubbed, I've been rubbed, I've been scrubbed. I'm lovable, huggable, and eatable." Harry has many of the same qualities. After the Henderson family brings him home, he breaks up a lot of the furniture, the stairs, and the walls, but only because he's clumsy. His favorite pastime is watching TV.

There is a dumb subplot, really dumb, about a professional Bigfoot hunter (David Suchet) who dreams only of killing Harry. Suchet skulks about the neighborhood, hiding in bushes, brandishing his rifle and engaging in debates with an old scientist (Don Ameche) who once saw Bigfoot and now runs a Bigfoot souvenir stand. Another fairly unnecessary supporting character is the nosy neighbor, played by Lainie Kazan.

Indeed, much of this movie is unnecessary. That's because William Dear, the director and co-writer, apparently decided right at the start to make *Harry and the Hendersons* into a predigested sitcom instead of exploring the Bigfoot idea more thoughtfully. If we ever have wondered if Bigfeet exist, and how they survive, and what they think about, we won't learn the answers here: This movie's basic insight is that Bigfoot is a tall Cabbage Patch doll with hair.

Too bad. There are some nice moments in the movie, contributed by John Lithgow and Melinda Dillon, as the adult Hendersons, and by Ameche and Bigfoot. But they're offset by the obnoxious qualities of the Henderson kids (Margaret Langrick and Joshua Rudoy), who seem to be aiming for Drew Barrymore but hitting Dennis the Menace. Little kids probably will like this movie, especially if they haven't seen *E. T.*

Note: Rick Baker's effective Bigfoot costume is inhabited by an actor named Kevin Peter Hall, who thus joins the David Prowse Fan Club, named for the man inside the Darth Vader uniform.

Harry and Tonto ★ ★ ★ ★

PG, 115 m., 1974

Art Carney (Harry), Ellen Burstyn (Shirley), Chief Dan George (Indian), Geraldine Fitzgerald (Jessie). Directed and produced by Paul Mazursky. Screenplay by Mazursky and Josh Greenfield.

Paul Mazursky's *Harry and Tonto* tells the story of a feisty seventy-two-year-old who is carried forcibly from his New York apartment one step ahead of the wrecker's ball. He was happy with his life in the city (apart from the four muggings so far this year) and content to talk to his old cronies and to his cat, Tonto. But life without a home isn't easy. He goes for a while to live with his son on Long Island, where he's welcomed, sort of, into a household on the edge of insanity. One of his grandsons thinks the other one is crazy. The other won't respond because, you see, he has taken a vow of silence. Harry sizes up the situation, packs Tonto in a carrying case, and hits the road. The road becomes a strange and wonderful place for Harry, mostly because of his own resilient personality. He's played by Art Carney as a man of calm philosophy, gentle humor, and an acceptance of the ways people can be. He is also not a man in a hurry. When he can't carry Tonto onto an airplane, he takes the bus. When the bus can't wait for Tonto to relieve himself, he buys a used car and picks up hitchhikers.

One of them is a young girl who becomes his friend. She talks of her life, and he talks of his, including his long-ago romance with a member of the Isadora Duncan troupe. The last he'd heard of her, she was living in Peru, Indiana, as the wife of a pharmacist. The girl talks him into stopping in Indiana and looking the old woman up. And he does so, in a scene of rare warmth and tenderness. The woman, Jessie (played by Geraldine Fitzgerald), has a very shaky memory, but she does recall being a dancer, and in the calm of the recreation room at her nursing home, the old couple dances together one last time.

And then Harry's back on the road to Chicago, where he has a daughter who runs a bookstore. He spends a few days with her, walking on the beach and talking things over. His silent grandson has broken his vow and flown to Chicago to try to talk the old man into coming back to New York. But, no, Harry doesn't think he will. ("You're talking now?" he asks his grandson. "Garbo speaks," the kid shrugs.)

He heads vaguely westward. His young hitchhiker has fallen in love with his grandson, and they think they'll aim for a commune in Colorado. Harry gives them a lift because that's more or less where he's going, but he declines, just now, to join the commune. He gives them his car, hitches a ride with a Las Vegas hooker, is (to his vast surprise) seduced by her, has a good time in Vegas, and, alas, is arrested for having a few too many.

This leads to the film's most hilarious scene. Harry is tossed into a cell already occupied by an ancient Indian (Chief Dan George) who has been arrested for practicing medicine without a license. The two old men gravely discuss recent television shows and the problem of bursitis, and the chief cures Harry's aching shoulder in return for an electric blender. Chief Dan George is so solemn, so understated, with Mazursky's dialogue that the result is a great comic scene.

Harry and Tonto drift on West toward the Pacific, and we begin to get the sense that this hasn't been your ordinary road picture, but a sort of farewell voyage by a warm and good old man who is still, at seventy-two, capable of being thankful for the small astonishments offered by life. The achievement is partly Mazursky's, partly Carney's.

Mazursky has established himself as the master of a kind of cinema he calls "serious comedy"—movies that make us laugh and yet have a special attitude toward their material and American society. His earlier films have included *Bob & Carol & Ted & Alice* and the remarkable *Blume in Love*.

Art Carney has, of course, fashioned a distinguished career for himself on the stage after all those years as Norton on "The Honeymooners." Here, he flowers as a movie star. The performance is totally original, all his own, and worthy of the Academy Award it received. It's not easy to make comedies that work as drama, too. But Carney's acting is so perceptive that it helps this material succeed.

Heart Beat ★ ★ 1/2

R, 109 m., 1980

Nick Nolte (Neal Cassady), Sissy Spacek (Carolyn Cassady), John Heard (Jack Kerouac). Directed by John Byrum and produced by Alen Greisman and Michael Shamberg. Screenplay by Byrum.

Jack Kerouac's novel *On the Road* announced an end to the Eisenhower years and the beginning of the narcissistic, rebellious sixties. It told the story of the first beatniks, those dropouts from the middle class who rode the highways from Maine to Mexico and raised hell, wrote poetry, loved unwisely, drank too well, and did the basic engineering on the life-style that would eventually be run to exhaustion by the hippies. Kerouac's novel starred a heroic proto-beat named Dean Moriarty, based on the legendary underground figure Neal Cassady. In *Heart Beat* we get the story of Neal and Jack and Neal's wife. Sort of.

The movie's based on a memoir written a few years ago by Carolyn Cassady, who was not one of the heroes of *On the Road*, and who, it now appears, had good reason to be less than enchanted with the beatnik lifestyle. The wives of famous men often have unique outlooks on their wonderful opportunities to live so close to greatness; when Bennett Cerf, visiting the James Joyces in Paris, described Joyce as a genius, Mrs. Joyce dryly replied, "That's all very well for *you* to say—*you* don't have to live with the bloody man." Carolyn Cassady's *Heart Beat* comes from the same fervent neighborhood of the soul.

But this movie is another matter altogether. How closely it resembles the facts I cannot say, but it paints a portrait of Jack and Neal as good buddies who drank, sang, hitchhiked, lied, and fought their way around the America of the late 1940s (Ker ouac described himself and Cassady as "furtives"), and then both fell in love with Carolyn. She married Neal, who stayed at home, sometimes, between time on the road with Jack and a great deal of additional time spent on applied research into alcoholism. Jack was a drunk, too, and a lot of the movie deals with their attempts to patch things together in the little postwar suburban house in San Francisco where Carolyn tried to maintain a home.

This is not exactly the story we have in memory from the Kerouac legend, and there were long stretches of *Heart Beat* during which I found myself wishing instead for a film version of *On the Road.* That's unfair, I guess—but what is director John Byrum trying to do in *this* movie? I'm not sure. The movie's a triumph of art direction, all right; the locations, clothes, lighting, moods, music, and whole tones of the performances are designed to throw a kind of nostalgic drop cloth over the story, and we're constantly invited to read greater significance into dialogue and gestures because they took place during those now-lost times.

Fine, except that the significance doesn't seem to be there. *Heart Beat* seems to exist almost entirely as a matter of style. The characters are wonderfully well played by Nick Nolte, Sissy Spacek, and John Heard—they have scenes together in which the round-robin of everyday dialogue is almost poetic—but nobody has given their characters anything to do except to be. They exist, we watch them, the decor is inspired, that's it.

The attempts to add other characters from the period are mostly misguided. A character named Ira, inspired by Allen Ginsberg (who forbade use of his name), is so awkwardly drawn he comes off as a fifties' satire of a beatnik poet. Jazz musicians are so artfully "cool" they're paralytic. Jack and Neal move through the worlds of coffee houses and jazz clubs as if they were backdrops, not habitations.

What finally happens is that the whole period—the conformist fifties as well as the rebellious beats—gets frozen into the same flashback. *Everything* becomes part of the film's nostalgic memory. The film seems to treasure the conformity of American mainstream society if only because it provides such an ideal contrast to Neal and Jack. This movie treats its events as so long ago, so finished and done with and bathed in a yellowing afterglow, that we don't sense the very passion and rebelliousness it's supposed to be about. What an irony for the first serious film about the Beats.

Heartbreakers ★ ★ ★ ½

R, 98 m, 1985

Peter Coyote (Arthur Blue), Nick Mancuso (Eli Kahn), Carole Laure (Liliane), Max Gail (King), Carol Wayne (Cathy), James Laurenson (Terry Ray), Jamie Rose (Libby), Kathryn Harrold (Syd). Directed by Bobby Roth and produced by Bob Weis and Roth. Screenplay by Roth.

You can only play the field so long. Then you get stuck in it. You become a person so adept at avoiding commitment that it eventually becomes impossible for you to change your own rules, and so there you are, trapped in your precious freedom. Bobby Roth's *Heartbreakers* is about a group of people like that, a mixed bag of loners that includes a couple of artists, a businessman, a gallery owner, an aerobics instructor, and a model who specializes in telephone sex. During the course of a few weeks, their lives cross in ways that make it particularly hard for each one of them to deny his own unhappiness.

The movie stars Peter Coyote as an angry young artist and Nick Mancuso as his best friend, a businessman who is confused about women and a great many other things. They've been pals for a long time, through good times and bad, but the one thing they've never been able to do is break down and talk about what they're really feeling. During the course of the film, they both fall in love with a beautiful young woman (Carole Laure) who works in an art gallery, and whose body is available but whose mind always seems to be somewhere else.

These three characters are in a movie populated with a lot of other interesting characters, the sort of mixed bag of people who find themselves thrown together in a big city like Los Angeles. Kathryn Harrold plays Coyote's long-time lover, who finally can't take his irresponsibility any longer and moves in with another artist (Charles King), who is big and powerful but surprisingly gentle—his character is developed against type, in interesting ways. Jamie Rose plays an aerobics instructor who is attracted to

Mancuso, but he is attracted to Laure, although not in a way that is likely to get him anywhere.

All of the threads of these lives seem to come together during one long night that Mancuso and Coyote spend with the busty, mid-thirties blonde who models for Coyote's kinky paintings. She is played by Carol Wayne, who had regular walk-ons on the Johnny Carson program until she drowned in Mexico not long after completing her work on this movie. Her performance is so good, so heartbreaking, if you will, that it pulls the whole movie together; her character's willingness to talk about what she really feels places the other characters in strong contrast.

When we first see her, she's an enigma at the edge of the screen—a seemingly dumb blonde who dresses up in leather to model for Coyote's strange, angry paintings. Later, the two men, adrift and unhappy about their respective love lives, end up in her apartment, and what begins as a *ménage à trois* ends up as her own startlingly direct confessional. She makes a frank assessment of her body, her appearance, her prospects. She talks about what she hoped for from life, and what she has received. There is an uncanny feeling that, to some degree, we are listening here to the real Carol Wayne, the real person beneath the image on the Carson show. It is one of the best movie scenes in a long time.

The rest of the movie is also very good, in the way it examines the complex relationships in its Los Angeles world of art, sex, and business, and in the way it shows how arid the Mancuso-Coyote buddy relationship is. The people in this movie might seem glamorous if you glimpsed just a small corner of their lives. But *Heartbreakers* sees them whole, and mercilessly.

The Heartbreak Kid ★ ★ ★ ½
PG, 106 m., 1972

Charles Grodin (Lenny), Cybill Shepherd (Kelly), Jeannie Berlin (Lila), Eddie Albert (Mr. Corcoran), Audra Lindley (Mrs. Corcoran). Directed by Elaine May and produced by Edgar J. Scherick. Screenplay by Neil Simon.

We know as early as the wedding scene—which opens the film—that Elaine May's *The Heartbreak Kid* was directed with a sure feeling for how comedy can edge over into satire and then tragedy. Both of Lila's parents are determined to give her away. They flank her, each clutching an arm, and attempt to march down the aisle in their living room. But it won't do: The folding chairs are too close together.

The honeymoon which follows is, to put it mildly, a disaster. Lenny begins to tire of his new bride during the drive to Miami Beach. She smears egg salad all over her face while eating a sandwich. She sings the same songs over and over. Somewhat ominously, she has saved herself for her wedding night.

In Miami Beach, disaster strikes. Lila gets a terrific sunburn and is confined to the hotel room, immersed in lotion and pain. Lenny goes down to the beach alone, spreads out his towel, stretches out, and is confronted by his destiny. His destiny is named Kelly. She is a blonde Nordic goddess from Minnesota, dedicated to twisting men around her little finger as a form of mild amusement. Lenny is thunderstruck with love and decides on the spot that he must divorce Lila, journey to Minnesota, and marry this creature.

That is the premise of *The Heartbreak Kid*, and maybe only Elaine May and the author of the screenplay, Neil Simon, could make such a hurtful situation funny, and still somewhat true. The movie is about how we do violence to each other with our egos—how everybody does, except for the poor nebbishes like Lila. She does violence only to egg salad. The movie has a way of making us laugh while it hurts, because it makes Lenny into such a blunt object of egotism, desire, and upward mobility.

But in a lot of ways the most interesting character in the movie is Kelly (as played by Cybill Shepherd). She's so inapproachably beautiful that, in a way, all she *can* do with men is tease and taunt them—they're too hypnotized to treat her as if she were alive and accessible. She has a couple of husky athletes to carry her books, and a rich daddy who'd do anything for her (he's actually helpless when she smiles at him). And, inside, she hungers for love more, even, than Lenny.

Lenny is headed for heartbreak, all right, I don't think he really believes in the possibility of love—not for himself. He's into the acquisition of inaccessible goals; maybe the only reason he married Lila was because she *did* save herself. Now there are new peaks to climb. But Lenny's victories are so lonely; we see him at the movie's end, confronted with the fact that he would rather desire than possess.

Jeannie Berlin (Elaine May's daughter) is wonderful as Lila. She has enough acting confidence to be able to go too far and still make us believe; she can get away with smearing that egg salad around for several seconds after common sense says she should stop. Charles Grodin, as her husband, is good as a kind of Dustin Hoffman-as-overachiever; in this role we can find the genesis of many of his later roles.

The movie doesn't constantly bow to Neil Simon's script (as most movie versions of his work do). Elaine May is willing to improvise, to indulge (and exploit) quirks in acting style, and to examine social hypocrisy with a kind of compulsive ferocity. It's a comedy, but there's more in it than that; it's a movie about the ways we pursue, possess, and consume each other as sad commodities.

Heartbreak Ridge ★ ★ ★
R, 130 m., 1986

Clint Eastwood (Highway), Marsha Mason (Aggie), Everett McGill (Major Powers), Moses Gunn (Sergeant Webster), Eileen Heckart (Little Mary), Bo Svenson (Roy Jennings), Mario Van Peebles (Stitch). Peter Koch (Swede). Directed and produced by Clint Eastwood. Screenplay by James Carabatsos.

Clint Eastwood's *Heartbreak Ridge* uses an absolutely standard plot, and makes it special with its energy, its colorful characters, and its almost poetic vulgarity. We have seen this story in a hundred other movies, where the combat-hardened veteran, facing retirement, gets one last assignment to train a platoon of green kids and lead them into battle. But Eastwood, as the producer, director, and star, caresses the material as if he didn't know B movies have gone out of style.

He plays a character named Tom Highway, nicknamed Gunney, a hard-drinking loser who has sacrificed everything—wife, family, friends, reputation—on the altar of the Corps. We meet him in a title sequence that seems directly inspired by *Dirty Harry*; he's in a drunk tank, smoking a cigar and telling tall tales, when a brawny giant attacks him. Eastwood hands his cigar to a bystander, creams the bully, and reaches for his cigar again (just as Dirty Harry finishes eating his hot dog after the opening shoot-out).

The opening scene promises his fans that *Heartbreak Ridge* will provide the violent Eastwood persona they have come to love. What's surprising is that Eastwood doesn't let Tom Highway stride through the picture beating up everybody in sight, and winning the war single-handedly. Instead, the movie is more of a tour through Highway's memories, a last hurrah for a combat veteran who won the Medal of Honor when he was a kid, and has been trying to lose it ever since.

Highway gets assigned to his old outfit, has a reunion with the veteran master sergeant he fought with in Korea, and is chewed out by the Annapolis grad (Everett McGill) who now heads the battalion and wants to run everything by the book. Highway is assigned to a platoon of misfits and malcontents, including a bright black kid (Mario Van Peebles), who wants to be a rock-and-roll singer, and a gigantic Swede (Peter Koch), who he is going to have to fight if he wants to win control of his new command.

There is also the reunion with his former wife (Marsha Mason), who couldn't take the weeks and months of waiting at home, watching the evening news for a glimpse of her husband in Vietnam. We can almost predict her dialogue; Highway was always more married to the Corps than he was to her.

The movie has a brisk, rough-and-tumble pace, with a knock-down fight every fifteen minutes or so. Highway may be over fifty, but of course he can still outfight any man alive, and there is one brutal scene in which he stands his ground and simply outtalks an opponent, his words as hard as his fists.

Nothing in *Heartbreak Ridge* is very subtle, and I wasn't surprised to learn that the shooting schedule lasted less than eight weeks—lightning speed for a movie including basic training and combat scenes. There is a certain raw energy in filmmaking at this pace, however; the actors swagger through their roles instead of chewing them, and there is never more subtlety than the plot can support.

It's easy to spot Eastwood, the director, as he cuts corners. The battalion only seems to support two platoons, for example, and its base seems limited to a few quonset huts.

Even the climactic battle scenes are budget-basement: Highway leads his men into action on Grenada, where they liberate some medical students.

And yet *Heartbreak Ridge* has as much energy and color as any action picture of 1986, and it contains truly amazing dialogue. Some people may be offended by the scatological and ancestral generalities in Highway's speech, but I was mostly amused by his flights of verbal invention. (The U.S. Marine Corps intended to use this film at benefits for its "Toys for Tots" program, but withdrew its support after screening it, presumably because the characters talked too much like Marines.)

Heartbreak Ridge is Eastwood's thirteenth picture as a director, and by now he is a seasoned veteran behind the camera. He has starred in all but one of his films, and who knows Eastwood better? This time he makes himself look old, ragged, and scarred, with a lot of miles behind him. He uses harsh lighting to make his face into a fierce icon. He speaks in a low rasp. He seems to be aiming for the kind of scuzzy, fast-paced vitality of a low-budget Sam Fuller picture, and he gets it. *Heartbreak Ridge* doesn't aim as high as most current high-tech action movies, but it hits its target.

Heartburn ★ ★
R, 109 m., 1986

Meryl Streep (Rachel), Jack Nicholson (Mark), Jeff Daniels (Richard), Maureen Stapleton (Vera), Stockard Channing (Julie), Richard Masur (Arthur), Catherine O'Hara (Betty). Directed by Mike Nichols and produced by Nichols and Robert Greenhut. Screenplay by Nora Ephron.

Maybe Nora Ephron should have based her story on somebody else's marriage. That way, she could have provided the distance and perspective that good comedy needs. Instead, she based *Heartburn*—first her novel and now her screenplay—on her own marriage. And she apparently had too much anger to transform the facts into entertaining fiction. This is a bitter, sour movie about two people who are only marginally interesting.

The characters are Rachel, a New York writer, and Mark, a Washington political columnist. The originals for the characters are Ephron and Watergate journalist Carl Bernstein, whom she married and then divorced when she learned he was having affairs. In the movie, the characters are played by Meryl Streep and Jack Nicholson, and just by seeing their names on the marquee you'd figure the movie would have to be electrifying. But it's not. Here is the story of two people with no chemistry, played by two actors with great chemistry. The only way they can get into character is to play against the very things we like them for.

Streep seems dowdy and querulous. Nicholson seems to be a shallow creep. Their romance never seems real, never seems important and permanent. So when he starts fooling around, we don't feel the enormity of the offense. There's not much in their marriage for him to betray.

The story: Rachel meets Mark and it's love at first sight, but it's not the kind of loin-churning passion we felt when Nicholson met Kathleen Turner in *Prizzi's Honor*. It's more of a low-grade fever, something to be treated with aspirin—or marriage.

On her wedding day, Rachel takes to the bedroom of her father's apartment and refuses to emerge for hours. Her reluctance is touching at first, then comic, and finally annoying. After the ceremony, they move into a handyman special in Georgetown (affordable because it recently had a fire), and the joke is that the renovations to the house will last longer than their marriage.

There are scenes set in the thickets of Washington gossip, where Catherine O'Hara plays the reigning bitch goddess, and other scenes of domesticity, as when Nicholson wonders why the carpenters have not supplied a doorway from the kitchen to the rest of the house.

Here and there, we see glimpses of the greatness of both Nicholson and Streep, who on an ordinary day with a decent script can act circles around anybody. There's a scene in a maternity ward where Streep comes out of anesthesia and turns to see Nicholson standing there holding their baby. She asks if it's theirs, and the goofy grin on his face is a moment of pure joy.

There's another moment where they sing nursery rhymes to each other. And a moment when Nicholson sits by her bed and cries, because he knows that the flaw in his character will make it impossible for him to function responsibly as a husband and father.

Those moments are adrift in a sea of ennui. *Heartburn* is punctuated by scenes that feel like the director, Mike Nichols, is marking time. Was Bernstein's dislike for the project so great that the filmmakers prudently left out all of the really good stuff? If I were Bernstein, I would rather be portrayed as a colorful rake than as the hapless fall guy in this movie. If they're going to remember you at all, it's not going to be for being unmemorable.

Heartburn not only misses in its treatment of the two central characters, it also fails to give us a real sense of the New York-Washington media axis. The O'Hara character comes closest; I guess she's supposed to be a cross between celebrity reporter Barbara Howar and Washington gossip columnist Diana McLellan. She puts the right spin in her sly reports of the latest transgressions and infidelities.

But Nicholson never seems to be a Washington columnist. Most of the time, he doesn't have much to say. The Streep character is supposed to be some kind of a food writer, but what we totally miss is the manic desperation of the typical New York free-lancer. She seems too placid and laid back. She ought to be pitching projects and trying to get big advances.

When she wrote the screenplay, Ephron missed a bet by not writing in some scenes in which her character meets with a New York publisher and tries to pitch a comic novel in which she rips the lid off of her marriage to a famous journalist. If we're going to base a story on a real marriage, let's go all the way.

After we've eviscerated the philandering husband, why stop before we get to the part where the ex-wife violates her own privacy and that of her children in a bid for revenge, the bestseller list and a sale to the movies? And what about the ex-husband's offer to sue? I had the strangest feeling that *Heartburn* ended just when it was starting to get interesting.

Heartland ★ ★ ★ ★

PG, 95 m., 1981

Conchata Ferrell (Elinore Randall), Rip Torn (Clyde Stewart), Barry Primus (Jack), Lilia Skala (Grandma), Megan Folsom (Jerrine). Directed by Richard Pearce and produced by Annick Smith, Michael Hausman, and Beth Ferris. Screenplay by Ferris.

Richard Pearce's *Heartland* is a big, robust, joyous movie about people who make other movie heroes look tentative. It takes place in 1910, out in the unsettled frontier lands of Wyoming, and it's about a determined young widow who packs up her daughter and moves out West to take a job as the housekeeper on a ranch. At first she is completely baffled by the rancher who has hired her ("I can't talk about anything with that man"), but in the end she marries him and digs in to fight an endless battle with the seasons, the land, and the banks.

A movie newcomer named Conchata Ferrell plays the widow, Elinore Randall. She's a big-boned, clear-eyed, wide-hipped woman of about thirty who makes us realize that most of the women in Westerns look as if they're about to collapse under the strain. She is extremely clear about her motivations. She gives a full day's work for a full day's pay, but she is tired of working for others, and would like to own her own land someday. She does not, however, speak endlessly about her beliefs and ambitions, because *Heartland* is a movie of few words. That is partly because of the character of Clyde Stewart (Rip Torn), the rancher she goes to work for. He hardly ever says anything. He is a hard man, a realist who knows that the undisciplined Western land can break his back. But he is not unkind, and in the scene where he finally proposes to marry her, his choice of words contains understated wit that makes us smile.

Everything in this movie affirms life. Perhaps that is why *Heartland* can also be so unblinking in its consideration of death. The American West was not settled by people who spent all their time baking peach cobbler and knitting samplers, and this movie contains several scenes that will shock some audiences because of their forthright realism. We see a pig slaughtered, a calf birthed, cattle skinned, and a half-dead horse left out in the blizzard because there is simply nothing to feed it.

All of *Heartland* is stunningly photographed on and around a Montana ranch. (The movie is based on the real life of a settler named Elinore Randall Stewart.) It contains countless small details of farming life, put in not for "atmosphere" but because they work better than dialogue to flesh out the characters. The desolation of the frontier is suggested in small vignettes, such as one involving a family that could get this far and no farther, and lives huddled inside a small wagon. Among the many scenes that delight us with their freshness is one moment right after the wedding, when Ferrell realizes she got married wearing her apron and work boots, and another when she is about to give birth and her husband rides off into the storm to fetch the midwife from the next farm. We settle back here in anticipation of the obligatory scene in which the midwife arrives and immediately orders everyone to boil hot water, lots of it—but this time we're surprised. The husband returns alone; the midwife was not at her farm. Quiet little developments like that help expose the weight of cliché that holds down most Westerns.

In a movie filled with wonderful things, the very best thing in *Heartland* is Conchata Ferrell's voice. It is strong, confident, clear as a bell, and naturally musical. It is a fine instrument, bringing authenticity to every word it says. It puts this movie to a test, because we could not quite accept that voice saying words that sounded phony and contrived. In *Heartland*, we never have to.

Heat and Dust ★ ★ ★

R, 130 m., 1983

Julie Christie (Anne), Zakir Hussain (Inder Lal), Greta Scacchi (Olivia), Shashi Kapoor (The Nawab). Directed by James Ivory and produced by Ismail Merchant. Screenplay by Ruth Prawer Jhabvala.

Forster suggested in *A Passage to India* that the subcontinent would forever be beyond the understanding of Western minds, and that attempts to impose European ways upon it were bound to be futile and likely to be ridiculous. *Heat and Dust* makes the same argument by telling us two love stories, one set in the 1920s, the other set in the present day.

The heroine of the earlier love story is Olivia Rivers (Greta Scacchi), a free spirit whose independent ways do not fit in with the hidebound values of the British. Her husband demands that she conform, that she stay with the other British wives, share their values and interests, and keep India itself at arm's length. Olivia does not see it that way. She explores on her own. She becomes fascinated by India. Eventually she has an affair with the local Nawab (Shashi Kapoor), who is beguiling, attractive, cheerfully sophisticated, and possibly a murderer. When she becomes pregnant with his child, the whole fabric of British-Indian relationships is torn, because—depending on the point of view—*both* of the lovers have lowered themselves.

The second love story involves Olivia's great-niece, Anne (Julie Christie). Fascinated by hints about the long-ago family scandal, she follows Olivia's footsteps out to India and does her own exploring and has her own affair. There comes a moment in the movie when we realize, with a little shock, what the movie is really about. It's an effective scene; soon after Anne arrives at a decision about her own pregnancy, she visits the isolated cottage where the disgraced Olivia went to spend her confinement.

As Anne dreamily moves among the memories of the past, we realize that India and England, the East and the West, are not quite the issues here: that both women were made social outcasts from both societies in two different periods, simply because of biological facts. East is East and West is West, and never the twain shall meet—except possibly in a shared enthusiasm for sexist double standards.

Heat and Dust contains wonderful sights and sounds and textures. It is seductive, treating both of its love stories with seriousness; these are not romances, but decisions to dissent. It is fully at home in its times and places (the director, James Ivory, and the producer, Ismail Merchant, have spent twenty years making films about the British in India). And when it is over, we're a little surprised to find that it is angry, too. Angry that women of every class and every system, women British and Indian, women of the 1920s and of the 1980s, are always just not quite the same caste as men.

Heaven ★ ★

PG-13, 80 m., 1987

A documentary directed by Diane Keaton and produced by Joe Kelly.

It was Edward Lear, that romantic old Victorian, who painted the best portrait of the hereafter that I have ever read. Writing to his friend Fortescue in his own creative spelling, he hoped that, "In the next eggzi stens you and I and my lady may be able to sit for placid hours under a lotus tree eating of ice cream and pelican pie, with our feet in a hazure coloured stream and with the birds and beasts of paradise a sporting around us."

Since not one of us knows exactly what awaits us after this life, that definition, I think, satisfies me as well as any, even though I have never tasted pelican. But other people have other notions of the sweet by and by, and in *Heaven*, Diane Keaton assembles a large number of them and asks them such questions as: What is heaven? Is there sex in heaven? How do you get to heaven? How do you get to hell?

Some of the answers she receives are memorable, or funny, or moving. Most are not; most are simply opinions from random subjects who have no particular credentials—except, of course, that like all of us they will someday either be, or not be, in heaven.

But there's more to the film than a simple Q & A. Keaton also assembles old film footage showing how heaven was visualized in previous films. And she photographs her subjects in a sort of angelic limbo, as if they were in heaven's waiting room.

But heaven's real waiting room, as we all know, is Palm Springs, California. And *Heaven* is an idea for a movie that is not quite realized. The weakness, I think, is in Keaton's excessive attention to visual detail. She has gone to a lot of effort to create her abstract sets, her heavenly decor in which the people seem almost like exhibits. But that has given her subjects time to think about their answers, some of which seem too clever, too thought out.

Perhaps a sloppier film would have been a better idea. I can imagine the "Candid Camera" approach, in which people would have been invited to talk about life and death in a totally unself-conscious way. That might have produced more spontaneity, and even more truth, than the deliberate artiness of *Heaven*.

Even so, there are moments in *Heaven* I am glad I saw. Some of the old film clips, for example, of angels being issued their wings. A debate between a believer and an atheist. And the utter certainty of some of the subjects, who know for sure what cannot, by definition, be known at all. There is enough good stuff in *Heaven* to supply a short film of thirty or forty minutes, but at eighty minutes Keaton runs out of inspiration as well as material.

The other night, I was showing a film called *Gates of Heaven* to some people. It is, as faithful readers will know, one of my favorite films, a 1977 documentary by Errol Morris about people involved in the operation of two California pet cemeteries.

Toward the end of the film, one woman speaks of her certainty that she will meet her dead dog in heaven. She says: "There's your dog. Your dog's dead. But what happened to the thing that made it move? There had to be something, didn't there?" And in those simple words are summarized the final mystery of life for all of us. *Heaven* never quite achieves a moment like that.

Heaven Help Us ★ ★ ½

R, 103 m., 1985

Andrew McCarthy (Michael Dunn), Mary Stuart Masterson (Danni), Kevin Dillon (Rooney), Malcolm Danare (Caesar), Donald Sutherland (Brother Thadeus), John Heard (Brother Timothy). Directed by Michael Dinner and produced by Don Wigutow and Mark Carliner. Screenplay by Charles Purpura.

If you remember those little clickers that the nuns used to use, you'll know why I liked the beginning of *Heaven Help Us* so much—and why I had such mixed feelings about the rest of it. The clickers were dime-store crickets that made a nice, loud click, perfect for signaling a First Communion class so all the kids would stand up at the same time, and kneel at the same time, and start filing down the aisle together. In an opening scene of the movie, a kid has his own clicker, and uses it to sabotage the nun's signals, so that the whole class is bobbing like a yo-yo. I thought that was funny, and I thought it set the tone for an affectionate, nostalgic, funny look back at Catholic school education in Brooklyn in the 1960s—sort of a cross between *Do Black Patent Leather Shoes Really Reflect Up?* and *Sister Mary Agnes Explains It All for You.* Unfortunately, what the movie turns into is more like a cross between *Stalag 17* and *Porky's*, as sadistic teachers beat every last glimmer of spirit out of students, and kids establish new indoor records in self-abuse.

Because *Heaven Help Us* does not have the

slightest ambition to be a serious movie about Catholic high schools, I can't understand why the classroom scenes are so overplayed. As the sadistic teaching brother (Jay Patterson) slams his students against the blackboard, all we're really watching is a lapse in judgment by the moviemakers. The scenes are so ugly and depressing that they throw the rest of the movie out of balance. And that's too bad, because here and there in this movie are moments of real insight and memory. There's a special charm in the sweet, shy romance between a student (Andrew McCarthy) and the daughter (Mary Stuart Masterson) of the local soda fountain owner. I also liked the character named Caesar (Malcolm Danare), who pretends to be a snotty intellectual, as a defense against the heat he gets because he's smart.

The strange thing about the movie is the way the moments of inspiration raise our hopes, and then disappoint them. Take the scene where the school plays host to the nearby Catholic girls' school at a dance. The boys and girls are lined up on opposite sides of the room, and then an earnest little priest (Wallace Shawn, from *My Dinner with André*) stands up on the stage and delivers a lecture on "The Evils of Lust," gradually warming to his subject. The idea of the scene is funny, and it has a certain amount of underlying truth (I remember a priest once warning my class, "Never touch yourselves, boys"—without telling us where). But Shawn's speech climbs to such a hysterical pitch that it goes over the top, and the humor is lost; it simply becomes weird behavior.

Heaven Help Us has assembled a lot of the right elements for a movie about a Catholic boys' high school—the locations, the actors, and a lot of the right memories. But it has not found its tone. Maybe the filmmakers just never did really decide what they thought about the subject. For their penance, they should see *Rock and Roll High School.*

Heaven's Gate ½★
R, 220 m., 1981

Kris Kristofferson (Averill), Christopher Walken (Champion), John Hurt (Irvine), Sam Waterston (Canton), Brad Dourif (Eggleston), Isabelle Huppert (Ella), Joseph Cotten (Reverend Doctor), Jeff Bridges (John), Gordana Rashovich (Widow Kovach). Directed by Michael Cimino and produced by Joann Carelli. Screenplay by Cimino.

We begin with a fundamental question: Why is *Heaven's Gate* so painful and unpleasant to look at? I'm not referring to its content, but to its actual visual texture: This is one of the ugliest films I believe I have ever seen. Its director, Michael Cimino, opens his story at Harvard, continues it in Montana, and closes it aboard a ship. And yet a grim industrial pall hangs low over everything. There are clouds and billows of dirty yellow smoke in every shot that can possibly justify it, and when he runs out of smoke he gives us fog and such incredible amounts of dust that there are whole scenes where we can barely see anything. That's not enough. Cimino also shoots his picture in a maddening soft focus that makes the people and places in this movie sometimes almost impossible to *see.* And then he goes after the colors. There's not a single primary color in this movie, only dingy washed-out sepia tones.

I know, I know: He's trying to demystify the West, and all those other things hotshot directors try to do when they don't really want to make a Western. But this movie is a study in wretched excess. It is so smoky, so dusty, so foggy, so unfocused and so brownish yellow that you want to try Windex on the screen. A director is in deep trouble when we do not even enjoy the primary act of looking at his picture.

But Cimino's in deeper trouble still. *Heaven's Gate* has, of course, become a notorious picture, a boondoggle that cost something like $36 million and was yanked out of its New York opening run after the critics ran gagging from the theater. Its running time, at that point, was more than four hours. Perhaps length was the problem? Cimino went back to the editing room, while a United Artists executive complained that the film had been "destroyed" by an unfairly negative review by *New York Times* critic Vincent Canby. Brother Canby was only doing his job. If the film was formless at four hours, it was insipid at 140 minutes. At either length it is so incompetently photographed and edited that there are times when we are not even sure which character we are looking at. Christopher Walken is in several of the initial Western scenes before he finally gets a closeup and we see who he is. John Hurt wanders through various scenes to no avail. Kris Kristofferson is the star of the movie, and is never allowed to generate enough character for us to miss him, should he disappear.

The opening scenes are set at Harvard (well, they were actually shot in England, but never mind). They show Kristofferson, Hurt, and other idealistic young men graduating in 1870 and setting off to civilize a nation. Kristofferson decides to go West, to help develop the territory. He explains this decision in a narration, and the movie might have benefited if he'd narrated the whole thing, explaining as he went along. Out West, as a lawman, he learns of a plot by the cattlebreeders' association to hire a private army and assassinate 125 newly arrived European immigrants who are, it is claimed, anarchists, killers, and thieves. Most of the movie will be about this plot, Kristofferson's attempts to stop it, Walken's involvement in it, and the involvement of both Kristofferson and Walken in the private life of a young Montana madam (Isabelle Huppert).

In a movie where nothing is handled well, the immigrants are handled very badly. Cimino sees them as a mob. They march onscreen, babble excitedly in foreign tongues, and rush off wildly in all directions. By the movie's end, we can identify only one of them for sure. She is the Widow Kovach, whose husband was shot dead near the beginning of the film. That makes her the emblem of the immigrants' suffering. Every time she steps forward out of the mob, somebody respectfully murmurs "Widow Kovach!" in the subtitles. While the foreigners are hanging onto Widow Kovach's every insight, the cattlemen are holding meetings in private clubs and offering to pay their mercenaries $5 a day plus expenses and $50 for every other foreigner shot or hung. I am sure of those terms because they are repeated endlessly throughout a movie that cares to make almost nothing else clear.

The ridiculous scenes are endless. Samples: Walken, surrounded by gunmen and trapped in a burning cabin, scribbles a farewell note in which he observes that he is trapped in the burning cabin, and then he signs his full name so that there will be no doubt who the note was from. Kristofferson, discovering Huppert being gang-raped by several men, leaps in with six-guns in both hands and shoots all the men, including those aboard Huppert, without injuring her. In a big battle scene, men make armored wagons out of logs and push them forward into the line of fire, even though anyone could ride around behind and shoot them. There is more. There is much more. It all adds up to a great deal less. This movie is $36 million thrown to the winds. It is the most scandalous cinematic waste I have ever seen, and remember, I've seen *Paint Your Wagon.*

The Hidden ★ ★ ★

R, 98 m., 1987

Michael Nouri (Tom Beck), Kyle MacLachlan (Lloyd Gallagher), Ed O'Ross (Cliff Willis), Clu Gulager (Ed Flynn), Claudia Christian (Brenda Lee), Clarence Felder (John Masterson). Directed by Jack Sholder and produced by Robert Shaye. Screenplay by Bob Hunt.

The Hidden opens with a brutal bank robbery and a violent chase scene, and for a moment I thought I was in for another routine cop movie, but then I saw the funny look in the eyes of the bank robber, and I wasn't so sure. Here was a guy who seemed to be receiving secret transmissions. Aiming his car at a police barricade, he allowed a little smile to flicker on his lips, and when the cops aimed a hail of bullets at him, he took dozens of hits and yet still stayed on his feet and laughed at them.

Back at headquarters, Michael Nouri plays the cop assigned to the case. He wants to catch this guy, who has been responsible for an incredible string of violent crimes, but he's not so happy when an FBI man turns up and assigns himself to the case. The federal agent is played by Kyle MacLachlan, the clean-cut kid from *Blue Velvet,* and he looks just as clean-cut this time, but he, too, has a strange light in his eyes. Nouri discovers the key to this mystery about half an hour after we've figured it out for ourselves. Both the killer and the so-called FBI agent are from another planet. "Are we talking spaceman here?" Nouri asks, and we are.

The Hidden takes this situation and makes a surprisingly effective film out of it, a sleeper that talks like a thriller and walks like a thriller, but has more brains than the average thriller. It also has a sense of humor, and some subtle acting by MacLachlan, whose assignment is to play a character who is always just a beat out of step.

Jeff Bridges had a similar challenge in *Starman*, where he played an alien who cloned a human body and then tried to find his way around in it. MacLachlan takes a different approach, playing his alien with a certain strange reserve, as if he's trying the controls very lightly, afraid of going into a spin.

At first, Nouri naturally assumes this FBI guy is simply another weirdo. As he gradually begins to believe the story, his problem is to deal with his fellow cops, who don't believe in spacemen. Meanwhile, the killer moves from one host body to another, taking a guided tour of earth life-forms (his hosts include a dog and a stripper). The movie was directed by Jack Sholder, whose last film was *A Nightmare on Elm Street, Part Two.* I don't know what I was expecting, but certainly not this original and efficient thriller.

The Hidden Fortress ★ ★ ★ ★

NO MPAA RATING, 139 m., 1958

Toshiro Mifuene (General Rokurota Makabe), Misa Uehara (Princess Yukihime), Takashi Shimura (General Nagakura), Susumu Fujita (General Tadokoro). Directed by Akira Kurosawa and produced by Kurosawa and Masumi Rumimoro. Screenplay by Kurosawa and Rumimoro.

The Hidden Fortress is grand, bold moviemaking—a Japanese adventure classic that combines elements of samurai films, Westerns, and myths of heroes and commoners. It does something else, too. It reveals many of the sources of the *Star Wars* movies so clearly that you can almost see R2D2, C3PO, and Princess Leia there on the screen. Now that we've had two sequels to *Star Wars*, how about this as a prologue?

The movie was made in 1958 by Akira Kurosawa, the greatest of Japanese directors, and it attracted a lot of attention at the time. It was the first Japanese movie in Cinemascope, it was one of the most expensive Japanese movies ever made, and it confirmed Kurosawa's role as a master of adventure epics. His *Seven Samurai* (1954) inspired Hollywood's *Magnificent Seven*, but it took George Lucas to use *The Hidden Fortress* as the starting point for the most popular American movies ever made.

The irony is that *The Hidden Fortress* has hardly been seen in this country. A much-shortened version had brief engagements in the early 1960s, but then it went out of release and the rights were allowed to lapse until late in 1983, when, for the first time, this uncut 139-minute version was brought to America. The best video version is the Criterion Collection's laserdisc, with a letterboxed format so Kurosawa's entire widescreen compositions are visible.

The debt of the *Star Wars* pictures to Kurosawa is obvious almost from the opening shots, when two hapless Army underlings, one short, one tall, stagger through an empty landscape bemoaning their fates. Then the other story elements fall into place: a brave, outcast warrior general; a proud and fierce princess who is forced to disguise herself as a commoner; a feared military leader who first opposes the princess's cause but then supports it; a mysterious hidden fortress that must be captured, defended, or destroyed; and, of course, chases and swordfights and appeals to tradition and history.

Does all of this sound more than vaguely familiar? Lucas gives full credit: He told Kurosawa he saw the movie in film school, never forgot it, and used the characters of the two foot soldiers as an inspiration for his two inseparable androids.

Kurosawa has made better movies, but never one more filled with humor and energy. His story isn't made into a dirge about honor and violence, but into a celebration of high spirits. The two foot soldiers enlist in the service of the general (Toshiro Mifune) without knowing who he is or that the woman accompanying him is their princess. They all conspire to move a wagonload of gold from one kingdom to another, concealing the gold inside sticks of firewood and hiding themselves in a procession to a firewood festival. There are close scrapes, double-crosses, cases of mistaken identity, and a thrilling lance-fight between Mifune and that other great Japanese star, Susumu Fujita. An overnight stop in a rowdy frontier town will remind you of the saloon planet in *Star Wars*.

There are also several breathtakingly great individual shots. One comes early in the film, when thousands off prisoners riot and run crazily down a long, sweeping flight of steps, overwhelming their captors. Another comes during the duel with lances, when the troops in the background are choreographed to mirror every move of the fight with their own body movements. And there's the firewood festival, with waves of celebrants dancing around the flames in a pagan dream. Seeing *The Hidden Fortress* is like visiting the wellspring of the Force.

High Anxiety ★ ★ ½
PG, 92 m., 1978

Mel Brooks (Dr. Thorndyke), Madeline Kahn (Victoria Brisbane), Cloris Leachman (Nurse Diesel), Harvey Korman (Dr. Montague), Ron Carey (Brophy), Howard Morris (Professor Lillolman), Murphy Dunne (Piano Player), Ira Miller (Psychiatrist). Directed and produced by Mel Brooks. Screenplay by Brooks, Ron Clark, Rudy DeLuca, and Barry Levinson.

One of the problems with Mel Brooks's *High Anxiety* is that it picks a tricky target: It's a spoof of the work of Alfred Hitchcock, but Hitchcock's films are often funny themselves. And satire works best when its target is self-important. It's easy for the *National Lampoon* to take on the *Reader's Digest*. But can you imagine a satire *of* the *National Lampoon*?

Almost all of Hitchcock's fifty-three or so films have their great moments of wit. And wit—the ability to share a sense of subtle fun with an audience—is not exactly Mel Brooks's strong point. He takes such key Hitchcock moments as the shower scene from *Psycho*, the climbing scene from *Vertigo*, and the shooting in *North by Northwest* and he clobbers them. It's not satire; it's overkill. Maybe it wasn't such a hot idea for Brooks to spoof Hitchcock in the first place. What he's done, though, is to go ahead and take the Hitchcock material, and almost bury his own comic talent in the attempt to fit things into his satirical formula. The best moments in *High Anxiety* come not when Brooks is being assaulted in the shower with a rolled-up newspaper, but when Brooks leaves Hitchcock altogether and does his own crazy, brilliant stuff.

Take, for example, a moment when dramatic music overwhelms the sound track while Brooks and his chauffeur are driving down a Los Angeles freeway. They look at each other, puzzled, and then we see the Los Angeles Symphony Orchestra performing in a bus in the next lane. Sure, he's pulled the same gag before (Count Basie turning up in the desert in *Blazing Saddles)*, but it still works. Another Brooks specialty that works again this time is the casting of Cloris Leachman in variations of a neo-Nazi sadist. In *Young Frankenstein*, she was Frau Blucher, whose very name made horses whinny with fright. Now she's Nurse Diesel, sinister presence at the Institute for the Very, *Very* Nervous, where Brooks has been hired as the new director. She has a closet full of whips and chains, and walks around as if her nurse's uniform covered a cast-iron corset. It's funny . . . but because it comes from Brooks and Leachman, not because it has much to do with Hitchcock.

Here's an example of why Hitchcock is so spoof-proof. At the end of *High Anxiety*, a victim dangles from the top of a tower for what seems like minutes on end, hanging at times by a single leg. Brooks is having fun with the way Hitchcock plays with his scenes of climactic violence. Fine. But remember Hitchcock's wonderful 1972 movie *Frenzy*? There's that strangling in it that goes on and on and on, played very straight, until we finally realize that Hitchcock is slyly giving us our money's worth by playing with the scene beyond all the possibilities of realism.

Brooks has made a specialty of movie satires: *Blazing Saddles*, *Young Frankenstein*, and *Silent Movie*. But they took on well-chosen targets. It's one thing to kid the self-conscious seriousness of a Western or a horror movie. It's another to take on a director of such sophistication that half the audience won't even get the in-jokes the other half is laughing at.

History of the World—Part I ★ ★
R, 90 m., 1981

Mel Brooks (Moses, Comicus, Torquemada, Jacques, Louis XVI), Dom DeLuise (Nero), Madeline Kahn (Empress Nympho), Harvey Korman (Count De Monet), Cloris Leachman (Madame Defarge), Ron Carey (Swiftus), Mary-Margaret Humes (Miriam). Directed and produced by Mel Brooks. Screenplay by Brooks.

Mel Brooks's movie *History of the World—Part I* is a rambling, undisciplined, sometimes embarrassing failure from one of the most gifted comic filmmakers around. What went wrong? Brooks never seems to have a clear idea of the rationale of his movie—so there's no confident narrative impetus to carry it along. His "history" framework doesn't have an approach or point of view; it's basically just a laundry-line for whatever gags he can hang on it.

What *is* this bizarre grab bag? Is it a parody of old Biblical, Roman, and French historical epics? Sometimes. Is it one-shot, comedy revue blackouts? Sometimes. Is it satire aimed at pompous targets? Sometimes. But most of the time it's basically just expensive sets sitting around waiting for Brooks to do something funny in front of them.

Brooks seems to rely on his own spontaneous comic genius in this film, and genius, even when you have it, is not something to be relied upon. He provides isolated moments that are indeed hilarious, moments that find an inspired image and zing us with it (as when a slave boogies through the streets of ancient Rome with a loud transistor radio glued to his ear). But as the movie creeps on, we realize that the inspirations are going to be rare, and that Brooks has not bothered to create a framework for the movie or to people it with characters. It's all just cardboard comic cutouts.

The film has another serious problem: It is in unfunny bad taste. That sounds strange coming from me. I've always enjoyed Brooks's ventures into taboo subject matter, and I still think his "Springtime for Hitler" from *The Producers* and the celebrated campfire scene in *Blazing Saddles* were hilarious. He seemed to be demonstrating that you could get away with almost anything in a movie, if you made it funny enough. (Told that *The Producers* was vulgar, he once responded loftily, "It rises *below* vulgarity.") But this time, the things he's trying to get away with aren't funny. There is, for example, the movie's tiresome series of jokes about urination. There must be comic possibilities in the subject (and he finds one when he shows a Stone Age critic's method of reviewing a cave painting), but there is nothing inherently funny about urination, and Brooks proves it here, again and again.

There also is nothing inherently funny about Jews, Catholics, nuns, blacks, and gays. They can all conceivably provide the makings of comedy, of course, but in *History of the World* Brooks doesn't have the patience to introduce a character and then create a comic situation *about* him. He introduces the character and expects us to laugh at the character himself. Example. Instead of developing a comic situation around Orthodox Jews, he simply shows us some, complete with beards and hats, their heads stuck through a stockade, and expects us to laugh. But while we might laugh with Brooks at a comic situation, we have no reason to laugh *at* people just because of their appearance or religion.

The same thing goes wrong with Brooks's big production number in this movie, "The Inquisition," featuring a song-and-dance team of medieval monks, and a chorus line of nuns who splash in a pool, Busby Berkeley-style. We're supposed to laugh at the shocking juxtaposition of religious images and Hollywood corn. But Brooks never gives us an additional comic level, one where he's making funny points about the images. When he dresses up like a monk and then dances like Donald O'Connor, that's only funny for a second. If we knew anything about the monk as a comic character, the scene could build. Instead, it just continues.

History of the World—Part I was fairly expensive to produce, but it exists on the level of quick, disposable, television. It thumbs its nose at icons that have lost their taboo value for most of us, and between the occasional good laughs, we're a little embarrassed that the movie is so dumb and predictable. God knows Mel Brooks is straining for yuks up there on the screen, but he's like the life of the party who still has the lampshade on his head when everybody else is ready to go home.

The Hitcher no stars

R, 98 m., 1985

C. Thomas Howell (Jim Halsey), Rutger Hauer (John Ryder), Jennifer Jason Leigh (Nash). Directed by Robert Holman and produced by Kip Oham. Screenplay by Eric Red.

The Hitcher begins and ends with the same sound, of a match being struck and flaring into flame. At the beginning of the film, the sound is made by the villain, a hitchhiker who is a mass-murderer. At the end of the film, the sound is made by the hero, a young man whose life has been spared so that he can become the special victim of the hitchhiker. The movie seems to be telling us, by the use of the sounds and in several other ways, that the killer and the hero have developed some kind of deep bond through their experiences together.

The victim's identification with his torturer is not a new phenomenon. In many of the hostage cases in recent years, some of the captives have adopted the viewpoints of their jailers. What is particularly sick about *The Hitcher* is that the killer is not given a viewpoint, a grudge, or indeed even a motive. He is deliberately presented as a man without a past, without a history, who simply and cruelly hurts and kills people. Although he spares the movie's young hero, he puts him through a terrible ordeal, framing him as a mass murderer and trapping him in a Kafkaesque web of evidence, until even the hero himself despairs of getting anyone to tell his story.

At the end of the movie, there is of course a scene of vengeance, in which the two men meet in final combat. And yet this showdown does not represent a fight between good and evil, because the movie suggests—and one of the characters even says—that there is something weird going on between the two men. The implication is that they have formed some kind of half-acknowledged sadomasochistic relationship. The death of the villain is not the hero's revenge, but the conclusion that the villain has been setting up for himself all along.

This unhealthy bond between the young hero (played by C. Thomas Howell) and the older killer (the cold-eyed Rutger Hauer) is developed in a movie which proves a horrible fate for its only major female character. As Howell flees down desert highways from the violence of Hauer, he is befriended by a young waitress (Jennifer Jason Leigh). She believes that he is innocent, and goes on the run with him. But the movie does not develop into a standard story of teen-agers in love.

The Howell character scarcely seems to notice Leigh as a human being; of course, he has a great deal else on his mind. She wants to sleep with him one night, but the scene is only a set-up for a later scene in which Hauer slips into her bed. And her death—she is tied hand and foot between two giant trucks and pulled in two—is so grotesquely out of proportion with the main business of this movie that it suggests a deep sickness at the screenplay stage.

There are other disgusting moments, as when a police dog feasts on the blood dripping from its master's neck, or when Howell finds a human finger in his french fries. Nothing else quite betrays the cynicism of this movie, however, as the scene in which Jennifer Jason Leigh and Howell are being chased by a helicopter, which is shot down in flames by Hauer. This scene takes on a grisly double meaning when you reflect that Leigh is the daughter of Vic Morrow, the actor who died in a tragic helicopter stunt gone wrong.

The Hitcher grants the Hauer character almost supernatural powers; he always seems to anticipate what Howell will do next. Although that makes the movie impossible to accept on a realistic level, it didn't bother me. I could see that the film was meant as an allegory, not a documentary. But on its own terms, this movie is diseased and corrupt. I would have admired it more if it had found the courage to acknowledge the real relationship it was portraying between Howell and Rutger, but no: It prefers to disguise itself as a violent thriller, and on that level it is reprehensible.

Hollywood Shuffle ★ ★ ★

R, 82 m., 1987

Robert Townsend (Bobby Taylor), Anne-Marie Johnson (Lydia), Helen Martin (Grandmother), Starletta Dupois (Mother), Craigus R. Johnson (Stevie), Domenick Irrera (Manvacum). Directed and produced by Robert Townsend. Screenplay by Townsend.

The story behind *Hollywood Shuffle* is more thrilling than anything on the screen. It's the story of Robert Townsend, young black actor from Chicago, talented, ambitious, who wins supporting roles in *Cooley High*, *Streets of Fire*, and *A Soldier's Story* but fails to gain stardom in a Hollywood where most roles for blacks are stereotypes and the rest go to people named Murphy, Pryor, and Glover.

In the ordinary course of events, Townsend would continue to make the weary rounds from one casting agent to another, auditioning for one forgettable role after another, paying the rent by waiting tables, until he was finally discovered or—more likely—quit the business and got a daytime job.

Townsend knew that routine as well as anyone, but he decided to break out of it. So he made his own movie. The saga of his production has been well-publicized: He begged cinematographers for leftover film, borrowed every dollar he could find, talked cast and crew into working for deferred payments, and somehow made an expensive-looking movie for less than $100,000. The comparisons are being drawn to Spike Lee, another young black filmmaker who broke the rules and had a hit with *She's Gotta Have It*.

It's a cliché that young novelists write their first novels about young novelists writing their first novels. Townsend's *Hollywood Shuffle* falls within this tradition. It is a movie about a young man much like Townsend, who makes the rounds, fights stereotypes, and dreams of the day when there will be a black Rambo.

The movie begins with Townsend working in a hot dog stand owned by a couple of negative thinkers who don't believe he can be successful as an actor. He defies their expectations and gets a job in a movie, but then he walks off the set; with his grandmother and his younger brother looking on, he just can't bring himself to mouth the street-talk clichés of his character, a gang member. This action inspires a series of fantasies in which Townsend sees himself in war movies, Westerns, and slice-of-life dramas, and even imagines a TV show in which two soul brothers are the feuding critics and give movies the finger as well as their thumbs.

There are a lot of good laughs in *Hollywood Shuffle*, and the movie certainly functions as a showcase for Townsend—who has a strong screen presence and will doubtless, using this film as a calling card, win some of the movie roles he dreams about. The movie has its problems, however. Many of the skits run on too long after we've long since gotten the jokes. Some of the supporting performances are wooden and under-written. And many of the stereotypes Townsend protests against haven't been used in Hollywood movies in decades. His attacks on them will be the first time some viewers have seen the stereotypes at all.

I suspect many of these problems are the direct result of the movie's low budget, hurried shooting schedule, and limited supply of film. When one take of a scene was acceptable, Townsend must have been inclined to accept it, rather than to waste precious film stock in trying to make it better. Under the circumstances, *Hollywood Shuffle* is an artistic compromise but a logistical triumph, announcing the arrival of a new talent whose next movie should really be something.

Home of the Brave ★ ★ ★ ½

NO MPAA RATING, 90 m., 1986

A concert documentary directed by Laurie Anderson and produced by Paula Mazur. Screenplay by Anderson.

Laurie Anderson once spoke, in a wondering voice, of the plight of human sperm: "Hundreds of thousands of tiny specks, all knowing exactly the same thing." Her performances are filled with insights like that. She doesn't make them to supply us with information, but to create a tone, an attitude. She is engulfed by the enormous mysteries of nature, and yet the human life around her seems more and more banal. Civilization is an assembly line to hell.

In retaliation, she weaves dream-images out of songs and symbols and electronic noises. She calls herself a "performance artist" rather than a musician. And although all musicians are performance artists, I think I know what she means. She does not give concerts. She attempts to create in her audiences a more open, wondering state of mind.

Home of the Brave is a ninety-minute documentary based on one of her performances. Large parts of it will be familiar to anyone who has seen her in person, but the film has a somewhat different feel than her live performances. As a backdrop to her music, Anderson uses a large rear-projection screen that sometimes relays messages made up of technological clichés and sometimes uses film loops to show the same images over and over.

The images have a hypnotic quality. Crudely drawn sheep jump over and over, again and again, or boats steam past a rusty bridge or—as she talks about the sperm—we see little tadpoles earnestly swimming upstream, one of them breaking away every once in a while for a loop-the-loop. The images are deliberately crude and machine--

made. The film loops are so short that they announce themselves. We can see that the same images are being recycled in a circle, and the feeling is sort of poignant: All those sperm, all that effort, all for nothing.

In front of these images, the Laurie Anderson Band performs. With her short, spiky hair and her athletic grace, Anderson sometimes seems more like a craftsman than a singer. She moves in a kind of robot choreography, and she likes to seem deadpan. She takes the hand-held mike and wanders the stage, reciting parables and slices of bizarre information. She likes phrases such as "This just in . . .," as if she were at the anchor desk for the death of the world. She uses strange lighting effects to create instants of magic.

She was one of the first to use voice synthesizers, which lower the tone of her voice while maintaining the same speed of speech. The effect is sort of big-brotherish; she seems official, detached, a voice made from a machine, speaking words as objects. Behind her, the rhythms are seductive, statements made over and over until they lull us into her mind state.

There are times when Anderson seems like an anti-performance artist, times when she cuts off a song or interrupts a progression just as it is threatening to develop into melody and entertainment. But the effect is not dry and antiseptic, as it is with some ultra-modern music. Every song has a soul of wit and an edge of rebellion.

It's strange. You can't put your finger on it, but after you see it, you have the feeling that your perception of things has been skewed slightly. Anderson is saying: We're surrounded by bankrupt images and music that is fascist noise, and they're pouncing away at us, trying to break us down, to kill the spark, but if we keep two things we will be able to survive and complete our journeys. Those two things are a sense of wonder and the ability to laugh back.

Honkytonk Man ★ ★ ★

PG, 123 m., 1982

Clint Eastwood (Red Stovall), Kyle Eastwood (Whit), John McIntire (Grandpa), Alexa Kenin (Marlene), Verna Bloom (Emmy). Directed and produced by Clint Eastwood.

Clint Eastwood produced and directed *Honkytonk Man*, and stars in it as a Depression-era loser who drifts through the South with his young nephew, aiming eventually to get to Nashville and maybe get on the Grand Ol' Opry. The movie's credits say the screenplay is by Clancy Carlile, based on his own novel, but in speculating on what drew Eastwood to this project, I came across this entry in Ephraim Katz's *Film Encyclopedia:*

"Eastwood, Clint. Actor, director. Born on May 31, 1930, in San Francisco. A child of the Depression, he spent his early boyhood trailing a father who pumped gas along dusty roads all over the West Coast . . ."

The entry goes on to list the usual odd jobs (logger, steel-furnace stoker) that all actors seem to hold down on their way to stardom, but I'd read enough to support my intuition that *Honkytonk Man* means a lot to Eastwood in ways that may not be immediately apparent. This is a sweet, whimsical, low-key movie, a movie that makes you feel good without pressing you too hard. It provides Eastwood with a screen character who is the complete opposite of the patented Eastwood tough guys and provides a role of nearly equal importance for his son, Kyle, as a serious, independent and utterly engaging young nephew named Whit. What happens to them on the road is not quite as important in this movie as what happens between them.

The movie starts with Eastwood drunk behind the wheel of a big 1930s touring car, knocking over the windmill on his latest return to the old homestead. He's sort of a Hank Williams type. His family has seen this act before. They put him to bed and hide the bottle. The next day, with an ominous cough, Eastwood talks about his dream of heading for Nashville and cashing in some old IOUs. He's a singer and a songwriter, luckless but not untalented, and he thinks he could make it onto the Opry. He wants to take the kid along. After some hesitation, the kid's mother (Verna Bloom) agrees, mostly because she hopes her son can ride herd on Eastwood and keep him reasonably sober. She makes her son promise not to drink or fool around with women (thus putting her finger unerringly on one thing he did the night before, and another that he hopes to do as soon as possible). Old grandpa (John McIntire) also decides to go along for the ride; he's got some people in Tennessee he hasn't seen in forty years.

The road part of the picture is picaresque, photographed through a haze of romance and nostalgia, and spiced up with a visit to a gambling house and an encounter with a very individualistic young woman (Alexa Kenin) who also decides to join the traveling party. She has an amazing gift for couching the most ordinary sentiments in romantic prose. The movie's best scenes are the ones Eastwood plays in Nashville, during an audition at the Opry and, later, in a recording studio. He sings his songs with the kind of bone-weariness that doesn't hurt the right kind of country song, and there's a special moment in the studio when a supporting musician lends a hand. The movie turns out to be about realizing your dreams after all, which is sort of a surprise in a story where even the high points are only bittersweet.

This is a special movie. In making it, Eastwood was obviously moving away from his Dirty Harry image, but that's nothing new; his spectacular success in violent movies tends to distract us from his intriguing and challenging career as the director and star of such offbeat projects as *Bronco Billy* and *Play Misty For Me.* He seems to have a personal stake in this story, and we begin to feel it, too. Sometimes the simplest country songs are just telling the facts.

Hoosiers ★ ★ ★ ★

PG, 114 m., 1987

Gene Hackman (Norman Dale), Barbara Hershey (Myra Fleener), Dennis Hopper (Shooter), Sheb Wooley (Cletus), Fern Persons (Opal Fleener), Chelcie Ross (George), Robert Swan (Rollin), Michael O'Guinne (Rooster). Directed by David Anspaugh and produced by Carter De Haven and Angelo Pizzo. Screenplay by Pizzo.

I was a sportswriter once for a couple of years in downstate Illinois. I covered mostly high school sports, and if I were a sportswriter again, I'd want to cover them again. There is a passion to high school sports that transcends anything that comes afterward; nothing in pro sports equals the intensity of a really important high school basketball game.

Hoosiers knows that. This is a movie about a tiny Indiana high school that sends a team all the way to the state basketball finals in the days when schools of all sizes played in the same tournaments and a David could slay a Goliath. The school in the movie is so small that it can barely field a team, especially after the best player decides to drop out. Can schools this small actually become state champs? Sure. That's what high school sports are all about.

Hoosiers is a comeback movie, but it's not simply about a comeback of this small team, the Hickory Huskers. It's also about the comeback of their coach, a mysterious middle-age guy named Norman Dale (Gene Hackman), who seems to be too old and too experienced to be coaching in an obscure backwater like Hickory.

And it's also the comeback story of Shooter, the town drunk (played by Dennis Hopper, whose supporting performance won an Oscar nomination). Everybody in this movie seems to be trying to start over in life, and, in a way, basketball is simply their excuse.

Hoosiers has the broad overall structure of most sports movies: It begins with the problem of a losing team, introduces the new coach, continues with the obligatory training sequences and personality clashes, arrives at the darkest hour, and then heads toward triumph. This story structure is almost as sacred to Hollywood as basketball is to Indiana.

What makes *Hoosiers* special is not its story, however, but its details and its characters. Angelo Pizzo, who wrote the original screenplay, knows small-town sports. He knows all about high school politics and how the school board and the parents' groups always think they know more about basketball than the coach does. He knows about gossip, scandal, and vengeance. And he knows a lot about human nature.

All of this knowledge, however, would be pointless without Hackman's great performance at the center of this movie. Hackman is gifted at combining likability with complexity—two qualities that usually don't go together in the movies. He projects all of the single-mindedness of any good coach, but then he contains other dimensions, and we learn about the scandal in his past that led him to this one-horse town. David Anspaugh's direction is good at suggesting Hackman's complexity without belaboring it.

Hickory High School is where Hackman hopes to make his comeback, but he doesn't think only of himself. He meets Shooter (Hopper), the alcoholic father of one of his team members, and enlists him as an assistant coach with one stipulation: no more drinking. That doesn't work. In a way, Hackman knows it won't work, but by involving Shooter once again in the life of the community, he's giving him a reason to seek the kind of treatment that might help.

Hackman finds that he has another project on his hands, too: the rehabilitation of his heart. He falls in love with a teacher at the school (Barbara Hershey), and their relationship is interesting, as far as it goes, although it feels like key scenes have been cut out of the romance. Maybe another movie could have been made about them; this movie is about basketball.

The climax of the movie will come as no great surprise to anyone who has seen other sports movies. *Hoosiers* works a magic, however, in getting us to really care about the fate of the team and the people depending on it. In the way it combines sports with human nature, it reminded me of another wonderful Indiana sports movie, *Breaking Away*. It's a movie that is all heart.

Hope and Glory ★ ★ ★

PG-13, 118 m., 1987

Sebastian Rice Edwards (Bill), Geraldine Muir (Sue), Sarah Miles (Grace), David Hayman (Clive), Sammi Davis (Dawn), Derrick O'Connor (Mac), Susan Wooldridge (Molly), Jean-Marc Barr (Bruce), Ian Bannen (Grandfather). Directed, produced, and written by John Boorman.

Maybe there is something in the very nature of war, in the power of guns and bombs, that appeals to the imagination of little boys. Bombers and fighter planes and rockets and tanks are thrilling at that age when you are old enough to understand how they work, but too young to understand what they do. John Boorman's *Hope and Glory* is a film about that precise season in the life of a young British boy who grows up in a London suburb during the Second World War.

The boy (Sebastian Rice Edwards), probably meant to be Boorman himself, is bright and curious, and although he is sad when his dad goes away in uniform, there are certain consolations, such as the nightly German air raids that leave real pieces of shrapnel in the garden—some of them still hot from explosions, and all of them very collectible.

For his mother (Sarah Miles, in one of the best performances of her career), life is not so simple, but it has its consolations. Left to raise the family after her husband is drafted, she deals distractedly with rebellion in the ranks of her children, particularly from a teen-age daughter whose sexual awakening has been hastened by the arrival of Canadian troops who are training in the neighborhood.

Hope and Glory is first of all a painstaking re-creation of the period. All the cars and signs and clothes look right, and there are countless small references to wartime rationing, as when the older sister draws seams on her legs to make fake nylons. But after re-creating the period, Boorman also reconstructs the very feeling that was in the air.

The nightly routine of air raids quickly loses its novelty, and Miles has to shake her sleepyheads to get them out of bed and into the backyard bomb shelter. One night, they don't make it, and crouch in the hall closet as the bombs fall closer and closer. The next one, they whisper, will either hit them or not—but it misses, and hits the house of a mean old lady down the street, creating a great fire and drawing lots of exciting fire engines.

There is something almost perverse in the way Boorman defines his point of view. He is not concerned in this film about the tragedy of war, or the meaning of war, but only with the specific experience of war for a grade school boy. Drawing from his own autobiographical memories, he has not given the little boy in the movie any more insights than such a little boy should have. His approach is especially effective in a scene where the boy witnesses his sister making out with a soldier; he looks, and does not quite understand, and looks away, perhaps sensing that this is a chapter that has not yet opened for him.

Toward the end of the film, the locale changes; the family goes to stay in the country with Miles's grandparents, and existence there seems more idyllic than in the city. Probably this is the way Boorman remembers it; going to the country is not an escape from bombs, but a chance to float on the river and run in the pastures.

Wartime is always a time, on the domestic

front, of personal upheaval. There is a quiet, touching subplot in *Hope and Glory* about a choice Sarah Miles made when she got married. She married out of common sense, not out of love, and although she is still best friends with the man she loved, she is faithful to her absent husband. This situation leads to one of the film's best scenes, when the daughter confesses her love for a Canadian airman—and reveals that she is pregnant. The mother tells her daughter she must be true to her heart, and follow love wherever it leads, and we know that is exactly what she did not do.

Hope and Glory was an enormous success in England, where every frame must have its special memories for British audiences. Through American eyes, it is a more universal film, not so much about war as about memory. When we are young, what happens is not nearly as important as what we think happens. Perhaps that's true even when we are not so young.

Housekeeping ★ ★ ★ ★

PG, 117 m., 1988

Christine Lahti (Sylvie), Sara Walker (Ruth), Andrea Burchill (Lucille), Anne Pitoniak (Aunt Lily), Barbara Reese (Aunt Nona). Directed by Bill Forsyth and produced by Robert F. Colesberry. Screenplay by Forsyth.

In a land where the people are narrow and suspicious, where do they draw the line between madness and sweetness? Between those who are unable to conform to society's norm, and those who simply choose not to, because their dreamy private world is more alluring? That is one of the many questions asked, and not exactly answered, in Bill Forsyth's *Housekeeping,* which was one of the strangest and best films of 1988.

The movie, set some thirty or forty years ago in the Pacific Northwest, tells the story of two young girls who are taken on a sudden and puzzling motor trip by their mother to visit a relative. Soon after they arrive, their mother commits suicide, and before long her sister, their Aunt Sylvie, arrives in town to look after them.

Sylvie, who is played by Christine Lahti as a mixture of bemusement and wry reflection, is not an ordinary type of person. She likes to sit in the dusk so much that she never turns the lights on. She likes to go for long, meandering walks. She collects enormous piles of newspapers and hundreds of tin cans—carefully washing off their labels and then polishing them and arranging them in gleaming pyramids. She is nice to everyone and generally seems cheerful, but there is an enchantment about her that some people find suspicious.

Indeed, even her two young nieces are divided. One finds her "funny," and the other loves her, and eventually the two sisters will take separate paths in life because they differ about Sylvie. At first, when they are younger, she simply represents reality to them. As they grow older and begin to attend high school, however, one of the girls wants to be "popular," and resents having a weird aunt at home, while the other girl draws herself into Sylvie's dream.

The townspeople are not evil, merely conventional and "concerned." Parties of church ladies visit, to see if they can "help." The sheriff eventually gets involved. But *Housekeeping* is not a realistic movie, not one of those disease-of-the-week docudramas with a tidy solution. It is funnier, more offbeat, and too enchanting to ever qualify on those terms.

The writer-director, Bill Forsyth, has made all of his previous films in Scotland (they make a list of whimsical, completely original comedies: *Gregory's Girl, Local Hero, Comfort and Joy, That Sinking Feeling*). For his first North American production, he began with a novel by Marilynne Robinson that embodies some of his own notions, such as that certain people grow so amused by their own conceits that they cannot be bothered to pay lip service to yours.

In Christine Lahti, he has found the right actress to embody this idea. Although she has been excellent in a number of realistic roles (she was Gary Gilmore's sister in *The Executioner's Song,* and Goldie Hawn's best friend in *Swing Shift*), there is something resolutely private about her, a sort of secret smile that is just right for Sylvie. The role requires her to find a delicate line; she must not seem too mad or willful, or the whole charm of the story will be lost. And although there are times in the film when she seems to be indifferent to her nieces, she never seems not to love them.

Forsyth has surrounded that love with some extraordinary images, which help to create the magical feeling of the film. The action takes place in a house near a lake that is crossed by a majestic, forbidding railroad bridge, and it is a local legend that one night decades ago, a passenger train slipped ever so lazily off the line and plunged down, down into the icy waters of the frozen lake. The notion of the passengers in their warm, well-lit carriages, plunging down to their final destination, is one that Forsyth somehow turns from a tragedy into a notion of doomed beauty. And the bridge becomes important at several moments in the film, especially the last one.

The pastoral setting of the film (in British Columbia) and the production design by Adrienne Atkinson are also evocative; it is important that the action takes place in a small, isolated community, in a place cut off from the world where whimsies can flourish and private notions can survive. At the end of the film, I was quietly astonished; I had seen a film that could perhaps be described as being about a madwoman, but I had seen a character who seemed closer to a mystic, or a saint.

House of Games ★ ★ ★ ★

R, 102 m., 1987

Lindsay Crouse (Margaret Ford), Joe Mantegna (Mike), Mike Nussbaum (Joey), Lilia Skala (Dr. Littauer), J.T. Walsh (Businessman), Jack Wallace (Bartender). Directed by David Mamet and produced by Michael Hausman. Screenplay by Mamet.

This movie is awake. I have seen so many films that sleepwalk through the debris of old plots and secondhand ideas that it was a constant pleasure to watch *House of Games*, a movie about con men that succeeds not only in conning its viewers, but also in creating a series of characters who seem imprisoned by the need to con or be conned.

The film stars Lindsay Crouse as a psychiatrist who specializes in addictive behavior, possibly as a way of dealing with her own compulsions. One of her patients is a gambler who fears he will be murdered over a bad debt. Crouse walks through lonely night streets to the neon signs of the House of Games, a bar where she thinks she can find the gambler who has terrorized her client. She wants to talk him out of enforcing the debt.

The gambler (Joe Mantegna) has never heard anything like this before. But he offers her a deal: If she will help him fleece a high-roller Texan in a big-stakes poker game, he will tear up the marker. She does so. She also becomes fascinated by the back-room reality of these gamblers who have reduced life to a knowledge of the odds. She comes back the next day, looking for Mantegna. She tells him she wants to learn more about gamblers and con men, about the kind of man he is. By the end of this movie, does she ever.

House of Games was written and directed by David Mamet, the playwright *(Glengarry Glen Ross)* and screenwriter *(The Untouchables)*, and it is his directorial debut. Originally it was intended as a big-budget movie with an established director and major stars, but Mamet took the reins himself, cast his wife in the lead and old acting friends in the other important roles, and shot it on the rainy streets of Seattle. Usually the screenwriter is insane to think he can direct a movie. Not this time. *House of Games* never steps wrong from beginning to end.

The plotting is diabolical and impeccable, and I will not spoil the delight of its unfolding by mentioning the crucial details. What I can mention are the performances, the dialogue, and the setting. When Lindsay Crouse enters the House of Games, she enters a world occupied by characters who have known each other so long and so well, in so many different ways, that everything they say is a kind of shorthand. At first we don't fully realize that, and there is a strange savor to the words they use. They speak, of course, in Mamet's distinctive dialogue style, an almost musical rhythm of stopping, backing up, starting again, repeating, emphasizing, all the time with the hint of deeper meanings below the surfaces of the words. The leading actors, Joe Mantegna and Mike Nussbaum, have appeared in countless performances of Mamet plays over the years, and they know his dialogue the way other actors grow into Beckett or Shakespeare. They speak it as it is meant to be spoken, with a sort of aggressive, almost insulting, directness. Mantegna has a scene where he "reads" Lindsay Crouse—where he tells her about her "tells," those small giveaway looks and gestures that poker players use to read the minds of their opponents. The way he talks to her is so incisive and unadorned it is sexual.

These characters and others live in a city that looks, as the Seattle of *Trouble in Mind* did, like a place on a parallel time track. It is a modern American city, but like none we have quite seen before; it seems to have been modeled on the paintings of Edward Hopper, where lonely people wait in empty public places for their destinies to intercept them. Crouse is portrayed as an alien in this world, a successful, best-selling author who has never dreamed that men like this exist, and the movie is insidious in the way it shows her willingness to be corrupted.

There is in all of us a fascination for the inside dope, for the methods of the confidence game, for the secrets of a magic trick. But there is an eternal gulf between the shark and the mark, between the con man and his victim. And there is a code to protect the secrets. There are moments in *House of Games* when Mantegna instructs Crouse in the methods and lore of the con game, but inside every con is another one.

I met a woman once who was divorced from a professional magician. She hated this man with a passion. She used to appear with him in a baffling trick where they exchanged places, handcuffed and manacled, in a locked cabinet. I asked her how it was done. The divorce and her feelings meant nothing compared to her loyalty to the magic profession. She looked at me coldly and said, "The trick is told when the trick is sold." The ultimate question in *House of Games* is, who's buying?

The House on Carroll Street ★ ★ ★
PG, 101 m., 1988
(See related Film Clip, p. 761.)

Kelly McGillis (Emily), Jeff Daniels (Cochran), Mandy Patinkin (Salwen), Jessica Tandy (Miss Venable), Jonathan Hogan (Alan), Remak Ramsay (Senator Byington), Ken Welsh (Hackett), Christopher Rhode (Stefan). Directed and produced by Peter Yates. Screenplay by Walter Bernstein.

There is a kind of movie sequence which Alfred Hitchcock always did well, and which most later directors have chosen not to do at all. It involves the hero discovering information by being nosy. Little or no dialogue is used. Most of what the hero sees is in long-shot, and we can sometimes not quite make out all of the details. Half-heard words float on the air. What is being spied on is none of the hero's business, but he cannot resist the human need to be a spy, and neither can we.

The crucial developments in *The House on Carroll Street* are established with such a sequence, and so well is it handled that it casts a sort of spell over the movie. The time is the early 1950s, the height of McCarthyism. The heroine (Kelly McGillis) is a young woman who has just lost her job at a magazine, after refusing to testify before the House Un-American Activities Committee. Desperate for work, she takes a job reading aloud to an old lady. One afternoon, walking in the lady's garden, she sees some figures moving in the tall back windows of the house on the other side of the yard.

She is intrigued. She moves closer, hiding behind the branch of a tree. She overhears an argument. She can tell that something is wrong, but does not know what it could be. Later, on the street, she sees a young man who was standing in the window. She tries to engage him in conversation, but he resists. Eventually, piecing together a clue here and a word there, she becomes convinced that the people in the house are smuggling Nazi war criminals into the United States, and that they have friends in high places.

There is more. Because the McGillis character is presumably a dangerous radical, she is being tailed by the FBI (there is a hint here of the opening scenes of *Notorious*). The important friends of the Nazis might want to smear her as a Commie, to confuse the trail. The Nazis begin to suspect what she knows. The old lady becomes a valuable ally. And in another echo from *Notorious*, she and one of the FBI men fall in love.

He's played by Jeff Daniels, that dependable, open-faced middle American from *Something Wild* and *Terms of Endearment*. Hey, maybe she is a Commie, but she sure is pretty. He is attracted to her, is disturbed when she is harassed by a search of her home, begins to trust her, and eventually becomes her ally in the fight against the Nazis and their protectors.

As thriller plots go, *The House on Carroll Street* is fairly old-fashioned, which is one of its merits. This is a movie where casting is important, and it works primarily because McGillis, like Ingrid Bergman in *Notorious*, seems absolutely trustworthy. She becomes the island of trust and sanity in the midst of deceit and treachery. The movie advances slowly enough for us to figure it out along with McGillis (or sometimes ahead of her), and there is a nice, ironic double-reverse in the fact that the government is following a good person who seems evil, and discovers evil people who seem good.

What is particularly welcome about the movie is that it's not high-tech. It not only takes place in the 1950s, but is happy there. We don't get the slam-bang cynicism of most characters in modern movies, and after awhile I began to figure out why. This movie takes place so long ago that the characters in it have never had their imaginations boiled by full immersion in the thriller culture of recent decades. They're still sort of sweet and innocent, and believe everybody is basically good, and are shocked when they're wrong. Maybe that's the movie's ultimate twist.

The Howling ★ ★

R, 91 m., 1981

Dee Wallace (Karen White), Patrick Macnee (Dr. Waggner), Kevin McCarthy (Fred), Slim Pickens (Sam), Dennis Dugan (Chris), Belina Balaski (Terry), John Carradine (Eric). Directed by Joe Dante and produced by Michael Pinell and Jack Conrad. Screenplay by John Sayles.

Now for America's favorite newspaper team, Uncle Roger and Little Jimmy. As we join them inside the Movie Lab, we hear . . .

(Whoo! Whoooo!)

I'm ol' Uncle Roger, and this is Little Jimmy!

(Arf! Barf!)

What's in the news today, Unca' Rog???

Well, Little Jimmy . . . new movie in town . . . name of *The Howling*.

(Whoooo! Chortle, chortle. Siren sound. Growwwwwl.)

What's it about???

Werewolves! Little Jimmy. Mean, nasty animals . . . story here . . . about a girl who went OUT ON A DATE . . . didn't know the guy too well . . . one thing led to another . . . the guy GROWS FANGS, Little Jimmy . . . starts dripping saliva all over her Gloria Vanderbilts.

(Whoooo!!)

Holy Alpo, Unca' Rog! What happened then!

Girl turns to the guy . . . doesn't know what to say . . . says, "GET YOUR HANDS OFF OF ME!" Werewolf . . . hardly listens. Doesn't SEEM TO HEAR!

Awful things can happen on a date, Unca' Rog.

Right, Little Jimmy. She said . . . she'd been out on dates with a wolf before . . . BUT NEVER A WEREWOLF!

What else happened?

(Pant, pant.)

Weird CALIFORNIA CULT, Little Jimmy. Up the coast from the big city. People . . . sitting around campfires . . . singing songs . . . getting their heads back together. One wanders off into the underbrush . . . NEVER SEEN AGAIN!

Holy lurking terrors!

Says here . . . this broad who was a TV ANCHORWOMAN. Investigating weird cults. Went into one of those adult movie arcades with the doors that lock from the inside . . . you know, Little Jimmy?

Two bits in the slot?

Right, Little Jimmy. Gets in there . . . locks the door . . . lights off . . . guy standing there in the dark . . . she wants to GET THE STORY. Guy says, "Turn around."

(Snaaaarrll!!!)

What happened then???

GUY'S A WEREWOLF! Cop comes in, blasts hell out of the private viewing booth . . . they take the body to the morgue . . . next day, the BODY IS MISSING! Says here . . . CLAW marks on the inside of the stainless steel door!

Holy Toledo Steel Works!

There's more. Broad follows the trail to the cult's summer camp . . . advice of her psychiatrist . . . turns out . . . WEREWOLVES are running the camp. She's not just hearing things . . . the underbrush DOES have noises in it.

What next?

Guy says . . . tells her . . . says, "I want to give you a piece of my mind!"

Does he?

GIVES HER . . . a piece of his mind. Pulls it out and gives it to her. Nauseating. Research indicates . . . if you're bitten by a werewolf, so long, baby . . . you ARE a WEREWOLF. Legendary story . . . they come out only at night . . . NOT TRUE. Can come out anytime. Daytime not safe.

(Barf!)

Unca' Rog?

Yes, Little Jimmy?

What's the SCARIEST THING in this movie?

In the whole movie?

The MOST AWFUL THING in the whole movie, please, please, tell me, please?

All right . . . you asked for it . . . WORST thing . . . you've ever seen . . . MOST DISGUSTING SIGHT in the history of films . . . you don't believe what you're seeing . . . here is comes, Little Jimmy: Before your VERY EYES . . . this movie CHANGES INTO A DOG!

Holy White Fang!!! Is it worth seeing?

Yes, Little Jimmy, in a sense, it is. Ridiculous . . . yes. Comical at times . . . yes. Silliest film seen in some time by the Animals Movies Critics' Team. BUT . . . great special effects as men BECOME werewolves. WOMEN, too. Before your eyes. Done with . . . says here . . . HYDRAULICS! Sensational!

Is it worth my money?

It sure is, Little Jimmy. Says here . . . worth your money, IF you get it two for one.

The Hunger ★ 1/2
R, 100 m., 1983

Catherine Deneuve (Miriam), David Bowie (John), Susan Sarandon (Sarah), Cliff De Young (Tom). Directed by Tony Scott. Screenplay by Ivan Davis and Michael Thomas.

The Hunger is an agonizingly bad vampire movie, circling around an exquisitely effective sex scene. Sorry, but that's the way it is, and I have to be honest. The seduction scene involves Catherine Deneuve, as an age-old vampire, and Susan Sarandon, as her latest victim. There was a great deal of controversy while the movie was being made (all sorts of rumors about closed sets, etc.), but the scene as it now appears isn't raunchy or *too* explicit—just sort of dreamily erotic. I mention the scene so prominently because it's one of the few scenes that really work in *The Hunger,* a movie that has been so ruthlessly overproduced that it's all flash and style and no story. Well, there's probably a story moping about somewhere within all the set decoration. It seems to involve Deneuve as a vampire of vaguely Egyptian origins, whose latest partner (David Bowie) is giving out on her after three or four centuries.

After an initial orgy of fancy camerawork, the movie settles down into the story of Bowie's final days. He has that chronic vampire disease where you age suddenly. He needs a lot of blood to keep going. He appeals to a medical researcher (Sarandon) for help, but she brushes him off, and by the time she realizes he's serious, he looks like Methuselah. Then Sarandon visits the lavish town house where Deneuve and Bowie live, and that's where a glass of sherry leads to the seduction scene.

I've got to be honest about this scene. Part of its interest lies in the fact that Catherine Deneuve *herself,* and Susan Sarandon *herself,* are acting in the scene. That gives it a level of reality that would be lacking in a porno film, even a much more explicit one. Because we know that famous actresses don't usually agree to appear in scenes such as this, we're aware of the chance they're taking—and the documentary reality of the scene gives it an effectiveness all its own. Deneuve, of course, has made a career out of the contrast between her cool, perfect beauty and the strange, erotic predicaments her characters get involved in. (Remember *Belle de Jour?*) Sarandon's scene by the window in *Atlantic City,* bathing herself with lemons, created great sultriness. But *The Hunger* approaches its big scene on an altogether different level, with understatement, awkward little pauses in conversation, and a canny awareness of our own curiosity about whether Deneuve and Sarandon really will go ahead with this scene, or whether the director will cut away to the usual curtains blowing in the wind.

Well, he doesn't, but it's about the only time in the whole movie there aren't curtains blowing in the wind. This movie has so much would-be elegance and visual class that it never quite happens as a dramatic event. There's so much cross-cutting, so many memories, so many apparent flashbacks, that the real drama is lost—the drama of a living human being seduced into vampirism. In Herzog's *Nosferatu,* we felt some of the blood-scented lure of eternal death-in-life. Here, it's just—how would an ad put it?—Catherine Deneuve for Dracula.

I

I Never Promised You a Rose Garden

★ ★ ★

R, 90 m., 1977

Kathleen Quinlan (Deborah), Bibi Andersson (Dr. Fried), Ben Piazza (Mr. Blake), Lorraine Gary (Mrs. Blake), Michael McGuire (McPherson), Reni Santoni (Hobbs), Susan Tyrrell (Kitty), Robert Viharo (Anterrabae). Directed by Anthony Page and produced by Terence F. Deane, Daniel H. Blatt, and Michael Hausman. Screenplay by Gavin Lambert and Lewis John Carlino.

I'm becoming suspicious of movies that assure us mental illness can be cured if the victim "wants" to be cured, or assume that mental illness is not illness at all—because in an insane world the only sane people are the crazies. *I Never Promised You a Rose Garden* doesn't altogether avoid the first assumption, but it firmly rejects the second, and it gives us a heroine so convincingly real we finally believe perhaps she *could* cure herself.

The heroine is well known to the millions of readers of Joanne Greenberg's novel, which began as a cult paperback and became a durable bestseller. She is Deborah, sixteen, schizophrenic, child of an affluent home, but inhabitant of a personal fantasy. After a suicide attempt, she spends three years in a mental institution, coming close to self-destruction more than once, but finally surviving through her own efforts and those of a psychiatrist who really attempts to understand her.

We are given only sketchy information about what drove her to attempt suicide—her parents didn't understand her, she's filled with guilt because she believes she tried to kill a younger sister—but her fantasies are shown in much greater detail. As visualized in the film, they seem to be inspired by the paintings of Frank Frazetta: A race of muscular young people, clothed in furs and feathers, ride giant horses across the desert and want her to join them.

This alternative universe is so much more romantic and seductive than the real world, which for Deborah becomes Ward D of the mental institution. It's a women's ward, filled with the "worst" cases. Some of the patients do indeed seem to be totally within their private hells, but others (like the loud and often cheerful Kitty) have a reservoir of common sense. Deborah is wary, here, and often silent; she's properly afraid of the sinister male attendant Hobbs, but the turning point in her cure comes when she can admit of the other attendant, McPherson: "I like him. He treats me like I'm a real person." That touch of reality from outside is the first crack in the totality of her fantasies.

The psychiatrist is Dr. Fried, played by Bibi Andersson with sympathy and fortitude: She listens, encourages, supports, suggests, doesn't push. And over a period of three years Deborah is finally able to open herself to the world outside her dreams, to send her phantom gods galloping out into the desert without her.

I Never Promised You a Rose Garden has been compared, of course, to *One Flew Over the Cuckoo's Nest,* which first defied a kind of unwritten Hollywood superstition. That superstition was that movies about mental illness wouldn't succeed at the box office, that they were too depressing. *Cuckoo's Nest* wasn't filmed for years because of that taboo, and *Rose Garden* probably couldn't have been made if it hadn't been for *Cuckoo's Nest*'s great success.

One big difference between the two

movies is that R.P. McMurphy, in *Cuckoo*, was, in fact, sane. Deborah is not. *Cuckoo* celebrates McMurphy's cosmic sanity, and so has room for the dimensions of Jack Nicholson's manic performance. *Rose Garden* celebrates, instead, very small victories (and one of its most poignant moments comes when Deborah, burning herself with a cigarette, realizes with triumph that she actually feels pain—that her mind has let the reality in).

This is difficult material to bring to life, but a young actress named Kathleen Quinlan does it with heart and sensitivity. There were opportunities here for climbing the walls and chewing the scenery, I suppose, but her performance always finds the correct and convincing human note.

And it's the skill with which Miss Quinlan (and Bibi Andersson) follow that thread of characterization that makes the movie work. Otherwise, those desert fantasies and all those feathers and fur might have been fatally distracting. But because Deborah seems to regard them with a sober fatalism, we can almost accept them; and because she never expresses any emotions that don't seem to grow right out of the situations she finds herself in, we always accept her.

I Never Sang for My Father ★ ★ ★ ★
PG, 92 m., 1971

Melvyn Douglas (Tom), Gene Hackman (Gene), Dorothy Stickney (Margaret), Estelle Parsons (Alice, The Sister), Elizabeth Hubbard (Peggy). Directed and produced by Gilbert Cates. Screenplay by Robert Anderson.

At the beginning and again at the end of *I Never Sang for My Father*, we see a grainy snapshot of an old man and a middle-aged man, arms thrown about each other's shoulders, peering uncertainly into the camera as if they're not quite sure what drew them out into the sunshine to pose this day. And we hear Gene Hackman's voice: "Death ends a life. But it does not end a relationship." This film takes that simple fact and uses it to make a poignant and ultimately tragic statement about parents and children, life and death, and all the words that go unspoken. The man is played by Melvyn Douglas, and Hackman plays his son, and the film is about the fierce love they bear for each other, and about their inability to communicate that love, or very much of anything else.

The story takes place at a time when the old man's life is ending, but he won't admit it, and when the younger man's life is about to permit a new beginning. The old man is eighty-one, and a long time ago he was the mayor and the school board president—one of the town's most important citizens. But now he has largely been forgotten, left to live a comfortable life in the rambling old family home. He lives there with his wife and his memories, and a fierce possessiveness for his son.

What he wants from the son is a show of devotion. He doesn't communicate with him; indeed, he spends a lot of time falling asleep in front of the television set. But he wants him there, almost as a hostage, because he has a hunger for affection left over from his own neglected childhood. The son tries to go through the motions. But his own wife died a year ago, and now, at forty-four, he has decided to marry a woman doctor who lives in California. This will mean leaving the hometown, and that would be heresy to his father.

The situation becomes urgent when the old man's wife dies. He seems to accept the death as an inconvenience, transferring his grief to memories of his own mother's death half a century before. But his dependence upon his son becomes almost total. His daughter (Estelle Parsons) comes home for the funeral; in a fit of rage, the old man had banished her for marrying a Jew. Now she explains to Hackman, with an objectivity that sounds cruel but springs from love, that an arrangement is going to have to be made about their father. He can't live in the big house by himself.

The trouble is, his pride makes him refuse to hire the housekeeper he could easily afford. He expects his son to watch over him. And Hackman has not gathered the courage to reveal his marriage plans. He goes to look at a couple of old peoples' homes, but he finds them depressing and he knows his father would never, ever, go to one. So there you have the son's dilemma. The father should not live alone. A nursing home seems impossible. For a moment, the children consider gaining power of attorney and insisting on a housekeeper. But then, in a scene of remarkable emotional impact, the son watches as his father finally breaks down and reveals his grief, and the son invites him to come and live in California. But that, of course, is also unacceptable to the old man, whose pride will not allow him to admit that others could make his decisions, and whose stubbornness makes him insist on having everything his way, no matter what.

These bare bones of plot hardly give any hint of the power of this film. I've suggested something of what it's about, but almost nothing about the way the writing, the direction, and the performances come together to create one of the most unforgettably human films I can remember.

Robert Anderson's screenplay is from his autobiographical play, and it rings with truth. His dialogue is direct and revealing, without the "literary" touches or sophistication that could have sabotaged the characters. Eugene O'Neill was writing a different kind of dialogue for different purposes in *Long Day's Journey into Night*, a somewhat similar work that comes to mind. But for Anderson's story, which depends on everyday realism and would find symbolism dangerous, the unadorned dialogue is essential.

Gilbert Cates's direction also respects the fact that this is a movie about visual style or any other fashionably cinematic self-consciousness. With the exception of an inappropriate song which sneaks onto the sound track near the film's beginning, Cates has directed solely to get those magnificent performances onto the screen as movingly as possible. Much of the film is just between the two of them and the characters seem to work so well because Douglas and Hackman respond to each other in every shot; the effect is not of acting, but as if the story were happening right now while we see it.

The film tells us that death ends a life, but not a relationship. That's true of all close and deep human relationships; when one person dies, the other continues long afterwards to wonder what could have been said between them, but wasn't.

I Never Sang for My Father has the courage to remain open-ended; the father dies, but the problems between father and son remain unresolved. That is really more tragic than the fact of death, because death is natural, but human nature cries out that parents and children should understand each other.

I Spit on Your Grave no stars
R, 98 m., 1980

With Camille Keaton, Eron Tabor, Richard Pace, and Anthony Nichols. Directed by Meir Zarchi and produced by Joseph Zbeda. Screenplay by Zarchi.

I Spit on Your Grave is a vile bag of garbage that is so sick, reprehensible, and contemptible that I can hardly believe it played in respectable theaters. But it did. Attending it was one of the most depressing experiences of my life.

This is a film without a shred of artistic distinction. It lacks even simple craftsmanship. There was no possible motive for exhibiting it, other than the totally cynical hope that it might make money. And it did make money: When I saw it at 11:20 A.M. on a Monday, the theater contained a larger crowd than usual.

It was not just a large crowd, it was a profoundly disturbing one. I do not often attribute motives to audience members, nor do I try to read their minds, but the people who were sitting around me on that Monday morning made it easy for me to know what they were thinking. They talked out loud. And if they seriously believed the things they were saying, they were vicarious sex criminals.

The story of *I Spit on Your Grave* is told with moronic simplicity. A girl goes for a vacation in the woods. She sunbathes by a river. Two men speed by in a powerboat. They harass her. Later, they tow her boat to a rendezvous with two of their buddies. They strip the girl, beat her, and rape her again. She crawls home. They are already there, beat her some more, and rape her again.

Two weeks later, somewhat recovered, the girl lures one of the men out to her house, pretends to seduce him, and hangs him. She lures out another man and castrates him, leaving him to bleed to death in a bathtub. She kills the third man with an axe and disembowels the fourth with an outboard engine. End of movie.

These horrible events are shown with an absolute minimum of dialogue, which is so poorly recorded that it often cannot be heard. There is no attempt to develop the personalities of the characters—they are, simply, a girl and four men, one of them mentally retarded. The movie is nothing more or less than a series of attacks on the girl and then her attacks on the men, interrupted only by an unbelievably grotesque and inappropriate scene in which she enters a church and asks forgiveness for the murders she plans to commit.

How did the audience react to all of this? Those who were vocal seemed to be eating it up. The middle-aged, white-haired man two seats down from me, for example, talked aloud. After the first rape: "That was a good one!" After the second: "That'll show her!" After the third: "I've seen some good ones, but this is the best." When the tables turned and the woman started her killing spree, a woman in the back row shouted: "Cut him up, sister!" In several scenes, the other three men tried to force the retarded man to attack the girl. This inspired a lot of laughter and encouragement from the audience.

I wanted to turn to the man next to me and tell him his remarks were disgusting, but I did not. To hold his opinions at his age, he must already have suffered a fundamental loss of decent human feelings. I would have liked to talk with the woman in the back row, the one with the feminist solidarity for the movie's heroine. I wanted to ask if she'd been appalled by the movie's hour of rape scenes. As it was, at the film's end I walked out of the theater quickly, feeling unclean, ashamed, and depressed.

This movie is an expression of the most diseased and perverted darker human natures. Because it is made artlessly, it flaunts its motives: There is no reason to see this movie except to be entertained by the sight of sadism and suffering. As a critic, I have never condemned the use of violence in films if I felt the filmmakers had an artistic reason for employing it. *I Spit on Your Grave* does not. It is a geek show. I wonder if its exhibitors saw it before they decided to play it, and if they felt as unclean afterward as I did.

I Wanna Hold Your Hand ★ ★ ½

PG, 104 m., 1978

Nancy Allen (Pam), Bobby DiCicco (Tony), Marc McClure (Larry), Susan Kendall Newman (Janis), Theresa Saldana (Grace), Wendie Jo Sperber (Rosie), Will Jordan (Ed Sullivan). Directed by Robert Zemeckis and produced by Tamara Asseyev and Alex Rose. Screenplay by Zemeckis and Bob Gale.

I Wanna Hold Your Hand is a goofy, funny, slapstick movie about the day the Beatles invaded America—and especially about a bunch of kids who are determined to see them, no matter what. It's silly, it doesn't always make sense, but it's fun. And it has a nice anarchic touch: There is something inspired about the image of a crazed teenager scaling a television tower to knock the Beatles off the air, and having the ax blasted from his hand by a lightning bolt from that big Beatles fan in the sky.

The movie is put together sort of like *American Graffiti*: We meet the teen-age heroes as they jam into a record store to buy the first Beatles album, and then we follow them as they attempt literally anything to get past police lines and security guards and into the presence of the Beatles. Today's teenagers are likely to ask: Were kids *really* that crazy about the Beatles? Yes, today's teenagers . . . yes, they were.

But the movie's not a sociological document. It's a series of slapstick chases inspired, I suspect, by the Hollywood tradition of screwball comedies. Some of the scenes work, some don't, but the director, Robert Zemeckis, doesn't stop for breath. Many of the best moments star a kid named Bobby DiCicco, who bills himself as the world's foremost Beatles fan, and is capable of crashing through elevator doors and swinging like a crazed Tarzan from a cable above the heads of Ed Sullivan's audience.

There's also a pudgy girl (Wendie Jo Sperber) who suffers from the most agonizing torture a teen-ager can experience: knowing the answer to the question being asked on the radio that will win you two free tickets to the "Ed Sullivan Show," and *not being able to get to a telephone!* In her desperation to call in with the answers to tricky questions ("Who is both the youngest and the oldest Beatle?"*), she leaps from speeding cars and throws loose change at telephones like a maniac.

The movie does a fairly good job of remembering how people talked, looked, and dressed in 1964 (incredible as it may seem, guys had short hair and hardly anybody wore blue jeans). One funny scene has a long-haired Beatles fan being told by his obviously sadistic father that he can have two tickets to the Sullivan show—but only if he gets his hair cut. A point-of-view shot shows the barber leaning ominously over him . . . with a patch over one eye.

We never really see the Beatles in the film, but we do see kinescopes of their actual TV appearance (very well coordinated with the movements of doubles on the studio stage). And we hear more than a dozen Beatles songs, and even see what are supposed to be John's shoes. That's in the scene I liked best, in which one girl actually does get into the Beatles' empty suite at the Plaza, and orgiastically touches the glasses *they* drank from, and the chairs *they* sat in, the beds *they* rumpled and, my God, even the cigarette butts *they* left behind . . . .

*(*Answer: Ringo, the oldest in years but youngest in terms of service.)*

Iceman ★ ★ ★ ★

PG, 99 m., 1984

Timothy Hutton (Dr. Shephard), John Lone (Iceman), Lindsay Crouse (Dr. Diane Brady). Directed by Fred Schepisi and produced by Norman Jewison and Patrick Palmer. Screenplay by John Drimmer and Chip Proser.

Iceman begins in almost exactly the same way as both versions of *The Thing,* with a team of Arctic scientists chopping a frozen mammal out of the ice. But somehow we're more interested in this discovery because the frozen object isn't simply a gimmick at the beginning of a horror picture; it is presented with real curiosity and awe.

What is it? As a helicopter lifts the discovery aloft, we can glimpse its vague, shadowy outline through the block of 40,000-year-old ice. It seems almost to be a man, with its arms outstretched. If we remember Fellini's *La Dolce Vita,* we're reminded of its famous opening scene, as the helicopter flew above Rome with the statue of Christ. In both cases, a contrast is made between the technological gimmicks of man and an age-old mystery. In both cases, also, we're aware that we are in the hands of a master director. *Iceman* is by Fred Schepisi, the Australian who made *The Chant of Jimmy Blacksmith* and Willie Nelson's *Barbarosa.* Both of those movies were about men who lived entirely apart from modern society, according to rules of their own, rules that we eventually realized made perfect sense (to them, at least). Now Schepisi has taken that story idea as far as it will go.

The block of ice is thawed. As each drop of water trickles down a stainless-steel table to the floor, we feel a real excitement. We're about to discover something, just as we were when the apes found the monolith in *2001.* Inside the block of ice is a Neanderthal man, perfectly preserved, frozen in an instant with his hands pushing out and his mouth open in a prehistoric cry of protest. Such a discovery is at least theoretically possible; mastodons have been found in Russia, frozen so quickly in a sudden global catastrophe that the buttercups in their stomachs had still not been digested. Why not a man? Of course, the man's cell tissue would have been destroyed by the freezing process, right? Not according to *Iceman,* which advances an ingenious theory.

The scene in which the Neanderthal is brought back to life is one of those emergency room dramas we're familiar with from the TV medical shows, with medics pounding on the chest and administering electrical shocks. Then the movie leaves the familiar, and begins an intriguing journey into the past of the man. The Neanderthal (his name sounds like "Charlie") is placed in a controlled environment. Two scientists (Timothy Hutton and Lindsay Crouse) establish a relationship with him. Elementary communication is started—although here the movie makes a basic error in showing the scientists teaching Charlie to speak English, when of course they would want to learn his language instead.

The rest of the movie develops a theory about how Charlie was frozen and what he was looking for when that surprising event took place. There is also an argument between two branches of science: Those who are more interested in what they can learn from Charlie's body and those who want to understand his mind. This conflict seems to have been put in to generate suspense (certainly no responsible scientist, presented with a living Neanderthal man, would suggest any experiment that would endanger his life). But never mind; before it turns into conflict between good and evil, *Iceman* departs in an unexpected, mystical direction.

This movie is spellbinding storytelling. It begins with such a simple premise and creates such a genuinely intriguing situation that we're not just entertained, we're drawn into the argument. What we feel about Charlie reflects what we feel about ourselves. And what he knows—that we've forgotten—illuminates the line between man the fire-builder, and man the stargazer. Think how much more interesting *The Thing* would have been if its frozen life form had been investigated rather than destroyed, and you have an idea of *Iceman*'s appeal.

The Idolmaker ★ ★ ★
PG, 117 m., 1980

Ray Sharkey (Vince Vacarri), Tovah Feldshuh (Brenda Roberts), Peter Gallagher (Cesare), Paul Land (Tommy Dee), Joe Pantoliano (Gino Pilate). Directed by Taylor Hackford and produced by Gene Kirkwood and Howard W. Koch, Jr. Screenplay by Edward Di Lorenzo.

At the core of *The Idolmaker*, making it a better film than it might otherwise have been, is the hungry, lonely ego of the movie's hero, Vince Vacarri. He has all the skills necessary to become a rock 'n' roll idol, especially in the late-1950s world of Top Forty payola and prefabricated stars. But he doesn't have the looks. He so desperately wants stardom, though, that he tries to have it vicariously, through the "idols" he painstakingly manufactures. Maybe that makes *The Idolmaker* sound more serious than it is, but it's that core of obsession in the Ray Sharkey performance that takes a movie that might have been routine and makes it interesting. This is not a dazzlingly original idea, but the movie understands its passions well enough to entertain us with them.

The "idolmaker" of the title is based, I understand, on the real-life character of Bob Marcucci (listed as the film's "technical adviser"). He is the Philadelphia Svengali who discovered, coached, and managed Frankie Avalon and Fabian, quarterbacking them to stardom. If this movie can be believed, he was a rock 'n' roll puppetmaster, supplying the lines, the songs, the delivery and—most importantly—the stage mannerisms and "look" of his personalities.

The movie moves the story to Brooklyn, and borrows heavily from the clichés of show-biz rags to riches movies: Not only is it lonely at the top in this movie . . . it's lonely at the bottom, too, for practice. The Sharkey character manufactures his first rock star (Paul Land) out of a little raw talent, an unshaped stage presence, and sheer energy. One of the movie's most engaging scenes shows Land at a high school record hop, doggedly pantomiming his first record while Sharkey, backstage, goes through the same motions.

Land does a good job of playing the movie's first rock singer—a spoiled, egotistical creation renamed "Tommy Dee." We can predict what will happen. He'll be pushed to the top by Sharkey, develop an inflated opinion of himself, and think he did it all alone. That's exactly what happens, but Land moves through these stages with a conviction that makes them seem fairly new, even while we're recognizing them.

Meanwhile, Sharkey has another discovery waiting in the wings. He spots a busboy (Peter Gallagher) in his brother's restaurant. The guy can't keep time, can't sing, and has one enormous hairy eyebrow all the way across his face. No problem: Sharkey pounds rhythm into him, grooms him, renames him Caesare and fast-talks him onto the movie's version of "American Bandstand." It turns out that this kid *does* have a natural rapport with the prepubescent girls in his audiences, and he's on his way.

None of this would work if *The Idolmaker* didn't have convincing actors playing the two rock singers. It does. Land and Gallagher can sing and move well enough to convince us they're plausible teen idols. They can also act well enough to modulate their stage performances—they start out terrible and work their way up to levels that Fabian himself must only have dreamed about. And the movie has fun with its production numbers. The songs are all standard late-fifties rock dreck (but newly composed for the movie), but the stage performances are a little sneaky. They're not as ridiculous as many of the late-fifties adolescent heroes actually were; they seem to owe a lot not only to Elvis (naturally) but also to such performers of a decade later as Mick Jagger.

All of this is not to say that *The Idolmaker* is a masterpiece. But it is a well-crafted movie that works, that entertains, and that pulls us through its pretty standard material with the magnetism of the Ray Sharkey performance. Because we sense his hungers, his isolations, and his compulsive needs, we buy scenes that might otherwise have been unworkable.

In the Mood ★ ★ ★

PG-13, 98 m., 1987

Patrick Dempsey (Sonny Wisecarver), Talia Balsam (Judy), Beverly D'Angelo (Francine). Directed by Phil Alden Robinson and produced by Gary Adelson and Karen Mack. Screenplay by Robinson.

Sonny Wisecarver must have been some kinduva guy. When he was fifteen, he ran off with one older woman, and after they hauled him back and put him on probation, he ran off with another one. He made a lot of headlines back in 1944, after the tabloids named him "Woo Woo Wisecarver." What was the kid's secret?

Maybe it was just that he was so darn nice, and yet had a spark of rebellion that allowed him to see himself in ways that fifteen-year-olds ordinarily do not see themselves—for example, as the husband of a twenty-two-year-old with a couple of kids and a mean bastard of a common-law spouse at home.

As the movie opens, Sonny (Patrick Dempsey) is the captive of his dispirited parents, who occupy their home as if they had been sentenced to it. Across the street, there's music and fun, as Judy (Talia Balsam), the older woman, hosts a dance party every afternoon while her old man is away. Sonny drops in one day, and right away there's a spark between them. Before long they are friends, and then they are kissing, and then Sonny thinks up the plan for their escape to another state, where they are married.

There are a lot of headlines after they're brought back to California to face the law, but after he is sentenced to a youth camp, Sonny escapes and falls into the arms of another older woman (Beverly D'Angelo). She invites him for a cup of coffee. He resists, she smiles, there is another spark, and he's back in the headlines.

In order to make this movie at all, the right note had to be found. The Wisecarver story, which is based on fact, is filled with hazards for the wrong script. It could be distasteful, contrived, creepy. Phil Alden Robinson, who wrote and directed it, has made it charming by finding the essential sweetness in all of his characters. Sonny and his women run off together not out of unbridled lust, but because they are nice people in a cold world, and because it seemed like a good idea at the time.

A kid named Patrick Dempsey is the perfect choice to play Sonny. He's got the wisecracking spirit of one of Neil Simon's autobiographical heroes, but he also has a certain saintly simplicity, a way of not seeing all the things that could go wrong. Talia Balsam, as his first love, does a wonderful job of revealing just enough of the hurt and suffering in her life, the hard knocks she has taken while still retaining a kind side. Beverly D'Angelo, as the second woman, is a little older and a little wiser, and Woo Woo Wisecarver is already famous when she meets him, but she's also an innocent, and she can't understand why the newspapers and the courts would make such a big deal out of this nice kid.

The movie is comfortably set in its period, the mid-1940s of Roosevelt and rationing, Glenn Miller and Woody Herman, and a national hunger for headlines that were not about the war. The period is established without being allowed to overcome the picture, which finds a gentle offhand way to get its laughs; usually we're laughing, not at punch lines, but at human nature. The movie ends with a title card informing us that Sonny Wisecarver is alive and well and sends us his best regards, and that's sort of the ending the whole story was pointing to. The saga of Woo Woo Wisecarver was the best kind of sensational scandal, in which everybody got distracted from their problems and nobody really got hurt.

The Incredible Shrinking Woman ★ ★ ½

PG, 88 m., 1981

Lily Tomlin (Pat Kramer and Judith Beasley), Charles Grodin (Vance Kramer), Ned Beatty (Dan Beame), Henry Gibson (Dr. Nortz). Directed by Joel Schumacher and produced by Hank Moonjean. Screenplay by Jane Wagner.

This is a terrific movie for kids and teenagers. It's a melancholy fact of the times we live in that any movie of even moderate ambition is supposed to become a blockbuster—and that "family movies," with few exceptions, are inane, innocent, and boring. But *The Incredible Shrinking Woman* is not inane, is sometimes wickedly knowing, and is only periodically boring. It strikes a note of quiet desperation that appeals to the teen-ager in all of us. When Lily Tomlin's character has shrunk to twenty-four inches in height and is desperately screaming for help because she is about to be flushed down the garbage disposal unit— who among us cannot say he has felt exactly the same way?

I suppose that at some basic level *The Incredible Shirnking Woman* is a protest against the lot of the housewife in American society. As Lily Tomlin slaves away in her suburban dream home, her husband (Charles Grodin) gets big raises and promotions for advertising home-care products. And eventually one of those products (was it the dye? detergent? glue?) causes Lily Tomlin to start shrinking. One of the intriguing things about the movie is that the smaller Tomlin gets, the more people treat her like a child. She even winds up living in a doll's house. I would like to argue that this is a dilemma not limited to housewives. A lot of people know this feeling. Kids can identify with the maddening sensation that they are smaller than everyone else in the world and *no one is listening!* Teen-agers have grown accustomed to being stuck down the garbage disposal of life: Nobody wants them around, and most people would probably like to hit a switch and make them disappear.

So there's a certain poignant comedy in *The Incredible Shrinking Woman* that strikes some chords. The movie is also funny in its visual approach, showing us a suburban world in which everything is done in hideously jolly colors and everybody, even the TV anchorman, wears peach blazers. America in this movie looks like a gigantic paint-color chart.

It's too bad, I suppose, that *The Incredible Shrinking Woman* succeeds on the levels I've mentioned without ever breaking through to become a really inspired comedy. Lily Tomlin is such a funny woman that we expect her to hit home runs in every movie. She doesn't in this one, but she does something almost as hard. She creates a character that is halfway believable, in the midst of chaos. She causes us to feel a certain comic sympathy for her plight. And, for that matter, she inhabits a plight that is interesting. Most "family movies" these days are uninspired, moronic, and directed and acted without any visible style. *The Incredible Shrinking Woman* at least has an intelligence behind it. It is engaging a lot of the time and funny some of the time, especially when a gorilla helps the two-inch-tall Tomlin escape from captivity.

Indiana Jones and the Temple of Doom ★ ★ ★ ★

PG, 118 m., 1984

Harrison Ford (Indiana Jones), Kate Capshaw (Willie Scott), Ke Huy Quan (Short Round), Amrish Puri (Mola Ram), Philip Stone (Captain Blumburtt), Roshan Seth (Chattar Lal). Directed by Steven Spielberg and produced by George Lucas. Screenplay by Willard Huyck and Gloria Katz.

Steven Spielberg's *Indiana Jones and the Temple of Doom* is one of the greatest Bruised Forearm Movies ever made. You know what a Bruised Forearm Movie is. That's the kind of movie where your date is always grabbing your forearm in a viselike grip, as unbearable excitement unfolds on the screen. After the movie is over, you've had a great time but your arm is black-and-blue for a week. This movie is one of the most relentlessly nonstop action pictures ever made, with a virtuoso series of climactic sequences that must last an hour and never stop for a second. It's a roller coaster ride, a visual extravaganza, a technical triumph, and a whole lot of fun. And it's not simply a retread of *Raiders of the Lost Ark,* the first Indiana Jones movie. It works in a different way, and borrows from different traditions.

Raiders was inspired by Saturday afternoon serials. It was a series of cliffhanging predicaments, strung out along the way as Indiana Jones traveled from San Francisco to Tibet, Egypt, and other romantic locales. It was an exotic road picture. *Indiana Jones* mostly takes place on one location, and belongs more to the great tradition of the Impregnable Fortress Impregnated. You know the kind of fortress I'm talking about. You see them all the time in James Bond pictures. They involve unbelievably bizarre hideaways, usually buried under the earth, beneath the sea, on the moon, or inside a volcano. They are ruled over by megalomaniac zealots who dream of conquest, and they're fueled by slave labor. Our first glimpse of an Impregnable Fortress is always the same: An ominous long shot, with Wagnerian music, as identically uniformed functionaries hurry about their appointed tasks.

The role of the hero in a movie like this is to enter the fortress, steal the prize, and get away in one piece. This task always involves great difficulty, horrendous surprises, unspeakable dangers, and a virtuoso chase sequence. The very last shots at the end of the sequence are obligatory: The fortress must be destroyed. Hopefully, there will be great walls of flame and water, engulfing the bad guys as the heroes race to freedom, inches ahead of certain death.

But enough of intellectual film criticism. Let's get back to Indiana Jones. As *Temple of Doom* opens, Indiana is in a nightclub somewhere in Shanghai. Killers are after him. He escapes in the nick of time, taking along a beautiful nightclub floozy (Kate Capshaw), and accompanied by his trusty young sidekick, Short Round (Ke Huy Quan). Their getaway leads them into a series of adventures: A flight over the Himalayas, a breathtaking escape from a crashing plane, and a meeting with a village leader who begs Indiana to find and return the village's precious magic jewel—a stone which disappeared along with all of the village's children. Indiana is a plucky chap and agrees. Then there's a dinner in the palace of a sinister local lord. The dinner scene, by the way, also is lifted from James Bond, where it's an obligatory part of every adventure: James is always promised a sure death, but treated first to an elegant dinner with his host, who boasts of his power and takes inordinate pride in being a sophisticated host. After Indiana and Willie retire for the night, there's the movie's only slow sequence, in which such matters as love are discussed. (Make some popcorn.) Then the movie's second half opens with a breathtaking series of adventures involving the mines beneath the palace—mines that have been turned into a vision of hell.

The set design, art direction, special effects, and sound effects inside this underground Hades are among the most impressive achievements in the whole history of Raiders and Bond-style thrillers. As dozens of little kids work on chain gangs, the evil maharajah keeps them in slavery by using the sinister powers of the missing jewel and its two mates. Indiana and his friends look on in astonishment, and then Indiana attempts to steal back the jewel. Some of the film's great setpieces now take place: Human victims are lowered into a subterranean volcano in a steel cage, weird rituals are celebrated, and there is a chase scene involving the mine's miniature railway. This chase has to be seen to be believed. Spielberg has obviously studied Buster Keaton's *The General*, that silent classic that solved the obvious logistic problem of a chase on railway tracks (i.e., what to do about the fact that one train seemingly always has to be behind the other one). As Indiana and friends hurtle in the little out-of-control mine car, the pursuers are behind, ahead, above, below, and beside them, and the scene will wring you out and leave you breathless. *Indiana Jones and the Temple of Doom* makes no apologies for being exactly what it is: Exhilarating, manic, wildly imaginative escapism.

No apologies are necessary. This is the most cheerfully exciting, bizarre, goofy, romantic adventure movie since *Raiders*, and it is high praise to say that it's not so much a sequel as an equal. It's quite an experience. You stagger out with a silly grin—and a bruised forearm, of course.

Infra-Man ★ ★ ½

PG, 92 m., 1976

Li Hsiu-hsien, Wang Hsieh, Yuan Man-tzu, Terry Liu, Tsen Shu-yi, Huang Chien-lung, Lu Sheng. Directed by Hua Shan and produced by Rumme Shaw.

Within the first four mintues of *Infra-Man*, (a) a giant flying lizard attacks a school bus, (b) the Earth cracks open, (c) Hong Kong is destroyed by flames, (d) mountains disintegrate to reveal the forms of reptilian monsters with blinking yellow eyes, (e) the Professor announces that a twenty-million-year-old woman is unleashing the hibernating monsters upon civilization, (f) the Science Headquarters is shaken by a second quake, (g) the Mutants awake, and (h) the Professor, obviously shaken, informs a secret meeting of world leaders, "This situation is so bad that it is the worst that ever has been!"

No doubt about it: This is a case for Infra-Man. In his secret laboratory far beneath the

Science Headquarters, the Professor explains to a brave volunteer: "We will wire your arms and legs with powerful transistors and death rays. You will be powered by a tiny nuclear reactor. Unfortunately, the operation will be very painful and you may die."

And so we're off and running, in the best movie of its kind since *Invasion of the Bee Girls*. I'm a pushover for monster movies anyway, but *Infra-Man* has it all: Horrendous octopus men, a gigantic beetle man with three eyes who sprays his victims with sticky cocoons, savage robots with coiled spring necks that can extend ten feet, a venomous little critter that looks like a hairy mutant footstool, elaborately staged karate fights, underground throne rooms, damsels in distress, exploding volcanoes, and a whip-cracking villainess named Princess Dragon Mom (Philip Wylie, please note).

The movie's totally, almost joyfully absurd, and a victim of John Carter's Syndrome. You remember J.C.S., based on the logical oversight in Edgar Rice Burrough's books about John Carter of Mars. After whole chapters of galloping across the Martian desert on his Martian steed and fighting off enemies in sword fights, John Carter finally says to hell with it, pulls out a ray gun, and fries everybody.

Same here. Gigantic mutant monsters with built-in death rays attack Infra-Man, who can hurl lightning bolts from the soles of his feet, and what do they do? They have a karate fight. After ten minutes of chopping and socking and doing acrobatic flips, THEN they zap each other.

No matter, *Intra-Man* contains terrific moments. In one cliff-hanging scene, for example, the Professor has Infra-Man wired up on the operating table when Science Headquarters is attacked by gigantic mutant arms. That's right, arms: no body, just arms. The arms squirm all over the headquarters, knocking off the power supply. The Professor shouts into his radio: "You have one minute to restore power before Infra-Man dies!"

His aide struggles toward a red power switch. He is knocked unconscious by an arm. Shot of a stopwatch ticking away the seconds. He regains consciousness, struggles some more. The arm attacks again. With ten seconds to go, soldiers burst into the room with a power saw and cut the arm in half. The switch is thrown and Infra-Man lives.

There are other good things. Lines like, "We are doing this for the children of the world." Or, "The clouds will cut off the sun and deprive Infra-Man of his power source." Or, "Drop the Earthling to her doom—she will melt at 3,000 degrees." The movie even looks good: It's a classy, slick production by the Shaw Brothers, the Hong Kong kung fu kings. When they stop making movies like *Infra-Man*, a little light will go out of the world.

Innerspace ★ ★ ★

PG, 120 m., 1987

Dennis Quaid (Tuck Pendleton), Martin Short (Jack Putter), Meg Ryan (Lydia Maxwell), Kevin McCarthy (Scrimshaw), Fiona Lewis (Dr. Canker), Vernon Wells (Mr. Igoe), Robert Picardo (The Cowboy). Directed by Joe Dante and produced by Michael Finnell. Screenplay by Jeffrey Boam and Chip Proser.

I would have loved to eavesdrop on the script conferences for *Innerspace*. Here is an absurd, unwieldy, overplotted movie that is nevertheless entertaining—and some of the fun comes from the way the plot keeps laying it on.

The movie stars Dennis Quaid as a daring but irresponsible test pilot who signs up for a bizarre mission: He will be placed inside a capsule, which will be reduced in size until it is smaller than a molecule, and then the capsule will be injected into a rabbit. (If the experiment is a success, future surgeons could operate from inside their patients' diseased organs.)

High-tech thieves want to steal the technology of Quaid's employers, and send a squad of hit men to steal the syringe that contains his capsule. A scientist flees with the syringe to a nearby shopping mall, where in desperation he plunges the needle into Martin Short, and injects Quaid's capsule where the sun don't shine.

Are you following this? Quaid uses a communications system to talk from within Short's head. At first Short thinks he's hearing things, but then Quaid tells him the whole story, and enlists Short's aid in a desperate effort to outwit the bad guys and restore Quaid to normal size before his oxygen runs out.

There are complications—a lot of them—mostly centering around Meg Ryan, as

Quaid's estranged girlfriend. Short, with Quaid inside of him, has to convince Ryan of what's happening. And in the process, of course, he gets a crush on her—with Quaid eavesdropping on every word and heartbeat. It's a new twist on the old gag about the Siamese twin who wanted a moment alone with his girl.

This plot is not only unbelievable, but almost unworkable, especially when much is made of the intrigues of the villains. The complications grow so labyrinthine that the movie drags at times; it could have benefited from some fairly severe editing. And yet I liked *Innerspace* all the same, for the special effects and especially for the performances by Quaid and Short.

This was Short's comeback film after the unhappy experience of *The Three Amigos*. At last he shows what he can do in a film, realizing the promise of his peculiar but fascinating work on "Saturday Night Live." He gives us a little of his SNL schtick in a weird, off-balance dance, but basically he's playing a very confused straight man in this film, and he is always fun to watch.

Working inside Short in his tiny capsule, Quaid has a tougher role because he can't get physical. All of his actions have to be taken through the instrument of Short's body, and there are wonderful scenes where he uses rhetoric to inspire this nerd to act like a hero.

I wish I knew more about how they achieved the special effects. Some of the scenes inside the human bloodstream look like fairly straightforward, computer-generated animation. But there is a sequence involving the heart that has an uncanny reality to it, as if Quaid's capsule had been combined with actual footage of a beating heart, taken with miniaturized cameras.

Innerspace never quite knows whether to be a comedy or a thriller, and I never quite cared which way it went. The performances are so engaging and the effects are so enthusiastic that even when the movie runs long, it's only because it has too many ideas. In fact, it has one idea too many, leading to a howling logical error: When Quaid wants a drink, he asks Short to chug some Jack Daniel's—and then intercepts the booze on its way past the miniaturized capsule. But Quaid himself is as small as a molecule of the whiskey he wants to drink. I've felt that way myself some mornings.

Insignificance ★ ★ ★

R, 110 m., 1985

Theresa Russell (The Actress), Tony Curtis (The Senator), Gary Busey (The Ballplayer), Michael Emil (The Professor), Will Sampson (Elevator Man). Directed by Nicholas Roeg and produced by Jeremy Thomas. Screenplay by Terry Johnson.

The premise is not too unlikely. Imagine that during one hot and steamy night in a New York City hotel room, the lives of these people crossed paths: Marilyn Monroe, Senator Joe McCarthy, Joe DiMaggio, and Albert Einstein. The key linking element is, of course, Monroe, a woman of such undefinable and ethereal appeal that her real life did indeed encompass such husbands as DiMaggio and Arthur Miller, such admirers as Norman Mailer and Laurence Olivier, such friends as Jack Kennedy and Robert Mitchum. Her address book, which disappeared mysteriously after she died, no doubt included names from such unexpected corners of America that DiMaggio, Einstein, and McCarthy would only have been starters.

But imagine, all the same, that long and steamy night and that hotel room, and you have the substance of *Insignificance*, which was first a play on the London stage and is now one of the last sorts of films I would have expected Nicholas Roeg to direct. Roeg is a master of baroque visuals and tangled plot lines. His *Don't Look Now* still has people trying to explain that Venetian dwarf in the red raincoat, and his credits include at least one good film, *Eureka*, that was not quite sure whether it was a dream.

Insignificance is a film in which almost all the audacity is contained by the premise—that these four most famous figures of the 1950s met during one long night. Grant Roeg that much, and he gives us a fairly realistic film most of the rest of the way. The characters are never actually given their real names in the film, but there seems to be little doubt who they're meant to be, especially when Einstein and Monroe work out the theory of relativity together, using a flashlight, a few simple props, and some almost perfect dialogue.

Monroe is played in the film by Theresa Russell, who is *still* only about twenty-six years old, and who already has appeared in such landmarks as *Straight Time*, *The Last*

Tycoon, and *Bad Timing*. She doesn't really look very much like Monroe, but what does it matter? The blonde hair and the red lips are there, and so is the manner, which has been imitated so often, and so badly, that the imitators prove that Monroe was a special case. Russell doesn't imitate. She builds her performance from the ground up, and it works to hold the movie together.

Tony Curtis has a lot of fun as the hard-drinking, paranoic senator. He has turned, in his middle years, into a glorious ham, willing to take the chance of appearing ridiculous in order to reach for the farther edges of a performance. His theories about the Russians in this film are little masterpieces of dialogue. Gary Busey is the ballplayer, stolid and not quite comprehending his famous wife, and Michael Emil is a wonderful Einstein, sweet and childlike, and closest of all of them to Monroe's own personality.

I am not quite sure, however, what the point of the movie is. It's more of an acting and writing tour de force than a statement on sports, politics, sex symbol, or relativity. It begins by imagining its remarkable meetings, and ends by having created them. It's all process, no outcome. I think in this case that's OK.

Interiors ★ ★ ★ ★

PG, 93 m., 1978

Kristin Griffith (Flyn), Marybeth Hurt (Joey), Richard Jordan (Frederick), Diane Keaton (Renata), E.G. Marshall (Arthur), Geraldine Page (Eve), Maureen Stapleton (Pearl), Sam Waterston (Mike). Directed by Woody Allen and produced by Charles H. Joffe. Screenplay by Allen.

Yes, the opening *does* remind us of Bergman: The static shots, held for a moment's contemplation, of the rooms and possessions of a family. But then people enter the rooms, and their lives and voices have a particularly American animation; Woody Allen is right to say that his drama, *Interiors*, belongs more in the tradition of Eugene O'Neill than of Ingmar Bergman. But what's this? Here we have a *Woody Allen* film, and we're talking about O'Neill and Bergman and traditions and influences? Yes, and correctly. Allen, whose comedies have been among the cheerful tonics of recent years, is astonishingly assured in his first drama.

He gives us a time of crisis in a family, and develops it in counterpoint with the countless smaller joys and crises that are a family. He is very spare: Every scene counts, and the dialogue has the precision of a J.D. Salinger short story. There's nothing thrown in for effect unless the effect contributes specifically to the direction of the complete film.

Allen's central character is the family's mother, Eve, played by Geraldine Page as a heartbreaking showdown between total self-confidence in the past and catastrophic breakdown in the present. She is a designer, and her rooms are some, but not all, of the interiors of the title. She aims for a cool perfectionism in her rooms, for grays and greens and pale blues, for a look of irreproachable sterility. Her science and art is to know the correct place for a lamp, within a fraction of an inch.

She is married to a wealthy lawyer (E.G. Marshall). She has three daughters: A poet (Diane Keaton), a movie star (Kristin Griffith), and a searcher for meaningful occupation (Marybeth Hurt). Keaton lives with an alcoholic would-be novelist (Richard Jordan). Hurt lives with a filmmaker (Sam Waterston). Marshall announces that he wants a trial separation from Page, and later introduces a woman he's met on a cruise and wants to marry (Maureen Stapleton).

There you have them, the eight people of this movie. Allen, who thought nothing in *Annie Hall* of producing Marshall McLuhan from behind a theater lobby display for a comic walk-on, isolates his characters in *Interiors* so thoroughly, we're reminded of O'Neill's family in *Long Day's Journey Into Night*, coming and going in an old house with no access to any world outside.

There are hurts in this family that have been buried for years, and guilts that still hold it together. One daughter finally blurts out an accusation against her mother, who had thought herself so perfect and yet was as capable as anyone of pettiness and cruelty. We get the feeling, indeed, that the family has been together much too long, and that family life is not necessarily a blessing.

If there is a common wish shared by all the characters in the film, it's to live a life of their own. The father, defending to his daughters his decision to marry a woman they call a "vulgarian," argues not unreasonably that he's paid the bills and maintained the household for years—that now, in his early sixties, he's *earned* his right to some years of his own choosing.

The others have earned their rights, too, but each at the expense of the others. That is how each sees it, anyway. The same charge passes again and again around the family circle: That if the others had not been so demanding, or selfish, or jealous, or vindictive, then *this* person would have been set free to realize himself or herself.

Allen treats these themes in scenes that have an elegant economy of expression. The scene around the dinner table, for example, as the father announces his decision to leave, is handled in a way that etches the feelings of every member of the family, in just the right tones of anger, disbelief, or defiance. Scenes involving the daughters and their men suggest in different ways that the problems of this family will not end in this generation.

The funniest and saddest scene begins with the father's second marriage; Maureen Stapleton is wonderful as the "vulgarian," sweeping in with her red gown and finding Page's rooms "so gray. . . ." The dinner table conversation this time allows Allen to regard the Stapleton character with a mixture of tenderness and satire so delicately balanced, it's virtuoso.

The wonderment is that it's "serious." Yes, it is, but to be serious is not always to be good, and a movie both serious and bad is a great depression for everyone. *Interiors* becomes serious by intently observing complex adults as they fend and cope, blame and justify. Because it illuminates some of the ways we all act, it is serious but not depressing; when it's over, we may even find ourselves quietly cheered that Allen has seen so clearly how things can be.

Invasion USA ½★

R, 108 m., 1985

Chuck Norris (Matt Hunter), Richard Lynch (Rostov), Melissa Prophet (McGuire), Alexander Zale (Nikko). Directed by Joseph Zito and produced by Menahem Golan and Yoram Globus. Screenplay by James Bruner and Chuck Norris.

You'd think maybe Chuck Norris would want to follow up his great action movie *Code of Silence* with another winner, but you'd be wrong. *Invasion U.S.A.* is a brain-damaged, idiotic thriller, not bad enough to be laughable. The movie is a production of the Cannon Group, which sometimes makes good movies and more often makes junk like this. The theory is that a big-name star like Norris will help the movie make money in the Third World. That theory has all but destroyed the box-office credibility of Charles Bronson, and Norris seems to be following in the same footsteps.

In *Code of Silence* he played a well-written character in a well-constructed story, and there were lots of thrilling stunts and good supporting performances. In *Invasion U.S.A.* he hardly even interacts with other people on the screen. He simply steps into the frame when needed and blows somebody away.

The movie is about an invasion of the United States by several boatloads of vicious killers, who come from somewhere (Cuba, maybe?) and leave their amphibious vehicles on the beach. They pile into a caravan of rented trucks and vans and spread out across Florida, using grenades, machine-guns, and bazookas to destroy anything that looks remotely like a wholesome American image. Examples: School buses full of kids; shopping malls; church services; and even suburban families decorating Christmas trees while singing "Hark! The Herald Angels Sing!"

The theory is that their random violence will unleash anarchy upon America, the rule of law will collapse, and government will fall, and then they will take over. Who are they? Their leader, named Rostov, sometimes seems Russian, usually sounds American. His followers are sometimes Oriental, sometimes Latino, usually anonymous.

Chuck Norris works for "the agency," and is brought out of retirement to fight the threat, but as usual he insists on two specific working conditions: He works alone, and he drives his own pickup truck. (In one scene, he drives the truck through the wall of a shopping mall and mows down several terrorists, miraculously not hitting any civilians in the process.) He says as little as possible, and the role has no particular individual characteristics. He's just a mindless violence symbol.

He isn't the only one with no dimensions.

The movie's worst, most thankless role goes to Melissa Prophet, who plays a newspaper reporter. She stands around at the scenes of all the many violent crimes in this movie, snapping photographs and being angry. (Like many photographers in the movies, she acts as if photography consists of pointing the camera in the direction of the action and recording the largest possible view.)

This woman is angry at everyone. She spouts off to cops, badmouths security guards, and when Norris saves her life from savage terrorists she brushes his hand off her sleeve and bitterly snarls, "Thanks a lot, cowboy!" Never in the movie does she write or file a story or a photograph, and (this is most amazing) at no point does her presence in the movie make the slightest difference. She never interacts with anybody else for any purpose. She just stands around with her camera, being mad.

Is this a bad movie? Real bad.

Ironweed ★ ★ ★
R, 143 m., 1988

Jack Nicholson (Francis Phelan), Meryl Streep (Helen), Carroll Baker (Annie Phelan), Michael O'Keefe (Billy), Diane Venora (Peg), Fred Gwynne (Oscar Reo), Margaret Whitton (Katrina). Directed by Hector Babenco and produced by Keith Barish and Marcia Nasatir. Screenplay by William Kennedy.

At first the shape simply seems to be some old debris blown up against the side of a building, but then the shape stirs and we see that it is a man. At first we cannot quite make out his face, and when we can, and we see that the character is played by Jack Nicholson, there is a shock, for even in that first moment he seems to have been enveloped by the character. A little later in *Ironweed,* when we see Meryl Streep, there is a similar shock, not so much because of her appearance as because of her voice, which is an amalgam of high-class breeding and low-class usage.

Nicholson and Streep play drunks in *Ironweed,* and actors are said to like to play drunks, because it gives them an excuse for overacting, but there is not much visible "acting" in this movie; the actors are too good for that. Nicholson plays a man haunted by guilt from his past. He dropped and killed his baby son years ago, and has never forgiven himself. He left home soon after, and dropped like a stone until he hit the gutters of Albany, his hometown, where he still lives. Streep's guilt is less dramatic; she let herself down, or that is what she believes, for she does not understand that it is not her own fault she is a drunk.

Ironweed, directed by the Brazilian Hector Babenco, whose familiarity with the human sewers of Sao Paulo and Rio de Janeiro made *Pixote* one of the best films of 1981, is a movie of moods, locales, and voices. It is not much on plot, and even when something dramatic happens—when the Nicholson character returns home after many years to face his family—the scene is played for the silences as much as for the noises. It is probably a fault of the film that it contains so little drama; we quickly sense that hopelessness is a condition of this movie, that since alcoholism has been accepted as a fact of life, none of the other facts will be able to change. The movie generates little suspense and no relief.

And yet it is worth seeing as a chamber piece, an exercise in which two great actors expand their range and work together in great sympathy. Both Nicholson and Streep have moments as good as anything they have done. Nicholson's come in a graveyard scene at the beginning of the film, and in the long stretch after he returns to his home. Streep's come in a barroom fantasy scene, in which she sings as she remembers singing long ago, and in a confessional scene in a church where she tells the Virgin she is not a drunk, no matter what people say.

Nicholson's homecoming is all the more effective because Carroll Baker is so good as his wife, who has never remarried, who in her way does not blame him for what he has made of their lives, because he had his reasons. Baker was not nearly this impressive in her "first" career, many years ago, in movies ranging from *Baby Doll* to *The Carpetbaggers.* It may seem surprising to say that Baker holds the screen against Jack Nicholson, and yet she does.

The movie was shot mostly on location in upstate New York, and is set in the last years of the Depression. Its visual look is heightened realism, but Babenco also uses imaginary scenes, as he did in *Kiss of the Spider Woman.* As the drunk, hallucinatory Nicholson sees the face of a trolley driver he accidentally killed years ago, we begin to understand some of the chaos within his soaked brain.

Ironweed was released while *Barfly*, another movie about a Skid Row couple, was still playing around the country. Do the movies bear comparison? *Barfly*, with Mickey Rourke and Faye Dunaway, has more energy, more life and humor, and is more directly about advanced alcoholism. *Ironweed* carries a weight of memory and guilt, with drunkenness as a backdrop. I enjoyed *Barfly* more as a movie, but both films are well-acted. The difference is that in *Barfly* the characters scream a lot, and in *Ironweed* they listen a lot, to things we cannot hear.

Irreconcilable Differences ★ ★ ★ ½
PG, 112 m., 1984

Ryan O'Neal (Albert Brodsky), Shelley Long (Lucy Van Patten Brodsky), Drew Barrymore (Casey Brodsky), Sam Wanamaker (David Kessler), Allen Garfield (Phil Hanner), Hortensia Colorado (Maria Hernandez). Directed by Charles Shyer and produced by Arlene Sellers and Alex Winitsky. Screenplay by Nancy Myers and Shyer.

The opening moments of *Irreconcilable Differences* are not promising. A lawyer is advising his client about divorce—and when we see the client, she turns out to be a little girl. Her plan is to divorce her parents, because they have (she stumbles over the word) ir . . . ir . . . rec . . . con*cil*able differences. Right away, I was bracing myself for one of those smarmy movies about cute kids and mean parents. I could foresee the series this movie would inspire: "Kids' Court," with a different little plaintiff every week. It turns out that I was too cynical. *Irreconcilable Differences* is sometimes cute, and is about mean parents, but it also is one of the funnier and more intelligent movies of 1984, and if viewers can work their way past the ungainly title, they're likely to have a surprisingly good time.

The movie stars Drew Barrymore as the little girl. You may remember her from *E. T.*, when she hid E.T. in the closet with her stuffed animals. She has grown up just a little, but she still has that slight lisp and that air of preternaturally concentrated seriousness: She is the right actress for this role precisely because she approaches it with such grave calm. A kid trying to be funny would be a mistake. Her parents are played by Shelley Long of "Cheers," who is one of my favorite actresses, and Ryan O'Neal, who is not usually one of my favorite actors but is right for this role and good in it. They have a Meet-Cute while he is hitchhiking and she is returning her car to her tall, muscular boyfriend. It's love at first sight, even after Bink, the boyfriend, bursts into their motel room and figures out that his engagement is over.

O'Neal plans to be a great movie director. (His character seems inspired by Peter Bogdanovich, right down to the style of his glasses.) Long starts out to be a helpful wife and good mother, but then, after O'Neal's career hits the skids, she has great success as a writer. The point is that one parent or the other is always so busy, so successful, so much in demand, that the little girl gets overlooked. The only place she really feels loved and comfortable is when she goes home with the family's Mexican maid. So the kid sues for divorce. She wants to give the maid custody of herself. The parents are shocked. The media have a circus. The plot drifts dangerously toward a series of stagy confrontations, but avoids the obvious: This movie has been written with so much wit and imagination that even obligatory scenes have a certain freshness and style.

It also has a real edge, even a suggestion of bitterness, in its scenes about Hollywood. Although *Irreconcilable Differences* is a movie about family life, it's also a perceptive portrait of success and failure in Hollywood, with a good ear for the way people use the language of Leo Buscaglia to describe the behavior of Machiavelli.

The Drew Barrymore character sees right through all of this. She doesn't care about careers, she wants to be given a happy home and her minimum daily requirement of love, and, in a way, the movie is about how Hollywood (and American success in general) tends to cut adults off from the natural functions of parents. The theory is that kids will wait but a deal won't. Actually, it's just the opposite.

Ishtar ½★
PG-13, 105m., 1987

Warren Beatty (Lyle Rogers), Dustin Hoffman (Chuck Clarke), Isabelle Adjani (Shirra Assel), Charles Grodin (Jim Harrison). Directed by Elaine May and produced by Warren Beatty. Screenplay by May.

It's hard to play dumb. There's always the danger that a little fugitive intelligence will sneak out of a sideways glance and give the game away. The best that can be said for *Ishtar* is that Warren Beatty and Dustin Hoffman, two of the most intelligent actors of their generation, play dumb so successfully that on the basis of this film there's no evidence why they've made it in the movies.

Ishtar is a truly dreadful film, a lifeless, massive, lumbering exercise in failed comedy. Elaine May, the director, has mounted a multimillion-dollar expedition in search of a plot so thin that it could hardly support a five-minute TV sketch. And Beatty and Hoffman, good soldiers marching along on the trip, look as if they've had all wit and thought beaten out of them. This movie is a long, dry slog. It's not funny, it's not smart, and it's interesting only in the way a traffic accident is interesting.

The plot involves the two stars as ninth-rate songwriters who dream of becoming Simon and Garfunkel. They perform bad songs badly before appalled audiences. Their agent gets them a gig in Morocco, and once they're in Northern Africa, they become involved in the political intrigues of the mythical nation of Ishtar. Isabelle Adjani plays the sexy rebel who leads them down the garden path, and dependable Charles Grodin supplies the movie's only laughs as the resident CIA man.

The movie cannot be said to have a plot. It exists more as a series of cumbersome set pieces, such as the long, pointless sequence in the desert that begins with jokes about blind camels and ends with Hoffman and Beatty firing machine guns at a helicopter. It probably is possible to find humor in blind camels and helicopter gun-fights, but this movie leaves the question open.

As I was watching *Ishtar* something kept nagging at the back of my memory. I absorbed Hoffman and Beatty, their tired eyes, their hollow laughs, their palpable physical weariness as they marched through situations that were funny only by an act of faith. I kept thinking that I had seen these performances elsewhere, that the physical exhaustion, the vacant eyes, and the sagging limbs added up to a familiar acting style.

Then I remembered. The movie was reminding me of the works of Robert Bresson, the great, austere French director who had a profound suspicion of actors. He felt they were always trying to slip their own energy, their own asides, their own "acting" into his movies. So he rehearsed them tirelessly, fifty or sixty times for every shot, until they were past all thought and caring. And then, when they were zombies with the strength to do only what he required, and nothing more, he was satisfied.

That's what I got out of Beatty and Hoffman in *Ishtar.* There's no hint of Hoffman's wit and intelligence in *Tootsie,* no suggestion of Beatty's grace and good humor in *Heaven Can Wait,* no chemistry between two actors who should be enjoying the opportunity to act together. No life. I don't know if *Ishtar* was clearly a disaster right from the first, but on the evidence of this film, I'd guess it quickly became a doomed project and that going to the set every morning was more like a sentence than an opportunity. It's said this movie cost more than $40 million. At some point, maybe they should have spun off a million each for Hoffman and Beatty, supplied them with their own personal camera crews and allowed them to use their spare time making documentaries about what they were going through.

I've Heard the Mermaids Singing
★ ★ ★ ½
NO MPAA RATING, 85 m., 1987

Sheila McCarthy (Polly Vandersma), Paule Baillargeon (Gabrielle St-Peres), Ann-Marie McDonald (Mary Joseph), John Evans (Warren), Brenda Kamino (Japanese waitress), Richard Monette (Critic). Directed by Patricia Rozema and produced by Rozema and Alexandra Raffe. Screenplay by Rozema.

"I have heard the mermaids singing, each to each. I do not think that they will sing to me."
—T.S. Eliot, "The Love Song of J. Alfred Prufrock"

Don't we all know that feeling? That feeling that other people in other places are singing in the sunshine, but here in the shadows of our own miserable existence, the parade has passed us by. It is a key discovery of adult life that almost everyone else feels the same way, too, and that anyone who believes he's leading the parade is either stupid, mistaken, or a saint.

Polly (Sheila McCarthy), the heroine of *I've Heard the Mermaids Singing,* is a thirty-one-year-old Toronto woman who does not think the mermaids will sing to her. The most important thing in her life is photography, and sometimes she even dreams of the pictures she will take. But no one else has seen her work, and to all outward signs she is a winsome and lonely woman with few skills. Sometimes she gets office work through a temporary agency, but she isn't very good, and so it is with a certain amazement that she finds an employer who actually likes her.

The employer's name is Gabrielle (Paule Baillargeon), and she is an elegant French-Canadian woman who runs an art gallery in Toronto. Polly calls her "the Curator," and idolizes her. The Curator is able to overlook Polly's little lapses, such as turning letters into a sticky sea of correction fluid. And one night at a Japanese restaurant, she actually offers Polly a full-time job. Polly recalls that wonderful night, and other nights, on a homemade videotape that serves as the narration for the movie.

I've Heard the Mermaids Singing then develops into a much more subtle character study than the opening scenes might have prepared us for. Gabrielle, the Curator, reveals that her greatest regret in life is her inability to become a great painter; she sells the work of others, but she cannot paint. Polly asks to see some of her attempts, and is overwhelmed by them. But of course Polly has no confidence in her own taste, and so she smuggles one of the Curator's paintings into a show, where it is laboriously praised in impenetrable ArtSpeak by a hilarious caricature of a critic.

If the critic has validated the Curator's work, Polly thinks, maybe there is hope for her own photographs. So she sends them to Gabrielle anonymously, only to have them shot down as hopelessly inept. Her spirit is crushed. But there are more discoveries for her to make. She finds, for example, that Gabrielle has a lover, a woman named Mary, and that Mary, not Gabrielle, actually created the painting that the critic liked. It may be that the Curator lacks not only talent, but taste.

It is only gradually, while we're watching this movie, that we realize it is as much about Gabrielle as Polly, and that we are permitted to make discoveries about Gabrielle that Polly herself only dimly suspects. The movie was written and directed by Patricia Rozema, who uses a seemingly simple style to make some quiet but deep observations. What happens to Polly in the movie is easy to anticipate: She learns to trust in mermaids. What happens to Gabrielle is that she is closely observed and skillfully dissected.

When the movie is over, we leave thinking of Polly, and I have even read reviews in which the movie is treated entirely as Polly's story. That is partly because of Sheila McCarthy's extraordinary performance in the role; she has one of those faces that speaks volumes, and she is able to be sad without being depressing, funny without being a clown. She strikes just the right off-center note for the narration of the film; she must not seem too sure of herself, because the movie must not seem too sure of what it wants to say. It works by indirection, and Polly is actually only the instrument for the real story here, of a lonely and proud woman whose surfaces are flawless but whose sadness is deep.

If you see this movie and then have occasion to read "The Love Song of J. Alfred Prufrock," which contains lines that strike some readers with the force of a blow, reflect that the narrator of the poem is more like Gabrielle than Polly. More like the Curator, who has measured out her life in coffee spoons, who has seen the moment of her greatness flicker, who lacks the strength to force the moment to its crisis, who grows old. Polly is, I suspect, intended to be out there with the mermaids, neither stupid nor mistaken, but a saint.

J

Jagged Edge ★ ★ ★ ½
R, 108 m., 1985

Glenn Close (Teddy Barnes), Jeff Bridges (Jack Forester), Peter Coyote (Thomas Krasny), Robert Loggia (Sam Ransom). Directed by Richard Marquand and produced by Martin Ransohoff. Screenplay by Joe Eszterhas.

Directors like to talk about playing the audience like a piano, about making movies that are efficient machines for assaulting our emotions. *Jagged Edge* is a movie like that, a murder thriller which dangles one clue after another before our eyes, daring us to decide who committed the murder. The machinery in this movie is so efficient that we don't know the answer until the very last shot—and I'll be getting back to that last shot in a moment.

The film stars Jeff Bridges as a powerful San Francisco publisher whose wife is brutally murdered in their isolated oceanside home. After an investigation reveals that he stood to inherit his wife's entire fortune, he is arrested and charged with the murder. Glenn Close plays his defense attorney. At first, she insists she has retired from courtroom cases, but then Bridges convinces her that he is innocent. And before long, she is also convinced that they are in love.

The Close character stands at the center of the film. Is she defending the man she loves against the unjust charges against him? Or is she defending a cold-blooded killer, who might murder her just as he murdered his wife? There are moments in *Jagged Edge* when each of these possibilities seems convincing, but most of the time we just don't know. There's a lot of evidence on both sides.

Close's courtroom opponent is the assistant D.A. (Peter Coyote). They worked together a few years ago on a case where, she believes, he concealed evidence in order to win a conviction. Is he concealing evidence this time? There comes a time when we think he may be. And by then the film's tension is so tightly wound that we, and Close, don't know what to believe.

Jagged Edge is supremely effective at what it sets out to do—toy with the audience. It's another effective thriller from Richard Marquand, who made *Eye of the Needle.* The performances are good and the plot is watertight, as a whodunit must be. I have only one quarrel with the film, but it's a fairly substantial one. The movie *only* wants to keep us guessing. The characters are developed only in ways intended to string us along. Any behavior is possible if it will further the plot. There's no sense of reality beneath the gleaming surface.

Even that would be all right, if the movie didn't reveal the identity of the real killer in the final shot. Here's my theory: In a movie which exists only to tantalize us with clues and deceptive evidence, we *shouldn't* find out who the killer was—because that should be what we're arguing about as we leave the theater. Once the killer is unmasked, his crime reflects on everything else we know about his character, and that's more realism than you really need in a well-oiled machine.

NOTE: As this movie went into wide release, a strange thing happened. People started to get confused about the identity of the real killer. Even though there is a close-up of his face, the shot is taken from such an oblique angle that some viewers were confused, and I got letters and phone calls suggesting at least three possible villians. I imagine a VCR freeze-frame will solve the mystery.

Jaws ★ ★ ★ ★
PG, 124 m., 1975

Roy Scheider (Brody), Robert Shaw (Quint), Richard Dreyfuss (Hooper), Lorraine Gary (Ellen Brody), Murray Hamilton (Mayor). Directed by Steven Spielberg and produced by Richard Zanuck and David Brown. Screenplay by Peter Benchley and Carl Gottleib.

Steven Spielberg's *Jaws* is a sensationally effective action picture—a scary thriller that works all the better because it's populated with characters that have been developed into human beings we get to know and care about. It's a film that's as frightening as *The Exorcist,* and yet it's a nicer kind of fright, somehow more fun because we're being scared by an outdoor-adventure saga instead of by a brimstone-and-vomit devil.

The story, as I guess everyone knows by now, involves a series of attacks on swimmers by a great white shark, the response of the threatened resort island to its loss of tourist business, and, finally, the epic attempt by three men to track the shark and kill it. There are no doubt supposed to be all sorts of levels of meanings in such an archetypal story, but Spielberg wisely decides not to underline any of them. This is an action film content to stay entirely within the perimeters of its story, and none of the characters has to wade through speeches expounding on the significance of it all. Spielberg is very good, though, at presenting those characters in a way that makes them individuals. Before the three men get on that leaky old boat and go forth to do battle with what amounts to an elemental natural force, we know them well enough to be genuinely interested in the ways they'll respond. There's Brody (Roy Scheider), the police chief, who came to the island from New York looking, so he thought, for a change from the fears of the city. There's Quint (Robert Shaw), a caricature of the crusty old seafaring salt, who has a very particular personal reason for hating sharks. And there's Hooper (Richard Dreyfuss), the rich kid turned oceanographer, who knows best of all what a shark can do to a man, and yet is willing to get into the water with one.

All three performances are really fine. Scheider is the character most of us identify with. He's actually scared of the water, doesn't like to swim and, when he sees the giant shark swim past the boat for the first time, we believe him when he informs Quint, very sincerely, "We need a bigger boat." Shaw brings a degree of cheerful exaggeration to his role as Quint, stomping around like a cross between Captain Queeg and Captain Hook, and then delivering a compelling five-minute monologue about the time the *Indianapolis* went down and he was one of more than 1,000 men in the water. By the time rescue came, two-thirds of them had been killed by sharks.

Probably the most inspired piece of casting in the movie is the use of Richard Dreyfuss as the oceanographer. He made this film soon after playing the driven, scheming, overwhelmingly ambitious title character in *The Apprenticeship of Duddy Kravitz,* and the nice kid, college-bound, in *American Graffiti.* Here he looks properly young, engaging, and scholarly, and introduces the technical material about sharks in a way that reinforces our elemental fear of them.

Which brings us to the shark itself. Some of the footage in the film is of an actual great white shark. The rest uses a mechanical shark patterned on the real thing. The illusion is complete. We see the shark close up, we look in its relentless eye, and it just plain feels like a shark. *Jaws* is a great adventure movie of the kind we don't get very often any more. It's clean-cut adventure, without the gratuitous violence of so many action pictures. It has the necessary amount of blood and guts to work—but none extra. And it's one hell of a good story, brilliantly told.

Jaws the Revenge no stars
PG-13, 87 m., 1987

Lorraine Gary (Ellen Brody), Lance Guest (Michael), Mario Van Peebles (Jake), Karen Young (Carla), Michael Caine (Hoagie), Judith Barsi (Thea). Directed and produced by Joseph Sargent. Screenplay by Michael de Gusman.

Jaws the Revenge is not simply a bad movie, but also a stupid and incompetent one—a ripoff. And that's a surprise, because the film is the fourth in a series that has served Universal Pictures long and well, and the movie stars Lorraine Gary, the wife of the studio's chief executive officer. Wasn't there someone in charge of assuring that the film was at least a passable thriller, however bad? I guess not.

The plot centers on the character of Ellen Brody, who, you may recall, was the wife of the Roy Scheider character in the first and second *Jaws* movies. Now she is a widow, and her son has his dad's old job at the police department. The story opens at Christmas, as the son is eaten by a shark right off Martha's Vineyard, while a children's choir drowns out his screams with Christmas carols.

Mrs. Brody (Gary) flees in horror to the Bahamas, where her other son (Lance Guest) works as, you got it, a marine biologist. She pleads with him not to go into the water, but he argues that the great white shark has never been seen in warm waters. Not long after, the shark is seen, having made the trip from Martha's Vineyard to the Bahamas in three days.

Mrs. Brody, meanwhile, falls in love with a local pilot (Michael Caine), and there is a subplot about how her son is jealous of this new man in his mother's life. This jealousy, like every other plot device in the movie, is left unresolved at the end, but so what? The screenplay is simply a series of meaningless episodes of human behavior, punctuated by shark attacks.

Since we see so much of the shark in the movie, you'd think they would have built some good ones. They've had three earlier pictures for practice. But in some scenes the shark's skin looks like canvas with acne, and in others all we see is an obviously fake shark head with lots of teeth.

The shark models have so little movement that at times they seem to be supporting themselves on boats, instead of attacking them. Up until the ludicrous final sequence of the movie, the scariest creature in the film is an eel.

What happens at the end? Ellen Brody has become convinced that the shark is following her. It wants revenge against her entire family. Her friends pooh-pooh the notion that a shark could identify, follow, or even care about one individual human being, but I am willing to grant the point, for the benefit of the plot. I believe that the shark wants revenge against Mrs. Brody. I do. I really do believe it. After all, her husband was one of the men who hunted this shark and killed it, blowing it to bits. And what shark wouldn't want revenge against the survivors of the men who killed it?

Here are some things, however, that I do not believe:

• That Mrs. Brody could be haunted by flashbacks to events where she was not present and that, in some cases, no survivors witnessed.

• That the movie would give us one shark attack as a dream sequence, have the hero wake up in a sweat, then give us a second shark attack, and then cut to the hero awake in bed, giving us the only thing worse than the old "it's only a dream" routine, which is the old "is it a dream or not?" routine.

• That Mrs. Brody would commandeer a boat and sail out alone into the ocean to sacrifice herself to the shark, so that the killing could end.

• That Caine's character could or would crash-land his airplane at sea so that he and two other men could swim to Mrs. Brody's rescue.

• That after being trapped in a sinking airplane by the shark and disappearing under the water, Caine could survive the attack, swim to the boat, and climb on board—not only completely unhurt but also wearing a shirt and pants that are not even wet.

• That the shark would stand on its tail in the water long enough for the boat to ram it.

• That the director, Joseph Sargent, would film this final climactic scene so incompetently that there is not even an establishing shot, so we have to figure out what happened on the basis of empirical evidence.

There is one other thing I can't believe about *Jaws the Revenge*, and that is that on March 30, 1987, Michael Caine passed up his chance to accept his Academy Award in person because of his commitment to this movie. Maybe he was thinking the same thing as the marine biologist in the movie, which is that if you don't go right back in the water after something terrible happens to you, you might be too afraid to ever go back again.

Jean de Florette ★ ★ ★ ½
PG, 121 m., 1987
(See also *Manon of the Spring*)

Gerard Depardieu (Jean de Florette), Yves Montand (Cesar Soubeyran), Daniel Auteuil (Ugolin), Elisabeth Depardieu (Aimee), Ernestine Mazurowna (Manon). Directed by Claude Berri and produced by Pierre Grunstein. Screenplay by Berri and Gerard Brach.

If you were to walk into the middle of *Jean de Florette*, you would see a scene that might mislead you.

In the middle of a drought, a farmer is desperate to borrow a mule to help haul water from a nearby spring. He asks his neighbor for the loan of the animal. The neighbor is filled with compassion and sympathy, but simply cannot do without his mule, which he needs in order to farm his own land and provide for his own family. As the neighbor rejects the request, his face is so filled with regret you'd have little doubt he is one of the best of men.

Actually, he is a thief. And what he is stealing is the joy, the hope, and even the future of the man who needs the mule. *Jean de Florette* is a merciless study in human nature, set in Provence in the 1920s. It's the story of how two provincial French farmers systematically destroy the happiness of a man who comes out from the city to till the land.

The man from the city is Jean de Florette, a hunchback tax collector played by Gerard Depardieu, that most dependable of French actors. When he inherits a little land in Provence, he is only too happy to pack up his loyal wife and beautiful child and move to the country for a new beginning. He wants to raise vegetables and rabbits on the land, which, according to the map, includes a freshwater spring.

His neighbors have other ideas. The old local farmer (Yves Montand) and his son (Daniel Auteuil) long have had their eyes on that land, and they realize if they can discourage the newcomer they can buy the land cheap. So they do what is necessary. They block the spring with concrete, conceal its location, and wait to see what happens.

At first, nothing much happens. There are steady rains, the vegetables grow, and the rabbits multiply. Then comes the drought, and Depardieu is forced to bring water from a neighboring well, using his mule and his own strength, turning himself into a beast of burden. From morning to night he plods back and forth under the burning sun, and his wife helps when she can, but the burden is too much and the land surely will die. It is then that he asks for the loan of Auteuil's mule, and is turned down.

The director, Claude Berri, does not tell this story as a melodrama; all of the motives are laid out well in advance, and it is perfectly clear what is going to happen. The point of the film is not to create suspense, but to capture the relentlessness of human greed, the feeling that the land is so important the human spirit can be sacrificed to it.

To create this feeling, Berri stands well back with his camera. There are not a lot of highly charged closeups, to turn the story into a series of phony high points. Instead, many of the shots are surrounded by the landscape and the sky, and there is one enormously dramatic set piece when the sky fills up with rain clouds, and the thunder roars and the rain seems about to come. And then, as Depardieu and his family run outside to feel it against their faces, the rain falls elsewhere and Depardieu shakes his fist at the heavens and asks God why he has been forsaken.

But God has not double-crossed him, his neighbors have. And the enormity of their crime is underlined by the deliberate pace of this film, which is the first installment of a two-part epic (the second part is *Manon of the Spring*). We realize here that human greed is patient, and can wait years for its reward. And meantime daily life goes on in Provence, and neighbors pass the time of day and regret that it is impossible to make a loan of a mule.

Jeremiah Johnson ★ ★ ★
PG, 108 m., 1972

Robert Redford (Jeremiah Johnson), Will Geer (Bear Claw), Stefan Gierasch (Del Gue), Allyn Ann McLerie (Crazy Woman), Delle Bolton (Swan), Charles Tyner (Robidoux). Directed by Sydney Pollack and produced by Joe Wizan. Screenplay by John Milius and Edward Anhalt.

If Thoreau had been a violent man, angry and unforgiving, *Jeremiah Johnson* might have been made from one of his books. Like

Walden, it's the story of a man who goes alone into the wilderness to live by his hands and wits. It is good at showing us this man and the ways by which he survives; but not so good when it ventures into Indian myth and magic, and edges up to vast universal questions.

There's a sense in which movies like this should be rough-hewn and a little inarticulate. When a man makes up his mind to go into the mountains and say to hell with civilization, it's cheating a little to frame him against spectacular landscapes as if he were a particularly heroic tour guide. It may also be cheating to cast Robert Redford in the title role; he projects a kind of intellectual, winsome handsomeness that doesn't really belong in such a simple character.

Still, the movie does approach its subject with a certain dogged honesty; it agrees for the most part to coexist with the rhythms of the wilderness, and not go for big, phony climaxes (it is so studiously low-keyed, indeed, that it seems to end four or five times before it really does). The humor is direct and folksy, as when an old trapper asks Jeremiah if he can skin a grizzly. Jeremiah says he can, and so the trapper lures a grizzly into the cabin with Jeremiah, jumps out the back window and shouts, "Start skinnin'!"

The humor is direct, and so is the violence. Director Sydney Pollack approaches his scenes head-on. He doesn't deal in the choreography of violence, like Peckinpah, or the fetish of violence, like the Kubrick of *A Clockwork Orange*. Instead, his violent scenes are brutally short and forcible. Death occurs suddenly, and is absorbed by the emptiness of the mountain range.

The story follows Jeremiah as he makes a roughly circular journey through high mountain ranges and passes. He nearly starves the first winter, until the old trapper (Will Geer, looking like Father Christmas in his fur parka) has mercy on him. He forms brief friendships and partnerships with some of the other outcasts of the mountains; he has hostile encounters with Crow Indians and friendly ones with Flatheads; and as the result of a misunderstanding he finds himself married to the daughter of a Flathead chief. The marriage sets up the movie's most absorbing sequences. Jeremiah has earlier become a sort of guardian for a young boy, and now the three of them set up housekeeping. Pollack gets a kind of poetic documentary rhythm going as they clear a space, cut some trees, and build a cabin. Their long weeks of work are followed by a clumsy football game in which the three of them, so different from one another, show that they've become a family.

It is after this section of the movie that things begin to go a little wrong. Without telling you everything that happens (because that would remove the necessary shock value), I can say that Jeremiah runs up against a host of impenetrable wilderness mysteries, undying Indian blood feuds and, yes, fate itself. In the end he becomes a mysterious and legendary figure, a man of the mountains, who is too symbolic to suit me.

Still, as the portrait of a man who turns his back on society, *Jeremiah Johnson* is a finely felt and beautiful film. And the scenery is particularly beautiful. I say that with a certain sense of pain; I made a vow never to praise a movie because "the scenery is beautiful." The scenery is always beautiful in movies. Liking a movie because of its beautiful scenery is like buying a car because its tires are round. And yet . . . the movie was shot on location in the national forests of Utah, and there are moments in it that make *Doctor Zhivago* look cramped for space.

The Jewel of the Nile ★ ★ ★

PG, 105 m., 1985

Michael Douglas (Jack Coltan), Kathleen Turner (Joan Wilder), Danny DeVito (Ralph), Avner Eisenberg (Holy Man), Spiros Focas (Omar). Directed by Lewis Teague and produced by Michael Douglas. Screenplay by Mark Rosenthal and Lawrence Konner.

The Jewel of the Nile is more silliness in the tradition of *Romancing the Stone*, which in its turn was a funny action comedy inspired by the Indiana Jones epics. We walk into the theater expecting absolutely nothing of substance, and that's exactly what we get, served up with high style. The movie reassembles three key cast members—Michael Douglas, Kathleen Turner, and Danny DeVito—and goes on to a fourth inspired casting decision with the addition of Avner Eisenberg as a holy man of gentle goofiness.

Movie industry gossip had it that Kathleen Turner didn't particularly want to make this sequel, and that even Michael Douglas, who produces as well as stars, thought it might be best to quit while he was ahead. But the original contract specified a sequel, and it's to everybody's credit that *The Jewel of the Nile* is an ambitious and elaborate attempt to repeat the success of the first movie; it's not just a ripoff.

Even so, it lacks some of the pleasures of *Romancing*, especially the development of the romance between Douglas and Turner. This time, as the movie opens, they're old friends, unwinding in Cannes and reminiscing about the good times they had in South America. Perhaps sensing that there is nowhere to go with this essentially stable relationship, the movie plunges them almost immediately into Middle East intrigue.

A fabulously wealthy Arab (Spiros Focas) invites Turner to travel with him to his homeland, for reasons as vague as they are fascinating. Douglas temporarily drops out; after a manufactured spat, he decides he'd rather sail his boat through the Mediterranean. Turner is quickly involved in danger as the Arab reveals plans to usurp the role of a legendary holy man, and Douglas becomes an ally of the great spiritual leader, who is known as the Jewel of the Nile. (Danny DeVito is somewhat lost in all of this, and left for long stretches of the film to wander through the desert and suffer meaningless tortures in lieu of a clearly defined role.)

The Jewel of the Nile expends amazing resources on some of its scenes, including a gigantic spiritual meeting in the desert that is staged as a cross between a rock concert and the Nuremberg Rally. What makes the Middle Eastern stuff work, however, is the performance of Eisenberg, who is a true comic discovery. He has some of the same cynical innocence we sensed in the Harold Ramis character in *Ghostbusters:* he's very wise and very innocent. Some of his best moments involve his bewildering cross-cultural dialogue: he speaks in vast metaphysical concepts which are unexpectedly interrupted with 1985 slang and pop sociology.

Meanwhile, Douglas and Turner have fun with two of the broadest roles in recent memory. They fight, they make up, they wisecrack in the face of calamity. And they make an ideally matched comedy team. Just as Woody Allen and Diane Keaton always seem to be on the same wavelength in their comic dialogues, so do Douglas and Turner, in their own way, seem well matched. It seems clear that they like each other and are having fun during the parade of ludicrous situations in the movie, and their chemistry is sometimes more entertaining than the contrivances of the plot.

My favorite moment between them comes as they hang by their hands over a rat-pit, while acid gnaws away at the ropes which suspend them above certain doom. Sure, this scene owes something to *Raiders of the Lost Ark.* But what's new about it this time is the dialogue, the way they break down and confess they love each other and make marriage plans as death inexorably approaches. And then, when DeVito appears and might possibly save them, there is some business with a ladder that is followed by dialogue so perfectly timed that I laughed not so much in amusement as in delight at how well the mechanisms of the scene fell together.

For all of those pleasures, *The Jewel of the Nile* is a slight and lightweight entertainment. How could it be otherwise? And it is not quite the equal of *Romancing the Stone.* That's not a surprise. For what it is, though, it's fun. And for what it's worth, Douglas and Turner could keep on working in this tradition forever, giving us a 1980s version of the Crosby and Hope *Road* pictures. I guess they don't want to, though, and perhaps that's just as well. What I hope is that a casting director sees Avner Eisenberg for what he is, the most intriguing comedy discovery in a long time.

Jo Jo Dancer, Your Life Is Calling

★ ★ ★

R, 97 m., 1986

Richard Pryor (Jo Jo), Debbie Allen (Michelle), Paula Kelly (Satin Doll), Billy Eckstine (Johnny Barnett), Art Evans (Arturo), J.J. Barry (Sal), Barbara Williams (Dawn), Carmen McRae (Grandmother), Diahnne Abbott (Mother), Scoey Mitchell (Father), E'Lon Cox (Little Jo Jo). Directed and produced by Richard Pryor. Screenplay by Rocco Urbisci, Paul Mooney, and Pryor.

Richard Pryor says that *Jo Jo Dancer, Your Life Is Calling* is not really his autobiography, and I believe him. But the movie is clearly inspired by the journey he has taken since that day in 1980 when he almost killed himself in a drug-related accident. There is pain in this movie, and truth, and also a lot of warmth and nostalgia. There is a certain incompleteness in the ending of the film, however; it seems to close without a third act. But Pryor has said there may be a sequel, and perhaps that's where the rest of the story will be told.

Jo Jo Dancer begins when its hero already is an entertainment superstar. We track him restlessly around his luxurious Hollywood home as he calls a drug dealer and sets up a party, all the time claiming that he's off drugs. He throws bottles and paraphernalia into the fireplace, screams to himself that he's gotta stop, and then decides to do cocaine one last time. The rest of the scene is borrowed from the headlines, as Jo Jo is raced into an emergency room with burns over most of his body.

He faces a turning point. Will he choose to live, or die? Jo Jo's alter ego separates from his body, looks down at the bandages, and says, "Jo Jo, what have you done to us this time?" And then the alter ego embarks on a trip back through Jo Jo's life and the memories that will die if the body dies.

We see little Jo Jo being raised in a small Ohio town, where his grandmother runs a whorehouse, and his mother is one of the girls. We see the affection he receives, but also the conflicting signals about sex, race, and booze. Later, after his mother has married, there is tension at home after Jo Jo announces that he thinks he could become a nightclub comedian. There are painful scenes of his first stumbling attempts to entertain an audience, and then the night when he talks back to a drunk and begins to find his own onstage voice.

This early show business material supplies the most heartfelt material in the film, and some of its best characters, especially a stripper named Satin Doll (Paula Kelly), who befriends Jo Jo and gets him his first job. Backstage, we meet the boozy old emcee (Art Evans), and the veteran trouper (Billy Eckstine). There is a great sequence where Pryor, dressed in drag, pulls out a fake pistol and tries to bluff the club's Mafia owners into paying him his salary.

There's an abrupt transition from these early scenes, which seem bathed in a glow of nostalgia and gratitude, and later scenes in which Jo Jo starts to make it big and is introduced to the Beverly Hills cocaine scene. Along the way, there have been several wives, one too frightened to leave her hometown, one so mercenary she comes along only for the money, one a white girl who likes cocaine too much. None of the relationships seems real, because Jo Jo doesn't seem real himself.

That's a point Pryor makes at the end of the film, in an onstage routine that represents his comeback nightclub act after he recovers from his accident. These passages are a reminder of *Richard Pryor Live on the Sunset Strip* and *Richard Pryor Here and Now*, his two post-cocaine concert films. He talks about always feeling that he didn't belong, always needing the instant confidence that came from booze and drugs, until finally they took away everything they had promised him.

The problem with the final onstage scene is that it's too self-contained. It doesn't take the dramatic chances that the rest of the movie is so willing to risk. It shows Pryor the performer, instead of continuing the story of Jo Jo the character. The structure of the movie leads us to a place where we expect some sort of redemption and re-evaluation from the character, but it's not there and we miss it. Maybe the sequel will show Jo Jo learning to live without drugs.

All the same, Pryor has taken some major risks in this movie. He has played straight and honest with his story, but he also has shown that he has a real gift as a director; the narrative scenes in the movie have a conviction and an interest that grow and hold us. This isn't a heartfelt amateur night, but a film by an artist whose art has become his life.

Johnny Dangerously ★ ★

PG-13, 90 m., 1984

Michael Keaton (Johnny), Joe Piscopo (Danny Vermin), Marilu Henner (Lil), Maureen Stapleton (Mom Kelly), Peter Boyle (Jocko), Griffin Dunne (D.A.), Glynnis O'Connor (Sally). Directed by Amy Heckerling and produced by Michael Hertzberg. Screenplay by Norman Steinberg, Bernie Kukoff, Harry Colomby, and Jeff Harris.

The opening scenes of *Johnny Dangerously* are so funny you just don't see how they can keep it up. And you're right: They can't. But they make a real try. The movie wants to do for gangster films what *Airplane!* did for *Airport,* and *Top Secret* did for spy movies. It has its work cut out; this formula consumes comic inspiration at an exhausting rate, and the gangster movie is not exactly an original target for satire. What distinguishes *Johnny Dangerously* from the other attempts in this direction is the caliber of the actors: This is a high-class cast, having fun with the material, and bringing a certain reality to some of the characters almost in spite of themselves.

Michael Keaton, from *Mr. Mom,* plays Johnny as a sweet, sort of gentle gangster who doesn't see any need to stir things up. His archenemy is Danny Vermin, played by Joe Piscopo, and there are a lot of other interesting characters around, including Marilu Henner as a sex bomb who spends some of her most intimate moments on top of a piano; Peter Boyle as an eminently reasonable mob patriarch, and Maureen Stapleton as Johnny's long-suffering mom.

The movie begins with the promise that it will grow into a great comedy. There's a title song out of left field, sung by Weird Al Yankovich, and then we see Johnny as a middle-aged pet store owner, stamping prices on his animals using one of those tape labeling machines they use in grocery stores. A kid tries to shoplift, and that inspires Johnny to remember the days when he began his own career in crime. The flashback then develops more or less along standard gangster movie lines, with of course a comic twist on every cliché. It's a little dizzying trying to spot all of the cameo roles as they go by; everybody who wandered onto the 20th Century Fox lot must have been hired to walk through this movie. But what gradually occurs to us is that we aren't laughing as often; the movie keeps trying, but it runs out of steam.

Too bad. And especially too bad for Joe Piscopo, who is such an accomplished mimic that he once literally had me thinking I was watching Jerry Lewis on "Saturday Night Live." Since masters of disguise are a fixture in gangster movies, why didn't they let Piscopo play a most-wanted criminal who was desperately trying to alter his appearance, and kept running up against incompetent gangland plastic surgeons? He plays Danny Vermin well enough, but the role seems rather limiting.

Johnny Got His Gun ★ ★ ★ ★

R, 111 m., 1971

Timothy Bottoms (Joe Bonham), Kathy Fields (Kareen), Jason Robards (Joe's Father), Diane Varsi (Fourth Nurse), Donald Sutherland (Jesus Christ), Eduard Franz (General Tillery). Directed by Dalton Trumbo and produced by Bruce Campbell. Screenplay by Trumbo.

I've never much liked anti-war films. They've never much stopped war, for one thing. For another, they attract hushed and reverential praise which speaks of their universality and the urgency of their messages. Most anti-war films come so burdened with universality and urgency that the ads for them read like calls to sunrise services.

Dalton Trumbo's *Johnny Got His Gun* smelled like that kind of anti-war film. It came out of the Cannes Film Festival with three awards and a slightly pious aroma, as if it had been made for joyless Student Peace Union types of thirty-five years ago. But it isn't like that at all. Trumbo has taken the most difficult sort of material—the story of a soldier who lost his arms, his legs, and most of his face in a World War I shell burst—and handled it, strange to say, in a way that's not so much anti-war as pro-life. Perhaps that's why I admire it. Instead of belaboring ironic points about the "war to end war," Trumbo remains stubbornly on the human level. He lets his ideology grow out of his characters, instead of imposing it from above. In this sense, his film resembles Joseph Losey's *King and Country* which also turned its back on the war in order to consider one ordinary, unremarkable soldier.

Trumbo's soldier is Joe Bonham (Timothy Bottoms), who comes from an American background that is clearly modeled on Trumbo's own. The boy works in a bakery, supports his mother and sisters after his father's death, is in love with an open-faced and sweet Irish girl, and enlists in the army because "it's the sort of thing a fellow ought to do, when his country is in trouble." Months later, he's sent on a patrol into no-man's land to bury a corpse that was offending a colonel's nose. A shell lands near him, and he wakes up in a hospital.

The army is convinced he has no conscious mind. They decide to keep him alive simply to learn from him. But he can think, and gradually the enormity of his injuries is revealed to him. He is literally the prisoner of his mind, for years, until he finds a way of communicating with a sympathetic nurse (Diane Varsi).

Trumbo uses flashbacks and fantasies to make Joe alive for us, while he exists in a living death. The most charming flashback is the first, when Joe and his girl kiss in her living room and are interrupted by her father. He's an old Wobbly who sends them both into the bedroom, and there is a love scene of such tenderness and beauty that its echoes resound through the entire film. Other scenes develop Joe's relationship with his father (Jason Robards) and with Jesus Christ (Donald Sutherland), whom he consults in fantasies. Christ really doesn't have much to suggest; he has no answers, in Joe's fantasies, because there are no answers.

The movie ends with no political solutions and without, in fact, even a political position. It simply states a case. Here was a patriotic young man who went off and was grievously wounded for no great reason, and whose conscious mind remains a horrible indictment of the system that sent all the young men away to kill each other. The soldier's own answer to his situation seems like the only possible one. He wants them to put him in a sideshow, where, as a freak, he can cause people a moment's thought about war. If they won't do that, he wants them to kill him. The army won't do either, of course.

The Journey of Natty Gann ★ ★ ★

PG, 101 m., 1985

Meredith Salenger (Natty Gann), John Cusack (Harry Slade), Ray Wise (Natty's Father). Directed by Jeremy Kagan and produced by Mike Lobell. Screenplay by Jeanne Rosenberg.

There is one sense in which I cannot stand any movie involving a child and an animal. I am acutely aware of the possibilities for manipulating the story in order to gain unearned emotional payoffs. There is another sense in which I cannot resist a story about a child and an animal—if it is done intelligently, bravely, and without cheap sentiment.

The Journey of Natty Gann falls into the second category. It begins with potentially lethal ingredients: A young girl is joined by a glorious wolf on a cross-country odyssey in search of her missing father. Along the way, she is befriended by another teen-age drifter, threatened by tough kids and railway cops, and faced with one setback after another. This is the sort of story that used to be routinely trashed by the Walt Disney people, who would turn it into sentimental melodrama. Amazingly, then, *The Journey of Natty Gann* is a Disney production, more evidence of the fresh winds blowing through the studio.

The movie stars Meredith Salenger, a solemn-faced newcomer, as Natty Gann, the young teen-age daughter of a Chicago working-class stiff (Ray Wise). The time is the Depression. Jobs are scarce and dollars are few. When Wise gets a chance at a good-paying lumberman's job in the Northwest, he decides to take it. The bus is pulling out, Natty is nowhere to be found, and he decides to leave her in the care of a boarding-house owner and send for her later.

It appears to Natty that he is never going to send for her, and the reformatory beckons. She hops on a freight train and heads west in a forlorn search for her father, and most of the movie concerns her adventures along the way. Her great moment comes when she is lost and alone in a rainstorm in a forest, and a wolf approaches her and, amazingly, curls up at her side. With the wolf as a companion, she is understandably protected from many of the dangers of the road, and she makes it out West and also makes a friend, Harry (John Cusack), another teen-ager riding the rails.

The film's photography is magnificent, as the girl, the boy, and the wolf make their way through the Rockies and into the Northwest. More to the point is the relationship between Natty and her wolf. The movie was written by Jeanne Rosenberg, co-author of *The Black Stallion*, and again this time there is a real, fundamental feeling for the reality of a relationship between a human and a beast. The wolf looks longingly into the forest, but stays by the girl's side, and there is a thrilling sequence in which both of them jump a freight train—a close call.

This is the kind of movie that younger teen-agers might like a lot, if they have not already been broken down by the corrupt cynicism of so many Hollywood "teen-age" movies. It is about dreams and fears and dangers, love and determination. And it does justice to those qualities.

Julia and Julia ★ ★ ★
R, 98 m., 1988

Kathleen Turner (Julia), Gabriel Byrne (Paolo), Sting (Daniel), Gabriele Ferzetti (Paolo's Father), Angela Goodwin (Paolo's Mother), Lidia Broccolino (Carla), Alexander Van Wyk (Marco). Directed by Peter Del Monte and produced by Francesco Pinto and Gaetano Stucchi. Screenplay by Silvia Napolitano, Sandrea Petraglia, and Del Monte.

Julia and Julia tells one of those nightmare stories, like *The Trial*, where the hero is condemned to live in a world in which absolutely nothing can be counted on. The story unfolds as a series of surprises, and since even the first surprise is crucial to the plot, I frankly don't see any way to review the film without spoiling some of the effect. I will, however, carry on, but I advise you not to read any further if you plan to see the film.

The story begins on the wedding day of its heroine, Julia, who is played by Kathleen Turner as a sweet and rather moony young woman not at all like the smart, aggressive characters she usually creates. It is a beautiful day in Italy, in a sunlit garden where even the trees seem to bow in happiness, but a few hours later Julia and her new husband (Gabriel Byrne) are involved in a road accident, and Byrne is killed.

You see what I mean about not reading any further. Yet how can I review the film at all without discussing such details? And there are more to follow. Turner, an American, decides to stay in Italy. She moves into a small apartment across the street from the large flat that was to be her home. Time passes. One day something strange happens, which the movie shows but does not explain. She passes through some kind of dimension into a different time scheme, a parallel path in which things turned out differently, and her husband did not die, and they have a small boy.

The sequence in which she discovers this is wonderful. She goes to her little flat, which is occupied by a strange woman who insists she has always lived there. She sees lights in the large flat across the street, which she had always refused to sell. Trembling, she climbs the stairs to find Byrne at home with their son, and everyone treating her as if she had been with them all along and none of her tragic memories had ever taken place.

She is, of course, shattered. She does not know how this could have happened, and there is no one she can discuss it with without appearing insane (although I kept wishing she wouldn't internalize everything). She is pathetically grateful to have her happiness back until one moment, completely without warning, when she is plunged back into her other, tragic lifetime. Then she is flipped back to happiness again, sort of like a ping-pong ball of fate, and there is the complication of a lover (played by Sting), whom she apparently has taken in her "happy" lifetime. (The rule at the center of these paradoxes is that she always remembers all of the sad lifetime, but only remembers those parts of the happy one that we actually see her experiencing.)

What's going on here? Don't ask me—and don't ask the movie, either. Even the simplest explanation, of parallel time tracks, is one I've borrowed out of old science-fiction novels. *Julia and Julia* wisely declines to offer any explanation at all, preferring to stay completely within Julia's nightmares as she experiences them.

The construction of the story is ingenious and perverse, and has a kind of inner logic of its own, and if there is a flaw, it's that no woman could endure this kind of round-trip more than once, if that much, before being emotionally shattered. I was reminded of Kathleen Turner's work in *Peggy Sue Got Married*, in which she traveled back in time to her own adolescence; think how much more disturbing it would be to travel sideways into the happiness you thought you'd lost.

This is the kind of movie that proves unbearably frustrating to some people, who demand explanations and resent obscurity. I have seen so many movies in which absolutely everything could be predicted that I found *Julia and Julia* perversely entertaining.

NOTE: This movie wins a footnote in cinematic history as the first feature shot entirely in High-Definition Television and then transferred to film. How does it look? There are a few moments when quick movements seem to trail their shadows behind them, but in general, the quality is comparable to a 16-millimeter print blown up to 35-millimeter. Although the film lacks the sharpness and clarity of a true 35-millimeter print, the result is much better than any previous TV-to-film transfer I've seen.

Jumpin' Jack Flash ★ ★
PG-13, 98 m., 1986

Whoopi Goldberg (Terry Doolittle), Stephen Collins (Marty Phillips), Carol Kane (Cynthia Sparks), John Wood (Jeremy Talbot), Roscoe Lee Browne (Archer Lincoln), Annie Potts (Liz Carlson). Directed by Penny Marshall and produced by Lawrence Gordon and Joel Silver. Screenplay by David H. Franzoni, J.W. Melville, Patricia Irving, and Christopher Thompson.

Whoopi Goldberg is the only original or interesting thing about *Jumpin' Jack Flash.* And she tries, but she's not enough. They've harnessed her to an exhausted screenplay—an anthology of old ideas and worn-out clichés—and although she strains with all her heart to pump energy into the movie, it's a lost cause.

There is nothing here to care about, except for her, and even then there's a catch: Her character is so self-contained, so cut off from the other people in the movie, that even when she is generating energy, the rest of the characters hardly seem to notice.

Goldberg plays a computer operator in a big New York bank, and it's a standing joke in her department that her computer terminal sometimes picks up Russian television. One day, it picks up another signal from Russia: a desperate cry for help from a man who signs himself Jumpin' Jack Flash. That is also the name of a Rolling Stones tune, and he challenges Goldberg to figure out his secret password key on the basis of that one clue.

She tries out a lot of passwords—including the first names of all of Mick Jagger's girlfriends—before she finally stumbles over the right one. Then she finds herself in the middle of an international intrigue. Jack Flash is the pseudonym for a British agent who's marooned in Russia and desperate to get information from the British Embassy that may allow him to escape. He wants Goldberg to help him. Then why the goofy business of the password? To make sure she's smart, he says. To kill time with meaningless cuteness, I say.

In the course of the movie, Goldberg will nearly fall off the roof of the British Embassy, and will get shot at by spies, chased by hit men, and dragged in a runaway phone booth. She will crash an embassy ball dressed like Tina Turner, outsmart the British computers, carry on war with her boss at the bank, break into Elizabeth Arden's, and fall in love through the computer with Jack Flash. What she will not do is play a single scene with another actor in which the basis of the dialogue is simple human conversation. (She comes closest to that over the computer.)

What's going on here? Did they think that Goldberg was simply too odd, too original, too unconventional to appear in a movie where she interacts on an everyday human basis? Her character lives alone, seems to have no real friends, and is treated by the screenplay at arm's length. This is a waste not only of talent, but also of warmth and charm: Despite everything, Goldberg survives this movie as a likable, interesting, warm, and infectiously funny person.

There's so much to like about her. I thought she was wonderful in *The Color Purple,* but that movie is a different case and belongs in a different category. *Jumpin' Jack Flash* is simply a creatively bankrupt package deal through which a lot of people will make money and Goldberg's career will receive a setback. Yet, I *still* liked her. She has that husky, warm voice filled with much humor and so many smarts. And she has life in her eyes and real pluck. Put her in a movie with a plot we could care about, and you'd have something.

What's surprising about *Jumpin' Jack Flash,* which had no fewer than four screenplay writers, is that anybody was interested enough in this material to even write it in the first place. This is the eighties. We've all been around. We've seen a few movies and a little TV. All of this spy business would be desperately uninteresting even in a movie that was written and directed with competence. Under the shaky hand of director Penny Marshall, the story doesn't even achieve coherence.

Maybe somebody thought Goldberg's talent was so great that she could save this movie and even turn it into something. Maybe even Goldberg thought so. I've got news for her. An actor choosing a screenplay should think just like a chess master or a tennis player: You only get better by playing above your head.

K

Kagemusha ★ ★ ★ ★
PG, 160 m., 1980

Tatsuya Nakadai (Shingen and Kagemusha), Tsutomu Yamazaki (Nobukado), Kenichi Hagiwara (Katsuyori), Jinpachi Nezu (Bodyguard), Shuji Otaki (Fire General). Directed by Akira Kurosawa and produced by Kurosawa and Tomoyuki Tanaka. Screenplay by Kurosawa and Masato Ide.

Kagemusha, we learn, means "shadow warrior" in Japanese, and Akira Kurosawa's great film tells the story of a man who becomes the double, or shadow, of a great warrior. It also teaches the lesson that shadows or appearances are as important as reality, but that men cannot count on either shadows or reality.

Kagemusha is a samurai drama by the director who most successfully introduced the genre to the West (with such classics as *The Seven Samurai* and *Yojimbo*), and who, at the age of seventy, made an epic that dares to wonder what meaning the samurai code—or any human code—really has in the life of an individual man. His film is basically the story of one such man, a common thief who, because of his astonishing resemblance to the warlord Shingen, is chosen as Shingen's double. When Shingen is mortally wounded in battle, the great Takeda clan secretly replaces him with the double—so their enemies will not learn that Shingen is dead. Thus begins a period of three years during which the kagemusha is treated by everyone, even his son and his mistresses, as if he were the real Shingen. Only his closest advisers know the truth.

But he is not Lord Shingen. And so every scene is undercut with irony. It is important that both friends and enemies believe Shingen is alive; his appearance, or shadow, creates both the respect of his clan and the caution of his enemies. If he is unmasked, he is useless; as Shingen's double, he can send hundreds of men to be killed, and his own guards will willingly sacrifice their lives for him. But as himself, he is worthless, and when he *is* unmasked, he's banished into the wilderness.

What is Kurosawa saying here? I suspect the answer can be found in a contrast between two kinds of scenes. His film contains epic battle scenes of astonishing beauty and scope. And then there are the intimate scenes in the throne room, the bedroom, the castles, and battlefield camps. The great battle scenes glorify the samurai system. Armies of thousands of men throw themselves heedlessly at death, for the sake of pride. But the intimate scenes undermine that glorious tradition; as everyone holds their breath, Shingen's double is tested in meetings with his son, his mistresses, and his horse. They know him best of all. If they are not fooled, all of the panoply and battlefield courage is meaningless, because the Tanaka clan has lost the leader who is their figurehead; the illusion that he exists creates the clan's reality.

Kurosawa made this film after a decade of personal travail. Although he is often considered the greatest living Japanese director, he was unable to find financial backing in Japan when he first tried to make *Kagemusha*. He made a smaller film, *Dodeskaden*, which was not successful. He tried to commit suicide, but failed. He was backed by the Russians and went to Siberia to make beautiful *Dersu Uzala* (1976), about a man of the wilderness. But *Kagemusha* remained his obsession, and he was finally able to make it only when Hollywood directors Francis Ford Coppola and George Lucas helped hi.wam find U.S. financing.

The film he finally made is simple, bold, and colorful on the surface, but very thoughtful. Kurosawa seems to be saying that great human endeavors (in this case, samurai wars) depend entirely on lavumbers of men sharing the same fantasies or beliefs. It is entirely unimportant, he seems to be suggesting, whether or not the beliefs are based on reality—all that matters is that men accept them. But when a belief is shattered, the result is confusion, destruction, and death. At the end of *Kagemusha,* for example, the son of the real Lord Shingen orders his troops into a suicidal charge, and their deaths are not only unnecessary but meaningless, because they are not on behalf of the sacred person of the warlord.

There are great images in this film: Of a breathless courier clattering down countless steps, of men passing in front of a blood-red sunset, of a dying horse on a battlefield. But Kurosawa's last image—of the dying kagemusha floating in the sea, swept by tidal currents past the fallen standard of the Takeda clan—summarizes everything: ideas and men are carried along heedlessly by the currents of time, and historical meaning *seems* to emerge when both happen to be swept in the same way at the same time.

The Karate Kid ★ ★ ★ ★

PG, 126 m., 1984

Ralph Macchio (Daniel), Noriyuki "Pat" Morita (Miyagi), Elisabeth Shue (Ali), Martin Kove (Kreese), William Zabka (Johnny). Directed by John G. Avildsen and produced by Jerry Weintraub. Written by Robert Mark Kamen.

I didn't want to see this movie. I took one look at the title and figured it was either (a) a sequel to *Toenails of Vengeance,* or (b) an adventure pitting Ricky Schroeder against the Megaloth Man. I was completely wrong. *The Karate Kid* was one of the nice surprises of 1984—an exciting, sweet-tempered, heartwarming story with one of the most interesting friendships in a long time. The friends come from different worlds. A kid named Daniel (Ralph Macchio) is a New Jersey teen-ager who moves with his mother to Los Angeles. An old guy named Miyagi (Pat Morita) is the Japanese janitor in their apartment building. When Daniel starts to date the former girlfriend of the toughest kid in the senior class, the kid starts pounding on Daniel's head on a regular basis. Daniel tries to fight back, but this is a Southern California kid, and so of course he has a black belt in karate. Enter Mr. Miyagi, who seems to be a harmless old eccentric with a curious hobby: He tries to catch flies with chopsticks. It turns out that Miyagi is a karate master, a student not only of karate fighting but of the total philosophy of the martial arts. He agrees to take Daniel as his student.

And then begins the wonderful center section of *The Karate Kid,* as the old man and the kid from Jersey become friends. Miyagi's system of karate instruction is offbeat, to say the least. He puts Daniel to work shining cars, painting fences, scrubbing the bottoms of pools. Daniel complains that he isn't learning karate, he's acting as free labor. But there is a system to Mr. Miyagi's training.

The Karate Kid was directed by Ralph Avildsen, who made *Rocky.* It ends with the same sort of climactic fight scene; Daniel faces his enemies in a championship karate tournament. But the heart of this movie isn't in the fight sequences, it's in the relationships. And in addition to Daniel's friendship with Miyagi, there's also a sweet romantic liaison with Ali (Elisabeth Shue), who is your standard girl from the right side of town and has the usual snobbish parents.

Macchio is an unusual, interesting choice for Daniel. He's not the basic handsome Hollywood teen-ager but a thin, tall, intense kid with a way of seeming to talk to himself. His delivery always sounds natural, even offhand; he never seems to be reading a line. He's a good, sound, interesting lead, but the movie really belongs to Pat Morita, an actor who has been around a long time (he was Arnold on "Happy Days") without ever having a role anywhere near this good. Morita makes Miyagi into an example of applied serenity. In a couple of scenes where he has to face down a hostile karate coach, Miyagi's words are so carefully chosen they don't give the other guy any excuse to get violent; Miyagi uses the language as carefully as his hands or arms to ward off blows and gain an advantage. It's refreshing to see a completely original character like this old man. *The*

Karate Kid is a sleeper with a title that gives you the wrong idea: It's one of 1984's best movies.

The Killing Fields ★ ★ ★ ★
R, 139 m., 1984

Sam Waterston (Sydney Schanberg), Dr. Haing S. Ngor (Dith Pran), John Malkovich (Al Rockoff), Craig T. Nelson (Military Attaché), Athol Fugard (Dr. Sundesval). Directed by Roland Joffe and produced by David Puttnam. Screenplay by Bruce Robinson.

There's a strange thing about stories based on what the movies insist on calling "real life." The haphazard chances of life, the unanticipated twists of fate, have a way of getting smoothed down into Hollywood formulas, so that what might once have happened to a real person begins to look more and more like what might once have happened to John Wayne. One of the risks taken by *The Killing Fields* is to cut loose from that tradition, to tell us a story that does not have a traditional Hollywood structure, and to trust that we'll find the characters so interesting that we won't miss the cliché. It is a risk that works, and that helps make this into a really affecting experience.

The "real life" story behind the movie is by now well-known. Sydney Schanberg, a correspondent for the *New York Times,* covered the invasion of Cambodia with the help of Dith Pran, a local journalist and translator. When the country fell to the communist Khmer Rouge, the lives of all foreigners were immediately at risk, and Schanberg got out along with most of his fellow Western correspondents. He offered Pran a chance to leave with him, but Pran elected to stay. And when the Khmer Rouge drew a bamboo curtain around Cambodia, Pran disappeared into a long silence. Back home in New York, Schanberg did what he could to discover information about his friend; for example, he wrote about four hundred letters to organizations like the Red Cross. But it was a futile exercise, and Schanberg had given up his friend for dead, when one day four years later word came that Pran was still alive and had made it across the border to a refugee camp. The two friends were reunited, in one of the rare happy endings that come out of a period of great suffering.

As a human story, this is a compelling one. As a Hollywood story, it obviously will not do because the last half of the movie is essentially Dith Pran's story, told from his point of view. Hollywood convention has it that the American should fight his way back into the occupied country (accompanied by renegade Green Berets and Hell's Angels, and Rambo, if possible), blast his way into a prison camp, and save his buddy. That was the formula for *Uncommon Valor* and *Missing in Action,* two box-office hits, and in *The Deer Hunter* one friend went back to Vietnam to rescue another. Sitting in New York writing letters is not quite heroism on the same scale. And yet, what else could Schanberg do? And, more to the point, what else could Dith Pran do, in the four years of his disappearance, but try to disguise his origins and his education, and pass as an illiterate peasant—one of the countless prisoners of Khmer Rouge work camps? By telling his story, and by respecting it, *The Killing Fields* becomes a film of an altogether higher order than the Hollywood revenge thrillers.

The movie begins in the early days of the journalistic coverage of Cambodia. We meet Schanberg (Sam Waterston) and Pran (played by Dr. Haing S. Ngor, whose own story is an uncanny parallel to his character's), and we sense the strong friendship and loyalty that they share. We also absorb the conditions in the country, where warehouses full of Coca-Cola are blown up by terrorists who know a symbolic target when they see one. Life is a routine of hanging out at cafes and restaurants and official briefings, punctuated by an occasional trip to the front, where the American view of things does not seem to be reflected by the suffering that the correspondents witness.

The whole atmosphere of this period is suggested most successfully by the character of an American photographer, played by John Malkovich as a cross between a dopehead and a hard-bitten newsman. He is not stirred to action very easily, and still less easily stirred to caring, but when an occasion rises (for example, the need to forge a passport for Pran), he reveals the depth of his feeling. As the Khmer Rouge victory becomes inevitable, there are scenes of incredible tension, especially one in which Dith Pran saves the lives of his friends by some desperate fast talking with the cadres of adolescent rebels who would just as soon shoot them. Then there is the confusion of the evacuation of the U.S. Embassy and a last glimpse of Dith Pran before he disappears for four years.

In a more conventional film, he would, of course, have really disappeared, and we would have followed the point of view of the Schanberg character. But this movie takes the chance of switching points of view in midstream, and the last half of the film belongs to Dith Pran, who sees his country turned into an insane parody of a one-party state, ruled by the Khmer Rouge with instant violence and a savage intolerance for any reminders of the French and American presence of the colonial era. Many of the best scenes in the film's second half are essentially played without dialogue, as Pran works in the fields, disguises his origins, and waits for his chance.

The film is a masterful achievement on all the technical levels—it does an especially good job of convincing us with its Asian locations—but the best moments are the human ones, the conversations, the exchanges of trust, the waiting around, the sudden fear, the quick bursts of violence, the desperation. At the center of many of those scenes is Dr. Haing S. Ngor, a non-actor who was recruited for the role from the ranks of Cambodian refugees in California, and who brings to it a simple sincerity that is absolutely convincing. Sam Waterston is effective in the somewhat thankless role of Sydney Schanberg, and among the carefully drawn vignettes are Craig T. Nelson as a military attaché and Athol Fugard as Dr. Sundesval.

The American experience in Southeast Asia has given us a great film epic *(Apocalypse Now)* and a great drama *(The Deer Hunter)*. Here is the story told a little closer to the ground, of people who were not very important and not very powerful, who got caught up in events that were indifferent to them, but never stopped trying to do their best and their most courageous.

King Lear ★ ★ ★

PG, 138 m., 1972

Paul Scofield (King Lear), Irene Worth (Goneril), Jack MacGowran (Fool), Alan Webb (Gloucester), Cyril Cusack (Albany), Patrick Magee (Cornwall), Robert Lloyd (Edgar), Tom Fleming (Kent), Susan Engel (Regan), Annelise Gaboid (Cordelia). Directed by Peter Brook. Screenplay by Brook.

Peter Brook's *King Lear* occupies a barren kingdom frozen in the middle of a winter that chills souls even more than bodies. He is not his own master; he gives away his power and then discovers, with a childlike surprise, that he can no longer exercise it. Burdened by senility and a sense of overwhelming futility, he collapses gratefully into death.

It is important to describe him as Brook's Lear, because he is not Shakespeare's. *King Lear* is the most difficult of Shakespeare's plays to stage, the most complex and, to my mind, the greatest. There are immensities of feeling and meaning in it that Brook has not even touched. And for Shakespeare's difficulties of staging, he has substituted his own cinematic decorations.

This is not to say that his film is not a brave and interesting effort in its own right. Peter Brook is not constitutionally able to direct "screen versions" of someone else's work. The vision must be his own, even if that means Shakespeare finishes second; this is not so much a film of *King Lear* as a film about it, with Brook's critical analysis of the play suggesting his directorial strategy.

His approach was suggested by *Shakespeare Our Contemporary*, a controversial book by the Polish critic Jan Kott. In Kott's view, *King Lear* is a play about the total futility of things. The old man Lear stumbles ungracefully toward his death because, simply put, that's the way it goes for most of us. To search for meaning of philosophical consolation is to kid yourself.

I suppose every age has attempted to redefine Shakespeare in terms of its own preoccupations, and the Brook-Kott version of *Lear* is certainly fashionable and modern. But it gives us a film that severely limits Shakespeare's vision, and focuses our attention on his more nihilistic passages while ignoring or sabotaging the others.

There is a great deal of goodness in *King Lear*. There is the old king himself, "more sinned against than sinning," whose cruelties are the result of misplaced love. There is Cordelia, the most touchingly sincere heroine in all of Shakespeare. There is Edgar, totally devoted to the father who has disowned him, and Kent, who serves Lear out of love. And there are the moments when Lear shakes off his sense of doom and hurls taunts at the gods, or tells his beloved Cordelia that their suffering will pass and they will once again live like the songbirds and dabble in the gossip of the court. Lear even seems to die convinced that Cordelia lives; she does not, but his last conscious impulse is one of hope and faith. Perhaps that is Shakespeare's final thought: that the ability to hope is what makes us human, even if, in fact, our hopes are futile.

This is a great humanistic assertion, and it has no place in the Peter Brook film. He omits or rearranges dialogue and scenes in order to make the evil daughters, Regan and Goneril, ambiguous in their villainy. He gives us a Cordelia who is not as perfect as she should be. He gives us a Lear who is only a figure of pity, not (as he was in Shakespeare) also sometimes a figure of greatness. He gives us a world so grim we might as well be dead.

Lear is played by Paul Scofield, whose beard and large, sad eyes make him look distractingly like the middle-aged Hemingway. Perhaps because of Brook's direction, Scofield's readings are often uninflected and exhausted. He reads Shakespeare's poetry the way Mark Twain said women use profanity: "They know the words, but not the music." The acting style suits Brook's ideas about the play, but leaves Lear diminished as a character.

Shakespeare's *Lear* survives in his play and will endure forever. Brook's *Lear* is a new conception, a rethinking, and a critical commentary on the play. It is interesting precisely because it contrasts so firmly with Shakespeare's universe; by deliberately omitting all faith and hope from Lear's kingdom, it paradoxically helps us to see how much is there.

The King of Comedy ★ ★ ★

PG, 101 m., 1983

Robert De Niro (Rupert Pupkin), Jerry Lewis (Jerry Langford), Diahnne Abbott (Rita), Sandra Bernhard (Masha), Ed Herlihy (Himself). Directed by Martin Scorsese. Screenplay by Paul Zimmerman.

Martin Scorsese's *The King of Comedy* is one of the most arid, painful, wounded movies I've ever seen. It's hard to believe Scorsese made it; instead of the big-city life, the violence and sexuality of his movies like *Taxi Driver* and *Mean Streets,* what we have here is an agonizing portrait of lonely, angry people with their emotions all tightly bottled up. This is a movie that seems ready to explode—but somehow it never does. That lack of release seriously disturbed me the first time I saw *The King of Comedy.* I kept straining forward, waiting for the movie to let loose, and it kept frustrating me. Maybe that was the idea. This is a movie about rejection, with a hero who never admits that he has been rejected, and so there is neither comic nor tragic release—just the postponement of pain.

I left that first screening filled with dislike for the movie. Dislike, but not disinterest. Memories of *The King of Comedy* kept gnawing at me, and when people asked me what I thought about it, I said I wasn't sure. Then I saw the movie a second time, and it seemed to work better for me—maybe because I was able to watch without any expectations. I knew it wasn't an entertainment, I knew it didn't allow itself any emotional payoffs, I knew the ending was cynical and unsatisfactory, and so, with *those* discoveries no longer to be made, I was free to simply watch what was on the screen.

What I saw the second time, better than the first, were the performances by Robert De Niro, Jerry Lewis, Diahnne Abbott, and Sandra Bernhard, who play the movie's most important characters. They must have been difficult performances to deliver, because there's almost no feedback in this movie. The actors can't bounce emotional energy off each other, because nobody *listens* in this film; everybody's just waiting for the other person to stop talking so they can start. And everybody's so emotionally isolated in this movie that they don't even seem able to guess what they're missing.

The movie stars De Niro, as Rupert Pupkin, a nerdish man in his thirties who fantasizes himself as a television star. He practices in his basement, holding condescending conversations with life-size cardboard cutouts of Liza Minnelli and Jerry Lewis. His dream is to get a stand-up comedy slot on the late-night talk show hosted by Lewis (whose name in the movie is Jerry Langford). The movie opens with

Rupert's first meeting with Jerry; he barges into Jerry's limousine and is immediately on an obnoxious first-name basis. Jerry vaguely promises to check out Rupert's comedy routine, and the rest of the movie is devoted to Rupert's single-minded pursuit of fame. He arrives at Jerry's office, is politely brushed off, returns, is ejected, arrives at Jerry's country home with a "date" in tow, is ejected again, and finally decides to kidnap Jerry.

This *sounds* like an entertaining story, I suppose, but Scorsese doesn't direct a single scene for a payoff. The whole movie is an exercise in *cinema interruptus;* even a big scene in a bar, where Rupert triumphantly turns on the TV set to reveal himself on television, is deliberately edited to leave out the payoff shots—reaction shots of the amazed clientele. Scorsese doesn't want laughs in this movie, and he also doesn't want release. The whole movie is about the inability of the characters to get any kind of a positive response to their bids for recognition.

The King of Comedy is not, you may already have guessed, a fun movie. It is also not a bad movie. It is frustrating to watch, unpleasant to remember, and, in its own way, quite effective. It represents an enormous departure for Scorsese, whose movies teemed with life before he filmed this emotional desert, and whose camera used to prowl restlessly before he nailed it down this time. Scorsese and De Niro are the most creative, productive director/actor team in the movies right now, and the fact that they feel the freedom to make such an odd, stimulating, unsatisfying movie is good news, I guess. But *The King of Comedy* is the kind of film that makes you want to go and see a Scorsese movie.

The King of Marvin Gardens ★ ★ ★

R, 104 m., 1972

Jack Nicholson (David Staebler), Bruce Dern (Jason Staebler), Ellen Burstyn (Sally), Julia Anne Robinson (Jessica), Scatman Crothers (Lewis), Charles Levine (Grandfather). Directed and produced by Bob Rafelson. Screenplay by Jacob Brackman.

Bob Rafelson's *The King of Marvin Gardens* is a perversely satisfying movie—it works after going out of its way not to—and a very eccentric one. It backs into its real subject in much the same way that *Five Easy Pieces,* Rafelson's previous film, did. Only after it's over do some of its scenes and moments fall into place; for much of the way we've been disoriented and the story has been suspended somewhere in midair. As someone wrote about a totally dissimilar movie, Paul Morrissey's *Trash,* it's the kind of film you want to walk out of, and then when it's over you want to see it again.

The movie opens and closes with autobiographical monologues being delivered by an all-night talk jockey (Jack Nicholson) into the loneliness of the FM airwaves. He works in a darkened studio, stopping sometimes to search for words, and it's evident that his broadcasts tear something loose from deep inside. It's possible, indeed, that he says more on the radio (or into his tape recorder) in this movie than he ever gets around to saying in the actual situations he finds himself in. He's tentative, unsure, private. His radio fantasies often involve his brother, Jason (Bruce Dern), who lives in Atlantic City, New Jersey, and does mysterious but glorious things there. After a long silence, Jason himself calls his brother and tells him to hustle down to Atlantic City because there are big deals cooking. They're going to buy an island near Hawaii and develop it into a resort. Sure.

Most of the movie takes place in Atlantic City, where the metaphor of a Monopoly game is employed a little too persistently, I thought. There's the Boardwalk, of course, and Marvin Gardens itself; but there are also Jason's attempts to buy a hotel, and the fact that he's in jail when we first meet him. This stuff is worked in quietly enough by Jacob Brackman's script, however, that it doesn't really distract.

Jason is living with a blonde on the far side of the hill (Ellen Burstyn) and her stepdaughter, a blonde coming up fast on this side (Julia Anne Robinson). A great deal of the movie is about the unacknowledged sexual competition between the two women, but this (like a few other things) becomes important only gradually. Most of the action seems to involve a disagreement between Jason, who turns out to be a minor hood, the mysterious Lewis, who is the black rackets boss and moneyman in town. Jason's deals are based on reckless confidence in Lewis's money, and Lewis isn't going along.

Until the movie's end, when everything

falls together with a really stunning force, Rafelson and Brackman seem to be going for a series of set-pieces. There is an unhappy lobster dinner with two Japanese investors reputed to have money; they wear their lobster-proof bibs happily, but don't come through. There's the matter of the older blonde marching into the hotel next door to take a bath ("Hell, you told me you *owned* the damn place," she says, then Jason explains the deal is still at the stage of "negotiations over language.")

And there is a truly fine scene, almost surrealistic, in which the stepmother concedes the sexual sweepstakes to her stepdaughter and throws all of her clothes and makeup apparatus into a bonfire on the beach. Even her false eyelashes. "They're made out of mink hairs, did you know that?" she says. "For twenty years I've been wearing animal hairs on my face."

The movie's performances are as good as we've come to expect from the somewhat incestuous BBS Productions. Rafelson had directed three movies for the company before this one, and Nicholson had acted in three and directed one *(Drive, He Said,* in which Dern was wonderfully uptight and focused as the basketball coach). These people have worked together often enough that they have a kind of BBS feel for scenes, if you will; Nicholson and Dern work with each other as easily as any two actors. Ellen Burstyn succeeds in a difficult task; she has to make her performance striking enough to justify the movie's ending, but she can't push *too* far or we'll know too much, too soon.

For the rest, all I can say is that *The King of Marvin Gardens* is an original, individual, and often frustrating movie that takes a lot of chances and wins on about sixty percent of them. There are scenes (including a simulated Miss America pageant in a deserted hall and a horseback confrontation between Nicholson and Dern) that are hopelessly affected. There are others, including Dern's blurted-out declaration of his love for his brother, that are deeply affecting.

King of the Gypsies ★ ★ ★
R, 112 m., 1978

Sterling Hayden (King Zharko Stepanowicz), Shelley Winters (Queen Rachel), Susan Sarandon (Rose), Judd Hirsch (Groffo), Eric Roberts (Dave), Brooke Shields (Tita), Annette O'Toole (Persa). Directed by Frank Pierson and produced by Dino and Federico De Laurentiis. Screenplay by Pierson.

It's impossible to see *King of the Gypsies* and not to be reminded of *The Godfather.* The film stories have uncanny parallels, and that's all the more interesting because Peter Maas's book *King of the Gypsies* is based on fact: Reality is chasing fiction this time.

Both stories deal with grizzled, wise, and unshakably traditional old patriarchs. Both have sons who cannot quite fill their father's shoes. Instead of the still younger son in *The Godfather, King of the Gypsies* gives us a grandchild—but in both films this character is powerfully lured by the attractions of middle-class American affluence, he leaves the ethnic group to take a WASP girl as his lover, and he eventually does accept the responsibility of leading his clan.

The movies even feel rather the same, with their elegiac music, their ancient rituals, their stately processions of classic autos, their obsessions with the secrets of the clan. It must have taken a certain amount of courage for Frank Pierson, the screenwriter and director, to venture into territory already inhabited by cinematic landmarks, and yet he gets away with it: *King of the Gypsies* is poetic and violent and memorable, and it gives us the first authentic movie glimpse of American gypsy culture.

The story's about a transfer of power within the Stepanowicz family, gypsies living in the New York area. The old patriarch, the gypsy king, is dying (although Sterling Hayden plays the role with so much zest it's hard to believe that). The son (Judd Hirsch) is an alcoholic, a horse player, an unfit man to become king. But the grandson (Eric Roberts) is another story: He's smart, cunning, handsome, and ambitious. Unfortunately, he's also halfway assimilated into mainstream culture. He's not at all sure he even wants to be king of the gypsies.

He is sure, though, that his father is cruel and worthless, and that his mother (Susan Sarandon) should try to free herself from him. She doesn't; life outside the gypsy society is unthinkable to her. In one of the movie's central confrontations, she faces her son after having sold her daughter into marriage for $6,000 to pay her husband's gambling debts.

In *The Godfather*, Al Pacino was lured away from the Mafia clanship by the WASP attractions of Diane Keaton. In *King of the Gypsies*, Eric Roberts falls for Annette O'Toole. As an outsider, she presents a basic threat not only to the gypsy society but also to the continuity of the Stepanowicz family.

Peter Maas's original book revealed things that gypsies would no doubt much rather have kept secret. Frank Pierson explores some of those same secrets, but his film isn't just an exposé; it has a sense of life and humor, as when Sarandon takes her son into a jewelry store and trains him as a con man by having him swallow a diamond.

The movie is above all an elegy to a passing way of life, to a society of people who've endured and prevailed as outsiders in so many different Western cultures. Gypsies have lived by choice outside the law, have been blamed no doubt for countless things they did not do, have preserved a fierce pride. *King of the Gypsies* suggests that gypsy culture may finally fall, not to laws and discrimination and persecution, but to that most insidious influence of all, the seductive middle class way of life.

Kiss of the Spider Woman ★ ★ ★ ½

R, 119 m., 1985

William Hurt (Luis Molina), Raul Julia (Valentin), Sonia Braga (Leni/Marta/Spider Woman), Jose Lewgoy (Warden). Directed by Hector Babenco and produced by David Weidman. Screenplay by Leonard Schrader.

Kiss of the Spider Woman tells one of those rare and entrancing stories where one thing seems to happen while another thing is really happening. There are passages in the movie that seem to be absolutely self-contained, and then a word or gesture will reveal that they have depths we can only guess. By the end of the film, what started out as a contest between two opposite personalities has expanded into a choice between two completely different attitudes toward life. And the choice is not sexual, although for a long time it seems so. It is between freedom and slavery.

The movie opens in a prison cell, somewhere in South America. A man is telling a story. The story is a lurid intrigue that seems pieced together from fragments and memories of countless old *film noir* melodramas—from those movies of the 1940s where the woman had lips that could kill, and the men were dying to kiss them. Only gradually does the reality of the film reveal itself: We are in a cramped, depressing prison cell, and the storyteller is a prisoner, trying to pass the days by escaping into fantasy.

His name is Luis. He is played by William Hurt as an affected homosexual, a window dresser who has been jailed for sex offenses. His cellmate is Valentin (Raul Julia), a bearded, macho political prisoner who has nothing but contempt for Luis's stories—not to mention his sexuality and his politics. But as Luis calmly explains, unless someone gives him a key to walk out of his prison, he will continue to escape in any way he can.

As he continues to weave his verbal movie plots, the movie uses fantasy scenes to depict them. There is a Nazi crime melodrama, and a thriller about a spider woman, and the woman in both of them is played by the same actress (Sonia Braga). Later in the film, she will also appear as Valentin's lover; reality and fantasy are by then thoroughly mixed.

What *Kiss of the Spider Woman* at first seems to be about is the changing nature of the relationship between two very different men who have been locked together in the same cell. They are opposites in every way. But they share the same experiences, day after day, and that gives them a common bond. Gradually, an affection grows between them, and we assume that the movie will be about the ways in which they learn to accept each other. Only gradually, mysteriously, do we realize that the movie is about a good deal more. Details of the plot are revealed so subtly and so surprisingly that I will say nothing more, except that the film does not lead in the directions we anticipate.

The performances are wonderful. The director, Hector Babenco, is a Brazilian, but he has directed his American stars in English without falling prey to the occasional loss of tone you sometimes hear as foreigners work in unfamiliar languages. William Hurt, who won the Academy Award and best actor award at Cannes for this film, creates a character utterly unlike anyone else he has ever played—a frankly theatrical character, exaggerated and mannered—and yet he never seems to be reaching for effects. Raul Julia, sweaty and physical in the early scenes, gradually reveals a poetry that makes the whole movie work. And Sonia Braga, called upon to satirize bad acting, makes a perfect spider woman.

Every decade seems to be dominated by the cinema of a different country (in addition to Hollywood, of course, a country of its own). In the 1950s it was Italy. In the 1960s, France. In the 1970s, Germany. In the 1980s, Brazil and Australia seem to be the centers of the most exciting work. Babenco's previous credits include the heartbreaking *Pixote* about a child growing up on the streets of San Paolo. *Kiss of the Spider Woman* is another film of insights and surprises.

Klute ★ ★ ★ ½

R, 114 m., 1971

Jane Fonda (Bree Daniel), Donald Sutherland (John Klute), Charles Cioffl (Frank Ligouri), Dorothy Tristan (Arlyn Page). Directed and produced by Alan J. Pakula. Screenplay by Andy K. and Dave Lewis.

What is it about Jane Fonda that makes her such a fascinating actress to watch? She has a sort of nervous intensity that keeps her so firmly locked into a film character that the character actually seems distracted by things that come up in the movie. You almost have the feeling, a couple of times in *Klute*, that the Fonda character had other plans and was just leaving the room when this (whatever it is) came up.

The movie is about a skilled, intelligent, cynical, and personally troubled New York call girl who does not, for once, have a heart of gold. She never feels anything when she's with a man, she tells her shrink, but she does experience a sense of professional pride when she's able to satisfy a client. And some of her clients have very complicated needs, which challenge the girl's imaginative acting ability. One old garment industry tycoon, for example, has spent all his life making clothes. But he fantasizes an idealistic sort of pre-World War I existence in Europe, in Vienna maybe, and the girl describes it to him in quiet, warm images while she disrobes. He never touches her.

The girl's name is Bree, and the movie should probably be titled *Bree* instead of *Klute*, because the Fonda character is at the center. John Klute (played by Donald Sutherland) is a policeman who has come to New York, free lance, to try to settle a missing persons case. It appears that the missing man may still be alive, and may be the source of obscene letters and telephone calls Bree has been receiving. Bree initially refuses to talk to Klute, but she eventually does confide in him, mostly because she's frightened by midnight prowlers and wants his protection. The film examines their somewhat strange relationship, and at the same time functions on another level as a somewhat awkward thriller.

There are scary shots of the prowler, for example, and shots of hands gripping a mesh fence—shots that are not very satisfactory because the wrong point of view is established. One thing about a thriller is that the threat should always be seen from the point of view of the threatened. We don't like looking over the killer's shoulder at his victim; shots like that interfere with our desire to identify with the victim and be scared in a satisfactory way.

Klute doesn't scare us very satisfactorily, maybe because it's kind of schizo. The director is Alan Pakula, whose concern is all too much with plot, and it gets in the way of the unusual and interesting relationship between Bree and Klute. But how *do* you develop a relationship between a prostitute with hang-ups and a square suburban cop? *Klute* does it by making the cop into a person of restraint and dignity, a man who is genuinely concerned about this girl he's met. His attitude is what makes their love relationship so absorbing. Usually, in the movies, it's just assumed the lovers were drawn toward each other by magnetism or concealed springs or something.

The scenes between Fonda and Sutherland are very good, then, and Bree is further developed in scenes showing her trying to get out of the trade and into something straight. She takes acting lessons, she auditions to model for cosmetics ads. She talks to her shrink (in scenes that sound improvised and exhibit Fonda's undeniable intelligence).

Intelligence. I suppose that's the word. In *Klute* you don't have two attractive acting vacuums reciting speeches at each other. With Fonda and Sutherland, you have actors who understand and sympathize with their characters, and you have a vehicle worthy of that sort of intelligence. So the fact that the thriller stuff doesn't always work isn't so important.

Koyaanisqatsi ★ ★ ★

NO MPAA RATING, 87 m., 1983

Produced and directed by Godfrey Reggio.

ko·yaa·nis·qatsi, n. (Hopi). 1. crazy life. 2. life in turmoil. 3. life disintegrating. 4. life out of balance. 5. a state of life that calls for another way of living.

I give the definition because it is the key to the movie. Without it, you could make a sincere mistake. *Koyaanisqatsi* opens with magnificent images out of nature: great canyons and limitless deserts and a world without man. Through the use of speeded-up images, clouds climb the sides of mountains and speed across the sky, their shadows painting the landscape. Then the movie turns to images of smokestacks, factories, and expressways. There is an assumption on the part of the filmmaker, Godfrey Reggio, that we'll immediately get the message. And the message, I think, is that nature is wonderful, but that American civilization is a rotten despoiler that is creating a "crazy life."

But I am irreverent, and given to my own thoughts during the film. After I have admired its visionary photography (this is a beautiful movie) and fallen under the spell of its music (an original sound track by the distinguished composer Philip Glass), there is still time to think other thoughts, such as:

This film has one idea, a simplistic one. It contrasts the glory of nature with the mess made by man. But man *is* a messy beast, given to leaving reminders of his presence all over the surface of planet Earth. Although a Hopi word is used to evoke unspoiled nature, no Hopis are seen, and the contrast in the movie doesn't seem to be between American Indian society and Los Angeles expressways, but between expressways and a beautiful world *empty* of man. Thanks, but no thanks.

I had another problem. *All* of the images in this movie are beautiful, even the images of man despoiling the environment. The first shots of smokestacks are no doubt supposed to make us recoil in horror, but actually I thought they looked rather noble. The shots of the expressways are also two-edged. Given the clue in the title, we can consider them as an example of life out of control. *Or*—and here's the catch—we can marvel at the fast-action photography and reflect about all those people moving so quickly to their thousands of individual destinations. What a piece of work is a man! And what expressways he builds!

Koyaanisqatsi, then, is an invitation to knee-jerk environmentalism of the most sentimental kind. It is all images and music. There is no overt message except the obvious one (the Grand Canyon is prettier than Manhattan). It has been hailed as a vast and sorrowful vision, but to what end? If the people in all those cars on all those expressways are indeed living crazy lives, their problem is not the expressway (which is all that makes life in L.A. manageable) but perhaps social facts such as unemployment, crime, racism, drug abuse, and illiteracy—issues so complicated that a return to nature seems like an elitist joke at their expense. Having said that, let me add that *Koyaanisqatsi* is an impressive visual and listening experience, that Reggio and Glass have made wonderful pictures and sounds, and that this film is a curious throwback to the 1960s, when it would have been a short subject to be viewed through a marijuana haze. Far-out.

L

La Bamba ★ ★ ★
PG-13, 108 m., 1987

Lou Diamond Phillips (Ritchie Valens), Esai Morales (Bob Morales), Rosana De Soto (Connie Valenzuela), Elizabeth Pena (Rosie Morales), Danielle von Zerneck (Donna Ludwig), Joe Pantoliano (Bob Keene). Directed by Luis Valdez and produced by Taylor Hackford and Bill Borden. Screenplay by Valdez.

La Bamba opens with a sequence that at first seems like a memory. Some teen-age boys are playing basketball in a school yard. Far overhead, a light plane drones through the sky. The colors of this scene are all washed out, as in an old memory, and the voices sound far away. There is slow motion. Another airplane appears. The basketball game continues. We are lulled by the feeling of a slow summer afternoon. Then the two planes collide and fall into the school yard below.

Because *La Bamba* is the story of Ritchie Valens, we assume this is his memory. But he was not present when the planes fell, and the scene represents how he might have imagined it. One of his friends was killed that day. He always assumed that if he had been in the school yard, he would have been killed, too. That was why he never liked to take airplanes.

The scene itself is very effective. But I wonder if it is the right way to open *La Bamba*. Everyone who goes to the movie will know that Valens died in an airplane crash with Buddy Holly and the Big Bopper on February 3, 1959, the day the music died. The opening scene is followed by several other references to Valens's fear of flying, and the effect is to put the whole movie under a cloud, to weigh down every scene with the knowledge of impending death.

That robs *La Bamba* of a quality I think it could use: the sense of fun. This is a sincere, well-acted movie about the short life of a minor rock & roll star, and by the time it's over we almost have the feeling Valens would have been surprised not to have died in a crash.

He is played by Lou Diamond Phillips as a serious, introspective, intensely focused young man who wanted to play his music more than anything else in life. His dedication amounts almost to an obsession. He never seems to really let go.

Valens had only three hit songs. His public career lasted less than six months. He died before he was eighteen. There isn't a wealth of material to draw from as there was for *The Buddy Holly Story.* So Luis Valdez, the director, fleshes out the story with information about Valens's family, especially his hardworking, cheerful mother (Rosana De Soto) and his half brother (Esai Morales), who both supports him and resents him.

Valens's real surname was Valenzuela. He was a Mexican-American, raised for a time in migrant labor camps, and he idolized the older brother who would appear from time to time on a glamorous motorcycle. But he admired music more and began to sing wherever he could find work in Los Angeles in the late 1950s. After the family moved into the city, and Valens got a girlfriend—a blond Anglo named Donna, whose parents didn't approve of Valens, inspiring "Donna," one of his hits. He had some of the usual adventures of growing up, and the movie makes much of a trip he and his brother took to Tijuana, where Valens was less interested in the girls than in the band (in the movie it is, of course, playing "La Bamba").

Once Valens is discovered by a minor

record producer (Joe Pantoliano), his career goes surprisingly well. He records a song, it is a hit, he is invited by Alan Freed to appear in one of his pioneering rock & roll stage shows in Brooklyn and two other hits follow fairly quickly. Valens makes one crucial artistic decision: Although he doesn't speak Spanish, he insists on recording "La Bamba" in Spanish, using the irrefutable logic that if Nat King Cole could record in Spanish, he could, too.

Valens's last tour is handled is an almost perfunctory manner. We know how the movie will end, anyway. The Big Bopper circulates backstage, saying "Hello, baby!" to everyone he meets. Buddy Holly sings "Crying, Waiting, Hoping." They go out to the airport in a snowstorm, Holly flips a coin, and Valens calls heads and wins his place on the fated plane. Still to come, no doubt, is a movie about the Big Bopper. And why not one called *Rock & Roll Pilot* ("He Was at the Controls the Day the Music Died!")?

This is a good small movie, sweet and sentimental, about a kid who never really got a chance to show his stuff. The best things in it are the most unexpected things: the portraits of everyday life, of a loving mother, of a brother who loves and resents him, of a kid growing up and tasting fame and leaving everyone standing around at his funeral shocked that his life ended just as it seemed to be beginning.

La Cage aux Folles ★ ★ ★ ★

R, 91 m., 1979

Ugo Tognazzi (Renato), Michel Serrault (Zaza), Michel Galabru (Charrier), Claire Maurier (Simone), Remy Laurent (Laurent), Benny Luke (Jacob). Directed by Edouard Molinaro and produced by Marcello Danon. Screenplay by Francis Veber and Molinaro.

La Cage aux Folles are "birds of a feather," which are precisely and hilariously what do not flock together in this wonderful comedy from France. It's about the gay owner of a scandalous nightclub in St. Tropez, his transvestite lover, and how the owner reacts after his son returns home one day and announces he's going to marry . . . a girl!

But that's not *really* what it's about: This is basically the first sitcom in drag, and the comic turns in the plot are achieved with such clockwork timing that sometimes we're laughing at what's funny and sometimes we're laughing at the movie's sheer comic invention. This is a great time at the movies.

The nightclub owner is played by Ugo Tognazzi, that grizzled Italian veteran of so many macho roles, and he has lived for twenty years with a drag queen (Michel Serrault) who stars in the club. They're like an old married couple, nostalgic and warm one minute, fighting like cats and dogs the next. Tognazzi sired the son all those years ago and has raised him with the help of "Auntie" Serrault and their live-in "maid," a wickedly funny black transvestite who has perhaps the movie's funniest moment.

Tognazzi and Serrault have trouble at first accepting the notion that their treasured young man is going to get married. They have more trouble, however, accepting the notion that the intended bride is the daughter of the Minister of Moral Standards—and that the in-laws are planning to come to dinner.

This dilemma inspires the film's hilarious middle section, in which Tognazzi's garishly bizarre apartment is severely redecorated in crucifixes and antiques, and Serrault is gently asked by the son if he'd mind being gone for the evening: "I told them my father was a Cultural Attache; what'll they think when they find out he lives with a drag queen?"

Tognazzi, meanwhile, goes to visit the woman who bore his son two decades ago, to ask her to portray the mother for one night. She agrees. Too bad, because in the course of the uproariously funny dinner party, at least two reputed mothers are produced, one of them suspiciously hairy around the chest.

Describing a comedy is always a risky business; the bare plot outline is, of course, no hint as to how funny a film is, and to steal the jokes is a misdemeanor. What I can say, though, is that *La Cage aux Folles* gets the audience on its side with immediate ease; it never betrays our confidence; it astonishes us with the inspiration and logic it brings to ringing changes on the basic situation.

And it contains several classic sequences. The best is perhaps the one in which Tognazzi coaches Serrault on how to act "macho," an attribute that apparently consists of knowing how to butter your toast with manly firmness. There's also that extended dinner scene that begins with the Minister of

Moral Standards discovering that . . . Greek boys . . . are doing . . . *something* . . . on his soup plate . . . and builds from there.

Lady in White ★ ★ ★
PG-13, 112 m., 1988 ✓

Lukas Haas (Frankie), Len Cariou (Phil), Alex Rocco (Angelo), Katherine Helmond (Amanda), Jarresson (Geno), Renata Vanni (Mama Assunta), Angelo Bertolini (Papa Charlie), Joelle Jacobi (Melissa), Jared Rushton (Donald), Gregory Levinson (Louie). Directed by Frank LaLoggia and produced by Andrew G. La Marca and LaLoggia. Screenplay by LaLoggia.

Lady in White tells a classic ghost story in such an everyday way that the ghost is almost believable, and the story is actually scarier than it might have been with a more gruesome approach. The film creates a run-of-the-mill small town, populates it with ordinary folks, gives us a bright grade-school kid as the hero, and then plunges into a tale of murder and revenge.

We have been this way before in countless other movies, but not often with so much style, atmosphere, and believable human nature. Frank LaLoggia, who wrote and directed *Lady in White*, knows that ghosts are more frightening when they appear in the midst of everyday life. He also knows that horror stories work best when they play by the rules of conventional morality and reality. The reason movies like the *Friday the 13th* efforts grow old and boring is they permit pure anarchy, in which anything can happen, and therefore, it's no use for us to hope, or care, about the characters.

This film's story stars Lukas Haas as Frankie, an inquisitive kid with an active imagination who has a cruel trick played on him one night. Some other kids lure him into the school cloakroom and lock him in, and as the night grows darker and the moon rises, he realizes that no one knows where to look for him. Then an eerie thing happens. He sees a ghost, the ghost of a young girl about his age, who seems restless and tragic, as ghosts must—because why would they wander the earth unless a great injustice remained unsettled?

Frankie even speaks with the ghost, but then, not long after, the cloakroom has another visitor, a masked man who fishes down in the heating duct for something, and who almost kills Frankie, but finally lets him loose. Who is this strange man? Is he a ghost or a real human being? Students of the Law of Economy of Movie Character Development will figure out soon enough that the masked man is obviously the only character in the movie who has no other reason for being on the screen, but by then it's already too late to save Frankie from possible doom.

The peculiar thing about these goings-on, we discover, is that they really do exist on two levels: There is indeed a ghost in the movie, and also a real, live killer. And on a parallel track, there is the ghostly Lady in White who is said to wander the town at night, and also the weird Amanda (Katherine Helmond), a spinster whose home reminded me of that lonely closed room in *Great Expectations* where Miss Havisham kept her wedding cake.

All of these bizarre events are anchored in reality by the strong, commonsense performances of Lukas Haas, and by Alex Rocco as his father, and Len Cariou as a family friend. There are lots of small-town details in the movie, conversations that exist for no other reason than to establish the everyday reality against which the haunted events of the night take place. The movie does a good job of telling a very complicated story that accounts for the various ghosts and other midnight apparitions, and yet it is not shy when it comes to special effects and cliff-hanging endings.

It's kind of tricky, reviewing a movie like this. Almost nothing I can say will accurately reflect the tone of the film. I can write about ghosts and killers and strange old ladies, and I could be describing a much different film. But *Lady in White*, like most good films, depends more on style and tone than it does on story, and after a while, it's the whole insidious atmosphere of the film that begins to envelop us. Like the best ghost stories of M.R. James and Oliver Onions, who were the best in their classic field, *Lady in White* is finally not really about being frightened by ghosts, but about feeling pity for them.

Lady Sings the Blues ★ ★ ★
R, 144 m., 1972

Diana Ross (Billie Holiday), Billy Dee Williams (Louis McKay), Richard Pryor (Piano Man), James Callahan (Reg Hanley), Paul Hampton (Harry), Virginia Capers (Mama Holiday). Directed by Sidney J. Furie and produced by Berry Gordy. Screenplay by Terence McCloy, Chris Clark, and Suzanne de Passa.

My first reaction when I learned that Diana Ross had been cast to play Billie Holiday was a quick and simple one: I didn't think she could do it. I knew she could sing, although not as well as Billie Holiday and certainly not in the same way, but I couldn't imagine Diana Ross reaching the emotional highs and lows of one of the more extreme public lives of our times. But the movie was financed by Motown, and Diana Ross was Motown's most cherished property, so maybe the casting made some kind of commercial sense. After all, Sal Mineo played Gene Krupa.

All of those thoughts were wiped out of my mind within the first three or four minutes of *Lady Sings the Blues,* and I was left with a feeling of complete confidence in a dramatic performance. This was one of the great performances of 1972.

And there is no building up to it. The opening scene is one of total and unrelieved anguish; Billie Holiday is locked into prison, destitute and nearly friendless, and desperately needing a fix of heroin. The high, lonely shriek which escapes from Ross in this scene is a call from the soul, and we know this isn't any "screen debut" by a Top 40 star; this is acting.

It was probably inevitable that the movie itself would follow the tried-and-true formula of most of the musical biographies of the last twenty years. The genre is well-established, and since most of the musicians they've made movies about have had unhappy privates lives, there's the problem of making downhill look like uphill, at least sometimes. This is usually handled (and it is again this time) by showing the performer hitting bottom, rebounding into the arms of friends, being nursed back to health, and making a spectacular comeback performance at Carnegie Hall, or at least the Palace. The formula is so firmly established that stars even seem to follow it consciously, and we're left with tantalizing possibilities: Did Judy Garland play the Palace for the last time to give the proper form to her biography? You gotta go out in triumph, no matter what happens before.

Lady Sings the Blues has most of the clichés we expect—but do we really mind clichés in a movie like this? I don't think so. There's the childhood poverty, the searching for love, the unhappy early sexual experiences, the first audition, the big break, the years of climbing to the top, the encounter with hard drugs, the fall, the comeback, the loyal lover . . . we know the scenes by heart.

What brings the movie alive is the performance that Diana Ross, and director Sidney J. Furie, bring to the scenes. As a gangly adolescent set out to work as a maid in a whorehouse, Ross somehow manages to look gangly and adolescent. When she is transformed into a great beauty later in the film, it IS a transformation, because she was brave enough, and good enough, to really look awful at first: "You got a long way to go," the madam tells her accurately, "before anybody gonna pay $2 for an hour of your time."

The movie is filled with many of the great Billie Holiday songs, and Ross handles them in an interesting way. She doesn't sing in her own style, and she never tries to imitate Holiday, but she sings somehow in the manner of Holiday. There is an uncanny echo, a suggestion, and yet the style is a tribute to Billie Holiday, not an impersonation. The songs do slow the movie down quite a bit, and it feels long at over two hours, but the Billie Holiday music is really the occasion, so I suppose I shouldn't complain.

Lassiter ★ ★ ★
R, 100 m., 1984

Tom Selleck (Lassiter), Jane Seymour (Sara), Lauren Hutton (Kari), Bob Hoskins (Becker). Directed by Roger Young and produced by Albert S. Ruddy. Screenplay by David Taylor.

Here's a basic rule about thrillers: Style is a lot more important than plot. What happens isn't nearly as important as how it happens and who it happens to—and if you doubt me, think back over to your favorite James Bond movies. *Lassiter* is a good example. Here's a movie with a plot spun out of thin air. That doesn't matter, though, because the movie is acted and directed with such style that we have fun slogging through the silliness. And part of the fun comes from watching Tom Selleck, the hero of "Magnum, P.I.," in a movie that does him justice. He was wasted in *High Road to China*, which looked like a *Raiders of the Lost Ark* rip-off with Selleck plugged into the Harrison Ford role. *Lassiter* is a movie that seems to have been made with Selleck in mind, and he delivers—he's clearly one of the few actors capable of making the leap from TV to the big screen.

The movie stars Selleck as Nick Lassiter, an American thief in London on the eve of World War II. A hardheaded police inspector (Bob Hoskins) gets the goods on him and makes him a flat offer: Either Lassiter breaks into the German Embassy and steals $10 million in jewels, or he goes into the slammer. Lassiter goes for the jewels. That involves seducing the kinky, sadistic German countess (Lauren Hutton) who has the diamonds in her bedroom inside the well-guarded embassy. The movie misses a bet here: It spends a lot of time establishing the Hutton character (who has an unusual taste for blood), and we see her killing one of her bed partners. Yet when Lassiter finally goes to bed with her, the movie cuts to the morning after instead of showing how he survived the night. And there's no big final confrontation with the countess; at a crucial moment, Lassiter knocks her cold, and that's that.

Other characters are handled more carefully. We meet Lassiter's sweet girlfriend (Jane Seymour, looking more than ever like a perfect porcelain portrait); Hoskins, who played the mob boss in *The Long Good Friday*, and assorted creeps. Selleck occupies this world effortlessly. He is a big man, and yet he moves gracefully, wears a tuxedo well, makes charming small talk, doesn't seem to be straining himself during the fight scenes, and, in general, stands at the center of a lot of action as if he belonged there. He would make a good James Bond. *Lassiter* knows that, and knows that style and movement are a lot more important than making sense of everything. I squirm when the action stops in a thriller while the characters explain everything to one another; I think of those speeches as memos from the screenwriter to the director. *Lassiter* stops for nothing.

The Last Detail ★ ★ ★ ★

R, 104 m., 1974

Otis Young (Mulhall), Jack Nicholson (Buddusky), Randy Quaid (Meadows), Carol Kane (Prostitute), Michael Moriarty (Marine O D). Directed by Hal Ashby and produced by Gerald Ayres. Screenplay by Robert Towne.

Meadows is a big hulk of a kid who compulsively shoplifts candy bars and peanut butter sandwiches and eats them for consolation. He has been in the navy only long enough to get busted for stealing a charity box with forty bucks inside, for which he has been sentenced to eight years in the Portsmouth naval brig. Buddusky and Mulhall are the two navy lifers assigned to transport him to Portsmouth, and *The Last Detail* is the story of how they travel there on a series of trains, buses, and drunks. It's a very good movie—and the best thing in it is Jack Nicholson's performance as Buddusky. Nicholson, always one of the most interesting of actors, does in *The Last Detail* what he did in *Easy Rider*. He creates a character so complete and so complex that we stop thinking about the movie and just watch to see what he'll do next.

What he tries to do is show the kid a good time. Now a good time, by Buddusky's standards, is not everybody's idea of a good time. It involves great volumes of time spent drinking great volumes of beer. It involves bitching about the system instead of doing something about it. But it also involves some small measure of human sympathy: Buddusky is personally affronted that the kid is going to be locked up for eight years before his life as a man has even begun.

Mulhall (Otis Young), the other member of this shore patrol, is a serious black man who has spent a lot of years working for his seniority and his retirement rights, and is not going to forfeit everything just by letting one dumb kid escape. But he goes along, within limits, and they take off the kid's handcuffs and try to give him some taste of life. They get him drunk in Washington and take him to a red-light house in New York—and the funny thing is, the kid goes along mostly to please them.

He might be described as a totally unformed youth. He's played superbly by Randy Quaid, who you might remember as the kid with the bottle in his sport coat pocket in *The Last Picture Show*—the grinning kid in the corner who took Cybill Shepherd skinny-dipping in the next county. His character is the only one that changes in the movie. What happens is that he learns in a very tentative way to assert himself—even to value himself, and make a token protest against his fate.

The direction is by Hal Ashby. How good this movie really is can be gauged by comparing it to *Cinderella Liberty*, another navy movie based on a novel by the same author, Darryl Ponicsan. Both movies have similar world views, and the stories in both move somewhat relentlessly toward inevitable conclusions. But *Cinderella Liberty* just can't be believed, and in *The Last Detail*, we always have the sense that these people are plausible individuals: each limited in his own way, but each somehow coping with life. The movie is ultimately pretty sad, but for most of the way it alternates between being poignant and being very funny. Nicholson plays comedy better than most comedians, because with him the humor seems to well up from the real experiences of his character.

The Last Dragon ★ ★ ½
PG-13, 110 m., 1985

Taimak (Leroy), Vanity (Laura), Julius J. Carry III (Sho'Nuff), Chris Murney (Eddie). Directed by Michael Schultz and produced by Rupert Hitzig. Screenplay by Louis Venosta.

The Last Dragon opens with its hero learning from his karate master that he has at last reached the final level of realization; he no longer needs a master, because what remains to be learned can only be found within himself. When he achieves the final level, he will know it because of a glow all over his body. This is not an idle promise; by the end of the film, the hero glows like somebody who has just tapped into the wrong power lines. Setups like that are obligatory in karate movies; there's an unwritten law that the movie must begin with five minutes of solemn, portentous philosophy before the action can begin. Once past its prologue, however, *The Last Dragon* turns into a funny, high-energy combination of karate, romance, rock music, and sensational special effects. It's so entertaining that I could almost recommend it—if it weren't for an idiotic subplot about a gangster and his girlfriend, a diversion that brings the movie to a dead halt every eight or nine minutes.

The Last Dragon stars two remarkably attractive and likable actors, who have one name apiece. The hero is played by Taimak, a twenty-year-old karate student who has not acted before, but who has a natural screen presence, and the heroine is Vanity, the rock singer discovered by Prince and used as a warm-up act at some of his concerts prior to the *Purple Rain* tour. Of Vanity, let it be said that she has the sort of rapport with the camera that makes us like her instantly; she has a sunny smile, and an inner happiness, and in the middle of this plot about gangsters and night clubs and bloody fights, she floats serenely, a joy to behold. In the same year, Prince introduced two electrifying actresses, Appolonia Kotero from *Purple Rain*, and now Vanity.

There's another engaging actor in the movie, a man named Julius J. Carry III, who describes himself as the Shogun of Harlem, and who presides over a hilarious early scene where he marches into a movie theater full of Bruce Lee fans and threatens to fight everyone in the house. Taimak is in the front row, so loyal to the Bruce Lee mystique that he's eating his popcorn with chopsticks, and after he has a showdown with the Shogun, it becomes inevitable that they will have to endure a fight to the finish. Meanwhile, Vanity is working as a video disc jockey at a private club, and a gangster (Chris Murney) decrees that she should play a video he has produced, starring his girlfriend (Faith Prince, no relation). Vanity refuses, and she is rescued from the gangster's thugs not once but twice by the brave Taimak, who barehandedly demolishes the hitmen.

That sets up the movie's basic situation: Taimak must defeat both the Shogun and the gangster—and fall in love with the girl, of course. There are also some nice scenes involving Taimak's father, who proudly runs New York's best black pizza parlor, and his little brother, who is a lot more street-smart than the otherworldly karate master.

The Last Dragon surrounds this simple plot with a lot of technology. The movie is backed by Berry Gordy's Motown Records, which has supplied it with a digital sound track, and the scenes in the disco make much use of back-projected music videos and scenes from old Bruce Lee movies. This is an expensive, high tech production. But then there's that whole business of the gangsters. They've been borrowed from a hundred other movies, they say things that have been said a hundred other times, and they walk around draining the movie of its vitality. They're tired old clichés getting in the way of the natural energy of Taimak, Vanity, and the Shogun character. Take out the gangsters, pump up the Shogun role, give Taimak and Vanity a little more screen time, and you'd have a great entertainment instead of simply a great near-miss.

The Last Emperor ★ ★ ★ ★
PG-13, 160 m., 1987

John Lone (Pu Yi, adult), Joan Chen (Wan Jung), Peter O'Toole (Reginald Johnston), Ying Ruocheng (Governor), Victor Wong (Chen Pao Shen), Dennis Dun (Big Li), Ryuichi Sakamoto (Amakasu), Maggie Han (Eastern Jewel). Directed by Bernardo Bertolucci and produced by Jeremy Thomas. Screenplay by Mark Peploe and Bertolucci.

The boy was three when he first sat on the Dragon Throne as emperor of China, and seven when he abdicated. He had barely reached what in the West is considered the age of reason, and already events beyond his control had shaped his life forever. Bernardo Bertolucci's *The Last Emperor* tells the story of this child, named Pu Yi, in an epic that uses the life of one man as a mirror that reflects China's passage from feudalism through revolution to its current state of relatively peaceful transition.

This is a strange epic because it is about an entirely passive character. We are accustomed to epics about heroes who act on their society—Lawrence of Arabia, Gandhi—but Pu Yi was born into a world that allowed him no initiative. The ironic joke was that he was emperor of nothing, for there was no power to go with his title, and throughout the movie he is seen as a pawn and victim, acted upon, exploited for the purposes of others, valued for what he wasn't rather than for what he was.

The movie reveals his powerlessness almost at once; scenes of his childhood in the Forbidden City are intercut with scenes from later in his life, when the Chinese communists had taken power, and he was seized and held in a re-education camp, where a party official spent a decade talking him through a personal transition from emperor to gardener—which was Pu Yi's last, and perhaps happiest, occupation.

But the process in the communist jail actually starts many years earlier, in one of the most poignant scenes in the film, when young Pu Yi is given a bicycle and excitedly pedals it around the Forbidden City until he reaches its gates to the outer world, and is stopped by his own guards. He is an emperor who cannot do the one thing any other little boy in China could do, which was to go out of his own house.

Bertolucci is able to make Pu Yi's imprisonment seem all the more ironic because this entire film was shot on location inside the People's Republic of China, and he was even given permission to film inside the Forbidden City—a vast medieval complex covering some 250 acres and containing 9,999 rooms (only heaven, the Chinese believed, had 10,000 rooms). It is probably unforgivably bourgeois to admire a film because of its locations, but in the case of *The Last Emperor*, the narrative cannot be separated from the awesome presence of the Forbidden City, and from Bertolucci's astonishing use of locations, authentic costumes, and thousands of extras to create the everyday reality of this strange little boy.

There is a scene early in the film when Pu Yi, seated on the Dragon Throne, attended by his minders and servants, grows restless, as small boys will do. He leaps impatiently from his seat and runs toward the door of the throne room, where at first a vast billowing drapery (a yellow one—the color reserved for only the emperor) obstructs the view. Then the curtain is blown aside, and we see an incredible sight, thousands of the emperor's minions, all of them traditionally costumed eunuchs, lined up in geometric precision as far as the eye can see, all of them kowtowing to the boy.

After he formally abdicates power in 1912, Pu Yi remains on the throne, a figurehead maintained in luxury for the convenience of the real rulers of China. A Scottish tutor named Reginald Johnston (Peter O'Toole) comes out to instruct him in the ways of Europe, and the youth (played in manhood by John Lone) becomes an anglophile, dreaming of "escaping" to Cambridge.

Johnston advises him to escape instead into marriage, and he takes an empress (Joan Chen) and a concubine. In 1924, he is thrown out of the Forbidden City, and moves with his retinue back to his native Manchuria, then controlled by the Japanese. In a scene of great elegant irony, Bertolucci shows him in Western clothes, a cigarette in hand, leaning on a piano and crooning "Am I Blue?"

As World War II grows closer, Pu Yi grows increasingly irrelevant, except to the Japanese, who set him up briefly as their puppet in Manchuria. His wife becomes an opium addict and begins a dalliance with a lesbian Japanese spy, his old tutor returns to England, he gives himself over to a life of depravity and drifting, and then everything changes for him when the communists take control of China and he is captured by Russians who turn him over to their new allies.

We might expect the communists to sentence Pu Yi to death (a fate he himself confidently expected), but instead there is the reeducation process, complicated by the fact that this grown man has never done anything for himself and does not know how to tie his own shoes or turn off the tap after filling a glass with drinking water. When we see him at the end of the film, he is working as a gardener in Peking, and seems happy, and we assume that for him, at least, re-education was a success because it was essentially education in the first place, for a man whose whole life was directed toward making him impotent and irrelevant.

In Orson Welles's *Citizen Kane*, one of the tycoon's friends says, "I was there before the beginning—and now I'm here after the end." *The Last Emperor* ends with an extraordinary sequence, beyond the end, in which an elderly Pu Yi goes to visit the Forbidden City, which is now open to tourists. He sees a little boy sneak past the velvet rope and climb onto the Dragon Throne. Once that would have been a fatal offense. But the old man who was once the boy on that throne looks on, now, with a complex mixture of emotions. It is an inspired ending for the film, which never makes the mistake of having only one thing to say about the life of a man who embodied all the contradictions and paradoxes of twentieth-century China.

There aren't a lot of action scenes in *The Last Emperor*, and little enough intrigue (even the Japanese spy isn't subtle: "I'm a spy, and I don't care who knows it," she tells the empress on their first meeting). As in *Gandhi*, great historical changes take place during *The Last Emperor*, but, unlike Gandhi, the emperor has no influence on them. His life is a sad irony; his end is a bittersweet elegy. But it is precisely because so little "happens" in this epic that its vast and expensive production schedule is important. When we see those thousands of servants bowing to a little boy, for example, the image is effective precisely because the kowtowing means nothing to the boy, and the lives of the servants have been dedicated to no useful purpose.

Everything involving the life of Pu Yi was a waste. Everything except one thing—the notion that a single human life could have infinite value. In its own way, the Dragon Throne argued that, making an emperor into a god in order to ennoble his subjects. And in its own way, the Chinese revolution argued the same thing by making him into a gardener.

Last House on the Left ★ ★ ★ ½

R, 82 m., 1972

David Hess (Krug), Ludy Gratham (Phyllis), Sandra Cassell (Mari), Marc Sheffler (Junior), Jeramie Rain (Sadie), Fred Lincoln (Weasel), Gaylord St. James (Dr. Collingwood), Cynthia Carr (Mrs. Collingwood). Directed by Wes Craven and produced by Sean S. Cunningham. Screenplay by Craven.

Last House on the Left is a tough, bitter little sleeper of a movie that's about four times as good as you'd expect. There is a moment of such sheer and unexpected terror that it beats anything in the heart-in-the-mouth line since Alan Arkin jumped out of the darkness at Audrey Hepburn in *Wait Until Dark*.

I don't want to give the impression, however, that this is simply a good horror movie. It's horrifying, all right, but in ways that have nothing to do with the supernatural. It's the story of two suburban girls who go into the city for a rock concert, are kidnapped by a gang of sadistic escaped convicts and their sluttish girlfriend, and are raped and murdered. Then, in a coincidence even the killers find extreme, the gang ends up spending the night at the home of one of the girls' parents.

The parents accidentally find out the identities of the killers, because of a stolen locket and some blood-stained clothing in their baggage. Enraged, the father takes on the gang single-handedly and murders them. Does any of this sound familiar? Think for a moment. Setting aside the modern details, this is roughly the plot of Ingmar Bergman's *The Virgin Spring.*

The story is also based on a true incident, we're told at the beginning of the movie, but I have my doubts; I think the producers may simply be trying one of those "only the names have been changed" capers. What does come through in *Last House on the Left* is a powerful narrative, told so directly and strongly that the audience (mostly in the mood for just another good old exploitation film) was rocked back on its psychic heels.

Wes Craven's direction never lets us out from under almost unbearable dramatic tension (except in some silly scenes involving a couple of dumb cops, who overact and seriously affect the plot's credibility). The acting is unmannered and . . . natural, I guess. There's no posturing. There's a good ear for dialogue and nuance. And there is evil in this movie. Not bloody escapism, or a thrill a minute, but a fully developed sense of the vicious natures of the killers. There is no glory in this violence. And Craven has written in a young member of the gang (again borrowed on Bergman's story) who sees the horror as fully as the victims do. This movie covers the same philosophical territory as Sam Peckinpah's *Straw Dogs,* and is more hard-nosed about it: Sure, a man's home is his castle, but who wants to be left with nothing but a castle and a lifetime memory of horror?

The Last Metro ★ ★ ★

NO MPAA RATING, 133 m., 1980

Catherine Deneuve (Marion Steiner), Gerard Depardieu (Bernard Granger), Jean Poiret (Jean-Loup), Heinz Bennent (Lucas Steiner), Andrea Ferreol (Arlette), Paulette Dubost (Germaine), Jean-Louis Richard (Daxlat). Directed by Francois Truffaut. Screenplay by Truffaut, Suzanne Schiffman, and Jean-Claude Grumberg.

Francois Truffaut said he wanted to satisfy three old dreams by making *The Last Metro.* He wanted to take the camera backstage in a theater, to evoke the climate of the Nazi occupation of France, and to give Catherine Deneuve the role of a responsible woman. He has achieved the first and last dreams, but he doesn't evoke the occupation well enough to make *The Last Metro* more than a sentimental fantasy.

The film takes place backstage, and below-stage, at a theater in Paris. The theater's director is German Jew (Heinz Bennent) who already has fled from Nazi Germany and now, with the occupation of Paris, goes into permanent hiding in the basement of his theater. Upstairs, his wife (Deneuve) spreads the rumor that he has fled to South America. Then she relays his instructions as the theater attempts to save itself from bankruptcy by presenting a new production.

There are many other characters in the movie, which at times resembles Truffaut's history of a film production in *Day for Night.* Gerard Depardieu plays the leading man for the new production. The supporting cast includes a young woman who will do anything for a job in the theater, an older woman of ambiguous sexuality, an avuncular stage manager, a gay director, and a powerful critic who is such an evil monster that he must surely have been inspired by a close Truffaut friend. Most of the movie's events take place within the walls of the theater; this is a backstage film, not a war film. We see the rehearsals under way, with Bennent downstairs listening through an air duct. There are the romantic intrigues among the cast members. There are occasional walkthroughs by Nazis. There are moments of great danger, somewhat marred by the fact that Truffaut does not resolve them realistically. And there is an unforgivably sentimental ending that ties up everything without solving anything.

The problem, I think, is that Truffaut sees the Nazi presence in Paris simply as a plot device to create tension within his theatrical troupe. It is ever so much more dramatic if the show must go on despite raids, political directives, and an electrical blackout that requires the stagehands to power a generator by bicycle-power. It's all too cute. Nobody seems to *really* understand that there's a war on out there. And yet, within the unfortunate limitations that Truffaut sets for himself, he does deliver an entertaining movie.

Catherine Deneuve is as beautiful as ever, and as enigmatic (it is typical of her performance that at the end we have to wait for the screenplay to tell us who she does, or does not, really love). Depardieu is gangly and sincere, a strong presence. Bennent, as the husband downstairs, is wan and courageous in the Paul Henreid role. And the most fascinating character in the cast is of course the villain, Daxlat, the pro-Nazi critic. He at least seems in touch with the true evil that the others, and Truffaut, see as backdrop.

The Last Picture Show ★ ★ ★ ★
R, 114 m., 1971

Timothy Bottoms (Sonny), Jeff Bridges (Duane), Cybill Shepherd (Jacy Farrow), Ben Johnson (Sam the Lion), Cloris Leachman (Ruth Popper), Ellen Burstyn (Lois Farrow), Ellen Brennan (Genevieve), Bill Thurman (Coach Popper). Directed by Peter Bogdanovich and produced by Bert Schneider and Stephen J. Friedman. Screenplay by Larry McMurty and Bogdanovich.

There was something about going to the movies in the 1950s that will never be the same again. It was the decade of the last gasp of the great American movie-going habit, and before my eyes in the middle 1950s the Saturday kiddie matinee died a lingering death at the Princess Theater on Main Street in Urbana. For five or six years of my life (the years between when I was old enough to go alone, and when TV came to town) Saturday afternoon at the Princess was a descent into a dark magical cave that smelled of Jujubes, melted Dreamsicles, and Crisco in the popcorn machine. It was probably on one of those Saturday afternoons that I formed my first critical opinion, deciding vaguely that there was something about John Wayne that set him apart from ordinary cowboys. The Princess was jammed to the walls with kids every Saturday afternoon, as it had been for years, but then TV came to town and within a year the Princess was no longer an institution. It survived into the early 1960s and then closed, to be reborn a few years later as the Cinema. The metallic taste of that word, cinema, explains what happened when you put it alongside the name "Princess."

Peter Bogdanovich's *The Last Picture Show* uses the closing of another theater on another Main Street as a motif to frame a great many things that happened to America in the early 1950s. The theater is the Royal, and along with the pool hall and the all-night cafe it supplies what little excitement and community survives in a little West Texas crossroads named Anarene.

All three are owned by Sam the Lion, who is just about the only self-sufficient and self-satisfied man in town. The others are infected by a general malaise, and engage in sexual infidelities partly to remind themselves they are alive. There isn't much else to do in Anarene, no dreams worth dreaming, no new faces, not even a football team that can tackle worth a damn. The nourishing myth of the Western (*Wagonmaster* and *Red River* are among the last offerings at the Royal) is being replaced by nervously hilarious TV programs out of the East, and defeated housewives are reassured they're part of the "Strike It Rich" audience with a heart of gold.

Against this background, we meet two high school seniors named Sonny and Duane, who are the co-captains of the shameful football squad. We learn next to nothing about their home lives, but we hardly notice the omission because their real lives are lived in a pickup truck and a used Mercury. That was the way it was in high school in the 1950s, and probably always will be: A car was a mobile refuge from adults, frustration, and boredom. When people in their thirties say today that sexual liberation is pale compared to a little prayerful groping in the front seat, they are onto something.

During the year of the film's action, the two boys more or less survive coming-of-age. They both fall in love with the school's only beauty, a calculating charmer named Jacy who twists every boy in town around her little finger before taking this skill away with her to Dallas. Sonny breaks up with his gum-chewing girlfriend and has an unresolved affair with the coach's wife, and Duane goes off to fight the Korean War. There are two deaths during the film's year, but no babies are born, and Bogdanovich's final pan shot along Main Street curiously seems to turn it from a real location (which it is) into a half-remembered backdrop from an old movie. *The Last Picture Show* is a great deal more complex than it might at first seem, and this shot suggests something of its buried structure. Every detail of clothing, behavior, background music, and decor is exactly right for 1951—but that still doesn't explain the movie's mystery.

Mike Nichols's *Carnal Knowledge* began with 1949, and yet felt modern. Bogdanovich has been infinitely more subtle in giving his film not only the decor of 1951, but the visual style of a movie that might have been shot in 1951. The montage of cutaway shots at the Christmas dance; the use of an insert of Sonny's foot on the accelerator; the lighting and black and white photography of real locations as if they were sets—everything forms a stylistic whole that works. It isn't just a matter of putting in Jo Stafford and Hank Williams.

The Last Picture Show has been described as an evocation of the classic Hollywood narrative film. It is more than that; it is a belated entry in that age—the best film of 1951, you might say. Using period songs and decor to create nostalgia is familiar enough, but to tunnel down to the visual level and get that right, too, and in a way that will affect audiences even if they aren't aware how, is one hell of a directing accomplishment. Movies create our dreams as well as reflect them, and when we lose the movies we lose the dreams. I wonder if Bogdanovich's film doesn't at last explain what it was that Pauline Kael, and a lot of the rest of us, lost at the movies.

The Last Starfighter ★ ★ 1/2

PG, 100 m., 1984

Lance Guest (Alex Rogan), Dan O'Herlihy (Grig), Catherine Mary Stewart (Maggie), Barbara Bosson (Jane Rogan), Robert Preston (Centauri). Directed by Nick Castle and produced by Gary Adelson and Edward O. Denault. Screenplay by Jonathan Betuel.

The way to get rich, they say is to invent something that's cheap and habit-forming, and get a patent on it. I guess video games would qualify. Kids pump quarters into them by the hour, turning into video junkies as they watch gorillas climbing little electronic ladders. Are the games educational? Sure, if you want to grow up to be a professional video game player.

Those arcade video games had to come from somewhere, and *The Last Starfighter* has an interesting theory to explain why they seemed to pop up all over the world, almost overnight. They came from outer space. Just as I've always suspected. That's right, they were put on Earth by representatives of the Star League, who use them as testing devices. If you break a record on a video game, they come and get you and turn you into an intergalactic fighter pilot. Meanwhile, your place on Earth is taken by a robot.

The Last Starfighter starts in a trailer camp in California. We know it's in California because all the residents are fugitives from mainstream life-styles. A kid (Lance Guest) lives in the camp and sets a record on a Starfighter game, and a Star League recruiter (Robert Preston) whisks him into outer space to join the battle against the evil race of Ko-Dan. At first the kid is a little reluctant. He'd rather stay on Earth and neck with his girlfriend. But he's persuaded that he's all that stands between the Ko-Dan and intergalactic civilization as we know it. So he agrees to become a Starfighter, and is tutored by a wise old lizard-warrior named Grig, who is played by Dan O'Herlihy in makeup inspired by the heartbreak of psoriasis.

The Last Starfighter is not a terrifically original movie. The video game concept seems inspired by Walt Disney's *Tron*, and the battles in space are such close copies of the Star Wars movies that George Lucas might have a lawsuit. For example, when Grig gives the kids lessons in how to fire from the cockpit of his rocket, the cockpit's swivel chair looks directly inspired by the original *Star Wars*. If the movie isn't original in its special effects, it tries to make up for that in the trailer camp scenes. A large gallery of eccentric supporting actors is trotted onscreen, all with a few colorful lines to say, and there's a subplot about the love affair between the kid's girlfriend and the robot who has replaced the kid (every time the girl tries to lick his ear, he gets a short circuit).

This is all pretty lame material. *The Last Starfighter* is a well-made movie. The special effects are competent. The acting is good, and I enjoyed Robert Preston's fast-talking *Music Man* reprise (we've got trouble, right here in the galaxy) and the gentle wit of Dan O'Herlihy's extraterrestrial. But the final spark was missing, the final burst of inspiration that might have pulled all these concepts and inspirations and retreads together into a good movie.

The Late Show ★ ★ ★ ★
PG, 94 m., 1977

Art Carney (Ira Wells), Lily Tomlin (Margo), Bill Macy (Charlie Hatter), Eugene Roche (Ron Birdwell), Joanna Cassidy (Laura Birdwell), John Considine (Lamar), Howard Duff (Harry Regan), Ruth Nelson (Mrs. Schmidt). Directed by Robert Benton and produced by Robert Altman. Screenplay by Benton.

It's hard enough for a movie to sustain one tone, let alone half a dozen, but that's just what Robert Benton's *The Late Show* does. It's the story of a strangely touching relationship between two people. It's a violent crime melodrama. It's a comedy. It's a commentary on the private eye genre, especially its 1940s manifestations. It's a study of the way older people do a balancing act between weariness and experience. It's a celebration of that uncharted continent, Lily Tomlin.

And most of all, it's a movie that dares a lot, pulls off most of it, and entertains us without insulting our intelligence. What's quietly astonishing is that all of it starts with a woman coming to a private eye about a missing cat. The woman is played by Lily Tomlin, who somehow provides scatterbrained eccentricism with a cutting edge. The cat has been missing a couple of days, and she's worried. The private eye is played by Art Carney, who has seen it all twice, when once would have been too much.

He takes the case maybe because he could use the money, maybe because he's intrigued by the client, maybe because he's bored, maybe because he's been taking cases so long it's second nature. He doesn't give a damn about the cat. But then, in a series of plot developments so labyrinthine we should be taking notes, the missing cat leads to a mysterious robbery, a missing stamp collection, a fence with a house full of stolen goods, and a dead body that's in the . . .

But, no, I won't say where the body is, because the way Benton reveals it and then lets Lily Tomlin discover it (when all she was after was a Coke) is one of the movie's many pleasures. A friend of mine objected to the body, and to the movie's violence, as being unnecessary in a comedy. Well, *The Late Show* is a long way from being only a comedy, and the introductory shot of that body redeems any amount of gratuitous movie violence.

It's the case with most good detective fiction that the puzzle seems impossible to solve until the last chapter, when everything is made transparently clear. That's true here, with Art Carney providing a brilliant analysis of the connections and coincidences just when it's most irrelevant. But the plot's incidental to the movie's center, which has to do with Carney and Lily Tomlin.

You see, they're allowed to be people here. They're allowed to play characters who have no particular connection with clichés or stereotypes or characters who were successful in a box office hit last year. Yes, Carney's a private eye, but a particular one: Overweight and wheezing, hard of hearing, given to comments that only obliquely refer to the problem at hand.

And Lily Tomlin . . . well, her character employs a form of reasoning that has nothing to do with logic but a lot to do with the good reasons we have for behaving as we do. An example. Art Carney pretends to be mortally ill (never mind why). He is not (never mind why). His ruse has saved their lives (never mind how). Lily Tomlin is not pleased: She could have had a heart attack! Does he think it's funny, playing with his own friend's *emotions* that way? Doesn't he have any *consideration*?

Benton's screenplay is filled with lines that perfectly define their moments (and belong so securely to the characters that they seem to come from them, as some of them probably did). The way in which Tomlin explains why today is the *pits*, for example. The way Carney wonders if it would kill her, for chrissakes, to wear a dress once in a while. The way Carney's sometime partner talks to himself before he dies. The way the fence offers a bribe of a stereo set.

The Late Show is one of three movies from the late seventies that had their spiritual origins in the classic private eye films. The other two were Dick Richard's *Farewell, My Lovely* (in which Robert Mitchum demonstrated that he was born to play Philip Marlowe), and Robert Altman's *The Long Goodbye*, (in which Elliott Gould demonstrated that he was not).

Altman produced *The Late Show,* which is probably another way of saying he made it possible to be filmed, and Benton has brilliantly realized it. Maybe these three films about an all but extinct occupation are telling us something: That the more we become plastic and bland, the more we become fascinated by a strata in our cities we'd like to believe still exists, a society of loners and eccentrics, people brave and crazy and doomed, old private eyes and cat lovers. If they're OK, we're OK.

Legend ★ ★

PG, 89 m., 1986

Tom Cruise (Jack), Mia Sara (Lili), Tim Curry (Darkness), David Bennent (Gump), Alice Playten (Blix), Billy Barty (Screwball). Directed by Ridley Scott and produced by Arnon Milchan. Screenplay by William Hjortsberg.

Recent movies have created sort of a generic fantasy universe, made out of Muppets and swamps, strange beasts and evil tyrants, damsels and heroic lads, ancient prophecies and mythical legends. It's a world that seems inspired by ingredients from *Lord of the Rings,* the *Star Wars* movies, Dungeons and Dragons gamesmanship, tales of King Arthur, and the latest gimmicks from the special effects people. In a movie that works, these ingredients can be exciting and delightful. *Legend* does not work.

The movie is a big-budget British special effects extravaganza by Ridley Scott, the director of *Alien.* It tells of a time that is long, long ago, when unicorns roam the earth, and the powers of light and darkness are at war. An evil prince named Darkness lives in caverns far beneath the earth, scheming to blot the sun out of the lives of all the planet's creatures, and rule the gloom forever.

Earth itself is a sylvan place, filled with flowers and little glades and grassy clearings—but also with dread swamps and mouldy fens. Young lovers can kiss for an afternoon in a bath of sunshine, but fearsome storms come up suddenly, and lash the land with their fury. A race of evil little druids lives in the woods and spreads mischief wherever they venture. Their favorite pastime is frightening the unicorns.

Into this setting come our heroes, Jack and Lili. Jack (Tom Cruise) is a hero whose mission in life is to vanquish Darkness and allow the sun to prevail. Lili (Mia Sara) is the young woman he meets and falls in love with, but who is lured into the underworld and seduced by an exotic priestess into seemingly becoming evil. Will Jack save Lili and defeat Darkness? Or will the movie end unhappily? Can we vote more than once?

Let it be said that *Legend* is an impressive technical achievement. Ridley Scott is a perfectionist who takes infinite pains to make things look right. One problem is, the world of *Legend* is *itself* wrong for this material. To some degree, this is a fairy tale, and it needs a certain lightness of tone, a plucky cheerfulness, to really work. Like so many of the other recent sword and sorcery movies, it is so effective in rendering evil, so good at depicting the dire, bleak fates facing the heroes, that it's too dreary and gloomy for its own good.

Performances tend to get lost in productions like this. I particularly noticed how easily Tom Cruise got buried in the role of Jack. Here is the talented young actor from *Risky Business* where he came across as a genuine individual, and this time he's so overwhelmed by sets and special effects that his character could be played by anybody. Tim Curry, from *Rocky Horror Picture Show,* makes an effective Darkness—I liked his style—but, once again, the makeup people have done such a good job with his blazing eyes and gigantic horns that, in a way, almost any actor could be lurking inside there somewhere (only Curry's sensuous lips give him away).

Despite all its sound and fury, *Legend* is finally just a movie I didn't care very much about. All of the special effects in the world, and all of the makeup, and all of the great Muppet creatures, can't save a movie that has no clear idea of its own mission, and no joy in its own accomplishments.

The Legend of Hell House ★ ★ ★ ½

PG, 94 m., 1973

Pamela Franklin (The Medium), Roddy McDowall (Fisher), Clive Revill (Barrett), Gayle Hunnicutt (Ann Barrett). Directed by John Hough and produced by Albert Fennell and Norman T. Herman. Screenplay by Richard Matheson.

It is, we are told, the Mount Everest of haunted houses. It has defied every attempt to understand or defeat it. Its windows were bricked up against the sun years ago by its evil master, Belasco, who presided over the depraved orgies inside. When the relatives of his guests had the house broken into by police, twenty-seven bodies were found, but never Belasco's. The party was over.

The only previous psychic expedition to probe the house's secrets ended with every one dead except one, Fisher, known to be the most powerful physical medium of his time. Now he is back with a spiritual medium and with a rational scientist, Barrett, who insists all paranormal phenomena have scientific explanations. It sounds good until the door slams shut behind them in Hell House.

The Legend of Hell House manages to be several things at once. It's a supernatural thriller; it's a shocker, with things leaping out of corners and hurling chandeliers, and it's an almost-convincing pseudoscientific study of psychic events.

The last was the trademark of the movie's author, Richard Matheson, who also wrote the book *Hell House* (which I liked more than *The Exorcist*). Matheson labored for years in the elusive territory between straight science fiction and the supernatural horror genre, developing a kind of novel in which vampires, ghouls, and the occult are treated as if they came under ordinary scientific classifications.

There was, for example, the Matheson classic *I Am Legend* (remade somewhat unhappily as *The Omega Man*, with Charlton Heston). In that one, a single normal man held hundreds of vampires (or were they werewolves?) at bay by figuring out the scientific reasons for old medieval antivampire measures like mirrors, crucifixes, and garlic. The Matheson novels of the 1950s and early 1960s anticipated pseudorealistic fantasy novels like *Rosemary's Baby* and *The Exorcist*.

And now here he is again with a tightly wound and really scary story, which has been directed by John Hough with a great deal of sympathy for the novel's spirit. A suitable Belasco House has been found, complete with library, upstairs bedrooms, and a chapel, which seems to be the source of all evil. The screenplay didn't have room (or perhaps couldn't find a visual equivalent?) for the steam room that suddenly filled with malevolent slime, but you can't have everything.

Roddy McDowall, looking like an owlishly haunted Andy Warhol, plays the sole survivor from the last team. Pamela Franklin is the young innocent who believes psychic events are God's manifestation on Earth. And Clive Revill and Gayle Hunnicutt, as husband and wife, move a large and curious machine into the manor.

He believes, you see, that there is no such thing as life after death, and that psychic happenings merely reflect electrical currents emanated by certain gifted persons. Belasco House is nothing but a vast psychic battery which has stored up the energies of all the evil people who lived and died there; his machine will ground the current and leave the house empty of energy. It all sounds promising, until the machine's dials begin to pick up energy emissions on their own . . . .

Less Than Zero ★ ★ ★ ★

R, 100 m., 1987

Andrew McCarthy (Clay), Jami Gertz (Blair), Robert Downey, Jr. (Julian), James Spader (Rip), Tony Bill (Bradford Easton), Nicholas Pryor (Benjamin Wells), Donna Mitchell (Elaine Easton), Michael Bowen (Hop), Sarah Buxton (Markie). Directed by Mark Kanievska and produced by Jon Avnet and Jordan Kerner. Screenplay by Harley Peyton.

George Carlin was once asked how cocaine made you feel, and he answered: "It makes you feel like having some more cocaine." That inescapable fact is at the bottom of *Less Than Zero,* a movie that knows cocaine inside out and paints a portrait of drug addiction that is all the more harrowing because it takes place in the Beverly Hills fast lane, in a world of wealth, sex, glamour, and helpless self-destruction.

The movie is about three very rich kids who graduate from the same high school. How rich? As a graduation present, the father of one of the kids sets him up in the recording industry. The character's name is Julian, and he is played by Robert Downey, Jr., as a slick, smart, charming young man who takes less than a year to lose everything. His best friend in high school was Clay, played by Andrew McCarthy. Clay, who wears a tie even in Southern California, goes off to an Ivy League university, leaving behind his girlfriend, Blair (Jami Gertz). By Thanksgiving, Downey and Gertz are sleeping together and doing cocaine together, and by Christmas, a terrified Gertz is calling McCarthy and begging him to come home and rescue Downey, who is in very big trouble.

The problem is, you cannot rescue someone who is addicted to drugs. You can lecture them, to no point, and plead with them, to no avail, but essentially, an outsider is powerless over someone else's addiction. Downey is clearly out of control and headed for bottom. He has lost the recording studio, spent all his money, made a half-hearted stab at a rehab center, gone back to using, and been banished from his home by his father, who practices tough love and tells him, "You can lead your life any way you want, but stay the hell out of mine."

The first hint of this movie's power comes during a Christmas party scene. McCarthy, back from the East, tries to talk to his old friend and his former girlfriend, but they're stoned, and talk too fast and too loud, almost mechanically, and have tiny attention spans. Later, Gertz begs McCarthy to help Downey—but what can he do? And then the movie's long middle section functions almost as a documentary of the Beverly Hills fast track, of private clubs that open at midnight, of expensive cars and smooth drug dealers and glamorous hangers-on, and the quiet desperation of a society of once-bright, once-attractive, once-promising young people who talk about a lot of things but essentially think only about cocaine.

The movie's three central performances are flawless, by Jami Gertz, as the frightened girl who witnesses the disintegration of her friend; Andrew McCarthy, as the quiet, almost cold, witness from outside this group; and especially by Robert Downey, Jr., whose acting here is so real, so subtle, and so observant that it's scary.

His life in the film revolves around the will of a fourth character, his drug dealer (James Spader). He owes the dealer $50,000 and has no money and no prospects, and the most frightening thing about his situation is that the Spader character is actually fairly reasonable, as these characters go. "I'm not the problem," Spader tells McCarthy. "Julian is the problem." He has extended much more credit than he would usually permit, out of "friendship," but now Downey is at the end of the line.

The movie's last thirty minutes are like a kick in the gut, as Downey spirals through the ultimate results of his addiction. He appeals to his father, to his friends, and even to his dealer, and the fact is, he gets more help than perhaps he deserves. He makes firm resolutions to stop using, and vague plans to "get back into rehab," and his friends stand by him as much as they can. The movie's outcome reflects, more or less accurately, what awaits most cocaine addicts who do not get clean.

If this description of *Less Than Zero* makes it sound like a downbeat retread of *The Lost Weekend,* that's because I haven't described the movie's visual style. Director Mark Kanievska and cinematographer Ed Lachman have photographed Beverly Hills, Bel Air, and Palm Springs the way they look in high-priced fashion ads and slick TV commercials. The water in the pools is always an azure blue. The homes look like sets. The people look like models. The discos look like music videos. The whole movie looks brilliantly superficial, and so Downey's predicament is all the more poignant: He is surrounded by all of this, he is in it and of it, and he cannot have it. All he wants to have is a good time, but he is trapped in a paradox: Cocaine is the good time that takes itself away.

Lethal Weapon ★ ★ ★ ★
R, 110 m., 1987

Mel Gibson (Martin Riggs), Danny Glover (Roger Murtaugh), Gary Busey (Joshua), Mitchell Ryan (The General), Tom Atkins (Michael Hunsaker), Darlene Love (Trish Murtaugh), Traci Wolfe (Rianne Murtaugh). Directed by Richard Donner and produced by Donner and Joel Silver. Screenplay by Shane Black.

Lethal Weapon is another one of those Bruised Forearm Movies, like *Raiders of the Lost Ark,* a movie where you and your date grab each other's arm every four minutes and you end up black and blue and grinning from ear to ear. It's a buddy movie about two homicide cops who chase a gang of drug dealers all over Southern California, and the plot makes an amazing amount of sense, considering that the action hardly ever stops for it.

The cops are played by Danny Glover, as a homebody who has just celebrated his fiftieth birthday, and Mel Gibson, as a crazed, wild-eyed rebel who has developed a suicidal streak since his wife was killed in a car crash. In the space of less than forty-eight hours, they become partners, share a family dinner, kill several people, survive a shoot-out in the desert, battle with helicopters and machine guns, toss hand grenades, jump off buildings, rescue Glover's kidnapped daughter, drive cars through walls, endure torture by electric shock, have a few beers, and repair the engine on Glover's boat—not in that order.

The movie's so tightly wound up, it's like a rubber band ready to snap. Richard Donner, the director, throws action scenes at us like hardballs, and we don't know when to duck. All of the elements of this movie have been seen many times before—the chases, the explosions, the hostage negotiations—but this movie illustrates a favorite belief of mine, which is that the subject of a movie is much less important than its style. I'm a guy who is bored by shoot-outs and chase scenes. I've seen it all. But this movie thrilled me from beginning to end.

Part of that is because I cared about the characters. Glover has had important roles for several years (in movies as different as *Places in the Heart* and *The Color Purple*), but this movie makes him a star. His job is to supply the movie's center of gravity, while all the nuts and weirdos and victims whirl around him. He's a family man, concerned about those gray hairs he sees in the mirror, not interested in taking unnecessary chances.

Gibson is the perfect counterpoint, with his wild hair, his slob clothing, and his emotional misery. It's a running gag in the movie that Gibson is so suicidal he doesn't care if he lives or dies—and that gives him a definite advantage in showdown situations. That's what happens in a scene where Gibson is up on a rooftop trying to reason with a jumper. I won't spoil the scene; I'll just say the movie ends with one of the few genuinely unexpected surprises in any recent action film.

The supporting cast is strong, and has to be, to stand out in the midst of the mayhem. Gary Busey, slimmed down and bright of eye, makes an appropriately hateful killer. And Traci Wolfe, as Glover's good-looking daughter, is cute when she gets a teen-age crush on Gibson. But most of the attention focuses on Glover and Gibson, and they work easily together, as if they were having fun, their eccentric personal rhythms supplying a counterpoint to the movie's roar of violence.

Now about that matter of style. In a sense, a movie like *Lethal Weapon* isn't about violence at all. It's about movement and timing, the choreography of bodies and weapons in time and space. In lesser movies, the people stand there and shoot at each other and we're bored. In a movie with the energy of this one, we're exhilarated by the sheer freedom of movement; the violence becomes surrealistic and less important than the movie's underlying energy level.

Richard Donner has directed a lot of classy pictures. My favorites are *Inside Moves*, *Ladyhawke*, and the original *Superman*, which is still the best. This time he tops himself.

Let's Spend the Night Together

★ ★ 1/2

PG, 94 m., 1983

Featuring The Rolling Stones. Directed by Hal Ashby and produced by Ronald L. Schwary.

It all comes down to the difference between a "concert film" and a documentary. *Let's Spend the Night Together* is essentially a concert film—a film recording an "ideal" Rolling Stones concert, put together out of footage shot at several outdoor and indoor Stones concerts. If that's what you want, enjoy this movie. I wanted more. I would have been interested in a film exploring the phenomenon of the Rolling Stones, who bill themselves as the greatest rock 'n' roll band in the world, and are certainly the most durable. I would have liked to know more about the staging of a modern rock concert, which is arguably the most sensually overpowering nonwartime spectacle in human history, and which may have been invented, in form and in its focus on a single charismatic individual, at Hitler's mass rallies. I would have liked to know more about Mick Jagger; how does it feel for an educated, literate, civilized man in his early forties, with a head for figures and a gift for contracts and negotiations, to strut with a codpiece before tens of thousands of screaming, drug-crazed fans?

Let's Spend the Night Together does not answer these questions—nor, to be fair, was it intended to. It is wall-to-wall music. The movie sells well in home video form; it's a cinematic Top Forty with Jagger and the Stones performing many of their best-known hits. But after a certain point it grows monotonous. At the beginning of the film I was caught up in the Stones' waves of sound energy, and fascinated by Jagger's exhilarating, limitless onstage energy. By the end of the film I was simply stunned, and not even "(Can't Get No) Satisfaction" could quite rouse me.

The movie was directed by Hal Ashby, a feature director whose credits include *Shampoo* and *The Last Detail.* It was reportedly photographed with twenty-one cameras, under the direction of cinematographers Caleb Deschanel and Gerald Feil. They've got a lot of good stuff on film, but they haven't broken any new ground. The best rock documentary is still *Woodstock* (1970), and the best concert film is probably Bette Midler's *Divine Madness* (1980). The Stones have been filmed more powerfully before, too, in *Gimme Shelter,* the stunning 1969 documentary of the Stones' Altamont concert, at which a man was killed.

The worst passages in *Let's Spend the Night Together* are the songs in which Ashby and his collaborators try to get seriously symbolic. There is, for example, a montage of images from a suffering world: starving children, a Buddhist monk immolating himself, the skeleton-like bodies of famine victims, decapitated heads of political prisoners, etc. The idea, I guess, is to provide visual counterpoint to the Stones' apocalyptic images. The effect is disgusting; this particular movie has not earned the right to exploit those real images.

The best passages involve Jagger, who is just about the whole show, with the exception of a truncated Keith Richards solo and a strange interlude during which would-be beauty queens invade the stage and dance along to "Honky Tonk Woman." Jagger is, as always, the arrogant hermaphrodite, strutting proudly before his fans and conducting the songs, the band, and the audience with his perfectly timed body movements. There is an exciting moment when he climbs down into the crowd and, carrying a hand-held mike, sings as he is lifted on a surge of security guards from one side of the auditorium to another.

It's fun, but it's about the only time we see the audience in this movie; Ashby apparently made a directorial decision to keep the audience in long-shot, making them into a collective, pulsating mass. But that limits his possibilities for setting up visual rhythms in his editing. In such landmarks rock films as *A Hard Day's Night* (1964) and *Woodstock,* the audience provided not only counterpoint but also emotional feedback. *Let's Spend the Night Together* seems to have been pretty closely calculated as just simply the record of a performance, and if that's what you want, that's what you get.

Lianna ★ ★ ★ ½
R, 110 m., 1983

Linda Griffiths (Lianna), Jane Hallaren (Ruth), Jon DeVries (Dick), Jo Henderson (Sandy), John Sayles (Jerry). Directed by John Sayles. Produced by Jeffrey Nelson and Maggie Renzi. Screenplay by Sayles.

Movies are good at showing us people who make great changes in their lives, but not so good at showing us the consequences of those changes. It's easier to present the sudden dramatic revelation than to follow through into all the messy complications in everyday life. John Sayles's *Lianna,* the story of a woman who discovers in her early thirties that she is a lesbian, follows through. Instead of being the simple, dramatic story of a woman who "comes out," it is the complex, interesting story of what happens then.

The woman is named Lianna (Linda Griffiths). When she was an undergraduate, she fell in love with her teacher—a pattern she is about to repeat. Her husband is a film professor and the father of their two small children. He tends to treat her like one of the children, lecturing to the general audience at the dinner table as if his wife was about as bright as the kids. He is a boor. Lianna, unhappy, tries to change her life. She signs up for a night class in child psychology, and finds herself attracted to the professor, a woman who has a quick sense of humor and really seems to care about her students.

The woman, Ruth (Jane Hallaren), has

been a lesbian for years, and is attracted to Lianna. But it is Lianna who makes the first, subtle moves, staying after class for a moment's chat, just as perhaps she did years ago with her husband. The two women become lovers fairly quickly, and although there are love scenes, the movie is not really about that side of their relationship. If *Personal Best* was an exploration of the physical aspects of lesbianism, *Lianna* explores the consequences. They are many. Lianna's husband throws her out and tries to block access to their children. Lianna's oldest friend, Sandy, is suddenly cold and distant. Ruth, a little surprised at the intensity of the affair, confesses that she has a long-standing relationship with another woman in another city. Lianna rents a room off-campus and begins a life-style that is free, yes, but also lonely and filled with guilt.

As *Lianna* looks into the large and small things that have changed in the life of its heroine, we become increasingly aware of the perception of the filmmaker, John Sayles, who wrote, directed, and edited. In this movie and his previous work, *Return of the Secaucus Seven,* he seems in touch with the kinds of changes that some Americans in their thirties are going through; his movies are cinematic versions of Gail Sheehey's *Passages.* He is attentive to what is said, what is worn, what attitudes are taken, what goes unsaid—and he is particularly interested, in both movies, in the ways that a generation raised to "do your own thing" now tries to decide when personal freedom ends and responsibility begins.

It's in that particular area that *Lianna* is a little shaky. It never quite dealt, I thought, with the issue of Lianna's two children. Although Lianna's lover is a child psychologist and Lianna herself seems to be a responsible and loving mother as the film opens, the kids are sort of left hanging. There are a couple of brief scenes with the kids, but no real resolution of the questions that a newly gay mother would have to answer. (Since the husband is presented as such a twerp, this absence of follow through is doubly bothering.) Still, in many other scenes, including two in which Lianna has a subtly class-conscious affair with a woman in the armed services, *Lianna* is an intelligent, perceptive movie. And the performances, especially by Griffiths and Hallaren, are so specific that we're never looking at "lesbians"—only at people.

Light of Day ★ ★ ★ ½
PG-13, 107 m., 1987

Michael J. Fox (Joe Rasnick), Gena Rowlands (Jeanette Rasnick), Joan Jett (Patti Rasnick), Jason Miller (Ben Rasnick), Michael McKean (Bu Montgomery), Thomas G. Waites (Smittie), Cherry Jones (Cindy). Directed by Paul Schrader and produced by Rob Cohen and Keith Barish. Screenplay by Schrader.

Early in *Light of Day,* a brother and sister go to their mother's birthday dinner at their parents' home. The atmosphere is charged with tension. At the table, the father sits silently in the calm before the storm. The mother begins to ask the blessing, and then her prayer turns into something more specific: She begins to ask God to forgive her daughter.

All hell breaks loose. The daughter runs from the table, and the brother follows her out of the house, trying to make peace. We can see that the two women are bitter enemies, although the mother probably would not see it that way; she uses prayer as a weapon, just as much as her daughter uses alienation and aggression.

This scene sets up the emotional conflict in *Light of Day,* which shows a family tearing itself apart despite the best efforts of the son, who wants to hold things together at almost any cost. This is a family drama, all right—but not one of those neat docudramas in which every character comes attached to a fashionable problem, and all the problems are solved in the same happy ending. The family in *Light of Day* is more like your average everyday unhappy family, in which the biggest problem is that some of the members quite simply hate each other.

Writer-director Paul Schrader tells his story against a working-class background in Cleveland. The parents (Gena Rowlands and Jason Miller) have worked hard for their share of suburban respectability. The children (Michael J. Fox and Joan Jett) play every night in a rock band, and although Fox has a daytime job in a factory, Jett's life is on hold until the sun goes down; she says rock 'n' roll is the most important thing in the world, and she means it.

Because she means it, life is not very healthy for her little boy, a son born out of wedlock by a father she refuses to name. It is this child that has driven the wedge between mother and daughter. And soon it becomes the focus of her relationship with her brother. When their band goes on a tour—sometimes playing for no more than a few bucks and free drinks—the child is left in cheap motel rooms, and Fox doesn't approve of that. Jett, filled with anger and defiance, won't listen to his objections, and Fox stands by helplessly, trying to be all things to all people.

His family is clearly a matriarchy, a battleground between two strong women. The father, played by Miller as a sensitive wimp, has long since given up, and now Fox is trying to play the peacemaker, the responsible one, almost the parent. Fox obviously idolizes his sister (and, in a way, his mother), and so there are painful moments, very well acted, in which he hurts because he cannot help these people he loves.

The movie is subtle in its construction. Schrader doesn't telegraph his ending in the first half-hour, and indeed the movie's one fault is that it sometimes seems without a clear direction. At first the film seems to be a blue-collar story. Then a family drama. Then a rock 'n' roll movie. But then we see that the rock band is going nowhere, and the center of the story turns back to the family, after the mother becomes seriously ill. And it's the illness that provides the payoff, in strong and painful bedside scenes between Gena Rowlands, Fox, and Jett.

This mother may be sick, but she knows exactly what she's doing, and Rowlands's acting is powerfully, heartbreakingly effective. The mother uses love, truth, insight, and a measure of cynical calculation in an attempt to control what will happen to her family if she dies. She has always been a controller, and the possibility of death only inspires her to new efforts.

Light of Day is told like a short story by Henry James or Raymond Carver, in which the last few moments and the final words throw everything else into focus. And there is so much pain and anger in the film's ending that we can speculate that this is the real material that Schrader only touched on in *Hard Core,* his 1977 film about a runaway daughter's rebellion against her strict fundamentalist family.

Light of Day arrived with an advance reputation as a rock 'n' roll film, and yet Joan Jett, the movie's one certified rocker, gives the most surprisingly good performance. In the bedside scene with Rowlands, she is acting in the big leagues; Rowlands is inspired and Jett rises to the same inspiration, and there's a rare, powerful chemistry. Fox, playing a weak, conciliatory character, is the right balance for these two strong women, and Miller, kept in the background in most of his scenes, has one searching speech in which he tries to explain what has happened to his family.

Schrader has been one of the most consistently interesting writers and directors of the last decade. Try to find the thread connecting his screenplays, such as *Taxi Driver* and *Raging Bull,* and his films as a director, such as *Blue Collar, Hard Core, American Gigolo, Cat People,* and *Mishima,* and what you come up with are wildly different characters with one thing in common: Their pasts keep them imprisoned, and shut them off from happiness in the present. Here is his most direct and painful statement of that theme.

Like Father, Like Son ★
PG-13, 99 m., 1987

Dudley Moore (Dr. Jack Hammond), Kirk Cameron (Chris Hammond), Margaret Colin (Ginnie Armbruster), Catherine Hicks (Dr. Amy Larkin), Patrick O'Neal (Dr. Armbruster), Sean Astin (Trigger), Cami Cooper (Lori Beaumont), Bill Morrison (Uncle Earl). Directed by Rod Daniel and produced by Brian Grazer and David Valdes. Screenplay by Lorne Cameron and Steven L. Bloom.

Like Father, Like Son is one of the most desperate comedies I've ever seen, and no wonder. The movie's premise doesn't work—not at all, not even a little, not even part of the time—and that means everyone in the movie looks awkward and silly all of the time. This plays less like a movie than like a penalty for the losers on a game show.

The film stars Dudley Moore and Kirk Cameron as father and son. Moore is a surgeon, Cameron is a high school student. One day, Moore unknowingly puts a few drops of a rare Indian "mind transference" potion into his Bloody Mary, and he and his son exchange their conscious minds. The surgeon is inside the teen-age body, and the teen-ager is inside the surgeon—although Moore's body still speaks with a British accent, and Cameron's body still sounds like a Southern California kid. If that seems like a slight inconsistency, it's mere chaff in the wind compared to the *really* yawning logical gap that the movie tries to ignore.

See if you can follow this. When you take the magic potion and look at another person, you exchange consciousnesses with that other person. The characters know this at the time. Therefore, if they don't like being in each other's bodies, why don't they just have Cameron's body drink the liquid and look at Moore's body, and then there would be a second transfer of minds, and the movie would be over, and the lights would go on, and we could get up and leave, and our lifetimes would have been enriched by the availability of the ninety-nine minutes of time that this movie goes on to plunder? Questions like that are fruitless, I suppose. *Like Father, Like Son* is based on an Idiot Plot, in which everyone has to be an idiot or the problem would be solved and the movie would be over. Actually, if the movie were funny, it wouldn't matter about the Idiot Plot. But this movie is dismally, painfully, not funny. The screenplay by Lorne Cameron and Steven L. Bloom makes a crucial miscalculation. It thinks the mind-transfer gimmick *itself* is funny. It is not. It is only the peg on which to hang funny incidents, of which this movie has one.

I will name the movie's single funny incident, because, lord knows, we have time. It occurs when Moore's body, inhabited by a teen-ager, tries to smoke and chew gum at the same time during the hospital's board meeting. Dudley Moore is a master of small-scale physical comedy, and he handles this scene well. The movie gives him nothing else of interest to do. He's lucky. Kirk Cameron doesn't even get one good scene. Think of the endless inventions of the Steve Martin-Lily Tomlin mind-sharing comedy *All of Me*, and you'll see how much is missing here.

The ineptness of the director, Rod Daniel, is sort of stunning. Look at the way he sets up one scene after another and then can't find the laugh, the punch line, or even the end of the scene. There was comic potential in a scene where Moore (inside the kid) goes out on a date to a rock concert with a teen-age girl. But all the movie gives us is Moore complaining about how loud the music is, and taking the girl home early. Meanwhile, Cameron (inside Moore) is being seduced by a sexy older woman, and sets the sofa on fire. Anyone reading this review could have directed at least one of these scenes better than Rod Daniel.

Perhaps the most pathetic aspect of the movie is the way it tries to cross one genre with another, in a shameless appeal to everybody. Would you believe that this movie contains a complete high school comedy, right down to the bully who picks on the hero? Would you believe there is a chase scene? Would you believe Dudley Moore is made to do a rip-off of Tom Cruise's dancing-on-the-furniture scene from *Risky Business*? You would? Yeah. Me too.

Little Big Man ★ ★ ★ ★

PG, 157 m., 1971

Dustin Hoffman (Jack Crabb), Faye Dunaway (Mrs. Pendrake), Martin Balsam (Merriweather), Richard Mulligan (General Custer), Chief Dan George (Old Lodge Skins), Jeff Corey (Wild Bill Hickok). Directed by Arthur Penn and produced by Stuart Millar. Screenplay by Calder Willingham.

Arthur Penn's *Little Big Man* is an endlessly entertaining attempt to spin an epic in the form of a yarn. It mostly works. When it doesn't—when there's a failure of tone or an overdrawn caricature—it regroups cheerfully and plunges ahead. We're disposed to go along; all good storytellers tell stretchers once in a while, and circle back to be sure we got the good parts.

It is the very folksiness of Penn's film that makes it, finally, such a perceptive and important statement about Indians, the West, and the American dream. There's no stridency, no preaching, no deep-voiced narrators making sure we got the point of the last massacre. All the events happened long, long ago, and they're related by a 121-year-old man who just wants to pass the story along. The yarn is the most flexible of story forms. Its teller can pause to repeat a point; he can hurry ahead ten years; he can forget an entire epoch in remembering the legend of a single man. He doesn't capture the history of a time, but its flavor. *Little Big Man* gives us the flavor of the Cheyenne nation before white men brought uncivilization to the West. Its hero, played by Dustin Hoffman, is no hero at all but merely a survivor.

Hoffman, or Little Big Man, gets around pretty well. He touches all the bases of the Western myth. He was brought West as a settler, raised as a Cheyenne, tried his hand at gunfighting and medicine shows, scouted the cavalry, experimented with the hermit life, was married twice, survived Custer's Last Stand, and sat at the foot of an old man named Old Lodge Skins, who instructed him in the Cheyenne view of creation.

Old Lodge Skins played by Chief Dan George with such serenity and conviction that an Academy Award was mentioned, doesn't preach the Cheyenne philosophy. It is part of him. It's all the more a part of him because Penn has allowed the Indians in the film to speak ordinary, idiomatic English. Most movie Indians have had to express themselves with an "um" at the end of every other word: "Swap-um wampum plenty soon," etc. The Indians in *Little Big Man* have dialogue reflecting the idiomatic richness of Indian tongues; when Old Lodge Skins simply refers to Cheyennes as "the Human Beings," the phrase is literal and meaningful and we don't laugh.

Despite Old Lodge Skins, however, Little Big Man doesn't make it as an Indian, or as a white man, either, or as anything else he tries. He looks, listens, remembers, and survives, which is his function. The protagonists in the film are two ideas of civilization: the Indian's and the white man's. Custer stages his bloody massacres and is massacred in turn, and we know that the Indians will eventually be destroyed as an organic community and shunted off to reservations. But the film's movement is circular, and so is its belief about Indians.

Penn has adopted the yarn form for a reason. All the characters who appear in the early stages of the film come back in the later stages, fulfilled. The preacher's wife returns as a prostitute. The medicine-quack, already lacking an arm, loses a leg (physician, heal thyself). Wild Bill Hickok decays from a has-been to a freak show attraction. Custer fades from glory to madness. Only Old Lodge Skins makes it through to the end not merely intact, but improved.

His survival is reflected in the film's structure. Most films, especially ones with violence, have their climax at the end. Penn puts his near at the center; it is Custer's massacre of an Indian village, and Little Big Man sees his Indian wife killed and his baby's head blown off. Penn can control violence as well as any American director (remember *Bonnie and Clyde* and *The Left Handed Gun*). He does here. The final massacre of Custer and his men is deliberately muted, so it doesn't distract from Old Lodge Skins's "death" scene.

But Custer stays dead, and Old Lodge Skins doesn't quite die ("I was afraid it would turn out this way"). So he leaves the place of death and invites Little Big Man home to have something to eat. Custer's civilization will eventually win, but Old Lodge Skins's will prevail. William Faulkner observed in his Nobel Prize speech that man will probably endure—but will he prevail? It's probably no accident that we don't smile when Old Lodge Skins explains the difference between Custer and the Human Beings.

The Little Drummer Girl ★ ★

R, 155 m., 1984

Diane Keaton (Charlie), Yorgo Voyagis (Joseph), Klaus Kinski (Kurtz), Sami Frey (Khalil). Directed by George Roy Hill and produced by Robert L. Crawford. Screenplay by Loring Mandel.

The Little Drummer Girl lacks the two essential qualities it needs to work: It's not comprehensible, and it's not involving. They made a real effort to pull of the daunting task of filming John Le Carre's labyrinthine bestseller, but the movie doesn't work. It is so jammed with characters and incidents and mystifications that everything seems to get equal, cursory attention. And not a single one of the characters comes alive. Not Kurtz, the brusque, scarred, touchingly human chief of Israeli intelligence, who was my favorite character in the book. Not Charlie, the American actress who is recruited by the Israelis to play a dangerous double game with a Palestinian terrorist. And certainly not Joseph, the man who is delegated to make Charlie fall in love with him. Those three characters, Kurtz and Charlie especially, are among the most vivid creations in recent fiction. In this movie version they are pale shadows of the people I imagined as I was turning the pages.

At least I have the advantage of having read the novel. If you haven't read the book, I suspect that a lot of *The Little Drummer Girl* will escape you, unless you focus on every piece of information with unwavering attention. The book was long and complicated, weaving a story of intrigue, double-cross, and betrayal. The movie is relatively long, but not long enough to do justice to Le Carre's plot. What's amazing is how many plot details are in the movie. Most of the characters turn up (even such minor walk-ons as Charlie's agent and the fake Red Cross men), and most of the twists and turns of the events are here. But the movie maintains a breathless pace to squeeze everything in; at the end we're stunned with information, but not moved by emotion. There is no time to linger on the emotional significance of the story—and surely what distinguished the Le Carre book was the way it combined a topical thriller with a deeper appreciation of the human issues involved in the Middle East.

Because the screenplay doesn't really provide the characters with time and space to grow and breathe, it may be unfair to criticize the actors: How much can you do with the Cliff's Notes edition of a story? Nevertheless, the movie has crucial failures in the two key roles. Diane Keaton's Charlie is not young enough, passionate enough or, if I may say so, sluttish enough, to recapture the wild, sloppy character in Le Carre's book. And Klaus Kinski's performance as Kurtz seems intended for a standard thriller. There is no sense of the man's past, of his intelligence, of his torn emotions, of the doubts he has about the job that Charlie is being asked to do.

What would have helped? Maybe the director, George Roy Hill, could have pared the story down to one specific element, such as Charlie's recruitment, training, and mission. Maybe we didn't need the scenes involving the capture of the red Mercedes, or the surveillance in the town square, or the stuff about Charlie's theatrical career in London. Even then, we'd be left with performances that did not resonate. It's not that Keaton and Kinski are bad actors, just that they were miscast. Unfortunately, there has hardly been another novel in recent years for which the casting of the movie version was more crucial.

Little Nikita ★ 1/2

PG, 97 m., 1988 ✓

Sidney Poitier (Roy Parmenter), River Phoenix (Jeff Grant), Richard Jenkins (Richard Grant), Caroline Kava (Elizabeth Grant), Richard Bradford (Konstantin Karpov), Richard Lynch (Scuba). Directed by Richard Benjamin and produced by Harry Gittes. Screenplay by John Hill and Bo Goldman.

The most important thing to understand about *Little Nikita* is that it represents a package—a story contrived to appeal to adults and teen-agers at the same time. This kind of cross-generational formula has been responsible for all those recent movies where dads and their sons switch identities, and all those other movies where today's teen-agers travel back in time to visit their parents' generation in the 1950s.

But it's also at work in a movie like this, where middle-aged FBI agent Sidney Poitier costars with all-American teen-ager River Phoenix for no reason more compelling than their combined marquee appeal. A package like this looks okay on paper, but goes nowhere. It turns all the characters into chess pieces, whose relationships depend on the plot, not on human chemistry. Since the plot is absurdly illogical, you're not left with much. *Little Nikita* stars Poitier as an FBI man who is making a routine check on River Phoenix, who wants to attend a military academy. When the computer tells Poitier that Phoenix's parents are dead, he suspects something. So do I. I suspect that neither Poitier nor the makers of this film know how computers work. See if you can follow this. Poitier types in the name of the River Phoenix character, "Jeff Grant." The computer comes up with "Richard and Elizabeth Grant," his parents, who both died sometime in the nineteenth century. The computer blinks the words "Does Not Compute!" on the screen, while Poitier looks thoughtful and decides to investigate further. What about the possibility that there are *other* people named Richard and Elizabeth Grant?

No matter. The plot moves on, and we discover that the Grants (played by Richard

Jenkins and Caroline Kava) are actually Russian agents, trained to pass as Americans and sent to the United States to live in San Diego, operate a nursery business, raise their son, and pretend to be ordinary citizens until the KGB needs them. Young Jeff has never suspected, of course, that his parents are Russian spies, maybe because they're clever (although they keep their Russian passports in a bureau drawer).

The plot marches on. A Russian agent (Richard Bradford) is dispatched to San Diego to give the Grants their orders. If he was trained in disguises in the same school as the Grants, he must have flunked out. He enters America by crossing the border at Tijuana, wearing a heavy black overcoat and a black fedora, and sporting a thick Russian accent. He is about as inconspicuous as Mr. T.

Meanwhile (there are a lot of meanwhiles in this movie), Poitier moves into the house across the street from the Grant nursery, becomes friendly with the family, informs young Jeff that his parents are Russian spies, and otherwise ingratiates himself. Everything leads up to the single most unbelievable chain of coincidences in recent movie history, when the entire plot depends on all the key characters accidentally boarding the same trolley car.

Because *Little Nikita* is impossible to believe, impossible even to accept as a plausible fantasy, it is impossible to care about. As a general rule, a thriller must have some sort of interior consistency; if anything can happen, how can we feel any suspense about what does happen? The script for this film has been assembled by writers John Hill and Bo Goldman and director Richard Benjamin with such carelessness and cheerful indifference that the characters, like the audience, are reduced to simply hanging around to see what will happen next.

The Living Daylights ★ ★

PG, 130 m., 1987

Timothy Dalton (James Bond), Maryam d'Abo (Kara), Joe Don Baker (Whitaker), Art Malik (Kamran Shah), Jeroen Krabbe (Koskov), John Rhys-Davies (Pushkin). Directed by John Glen and produced by Albert R. Broccoli. Screenplay by Richard Maibaum and Michael S. Wilson.

The raw materials of the James Bond films are so familiar by now that the series can be revived only through an injection of humor. That is, unfortunately, the one area in which the new Bond, Timothy Dalton, seems to be deficient. He's a strong actor, he holds the screen well, he's good in the serious scenes, but he never quite seems to understand that it's all a joke.

The correct tone for the Bond films was established right at the start, with Sean Connery's quizzical eyebrows and sardonic smile. He understood that the Bond character was so preposterous that only lightheartedness could save him. The moment Bond began to act like a real man in a real world, all was lost. Roger Moore understood that, too, but I'm not sure Dalton does.

Dalton is rugged, dark, and saturnine, and speaks with a cool authority. We can halfway believe him in some of his scenes. And that's a problem, because the scenes are intended to be preposterous. The best Bond movies always seem to be putting us on, to be supplying the most implausible and dangerous stunts in order to assure us they can't possibly be real. But in *The Living Daylights*, there is a scene where Bond and his girlfriend escape danger by sliding down a snow-covered mountain in a cello case, and damned if Dalton doesn't look as if he thinks it's just barely possible.

The plot is the usual grab-bag of recent headlines and exotic locales. Bond, who is assigned to help a renegade Russian general defect to the West, stumbles across a plot involving a crooked American arms dealer, the war in Afghanistan, and a plan to smuggle a half-billion dollars worth of opium. The story takes Bond from London to Prague, from mountains to deserts, from a chase down the slopes of Gibraltar, to a fight that takes place while Bond and his enemy are hanging out of an airplane. The usual stuff.

One thing that isn't usual in this movie is Bond's sex life. No doubt because of the AIDS epidemic, Bond is not his usual promiscuous self, and he goes to bed with only one, perhaps two, women in this whole film (it depends on whether you count the title sequence, where he parachutes onto the boat of a woman in a bikini). This sort of personal restraint is admirable, coming from Bond, but given his past sexual history surely it is the woman, not Bond, who is at risk.

The key female character is Kara (Maryam d'Abo), the Russian cellist, who gets involved in the plot with the Russian general, tries to work against Bond, and eventually falls in love with him. As the only "Bond girl" in the movie, d'Abo has her assignment cut out for her, and unfortunately she's not equal to it. She doesn't have the charisma or the mystique to hold the screen with Bond (or Dalton) and is the least interesting love interest in any Bond film.

There's another problem. The Bond films succeed or fail on the basis of their villains, and Joe Don Baker, as the arms-dealing Whitaker, is not one of the great Bond villains. He's a kooky, phony general who plays with toy soldiers and never seems truly diabolical. Without a great Bond girl, a great villain, or a hero with a sense of humor, *The Living Daylights* belongs somewhere on the lower rungs of the Bond ladder. But there are some nice stunts.

Local Hero ★ ★ ★ ★
PG, 112 m., 1983

Burt Lancaster (Happer), Peter Riegert (Mac), Peter Capaldi (Danny), Fulton McKay (Ben), Denis Lawson (Urquhart). Directed by Bill Forsyth and produced by David Puttnam. Screenplay by Forsyth.

Here is a small film to treasure; a loving, funny, understated portrait of a small Scottish town and its encounter with a giant oil company. The town is tucked away in a sparkling little bay, and is so small that everybody is well aware of everybody else's foibles. The oil company is run by an eccentric billionaire (Burt Lancaster) who would really rather have a comet named after him than own all the oil in the world. And what could have been a standard plot about conglomerates and ecology, etc., turns instead into a wicked study of human nature.

Ahe movie opens in Houston, but quickly moves to the fishing village of Ferness. The oil company assigns an earnest young American (Peter Riegert) and a whimsical Scot (Peter Capaldi) to go to Ferness, and buy it up, lock, stock, and beachline, for a North Sea oil-refining complex. This is a simpler job than it appears, since a lot of the locals are all too willing to soak the oil company for its millions of dollars, sell the beach, and go in search of the bright lights of Edinburgh. But there are complications. One of them is old Ben, the cheerful philosopher who lives in a shack on the beach. It turns out that the beach has been the legal property of Ben's family for four centuries, ever since an ancestor did a favor for the king. And Ben doesn't want to sell: "Who'd look after the beach then? It would go to pieces in a short matter of time."

The local negotiations are handled by the innkeeper, Urquhart (Denis Lawson). He also is the accountant, and sort of the mayor, I guess, and is so much in love with his pretty wife that they're forever dashing upstairs for a quickie. Meanwhile, Riegert and Capaldi fall under the spell of the town, settle into its rhythms, become wrapped up in its intrigues, and, in general, are co-opted by a place whose charms are seductive.

What makes this material really work is the low-key approach of the writer-director, Bill Forsyth, who also made the charming *Gregory's Girl* and has the patience to let his characters gradually reveal themselves to the camera. He never hurries, and as a result, *Local Hero* never drags: Nothing is more absorbing than human personalities, developed with love and humor. Some of the payoffs in this film are sly and subtle, and others generate big laughs. Forsyth's big scenes are his little ones, including a heartfelt, whiskey-soaked talk between the American and the innkeeper, and a scene where the visitors walk on the beach and talk about the meaning of life. By the time Burt Lancaster reappears at the end of the film, to personally handle the negotiations with old Ben, *Local Hero* could hardly have anything but a happy ending. But it's a fairly close call.

Lone Wolf McQuade ★ ★ ★ ½
107 m., 1983

Chuck Norris (J.J. McQuade), David Carradine (Rawley), Barbara Carrera (Lola), Robert Beltran (Kayo Ramas), Sharon Farrell (Molly), Leon Isaac Kennedy (Jackson). Directed by Steve Carver.

To really understand *Lone Wolf McQuade*, you have to go back to those original spaghetti Westerns that made Clint Eastwood a star. They weren't great movies, and some critics attacked them for trashing the classic forms of the Western. But they had presence, style, and energy, and at the center of them they had a perfectly realized hero in Clint Eastwood. He was called The Man With No Name. He dealt violence with implacable fury. He stood at the middle of the maelstrom and remained untouched. And, in his own way, he was powerfully charismatic. Eastwood and Sergio Leone, his director, created a new kind of Western, pared down to its bare essentials of men and guns, horses and deserts, sweat and flies, and rotgut.

Now comes Chuck Norris. He's been in a series of karate and kung fu movies that were almost always better than average—but not a lot better than average. (The best of them was *Eye for an Eye,* directed by Steve Carver, who also directed *McQuade.*) The most you could say for a Chuck Norris film was that it did not have downright contempt for its action audiences; it tried to be better than the interchangeable chop-socky movies from Hong Kong, and Norris made an energetic, likable star. What Norris was really looking for in all those pictures, I guess, was the right character. Like Eastwood's Man With No Name, he needed a personality that would fit, that would contain his kung fu skills and allow him ways of expression not limited to flying fists and deadly elbows. That's what he's found in *Lone Wolf McQuade.*

This is an action movie. It makes no apology for that. But it's high-style action. Norris plays J.J. McQuade, a renegade modern-day Texas Ranger who walks alone, likes to work with machine guns, deals out justice on the spot, and hardly ever says much of anything. The movie surrounds him with a gallery of interesting characters, played by colorful stars: David Carradine is Rawley, the evil local criminal and karate master; Barbara Carrera is lovely, as usual, as Carradine's wife and Norris's mistress; Robert Beltran plays Kaya Ramas, Norris's Mexican-American sidekick; Leon Issac Kennedy is the federal officer; grizzled L.Q. Jones lopes through a few scenes; and Sharon Farrell is counterpoint as Norris's former wife. All of these people are thrown together into a plot that is, of course, essentially meaningless. But the movie respects the plot, and keeps it moving, and a lot of excitement is generated.

Series characters always have one archetypal scene. With Eastwood, it was the time he killed three men with one bullet. Lone Wolf McQuade has a classic. He's shot. They think he's dead. They bury him in his supercharged, customized pickup truck. He comes to. Pours a beer over his head. Floors the accelerator and drives that mother right out of the grave. You get the idea.

The Lonely Guy ★ 1/2

R, 91 m., 1984

Steve Martin (Larry), Charles Grodin (Warren), Judith Ivey (Iris), Steve Lawrence (Jack), Robyn Douglass (Danielle), Dr. Joyce Brothers (Herself). Directed and produced by Arthur Hiller. Screenplay by Ed Weinberger and Stan Daniels.

I saw *The Lonely Guy* all by myself. It was one of those Saturday afternoons where the snow is coming down gray and mean, and you can't even get a decent recorded message on the answering machines of strangers.

There was a warm glow coming out of the windows of a tanning parlor. At a table in the window of a hot dog joint, three bums were laughing warmly, sharing a joke and a cup of coffee. I stuck my hands down deep into the pockets of my jeans and hunched my shoulders against the cold. I tried to force a smile to my frozen lips: Hey, I was going to the movies!

I walked up to the ticket booth of the Esquire theater and with a flourish presented my Plitt Theaters pass.

"What's this?" asked the ticket person.

"A pass to the Plitt Theaters," I said.

"I don't know," the person said. "I'll have to phone and check it out." I turned my back to the wind until the pass was verified, and then walked into the theater's priceless and irreplaceable Art Deco lobby, which cheered me somewhat.

"It's a shame they're tearing this theatre down," said a young woman to her date, as they swept past me on their way to the street. I ordered a box of popcorn, and went into the theater.

"Good luck," an usher told me. "You're going to need it."

He was right. *The Lonely Guy* is the kind of movie that seems to have been made to play in empty theaters on overcast January afternoons. It stars Steve Martin, an actor who inspires in me the same feelings that fingernails on blackboards inspire in other people. He plays a lonely guy. His girl leaves him, and he keeps losing the phone number of the only girl in New York who will talk to him. This could have been fun, if the movie were only a little more upbeat about his loneliness. But it isn't. *The Lonely Guy* is a dreary slog through morose situations, made all the worse by Martin's deadpan delivery, his slightly off-balance sense of timing, and his ability to make you cringe with his self-debasing smarminess. In a movie crawling with bad scenes, the worst is probably the bedroom scene with Iris (Judith Ivey), the above-mentioned only girl in New York who will talk to him. She has never had an orgasm. He convinces her that she will have an orgasm every time he sneezes. She fakes it by screaming "gesundheit!"

The Lonely Guy is the kind of movie that inspires you to distract yourself by counting the commercial products visible on the screen, and speculating about whether their manufacturers paid fees to have them worked into the movie. I counted two Diet 7-Ups, two Tabs, and Steve Martin.

The Lonely Passion of Judith Hearne

★ ★ ★

R, 110 m., 1988 ✓

Maggie Smith (Judith Hearne), Bob Hoskins (James Madden), Wendy Hiller (Aunt D'Arcy), Marie Kean (Mrs. Rice), Ian McNeice (Bernard), Alan Devlin (Father Quigley), Rudi Davies (Mary). Directed by Jack Clayton and produced by Peter Nelson and Richard Johnson. Screenplay by Nelson.

The most intimate moment in *The Lonely Passion of Judith Hearne* is one played between the heroine and a bottle of whiskey. She retreats to her lonely room in a sad Dublin boardinghouse and locks the door, then runs to her closet and finds the bottle where it has been hidden away during all the recent days of happiness, waiting quietly until she would need it again. She pours the drink quickly, and then all is chaos once again in her life, as we sense it has been so many times before.

Maggie Smith brings precise body language to this scene. She does not play it eagerly, or desperately, but with well-rehearsed precision, showing us that for the alcoholic Miss Hearne, this is a ritual. Smith's goal in the scene is to show us, without telling us, that this is not the first time Judith Hearne has admitted despair. And as the whiskey takes hold and the lonely spinster begins to sing to herself, her boozy joy is all the more depressing because it comes from defeat, not victory.

The realities of Miss Hearne's life are made clear a little at a time. She is poor, but respectable. She lives in rooming houses. She has few friends, and the family she is closest to tolerates her out of pity. She gives piano lessons, and dreams that some day a white knight will come riding out of the mist—a man to sweep her off her feet and make everything right again. In this dream she is frequently disappointed, and then the bottle comes out of the closet and her downward spiral continues. Since the only apparent joy in her life comes from drunkenness, there is even the possibility that she sets up her own failures—to give herself an excuse to drink.

This time, though . . . this time may be different. As *The Lonely Passion of Judith Hearne* opens, she has moved into another boardinghouse, and at breakfast she meets the brother of the landlady. His name is James (Bob Hoskins), and he has just come back from spending many years in America. She thinks America must be a wonderful place, and before long she thinks James must be a wonderful person. He seems lonely, too, and after some shy verbal sparring they go to Mass together and to the picture show.

Eventually it becomes clear that James is interested in Judith primarily for the money he thinks she must have—money she might invest in his own dream of an American-style hot dog stand, to cater to all the Yankee tourists in Dublin. There is even talk of marriage between the two people, before Judith finally sees through to James's real motives. Then she gets drunk, of course, but that is not the end of the movie, only the midpoint, because then James must question his own motives.

We sense that this sort of scenario has repeated itself, in one version or another, for many years in Judith Hearne's life. But since James is, in some ways, her last chance, the cruelty of his betrayal hits her harder and almost destroys her. And her suffering leads up to a crucial scene in which she is at last able to tell James, and herself, the exact reality of her life. The movie implies that by seeing herself clearly, she can begin to mend.

For Maggie Smith, the movie is a triumph, a performance to compare with *The Prime of Miss Jean Brodie* of twenty years ago. Bob Hoskins is very good, too, but his character is less clearly seen, and it might have been wise for the screenplay to make his actual feelings for Judith Hearne more clear. The movie's ending is courageous and moving, I suppose, but since it deals more with Judith's fate than with her drinking, it rather evades the issue. Courage and clarity will not heal Judith unless they come after sobriety—without which, for her, even the best intentions will end with another ritualistic search for the bottle in the back of the closet.

The Long Good Friday ★ ★ ★ ★

R, 118 m., 1982

Bob Hoskins (Harold Shand), Helen Mirrin (Victoria), Eddie Constantine (Charlie), Derek Thompson (Jeff), Bryan Marshall (Harris), Paul Freeman (Collin). Directed by John Mackenzie and produced by Barry Hanson. Screenplay by Barrie Keeffe.

Harold is as hard as a rock and he will crush you. He runs the London docks and he wants to put together the biggest real estate deal in Europe. He has Mafia money from America and the tacit cooperation of the London criminal organization. He's short, barrel-chested, with his thinning hair combed forward above a round face and teeth that always seem to be grinding. He cannot believe that in one weekend his whole world can come apart. Harold Shand is a hood, but he lives in a penthouse, anchors a world-class yacht in the Thames, has the love of an intelligent and tactful mistress and talks obsessively about the ten years of peace he has helped negotiate in the London underground. Then a bomb blows up his Rolls Royce, killing his chauffeur. Another bomb demolishes the lovingly restored landmark pub he owns. A third bomb is found inside Harold's Mayfair casino, but fails to detonate. Who is after him? Who is his enemy? And why has the enemy chosen this worst of all possible times to come after him—the Easter weekend when an American Mafioso is in town to consider investing millions in his real estate project?

The Long Good Friday, which is a masterful and very tough piece of filmmaking, eventually does answer these questions. But the point of the film isn't to analyze Harold Shand's problems. It's to present a portrait of this man. And I have rarely seen a movie character so completely alive. Shand is an evil, cruel, sadistic man. But he's a mass of contradictions, and there are times when we understand him so completely we almost feel affectionate. He's such a character, such an overcompensating Cockney, sensitive to the slightest affront, able to strike fear in the hearts of killers, but a pushover when his mistress raises her voice to him. Shand is played by a compact, muscular actor named Bob Hoskins, in the most-praised film performance of the year from England. Hoskins has the energy and the freshness of a younger Michael Caine, if not the good looks, of course. There are scenes where he hangs his enemies upside down from meat hooks and questions them about the bombings, and other scenes, moments later, where he solemnly kids with the neighborhood juvenile delinquents and tries to soft-talk the American out of his millions.

He's an operator. He's a con man who has muscled his way to the top by knowing exactly how things work and what buttons to push, and now here he is, impotent before this faceless enemy. *The Long Good Friday* tells his story in a rather indirect way, opening with a montage of seemingly unrelated events, held together by a hypnotic music theme. Everything is eventually explained. It's all a big misunderstanding, based on stupid decisions taken by Shand's underlings and misinterpreted by the IRA. But although we know the real story, and Harold Shand does, the IRA never does—and the movie's final shots are, quite simply, extraordinary close-ups, held for a long time, of Shand's ratlike face in close-up, as his eyes shift from side to side, and his mouth breaks into a terrified grin, and he realizes how it feels to get a dose of his own medicine. This movie is one amazing piece of work, not only for the Hoskins performance but also for the energy of the filmmaking, the power of the music, and, oddly enough, for the engaging quality of its sometimes very violent sense of humor.

The Long Goodbye ★ ★ ★
R, 112 m., 1973

Elliott Gould (Philip Marlowe), Nina van Pallandt (Eileen Wade), Sterling Hayden (Roger Wade), Mark Rydell (Marty Augustine), Henry Gibson (Dr. Verringer), David Arkin (Harry). Directed by Robert Altman and produced by Elliott Kastner. Screenplay by Leigh Brackett.

Robert Altman's *The Long Goodbye* attempts to do a very interesting thing. It tries to be all genre and no story, and it almost works. It makes no serious effort to reproduce the Raymond Chandler detective novel it's based on; instead, it just takes all the characters out of that novel and lets them stew together in something that feels like a private-eye movie.

The private eye is, I suppose, a fairly obsolete institution in our society. I'm not talking about the divorce case specialists and the missing persons guys; I'm thinking of the Chandler, Dashiell Hammett, Ross MacDonald kind of hired eye whose occupation takes him into glamorous danger and who subscribes to a weary private credo. The private eye as a fiction device was essentially a way to open doors; the best novels of Chandler and the others are simply hooks for a cynical morality.

Altman seems to understand this. He knows we don't care any more about the plot than he does; he agrees with Hitchcock that it doesn't even matter what the plot is about (as long as it's something). The important thing is the way the characters spar with each other. But Altman has added a twist: Instead of making his private eye into a cool, competent professional, he makes him into a 1950s anachronism. Philip Marlowe has been in a lot of movies, but never one in which he was more confused than he is in this one.

The story, or whatever you want to call it, involves a murder, a missing person, and an alcoholic writer with a bewitching blonde wife. There are also some gangsters and a cat. The writer and his wife are played with really fine style by Sterling Hayden and Nina van Pallandt—who not only demonstrates that she can act, but also that a real woman is infinitely more interesting on the screen than some starlet beauty-school graduate who should be leading the pompon team.

The middle of this mess is inhabited by Elliott Gould, as the chain-smoking, mumbling, disorganized Marlowe. It's a good performance, particularly the virtuoso ten-minute stretch at the beginning of the movie when he goes out to buy food for his cat. Gould has enough of the paranoid in his acting style to really put over Altman's revised view of the private eye.

Altman doesn't string his scenes together to tell a taut story, but he directs each scene as if he were. There's an especially memorable scene involving Philip Marlowe and a gangster (played by Mark Rydell, who is usually a director). The gangster smacks his girlfriend with a pop bottle and then snarls at Marlowe: "Now that's someone I *love.* Think what could happen to you." The scene sounds rather grim in print, I know, but in the movie it has a kind of hard-boiled desperation to it. It feels like it belongs in a private eye's life and so does the whole movie—right up to the ending, which is really off the wall.

Looking for Mr. Goodbar ★ ★ ★
R, 136 m., 1977

Diane Keaton (Theresa), Tuesday Weld (Katherine), William Atherton (James), Richard Kiley (Mr. Dunn), Richard Gere (Tony), Alan Feinstein (Martin), Tom Berenger (Gary), Priscilla Pointer (Mrs. Dunn). Directed by Richard Brooks and produced by Freddie Fields. Screenplay by Brooks.

There's one crucial thing that *Looking for Mr. Goodbar* doesn't make clear: Just because you find Mr. Goodbar doesn't necessarily mean you were looking for him. The heroine of Judith Rossner's bestseller *was* looking. Theresa was turned on to a particular flavor of self-destructive sexual experience, one involving possible danger to herself, and she played a role in bringing about her own death.

In Richard Brooks's film version, that masochistic impulse isn't considered as openly. He gives us a Theresa who drinks too much, sleeps around too much, and takes too many drugs—but she seems more of a hedonist than a masochist. She's looking for a combination of good times, good sex, and a father figure, for psychological reasons the movie makes all too abundantly clear. But she isn't looking for danger, mistreatment, or death. Maybe Brooks thought audiences would find Rossner's masochistic heroine too hard to understand. He has rewritten the story, in any event, into a cautionary lesson: Promiscuous young women who frequent pick-up bars and go home with strangers are likely to get into trouble.

Brooks hasn't improved the story by changing its focus, and he's distracted from the heart of the narrative by several unnecessary scenes. Theresa's fantasies, for example, are handled in ways that annoy viewers more than they intrigue them. And her home life—its broadly painted Freudian details right out of soap operas—could have just simply been dropped.

But, all the same, Brooks hasn't directed a bad picture. *Looking for Mr. Goodbar* is very much worth seeing, particularly for the Diane Keaton performance. And it's not fair to praise her while damning Brooks (as so many critics have done). Brooks and Keaton must have worked together to create such a great performance; it's just a shame that it's surrounded by perhaps half an hour of material that only distracts.

The performance creates a character who would have been unthinkable in the movies of thirty years ago: A young woman who spends her days teaching first grade to a classroom of deaf-mutes and her nights making herself available in singles bars. Women weren't allowed to be that complicated in the "women's pictures" that *Mr. Goodbar* has come such a long way from. They were ladies or they were tramps. Now they're allowed to be both, which has done wonders for the quality of the tramps you meet these days.

Diane Keaton suggests the motivation for her character almost independently from all those heavy-handed scenes in which her father stomps around the living room, and we get flashbacks of her tragic childhood. She suggests that Theresa is driven by a need to communicate on her own terms—and that those terms require her to have an advantage. She's great in a classroom of deaf-mutes, and great, too, with the men she picks up—men who are inarticulate because of insecurity, cultural short-changing, or too much booze. She delights in working people over verbally—in kidding them, mocking them, putting them down, playing games with them. On the physical level, though, she needs constant reassurance.

This Theresa is a different woman from the Judith Rossner character, but she's an interesting one. And Keaton plays her wonderfully, with a light touch you'd think would be impossible with this material. She's always moving. She choreographs every situation, and only eventually do we realize she's dancing out of the way. Her voice is liquid and funny, tossing off asides because they cut more deeply that way. The performance and the character are fully realized, even in this movie that finds room for so many loose ends and dead ends.

Then there's that ending that bothers me. On a New Year's Eve, she makes a fatal decision in choosing the next guy she's going to take home. *We* know she's made the wrong decision because Brooks abandons her point of view to show us a scene in which the guy is established as unbalanced and hostile. But she doesn't know that and gets killed because she doesn't. Her lack of knowledge is exactly the issue here: In the book, Theresa might have picked up the guy *because* she knew he'd be trouble.

What we get (and I quote from someone walking out of the screening ahead of me) is "another one of those movies that are supposed to be all filled with significance because the person gets killed at the end." What we might have gotten is a movie about a character obsessed, and fascinated, by what the end might be. Even a movie about how she got to be that way.

The Lords of Discipline ★ ★

R, 103 m., 1983

David Keith (Will), Robert Prosky (Bear), G.D. Spradlin (General Durrell), Barbara Babcock (Abigail), Michael Biehn (Alexander), Rick Rossovich (Pig), Mark Breland (Pearce). Directed by Frank Roddam and produced by Herb Jaffe and Gabriel Katzka. Screenplay by Thomas Pope and Loyd Fonvielle.

I knew the military school in *Taps* (1981) was a fiction, but I didn't mind, because it was a fiction that worked to support a group of compelling characters. I also know that the military school in *The Lords of Discipline* is a fiction, and this time I *do* mind, because the whole function of the school here is to provide a framework for a nasty, cruel little thriller.

The movie takes place in the South, in the mid-1960s. A famous private military academy is struggling to haul itself into the twentieth century. A few cadets have been admitted who "don't belong," including a kid too gauche to fit in with the polished cadets, and another kid who is the school's first black. The story is told mostly through the eyes of one cadet who stands up for the underdogs. He's played by David Keith, who was the naval officer's candidate who hanged himself in *An Officer and a Gentleman.*

The school is a little odd. Although it has a magnificent, galleried library (where secret notes are hidden in the pages of Spengler's *The Decline of the West*), it apparently has no classrooms, no academic program, and no faculty members except two: the school's president, a slimy retired general (G.D. Spradlin), and a crusty old colonel named Bear (Robert Prosky), who lights a cigar every time he has anything to say. Keith is elected head of the cadet corps and determines to protect the rights of the misfit and the black. But then he begins to hear about a mysterious organization named "The Ten," a secret society within the school; its origins lost in the mists of time, its duty to "protect" the school's sacred honor against contamination by undesirable elements. Before long, it's Keith against "The Ten."

The Lords of Discipline starts out fairly well, and David Keith and the other actors in the movie are good, convincing performers. So it's only gradually that we realize the movie is essentially a ridiculous revenge melodrama. There's a scene where a cadet plunges to his death from the top of a school building, but that's nothing compared to the really creepy scenes where the black student is cut with a razor blade, attacked in a shower, and finally—in an offensively gratuitous scene—kidnapped, held in an old plantation, and tortured with electrical charges to his genitals. There's a funny thing about the way the movie handles that scene. David Keith tracks down the kidnappers, looks in a window, sees the electrical shock torture, sees the masked members of "The Ten" pour gasoline over the helpless student, sees them set a rag on fire and dangle it over him, watches all that happen, and *then* tries to stop the torture. Why didn't he act sooner? I'm afraid the answer, a sick one, is that the movie was so happy to linger over the scene that it didn't want to interrupt the sadism with a quick rescue. This is not a nice movie.

The Lost Boys ★ ★ ½

R, 97 m., 1987

Jason Patric (Michael), Corey Haim (Sam), Dianne Wiest (Lucy), Barnard Hughes (Grandpa), Ed Herrmann (Max), Kiefer Sutherland (David), Jami Gertz (Star), Corey Feldman (Edgar Frog), Jamison Newlander (Alan Frog). Directed by Joel Schumacher and produced by Harvey Bernhard. Screenplay by Janice Fischer, James Jeremias, and Jeffrey Boam.

The Lost Boys in this movie are vampires, teen-age vampires, and of course there is a lost girl, too, but why mention her? They hang from the ceiling of their lair, in the ruins of an old hotel, and at night they go out to cruise the boardwalk of Santa Cruz, Mass Murder Capital of the World. When a new kid moves to town, the lost boys look threatening but the lost girl looks just great.

From this beginning, Joel Schumacher has devised an ambitious entertainment that starts out well but ends up selling its soul. There is a moment, early in this film, when it seems to have a handle on its characters and the after-dark teen-age world they inhabit. But the ending of the film is just another one of those by-the-numbers action climaxes, in which the movie is over when all the bad guys are dead. Has there been an action thriller recently in which the last twenty minutes weren't phoned in from the depository of bankrupt clichés?

The movie stars Jason Patric as Michael, a bright kid who moves to town with his widowed mother (Dianne Wiest) and little brother. Right away he meets a nice local man (Edward Herrmann), who comes calling on his mother. Before long he sees the great-looking girl (Jami Gertz), and not long after he sees the pack of lost boys, led by Kiefer Sutherland. The girl invites him to join them.

The Frog Brothers try to warn him. They're a couple of bright kids who run a comic book store on the carnival boardwalk. They give him a couple of comic books about vampires, and offer their services if any vampires need to be killed, but Michael doesn't believe in vampires and doesn't make the connection until it's too late.

At about this point, the movie feels like it's going somewhere. But then the plot starts getting very complicated, with the adult romance between Wiest and Herrmann and the teen-age romance between Patric and Gertz, and the vampire intrigues of Sutherland. Because everything looks so good (the movie was photographed in rich dark colors by Michael Chapman), we almost give it the benefit of the doubt: The high quality of the photography and acting had me wondering if perhaps this wouldn't develop into a genuinely frightening and interesting vampire story. But no such luck. It is no longer a virtue in mainstream Hollywood to bring any genuine, unsettling imagination to a commercial movie.

If you really stop to think about it, a bunch of vampire teen-agers would be a terrible shame, a tragedy, a heartbreaking loss of innocence for them, let alone their victims. Am I silly to take them seriously? Maybe so. The movie doesn't. It lacks the sense of dread that creeps out from the pages of a novel like Anne Rice's *Interviews with the Vampire*, and substitutes instead the same old cornball, predictable action climax, everybody chasing everybody around with lots of screams and special effects gore. Sometimes I think modern advances in special effects technology can be directly blamed for the collapse of original screenwriting.

There's some good stuff in the movie, including a cast that's good right down the line, and a willingness to have some fun with teen-age culture in the Mass Murder Capital. But when everything is all over there's nothing to leave with, no real horrors, no real dread, no real imagination. Just technique at the service of formula.

Lost in America ★ ★ ★ ★

R, 90 m., 1985

Albert Brooks (David Howard), Julie Hagerty (Linda Howard), Garry K. Marshall (Casino Boss), Art Frankel (Job Counselor). Directed by Albert Brooks and produced by Marty Katz. Screenplay by Brooks and Monica Johnson.

Every time I see a Winnebago motor home, I have the same fantasy as the hero of *Lost in America*. In my dream, I quit my job, sell everything I own, buy the Winnebago, and hit the open road. Where do I go? Look for me in the weather reports. I'll be parked by the side of a mountain stream, listening to Mozart on compact discs. All I'll need is a wok and a paperback.

In *Lost in America*, Albert Brooks plays an advertising executive in his thirties who realizes that dream. He leaves his job, talks his wife into quitting hers, and they point their Winnebago down that long, lonesome highway. This is not, however, a remake of *The Long, Long Trailer.* Brooks puts a different spin on things. For example, when movie characters leave their jobs, it's usually because they've been fired, they've decided to take an ethical stand, or the company has gone broke. Only in a movie by Brooks would the hero quit to protest a "lateral transfer" to New York. There's something intrinsically comic about that: He's taking a stand, all right, but it's a narcissistic one. He's quitting because he wants to stay in Los Angeles, he thinks he deserves to be named vice president, and he doesn't like the traffic in New York.

Lost in America is being called a yuppie comedy, but it's really about the much more universal subjects of greed, hedonism, and panic. What makes it so funny is how much we can identify with it. Brooks plays a character who is making a lot of money, but not enough; who lives in a big house, but is outgrowing it; who drives an expensive car, but not a Mercedes-Benz; who is a top executive, but not a vice president. In short, he is a desperate man, trapped by his own expectations.

On the morning of his last day at work, he puts everything on hold while he has a long, luxurious telephone conversation with a Mercedes dealer. Brooks has great telephone scenes in all of his movies, but this one perfectly captures the nuances of consumerism. He asks how much the car will cost—including *everything.* Dealer prep, license, sticker, add-ons, extras, *everything.* The dealer names a price.

"That's *everything?*" Brooks asks.

"Except leather," the dealer says.

"For what I'm paying, I don't get leather?" Brooks asks, aghast.

"You get Mercedes leather."

"*Mercedes* leather? What's that?"

"Thick vinyl."

This is the kind of world Brooks is up against. A few minutes later, he's called into the boss's office and told that he will not get the promotion he thinks he deserves. Instead, he's going to New York to handle the Ford account. Brooks quits, and a few scenes later, he and his wife (Julie Hagerty) are tooling the big Winnebago into Las Vegas. They have enough money, he conservatively estimates, to stay on the road for the rest of their lives. That's before she loses their nest egg at the roulette tables.

Lost in America doesn't tell a story so much as assemble a series of self-contained comic scenes, and the movie's next scene is probably the best one in the movie. Brooks the adman tries to talk a casino owner (Garry K. Marshall) into giving back the money. It doesn't work, but Brooks keeps pushing, trying to sell the casino on improving its image ("I'm a high-paid advertising consultant. These are professional opinions you're getting.") There are other great scenes, as the desperate couple tries to find work to support themselves: An interview with an unemployment counselor, who listens, baffled, to Brooks explaining why he left a $100,000-a-year job because he couldn't "find himself." And Brooks's wife introducing her new boss, a teen-age boy.

Lost in America has one strange flaw. It doesn't seem to come to a conclusion. It just sort of ends in midstream, as if the final scenes were never shot. I don't know if that's the actual case, but I do wish the movie had been longer and had arrived at some sort of final destination. What we do get, however, is observant and very funny. Brooks is especially good at hearing exactly how people talk, and how that reveals things about themselves. Take that line about "Mercedes leather." A lot of people would be very happy to sit on "Mercedes leather." But not a Mercedes owner, of course. How did Joni Mitchell put it? "Don't it always seem to go, that you don't know what you've got, till it's gone."

Louie Bluie ★ ★ ★ ½

NO MPAA RATING, 75 m., 1985

A documentary featuring Howard Armstrong and Ted Bogan. Directed and produced by Terry Zwigoff.

It was back in 1970 when the Earl called me up and said I should be at his bar on Monday night because he had something special, a band called Martin, Bogan, and the Armstrongs. "Don't ask any questions," he said. "Just be here." I was there, and I returned week after week for more than a year, along with a loyal cult who packed the place.

Martin, Bogan, and one of the Armstrongs were black men in their sixties and seventies (the other Armstrong, a son, played bass). They looked like a blues band, but they didn't play the blues, and in fact it was hard to figure out exactly what they did play. They did all the Mills Brothers standards, such as "Lazy River" and "Paper Doll," and they sang "Lady Be Good" and an unprintable version of "Sweet Georgia Brown." Howard Armstrong stood up and did fiddle solos on songs such as "Turkey in the Straw," and brought the house down.

Sixteen years later, those Monday sessions blur into a smoky series of hot summer nights when the sweet lyrics of Armstrong's fiddle danced above Martin's guitar and Bogan's mandolin, and they took turns on the vocals, including Martin's composition of "The Barnyard Dance" and Armstrong's pseudo-Hawaiian love songs. Toward the end of the evening, Ted Bogan would sing "Summertime" with such unadorned purity that you knew, quite simply, that you would never, ever, hear that great song sung better by anyone, anywhere.

Martin, Bogan, and the Armstrongs stopped playing together in the mid-1970s, and a few years later the Earl of Old Town closed its doors. When I would run into Earl Pionke, I would ask him about them and he would have vague reports that they were in Detroit, or Tennessee. Then word came that Carl Martin, who always scowled the fiercest when he was singing the funniest lyrics, had died.

And that was the situation when I went to the 1985 Telluride Film Festival, up in the San Juan range of the Rockies, and there on Main Street I saw Howard Armstrong with his beret and all that hip jewelry around his neck, checking out the scene and giving free advice to Ted Bogan, who was nodding and not listening, just like he always did when Armstrong talked to him during the sets at the Earl.

The story of how they got to Telluride is an

amazing one, and it explains the existence of *Louie Bluie*, an equally amazing music documentary film.

Terry Zwigoff, a music lover who went on to produce and direct *Louie Bluie*, was an avid collector of old jazz and blues recordings. He liked the sound on an old 1930s disc that was by somebody named Louie Bluie who never recorded before or since, and after years of searching he found out that Louie Bluie was Howard Armstrong, and his group, one of the first (and now one of the last) of the traditional black string bands, was still around.

Zwigoff tracked down Armstrong, who had moved to Detroit, and talked Armstrong and Bogan into appearing in a film, and *Louie Bluie* is that film, filled with music and life and humor, but also with an extraordinary portrait of Howard Armstrong, who is an artist, poet, composer, violin virtuoso, storyteller, and tireless womanizer (according to many of his stories).

The movie is loose and disjointed, and makes little effort to be a documentary about anything. Mostly, it just follows Armstrong around as he plays music with Bogan, visits his Tennessee childhood home, and philosophizes on music, love, and life. The film occasionally turns to the pages of the semi-pornographic journals Armstrong has kept through the years, filled with lurid cartoons and bawdy poems and his observations of life. Armstrong is a natural artist, and he remembers making his first colors out of dyes wrung out of crepe paper.

There is a lot of music in the movie, including some I could do without. (Armstrong likes his Hawaiian and German songs much better than I do.) There is also an enigma to consider: the relationship of Bogan and Armstrong, who have known each other and played together for almost seventy years, despite the fact that Armstrong is almost always on Bogan's case, and Bogan's eyes always seem to be looking for the nearest exit. *Louie Bluie* peers into the areas where nothing is certain, except that these people live and strive and laugh and make music. It is a wonderful film.

Love Letters ★ ★ ★ ½

R, 98 m., 1984

Jamie Lee Curtis (Anna), James Keach (Oliver), Amy Madigan (Wendy), Matt Clark (Mr. Winter). Directed by Amy Jones and produced by Roger Corman. Screenplay by Jones.

Love Letters teaches this lesson: Passion can exist between two people who know their relationship is wrong, but love cannot exist, because love demands to know that it is right. The movie stars Jamie Lee Curtis, in the best performance she has ever given, as Anna, a bright young woman who has an affair with a married man. She tries to make herself see their relationship as existing above conventional morality, but she can't, not after she sees the man's wife and kids.

The affair begins at a crossroads in her life. She's an announcer for a public radio station in San Francisco, and within a period of a few weeks her mother dies, and she gets a job offer from a larger station. She doesn't take the job, though, because something else happens. She meets a photographer (James Keach), who is a sensitive, intelligent, married man, and feels powerfully drawn to him. And she finds her mother's love letters, which reveal that her mother once had an affair. The old letters are used as a counterpoint to the events in the present. They're read on the sound track in the voice of the man who wrote them—a man we don't meet until the movie is almost over. They are letters about love, separation, loneliness, and loyalty. Anna learns to her astonishment that her mother continued the affair for years and years during her marriage, finally ending it only because she had decided to stay with her husband.

We meet the husband, Anna's father. He is a self-pitying alcoholic who believes he was never good enough for Anna's mother, and who smothers Anna with neurotic demands. What happens then is fascinating, and the movie treats it with great intelligence. Anna is already attracted to the James Keach character. Now, reading the old love letters, she begins to develop a romantic idea about affairs. She hates her father, and so, perhaps, did her mother. Her mother cheated on her father—and so will she, by having an affair with Keach. She will become the same kind of noble, romantic outsider that the author of the love letters must have been.

All of this is handled with as much subtlety as Ingmar Bergman brought to similar situations in *Scenes from a Marriage.* This isn't a soap opera romance; it's an investigation into how we can intellectualize our way into situations where our passions are likely to ta3er. Anna and the photographer spend happy times together. They are "in love." Anna thinks she only wants an affair, but she grows possessive in spite of herself. And when she spies on Keach's family, she sees that his wife is a good woman and there is love in their home. Her life refuses to parallel the love letters.

Love Letters was written and directed by Amy Jones, whose previous credit was *The Slumber Party Massacre.* This is perhaps another case of a young filmmaker beginning with exploitation movies and finally getting the chance to do ambitious work. What she accomplishes here is wonderful. She creates a story of passion that is as absorbing as a thriller. She makes a movie of ideas that never, ever, seems to be just a message picture. And she gives Jamie Lee Curtis the best dramatic role of her career; this role, side-by-side with Curtis's inspired comic acting in *Trading Places,* shows her with a range we couldn't have guessed from all her horror pictures. *Love Letters* is one of those treasures that slips through once in a while: A movie that's as smart as we are, that never goes for cheap shots, that's about passion but never blinded by it.

Love Story ★ ★ ★ ★
PG, 100 m., 1970

Ali MacGraw (Jenny Cavilleri), Ryan O'Neal (Oliver Barrett IV), Ray Milland (Oliver Barrett III), John Marley (Phil Cavilleri). Directed by Arthur Hiller and produced by Howard G. Minsky. Screenplay by Erich Segal.

I read *Love Story* one morning in about fourteen minutes flat, out of simple curiosity. I wanted to discover why five and a half million people had actually bought it. I wasn't successful. I was so put off by Erich Segal's writing style, in fact, that I hardly wanted to see the movie at all. Segal's prose style is so revoltingly coy—sort of a cross between a parody of Hemingway and the instructions on a soup can—that his story is fatally infected.

The fact is, however, that the film of *Love Story* is infinitely better than the book. I think it has something to do with the quiet taste of Arthur Hiller, its director, who has put in all the things that Segal thought he was being clever to leave out. Things like color, character, personality, detail, and background. The interesting thing is that Hiller has saved the movie without substantially changing anything in the book. Both the screenplay and the novel were written at the same time, I understand, and if you've read the book, you've essentially read the screenplay. Nothing much is changed except the last meeting between Oliver and his father; Hiller felt the movie should end with the boy alone, and he was right. Otherwise, he's used Segal's situations and dialogue throughout. But the Segal characters, on paper, were so devoid of any personality that they might actually have been transparent. Ali MacGraw and Ryan O'Neal, who play the lovers on film, bring them to life in a way the novel didn't even attempt. They do it simply by being there, and having personalities.

The story by now is so well-known that there's no point in summarizing it for you. I would like to consider, however, the implications of *Love Story* as a three-, four- or five-handkerchief movie, a movie that wants viewers to cry at the end. Is this an unworthy purpose? Does the movie become unworthy, as *Newsweek* thought it did, simply because it has been mechanically contrived to tell us a beautiful, tragic tale? I don't think so. There's nothing contemptible about being moved to joy by a musical, to terror by a thriller, to excitement by a Western. Why shouldn't we get a little misty during a story about young lovers separated by death?

Hiller earns our emotional response because of the way he's directed the movie. The Segal book was so patently contrived to force those tears, and moved toward that object with such humorless determination, that it must have actually disgusted a lot of readers. The movie is mostly about life, however, and not death. And because Hiller makes the lovers into individuals, of course we're moved by the film's conclusion. Why not?

Love Streams ★ ★ ★ ★

PG-13, 141 m., 1984

Gena Rowlands (Sarah Lawson), John Cassavetes (Robert Harmon), Diahnne Abbott (Susan), Seymour Cassel (Jack Lawson), Margaret Abbott (Margarita). Directed by John Cassavetes and produced by Menahem Golan and Yoram Globus. Screenplay by Ted Allan and Cassavetes.

John Cassavetes's *Love Streams* is the kind of movie where a woman brings home two horses, a goat, a duck, some chickens, a dog, and a parrot, and you don't have the feeling that the screenplay is going for cheap laughs. In fact, there's a tightening in your throat as you realize how desperate an act you're witnessing, and how unhappy a person is getting out of the taxi with all those animals. The menagerie scene occurs rather late in the film, after we've already locked into Cassavetes's method. This is a movie about mad people, and they are going to be acting in crazy ways, but the movie isn't going to let us off the hook by making them funny or picaresque or even symbolic (as in *King of Hearts*). They are, quite simply, desperate.

The brother, Robert (played by Cassavetes), is a writer who lives up in the Hollywood Hills in one of those houses that looks like *Architectural Digest* Visits a Motel. He writes trashy novels about bad women. A parade of hookers marches through his life; he gathers them by the taxi load, almost as a hobby, and dismisses them with lots of meaningless words about how he loves them, and how they're sweethearts and babies and dolls. The circular drive in front of his house is constantly filled with the cars of the lonely and the desperate. He is an alcoholic who stays up for two or three days at a stretch, as if terrified of missing one single unhappy moment. The sister, Sarah (Gena Rowlands), is as possessive as her brother is evasive. She is in the process of a messy divorce from her husband (Seymour Cassel), and her daughter is in flight from her. Rowlands thinks that maybe she can buy love: First she buys the animals, later she talks about buying her brother a baby, because that's what he "needs."

At least Cassavetes and Rowlands can communicate. They share perfect trust, although it is the trust of two people in the same trap. There are other characters in the movie that Cassavetes talks at and around, but not with. They include a bemused young singer (Diahnne Abbott) who goes out with Cassavetes but looks at him as if he were capable of imploding, and a former wife (Michele Conway) who turns up one day on the doorstep with a small boy and tells him: "This is your son." The way Cassavetes handles this news is typical of the movie. The woman wonders if maybe he could baby sit for a weekend. He says he will. He brings the kid into the house, scares him away, chases him halfway down Laurel Canyon, brings him back, pours him a beer, has a heart-to-heart about "Women, Life and Marriage," and then asks the kid if he'd like to go to Vegas. Cut to Vegas. Cassavetes dumps the kid in a hotel room and goes out partying all night. He is incapable of any appropriate response to a situation requiring him to care about another human being. He fills his life with noise, hookers, emergencies, and booze to drown out the insistent whisper of duty.

The movie is exasperating, because we never know where we stand or what will happen next. I think that's one of its strengths: There's an exhilaration in this roller coaster ride through scenes that come out of nowhere. This is not a docudrama or a little psychological playlet with a lesson to be learned. It is a raw, spontaneous life, and when we laugh (as in the scene where Cassavetes summons a doctor to the side of the unconscious Rowlands), we wince.

Viewers raised on trained and tame movies may be uncomfortable in the world of Cassavetes; his films are built around lots of talk and the waving of arms and the invoking of the gods. Cassavetes has been making these passionate personal movies for twenty-five years, ever since his *Shadows* helped create American underground movies. His titles include *Minnie and Moskowitz* (in which Rowlands and Cassel got married), *Faces*, *A Woman Under the Influence*, *The Killing of a Chinese Bookie*, *Gloria*, *Opening Night*, and *Husbands*. Sometimes (as in *Husbands*) the wild truth-telling approach evaporates into a lot of empty talk and play-acting. In *Love Streams*, it works.

Lovesick ★ ★ ★
PG, 94 m., 1983

Dudley Moore (Saul Benjamin), Elizabeth McGovern (Chloe Allen), Alec Guinness (Sigmund Freud), Wallace Shawn (Otto Jaffe), Ron Silver (Ted Caruso), Larry Rivers (Jac Applezweig), John Huston (Dr. Geller). Directed by Marshall Brickman and produced by Charles Okun. Screenplay by Brickman.

The notion of a psychiatrist falling in love with his patient is not exactly new, but there are whole moments at a time when it *seems* new in *Lovesick*, a comedy where the psychiatrist is played by Dudley Moore and his patient is Elizabeth McGovern. They should not fall in love. It is against all the rules. It is also in violation of all the ethics of Moore's profession. But what is he to do when she turns those wide, grave eyes upon him and asks for his help? Moore actually hears about McGovern before he meets her. He gets a visit from a colleague (Wallace Shawn, who had dinner with André). Shawn needs help. He's head over heels with the woman and can't stop himself. Moore disapproves, until Shawn leaves and he himself meets McGovern. Then he is instantly smitten.

The scene in which he is smitten illustrates some of the best and worst qualities of this movie. Dudley Moore is very good at what directors call "reaction shots"—shots where we watch an actor watching someone else. In *Lovesick*, Moore's reactions as he gazes upon McGovern are comic and helpless. Her close-ups are fun, too. We find ourselves in sympathy with them. But the development of the scene is interrupted by an annoying device used throughout the film by Marshall Brickman, the director. He stops everything for a fantasy sequence in which Moore imagines that he goes around his desk and kisses McGovern, and that she responds, and that Sigmund Freud magically appears to chastise him.

Brickman, who has written for Woody Allen, may be developing a device here that was first used in *Annie Hall*. (Remember the scene where Marshall McLuhan appeared in a theater lobby and answered a man's question?) Here, though, it doesn't work. Freud (played by Alec Guinness) appears several times during the movie, and although the gimmick no doubt seemed like a clever way to illustrate the subconscious, it brings everything grinding to a dead standstill.

It's not fatal, though, to a movie with a lot of other nice things in it. I really enjoyed the rapport between Moore and McGovern—she so limpid in her unstudied sexuality; he so dreadfully serious about the burden of his love—as if the fact that he loves her is a cross he must bear. The movie is populated with a lot of interesting supporting performances, too. In fact, you can tell it's a New York film, and you can almost guess that it comes from someone in the Woody Allen orbit because of the fun it has with celebrity cameos; the actors, professional and not, who appear in this film include not only Shawn but Alan King, artist Larry Rivers, director Gene Saks, playwright Renee Taylor, director John Huston, and several actual New York shrinks.

Lovesick isn't a great comedy but it's not a bad one. And it's a reminder that Dudley Moore is a gifted and very likable comic actor. I suppose that like all great comedians, he has urges to play serious roles, but after the dreadful *Six Weeks* (in which his principal mistake was to appear), here he is in the lovesick territory of *10* and *Arthur*. It's where he belongs.

Lucas ★ ★ ★ ★
PG-13, 99 m., 1985

Corey Haim (Lucas), Kerri Green (Maggie), Charlie Sheen (Cappie), Courtney Thorne-Smith (Alise), Guy Bond (Coach). Directed by David Seltzer and produced by Lawrence Gordon and David Nicksay. Screenplay by Seltzer.

The first loves of early adolescence are so powerful because they are not based on romance, but on ideals. When they are thirteen and fourteen, boys and girls do not fall in love with one another because of all the usual reasons that are celebrated in love songs; they fall in love because the other person is perfect. Not smart or popular or good-looking, but *perfect*, the embodiment of all good.

The very name of the loved one becomes a holy name, as you can see in *Lucas*, when the hero says, "Maggie. Is that short for Margaret?" And then hugs himself to find that it is, because he suddenly realizes that Margaret is the most wonderful name in all the world.

Everybody grows up, and sooner or later love becomes an experience that has limits and reasons. *Lucas* is a movie that takes place before that happens. It is about a very smart kid who looks a little too short and a little too young to be in high school, and when you tell him that, he nods and solemnly explains that he is "accelerated."

One summer day, while riding his bike through the leafy green of a suburb north of Chicago, he sees a red-haired girl practicing her tennis swing. He stops to speak to her, and before long they are fast friends who sit cross-legged in the grass, knees touching knees, and talk about things that begin with capital letters, like Life and Society and Art.

Lucas loves Maggie, but she is just a little older and more mature than he, and has her eye on a member of the football team. Lucas believes, of course, that the whole value system of football and cheerleaders and pep rallies is corrupt. Maggie says she agrees. But how can she argue when the football hero notices her, breaks up with his girlfriend, and asks her if he can have a kiss?

To describe this situation is to make *Lucas* sound like just one more film about teen-age romance. But it would be tragic if this film got lost in the shuffle of "teen-age movies." This is a movie that is as pure and true to the adolescent experience as Truffaut's *The 400 Blows.* It is true because it assumes all of its characters are intelligent, and do not want to hurt one another, and will refuse to go along with the stupid, painful conformity of high school.

The film centers around the character of Lucas, a skinny kid with glasses and a shock of unruly hair and a gift for trying to talk himself into situations where he doesn't belong. Lucas is played by Corey Haim, who was Sally Field's son in *Murphy's Romance,* and he does not give one of those cute little boy performances that get on your nerves. He creates one of the most three-dimensional, complicated, interesting characters of any age in any recent movie, and if he can continue to act this well he will never become a half-forgotten child star but will continue to grow into an important actor. He is that good.

But the film's other two major actors are just as effective. Kerri Green, who was in *The Goonies,* is so subtle and sensitive as Maggie that you realize she isn't just acting, she understands this character in her heart. As the football hero, Charlie Sheen in some ways has the most difficult role, because we're primed to see him in terms of clichés—the jock who comes along and wins the heart of the girl. Sheen doesn't play the character even remotely that way. It is a surprise to find that he loves Lucas, that he protects him from the goons at school, that although he has won Maggie away from Lucas, he cares very deeply about sparing the kid's feelings.

The last third of the movie revolves around a football game. So many films have ended with the "big match" or the "big game," that my heart started to sink when I saw the game being set up. Surely *Lucas* wasn't going to throw away all its great dialogue and inspired acting on another formula ending? Amazingly, the movie negotiates the football game without falling into predictability. Lucas finds himself in uniform and on the field under the most extraordinary circumstances, but they are plausible circumstances, and what happens then can hardly be predicted.

There are half a dozen scenes in the movie so well-done that they could make little short films of their own. They include: The time Lucas and Maggie listen to classical music and discuss her name; the scene between Maggie and the football hero in the high school's laundry room; the scene in which Lucas is humiliated at a school assembly, and turns the situation to his advantage; the way in which he takes the news that he will not be going to the dance with Maggie; and the very last scene in the whole movie, which is one of those moments of perfect vindication that makes you want to cry.

Lucas was written and directed by David Seltzer, who has obviously put his heart into the film. He has also used an enormous amount of sensibility. In a world where Hollywood has cheapened the teen-age years into predictable vulgarity, he has remembered how urgent, how innocent, and how idealistic those years can be. He has put values into this movie. It is about teen-agers who are learning how to be good to each other, to care, and not simply to be filled with egotism, lust, and selfishness—which is all most Hollywood movies think teen-agers can experience. *Lucas* is one of the year's best films.

Lust in the Dust ★ ★
R, 90 m., 1985

Tab Hunter (Abel), Divine (Rosie), Lainie Kazan (Marguerite), Geoffrey Lewis (Hard Case), Cesar Romero (Father Garcia), Gina Gallego (Ninfa). Directed by Paul Bartel and produced by Allan Glaser and Tab Hunter. Screenplay by Philip John Taylor.

Lust in the Dust would have worked better with Divine in the Tab Hunter role. Divine was born to play Tab Hunter, a claim Hunter himself has not been able to make for several years. And Divine wouldn't have made the mistake Hunter makes, of playing his Western gunslinger as a Clint Eastwood type. Divine would have chewed the scenery before shooting at it, and *Lust in the Dust* might have been funny all the way through, instead of just for the first twenty minutes.

The movie is a comedy Western, deliberately camp, starring Tab Hunter as a silent cowboy with no name, Divine as a hapless wanderer in the desert who wants to be a saloon singer, and Lainie Kazan as the owner of the only saloon in the miserable little town of Chili Verde. Divine is, of course, the well-known transvestite who has starred in lots of John Waters's movies (including *Polyester,* where the audience was issued Scratch 'n' Sniff cards). Divine usually goes for hysterical overacting, but this time she plays a timid, wistful soul, and it doesn't work as well. We need her slinging people out the saloon doors.

The movie is apparently intended as a satire on several different classic Westerns, including *Duel in the Sun,* but a funny thing happens at about the halfway point: It settles down and starts to get involved in its story. And since we don't care about the story, that's a mistake. The movie should have continued to go for the one-liners. As it is, we get this impenetrable story about a missing treasure map, and when they find the map, believe me, it's not a pretty sight.

Good things in the movie include a rousing, high-spirited performance by Kazan, who has abandoned forever her former images and has developed into an effective comedy performer; a TV producer should take a look at this movie and develop a sitcom around her (but not a comedy Western, please!). Hunter underplays until he is almost not present in some of the scenes, Divine is misused. Cesar Romero is a distraction as the local priest, and a young saloon waitress (Gina Gallego) has what used to be called the Lainie Kazan role.

The movie was directed by Paul Bartel, whose previous credit is *Eating Raoul.* Like most of the people associated with the movie, including Tab Hunter (who shares the producer's credit), he seems convinced that simply combining Divine, Kazan, and Hunter in the same room would create a fissionable comic mass. Before he shut the door, he should have also thrown in a screenplay.

M

M*A*S*H ★ ★ ★ ★

R, 116 m., 1970

Donald Sutherland (Hawkeye), Elliott Gould (Trapper John), Tom Skerritt (Duke), Sally Kellerman (Hot Lips Hoolihan), Robert Duvall (Major Burns), Jo Ann Pflug (Lieutenant Dish), Rene Auberjonois (Dago Red). Directed by Robert Altman and produced by Ingo Preminger. Screenplay by Ring Lardner, Jr.

One of the reasons *M*A*S*H* is so funny is that it's so desperate. It is set in a surgical hospital just behind the front lines in Korea, and it is drenched in blood. The surgeons work rapidly and with a gory detachment, sawing off legs and tying up arteries, and making their work possible by pretending they don't care. And when they are at last out of the operating tent, they devote their lives to remaining sane. The way they do that, in *M*A*S*H,* is to be almost metaphysically cruel. There is something about war that inspires practical jokes and the heroes (Donald Sutherland, Elliott Gould, and cronies) are inspired and utterly heartless. They sneak a microphone under the bed of Major "Hot Lips" Hoolihan, and broadcast her lovemaking to the entire camp. They drug a general and photograph him in a brothel.

We laugh, not because *M*A*S*H* is Sgt. Bilko for adults, but because it is so true to the unadmitted sadist in all of us. There is perhaps nothing so exquisite as achieving (as the country song has it) sweet mental revenge against someone we hate with particular dedication. And it is the flat-out, poker-faced hatred in *M*A*S*H* that makes it work. Most comedies want us to laugh at things that aren't really funny; in this one we laugh precisely because they're not funny. We laugh, that we may not cry.

But none of this philosophy comes close to the insane logic of *M*A*S*H,* which is achieved through a peculiar marriage of cinematography, acting, directing, and writing. The movie depends upon timing and tone to be funny. I had an opportunity to read the original script, and I found it uninteresting. It would have been a failure, if it had been directed like most comedies; but Ring Lardner, Jr., wrote it, I suspect, for exactly the approach Robert Altman used in his direction, and so the angle of a glance or the timing of a pause is funnier than any number of conventional gag lines. This is true, for example, in the football game between the surgeons and the general's team. The movie assumes, first of all, that we are intimate with the rules of football. We are. The game then becomes doubly funny, not just because the *M*A*S*H* boys have recruited a former pro as a ringer for their side, but because their victory depends upon legal cheating (how about a center-eligible play?). The audience's laughter is triumphant, because our guys have outsmarted the other guys. Another movie might have gone for purely physical humor in the scene (big guy walks over little guy, etc.) and blown it.

The performances have a lot to do with the movie's success. Elliott Gould and Donald Sutherland are two genuinely funny actors; they don't have to make themselves ridiculous to get a laugh. They're funny because their humor comes so directly from their personalities. They underplay everything (and Sutherland and Gould trying to downstage each other could eventually lead to complete paralysis).

Strangely enough, they're convincing as surgeons. During operations, covered with blood and gore, they mutter their way through running commentaries that sound totally professional. Sawing and hacking away at a parade of bodies, they should be driving us away, but they don't. We can take the unusually high gore-level in *M*A*S*H* because it is originally part of the movie's logic. If the surgeons didn't have to face the daily list of maimed and mutilated bodies, none of the rest of their lives would make any sense. When they are matter-of-factly cruel to "Hot Lips" Hoolihan, we cannot quite separate that from the matter-of-fact way they've got to put wounded bodies back together again. "Hot Lips," who is all Army professionalism and objectivity, is less human because the suffering doesn't reach her.

I think perhaps that's what the movie is about. Gould and Sutherland and the members of their merry band of pranksters are offended because the Army regulars don't feel deeply enough. "Hot Lips" is concerned with protocol, but not with war. And so the surgeons, dancing on the brink of crack-ups, dedicate themselves to making her *feel* something. Her façade offends them; no one could be unaffected by the work of this hospital, but she is. And so if they can crack her defenses and reduce her to their own level of dedicated cynicism, the number of suffering human beings in the camp will go up by one. And even if they fail, they can have a hell of a lot of fun trying. Also, of course, it's a distraction.

Macbeth ★ ★ ★ ★

R, 139 m., 1972

Jon Finch (Macbeth), Francesca Annis (Lady Macbeth), Martin Shaw (Banquo), Nicholas Selby (Duncan), John Stride (Ross), Stephen Chase (Malcolm), Paul Shelley (Donalbain), Terence Bayler (Macduff). Directed by Roman Polanski and produced by Andrew Braunsberg. Screenplay by Polanski and Tenneth Tynan.

We have all heard it a hundred times, Macbeth's despairing complaint about life: ". . . it is a tale told by an idiot, full of sound and fury, signifying nothing." But who has taken it more seriously than Roman Polanski, who tells his bloody masterpiece at precisely the level of the idiot's tale?

Macbeth always before seemed reasonable, dealing with a world in which wrongdoing was punished and logic demonstrated. Macbeth's character was not strong enough to stand up under the weight of the crime he committed, so he disintegrated into the fantasies of ignorant superstition, while his flimsy wife went mad.

It all seemed so clear. And at the proper moment, the forces of justice stepped forward, mocked the witches' prophecies which deluded poor Macbeth and set things right for the final curtain. There were, no doubt, those who thought the play was about how Malcolm became king of Scotland.

But in this film Polanski and his collaborator, Kenneth Tynan, place themselves at Macbeth's side and choose to share his point of view, and in their film there's no room at all for detachment. All those noble, tragic Macbeths—Orson Welles and Maurice Evans and the others—look like imposters now, and the king is revealed as a scared kid.

No effort has been made to make Macbeth a tragic figure, and his death moves us infinitely less than the murder of Macduff's young son. Polanski places us in a visual universe of rain and mist, of gray dawns and clammy dusks, and there is menace in the sound of hoofbeats but no cheer in the cry of trumpets. Even the heroic figure of Macduff has been tempered; now he is no longer the instrument of God's justice, but simply a man bent on workaday revenge. The movie ends with the simple fact that a job has been done: Macbeth got what was coming to him.

Polanski has imposed this vision on the film so effectively that even the banquet looks like a gang of highwaymen ready to wolf down stolen sheep. Everyone in the film seems to be pushed by circumstances; there is small feeling that the characters are motivated by ideas. They seem so ignorant at times that you wonder if they understand the wonderful dialogue Shakespeare has written for them. It's as if the play has been inhabited by Hell's Angels who are quick studies.

All of this, of course, makes Polanski's *Macbeth* more interesting than if he had done your ordinary, respectable, awe-stricken tiptoe around Shakespeare. This is an original film by an original film artist, and not an "interpretation." It should have been titled *Polanski's Macbeth,* just as we got *Fellini Satyricon.*

I might as well be honest and say it is impossible to watch certain scenes without thinking of the Charles Manson case. It is impossible to watch a film directed by Roman Polanski and not react on more than one level to such images as a baby being "untimely ripped from his mother's womb." Indeed, Polanski adds his own trim conclusion after Shakespeare's, with a final scene in which Malcolm, now crowned king, goes to consult the same witches who deceived Macbeth. Polanski's characters resemble Manson: They are anti-intellectual, witless, and driven by deep, shameful wells of lust and violence.

Why did Polanski choose to make *Macbeth,* and why this *Macbeth*? I have no way of guessing. This is certainly one of the most pessimistic films ever made, and there seems little doubt that Polanski intended his film to be full of sound and fury—which it is, to the brim—and to signify nothing.

It's at that level that Polanski is at his most adamant: The events that occur in the film must not be allowed to have significance. Polanski and Tynan take only small liberties with Shakespeare, and yet so successfully does Polanski orchestrate *Macbeth*'s visual content that we come out of the film with a horrified realization. We didn't identify with either Macbeth or Macduff in their final duel. We were just watching a sword-fight.

Mad Max Beyond Thunderdome

★ ★ ★ ★

R, 115 m., 1985

Mel Gibson (Mad Max), Tina Turner (Aunty Entity), Frank Thring (Collector), Angelo Rossitto (Master), Paul Larsson (Blaster), Angry Anderson (Ironbar). Directed and produced by George Miller. Co-directed by George Ogilvie. Screenplay by Miller and Terry Hayes.

It's not supposed to happen this way. Sequels are not supposed to be better than the movies that inspired them. The third movie in a series isn't supposed to create a world more complex, more visionary, and more entertaining than the first two. Sequels are supposed to be creative voids. But now here is *Mad Max Beyond Thunderdome,* not only the best of the three Mad Max movies, but one of the best films of 1985.

From its opening shot of a bizarre vehicle being pulled by camels through the desert, *Mad Max Three* places us more firmly within its apocalyptic postnuclear world than ever before. We are some years in the future; how many, it is hard to say, but so few years that the frames and sheet metal of 1985 automobiles are still being salvaged for makeshift new vehicles of bizarre design. And yet enough years that a new society is taking shape. The bombs have fallen, the world's petroleum supplies have been destroyed, and in the deserts of Australia, mankind has found a new set of rules and started on a new game.

The driver of the camels is Mad Max (Mel Gibson), former cop, now sort of a free-lance nomad. After his vehicle is stolen and he is left in the desert to die, he makes his way somehow to Bartertown, a quasi-Casablanca hammered together out of spare parts. Bartertown is where you go to buy, trade, or sell anything—or anybody. It is supervised by a Sydney Greenstreet-style fat man named the Collector (Frank Thring), and ruled by an imperious queen named Aunty Entity (Tina Turner).

And it is powered by an energy source that is, in its own way, a compelling argument against nuclear war: In chambers beneath Bartertown, countless pigs live and eat and defecate, and from their waste products, Turner's soldiers generate methane gas. This leads to some of the movie's most memorable moments, as Mad Max and others wade knee-deep in piggy-do.

Tina Turner herself lives far above the masses, in a birds'-nest throne room perched high overhead. And as Mad Max first visits Turner's sky palace, I began to realize how completely the director, George Miller, had imagined this future world. It has the crowding and the variety of a movie crossroads, but it also has a riot of hairstyles and costume design, as if these desperate creatures could pause from the daily struggle for survival only long enough to invent new punk fashions. After the clothes, the hair, the crowding, the incessant activity, the spendthrift way in which Miller fills his screen with throwaway details, Bartertown becomes much more than a movie set—it's an astounding address of the imagination, a place as real as Bogart's Cas ablanca or Orson Welles's Xanadu or the Vienna of *The Third Man.* That was even before the movie introduced me to Thunderdome, the arena for Bartertown's hand-to-hand battles to the death.

Thunderdome is the first really original movie idea about how to stage a fight since we got the first karate movies. The "dome" is a giant upside-down framework bowl. The spectators scurry up the sides of the bowl, and look down on the fighters. But the combatants are not limited to fighting on the floor of the arena. They are placed on harnesses with long elastic straps, so that they can leap from top to bottom and from side to side with great lethal bounds. Thunderdome is to fighting as three-dimensional chess is to a flat board. And the weapons available to the fighters are hung from the inside of the dome: Cleavers, broadaxes, sledge-hammers, the inevitable chainsaw.

It is into Thunderdome that Mad Max goes for his showdown with Aunty Entity's greatest warrior, and George Miller's most original creation, a character named Master-Blaster, who is actually two people. Blaster is a giant hulk of a man in an iron mask. Master is a dwarf who rides him like a chariot, standing in an iron harness above his shoulders. The fight between Mad Max and Master-Blaster is one of the great creative action scenes in the movies.

There is a lot more in *Mad Max Beyond Thunderdome*. The descent into the pig world, for example, and the visit to a sort of postwar hippie commune, and of course the inevitable final chase scene, involving car, train, truck, cycle, and incredible stunts. This is a movie that strains at the leash of the possible, a movie of great visionary wonders.

Making Mr. Right ★ ★ ★ 1/2

PG-13, 98 m., 1987

John Malkovich (Jeff/Ulysses), Ann Magnuson (Frankie), Glenne Headly (Trish), Ben Masters (Steve), Laurie Metcalf (Sandy), Robert Trebor (Tuxedo Salesman). Directed by Susan Seidelman and produced by Mike Wise and Joel Tuber. Screenplay by Floyd Byars and Laurie Frank.

Making Mr. Right is about a scientist who invents a remarkably lifelike android in his own image and about an ad executive who begins to like the android more than the scientist. These raw materials easily could have been turned into a fairly dreary movie, but not this time. Instead, we get a smart, quick-witted, and genuinely funny movie.

A lot of the movie's smarts come from John Malkovich, who plays the dual role of the scientist and the android, and a newcomer named Ann Magnuson, who plays the account executive with a pert intelligence that reminded me of Susan Hayward or Gloria Grahame. Both actors see right through their roles, know what's funny and what's important, and are able to put a nice spin even on the obligatory scenes.

That's true, for example, during the sweet, tentative moments when the android begins to fall for the woman. Malkovich provides just the right amount of inept clumsiness for the android, which sometimes has trouble getting its mind-body coordination in line. Like Jeff Bridges in *Starman*, he's able to meet the tricky challenge of moving in an uncoordinated way without looking merely ridiculous.

Magnuson is fun, too, with her high heels and designer outfits, clipboards and speculative looks. She has an instantly combative relationship with the scientist who invented the android, and it's made trickier because as the android grows more human, the scientist subtly grows more robotic.

Making Mr. Right was directed by Susan Seidelman, whose previous credits are *Smithereens*, which I didn't much like, and *Desperately Seeking Susan*, which was much more assured. With this film, she hits her stride as a comedy director who would rather be clever than obvious, who allows good actors such as Malkovich to go for quiet effects rather than broad, dumb clichés.

Another comedy depending on dual and mistaken identities is *The Secret of My Success*. Seeing the two movies is instructive because they take such different approaches to the challenge of identity. *Secret* has lots of moments when characters don't realize exactly who they're talking to, and it creates those moments out of the stupidity of the characters. In *Mr. Right*, there are scenes where the scientist and the android are mistaken for one another, and Seidelman uses the misunderstandings to make comic points about the personalities of her characters: They make wrong assumptions because of who they are, instead of because of how stupid they are. It makes all the difference in the world.

Seidelman also has fun populating the outskirts of her plot with good character actors, especially Robert Trebor as the tuxedo salesman. You may remember him as the smarmy, sweating porno store operator in *52 Pick-Up.* The distance between these two good performances is impressive.

At one point in *Making Mr. Right,* we see a theater marquee in the background advertising *The Parent Trap.* That was, of course, the movie where Hayley Mills played twins, thanks to trick photography. Malkovich is often seen onscreen with himself in this movie, but I never noticed any seams or glitches, and I was grateful to Seidelman for not providing any moments that were intended merely to exploit the trick.

Man of Iron ★ ★ ★ ★

RATING, 140 m., 1980

Jerzy Radziwilowicz (Tomczyk), Krystyna Janda (Agnieszka), Marian Opania (Winkiel), Lech Walesa (As himself). Directed by Andrzej Wajda. Screenplay by Aleksander Scibor-Rylski.

As a youth of thirteen, the Polish filmmaker Andrzej Wajda lived in a small town where he witnessed German troops lead thousands of Polish army officers to their deaths in concentration camps. As a young student after the war, he lived through the repressive Stalinist years. In the 1950s he made his first films, betraying a spirit that the Party ideologues found too individualistic for their taste. In a speech in 1981 at American University in Washington, D.C., he quoted from "the best review I've ever had." It was from a confidential 1976 Polish censor's report:

. . . politically and ideologically he is not on our side. He has taken the position, often found among artists, of a "neutral judge" of history and today's times—believing that he has the right . . . to apply the gauge of humanism and morals to all the problems of the world and that he doesn't need Marxism nor any other philosophical-social system to do it.

Wajda is at it again, judging history, applying the gauge of humanism, not requiring Marxism, in *Man of Iron,* his extraordinary film about the birth of the Polish Solidarity labor movement. This film is a marriage between a fictional story and actual events, and Wajda took his cameras and his actors right into the firestorm of the Gdansk demonstrations to record the victorious Solidarity agreement at the Lenin Shipyard.

Wajda is in a strange position in Poland. He and Krystof Zanussi are the only two Polish directors still in Poland who have international reputations. He is honored all over the world, but at home the authorities are a little reluctant to give him his head; his films do not promote domestic tranquility.

Man of Iron, filmed during the tumultuous days of relative freedom when Solidarity seemed to hold all the cards, was permitted to be flown out of Warsaw during the closing days of the 1981 Cannes Film Festival, where it won the Grand Prize.

It's a sequel of sorts to Wajda's *Man of Marble* (1976), although you needn't have seen the earlier film, which was about a labor leader during the years of repressive policies in Poland. This film is about the same man's son, who is a Solidarity leader a few steps down in influence from Lech Walesa. Wajda follows his fictional characters into the center of real events (it's sometimes hard to tell where fiction ends and documentary begins), and he uses a broadcast newsman as an interviewer—a technique that allows his film to go places and ask questions that would be difficult to cover in "pure" fiction.

Exactly the same two techniques—the use of a character who is a journalist, and the juxtaposition of a fictional story with actual events—were used by Haskell Wexler in *Medium Cool,* the film about the 1968 Democratic convention demonstrations in Chicago. The approach leaves some ragged edges, but when you are filming at the cutting edge of history you can't stop for rewrites.

Wajda's film is not a polemic, however. That humanist streak, complained of by the state censors, sneaks through even at the expense of the Solidarity politics he wants to celebrate. Wajda is an artist first, a reporter second or third, and not really a very good propagandist. And the best things in *Man of Iron* are the purely personal moments, the scenes where Wajda is concerned with the human dimensions of his characters rather than their ideological struggles.

Those dimensions come through most clearly in the character of Winkiel (Marian Opania), the alcoholic journalist who is sent by the party bosses in Warsaw to spy on Solidarity in the guise of a radio reporter. Winkiel had his own values once. Meeting the son of the old labor leader, he remembers the father. Arriving in Gdansk, Winkiel discovers to his horror that the area has been declared dry because of the troubles—he can't get booze. A party agent slips him a bottle of vodka, but Winkiel breaks it on the bathroom floor, and in a scene that will profoundly affect the way we understand his later actions, he desperately tries to soak up some of the vodka with a towel. He is a man whose spirit is broken, a man prepared to be a spy. The most moving of the several stories in *Man of Iron* concerns his gradual rediscovery of his old values, until he finally decides to side with the workers and to abandon his undercover role.

Man of Iron is a fascinating and courageous document—a film of dissent made because of, or in spite of, the upheaval in Poland.

In that speech in 1981, Wajda closed with these words: *Someone once asked me a naive question. It's a question often asked of very old writers: Do you feel that you've helped to make history? My answer is this. I don't know whether I helped make it. I know I didn't stand with my hands folded. I didn't look on indifferently as history was being made.*

The Man Who Would Be King

★ ★ ★ ★

PG, 129 m., 1975

Sean Connery (Daniel Dravot), Michael Caine (Peachy Carnahan), Christopher Plummer (Kipling), Saeed Jaffrey (Billy Fish), Shakira Caine (Roxanne). Directed by John Huston and produced by John Foreman. Screenplay by Huston and Gladys Hill.

John Huston's *The Man Who Would Be King* is swashbuckling adventure, pure and simple, from the hand of a master. It's unabashed and thrilling and fun. The movie invites comparison with the great action films like *Gunga Din* and *Mutiny on the Bounty*, and with Huston's own classic *Treasure of the Sierre Madre:* We get strong characterizations, we get excitement, we even get to laugh every once in a while.

The action epics of the last twenty years seem to have lost their sense of humor; it's as if once the budget goes over five million dollars, directors think they have to be deadly serious. *Lawrence of Arabia* was a great movie, but introspective and solemn, and efforts such as *Dr. Zhivago* and *War and Peace* never dared to smile. Huston's movie isn't like that. It reflects his personality and his own best films; it's open, sweeping, and lusty—and we walk out feeling exhilarated.

Huston waited a long time to make this film, and its history is a Hollywood legend. He originally cast Bogart and Gable, but then Bogart died. In the early 1960s, he planned to make it with Gable and Michael Caine—but then Gable died, and the project was shelved until 1975. Maybe it's just as well. We need movies like this more now than we did years ago, when Hollywood wasn't shy about straightforward action films. And Huston's eventual casting of Michael Caine and Sean Connery is exactly right.

They work together so well, they interact so easily and with such camaraderie, that watching them is a pleasure. They never allow themselves to be used merely as larger-than-life heroes, photographed against vast landscapes. Kipling's story, and Huston's interpretation of it, requires a lot more than that; it requires acting of a subtle and difficult sort, even if the sheer energy of the movie makes it look easy.

The two of them play former British soldiers who vow to march off into Afghanistan or somewhere and find a kingdom not yet touched by civilization. With their guns and training, they think they'll be able to take over pretty easily, manipulate the local high priests, and set themselves up as rulers. They tell their plan to an obscure colonial editor named Kipling (played very nicely by Christopher Plummer) and then they set off into the mountains. After the obligatory close calls, including an avalanche that somehow saves their lives, they find their lost land and it's just as they expected it would be.

The natives aren't too excited by their new rulers at first, but a lucky Masonic key chain saves the day—never mind how—and Connery finds himself worshiped as a deity. He even gets to like it, and condescends to Caine, who remains a Cockney and unimpressed. The movie proceeds with impossible coincidences, untold riches, romances and betrayals, and heroic last words and—best of all—some genuinely witty scenes between Connery and Caine, and when it's over we haven't learned a single thing worth knowing and there's not even a moral, to speak of, but we've had fun. It's great that someone still has the gift of making movies like this; even Huston, after thirty years, must have wondered whether he still knew how.

The Man With Two Brains ★ ★
R, 91 m., 1983

Steve Martin (Dr. Hfuhruhurr), Kathleen Turner (Dolores), David Warner (Dr. Necessiter), Paul Benedits (Butler). Directed by Carl Reiner and produced by David V. Picker and William E. McEuen. Written by Reiner, Steve Martin, and George Gipe.

Steve Martin and Carl Reiner continue their tour of ancient movie genres with *The Man With Two Brains,* which does for Mad Scientist movies what *Dead Men Don't Wear Plaid* did for private eye pictures, which is to say, not very much. Some of the gags depend on a familiarity with classics like *Donovan's Brain, Bride of Frankenstein*—and even, in this case, Mel Brooks's *Young Frankenstein.* Other gags depend on Steve Martin's comic personality, as a guy whose elevator doesn't go all the way to the top floor. I've never found Steve Martin irresistibly funny. There's something stolid about his approach to humor, something deliberately half-paced and mannered that seems designed to be subtly irritating. I guess it's a tribute to *The Man With Two Brains* that I found myself laughing a fair amount of the time, despite my feelings about Martin. This is not a great comedy but it has scenes that don't know that.

Martin plays a brain surgeon named Dr. Michael Hfuhruhurr. The moment I heard the name I knew we were in trouble, and, sure enough, the movie never tires of making jokes based on his funny name. Since the First Law of Comedy should be *No funny names are funny unless they are used by W.C. Fields or Groucho Marx,* the name jokes are an exercise in futility. Hfuhruhurr has perfected something called the cranial screw-top method of brain surgery, and uses it to save the life of a beautiful young woman (Kathleen Turner) whom he's hit with his Mercedes. The woman, alas, turns out to be a gold digger. She seduces the gardener but refuses to have sex with Hfuhruhurr, who in his frustration falls in love with the brain of another young woman—a brain that has been pickled in a jar in the Vienna laboratory of the eccentric Dr. Necessiter (David Warner).

And so on. The movie uses the basic approach established by Brooks in *Young Frankenstein:* sight gags, cross-references, scatalogical puns, broad plotting, running gags, and so on. It filters its material through Martin's peculiar style, which is, I think, not light-footed enough. Martin is the kind of comedian who chews every line, lingering even on the throwaways.

Turner, seen in *Body Heat,* has a nice teasing quality as the hot-and-cold sexpot. David Warner (remember him from *Morgan* all those years ago?) makes a suitably cadaverous mad scientist. But the cast somehow seems underpopulated, and the characters are underdeveloped. That's one of the weaknesses of genre satires: The filmmakers depend on our knowledge of past characters as a substitute for creating new ones. And since comedy grows out of inappropriate behavior, and our notions of inappropriate behavior depend on what we know about people, the jokes all boil down to the fact that the characters in old Mad Scientist movies wouldn't behave like the characters in this one. So what?

The Manchurian Candidate ★ ★ ★ ★
PG-13, 126 m., 1962

Frank Sinatra (Bennett Marco), Laurence Harvey (Raymond Shaw), Janet Leigh (Rosie), Angela Lansbury (Raymond's Mother), Henry Silva (Chunjin), James Gregory (Senator John Iselin), Leslie Parrish (Jocie), John McGiver (Senator Thomas Jordan), Khigh Dhiegh (Yen Lo), James Edwards (Corporal Melvin). Directed by John Frankenheimer and produced by George Axelrod and Frankenheimer. Screenplay by Axelrod.

Here is a movie that was made more than twenty-five years ago, and it feels as if it were made yesterday. Not a moment of *The Manchurian Candidate* lacks edge and tension and a cynical spin—and what's even more surprising is how the film now plays as a political comedy, as well as a thriller. After being suppressed for a quarter of a century, after becoming an unseen legend that never turned up on TV or on home video, John Frankenheimer's 1962 masterpiece now reemerges as one of the best and brightest of modern American films.

The story is a matter of many levels, some of them frightening, some pointed with satirical barbs. In a riveting opening sequence, a group of American combat infantrymen are shown being brainwashed by a confident Chinese communist hypnotist, who has them so surely under his control that one man is ordered to strangle his buddy, and cheerfully complies.

Two members of the group get our special attention: the characters played by Frank Sinatra and Laurence Harvey. Harvey seems to be the main target of the Chinese scheme, which is to return him to American society as a war hero, and then allow him to lead a normal life until he is triggered by a buried hypnotic suggestion, and turned into an assassin completely brainwashed to take orders from his enemy controller. Harvey does indeed re-enter society, where he is the son of a Republican dowager (Angela Lansbury), and the stepson of her husband (James Gregory). Gregory is a leading candidate for his party's presidential nomination, and more than that I choose not to reveal. Meanwhile, Sinatra also returns to civilian life, but he is haunted by nightmares in which he dimly recalls the terrifying details of the brainwashing. He contacts Harvey (who is not, we must remember, a conscious assassin, but merely a brainwashed victim). Sinatra also becomes central to a Pentagon investigation of a possible plot that affected all the members of his platoon—which disappeared on patrol and returned telling the same fabricated story.

Midway in his investigation, Sinatra meets and falls in love with a woman played by Janet Leigh, and their relationship provides the movie with what looks to me like a subtle, tantalizing suggestion of an additional level of intrigue. They meet in the parlor car of a train, where Sinatra, shaking, cannot light a cigarette and knocks over the table with his drink on it. Leigh follows him to the space between cars, lights a cigarette for him, and engages him in a very weird conversation, after which they fall in love and she quickly ditches her fiancé. What's going on here? My notion is that Sinatra's character is a Manchurian killer, too—one allowed to remember details of Harvey's brainwashing because that would make him seem more credible. And Leigh? She is Sinatra's controller.

This possible scenario simply adds another level to a movie already rich in intrigue. The depths to which the Lansbury character will sink in this movie must be seen to be believed, and the actress generates a smothering "momism" that defines the type. By the end of the film, so many different people have used so many different strategies on Harvey's overtaxed brain that he is almost literally a zombie, unable to know what to believe, incapable of telling who can be trusted.

The Manchurian Candidate got glowing reviews when it was first released in 1962. (Pauline Kael wrote: "It may be the most sophisticated political satire ever made in Hollywood.") But then it was shelved in a dispute between United Artists and Sinatra. For more than twenty-five years, memories of *The Manchurian Candidate* have tantalized those who saw it at the time. Was it really as good as it seemed? It was.

Manhattan ★ ★ ★ ½

R, 96 m., 1979

Woody Allen (Isaac Davis), Diane Keaton (Mary Wilke), Michael Murphy (Yale), Mariel Hemingway (Tracy), Meryl Streep (Jill), Anne Byrne (Emily), Karen Ludwig (Connie), Michael O'Donoghue (Dennis). Directed by Woody Allen and produced by Charles H. Joffe. Screenplay by Allen and Marshall Brickman.

The overture is filled with brash confidence: Gershwin's "Rhapsody in Blue," played over powerful black-and-white visions of Manhattan and its skyline, and the mighty bridges leaping out to it from the provinces. The voice is filled with uncertainty and hesitation: "Chapter One. . . ."

The voice is Woody Allen's, of course, and we find ourselves laughing—actually laughing *already*—on the words "Chapter One," because the Allen character is so firmly established in our imaginations that we supply the rest of the joke ourselves. "Chapter One," yes, but Woody's the definitive vulnerable artist with giant dreams, and so of course he begins with confidence but will be mired in self-doubt long, long before Chapter Two.

A great deal of the success of Allen's *Manhattan* depends on how well he has established that Woody persona. Because we believe we know him (or the character he plays), we supply additional dimensions to the situations on the screen. A movie that might seem sketchily fleshed-out in other hands becomes a great deal more resonant in Allen's: This is a variation on a familiar theme.

And the Gershwin is a masterstroke. Woody Allen populates his film with people who are at odds with their own visions of themselves. They've been so sold, indeed, on the necessity of seeming true and grave and ethical that even their affairs, their deceptions, have to be discussed in terms of "values" and "meanings"—the dialogue in this film was learned in psychoanalysis. Their rationalizations double back upon themselves, and then, clear as a bell on the sound track, there are the Gershwin songs. "S'Wonderful" and "Embraceable You" and "Sweet and Low Down" and "I've Got a Crush on You" . . . written as if love were *simple*, for chrissakes, and you actually could "fall" in love when we all know it's more a matter of pulling yourself up, hand over hand, out of a pit of snapping emotions. In Allen's earlier films, middle-class society was usually the contrast to the Woody character's hang-ups and fantasies. This time, brilliantly, he sets his entire story in a "real" world—and uses the music as the counterpoint. No wonder it's deliberately loud and dominating; Gershwin is the second most important person in this film.

Allen's humor has always been based on the contrast between his character ("Woody," spectacled, anemic, a slob, incredibly bright and verbal, tortured by self-doubt) and his goals (writing a great novel, being like Bogart, winning the love of beautiful women). The fact that he thinks he can achieve his dreams (or that he *pretends* he thinks he can) makes him lovable. It is amazing, for example, how many women believe they are unique because they find Woody sexy.

What Allen does in *Manhattan* is to treat both the Woody character and the goals with more realism, and to deal with them in an urban social setting we can recognize. He was already doing this in *Annie Hall*, the comedy the critics said was "really" serious—as if comedy were not already serious enough. His earlier movies were made from farce, slapstick, stand-up verbal wit, satire, and the appeal of the Woody character. *Annie Hall* and *Manhattan* are made from his observations about the way we talk and behave, and the fearsome distances between what we say and what we mean, and how we behave and how we mean to behave.

The story follows several characters through several affairs. Woody himslf is twice-divorced as the movie opens—most recently from a lesbian who is writing a book that will tell all about their marriage. He is having an affair with a seventeen-year-old girl (Mariel Hemingway). His best friend, Yale (Michael Murphy), is married and is having an affair with a girl he met at a party (Diane Keaton). But Murphy has doubts about the relationship, and so subtly tries to shift Keaton to Allen, who in the meantime thinks he wants to ditch the seventeen-year-old. Inevitably, Woody and Keaton begin to fall in love, and their courtship is photographed against magnificent Manhattan backdrops. And once this is all set up, of course, it goes topsy-turvy.

The relationships aren't really the point of the movie: It's more about what people say during relationships—or, to put it more bluntly, it's about how people lie by technically telling the truth. *Manhattan* is one of the few movies that could survive a sound track of its dialogue; a lot of it, by Allen and Marshall Brickman, has the kind of convoluted intellectual cynicism of the early Nichols and May (and a lot of the rest of it consists of great one-liners).

Manhattan has been almost routinely praised by the New York critics as "better than *Annie Hall.*" I don't think so. I think it goes wrong in the very things the New York critics like the most—when, in the last forty-five minutes or so, Allen does a subtle turn on his material and gets serious about it. I'm most disturbed by the final scene between Woody and Mariel Hemingway. It's not really thought out; Allen hasn't found the line between the irony the scene needs and the sentiment he wants his character to feel. The later scenes involving the Michael Murphy character are also not as good as the early ones; the character is seen correctly for humor, but hasn't been developed completely enough to bear the burden of confession.

And yet this is a very good movie. Woody Allen is . . . Woody, sublimely. Diane Keaton gives us a fresh and nicely edged New York intellectual. And Mariel Hemingway deserves some kind of special award for what's in some ways the most difficult role in the film. It wouldn't do, you see, for the love scenes between Woody and Mariel to feel awkward or to hint at cradle-snatching or an unhealthy interest on Woody's part in innocent young girls. But they don't feel that way: Hemingway's character has a certain grave intelligence, a quietly fierce pride, that, strangely enough, suggest that even at seventeen she's one Woody should be thinking of during Gershwin's "Someone to Watch Over Me."

Note: The video version of Manhattan *was released with black bands at the top and bottom to preserve the wide-screen composition of the film. This unusual decision reflects Allen's perfectionism—and provides an eye-opening demonstration of how much is lost when other wide-screen formats are squeezed into the video frame.*

The Manhattan Project ★ ★ ★ ★

PG-13, 118 m., 1986

John Lithgow (John Mathewson), Christopher Collet (Paul Stephens), Cynthia Nixon (Jenny Anderman), Jill Eikenberry (Elizabeth Stephens). Directed by Marshall Brickman and produced by Brickman and Jennifer Ogden. Screenplay by Brickman and Thomas Baum.

The kid is really smart, but like a lot of smart kids he has learned to hide it, to lay back and observe and keep his thoughts to himself. When the new scientist arrives in town and starts to date the kid's mother, and then tries to make pals by taking the kid on a tour of the research lab where he works, the kid keeps his eyes open and his mouth shut. But he knows the lab is devoted to nuclear weapons research, and he's kind of insulted that the scientist would try to deceive him.

That's the setup for *The Manhattan Project*, a clever, funny, and very skillful thriller about how the kid builds his own atomic bomb. This is not, however, another one of those teen-age movies about bright kids and science projects. There have been some good movies in that genre—I liked *WarGames* and *Real Genius*—but this isn't really a teen-age movie at all, it's a thriller. And it's one of those thrillers that stays as close as possible to the everyday lives of convincing people, so that the movie's frightening aspects are convincing.

The kid is played by Christopher Collet. He is very, very smart. We know that not just because we are told so, but because the movie has lots of subtle, sometimes funny little ways of demonstrating it—as when the kid solves a puzzle in three seconds flat, just as we were trying to understand it.

The kid lives with his mother (Jill Eikenberry) in an upstate New York college town. John Lithgow plays the scientist who moves into the town and starts to date Eikenberry and makes friends with the kid. The movie is very sophisticated about the relationship between Collet and Lithgow. This isn't a case of the two men competing for the affections of the mother; indeed, there are times when these two bright, lonely males seem to have more in common with each other.

In particular, the Lithgow character isn't allowed to fall into clichés. He isn't a mad scientist, and he isn't a heartless intellectual: He's just a smart man trying to do his job well and still have some measure of simple human pleasure.

After Collet is given his tour of the "research center," he tells his girlfriend (Cynthia Nixon) that he's a little insulted that they thought they could fool him. He knows a bomb factory when he sees one. And so, to prove various things to various people, the kid figures out a way to sneak into the plant, steal some plutonium, and build his own nuclear bomb. He wants to enter it in a New York City science fair.

I love it when movies get very detailed about clever schemes for outsmarting people. *The Manhattan Project* invites us to figure out things along with Collet, as he uses his girlfriend as a decoy and outsmarts the security guards at the plant. Inside, he has it all figured out: how to baffle the automatic alarms, how to anticipate what the guards are going to do, how to get in and out without being detected.

The long closing sequence is probably too predictable, as Lithgow and the federal authorities try to convince the kid to take his bomb out of the science fair and allow them to disarm it before he vaporizes the city. Even here, the movie doesn't depend on ordinary thriller strategies; a lot depends not only on the relationship between the kid and the scientist, but on how they think alike and share some of the same goals.

The Manhattan Project was co-written and

directed by Marshall Brickman, the sometime Woody Allen collaborator (*Annie Hall*, *Manhattan*) whose own films include *Lovesick* and *Simon*. This movie announces his arrival into the first ranks of skilled American directors. It's a *tour de force*, the way he combines everyday personality conflicts with a funny, oddball style of seeing things, and wraps up the whole package into a tense and effective thriller. It's not often that one movie contains so many different kinds of pleasures.

Mannequin ½★
PG, 90 m., 1987

Andrew McCarthy (Jonathan), Kim Cattrall (Emmy), Estelle Getty (Mrs. Timkin), Meshach Taylor (Hollywood), G.W. Bailey (Felix), James Spader (Richards), Carole Davis (Roxie), Steve Vinovich (B.J. Wert). Directed by Michael Gottlieb and produced by Art Levinson. Screenplay by Gottlieb and Edward Rugoff.

This movie is a real curiosity. It's dead. I don't mean it's bad. A lot of bad movies are fairly throbbing with life. *Mannequin* is dead. The wake lasts two hours, and then we can leave. Halfway through, I was ready for someone to lead us in reciting the rosary.

The movie stars Andrew McCarthy and Kim Cattrall, actors I have admired before and will, no doubt, admire again. In years to come, they will probably look back on this project with a rueful smile and a shrug, much as Paul Newman must remember *The Silver Chalice*.

In *Mannequin*, McCarthy plays a hapless young man who is fired from one job after another, and Cattrall plays an Egyptian princess who is reincarnated as a dummy in a Philadelphia department store window. When she comes to life, she gives him the inspiration to decorate great windows, and that gives him confidence in himself. I am not leaving out very much here.

The supporting characters have been recycled out of failed sitcoms: Felix, the dim-witted night watchman, who spends most of his time talking to his dog. Hollywood, the flamboyantly gay black window dresser, who becomes the hero's only friend. Mrs. Timkin, the good-hearted owner of the department store. Roxie, the hero's bitchy former girlfriend, who is jealous of the dummy. And so on.

All of these people do exactly what we expect them to do, exactly when we expect them to do it. They also sputter a lot. People sputter all the time in pulp fiction. Have you ever really seen anyone sputter in life? If I am not mistaken, there is even a character in this movie who says, "Why . . . why . . . you . . . you . . ." It's not often you get that line anymore.

The gimmick in the movie is that the mannequin can only come to life when McCarthy is watching her. This rule is enforced rather loosely. For example, when they ride down the street on his motorcycle, she only freezes up when other characters in the movie see her. Miscellaneous passersby don't count. Left unexplained is how she managed to leave ancient Egypt and land in 1987 understanding the language and nuances of modern-day Philadelphia.

Studying the press material for *Mannequin*, I learned that Michael Gottlieb, the director, got the idea for this movie five years ago when he was walking down Fifth Avenue and thought he saw a mannequin move in the window of Bergdorf Goodman. Just thought you'd like to know.

Manon of the Spring ★ ★ ★ ★
PG, 113 m., 1987
(See also *Jean de Florette*)

Yves Montand (Cesar Soubeyran), Daniel Auteuil (Ugolin), Emmanuelle Beart (Manon), Hippolyte Girardot (Schoolteacher), Elisabeth Depardieu (Aimee), Gabriel Bacquier (Victor). Directed by by Claude Berri and produced by Pierre Grunstein. Screenplay by Berri and Gerard Brach.

There is something to be said for a long story that unfolds with an inexorable justice. In recent movies, we've become accustomed to stories that explode into dozens of tiny, dim-witted pieces of action, all unrelated to each other. Cars hurtle through the air, victims are peppered with gunshot holes, heroes spit out clever one-liners, and at the end of it all, what are we left with? Our hands close on empty air.

Manon of the Spring, which is the conclusion of the story that began with *Jean de Florette*, is the opposite kind of movie. It moves with a majestic pacing over the affairs of four generations, demonstrating that the sins of the fathers are visited upon the children. Although *Manon* is self-contained and can be understood without having seen *Jean de Florette,* the full impact of this work depends on seeing the whole story, right from the beginning; only then does the ending have its full force.

In the first part of the story, as you may recall, a young hunchbacked man from Paris (Gerald Depardieu) came with his wife and infant daughter to farm some land he had inherited in a rural section of France. The locals did not greet him kindly, and one of the local patriarchs (Yves Montand) sabotaged his efforts by blocking the spring that fed his land. The young man worked morning to night to haul water for his goats and the flowers he wished to grow, but in the end the effort killed him. Montand and his worthless nephew (Daniel Auteuil) were then able to buy the land cheaply.

Montand's plot against the hunchback was incredibly cruel, but the movie was at pains to explain that Montand was not gratuitously evil. His most important values centered around the continuity of land and family, and in his mind, his plot against Depardieu was justified by the need to defend the land against an "outsider." As *Manon of the Spring* opens, some years later, the unmarried and childless Montand is encouraging his nephew to find a woman and marry, so the family name can be continued.

The nephew already has a bride in mind: the beautiful Manon (Emmanuelle Beart), daughter of the dead man, who tends goats on the mountainside and lives in poverty, although she has received a good education. Unfortunately for the nephew, he has a rival for her affections in the local schoolteacher. As the story unfolds, Manon discovers by accident that the nephew and his uncle blocked her father's spring—and when she accidentally discovers the source of the water for the whole village, she has her revenge by cutting off the water of those who killed her father.

All of this takes place with the implacable pace of a Greek tragedy. It sounds more melodramatic than it is, because the events themselves are not the issue here—the director, Claude Berri, has a larger point he wants to make, involving poetic justice on a scale that spans the generations. There are surprises at the end of this film that I do not choose to reveal, but they bring the whole story full circle, and Montand finally receives a punishment that is perfectly, even cruelly, suited to his crime.

Apart from its other qualities, *Manon of the Spring* announces the arrival of a strong and beautiful new actress from France in Emmanuelle Beart. Already seen in *Date With an Angel,* a comedy in which she supplied the only redeeming virtue, she is very effective in this central role, this time as a sort of avenging angel who punishes the old man and his nephew by giving them a glimpse of what could have been for them, had they not been so cruel.

The Marriage of Maria Braun

★ ★ ★ ★

R, 120 m., 1979

Hanna Schygulla (Maria Braun), Klaus Lowitsch (Hermann Braun), Ivan Desny (Oswald), Gottfried John (Willi), Gisela Uhlen (Mother), R.W. Fassbinder (Peddler). Directed and produced by Rainer Werner Fassbinder. Screenplay by Peter Marthescheimer and Pea Frohlicj.

Rainer Werner Fassbinder had been working his way toward this film for years, ever since he began his astonishingly prodigious output with his first awkward but powerful films in 1969. His films were always about sex, money, and death, and his method was often to explore those three subjects through spectacularly incompatible couples (an elderly cleaning woman and a young black worker, a James Dean look-alike and a thirteen-year-old girl, a rich gay about town and a simple-minded young sweepstakes winner).

Whatever his pairings and his cheerfully ironic conclusions, though, there was always another subject lurking in the background of his approximately thirty-three (!) features. He gave us what he saw as the rise and second fall of West Germany in the three postwar decades—considered in the context of the overwhelming American influence on his country.

With the masterful epic *The Marriage of Maria Braun,* he made his clearest and most cynical statement of the theme, and at the same time gave us a movie dripping with period detail, with the costumes and decor he was famous for, with the elegant decadence his characters will sell their souls for in a late-1940s economy without chic retail goods.

Fassbinder's film begins with a Germany torn by war and ends with a gas explosion and a soccer game. His ending may seem arbitrary to some, but in the context of West German society in the 1970s it may only be good reporting. His central character, Maria Braun, is played with great style and power by Hanna Schygulla, and Maria's odyssey from the war years to the consumer years provides the film's framework.

The film opens as Maria marries a young soldier, who then goes off to battle and presumably is killed. It follows her during a long period of mourning, which is punctuated by a little amateur hooking (of which her mother tacitly approves) and then by a tender and very carefully observed liaison with a large, strong, gentle black American soldier whom she really likes—we guess.

The soldier's accidental death, and her husband's return, are weathered by Maria with rather disturbing aplomb, but then we begin to see that Maria's ability to feel has been atrophied by the war, and her ability to be surprised has withered away. If war makes any plans absolutely meaningless, then why should one waste time analyzing coincidences?

Fassbinder has some rather bitter fun with what happens in the aftermath of the soldier's death (the lovestruck, or perhaps just shellshocked, husband voluntarily goes to prison, and Maria rises quickly in a multinational corporation). The movie is more realistic in its treatment of characters than Fassbinder sometimes is, but the events are as arbitrary as ever (and why not—events only have the meanings we assign to them, anyway).

The mini-apocalypse at the end is a perfect conclusion (an ending with "meaning" would have been obscene for this film) and then I think we are left, if we want it, with the sum of what Fassbinder has to say about the rebuilding of Germany: We got the stores opened again, but we don't know much about the customers yet.

Mask ★ ★ ★ ½

PG-13, 120 m., 1985

Cher (Rusty Dennis), Eric Stoltz (Rocky Dennis), Sam Elliott (Gar), Estelle Getty (Evelyn), Richard Dysart (Abe), Laura Dern (Diana). Directed by Peter Bogdanovich and produced by Martin Starger. Screenplay by Anna Hamilton Phelan.

When we see him for the first time, it's a glimpse through his bedroom window, half-reflected in a mirror. A second later, we see him more clearly, this teen-age boy with the strange face. We are shocked for a second, until he starts to talk, and then, without effort, we accept him as a normal kid who has had an abnormal thing happen to him. The name of his disease is craniodiaphyseal dyaplasia, and it causes calcium deposits on his skull that force his face out of shape. "What's the matter?" he likes to ask. "You never seen anyone from the planet Vulcan before?"

The kid's name is Rocky Dennis, and his mother is named Rusty. She is not your normal mom, either. She rides with a motorcycle gang, abuses drugs, shacks up with gang members, and has no visible means of employment. But within about ten minutes, we know that she is the ideal mom for Rocky. That's in the scene where the school principal suggests that Rocky would be better off in a "special" school, and she tells the principal he is a jerk, her son is a good student with good grades, and here is the name of her lawyer.

Movies don't often grab us as quickly as *Mask* does. The story of Rocky and Rusty is absorbing from the very first, maybe because the movie doesn't waste a lot of time wringing its hands over Rocky's fate. *Mask* lands on its feet, running. The director, Peter Bogdanovich, moves directly to the center of Rocky's life—his mother, his baseball cards, his cocky bravado, his growing awareness of girls. Bogdanovich handles *Mask* a lot differently than a made-for-TV movie would have, with TV's disease-of-the-week approach. This isn't the story of a disease, but the story of some people. And the most extraordinary person in the movie, surprisingly, is not Rocky, but his mother. Rusty Dennis is played by Cher as a complicated, angry, high-energy woman with a great capacity to love her son and encourage him to live as fully as he can. Rocky is a great kid, but because he succeeds so well at being a teen-ager, he is not a special case like, say, the Elephant Man. He is a kid with a handicap. It is a tribute to Eric Stoltz, who plays the role beneath the completely convincing makeup of Michael Westmore, that we accept him on his own terms.

Cher, on the other hand, makes Rusty Dennis into one of the most interesting movie characters in a long time. She is up front about her life-style, and when her son protests about her drinking and drugging, she tells him to butt out of her business. She rides with the motorcycle gang, but is growing unhappy with her promiscuity, and is relieved when the guy she really loves (Sam Elliott) comes back from a trip and moves in. She is also finally able to clean up her act, and stop drinking and using, after Rocky asks her to; she loves him that much.

Mask is based on a true story, and that doesn't come as a surprise: Hollywood wouldn't have the nerve to make a fictional tearjerker like this. The emotional peak of the movie comes during a summer that Rocky spends as an assistant at a camp for the blind. He falls in love with a blind teenager (Laura Dern), who feels his face and says he looks all right to her, and they have some of that special time together that only teen-agers can have: time when love doesn't mean sex so much as it means perfect agreement on the really important issues, like Truth and Beauty. Then the girl's parents come to pick her up, and their reaction to Rocky comes as a shock to us, a reminder of how completely we had accepted him.

Mask is a wonderful movie, a story of high spirits and hope and courage. It has some songs in it, by Bob Seger, and there was a lot of publicity about the fact that Peter Bogdanovich would rather the songs were by Bruce Springsteen. Let me put it this way: This is a movie that doesn't depend on its sound track. It works because of the people it's about, not because of the music they listen to.

Masquerade ★ ★ ★

R, 91 m., 1988 ✓

Rob Lowe (Tim Whalan), Meg Tilly (Olivia Lawrence), Kim Cattrall (Brooke Morrison), Doug Stewart (Mike McGill), John Glover (Tony Gateworth), Dana Delany (Anne Briscoe), Erik Holland (Chief of Police), Brian Davies (Granger Morrison), Barton Heyman (Tommy McGill), Bernie McInerney (Harland Fitzgerald). Directed by Bob Swaim and produced by Michael I. Levy. Screenplay by Dick Wolf.

"The problem with us," one of her relatives tells her, "is that we have too much money." They do. The whole family is rich, and now here is young Olivia, fresh out of school, single, an orphan, with a bank balance of $200 million. She's a target for every gold digger in the Hamptons. But even Olivia should not have to endure the way men treat her in *Masquerade,* which is a thriller in the shape of a Chinese puzzle box: Every time she solves one mystery, there's another one hidden inside it.

The movie's first mystery is Olivia herself, played by Meg Tilly in a very particular way that was slightly distracting at first, until I began to realize how well-chosen it was for the part. Tilly, who can be sharp-edged and observant, is a little dreamy this time. She talks in a breathy voice that seems filled with afterthoughts, and she comes across as innocent and passive.

Her character has not had an easy life. Her father died when she was twelve, and her mother has died just a few months before the story opens. She lives in a mansion in the Hamptons (one of her nine homes) with her mother's fourth husband, a drunken lout played with cheerful hatefulness by John Glover. She hates him, but there's no way to get him out of the house; he's protected by her mother's will.

Back home after school, Olivia drifts into a round of idle days and evenings filled with parties and dances. She runs into Mike (Doug Savant), the boy she promised to marry when she was twelve. He's now one of the local cops, forever on the other side of the divide between the rich and the poor. "Some dreams don't die," he tells her, but she tells him gently that it wasn't meant to be. Then one night at a dance she meets Tim (Rob Lowe), the handsome skipper of the racing sailboat owned by a local millionaire.

Tim has been sleeping with the millionaire's wife, but it's love at first sight when he sees Olivia. Before long they're holding hands on the beach and even committing the ultimate transgression: public fraternization between members and employees at the yacht club. Glover, the stepfather, is savage in his disapproval of the penniless sailor. He goes away for the weekend, the young couple sleep together in her house, Glover unexpectedly bursts in drunkenly, there is a struggle, and Tim shoots him dead.

That's what happens, all right, but what really happens is a lot more complicated. Because *Masquerade* depends so surely upon its many surprises, I won't reveal any more of the plot, except to say that Olivia tries to cover up for the man she loves, and Mike, the local cop, seems to go along with the cover-up for complicated motives going back to his original love for her.

If all of this sounds needlessly complicated (sort of a "Deathstyles of the Rich and Famous"), director Bob Swaim and writer Dick Wolf are sure-footed in their storytelling. One by one, the curtains of deception and intrigue are pulled back, and the most tantalizing thing about their method is that they always keep young Olivia in the dark. While evil currents swirl around her, while the people she trusts turn treacherous, she remains in a kind of innocent cocoon, gullible and deluded. That's why Meg Tilly's acting style is the right choice for the movie. Her dreaminess, which at first seems distracting, becomes an important part of the suspense, because while she drifts in her romantic reverie, a sweet smile on her face, we're mentally screaming at her to wake up and smell the coffee.

The other performances are mostly adequate. Rob Lowe is rather boxed in by the complicated things the plot does with his character, and Doug Savant goes through some interesting changes as the local cop. I was disappointed, though, by John Glover's evil stepfather. Glover was a superb villain in John Frankenheimer's *52 Pickup* (1987), suave and oily, but this time he overplays the drunk routine and lurches around the house so grotesquely that we fear more for his balance than Tilly's life.

This is Bob Swaim's third film, after the great *La Balance* and the intriguing *Half Moon Street.* Like both of those films, it has its roots in the crime melodramas of the 1940s—when movies were about attractive victims, rather than attractive killers. The notion of placing a complete innocent at the center of the frame, and then surrounding her with menace, is a little old-fashioned, in a way; many recent films have preferred all-powerful heroes and heroines who destroy anyone who crosses them. But in Roman Polanski's *Frantic,* Peter Yates's *The House on Carroll Street,* and now *Masquerade,* we're seeing a rebirth of the innocent bystander.

Maurice ★ ★ ★

R, 140 m., 1987

James Wilby (Maurice), Hugh Grant (Clive), Rupert Graves (Scudder), Denholm Elliott (Dr. Barry), Simon Callow (Mr. Ducie), Billie Whitelaw (Mrs. Hall), Ben Kingsley (Lasker-Jones). Directed by James Ivory and produced by Ismail Merchant. Screenplay by Kit Hesketh-Harvey and Ivory.

Maurice tells the story of a young English homosexual who falls in love with two completely different men—and in their differences is the whole message of the movie, a message I do not agree with. Yet because the film is so well made and acted, because it captures its period so meticulously, I enjoyed it even in disagreement.

This is the first film from the team of James Ivory and Ismail Merchant since *A Room With a View,* and is based once again on a novel by E.M. Forster. Both books are about the gulf between idealistic romance and immediate physical passion, but otherwise they could not be more dissimilar. *Maurice,* written in 1913, was Forster's attempt to deal in fiction with his own homosexuality, and he suppressed the novel until after his death.

The story takes place in the years before World War I, when homosexuality was outlawed in Britain, and exposure meant disgrace and ruin. At Cambridge, two undergraduates become close friends, and then one day, in a moment of risk, one tells the other that he loves him.

The man declaring his love is Clive (Hugh Grant), an aristocrat who can look forward to a lifetime of wealth, privilege, and perhaps public office. The man he loves is Maurice (James Wilby), also well-born, who may go into the stock market. At first Maurice is shocked and repelled by what his friend says, but later that night he climbs in the window to give him a quick, passionate kiss and whisper, "I love you."

From the first, their ideas about love are opposite. Clive is not much interested in the physical expression of love; he thinks it will "lower" them. His notions are more platonic and idealistic. Maurice, once he has been introduced to the idea of love between men, becomes a passionate romantic, and before long Clive, the pursuer, becomes the pursued.

Clive fears exposure and disgrace. He sees homosexuality as something to be battled and overcome, and he breaks off with Maurice to marry, assume his family responsibilities, and go into politics. At first Maurice is shattered, and there are tragicomic scenes in which he seeks help from a hypnotist and the family doctor. Then he has a physical encounter of astonishing passion with Scudder (Rupert Graves), the roughhewn gamekeeper on Clive's estate, and eventually both men determine to risk everything, throw their reputations to the wind, and live together as lovers.

Merchant and Ivory tell this story in a film so handsome to look at and so intelligently acted that it is worth seeing just to regard the production. Scene after scene is perfectly created: a languorous afternoon floating on the river behind the Cambridge colleges; a desultory cricket game between masters and servants; the daily routine of college life; visits to country estates and town homes; the settings of the rooms. The supporting cast (Ben Kingsley, Simon Callow, Billie Whitelaw, Denholm Elliott) is unusually strong, and although some people might find Wilby unfocused in the title role, I thought he was making the right choices, portraying a man whose real thoughts were almost always elsewhere.

The problem in the movie is with the gulf between his romantic choices. His first great love, Clive, is a person with whom he has a great deal in common. They share minds as well as bodies. Scudder, the gamekeeper, is frankly portrayed as an unpolished working-class lad, handsome but simple. In the England of 1913, with its rigid class divisions, the two men would have had even less in common than the movie makes it seem, and the real reason their relationship is daring is not because of sexuality but because of class.

Apart from their sexuality, they have nothing of substance to talk about with each other in this movie. No matter how deep their love, I suspect that within a few weeks or months the British class system would have driven them apart.

In ignoring this reality, Forster and Ivory seem to be making the idealistic statement that love conquers all. Sometimes it does. Not usually. Physical sexuality is an important part of everyone, but, especially after the first passion has cooled, it is not the most important part. There comes a time when people need to simply talk to one another, to coexist as companions, and I doubt if that time could ever come between Maurice and Scudder.

By arguing that their decision to stay together was a good and courageous thing, *Maurice* seems to argue that the most important thing about them was their homosexuality. Perhaps in the dangerous atmosphere of homophobia in the England of seventy-five years ago, that might have seemed the case. But this film was made in 1987, and shares the same limited insight.

McCabe and Mrs. Miller ★ ★ ★ ★

R, 120 m., 1971

Warren Beatty (McCabe), Julie Christie (Mrs. Miller), Rene Auberjonois (Shehan), Hugh Millais (Butler), Michael Murphy (Sears), William Devane (Lawyer). Directed by Robert Altman and produced by David Foster and Mitchell Brower. Screenplay by Altman and Brian McKay.

McCabe rides into the town of Presbyterian Church under a lowering sky, dismounts, takes off his buffalo-hide coat, puts on his bowler hat, and mumbles something under his breath that we can't quite make out, but the tone of voice is clear enough. This time, he's not going to let the bastards grind him down. He steps off through the mud puddles to the only local saloon, throws a cloth on the table, and takes out a pack of cards, to start again. His plan is to build a whorehouse with a bathhouse out in back, and get rich. By the end of the movie, he will have been offered $6,250 for his holdings, and he will be sitting thoughtfully in a snowbank, dead, as if thinking it all over.

And yet Robert Altman's *McCabe and Mrs. Miller* doesn't depend on that final death for its meaning. It doesn't kill a character just to get a trendy existential feel about the meaninglessness of it all. No, McCabe doesn't find it meaningless at all, and once Mrs. Miller explains the mistake he made in his reasoning, he rides all the way into the next town to try to sell his holdings for half what he was asking, because he'd rather not die.

Death is very final in this Western, because the movie is about life. Most Westerns are about killing and getting killed, which means they're not about life and death at all. We spend a time in the life of a small frontier town, which grows up before our eyes out of raw, unpainted lumber and tubercular canvas tents. We get to know the town pretty well, because Altman has a gift for making movies that seem to eavesdrop on activity that would have been taking place anyway.

That was what happened in *M*A*S*H*, where a lot of time didn't have to be wasted in introducing the characters and explaining the relationships between them, because the characters already knew who they were and how they felt about each other. In a lot of movies, an actor appears on the screen and has no identity at all until somebody calls him "Smith" or "Slim," and then he's Smith or Slim. In *McCabe and Mrs. Miller*, Altman uses a tactfully unobtrusive camera, a distinctive conversational style of dialogue, and the fluid movements of his actors to give us people who are characters from the moment we see them; we have the sense that when they leave camera range they're still thinking, humming, scratching, chewing, and nodding to each other in the street.

McCabe and Mrs. Miller are an organic part of this community. We are aware, of course, that they're played by Warren Beatty and Julie Christie, but rarely have stars been used so completely for their talents rather than their fame. We don't ever think much about McCabe being Warren Beatty, and Mrs. Miller being Julie Christie; they're there along with everybody else in town, and the movie just happens to be about their lives.

Because the movie is about a period in the lives of several people (and not about a series of events that occur to one-dimensional characters), McCabe and Mrs. Miller change during the course of the story. Mrs. Miller is a tough Cockney madam who convinces McCabe that he needs a competent manager for his whorehouse: How would *he* ever know enough about managing women? He agrees, and she lives up to her promise, and they're well on their way to making enough money for her to get out of this dump of a mining town and back to San Francisco, where, she believes, a woman of her caliber belongs.

All of this happens in an indoor sort of a way, and by that I don't mean that the movie looks like it was shot on a sound stage. The outdoors is always there, and people are always coming in out of it and shaking the rain from their hats, and we see the trees whipping in the wind through the windows. But it's a wet autumn and then a cold winter, so people naturally congregate in saloons and grocery stores and whorehouses, and the climate forces a sense of community. Then the enforcers come to town: The suave, Scottish-accented Butler, who kills people who won't sell out to the Company, and his two sidekicks. One of them is slack-jawed and mean, and the other is a nervous blond kid with the bare makings of a mustache. On the suspension bridge that gets you across the river to the general store, he kills another kid—a rawboned, easygoing country kid with a friendly smile—and it is one of the most affecting and powerful deaths there ever has been in a Western.

The final hunt for McCabe takes place in almost deserted streets, because the church is burning down and everybody is out at the edge of town trying to save it. The church burns during a ghostly, heavy daylight snowstorm: fire and ice. And McCabe almost gets away. Mrs. Miller, who allowed him into her bed but always, except once, demanded five dollars for the privilege, caught on long before he did that the Company would rather kill him than go up $2,000. She is down at the foot of town, in Chinatown, lost in an opium dream while the snow drifts against his body. *McCabe and Mrs. Miller* is like no other Western ever made.

Mean Streets ★ ★ ★ ★

R, 110 m., 1974

Robert De Niro (Johnny Boy), Harvey Keitel (Charlie). Directed by Martin Scorsese and produced by Jonathan T. Taplin. Screenplay by Scorsese and Mardik Martin.

Martin Scorsese's *Mean Streets* isn't so much a gangster movie as a perceptive, sympathetic, finally tragic story about how it is to grow up in a gangster environment. Its characters (like Scorsese himself) have grown up in New York's Little Italy, and they understand everything about that small slice of human society except how to survive in it. The two most important characters, Charlie and Johnny Boy, move through the Mafia environment almost because it's expected of them. Charlie is a Catholic with pathological guilt complexes, but because the mob is the family business, he never quite forces himself to make the connection between right and wrong and what he does. Not that he's very good at being a Mafioso: He's twenty-seven, but he still lives at home; he's a collector for his uncle's protection racket, but the collections don't bring in much. If he has any luck at all, he will be able to take over a bankrupt restaurant.

He is, at least fitfully, a realist. Johnny Boy, on the other hand, is a violent, uncontrolled product of romanticized notions of criminal street life. Little Italy is all around him, and yet he seems to have formed his style and borrowed half his vocabulary from the movies. He contains great and ugly passions, and can find no way to release them except in sudden violent bursts. Charlie is in love with Johnny Boy's sister, and he also feels a dogged sense of responsibility for Johnny Boy: He goes up on a roof one night when Johnny is shooting out streetlights and talks him down. At least Johnny releases his angers in overt ways. Charlie suppresses everything, and sometimes in desperation passes his hand through a flame and wonders about the fires of hell. He takes his Catholicism literally.

Scorsese places these characters in a perfectly realized world of boredom and small joys, sudden assaults, the possibility of death, and the certainty of mediocrity. He shot on location in Little Italy, where he was born and where he seems to know every nuance of architecture and personality, and his story isn't built like a conventional drama: It emerges from the daily lives of the characters. They hang out. They go to the movies. They eat, they drink, they get in sudden fights that end as quickly as a summer storm. Scorsese photographs them with fiercely driven visual style. We never have the sense of a scene being set up and then played out; his characters hurry to their dooms while the camera tries to keep pace. There's an improvisational feel even in scenes that we know, because of their structure, couldn't have been improvised.

Scorsese got the same feel in his first feature, *Who's That Knocking at My Door?* (1967). *Mean Streets* is a sequel, and Scorsese gives us the same leading actor (Harvey Keitel) to assure the continuity. In the earlier film, he was still on the edge of life, of sex, of violence. Now he has been plunged in, and he isn't equal to the experience. He's not tough enough to be a Mafia collector (and not strong enough to resist). Johnny Boy is played by Robert De Niro and it's a marvelous performance, filled with urgency and restless desperation.

The movie's scenes of violence are especially effective because of the way Scorsese stages them. We don't get spectacular effects and skillfully choreographed struggles. Instead, there's something realistically clumsy about the fights in this movie. A scene in a pool hall, in particular, is just right in the way it shows its characters fighting and yet mindful of their suits (possibly the only suits they have). The whole movie feels like life in New York; there are scenes in a sleazy nightclub, on fire escapes, and in bars, and they all feel as if Scorsese has been there.

Melvin and Howard ★ ★ ★ ½

R, 95 m., 1980

Paul Le Mat (Melvin Dummar), Jason Robards (Howard Hughes), Mary Steenburgen (Lynda Dummar), Pamela Reed (Bonnie Dummar), Michael J. Pollard (Little Red), Charles Napier (Man with Envelope), Robert Ridgely (TV Host), Melvin Dummar (Depot Counterman). Directed by Jonathan Demme and produced by Art Linson and Don Phillips. Screenplay by Bo Goldman.

Melvin Dummar is the man who claimed he gave a lift to a doddering old hitchhiker, loaned him a quarter, and was left $156 million in the hitchhiker's will. If he was telling the truth, the hitchhiker was Howard Hughes. But Jonathan Demme's wonderful comedy *Melvin and Howard* doesn't depend on whether the so-called Mormon Will was really written by Hughes. That hardly matters. This is the story of a life lived at the other end of the financial ladder from

Hughes. It sees Dummar as the kind of American hero who is celebrated for being so extraordinarily ordinary.

For what, after all, constitutes heroism? And why shouldn't Dummar be considered a hero? We learn from this movie that he ventured single-handedly into the jungle of American consumerism, and lived. We see his major battles. Here's a guy who was married three times (twice to the same woman, the second time with the "Hawaiian War Chant" playing in an all-night Vegas chapel). He had three cars and a boat repossessed, he went from being Milkman of the Month to hauling his first wife off a go-go stage, he loved his children, did not drink or smoke, and stood at the brink of losing his gas station franchise on the very day when a tall, blond stranger dropped what looked a lot like Hughes's last will and testament into his life.

The genius of *Melvin and Howard* is that it is about Melvin, not Howard. The film begins and ends with scenes involving the Hughes character, who is played by Jason Robards as a desert rat with fading memories of happiness. Dummar stops in the desert to answer a call of nature, finds Hughes lying in the sagebrush, gives him a ride in his pickup truck, and gets him to sing. For reasons of his own, Hughes sings "Bye, Bye Blackbird": *Got no one to love and understand me . . . oh, what hard-luck stories they all hand me.*

Robards is a chillingly effective Hughes. But this movie belongs to Paul Le Mat, as Dummar. Le Mat played the round-faced hot-rodder in *American Graffiti,* and Dummar is the kind of guy that character might have grown up to be. He is pleasant, genial, simple of speech, crafty of mind, always looking for an angle. He angles for Milkman of the Month, he plots to get his wife on a TV game show, he writes songs like "Santa's Souped-Up Sleigh," he plays the slots at Vegas and goes through his life asking only for a few small scores.

When he gets a big score—named the beneficiary of a $156 million will that seems to have been signed by Hughes—he hardly knows what to do. Long-lost relatives and new-found friends turn up by the dozens, and press conferences are held in front of his gas station. There is a court trial, but the movie never really addresses itself to the details of the Hughes will court case. It goes instead for the drama and for the effect on Dummar and his family.

This is a slice of American life. It shows the flip side of Gary Gilmore's Utah. It is a world of mobile homes, Pop Tarts, dust, kids, and dreams of glory. It's pretty clear how this movie got made. The producers started with the notion that the story of the mysterious Hughes will might make a good courtroom thriller. Well, maybe it would have. But my hunch is that when they met Dummar, they had the good sense to realize that they could get a better—and certainly a funnier—story out of what happened to him between the day he met Hughes and the day the will was discovered. Dummar is the kind of guy who thinks they oughta make a movie out of his life. This time, he was right.

Mephisto ★ ★ ★ ★

NO MPAA RATING, 135 m., 1981

Klaus Maria Brandauer (Henrik Hofgon), Krystyna Janda (Barbara Bruckner), Ildiko Bansagi (Nicolette Von Hiebuhr), Karin Boyd (Juliette Martens). Directed and produced by Istvan Szabo. Screenplay by Szabo and Peter Dobel.

There are times in *Mephisto* when the hero tries to explain himself by saying that he's only an actor, and he has that almost right. *All* he is, is an actor. It's not his fault that the Nazis have come to power, and that as a German speaking actor he must choose between becoming a Nazi and being exiled into a foreign land without jobs for German actors. As long as he is acting, as long as he is not called upon to risk his real feelings, this man can act his way into the hearts of women, audiences, and the Nazi power structure. This is the story of a man who plays his life wearing masks, fearing that if the last mask is removed, he will have no face.

The actor is played by Klaus Maria Brandauer in one of the greatest movie performances I've ever seen. The character, Henrik, is not sympathetic, and yet we identify with him because he shares so many of our own weaknesses and fears. Henrik is not a very good actor or a very good human being, but he is good enough to get by in ordinary times. As the movie opens, he's a socialist, interested in all the most progressive new causes, and is even the proud lover of a black woman. By the end of the film, he has learned that his liberalism was a taste, not a conviction, and that he will do anything, flatter anybody, make any compromise, just to hear applause, even though he knows the applause comes from fools.

Mephisto does an uncanny job of creating its period, of showing us Hamburg and Berlin from the 1920s to the 1940s. And I've never seen a movie that does a better job of showing the seductive Nazi practice of providing party members with theatrical costumes, titles, and pageantry. In this movie, not being a Nazi is like being at a black tie ball in a brown corduroy suit. Hofgon, the actor, is drawn to this world like a magnet. From his ambitious beginnings in the provincial German theater, he works his way up into more important roles and laterally into more important society. All of his progress is based on lies. He marries a woman he does not love, because her father can do him some good. When the rise of the Nazis destroys his father-in-law's power, he leaves his wife. He continues all this time to maintain his affair with his black mistress. He has a modest, but undeniable, talent as an actor, but prostitutes it by playing his favorite role, Mephistopheles in *Faust*, not as he could but as he calculates he should.

The obvious parallel here is between the hero of this film and the figure of tragedy who sold his soul to the devil. But *Mephisto* doesn't depend upon easy parallels to make its point. This is a human story, and as the actor in this movie makes his way to the top of the Nazi propaganda structure and the bottom of his own soul, the movie is both merciless and understanding. This is a weak and shameful man, the film seems to say, but then it cautions us against throwing the first stone.

Mephisto is not a German but a Hungarian movie, directed by the talented Istvan Szabo, who has led his country's cinema from relative obscurity to its present position as one of the best and most innovative film industries in Europe. Szabo, in his way, has made a companion film to Fassbinder's *The Marriage of Maria Braun.* The Szabo film shows a man compromising his way to the top by lying to himself and everybody else, and throwing aside all moral standards. It ends as World War II is under way. The Fassbinder film begins after the destruction of the war, showing a woman clawing her way out of the rubble and repeating the same process of compromise, lies, and unquestioning materialism.

Both the man in the Szabo film and the woman in the Fassbinder film maintain one love affair all through everything, using their love (he for a black woman, she for a convict) as a sort of token contempt for a society whose corrupt values they otherwise completely accept. The fact that they *can* still love, of course, makes it impossible for them to quite deceive themselves. That is the price they pay for their deals with the devil.

Merry Christmas, Mr. Lawrence

★ ★ 1/2
R, 122 m., 1983

David Bowie (Celliers) Tom Conti (Colonel Lawrence), Ryuichi Sakamoto (Captain Yonoi), Takeshi (Sergeant Hara), Jack Thompson (Hicksley-Ellis). Directed by Nagisa Oshima and produced by Jeremy Thomas. Screenplay by Oshima and Paul Mayersberg.

Here's a movie that is even stranger than it was intended to be. *Merry Christmas, Mr. Lawrence* is about a clash between two cultures (British and Japanese) and two styles of military service (patriotic and pragmatic). That would be enough for any movie, and there are scenes when it *is* enough, and the movie works pretty well. But then the movie makes another contrast that doesn't work so well, a contrast between basic views of theatrical acting styles. British tradition suggests that, everything else being equal, actors should behave as if they were real people in a real situation. The Japanese tend toward a more overwrought acting style, made of screams and grimaces, histrionics and dramatizations. Each tradition works well enough in a movie where it is the only tradition. But in a movie where British and Japanese are on the screen at the same time and are apparently sharing the same reality, the results look odd, and eventually undermine the film. We wonder, in some small irreverent corner of our minds, whether the soft-spoken British *notice* that the Japanese rant and rave over everything, including the weather, and whether the Japanese, in turn, find the British catatonic.

The movie is by Nagisa Oshima, the best-known of the younger Japanese directors, whose notorious *In the Realm of the Senses* (1976) began with a love affair between a businessman and a geisha and ended in a bloodbath of castration and suicide. He is clearly fascinated by relationships between authorities and victims, and that's the subject here. The time is 1942, in a Japanese prison camp on Java, and the story concentrates on two pairs of officers. The British are Celliers (David Bowie), very upper crust, duty-bound, guilt-ridden, and Lawrence (Tom Conti), sensitive, bilingual, trying to translate not only the words but the values of the two races. The Japanese are Yonoi (Ryuichi Sakamoto) of the warrior class, filled with pride and glory, and Hara (Takeshi), a sort of Japanese Falstaff with a streak of sadism. How these two pairs get along together will determine the fate of the British (which is complicated by their nominal leader, a blustering bully played by Jack Thompson).

The movie develops the situation in a series of scenes that owe something to *Bridge Over the River Kwai*. Rules are made, forgotten, broken, then strictly enforced. Enemies admit at weak moments that we are all human beings, after all. But then there's a breach of protocol and a crackdown from the top. The most rigid officers on each side (Celliers and Yonoi) have a sort of admiration for each other, which turns into a contest of wills. This is interesting material, especially since Oshima plunges a little more deeply into the psychology of his characters than your average prisoner-of-war movie is likely to. There are hints of a homosexual attraction between Celliers and Yonoi, eventually leading to one of the movie's most awkward moments—a parting in which the British soldier actually seems to be saying that both sides were right in the war and both sides were wrong.

It's awkward, not because of the subject matter, because of the contrasting acting styles. Here are two men trying to communicate in a touchy area and they behave as if they're from different planets. The overstatement in the Japanese acting ruins the scene. It's strange: Japanese acting styles never bother me in all-Japanese movies (especially not when they're modulated, as in the contemporary films of Kurosawa). It's only when you have actors who are clearly on different wavelengths that the Japanese histrionics become distracting. What this movie needed was a diplomatic acting coach.

Metropolis ★ ★ ★ ★

NO MPAA RATING, 120 m., 1926, 1984 (Sound version)

Alfred Abel (Leader), Gustay Frohlich (His Son), Brigitte Helm (Maria), Rudolf Klein-Rogge (Rotwang), Heinrich George (Foreman). Directed by Fritz Lang. Screenplay by Lang and Thea Von Harbou. New sound track by Giorgio Moroder.

Fritz Lang's 1926 film *Metropolis* is one of the great achievements in the silent era, a work so audacious in its vision and so angry in its message that it is, if anything, more powerful today than when it was made. But it is rarely seen today; even in the era of insatiable home TV watching, silent films are condemned to the hinterlands of film societies and classrooms.

That is a great loss. Lang's movie is one of the great overwrought fantasies of German Expressionism, a story of a monstrous twenty-first-century city in which the workers labor like robots in their subterranean factories, while the privileged classes dance the night away, far above. The plot is broad melodrama: The son of the ruler of Metropolis visits the underground city and falls in love with a revolutionary named Maria, who makes impassioned speeches against the tyrants above. But the ruler orders a mad scientist to provide his new robot with Maria's face, creating a false Maria who will mislead the workers. Some of the individual scenes are amazing in their visual power, especially our first sight of the workers marching to their jobs, and a bizarre Art Deco factory wall where the humans are treated as parts of the machines. The movie was widely influential: The scene where the robot is turned into the false Maria was the inspiration for all the 1930s transformations of Frankenstein's monsters. Yet the original *Metropolis* is hardly known to today's filmgoers.

But now Giorgio Moroder, the composer of "Flashdance—What a Feeling" and the sound tracks for such movies as *Cat People,* has resurrected *Metropolis*, discovered or reconstructed some of its missing scenes, added some color tinting, and released it with a sound track of 1984 pop music. When this version of the movie was premiered at the 1984 Cannes Film Festival, it was sold primarily for its possibilities as a midnight cult film. In some sort of weird cultural inversion, Pat Benatar and Adam Ant would be used to sell Fritz Lang.

After you've seen the film with its new sound track, however, the notion seems almost sane. Silent films have always been accompanied by some sort of musical accompaniment—everything from orchestras to solo pianos. And in recent years such silent classes as *Napoleon* and *Peter Pan* have been resurrected with new scores. This is even the second time around for *Metropolis,* which was given a track of electronic music by the BBC in the 1970s. Moroder, however, has gone all the way and tarted up *Metropolis* with the same kinds of songs you'd expect to hear on MTV—he treats *Metropolis* like a music video. The film is too strong and original to be reduced to a formula, however; it absorbs the sound track, instead of being dominated by it, and the result is a film that works and a sound track that is an addition.

Some purists will not approve of Moroder's choice in music. Kevin Thomas of the *Los Angeles Times* was especially offended by the use of songs with words ("which sound especially silly because they're so painfully redundant"), but the words didn't bother me because, frankly, I didn't find myself listening to them. They are part of the background, and Fritz Lang's great film, so lovingly reconstructed, is the magnificent foreground.

Micki & Maude ★ ★ ★

PG-13, 115 m., 1984

Dudley Moore (Rob Salinger), Amy Irving (Maude Salinger), Ann Reinking (Micki Salinger), Richard Mulligan (Leo Brody), Lu Leonard (Nurse Verbeck). Directed by Blake Edwards and produced by Tony Adams. Screenplay by Jonathan Reynolds.

The key to the whole thing is Dudley Moore's absolutely and unquestioned sincerity. He loves both women. He would do anything to avoid hurting either woman. He wants to do the right thing but, more than that, he wants to do the kind thing. And that is how he ends up in a maternity ward with two wives who are both presenting him with baby children. If it were not for those good qualities in Moore's character, qualities this movie goes to great lengths to establish, *Micki & Maude* would run the risk of turning into tasteless and even cruel slapstick. After all, these are serious matters we're talking about. But the triumph of the movie is that it identifies so closely with Moore's desperation and his essentially sincere motivation that we understand the lengths to which he is driven. That makes the movie's inevitable climax even funnier.

As the movie opens, Moore is happily married to an assistant district attorney (Ann Reinking) who has no desire to have children. Children are, however, the only thing in life that Moore himself desires; apart from that one void, his life is full and happy. He works as a reporter for one of those TV magazine shows where weird people talk earnestly about their constitutional rights to be weird: For example, nudists defend their right to bear arms. Then he meets a special person, a cello player (Amy Irving) who has stepped in at the last moment to play a big concert. She thinks he has beautiful eyes, he smiles, it's love, and within a few weeks Moore and Irving are talking about how they'd like to have kids. Then Irving gets pregnant. Moore decides to do the only right thing, and divorce the wife he loves to marry the pregnant girlfriend that he also loves. But then his wife announces that she's pregnant, and Moore turns, in this crisis of conscience, to his best friend, a TV producer wonderfully played by Richard Mulligan. There is obviously only one thing he can do: become a bigamist.

Micki & Maude was directed by Blake Edwards, who also directed Moore in *10,* and who knows how to build a slapstick climax by one subtle development after another. There is, for example, the fact that Irving's father happens to be a professional wrestler, with a lot of friends who are even taller and meaner than he is. There is the problem that Moore's original in-laws happen past the church where he is having his second wedding. Edwards has a way of applying absolute logic to insane situations, so we learn, for example, that after Moore tells one wife he works days and the other one he works nights, his schedule works out in such a way that he begins to get too much sleep.

Dudley Moore is developing into one of the great movie comedians of his generation.

Micki & Maude goes on the list with *10* and *Arthur* as screwball classics. Moore has another side as an actor, a sweeter, more serious side, that shows up in good movies like *Romantic Comedy* and bad ones like *Six Weeks,* but it's when he's in a screwball comedy, doing his specialty of absolutely sincere desperation, that he reaches genius. For example: The last twenty minutes of *Micki & Maude,* as the two pregnant women move inexorably forward on their collision course, represents a kind of filmmaking that is as hard to do as anything you'll ever see on a screen. The timing has to be flawless. So does the logic: One loose end, and the inevitability of a slapstick situation is undermined. Edwards and Moore are working at the top of their forms here, and the result is a pure, classic slapstick that makes *Micki & Maude* a real treasure.

A Midsummer Night's Sex Comedy

★ ★

PG, 88 m., 1982

Woody Allen (Andrew), Mia Farrow (Ariel), Jose Ferrer (Leopold), Julie Hagerty (Dulcy), Tony Roberts (Maxwell), Mary Steenburgen (Adrian). Directed by Woody Allen and produced by Robert Greenhut. Screenplay by Allen.

The further north you go in summer, the longer the twilight lingers, until night is but a finger drawn between the dusk and the dawn. Such nights in northern climes are times of revelry, when lads and maids frolic in the underbrush to the pipes of Pan. Woody Allen's *A Midsummer Night's Sex Comedy* sneaks up rather suspiciously on this tradition; his men and women are rationalists, belong to such professions as finance, medicine, and psychiatry, and are nonchalant in the face of such modern inventions as flying bicycles. And yet here they all are, out in the country for the weekend. They gather at a little cottage somewhere in upstate New York, arriving by carriage or primitive auto, and in no time at all they are deeply unhappy about each other's sex lives. The host and hostess are Woody Allen and Mary Steenburgen. He is a stockbroker and she is his shy and sweet wife. The guests include Jose Ferrer, as an egotistical scientist, Mia Farrow, as his fiancée, Tony Roberts as a doctor, and Julie Hagerty as his abundantly sexed nurse.

During the course of their long weekend, many themes emerge, but the most common one is the enigma of male jealousy. Look at these three men, each one paired with the wonderful woman of his dreams. Allen, a part-time crackpot inventor, has a wife who loyally supports his experiments. Ferrer, an aging genius with a monstrous ego, has a beautiful young woman to hang on his arm. Roberts, an insatiable satyr, has a nubile nurse panting with desire. Are all three men happy and satiated? Not a chance. It is the most inevitable thing in the world that each man should be consumed with lust for one or more of the other women. It is not enough to have a bird in the hand; one must also have another bird in the bush. Or, as David Merrick once observed, "It is not enough for me to succeed. My enemies must fail."

From this simple and intriguing little situation, Woody Allen spins a rondelet of sexual intrigue and frustration. The basic developments: Allen pines away with the thought that he could once have made love to Farrow, but declined the chance. Ferrer conspires to meet Hagerty in the woods. Roberts attempts to seduce Farrow. And, through it all, Steenburgen steadfastly hopes for the best from everybody. To pass the time in between assignations and intrigues, the couples picnic, go for walks in the woods and express curiosity in Allen's latest inventions, which, in addition to the flying bicycle, include a metal sphere that can provide a magic lantern show that remembers the past and foresees the future.

This all sounds very charming and whimsical, and it is—almost paralyzingly so. *A Midsummer Night's Sex Comedy* is so low-key, so sweet and offhand and slight, there are times when it hardly even seems happy to be a movie. I am not quite sure what Allen had in mind when he conceived this material, but in addition to the echoes of Shakespeare and of Bergman's *Smiles of a Summer Night,* there are suggestions of John Cheever's Wapshots, Doctorow's *Ragtime* and Jean Renoir films in which nice people do nice things to little avail. This is not a "Woody Allen film," then. It is not a brash comedy, it does not really contain the Woody Allen persona, and I guess Woody wanted it that way; he says he wants to try new things instead of giving people the same old stuff all the time. It is our misfortune that he arrived at that decision just after making *Annie Hall* and *Manhattan,* two wonderful films that brought his same old stuff to an exciting new plateau.

Now, with *Stardust Memories* and this film, he seems rudderless. I don't object to *A Midsummer Night's Sex Comedy* on grounds that it's different from his earlier films, but on the more fundamental ground that it's adrift. There doesn't seem to be a driving idea behind it, a confident tone to give us the sure notion that Allen knows what he wants to do here. It's a tip-off that the story is lacking in both sex and comedy. If the film seems at a loss to know where to turn next, the ending is particularly unsatisfactory. It involves a moment of fantasy or spirituality in which one of the movie's most rational characters dies and turns into a spirit of light, and bobs away on the twilight breeze. I don't object to the development itself, but to the way Allen handles it, so briefly and incompletely that it ends the film with what can only be described as a whimsical anticlimax.

There are nice small moments here and reflective, quiet performances, and a few laughs and smiles. But when we see Woody pedaling furiously to spin the helicopter blades of his flying bicycle, we're reminded of what we're missing. Woody doesn't have to be funny in every shot and he doesn't have to become another Mel Brooks, but he should allow himself to be funny when he feels like it, without apology, instead of receding into cuteness. I had the feeling during the film that Woody Allen was soft-pedaling his talent, was sitting on his comic gift, was trying to be somebody that he is not—and that, even if he were, would not be half as wonderful a piece of work as the real Woody Allen.

Mishima ★ ★ ★ ★

R, 121 m., 1985

Ken Ogato (Yukio Mishima), Mashayuki Shionoya (Morita), Hiroshi Mikami (First Cadet), Naoko Otani (Mother). Directed by Paul Schrader and produced by Mata Yamamoto and Tom Luddy. Screenplay by Paul and Leonard Schrader.

The Japanese author Yukio Mishima seems to have thought of his life as a work of art, and more than anyone since Hemingway he got other people to think of it that way, too. He was a brilliant self-promoter who not only wrote important novels and plays, but also cultivated the press, posed for beefcake photographs, and founded his own private army. He was an advocate of a return to medieval Japanese values, considered himself a samurai, and died on schedule and according to his own plan: After occupying an Army garrison with some of his soldiers, he disemboweled himself while being beheaded by a follower.

Mishima's life obviously supplies the materials for a sensationalistic film. Paul Schrader has not made one. Instead, his *Mishima* takes this most flamboyant of writers and translates his life into a carefully structured examination of three different Mishimas: Public, private, and literary.

The film begins with the public Mishima, a literary superstar who begins the last day of his life by ritualistically donning the uniform of his private army. From time to time during the film, we return to moments from that final day, as Mishima is jammed somewhat inelegantly into a tiny car and driven by his followers to an appointment with a Japanese general. The film ends with Mishima holding the general hostage, and winning the right to address the troops of the garrison (who must have been just as astonished as if Norman Mailer turned up at West Point). Although the film ends with Mishima's ritual suicide, it is not shown in the graphic detail that's popular in recent films; Schrader wisely realizes that too much blood would destroy the mood of his film and distract attention from the idea behind Mishima's death.

Mishima's last day is counterpointed with black-and-white sequences showing his childhood and adolescence, and with gloriously stylized color dramatizations of scenes from his novels, *Temple of the Golden Pavilion, Kyoko's House,* and *Runaway Horses.* The scenes from the novels were visualized by designer Eiko Ishioka, who seems to have been inspired by fantasy scenes from early Technicolor musicals. They don't summarize Mishima's novels so much as give us an idea about them; as we see the ritualistic aspects of his fantasies, we are seeing Japan through his eyes, as he wished it to be.

The black-and-white biographical sequences show a little boy growing up into a complicated man. Young Yukio, raised by his mother and his grandmother, was a lonely outcast with a painful stammer, and we can see in the insecurities of his youth impulses that led him to build his muscles, to leap for literary glory, and to wrap himself in the samurai ethic.

Mishima is a rather glorious project, in these days of pragmatic commercialism and rank cynicism in the movie industry. Although a sensationalized version of his life might have had potential at the box office (and although Schrader, author of *Taxi Driver*, director of *American Gigolo*, would have been quite capable of directing it), this is a much more ambitious and intellectual film.

It challenges us to think about Mishima, instead of simply observing the strange channels of his life. What did he prove, on the day when his life ended according to plan? That he was willing to pay the ultimate price to transform his life into an artistic statement—and also, perhaps, that some of his genius was madness. Was it worth it? Who can say who is not Mishima?

Missing ★ ★ ★

R, 122 m., 1982

Jack Lemmon (Ed Horman), Sissy Spacek (Beth Horman), Melanie Mayron (Terry Simon), John Shea (Charles Horman), Charles Cioffi (Capt. Tower), David Clennon (Consul Putnam). Directed by Constantin Costa-Gavras and produced by Edward and Mildred Lewis. Screenplay by Costa-Gavras and Donald Stewart.

Much has already been written about the bravery of *Missing*, which dares, we are told, to make a specific attack on American policies in Chile during and after the Allende regime. I wish the movie had been even braver—brave enough to risk a clear, unequivocal, uncompromised statement of its beliefs, instead of losing itself in a cluttered mishmash of stylistic excesses. This movie might have *really* been powerful, if it could have gotten out of its own way.

The story involves the disappearance in the early 1970s of a young American journalist in a country (not named) that is obviously intended to be Chile. The young man and his wife (played by John Shea and Sissy Spacek) have gone down there to live, write, and absorb the local color. But then a civil war breaks out, martial law is declared, troops roam the streets, and one day soldiers come and take the young man away. The movie is the record of the frustrating attempts by Spacek and her father-in-law (Jack Lemmon) to discover what happened to the missing man. It suggests that the young American might have been on some sort of informal hit list of left-wing foreign journalists, that he was taken away and killed, and that (this is the controversial part) American embassy officials knew about his fate and may even have been involved in approving his death.

If that was indeed the case, then it is a cause for great anger and dismay. And the best scenes in *Missing*—the ones that make this movie worth seeing despite its shortcomings—are the ones in which Spacek and Lemmon hack their way through a bureaucratic jungle in an attempt to get someone to make a simple statement of fact. Those scenes are masterful. The U.S. embassy officials are painted as dishonest weasels, shuffling papers, promising immediate action, and lying through their teeth. Lemmon and Spacek are about as good an example of Ordinary Americans as you can find in a movie, and their flat voices and stubborn determination and even their initial dislike for one another all ring exactly true. If *Missing* had started with the disappearance of the young man, and had followed Spacek and Lemmon in a straightforward narrative as they searched for him, this movie might have generated overwhelming tension and anger. But the movie never develops the power it should have had, because the director, Constantin Costa-Gavras, either lacked confidence in the strength of his story, or had too much confidence in his own stylistic virtuosity. He has achieved the unhappy feat of upstaging his own movie, losing it in a thicket of visual and editing stunts.

Let's begin with the most annoying example of his meddling. *Missing* contains scenes that take place before the young man disappears. We see his domestic happiness with his wife and friends, we see him reading from *The Little Prince* and making plans for the future. The fact that this material is in the movie suggests, at least, that the story is being told by an omniscient author, one who can also tell us, if he wishes to, what happened to the victim. But he does not. Costa-Gavras shows us all sorts of ominous warnings of approaching trouble (including a lot of loose talk by American military men who are not supposed to be in the country, but are, and all but claim credit for a coup). He shows us a tragic aftermath of martial law, guns in the streets, vigilante justice, and the chilling sight of row after row of dead young men, summarily executed by the new junta. But he does not show us what happened to make the film's hero disappear. Or, rather, he shows us several versions—visual fantasies in which the young husband is arrested at home by a lot of soldiers, or a few, and is taken away in this way or that. These versions are pegged to the unreliable eyewitness accounts of the people who live across the street. They dramatize an uncertain human fate in a time of upheaval, but they also distract fatally from the flow of the film.

By the time *Missing* begins its crucial last half-hour, a strange thing has happened. We care about this dead American, and his wife and father, almost *despite* the movie. The performances of Spacek and Lemmon carry us along through the movie's undisciplined stylistic displays. But at the end of the film, there isn't the instant discharge of anger we felt at the end of Costa-Gavras's great *Z* (1968), because the narrative juggernaut of that film has been traded in for what is basically just a fancy meditation on the nature of reality. Something happened to the missing young man (his story is based on real events). Somebody was guilty, and somebody was lying, and he was indeed killed. But *Missing* loses its way on the road to those conclusions, and at the end Lemmon and Spacek seem almost to mourn alone, while the crew is busy looking for its next shot.

The Mission ★ ★ ½

PG, 126 m., 1986

Robert De Niro (Mendoza), Jeremy Irons (Gabriel), Ray McAnally (Altamirano), Aidan Quinn (Felipe), Cherie Lunghi (Carlotta), Ronald Pickup (Hontar). Directed by Roland Joffe and produced by Fernando Ghia and David Puttnam. Screenplay by Robert Bolt.

The Mission feels exactly like one of those movies where you'd rather see the documentary about how the movie was made. You'd like to know why so many talented people went to such incredible lengths to make a difficult and beautiful movie—without any of them, on the basis of the available evidence, having the slightest notion of what the movie was about. There isn't a moment in *The Mission* that is not watchable, but the moments don't add up to a coherent narrative. At the end, we can sort of piece things together, but the movie has never really made us care.

The action takes place in South America, in the eighteenth century. Two great colonial forces are competing for the hearts and minds of the native Indians. On the one hand, there are the imperialist plunderers, who want to establish a trade in riches and slaves. On the other hand, there are the missionaries, who want to convert the Indians to Christ.

The central figure in the movie is Mendoza (Robert De Niro), who begins as the first kind of imperialist and ends as the second. Early in the film, he is a slave-trader, a man of the flesh, but after he kills his brother in a flash of anger, he yearns for redemption, and he gets it from the missionaries who assign him an agonizing penance: He must climb a cliff near a steep waterfall, dragging behind him a net filled with a heavy weight of armor. Again and again De Niro strives to scale the dangerous height, until finally all of the anger and sin is drained from him, and he becomes a missionary at a settlement run by Gabriel (Jeremy Irons).

The movie now develops its story through the device of letters which explain what happened to the mission settlement. The missionaries dream of a society in which Christian natives will live in harmony with the Spanish and Portuguese. But the colonial governors find this vision dangerous; they would rather enslave the Indians than convert them, and they issue orders for the mission to be destroyed. Irons and De Niro disagree on how to meet this threat: Irons believes in prayer and passive resistance, and De Niro believes in armed rebellion.

In the end, neither approach is effective, and the movie concludes in a confusing series of scenes in which badly choreographed battle sequences are intercut with Irons's final religious services. It is a measure of the film's disorganization that at the end, when it is crucial that we understand who the Indians are fighting, and how the battle is going, mere chaos takes over the screen, and the actors stagger out of clouds of smoke as if they're looking for directions.

The Mission was produced by David Puttnam and Roland Joffe, the same team that made the great film *The Killing Fields*. That film was fired by a pure, burning anger against a great injustice, and it had a dramatic center in the life and saga of Haing S. Ngor, the Cambodian doctor who survived the occupation of his land and eventually lived to find freedom. Ngor's story was a magnet that pulled us through the film. *The Mission* has no similar pull; indeed, it hardly seems to have a center, and feels like a massive, expensive film production that, once set in motion, kept going under its own momentum even though nobody involved had a clear idea of its final direction.

I suggested that no single shot in the movie is without interest. That is probably true. The locations are spectacular—especially a waterfall that supplies the great opening image of a crucified missionary floating to his doom. The actors are effective in their individual scenes. The mysterious atmosphere of the forest seeps into the story and lends it a certain mysticism. All that was needed to pull these elements together was a structure that would clearly define who the characters were, what they stood for, and why we should care about them. Unfortunately, that is all that is missing.

Mommie Dearest ★

PG, 129 m., 1981

Faye Dunaway (Joan Crawford), Diana Scarwid (Christina, adult), Steve Forrest (Greg Savitt), Howard Da Silva (L.B. Mayer), Mara Hobel (Christina, child), Autanya Alda (Carol Ann). Directed by Frank Perry and produced by Frank Yablans. Screenplay by Yablans, Perry, Tracy Hotchner, and Robert Getchell.

I can't imagine who would want to subject themselves to this movie. *Mommie Dearest* is a painful experience that drones on endlessly, as Joan Crawford's relationship with her daughter, Christina, disintegrates from cruelty through jealousy into pathos. It is unremittingly depressing, not to any purpose of drama or entertainment, but just to depress. It left me feeling creepy. The movie was inspired, of course, by a best-selling memoir in which adopted daughter Christina Crawford portrayed her movie-star mother as a grasping, sadistic, alcoholic wretch whose own insecurities and monstrous ego made life miserable for everyone around her. I have no idea if the book's portrait is an accurate one, but the movie is faithful to it in one key sense: It made life miserable for me.

Mommie Dearest repeats the same basic dramatic situation again and again. Baby Christina tries to do the right thing, tries to be a good girl, tries to please Mommie, but Mommie is a manic-depressive who alternates between brief triumphs and long savage tirades, infecting her daughter with resentment and guilt. In scene after scene, we are invited to watch as Joan Crawford screams at Christina, chops her hair with scissors, beats her with a wire coat hanger and, on an especially bad day, tackles her across an end table, hurls her to the carpet, bangs her head against the floor, and tries to choke her to death. Who wants to watch this?

This material is presented essentially as sensationalism. The movie makes no attempt to draw psychological insights from the life of its Joan Crawford—not even through the shorthand Freudianism much beloved by Hollywood. Mommie is a monster, that's all, and there's some mention of her unhappy childhood. Christina is a brave, smiling, pretty, long-suffering dope who might inspire more sympathy if she were not directed (in both her childhood and adult versions) to be distant and veiled.

The movie doesn't even make narrative sense. Success follows crisis without any pattern. At one moment, Joan is in triumph after winning the Oscar for *Mildred Pierce*. In the very next scene she goes so berserk we want to scrape her off the screen with a spatula. The scenes don't build, they just happen. Another example: After an especially ugly fight, Joan sends Christina to a convent school. There's a scene where the mother superior welcomes her and promises to reform her. One scene later, Christina checks out of the school, and the nun wishes her godspeed. No mention of what happened in the school, how it affected Christina, or whether the nun changed her opinion of the girl.

The movie also offers few insights into Crawford's relationships with others. There's a loyal housekeeper, but never a scene where Crawford speaks personally with her. There is a lover and a third husband, both enigmas. Crawford's acting career is treated mostly in ellipses. The sets look absolutely great, Faye Dunaway's impersonation of Crawford is stunningly suggestive and convincing, and little Mara Hobel, as Baby Christina, handles several difficult moments very well. But to what end? *Mommie Dearest* is a movie that knows exactly how it wants to look, but has no idea what it wants to make us feel.

Mona Lisa ★ ★ ★ ★
R, 104 m., 1986

Bob Hoskins (George), Cathy Tyson (Simone), Michael Caine (Mortwell), Clarke Peters (Anderson), Kate Hardie (Cathy), Robbie Coltrane (Thomas). Directed by Neil Jordan and produced by Stephen Wooley and Patrick Cassavetti. Screenplay by Jordan and David Leland.

You can tell how much they will eventually like each other by how much they hate each other at first. His name is George. He's a short, fierce, bullet-headed foot-soldier in the London underworld, and he's just gotten out of prison. Her name is Simone. She's a tall, beautiful black woman who works as a high-priced call girl. George goes to Mortwell, who runs the mob, looking for a job. He is assigned to drive Simone around to expensive hotels and private homes and to wait for her while she conducts her business. He is also supposed to protect her if anything goes wrong.

At first he seems hopelessly unsuited to his job. He wears the wrong clothes, and stands out like a sore thumb in the lobbies of hotels like the Ritz. She can't believe she's been saddled with this misfit. He thinks she is stuck-up and cold, and puts on too many airs for a whore. They are at each other's throats day and night, fighting about everything, until eventually they realize they enjoy their arguments; they are entertained by one another.

That's the set-up for *Mona Lisa*, a British film set in the tattered precincts of Soho, where vice lords run sordid clubs where bewildered provincial girls sell themselves to earn money for drugs. Simone now operates at a higher level in the sex business, but she never forgets where she started, and sometimes she orders George to cruise slowly in the big Rolls Royce, as she searches for a young girl who used to be her friend when they were on the streets together, and who is still the slave, she fears, of a sadistic pimp. These nighttime journeys are a contrast to her usual routine, which involves visiting wealthy bankers, decadent diplomats, and rich Middle Eastern investors who live on the most expensive streets of Hampstead. George drives her, argues with her, speculates about her, and falls in love with her. And when she asks him to help find the missing girl, he risks his life for her.

Mona Lisa stars Bob Hoskins as George. You may remember him as the ferocious little mob boss in *The Long Good Friday*, where he had it all fixed up to go respectable and then someone started blowing up his pubs. Hoskins is one of the very best new British actors, and this is a great performance—it won him the best actor award at the 1986 Cannes Film Festival. Simone is played by Cathy Tyson, and she is elegant and cool and yet able to project the pain that is always inside. The relationship of their characters in the film is interesting, because both people, for personal reasons, have developed a style that doesn't reveal very much. They have walls, and friendship means being able to see over someone else's wall while still keeping your own intact.

The third major character in the movie, and the third major performance, is by Michael Caine, as Mortwell, the vice boss. In the more than twenty years since I first saine in a movie, I don't believe I've seen him in a bad performance more than once or twice. And I've rarely seen him doing the same thing, which is strange, since in one way or another he usually seems to %.evlook and talk like Michael Caine—and yet with subtle differences that are just right for the role. In *Mona Lisa*, he plays one of his most evil villains, a slimebag who trades in the lives and happiness of naive young girls, and he plays the character without apology and without exaggeration, as a businessman. That's why Mortwell is so creepy.

The movie plot reveals itself only gradually. At first *Mona Lisa* seems to be a character study, the story of George and Simone and how they operate within the call-girl industry. After we find out how important the missing girl is to Simone, however, the movie becomes a thriller, as George descends into gutters to try to find her and bring her back to Simone. The movie's ending is a little too neat for my taste. But in a movie like this, everything depends on atmosphere and character, and *Mona Lisa* knows exactly what it is doing.

The Money Pit ★
PG-13, 90 m., 1986

Tom Hanks (Walter Fielding), Shelley Long (Anna Crowley), Alexander Godunov (Max Beissart), Maureen Stapleton (Estelle), Joe Mantegna (Art Shirk), Philip Bosco (Curly Shirk), Josh Mostell (Schnittman), Yakov Smirnoff (Shatov). Directed by Richard Benjamin and produced by Frank Marshall, Kathleen Kennedy, and Art Levinson. Screenplay by David Giler.

In a movie called *Big Deal on Madonna Street,* a gang of crooks was trying to break through a wall into a bank building. They rigged up a system that was going to penetrate the wall, and braced it against another wall, and of course it was the other wall that collapsed. Their surprise when that happened was one of the biggest laughs in the movie.

However, if the entire movie had consisted of the same gag, repeated over and over again, with the gadget breaking through the wrong wall a dozen times, I think the original laughter would have eventually collapsed into quiet desperation. That is what happens with *The Money Pit,* a movie that contains one funny scene, and more than an hour of running time to kill.

The movie stars Tom Hanks and Shelley Long as a couple who need to find a house in a hurry. They've been living in the Manhattan apartment of her former husband (Alexander Godunov, as a symphony conductor), but now he throws them out and they take the only place they can find—a country estate at a suspiciously low price. Sure, it needs a little work. All older houses need a little work. But Hanks begins to suspect something is seriously wrong when he slams the front door, and it falls off its hinges.

Ha, ha. In the course of this movie, we will also see a staircase collapse, a bathtub fall through the floor, and several walls reduced to piles of rubble. That's before the craftsmen arrive to repair the building. They have a standard answer to how long everything will take: "Two weeks," they say, snickering up their sleeves. They demand cash advances and then drive off in their Cadillacs and Porsches, maybe never to be seen again.

If the movie had made the carpenters, plumbers, and electricians into interesting characters, it might have been able to save itself. But one contractor (Joe Mantegna) is onscreen so little he seems like an afterthought, and the other one (Philip Bosco) is never developed into much more than a genial presence.

Instead, we get one monotonous sight gag after another. The most irritating is the one where Hanks falls through the floor and is pinned, halfway down, by a rug. He can't move. All he can do is scream for help, but when Long finally arrives at the house, he screams all the wrong things, until we aren't laughing, we're groaning. Didn't it occur to anybody that the smarter the characters were, the funnier their troubles would be? Make them into idiots, and who cares if their house falls down?

There is just the beginning of a comic idea with the Godunov character. He exhibits a certain wry charm, as a conceited conductor who thinks himself to be altogether the most brilliant person in the world. His scenes with Shelley Long are among the movie's few pleasant interludes, if only because he's so cheerful about his absolute cynicism.

But the house is a disaster in more ways than one. Sure, it's a triumph of art direction. The Hollywood artisans who designed it deserve some sort of medal, for the neat stunts they think up and the great tricks they're able to pull. There is even one sustained Rube Goldberg-type gag that is really funny, as an incredible chain of events unfolds with meticulous precision. But one gag does not a comedy make, and if they'd spent the time on the characters that they spent on building the house, they might have really had something here.

Monty Python's Meaning of Life
★ ★ ½
R, 103 m., 1983

Written and starring: Graham Chapman, John Cleese, Terry Gilliam, Eric Idle, Terry

Jones, and Michael Palin. Directed by Terry Jones and produced by John Goldstone.

Halfway through *Monty Python's Meaning of Life,* the thought struck me that One-Upmanship was a British discovery. You remember, of course, the book and movie *(School for Scoundrels)* inspired by Stephen Potter's theory of One-Upmanship, in which the goal of the practitioner was to One-Up his daily associates and, if possible, the world. A modern example:

Victim: I've just been reading Gabriel Garcia Marquez's *Chronicle of a Death Foretold* in *Vanity Fair* magazine.

One-Upman: Really? I'm afraid I missed it.

Victim: But Garcia Marquez is brilliant.

One-Upman: No doubt, dear fellow, but my subscription ran out in 1939.

I use this illustration as an approach to *Monty Python's Meaning of Life,* which is a movie that seems consumed with a desire to push us too far. This movie is so far beyond good taste, and so cheerfully beyond, that we almost feel we're being One-Upped if we allow ourselves to be offended. Take, for example, the scene featuring projectile vomiting. We don't get just a little vomit in the scene, as we saw in *The Exorcist.* No sir, we get gallons of vomit, streams of it, all a vile yellow color, sprayed all over everybody and everything in a formal dining room. The first reaction of the non-Upman is *"Yech!"* But I think the Python gang is working at another level. And, given the weakness of movie critics for discussing what "level" a movie "works" on, I find myself almost compelled to ask myself, "At what 'level' *does* the projectile vomiting 'work'?" And I think the Python One-Up reply would be, dear fellow, that it rises above vulgarity and stakes out territory in the surrealistic. Anyone who takes the vomiting literally has missed the joke; the scene isn't about vomiting, but about the lengths to which Python will go for a laugh.

There are other scenes in equally poor taste in this movie, which has a little something to offend everybody. And I mean *really* offend them: This isn't a Mel Brooks movie, with friendly little ethnic in-jokes. It's a barbed, uncompromising attack on generally observed community standards. Does the attack work? Only occasionally. The opening sequence of the film is one of its best, showing the overworked old clerks in an insurance company staging a mutiny. After they've gained control of their shabby old stone building, the movie does a brilliant turn into surrealism, the building becomes a ship, and the clerks weigh anchor and set sail against the fleets of modern high-rises, firing their filing cabinets like cannons. It's a wonderful sequence.

I also liked a scene set on a military parade ground, and a joke involving a tankful of fish, and a cheerfully unfair rugby match between two teams, one made up of twelve small schoolboys, the other with eighteen schoolmasters, all huge. Balanced against these bright moments is the goriest scene in Python history, showing a liver being removed from a transplant "volunteer" by brute force. There are also a lot of religious jokes, some straightforward sexism, and the above-mentioned vomiting sequence.

By admitting to being offended by some of the stuff in this movie, I've been One-Upped. By liking the funny stuff, I've been One-Upped again. ("But you liked the jokes that were in good taste? Jolly good!") But I'm a good loser, and I don't mind being One-Upped. In fact, let's say this is a tennis match, and the Pythons are the winners. Here, I'll hold down the net while they jump over to shake hands with me. Whoops!

Moonlighting ★ ★ ★ ★

PG, 97 m., 1982

Jeremy Irons (Nowak), Eugene Lipinski (Banaszak), Jiri Stanislav (Wolski), Eugeniusz Haczkiewicz (Kudaj). Directed by Jerzy Skolimowski and produced by Mark Shivas and Skolimowski. Screenplay by Skolimowski.

Moonlighting is a wickedly pointed movie that takes a simple little story, tells it with humor and truth, and turns it into a knife in the side of the Polish government. In its own way, this response to the crushing of Solidarity is as powerful as Andrezej Wajda's *Man of Iron.* It also is more fun. The movie takes place in London, during the weeks just before and after the banning of the Solidarity movement in Poland. It begins, actually, in Warsaw, with a mystifying scene in which a group of plotters are scheming to smuggle some hardware past British customs.

They're plotters, all right; their plot is to move into a small house in London and remodel it, knocking out walls, painting ceilings, making it into a showplace for the Polish government official who has purchased it. The official's plan is simplicity itself: By bringing Polish workers to London on tourist visas, he can get the remodeling done for a fraction of what British workman would cost him. At the same time, the workers can earn good wages that they can take back to Poland and buy bicycles with. The only thing nobody counts on is the upheaval after Solidarity is crushed and travel to and from Poland is strictly regulated.

Jeremy Irons, of *The French Lieutenant's Woman,* plays the lead in the film. He's the only Polish workman who can speak English. Acting as foreman, he guides his team of men through the pitfalls of London and safely into the house they're going to remodel. He advises them to keep a low profile, while he ventures out to buy the groceries and (not incidentally) to read the newspapers. When he finds out about the crisis in Poland, he keeps it a secret from his comrades. The daily life of the renovation project falls into a pattern, which the film's director, Jerzy Skolimowski, intercuts with the adventures of his hero. Jeremy Irons begins to steal things: newspapers, bicycles, frozen turkeys. He concocts an elaborate scheme to defraud the local supermarket, and some of the movie's best scenes involve the subtle timing of his shoplifting scam, which involves the misrepresentation of cash-register receipts. He needs to steal food because he's running out of money, and he knows his group can't easily go home again. There's also a quietly hilarious, and slightly sad, episode involving a salesgirl in a blue jeans store. Irons, pretending to be more naive than he is, tries to pick the girl up. She's having none of it.

Moonlighting invites all kinds of interpretations. You can take this simple story and set it against the events of the last two years, and see it as a kind of parable. Your interpretation is as good as mine. Is the house itself Poland, and the workmen Solidarity—rebuilding it from within, before an authoritarian outside force intervenes? Or is this movie about the heresy of substituting Western values (and jeans and turkeys) for a home-grown orientation? Or is it about the manipulation of the working classes by the intelligentsia? Or is it simply a frontal attack on the Communist Party bosses who live high off the hog while the workers are supposed to follow the rules?

Like all good parables, *Moonlighting* contains not one but many possibilities. What needs to be insisted upon, however, is how much *fun* this movie is. Skolimowski, a Pole who has lived and worked in England for several years, began writing this film on the day that Solidarity was crushed, and he filmed it, on a small budget and with a small crew, in less than two months: He had it ready for the 1982 Cannes Film Festival where it was a major success. It's successful, I think, because it tells an interesting narrative in a straightforward way. Skolimowski is a natural storyteller. You can interpret and discuss *Moonlighting* all night. During the movie, you'll be more interested in whether Irons gets away with that frozen turkey.

Moonstruck ★ ★ ★ ★
PG, 100 m., 1987

Cher (Loretta Castorini), Nicolas Cage (Ronny Cammareri), Vincent Gardenia (Cosmo Castorini), Olympia Dukakis (Rose Castorini), Danny Aiello (Johnny Cammareri), Julia Bovasso (Rita Cappomaggi), John Mahoney (Perry), Louis Guss (Raymond Cappomaggi), Feodor Chaliapin (Old Man). Directed by Norman Jewison and produced by Patrick Palmer and Jewison. Screenplay by John Patrick Shanley.

"When the moon hits your eye, like a big-a pizza pie—that's amore!"—Dean Martin

The most enchanting quality about *Moonstruck* is the hardest to describe, and that is the movie's tone. Reviews of the movie tend to make it sound like a madcap ethnic comedy, and that it is. But there is something more here, a certain bittersweet yearning that comes across as ineffably romantic, and a certain magical quality that is reflected in the film's title.

The movie stars Cher, as an Italian-American widow in her late thirties, but she is not the only moonstruck one in the film. There is the moonlit night, for example, that her wise, cynical mother (Olympia Dukakis) goes out for dinner by herself, and meets a middle-aged university professor (John Mahoney) who specializes in seducing his young students, but who finds in this mature woman a certain undeniable sexuality. There is the furtive and yet somehow sweet affair that Cher's father (Vincent Gardenia) has been carrying on for years with the ripe, disillusioned Anita Gillette.

And at the heart of the story, there is Cher's astonishing discovery that she is still capable of love. As the movie opens, she becomes engaged to Mr. Johnny Cammareri (Danny Aiello), not so much out of love as out of weariness. But after he flies to Sicily to be at the bedside of his dying mother, she goes to talk to Mr. Johnny's estranged younger brother (Nicolas Cage), and is thunderstruck when they are drawn almost instantly into a passionate embrace.

Moonstruck was directed by Norman Jewison and written by John Patrick Shanley, and one of their accomplishments is to allow the film to be about all of these people (and several more, besides). This is an ensemble comedy, and a lot of the laughs grow out of the sense of family that Jewison and Shanley create; there are, for example, small hilarious moments involving the exasperation that Dukakis feels for her ancient father-in-law (Feodor Chaliapin), who lives upstairs with his dogs. (In the course of a family dinner, she volunteers: "Feed one more bite of my food to your dogs, old man, and I'll kick you to death!")

As Cher's absent fiancé lingers at his mother's bedside, Cher and Cage grow even more desperately passionate, and Cher learns the secret of the hatred between the two brothers: One day Aiello made Cage look the wrong way at the wrong time, and he lost his hand in a bread-slicer. Now he wears an artificial hand, and carries an implacable grudge in his heart.

But grudges and vendettas and old wounds and hatreds are everywhere in this film. The mother knows, for example, that her husband is having an affair with another woman. She asks from the bottom of her heart why this should be so, and a friend replies, "Because he is afraid of dying." She sees at once that this is so. But does that cause her to sympathize with her husband? Hardly. One night he comes home. She asks where he has been. He replies, "Nowhere." She tells him she wants him to know one thing: "No matter where you go, or what you do—you're gonna die."

Some of these moments are so charged with tension they remind us of the great opening scenes of *Saturday Night Fever* (and the mother from that movie, Julie Bovasso, is on hand here as an aunt). But all of the passion is drained of its potential for hurt, somehow, by the influence of the moon, which has enchanted these people and protects them from the consequences of their frailties. Jewison captures some of the same qualities of Ingmar Bergman's *Smiles of a Summer Night*, in which nature itself conspires with lovers to bring about their happiness.

The movie is filled with fine performances—by Cher, 1987's Best Actress Oscar winner, never funnier or more assured; by Olympia Dukakis (who was named Best Supporting Actress) and Vincent Gardenia, as her parents, whose love runs as deep as their exasperation, and by Nicolas Cage as the hapless, angry brother, who is so filled with hurts he has lost track of what caused them. In its warmth and in its enchantment, as well as in its laughs, this is the best comedy in a long time.

The Morning After ★ ★ ★

R, 103 m., 1986

Jane Fonda (Alex), Jeff Bridges (Turner), Raul Julia (Manero), Diane Salinger (Isabel), Richard Foronjy (Sergeant Greenbaum), Geoffrey Scott (Bobby), Bruce Vilanch (Bartender). Directed by Sidney Lumet and produced by Bruce Gilbert. Screenplay by James Hicks.

If an ordinary person woke up in the morning feeling the way a drunk feels with a hangover, they'd call an ambulance and check themselves into the emergency room. I'm not talking about your average garden-variety office-party hangover. I'm thinking of one of those mornings when you pick up the phone and somebody says hello and you're stuck for an answer.

That's how Jane Fonda feels in the first scene of *The Morning After*. She crawls out of bed and looks in the mirror and sloshes some gin into a glass and wonders about the guy she woke up with. She wonders things like, who is he? She has apparently had a lot of mornings like this. She doesn't realize how bad things really are until she notices the guy has a knife stuck in his chest.

Did she kill him? She knows no cop is

going to believe her story, and so she tries to erase all the evidence of her visit—all the fingerprints and bloodstains. And then she wanders back out into the blinding Los Angeles light, and in a shot from high overhead, she looks like a laboratory animal, trapped in some kind of a test.

This feels like the beginning of an extraordinary thriller. Unfortunately, *The Morning After* never lives up to its early promise—not as a thriller, anyway. The plot has some yawning gaps in it, and thriller plots should be watertight. But *The Morning After* is worth seeing anyway, because of the characters that it develops, and the performances of Fonda and Jeff Bridges in the two leads.

She plays an alcoholic actress who is long past her prime. He plays an ex-cop who happens to be repairing his car at the airport parking lot when she tumbles into his backseat and pleads with him to get her away from there, fast. The mere presence of Jeff Bridges in this movie is sort of a tease; we remember him from *Jagged Edge*, when he was one of the prime suspects, and we wonder if it's a coincidence that he happens along this time.

Bridges lives in a Quonset hut, where he fixes things like toasters. This is all Fonda needs. She moves in the fast lane—her friends are bartenders and drag queens, and her estranged husband (Raul Julia) is the classiest hairdresser in Beverly Hills. What does she need with a small appliance repairman? But Bridges is sure and steady, and she needs a friend. Of course it goes without saying that they fall in love.

The plot of *The Morning After* is not nearly as good as the everyday lives of these characters; indeed, I can imagine a movie which would leave out the murder and simply follow the natural human development of the relationship between Fonda and Bridges. The thriller stuff isn't necessary, but as long as they put it in, couldn't they have worked just a little harder and made it plausible? Why, for example, didn't the cops find the bloody sheets under Fonda's sink?

The whole murder plot gets such sloppy handling that maybe I shouldn't have been surprised by the big scene in which the identity of the murderer is revealed. I've seen a lot of revelations in a lot of murder movies, but rarely one as unsubtle as this one, where the plot secrets are simply blurted out in an unlikely speech. (Maybe I should be more grateful; I understand that this very scene—implausible and awkward as it is—was reshot because the original version was worse.)

It would be a mistake, however, to dismiss this movie just because the plot is so shaky. I think it's worth considering because of the performances. Fonda and Bridges are wonderful in the film, and their relationship, based on secrets and resentments and private agendas, gets really interesting. They feel good together, and they have some dialogue that seems more alive than most romantic talk in the movies.

I liked what they did with the characters, and I also liked what Sidney Lumet has done with the look of the movie. He creates a Los Angeles made out of great flat planes of cold pastels, and threatening sunlit open spaces. He pins the hungover Fonda on this canvas like a butterfly on the wall, and the visuals make the whole first hour of the movie much more threatening than it deserves to be. Too bad they couldn't have done something about the screenplay.

Moscow on the Hudson ★ ★ ★ ★

R, 115 m., 1984

Robin Williams (Vladimir Ivanoff), Maria Conchita Alonso (Lucia Lombardo), Cleavant Derricks (Witherspoon), Alejandro Rey (Orlando Ramirez). Directed and produced by Paul Mazursky. Screenplay by Mazursky and Leon Capetanos.

Mike Royko likes to make fun of foreign-born taxi drivers. He uses a lot of phonetic spellings to show how funny dey speeka da Engleesh. Maybe he's missing out on some good conversations. Have you ever *talked* to a taxi driver from Iran or Pakistan or Africa? I have, and usually I hear a fascinating story about a man who has fled from poverty or persecution, who in some cases has left behind a thriving business, and who is starting out all over again in this country. I also usually get the name of a good restaurant.

I thought of some of those experiences while I was watching Paul Mazursky's *Moscow on the Hudson*, a wonderful movie about a man who defects to the United States. His name is Vladimir Ivanoff, he plays the saxophone in a Russian circus, and when the circus visits New York, he falls in love with the United States and defects by turning himself in to a security guard at Bloomingdale's. The Russian is played by Robin Williams, who disappears so completely into his quirky, lovable, complicated character that he's quite plausible as a Russian. The movie opens with his life in Moscow, a city of overcrowded apartments, bureaucratic red tape, long lines for consumer goods, secret pleasures like jazz records, and shortages so acute that toilet paper has turned into a currency of its own. The early scenes are eerily convincing, partly because Williams plays them in Russian. This isn't one of those movies where everybody somehow speaks English. The turning point of the movie occurs in Bloomingdale's, as so many turning points do, and Ivanoff makes two friends right there on the spot: Witherspoon, the black security guard (Cleavant Derricks) and Lucia, the Italian salesclerk (Maria Conchita Alonso).

They're a tip-off to an interesting casting decision by Mazursky, who populates his movie almost entirely with ethnic and racial minorities. In addition to the black and the Italian, there's a Korean taxi driver, a Cuban lawyer, a Chinese anchorwoman, all of them reminders that all of us, except for American Indians, came from somewhere else. Ivanoff moves in with the security guard's family, which greatly resembles the one he left behind in Moscow, right down to the pious grandfather. He gets a job selling hot dogs from a pushcart, he works his way up to driving a limousine, and he falls in love with the salesclerk from Italy. That doesn't go so well. She dreams of marrying a "real American," and Ivanoff, even after he trims his beard, will not quite do.

Moscow on the Hudson is the kind of movie that Paul Mazursky does especially well. It's a comedy that finds most of its laughs in the close observations of human behavior, and that finds its story in a contemporary subject Mazursky has some thoughts about. In that, it's like his earlier films *An Unmarried Woman* (women's liberation), *Harry and Tonto* (growing old), *Blume in Love* (marriage in the age of doing your own thing), and *Bob & Carol and Ted & Alice* (encounter groups). It is also a rarity, a patriotic film that has a liberal, rather than a conservative, heart. It made me feel good to be an American, and good that Vladimir Ivanoff was going to be one, too.

The Mosquito Coast ★ ★

PG, 118 m., 1986

Harrison Ford (Allie Fox), Helen Mirren (Mother), River Phoenix (Charlie), Martha Plimpton (Emily), Andre Gregory (Mr. Spellgood), Butterfly McQueen (Ma Kennywock), Dick O'Neil (Tim Polski), Conrad Roberts (Mr. Haddy). Directed by Peter Weir and produced by Jerome Hellman. Screenplay by Paul Schrader.

Some kinds of bores you will tolerate, and other kinds you will not. *The Mosquito Coast* has the misfortune to be about the second kind of bore—about a man who is zealous in the pursuit of his obsessions long, *long* after they have ceased to interest anyone else.

The man's name is Allie Fox, and he is convinced that the American civilization is coming apart at the seams. Acting on his fears, Allie packs up his wife and children and moves them into the rain forests of Central America, where he plans to establish a new civilization. This man is not without intelligence; he has invented, for example, a new kind of machine for making ice, and nobody can say he is not handy with his hands. But he shares the common fault of many utopians; he wants to create a society in which men will be free—but free only in the way he thinks they should be free.

Allie Fox is played in *The Mosquito Coast* by Harrison Ford, and it is one of the ironies of the movie that he does very good work. Ford gives us a character who has tunnel vision, who is uncaring toward his family or anyone else, who is totally lacking in a sense of humor, who is egocentric to the point of madness. It is a brilliant performance—so effective indeed, that we can hardly stand to spend two hours in the company of this consummate jerk.

There have been other madmen in other movies who tried to find their vision in these same rain forests. I think immediately of *Aguirre, the Wrath of God*, and *Fitzcarraldo*, two movies by Werner Herzog about crazed eccentrics who pressed on into the jungle, driven by their obsessions. Those movies were so much more watchable than *The Mosquito Coast* because they created characters (both played by Klaus Kinski) who were mad with a flamboyant, burning intensity. Allie Fox's madness is more of a drone, an unending complaint against the way things are. It is painful to watch him not because he is mad, but because he is boring—one of those nuts who will talk all night long without even checking to see if you're listening.

The movie is based on a novel by Paul Theroux, in which the narrator is Fox's teenage son, Charlie. Through Charlie's eyes, we gradually see the father turning from an idealist into an obsessive, and we also see Charlie becoming a man in the process of dealing with that change. In the movie, Charlie (River Phoenix) is still the narrator, but what he tells us on the sound track isn't reinforced by what we see on the screen; Charlie recedes into the family, and becomes just one more hapless victim to be dragged through the jungle by his father.

Another mysterious character in the movie is Mother (Helen Mirren), the wife, who stands by mutely and uncomplainingly while Allie Fox subjects her family to dangerous and pointless experiences. What does she feel? What does she really think? Apart from one welcome outburst, we never know. Mirren has said that the character was opposite to everything in her own nature, and that she played Mother by trying to become completely passive. Well, that's probably the only strategy that would have worked, but it leaves enormous questions about Mother's thoughts and fears—questions this movie is not prepared to answer.

The Mosquito Coast was directed by Peter Weir, an Australian who has made great films about the silences and mysteries of nature. In *Picnic at Hanging Rock*, he showed us a group of giggling schoolgirls on a day's outing, who are mysteriously lost somewhere within a vast prehistoric rock formation; the movie provided no answer to its mystery except for an awesome silence.

In that film and throughout his career, Weir has been able to capture the majesty of nature—and the production values in *The Mosquito Coast* are impressive, especially in a scene where a typhoon threatens to sweep away Ford's fragile settlement on a threatened beach.

The movie has been directed and acted so well, in fact, that almost all my questions have to do with the script: Why was the hero made so uncompromisingly hateful? The screenplay is by Paul Schrader, whose own movies (*Hard Core*, *Mishima*) and screenplays (*Taxi Driver*) are often about men obsessed with their own narrow range of vision. But Schrader's characters always have some measure of humanity that is lacking here.

Weir's previous movie was *Witness*, also with Harrison Ford, and also about a contrast between modern and utopian sensibilities. Ford played the cop who came to live with and understand an Amish farm community. He fell in love with a young woman whose father was rigid and uncompromising, so utterly sure of his own infallibility that he was heedless of the unhappiness he caused to others. *The Mosquito Coast*, unfortunately, is all about the father.

Motel Hell ★ ★ ★

R, 106 m., 1980

Rory Calhoun (Farmer Vincent), Paul Linke (Bruce Smith), Nancy Parsons (Ida Smith), Nina Axelrod (Terry), Wolfman Jack (Reverend Billy), Elaine Joyce (Edith Olson). Directed by Kevin Connor and produced by Steven-Charles Jaffe and Robert Jaffe. Screenplay by Jaffe and Jaffe.

Motel Hell satirizes a whole sub-basement genre of American movies that a lot of lucky people may never even have seen. I call them Sleazoid Movies; films that deliberately test our sensibilities, and our stomachs, by the subhuman and nauseating behavior of the characters on the screen. The genre includes *The Texas Chainsaw Massacre*, *The Hills Have Eyes*, *The Honeymoon Killers*, *Night of the Living Dead*, and *Last House on the Left*.

These films are not to be confused with those of a neighboring genre, the Women in Danger films, which spew hatred of women. Sleazoid movies seem to exist on the edge of self-parody, and their ambition is to be to the cinema what the geek show is to the circus. They're not antiwoman, they're antitaste, and their characters sink into moronic, bestial savagery. They touch on the ultimate horror of people degraded into subhuman, animalistic behavior. Some of these films, I should add, are not without merit—although this isn't the place to launch into a defense of them.

What *Motel Hell* brings to this genre is the refreshing sound of laughter. This movie *is* disgusting, of course; it's impossible to satirize this material, I imagine, without presenting the subject matter you're satirizing. But *Motel Hell* is not nearly as gruesome as the films it satirizes, and it finds the right stylistic note for its central characters, who are simple, cheerful, smiling, earnest, and resourceful cannibals.

Motel Hell (the second "e" on the neon sign has gone out) is a ramshackle place that seems to be located in the same redneck backwoods where Russ Meyer's characters all live. It is operated by friendly Farmer Vincent (Rory Calhoun) and his sister (Nancy Parsons). The district is patrolled, none too adroitly, by a relative (Paul Linke), who is the sheriff, but sees nothing wrong with burying the victims of a motorcycle crash without benefit of investigation or autopsy.

That's just as well, because Farmer Vincent's specialty is burying people. He just doesn't wait until they're dead. He waylays unsuspecting travelers, knocks them unconscious, buries them up to their necks in his secret garden, fattens them up with cattle feed, and then slaughters them, smokes them in his smokehouse, and sells them as sausage at his roadside stand. His cheerful motto: "It takes all kinds of critters . . . to make Farmer Vincent's fritters."

All right now, of *course* this is disgusting. But hold on just a dagbone minute, as Farmer Vincent might say. It isn't simply the subject matter of Sleazoid Movies that makes them reprehensible, it's their low opinion of human nature, their acquiesence in the proposition that the world is essentially an evil place. *Motel Hell*, with Rory Calhoun looking like a Norman Rockwell model in his bib overalls, pushes this material so far in such unlikely directions that, incredibly, it works as satire. A lot of horror movies used to work that way. We went to be scared, sure, but we also went to laugh, enjoying the delicious self-indulgence with which Vincent Price or Christopher Lee hammed it up. But horror movies stopped being funny. And now they're mostly just depressing, disgusting exercises in depravity.

Motel Hell is a welcome change-of-pace; it's to *Chainsaw Massacre* as *Airplane!* is to *Airport*. It has some great moments, including a duel fought with chainsaws, a hero swinging to the rescue on a meathook, and Farmer Vincent's dying confession of the shameful secret that he concealed for years. These moments illuminate the movie's basic and not very profound insight, which is that most of the sleazoids would be a lot more fun if they didn't take themselves with such gruesome solemnity.

Mother's Day no stars

R, 98 m., 1980

With Nancy Hendrickson, Deborah Luce, Tiana Pierce, Holden McQuire, Billy Ray McQuade, and Rose Ross.

Mother's Day is a reprehensible specimen of the geek film, so-called because such films are about the activities of that subcategory of humans formerly found in the carnival sideshows, biting the heads off chickens. Like the geeks of old, a film such as this will stoop to anything in its attempt to disgust its audiences. And the audiences for geek films are not easily disgusted. After the first five minutes of *Mother's Day*—after the shot of blood spurting from the severed neck of the movie's first victim—I was ready to walk out. But no, that would have been too easy. I determined to stick this one out.

The plot: A demented old woman lives in a shack in the woods with her two cretinous sons. Their entertainment is to capture unwary campers and torture, rape, and kill them for the delight of their mother. In between, they behave like pigs. A typical dinner scene involves one of the sons shooting a can of pressurized cheese whip down his throat.

Near the beginning of the film (but after the first beheading), three young women, former college classmates, go camping in the woods. They are imprisoned inside their sleeping bags and dragged back to the shack, where they are assaulted, raped, cut up, beaten, and forced to watch unspeakable acts. The mother cackles with glee. The actresses scream relentlessly.

Later in the film, after one of the girls is dead, the two survivors come back for revenge. (This sort of "eye for an eye" conclusion is apparently a ghastly attempt at fairness on the part of the geeks who make these movies.) The girls get their revenge. In one sequence, one of the sons is stabbed with a hatchet. His brother has a can of Drano poured down his throat, and is hit over the head with a television set. Viewers can look in through the TV screen as the victim is electrocuted. The question of why anybody of any age would possibly want to see this film remains without an answer.

The Muppet Movie ★ ★ ★ ½
G, 94 m., 1979

Jim Henson (Kermit, Rowlf, Dr. Teeth, and Waldorf), Frank Oz (Miss Piggy, Fozzie Bear, Animal, and Sam), Jerry Nelson (Floyd Pepper, Crazy Harry, Robin the Frog, and Lew Zealand), Richard Hunt (Scooter, Statler, Janice, Sweetums, and Beaker), Dave Goelz (The Great Gonza, Zoot, and Dr. Bunsen Honeydew). Directed by James Frawley and produced by Jim Henson. Screenplay by Jerry Juhl and Jack Burns.

Jolson sang, Barrymore spoke, Garbo laughed, and now Kermit the Frog rides a bicycle. *The Muppet Movie* not only stars the Muppets but, for the first time, shows us their feet. And if you can figure out how they were able to show Kermit pedaling across the screen, then you are less a romantic than I am: I prefer to believe he did it himself.

He's pedaling on his way to Hollywood, and *The Muppet Movie* itself is one of those origin stories so beloved by comic books. We've learned how Spiderman came into his extraordinary powers, and now here are the earliest days of the Muppets.

Kermit, we learn, was born in a swamp. Well, maybe we coulda guessed it. And he was born with an ability somewhat unusual to frogs: a talent for playing the guitar. We encounter him sitting on a log and singing one of the movie's several Paul Williams songs, and for just a second we wonder where Jim Henson is. That's because Kermit is quite clearly surrounded by water, and we can't for the life of us figure out where they hid the Muppeteer.

It turns out Henson was sitting in a watertight compartment and communicating with the rest of the crew via walkie-talkie, and that Kermit's hands on the banjo were animated by remote control, and that all sorts of technology went into making the Muppets move, but after that first second we quit wondering: This is magic, after all, so who *wants* to know where Henson is?

Dom DeLuise, on the other hand, wants to know where Kermit is. DeLuise comes rowing through the swamp in a rowboat and hears Kermit's song and reveals himself to be a big Hollywood agent with a copy of *Variety* in his boat. And, wouldn't you know, *Variety* has an ad for singing frogs in it. So of course Kermit leaves his swamp behind and commences a cross-country odyssey to Hollywood to make his audition.

He makes his trip mostly in a late-1940s Studebaker, one of those models that looked like it was going in both directions simultaneously, and the trip would have been a happy one except for one thing: Kermit is pursued by an evil fast-food magnate (Charles Durning) who wants him to sign on as the trademark of a chain of French-fried frogs' legs restaurants. It is one of the movie's more poignant ironies that no sooner does Kermit obtain legs than humans find an unsavory use for them.

Durning and DeLuise are two of the several humans in the film. The format makes absolutely no distinction between the Muppets and other forms of life, so we meet such humans as Mel Brooks, Bob Hope, Carol Kane, Steve Martin, Richard Pryor, Telly Savalas, Orson Welles, and, in their last film appearance before their deaths, Edgar Bergen and Charlie McCarthy.

We also meet, of course, Miss Piggy, who falls instantly and incurably in love with Kermit. And we get to know all the Muppets better than we could on their television show. They turn out, somehow, to have many of the same emotions and motivations that we do. They are vain and hopeful, selfish and generous, complicated and true. They mirror ourselves, except that they're a little nicer.

The Muppets Take Manhattan ★ ★ ★
G, 94 m., 1984

With guest stars Dabney Coleman, Joan Rivers, Liza Minelli, and John Landis. Directed by Frank Oz and produced by David Lazer. Written by Oz and Jim Henson.

Dear Kermit,

I hope you will take this in the right spirit. I know you've been tortured for some years now by an identity crisis, ever since you were discovered sitting on that log down in the swamp, strumming on your ukulele. Stardom happened almost overnight, and here you are in your third starring vehicle, *The Muppets Take Manhattan.* Yet you still don't know who you really are.

You are obviously not a frog. You have

none of the attributes of a frog, except for your appearance and your name. In your first film, *The Muppet Movie,* you were sort of a greenish overgrown pop singer, an amphibian Frankie Avalon. In your second movie, *The Great Muppet Caper,* you were cast adrift in a plot that really belonged to the human guest stars. You basically had a supporting role, making the humans look good. Only in *The Muppets Take Manhattan,* your third film, do you really seem to come into your own. You take charge. You are the central figure in the plot, you do not allow yourself to get shouldered aside by Miss Piggy, and you seem thoroughly at home with the requirements of genre, stereotype, and cliché. In the 1940s, you would have been under contract to MGM.

The plot of your movie has been seen before. I doubt if that will come as news to you. *The Muppets Take Manhattan* is yet another retread of the reliable old formula in which somebody says "Hey, gang! Our senior class musical show is so good, I'll bet we could be stars on Broadway!" The fact that this plot is not original does not deter you, Kermit, nor should it. It's still a good plot.

I liked the scenes in which you persevered. I liked the way you went to New York and challenged the stubborn agents like Dabney Coleman, and upstaged Liza Minnelli in Sardi's. I especially liked the scenes where you supported yourself by waiting tables in a greasy spoon cafe with rats in the kitchen and a Greek owner who specialized in philosophical statements that didn't make any sense. I even liked Miss Piggy's scenes, especially her childhood memories. I gasped at the wedding scene, in which you finally married her. I refrained from speculating about your wedding night—and speculation is all your G-rated movie left me with.

In short, I liked just about everything about your movie. But what I liked best was your discovery of self. Kermit, you are no longer a frog with an identity crisis. You've found the right persona, old boy, and it will see you through a dozen more movies. It was clear to me from the moment you took your curtain call and basked in the spotlight. Kermit, this may come as a shock, but you're Mickey Rooney in a frog suit. Think about it. You're short. You're cute. You never say die. You keep smilin'. You have a philosophy for everything. You appear only in wholesome, G-rated movies. And sex bombs like Liza Minnelli only kiss you on the cheek.

One word of advice. Dump Miss Piggy. Stage a talent search for a Liza Minnelli Muppet. Mickey Rooney made a lot of movies with Liza's mother before you were hatched, Kermit, and now it's your turn. Move fast, kid, before you croak.

Murder on the Orient Express ★ ★ ★

PG, 128 m., 1974

Albert Finney (Hercule Poirot), Lauren Bacall (Mrs. Hubbard), Martin Balsam (Blanchi), Ingrid Bergman (Greta Ohlsson), Jacqueline Bisset (Countess Andrenyi), Jean-Pierre Cassel (Pierre Paul Michel), Sean Connery (Colonel Arbuthnot), John Gielgud (Beddoes), Wendy Hiller (Princess Dragomiroff), Anthony Perkins (Hector McQueen), Vanessa Redgrave (Mary Debenham), Richard Widmark (Ratchett), Rachel Roberts (Hildegarde Schmitt), Michael York (Count Andrenyi). Directed by Sidney Lumet and produced by John Brabourne and Richard Goodwin. Screenplay by Paul Deim.

There is a cry of alarm, some muffled French, a coming and a going in the corridor. Hercule Poirot, adjusting the devices that keep his hair slicked down and his mustache curled up, pauses for a moment in his train compartment. He lifts an eyebrow. He looks out into the hallway. He shrugs. The next morning, it's revealed that Ratchett, the hateful American millionaire, has been stabbed to death in his sleep. This is quite obviously a case for Poirot, the most famous detective in the world, and, over breakfast, he agrees to accept it. The list of suspects is long, but limited: It includes everybody on board the crack Orient Express, en route from Istanbul to Calais, and currently brought to a standstill by an avalanche of snow that has fallen across the track. Poirot arranges to begin a series of interviews and plunges himself (and the rest of us) into a net of intrigue so deep, so deceptive, and so labyrinthine that only Agatha Christie would have woven it. *Murder on the Orient Express* is a splendidly entertaining movie of the sort that isn't made any more: It's a classical whodunit, with all the clues planted and all of them visible, and it's peopled with a large and expensive collection of stars. Albert Finney, who plays Poirot, is the most impressive, largely because we can never for a moment be sure that he *is* Finney. His hair is slicked down to a patent-leather shine, his eyes have somehow become beady and suspicious, his French mustache is constantly quivering with alarm (real and pretended), and he scurries up and down the train like a paranoid crab. The performance is brilliant, and it's high comedy.

So is the movie, although it's careful never to make its essentially comic intentions get in the way of Miss Christie's well-oiled mystery. This isn't a "thriller," because we're not thrilled, or scared—only amused. The murder itself has a certain antiseptic, ritualistic quality, and the investigation is an exercise in sophisticated cross-examination and sputters of indignation. What I liked best about this movie is its style, both the deliberately old-fashioned visual strategies used by director Sidney Lumet, and the cheerful overacting of the dozen or more suspects.

They form a suitably bizarre menagerie and at first glance have nothing in common with one another. Bear with me please, and I'll work my way through the all-stars: Lauren Bacall is a particularly obnoxious American, Ingrid Bergman is an African missionary, Michael York and Jacqueline Bisset are Hungarian royalty, Jean-Pierre Cassel is the conductor, Sean Connery is an English officer returning from India, Vanessa Redgrave is his constant companion, John Gielgud is a veddy, veddy proper manservant to millionaire Richard Widmark, Wendy Hiller is an aloof Russian aristocrat, Anthony Perkins is Widmark's secretary, Rachel Roberts is a neo-Nazi ladies' maid, Martin Balsam is a director of the railroad line, and there are, believe it or not, others also under suspicion.

There are obviously big technical problems here: More than a dozen characters have to be introduced and kept alive, a very complicated plot has to be unraveled, and everything must take place within the claustrophobic confines of the railway car. Lumet overcomes his difficulties in great style, and we're never for a moment confused (except when we're supposed to be, which is most of the time).

There is hardly anything more I can tell you, or even hint, about the plot, except that nothing is as it seems (and you knew that already about a movie based on an Agatha Christie book). The movie provides a good time, high style, a loving salute to an earlier period of filmmaking, and an unexpected bonus: It ends with a very long scene in which Poirot asks everyone to be silent, please, while he explains his various theories of the case. He does so in great detail, and it's fun of a rather malicious sort watching a dozen high-priced stars keep their mouths shut and just listen while Finney masterfully dominates the scene.

Murphy's Romance ★ ★ ★

PG-13, 107 m., 1985

Sally Field (Emma Moriarty), James Garner (Murphy Jones), Brian Kerwin (Bobby Jack), Corey Haim (Jake), Dennis Burkley (Freeman Coverly), Georgann Johnson (Margaret). Directed by Martin Ritt and produced by Laura Ziskin. Screenplay by Harriet Frank, Jr., and Irving Ravetch.

From the moment Sally Field pilots her battered old pickup into town and parks her kid out at the farm and walks into James Garner's drugstore and they lay eyes on each other for the first time, it's pretty clear that they are going to have to fall in love with each other and get married. All you have to do is look at them to see that.

Murphy's Romance takes almost two hours to arrive at the conclusion that takes us two minutes, but that doesn't mean this is a predictable movie. The whole point of this movie is how it looks at those characters, and listens to them, and allows them to live in a specific time and place. If they knew what we know, it would spoil all the fun, as they flirt and pout and spar and circle each other, and survive the sudden and unexpected appearance of Sally Field's no-good ex-husband.

His name is Bobby Jack, and Field describes him in a sentence: "How come you were never as good on your feet as you were between the sheets?" He's an immature, sweet-talking con man without a responsible bone in his body. He turns up one day, and moves in, and Field lets him stay because it means a lot to their son, Jake.

At first it appears that Bobby Jack's arrival is going to cause problems for the budding relationship between Emma and Murphy (Field and Garner). But Emma keeps on inviting Murphy to stay to dinner, and Murphy reads the situation correctly: Emma may be stuck with Bobby Jack, but she is stuck on Murphy.

Murphy is quite a guy. He figures he has a lot of knowledge about human nature, and he's not shy about sharing it. He doesn't take himself too seriously, but he likes to pretend that he does. He speaks thoughtfully, moves deliberately, and lets you know what a character he is by parking his mint-condition 1928 Studebaker out in front of his drugstore. Garner plays this character in more or less his usual acting style, but he has been given such quietly offbeat dialogue by the screenwriters, Harriet Frank, Jr., and Irving Ravetch, that he comes across as a true original.

Sally Field is also not particularly original in her approach to the character Emma, who is a close relative of other Field heroines: plucky, quietly sensible in the face of calamity. Originality is not called for in this performance, anyway; it would have been a mistake to turn into a colorful character, instead of letting her proceed at her own speed. In the movie's key series of scenes—where Bobby Jack makes his move and Emma sneezes at him and then a surprise visitor turns up from Tulsa—the movie is saved from melodrama only by Field's matter-of-fact ability to take things as they come.

Then comes the ending, which is one of the most carefully and lovingly written passages in any recent movie. Much depends on exactly what Emma and Murphy say to each other, and how they say it, and what they don't say. The movie gets it all right.

Murphy's Romance was directed by Martin Ritt, who also directed Field's Oscar-winning performance in *Norma Rae* (and worked with her again in the less-than-successful *Back Roads*). Ritt specializes in movies about the rural South and Southwest (his credits also include *Sounder*, *Hud*, and *Conrack*), and one of the strengths of *Murphy's Romance* is the freedom he feels to simply pause, occasionally, and soak in the local color. Two examples: Listen carefully to the man who calls the bingo numbers, and the old man Murphy gives a lift to one day. They have particular voices and deliberate word choices, and they seem completely authentic. So, to a surprising degree, does the whole movie.

The Music Lovers ★ ★
R, 122 m., 1971

Richard Chamberlain (Tchaikovsky), Glenda Jackson (Nina Milukova), Max Adrian (Nicholas Rubenstein), Christopher Gable (Count Chiluvsky), Isabella Telezynska (Madame Von Meck). Directed and produced by Ken Russell. Screenplay by Melvyn Bragg.

Ken Russell's *The Music Lovers* is an involved and garish private fantasy which Russell, alas, presents to us as the life of Tchaikovsky. Poor Tchaikovsky. I know it is against the rules to complain that this or that detail may not be precisely accurate, or that Tchaikovsky may not have been dealt with in the fairest possible manner. I know, because I get letters from graduate students, that I must resolutely examine the film itself—or the "film itself" as they put it—and put aside considerations from real life. What difference does it matter whether Tchaikovsky actually existed as Russell portrays him—as long as Russell has made a good film?

Well, I suppose there's something to be said for that point of view, had Russell made a good film and not said it was about Tchaikovsky. But *The Music Lovers* is libelous not only to the composer but to his music. I am no composer, Lord knows, but I have a notion that even the greatest of composers must have spent most of their time hard at work composing. I doubt whether their great works came to them, full-blown, in moments of sexual, religious, political, or sporting ecstasy. I doubt whether any great work in any field of art "comes" to anybody. Great novels are not produced by automatic writing, so why should great symphonies be?

Russell apparently thinks they are. And so although his film is more visually daring and more sexually explicit than other biographies of composers, it rests on the same fallacious assumption: That a sunset, or a woman (or a man, in Tchaikovsky's case), or a famous naval victory, or something could inspire the composer to sit down and dash off a few inspired moments.

Lest you accuse me of exaggerating, let me just mention that Tchaikovsky's mental image, when the cannons roar in the "1812

Overture," is supposed to be a friend's head being blown off. Better we should have a movie in which Russell's image, during the same passage, is of his own head being blown off. We would save the head for last, of course, in order to deal with lesser extremeties of the minor works.

The Music Lovers is totally irresponsible, then, as a film about, or inspired by, or parallel to, or bearing a vague resemblance to, Tchaikovsky, his life and times. It is not, however, a complete failure. Ken Russell is a most deviously baroque director, sucking us down with him into his ornate fantasies of decadent interior decoration, until every fringe on every curtain has a fringe of its own, and the characters have fringes, too, and the characters elbow their way through a grotesque jungle of candlesticks, potted plant stands, incense sticks, old champagne bottles, and gilt edges, and it is almost certain that something is happening in the movie. But what?

My Beautiful Laundrette ★ ★ ★

R, 93 m., 1986

Daniel Day Lewis (Johnny), Saeed Jaffrey (Nasser), Roshan Seth (Papa), Gordon Warnecke (Omar), Shirley Ann Field (Rachel), Rita Wolf (Tania). Directed by Stephen Frears and produced by Sarah Radclyffe and Tim Bevan. Screenplay by Hanif Kureishi.

When people told me they'd seen *My Beautiful Laundrette* and it was a good movie, I had a tendency to believe them, for who would dare to make a bad movie with such an uncommercial title? The launderette in question is a storefront operation in one of the seedier areas of London, and it is losing money when a rich Pakistani decides to entrust its management to his nephew. But this is not the saga of a launderette. It is the story of two kinds of outsiders in modern London.

The film opens with some uneventful days in the life of its hero, Omar, who is a young man in need of a job. His father is an alcoholic journalist, once important and successful, now never far from the gin bottle. His uncle Nasser is one of the more successful members of the Pakistani community in London, a businessman who owns a chain of parking garages and storefront retail shops. He enjoys success in British terms: He has a big house in the country, an expensive car, and a British mistress.

Because a man cannot stand by and see a member of his family fail for lack of opportunity, he gives Omar a job in a parking garage, and later turns the launderette over to him. He also suggests that Omar should get married, perhaps even to his own daughter.

There is some doubt, however, about whether Omar will ever get married. Earlier in the film, we have witnessed a strange scene. Omar and friends have been stopped by a gang of punk neofascist Paki bashers, when Omar walks up fearlessly to their leader, Johnny, and greet him with affection. We discover that the two young men had been lovers, and before long Johnny abandons his gang to join with Omar in the operation of the launderette.

My Beautiful Laundrette refuses to commit its plot to any particular agenda, and I found that interesting. It's not about whether Johnny and Omar will remain lovers, and it's not about whether the launderette will be a success, and it's not about the drunken father or even about Nasser's daughter, who is so bored and desperate that during a cocktail party she goes outside and bares her breasts to Omar through the French doors: Anything to get away from the small talk.

The movie is not concerned with plot, but with giving us a feeling for the society its characters inhabit. Modern Britain is a study in contrasts, between rich and poor, between upper and lower classes, between native British and the various immigrant groups—some of which, like the Pakistanis, have started to prosper. To this mixture, the movie adds the conflict between straight and gay.

Their relationship encompasses some subtleties which the movie handles with great delicacy. Although Omar is a member of a non-white immigrant group and Johnny is Anglo-Saxon, the realities of their lives are that Omar will probably turn out to be more successful and prosperous than Johnny. He has the advantage of his uncle's capital, his family connections, and his own gift at business. Johnny is a true outsider with small prospects of success.

There is another outsider in the movie who shares his dilemma. She is Rachel,

Nasser's British mistress. Nasser remains married to his Pakistani wife, and although the two women are more or less known to one another, he keeps them in separate compartments of his life. There is a moment, though, during the opening ceremonies at the launderette, when the two women are accidentally in the same room at the same time, and it results in an extraordinary speech by Rachel, who with pride and dignity defends her position as Nasser's mistress by describing herself as a woman who has never had a break in life, who has always had to ask for what she wanted, and who deserves some small measure of happiness, just like everybody else.

A movie like this lives or dies with its performances, and the actors in *My Beautiful Laundrette* are a fascinating group of unknowns, with one exception—Shirley Anne Field, who plays Rachel, and who may be familiar from *Saturday Night and Sunday Morning* and other British films.

The character of Johnny may cause you to blink, if you've seen the wonderful *A Room with a View;* he is played by Daniel Day Lewis, the same actor who in that film plays the heroine's affected fiancé Cecil. Seeing these two performances side by side is an affirmation of the miracle of acting: That one man could play these two opposites is astonishing.

Omar is played by Gordon Warnecke, an actor unknown to me, as a bright but passive youth who hasn't yet figured out the strategy by which he will approach the world. He is a blank slate, pleasant, agreeable, not readily showing the sorrows and angers that we figure ought to be inside there somewhere. The most expansive character in the movie is Nasser (Saeed Jaffrey), an engaging hedonist who doesn't see why everyone shouldn't enjoy life with the cynical good cheer he possesses.

The viewer is likely to go through a curious process while watching this film. At first there is unfamiliarity: Who are these people, and where do they come from, and what sort of society do they occupy in England? We get oriented fairly quickly, and understand the values that are at work. Then we begin to wonder what the movie is about. It is with some relief that we realize it isn't "about" anything; it's simply some weeks spent with some characters in a way that tells us more about some aspects of modern Britain than we've seen before.

I mentioned *A Room with a View* because of the link with Daniel Day Lewis. There is another link between the two films. They are both about the possibility of opening up views—of being able to see through a window out of your own life and into other possibilities. Both films argue that you have a choice. You can accept your class, social position, race, sexuality, or prejudices as absolutes, and live entirely inside them. Or you can look out the window, or maybe even walk out the door.

My Bodyguard ★ ★ ★ ½

PG, 97 m., 1980

Chris Makepeace (Clifford), Adam Baldwin (Linderman), Matt Dillon (Moody), Ruth Gordon (Gramma), Martin Mull (Mr. Peache), John Houseman (Dobbs), Paul Quandt (Carson), Craig Richard Nelson (Griffith). Directed by Tony Bill and produced by Don Devlin. Screenplay by Alan Ormsby.

There is a terrifying moment in adolescence when suddenly some of the kids are twice as big as the rest of the kids. It is terrifying for everybody: For the kids who are suddenly tall and gangling, and for the kids who are still small and are getting beat up all the time. *My Bodyguard* places that moment in a Chicago high school and gives us a kid who tries to think his way out of it.

The kid's name is Clifford. He has everything going against him. He's smart, he's new in the school, he's slightly built. As he's played by Chris Makepeace, he is also one of the most engaging teen-age characters I've seen in the movies in a long time. Too many movie teen-agers have been sex-crazed *(Little Darlings)*, animalistic food-fighters *(Meat Balls)*, or hopelessly romanticized *(The Blue Lagoon)*. Clifford is basically just your normal, average kid.

He has just moved to Chicago with his family. His father (Martin Mull) is the new resident manager of the Ambassador East Hotel. His grandmother (Ruth Gordon) hangs out in the lobby and picks up old men in the bar. Life is great, backstage at a hotel (he gets his meals in the kitchen or sometimes in the Pump Room). But it's not so great at school. The movie sends Clifford to

Lake View High School, where he's immediately shaken down for his lunch money.

The extortionist (Matt Dillon) is the kind of kid we all remember from high school. He's handsome in an oily way, he's going through a severe case of adolescent sadism, he's basically a coward. His threat is that unless Clifford pays protection money, he'll sic the dreaded Linderman on him.

Linderman (Adam Baldwin) is a school legend, a big, hulking kid who allegedly killed his brother, raped a teacher, hit a cop, you name it. The movie's inspiration is to have Clifford *think* his way out of his dilemma—neutralizing Linderman by hiring him as a bodyguard. This is genius, and there's a wonderful scene where Clifford springs Linderman on the rest of the kids.

Then the movie takes an interesting turn. Clifford and Linderman become friends, and we learn some of the unhappy facts of Linderman's life. It turns out Linderman isn't the Incredible Hulk after all—he's just another kid going through growing pains and some personal tragedy. This whole middle stretch is the best part of the movie, developing a friendship in a perceptive and gentle way that's almost shocking in comparison with the idiotic, violent teen-agers so many movies have given us.

The ending is predictable (it's a showdown between Linderman and another tough kid). And there are some distractions along the way from Clifford's family. Martin Mull makes an interesting hotel manager, whimsical and charming. But the movie gets off track when it follows Ruth Gordon through some of her adventures, including a romantic collision with a hotel executive played by John Houseman. These scenes just don't seem part of the same movie: The hotel stuff is sitcom, while the stuff in the high school is fresh and inventive.

That seems to apply to the performances, too. One of the strengths of *My Bodyguard* is in the casting of the younger performers—Chris Makepeace, Adam Baldwin, Matt Dillon. They look right for their parts, but, more to the point, they *feel* right. Dillon exudes creepiness, Makepeace is plausible while thinking on his feet, Linderman is convincingly vulnerable and confused, and there's another kid, the solemn-faced, wide-eyed Paul Quandt, who steals a couple of scenes with his absolute certainty that the worst is yet to come.

My Bodyguard is a small treasure, a movie about believable characters in an unusual situation. It doesn't pretend to be absolutely realistic, and the dynamics of its big city high school are simplified for the purposes of the story. But this movie is fun to watch because it touches memories that are shared by most of us, and because its young characters are recognizable individuals, and not simplified cartoon figures like so many movie teen-agers.

My Brilliant Career ★ ★ ★ ½

NO MPAA RATING, 101 m., 1980

Judy Davis (Sybylia Melvyn), Sam Neill (Harry Beecham), Wendy Hughes (Aunt Helen), Robert Grubb (Frank Hawden), Max Cullen (Mr. McSwat), Pat Kennedy (Aunt Gussie). Directed by Gillian Armstrong and produced by Margaret Fink. Screenplay by Eleanor Witcombe.

What magic is it that sometimes allows young girls in backward districts to guess that they need not play along with the general ideas about a "woman's role"? I ask because three of my favorite writers—and now a fourth—discovered, more or less by themselves, that the possibilities in their lives were unlimited.

Two of the writers are famous: Willa Cather, who wrote of independent young women in Nebraska and points west, and Doris Lessing, whose *Children of Violence* series chronicles the liberation of a young woman from Rhodesia. The other two writers are not so well known, but the parallels in their lives are so astonishing that I'd like to sketch them, briefly, before moving on to an extraordinary film, *My Brilliant Career.* Their names are Olive Schreiner and Miles Franklin. They both led isolated childhoods in the nineteenth century, in the backwaters of the British Empire. And they both wrote novels about those lives at a very early age.

Olive Schreiner was raised on a farm in the Orange Free State, in South Africa. She learned Afrikaans along with English, read the Bible daily, and in her mid-teens wrote a classic novel, *The Story of an African Farm.* It was about the awakening of the spirit of a teen-age girl (herself, obviously) who did not see why her life had to be so limited just because she was a woman. Schreiner's later life was spent in intellectual and feminist circles in London (and for a time she filled the challenging position of being Havelock Ellis's mistress).

The other writer is someone I've just learned about recently: Miles Franklin, born in 1879 in rural Australia and raised on an isolated country station in the outback. At the age of sixteen she wrote a novel about her experiences, *My Brilliant Career.* It was published six years later in Edinburgh. Like Schreiner, Franklin became a feminist, traveled abroad in her twenties (and came to Chicago, where she and Alice Henry organized the Women's Trade Union League).

The Story of an African Farm is an established literary classic. *My Brilliant Career,* on the other hand, was relatively forgotten until a group of Australian women filmmakers made it into this remarkable film. It tells the story of a restless, high-spirited young woman whose temperament just isn't suited to the leftover Victorian standards of Australian country districts in the 1890s.

Franklin's novel is successful as a movie primarily because of a brilliant casting discovery. Judy Davis, who plays the film's heroine, is so fresh, unique, irreverent, and winning that she makes this material live. She's a young actress from Perth, a sometime pop and jazz singer, who was reportedly the second choice for the film's lead; if that's so, it was a completely fortunate second choice.

My Brilliant Career could have been just another feminist film. The director, Gillian Armstrong, could have gone to great lengths to explain the thinking and motivations of her character—and bored us in the meantime. But she doesn't. Instead, she makes her points through Judy Davis's presence and personality.

This isn't a movie that ends with any final answers or conclusions. Instead, it's about a young woman in a painful and continuing process of indecision. She's not considered by her family to be an ideal young woman at all—she's too independent, untamed, unreconciled to a woman's role. She doesn't automatically swoon at the attentions of every young man in the district. She's red-haired, freckled, feisty.

These qualities do appeal, however, to one young neighboring man, a farmer who's of two minds about her: He finds her independence appealing, and yet he tends to share the prevailing view about proper behavior for women. Can he overcome his narrow view and accept her? He does propose marriage. Can she overcome her headstrong independence and accept him? That's the film's key question, and *My Brilliant Career* is wise in never quite answering it.

The film is beautiful to look at. It was filmed on location in the outback, in warm natural colors, and the costumes and settings meticulously establish the period. But Judy Davis's performance establishes it even more, because she creates a complicated character so naturally that we feel the conflicts instead of having to understand them intellectually. This is the best kind of movie of ideas, in which the movie supplies the people and emotions and *we* come up with the conclusions.

My Dinner with André ★ ★ ★ ★

NO MPAA RATING, 110 m., 1981

Wallace Shawn (Wally), André Gregory (André), Jean Lenauer (Waiter), Roy Butler (Bartender). Directed by Louis Malle and produced by George W. George and Beverly Karp. Screenplay by Shawn and Gregory.

The idea is astonishing in its audacity: a film of two friends talking, just simply talking—but with passion, wit, scandal, whimsy, vision, hope, and despair—for 110 minutes. It sounds at first like one of those underground films of the 1960s, in which great length and minimal content somehow interacted in the dope-addled brains of the audience to provide the impression of deep if somehow elusive profundity. *My Dinner with André* is not like that. It doesn't use all of those words as a stunt. They are alive on the screen, breathing, pulsing, reminding us of endless, impassioned conversations we've had with those few friends worth talking with for hours and hours. Underneath all the other fascinating things in this film beats the tide of friendship, of two people with a genuine interest in one another.

The two people are André Gregory and Wallace Shawn. Those are their real names, and also their names in the movie. I suppose they are playing themselves. As the film opens, Shawn travels across New York City to meet Gregory for dinner, and his thoughts provide us with background: His friend

Gregory is a New York theater director, well-known into the 1970s, who dropped out for five years and traveled around the world. Now Gregory has returned, with wondrous tales of strange experiences. Shawn has spent the same years in New York, finding uncertain success as an author and playwright. They sit down for dinner in an elegant restaurant. We do not see the other customers. The bartender is a wraith in the background, the waiter is the sort of presence they were waiting for in *Waiting for Godot.* The friends order dinner, and then, as it is served and they eat and drink, they talk.

What conversation! André Gregory does most of the talking, and he is a spellbinding conversationalist, able to weave mental images not only out of his experiences, but also out of his ideas. He explains that he had become dissatisfied with life, restless, filled with anomie and discontent. He accepted an invitation to join an experimental theater group in Poland. It was *very* experimental, tending toward rituals in the woods under the full moon.

From Poland, he traveled around the world, meeting a series of people who were seriously and creatively exploring the ways in which they could experience the material world. They (and Gregory) literally believed in mind over matter, and as Gregory describes a monk who was able to stand his entire body weight on his fingertips, we visualize that man and in some strange way (so hypnotic is the tale) we share the experience.

One of the gifts of *My Dinner with André* is that we share so many of the experiences. Although most of the movie literally consists of two men talking, here's a strange thing: *We* do not spend the movie just passively listening to them talk. At first, director Louis Malle's sedate series of images (close-ups, two-shots, reacton shots) calls attention to itself, but as Gregory continues to talk, the very simplicity of the visual style renders it invisible. And like the listeners at the feet of a master storyteller, we find ourselves visualizing what Gregory describes, until this film is as filled with visual images as a radio play—*more* filled, perhaps, than a conventional feature film.

What Gregory and Shawn talk about is, quite simply, many of the things on our minds these days. We've passed through Tom Wolfe's Me Decade and find ourselves in a decade during which there will apparently be less for everybody. The two friends talk about inner journeys—not in the mystical, vague terms of magazines you don't want to be seen reading on the bus, but in terms of trying to live better lives, of learning to listen to what others are really saying, of breaking the shackles of conventional ideas about our bodies and allowing them to more fully sense the outer world.

The movie is not ponderous, annoyingly profound, or abstract. It is about living, and Gregory seems to have lived fully in his five years of dropping out. Shawn is the character who seems more like us. He listens, he nods eagerly, he is willing to learn, but—something holds him back. Pragmatic questions keep asking themselves. He can't buy Gregory's vision, not all the way. He'd like to, but this is a real world we have to live in, after all, and if we all danced with the druids in the forests of Poland, what would happen to the market for fortune cookies?

The film's end is beautiful and inexplicably moving. Shawn returns home by taxi through the midnight streets of New York. Having spent hours with Gregory on a wild conversational flight, he is now reminded of scenes from his childhood. In *that* store, his father bought him shoes. In that one, he bought ice cream with a girl friend. The utter simplicity of his memories acts to dramatize the fragility and great preciousness of life. He has learned his friend's lesson.

My Favorite Year ★ ★ ★ ½

PG, 92 m., 1982

Peter O'Toole (Alan Swann), Mark Linn-Baker (Benjy Stone), Jessica Harper (K.C. Downing), Joseph Bologna (King Kaiser), Lainie Kazan (Belle Corroca), Lou Jacobi (Uncle Morty). Directed by Richard Benjamin and produced by Michael Gruskoff. Screenplay by Norman Steinberg and Dennis Palumbo.

"Live? I can't go on *live!!* I'm a movie star—not an actor!"

Alan Swann is imploring them: Say it isn't so! He's an alcoholic British matinee idol, veteran of countless swashbuckling epics in which he faced fleets of pirates and waves of savage barbarians. Now he is being asked to accept the worst challenge of all: to appear on live television.

My Favorite Year is the story of an era when most television was live, and the great television stars were inventing the medium out of their own imaginations every Saturday night. The year is 1954. The program is "King Kaiser's Comedy Hour," obviously inspired by the old Sid Caesar and Imogene Coca programs. The British star, Alan Swann, is played by Peter O'Toole, but he could be Errol Flynn or John Barrymore or even O'Toole himself. The movie is told from the point of view of a young production assistant named Benjy (Mark Linn-Baker). His job is to shadow the great Alan Swann, get him everything he wants except booze, keep him out of trouble, and deliver him intact to the studio in time for the broadcast. Along the way, Benjy adds a priority of his own, his continuing courtship of his would-be girlfriend, K.C. (Jessica Harper).

Through Benjy's eyes, we see Swann as the great man he was, as the pathetic drunk he is, and as the hero he could become—if he survives the live telecast. We also gain some understanding of King Kaiser (Joseph Bologna), who is a big, beefy, not-too-bright guy who has an absolutely accurate understanding of his own comic talent. Translated, that means he knows what will work. What will get a laugh. He has no taste, of course; when he offends a girl, he sends her steaks instead of flowers, and he sends a business associate a gift of tires. But he's a physical comedian with a gift for pumping the laughter out of this frail new medium, and he's backed up by a whole crew of talented writers.

Swann, meanwhile, is backed up only by memories of his greatness and fears of performing in front of a live audience. But as O'Toole plays this character, he becomes one of the great comic inventions of recent movies. Swann is a drunk, but he has an uncanny ability to pass from coma through courtliness to heroics without ever quite seeming to gain consciousness. A character like Swann could probably only be played by someone who is both a great actor and a great ham, and O'Toole is both.

My Favorite Year is not a perfect movie. I could have done without the entire romantic subplot between Benjy and K.C. But I liked the movie's ability to move from one unexpected comic situation to another. That produces one of the best scenes, when Benjy takes Swann home to Brooklyn to meet his mother and weird Uncle Morty (Lainie Kazan and Lou Jacobi in hilarious performances). There is, to be sure, a force running through the movie's disorganization, and that force is O'Toole's charisma. He is so completely charming, so doomed, so funny, and so pathetically invincible as Swann that this movie succeeds despite its occasional unnecessary scenes.

N

Nadine ★ ★ ½
PG, 83 m., 1987
(See related Film Clip, p. 781.)

Jeff Bridges (Vernon Hightower), Kim Basinger (Nadine Hightower), Rip Torn (Buford Pope), Gwen Verdon (Vera), Glenne Headly (Renee), Jerry Stiller (Raymond Escobar). Directed by Robert Benton and produced by Arlene Donovan. Screenplay by Benton.

As a general rule, you hardly can go wrong with a movie that uses a woman's first name as its title. Right away you know the film is going to showcase an actress playing a character who is indomitable, eccentric, stubborn, determined, and with a heart as big as all outdoors. Let's make a list: *Camille, Gilda, Julia, Sophie's Choice, Carrie, Norma Rae, Hello, Dolly!, Cleopatra.* (You hardly ever get a movie with a man's first name, probably because of some obscure, sexist impulse we will examine at a later date.)

Nadine is the latest entry in this tradition, a movie about a down-home Texas woman (Kim Basinger) who makes the mistake of posing for the wrong pictures for the wrong photographer. He was going to send them to his personal friend, Mr. Hugh M. Hefner, but now it looks like they may wind up on the back of a truck-stop poker deck, so she wants to get them back.

This involves enlisting her soon-to-be-ex-husband (Jeff Bridges) in a scheme to break into the photographer's office and grab the incriminating negatives. But first she has to pry him loose from the clutches of his current fiancée, the Pecan Queen. And then there's the problem of the dead body they stumble over in the photographer's studio. That's the setup for what looks like a screwball comedy, sounds like a screwball comedy, and is intended to be a screwball comedy, but is not, alas, very funny.

Basinger and Bridges make a nice team, fighting and making up and trying not to get killed after they're trapped in a conspiracy to get rich off of secret Texas state highway plans. The movie surrounds them with colorful character actors, gives them lots of down-home dialogue, and adds the usual number of chases and showdowns and scenes where they have to escape on a creaky ladder over a certain drop to their deaths. It would seem to have all the right ingredients.

And yet I didn't laugh very much watching this movie. There were a couple of genuinely funny moments, but they didn't build and the movie didn't redeem itself by making me very interested in the characters. I kept getting the idea I was looking at fabricated behavior that didn't have any foundation in real people that the filmmakers cared about.

You'd almost think, though, that Basinger and Bridges could pull it off no matter what. Although Basinger still somehow is dismissed as a sexy blond (maybe because she is one), she is an actress of substantial talent and is right at home in Texas, as she showed in *Fool for Love.* Bridges is one of the most dependable Hollywood leading men, effortlessly likable, and they have a nice, easy chemistry together. But it doesn't add up to much.

Scene after scene just sort of sits there on the screen. The screenplay seems to be going through the motions. Stock supporting characters walk on, and they feel stock. They don't give the sense, as supporting characters should, of leading full lives just out of sight offscreen. Only Rip Torn, as one of the conspirators, seems convinced his character actually has a stake in the matters at hand.

This is the second movie Robert Benton has filmed in his home state of Texas; the other was *Places in the Heart*. He is obviously dealing with a lot of nostalgia here, and he has all the details right: the cars, the rhythm of the streets, the way rooms are furnished. What he doesn't have is much in the way of laughter. This is a curiously flat, unfinished, low-energy comedy, and what I liked the most was simply the ease with which Basinger and Bridges inhabited it.

The Name of the Rose ★ ★ ½
R, 128 m., 1986

Sean Connery (William of Baskerville), F. Murray Abraham (Bernardo Gui), Christian Slater (Adso of Melk), Elya Baskin (Severinus), Feodor Chaliapin, Jr. (Jorge de Burgos), William Hickey (Ubertino de Casale), Michael Lonsdale (The Abbot). Directed by Jean-Jacques Annaud and produced by Berno Eichinger. Screenplay by Andrew Birkin, Gerard Brach, Howard Franklin, and Alain Godard.

In my imagination, there are two kinds of monks and two kinds of monasteries. The first kind of monastery is a robust community of men who work hard and pray hard and are bronzed by the sun and have a practical sense of humor. They have joined the life of prayer with the life of the hands. The second monastery is a shuttered series of gloomy passages and dank cells where jealous, mean-spirited little men scamper about playing politics. Their prayers are sanctimonious and their nights are long and resentful.

In the first few scenes of *The Name of the Rose,* we realize that this will be a movie about a contest between the two kinds of monks. Here comes the first one now, striding across the open fields of the Middle Ages, his heavy wool habit little protection against the cold winds, his young novice walking at his side. His name is William of Baskerville, and he is portrayed by Sean Connery, who plays him as the first modern man, as a scholar-monk who understands all of the lessons of the past but is able to see them in a wider context than the others of his time.

One day, William arrives at a vast monastery, which crouches with foreboding on top of a steep hill. At its base, starving peasants wrestle for scraps of food, which are thrown down from the monk's kitchens. At its pinnacle is a great tower that has been arranged as a labyrinth; you might find anything up there—except the way out.

A series of murders is taking place in the monastery. William has a reputation as something of an investigator, and soon after his arrival he is involved in trying to identify the causes of death and to find the murderer. There are many suspects. Indeed, I cannot remember a single monk in this monastery who does not look like a suspect. The film has been cast to look like a cross between the grotesques of Fellini and the rat-faced devils scampering in the backgrounds of a tarot deck.

What we have here is the setup for a wonderful movie. What we get, unfortunately, is a very confused story, photographed in such murky gloom that sometimes it is hard to be sure exactly what is happening. William of Baskerville listens closely and nods wisely and pokes into out-of-the-way corners, and makes solemn pronouncements to his young novice. It is clear that he is onto something, but the screenplay is so loosely constructed that few connections are made between his conclusions and what happens next.

During the central sections of the film, the atmosphere threatens to overwhelm the action. *The Name of the Rose* was shot in a real monastery and on sets that look completely convincing, but unfortunately the film takes the "dark ages" literally and sets its events in such impenetrable gloom that sometimes it is almost impossible to see what is happening. The large cast of characters swims in and out of view while horrible events take place; a monk is found dead at the base of the tower, and another is drowned in a wine vat. William of Baskerville moves solemnly from one event to another, deliberately, wisely, but then the plot takes on a crazy rhythm of its own, as the Grand Inquisitor arrives to hold a trial and ancient secrets are discovered inside the labyrinth of the tower.

What this movie needs is a clear, spare, logical screenplay. It's all inspiration and no discipline. At a crucial moment in the film, William and his novice seem sure to be burned alive, and we have to deduce how they escaped because the movie doesn't tell us. There are so many good things in *The Name of the Rose*—the performances, the reconstruction of the period, the overall feeling of medieval times—that if the story had been able to really involve us, there would have been quite a movie here.

Nashville ★ ★ ★ ★

R, 159 m., 1975

Henry Gibson (Haven Hamilton), Ronee Blakely (Barbara Jean), Timothy Brown (Tommy Brown), Gwen Welles (Sueleen Gay), Michael Murphy (John Triplette), Shelley Duvall (L.A. Joan), Lily Tomlin (Linnea Reese), Ned Beatty (Delbert Reese), Scott Glenn (Pfc. Glenn Kelly), Keith Carradine (Tom Frank), Geraldine Chaplin (Opal), Karen Black (Connie White), Barbara Harris (Albuquerque). Directed and produced by Robert Altman. Screenplay by Joan Tewkesbury.

Robert Altman's *Nashville,* which was the best American movie since *Bonnie and Clyde,* creates in the relationships of nearly two dozen characters a microcosm of who we were and what we were up to in the 1970s. It's a film about the losers and the winners, the drifters and the stars in Nashville, and the most complete expression yet of not only the genius but also the humanity of Altman, who sees people with his camera in such a way as to enlarge our own experience. Sure, it's only a movie. But after I saw it I felt more alive, I felt I understood more about people, I felt somehow wiser. It's that good a movie.

The movie doesn't have a star. It does not, indeed, even have a lead role. Instead, Altman creates a world, a community in which some people know each other and others don't, in which people are likely to meet before they understand the ways in which their lives are related. And he does it all so easily, or seems to, that watching *Nashville* is as easy as breathing and as hard to stop. Altman is the best natural filmmaker since Fellini.

One of the funny things about *Nashville* is that most of the characters never have entrances. They're just sort of there. At times, we're watching an important character and don't even know, yet, why he's important, but Altman's storytelling is so clear in his own mind, his mastery of this complex wealth of material is so complete, that we're never for a moment confused or even curious. We feel secure in his hands, and apart from anything else, *Nashville* is a vurtuoso display of narrative mastery.

It concerns several days and nights in the lives of a very mixed bag of Nashville locals and visitors, all of whom, like the city itself, are obsessed with country music. Tennessee is in the midst of a presidential primary, and all over Nashville, there are the posters and sound trucks of a quasipopulist candidate, Hal Philip Walker, who seems like a cross between George Wallace and George McGovern. We never meet Walker, but we meet both his local organizer and a John Lindsay-type PR man. They're trying to round up country-western talent for a big benefit, and their efforts provide a thread around which some of the story is loosely wound.

But there are many stories here, and in the way he sees their connections, Altman makes a subtle but shrewd comment about the ways in which we are all stuck in this thing together. There are the veteran country stars like Haven Hamilton (Henry Gibson), who wears gaudy white costumes, is self-conscious about his short stature, is painfully earnest about recording a painfully banal Bicentennial song, and who, down deep, is basically just a good old boy. There is the reigning queen of country music, Barbara Jean (Ronee Blakely), who returns in triumph to Nashville after treatment at a burn center in Atlanta for unspecified injuries incurred from a fire baton (she's met at the airport by a phalanx of girls from TIT—the Tennessee Institute of Twirling—only to collapse again). There is the corrupted, decadent rock star, played by Keith Carradine, who is so ruthless in his sexual aggression, so evil in his need to hurt women, that he telephones one woman while another is still just leaving his bed, in order to wound both of them.

But these characters are just examples of the people we meet in *Nashville,* not the leads. Everyone is more or less equal in this film, because Altman sees them all with a judicious and ultimately sympathetic eye. The film is filled with perfectly observed little moments: The starstruck young soldier keeping a silent vigil by the bedside of Barbara Jean; the campaign manager doing a double-take when he discovers he's just shaken the hand of Elliott Gould ("a fairly well-known actor," Haven Hamilton explains, "and he used to be married to Barbra Streisand"); the awestruck BBC reporter describing America in breathless, hilarious hyperbole; the way a middle-aged mother of two deaf children (Lily Tomlin) shyly waits for an assignation with a rock singer; the birdbrained cheerfulness with which a young groupie (Shelley Duvall) comes to town to visit her dying aunt and never does see her, being distracted by every male over the age of sixteen that she mets.

The film circles around three motifs without, thankfully, ever feeling it has to make a definitive statement about any of them. Since they're all still very open subjects, that's just as well. What Altman does is suggest the ways in which we deal with them—really, in unrehearsed everyday life, not thematically, as in the movies. The motifs are success, women, and politics.

Success: It can be studied most fruitfully in the carefully observed pecking order of the country-and-western performers. There are ones at the top, so successful they can afford to be generous, expansive, well-liked. There are the younger ones in the middle, jockeying for position. There are what can only be described as the professional musicians at the bottom, playing thanklessly but well in the bars and clubs where the stars come to unwind after the show. And at the very bottom, there are those who aspire to be musicians but have no talent at all, like a waitress (Gwen Welles) who comes to sing at a smoker, is forced to strip, and, in one of the film's moments of heartbreaking truthfulness, disdainfully flings at the roomful of men the sweat socks she had stuffed into her brassiere.

Women: God, but Altman cares for them while seeing their predicament so clearly. The women in *Nashville* inhabit a world largely unaffected by the feminist revolution, as most women do. They are prized for their talent, for their beauty, for their services in bed, but not once in this movie for themselves. And yet Altman suggests their complexities in ways that movies rarely have done before. The Lily Tomlin character, in particular, forces us to consider her real human needs and impulses as she goes to meet the worthless rock singer (and we remember a luminous scene during which she and her deaf son discussed his swimming class). Part of the movie's method is to establish characters in one context and then place them in another, so that we can see how personality—indeed, basic identity itself—is constant but must sometimes be concealed for the sake of survival or even simple happiness.

Politics: I won't be giving very much away by revealing that there is an attempted assassination in *Nashville*. The assassin, a loner who takes a room in a boarding house, is clearly telegraphed by Altman. It's not Altman's style to surprise us with plot. He'd rather surprise us by revelations of character. At this late date after November 22, 1963, and all the other days of infamy, I wouldn't have thought it possible that a film could have anything new or very interesting to say on assassination, but *Nashville* does, and the film's closing minutes, with Barbara Harris finding herself, to her astonishment, on stage and singing, "It Don't Worry Me," are unforgettable and heartbreaking. *Nashville*, which seems so unstructured as it begins, reveals itself in this final sequence to have had a deep and very profound structure—but one of emotions, not ideas.

This is a film about America. It deals with our myths, our hungers, our ambitions, and our sense of self. It knows how we talk and how we behave, and it doesn't flatter us but it does love us.

National Lampoon's Animal House

★ ★ ★ ★

R, 109 m., 1978

John Belushi (Bluto), Tim Matheson (Otter), John Vernon (Dean Wormer), Verna Bloom (Mrs. Wormer), Thomas Hulce (Pinto), Cesare Danova (Mayor), Donald Sutherland (Jennings), Mary Louise Weller (Mandy), Stephen Furst (Flounder), Mark Metcalf (Neidermeier). Directed by John Landis and produced by Marry Simmons and Ivan Reitman. Screenplay by Harold Ramis, Douglas Kenney, and Chris Miller.

"What we need right now," Otter tells his fraternity brothers, "is a stupid, futile gesture on someone's part." And no fraternity on campus—on any campus—is better qualified to provide such a gesture than the Deltas. They have the title role in *National*

Lampoon's Animal House, which remembers all the way back to 1962, when college was simpler, beer was cheaper, and girls were harder to seduce.

The movie is vulgar, raunchy, ribald, and occasionally scatological. It is also the funniest comedy since Mel Brooks made *The Producers. Animal House* is funny for some of the same reasons the *National Lampoon* is funny (and Second City and Saturday Night Live are funny): Because it finds some kind of precarious balance between insanity and accuracy, between cheerfully wretched excess and an ability to reproduce the most revealing nuances of human behavior.

In one sense there has never been a campus like this movie's Faber University, which was apparently founded by the lead pencil tycoon and has as its motto "Knowledge is Good." In another sense, Faber University is a microcosm of . . . I was going to say *our society*, but why get serious? Let someone else discuss the symbolism of Bluto's ability to crush a beer can against his forehead.

Bluto is, of course, the most animalistic of the Deltas. He's played by John Belushi, and the performance is all the more remarkable because Bluto has hardly any dialogue. He isn't a talker, he's an event. His best scenes are played in silence (as when he lasciviously scales a ladder to peek at a sorority pillow fight).

Bluto and his brothers are engaged in a holding action against civilization. They are in favor of beer, women, song, motorcycles, *Playboy* centerfolds, and making rude noises. They are opposed to studying, serious thought, the Dean, the regulations governing fraternities, and, most especially, the disgusting behavior of the Omegas—a house so respectable it has even given an ROTC commander to the world.

The movie was written by *National Lampoon* contributors (including Harold Ramis, who was in Second City at the same time Belushi was), and was directed by John Landis. It's like an end run around Hollywood's traditional notions of comedy. It's anarchic, messy, and filled with energy. It assaults us. Part of the movie's impact comes from its sheer level of manic energy: When beer kegs and Hell's Angels come bursting through the windows of the Delta House, the anarchy is infectious. But the movie's better made (and better acted) than we might at first realize. It takes skill to create this sort of comic pitch, and the movie's filled with characters that are sketched a little more absorbingly than they had to be, and acted with perception.

For example: Tim Matheson, as Otter, the ladies' man, achieves a kind of grace in his obsession. John Vernon, as the Dean of Students, has a blue-eyed, rulebook hatefulness that's inspired. Verna Bloom, as his dipsomaniacal wife, has just the right balance of cynicism and desperation. Donald Sutherland, a paranoic early sixties pothead, nods solemnly at sophomoric truisms and admits he's as bored by Milton as everyone else. And stalking through everything is Bluto, almost a natural force: He lusts, he thirsts, he consumes cafeterias full of food, and he pours an entire fifth of Jack Daniels into his mouth, belches, and observes, "Thanks. I needed that."

He has, as I suggested, little dialogue. But it is telling. When the Delta House is kicked off campus and the Deltas are thrown out of school, he makes, in a moment of silence, a philosophical observation: "Seven years down the drain." What the situation requires, of course, is a stupid, futile gesture on someone's part.

The Natural ★ ★

PG, 134 m., 1984

Robert Redford (Roy Hobbs), Robert Duvall (Max Mercy), Glenn Close (Iris Gaines), Kim Basinger (Memo Paris), Wilford Brimley (Pop Fisher), Barbara Hershey (Harriet Bird), Robert Prosky (The Judge), Richard Farnsworth (Red Blow). Directed by Barry Levinson and produced by Mark Johnson. Screenplay by Roger Towne and Phil Dusenberry.

Why didn't they make a baseball picture? Why did *The Natural* have to be turned into idolatry on behalf of Robert Redford? Why did a perfectly good story, filled with interesting people, have to be made into one man's ascension to the godlike, especially when no effort is made to give that ascension meaning? And were the most important people in the god-man's life kept mostly offscreen so they wouldn't upstage him?

Let's begin at the end of *The Natural.* Redford plays Roy Hobbs, a middle-aged ballplayer making his comeback. It's the last out of the last inning of the crucial play-off game, and everything depends on him. He's been in a slump. Can his childhood sweetheart, Iris Gaines (Glenn Close), snap him out of it? She sends him a note revealing that her child is his son. The fact that he has not already figured this out is incredible. But he is inspired by the revelation. He steps to the plate. He has been having some trouble with his stomach. Some trouble, all right. A stain of blood spreads on his baseball shirt. It's a pretty badly bleeding stomach when it bleeds right through the skin. Roy swats a homer that hits the lights, and they all explode into fireworks, showering fiery stars upon him as he makes the rounds. In the epilogue, Roy plays catch with Iris and their son—a son who has not been allowed a single onscreen word—and a woman whose role has been to sit in the stands, wreathed in ethereal light, and inspire him.

Come on, give us a break. The last shot is cheap and phony. Either he hits the homer and then dies, or his bleeding was just a false alarm. If the bleeding was a false alarm, then everything else in the movie was false, too. But I guess that doesn't matter, because *The Natural* gives every sign of a story that's been seriously meddled with. Redford has been placed so firmly in the foreground that the prime consideration is to show him in a noble light. The people in his life—baseball players, mistresses, gamblers, crooks, sportswriters—seem grateful to share the frame with him. In case we miss the point, Redford is consistently backlit to turn his golden hair into a saintly halo.

The Natural could have been a decent movie. One reason that it is not: Of all its characters, the only one we don't want to know more about is Roy Hobbs. I'd love to get to know Pop Fisher (Wilford Brimley), the cynical, old team manager. Robert Duvall, as the evil sportswriter, Max Mercy, has had his part cut so badly that we only know he's evil because he practically tells us. Richard Farnsworth, as a kindly coach, has a smile that's more genuine than anything else in the movie. But you have to look quick. And what's with Glenn Close? She's the childhood sweetheart who doesn't hear from Roy after an accident changes the course of his life. Then she turns up years later, and when she stands up in the bleachers she is surrounded by blinding light: "Our Lady of Extra Innings." In the few moments she's allowed alone with Roy, she strikes us as complicated, tender, and forgiving. But even the crucial fact of her life—that she has borne this man's son—is used as a plot gimmick. If *The Natural* were about human beings and not a demigod, Glenn Close and Robert Redford would have spoken together, in the same room, using real words, about their child. Not in this movie.

As for the baseball, the movie isn't even subtle. When a team is losing, it makes Little League errors. When it's winning, the hits are so accurate they even smash the bad guy's windows. There's not a second of real baseball strategy in the whole film. The message is: Baseball is purely and simply a matter of divine intervention. At about the 130-minute mark, I got the idea that God's only begotten son was playing right field for the New York team.

Neighbors ★ ★ ★

R, 90 m., 1981

John Belushi (Earl Keese), Kathryn Walker (Enid Keese), Cathy Moriarty (Ramona), Dan Aykroyd (Vic). Directed by John G. Avildsen and produced by Richard D. Zanuck and David Brown. Screenplay by Larry Gelbart.

If there's one quality that middle-class Americans have in common, it's a tendency to be rigidly polite in the face of absolutely unacceptable behavior. Confronted with obnoxious rudeness, we freeze up, we get a nervous little smile, we allow our eyes to focus on the middle distance, and we cannot believe this is happening to us. It's part of our desire to avoid a scene. We'd rather choke to death in a restaurant than break a plate to attract attention. *Neighbors* is about one such man, Earl Keese (John Belushi). He is a pleasant, low-key dumpling of a fellow. He lives an uneventful life with an uneventful wife (Kathryn Walker). Then the neighbors move in, and there goes the neighborhood. They are everything we dread in neighbors. They are loud. They are blatant freeloaders. The man (Dan Aykroyd) is gung-ho macho. The woman (Cathy Moriarty, from *Raging Bull*) is oversexed and underloved. They park some kind of customized truck on their front lawn. They invite themselves to dinner.

There are compensations. For example,

the woman seems to be a nymphomaniac. That would be more of a compensation for Earl if he were not terrified of aggressive woman. Earl has not the slightest notion of how to deal with these next-door maniacs, and his wife's no help: She puts on her best smile and tries to handle the situation as if everyone were playing by Emily Post's rules. The story of the Keeses and their weird neighbors was first told in Thomas Berger's novel. It was obviously a launching pad for a movie, but what sort of movie? The relationships among these neighbors depend almost entirely on the chemistry of casting: For example, obnoxious Richard Benjamin could have moved in next to meek Donald Sutherland. In *Neighbors,* however, we get Belushi and Aykroyd. I think it was brilliant casting, especially since they divided the roles somewhat against our expectations. Belushi, the most animalistic animal in *Animal House,* plays the mild-mannered Keese. And Aykroyd, who often plays straight-arrows, makes the new neighbor into a loud neo-fascist with a back slap that can kill.

The movie slides easily from its opening slices of life into a surburban nightmare. We know things are strange right at the start, when Aykroyd extorts money from Belushi to get a carry-out Italian dinner, and then secretly cooks the spaghetti right in his own kitchen. Belushi sneaks out into the night to spy on Aykroyd and catches him faking it with Ragu, but is too intimidated to say anything. The whole movie goes like that, with Belushi so intimidated that he hardly protests even when he finds himself sinking into quicksand.

Meanwhile, the women are making their own strange arrangements, especially after the Keese's college-age daughter (Lauren-Marie Taylor) comes home from school and begins attracting Moriarty's attention. The movie operates as a satire of social expectations, using polite clichés as counterpoint to deadly insults (all delivered in pleasant conversational tones).

The first hour of *Neighbors* is probably more fun than the second, if only because the plot developments come as a series of surprises. After a while, the bizarre logic of the movie becomes more predictable. But *Neighbors* is a truly interesting comedy, an offbeat experiment in hallucinatory black humor. It grows on you.

Network ★ ★ ★ ★

R, 121 m, 1976

Faye Dunaway (Diana Christenson), William Holden (Alex Schumacher), Peter Finch (Howard Beale), Robert Duvall (Frank Hackett), Wesley Addy (Nelson Chaney), Ned Beatty (Arthur Jensen). Directed by Sidney Lumet and produced by Howard Gottfried. Screenplay by Paddy Chayefsky.

There's a moment near the beginning of *Network* that has us thinking this will be the definitive indictment of national television we've been promised. A veteran anchorman has been fired because he's over the hill and drinking too much and, even worse, because his ratings have gone down. He announces his firing on his program, observes that broadcasting has been his whole life, and adds that he plans to kill himself on the air in two weeks. We cut to the control room, where the directors and technicians are obsessed with getting into the network feed on time. There are commercials that have to be fit in, the anchorman has to finish at the right moment, the buttons have to be pushed, and the station break has to be timed correctly. Everything goes fine. "Uh," says somebody, "did you hear what Howard just said?" Apparently nobody else had.

They were all consumed with form, with being sure the commercials were played in the right order and that the sesgment was the correct length. What was happening—that a man has lost his career and was losing his mind—passed right by. It wasn't their job to listen to Howard, just as it wasn't his job to run the control board. And what *Network* seems to be telling us is that television itself is like that: An economic process in the blind pursuit of ratings and technical precision, in which excellence is as accidental as banality.

If the whole movie had stayed with this theme, we might have had a very bitter little classic here. As it is, we have a supremely well-acted, intelligent film that tries for too much, that attacks not only television but also most of the other ills of the 1970s. We are asked to laugh at, be moved by, or get angry about such a long list of subjects: Sexism and ageism and revolutionary ripoffs and upper-middle-class anomie and capitalist exploitation and Neilsen ratings and psychics and that perennial standby, the failure to communicate. Paddy Chayefsky's script isn't a bad one, but he finally loses control of it. There's just too much he wanted to say. By the movie's end, the anchorman is obviously totally insane and is being exploited by blindly ambitious programmers on the one hand and corrupt businessmen on the other, and the scale of evil is so vast we've lost track of the human values.

And yet, still, what a rich and interesting movie this is. Lumet's direction is so taut, that maybe we don't realize that it leaves some unfinished business. It attempts to deal with a brief, cheerless love affair between Holden and Dunaway, but doesn't really allow us to understand it. It attempts to suggest that multinational corporations are the only true contemporary government, but does so in a scene that slips too broadly into satire, so that we're not sure Chayefsky means it. It deals with Holden's relationship with his wife of twenty-five years, but inconclusively.

But then there are scenes in the movie that are absolutely chilling. We watch Peter Finch cracking up on the air, and we remind ourselves that *this* isn't satire, it was a style as long ago as Jack Paar. We can believe that audiences would tune in to a news program that's half happy talk and half freak show, because audiences *are* tuning in to programs like that. We can believe in the movie's "Ecumenical Liberation Army" because nothing along those lines will amaze us after Patty Hearst. And we can believe that the Faye Dunaway character could be totally cut off from her emotional and sexual roots, could be fanatically obsessed with her job, because jobs as competitive as hers almost require that. Twenty-five years ago, this movie would have seemed like a fantasy; now it's barely ahead of the facts.

So the movie's flawed. So it leaves us with loose ends and questions. That finally doesn't bother me, because what it does accomplish is done so well, is seen so sharply, is presented so unforgivingly, that *Network* will outlive a lot of tidier movies. And it won several Academy Awards, including those for Peter Finch, awarded posthumously as best actor; Chayevsky for his screenplay; Beatrice Straight, as best supporting actress; and Faye Dunaway, as best actress. Watch her closely as they're deciding what will finally have to be done about their controversial anchorman. The scene would be hard to believe—if she weren't in it.

Never Say Never Again ★ ★ ★ 1/2

PG, 137 m., 1983

Sean Connery (James Bond), Klaus Maria Brandauer (Largo), Max von Sydow (Blofeld), Barbara Carrera (Fatima Blush), Kim Basinger (Domino), Bernie Casey (Felix Leiter). Directed by Irwin Kershner and produced by Jack Schwartzman. Screenplay by Lorenzo Semple, Jr.

Ah, yes, James, it is good to have you back again. It is good to see the way you smile from under lowered eyebrows, and the way you bark commands in a sudden emergency, and it is good to see the way you look at women. Other secret agents may undress women with their eyes. You are more gallant. You undress them, and then thoughtfully dress them again. You are a rogue with the instincts of a gentleman.

It has been several years since Sean Connery hung it up as James Bond, several years since *Diamonds Are Forever*, and Connery's announcement that he would "never again" play special agent 007. What complex instincts caused him to have one more fling at the role, I cannot guess. Perhaps it was one morning in front of the mirror, as he pulled in his gut and reflected that he was in pretty damn fine shape for a man over fifty. And then, with a bow in the direction of his friend Roger Moore, who has made his own niche as a different kind of Bond, Sean Connery went back on assignment again.

The movie is called *Never Say Never Again*. The title has nothing to do with the movie—except why Connery made it—but never mind, nothing in this movie has much to do with anything else. It's another one of those Bond plots in which the basic ingredients are thrown together more or less in fancy. We begin with a threat (SPECTRE has stolen two nuclear missiles and is holding the world at ransom). We continue with Bond, his newest gadgets, his mission briefing. We meet the beautiful women who will figure in the plot (Barbara Carrera as terrorist Fatima Blush; Kim Basinger as the innocent mistress of the evil Largo). We meet the villains (Max van Sydow as Blofeld; Klaus Maria Brandauer as Largo). We visit exotic locations, we survive near-misses, and Bond spars with the evil woman and redeems the good one. All basic.

What makes *Never Say Never Again* more

fun than most of the Bonds is more complex than that. For one thing, there's more of a human element in the movie, and it comes from Klaus Maria Brandauer, as Largo. Brandauer is a wonderful actor, and he chooses not to play the villian as a cliché. Instead, he brings a certain poignancy and charm to Largo, and since Connery always has been a particularly human James Bond, the emotional stakes are more convincing this time.

Sean Connery says he'll never make another James Bond movie, and maybe I believe him. But the fact that he made this one, so many years later, is one of those small show-business miracles. There was never a Beatles reunion. Bob Dylan and Joan Baez don't appear on the same stage anymore. But here, by God, is Sean Connery as Sir James Bond. Good work, 007.

The Neverending Story ★ ★ ★

PG, 94 m., 1984

Barret Oliver (Bastian), Noah Hathaway (Atreyu), Tami Stronach (Empress), Moses Gunn (Cairon). Directed by Wolfgang Petersen and produced by Bernd Eichinger and Dieter Geissler. Screenplay by Petersen and Weigel.

How's this for a threat? The kingdom of Fantasia is about to be wiped out, and the enemy isn't an evil wizard or a thermonuclear device, it's Nothingness. That's right, an inexorable wave of Nothingness is sweeping over the kingdom, destroying everything in its path. Were children's movies this nihilistic in the old days?

The only thing standing between Fantasia and Nothingness is the faith of a small boy named Bastian (Barret Oliver). He discovers the kingdom in a magical bookstore, and as he begins to read the adventure between the covers, it becomes so real that the people in the story know about Bastian. How could that be? Well, that's the very first question Bastian asks. This is a modern kid with quite a healthy amount of skepticism, but what can he do when he turns the page and the Child Empress (Tami Stronach) is begging him to give her a name so that Fantasia can be saved?

The idea of the story within a story is one of the nice touches in *The Neverending Story.* Another one is the idea of a child's faith being able to change the course of fate. Maybe not since the kids in the audience were asked to save Tinker Bell in *Peter Pan* has the outcome of a story been left so clearly up to a child's willingness to believe. There is a lot we have to believe in *The Neverending Story,* and that's the other great strength of this movie. It contains some of the more inventive special effects work of a time when battles in outer space, etc., have grown routine. Look for example, at *The Last Starfighter,* where the special effects are competent but never original—all the visual concepts are ripped off from *Star Wars*—and then look at this movie, where an entirely new world has been created.

The world of Fantasia contains creatures inspired by Alice in Wonderland (a little man atop a racing snail), the Muppets (a cute dragon-dog that can fly), and probably B.C. (a giant made of stone, who snacks on quartz and rumbles around on his granite tricycle). Many of the special effects involve sophisticated use of Muppet-like creatures (there are scenes that reminded me of *The Dark Crystal*). They are, in a way, more convincing than animation, because they exist in three dimensions and have the same depth as their human co-stars. And that illusion, in turn, helps reinforce the more conventional effects like animation, back projection, and so on. The world of this movie looks like a very particular place, and the art direction involved a lot of imagination. The movie's director, Wolfgang Petersen, is accustomed to creating worlds in small places; his last film, *Das Boot (The Boat),* took place almost entirely within a submarine.

Within the world of Fantasia, a young hero (Noah Hathaway) is assigned to complete a hazardous quest, sneak past the dreaded portals of some stone amazons, and reach the Ivory Tower, where he will receive further instructions from the empress. In most movies, this quest would be told in a straightforward way, without the surrounding story about the other little boy who is reading the book. But *The Neverending Story* is *about* the unfolding of a story, and so the framing device of the kid hidden in his school attic, breathlessly turning the pages, is interesting. It lets kids know that the story isn't just somehow happening, that storytelling is a neverending act of the imagination.

New York, New York ★ ★ ★

PG, 163 m., 1977

Liza Minnelli (Francine Evans), Robert De Niro (Jimmy Doyle), Lionel Stander (Tony Harwell), Barry Primus (Paul Wilson), Mary Kay Place (Berenice), Georgie Auld (Frankie Harte). Directed by Martin Scorsese and produced by Irwin Winkler and Robert Chartoff. Screenplay by Earl MacRauch and Mardik Martin.

Martin Scorsese's *New York, New York* never pulls itself together into a coherent whole, but if we forgive the movie its confusions we're left with a good time. In other words: Abandon your expectations of an orderly plot, and you'll end up humming the title song. The movie's a vast, rambling, nostalgic expedition back into the big band era, and a celebration of the considerable talents of Liza Minnelli and Robert De Niro.

She plays a sweet kid with a big voice who starts as a band vocalist and ends up as a movie star. He plays an immature, aggressive, very talented saxophone player whose social life centers around the saloon fights. A generation before Punk Rock, here's Punk Swing. They get married for reasons the movie never makes quite clear (oh, they're in love, all right, but he's so weird it's a miracle she'll have him). And then their marriage starts to disintegrate for reasons well hallowed in show biz biographies: Her success, his insecurity, his drinking, their child.

De Niro comes on as certifiably loony from the start, and some of the movie's best scenes are counterpoint between his clowning and her rather touching acceptance of it. Maybe because he's really shy underneath, he likes to overact in social situations. He's egotistical, self-centered, inconsiderate, and all sorts of other things she should leave him because of, and there are times when the Minnelli character is so heroically patient that it's gotta be love. The movie doesn't really explore the nuances of their personalities, though; the characters are seen mostly by their surfaces, and they inhabit a cheerfully phony Hollywood back-lot New York. Scorsese, who knows how to shoot New York in California so it looks real (see *Mean Streets*), is going for a frankly movie feel with his sets and decors, and especially with his colors, which tend toward lurid rotogravure.

The look is right for the movie's musical scenes, and there are a lot of them: We start with a loving re-creation of V-J Day, with Tommy Dorsey's orchestra playing all the obligatory standards and De Niro trying with desperate zeal to pick up Minnelli. And then maybe half of the movie from then on will be music, mostly very good music (the movie's new songs deserve comparison with the old standards), and wonderfully performed. That Liza Minnelli has not been making an annual musical for the last decade is our loss; she's hauntingly good and so much more, well, human than Barbra Streisand.

It's a good thing the movie inhabits a familiar genre, though, because the fact that we've seen dozens of other musical biographies helps us fill in the gaps in this one. And there are a lot of them; the movie originally came in at something like four hours, and the cuts necessary to get it down to a more commercial length are responsible for a lot of confusion. The confusions, as I've suggested, can be forgiven because the movie has so many good things in it. And in the video version, to make amends, they've put back two musical numbers that weren't seen in the theater. But the ending is still puzzling. We've seen De Niro, totally unable to deal with the fact that he's become a father, tearfully (and amusingly) end their marriage right there in the maternity ward. Six years pass, there are Liza's great final production numbers, and then they have a backstage reunion after her night of triumph. Great, we're thinking, we've been here before, we relish the obligatory romantic reunion scene in the dressing room. But, no, he leaves. Then he calls her from a pay phone: He can't stand the people she's with, but would she like to sneak out, meet by the stage door, eat some Chinese food, and talk about themselves? Sure, she would. He waits outside the door. She approaches it from inside, pauses, sees no one there, and goes back to her dressing room. End of movie (with a nicely evocative night street scene). But did she change her mind and *decide* not to go out and meet him, or did she expect him to be waiting *inside* the door—and assume the cocky S.O.B. had stood her up again? This particular confusion is hard to forgive.

So the movie's flawed. It's not Scorsese's best work, or De Niro's (there are scenes in which his personality quirks and bizarre behavior make him seem uncannily like his Travis Bickle in Scorsese's *Taxi Driver*). Liza Minnelli's musical numbers are wondrous, as I've said, but the movie doesn't provide her with a character as fully understood as *Cabaret* did. So I guess we go to *New York, New York* to enjoy the good parts, and spend just a moment regretting the absence of a whole.

A Nightmare on Elm Street 3: Dream Warriors ★ 1/2
R, 96 m., 1987

Craig Wasson (Dr. Neil Goldman), Heather Langenkamp (Nancy Thompson), Patricia Arquette (Kristen Parker), Larry Fishburne (Max), Priscilla Pointer (Elizabeth Simms), Robert Englund (Freddy Krueger). Directed by Chuck Russell and produced by Robert Shaye. Screenplay by Wes Craven.

The *Nightmare on Elm Street* series has a reputation in the movie business as sort of a high-rent answer to the *Friday the 13th* saga, and this third episode lives up to the billing. It's slick, it has impressive production values, and the acting is appropriate to the material. So why did I find myself so indifferent to the movie? Maybe because it never generated any sympathy for its characters. This is filmmaking by the numbers, without soul.

A great horror film begins with its characters and establishes their humanity. We have to care for them before the shocks can begin, or otherwise even the best special effects will be exercises in technology. Make a list of your favorite horror films, from *Nosferatu* to *The Exorcist*, and you'll remember the people who were involved. One reason Sigourney Weaver deserved her Oscar nomination for *Aliens* is because she brought a solid foundation of sympathy to a character surrounded by props.

In *A Nightmare on Elm Street 3: Dream Warriors* (which has the longest title in several years), I never felt that sympathy. All the characters seemed adrift in a machine-made script, a script devised as a series of pegs to hang the special effects on. The story involves the surviving "Elm Street children," whose parents, we learn, were vigilantes who cornered a child-killer down in the old junkyard and burned him alive. (If you live on Elm Street, ask yourself: Does this sound like your neighbors?)

According to a mysterious nun who's always hanging around, the body of that man was not buried in consecrated ground. Therefore, his ghost haunts the dreams of the children. And thanks to the psychic ability of one of the children, they all can enter each other's dreams. I'm not sure how this child's psychic gift works, but I think it's something like a computer network in which each kid's input reads out on everybody's screen.

All of the kids have horrible nightmares, of course, and they've been brought together at a local psychiatric hospital, where the brave young doctor (Craig Wasson) and the new dream specialist (Heather Langenkamp) believe the kids' stories and try to help them. That involves, of course, entering the mutual dream and engaging in hand-to-hand combat with the child-killer's ghost, while simultaneously trying to discover his bones and douse them with holy water.

I never really cared about the kids, however. The byplay between the doctors and administrators was assembled from standard institutional clichés. A couple of the nightmare moments had good special effects, especially when one of the kids is seduced by a naked nurse, then strapped to a bed with human tongues and suspended above a fiery pit. In light of the controversy over *Angel Heart* I kept wondering if the movie would have gotten an X rating if the kid had been played by Lisa Bonet.

If some of the special effects are good, the movie also contains a classic line of dialogue. The child-killer, we learn, was conceived after his mother was held captive in a madhouse; he is therefore, and I quote, "the bastard son of a hundred maniacs." Now that would make a great title for a movie.

9 1/2 Weeks ★ ★ ★ 1/2
R, 113 m., 1985

Kim Basinger (Elizabeth), Mickey Rourke (John). Directed by Adrian Lyne and produced by Anthony Rufus Isaacs and Zalman King. Screenplay by Patricia Knop, King, and Sarah Kernochan.

9 1/2 Weeks arrived in a shroud of mystery

and scandal, already notorious as the most explicitly sexual big-budget movie since *Last Tango in Paris.* I went expecting erotic brinksmanship (how far *will* its famous stars go in the name of their art?) and came away surprised by how thoughtful the movie is, how clearly it sees exactly what really happens between its characters.

That's not to say the movie isn't sexy. I suppose a project of this sort depends crucially on the chemistry between its actors, and Kim Basinger and Mickey Rourke develop an erotic tension in this movie that is convincing, complicated, and sensual.

In the film, they play strangers who meet one day in a Chinese grocery store in Manhattan—Elizabeth, the smart, pretty assistant in a Soho art gallery, and John, the smiling, enigmatic commodities broker. Their first meeting is crucial to the entire film, and it is a quiet masterpiece of implication. She waits by a counter. Senses someone is standing behind her. Turns, and meets his eyes. He smiles. She turns away. Is obviously surprised by how much power was in their exchange of glances. She hesitates, turns back, meets his eyes again, almost boldly, and then turns away again. And a few minutes later looks at him very curiously as he walks away along the street.

They meet again, of course, and that is the beginning of their relationship, as chronicled first in a best-selling novel and now in this movie by Adrian Lyne, the director of *Flashdance.* It is clear from the start that they aren't going to follow an orthodox pattern of courtship and romance. He offers her, quite boldly, an experimental erotic relationship. The first time he touches her seriously, it is to tie a blindfold around her eyes. They advance into arenas of lovemaking often described in the letters column in *Penthouse* magazine, and Elizabeth, for the most part, is prepared to let John call all the shots. He wants to be in control, and as she surrenders to him, she abandons herself into dreamy erotic absentmindedness.

John is nothing if not inventive. In one scene, he blindfolds her and feeds her all kinds of strange foods, sweet and sour, different textures, each one a surprise to her lips, and it's astonishing the way the movie makes this visual scene so tactile. John calls her at unexpected times, orders her to unorthodox rendezvous, and as she follows his instructions they both seem to retreat more deeply into their obsession.

The movie contrasts their private life with the everyday world of her work: With the small talk and gossip of the art gallery, with a visit she pays to an old artist who lives like a hermit in the woods, with the intrigue as her ex-husband dates another woman in the gallery. This everyday material is an interesting strategy: It makes it clear that the private life of Elizabeth and John is a conscious game they're playing outside of the real world, and not just a fantasy in a movie where reality has been placed on hold.

Eventually, it is Elizabeth's hold on the real world that redeems the movie—makes it more than just a soft-core escapade—and sets up the thoughtful and surprising conclusion. So long as it is understood that she and John are engaged in a form of a game, and are conspiring in a sort of master-slave relationship for their mutual entertainment, Elizabeth has no serious objections. But as some of John's games grow more challenging to her own self-respect, she rebels. Does he want to engage her mind and body in an erotic sport, or does he really want to edge her closer to self-debasement? There are two times that Elizabeth draws the line, and a third time when she chooses her own independence and self-respect over what begins to look like his sickness.

That's what makes the movie fascinating: Not that it shows these two people entering a bizarre sexual relationship, but because it shows the woman deciding for herself what she will, and will not, agree to. At the end of *9½ Weeks,* there is an argument, not for sexual liberation, but for sexual responsibility.

I have a few problems with certain scenes in the film. There is a moment when John and Elizabeth run through the midnight streets of a dangerous area of Manhattan, chased by hostile people, and finally take refuge in a passageway where they make love in the rain. The scene owes more to improbable gymnastic events than to the actual capabilities of the human body.

There is another scene in which John and Elizabeth go into a harness shop, and John selects and purchases a whip, while the shop employees do double-takes and Elizabeth stands wide-eyed, while he whooshes it through the air. There is no subsequent scene in which the whip is used. I do not argue that there should be; I only argue that in a movie like this, to buy a whip and not use it is like Camille coughing in the first reel and not dying in the last.

Any story like *9½ Weeks* risks becoming very ridiculous. The actors are taking a chance in appearing in it. Plots like this make audiences nervous, and if the movie doesn't walk a fine line between the plausible and the bizarre, it will only find the absurd. A lot of the success of *9½ Weeks* is because Rourke and Basinger made the characters and their relationship convincing.

Rourke's strategy is to never tell us too much. He cloaks himself in mystery, partly for her fascination, partly because his whole approach depends on his remaining a stranger. Basinger's strategy is equally effective, and more complicated. Physically, she looks sensuous and luscious; if you saw her in *Fool for Love,* you won't be surprised by the force of her appearance here. But if she'd just presented herself as the delectable object of all of these experiments, this would have been a modeling job, not an acting job.

In the early scenes, while she's at work in the gallery, she does a wonderful job of seeming distracted by this new relationship; her eyes cloud over and her attention strays. But one of the fascinations of the movie is the way her personality gradually emerges and finds strength, so that the ending of the film belongs completely to her.

The Hitcher, is also about a sadomasochistic relationship between a stronger personality and a weaker one. Because it lacks the honesty to declare what it is really about, and because it romanticizes the cruel acts of its characters, it left me feeling only disgust and disquiet. *9½ Weeks* is not only a better film, but a more humanistic one, in which it is argued that sexual experimentation is one thing, but the real human personality is something else, something incomparably deeper and more valuable—and more erotic.

1984 ★ ★ ★ ½
R, 117 m., 1984

John Hurt (Winston Smith), Richard Burton (O'Brien), Suzanna Hamilton (Julia), Cyril Cusack (Charrington), Gregor Fisher (Parsons). Directed by Michael Radford and produced by Simon Perry. Screenplay by Radford.

George Orwell made no secret of the fact that his novel *1984* was not really about the future but about the very time he wrote it in, the bleak years after World War II when England shivered in poverty and hunger. In a novel where passion is depicted as a crime, the greatest passion is expressed, not for sex, but for contraband strawberry jam, coffee, and chocolate. What Orwell feared, when he wrote his novel in 1948, was that Hitlerism, Stalinism, centralism, and conformity would catch hold and turn the world into a totalitarian prison camp. It is hard, looking around the globe, to say that he was altogether wrong.

Michael Radford's brilliant film of Orwell's vision does a good job of finding that line between the "future" world of 1984 and the grim postwar world in which Orwell wrote. The movie's 1984 is like a year arrived at through a time warp, an alternative reality that looks constructed out of old radio tubes and smashed office furniture. There is not a single prop in this movie that you couldn't buy in a junkyard, and yet the visual result is uncanny: Orwell's hero, Winston Smith, lives in a world of grim and crushing inhumanity, of bombed factories, bug-infested bedrooms, and citizens desperate for the most simple pleasures.

The film opens with Smith rewriting history: His task is to change obsolete government documents so that they reflect current reality. He methodically scratches out old headlines, obliterates the photographs of newly made "unpersons," and attends mass rallies at which the worship of Big Brother alternates with numbing reports of the endless world war that is still going on somewhere, involving somebody. Into Smith's world comes a girl, Julia, who slips him a note of stunning force. The note says, "I love you." Smith and Julia become revolutionaries by making love, walking in the countryside, and eating strawberry jam. Then Smith is summoned to the office of O'Brien, a high official of the "inner party," who seems to be a revolutionary too, and gives him the banned writings of an enemy of the state.

This story is, of course, well known. *1984* must be one of the most widely read novels of our time. What is remarkable about the movie is how completely it satisfied my feelings about the book; the movie looks, feels, and almost tastev smells like Orwell's bleak and angry vision. John Hurt, with his scrawny body and lined and weary face, makes the perfect Winston Smith; and Richard Burton, looking so old and weary in this film that it is little wonder he died soon after finishing it, is the immensely cynical O'Brien, who feels close to people only while he is torturing them. Suzanna Hamilton is Julia, a fierce little war orphan whose rebellion is basically inspired by her hungers.

Radford's style in the movie is an interesting experiment. Like Chaplin in *Modern Times,* he uses passages of dialogue that are not meant to be understood—nonsense words and phrases, garbled as they are transmitted over Big Brother's primitive TV, and yet listened to no more or less urgently than the messages that say something. The 1954 film version of Orwell's novel turned it into a cautionary, simplistic science fiction tale. This version penetrates much more deeply into the novel's heart of darkness.

Nine to Five ★ ★ ★

PG, 111 m., 1980

Jane Fonda (Judy Bernly), Lily Tomlin (Violet Newstead), Dolly Parton (Doralee Rhodes), Dabney Coleman (Franklin Hart, Jr.), Sterling Hayden (Tinsworthy), Elizabeth Wilson (Roz). Directed by Colin Higgins and produced by Bruce Gilbert. Screenplay by Higgins and Patricia Resnick.

Nine to Five is a good-hearted, simple-minded comedy that will win a place in film history, I suspect, primarily because it contains the movie debut of Dolly Parton. She is a natural-born movie star, a performer who holds our attention so easily that it's hard to believe it's her first film. The movie has some funny moments, and then it has some major ingredients that don't work, including some of its fantasy sequences. But then it also has Dolly Parton. And she contains so much energy, so much life and unstudied natural exuberance that watching her do anything in this movie is a pleasure. Because there have been so many Dolly Parton jokes (and doubtless will be so many more), I had better say that I'm not referring to her sex appeal or chest measurements. Indeed, she hardly seems to exist as a sexual being in the movie. She exists on another plane, as Monroe did: She is a center of life on the screen.

But excuse me for a moment while I regain my composure. *Nine to Five* itself is pleasant entertainment, and I liked it, despite its uneven qualities and a plot that's almost too preposterous for the material. The movie exists in the tradition of 1940s screwball comedies. It's about improbable events happening to people who are comic caricatures of their types, and, like those Forties movies, it also has a dash of social commentary. The message has to do with women's liberation and, specifically, with the role of women in large corporate offices. Jane Fonda, Lily Tomlin, and Dolly Parton all work in the same office. Tomlin is the efficient office manager. Fonda is the newcomer, trying out her first job after a divorce. Parton is the boss's secretary, and everybody in the office thinks she's having an affair with the boss. So the other women won't speak to her.

The villain is the boss himself. Played by Dabney Coleman, he's a self-righteous prig with a great and sincere lust for Dolly Parton. She's having none of it. After the movie introduces a few social issues (day care, staggered work hours, equal pay, merit promotion), the movie develops into a bizarre plot to kidnap Coleman in an attempt to win equal rights. He winds up swinging from the ceiling of his bedroom, attached by wires to a garage-door opener. Serves him right, the M.C.P. This whole kidnapping sequence move so far toward unrestrained farce that it damages the movie's marginally plausible opening scenes. But perhaps we don't really care. We learn right away that this is deliberately a lightweight film, despite its superstructure of social significance. And, making the necessary concessions, we simply enjoy it.

What I enjoyed most, as you have already guessed, was Dolly Parton. Is she an actress? Yes, definitely, I'd say, although I am not at all sure how wide a range of roles she might be able to play. She's perfect for this one—which was, of course, custom-made for her. But watch her in the scenes where she's not speaking, where the action is elsewhere.

She's always in character, always reacting, always generating so much energy we expect her to fly apart. There's a scene on a hospital bench, for example, where Tomlin is convinced she's poisoned the boss, and Fonda is consoling her. Watch Dolly. She's bouncing in and out, irrepressibly. What is involved here is probably something other than "acting." It has to do with what Bernard Shaw called the "life force," that dynamo of energy that some people seem to possess so bountifully. Dolly Parton simply seems to be having a great time, ready to sweep everyone else up in her enthusiasm, her concern, her energy. It's some show.

No Man's Land ★ ★ ★
R, 107 m., 1987

D.B. Sweeney (Benjy Taylor), Charlie Sheen (Ted Varrick), Lara Harris (Ann Varrick), Randy Quaid (Lieutenant Bracey), Bill Duke (Malcolm), R.D. Call (Frank Martin), Arlen Dean Snyder (Lieutenant Loos), M. Emmet Walsh (Captain Haun). Directed by Peter Werner and produced by Joseph Stern and Dick Wolf. Screenplay by Wolf.

The lieutenant wants the new patrolman to do undercover work for a couple of reasons: The kid knows all about Porsches, and he's so new on the force that he doesn't act like a cop. There are two things the lieutenant doesn't take into account: The kid really loves Porsches, and he doesn't think like a cop. By the end of *No Man's Land,* those two items have gotten everybody into a lot of trouble.

The young cop, played by D.B. Sweeney, is a fresh-faced rookie who spends all of his free time rebuilding old cars. The lieutenant wants him to infiltrate a Porsche dealership run by a rich kid (Charlie Sheen). The dealership seems to be a front for a car-theft and chop-shop operation, and the previous cop who infiltrated it has been murdered. The lieutenant is convinced that Sheen pulled the trigger.

Sweeney gets the job after he passes a couple of tests; he proves he knows all about repairing Porsches, and during a fast trip down the hairpin turns in the hills above Los Angeles, he proves to Sheen that he can drive one, too. You'd think that Sheen would be on the alert for another undercover cop, having just discovered one, but he trusts Sweeney and before long the two men have become friends.

It's a complicated friendship. Sweeney, from a working-class background, is impressed by Sheen's style and wealth, by the fancy discos and private clubs he hangs out in, and by the expensive cars he lets Sweeney drive. He is also impressed by Sheen's sister (Lara Harris), and after they fall in love, he becomes convinced that there's no way Sheen could have murdered a cop.

Randy Quaid, as the lieutenant, worries that his undercover guy is falling for a con job. "You're not going native, are you?" he asks. He's right; the kid hasn't been on the force long enough to develop good police instincts, and he falls under the influence of the charismatic Sheen. That leads him into a no man's land, halfway between the criminals and the law, and as he tries to do the right thing and juggle his conflicting loyalties, a tragic situation begins to develop.

No Man's Land is better than the average thriller because it is interested in these moral questions—in the way that money and beautiful women and fast cars look more exciting than good police work. The screenplay, by Dick Wolf, is subtle in the way it develops its temptations for Sweeney. He is seduced by Sheen's style and flash. And Sheen creates his character as a very complicated young man. True, he's rich, and doesn't need to steal and kill. But like the members of that Billionaire Boys' Club out in L.A., he is attracted to risk. And eventually he gets way in over his head.

The climax of the movie is fascinating in the way it uses a *really* corrupt cop to create a situation in which the two friends are faced with the consequences of their actions. By the end of the film, Sweeney and Sheen both possess all the facts, and in a way, they both understand all the facts. They think there must be a way they can work this thing out. But maybe there isn't. Like the *film noir* thrillers of the 1940s, *No Man's Land* is about ordinary people with flawed characters, who fall to temptation and pay for it.

The performances are very good, by Sheen (who played the narrator in *Platoon*), and especially by Sweeney, who at first seems lost in his role, until we realize that's the character he's playing. The director is Peter Werner, who creates a real sense of materialistic subculture in which $60,000 automobiles are the proof of personal worth (offered a chance to steal another expensive import, Sheen scornfully says, "I only steal Porsches"). The movie has lots of scenes of Sheen and Sweeney stealing cars, and it dwells on the details of their crimes, and the reckless way they risk capture. This is a movie about how money and excitement generate a seduction that can change personal values; it's better and deeper than you might expect.

No Mercy ★ ★ ★

R, 107 m., 1986

Richard Gere (Eddie Jillette), Kim Basinger (Michel Duval), Jeroen Krabbe (Losado), George Dzunda (Stemkowski), Joe Basaraba (Collins), William Atherton (Deneneux). Directed by Richard Pearce and produced by D. Constantine Conte. Screenplay by Jim Carabatsos.

I could go two ways. I could say that *No Mercy* is a dumb formula thriller, or I could go the other way, and talk about the movie's style and energy. I think I'll go the second way, because whatever this movie is, it's not boring. It doesn't take shortcuts and it delivers on its grimy, breathless action sequences.

The plot has the footprints of other movies all over it: A cop's partner is murdered. A beautiful blonde is involved. The cop follows the blonde to New Orleans, and discovers she belongs to a sleazy vice boss. He tries to arrest her, they become handcuffed to one another, he loses the key, the villain's goons try to kill them, and they escape into the bayou country with nothing more than her torn blouse standing between them and the alligators. Meanwhile, they're falling in love. So what do you want for six bucks?

It's easy to make fun of the plot, but what's a plot for? In a thriller like *No Mercy*, it exists for one simple reason, to provide the characters with something to do while they attempt to make themselves interesting. And the really remarkable thing about this movie is the genuine chemistry that is generated, not only between Richard Gere and Kim Basinger, who are on either end of the handcuffs, but also between both of them and the movie's two principal bad guys: An effete rich Southerner played by William Atherton, and a sadistic neo-Nazi vice lord, played by the Dutch actor Jeroen Krabbe.

Thrillers are often only as good as their villains. The Krabbe character seems seriously confused about time and place; I never understood what he was doing in the bayou with his Dr. Strangelove act, and I don't think his redneck followers did, either. But he makes a very satisfactory villain, especially after we learn that the Basinger character was heartlessly sold to him when she was only a child, and has been his slave ever since.

The Richard Gere character figures this out only belatedly. At first he thinks she's another one of this guy's hookers, used to lure his partner to his doom. But there is nothing like being handcuffed to Kim Basinger in the middle of a swamp to concentrate the mind, and eventually he can see that she is a victim. His realization comes at a delicately handled, understated turning point; he learns, almost by accident, that she has never learned to read, and we can see in his eyes that this touches him.

Gere is interesting all through the movie. As it happened, I'd just seen him again in *American Gigolo* a few days before I saw *No Mercy*, and so at first I was cross referencing his standard mannerisms, like that way he struts across the screen. Then he sold me on the character, and I stopped thinking about Richard Gere and started caring about what was going to happen next.

With Basinger, that process was even easier. Although she fits all of the usual requirements for a movie sexpot, there is within her the genuine soul of an artist, and she throws herself into this role so convincingly that there is real pathos in her history. There is enough conviction in their relationship that it carries over even into the obligatory bloodbath that ends the film, and I found myself caring about them even while on another level I was running an inventory on the special effects.

The movie's climax, a shoot-out in a flophouse across the river from New Orleans, is an anthology of action clichés and a few fresher touches, such as the villain's ability to ram through walls. It's always a shame when a movie bothers to create interesting characters and then discards them in a high-tech climax. But up until then, *No Mercy* has been an above-average *film noir* and its creepy feeling for the backstreets of New Orleans and the sultry evil of its red-light suburbs got under my skin.

No Way Out ★ ★ ★ ★
R, 114 m., 1987

Kevin Costner (Tom Farrell), Gene Hackman (David Brice), Sean Young (Susan Atwell), Will Patton (Scott Pritchard), Howard Duff (Senator Duvall), George Dzundza (Sam Hesselman), Jason Bernard (Major Donovan), Iman (Nina Beka). Directed by Roger Donaldson and produced by Laura Ziskin and Robert Garland. Screenplay by Garland.

No Way Out is one of those thrillers like *Jagged Edge,* where the plot gives us a great deal of information, but the more we know, the less we understand. It's like a terrifying jigsaw puzzle. And because the story is so tightly wound and the performances are so good, I found myself really caring about the characters. That's the test of a good thriller: When you stop thinking about the mechanics of the plot and start caring about the people. The movie begins with the same basic situation that was always one of Alfred Hitchcock's favorites: An innocent man stands wrongly accused of a crime, and all the evidence seems to point right back to him. In *No Way Out,* there are a couple of neat twists. One is when the innocent man is placed in charge of the investigation of the crime.

The man is played by Kevin Costner in a performance I found a lot more complex and interesting than his work in *The Untouchables.* He plays a career Navy man who is assigned to the personal staff of the secretary of defense (Gene Hackman). Hackman and his devoted assistant (Will Patton) want Costner to handle some sensitive assignments for them involving the secretary's pet defense projects.

All of those details are handled in the first few minutes, and then the movie springs a genuine erotic surprise. Costner goes to a diplomatic reception to meet Hackman. There is a beautiful young woman at the party. Their eyes meet. The chemistry is right. They leave almost immediately, and the woman throws herself at Costner in hungry passion.

They have an affair. The woman (Sean Young) is friendly, but mysterious, and eventually Costner finds out why: She is also Hackman's mistress. And that leads to the night when Hackman attacks her in a jealous rage, and she dies. Because Costner saw Hackman going into her apartment as he was leaving, he knows who committed the crime. But there are reasons why he cannot say what he knows. And then Patton determines to mastermind a cover-up and enlists Costner.

At about this point you may be thinking I have revealed too much of the plot. I haven't. *No Way Out* is truly labyrinthine and ingenious. The director, Roger Donaldson, sometimes uses two or three suspense-building devices at the same time, such as when a search of the Pentagon coincides with Costner's attempt to obtain evidence against Hackman, and the slow progress of a computer that may, or may not, enhance a photograph that could hang Costner.

A lot of what goes on in the film is psychological and not merely plot-driven. For example, there's the interesting performance of Patton, who says early on that he would willingly sacrifice his life for Hackman and who is later revealed to have more than one reason for his devotion. There's another good performance by George Dzundza (*The Deer Hunter*) as the wheelchair-bound Pentagon computer expert, trying to be a nice guy without ever really understanding what he's in the middle of.

The movie contains some of the ingredients I have declared myself tired of in recent thrillers, including a couple of chases. But here the chases do not exist simply on their own accord; they grow out of the logic of the plot. And as the plot moves on it grows more and more complex, until a final twist that some people will think is simply gratuitous but that does fit in with the overall logic.

Movies such as this are very hard to make. For proof, look at the wreckage of dozens of unsuccessful thrillers every year. *No Way Out* is a superior example of the genre, a film in which a simple situation grows more and more complex until it turns into a nightmare not only for the hero but also for everyone associated with him. At the same time, it respects the audience's intelligence, gives us a great deal of information, trusts us to put it together, and makes the intellectual analysis of the situation one of the movie's great pleasures.

Nobody's Fool ★ ★
PG-13, 107 m., 1986

Rosanna Arquette (Cassie), Eric Roberts (Riley), Mare Winningham (Pat), Jim Young (Billy), Louise Fletcher (Pearl), Gwen Welles (Shirley), J.J. Hardy (Ralphy), Stephen Robolowsky (Kirk). Directed by Evelyn Purcell and produced by James C. Katz and Jon S. Denny. Screenplay by Beth Henley.

Nobody's Fool is about a wide-eyed young girl who falls for her boyfriend's line and gets stuck with his baby while he goes off and marries a rich kid. We meet her shortly after she has given up the child for adoption and is trying to piece her life back together. She works as a waitress at a small-town bar and acts goofy all the time so nobody will know how much she was hurt.

Her name is Cassie, and she is played by Rosanna Arquette, who is one of my favorite actresses, but who is best when she plays against her inclinations. Cassie is perhaps too close to an idea Arquette has of herself, and so we don't feel enough pain in those early scenes. Cassie seems odd, rather than suffering.

There's a summer theater in the town, and she goes with her best friend (Mare Winningham) to see *The Tempest.* What she sees instead are the deep blue eyes of the lighting director (Eric Roberts). After the show, she forgets her purse, but he has found it for her, and as he looks at her she begins to feel strange. Later she complains to her friend, "He looks at me so funny."

He is in love. She is wary. They go out on a date, and eventually the truth about both of their past lives comes out: He's been just as messed up as she is. I got the impression that at some level the movie was trying to tell the story of two confused people who were getting a second chance at love, but the problem instead becomes: Is this guy really the right second chance that she needs? He seems distant and manipulative and filled with himself, and she's such a waif that she seems unprotected.

Another problem is caused by the flashback structure of Beth Henley's screenplay. We begin in the present, and then begin to get glimpses of the traumatic events in Cassie's past, leading up to a touching, pathetic scene in a restaurant where Cassie is wearing balloons and has a birthday candle on her hat. She tells her boyfriend she's pregnant, and he does not learn this news with joy. She wanders out into the parking lot, her balloons sagging, and we really feel for her. But wouldn't this scene have been more effective higher up in the film, and wouldn't the whole film have had a clearer emotional line if it had been told chronologically?

Sometimes flashbacks are a useful form of storytelling, but what is happening in Cassie's life is basically so simple that they come across in *Nobody's Fool* as just a writer's conceit. She has been disappointed in love, betrayed by her lover, survived a traumatic experience, and is now considering whether to take a chance on this new man—and maybe go to Los Angeles with him and start all over. This story is the very soul of straightforwardness, and the flashbacks simply delay the time when we know why we should feel real sympathy for the Arquette character.

There's another problem, and that's the lack of any convincing magnetism between Arquette and Roberts. They both give interesting performances—he's trying something new with his gentler, quieter tone—but their characters, as written, don't generate the feeling of inevitability that you need between real lovers. When we don't know why a woman's past is tragic and we can't see how her future would be good for her, it's not easy for us to get swept along by her progress.

Nobody's Fool has some smaller elements in it that deserve mention. One is the character of Cassie's fat, obnoxious kid brother (J.J. Hardy), who steals every scene he is in. Just the way he squeezes his pet frog should be enough to inspire Henley to write a whole movie about him. I also liked Jim Young's performance as the cold former boyfriend and Stephen Tobolowsky as the summer theater director whose special cross in life is the acting class he has to conduct for the local would-be actors. The whole movie, in fact, is filled with good small moments; it's the big moments that don't seem convincing.

Norma Rae ★ ★ ★
PG, 114 m., 1979

Sally Field (Norma Rae), Ron Liebman (Reuben), Beau Bridges (Sonny), Pat Hingle (Father), Barbara Baxley (Mother), Gail Strickland (Bonnie). Directed by Martin Ritt and produced by Tamara Asseyev and Alex

Rose. Screenplay by Irving Ravetch and Harriet Frank, Jr.

We're sometimes unfair to our movie actresses, and Sally Field's extraordinary performance in *Norma Rae* helps dramatize it. Most new actresses come up through television and its lame-brained sexist stereotyping. And most of the female TV stars have their moment of glory and then become unfairly categorized in our memories. Be honest: Didn't we think of Sally Field as the Flying Nun before this Oscar-winning performance?

For any actress, an opportunity to star on TV has to be great. But the opportunity to escape TV and appear in a challenging movie has to be a godsend. Jill Clayburgh got her chance with *An Unmarried Woman.* Here it's Sally Field's turn. And as the plain-spoken, spunky Southern textile worker in Martin Ritt's *Norma Rae,* she quite simply surpassed our expectations.

The performance is at the heart of the movie, because this isn't a film about labor unions or mill working conditions; it's about a woman of thirty-one learning to grow into her own potential.

She has a couple of kids—one out of wedlock, the other orphaned by a brawling father—and a few boyfriends here and there, and she's never taken much time to think about the value of her life. Like everyone in the town, she works in the textile mill, which has no union, pays minimum wages, has few benefits, and does little or nothing about brown lung disease.

Then a union organizer (Ron Liebman) from New York turns up in town. He finds precious little support, and almost none from Norma Rae; she's too absorbed in a whirlwind courtship and marriage with a local good ol' boy (Beau Bridges) who promises to bring his check home on Fridays and not chase around. She marries him, mostly out of affection and convenience.

But then the organizer begins to make a little sense to her. She grows less blind to the conditions at the mill. She gets angry when her father drops dead on an assembly line. She goes to a couple of meetings at which Liebman harangues his handful of recruits. She becomes a recruit herself, a volunteer organizer, and eventually it's taking up all of her time.

Her new husband complains—but both she and the movie tend to ignore him. The marriage, indeed, seems almost peripheral to the movie's central story, which is about the way she slowly opens her eyes to herself and her world. Liebman puts it simply: "You're too smart to do what you're doing to yourself."

She eventually agrees. And we're sort of set up for a situation where Norma Rae and the organizer fall in love with each other. But they don't; the movie is steadfast in its determination to show Norma Rae growing because of her own thought and will—not under the influence of yet another sexual liaison.

That's what makes the movie so special. It has all sorts of plot problems (especially involving the marriage), and there are scenes that don't quite fit together, and moments that don't sound right. But the character of Norma Rae is so deeply seen and realized, and played by Sally Field with such conviction, that we accept her in spite of our doubts about other things. In the tenth year of her acting career, Sally Field has made a remarkable debut.

North Dallas Forty ★ ★ ★ ½

R, 117 m., 1979

Nick Nolte (Phil Elliott), Mac Davis (Maxwell), Charles Durning (Coach Johnson), Dayle Haddon (Charlotte), Bo Svenson (Jo Bob), Steve Forrest (Conrad Hunter), G.D. Spradlin (B.A.), John Matuszak (O.W. Shaddock). Directed by Ted Kotcheef and produced by Frank Yablans. Screenplay by Yablans, Kotcheef, and Peter Gent.

North Dallas Forty is about pro football the way *Network* was about television. It's about the ways large and competitive institutions grind up people and spit them out. The guy who gets spit out in this movie is Phil Elliott, whose coach tells him he has the best hands in football, but a "bad attitude." Elliott is played by Nick Nolte in a muscular and compelling performance: After this movie, people began to take Nolte seriously.

The movie is not really a sports film. It doesn't share the patented formula of the routine sports movie, in which everything depends on the bravura final match, or game, or race. The film does lead up to an important game, yes—North Dallas plays

Chicago for a divisional championship—but by then we're so involved in the human drama that we almost don't care who wins.

The drama revolves around the Nolte character and his best friend, a quarterback played by Mac Davis. They play football very hard and very well. Off the field, they regard the business of football with a profound cynicism, and they assault themselves with boozing, drugs, all-night partying, and bleak thoughts about what they will do when the day comes when they finally cannot play any longer.

Characters in the movie talk, at times, about words like "play" and "game." Is professional football a game? Not according to John Matuszak, in real life an Oakland Raider, who in one of the movie's most electrifying scenes has a shouting match with a coach in the locker room. At *some* point, he screams, football for the players must be more than a business—must be a cause, a spirit. In the fourth quarter, when you're cold and hurt and exhausted, the game plan means nothing, but your desire means everything.

The North Dallas management doesn't quite see it that way. The owners and coaches are detached, scientific, quite prepared to see a player shoot up pain-killers and run the risk of permanently crippling himself. Nolte himself is prepared to do that. But the management doesn't like him. He's a wiseass. He has the wrong attitude. He's childish. Their ideal football player would be someone like the fearsome Jo Bob Priddy (Bo Svenson), who is not in fact as good a player as Nolte, but has a magnificently simpleminded "correct" attitude.

The pressures put Nolte in a vise: He loves playing, he cannot envision himself not playing, he even understands the management attitude if only they knew it. But age and wear and cynicism are closing in, and he finds himself, half astonished, in love with a woman. She represents a kind of settling down that football has given him license to avoid, and the movie uses the relationship as a counterpoint to a week of training and a climactic game.

The football scenes are brutally real; the locker room scenes are totally authentic. There are obscenities and violence and pain, and a clear view of how the "adults"—the coaches—manipulate their strong, fearsome, and intimidated employees. "*We're* not the team," Nolte shouts at the owner. "*You're* the team. We're only the equipment—like the jockstraps and the helmets."

The movie is funny at times, especially during the lecture meetings where the players, openly contemptuous, listen to such dim inspirational insights as that, if God had really meant all men to be equal, he wouldn't have called us the human "race." God, for example, clearly meant for North Dallas to be more equal than Chicago.

Those kinds of details, and the scenes of the players' agents and the parties and the practice sessions, have a convincing documentary feel. Holding it all together, making it work, forcing us to get involved, is the Nolte character. It's a tribute to this movie that we would probably care as much about Nolte if he were *not* a football player. What he's facing is common in so many parts of American society; in so many of the things we do and the jobs we have, at some ultimate level we are just simply part of somebody else's business.

Nosferatu ★ ★ ★ ★

R, 63 m., 1979

Klaus Kinski (Count Dracula), Isabelle Adjani (Lucy Harker), Bruno Ganz (Jonathan Harker). Directed, produced, and written by Werner Herzog.

Set aside for the moment the details of the Dracula story. They've lost their meaning. They've been run through a thousand vampire movies too many. It's as easy these days to play Dracula as Santa Claus. The suit comes with the job. The kids sit on your knee and you ask them what they want and this year they want blood.

Consider instead Count Dracula. He bears a terrible cross but he lives in a wonderful sphere. He comes backed by music of the masters and dresses in red and black, the colors De Sade found finally the most restful. Dracula's shame as he exchanges intimacies and elegant courtesies with you is that tonight or sometime soon he will need to drink your blood. What an embarrassing thing to know about someone else.

Werner Herzog's *Nosferatu* concerns itself with such knowledge. *Nosferatu.* A word for *the vampire.* English permits "vampire movies"—but a "nosferatu movie?" Say "vampire" and your lips must grin. The other word looks like sucking lemons. Perfect. There is nothing pleasant about Herzog's vampire, and this isn't a movie for Creature Feature fans. There are movies for people who like to yuk it up and make barfing sounds, God love 'em, while Christopher Lee lets the blood dribble down his chin, but they're not the audience for *Nosferatu.* This movie isn't even scary. It's so slow it's meditative at times, but it is the most evocative series of images centered around the idea of the vampire that I have ever seen—since F.W. Murnau's *Nosferatu,* which was made in 1922.

That is why we're wise to forget the details of the basic Dracula story. *Nosferatu* doesn't pay them heed. It is about the mood and *style* of vampirism, about the terrible seductive pity of it all. There is a beautiful passage early in the film showing the hero, Jonathan Harker, traveling from his home village to the castle of Dracula. The count has summoned him because he is considering the purchase of another home. Harker makes the journey by horse path. He enters into a high mountain pass filled with tenuous cloud layers that drift by a little too fast, as if God were sucking in his breath. The music is *not* your standard creepy Loony Tunes, but a fierce melody of exhilaration and dread. Deeper and deeper rides Harker into the cold gray flint of the peaks. Some will say this passage goes on too long and that nothing happens during it. I wish the whole movie were this empty.

Before long, we are regarding the count himself. He is played totally without ego by Klaus Kinski. The *count* has a monstrous ego, of course—it is Kinski who has none. There is never a moment when we sense this actor enjoying what a fine juicy cornpone role he has, with fangs and long sharp fingernails and a cape to swirl. No, Kinski has grown far too old inside to play Dracula like that: He makes his body and gaunt skull transparent, so the role can flicker through.

Sit through *Nosferatu* twice, or three times. Cleanse yourself of the expectation that things will happen. Get with the flow. This movie works like an LP record: You can't love the music until you've heard the words so often they're sounds. It's in German with English subtitles. It would be just fine with no subtitles, dubbed into an unknown tongue. The need to know what Dracula is saying at any given moment is a bourgeois affectation. Dracula is *always* saying, "I am speaking with you now as a meaningless courtesy in preface to the unspeakable event that we both know is going to take place between us sooner rather than later."

Nuts ★ ★

R, 115 m., 1987

Barbra Streisand (Claudia Draper), Richard Dreyfuss (Aaron Levinsky), Maureen Stapleton (Rose Kirk). Karl Malden (Arthur Kirk), Eli Wallach (Dr. Morrison), Robert Webber (Francis MacMillan), James Whitmore (Judge Murdoch). Directed by Martin Ritt and produced by Barbra Streisand. Screenplay by Tom Topor, Darryl Ponicsan, and Alvin Sargent.

If you were to meet this woman on the street, you wouldn't have much doubt she was nuts. She has that look in her eye, the one that suggests she can be reasonable one minute and lash out wildly the next. She is so filled with anger that the specific targets hardly matter; the whole world is her target.

Barbra Streisand does a good job of projecting that crazed wildness during the opening scenes of *Nuts,* but the problem is, the movie doesn't know where to go with it. This is not a movie like *One Flew Over the Cuckoo's Nest,* in which madness is seen as an antidote for regimentation. It aims lower, and accomplishes less. It's a courtroom drama, with all the conventional thrusts and parries of the legal system, and because the structure of the movie is so timid, Streisand's madness threatens to overwhelm it.

She plays a hooker who came from a conventional upper-middle-class home. We see her parents in the courtroom every day, and they're conventional, all right: They're played by Karl Malden and Maureen Stapleton as the picture of intelligent concern. Streisand has been charged with the murder of one of her clients, and her parents are in league with a psychiatrist (Eli Wallach) who thinks she should be committed "for her own good."

What Streisand knows is that she's likely to spend more time locked up in a psychiatric ward than in jail. She claims she's innocent—she killed in self-defense—but even if she's found guilty, at least she will be given a finite sentence with definite provisions. If she's found incompetent to stand trial by reason of insanity, she could be put away indefinitely. And so she fights for the right to be tried.

Her parents hire an expensive lawyer, but she assaults him and he leaves the case. Then she gets a public defender (Richard Dreyfuss), and treats him with hostility until she sees that he's on her side. The judge (James Whitmore) moves the sanity hearing into a closed courtroom, which is the scene of one earth-shaking revelation after another, none of which really surprise us.

We sort of know, don't we, that because the character is a hooker and yet is played by Barbra Streisand, she will turn out to be good at heart. We know she may have killed her customer, but there had to be more to the story than that. And we have a pretty good hunch that Malden and Stapleton have more complicated stories than it would first appear. All of these hunches pan out. But the movie's revelations are told in such dreary, clichéd, weather-beaten old movie terms that we hardly care.

The director, Martin Ritt, is not at the top of his form with this material. He uses the old gimmick of the Gradually Expanding Flashback. That's when we see just a flash of a past event, and then we see a little more, and eventually we see the whole event. Two different bathroom sequences are revealed in this way—one involving the Streisand character as a little girl, the other involving her bloody encounter with her victim.

Wouldn't you know that the childhood experiences are a perfect prediction of the night of murder? Isn't it almost inevitable that Malden, a stepfather, is also a child-molester? Doesn't Malden's $20 bill, slipped under the bathroom door, neatly foreshadow the way the john wants to pay her to take a bath? If all of psychiatry had been this simple, Freud wouldn't have been needed to devise it; the Brothers Grimm would have done.

As the courtroom drama slogs its weary way home, Streisand's authentic performance as a madwoman seems harder and harder to sustain. All the forces of do-good pop self-help are arrayed against her, pushing her character to become a reasonable, sweet, tragic victim. The problem is, the movie's opening scenes have been so wild and so unrestrained that the sanity hearing draws a wild card: It is quite possible, after all, that although this character was molested as a child, and although she killed in self-defense, she is *nevertheless* insane. *Nuts* is essentially just a futile exercise in courtroom clichés, surrounding a good performance that doesn't fit.

O

Off Beat ★ ★ ★ ½
PG, 93 m., 1986

Judge Reinhold (Joe Gower), Meg Tilly (Rachel Wareham), Cleavant Derricks (Abe Washington), Joe Mantegna (Pete Peterson), Jacques D'Amboise (August), Amy Wright (Mary Ellen), John Turturro (Pepper), Harvey Keitel (Bank Robber), Julie Bovasso (Mrs. Wareham). Directed by Michel Dinner and produced by Joe Roth and Harry Ufland. Screenplay by Mark Medoff.

It's been a long time since I've found the characters in a comedy as sympathetic as they are in *Off Beat.* So many recent American comedies seem to hate their heroes, to want to make fun of them, but here is a movie about sweet, likable people who get into a funny situation and watch it grow funnier the more they try to escape from it. *Off Beat* is a movie with a sharp edge and more than a little hostility, but the overall feeling is sort of warm and romantic.

It's about this librarian named Joe (Judge Reinhold) who is going nowhere with his life. He puts on his roller skates and rolls back and forth in the stacks of the New York Public Library, feeding a conveyor belt with books for people he never sees. His promotion is blocked by the hateful Mr. Pepper (John Turturro), who is a Pee Wee Herman clone; his girlfriend has just left him, and he spends his evenings drowning his sorrows, drinking with his best friend, a black cop named Washington (Cleavant Derricks).

One day he screws up one of Washington's undercover assignments, and so he owes him one. And here is what Washington wants him to do: Having been assigned to audition for the dance line in a police department charity show, he wants Joe to go to the audition for him. Joe protests, but it's no use, and that's how he gets into the peculiar position of impersonating a police officer *and* a dancer, both at once.

The audition is not a happy event. Most of the cops are angry about having to be there. Joe figures he can flunk the audition, and that'll be that, but then his eyes meet the eyes of a high-spirited woman cop (Meg Tilly), and he decides to stick around. *Off Beat* will be the story of their love affair, cross-cut with such other matters as a bank robbery, backstage intrigue at the library, the hostility of the other cops, and the problems Joe walks into by wearing a police uniform around the streets of New York.

The movie has a more ingenious plot than is usually the case in modern comedies; it's not just a straight line from beginning to end, but a series of little character studies and quiet dialogue passages and small insights into human nature. Holding the elements together is the strong chemistry between Judge Reinhold (who was Eddie Murphy's partner in *Beverly Hills Cop*) and Meg Tilly (who won an Academy Award nomination for *Agnes of God,* but is ten or twenty times more interesting in this film). What's nice is that they approach each other out of vulnerability. There isn't that feeling you sometimes get with the big stars, that *of course* people are going to be attracted to them. They both seem a little flattered to be so much in love. It creates a good feeling.

But the movie isn't all sweetness. It contains one of the single most explosive and surprising comic moments of any movie in a long time, when a hostile cop delivers a brutal insult to Meg Tilly, and she responds appropriately. More than that I won't say, but the moment gets a laugh that grows out of shock, surprise, and the perfect timing of what happens.

Off Beat is filled with good character actors, bringing more dimensions to their characters than the roles might otherwise permit. Among them are Harvey Keitel as a bank robber, Julie Bovasso as Tilly's mother, and Joe Mantegna as a cop who hates ballet instructors.

At the center of everything, Reinhold and Tilly make a wonderful romantic couple. There is a real magic about the scene where they have a quiet dinner and then begin to dance. Reinhold became a star of sorts in *Beverly Hills Cop*, just by having a good role in a hit movie, but this time he carries the show, and gives promise of being around for a long time, probably in more of these Everyman roles that Jack Lemmon plays so well. Meg Tilly has been in wildly uneven movies over the years (and I was not one of the admirers of *Agnes of God*, her most prestigious film to date). This time, allowed to play a fairly tough and complicated character, she suddenly blossoms. She's never been more appealing.

Off Beat probably sounds contrived. The plot is filled with predictable devices and contrived meetings and wild coincidences, and elements that seem borrowed from other films. What's surprising is how original it all seems, maybe because the director, Michael Dinner, seems to really care for his characters.

An Officer and a Gentleman

★ ★ ★ ★

R, 126 m., 1982

Richard Gere (Zack Mayo), Debra Winger (Paula Pokrifki), Lou Gossett, Jr. (Sergeant Foley), David Keith (Sid Worley), Robert Loggia (Byron Mayo), Lisa Blount (Lynette), Lisa Eilbacher (Casey Seeger). Directed by Taylor Hackford and produced by Martin Elfand. Screenplay by Douglas Day Stewart.

An Officer and a Gentleman is the best movie about love that I've seen in a long time. Maybe that's because it's not about "love" as a Hollywood concept, but about love as growth, as learning to accept other people for who and what they are. There's romance in this movie, all right, and some unusually erotic sex, but what makes the film so special is that the sex and everything else is presented within the context of its characters finding out who they are, what they stand for—and what they will *not* stand for.

The movie takes place in and around a Naval Aviation Officer Candidate School in Washington state. Every thirteen weeks, a new group of young men and women come here to see if they can survive a grueling session of physical and academic training. If they pass, they graduate to flight school. About half fail. Across Puget Sound, the local young women hope for a chance to meet an eligible future officer. They dream of becoming officers' wives, and in some of their families, we learn, this dream has persisted for two generations.

After the first month of training, there is a Regimental Ball. The women turn out with hope in their hearts and are sized up by the candidates. A man and a woman (Richard Gere and Debra Winger) pair off. We know more about them than they know about one another. He is a loner and a loser, whose mother died when he was young and whose father is a drunk. She is the daughter of an officer candidate who loved and left her mother twenty years before. They dance, they talk, they begin to date, they fall in love. She would like to marry him, but she refuses to do what the other local girls are willing to do—get pregnant or fake pregnancy to trap a future officer. For his part, the man is afraid of commitment, afraid of love, incapable of admitting that he cares for someone. All he wants is a nice, simple affair, and a clean break at the end of OCS.

This love story is told in counterpoint with others. There's the parallel affair between another candidate and another local girl. She *is* willing to trap her man. His problem is, he really loves her. He's under the thumb of his family, but he's willing to do the right thing, if she'll give him the chance.

All of the off-base romances are backdrops for the main event, which is the training program. The candidates are under the supervision of a tough drill sergeant (Lou Gossett, Jr.) who has seen them come and seen them go and is absolutely uncompromising in his standards. There's a love-hate relationship between the sergeant and his trainees, especially the rebellious, resentful Gere. And Gossett does such a fine job of fine-tuning the line between his professional standards and his personal emotions that the performance deserves its Academy Award.

The movie's method is essentially to follow its characters through the thirteen weeks, watching them as they change and grow. That does wonders for the love stories, because by the end of the film we know these people well enough to care about their decisions and to have an opinion about what they should do. In the case of Gere and Winger, the romance is absolutely absorbing because it's so true to life, right down to the pride that causes these two to pretend they don't care for each other as much as they really do. When it looks as if Gere is going to throw it all away—is going to turn his back on a good woman who loves him, just because he's too insecure to deal with her love—the movie isn't just playing with emotions, it's being very perceptive about human behavior.

But maybe I'm being too analytical about why *An Officer and a Gentleman* is so good. This is a wonderful movie precisely because it's so willing to deal with matters of the heart. Love stories are among the rarest of movies these days (and when we finally get one, it's likely to involve an extra-terrestrial). Maybe they're rare because writers and filmmakers no longer believe they understand what goes on between modern men and women. *An Officer and a Gentleman* takes chances, takes the time to know and develop its characters, and by the time this movie's wonderful last scene comes along, we know exactly what's happening, and why, and it makes us very happy.

Oh, God! ★ ★ ★ ½
PG, 104 m., 1977

George Burns (God), John Denver (Jerry Landers), Teri Garr (Bonnie Landers), Donald Pleasence (Dr. Harmon), Ralph Bellamy (Sam Raven), William Daniels (George Summers), Paul Sorvino (Reverend Williams), Dinah Shore (Dinah). Directed by Carl Reiner and produced by Jerry Weintraub. Screenplay by Larry Gelbart.

Carl Reiner's *Oh, God!* is a treasure of a movie: A sly, civilized, quietly funny speculation on what might happen if God endeavored to present himself in the flesh yet once again to forgetful Man. He comes back this time looking and talking a great deal like George Burns, an improvement on his earlier cinematic incarnations. And as his contact on Earth, he selects a common man—John Denver, to the manner born.

Part of the movie's charm is in the way it surprises us by treating its subject matter with affection and respect. I went expecting blasphemous jokes and cheap shots at religion, since serious subjects so rarely make it into comedies these days except as targets. But no: *Oh, God!* is lighthearted, satirical, and humorous and (that rarest of qualities) in good taste.

It also makes you feel good, in the way some of the Frank Capra comedies did. The John Denver character becomes a contemporary version of Mr. Smith, John Doe, Mr. Deeds, and those other Capra heroes who prevailed because they were decent, honest, and true. Once Denver gets over his initial astonishment at being selected as God's spokesman, he makes a good job of it, justifying God's faith in the common man, which He, after all, put into production.

God is careful, throughout the movie, to make his reasoning clear. Why did he pick Denver? "You're like the lady who's the millionth person across the bridge and gets to meet the governor. You're better than some people, and worse than others, but you came across the bridge at the right time." The message God wants to remind His creatures of is a simple one: That things *can* turn out all right, although they will not necessarily or automatically do so. That we have everything here on Earth that we need to bring a happy ending to our story. And that we should try being a little nicer to one another.

Carl Reiner's credits as a director include the immortal *Where's Poppa?* (1970), a masterpiece of comic bad taste. So there was reason to anticipate a showdown again this time between the sacred and the profane. As an idea, indeed, *Oh, God!* must have seemed almost impossibly supplied with ways to go wrong. But it doesn't. Reiner is superb at establishing the right tone for this very difficult material, and the casting of George Burns as God is an inspiration.

"I took this form," God explains, "because if I showed myself to you as I am, you wouldn't be able to comprehend me." He chose his form well. God, as Burns, recalls some of his miracles (the 1969 Mets), some of his mistakes (tobacco, giraffes, and avocados—"I made the seeds too big"), and some common misconceptions about Himself ("To tell you the truth, I spent the first five days thinking and created everything on the sixth"). And he has such quiet authority, such wonderfully understated humor, such presence. John Denver, too, is well-cast: Sincere, believable, with that face so open and goofy. They work with Reiner, and with Larry Gelbart's screenplay, to create a movie that takes a really risky comic gamble, and wins.

Oh, God! Book II ★ ★
PG, 94 m., 1980

George Burns (God), Louanne (Tracy), Suzanne Pleshette (Paula), David Birney (Don), John Louie (Shingo), Anthony Holland (Dr. Newell). Directed and produced by Gilbert Cates. Screenplay by John Greenfield, Hal Goldman, Fred S. Fox, Seaman Jacobs, and Melissa Miller.

Oh, God! Book II qualifies as a sequel only because of its title and the irreplaceable presence of George Burns in the title role. Otherwise, it seems to have lost faith in the film it's based on. It begins with the same great idea for a movie (what would happen if God personally came down to earth and got involved in the affairs of men?), but it winds up as a third-rate situation comedy, using its subject as a gimmick.

Neither of the *Oh, God!* movies is, of course, seriously religious; they create God as a sort of ancient Will Rogers on a Christmas card by Norman Rockwell, and then give him lots of cute lines and paradoxical comic insights. But the original film—with God appearing to a supermarket manager played by John Denver—did at least follow through on its basic premise. What if God really did turn up in the checkout line? How do you behave when God blows the whistle and challenges you to test his rules?

Oh, God! Book II doesn't seem willing to devote a whole movie to the same subject; it uses God as basically just a *deus ex machina*. He is, of course, enormously appealing, and George Burns is rich and understated in the role. But after he appears to a little girl named Tracy (played by a very little actress named Louanne), the movie uses him as a springboard for scenes involving the little girl, her parents, her school, her psychiatrist—everything except what we'd really enjoy—more scenes with God.

Tracy's basic problem, it appears, is that she can see God and talk with him, but nobody else can. Her parents and teachers think she's talking to herself. God asks her to organize an advertising campaign to promote his image on earth, and she comes up with a slogan ("Think God") which her little playmates plaster on every open space in town. But, meanwhile, a psychiatrist (Anthony Holland) determines that Tracy's got serious problems.

There are other sitcom-style distractions. Tracy's parents (Suzanne Pleshette and David Birney) are divorced. Tracy doesn't like her daddy's new girlfriend. The principal at school is a meanie. And so on. The movie's screenplay was written by no less than five collaborators, but they were so bankrupt of ideas that some scenes have a quiet desperation to them. For example: There's an awkward TV newscast staged in the movie, with Hugh Downs as the avuncular anchorman and none other than Dr. Joyce Brothers giving her opinion that little Tracy may, indeed, have seen God. It would be sad enough if the movie were using Downs and Brothers for laughs—but, God help us, they're brought in as authority figures.

There is, however, one additional small treasure in this movie, a supporting performance by Mari Gorman, who steals every scene she's in, playing Tracy's grade school teacher, Miss Hudson. She has a weird kind of off-balance walk and out-of-time speaking style that's infectious and funny. It's amazing that a movie so devoid of comic imagination would allow itself to play around with such an offbeat supporting performance. If Gorman had played, say, Tracy's mother—and if the rest of the movie had been equally willing to take chances with its approach—*Book II* could have been worth seeing.

Oh, God! You Devil ★ ★ ★ ½
PG, 96 m., 1984

George Burns (God and Harry), Ted Wass (Bobby Shelton), Roxanne Hart (Wendy), Ron Silver (Gary). Directed by Paul Bogart and produced by Robert M. Sherman. Screenplay by Andrew Bergman.

The *God* pictures are ideal for sequels; after

all, the leading character has no beginning and no end. But sequels have a way of ripping off profitable ideas without anything new to say. They grow so dreary and pale that we forget why we liked the original picture in the first place. That's why *Oh, God! You Devil* is such a delight. Here is George Burns's third God movie, and not only does it have as much humor, warmth, and good cheer as the first—it actually has a better story. The story involves a young man who was placed under God's protection when he was a little baby; he had a fever, and his father's prayers were answered. The kid has grown up into an unsuccessful musician, and one day while he's performing at some dumb wedding reception, he meets an unusual guest, one Harry O. Tophet, who is, of course, the devil. Harry makes the kid an offer he should, but does not, refuse, and before long the kid is the top rock superstar in the world.

Of course, there's a catch. He has to assume the identity of another musician—an existing superstar whose deal with the devil has just run out. And worst of all, he has to remember his previous life, including the wife he loved and the child they were expecting. This whole balancing act between success and loss is unexpectedly touching, and gives the movie a genuine human heart.

Meanwhile, the devil basks in his acquisition, and then God gets into the act when the rock star prays to be released from his deal with the devil.

It's here that we get what we've been waiting for all through the picture, the scenes where God and the devil, both played by George Burns, appear on the same screen. Dual appearances through trick photography are, of course, an old Hollywood standby, but what's fun here is the way Burns plays scenes with himself: This casting was made in heaven.

Oh, God! You Devil has two different kinds of successful elements. The Burns stuff is all superb, especially when the devil reflects whimsically about the evils he's unleashed upon the earth. But the other story—the story starring Ted Wass as the condemned rock star—has an authenticity of its own. Like Warren Beatty's *Heaven Can Wait*, it starts with a fantastical idea and then develops it along plausible human lines. For the first time in the God pictures, we care so much about the human characters that it really does make a difference what God does; it's not just a celestial vaudeville act.

On Golden Pond ★ ★ ★ ★

PG, 109 m., 1981

Katharine Hepburn (Ethel Thayer), Henry Fonda (Norman Thayer, Jr.), Jane Fonda (Chelsea), Doug McKeon (Billy Ray), Dabney Coleman (Bill Ray). Directed by Mark Rydell and produced by Bruce Gilbert. Screenplay by Ernest Thompson.

Simple affection is so rare in the movies. Shyness and resentment are also seldom seen. Love is much talked-about, but how often do we really believe that the characters are in love and not simply in a pleasant state of lust and like? Fragile emotions are hard to portray in a movie, and the movies that reach for them are more daring, really, than movies that bludgeon us with things like anger and revenge, which are easy to portray.

On Golden Pond is a treasure for many reasons, but the best one, I think, is that I could believe it. I could believe in its major characters and their relationships, and in the things they felt for one another, and there were moments when the movie was witness to human growth and change. I left the theater feeling good and warm, and with a certain resolve to try to mend my own relationships and learn to start listening better. All of those achievements are small miracles for any movie, but especially for this one, which began as a formula stage play and still contains situations and characters that are constructed completely out of cardboard.

The story of *On Golden Pond* begins with the arrival of an old, long-married couple (Henry Fonda and Katharine Hepburn) at the lakeside cottage where they have summered for many years. They know each other very well. Hepburn, of course, knows Fonda better than he knows her—or himself, for that matter. Fonda is a crotchety, grouchy old professor whose facade conceals a great deal of shyness, we suspect. Hepburn knows that. Before long, three more people turn up at the pond: Their daughter (Jane Fonda), her fiancé (Dabney Coleman), and his son (Doug McKeon).

That's the first act. In the second act, the conflicts are established. Jane Fonda feels that her father has never really given her her due—he wanted a son, or perhaps he never really understood how to be a father, anyway. Jane tells her parents that she's spending a month in Europe with Coleman, and, ah, would it be all right if they left the kid at the lake? Hepburn talks the old man into it. In the central passages of the movie, the old man and the kid grudgingly move toward some kind of communication and trust. There is a crisis involving a boating accident, and a resolution that brings everybody a lot closer to the realization that life is a precious and fragile thing. Through learning to relate to the young boy, old Fonda learns, belatedly, how to also trust his own daughter and communicate with her: The kid provides Henry with practice at how to be a father. There is eventually the sort of happy ending that some people cry through.

Viewed simply as a stage plot, *On Golden Pond* is so predictable we can almost hear the gears squeaking. Forty-five minutes into the movie, almost everyone in the audience can probably predict more or less what is going to happen to the characters, emotionally. And yet *On Golden Pond* transcends its predictability and the transparent role of the young boy, and becomes a film with passages of greatness.

This is because of the acting, first of all, but also because Ernest Thompson, who wrote such a formula play, has furnished it with several wonderful scenes. A conversation between old Henry Fonda and young Coleman is an early indication that this is going to be an unusual movie: A man who is forty-five asks a man who is eighty for permission to sleep in the same room with the man's daughter, and after the old man takes the question as an excuse for some cruel put-downs, the conversation takes an altogether unexpected twist into words of simple truth. That is a good scene. So are some of the conversations between Hepburn and Fonda. And so are some remarkable scenes involving the boating accident, in which there is no doubt that Hepburn, at her age, is doing some of her own stunts. It's at moments like this that stardom, acting ability, character, situation—and what the audience already knows about the actors—all come together into an irreplaceable combination.

As everybody knows, this is the first film in which Hepburn and the two Fondas have acted in any combination with one another. Some reviews actually seem to dismiss the casting as a stunt. I believe it adds immeasurably to the film's effect. If Hepburn and Henry Fonda are legends, seen in the twilight of their lives, and if we've heard that Jane and Henry have had some of the same problems offscreen that they have in this story—does that make the movie simple gossip? No, not if the movie deals honestly with the problems, as this one does. As people, they have apparently learned something about loving and caring that, as actors, they are able to communicate, even through the medium of this imperfect script. Watching the movie, I felt I was witnessing something rare and valuable.

On the Edge ★ ★ ★ ½

PG-13, 112 m., 1986

Bruce Dern (Wes Holman), John Marley (Elmo Glidden), Bill Bailey (Flash), Jim Haynie (Owen Riley). Directed by Rob Nilsson and produced by Jeffrey Hayes and Nilsson. Screenplay by Nilsson.

There is some mention that Wes Holman has been coaching for the last twenty years, but more likely he has been brooding. He is a thin, wiry man with a bushy beard and burning eyes. When we see him for the first time, he is watching some runners race up the side of a mountain. Just by the way he looks at the mountain, we can tell how important it is to him. Of course, the dramatic music doesn't hurt.

As Wes Holman was turning to walk back down the road, I was settling down into my seat, convinced that I was doomed to witness yet another formula sports picture. The film would follow Holman's masochistic training regime, and then the climax would be his amazing comeback and victory. It would all be very predictable, I thought, but I was wrong. *On the Edge* may have a familiar formula, but it is an angry, original, unpredictable movie. And it's not about winning. It's about the reasons that athletes carry in their hearts after all strength and reason have fled.

The movie stars Bruce Dern, in one of his best performances, as Holman, a great runner who was banned from amateur athletics twenty years ago after he attempted to expose clandestine payoffs to athletes. He was no more dishonest than anyone else, but he rocked the boat, insisting that amateurism in athletics was the way the rich kept the poor from competing.

Now the runner has come back to prove something. He wants to run the Cielo-Sea Race, the second oldest in America, a grueling race over the mountains from Mill Valley to the Pacific. It's a point-to-point race, which means the runner can follow any path he chooses, as long as he passes a few checkpoints. Holman, running in the older-than-forty age group, figures he can win the race, especially if he can persuade his old coach to help him.

The coach is played magnificently by the late John Marley, in his last role. He is one of the two great old men in the movie. The other, playing Holman's father, is the West Coast radical union organizer Bill Bailey, in his first dramatic role. The age shift in this movie is interesting; instead of a kid with a father figure, Holman is a bitter, grown man who wants to prove something once again to the men who were so important to him years ago.

The middle portions of the movie alternate between the training sequences and episodes from Holman's private life. He moves into makeshift quarters on an old dredging boat. He visits his father's junkyard and sits down to eat with a table full of old leftists. He spends time in the bar where his old coach hangs out. The movie creates a real sense of place: These aren't Hollywood locations but rooms where human voices sound at home.

The race is as exciting as it should be. But the ending is something else again. Never mind who wins. At the end, it's not winning that counts. It's making a statement about sports, about why hundreds of people train for a year so that one of them can win and the rest can lose. The last few minutes of *On the Edge* are surprisingly moving, as the film makes its point with great dramatic images.

On the Edge was directed by Rob Nilsson, whose earlier credits include *Northern Lights,* the independent film about the farmer-labor movement in Minnesota. Here he combines his politics with adequate financing and creates a powerful movie. What's best about it is that the sports don't overwhelm everything else. Winning is not the only thing for Wes Holman and his friends. Or, to be more precise, placing first is not the same as winning.

On the Road Again ★ ★ ★

PG, 119 m., 1980

Willie Nelson (Buck), Dyan Cannon (Viv), Amy Irving (Lily), Slim Pickens (Garland), Joey Floyd (Jamie), Mickey Rooney, Jr. (Cotton). Directed by Jerry Schatzberg and produced by Sydney Pollack and Gene Taft. Screenplay by Carol Sobieski, William D. Wittliff, and John Binder.

The plot of Willie Nelson's *Honeysuckle Rose** is just a slight touch familiar, maybe because it's straight out of your basic country and western song. To wit: The hero, a veteran country singer still poised at the brink of stardom after twenty-five years on the road, won't listen to his wife's pleas that he leave the road and settle down with her and their son. Meanwhile, the band's guitarist, who is also the singer's best friend, retires. A replacement is needed, and the singer hires the best friend's daughter.

She is a shapely young lady who has had a crush on the singer since she was knee-high to a grasshopper. Once they go out on the road again, the singer and the best friend's daughter start sleeping with one another. This situation causes anguish for the singer, the daughter, the best friend, the wife, the son, and the band. But after going down to Mexico to slug back some tequila and think it over, the singer returns to his wife and the best friend's daughter wisely observes: "Anything that hurts this many people can't be right."

This story is totally predictable from the opening scenes of *Honeysuckle Rose,* which is a disappointment; the movie is sly and entertaining, but it could have been better. Still, it has its charms, and one is certainly the presence of Willie Nelson himself, making his starring debut at the age of forty-seven and not looking a day over sixty. He's grizzled, grinning, sweet-voiced and pleasant, and a very engaging actor. (He gave promise of that with a single one-liner in his screen debut in *Electric Horseman,* expressing his poignant desire for the kind of girl who could suck the chrome off a trailer hitch.)

The movie also surrounds Nelson with an interesting cast: Dyan Cannon is wonderful as Willie's long-suffering wife, a sexy fortyish earth-woman with streaked hair and a wardrobe from L.L. Bean. She survives the test of her big scene, an archetypical C&W confrontation in which she charges onstage to denounce her husband and his new girlfriend.

Amy Irving is not quite so well-cast as the girlfriend; she has too many scenes in which she gazes adoringly at Willie—who, on the other hand, hardly ever gazes adoringly at her. Slim Pickens, who should be registered as a national historical place, is great as the best friend. And there is a hilarious bit part, a fatuous country singer, played by Mickey Rooney, Jr.

Mercifully, the movie doesn't drag out its tale of heartbreak into a C&W soap opera. Instead, director Jerry Schatzberg *(Scarecrow)* uses an easy-going documentary style to show us life on the band bus, at a family reunion, and backstage at big concerts. All of these scenes are filled to overflowing with colors; this is one of the cheeriest, brightest looking movies I've ever seen, starting with Willie's own amazing costumes and including the spectrum at the concerts, reunions, picnics, etc. Half the movie seems to be shot during parties, and although we enjoy the texture and detail we sometimes wonder why so little seems to be happening.

The movie remains resolutely at the level of superficial cliché, resisting any temptation to make a serious statement about the character's hard-drinking, self-destructive life-style; this isn't a movie like *Payday*, in which Rip Torn re-created the last days of the dying Hank Williams. *Honeysuckle Rose* has the kind of problems that can be resolved with an onstage reconciliation in the last scene: Willie and Dyan singing a duet together and everybody knowing things will turn out all right.

If there's an edge of disappointment coming out of the movie, maybe it's inspired by that simplicity of approach to complicated problems. Willie Nelson has lived a long time, experienced a lot, and suffered a certain amount on his way to his current success, and my hunch is that he knows a lot more about his character's problems in this movie than he lets on. Maybe the idea was to film the legend and save the man for later.

*Retitled *On the Road Again* for TV and cassette.

Once Upon a Time in America

★ —short version

★ ★ ★ ★ —original version

R, 137 m., 227 m., 1984

Robert De Niro (Noodles), James Woods (Max), Elizabeth McGovern (Deborah), Treat Williams (Jimmy), Tuesday Weld (Carol), Burt Young (Joe). Directed by Sergio Leone and produced by Arnon Milchan. Screenplay by L. Benvenuti, P. De Bernardo, E. Medioli, F. Arcalli, F. Ferrini, Leone, and S. Kaminski.

This was a murdered movie, now brought back to life on cassette. Sergio Leone's *Once Upon a Time in America*, which in its intended 227-minute version is an epic poem of violence and greed, was chopped by ninety minutes for U.S. theatrical release into an incomprehensible mess without texture, timing, mood, or sense. The rest of the world saw the original film, which I saw at the Cannes Film Festival. In America, a tragic decision was made. When the full-length version (now available in cassette form) played at the 1984 Cannes Film Festival, I wrote:

"Is the film too long? Yes and no. Yes, in the sense that it takes real concentration to understand Leone's story construction, in which everything may or may not be an opium dream, a nightmare, a memory, or a flashback, and that we have to keep track of characters and relationships over fifty years. No, in the sense that the movie is compulsively and continuously watchable and that the audience did not stir or grow restless as the epic unfolded."

The movie tells the story of five decades in the lives of four gangsters from New York City—childhood friends who are merciless criminals almost from the first, but who have a special bond of loyalty to each other. When one of them breaks that bond, or thinks he does, he is haunted by guilt until late in his life, when he discovers that he was not the betrayer but the betrayed. Leone's original version tells this story in a complex series of flashbacks, memories, and dreams. The film opens with two scenes of terrifying violence, moves to an opium den where the Robert De Niro character is seeking to escape the consequences of his action, and then establishes its tone with a scene of great power: A ceaselessly ringing telephone, ringing forever in the conscience of a man who called the cops and betrayed his friends. The film moves back and forth in a tapestry of episodes, which all fit together into an emotional whole. There are times when we don't understand exactly what is happening, but never a time when we don't feel confidence in the film's narrative.

That version was not seen in American theaters, although it is now available on cassette. Instead, the whole structure of flashbacks was junked. The telephone rings once. The poetic transitions are gone. The movie has been wrenched into apparent chronological order, scenes have been thrown out by the handful, relationships are now inexplicable, and the audience is likely to spend much of its time in complete bewilderment. It is a great irony that this botched editing job was intended to "clarify" the film.

Here are some of the specific problems with the shortened version. A speakeasy scene comes before a newspaper headline announces that Prohibition has been ratified. Prohibition is then repealed, on what feels like the next day but must be six years later. Two gangsters talk about robbing a bank in front of a woman who has never been seen before in the film; they've removed the scene explaining who she is. A labor leader turns up, unexplained, and involves the gangsters in an inexplicable situation. He later sells out, but to whom? Men come to kill De Niro's girlfriend, a character we've hardly met, and we don't know if they come from the mob or the police. And here's a real howler: At the end of the shortened version, De Niro leaves a room he has never seen before by walking through a secret panel in the wall. How did he know it was there? In the long version, he was told it was there. In the short version, his startling exit shows simple contempt for the audience.

Many of the film's most beautiful shots are missing from the short version, among them a bravura moment when a flash-forward is signaled by the unexpected appearance of a Frisbee, and another where the past becomes the present as the Beatles' "Yesterday" sneaks into the sound track. Relationships are truncated, scenes are squeezed of life, and I defy anyone to understand the plot of the short version. The original *Once Upon a Time in America* gets a four-star rating. The shorter version is a travesty.

One Flew Over the Cuckoo's Nest

★ ★ ★

R, 129 m., 1975

Jack Nicholson (R.P. McMurphy), Louise Fletcher (Nurse Ratched), Will Sampson (The Chief), William Redfield (Harding), Brad Dourif (Billy), Sydney Lassick (Cheswick), Scatman Crothers (Turkle), Dean R. Brooks (Dr. Spivey), Danny DeVito (Martini). Directed by Milos Forman and produced by Saul Zaentz and Michael Douglas. Screenplay by Lawrence Hauben and Bo Goldman.

Milos Forman's *One Flew Over the Cuckoo's Nest* is a film so good in so many of its parts that there's a temptation to forgive it when it goes wrong. But it does go wrong, insisting on making larger points than its story really should carry, so that at the end, the human qualities of the characters get lost in the significance of it all. And yet there are those moments of brilliance. If Forman was preaching a parable, the audience seemed in total agreement with it, and I found that a little depressing: It's a lot easier to make noble points about fighting the establishment, about refusing to surrender yourself to the system, than it is to closely observe the ways real people behave when they're placed in an environment like a mental institution.

That sort of observation, when it's allowed to happen, is what's best about *One Flew Over the Cuckoo's Nest*. We meet a classic outsider—R.P. McMurphy, a quintessentially sane convict sent to the institution as a punishment for troublemaking—whose charisma and gall allow him to break through to a group of patients who've mostly fallen into a drugged lethargy. Their passive existence is reinforced by the unsmiling, domineering Nurse Ratched, who lines them up for compulsory tranquilizers and then leads them through group therapy in a stupor.

McMurphy has no insights into the nature of mental illness, which is his blessing. He's an extroverted, life-loving force of nature who sees his fellow patients as teammates, and defines the game as the systematic defiance of Nurse Ratched and the system she personifies. In many of the best scenes in the film, this defiance takes the shape of spontaneous and even innocent little rebellions: During exercise period, the patients mill around aimlessly on a basketball court until McMurphy hilariously tries to get a game going.

He also makes bets and outrageous dares, and does some rudimentary political organizing. He needs the votes of ten patients, out of a possible eighteen, to get the ward schedule changed so they can all watch the World Series—and his victory is in overcoming the indifference the others feel not only toward the Series but toward existence itself. McMurphy is the life force, the will to prevail, set down in the midst of a community of the defeated. And he's personified and made totally credible by Jack Nicholson, in another of the remarkable performances that have made him the most interesting actor to emerge in the last two decades. Nicholson, manically trying to teach basketball to an Indian (Will Sampson) who hasn't even spoken in twelve years, sometimes succeeds in translating the meaning of the movie and Ken Kesey's novel into a series of direct, physical demonstrations.

That's when the movie works, and what it's best at. If Forman had stayed at that level—introducing his characters and making them real, and then seeing how they changed as they bounced off one another—*One Flew Over the Cuckoo's Nest* might have been a great film. It's a good one as it is, but we can see the machinery working. Take, for example, the all-night orgy that finally hands McMurphy over to his doom. He's smuggled booze and broads into the ward, and everyone gets drunk, and then the hapless Billy (Brad Dourif) is cheerfully bundled into a bedroom with a willing girl. Billy stutters so badly he can hardly talk, but he's engaging and intelligent, and we suspect his problems are not incurable. The next morning, as Nurse Ratched surveys the damage, Billy at first defies her (speaking without a stutter, which is too obvious) and then caves in when she threatens to tell his mother what he's done. Nurse Ratched and Billy's mother are old friends, you see (again, too obvious, pinning the rap on Freud and Mom). Billy commits suicide, and we're invited to stand around his pitiful corpse and see the injustice of it all—when all we've really seen is the plot forcing an implausible development out of unwilling subject matter.

Another scene that just doesn't work, because it's too heavily burdened with its purpose, occurs when McMurphy escapes, commandeers a school bus, and takes all the inmates of the ward on a fishing trip in a stolen boat. The scene causes an almost embarrassing break in the movie—it's Forman's first serious misstep—because it's an idealized fantasy in the midst of realism. By now, we've met the characters, we know them in the context of hospital politics, and when they're set down on the boat deck, they just don't belong there. The ward is the arena in which they'll win or lose, and it's not playing fair—to them, as characters—to give them a fishing trip.

Even as I'm making these observations, though, I can't get out of my mind the tumultuous response that *Cuckoo's Nest* received from its original audiences. Even the most obvious, necessary and sobering scenes—as when McMurphy tries to strangle Nurse Ratched to death—were received, not seriously, but with sophomoric cheers and applause. Maybe that's the way to get the most out of the movie—see it as a simple-minded antiestablishment parable—but I hope not. I think there are long stretches of a very good film to be found in the midst of Forman's ultimate failure, and I hope they don't get drowned in the applause for the bad stuff that plays to the galleries.

One from the Heart ★ ★

PG, 98 m., 1982

Frederic Forrest (Hank), Teri Garr (Frannie), Raul Julia (Ray), Nastassja Kinski (Leila), Lainie Kazan (Maggie), Harry Dean Stanton (Moe). Directed by Francis Ford Coppola and produced by Bernard Gersten.

Arriving after two years of sound and fury, after all the news items on the financial pages and alarms and excursions in the movie trade press, Francis Ford Coppola's *One from the Heart* is an interesting production but not a good movie. From Coppola, the brilliant orchestrator of *Apocalypse Now* and the Godfather films, it is a major disappointment. This must be the first movie in history to arrive with more publicity about its production techniques than about its stars. Everybody knows that Coppola used experimental video equipment to view and edit his movie, sealing himself into a trailer jammed with electronic gear so that he could see on TV what the camera operator was seeing through the lens. Of course the film itself was photographed on the same old celluloid that the movies have been using forever; Coppola used TV primarily as a device to speed up the process of viewing each shot and trying out various editing combinations. (Or, as an industry wisecrack had it, "He took an $8 million project and used the latest advances in video to bring it in for $23 million.")

If *One from the Heart* is the sort of film this process inspires, then Coppola should abandon it. But of course the process is neutral; films live or die according to an inner rhythm of their own. The most dismal thing about *One from the Heart* is that it lacks those rhythms. It is a ballet of graceful and complex camera movements occupying magnificent sets, and somehow the characters get lost in the process. There was never a moment in this film when I cared about what was happening to the people in it, and only one moment (a cameo by Allen Goorwitz as an irate restaurant owner) when I felt that an actor's spontaneity was able to sneak past Coppola's smothering style and into the audience.

The storyteller of *The Godfather* has become a technician here. There are chilling parallels between Coppola's obsessive control of this film and the character of Harry Caulfield, the wiretapper in Coppola's *The Conversation* (1973), who cared only about technical results and refused to let himself think about human consequences. Movies are a lot of different things, but most of the best ones are about people and for people, and *One from the Heart* pays little heed to the complexities of the human heart. Indeed, it seems almost on guard against the actors who occupy its carefully architectured scenes. They are hardly ever allowed to dominate. They are figures in a larger pattern, one that diminishes them, that sees them as part of the furniture. They aren't given many close-ups; they're often bathed in garish red glows or sickly blues and greens; they're placed in front of distractingly flamboyant sets or lost in badly choreographed crowds, and sometimes they're cut off in the middle of an emotion or a piece of business because the relentlessly programmed camera has business elsewhere.

I've neglected, in fact, to name the actors, or describe the characters they play. That's not so much of an oversight in a review of a film like this. The two main characters (Teri Garr and Frederic Forrest) inhabit a Las Vegas of disappointment, ennui, and glittering lights. For a brief time, they break out of their humdrum lives and meet new lovers (Raul Julia and Nastassja Kinski) who tease them with dreams and fantasies. The underlying story notion, I suppose, is that ordinary little people have a great night on the town, but the night and the town in Coppola's production so overwhelm them that they remain ordinary little people throughout.

There are small pleasures in this movie. One is Harry Dean Stanton's walk-through as the seedy owner of a junkyard, although Coppola resists showing us Stanton's most effective tool, his expressive eyes. Kinski, as a circus tightrope walker, has a beauty much more mature than in *Tess* and a wonderful moment when she explains "to make a circus girl disappear, all you have to do is blink your eyes." Garr is winsome, but her role makes her thanklessly passive, and Forrest (the Oscar nominee from *The Rose*) is almost transparent here, he's given such a nebbish to play.

One-Trick Pony ★ ★ ★ ½

R, 98 m., 1980

Paul Simon (Jonah), Blair Brown (Marion), Rip Torn (Walter Fox), Joan Hackett (Lonnie Fox), Allen Goorwitz (Cal Van Damp), Mare Winningham (Modeena), Lou Reed (Steve), Harper Simon (Young Jonah). Directed by Robert M. Young and produced by Michael Tannen. Screenplay and original music by Paul Simon.

One-Trick Pony is a wonderful movie, an affectionate character study with a lot of good music in it, and it's being sold in all the wrong ways to Paul Simon "fans." True, you'll like it if you *are* a Paul Simon fan, but does Paul Simon have "fans" anymore? He has lots of admirers, people who follow his music—but they're not necessarily prepared to race out into the night to see this movie, as fans of, say, Bruce Springsteen might be willing to do. And that's sort of the point of *One-Trick Pony*, which tells the story of a folk singer who used to have a lot more fans than he does today.

It's ironic, the way the movie's ad campaign seemed to have exactly missed the point of the movie. Ironic, but not unusual. And never mind: This movie was one of a lousy film year's few good films, a work that knows exactly what it's like to be a musician on tour. Jonah, the character Paul Simon wrote and plays, is a person drawn from life. If you are or ever have been a regular at a marginal local folk club, you've seen singers like Jonah many times.

He was very big in the 1960s. He wrote one of the songs that became an anthem for that decade. His music was an anti-war rallying point. But the sixties are long ago. And Jonah has continued to perform more or less in the same vein. He still travels the country by van, working with a small band. He still writes and arranges his own songs. He is still very good, for that matter—but he's out of date. He plays smaller and smaller clubs, and back home, in New York, his wife and child are both growing up without him.

There is a point, this movie argues, when a singer like Jonah stops being a brave individualist and becomes merely a middle-aged man hanging onto an obsolete self-image. That's the opinion held by Jonah's wife (Blair Brown), who loves him but wants a divorce. Jonah is sort of willing to try a change. He begins to deal with a "hitmaker" (Rip Torn) who sets him up with an arranger (Lou Reed) who can almost guarantee a Top 40 sound.

The movie does an effortless job of teaching us this aspect of the music business. We hear various versions of one of Jonah's songs: first as it sounds in a small club, then as it sounds during a very nervous audition session, and finally as it is gruesomely transformed, violins and all, into a prepackaged "hit." During this period we begin to feel sympathy with a certain nobility in Jonah's character. *One-Trick Pony* never forces its points, but we begin to understand why his way might be preferable to success.

The movie is filled with interesting, sharply drawn characters. Allen Goorwitz is brilliant in a hateful role as an egotistical monster who controls radio playtime. Joan Hackett, as Torn's sexually adventurous wife, goes after Jonah in simple, lustful boredom, but ends up trying to be his friend, to explain the realities of the situation they find themselves in. Brown plays the singer's wife as a complex woman who, in her thirties, still knows and feels why she married this man, but wonders how long he has to prove his point before her life is sidetracked.

And Simon is very good in the central role. The movie has a lot of music in it that he sings well and with love, but it also contains some very tricky dramatic moments. Halfway through, we begin to realize that it's about a lot more things than an aging folk hero. It is also about the generation that was young and politically active in the 1960s and now has been overtaken by the narcissism of the most brutally selfish and consumer-oriented period in American history. Many children of the sixties have been, of course, willing converts to the new culture of the Cuisinart. Others stick to what they used to believe in. In Jonah's case, it's folk music. Everybody's case is different.

The Onion Field ★ ★ ★ ★

R, 126 m., 1979

John Savage (Karl Hettinger), James Woods (Greg Powell), Franklyn Seales (Jimmy Smith), Ted Danson (Ian Campbell), Ronny Cox (Pierce Brooks), David Huffman (Phil Halpin), Christopher Lloyd (Jailhouse Lawyer), Diane Hull (Helen Hettinger), Priscilla Pointer (Chrissie Campbell). Directed by Harold Becker and produced by Walter Coblenz. Screenplay by Joseph Wambaugh.

Since *The Onion Field* will inevitably inspire comparisons with *In Cold Blood,* we might as well begin with a basic one: Both the book and the film of *In Cold Blood* restructured the order of real events in order to use the actual murders as a climax. The storytellers were having it both ways, by conveying dismay at the killings while at the same time using them for essentially fictional shock value.

The Onion Field does not do that. It is also based on real events—the 1963 kidnappings of Los Angeles police officers Karl Hettinger and Ian Campbell, and the eventual cold-blooded murder of Campbell. But Joseph Wambaugh, who wrote the book and personally controlled the film production, didn't reorder the facts to give us a dramatic burst of gunfire at the end. Instead, he places the deadly event of the murder in an onion field at about where it should occur, midway between the criminal preparations that led up to it and the longest single criminal court case in California history, which lasted more than seven years.

For Wambaugh (himself a former policeman), the trial, too, was a crime—and the fact of Campbell's murder had to be considered in the context of the legal travesties that followed it. That attention to the larger context of the kidnap-killing is one thing that makes *The Onion Field* so much more than another cop drama. This movie is about people, about how they behave and why, and about how small accidents and miscalculations can place people in situations they never dreamed of. Life is a very fragile thing; *The Onion Field* knows that in its bones.

The film moves betwen two basic, completely dissimilar, sets of characters: the two police officers, and the two third-rate hoods who would eventually be convicted of the crime. The cops aren't seen in quite the same sharp focus as the criminals—perhaps because, until the night of the onion field, little they had done in their lives had prepared them for what would follow.

Campbell (Ted Danson), the one who is killed, is seen almost as a memory: a tall, good-looking, black-haired Scottish-American with an obsession for bagpipes. Hettinger (John Savage from *The Deer Hunter*) is seen at the beginning as a cheerful, open-faced young man who will only later, after the onion field, develop very deep hurts and complications.

The hoods are seen more clearly. There's Greg Powell (James Woods), a street-wise smartass with a quick line of talk and an ability to paint situations so other people see them his way. And then there's Jimmy Smith (Franklyn Seales), a disturbed, insecure young black who is a perfect recruit for Powell. They make a suitable team. Powell creates criminal scenarios out of his fantasies; Smith finds them real enough to follow; and in some convoluted way Powell then follows Smith into them.

The Onion Field makes these two characters startingly convincing: It paints their manners, their speech, their environment, their indecisions in such a way that we can almost understand them as they blunder stupidly into their crimes.

It never quite captures the personality of Campbell, the man who will be killed, but in the aftermath of the killing it begins to develop disturbing insights into Hettinger, the survivor. In a dozen subtle ways he becomes an outcast in the department (he senses, perhaps correctly, that the other cops wonder how he could allow his partner to be killed). Eventually, punishing himself, seeking guilt, he becomes a shoplifter, and is caught and fired from the force. Savage's handling of a scene of near-suicide, late in the film, is so frightening we can hardly stand to watch it.

Those events take place as *The Onion Field* explores the bureaucratic nightmare of the criminal courts system. The case dragged on and on and on—Hettinger was called upon to testify in more than six different trials—and plea bargaining, delays, and continuances, and legal loopholes made the case into an impossible (and almost insoluble) tangle.

So there is a lot of ground for *The Onion Field* to cover. It covers it remarkably well, working both as a narrative and as Wambaugh's cry of protest against the complicated and maddening workings of the courts. The movie is actually a vindication for Wambaugh: He was so displeased with the Hollywood and TV treatments of his novels (especially *The Choirboys*) that he said he would never let this factual story be made into a movie unless he controlled the production.

He did, and he has made it into a strong and honorable film. His instinct in going with Harold Becker, a commercial director with little previous feature experience, was obviously a good one; the movie's craftsmanship is unobtrusive but fine. And the performances (especially James Woods's as Greg Powell) bring the characters into heartbreaking reality. This is a movie that, once seen, cannot be set aside.

Ordinary People ★ ★ ★ ★

R, 125 m., 1980

Donald Sutherland (Calvin), Mary Tyler Moore (Beth), Judd Hirsch (Berger), Timothy Hutton (Conrad), M. Emmet Walsh (Swim Coach), Elizabeth McGovern (Jeannine), Dinah Manoff (Karen). Directed by Robert Redford and produced by Ronald L. Schwary. Screenplay by Alvin Sargent.

Families can go along for years without ever facing the underlying problems in their relationships. But sometimes a tragedy can bring everything out in the open, all of a sudden and painfully, just when everyone's most vulnerable. Robert Redford's *Ordinary People* begins at a time like that for a family that loses its older son in a boating accident. That leaves three still living at home in a perfectly manicured suburban existence, and the movie is about how they finally have to deal with the ways they really feel about one another.

There's the surviving son, who always lived in his big brother's shadow, who tried to commit suicide after the accident, who has now just returned from a psychiatric hospital. There's the father, a successful Chicago attorney who has always taken the love of his family for granted. There's the wife, an expensively maintained, perfectly groomed, cheerful homemaker whom "everyone loves." The movie begins just as all of this is falling apart.

The movie's central problems circle almost fearfully around the complexities of love. The parents and their remaining child all "love" one another, of course. But the father's love for the son is sincere yet also inarticulate, almost shy. The son's love for his mother is blocked by his belief that she doesn't really love him—she only loved the dead brother. And the love between the two parents is one of those permanent facts that both take for granted and neither has ever really tested.

Ordinary People begins with this three-way emotional standoff and develops it through the autumn and winter of one year. And what I admire most about the film is that it really *does* develop its characters and the changes they go through. So many family dramas begin with a "problem" and then examine its social implications in that frustrating semifactual, docudrama format that's big on TV. *Ordinary People* isn't a docudrama; it's the story of these people and their situation, and it shows them doing what's most difficult to show in fiction—it shows them changing, learning, and growing.

At the center of the change is the surviving son, Conrad, played by a wonderfully natural young actor named Timothy Hutton. He is absolutely tortured as the film begins; his life is ruled by fear, low self-esteem, and the correct perception that he is not loved by his mother. He starts going to a psychiatrist (Judd Hirsch) after school. Things are hard for this kid. He blames himself for his brother's death. He's a semi-outcast at school because of his suicide attempt and hospitalization. He does have a few friends—a girl he met at the hospital, and another girl who stands behind him at choir practice and who would, in a normal year, naturally become his girlfriend. But there's so much turmoil at home.

The turmoil centers around the mother (Mary Tyler Moore, inspired casting for this particular role, in which the character masks her inner sterility behind a facade of cheerful suburban perfection). She does a wonderful job of running her house, which looks like it's out of the pages of *Better Homes and Gardens*. She's active in community affairs, she's an organizer, she's an ideal wife and mother—except that at some fundamental level she's selfish, she can't really give of herself, and she *has,* in fact, always loved the dead older son more. The father (Donald Sutherland) is one of those men who wants to do and feel the right things, in his own awkward way. The change he goes through during the movie is one of the saddest ones: Realizing his wife cannot truly care for others, he questions his own love for her for the first time in their marriage.

The sessions of psychiatric therapy are supposed to contain the moments of the film's most visible insights, I suppose. But even more effective, for me, were the scenes involving the kid and his two teen-age girlfriends. The girl from the hospital (Dinah Manoff) is cheerful, bright, but somehow running from something. The girl from choir practice (Elizabeth McGovern) is straightforward, sympathetic, able to be honest. In trying to figure them out, Conrad gets help in figuring himself out.

Director Redford places all these events in a suburban world that is seen with an understated matter-of-factness. There are no cheap shots against suburban life-styles or affluence or mannerisms: The problems of the people in this movie aren't caused by their milieu, but grow out of themselves. And, like it or not, the participants have to deal with them. That's what sets the film apart from the sophisticated suburban soap opera it could easily have become. Each character in this movie is given the dramatic opportunity to look inside himself, to question his *own* motives as well as the motives of others, and to try to improve his own ways of dealing with a troubled situation. Two of the characters do learn how to adjust; the third doesn't. It's not often we get characters who face those kinds of challenges on the screen, nor directors who seek them out. *Ordinary People* is an intelligent, perceptive, and deeply moving film.

Orphans ★ ★ ½
R, 115 m., 1987
(See related Film Clip, p. 745.)

Albert Finney (Harold), Matthew Modine (Treat), Kevin Anderson (Phillip), John Kellogg (Barney), Anthony Heald (Man in Park). Directed and produced by Alan J. Pakula and co-produced by Susan Solt. Screenplay by Lyle Kessler.

Orphans is a good play about behavior turned into a mediocre movie about nothing much at all. That is not intended as a criticism of the filmmakers, but simply as an observation about the nature of the material. Although it is possible to construct elaborate theories about this movie, you blink and they're gone. *Orphans* is not about a man who wants to be a father, or about boys who want to have a father, or about sublimated sexual desires, or the underlying bond between criminals and outcasts. It is about shouting and jumping around and posturing and eccentric behavior.

The movie stars Albert Finney as a Chicago gangster who travels to Newark with a briefcase full of negotiable bonds, and promptly gets drunk out of his mind in a tavern. He runs across Matthew Modine, a street punk, and instantly sentimentalizes him as a Dead-End Kid—perhaps out of some maudlin idea the gangster has of his own childhood. Finney gets even more drunk, and passes out, and wakes up tied to a chair. He has been kidnapped by Modine, who lives with his brother (Kevin Anderson) in a crumbling house in the middle of an urban wasteland.

Finney never loses his cool. He frees himself of his bonds and then, amazingly, does not take the opportunity to escape. Instead, he stays in the house, cleaning and painting it, and appoints himself to tutor the two brothers in the ways of the world. His task is to tame and domesticate Modine, who is too hot-tempered, and to free Anderson of self-imprisonment (the kid hasn't even been outdoors in years, because Modine has convinced him he's allergic to the outside world).

Modine has a stake in keeping his brother imprisoned. It gives him power and a godlike role in their small world. Finney works artfully, using object lessons, parables, and Q & A sessions, feeling his way, talking these kids into a new view of themselves. There is a lot of stage business for him to perform while he talks. He paints, does carpentry, plays with his gun, and watches while Anderson swings from the curtains and tumbles around the set like a monkey in a cage. Modine alternates between aggression and passivity; he takes a strong line at first, but eventually confesses his ignorance to the older man.

This sort of material is strong on the stage. You enter the same time and space as the actors; the lights go down, and the actors project great energy at the audience, which leaves feeling slightly more dangerous and alive than when it entered the room. It is a very satisfactory experience. Plays like Lyle Kessler's *Orphans* and Sam Shepard's *True West* (with its suite for pop-up toasters) can be considered as concerts for voices and movement. The playwright supplies the words and suggests the actions, and the actors cry and whisper, leap and crouch, fight and surrender, and reveal great hurts from their pasts. Along the way, it is important, of course, that they change, and that they discover some measure of the truth about themselves.

Actually, change and truth are the least important ingredients, because they are the most arbitrary and artificial—put in to make the behavior look like a real play. The actual physical and verbal behavior itself is the subject of the play. It is possible to construct elaborate theories about the meaning of *Orphans*, but on the stage, the play works as an exercise in human vitality in which the actors test their instruments. On screen, where the impact of their actual physical presence is missing, the material is revealed as a series of contrivances.

Albert Finney, who does an excellent job of portraying Harold the gangster, probably realizes this. He saw the play in Chicago, brought it to London and performed it triumphantly on the stage. Of course a movie had to be made of it, and he was happy to play his role again, but when I talked to him about the film, he spoke of the play almost entirely in stage actor's words, in terms of the opportunities it gave him rather than in the statement it made. That's the right approach.

The theater works best when it places the audience in the same box of space and time as the actors and the material. Movies work best when they break out of the box, when they spring free from the physical constraints of space and time—even in such a simple matter as the way the camera's point of view is free to roam. The problem of filming a play is as old as the cinema itself, and *Orphans* doesn't solve it—not that this play *could* be successfully filmed. Pakula and his actors do their best, but "out there" feels as much like "offstage" at the end as at the beginning.

Out of Africa ★ ★ ★ ★
PG, 153 m., 1985

Meryl Streep (Karen), Robert Redford (Denys), Klaus-Maria Brandauer (Bror), Michael Kitchen (Berkeley), Malick Bowens (Farah), Joseph Thiaka (Kamante), Stephen Kinyanjui (Kinyanjui), Michael Gough (Delamere), Suzanna Hamilton (Felicity). Directed and produced by Sydney Pollack. Screenplay by Kurt Luedtke.

Earlier, there was a moment when a lioness seemed about to attack, but did not. The baroness had been riding her horse on the veld, had dismounted, had lost her rifle when the horse bolted. Now the lioness seemed about to charge, when behind her a calm voice advised the baroness not to move one inch. "She'll go away," the voice said, and indeed the lioness did skulk away after satisfying its curiosity.

That scene sets up the central moment in Sydney Pollack's *Out of Africa,* which comes somewhat later in the film. The baroness is on safari with the man who owned the cool voice, a big-game hunter named Denys. They happen upon a pride of lions. Once again, the man assumes charge. He will protect them. But then a lion unexpectedly charges from another direction, and it is up to the baroness to fell it, with one shot that must not miss, and does not. After the man and woman are safe, the man sees that the woman has bitten her lip in anxiety. He reaches out and touches the blood. Then they hold each other tightly.

If you can sense the passion in that scene, then you may share my enjoyment of *Out of Africa,* which is one of the great recent epic romances. The baroness is played by Meryl Streep. The hunter is Robert Redford. These are high-voltage stars, and when their chemistry is wrong for romances (as Streep's was for *Falling in Love,* and Redford's for *The Natural*), it is very wrong. This time, it is right.

The movie is based on the life and writings of Baroness Karen Blixen, a Danish woman who, despairing that she would be single forever, married her lover's brother, moved to Kenya in East Africa, ran a coffee plantation on the slopes of Kilimanjaro, and later, when the plantation was bankrupt and the dream was finished, wrote books about her experiences under the name Isak Dinesen.

Her books are glories—especially *Out of Africa* and *Seven Gothic Tales*—but they are not the entire inspiration for this movie. What we have here is an old-fashioned, intelligent, thoughtful love story, told with enough care and attention that we really get involved in the passions between the characters.

In addition to the people Streep and Redford play, there is a third major character, Bror, the man she marries, played by Klaus Maria Brandauer. He is a smiling, smooth-faced, enigmatic man, who likes her well enough, after his fashion, but never seems quite equal to her spirit. After he gives her syphilis and she returns to Denmark for treatment, she is just barely able to tolerate his behavior—after all, he did not ask to marry her—until a New Year's Eve when he flaunts his infidelity, and she asks him to move out.

He turns up once more, asking for money, after Redford has moved his things into the baroness's farmhouse. The two men have a classic exchange. Brandauer: "You should have asked permission." Redford: "I did. She said yes."

The movie takes place during that strange blip in history when the countries of East Africa—Kenya, Uganda, the Rhodesias—were attracting waves of European settlers discontented with life at home in the years around World War I. The best land available to them was in the so-called white highlands of Kenya, so high up the air was cooler and there were fewer insects, and some luck could be had with cattle and certain crops.

The settlers who lived there soon settled into a hard-drinking, high-living regime that has been documented in many books and novels; they were sort of "Dallas" crossed with *Mandingo*. The movie steers relatively clear of the social life, except for a scene where Streep is snubbed at the local club, a few other scenes in town, and an extraordinary moment when she goes down on her knees before the British governor to plead for land for the Africans who live on her bankrupt farm.

Before that moment, she has not seemed particularly interested in Africans, except for an old overseer who becomes a close friend (and this is not true to the spirit of her book, where Africans are of great importance to her). Instead, she is much more involved in the waves of passion that sweep over the veld, as Redford passes through her life like a comet on a trajectory of its own.

He wants to move "his things" in, but does not want to move himself in. He wants commitment, but personal freedom. His ambiguity toward her is something like his ambiguity toward the land, which he penetrates with truck and airplane, leading tours while all the time bemoaning the loss of the virgin veld. Because *Out of Africa* is intelligently written, directed, and acted, however, we do not see his behavior as simply willful and spoiled, but as part of the contradictions he needs to stay an individual in a land where white society is strictly regimented.

The Baroness Blixen needs no such shields; she embodies sufficient contradictions on her own. In a land where whites are foreigners, she is a foreign white. She writes and thinks instead of gossiping and drinking. She runs her own farm. She scorns local gossip. In this hunter, she finds a spirit equal to her own, which is eventually the undoing of their relationship.

Out of Africa is a great movie to look at, breathtakingly filmed on location. It is a movie with the courage to be about complex, sweeping emotions, and to use the star power of its actors without apology. Sydney Pollack has worked with Redford before—notably in another big-sky epic, *Jeremiah Johnson*. He understands the special, somewhat fragile mystique of his star, who has a tendency to seem overprotective of his own image. In the wrong hands, Redford can look narcissistic. This time, he seems to have much to be narcissistic about.

Out of the Blue ★ ★ ★ ½

R, 94 m., 1982

Linda Manz (CeBe), Dennis Hopper (Don), Sharon Farrell (Kathy), Raymond Burr (Dr. Brean), Don Gordon (Charlie). Directed by Dennis Hopper and produced by Gary Jules Jouvenat. Screenplay by Leonard Yakir and Brenda Nielson.

Out of the Blue is one of the unsung treasures of independent films, a showcase for the maverick talents of two movie rebels: veteran actor Dennis Hopper, of *Easy Rider* and *Rebel Without a Cause*, and young, tough-talking Linda Manz, whose debut in *Days of Heaven* was so heartbreaking. Made in 1982, it never got a chance in commercial theaters. The movie is Hopper's comeback as a director. After the enormous international success of *Easy Rider* (1969) and the resounding thud of his next directorial effort, *Last Movie* (1971), he didn't direct again until this movie (he acted, in such films as *The American Friend* and *Apocalypse Now*). Originally hired just to act in *Out of the Blue*, he took over two weeks into production, rewrote the screenplay, found new locations and made this movie into a bitter, unforgettable poem about alienation.

Hopper is one of the movie's stars, playing an alcoholic truck driver whose semi-rig crashes into a school bus, kills children, and sends him to jail for six years. Manz plays his daughter, a leather-jacketed, punk teen-ager who combs her hair with shoe polish and does Elvis imitations. Her mother is played by Sharon Farrell as a small-town waitress who tries a reconciliation with Hopper when he gets out of prison but is undercut by her drug addiction. Manz is the centerpiece of the film. As she demonstrated in the magnificent pastoral romance *Days of Heaven*, she has a presence all her own. She's tough and hard-edged and yet vulnerable, and in this movie we can sometimes see the scared little kid beneath the punk bravado. She lives in a world of fantasy. All but barricaded into her room, surrounded by posters of Elvis and other teen heroes, she practices her guitar (she isn't very good) and dresses up in her dad's leather jacket. He's a hero to her. She doesn't buy the story that he was responsible for the deaths of those kids. And when he finally gets out of prison, she has a father at last—but only for a few days.

Hopper's touch as a director is especially strong in a pathetic scene of reunion, including the family's day at the overcast, gloomy beach, and a "party" that turns into a violent brawl dominated by the Hopper character's drunken friend (Don Gordon). The movie escalates so relentlessly toward its violent, nihilistic conclusion that when it comes, we believe it. This is a very good movie that simply got overlooked. When it premiered at the 1980 Cannes Film Festival, it caused a considerable sensation, and Manz was mentioned as a front-runner for the best actress award. But back in North America, the film's Canadian backers had difficulties in making a distribution deal, and the film slipped through the cracks.

The Outlaw Josey Wales ★ ★ ★
PG, 135 m., 1976

Clint Eastwood (Josey), Chief Dan George (The Old Indian), Sondra Locke (The Girl), John Vernon (Fletcher). Directed by Clint Eastwood and produced by Robert Daley. Screenplay by Phil Kaufman.

Clint Eastwood's *The Outlaw Josey Wales* is a strange and daring Western that brings together two of the genre's usually incompatible story lines. On the one hand, it's about a loner, a man of action and few words, who turns his back on civilization and lights out for the Indian nations. On the other hand, it's about a group of people heading West who meet along the trail and cast their destinies together. What happens next is supposed to be against the rules in Westerns, as if *Jeremiah Johnson* were crossed with *Stagecoach:* Eastwood, the loner, becomes the group's leader and father figure.

We meet his character, Josey Wales, just after the Civil War. He's an unreconstructed Southerner, bitter about the atrocities he's witnessed, refusing to surrender. When Northern troops cold-bloodedly murder some of his comrades, he mows down the Yankees with a Gatling gun and becomes a fugitive. So far, we're on familiar ground; Eastwood plays essentially the same character he's been developing since the *Dollar* Westerns. He says little, keeps his face in the shadows, has an almost godlike personal invulnerability, and lives by a code we have to intuit because he'd die rather than explain it aloud.

But then this character begins to come across other drifters and refugees in the unsettled postwar West. The first is an old Indian, played by Chief Dan George with such wonderfully understated wit that there should have been an Oscar nomination around somewhere. "I myself never surrendered," he explains to Josey Wales. "But they got my horse, and *it* surrendered." George achieves the same magical effect here that he did in *Harry and Tonto,* trading Mixmasters for Indian medicine in a jail cell: He's funny and dignified at once. He joins up with the outlaw Eastwood, and their relationship is a reminder of all those great second bananas from the Westerns of the 1940s—the grizzled old characters played by Gabby Hayes and Smiley Burnette. But Chief Dan George brings an aura to his role that audiences seem to respond to viscerally. He has his problems (he's humiliated, as an Indian, that he's grown so old he can no longer sneak up behind people), but he has a humanity that's just there, glowing. He's as open with his personality as Josey Wales is closed; it's a nice match.

Various, and inexhaustible, bounty hunters are constantly on the outlaw's trail, despite the Eastwood ability (in this movie as before) to wipe out six, eight, ten bad guys before they can get off a shot. Eastwood keeps moving West, picking up along the way a young Indian girl and then the survivors of a Kansas family nearly wiped out on their quest for El Dorado. The relationships in the group are easily established or implied. There's not a lot of talking, but everybody understands each other.

Eastwood is such a taciturn and action-oriented performer that it's easy to overlook the fact that he directs many of his movies—and many of the best, most intelligent ones. Here, with the moody, gloomily beautiful, photography of Bruce Surtees, he creates a magnificent Western feeling.

Outrageous Fortune ★ ★

R, 96 m., 1987

Bette Midler (Sandy), Shelley Long (Lauren), Peter Coyote (Michael), Robert Prosky (Korzenowski), John Schuck (Atkins), George Carlin (Frank). Directed by Arthur Hiller and produced by Ted Field and Robert W. Cort. Screenplay by Leslie Dixon.

In an interview in the *New York Times*, Leslie Dixon, the author of the screenplay for *Outrageous Fortune*, revealed some of the secrets of being a successful writer for the movies. You have to read a lot of successful screenplays, she said, and be familiar with what's out there, what's selling at the studios. On the basis of this movie, she has done her job well; *Outrageous Fortune* is a combination of comedy and chase, billed by the producers as "the first genuine female buddy action comedy."

Unfortunately, the movie is so busy cross-pollinating its genres that it never pauses for the kind of thought that might have made it really special, instead of just fitfully funny. This is a movie that has its commercial concept written all over it; it's so painstakingly crafted as a product that the messy spontaneity of life is rarely allowed to interrupt.

The film stars Bette Midler and Shelley Long as two would-be acting students who discover they're both having an affair with the same fellow student. Midler plays a brassy, vulgar veteran of movies with names like *Ninja Vixens*, and Long is a Yale graduate who has deep ideas about "Art." The man they have in common is played by Peter Coyote, as a slick, mysterious Romeo who turns out, alas, to be involved in espionage.

I say "alas" because this movie goes wrong the moment it introduces its counterspy plot. You can almost hear the standard clichés slamming into place. Midler and Long discover that their drama teacher is a spy (Robert Prosky), that Coyote is in the class to spy on him, that there are people who want to kill them, and that it's up to them to chase all over the Western states and endure untold physical risks until the mystery is solved.

Take away the specific details, and this is the same premise that sabotaged *Jumpin' Jack Flash*, another "genuine" female action comedy. What happens is, the screenplay gets so wound up with the action that there's no time to explore the characters or let them be funny on their own terms. Midler has some very funny moments in *Outrageous Fortune*, but they're inspired by the personality she brings to the movie, not the one that Dixon's screenplay supplies for her. Long, who doesn't come packaged with a pre-existing comic persona, seems adrift most of the time.

My advice to Leslie Dixon would be: After you've studied all those screenplays, ask yourself what's wrong with them, and you're likely to discover that they all begin with interesting characters and then march relentlessly into a series of clichés involving the CIA, the Russians, car chases, sinister plots, and colorful locations. Truly funny movies (here I include Midler's previous two films, *Down and Out in Beverly Hills* and *Ruthless People)* settle down in one location and explore their characters, finding humor in human nature instead of in a lot of expensive physical stunts.

Outrageous Fortune has a climax that must have been expensive and dangerous to film, but it's a waste of time. The plot requires Long to leap from one towering desert rock formation to another, while she's chased by the bad guys. The whole sequence breaks down for two reasons: (1) The stunt is so dangerous that it distracts from any latent comedy, and (2) we're so busy trying to spot when they're using the stunt doubles that we lose any remaining interest in the plot.

Overboard ★ ★ ★

PG, 113 m., 1987

Goldie Hawn (Joanna/Annie), Kurt Russell (Dean Proffit), Edward Herrmann (Grant Stayton III), Katherine Helmond (Edith Mintz), Michael Hagerty (Billy Pratt), Roddy McDowall (Andrew), Harvey Alan Miller (Dr. Korman). Directed by Garry Marshall and produced by Anthea Sylbert and Alexandra Rose. Screenplay by Leslie Dixon.

Overboard is one more twist on the old reliable story about the snob who learns how the other half lives. The formula is written in stone: The character is established as stuck-up, arrogant, and spoiled, and then something happens to bring reality crashing through the door. By the end of the movie, the hero has discovered humility, gratitude, and love.

The reason this formula has been around so long is that it's dependable, as Goldie Hawn cheerfully proves in *Overboard.* There is hardly a major development in this story that we can't predict thirty minutes in advance, but what does it matter when the performances are so much fun, and there are so many comic delights along the way? This is the kind of movie that not only could have been directed by Frank Capra or Preston Sturges, but may have been.

The movie stars Hawn as a rich, bitchy society lady who lives on a luxury yacht with her snotty husband (Edward Herrmann) and long-suffering butler (Roddy McDowall). When the yacht pulls into harbor for repairs, she hires a local carpenter (Kurt Russell) to remodel some of her closet space. Then she refuses to pay him because he didn't use cedar wood—and doesn't *everybody* know closets are constructed of cedar? In the disagreement that follows, she kicks Russell overboard and pitches in his tools after him.

Later that night, Goldie herself falls overboard, is struck by a garbage scow, and ends up in the local hospital with amnesia. Seeing her bedraggled photo on the TV news, Russell maps his revenge: He will claim Hawn as his own long-lost wife, and bring her down a notch or two by turning her into a domestic laborer and baby sitter for his four ill-behaved boys.

All together now, everybody, what happens next? Is there a scene of rebellion? And then a scene where Hawn shows how incompetent she is, even cleaning the windows with furniture polish? And a scene where Kurt and the boys play mean tricks on her? And a scene where she begins to change, just a little? And a scene where the boys get to like her? And a moment when she begins to feel she belongs with this family, and feels love and pride? And then a scene where her snotty husband turns up again? And a scene where she gets mad at Russell for having so cruelly deceived her?

If you cannot find each and every one of those scenes in *Overboard,* you're not even trying. The general outlines of this story—spoiled character is reformed by humbling experience—has even been followed before by Hawn herself in *Private Benjamin.* What makes *Overboard* special, however, is the genuine charm, wit, and warm energy that's generated by the entire cast and director Garry Marshall.

Hawn and Russell work well together, never overplaying scenes that could easily have self-destructed. The movie is filled with dozens of funny little moments, like the way McDowall arrives on time with the caviar and is bawled out for potentially being late. And the way Michael Hagerty, as Russell's best friend Billy, covers up when Hawn finds a pair of her own panties in Russell's truck and thinks they must belong to another woman ("I got lucky with one of them phone-for-sex gals").

If the ending of *Overboard* is reminiscent of *The African Queen,* maybe that's because the whole movie owes something to the Bogart-Hepburn relationship, in which a rude and crude man is civilized by a real lady. In *Overboard,* that development is cross-bred with the heartless bitch who is civilized by a real gentleman. It's kind of a nice process, and it makes a warm and funny movie.

P

Pale Rider ★ ★ ★
R, 113 m., 1985

Clint Eastwood (Preacher), Michael Moriarty (Hull Barret), Carrie Snodgress (Sarah Wheeler), Christopher Penn (Josh LaHood), Richard Dysart (Coy LaHood), Sydney Penny (Megan Wheeler), Richard Kiel (Club), Doug McGrath (Spider). Directed and produced by Clint Eastwood. Screenplay by Michael Butler and Dennis Shryack.

Clint Eastwood has become an actor whose moods and silences are so well-known that the slightest suggestion will do to convey an emotion. No actor is more aware of his own instrument, and Eastwood demonstrates that in *Pale Rider*, a film he dominates so completely that only later do we realize how little we really saw of him.

Instead of filling each scene with his own image and dialogue, Eastwood uses sleight of hand: We are shown his eyes, or a corner of his mouth, or his face in a shadow, or his figure with strong light behind it. He has few words. The other characters in the movie project their emotions upon him. He may indeed be the Pale Rider suggested in the title, whose name was death, but he may also be an avenging spirit, come back from the grave to confront the man who murdered him. One of the subtlest things in the movie is the way it plays with the possibility that Eastwood's character may be a ghost, or at least something other than an ordinary mortal.

Other things in the movie are not so subtle. In its broad outlines, *Pale Rider* is a traditional Western, with a story that has been told, in one form or another, a thousand times before. In a small California mining town, some independent miners have staked a claim to a promising lode. The town is ruled by a cabal of evil men, revolving around the local banker and the marshal, who is his hired gun. The banker would like to buy out the little miners, but, lacking that, he will use force to drive them off their land and claim it for his company.

Into this hotbed rides the lone figure of Eastwood, wearing a clerical collar and preferring to be called "Preacher." There are people here he seems to know from before. The marshal, for example, seems to be trying to remember where he has previously encountered this man. Eastwood moves in with the small miners, and becomes close with one group: a miner (Michael Moriarty) who lives with a woman (Carrie Snodgress) and her daughter (Sydney Penny). He urges the miners to take a stand and defend their land, and agrees to help them. That sets the stage for a series of violent confrontations.

As the film's director, Eastwood has done some interesting things with his vision of the West. Instead of making the miners' shacks into early American antique exhibits, he shows them as small and sparse. The sources of light are almost all from the outside. Interiors are dark and gloomy, and the sun is blinding in its intensity. The Eastwood character himself is almost always backlit, so we have to strain to see him, and this strategy makes him more mysterious and fascinating than any dialogue could have.

There are some moments when the movie's myth-making becomes self-conscious. In one scene, for example, the marshal's gunmen enter a restaurant and empty their guns into the chair where Eastwood had been sitting moments before. He is no longer there; can't they see that? In the final shoot-out, the Preacher has a magical ability to dematerialize, confounding the bad guys, and one shot (of a hand with a gun emerging from a water trough) should have been eliminated—it spoils the logic of the scene. But *Pale Rider* is, overall, a considerable achievement, a classic Western of style and excitement. Many of the greatest Westerns grew out of a director's profound understanding of the screen presence of his actors; consider, for example, John Ford's films with John Wayne and Henry Fonda. In *Pale Rider*, Clint Eastwood is the director, and having directed himself in nine previous films, he understands so well how he works on the screen that the movie has a resonance that probably was not even there in the screenplay.

The Paper Chase ★ ★ ★ ★
PG, 111 m., 1973

Timothy Bottoms (Hart), Lindsay Wagner (Susan), John Houseman (Kingsfield), Graham Beckel (Ford), Edward Herrmann (Anderson), Bob Lydiard (O'Connor). Directed by James Bridges and produced by Robert C. Thompson and Rodrick Paul. Screenplay by Bridges.

The Paper Chase is about an aggressive, very bright, terribly engaging first-year student at Harvard Law School. The movie respects its hero, respects the school, and most of all respects the venerable Professor Kingsfield, tyrant of contract law.

Kingsfield is really the movie's central character, even though John Houseman gets supporting billing for the role. Everything centers around his absolute dictatorship in the classroom and his icy reserve at all other times. He's the kind of teacher who inspires total dread in his students, and at the same time a measure of hero worship; he doesn't just know contract law, he wrote the book.

Into his classroom every autumn come several dozen would-be Harvard law graduates, who fall into the categories we all remember from school: (a) the drones, who get everything right but will go forth to lead lives of impeccable mediocrity; (b) the truly intelligent, who will pass or fail entirely on the basis of whether they're able to put up with the crap; (c) those with photographic memories, who can remember everything but connect nothing; (d) the students whose dogged earnestness will somehow pull them through; and (e) the doomed.

One of each of these types is in the study group of Hart, the movie's hero, and the one who is truly intelligent. He's a graduate of the University of Minnesota and somewhat out of place among the Ivy League types, but he does well in class because he really cares about the law. He also cares about Kingsfield, to the degree that he breaks into the library archives to examine the master's very own undergraduate notes.

Hart is played by Timothy Bottoms, the star of *The Last Picture Show*. Bottoms is an awfully good actor, and so natural and unaffected that he shows up the mannerisms of actors like Dustin Hoffman or Jon Voight. Bottoms never seems to try; he's just there, complete and convincing. He falls in love, fatefully, with Susan (Lindsay Wagner), who turns out to be, even more fatefully, Kingsfield's daughter. Their relationship is a little hard to follow in the film; we aren't sure why she treats him the way she does—after all, she loves the guy—and the movie jerks abruptly in bringing them back together after a split-up.

But that isn't fatal because the fundamental relationship in the movie is between Hart and Kingsfield. The crusty old professor obviously appreciates the intelligence and independence of his prize student, but he hardly ever lets his affection show; there's a great scene in the classroom where he calls Hart forward, offers him a dime, and says: "Call your mother and tell her you will never be a lawyer." Houseman is able to project subtleties of character even while appearing stiff and unrelenting; it's a performance of Academy Award quality, and resulted in an Oscar for Best Supporting Actor.

Lindsay Wagner, as the daughter, is also a surprise; she made her movie debut in the unfortunate *Two People*, which had Peter Fonda as a conscience-stricken Army deserter. She wasn't able to make much of an impression in that one, but *The Paper Chase* establishes her as an actress with class and the saving grace of humor.

What's best about the movie is that it considers interesting adults—young and old—in an intelligent manner. After it's over we almost feel relief; there are so many movies about clods reacting moronically to romantic and/or violent situations. But we hardly ever get movies about people who seem engaging enough to spend half an hour talking with (what would you say to Charles Bronson?). Here's one that works.

Paris, Texas ★ ★ ★ ★
R, 145 m., 1984

Harry Dean Stanton (Travis), Nastassja Kinski (Jane), Hunter Carson (Their Son), Dean Stockwell (Walt), Aurore Clement (Anne), Bernhard Wicki (Dr. Ulmer). Directed by Wim Wenders and produced by Don Guest. Screenplay by Sam Shepard.

A man walks alone in the desert. He has no memory, no past, no future. He finds an isolated settlement where the doctor, another exile, a German, makes some calls. Eventually the man's brother comes to take him back home again. Before we think about this as the beginning of a story, let's think about it very specifically as the first twenty minutes of a movie. When I was watching *Paris, Texas* for the first time, my immediate reaction to the film's opening scenes was one of intrigue: I had no good guesses about where this movie was headed, and that, in itself, was exciting, because in this most pragmatic of times, even the best movies seem to be intended as predictable consumer products. If you see a lot of movies, you can sit there watching the screen and guessing what will happen next, and be right most of the time.

That's not the case with *Paris, Texas*. This is a defiantly individual film, about loss and loneliness and eccentricity. We haven't met the characters before in a dozen other films. To some people, that can be disconcerting; I've actually read reviews of *Paris, Texas* complaining because the man in the desert is German, and that another character is French. Is it written that the people in movies have to be Middle Americans, like refugees from a sitcom?

The characters in this movie come out of the imagination of Sam Shepard, the playwright of rage and alienation, and Wim Wenders, a West German director who often makes "road movies," in which lost men look for answers in the vastness of great American cities. The lost man is played this time by Harry Dean Stanton, the most forlorn and angry of all great American character actors. We never do find out what personal cataclysm led to his walk in the desert, but as his memory begins to return, we learn how much he has lost. He was married, once, and had a little boy. The boy has been raised in the last several years by Stanton's brother (Dean Stockwell) and sister-in-law (Aurore Clement). Stanton's young wife (Nastassja Kinski) seems to have disappeared entirely in the years of his exile. The little boy is played by Hunter Carson, in one of the least affected, most convincing juvenile performances in a long time. He is more or less a typical American kid, despite the strange adults in his life. He meets Stanton and accepts him as a second father, but of course he thinks of Stockwell and Clement as his family. Stanton has a mad dream of finding his wife and putting the pieces of his past back together again. He goes looking, and finds Kinski behind the one-way mirror of one of those sad sex emporiums where men pay to talk to women on the telephone.

Paris, Texas is more concerned with exploring emotions than with telling a story. This isn't a movie about missing persons, but about missing feelings. The images in the film show people framed by the vast, impersonal forms of modern architecture; the cities seem as empty as the desert did in the opening sequence. And yet this film is not the standard attack on American alienation. It seems fascinated by America, by our music, by the size of our cities, and a land so big that a man like the Stanton character might easily get misplaced. Stanton's name in the movie is Travis, and that reminds us not only of Travis McGee, the private eye who specialized in helping lost souls, but also of lots of American Westerns in which things were simpler, and you knew who your enemy was. It is a name out of American pop culture, and the movie is a reminder that all three of the great German New Wave directors—Herzog, Fassbinder, and Wenders—have been fascinated by American rock music, American fashions, American mythology.

This is Wenders's fourth film shot at least partly in America (the others were *Alice in the Cities, The American Friend*, and *Hammett*). It also bears traces of *Kings of the Road*, his German road movie in which two men meet by chance and travel for a time together, united by their mutual inability to love and understand women. But it is better than those movies—it's his best work so far—because it links the unforgettable images to a spare, perfectly heard American idiom. The Sam Shepard dialogue has a way of allowing characters to tell us almost nothing about themselves, except for their most banal beliefs and their deepest fears.

Paris, Texas is a movie with the kind of passion and willingness to experiment that was more common fifteen years ago than it is now. It has more links with films like *Five Easy Pieces* and *Easy Rider* and *Midnight Cowboy*, than with the slick arcade games that are the box office winners of the 1980s. It is true, deep, and brilliant.

A Passage to India ★ ★ ★ ★

PG, 160 m., 1984

Judy Davis (Adela Quested), Victor Banerjee (Dr. Aziz), Peggy Ashcroft (Mrs. Moore), Alec Guinness (Godbole) James Fox (Fielding), Nigel Havers (Ronny Heaslop). Directed by David Lean and produced by John Brabourne and Richard Goodwin. Screenplay by Lean.

"Only connect!"—E.M. Forster

That is the advice he gives us in *Howard's End*, and then, in *A Passage to India*, he creates a world in which there are no connections, where Indians and Englishmen speak the same language but do not understand each other, where it doesn't matter what you say in the famous Marabar Caves, since all that comes back is a hollow, mocking, echo. Forster's novel is one of the literary landmarks of this century, and now David Lean has made it into one of the greatest screen adaptations I have ever seen.

Great novels do not usually translate well to the screen. They are too filled with ambiguities, and movies have a way of making all their images seem like literal fact. *A Passage to India* is especially tricky, because the central event in the novel is something that happens offstage, or never happens at all—take your choice. On a hot, muggy day, the eager Dr. Aziz leads an expedition to the Marabar Caves. One by one, members of the party drop out, until finally only Miss Quested, from England, is left. And so the Indian man and the British woman climb the last path alone, at a time when England's rule of India was based on an ingrained, semiofficial racism, and some British, at least, nodded approvingly at Kipling's "East is East, and West is West, and never the twain shall meet."

In Forster's novel, it is never clear exactly what it was that happened to Miss Quested after she wandered alone into one of the caves. David Lean's film leaves that question equally open. But because he is dealing with a visual medium, he cannot make it a mystery where Dr. Aziz is at the time; if you are offstage in a novel, you can be anywhere, but if you are offstage in a movie, you are definitely not where the camera is looking. So in the film version we know, or think we know, that Dr. Aziz is innocent of the charges later brought against him—of the attempted rape of Miss Quested.

The charges and the trial fill the second half of Lean's *A Passage to India*. Lean brings us to that point by a series of perfectly modulated, quietly tension-filled scenes in which Miss Quested (Judy Davis) and the kindly Mrs. Moore (Peggy Ashcroft) sail to India, where Miss Quested is engaged to marry the priggish local British magistrate in a provincial backwater. Both women want to see the "real India"—a wish that is either completely lacking among the locals, or is manfully repressed. Mrs. Moore goes walking by a temple pool by moonlight, and meets the earnest young Dr. Aziz, who is captivated by her gentle kindness. Miss Quested wanders by accident into the ruins of another temple, populated by sensuous and erotic statuary, tumbled together, overgrown by vegetation.

Miss Quested's temple visit is not in Forster, but has been added by Lean (who wrote his own screenplay). It accomplishes just what it needed, suggesting that in Miss Quested the forces of sensuality and repression run a great deal more deeply than her sexually constipated fiancé is ever likely to suspect. Meanwhile, we meet some of the other local characters, including Dr. Godbole (Alec Guinness), who meets every crisis with perfect equanimity, and who believes that what will be, will be. This philosophy sounds like recycled fortune cookies but turns out, in the end, to have been the simple truth. We also meet Fielding (James Fox), one of those tall, lonely middle-aged Englishmen who hang about the edges of stories set in the Empire, waiting until their destiny commands them to take a firm stand.

Lean places these characters in one of the

most beautiful canvases he has ever drawn (and this is the man who directed *Dr. Zhivago* and *Lawrence of Arabia*). He doesn't see the India travel posters and lurid postcards, but the India of a Victorian watercolorist like Edward Lear, who placed enigmatic little human figures here and there in spectacular landscapes that never seemed to be quite finished. Lean makes India look like an amazing, beautiful place that an Englishman can never quite put his finger on—which is, of course, the lesson Miss Quested learns in the caves.

David Lean is a meticulous craftsman, famous for going to any lengths to make every shot look just the way he thinks it should. His actors here are encouraged to give sound, thoughtful, unflashy performances (Guinness strains at the bit), and his screenplay is a model of clarity: By the end of this movie we know these people so well, and understand them so thoroughly, that only the most reckless among us would want to go back and have a closer look at those caves.

Patton ★ ★ ★ ★

PG, 171 m., 1970

George C. Scott (Patton), Karl Malden (Bradley), Stephen Young (Captain Hansen), Michael Strong (General Carver), Karl Michel Vogler (Rommel), Michael Bates (Montgomery). Directed by Franklin J. Schaffner and produced by Frank McCarthy. Screenplay by Francis Ford Coppola.

We have all of these things buried inside of us, waiting for a movie like *Patton* to release them. The reflex patriotism of World War II is still there, we discover, Vietnam has soured us on war, but not on that war. There is a small corner of our being that will always be thrilled by Patton's dash across Europe after the Germans, and we are still a little bit in admiration of heroes on his arrogant scale. And that is why, make no mistake, *Patton* is not an antiwar film. If I read one, I read half a dozen tortuous liberal rationalizations for this movie, written by people who liked it but felt guilty afterward. *Patton* is really against war, they said; by taking us almost inside the soul of the most fanatically military of all America's generals, *Patton* was supposed to fill us with distaste for militarism. It does not, of course. But neither is it a very hawklike movie. It is such an extraordinarily intelligent film, so sure of its purpose, that it makes war its medium but not its subject. It is not about war but about Patton at war, and it is one of the best screen biographies ever made.

Patton once said something to the effect that war was the supreme human activity because it forced men to operate at the ultimate limit of their abilities. This is not a very good justification for war, but it is a supreme test for men, and the action in *Patton* all takes place at the delicate balance point where the war meets the man. That was a basically brilliant idea in Francis Ford Coppola's original screenplay, but what makes it work so well in *Patton* is the performance of George C. Scott. He is absorbed into the role, and commands it. He is such a good actor that the movie doesn't have to explain a lot of things; we feel we know Patton and so we're sure of our footing. That's good, because it frees director Franklin J. Schaffner from a lot of cluttering props and plot lines. *Patton* is almost three hours long but it is a surprisingly uncomplicated movie, telling its story with clean, simple scenes and shots. Schaffner is at home here; one of the best things about his *Planet of the Apes* was the simplicity of style he found for it. If *Planet* had gotten complicated, we would have laughed at it.

The simplicity of *Patton* does not lead to any loss of subtlety; just the reverse. Because we are freed from those semiobligatory junk scenes that clutter up most war movies (the wife at home, the "human interest" drained from ethnic character actors, the battle scenes that are allowed to run too long because they cost so much) we can concentrate on the man, and we can even begin to believe we understand a warrior like this one. Because it's no good being hypocritical, I guess. Generals should be generals, and not lovable quasi-political figures like Ike or MacArthur. Patton's life was war (and how sad that really was) but he was honest enough to admit it, and the movie takes its stand on that point. And so although we deplore war we find ourselves respecting the movie; *Patton* is written and directed with integrity.

Beyond that, it's an awfully good movie, and one of its best features is the way it gets its laughs. There aren't any cheap laughs in *Patton*, but there are a lot of earned ones, all serving to flesh in our idea of this brilliant, obsessed man. And a lot of the humor is simply there, embodied in the Scott performance. It turns out *Patton* is exactly the war movie we didn't realize how much we wanted to see.

Peeping Tom ★ ★ ★ 1/2
NO MPAA RATING, 109 m., 1960

Carl Boehm (Mark Lewis), Moira Shearer (Vivian), Anna Massey (Helen Stephens), Maxine Audley (Mrs. Stephens), Edmond Knight (Arthur Baden), Bartlet Mullins (Mr. Peters). Directed and produced by Michael Powell. Screenplay by Leo Marks.

In 1960, the year in which the psychic violence of Hitchcock's *Psycho* aroused such a storm, a film named *Peeping Tom* was premiered in London, was savaged by all the major British critics, brought the career of its director nearly to an end, and was then all but forgotten. The director was Michael Powell, whose credits included *The Thief of Bagdad* and *The Red Shoes*, and who was to make only four more very low-budget films after this one. He had worked with Hitchcock in the 1920s but apparently had not learned the master's gift of disguising abnormal criminal behavior as entertainment.

Peeping Tom has remained a legendary but unseen film ever since its release and burial (Susan Sontag uses it as a reference point in *On Photography*), and now it's in the process of rediscovery. It was first seen in America at 1978's Telluride Film Festival and then was purchased for U.S. release by a group backed by Martin (*Taxi Driver*) Scorsese. Now it's on video.

Perhaps the delay of more than twenty years works in the film's favor. Its story of a lonely voyeur's sadistic killings was horrifying in 1960, and Powell's visual strategy was to cloak the story in lurid rotogravure colors and deliberately banal settings—but now the film's dated clothing, mannerisms, and locations give it an additionally creepy flavor. We're given a man whose crimes are committed through, by, and because of cameras—and it's as if those crimes have been developing in the lab all these years.

The film stars the open-faced, blond actor Carl Boehm, whose regular Teutonic features and neatly combed-back hair give him the curious look of being too straight, too regular. And of course he's the opposite. He works as an assistant movie cameraman and then comes home to the boardinghouse that used to be his father's home. Upstairs, in seclusion, his sick obsession is to run films of his murder victims—women he has photographed as he killed them.

One day, by chance, he meets the girl who lives downstairs (Anna Massey). And here we have a classic Hitchcock situation, in which a possible victim is in constant danger, we know it, and she doesn't. The girl becomes his confidant, to a degree, and he spares her ("I never want to photograph *you!*") while committing another murder and hiding the body on the set of a movie.

Massey learns from him that his father had been a perverted psychologist who wanted to record Boehm's entire childhood on film—and who filmed and tape recorded his childish screams of fright. As a man, the killer's crimes are often elaborate re-enactments of his childhood terrors.

Is the film as disgusting as the British critics found it? Yes, but it is also very moving, a case study that could have been simply sadistic but emerges (especially because of the Boehm performance) as a tragic record of a destroyed life. Perhaps that's why *Peeping Tom* was so disturbing to its first viewers: It is *not* distanced into "entertainment" like *Psycho*, but remains unforgivingly as the story of horrible crimes seen straight-on.

Peggy Sue Got Married ★ ★ ★ ★
PG-13, 103 m., 1986

Kathleen Turner (Peggy Sue), Nicholas Cage (Charlie), Barry Miller (Richard), Catherine Hicks (Carol), Joan Allen (Maddie). Directed by Francis Ford Coppola and produced by Paul R. Gurian. Screenplay by Jerry Leightling and Arlene Sarner.

We walk like ghosts through the spaces of our adolescence. We've all done it. We stroll unseen across the high school football field. We go back to the drive-in restaurants where we all hung out, all those years ago. We walk into a drugstore for some aspirin, and the magazine rack brings back a memory of sneaking a peek at a Playmate in 1959.

Certain times and places can re-create, with a headstrong rush, what it felt like to be seventeen years old—and we are sometimes more in touch with ourselves at that age than we are with the way we felt a year ago. Have you ever received a telephone message from somebody you were in love with when you were seventeen? And didn't it feel, for a second, as if it came from that long-ago teenager, and not from the adult who left it?

Peggy Sue Got Married is a lot of things—a human comedy, a nostalgic memory, a love story—but there are times when it is just plain creepy, because it awakens such vivid memories in us. It's about a woman who attends her twenty-fifth high school reunion, and passes out, and when she comes to it is 1958 and she inhabits her own teen-age body.

Those few details make the movie sound like *Back to the Future,* but give it some thought and you will see that *Peggy Sue* is not a clone, but a mirror image. In *Back to the Future,* the hero traveled backwards through time to meet his own parents when they were teen-agers. In *Peggy Sue* the heroine travels backwards to enter her own body as a teenager—and she enters it with her forty-two-year-old mind still intact.

What would you say, knowing what you know now, to the people you loved when you were seventeen? How would you feel if you picked up the telephone, and it was your grandmother's voice? Would you tell her she was going to die in another two years and three months? No, but you would know that, and wouldn't your heart leap into your throat, and wouldn't she wonder what was wrong with you, that you couldn't respond to her simple hello?

Peggy Sue Got Married provides moment after moment like that. It's like visiting a cemetery where all of the people are still alive. And yet it is a comedy. Frank Capra made comedies like this, in which the humor welled up out of a deep, even sentimental, drama of human emotions. There is a scene in the movie where the seventeen-year-old girl (with the mind of the forty-two-year-old woman) sits in the front seat of a car and necks with the teen-age boy that (she knows) she will marry and someday decide to divorce. Imagine kissing someone for the first time after you have already kissed them for the last time.

The movie stars Kathleen Turner, in a performance that must be seen to be believed. How does she play a seventeen-year-old? Not by trying to actually look seventeen, because the movie doesn't try to pull off that stunt (the convention is that the heroine looks adult to us, but like a teen-ager to the other characters). Turner, who is actually thirty-two, plays a teen-ager by making certain changes in her speech and movement: She talks more impetuously, not waiting for other people to reply, and she walks in that heedless teen-age way of those who have not yet stumbled often enough to step carefully. There is a moment when she throws herself down on her bed, and never mind what she looks like, it feels like a seventeen-year-old sprawled there. Her performance is a textbook study in body language; she knows that one of the symptoms of growing older is that you arrange your limbs more thoughtfully in repose.

The other important character in the movie is Charlie, her boyfriend and later her husband, played by Nicholas Cage. We meet him first as a local businessman in his early forties, and from the way he walks into a room you can tell he's the kind of man who inspires a lot of local gossip. He and his wife are separated and planning to divorce. When we see him again, he's the teen-age kid she's dating, and there are two delicate, wonderful scenes where she walks a tightrope, trying to relate to him as if she were a teen-ager, and as if she hadn't already shared his whole future.

That scene in the front seat of the car is a masterpiece of cross purposes; she actually wants to go all the way, and he's shocked—shocked not so much by her desire, as by a girl having the temerity to talk and act that way in the 1950s. "Jeez," he says, after she makes her move, "that's a guy's line."

The movie was directed by Francis Coppola, who seems to have been in the right place at the right time. The *Peggy Sue* project got traded around from one actor and director to another (Turner's role was originally cast with Debra Winger, and Coppola was the third director on the project). After several years in which he has tried to make technical and production breakthroughs on his movies, experimenting with new film processes and new stylistic approaches with honorable but uneven results, this time Coppola apparently simply wanted to make a movie, Permanent Recordand put some characters on the screen, and tell a story. He has, all right. This was one of the best movies of 1986.

Performance ★ ★ ½
R, 105 m., 1970

James Fox (Charles), Mick Jagger (Turner), Anita Pallenberg (Pherber), Michele Breton (Lucy), Ann Sidney (Dana), John Bindon (Moody). Directed by Donald Cammell and Nicolas Roeg. Screenplay by Cammell.

Performance is a bizarre, disconnected attempt to link the inhabitants of two kinds of London underworlds: pop stars and gangsters. It isn't altogether successful, largely because it tries too hard and doesn't pace itself to let its effects sink in. But it does have a kind of frantic energy, and it introduced Mick Jagger in a role that reinforced his stage image without copying it. The movie is really about images anyway. On its most fundamental plot level, it's about a gangster (James Fox) who is trying to disguise himself so that he can slip out of England on a forged passport. He meets the Jagger character by accident when he takes a basement room in a boarding house.

Jagger is introduced as a top star of two or three years ago who has "retired" and hidden away to work on his memoirs or something. Mostly he seems to have submerged himself in a hedonistic existence with two girls, a variety of drugs, and a cloying assortment of Eastern artifacts. Almost every shot in his apartment is aimed past candles, incense, wall hangings, tapestries, and all that, and half the time we're even getting the Turkish rug reflected in the mirror.

This is not exactly the environment your everyday white-collar gangster feels at home in, but Fox plays a strange character who never feels at home anywhere. His workaday style is to beat and threaten potential "protection" customers. But despite his enthusiasm, he isn't really accepted even by the boss (every gangster has a boss) and his associates. So Jagger's little corner of London seems much like any other to him, affording a hideout until he can get the passport and fly to New York. Alas, Jagger doesn't see it that way, and over the course of a day or two, the gangster is sucked down into a psychedelic whirlpool with Jagger and the two girls. One of them feeds him a hallucinogenic mushroom, after which the other dresses him in the unisex clothes they all wear, and then we get a lot of obligatory psychedelic photography showing the poor guy losing his identity, or his values, or in any event his inclination to escape.

The movie is so nervously edited that it doesn't stay around to develop the effects it introduces. That was a tendency with many semi-experimental British films of the early seventies; they were so concerned with reminding us they're movies that they don't do the work movies should. The first half of the movie is especially distracting. But after the gangster and the pop star meet, the editing and the story settle into a kind of consistency.

The surprise of the movie, and the reason to see it, is Mick Jagger's performance. It isn't simply good; it's a comment on his life and style. The ads emphasized his unisex appearance, and the role does so even more. When he slicks back his hair during a psychedelic fantasy, and seems to adopt the gangster's lifestyle, we're looking at acting insights of a very complex psychological order. Other than that, the movie is neither very good nor very bad. Interesting.

Permanent Record ★ ★ ★ ★
PG-13, 92 m., 1988 ✓

Alan Boyce (David Sinclair), Keanu Reeves (Chris Townsend), Michelle Meyrink (J.G.), Jennifer Rubin (Lauren), Pamela Gidley (Kim), Michael Elgart (Jake), Richard Bradford (Leo Verdell). Directed by Marisa Silver and produced by Frank Mancuso Jr. Screenplay by Jarre Fees, Alice Liddle, and Larry Ketron.

The opening shot of *Permanent Record* is ominous and disturbing, and we don't know why. In an unbroken movement, the camera tracks past a group of teen-agers who have parked their cars on a bluff overlooking the sea, and are hanging out casually, their friendship too evident to need explaining. There seems to be no "acting" in this shot, and yet it is superbly acted, because it feels so natural that we accept at once the idea that these kids have been close friends for a long time. Their afternoon on the bluff seems superficially happy, and yet there is a brooding quality to the shot, perhaps inspired by the lighting, or by the way the camera circles vertiginously above the sea below.

The following scenes unfold, it seems, almost without plan. We meet a couple of kids who play in a rock band together, and try to sneak into a recording studio, and are thrown out, and arrive at school late. We meet the high school principal, a man who is enormously intriguing because he reveals so little, and yet still succeeds in revealing goodness. We meet the crowd that these two kids hang out with, and we attend some auditions for a school production of *The Pirates of Penzance*. We are impressed by the fact that these teen-agers are intelligent, thoughtful, and articulate; they come from a different planet than most movie teen-agers.

To describe the opening scenes makes them seem routine, and yet they captured my attention with an intensity I still do not understand. The underlying mystery of many good movies is the way they absorb us in apparently unremarkable details, while bad movies can lose us even with car crashes and explosions. Marisa Silver, who directed this film, and Frederick Elmes, who photographed it, have done something very subtle and strong here, have seen these students and their school in a way that inescapably prepares us for something, without revealing what it is.

The kids all hang out together, but one begins to attract our attention more than the others. He is David (Alan Boyce), an intense, dark-eyed musician who everyone knows is gifted. He leads the rock band, gives lessons to his fellow musicians, and is arranging the music for the production of *Pirates*. In a scene of inexplicable tension, he is told by the principal (Richard Bradford) that he's won a scholarship to a great music school. He tries to seem pleased, but complains that he is so busy—too busy. Bradford quietly reminds him the scholarship isn't until next year.

And then . . . but here I want to suggest that if you plan to see the film, you should read no further and permit yourself its surprises. I began watching this film knowing absolutely nothing about it, and this is the kind of film where that is an advantage. Let the movie unfold like life. Save the review until later.

I found myself impressed, most of all, by the subtlety with which Silver and her writers (Jarre Fees, Alice Liddle, and Larry Ketron) develop David's worsening crisis. This is not a young man made unhappy by the usual problems of TV docudramas. He doesn't use drugs, his girlfriend isn't pregnant, he isn't flunking out of school, and he doesn't have an unhappy home life. But it becomes clear, especially in retrospect, that there is no joy in his life, and we see that most clearly in the understated scene in the bedroom of the girl he sometimes sleeps with. Any other couple who do what they do together, she suggests, would be said to be going together. He nods.

There is something missing here. Some kind of connection with other people. Some exultation in his own gifts and talents. Giving guitar lessons to his friend Chris (Keanu Reeves), he is a little impatient; Chris does not strive hard enough for excellence. David, who is admired by everyone in his school, who is the one singled out by his friends for great success, has a deep sadness inside himself because he is not good enough. And that leads to the scene in which one moment he is on the side of that high bluff, and the next moment he is not.

The rest of the movie is about his friends—about the gulf he has left behind, and about their sorrow, and their rage at him. Again and again, Silver and her writers find authentic ways to portray emotions. We never feel manipulated, because the movie works too close to the heart. Perhaps the best scene in the whole film is the one where Chris, drunk, drives his car into David's yard and almost hits David's younger brother, and then, when David's father comes out on the lawn to shout angrily at him, Chris falls into his arms, weeping and shouting, "I should have stopped him." And the father holds him.

Life goes on. The school production is held. There is a dramatic moment in which David is eulogized, and there is also the sense that years from now his friends will sometimes remember him, be angry with him, and wonder what would have become of him. This is one of the year's best films, and one reason for its power is that it clearly knows what it wants to do, and how to do it. It is not a film about the causes of David's death, and it does not analyze or explain. It is a film about the event, and about the memory of the event. The performances, seemingly artless, are appropriate to the material, and I was especially impressed by the way Bradford suggested so many things about the principal while seeming to reveal so little.

Permanent Record is Marisa Silver's second

feature, after the wonderful *Old Enough* (1984), which told the story of a friendship between two thirteen-year-old girls who were from opposite sides of the tracks but were on the same side of adolescence. In that film and this one, she shows that she has a rare gift for empathy, and that she can see right to the bottoms of things without adding a single gratuitous note.

Personal Best ★ ★ ★ ★
R, 124 m., 1982

Mariel Hemingway (Chris Cahill), Patrice Donnelly (Tory Skinner), Scott Glenn (Coach), Kenny Moore (Denny Stites). Directed and produced by Robert Towne. Screenplay by Towne.

Robert Towne's *Personal Best* tells the story of two women who are competitors for pentathlete berths on the 1980 U.S. Olympics team—the team that did not go to Moscow. The women are attracted to one another almost at first sight, and what begins as a tentative exploration develops into a love relationship. Then the romance gets mixed up with the ferocity of top-level sports competition.

What distinguishes *Personal Best* is that it creates *specific* characters—flesh-and-blood people with interesting personalities, people I cared about. *Personal Best* also seems knowledgeable about its two subjects, which are the weather of these women's hearts, and the world of Olympic sports competition.

It is a movie containing the spontaneity of life. It's about living, breathing, changeable people and because their relationships seems to be so deeply felt, so important to them, we're fascinated by what may happen next. The movie stars Mariel Hemingway and Patrice Donnelly as the two women track stars, Scott Glenn as their coach, and Kenny Moore as the Olympic swimmer who falls in love with Hemingway late in the film. These four people are so right for the roles it's almost scary; it makes us sense the difference between performances that are technically excellent and other performances, like these, that may sometimes be technically rough but always find the correct emotional note.

Mariel Hemingway plays a young, naive natural athlete. We sense that she always has been under the coaching thumb of her father, a perfectionist, and that her physical excellence has been won at the cost of emotional maturity. She knows everything about working out, and next to nothing about her heart, her sexuality, her own identity. She loses an important race at a preliminary meet, is sharply handled by the father, gets sick to her stomach, is obviously emotionally distraught.

Patrice Donnelly, as a more experienced athlete, tries to comfort the younger girl. In a dormitory room that night, they talk. Donnelly shares whatever wisdom she has about training and running and winning. They smoke a joint. They kid around. They arm wrestle. At this point, watching the film, I had an interesting experience. I did not already know that the characters in the film were homosexual, but I found myself thinking that the scene was so erotically charged that, "if Hollywood could be honest," it would develop into a love scene. Just then, it did! "This is scary," Donnelly says, and then she kisses Hemingway, who returns the kiss.

Personal Best is not simply about their romance, however, It is about any relationship in which the trust necessary for love is made to compete with the total egotism necessary for championship sports. *Can* two people love each other, and at the same time compete for the same berth on an Olympic team? Scott Glenn, the coach, doesn't think so. He accepts the fact of his two stars' homosexuality, but what bothers him is a suspicion that Donnelly may be using emotional blackmail to undercut Hemingway's performance.

This is a very physical movie, one of the healthiest and sweatiest celebrations of physical exertion I can remember. There is a lot of nudity in the film—not only erotic nudity, although there is some of that, but also locker room and steam room nudity, and messing around nudity that has an unashamed, kidding freshness to it. One scene that shocks some viewers occurs between Mariel Hemingway and Kenny Moore, when he gets up to go to the bathroom and she decides to follow along; the scene is typical of the kind of unforced, natural spontaneity in the whole film. The characters in *Personal Best* seem to be free to have real feelings. It is filled with the uncertainties, risks, cares, and rewards of real life, and it considers its characters' hearts and minds, and sees their sexuality as an expression of their true feelings for each other.

Personal Services ★ ★ ★ ½
R, 97 m., 1987

Julie Walters (Christine Painter), Alec McCowen (Wing Commander Morton), Shirley Stelfox (Shirley), Danny Schiller (Dolly), Victoria Hardcastle (Rose), Tim Woodward (Timms). Directed by Terry Jones and produced by Tim Bevan. Screenplay by David Leland.

I'm writing this review in London, where the papers for the last few days have been filled with the scandal of the Conservative member of Parliament who had to resign his constituency after being convicted of spanking two male prostitutes who were younger than twenty-one, which is the age of consent for homosexual spankings in Britain. (Female prostitutes can legally be spanked once they are sixteen. There'll always be an England.)

This morning on the radio, they interviewed Cynthia Payne, who said she was shocked that this fine public servant had to have his reputation ruined: "What's wrong with wanting to slap somebody's bottom once in a while, so long as no harm is done? We all have our peculiarities, we just cover them up, that's all." She sounded just like all other housewives on the call-in show.

This was the same Cynthia Payne who has become something of a folk legend over here for operating what the tabloids called "the House of Cyn," a brothel catering to middle-age and elderly gentlemen with rather specialized tastes. Nicknamed the "Luncheon Voucher Madame" because she sometimes charged as little as you'd pay for a nice plate of sausages-and-mashed, Payne was acquitted on her latest round of charges and greeted outside the law court by a street full of her cheering supporters.

Payne has always insisted she did not engage in sex herself and did not supply sex to her clients. Instead, there were naughty fashion shows featuring lace undies, see-through nighties, and leather corsets. Also available were such specialties as charging men for the privilege of doing the housework and weeding her garden. Military men and successful businessmen were especially keen for the humiliation; it took their minds off their responsibilities.

Personal Services, by the Monty Python veteran Terry Jones, is an attempt to explore the peculiarly mercenary world of Payne. She is called "Christine Painter" in the movie but nevertheless is listed as an adviser and went to New York on a public relations tour. She began as a waitress who invested her savings in cheap flats and only got into the brothel-keeping business because hookers paid their rent on time.

As the movie tells it, Payne never really even intended to go into business; she just kept running across nice gentlemen who liked a bit of naughtiness once in a while. She preferred older gentlemen; they caused less trouble and were more grateful. And, as she told the court, an evening at the "House of Cyn" simply involved having a few old friends over for a party. It was all very innocent; they preferred their crumpets with tea.

Personal Services is not a sensational movie, nor does it want to be. It is a study of banality, with flashes of genuine comedy, as when a retired war hero (Alec McCowen) takes the press on a tour of the House while singing the praises of transvestism.

The heroine is played by Julie Walters, seen in the Oscar-nominated title role of *Educating Rita* and she has it just right: the tight lips, polite reserve, the proper manner and bearing, all designed to keep passion and sex in different departments, where they belong.

The British law, on the other hand, comes across as more obsessed by sex than anyone at the madam's parties. Plainclothesmen infiltrate the goings-on and deliver breathless accounts of whips and leather knickers. Many of the clients are only too happy to go into the dock and testify to the underlying innocence of their particular hobbies, and by the end of the film there is the suggestion that the heroine probably will keep right on doing what she does best: having friends in for little parties. Which, as it turned out, was exactly what happened.

Picnic at Hanging Rock ★ ★ ★ ½
PG, 110 m., 1980

Rachel Roberts (Miss Appleyard), Dominic Guard (Fitzhubert), Helen Morse (Dianne), Jacki Weaver (Minnie). Directed by Peter

Weir and produced by James and Hal McElroy. Screenplay by Cliff Green.

Peter Weir's *Picnic at Hanging Rock* has something of the same sense of mystery and buried terror as Antonioni's *L'Aventura*—another film about a sudden and disquieting disappearance. But it's more lush and seductive than Antonioni's spare black-and-white images: Weir films an Australian landscape that could be prehistoric, that suggests that men have not come this way before . . . and that, quite possibly, they should not have come this time.

"This time" is 1900, when much of Australia remained unseen by European eyes, but when a staid and proper version of European culture had been established at such places as Appleyard College, presented here as a boarding school for proper young ladies. As is almost always the case in movies about proper boarding schools, an undercurrent of repressed sexuality runs through Appleyard, and especially through the person of its headmistress (Rachel Roberts).

We get a preliminary sense of that in the film's opening scenes, which show several of the young ladies preparing to spend the day picnicking at nearby Hanging Rock, a geological outcropping from time immemorial. And then there is the picnic itself, with the girls in their bonnets and parasols and immaculate white dresses, dappled in sunlight.

The film moves here at a deliberately lazy pace. The sun beats down, insects drone—and four of the young ladies, having climbed halfway up into the rock passages, are overcome by torpor. When they awake, three of them climb farther on, never to be seen again. The fourth, badly frightened, returns to the main group. A search is set into motion, and the local constable questions witnesses who saw the young girls later on in the day, but the mystery of their disappearance remains unsolved.

It's that very inconclusiveness, linked with later scenes in which the cruel nature of the headmistress is developed, that make *Picnic at Hanging Rock* so haunting. What's going on here, we ask, knowing there is no possible answer and half-pleased by the enigma. The film opens itself to our interpretations: Is the disappearance a punishment, real or imagined, for the girls' stirring sexuality? Is it a rebuke from the ancient landscape against the brash inroads of civilization? Or is it, as it was in the famous Antonioni film, a statement of nihilism: These people have disappeared, so might we, it all matters nothing, life goes on meaninglessly.

Picnic at Hanging Rock of course subscribes to none of those readings or to any reading. I've heard its ending described as inconclusive (it is) and frustrating (ditto). But *why not?* Do we want a rational explanation? Arrest and trial for vagabond kidnappers? An autopsy revealing broken necks? Poisonous snakes named as the culprits? If this film *had* a rational and tidy conclusion, it would be a good deal less interesting. But as a tantalizing puzzle, a tease, a suggestion of forbidden answer just out of earshot, it works hypnotically and very nicely indeed.

Pixote ★ ★ ★ ★

R, 127 m., 1981

Fernando Ramos da Silva (Pixote), Marilla Pera (Sueli), Jorge Juliao (Lilica), Gilberto Moura (Dito). Directed by Hector Babenco and produced by Sylvia B. Naves. Screenplay by Babenco and Jorge Duran.

Kids love to play by the rules. They're great at memorizing them. They repeat them to one another like ancient commandments. They never pause to question them. For the kids in *Pixote*, the rules apply to their lives in the streets as thieves, beggars, and child prostitutes. These kids are only ten or twelve years old, and at the beginning of *Pixote* we learn that there are hundreds of thousands of them living in the streets of Rio and Sao Paolo, Brazil, where more than half the population is younger than eighteen.

Pixote is the story of one of those chldren, called Pixote because he is small and wide-eyed and solemn-faced and the name seems to fit. He is not a bad kid, but he lives in a fearsome environment, in which all crimes, even the most violent, are part of the daily routine. Some of the children who commit these crimes are too young to even fully understand the gravity of taking a human life. To them, a gun or a knife is a coveted possession, a prize captured from the adult world, and to use it is to gain in stature.

There is no attempt to reform these kids. They're rounded up from time to time, after a particularly well-publicized theft, mugging, or killing. They're thrown into corrupt reformatories that act as schools for crime. For all of them, the overwhelming fact of their society—the only *law* they finally understand—is that they are immune from the full force of the law until they are eighteen. They almost seem to interpret this as a license to steal, a license revoked on their eighteenth birthday, when real life begins.

Hector Babenco's film follows Pixote and several other street children through a crucial passage in their lives. They survive, they steal, they engage in innocent entertainments, they impassively observe the squalor around them, they pass through reformatory jails, they sit on the beach and dream of the future, and their lives lead up to a moment of unplanned, almost accidental violence.

Babenco shot his film on location, on the streets and inside the slum rooms of Brazil's big cities. He also cast it from among the street children themselves. Twenty-one homeless, parentless children play themselves, more or less, in this movie, and the leading character (Fernando Ramos da Silva) is an untrained, uneducated young orphan who succeeds, in this film, in creating a performance of utterly convincing realism. The film's other great performance is by Marilla Pera, as the prostitute who adopts him. (Pera won the National Society of Film Critics award for best actress for this performance; da Silva returned to the streets and was killed by police bullets in 1988.)

Babenco's filmmaking method, of casting actual people to play themselves, and then shooting on the locations where they live and work, has been used before, most successfully by the Italian neorealists. Such films as Vittorio De Sica's *Bicyle Thief* and *Shoeshine* were cast with non-actors and shot on location, and they captured a freshness and actuality that influenced the look and feel of subsequent mainstream films: After the neorealists, there was a movement in the studio films of the 1950s and 1960s toward performances, dialogue, and sets that reflected more of real life and less of the stylized Hollywood fantasies of the 1930s.

De Sica's story lines, however, were heavily, if simply, plotted, and his films drew clear conclusions about the social injustices suffered by his characters. *Pixote* is just as angry and committed as *Bicyle Thief*, but it has more of a documentary freedom. Even though it is loosely based on a novel, Babenco's film sometimes seems to be following characters no matter what they're inclined to do or say.

The one scene in the film that does seem planned is the last one, of a prostitute nursing a mournful child at her breast—and that scene, of course, is directly from John Steinbeck's *The Grapes of Wrath*, where even at the time it seemed contrived and too obviously symbolic.

The film otherwise moves with the very rhythms of life itself. It shows evil deeds (thefts, muggings, killings) that have no evil perpetrators; both criminal and target are victims. And it shows a society that perpetrates a class of child criminals because it is incapable of even really *seeing* them clearly, let alone helping to improve their lives. *Pixote* is one of the very best realistic dramas of modern cinema.

Places in the Heart ★ ★ ★

PG, 110 m., 1984

Sally Field (Edna Spaulding), John Malkovich (Mr. Will), Danny Glover (Mose), Lindsay Crouse (Margaret Lomax), Ed Harris (Wayne Lomax), Amy Madigan (Viola Kelsey). Directed by Robert Benton and produced by Arlene Donovan. Screenplay by Benton.

The places referred to in the title of Robert Benton's movie are, he has said, places that he holds sacred in his own heart: The small town in Texas where he grew up, various friends and relatives he remembers from those days, the little boy that he once was, and the things that happened or almost happened. His memories provide the material for a wonderful movie, and he has made it, but unfortunately he hasn't stopped at that. He has gone on to include too much. He tells a central story of great power, and then keeps leaving it to catch us up with minor characters we never care about.

The main story stars Sally Field as a sheriff's widow who learns from the banker that times are hard and she should sell her farm and maybe board her kids with somebody else. She refuses. She will keep the farm and keep the kids, thank you, although she's not sure just how that will work. Then a black hobo comes knocking at the back door, asking for food, and he sort of insists that he is just the man to plant her acreage in cotton and farm it. He knows all there is to know about cotton. Since Field has no choice, she takes the man at his word, and he plants the cotton. Meanwhile, the banker, trying to solve a family problem and maybe help her at the same time, brings around a blind relative named Mr. Will, who will be a paying boarder. The three adults and the two kids form a little family that pulls together to make that farm work—and that is the central story of *Places in the Heart.*

Unfortunately, there are other stories. We meet Field's sister (Lindsay Crouse), and her brother-in-law (Ed Harris), and the local woman (Amy Madigan) he's having an affair with. Their stories function as counterpoint to the drama on the farm, but who cares? We learn just enough about the other characters to suspect that there might be a movie in their stories—but not this one, please, when their adulteries and betrayals have nothing to do with the main story.

Places in the Heart is the kind of movie where people tend to dismiss the parts they don't like. I've seen some reviews where the story of Field and the farm is the only part of the movie the critics refer to, as if Crouse, Harris, and Madigan had slipped their minds. That's wishful thinking. The subplot is there, and it's an unnecessary distraction, and it robs the movie of a lot of the sheer narrative power it would have had otherwise. It also robs us of a chance to learn more about the relationships among Field, the black farmer (Danny Glover), and the blind boarder (John Malkovich). What a group of unforgettable characters! What do they talk about in their evenings at home? Do they ever get into politics or philosophy? This is Texas in the Depression: How do they think the neighbors like the idea of a black man helping a white woman farm her land? The movie spends so much time watching the hanky-panky at the dances in town that when the Ku Klux Klan suddenly turns up in the movie, it's like it dropped out of a tree.

The movie's last scene has caused a lot of comment. It is a dreamy, idealistic fantasy in which all the characters in the film—friends and enemies, wives and mistresses, living and dead, black and white—take communion together at a church service. This is a scene of great vision and power, but it's too strong for the movie it concludes. *Places in the Heart* can't support such an ending, because it hasn't led up to it with a narrative that was straight and well-aimed as an arrow. The story was on the farm and not in the town, and although the last scene tries to draw them together, you can't summarize things that have nothing in common.

Planes, Trains and Automobiles

★ ★ ★ 1/2

R, 93 m., 1987

Steve Martin (Neal Page), John Candy (Del Griffith). Directed and produced by John Hughes. Screenplay by Hughes.

The letters in the title of *Planes, Trains and Automobiles* roar across the screen like a streamliner, and the movie itself has the same confidence. The movie tells the story of two travelers who share a modest wish in life, to fly from LaGuardia to O'Hare on schedule, and it follows with complete logic the chain of events that leads them to share a soggy bed in a cheap motel in Wichita.

The travelers are played by Steve Martin and John Candy, Martin as the fastidious, anal-compulsive snob, and Candy as the big, unkempt shower-ring salesman with a weakness for telling long stories without punch lines. Both actors are perfectly cast, not so much because they are physically matched to their roles as because the movie is able to see past their differences to an essential sweetness they share.

The film was written and directed by John Hughes, who previously specialized in high-quality teen-age movies such as *Sixteen Candles* and *The Breakfast Club*. One hallmark of Hughes's work is his insistence that his characters have recognizable human qualities; he doesn't work with a cookie cutter, and the teen-age roles he wrote for Molly Ringwald, Emilio Estevez, Ally Sheedy, Matthew Broderick, and others helped transform Hollywood's idea of what a teen-age movie could be. Hughes's comedies always contain a serious undercurrent, attention to some sort of universal human dilemma that his screenplay helps to solve.

All of which may seem a million miles away from Steve Martin and John Candy, whom we left on that beer-soaked mattress in Kansas ("You should have known what would happen when you left a six-pack on a vibrating mattress," Martin complains). But *Planes, Trains and Automobiles* is a screwball comedy with a heart, and after the laughter is over, the film has generated a lot of good feeling.

The story opens in Manhattan a few days before Thanksgiving, when Candy grabs a taxi that Martin thought was his. The two men meet again at a departure lounge at LaGuardia, where their flight to Chicago has been delayed by bad weather. Martin immediately recognizes the other man as the SOB who got his cab, and inevitably, when they finally board the plane, he finds himself bumped out of first class and wedged into a center seat next to the ample Candy.

The flight eventually takes off, only to be diverted to Wichita, where Candy has enough connections through the shower-ring business to get them a room—one room with one bed. This is the beginning of a two-day nightmare for the fastidious Martin, who at one point screams at Candy that he snores and smokes, his socks smell, and his jokes aren't funny. How bad are Candy's jokes? Martin pulls out all the stops. He'd rather attend an insurance seminar than listen to one more of them. During Martin's long outburst, the camera holds on Candy's face, and we see that he is hurt, not offended. He only wants to please, to make friends, and, as usual, he has tried too hard.

Back at the Wichita airport the next morning, Martin tries to dump Candy, but fate has linked them together. Through a series of horrible misadventures on trains, buses, semi-trailer trucks, and automobiles, they end up on a highway somewhere in southern Illinois, trying to explain to a state trooper why they are driving a car that has not only crashed but burned.

There are a lot of big laughs in *Planes, Trains and Automobiles*, including the moment when the two men wake up cuddled together in the motel room, and immediately leap out of bed and begin to make macho talk about the latest Bears game. The movie's a terrific comedy, but it's more than that, because eventually Hughes gives the Martin and Candy characters some genuine depth. We begin to understand the dynamics of their relationship, and to see that although they may be opposites, they have more in common than they know. This is a funny movie, but also a surprisingly warm and sweet one.

Platoon ★ ★ ★ ★

R, 119 m., 1986

Tom Berenger (Barnes), Willem Dafoe (Sergeant Elias), Charlie Sheen (Chris), Forest Whitaker (Big Harold), Francesco Quinn (Raah), John C. McGinaly (Sergeant O'Nill), Richard Edson (Sal), Kevin Dillon (Bunny). Directed by Oliver Stone and produced by Arnold Kopelson. Screenplay by Stone.

It was Francois Truffaut who said that it's not possible to make an anti-war movie, because all war movies, with their energy and sense of adventure, end up making combat look like fun. If Truffaut had lived to see *Platoon*, he might have wanted to modify his opinion. Here is a movie that regards combat from ground level, from the infantryman's point of view, and it does not make war look like fun.

The movie was written and directed by Oliver Stone, who fought in Vietnam and who has tried to make a movie about the war that is not fantasy, not legend, not metaphor, not message, but simply a memory of what it seemed like at the time to him.

The movie is narrated by a young soldier (Charlie Sheen) based on Stone himself; a middle-class college kid who volunteers for the war because he considers it his patriotic duty, and who is told, soon after he arrives in the combat zone, "You don't belong here." He believes it.

There are no false heroics in this movie, and no standard heroes; the narrator is quickly at the point of physical collapse, bedeviled by long marches, no sleep, ants, snakes, cuts, bruises, and constant, gnawing fear. In a scene near the beginning of the film, he is on guard duty when he clearly sees enemy troops approaching his position, and he freezes. He will only gradually, unknowingly, become an adequate soldier.

The movie is told in a style that rushes headlong into incidents. There is no carefully mapped plot to lead us from point to point, and instead, like the characters, we are usually disoriented. Anything is likely to happen, usually without warning. From the crowded canvas, large figures emerge: Barnes (Tom Berenger), the veteran sergeant with the scarred face, the survivor of so many hits that his men believe he cannot be killed; Elias (Willem Dafoe), another good fighter, but a man who tries to escape from the reality through drugs; Bunny (Kevin Dillon), the scared kid, who has become dangerous because that seems like a way to protect himself.

There is rarely a clear, unequivocal shot of an enemy soldier. They are wraiths, half-seen in the foliage, their presence scented on jungle paths, evidence of their passage unearthed in ammo dumps buried beneath villages. Instead, there is the clear sense of danger all around, and the presence of civilians who sometimes enrage the troops just by standing there and looking confused and helpless.

There is a scene in the movie that seems inspired by My Lai, although it does not develop into a massacre. As we share the suspicion that these villagers may, in fact, be harboring enemy forces, we share the fear that turns to anger, and we understand the anger that turns to violence.

Some of the men in *Platoon* have lost their bearings, are willing to kill almost anyone on the least pretext. Others still retain some measure of the morality of the situation. Since their own lives may also be at stake in their arguments, there is a great sense of danger when they disagree; we see Americans shooting other Americans, and we can understand why.

After seeing *Platoon*, I fell to wondering why Stone was able to make such an effective movie without falling into the trap Truffaut spoke about—how he made the movie riveting without making it exhilarating. Here's how I think he did it. He abandoned the choreography that is standard in almost all war movies. He abandoned any attempt to make it clear where the various forces were in relation to each other, so that we never know where "our" side stands and where "they" are. Instead of battle scenes in which lines are clearly drawn, his combat scenes involve 360 degrees. Any shot might be aimed at friend or enemy, and in the desperate rush of combat, many of his soldiers never have a clear idea of exactly who they are shooting at, or why.

Traditional movies impose a sense of order upon combat. Identifying with the soldiers, we feel that if we duck behind this tree or jump into this ditch, we will be safe from the fire that is coming from over there. In *Platoon*, there is the constant fear that any movement offers a fifty-fifty chance between a safe place or an exposed one. Stone sets up his shots to deny us the feeling that combat makes sense.

The Vietnam War is the central moral and political issue of the last quarter century for Americans. It has inspired some of the greatest recent American films: *Apocalyse Now, The Deer Hunter, Coming Home, The Killing Fields*. Now here is the film that, in a curious way, should have been made before any of the others. A film that says—as the Vietnam Memorial in Washington says—that before you can make any vast sweeping statements about Vietnam, you have to begin by understanding the bottom line, which is that a lot of people went over there and got killed, dead, and that is what the war meant for them.

Play It Again, Sam ★ ★ ★

PG, 85 m., 1972

Woody Allen (Allan), Diane Keaton (Linda), Tony Roberts (Dick), Jerry Lacy (Bogart), Susan Anspach (Nancy), Jennifer Salt (Sharon), Joy Bang (Julie), Viva (Jennifer). Directed by Herbert Ross and produced by Arthur P. Jacobs. Screenplay by Woody Allen.

Allan lives in an apartment furnished with movie trivia. He sleeps beneath a poster for *Across the Pacific*, shaves with *Casablanca* reflected in the mirror, and fries his eggs across from *The Big Sleep*. There is not a place in the apartment from which the names Mary Astor and Sydney Greenstreet cannot be read. He is a Humphrey Bogart fan. He is more than that. He is a Humphrey Bogart pupil.

Allan's wife moved out some weeks ago and is suing for divorce, so now there are only the two people living in the apartment: Allan and Bogie. Whenever Allan reaches a crisis in his life, Bogie appears. His snap-brim is pulled down low over his eyes, and the collar is turned up on his trench coat, and there is a gat in his pocket and a Chesterfield in his mug.

"Tell her your life has changed since you met her," Bogie advises. Allan turns toward the lovely brunette sitting next to him on the sofa. He turns back to Bogie. "She won't fall for that!" Allan says. "Oh no?" says Bogie. "Try it and see."

This is pretty high-class advice, but Allan is a mess around girls. He's your average, ordinary movie freak, perfectly at home in the dark cave of a revival theater, watching the airport scene from *Casablanca.* But get him away from the movies and he gets . . . nervous. His friends try to take him to the beach. "I hate the beach! I hate the sun!" he cries. "I'm pale and I'm redheaded! I don't tan—I stroke!"

You can see that he has problems, even with Bogie on his side. His friends, Linda and Dick, try to fix him up with girls, but he splashes himself with too much Canoe and then destroys his furniture during a seizure of nonchalance. After a while it begins to occur to him that he's in love with Linda, and she likes him, and Dick is always on the phone making real estate deals.

All of this is slightly less mad than your usual Woody Allen comedy, maybe because *Play It Again, Sam* is based on Woody's Broadway play, and with a play it's a little hard to work in material like a Howard Cosell play-by-play of an assassination in South America. Still, as comedies go, this is a very funny one. Woody Allen is one of those rare comedians who understands that humor can be based on pathos as well as sadism. While the high-pressure comics overwhelm us with aggressive humor, Woody is off in the bathroom somewhere being attacked by a hairdryer.

The notion of using a Bogart character is surprisingly successful. The Bogie imitation by Jerry Lacy is good, if not great, and the movie begins and ends with variations on that great *Casablanca* ending. That, and the movie's rather conventional Broadway plot structure, give it more coherence than the previous Woody Allen films, *Take the Money and Run* and *Bananas.* Maybe the movie has too much coherence, and the plot is too predictable; that's a weakness of films based on well-made Broadway plays. Still, that's hardly a serious complaint about something as funny as *Play It Again, Sam.*

Play Misty for Me ★ ★ ★ ★
R, 102 m., 1971

Clint Eastwood (Disc Jockey), Jessica Walter (Strange Woman), Donna Mills (Girlfriend), Don Siegel (Bartender). Directed by Clint Eastwood and produced by Robert Daley. Screenplay by Jo Heims and Dean Reisner.

The girl calls up every night at about the same time and asks the disc jockey to play "Misty" for her. Some nights he does. He's the all-night man on a small station in Carmel who plays records, reads poems, and hopes to make it someday in the big city. After work (and before work, for that matter) he drinks free at bars around town, places he sometimes mentions on the air. He had a steady girl for a while, but he's been free-lancing recently, and one night he picks up a girl in a bar. Or maybe she picks him up. She's the girl who likes "Misty." She is also mad. She insinuates herself into his life with a passionate jealousy, and we gradually come to understand that she is capable of violence. At the same time, the disc jockey's old love turns up in town, and he wants nothing more than to allow himself, finally, to quit playing the field and marry her. But the new girl doesn't see it that way. And she has this thing for knives.

Play Misty for Me is not the artistic equal of *Psycho,* but in the business of collecting an audience into the palm of its hand and then squeezing hard, it is supreme. It doesn't depend on a lot of surprises to maintain the suspense. There ARE some surprises, sure, but mostly the film's terror comes from the fact that the strange woman is capable of anything.

The movie was Clint Eastwood's debut as a director, and it was a good beginning. He must have learned a lot during seventeen years of working for other directors. In particular, he must have learned a lot from Don Siegel, who directed his previous four movies and has a bit part (the bartender) in this one. There is no wasted energy in *Play Misty for Me.* Everything contributes to the accumulation of terror, until even the ordinary, daytime scenes seem to have unspeakable things lurking beneath them.

In this connection, Eastwood succeeds in filming the first Semi-Obligatory Lyrical Interlude that works. The Semi-OLI, you'll recall, is the scene where the boy and girl walk in the meadow and there's a hit song on the sound track. In Eastwood's movie, he walks in the meadow with the girl, but the scene has been prepared so carefully that the meadow looks ominous. The grass looks muddy, the shadows are deep, the sky is gray, and there is a chill in the air. The whole visual style of the movie is strangely threatening.

The movie revolves around the character of the girl, who is played with an unnerving effectiveness by Jessica Walter. She is something like flypaper; the more you struggle against her personality, the more tightly you're held. Clint Eastwood, in directing himself, shows that he understands his unique movie personality. He is strong but somehow passive, he possesses strength but keeps it coiled inside. And so the movie, by refusing to release any emotion at all until the very end, absolutely wrings us dry. There is no purpose to a suspense thriller, I suppose, except to involve us, scare us, to give us moments of vicarious terror. *Play Misty for Me* does that with an almost cruel efficiency.

Plenty ★ ★ ★ ½
R, 119 m., 1985

Meryl Streep (Susan), Charles Dance (Raymond), Tracey Ullman (Alice), John Gielgud (Darwin), Sting (Mick), Ian McKellen (Sir Andrew), Sam Neill (Lazar). Directed by Fred Schepisi and produced by Edward R. Pressman and Joseph Papp. Screenplay by David Hare.

At the end of World War II, a young woman stands on a hilltop in France and, as the sun bathes her in golden light, she says, "There will be days and days and days like this." That image provides the last shot in *Plenty,* which is the story of how very wrong she was.

The woman is Susan Traherne, a young English fighter in the French Resistance. She is not very seasoned and perhaps not very good at her job, but she stays alive behind enemy lines and she has a brief, poignant love affair with one of the men who parachuted down out of the night sky to fight the Germans.

The movie opens with her days in France. It follows her through the next fifteen or twenty years, and ends with that painful flashback to a day when she thought the future had nothing but good things for her. But nothing else in her life is ever as important, as ennobling or as much fun as the war. She is, perhaps, a little mad. She confesses at one point that she has a problem: "Sometimes I like to lose control."

The movie stars Meryl Streep as Susan and it is a performance of great subtlety; it is hard to play an unbalanced, neurotic, self-destructive woman, and do it with such gentleness and charm. Susan is often very pleasant to be around for the other characters in *Plenty,* and when she is letting herself lose control, she doesn't do it in the style of those patented movie mad scenes in which eyes roll and teeth are bared. She does it with an almost winsome urgency.

When she returns to England after the war, Susan makes friends almost at once. One of them is Alice (Tracey Ullman), a round-faced, grinning imp who seems born to the role of best pal. Another is Raymond (Charles Dance), a foreign service officer who is at first fascinated by her free, Bohemian lifestyle, and then marries her and becomes her lifelong enabler, putting up a wall of patience and almost saintly tolerance around her outbursts.

It is hard to say exactly what it is that troubles Susan. At first, David Hare's screenplay leads us to her own interpretation: That after the glory and excitement of the war, after the heroism and romance, it is impossible for her to return to civilian life and suffer the boring conversations of polite society. Later, we begin to realize there is something a little willful, a little cruel, in the way she embarrasses her husband on important occasions, always seeking to say the wrong thing at the wrong time. Finally, we tend to agree with him when he explodes that she is cruel and brutish, and ungrateful to those who have put up with her.

But then there is an epilogue—a strange, furtive meeting with the boy, the parachutist, she made love with twenty years earlier. It is bathed in the cold, greenish-gray light of the saddest part of an autumn afternoon, and there is such desperation in the way they both realize that nothing will ever, ever touch them again the way the war did.

Plenty is finally not a statement about war, or foreign service, or the British middle class, but simply the story of this flawed woman who once lived intensely, and now feels that she is hardly living at all.

The performances in the movie supply one brilliant solo after another; most of the big moments come as characters dominate the scenes they are in. Streep creates a whole character around a woman who could have simply been a catalog of symptoms. Charles Dance has a thankless role, I suppose, as her long-suffering husband, but manages to suggest that he is decent as well as duped. Sting plays a nondescript young man who unsuccessfully attempts to father her child. John Gielgud has three brief scenes and steals them all.

The movie is written, acted, and directed (by Fred Schepisi) as a surface of literacy and brittle wit, beneath which lives the realization that life can sometimes be pointless and empty and sad—and that there can be days and days and days like that.

Police Academy **no stars**
R, 97 m., 1984

Steve Guttenberg (Carey Mahoney), Kim Cattrall (Karen Thompson), G.W. Bailey (Lieutenant Harris), Bubba Smith (Moses Hightower), Georgina Spelvin (Hooker). Directed by Hugh Wilson and produced by Paul Maslansky. Screenplay by Neal Israel, Pat Proft, and Wilson.

Once upon a time there was a movie named *Airplane!* which had a clever notion: Wouldn't it be fun to satirize all of those *Airport* movies by combining their clichés into one gloriously confused mess, typecasting the movie with walking stereotypes, and going for every corny gag in the book? They were right. It was a great idea, and it made a very funny movie. It also inspired a dreary series of clones and rip-offs, including *Young Doctors in Love* and *Jekyll and Hyde—Together Again.* Now comes without any doubt the absolute pits of this genre, the least funny movie that could possibly have been inspired by *Airplane!* or any other movie.

It's really something. It's so bad, maybe you should pool your money and draw straws and send one of the guys off to rent it so that in the future, whenever you think you're sitting through a bad comedy, he could shake his head, and chuckle tolerantly, and explain that you don't know what bad is. This is the kind of movie where they'll bring a couple of characters onscreen and begin to set up a joke, and then, just when you realize you can predict exactly what's going to happen . . . not only doesn't it happen, but nothing happens—they just cut to some different characters! If there's anything worse than a punch line that doesn't work, it's a movie that doesn't even bother to put the punch lines in.

Among the many questions raised by *Police Academy*, the easiest is: What genre does this movie think it's satirizing? Are there any other movies about police academies? That hardly matters, since the academy in this movie resembles no police academy known to modern man, and seems, indeed, to be modeled after a cross between basic training and prep school. All of the trainee cops live on campus together, in big dorms. The head of the academy is sort of like the headmaster. The campus is green and leafy and peaceful and altogether unlike, I suspect, the training experience undergone by any real police officers.

In a movie this bad, one plot element is really idiotic. It involves the casting of Bubba Smith as a giant black recruit who only has to look at a guy, and his knees start to tremble. This is funny? Don't they know that in comedy, you need a twist—like, why not make Bubba Smith a pathological coward who's afraid of everybody? Now right there is one good idea more than you can find in this entire movie.

Poltergeist ★ ★ ★
PG, 114 m., 1982

Craig T. Nelson (Steve), Jobeth Williams (Diane), Beatrice Straight (Dr. Lesh), Dominique Dunne (Dana), Oliver Robins (Robbie), Heather O'Rourke (Carol Anne). Directed by Tobe Hooper and produced by Steven Spielberg and Frank Marshall. Screenply by Spielberg, Michael Grais, and Mark Victor.

Special effects in the movies have grown so skilled, sensational, and scary that they sometimes upstage the human actors. And they often cost a lot more. In *Poltergeist*, for example, the cast is made up of relatively unknown performers, but that's all right because the real stars are producer Steven Spielberg *(Raiders of the Lost Ark)*, director Tobe Hooper *(The Texas Chainsaw Massacre)*, and their reputations for special effects and realistic violence. Their names on this horror film suggest that its technology will be impeccable. And they don't disappoint us. This is the movie *The Amityville Horror* dreamed of being. It begins with the same ingredients (a happy American family, living in a big, comfortable house). It provides similar warnings of doom (household objects move by themselves, the weather seems different around the house than anywhere else). And it ends with a similar apocalypse (spirits take total possession of the house, and terrorize the family). Even some of the special effects are quite similar, as when greasy goo begins to ooze around the edges of a doorjamb.

But *Poltergeist* is an effective thriller, not so much because of the special effects, as because Hooper and Spielberg have tried to see the movie's strange events through the eyes of the family members, instead of just standing back and letting the special effects overwhelm the cast along with the audience. The movie takes place in Spielberg's favorite terrain, the American suburb (also the locale of parts of *Close Encounters*, *Jaws*, and *E.T.*). The haunted house doesn't have seven gables, but it does have a two-car garage. It is occupied by a fairly normal family (two parents, three kids) and the movie begins on a somewhat hopeful note with the playing of "The Star Spangled Banner" as a TV station signs off.

The opening visuals, however, are somewhat ominous. They're an extreme close-up of a TV screen, filled with the usual patriotic images (Iwo Jima, the Lincoln Memorial). Why so close? We're almost being invited to look between the dots on the screen and see something else. And indeed, the family's youngest daughter, an open-faced, long-haired, innocent little cherub, begins to talk to the screen. She's in touch with the "TV people." Before long she disappears from this plane of existence and goes to live with the TV people, wherever they are. Weird events begin to happen in the house. An old tree behaves ominously. The swimming pool seems to have a mind of its own. And the villains are the same people who were the bad guys in Spielberg's *Jaws*—the real estate developers. This time, instead of encouraging people to go back into the water, they're building a subdivision on top of an old graveyard.

This is all ridiculous, but Hooper and Spielberg hold our interest by observing the everyday rituals of this family so closely that, since the family seems real, the weird events take on a certain credibility by association. That's during the first hour of the movie. Then all hell breaks loose, and the movie begins to operate on the same plane as *Alien* or *Altered States*, as a shocking special effects sound-and-light show. A closet seems to exist in another dimension. The swimming pool is filled with grasping, despairing forms of the undead. The search for the missing little girl involves a professional psionics expert, and a lady dwarf who specializes in "cleaning" haunted homes. Nobody ever does decide whether a poltergeist really is involved in the events in the house, or who the poltergeist may be, but if that doesn't prevent them from naming the movie *Poltergeist* I guess it shouldn't keep us from enjoying it.

The Pope of Greenwich Village

★ ★ ★

R, 122 m., 1984

Eric Roberts (Paulie), Mickey Rourke (Charlie), Daryl Hannah (Diane), Geraldine Page (Mrs. Ritter), Kenneth McMillan (Barney), Tony Musante (Pete), Burt Young (Bedbug Eddie). Directed by Stuart Rosenberg and produced by Gene Kirkwood. Screenplay by Vincent Patrick.

Everybody is very ethnic in *The Pope of Greenwich Village*. They all wave their hands a lot, and hang out on street corners, and have uncles in the Mafia. They have such bonds of blood brotherhood, a cousin to them is closer than your mother is to you. And they've always got some kind of con game going on the side. Take Paulie, for example. He knows this racehorse that's selling for $15,000, only the joke is, this is a champion horse because it was sired with sperm stolen directly from the winner of the Belmont. Paulie explains about the horse while he has his mouth full of a hero sandwich that's a yard long. His cousin, Charlie, tells him he's crazy. That is a compliment in this family.

Paulie and Charlie have just been fired from their jobs at a restaurant for stealing from the management. Charlie is hard up. He can no longer support his girlfriend, a long-limbed, blonde aerobics instructor who seems attracted to his exotic ethnic charm. Paulie has the answer to their problems. He will buy the future champion racehorse with money from a juice loan and then pay off the loan by cracking a safe he has heard about. There is only one problem with this plan. The safe belongs to the Mafia godfather of Greenwich Village, and if he finds out who did it, not even Paulie's uncle in the Mafia can save them. Meanwhile, Charlie's girlfriend is pregnant, Paulie's car has been towed, a cop has killed himself falling down an elevator shaft, and on the sound track Frank Sinatra is singing "Summer Wind."

The Pope of Greenwich Village bills itself as a drama and is structured like a crime thriller, but I categorize it as basically a Behavior Movie. The real subject of the movie is the behavior of the characters, and the story is essentially an excuse for showboat performances. This movie is an actor's dream, and the actors involved are Eric Roberts, fresh from his triumph in *STAR 80,* as Paulie; Mickey Rourke, the hero of *Diner,* as Charlie; Daryl Hannah, right after her hit in *Splash,* as the aerobics instructor; and the usual supporting types like Tony Musante as the uncle, Burt Young—stuffing his face with pasta—as the godfather, and Geraldine Page as the tough-talking mother of the dead cop. Also, Kenneth McMillan has a well-acted key role as an old safecracker who gets caught in the middle of the whole deal.

There are times when *The Pope of Greenwich Village* seems to aspire to some great meaning, some insight into crime like *The Godfather* had. But the tip-off is the last shot, where the boys have a happy-go-lucky walk down the street and into a freeze-frame, while Sinatra is trotted out for his third encore. This movie is not really about anything except behavior, and the only human drama in it is the story of the safecracker and his family. That doesn't mean it's not worth seeing. The behavior is well-observed, although Eric Roberts has a tendency to go over the top in his mannered performance, and the last two scenes are highly unlikely. It's worth seeing for the acting, and it's got some good laughs in it, and New York is colorfully observed, but don't tell me this movie is about human nature, because it's not; it's about acting.

Popeye ★ ★ ★ ½

PG, 114 m., 1980

Robin Williams (Popeye), Shelly Duvall (Olive Oyl), Ray Walston (Poopdeck Pappy), Paul Dooley (Wimpy), Paul L. Smith (Bluto), Richard Libertini (Geezil). Directed by Robert Altman and produced by Robert Evans. Screenplay by Jules Feiffer.

One of Robert Altman's trademarks is the way he creates whole new worlds in his movies—worlds where we somehow don't believe that life ends at the edge of the screen, worlds in which the main characters are surrounded by other people plunging ahead at the business of living. That gift for populating new places is one of the richest treasures in *Popeye,* Altman's musical comedy. He takes one of the most artificial and limiting of art forms—the comic strip—and raises it to the level of high comedy and high spirits.

And yet *Popeye* nevertheless remains true to its origin on the comic page, and in those classic cartoons by Max Fleischer. A review of this film almost has to start with the work of Wolf Kroeger, the production designer, who created an astonishingly detailed and rich set on the movie's Malta locations. Most of the action takes place in a ramshackle fishing hamlet—"Sweethaven"—where the streets run at crazy angles up the hillsides, and the rooming houses and saloons lean together dangerously.

Sweethaven has been populated by actors who look, or are made to look, so much like their funny-page originals that it's hardly even jarring that they're *not* cartoons. Audiences immediately notice the immense forearms on Robin Williams, who plays Popeye; they're big, brawny, and completely convincing. But so is Williams's perpetual squint and his lopsided smile. Shelly Duvall, the star of so many other Altman films, is perfect here as Olive Oyl, the role she was born to play. She brings to Olive a certain . . . dignity, you might say. She's not lightly scorned, and although she may tear apart a room in an unsuccessful attempt to open the curtains, she is fearless in the face of her terrifying fiancé, Bluto. The list continues: Paul Smith (the torturer in *Midnight Express*) looks ferociously Bluto-like, and Paul Dooley (the father in *Breaking Away*) is a perfect Wimpy, forever curiously sniffing a hamburger with a connoisseur's fanatic passion. Even the little baby, Swee' Pea, played by Altman's grandson, Wesley Ivan Hurt, looks like typecasting.

But it's not enough that the characters and the locations look their parts. Altman has breathed life into this material, and he hasn't done it by pretending it's camp, either. He organizes a screenful of activity, so carefully choreographed that it's a delight, for example to watch the moves as the guests in Olive's rooming house make stabs at the plates of food on the table.

There are several set pieces. One involves Popeye's arrival at Sweethaven, another a stop on his lonely quest for his long-lost father. Another is the big wedding day for Bluto and Olive Oyl, with Olive among the missing and Bluto's temper growing until steam jets from his ears. There is the excursion to the amusement pier, and the melee at the dinner table, and the revelation of the true identity of a mysterious admiral, and the kidnapping of Swee' Pea, and then the kidnapping of Olive Oyl and her subsequent wrestling match with a savage octopus.

The movie's songs, by Harry Nilssen, fit into all of this quite effortlessly. Instead of having everything come to a halt for the musical set pieces, Altman stitches them into the fabric. Robin Williams sings Popeye's anthem, "I Yam What I Yam" with a growling old sea dog's stubborness. Bluto's "I'm Mean" has an undeniable conviction, and so does Olive Oyl's song to Bluto, "He's Large." Shelly Duvall's performance as Olive Oyl also benefits from the amazingly ungainly walking style she brings to the movie.

Popeye, then, is lots of fun. It suggests that it *is* possible to take the broad strokes of a comic strip and turn them into sophisticated entertainment. What's needed is the right attitude toward the material. If Altman and his people had been the slightest bit condescending toward Popeye, the movie might have crash-landed. But it's clear that this movie has an affection for Popeye, and so much regard for the sailor man that it even bothers to reveal the real truth about his opinion of spinach.

Porky's ★ 1/2

R, 94 m., 1982

Dan Monahan (Pee Wee), Mark Herrier (Billy), Wyatt Knight (Tommy), Roger Wilson (Mickey), Kim Cattrall (Honeywell), Alex Karras (Sheriff), Susan Clark (Cherry Forever), Nancy Parsons (Ms. Balbricker). Directed by Bob Clark and produced by Don Carmody and Clark.

Porky's is another raunchy teen-age sex-and-food-fight movies. The whole genre seems fixated on the late 1950s and early 1960s, when the filmmakers, no doubt, were teen-agers. Do today's teen-agers really identify with jokes about locker rooms, Trojans, boobs, jockstraps, killer-dyke gym coaches, and barfing? Well, yes, probably they do. Teen-agers seem to occupy a time warp of eternally unchanging preoccupations. Hollywood originally entered that world with a certain innocence in the late 1950s with Pat Boone and beach part movies. That innocence is now long, long ago. Since *American Graffiti*, *National Lampoon's Animal House*, and *Meatballs*, the A.C.N.E.S. movie has turned cynical. You remember what A.C.N.E.S. stands for. It's an acronym for any movie about the dreaded Adolescent Character's Neurotic Eroticism Syndrome.

In *Porky's*, the male characters are neurotic about the usual three subjects: the size, experience, and health of their reproductive organs. The female characters, on the other hand, are seen almost entirely as an undiscovered species from a lost continent. They're whispered about, speculated about, spied upon, victimized, and, in general, feared. And it's not only Ms. Balbricker, the juggernaut gym coach, who's a heavy. All of the women in this movie are weird. One howls like a dog during sexual intercourse. Others lure unsuspecting horny teen-age boys into rooms with trapdoors, and dump them into alligator-infested waters.

In fact, the strangest thing about *Porky's* is how much it hates women. The only close friendships in the movie are between men. The movie even takes certain scenes that are usually clichés for female characters and assigns them to men. For example, you can hardly make a movie like this without a scene in which someone's caught nude in public. Remember Hot Lips in *M*A*S*H?* In *Porky's*, it's a kid named Pee Wee. He's caught with his pants down, chased into the woods, picked up by the cops, and deposited at the local drive-in hamburger stand, where he poses like September Morn.

Since the movie doesn't like women, its sex scenes all create fear and hostility, which prevents them from being funny (sex scenes *about* fear and hostility, on the other hand, can be very funny). Even in an easy scene like the one where the guys spy on the girls in the locker room, the director, Bob Clark, blows it. Peeping-tom scenes can be very funny (remember John Belushi on the ladder in *Animal House?*). Here, it's just smarmy. There's one other problem. None of the male actors in this movie look, sound, or act like teen-agers. They all look like overgrown preppies at their fraternity pledge class's fifth reunion. Jokes based on embarrassment never work unless we can identify with the embarrassed character. Here, the actors all seem to be just acting.

I see that I have neglected to summarize the plot of *Porky's*. And I don't think I will. I don't feel like writing one more sentence (which is, to be sure, all it would take).

The Possession of Joel Delaney ★ ★

R, 105 m., 1972

Shirley MacLaine (Norah), Perry King (Joel), Lisa Kohane (Terry), David Elliott (Peter). Directed by Warris Hussein. Screenplay by Matt Robinson and Grimes Grace.

What can you say about the possession of Joel Delaney, except that it gave him a hobby? Before his friend Tonio's spirit occupied his body, life was little more than a series of hos and hums for Joel. He was the kind of kid who kept his bedroom door shut, played old bongo music on his stereo, and complained of headaches. His big thing was to wrap himself up in a blanket and stare vacantly at the closet door. A guy like this is never going to make the Jaycee's list of the ten most up-and-coming young men in America, let's face it.

After he met Tonio, everything changed. Tonio was outgoing and dynamic; he had beheaded three girls in Central Park. Then Tonio died, alas, and Joel moved into Tonio's vacant apartment and was possessed by Tonio's spirit. Right away, he could speak Spanish with a Puerto Rican accent that would have required months at Berlitz. And he was given to dandy rages. He could snarl and squirm and scream and throw things, and the cops had to take him to Bellevue on more than one occasion. No more closet doors for Joel.

The Possession of Joel Delaney is not so much about Joel's new zest for living, however, as it is about Shirley MacLaine, who plays Joel's sister. She lives alone in Manhattan, and supplies the three necessary ingredients for any supernatural horror flick. (1) She is an unprotected female. (2) She has two young and helpless children. (3) In times of terror and emergency, when her life and the lives of her children are threatened by Puerto Rican voodoo, her immediate impulse is to flee to an isolated and abandoned beach house, miles from help.

After Ms. MacLaine finally catches on that her brother has been possessed by an evil spirit, she goes to a voodoo priest in Spanish Harlem, who attempts to lure Tonio's spirit from Joel's body. No dice. This scene is about the only good thing in the movie, however, because it's shot and edited in a scary, claustrophobic style and seems to reflect some research into the actual folklore of voodoo.

The rest of the movie is badly put together, with little feeling for suspense, and the final scenes in the beach house are in nauseatingly bad taste. Filmmakers should have enough imagination and enterprise to scare us without resorting to cheap tricks. Hitchcock could, and did. But Warris Hussein, who directed this film, is so bankrupt of imagination that he actually descends to a scene where the little boy is forced to disrobe and eat dog food. This is all because of the evil spirit in Joel's body, of course, but I don't care.

The Postman Always Rings Twice ★ ★ ½

R, 122 m., 1981

Jack Nicholson (Frank Chambers), Jessica Lange (Cora Papadakis), John Colicos (Nick Papadakis), Michael Lerner (Katz), John P. Ryan (Kennedy), Anjelica Huston (Madge). Directed by Bob Rafelson and produced by Charles Mulvehill and Rafelson. Screenplay by David Mamet.

The Postman Always Rings Twice is an absolutely superb mounting of a hollow and disappointing production. It shows a technical mastery of filmmaking, and we are dazzled by the performances, the atmosphere, the mood of mounting violence. But by the second hour of the film we've lost our bearings: What is this movie *saying* about its characters? What does it feel and believe about them? Why was it necessary to tell their stories? The movie is based on a hard-boiled, classic novel by James M. Cain, which has already inspired three previous films, including the famous 1946 John Garfield version. It isn't difficult to guess why the director, Bob Rafelson, wanted to make it again. On the basis of his key scenes, he was attracted by the physical violence in the story and he felt that in 1981 he could deal more frankly with Cain's sexual savagery.

He was right. His film contains passages of unusual physical power, including one in which Jack Nicholson and Jessica Lange make love (if that is the word) on a kitchen table. Nicholson plays a Depression-era drifter in the film, a cheap thief, and a con man. Lange is the bored and sensuous cook in a short-order joint run by her much older Greek husband, John Colicos. Passion flares between Nicholson and Lange almost the moment they first see one another, and their lovemaking is quick, brutal, uncontrolled, and animalistic.

Eventually, they kill Colicos—although not without the greatest difficulties. This is one of those films where blood, violence, and sheer weight of human bodies are made into Hitchcockian embarrassments. And then the two lovers are put on trial, are freed through a cynical arrangement between opposing insurance companies, and then arrive at an ironic fate. Along the way, there is a brief and totally inexplicable appearance by a woman lion tamer (Anjelica Huston), who seems to be visiting from another movie.

The movie is a triumph of atmosphere. Every last weathered Coke sign, every old auto and old overcoat and old cliché have been put in with loving care. And the performances have been cranked up to levels of trembling intensity. Jessica Lange, first seen in *King Kong*, this time submits to the embrace of a wanton monster. Jack Nicholson has never been seedier, shiftier, more driven. John Colicos, as the simple, alcoholic, ambitious Greek-American, provides a wonderfully textured performance. And yet, there is no feeling of tragedy in Colicos's death. No feeling of greatness in the romantic compulsion of Lange and Nicholson. No way to tell what the movie believes about their acquittal and eventual fate. A movie such as *Bonnie and Clyde* comes to mind. It also dealt with passion, crime, and money, but so clearly that at the end of the film we felt we knew the dying characters.

We never know the people in *The Postman Always Rings Twice*. They are kept rigidly imprisoned within a tradition of absolute naturalism: They exist, they eat, they sleep, they act. That would be acceptable if the filmmakers could stand outside their characters and have feelings about them. But I never believed that was the case. Rafelson and his collaborators have gone to infinite pains, successfully, to create a film that is wonderfully achieved on the level of production. But they have not filled it with the purposes of its characters.

Predator ★ ★ ★

R, 105 m., 1987

Arnold Schwarzenegger (Dutch), Carl Weathers (Dillon), Elpidia Carrillo (Anna), Bill Duke (Mac), Jesse Ventura (Blain), Sonny Landham (Billy), Richard Chaves (Poncho), R.G. Armstrong (General Phillips), Shane Black (Hawkins), Kevin Peter Hall (Predator). Directed by John McTiernan and produced by Lawrence Gordon, Joel Silver, and John Davis. Screenplay by Jim and John Thomas.

Predator begins like *Rambo* and ends like *Alien*, and in today's Hollywood, that's creativity. Most movies are inspired by only one previous blockbuster.

The movie stars Arnold Schwarzenegger as the leader of a U.S. Army commando team that goes into the South American jungle on a political mission and ends up dueling with a killer from outer space. This is the kind of idea that is produced at the end of a ten-second brainstorming session, but if it's done well, who cares?

Predator is filmed very well. It's a slick, high-energy action picture that takes a lot of its strength from its steamy locations in Mexico. The heroes spend most of their time surrounded by an impenetrable jungle, a green wall of majestic vistas populated by all sorts of natural predators in addition to the alien. I've rarely seen a jungle look more beautiful, or more convincing; the location effect is on a par with *Fitzcarraldo* and *The Emerald Forest.*

As the film opens, Schwarzenegger and his comrades venture into this jungle in search of South American officials who have been kidnapped by terrorists. They track and locate the fugitives, and move in for the kill. But as they find the bodies of team members skinned and hanging from trees, they begin to realize they're up against more than terrorists.

The predator of the movie's title is a visitor from space; that's established in the opening scene. What it is doing in the jungle is never explained. The creature lives in the trees, even though it seems to be a giant biped much too heavy to swing from vines. When Schwarzenegger finally grapples with it, we discover it is wearing a space suit, and that inside the suit is a disgusting creature with a mouth surrounded by little pincers to shove in the food.

Such details are important, of course. Stan Winston, who designed the creature, has created a beast that is sufficiently disgusting to justify Schwarzenegger's loathing for it. And the action moves so quickly that we overlook questions such as (1) Why would an alien species go to all the effort to send a creature to Earth, just so that it could swing from trees and skin American soldiers? Or, (2) Why would a creature so technologically advanced need to bother with hand-to-hand combat, when it could just zap Arnold with a ray gun? At one point in the movie, the creature removes its helmet so it can battle Arnold *mano-a-mano,* and I was cynical enough to assume that its motivation was not macho pride, but the desire to display Winston's special effects.

None of these logical questions are very important to the movie. *Predator* moves at a breakneck pace, it has strong and simple characterizations, it has good location photography and terrific special effects, and it supplies what it claims to supply: an effective action movie.

Students of trivia might want to note that the actor inside the predator costume is Kevin Peter Hall, who also occupies the Bigfoot costume in *Harry and the Hendersons.* This guy must really be a good sport.

Pretty Baby ★ ★ ★

R, 109 m., 1978

Brooke Shields (Violet), Keith Carradine (Bellocq), Susan Sarandon (Hattie), Frances Faye (Nell), Antonio Fargas (Professor), Matthew Anton (Red Top), Diana Scarwid (Frieda). Directed and produced by Louis Malle. Screenplay by Polly Platt.

Louis Malle's *Pretty Baby* was a pleasant surprise: After all the controversy and scandal surrounding its production, it turned out to be a good-hearted, good-looking, quietly elegiac movie. That was a coup for Malle, who sometimes seemed to dare himself to find acceptable ways of filming unacceptable subjects.

His subject this time is a twelve-year-old girl who is raised in the New Orleans brothel where her mother works. She plays in the garden, she rides a pony, she likes ragtime music, and one day she's auctioned off to the man who will deflower her. This is, of course, tragically perverted, but *Pretty Baby* itself is not a perverted film: It looks soberly, and with a good deal of compassion, at its period of history and the people who occupied it.

The pretty baby of the title is named Violet, and is played by Brooke Shields, as an extraordinarily beautiful child. Before anyone had seen *Pretty Baby,* Malle was being accused of exploiting that fact. But he's thoughtful and almost cautious in his approach: Given the film's subject matter and its obligatory sex scenes, Malle shows taste and restraint. And Shields really creates a character here; her subtlety and depth are astonishing.

Malle places her in an extraordinarily well-realized world, the Storyville section of New Orleans, circa 1917. The movie pays infinite attention to detail, and looks and feels accurate: We get to know the brothel so well, with its curving staircases and baroque furnishings, we almost feel we live there too. And we get to know the people, too, especially the strange and cynical brothel-keeper Madame Nell (Frances Faye), who observes at one point in her gravelly voice: "I am old. And I know one thing: Life is very long." An almost opaque line, but she invests it with infinite weariness.

She also keeps a well-run establishment, populated by hookers like Violet's mother

Hattie (Susan Sarandon), who dreams of escaping from the life and eventually succeeds: She marries a prosperous businessman from St. Louis, and moves north. She wants to take her daughter with her, but Violet won't go: For her, this house *is* a home. Violet has in the meantime gained a protector and confidant: Bellocq (Keith Carradine), the silent, eccentric photographer. He seems at first to feel no passion at all, as he takes his infinite pains to arrange the lights and shadows in which he poses the prostitutes. There is, we feel, the possibility that he's asexual. But he does have a special feeling for Violet. And on the night she is auctioned off, there are two long, anguished close-ups: Of Bellocq, and of the house's black piano player (Antonio Fargas). Both of them clearly feel the auction is an outrage. Neither one speaks out. They are both creatures of Storyville, and know how things are done.

After Hattie goes north, Violet stays in the house for a time, and then goes to live with Bellocq. Their relationship is, of course, a strange one, made more complicated by the fact that this experienced twelve-year-old prostitute is still just a little girl. One of the film's most heartbreaking scenes has Violet sitting under a tree, playing with her doll. She is pretending that the doll is herself and that she is her mother. There's such a curious mixture of resentment and envy in her game that we cringe.

Pretty Baby has been attacked in some quarters as child porn. It's not. It's an evocation of a time and a place and a sad chapter of Americana. The ragtime music and the blues that fill its sound track take on a deeper meaning, in the context of the story, and we are reminded that the artists who sang "Do You Know What It Means to Miss New Orleans?" knew very well, and perhaps for that reason missed it less than their listeners.

Pretty in Pink ★ ★ ★

PG-13, 96 m., 1985

Molly Ringwald (Andie Walsh), Harry Dean Stanton (Jack Walsh), Jon Cryer (Duckie Dale), Andrew McCarthy (Blane McDonoug), Annie Potts (Iona), James Spader (Steff McKee). Directed by Howard Deutch and produced by Lauren Shuler. Screenplay by John Hughes.

Although *Pretty in Pink* contains several scenes that are a great deal more dramatic, my favorite moments were the quietest ones, in which nothing was being said because a boy was trying to get up the courage to ask a girl out on a date, and she knew it, and he knew it, and still nothing was happening.

To be able to listen to such a silence is to understand the central dilemma of adolescence, which is that one's dreams are so much larger than one's confidence. *Pretty in Pink* is a movie that pays attention to such things. And although it is not a great movie, it contains some moments when the audience is likely to think, yes, being sixteen was exactly like that.

The movie stars Molly Ringwald as Andie Walsh, a poor girl from the wrong side of the tracks. Her mother bailed out of her life some years earlier, and she lives with her unemployed father (Harry Dean Stanton), whose first words after she wakes him one morning are, "Where am I?" Andie works in a record store in a downtown mall and wears fashions that seem thrown together by a collision between a Goodwill store and a 1950s revival.

Andie attends a high school where most of the kids are wealthy snobs, and she has a crush on a rich kid named Blane (Andrew McCarthy). Her best friends are Duckie (Jon Cryer), who is a case study of the kind of teenage boy who thinks he can clown his way into a girl's heart, and Iona (Annie Potts), a thirtyish sprite who affects one radical hairstyle after another.

The movie's plot is old, old, old. It's about how the rich boy and the poor girl love each other, but the rich kid's friends are snobs, and the poor girl doesn't want anyone to know what a shabby home she lives in, and about how they do find true love after all. Since the basic truths in the movie apply to all teen-agers, rich and poor, I wish the filmmakers had found a new plot to go along with them. Perhaps they could have made the lovers come from different ethnic groups, which wouldn't have been all that original, either, but at least would have avoided one more recycling of ancient Horatio Alger stories.

There is one other major problem with the movie, and that involves the character of Steff McKee (James Spader), the effete, chain-smoking rich snot who is Blane's best friend. He has been turned down several times by Andie and now pretends to be appalled that Blane would want to go out with such a "mutant." His snobbery almost shipwrecks the romance. Steff does have one great line of dialogue: "Money really means nothing to me. Do you think I'd treat my parents' house this way if it did?" But, as played by Spader, he looks much too old to be a teen-ager, and his scenes play uneasily for that reason. He seems more like a sinister twenty-five-year-old still lurking in the high school corridors, the Ghost of Proms Past.

Those objections noted, *Pretty in Pink* is a heartwarming and mostly truthful movie, with some nice touches of humor. The movie was written by John Hughes, who repeats the basic situation of his *Sixteen Candles*, which also starred Molly Ringwald as a girl who had a crush on a senior boy, and whose best friend was the class geek. But Ringwald grows with every movie into an actress who can project poignancy and vulnerability without seeming corny or coy, and her scenes here with Cryer and Potts have one moment of small truth after another.

The nicest surprise in the movie is the character created by Potts. The first time we see her, she's dressed in leather and chains, but the next time, she wears one of those beehive hairdos from the early 1960s. She is constantly experimenting with her "look," and when she finally settles on conservative good taste, the choice seems like her most radical so far.

Pretty in Pink is evidence, I suppose, that there must be a reason why certain old stories never seem to die. We know all the clichés, we can predict half of the developments. But at the end, when this boy and this girl, who are so obviously intended for one another, finally get together, there is great satisfaction. There also is the sense that Molly Ringwald just might have that subtle magic that will allow her, like young Elizabeth Taylor, to grow into an actress who will keep on breaking and mending boys' hearts for a long time.

Prick Up Your Ears ★ ★ ★ ★

R, 111 m., 1987

Gary Oldman (Joe Orton), Alfred Molina (Kenneth Halliwell), Vanessa Redgrave (Peggy Ramsay), Wallace Shawn (John Lahr), Lindsay Duncan (Anthea Lahr), Julie Walters (Elsie Orton), James Grant (William Orton). Directed by Stephen Frears and produced by Andrew Brown. Screenplay by Alan Bennett.

For all of their years together, Joe Orton and Kenneth Halliwell lived in a cramped room in the north of London, up near the Angel tube stop where everything seems closer to hell. Even after Orton became famous, even after his plays were hits and he was winning awards and his picture was in the papers, he came home to the tiny hovel where Halliwell was waiting. One night he came home and Halliwell hammered him to death and killed himself.

Prick Up Your Ears is the story of Orton and Halliwell and the murder. They say that most murderers are known to their victims. They don't say that if you knew the victims as well as the murderer did, you might understand more about the murder, but doubtless that is sometimes the case. This movie opens with a brutal, senseless crime. By the time the movie is over, the crime is still brutal, but it is possible to comprehend.

When they met, Orton was seventeen, Halliwell was twenty-five, and they both wanted to be novelists. They were homosexuals, but sex never seemed to be at the heart of their relationship. They lived together, but Orton prowled the night streets for rough trade and Halliwell scolded him for taking too many chances. Orton was, by all accounts, a charming young man—liked by everybody, impish, rebellious, with a taste for danger. Halliwell, eight years older, was a stolid, lonely man who saw himself as Orton's teacher.

He taught him everything he could. Then Orton used what he'd learned to write plays that drew heavily on their life together. His big hits were *Loot* and *What the Butler Saw*, and both are still frequently performed. But when Orton won the *Evening Standard*'s award for the play of the year—an honor like the Pulitzer Prize—he didn't take Kenneth to the banquet, he took his agent.

Halliwell began to feel that he was receiving no recognition for what he saw as the sacrifice of his life. He dabbled in art and constructed collages out of thousands of pictures clipped from books and magazines. But his shows were in the lobbies of the theaters presenting Joe's plays, and people were patronizing to him. That began to drive him mad.

Prick Up Your Ears is based on the biography that John Lahr wrote about Orton, a biography that has become famous for discovering a private life so different from the image seen by the public.

Homosexuality was a crime in the 1960s in England, but Orton was heedless of the dangers. In fact, he seemed to enjoy danger. Perhaps that was why he kept Halliwell around, because he sensed the older man might explode. More likely, though, he kept him out of loyalty and indifference and didn't fully realize how much he was hurting him. One of the early scenes in the film shows Halliwell skulking at home, angry because Orton is late for dinner.

The movie is good at scenes like that. It has a touch for the wound beneath the skin, the hurt that we can feel better than the person who is inflicting it. The movie is told as sort of a flashback, with the Lahr character interviewing Orton's literary agent and then the movie spinning off into memories of its own.

The movie is not about homosexuality, which it treats in a matter-of-fact manner. It is really about a marriage between unequal partners. Halliwell was, in a way, like the loyal wife who slaves at ill-paid jobs to put her husband through medical school, only to have the man divorce her after he's successful because they have so little in common—he with his degree, she with dishwater hands.

The movie was written by Alan Bennett, a successful British playwright who understands Orton's craft. He bases one of his characters on Lahr (played by Wallace Shawn), apparently as an excuse to give Orton's literary agent (Vanessa Redgrave) someone to talk to. The device is awkward, but it allows Redgrave into the movie, and her performance is superb: aloof, cynical, wise, unforgiving.

The great performances in the movie are, of course, at its center. Gary Oldman plays Orton and Alfred Molina plays Halliwell, and these are two of the best performances of 1987. Oldman you may remember as Sid Vicious, the punk rock star in *Sid & Nancy.* There is no point of similarity between the two performances; like a few gifted actors, he is able to re-invent himself for every role. On the basis of these two movies, he is the best young British actor around. Molina has a more thankless role as he stands in the background, overlooked and misunderstood. But even as he whines we can understand his feelings, and by the end we are not very surprised by what he does.

The movie was directed by Stephen Frears, whose previous movie, *My Beautiful Laundrette,* also was about a homosexual relationship between two very different men: a Pakistani laundry operator and his working-class, neofascist boyfriend. Frears makes homosexuality an everyday thing in his movies, which are not about his characters' sexual orientation but about how their underlying personalities are projected onto their sexuality and all the other areas of their lives.

In the case of Orton and Halliwell, there is the sense that their deaths had been waiting for them right from the beginning. Their relationship was never healthy and never equal, and Halliwell, who was willing to sacrifice so much, would not sacrifice one thing: recognition for his sacrifice. If only Orton had taken him to that dinner, there might have been so many more opening nights.

Prime Cut ★ ★ ★

R, 86 m., 1972

Lee Marvin (Nick Devlin), Gene Hackman ("Mary Ann"), Angel Tompkins (Clarabelle), Gregory Walcott (Weenie), Sissy Spacek (Poppy), William Morey (Shay). Directed by Michael Ritchie and produced by Joe Wizan. Screenplay by Robert Dillon.

Prime Cut is a movie about an enforcer for the Chicago mob (Lee Marvin) who goes to Kansas City to collect a debt. So we expect a seamy journey into the guts of the city, right? But it doesn't quite work out like that. *Prime Cut* is very different from the usual gangster movie; it's put together almost like a comic strip, with all of the good and bad things that implies, and the Marvin character has more in common with superheroes than with mobsters.

We're almost on the familiar terrain of "Steve Canyon." All of the characters are caricatures, with nicknames and gimmicks to help us identify them. There's "Mary

Ann" himself, a Kansas City dealer in prostitutes played by Gene Hackman. There's Weenie (Gregory Walcott), so-called because of his habit of carrying wieners around in his pocket—some of them made out of the ground-up bodies of his enemies. And there's Clarabelle (Angel Tompkins), who is Mary Ann's wife and lives in a luxurious houseboat with a mirror on the bedroom ceiling. Clearly, this is not the turf of Cagney and Bogart.

Prime Cut is a fantasy in which everything is very simple and usually takes place outdoors, and in which the characters act toward each other with great directness and brutality. It may owe a little to Hitchcock, as so many thrillers do. There's a scene at a county fair, for example, where Marvin and a young girl played by Sissy Spacek are trying to escape Hackman's gunmen. They do it all out in the open, casually walking in front of a grandstand in full view of thousands, so the gunmen can't shoot.

This is followed by the great wheat-field chase, in which Marvin and the girl are pursued by a giant reaper. A telephoto lens is used to give the impression that the giant reaper is almost literally on top of them, and every so often there's a cut to the obscene sight of the reaper dropping another bundle of wheat. Marvin and friend are saved when his chauffeur rams a limousine into the reaper—which digests it.

It's interesting to note that during the fairgrounds chase and the reaper chase, Marvin never lets go of the girl's hand (even though both could run faster if they weren't holding hands—and could even split up to avoid the reaper). This is a whammo visual signal of the movie's total male chauvinist orientation, which became clear much earlier during Gene Hackman's "cattle auction." The cattle, you see, are fresh, naked young girls, held in pens filled with straw. They have been raised in a special "orphanage," are certified to be virgin, and can be bought to stock your local bordello. Far-out.

Now you begin to see why *Prime Cut* is like a comic strip. It is broken up into several large set-pieces (the introduction, the trip to Kansas City, Marvin's rescue of one of the orphan girls, a couple of love scenes, the fairgrounds, the reaper, and a gunfight). This structure is a lot less complex than those in the gangster movies we're used to, and makes *Prime Cut* seem larger than ordinary movie life. The colors are clearer, and the characters act and react only to each other's giant-sized images. It's fun, in a way.

Prince of the City ★ ★ ★ ★

R, 167 m., 1981

Treat Williams (Daniel Ciello), Jerry Orbach (Gus Levy), Richard Foronjy (Joe Marinaro), Don Billett (Bill Mayo), Jenny Marino (Dom Bando), Bob Balaban (Sentimassino), Lindsay Crouse (Carla Ciello). Directed by Sidney Lumet and produced by Burtt Harris. Screenplay by Jay Presson Allen and Lumet.

He will not rat on his partners. This is his bottom line. He will talk to investigators about all the other guys he knows things about. He will talk about how narcotics cops get involved in the narcotics traffic, how they buy information with drugs, how they string out addicts and use them as informers, how they keep some of the money and some of the drugs after big busts. He will tell what he knows about how the other cops do these things. But he will not talk about his partners in his own unit. This is his code, and, of course, he is going to have to break it.

That is the central situation of Sidney Lumet's *Prince of the City.* While you are watching it, it's a movie about cops, drugs, and New York City, in that order. After the film starts to turn itself over in your mind, it becomes a much deeper piece, a film about how difficult it is to go straight in a crooked world without hurting people you love.

Drugs are a rotten business. They corrupt everyone they come into contact with, because they set up needs so urgent that all other considerations are forgotten. For addicts, the need is for the drug itself. For others, the needs are more complex. The members of the special police drug unit in *Prince of the City,* for example, take on an envied departmental status because of their assignment. They have no hours, no beats, no uniforms. They are elite free-lancers, modern knights riding out into the drug underworld and establishing their own rules. They do not look at it this way, but their status depends on drugs. If there were no drugs and no addicts, there would be no narcs, no princes of the city. Of course, their jobs are also cold, dirty, lonely, dangerous, thankless, and never finished. That is the other side of the deal, and that helps explain why they will sometimes keep the money they confiscate in a drug bust. It's as if they're levying their own fines. It also explains why they sometimes supply informers with drugs: They know better than anyone how horrible the addict's life can be. "A junkie can break your heart," the hero of this movie says at one point, and by the movie's end we understand what he means.

The film is based on a book by Robert Daley about Bob Leuci, a New York cop who cooperated with a 1971 investigation of police corruption. In the movie, Leuci is called Ciello, and he is played by Treat Williams in a demanding and grueling performance. Williams is almost always onscreen, and almost always in situations of extreme stress, fatigue, and emotional turmoil. We see him coming apart before our eyes. He falls to pieces not simply because of his job, or because of his decision to testify, but because he is in an inexorable trap and he *will* sooner or later have to hurt his partners.

This is a movie that literally hinges on the issue of perjury. And Sidney Lumet and his co-writer, Jay Presson Allen, have a great deal of respect for the legal questions involved. There is a sustained scene in this movie that is one of the most spellbinding I can imagine, and it consists entirely of government lawyers debating whether a given situation justifies a charge of perjury. Rarely are ethical issues discussed in such detail in a movie, and hardly ever so effectively.

Prince of the City is a very good movie and, like some of its characters, it wants to break your heart. Maybe it will. It is about the ways in which a corrupt modern city makes it almost impossible for a man to be true to the law, his ideals, and his friends, all at the same time. The movie has no answers. Only horrible alternatives.

The Princess Bride ★ ★ ★ ½

PG, 98 m., 1987

Cary Elwes (Westley), Mandy Patinkin (Inigo Montoya), Chris Sarandon (Humperdinck), Christopher Guest (Count Rugen), Wallace Shawn (Vizzini), Andre the Giant (Fezzik), Fred Savage (Grandson), Robin Wright (Princess Bride), Peter Falk (Grandfather), Peter Cook (Clergyman), Billy Crystal (Miracle Max). Directed by Rob Reiner and produced by Andrew Scheinman and Reiner. Screenplay by William Goldman.

The Princess Bride begins as a story that a grandfather is reading out of a book. But already the movie has a spin on it, because the grandfather is played by Peter Falk, and in the distinctive quality of his voice we detect a certain edge; his voice seems to contain a measure of cynicism about fairy stories, a certain awareness that there are a lot more things in heaven and earth than have been dreamed of by the Brothers Grimm.

The story he tells is about a beautiful princess (Robin Wright) who scornfully orders around a farm boy (Cary Elwes) until the day when she realizes, thunderstruck, that she loves him. She wants to live happily ever after with him, but then evil forces intervene, and she is kidnapped and taken far away across the lost lands, while he is killed.

"Is this story going to have a lot of kissing in it?" Falk's grandson asks. Well, it's definitely going to have a lot of Screaming Eels. The moment the princess is taken away by agents of the evil Prince Humperdinck (Chris Sarandon), *The Princess Bride* reveals itself as a sly parody of sword and sorcery movies, a film that somehow manages to exist on two levels at once: While younger viewers will sit spellbound at the thrilling events on the screen, adults, I think, will be laughing a lot.

In its own peculiar way, *The Princess Bride* resembles *This Is Spinal Tap*, an earlier film by the same director, Rob Reiner. Both films are funny not only because they contain comedy, but because Reiner does justice to the underlying form of his story. *Spinal Tap* looked and felt like a rock documentary—and *then* it was funny. *The Princess Bride* looks and feels like *Legend*, or any of those other quasi-heroic epic fantasies, and *then* it goes for the laughs.

Part of the secret is that Reiner never stays with the same laugh very long. There are a lot of people for his characters to meet as they make their long journey, and most of them are completely off the wall. There is, for example, a band of three brigands led by Wallace Shawn as a scheming little conniver, and including Andre the Giant as Fezzik the Giant, a crusher who may not necessarily have a heart of gold. It is Shawn who tosses the Princess Bride to the Screaming Eels, with great relish.

Another funny episode involves Mandy Patinkin as Inigo Montoya, heroic swordsman with a secret. And the funniest sequence in the film stars Billy Crystal and Carol Kane, both invisible behind makeup, as an ancient wizard and crone who specialize in bringing the dead back to life. (I hope I'm not giving anything away; you didn't expect the princess's loved one to stay dead indefinitely, did you?)

The Princess Bride was adapted by William Goldman from his own novel, which he says was inspired by a book he read as a child, but which seems to have been cheerfully transformed by his wicked adult imagination. It is filled with good-hearted fun, with performances by actors who seem to be smacking their lips, and by a certain true innocence that survives all of Reiner's satire. And also, it does have kissing in it.

Private Benjamin ★ ★ ★
R, 110 m., 1980

Goldie Hawn (Judy Benjamin), Eileen Brennan (Captain Lewis), Armand Assante (Henri Tremont), Robert Webber (Colonel Thornbush), Sam Wanamaker (Teddy Benjamin), Barbara Barrie (Harriet Benjamin), Harry Dean Stanton (Sergeant Ballard), Albert Brooks (Yale Goodman). Directed by Howard Zieff and written and produced by Nancy Meyers, Charles Shyer, and Harvey Miller.

Howard Zieff's *Private Benjamin* is an appealing, infectious comedy starring Goldie Hawn as Judy Benjamin, a Jewish-American princess, breathless with joy on the day of her second marriage. She has a real catch: He's named Yale, he's a professional man, he wants his study done in mushroom colors. Alas, he dies in the throes of passion on his wedding night (something his grieving mother discovers when Judy solemnly repeats his last words). And Judy goes into mourning.

What's she to do? She calls in to an all-night talk show and is promised a solution by another caller. The next day, we meet the guy with the answer. Played by Harry Dean Stanton, that wonderful character actor who could be Robert Mitchum's sneaky cousin, the guy turns out to be an Army recruiter. And he solemnly paints a picture of Army life that has Judy signing up. Her subsequent shocks of discovery provide the great laughs of the movie's best scenes. She solemnly explains to a captain (Eileen Brennan) that she *did* sign up with the Army, yes, but with another Army. Where, she asks, are the private condo living quarters the recruiter promised her? And surely the Army could have afforded some draperies? In no time at all, she's cleaning the latrines with her electric toothbrush.

This is an inspired idea for a movie comedy, and Goldie Hawn has a lot of fun with it. She finds just the right note for her performance, poised halfway between the avaricious and the slack-jawed, the calculating and the innocent. She makes some kind of impression on everyone she runs up against (or into), especially Robert Webber as the square-jawed Colonel Thornbush, commander of the Army's elite paratroop unit, the Thornbushers.

It's at about this point that the movie seems to lose its unique comic direction and turn into a more or less predictable combination of service comedy and romantic farce. After Judy's parents try to rescue her from the Army, she suddenly decides to stay and stick it out. She turns into a passable soldier. She almost inadvertently captures the entire Red team and makes them Blue prisoners of war during war games. And she is invited to join the Thornbushers by Colonel Thornbush himself (who turns out to have an alternative in mind if Judy doesn't want to jump at 13,000 feet).

Along the way, she meets a sexy and eligible French bachelor who's a gynecologist. After she blackmails Thornbush into sending her to Allied Army headquarters in Paris, she falls in love with the Frenchman (Armand Assante), and gets involved in Gallic romantic intrigues. It turns out that her would-be third husband is more interested in Sunday morning soccer games and cute little downstairs maids than in the kind of marriage Judy Benjamin was brought up to desire.

This stuff is occasionally funny, but it's kind of predictable. It turns *Private Benjamin* into areas that are too familiar: We've all seen the comic situations that grow out of the courtship with the Frenchman, and we'd really rather have seen more stuff of Private

Benjamin in the Army. The movie would have been better off sticking with Goldie Hawn as a female Beetle Bailey and forgetting about the changes that allow her to find self-respect, deal with the Frenchman, etc. Still, *Private Benjamin* is refreshing and fun. Goldie Hawn, who is a true comic actress, makes an original, appealing character out of Judy Benjamin, and so the movie feels alive—not just an exercise in gags and situations.

Prizzi's Honor ★ ★ ★ ★

R, 129 m., 1985

Jack Nicholson (Charley Partanna), Kathleen Turner (Irene Walker), Anjelica Huston (Maerose), Robert Loggia (Eduardo Prizzi), John Randolph (Pop Partanna), William Hickey (Don Carrado Prizzi), Lee Richardson (Dominic). Directed by John Huston and produced by John Foreman. Screenplay by Richard Condon and Janet Roach.

John Huston's *Prizzi's Honor* marches like weird and gloomy clockwork to its relentless conclusion, and half of the time, we're laughing. This is the most bizarre comedy in many a month; a movie so dark, so cynical, and so funny that perhaps only Jack Nicholson and Kathleen Turner could have kept straight faces during the love scenes. They do. They play two professional Mafia killers who meet, fall in love, marry, and find out that the mob may not be big enough for both of them.

Nicholson plays Charley Partanna, a soldier in the proud Prizzi family, rulers of the East Coast, enforcers of criminal order. The godfather of the Prizzis, Don Corrado, is a mean little old man who looks like he has been freeze-dried by the lifelong ordeal of draining every ounce of humanity out of his wizened body. To Don Corrado (William Hickey), nothing is more important than the Prizzis' honor—not even another Prizzi. Charley Partanna is the Don's grandson. He has been raised in this ethic, and accepts it. He kills without remorse. He follows orders. Only occasionally does he disobey the family's instructions, as when he broke his engagement with Maerose Prizzi (Anjelica Huston), his cousin. She then brought disgrace upon herself and, as the movie opens, is in the fourth year of self-imposed exile. But she is a Prizzi, and does not forget, or forgive.

The movie opens like *The Godfather,* at a wedding. Charley's eyes roam around the church. In the choir loft, he sees a beautiful blonde (Kathleen Turner). She looks like an angel. At the reception, he dances with her once, and then she disappears. Later that day, there is a mob killing. Determined to find out the name of the blonde angel, Charley discovers even more—that she was the California hitman, brought in to do the job. He turns to Maerose for advice. She counsels him to go ahead: After all, it's good to have interests in common with your wife.

Charley flies to the coast, setting up a running gag as they establish a transcontinental commute. There is instant, electrifying chemistry between the two of them, and the odd thing is, it seems halfway plausible. They're opposites, but they attract. Nicholson plays his hood as a tough Brooklynite; he uses a stiff upper lip, like Bogart, and sounds simple and implacable. Turner, who is flowering as a wonderful comic actress, plays her Mafia killer like a bright, cheery hostess. She could be selling cosmetics.

What happens between them is best not explained here, since the unfolding of the plot is one of the movie's delights. The story is by Richard Condon, a novelist who delights in devious plot construction, and here he takes two absolutes—romantic love and the Prizzis' honor—and arranges a collision between them. Because all of the motivations are so direct and logical, the movie is able to make the most shocking decisions seem inevitable.

John Huston directed this film right after *Under the Volcano,* and what other director could have put those two back-to-back? It is one of his very best films, perhaps because he made it with friends; Condon is an old pal from Ireland, Anjelica Huston is, of course, his daughter, and Nicholson has long been Anjelica's lover. Together they have taken a strange plot, peopled it with carefully overwrought characters, and made *Prizzi's Honor* into a treasure.

Project X ★ ★ ★
PG, 115 m., 1987

Matthew Broderick (Jimmy), Helen Hunt (Teri), Bill Sadler (Dr. Carroll), Johnny Ray McGhee (Robertson), Jonathan Stark (Sergeant Krieger), Willie (Virgil). Directed by Jonathan Kaplan and produced by Walter F. Parkes and Lawrence Lasker. Screenplay by Stanley Weiser.

W.C. Fields hated to appear in the same scene with a baby, an animal, or a plunging neckline. He was afraid of being upstaged. Virgil, the gifted chimpanzee in *Project X*, does not quite upstage Matthew Broderick, but it's one of the strengths of this movie that he deserves co-star billing.

We meet Virgil, an African primate, as he's being shipped to America for a career at the University of Wisconsin's psychology department. As played by a charismatic chimp named Willie, he turns out to be a surprisingly clever little fellow, who picks up sign language from his trainer (Helen Hunt). Then his research project loses its funding, and Virgil is shipped off under mysterious circumstances to an Air Force base in Florida, where he will train on a flight simulator.

That's where Broderick comes in. He's a troublemaking would-be pilot who is assigned to the chimp project as punishment. Once there, he turns out to be naturally gifted at identifying with the animals, and after he discovers that Virgil speaks sign language, they develop a trusting relationship. Then Broderick discovers the secret purpose of the chimp research: First, the chimps are trained to operate flight simulators, and then they're exposed to lethal doses of radiation to find out how that might affect the performance of human pilots during a nuclear war.

There is a large logical flaw in this experiment, and, to give *Project X* fair credit, Broderick himself points it out: The difference between chimps and human pilots is that the humans would know they had been exposed to lethal radiation and that knowledge would affect their performance, but the chimps' behavior wouldn't be affected.

After the threat to Virgil's life is established, the movie turns into a thriller. Can Virgil be saved? Will Broderick destroy his career? What would happen if the chimps discovered that the experiment was designed to kill them? The last third of this movie contains so many surprises that it would be unfair for me to even hint at them.

Project X is not a great movie because its screenplay doesn't really try for greatness. It's content to be a well-made, intelligent entertainment aimed primarily, I imagine, at bright teen-agers. It works on that level. More complicated issues might have confused it. And if the movie had been forced to stay within the bounds of what a chimpanzee, even a smart one, can really do, we would have lost the story's climax, which is a lot of fun but completely implausible in the real world.

Psycho II ★ ★ ½
R, 113 m., 1983

Anthony Perkins (Norman Bates), Vera Miles (Lila), Meg Tilly (Mary), Robert Loggia (Dr. Raymond), Dennis Franz (Toomey), Hugh Gillan (Sheriff Hunt). Directed by Richard Franklin and produced by Hilton A. Green. Screenplay by Tom Holland.

The first thing is to put Alfred Hitchcock's original 1960 *Psycho* right out of your mind. There will never be another movie like it, and no sequel could possibly capture its unique charms. If you've seen *Psycho* a dozen times and can recite the shots in the shower scene by heart, *Psycho II* is just not going to do it for you. But if you can accept this 1983 movie on its own terms, as a fresh start, and put your memories of Hitchcock on hold, then *Psycho II* begins to work. It's too heavy on plot and too willing to cheat about its plot to be really successful, but it does have its moments, and it's better than your average, run-of-the-mill slasher movie.

Norman Bates, having been judged not guilty by reason of insanity back in 1960, has responded well to psychiatric treatment. He is released. Because of a "state budget cutback," however, there will be no halfway house to ease his transition back into society's mainstream, and no social worker to drop in from time to time. Instead, Norman's all on his own—and he moves back into that Gothic house of horrors up on the hill above the Bates Motel. The movie's homecoming scenes strike a nerve. After all, that *is* the Bates Motel, and few images of Sir Alfred's long career have remained more indelibly etched in the memories of moviegoers. Perkins plays Bates about the same as the last time we saw him, with perhaps a few additional twitches. But he's a more sympathetic character this time, more mellow, more subdued. He still is, of course, as nutty as a fruitcake. He gets a job washing dishes at the local diner, and he makes friends with a waitress named Mary (Meg Tilly), who agrees to move into the Bates home and become his roommate. And then, in Norman's words, it starts again. His "mother," long dead (as we have every reason to recall), begins telephoning him. There are some unexplained murders. The plot thickens, but I'll end my description right here, to preserve the movie's many, many, many, secrets.

Is *Psycho II* worth seeing? It is a craftsmanlike piece of filmmaking with a suitably flaky performance by Perkins, but it isn't really a sequel to *Psycho.* It continues the story, but not the spell. And it never really establishes the other characters very well. Meg Tilly, as Norman's friend, is too laid-back and dreamy to hold her own against Norman Bates *and* a fresh slasher mystery. Vera Miles, as a woman with a fierce hatred of Norman, never quite crosses the line from indignation to insanity. In a movie full of half-sketched characters and half-explained developments, Norman Bates is just too mesmerizing to fit in very easily. But then I should have guessed the sequel wouldn't make it—right from the pretitle sequence, in which Hitchcock's original shower scene is shown, but is allowed to end before the shot of the blood going down the drain! Is nothing sacred?

Psycho III ★ ★ ★
R, 93 m., 1986

Anthony Perkins (Norman Bates), Diana Scarwid (Maureen), Jeff Fahey (Duane), Roberta Maxwell (Tracy), Hugh Gillin (Sheriff Hunt), Lee Garlington (Myrna). Directed by Anthony Perkins and produced by Hilton A. Green. Screenplay by Charles Edward Pogue.

How well we remember Norman Bates. Tens of thousands of movie characters have come and gone since 1960, when he made his first appearance in *Psycho,* and yet he still remains so vivid in the memory, such a sharp image among all the others that have gone out of focus.

Most movies are disposable. *Psycho* supplied us with the furnishings for nightmares. "Dear Mr. Hitchcock," a mother wrote the master, "after seeing your movie my daughter is afraid to take a shower. What should I do?" Send her to the dry cleaners, Hitch advised her.

In *Psycho III,* there is one startling shot that completely understands Norman Bates. Up in the old gothic horror house on the hill, he has found a note from his mother, asking him to meet her in Cabin Number Twelve. We know that although his mother may have frequent conversations with him, she is in no condition to write him a note. Norman knows that, too. He stuffed her himself. As he walks down the steps and along the front of the Bates Motel toward his rendezvous, the camera tracks along with him, one unbroken shot, and his face is a twitching mask of fear.

The face belongs to Anthony Perkins, who is better than any other actor at reflecting the demons within. Although his facial expressions in the shot are not subtle, he isn't overacting; he projects such turmoil that we almost sympathize with him. And that is the real secret of Norman Bates, and one of the reasons that *Psycho III* works as a movie: Norman is not a mad-dog killer, a wholesale slasher like the amoral villains of the Dead Teen-ager Movies. He is at war with himself. He is divided. He, Norman Bates, wants to do the right thing, to be pleasant and quiet and pass without notice. But also inside of him is the voice of his mother, fiercely urging him to kill.

At the beginning of *Psycho III,* only a short time has passed since the end of *Psycho II.* In a nearby convent, a young novice (Diana Scarwid) blames herself when an older nun falls to her death. She runs out into the night, gets a ride with a sinister motorist (Jeff Fahey), and ends up at the Bates Motel. Fahey arrives there, too, and is hired as a night clerk. Other people also turn up: an investigative reporter who wants to do a story on Norman; a local woman who gets drunk and is picked up by Fahey; and finally a crowd of rowdies back for their high school reunion.

By the end of the movie, many of these people will be dead—and because this is a tragedy, not a horror story, some of the dead ones won't deserve it, and others will survive unfairly.

The movie was directed by Perkins, in his filmmaking debut. I was surprised by what a good job he does. Any movie named *Psycho III* is going to be compared to the Hitchcock original, but Perkins isn't an imitator. He has his own agenda. He has lived with Norman Bates all these years, and he has some ideas about him, and although the movie doesn't apologize for Norman, it does pity him. For the first time, I was able to see that the true horror in the *Psycho* movies isn't what Norman does—but the fact that he is compelled to do it.

There are a couple of scenes that remind us directly of Hitchcock, especially the scene where the local sheriff dips into the ice chest on a hot day, and doesn't notice that some of the cubes he's popping into his mouth have blood on them. Perkins permits himself a certain amount of that macabre humor, as when he talks about his hobby ("stuffing things") and when he analyzes his own case for the benefit of the visiting journalist. But the movie also pays its dues as a thriller, and there is one shocking scene that is as arbitrary, unexpected, tragic, and unfair as the shower scene in *Psycho.* Only one, but then one of those scenes is enough for any movie.

The Purple Rose of Cairo ★ ★ ★ ★

PG, 87 m., 1985

Mia Farrow (Cecilia), Jeff Daniels (Tom Baxter/Gil Shepherd), Danny Aiello (Monk), Van Johnson (Larry), Alexander H. Cohen (Raoul Hirsh). Directed by Woody Allen and produced by Robert Greenhut. Screenplay by Allen.

About twenty minutes into Woody Allen's *The Purple Rose of Cairo,* an extraordinary event takes place. A young woman has been going to see the same movie over and over again, because of her infatuation with the movie's hero. From his vantage point up on the screen, the hero notices her out in the audience. He strikes up a conversation, she smiles and shyly responds, and he abruptly steps off the screen and into her life. No explanation is offered for this miraculous event, but then perhaps none is needed: Don't we spend our lives waiting for the same thing to happen to us in the movies?

Life, of course, is never as simple and dreamy as the movies, and so the hero's bold act has alarming consequences. The movie's other characters are still stranded up there on the screen, feeling angry and left out. The Hollywood studio is aghast that its characters would suddenly develop minds of their own. The actor who *played* the hero is particularly upset, because now there are two of him walking around, one wearing a pith helmet. Things are simple only in the lives of the hero and the woman, who convince themselves that they *can* simply walk off into the sunset, and get away with this thing.

The Purple Rose of Cairo is audacious and witty and has a lot of good laughs in it, but the best thing about the movie is the way Woody Allen uses it to toy with the very essence of reality and fantasy. The movie is so cheerful and open that it took me a day or two, after I'd seen it, to realize how deeply Allen has reached this time. If it is true, and I think it is, that most of the time we go to the movies in order to experience brief lives that are not our own, then Allen is demonstrating what a tricky self-deception we practice. Those movie lives consist of *only* what is on the screen, and if we start thinking that real life can be the same way, we are in for a cruel awakening.

The woman in the movie is played by Mia Farrow as a sweet, rather baffled small-town waitress whose big, shiftless lug of a husband bats her around. She is a good candidate for the magic of the movies. Up on the screen, sophisticated people have cocktails and plan trips down the Nile and are recognized by the doormen in nightclubs. The hero in the movie is played by Jeff Daniels (who was Debra Winger's husband in *Terms of Endearment*). He is a genial, open-faced smoothie with all the right moves, but he has a problem: He *only* knows what his character knows in the movie, and his experience is literally limited to what happens to his character in the plot. This can cause problems. He's great at talking sweetly to a woman, and holding hands, and kissing—but just when the crucial moment arrives, the movie fades out, and therefore, alas, so does he.

Many of Allen's best moments come from exploring the paradox that the movie character knows nothing of real life. For example, he can drive a car, because he drives one in the movie, but he can't start a car, because he doesn't turn on the ignition in the movie. Mia Farrow thinks maybe they can work this out. They can learn from each other. He can learn real life, and she can learn the romance of the movies. The problem is, both of them are now living in real life, where studio moguls and angry actors and snoopy reporters are making their life miserable.

Allen's buried subject in *The Purple Rose of Cairo* is, I think, related to the subjects of his less successful movies, *Stardust Memories* (1980) and *Zelig* (1983). He is interested in the conflicts involving who you want to be, and who other people want you to be. *Stardust* was about a celebrity whose fame prevented people from relating to anything but his image. *Zelig*, the other side of the coin, was about a man whose anonymity was so profound that he could gain an identity only by absorbing one from the people around him. In *Purple Rose*, the movie hero has the first problem, and the woman in the audience has the second, and when they get together, they still don't make one whole person, just two sad halves.

Purple Rose is delightful from beginning to end, not only because of the clarity and charm with which Daniels and Farrow explore the problems of their characters, but also because the movie is so intelligent. It's not brainy or intellectual—no one in the whole movie speaks with more complexity than your average 1930s movie hero—but the movie is filled with wit and invention, and Allen trusts us to find the ironies, relish the contradictions, and figure things out for ourselves. While we do that, he makes us laugh and he makes us think, and when you get right down to it, forget about the fantasies; those are two of the most exciting things that could happen to anybody in a movie. The more you think about *The Purple Rose of Cairo*, and about the movies, and about why you go to the movies, the deeper the damned thing gets.

Q

Q ★ ★ 1/2
R, 92 m., 1982

Michael Moriarty (Quinn), Candy Clark (Girlfriend), David Carradine (Detective), Richard Roundtree (Detective), Ed Kovens (Crook). Directed by Larry Cohen and produced by Samuel Z. Arkoff. Screenplay by Cohen.

A few days after *Q* was screened at the Cannes Film Festival (under its original title, *The Winged Serpent*), the following conversation took place between Samuel Z. Arkoff, the film's producer, and Rex Reed, the critic:

Reed: Sam! I just saw *The Winged Serpent!* What a surprise! All that dreck—and right in the middle of it, a great Method performance by Michael Moriarty!
Arkoff: The dreck was my idea.

I believe him. Arkoff has been producing films for thirty years now, and even if he *was* honored with a retrospective at the Museum of Modern Art, his heart still lies with shots of a giant flying lizard attacking a woman in a bikini on top of a Manhattan skyscraper. He's just that kinda guy. There are, in fact, several shots in *Q* that owe their ancestry to Sam Arkoff. I am aware, of course, that Larry Cohen gets credit for having written and directed this movie, but where would Cohen or any other director be without the rich heritage of a quarter-century of American-International Pictures made by Sam Arkoff? Here are examples of the shots I have in mind:

• The camera looks straight down at terrified citizens fleeing from a menace. They run crazily across the street. Some run away from the camera, some toward it, so that you can't tell for sure where the menace is, and the shot can be intercut with shots of a menace approaching from any direction.

• The hero empties his machine gun into the giant serpent and turns away from a window to issue orders: "Everybody hold your positions!" Just then the serpent reappears behind him.

• There are False Serpent Alarms in which people get hit from behind by toy birds, chairs, and their boyfriends.

• David Carradine says, "He doesn't die easy."

You get the idea. *Q* is another silly monster movie. But think how long it's *been* since we had another silly monster movie. There was a time during the golden age of Sam Arkoff's career when there were lots of monster movies. Remember, for example, *Attack of the Crab Monsters*, *The Viking Women and the Sea Serpent*, *Creature from the Haunted Sea*, and *Wasp Woman*. But in the last few years Creature Features have been replaced by Dead Teen-ager Movies, and instead of awful special effects of a monster going berserk, we get worse shots of a homicidal maniac going berserk.

Q returns to the basic formula, in which a prehistoric creature terrorizes the city. In this case, the creature is a Quetzalcoatl, a mythical Aztec monster with wings *and* four claws. It apparently has been brought back into existence in connection with some shady human sacrifices at the Museum of National History (although this particular subplot is very muddled). It lives in a nest at the top of the Chrysler Building, lays eggs, and terrorizes helpless New Yorkers, who are not sure if this is a real monster or another crazy circulation stunt by Rupert Murdoch.

Rex Reed was right, though, about the Method performance by Michael Moriarty. In the middle of this exploitation movie, there's Moriarty, rolling his eyes, improvising dialogue, and acting creepy. He's fun to watch, especially in the scene where he names his terms for leading the cops to the lizard. The cast also includes David Carradine, Richard Roundtree, and Candy Clark, good actors all, but you have to be *awfully* good not to be upstaged by the death throes of a dying Quetzalcoatl.

Still to be answered: How did *one* Quetzalcoatl get pregnant?

Quest for Fire ★ ★ ★ ½
R, 100 m., 1982

Everett McGill (Noah), Ron Perlman (Amoukar), Nameer El-Kadi (Gaw), Rae Dawn Chong (Ika). Directed by Jean-Jacques Annaud and produced by John Kemeny and Denis Heroux. Screenplay by Gerard Brach.

There are basically two ways to regard *Quest for Fire.* The movie is either (a) the moving story of how scattered tribes of very early men developed some of the traits that made them human, or (b) a laughable caveman picture in which a lot of lantern-jawed actors jump around in animal skins, snarling and swinging clubs at one another. During the movie's opening scenes, I found myself seeing it in the second way, as a borderline comedy. But then these characters and their quest began to grow on me, and by the time the movie was over I cared very much about how their lives would turn out.

Other viewers report some of the same confusion. The movie has been compared with such varied works of art as *2001: A Space Odyssey* and *Alley Oop.* The question, I suppose, is whether you can make your own leap of imagination into the world of the movie—whether you're willing to identify with these beetle-browed ancestors who made more important discoveries, in their way, than all of the Nobel laureates put together. I found I *was* willing, and I was a little surprised at how much affection the movie generated.

Quest for Fire was shot on rugged locations in Canada and Scotland and takes place at the dawn of man. It introduces us to a tribe of primitive men who guard their most precious possession, which is fire. They know how to tend it and how to use it, but not how to make it. And after a jealous tribe of less-advanced creatures attacks them and destroys their fire, three men set out on an odyssey to seek another tribe that possesses fire and to steal it from them. Along the way, there are terrifying adventures. A saber-toothed tiger chases the men up into a tree and keeps them there for days. On another occasion, the heroes are trapped between an unfriendly tribe of apes and a herd of mastodons. In each situation, the men realize that simply running away won't work; they can't run fast or far enough. And so they slowly and painfully figure out a solution to their dilemma. Climbing the tree, for example, is rather obvious, but their solution to the mastodon problem is a brave inspiration.

Eventually the men discover another tribe, a more advanced tribe that lives in primitive huts and knows how to make fire and has even developed arts (they decorate themselves with mud, and their clay pots have drawings of animals scratched on them). The leader of the wanderers lusts after one of the women of the new tribe, and after a strange initiation ceremony he has sex with her. Soon he will make one of his greatest discoveries: The difference between lust and love and how it leads to the difference between isolation—and loneliness.

Quest for Fire compresses prehistory quite radically, of course. It's a little much to expect that one man in one span of a few weeks could make the scientific, emotional, and tactical discoveries that take place in the movie. Our progress as a race must have been slower than that (although Loren Eiseley writes in his books of the amazing explosion of the size of the human brain in just a handful of generations). *Quest for Fire* isn't science, though, it's an imaginary re-creation of our past, and it uses history for inspiration, not as a data source. The only two technical advisers listed in the credits are, appropriately, a novelist and a scientific popularizer: Anthony Burgess created the special primitive languages in the film, and Desmond Morris choreographed the body language and gestures.

I suggested earlier that there's probably a temptation to laugh during *Quest for Fire,* especially during such touchy scenes as the one in which early woman teaches early man that it *wasn't* as good for her as it was for him. I smiled during those scenes. But, thinking over my response, I realize that I wasn't smiling at the movie, but at the behavior of the characters. Man is a comic beast. For all of our dignity, we are very simple in many of our wants and desires, and as we crawled out of the primeval sludge and started our long trek toward civilization, there must have been many more moments of comedy than of nobility.

Quest for Fire cheerfully acknowledges that, and indeed some of its best scenes involve man's discovery of laughter. When one of the primitive tribesmen is hit on the head by a small falling stone, the woman from the other tribe laughs and laughs. Our heroes are puzzled: They haven't heard such a noise before. But it strikes some sort of deep chord, I guess, because later, one of the tribesmen deliberately drops a small stone on his friend's head, and then everybody laughs: The three men together with the woman who taught them laughter. That's human. The guy who got hit on the head is, of course, a little slow to join in the laughter, but finally he goes along with the joke. That's civilization.

R

Racing with the Moon ★ ★ ★ ½
PG, 108 m., 1984

Sean Penn (Hopper), Elizabeth McGovern (Caddie), Nicolas Cage (Nicky), Suzanne Adkinson (Sally), Julie Phillips (Alice). Directed by Richard Benjamin and produced by Alain Bernheim and John Kohn. Screenplay by Steven Kloves.

I'd like to start with a hypothetical question: How long has it been since you went to a movie that ended with the words "I love you"? For me, it had been a very long time, and one of the simpler pleasures of *Racing with the Moon* was to observe the movie marching inevitably toward those three words. A deeper pleasure was that the movie arrived there with grace and charm.

The story takes place in California in 1943, with the United States at war and teen-agers volunteering for the service. We meet a couple of high school kids, Hopper and Nicky, who are pinspotters down at the bowling alley and otherwise spend their time cutting classes, shooting pool, hitching rides on trains, and talking about the meaning of life. We are reminded of Tom and Huck. One night Hopper goes to the movies. His eyes meet the girl who is selling him his ticket, and he is thunderstruck by her. Her name is Caddie. Nicky already has a girlfriend, a plump little blonde named Sally. Hopper starts a campaign to win Caddie's heart, by slipping her flowers anonymously and tracking her down in the high school library. It appears that Caddie is a rich kid who lives in the house on the hill. But she likes Hopper anyway, and he likes her, and *Racing with the Moon* turns into a love story.

So far, what we have here is a movie that could go in several different directions. It could be sappy, it could be great, it could be dripping with so much nostalgia that it would feel like a memory even while we were watching it. *Racing with the Moon* doesn't fall into the *Summer of '42* nostalgia trap, but tries to be honest with its romantic characters. The performers are probably the reason that approach works so well. The three leading actors are Sean Penn and Elizabeth McGovern, as the young lovers, and Nicolas Cage, as Penn's friend. It's a pleasure to watch them work.

Penn, in particular, shows a whole side we didn't see in movies like *Bad Boys* or, needless to say, *Fast Times at Ridgemont High.* He's somehow better-looking than before, and more relaxed and confident. He doesn't come across with a lot of distracting self-importance. He plays the kind of kid who uses a rough exterior—smoking and shooting pool—as a kind of cover-up for the intelligence and sensitivity underneath, and one of the movie's best quiet moments comes when he reveals how well he can play the piano. McGovern, who had such a sweet face and such a wicked charm as the mistress in *Ragtime*, seems younger here. She has a secret she keeps from Penn, but only because she loves him. The way she plays against him is fun to watch: She's not a flirt and she's not coy, but instead she's open with this kid and has fun teasing him; there's a scene where she sets him up for a date with her girlfriend, and it's written and choreographed so carefully that it takes you back to any soda fountain you may ever have inhabited. Cage is good, too, reckless and self-destructive and dreamy, and by the end of the movie we really have a feeling for their complex relationships with each other.

Racing with the Moon is a movie like *Valley*

Girl or *Baby, It's You,* a movie that is interested in teen-agers and willing to listen to how they talk and to observe, with great tenderness, the fragility and importance of their first big loves. It's easy to end a movie with "I love you," but it's hard to get there honestly.

Radio Days ★ ★ ★ ★
PG, 88 m., 1987

Mia Farrow (Sally White), Seth Green (Joe), Michael Tucker (Father), Josh Mostel (Abe), Tito Puente (Bandleader), Danny Aiello (Rocco), Diane Keaton (New Year's Singer), Wallace Shawn (Masked Avenger), Dianne Wiest (Bea). Directed by Woody Allen and produced by Robert Greenhut. Screenplay by Allen.

I can remember what happened to the Lone Ranger in 1949 better than I can remember what happened to me. His adventures struck deeply into my imagination in a way that my own did not, and as I write these words there is almost a physical intensity to my memories of listening to the radio. Television was never the same. Television shows happened in the TV set, but radio shows happened in my head.

That is one of the truths that Woody Allen evokes in *Radio Days,* his comedy about growing up in the 1940s. Another one is that glamor and celebrity meant something in those days. And for millions of people living in ordinary homes in ordinary neighborhoods, the radio brought images of beings who lived in a shimmering world of penthouses and nightclubs, in dressing rooms and boudoirs.

The hero of *Radio Days* is an ordinary person like that: an adolescent Jewish kid who grows up in Brooklyn in a house full of relatives and listens passionately to the radio. But the movie is not simply his story. It is also the story of 1940s radio itself, and it recreates many of the legends that he remembers hearing.

For example, the story of the burglars who answered the phone in a house they were burgling and won the jackpot on "Name That Tune," and the prizes were delivered the next day to their bewildered victims. Or the embarrassing plight of the suave radio host who liked to play around and got locked on the roof of a nightclub with the cigarette girl. Or the way the macho heroes of radio adventure serials turned out, in real life, to be short little bald guys. (The one legend Allen leaves out is the scandal of the kiddie-show host who growled "That oughta hold the little bastards" into an open mike.)

Radio Days cuts back and forth between the adolescent hero's working-class neighborhood in Brooklyn and the glamorous radio world of Manhattan. And, like radio, it jumps easily from one level of reality to another. There are autobiographical memories of relatives and school, neighbors and friends, and then there are the glittering radio legends that seeped into these ordinary lives.

Allen is not concerned with creating a story with a beginning and an end, and his movie is more like a revue in which drama is followed by comedy and everything is tied together by music, by dozens of lush arrangements of the hit songs of the 1940s. He has always used popular music in his movies (remember the opening of *Manhattan*?), but never more than this time, where the muscular, romantic confidence of the big-band sound reinforces every memory with the romance of the era.

There are so many characters in *Radio Days,* and they are in so many separate vignettes, that it's hard to give a coherent description of the plot or plots. In form and even in mood, the movie it's closest to is Federico Fellini's *Amarcord,* which also was a memory of growing up—of family, religion, sex, local folk legends, scandalous developments, and intense romantic yearnings, underlined with wall-to-wall band music. In a way, both films have nostalgia itself as one of their subjects. What they evoke isn't the long-ago time itself, but the memory of it. There is something about it being past and gone and irretrievable that makes it more precious than it ever was at the time.

As part of this nostalgic feeling, Allen seems to have made a deliberate attempt to use as many of his former actors as possible. The movie is a roll call of casts from earlier films, from Mia Farrow and Diane Keaton to Tony Roberts, Danny Aiello, Dianne Wiest, Jeff Daniels, and Wallace Shawn. And viewers with good memories will notice there also are many actual radio veterans in the movie, such as Don Pardo and Kitty Carlisle, and the shadows of others, such as Bill Stern, whose inspirational parables about sports heroes are mercilessly satirized.

The one actor who is not visible is Allen. But his teen-age alter ego (Seth Green) provides a memory of young Allen in *Take the Money and Run*, and then there is Allen's own voice on the sound track, evoking those golden days of yesteryear. There also is the Allen irreverence in several moments of absolutely inspired comedy, such as a classroom show-and-tell session, or the time the young hero collects dimes for Israel and then spends them on a boxtop secret decoder ring and has to face the rabbi's wrath.

Radio Days is so ambitious and so audacious that it almost defies description. It's a kaleidoscope of dozens of characters, settings, and scenes—the most elaborate production Allen has ever made—and it's inexhaustible, spinning out one delight after another. Although there is no narrative thread from beginning to end, there is a buried emotional thread. Like music, the movie builds toward a climax we can't even guess is coming, and then Allen finds the perfect images for the last few minutes, for a bittersweet evocation of goodbye to all that.

His final moments are staged on a set representing a rooftop on Times Square, with a smoker puffing his cigarette on a Camel billboard, while in another direction a giant neon top hat is lifted and lowered. This set is so overblown and romantic, it's like the moment in *Amarcord* when all of the townspeople get into boats and go out to watch the great ocean liner go past, and we see that the liner is obviously a prop—a vast, artificial Christmas tree of shimmering lights and phony glory. Allen finds the same truth that Fellini did: What actually happens isn't nearly as important as how we remember it.

Raggedy Man ★ ★ ★ ½

PG, 94 m., 1981

Sissy Spacek (Nita), Eric Roberts (Teddy), Sam Shepard (Bailey), R.G. Armstrong (Rigby). Directed by Jack Fisk and produced by Burt Weissbourd and William D. Wittliff. Screenplay by Wittliff.

Raggedy Man remembers the small-town years of World War II so exactly that, although not yet born when the war broke out, I found myself remembering things I didn't even know I knew. Things like the way kids zoomed around dusty backyards, making their arms into airplane wings and imitating the noises of dive bombers. Like the Andrews Sisters singing "Rum and Coca-Cola" on the radio. Like the absolutely correct detail of a plaster-of-paris plaque on the wall, with a child's hand print immortalized on it. Remember?

Sissy Spacek stars as the sole switchboard operator of a small-town telephone company somewhere in the wilds of Texas. She lives in a small white frame house with a slamming screen door, and tries to raise her two sons, who are almost too small to support such grown-up names as Henry and Harry. The question of her husband is a mystery. Spacek hates her job, but she can't leave it: Mr. Rigby, the president of the telephone company, barks that this is wartime and her job is "frozen." Right, and she's frozen in it, until one day a young sailor (Eric Roberts) comes looking for a pay phone so he can call home. He's got a few days' leave, and has hitchhiked for hundreds of miles on the hopes of seeing his fiancée. The phone call reveals that she has taken up with a new beau. Roberts is crestfallen. Spacek kindly offers him some coffee. More or less, a little at a time, they fall in love.

These surface events of small-town life are wonderfully observed in *Raggedy Man*, which never pushes the romance between Spacek and Roberts too far: They remain decent, sensitive, courteous people, a little shy in the presence of large emotions. The town gossips about the woman taking up with the sailor, but people will gossip. (Nobody knows that better than the telephone operator!) Unfortunately, *Raggedy Man* has a whole additional level of plotting that is not nearly as rewarding as the events I've already described. There is, for example, the mystery of the "raggedy man" himself, a strange, scarecrow character who hangs about in the background of several scenes and has a disconcerting way of disappearing just when you want to get a closer look at him. There's also the matter of the town louts, who inhabit the beer hall and lust after the slim, young telephone operator.

These two plot strands lead up to a climactic ending that, quite frankly, I thought was unnecessary. Without giving away several secrets that the movie itself takes very seriously, I can say that *Raggedy Man* would have pleased me more if it had completely avoided its violent conclusion—and if the raggedy man himself had been left totally out of the story, the movie, and especially the symbolism.

Such regrets still leave my affection for this movie pretty much untouched. The Sissy Spacek performance is a small jewel: She has the words, the movements, the very tilt of her face, down just right. There's a scene where she puts music on the radio and dances with a broom, and another scene where she has a serious talk with her two little boys, and they're nearly perfect scenes. So is another one, where Roberts takes the two boys to a carnival. Roberts himself is a revelation: He is often overwrought in his acting; here, playing more quietly, he expresses great reserve of tenderness and strength, and is very effective.

Raggedy Man was Sissy Spacek's first movie after she won the Academy Award for *Coal Miner's Daughter,* and the first movie directed by her husband, Jack Fisk. (She met him when he was the art director for her first starring movie, *Badlands,* back in 1973.) The movie was made with a lot of love and startingly fresh memories of the early 1940s, and reminds us once again that Spacek is a treasure.

Raging Bull ★ ★ ★ ★

R, 119 m., 1980

Robert De Niro (Jake La Motta), Cathy Moriarty (Vickie La Motta), Joe Pesci (Joey), Frank Vincent (Salvy), Nicholas Colasanto (Tommy Como), Theresa Saldana (Lenore), Frank Adonis (Patsy), Mario Gallo (Mario). Directed by Martin Scorsese and produced by Irwin Winkler and Robert Chartoff. Screenplay by Paul Schrader and Mardik Martin.

Martin Scorsese's *Raging Bull* is a movie about brute force, anger, and grief. It is also, like several of Scorsese's other movies, about a man's inability to understand a woman except in terms of the only two roles he knows how to assign her: virgin or whore. There is no room inside the mind of the prizefighter in this movie for the notion that a woman might be a friend, a lover, or a partner. She is only, to begin with, an inaccessible sexual fantasy. And then, after he has possessed her, she becomes tarnished by sex. Insecure in his own manhood, the man becomes obsessed by jealousy—and releases his jealousy in violence.

It is a vicious circle. Freud called it the "madonna-whore complex." Groucho Marx put it somewhat differently: "I wouldn't belong to any club that would have me as a member." It amounts to a man having such low self-esteem that he (a) cannot respect a woman who would sleep with him, and (b) is convinced that, given the choice, she would rather be sleeping with someone else. I'm making a point of the way *Raging Bull* equates sexuality and violence because one of the criticisms of this movie is that we never really get to know the central character. I don't agree with that. I think Scorsese and Robert De Niro do a fearless job of showing us the precise feelings of their central character, the former boxing champion Jake La Motta.

It is true that the character never tells us what he's feeling, that he is not introspective, that his dialogue is mostly limited to expressions of desire, fear, hatred, and jealousy. But these very limitations—these stone walls separating the character from the world of ordinary feelings—tell us all we need to know, especially when they're reflected back at him by the other people in his life. Especially his brother and his wife, Vickie.

Raging Bull is based, we are told, on the life of La Motta, who came out of the slums of the Bronx to become middleweight champion in the 1940s, who made and squandered millions of dollars, who became a pathetic stand-up comedian, and finally spent time in a prison for corrupting the morals of an underage girl. Is this the real La Motta? We cannot know for sure, though La Motta was closely involved with the production. What's perhaps more to the point is that Scorsese and his principal collaborators, actor Robert De Niro and screenwriter Paul Schrader, were attracted to this material. All three seem fascinated by the lives of tortured, violent, guilt-ridden characters; their previous three-way collaboration was the movie *Taxi Driver.*

Scorsese's very first film, *Who's That Knocking at My Door* (1967), starred Harvey Keitel as a kid from Little Italy who fell in love with a girl but could not handle the facts of her previous sexual experience. In its sequel, *Mean Streets* (1972), the same hang-up was explored, as it was in *Taxi Driver,* where the De Niro character's madonna-whore complex tortured him in sick relationships with an inaccessible, icy blonde, and with a young prostitute. Now the filmmakers have returned to the same ground, in a film deliberately intended to strip away everything but the raw surges of guilt, jealousy, and rage coursing through La Motta's extremely limited imagination.

Raging Bull remains close to its three basic elements: a man, a woman, and prizefighting. La Motta is portrayed as a punk kid, stubborn, strong, and narrow. He gets involved in boxing, and he is good at it. He gets married, but his wife seems almost an afterthought. Then one day he sees a girl at a municipal swimming pool and is transfixed by her. The girl is named Vickie, and she is played by Cathy Moriarty as an intriguing mixture of unstudied teen-ager, self-reliant survivor, and somewhat calculated slut.

La Motta wins and marries her. Then he becomes consumed by the conviction she is cheating on him. Scorsese finds a way to visually suggest his jealousy: From La Motta's point of view, Vickie sometimes floats in slow motion toward another man. The technique fixes the moment in our minds; we share La Motta's exaggeration of an innocent event. And we share, too, the La Motta character's limited and tragic hang-ups. This man we see is not, I think, supposed to be any more subtle than he seems. He does not have additional "qualities" to share with us. He is an engine driven by his own rage. The equation between his prizefighting and his sexuality is inescapable, and we see the trap he's in: La Motta is the victim of base needs and instincts that, in his case, are not accompanied by the insights and maturity necessary for him to cope with them. The raging bull. The poor sap.

Ragtime ★ ★ ★ ½
PG, 156 m., 1981

Howard E. Rollins, Jr. (Coalhouse Walker), James Cagney (Rhinelander Waldo), Brad Dourif (Younger Brother), Mary Steenburgen (Mother), James Olson (Father), Elizabeth McGovern (Evelyn Nesbit), Kenneth McMillan (Willie Conklin), Pat O'Brien (Delmas), Mandy Patinkin (Tateh), Moses Gunn (Booker T. Washington). Directed by Milos Forman and produced by Dino De Laurentiis. Screenplay by Michael Weller.

Milos Forman apparently made a basic decision very early in his production of E.L. Doctorow's best-selling novel, *Ragtime.* He decided to set aside the book's kaleidoscopic jumble of people, places, and things, and concentrate on just one of the several narrative threads. Instead of telling dozens of stories, his film is mostly concerned with the story of Coalhouse Walker, Jr., a black piano player who insists that justice be done after he is insulted by some yahoo volunteer firemen.

Doctorow's novel was an inspired juggling act involving both actual and fictional characters, who sometimes met in imaginary scenes of good wit and imagery. The Coalhouse story was more or less equal with several others. A film faithful to the book would have had people walking in and out of each other's lives in an astonishing series of coincidences. That might have been a good film, too. It might have looked a little like Robert Altman's *Nashville* or *Buffalo Bill,* and indeed Altman was the first filmmaker signed to direct *Ragtime.* But we will never see what Altman might have done, and Forman decided to do something different. He traces the ways in which Coalhouse Walker enters and affects the lives of an upstate New York family in the first decade of the century. The family lives in White Plains, N.Y., in a vast and airy old frame manor, and it consists of Father, Mother, and Younger Brother, with walk-ons by a grandfather and a young son.

For Younger Brother, the sirens of the big city call, in the form of an infatuation with the chorus girl Evelyn Nesbit (Elizabeth McGovern). That's before the saga of Coalhouse Walker alters his life. Coalhouse (in a superb performance by Howard E. Rollins, Jr.) meets the family by accident, or maybe by fate. A young black woman gives birth to Coalhouse's son, and then the family takes in both the woman and her son, hiring her as their maid. Coalhouse comes calling. He wants to marry the mother of his child. He has earned enough money. Everything's all set for the ceremony, when an event takes place that changes everything. The local volunteer firemen, enraged that a black man would own his own Model T, block the car's way in front of their station. They pile horse manure on the front seat. And Coalhouse, quite simply, cannot rest until he sees his car restored to him in its original condition.

The story develops quickly into a confrontation. Coalhouse barricades himself into New York's J. Pierpont Morgan Library, and issues a set of demands. The library is surrounded by police and guardsmen, led by Police Commissioner Rhinelander Waldo (the great James Cagney, out of retirement). Father (James Olson) gets drawn into negotiations, and Younger Brother (Brad Dourif) is actually one of Coalhouse's lieutenants, in blackface disguise. Meanwhile, Mother is running off with a bearded immigrant who started out making cutout silhouettes on the streets and is now one of the first film directors.

The story of *Ragtime,* then, is essentially the story of Coalhouse Walker, Jr. Forman, a Czechoslovakian with an usually keen eye for American society—his credits include *One Flew Over the Cuckoo's Nest* and *Hair!*—has made a film about black pride and rage and . . . not *only* white racism, which we sort of expect, but also white liberalism.

The great achievement of *Ragtime* is in its performances, especially Rollins and the changes he goes through in this story, from youthful romantic love to an impassioned cry "Lord, why did you fill me with such rage?" Olson, quiet and self-effacing, is subtly powerful as Father. Mary Steenburgen is clear-voiced, primly ethical Mother who springs a big surprise on everyone. Pat O'Brien has two great scenes as a corrupt, world-weary lawyer. Kenneth McMillan blusters and threatens as the racist fire chief. And when Cagney tells him "people tell me . . . you're slime," there is the resonance of movie legend in his voice.

Ragtime is a loving, beautifully mounted, graceful film that creates its characters with great clarity. We understand where everyone stands, and most of the time we even know why. Forman surrounds them with some of the other characters from the Doctorow novel (including Harry Houdini, Teddy Roosevelt, and Norman Mailer as the architect Sanford White), but in the film they're just atmosphere—window dressing. Forman's decision to stick with the story of Coalhouse is vindicated, because he tells it so well.

Raiders of the Lost Ark ★ ★ ★ ★

PG, 115 m., 1981

Harrison Ford (Indy), Ronald Lacey (Teht), John Rhys-Davies (Sallah), Karen Allen (Marion), Wolf Kahler (Dietrich). Directed by Steven Spielberg and produced by Frank Marshall. Executive producers, George Lucas and Howard Kazanjian. Screenplay by Lucas and Phillip Kaufman.

Raiders of the Lost Ark is an out-of-body experience, a movie of glorious imagination and breakneck speed that grabs you in the first shot, hurtles you through a series of incredible adventures, and deposits you back in reality two hours later—breathless, dizzy, wrung-out, and with a silly grin on your face. This movie celebrates the stories we spent our adolescence searching for in the pulp adventure magazines, in the novels of Edgar Rice Burroughs, in comics—even in the movies. There used to be a magazine named *Thrilling Wonder Stories,* and every shot in *Raiders of the Lost Ark* looks like one of its covers. It's the kind of movie where the hero gets out of bed wondering what daring exploits and astonishing, cliff-hanging, death-defying threats he will have to survive in the next ten seconds.

It's actually more than a movie; it's a catalog of adventure. For locations, it ticks off the jungles of South America, the hinterlands of Tibet, the deserts of Egypt, a hidden submarine base, an isolated island, a forgotten tomb—no, make that *two* forgotten tombs—and an American anthropology classroom. For villains, it has sadistic Nazis, slimy gravediggers, drunken Sherpas, and scheming Frenchmen. For threats, it climaxes with the wrath of God, and leads up to that spectacular development by easy stages, with tarantulas, runaway boulders, hidden spears, falling rock slabs, burning airplanes, runaway trucks, sealed tombs, and snakes. Lots of snakes. For modes of conveyance, it looks like one of those old world's fair panoramas of transportation: It has horse carts, biplanes, motorcycles, submarines, ships, horse, trains, and trucks. No bicycles.

For heroes, it has Indiana Jones (Harrison Ford) and his former and future girlfriend, Marion (Karen Allen). She's the kind of girl . . . well, to make a long story short, when they first met ten years ago, Indiana deflowered her, and that made her so mad at men that she moved to the mountains of Tibet, opened a bar, and started nightly drinking contests with the Sherpas. She'll never forgive him, almost.

The time is 1936. Indy is an American anthropologist who learns that the Nazis think they've discovered the long-lost resting place of the Ark of the Covenant, the golden casket used by the ancient Hebrews to hold the Ten Commandments. Indy's mission: Beat the Nazis to the prize. He flies to Tibet, collects Marion and a priceless medallion that holds the secret of the Ark's location, and then tries to outsmart the Nazis. What is a little amazing about *Raiders of the Lost Ark* is that this plot somehow holds together and makes some sense, even though it functions primarily as a framework for the most incredible series of action and stunt set-pieces I've ever seen in a movie. Indiana and Marion spend the entire film hanging by their fingernails—literally, at one point, over a pit of poisonous snakes.

They survive a series of gruesome and dreadful traps, pitfalls, double-crosses, ambushes, and fates worse than death (of which this movie suggests several). And Indiana engages in the best chase scene I've seen in a film. (I include, in second place, the chase from *The French Connection*, with *Bullitt* in third.) The chase involves a truck, three jeeps, a horse, a motorcycle, and an awesomely difficult stunt in which a character is required to make a 360-degree turn of the speeding truck. All of these spectacles are achieved with flawless movie technology brought to a combination of stunts, special visual effects, and sheer sweat. The makers of this film have covered similar ground before, if perhaps never so fluently; George Lucas, the executive producer, gave birth to the *Star Wars* movies, and Steven Spielberg, the director, made *Jaws* and *Close Encounters*. The rest of the all-star crew's work includes photography by veteran British cinematographer Douglas Slocombe, appropriately stirring and haunting music by *Star Wars* composer John Williams, sets by *Star Wars* production designer Norman Reynolds and art director Les Dilley, and countless wonderments by Richard Edlund, who supervised the visual effects.

Two things, however, make *Raiders of the Lost Ark* more than just a technological triumph: its sense of humor and the droll style of its characters. This is often a funny movie, but it doesn't get many of its laughs with dialogue and only a few with obvious gags (although the biggest laugh comes from the oldest and most obvious gag, involving a swordsman and a marksman). We find ourselves laughing in surprise, in relief, in incredulity at the movie's ability to pile one incident upon another in an inexhaustible series of inventions. And the personalities of the central characters are enormously winning. Harrison Ford, as Indy Jones, does not do a reprise of his *Star Wars* work. Instead he creates a taciturn, understated, stubborn character who might be the Humphrey Bogart of *Treasure of the Sierra Madre* with his tongue in his cheek. He survives fires, crushings, shootings, burnings. He really hates snakes. Karen Allen plays the female lead with a resilient toughness that develops its own charm. She can handle herself in any situation. She *really* hates snakes.

Raiders of the Lost Ark is a swashbuckling adventure epic in the tradition of *Star Wars*, *Superman*, the James Bond pictures, and all the other multimillion-dollar special effects extravaganzas. It wants only to entertain. It succeeds. Watch it with someone you know fairly well. There will be times during the film when it will be necessary to grab somebody.

Raising Arizona ★ 1/2

PG-13, 103 m., 1987

Nicolas Cage (H.I.), Holly Hunter (Ed), Trey Wilson (Nathan Arizona, Sr.), John Goodman (Gale), William Forsythe (Evelle), Sam McMurray (Glen), Frances McDormand (Dot). Directed by Joel Coen and produced by Ethan Coen. Screenplay by Coen and Coen.

I have a problem with movies where everybody talks as if they were reading out of an old novel about a bunch of would-be colorful characters. They usually end up sounding silly. For every movie like *True Grit* that works with lines like "I was determined not to give them anything to chaff me about," there is a *Black Shield of Falworth*, with lines like "Yonder lies duh castle of my fadder."

Generally speaking, it's best to have your characters speak in strong but unaffected English, especially when your story is set in the present. Otherwise they'll end up distracting the hell out of everybody.

That's one of the problems with *Raising Arizona.* The movie is narrated by its hero, a man who specializes in robbing convenience stores, but it sounds as if he just graduated from the Rooster Cogburn School of Elocution. There are so many "far be it from me's" and "inasmuches" in his language that he could play Ebenezer Scrooge with the same vocabulary—and that's not what you expect from a two-bit thief who lives in an Arizona trailer park.

Maybe, of course, he just happens to talk that way. Even in this age of homogenized culture, a few people do retain distinctive and colorful speech patterns. That would be a good theory except that everyone in *Raising Arizona* talks funny. They all elevate their dialogue to an arch and artificial level that's distracting and unconvincing and slows down the progress of the film.

And what *Raising Arizona* needs more than anything else is more velocity. Here's a movie that stretches out every moment for more than it's worth, until even the moments of inspiration seem forced. Since the basic idea of the movie is a good one and there are talented people in the cast, what we have here is a film shot down by its own forced and mannered style.

The movie stars Nicolas Cage as the guy who sticks up all-night grocery stores, and Holly Hunter as the policewoman who falls in love with him while taking his mug shots. After he gets out of prison for what he hopes is the last time, they get married and set up their little home, and then discover that they cannot have children. Meanwhile, there have been stories in the paper about a local furniture czar, Nathan Arizona, whose wife took a fertility drug and had quints. Hunter convinces Cage that anybody with five kids is not going to miss one of them, and Cage steals into the Arizona home to kidnap one of the infants.

The movie has some fun with the bombastic Arizona (played like a used-car huckster by Trey Wilson), and it also contains some charming moments involving the photogenic child who has been cast as the kidnapping victim. But then there's a silly subplot about a couple of escaped cons, and an even more ridiculous development involving some kind of superhero Hell's Angel, who roars through town like a messenger from hell.

The movie cannot decide if it exists in the real world of trailer parks and 7-Elevens and Pampers, or in a fantasy world of characters from another dimension. It cannot decide if it is about real people, or comic exaggerations. It moves so uneasily from one level of reality to another that finally we're just baffled. Comedy often depends on frustrating the audience's expectations. But how can it work when we don't have a clue about what to expect—when the movie itself doesn't know what is possible and what is not?

Raising Arizona is the new work by the Coen brothers, Joel and Ethan, whose previous film was the superb thriller *Blood Simple.* That was a movie that pushed reality as far as it could go within the rigid confines of a well-made thriller. *Raising Arizona* needs the same kind of restraint. It's all over the map. If the same story had been told straight, as a comic slice of life, it might have really worked. I kept thinking of Jonathan Demme's *Melvin and Howard,* the film about the gas station owner and the billionaire, in which equally unlikely events happened but were very funny because they were allowed to be believable.

Rambo: First Blood Part II ★ ★ ★

R, 90 m., 1985

Sylvester Stallone (Rambo), Richard Crenna (Trautman), Charles Napier (Murdock), Steven Berkoff (Podovsky). Directed by George P. Cosmatos and produced by Buzz Feitshans. Screenplay by Stallone and James Cameron.

Rambo, subtitled *First Blood Part II* and continuing the adventures of Sylvester Stallone's one-man army, is two movies in one. First there's a hard-boiled, high-energy, violent action picture, which will probably find a large and enthusiastic audience. Lurking beneath the action is a political statement accusing the U.S. government of such base political motives that I was, quite simply, astonished. *Rambo* is not left wing or right wing, but belongs to the paranoid wing of American politics, in which villains left and right crawl under the covers together and conspire to annihilate John Rambo.

If you saw the original *First Blood,* which was a big hit, you remember Rambo. He is a returned Vietnam hero, a superbly trained fighting machine who is considered by his superior officers to be the finest soldier they have ever seen. But Rambo becomes unhinged by civilian life, and by the insults which he believes society is heaping on men like himself, who risked their lives to fight the war. So Rambo reverts to his military training and turns into a one-man army dedicated to destroying the establishment that does not honor him.

At the end of *First Blood,* Rambo was captured after blowing up half a town and wiping out countless civilian and military authorities. If anyone had been keeping count, he would have qualified as the nation's most prolific mass killer. In the opening scenes of *Rambo,* he is breaking rocks on a chain gang when his old superior officer (Richard Crenna) arrives with a mission: Rambo is needed to parachute into Southeast Asia and scout out a suspected POW compound holding missing Americans. Any questions, Rambo? "Only one," he tells Crenna. "This time, do we get to win?"

His question places *Rambo* squarely within the revisionist genre of Vietnam movies, in which the war is refought with a happy ending. *Uncommon Valor,* the two *Missing in Action* movies, and this film are all about missions to free American MIAs and kill countless Asian soldiers. The basic assumption is that we lost the war because "the politicians" prevented men like Rambo from doing what they were trained to do. And indeed, again this time he has his hands tied: he's only supposed to take pictures, not engage in violence. Needless to say, if they only want pictures, they've picked the wrong mass murderer for the job.

Rambo's mission is outlined by a suspicious American intelligence officer (the square-jawed, rugged Charles Napier, a favorite of Russ Meyer *and* Jonathan Demme). Only after Rambo parachutes into the night does it become clear that Napier doesn't really want the mission to succeed. In logic so impenetrable that I would love to have somebody run it past me again, the movie argues that it would be politically embarrassing for American MIAs to be found at this late date, and that therefore it would be best if Rambo's mission fails. If he *does* come back with photos, they'll be suppressed. In that case, I was wondering, why sponsor the mission in the first place—and especially with a loose cannon like Rambo? No matter; the movie turns into an efficient action picture, with Rambo wiping out legions of North Vietnamese and Russians with a variety of weapons, including explosive-tipped arrows. Back at headquarters, Napier does all he can to sabotage the mission, but it becomes clear that Rambo could have won the Vietnam war by himself, had he been unleashed, and everything leads to a big climax, a helicopter dogfight. The strange thing about *Rambo* is that it works despite its politics. Its conspiracy theory is so angry and so unlikely that we tend to ignore it, sit back, and enjoy the action.

Ran ★ ★ ★ ★

R, 160 m., 1985

Tatsuya Nakadai (Lord Hidetora), Akira Terao (Taro, Eldest Son), Jinpachi Nezu (Jiro, Second Son), Daisuke Ryn (Sahuro, Youngest Son), Mjeko Harada (Lady Kaede, Taro's Wife), Yoshiko Miyazaki (Lady Sue, Jiro's Wife), Masayuki Yui (Tango, Hidetora's Servant), Peter (Kyoami, The Fool). Directed by Akira Kurosawa and produced by Serge Silberman and Masato Hara. Screenplay by Hideo Oquino, Masato Ide, and Kurosawa.

One of the early reviews of Akira Kurosawa's *Ran* said that he could not possibly have directed it at an earlier age. My first impression was to question that act of critical omnipotence. Who is to say Kurosawa couldn't have made this film at fifty or sixty, instead of at seventy-five, as he has? But then I thought longer about *Ran,* which is based on Shakespeare's *King Lear* and on a similar medieval samurai legend. And I thought about Laurence Olivier's Lear and about the *Lear* I recently saw starring Douglas Campbell and I realized that age is probably a prerequisite to fully understanding this character. Dustin Hoffman might be able to play Willy Loman by aging himself with makeup, but he will have to wait another twenty years to play Lear.

The character contains great paradoxes, but they are not the paradoxes of youth; they spring from long habit. Lear has the arrogance of great power, long held. He has wide knowledge of the world. Yet he is curiously innocent when it comes to his own children; he thinks they can do no wrong, can be trusted to carry out his plans. At the end, when his dreams have been broken, the character has the touching quality of a childlike innocence that can see breath on lips that are forever sealed, and can dream of an existence beyond the cruelties of man. Playing Lear is not a technical exercise. I wonder if a man can do it who has not had great disappointments and long dark nights of the soul.

Kurosawa has lived through those bad times. Here is one of the greatest directors of all time, out of fashion in his own country, suffering from depression, nearly blind. He prepared this film for ten years, drawing hundreds of sketches showing every shot, hardly expecting that the money would ever be found to allow him to make the film. But a deal was finally put together by Serge Silberman, the old French producer who backed the later films of Luis Bunuel (who could also have given us a distinctive Lear). Silberman risked his own money; this is the most expensive Japanese film ever made, and, yes, perhaps Kurosawa could not have made it until he was seventy-five.

The story is familiar. An old lord decides to retire from daily control of his kingdom, yet still keep all the trappings of his power. He will divide his kingdom in three parts among his children. In *Ran,* they are sons, not daughters. First, he requires a ritual statement of love. The youngest son cannot abide the hypocrisy, and stays silent. And so on.

The Japanese legend which Kurosawa draws from contains a famous illustration in which the old lord takes three arrows and demonstrates that when they are bundled, they cannot be broken, but taken one at a time, they are weak. He wishes his sons to remain allies, so they will be strong, but of course they begin to fight, and civil war breaks out as the old lord begins his forlorn journey from one castle to another, gradually being stripped of his soldiers, his pride, his sanity.

Nobody can film an epic battle scene like Kurosawa. He has already abundantly demonstrated that in *The Seven Samurai,* in *Yojimbo,* in *Kagemusha.* In *Ran,* the great bloody battles are counterpointed with scenes of a chamber quality, as deep hatreds and lusts are seen to grow behind the castle's walls.

King Lear is a play that centers obsessively around words expressing negatives. "Nothing? Nothing will come of nothing!" "Never, never, never." "No, no, no, no, no." They express in deep anguish the king's realization that what has been taken apart will never be put together again, that his beloved child is dead and will breathe no more, that his pride and folly have put an end to his happiness. Kurosawa's film expresses that despair perhaps more deeply than a Western film might; the samurai costumes, the makeup inspired by Noh drama, give the story a freshness that removes it from all our earlier associations.

Ran is a great, glorious achievement. Kurosawa must often have associated himself with the old lord as he tried to put this film together, but in the end he has triumphed, and the image I have of him, at seventy-five, is of three arrows bundled together.

Re-Animator ★ ★ ★

NO MPAA RATING, 95 m., 1985

Jeffrey Combs (Herbert West), Bruce Abbott (Dan Cain), Barbara Crampton (Megan Halsey), David Gale (Dr. Carl Hill), Robert Sampson (Dean Halsey), Gerry Glack (Mace), Carolyn Purdy-Gordon (Dr. Harrod). Directed by Stuart Gordon and produced by Brian Yuzna. Screenplay by Dennis Paoli, William J. Morris, and Gordon.

One of the most boring experiences on Earth is a trash movie without the courage of its lack of convictions. If it only wants to be cynical, it becomes lifeless in every moment—a bad dream on the screen. One of the pleasures of the movies, however, is to find a movie that chooses a disreputable genre and then tries with all its might to transcend the genre, to go over the top into some kind of artistic vision, however weird.

Stuart Gordon's *Re-Animator* is a pleasure like that, a frankly gory horror movie that finds a rhythm and a style that make it work in a cockeyed, offbeat sort of way. It's charged up by the tension between the director's desire to make a good movie and his realization that few movies about mad scientists and dead body parts are ever likely to be very good. The temptation is to take a camp approach to the material, to mock it, as Paul Morrissey did in *Andy Warhol's Frankenstein.* Gordon resists that temptation, and creates a livid, bloody, deadpan exercise in the theater of the undead.

Seeing this movie at the Cannes Film Festival, I walked in with no particular expectations, except that I hoped *Re-Animator* would be better than the festival's run-of-the-mill exploitation films. I walked out somewhat surprised and reinvigorated (if not re-animated) by a movie that had the audience emitting taxi whistles and wild goat cries. In its own way, on its own terms, in its corrupt genre, this movie worked as well as any other movie in the festival.

I was reminded of Pauline Kael's sane observation: "The movies are so rarely great art, that if we can't appreciate great trash, there is little reason for us to go."

The movie's story involves . . . but why bother? In the ads, the hero was described as having a good head on his shoulders, and another one in the laboratory dish in front of him. That more or less captures the essence of *Re-Animator.* Driven by an insane desire to vindicate himself by creating living beings out of dead body parts, a scientist uses his intelligence to burrow more and more deeply into sheer madness.

Gordon's direction, and particularly his use of special effects, will come as no surprise to anyone who saw his famous *Warp* trilogy onstage. He borrows from the traditions of comic-book art and B-grade thrillers, using his special effects not as set pieces for us to study, but as dazzling throwaways as the action hurtles ahead. By the end of the film, we are keenly aware that nothing of consequence has happened, but so what? We have been assaulted by a lurid imagination, amazed by unspeakable sights, blind-sided by the movie's curiously dry sense of humor. I guess that's our money's worth.

Real Genius ★ ★ ★ 1/2
PG-13, 105 m., 1985

Val Kilmer (Chris Knight), William Atherton (Professor Hathaway), Gabe Jarret (Mitch), Michelle Meyrink (Jordan Cochran), Jonathan Gries (Laslo [recluse]), Robert Prescott (Kent Torokvei), Severn Darden (Dr. Meredith). Directed by Martha Coolidge and produced by Brian Grazer. Screenplay by Neal Israel, Pat Profit, and Peter Torokvei.

It is probably not true that all American college students have been lobotomized and pumped full of sex hormones, although most movies treat them that way. Some students are more like the ones we meet in *Real Genius.* They are smart but socially uncertain and relativity is easier for them to understand than what to say on a first date. This is the first movie in a long time that's set on a college campus where the students are supposed to be intelligent. The campus is apparently Cal Tech, and the students are the next generation of great physicists, the kind who will write papers proving that everything we know is wrong.

The movie involves the saga of Mitch (Gabe Jarret), a brilliant high school student whose Science Fair project has revised the theory of laser beam technology. He is personally recruited by Prof. Hathaway (William Atherton), a famous physics professor who wants the kid to work in his personal laboratory. Once on campus, the kid meets the legendary Chris Knight (Val Kilmer), who was the most brilliant freshman in history, and who is now a junior whose mind is beginning to be cluttered by mischief. The two students room together—and there seems to be a third person in the room, a strange, wraith-like bearded figure who disappears into the clothes closet, and doesn't seem to be there when the door is flung open.

The professor is running a scam. He has a Defense Department contract for a sophisticated laser device so accurate that it could incinerate a single man on earth from a base in orbit. The professor is using his students as slave labor to do most of the work on the project while ripping off the government grant to build himself a new house. The students, meanwhile, have no idea they're working on a weapons system, and are more interested in using laser beams to lead everyone to a "Tanning Invitational" they've set up by turning a lecture hall into a swimming pool.

Real Genius allows every one of its characters the freedom to be complicated and quirky and individual. That's especially true of Jordan (Michelle Meyrink), a hyperactive woman student who talks all the time and never sleeps and knits things without even thinking about it, and follows Mitch into the john because she's so busy explaining something that she doesn't even notice what he's doing. I could recognize students like this from my own undergraduate days. One of the most familiar types on campus (and one of the rarest in the movies) is the self-styled eccentric, who develops a complex of weird personality traits as a way of clearing space and defining himself.

Real Genius was directed by Martha Coolidge, who made *Valley Girl,* one of the best and most perceptive recent teen-age movies. What I like best about her is that she gives her characters the freedom to be themselves. They don't have to be John Belushi clones, or fraternity jocks, or dumb coeds. They can flourish in all of their infinite variety, as young people with a world of possibilities and a lot of strange, beautiful notions. *Real Genius* contains many pleasures, but one of the best is its conviction that the American campus contains life as we know it.

Red Heat ★ ★ ★
R, 106 m., 1988 ✓
(See related Film Clip, p. 777.)

Arnold Schwarzenegger (Ivan Danko), James Belushi (Art Ridzik), Peter Boyle (Lou Donnelly), Ed O'Ross (Viktor Rostavili), Larry Fishburne (Lt. Stobbs), Gina Gershon (Cat Manzetti), Marjorie Bransfield (Waitress). Directed by Walter Hill and produced by Hill and Gordon Carroll. Screenplay by Harry Kleiner, Hill, and Troy Kennedy Martin.

Red Heat is not the first movie about a couple of very different cops, and it will not be the last, but as the formula goes, this is a superior example. It's an action picture with a sense of humor and slyly comic performances by Arnold Schwarzenegger and James Belushi, and it's an example of slick professionalism.

Hollywood calls movies like this "high concept" pictures, because you can summarize the plot in a few words, and the words could go like this: Schwarzenegger plays a tough Russian cop who follows a criminal to Chicago and teams up with Belushi as a Chicago slob who knows more about clout than *glasnost.* Take that line and you have the movie. All you have to do is plug in a plot and some shoot-outs and chase scenes.

The man who directed and co-wrote *Red Heat* is Walter Hill, and he is a master at doing just that. Hill specializes in male buddy and action movies, and he more or less reinvented this genre with *48 Hours* and its pairing of Nick Nolte and Eddie Murphy. One of the nice things about *Red Heat* is that it doesn't rip off Hill's earlier picture (except for the basic concept, of course), and finds new things to say about an odd couple of law enforcement.

The Schwarzenegger character is a straight-arrow Russian cop, all business, muscular and tough. The Belushi character is the kind of cop who doesn't believe in busting his buns every second of every day, and who is capable of advising his Soviet comrade to lighten up. He is assigned to Schwarzenegger as sort of a guide and bodyguard, and together they stumble across the usual assortment of weirdos and conspiracies.

What actually happens in the plot is fairly unimportant in movies like this. Style is everything, and if there is a rapport between the two stars, then everything else falls into place. *Red Heat* works because Schwarzenegger and Belushi are both basically comic actors; Arnold's whole career is based on his ability to see the humor in apparently hard-boiled situations. That doesn't mean the actors stand around cracking one-liners, but that even the straight sequences are setups for later payoffs, and you get the quiet feeling that both actors are amused by the material.

The premise is that Schwarzenegger, nicknamed Iron Jaw, would rather die than bend, and that Belushi would rather bend than die. Confronted with the capitalistic excesses of Chicago, Schwarzenegger has some conventional Russian criticisms, and Belushi responds with dialogue that often sounds adlibbed, even if it's not. The two of them both have to placate the hard-boiled chief of detectives (Peter Boyle), who issues stern warnings when they violate departmental procedure. At one point, Belushi is actually taken off the case, although that, of course, doesn't change any of his behavior. Boyle's role is the thankless one in the film; the stern chief is the oldest cliché in cop movies, with his obligatory lectures on protocol to tough cops who shift back and forth on their feet like guilty schoolboys.

The film is punctuated by violence, a great deal of violence, although most of it is exaggerated comic-book style instead of being truly gruesome. Walking that fine line is a speciality of Hill, who once simulated the sound of a fist on a chin by making tape recordings of pingpong paddles slapping leather sofas.

Reds ★ ★ ★ ½
PG, 200 m., 1981

Warren Beatty (John Reed), Diane Keaton (Louise Bryant), Edward Herrmann (Max Eastman), Jerzy Kosinski (Zinoviev), Jack Nicholson (Eugene O'Neill), Maureen Stapleton (Emma Goldman), Paul Sorvino (Louis Fraina), Gene Hackman (Pete Van Wherry). Directed and produced by Warren Beatty. Screenplay by Beatty and Trevor Griffiths.

The original John Reed was a dashing young man from Portland who knew a good story when he found one, and, when he found himself in the midst of the Bolshevik revolution, wrote a book called *Ten Days That Shook the World* and made himself a famous journalist. He never quite got it right again after that. He became embroiled in the American left-wing politics of the 1920s, participated in fights between factions of the Socialist Party and the new American Communist Party, and finally returned to Moscow on a series of noble fool's errands that led up, one way or another, to his death from tuberculosis and kidney failure in a Russian hospital. He is the only American buried within the Kremlin walls.

That is Reed's story in a nutshell. But if you look a little more deeply you find a man who was more than a political creature. He was also a man who wanted to be where the action was, a radical young intellectual who was in the middle of everything in the years after World War I, when Greenwich Village was in a creative ferment and American society seemed, for a brief moment, to be overturning itself. It is that personal, human John Reed that Warren Beatty's *Reds* takes as its subject, although there is a lot, and maybe too much, of the political John Reed as well. The movie never succeeds in convincing us that the feuds between the American socialist parties were much more than personality conflicts and ego-bruisings, so audiences can hardly be expected to care which faction is "the" American party of the left.

What audiences can, and possibly will, care about, however, is a traditional Hollywood romantic epic, a love story written on the canvas of history, as they used to say in the ads. And *Reds* provides that with glorious romanticism, surprising intelligence, and a consistent wit. It is the thinking man's *Dr. Zhivago*, told from the other side, of course. The love story stars Warren Beatty and Diane Keaton, who might seem just a tad unlikely as casting choices, but who are immediately engaging and then grow into solid, plausible people on the screen. Keaton is a particular surprise. I had somehow gotten into the habit of expecting her to be a touchy New Yorker, sweet, scared, and intellectual. Here, as a Portland dentist's wife who runs away with John Reed and eventually follows him halfway around the world, through blizzards and prisons and across icy steppes, she is just what she needs to be: plucky, healthy, exasperated, loyal, and funny.

Beatty, as John Reed, is also surprising. I expected him to play Reed as a serious, noble, heroic man for all seasons, and so he does, sometimes. But there is in Warren Beatty's screen persona a persistent irony, a way of kidding his own seriousness, that takes the edge off a potentially pretentious character and makes him into one of God's fools. Beatty plays Reed but does not beatify him: He permits the silliness and boyishness to coexist with the self-conscious historical mission.

The action in the movie takes Reed to Russia and back again to Portland, and off again with Louise Bryant (Keaton), and then there is a lengthy pause in Greenwich Village and time enough for Louise to have a sad little love affair with the morosely alcoholic playwright Eugene O'Neill (Jack Nicholson). Then there are other missions to Moscow, and heated political debates in New York basements, and at one point I'm afraid I entirely lost track of exactly why Reed was running behind a horsecart in the middle of some forgotten battle in an obscure backwater of the Russian empire. The fact is, Reed's motivation from moment to moment is not the point of the picture. The point is that a revolution is happening, human societies are being swept aside, a new class is in control—or so it seems—and for an insatiably curious young man, that is exhilirating, and it is enough.

The heart of the film is in the relationship between Reed and Bryant. There is an interesting attempt to consider her problems as well as his. She leaves Portland because she is sick unto death of small talk. She wants to get involved in politics, in art, in what's happening: She is so inexorably drawn to Greenwich Village that if Reed had not taken her there, she might have gone on her own. If she was a radical in Portland, however, she is an Oregonian in the Village, and she cannot compete conversationally with such experienced fast-talkers as the anarchist Emma Goldman (Maureen Stapleton). In fact, no one seems to listen to her or pay much heed, except for sad Eugene O'Neill, who is brave enough to love her but not smart enough to keep it to himself. The ways in which she edges toward O'Neill, and then loyally returns to Reed, create an emotional density around her character that makes it really *mean* something when she and Reed embrace at last in a wonderful tear-jerking scene in the Russian train station.

The whole movie finally comes down to the fact that the characters matter to us. Beatty may be fascinated by the ins and outs of American left-wing politics sixty years ago, but he is not so idealistic as to believe an American mass audience can be inspired to care as deeply. So he gives us people. And they are seen here with such warmth and affection that we sense new dimensions not only in Beatty and Keaton, but especially in Nicholson. In *Reds,* understating his desire, apologizing for his passion, hanging around Louise, handing her a poem, throwing her out of his life, he is quieter but much more passionate than in the overwrought *The Postman Always Rings Twice.*

As as for Beatty, *Reds* is his bravura turn. He got the idea, nurtured it for a decade, found the financing, wrote most of the script, produced, and directed and starred and still found enough artistic detachment to make his Reed into a flawed, fascinating enigma instead of a boring archetypal hero. I liked this movie. I felt a real fondness for it. It was quite a subject to spring on the capitalist Hollywood movie system, and maybe only Beatty could have raised $35 million to make a movie about a man who hated millionaires. I noticed, here at the end of the credits, a wonderful line that reads:

Copyright © MCMLXXXI Barclays Mercantile Industrial Finance Limited. John Reed would have loved that.

Repo Man ★ ★ ★

R, 92 m., 1984

Harry Dean Stanton (Bud), Emilio Estevez (Otto), Tracey Walter (Miller), Olivia Barash (Leila). Directed by Alex Cox and produced by Jonathan Wacks and Peter McCarthy. Screenplay by Cox.

Repo Man is one of those movies that slips through the cracks and gives us all a little weirdo fun. It is the first movie I know about that combines (1) punk teen-agers, (2) automobile repossessors, and (3) aliens from outer space. This is the kind of movie that baffles Hollywood, because it isn't made from any known formula and doesn't follow the rules. The movie begins with a mad scientist careening down a New Mexico road in his Chevy Malibu. He is stopped by a cop, who finds some really strange things happening in the car's trunk. Then the action moves to Los Angeles, where a punk kid (Emilio Estevez) is passing the time by going to dances and banging his head against other kids' heads, to demonstrate his affection.

The kid runs into a guy named Bud (Harry Dean Stanton), who is an auto repossessor. Bud tricks the kid into driving a repo car for him, and before long the kid is a full-time auto repossessor, learning the ropes. The ropes are pretty tough. Repo men, we learn, live their lives on the edge, operating under extreme tension that is caused partly by their working conditions and partly because as Stanton explains, "I've never known a repo man who didn't use a lot of speed." Harry Dean Stanton is one of the treasures of American movies. He has appeared in a lot of films without becoming a big star, but he has that total cynicism that brings jobs like repo into focus. In the movie, he and Estevez make a nice team; the beaten veteran and the cocky kid, and they cruise the streets looking for cars.

Meanwhile (and here I will be careful to respect some surprises in the story), the government is looking for that Chevy Malibu, because it is connected to the possibility that alien beings have visited the Earth. The feds put out a $10,000 reward for the car, which makes it the jackpot every repo man in L.A. is looking for. Hot on the trail of the car, Stanton and Estevez get into a duel with the famed Rodriguez brothers, known as the bandits of repo. All of this works very nicely, but what's best about *Repo Man* is its sly sense of humor. There are a lot of running gags in the movie, and the best of them involves generic food labels, of all things. (There is a moment involving some food in a refrigerator that gave me one of the biggest laughs I'd had at the movies in a long time.) The movie also has a special way of looking at Los Angeles, seeing it through Harry Dean Stanton's eyes as a wasteland of human ambitions where a few bucks can be made by the quick, the bitter, and the sly.

I saw *Repo Man* near the end of a busy stretch on the movie beat: Three days during which I saw more relentlessly bad movies than during any comparable period in memory. Most of those bad movies were so cynically constructed out of formula ideas and "commercial" ingredients that watching them was an ordeal. *Repo Man* comes out of left field, has no big stars, didn't cost much, takes chances, dares to be unconventional, is funny, and works. There is a lesson here.

Return of the Jedi ★ ★ ★ ★

PG, 133 m., 1983

Mark Hamill (Luke Skywalker), Harrison Ford (Han Solo), Carrie Fisher (Princess Leia), Billy Dee Williams (Lando Calrissian), Anthony Daniels (C-3PO), David Prowse (Darth Vader), James Earl Jones (Vader's Voice), Alec Guinness (Obi-Wan Kenobi). Directed by Richard Marquand and produced by Howard Kazanjian. Screenplay by Lawrence Kasdan and George Lucas.

Here is just one small moment in *Return of the Jedi*, a moment you could miss if you looked away from the screen, but a moment that helps explain the special magic of the Star Wars movies. Luke Skywalker is engaged in a ferocious battle in the dungeons beneath the throne room of the loathsome Jabba the Hutt. His adversary is a slimy, gruesome, reptilian monster made of warts and teeth. Things are looking bad when suddenly the monster is crushed beneath a falling door. And then (here is the small moment) there's a shot of the monster's keeper, a muscle-bound jailer, who rushes forward in tears. He is brokenhearted at the destruction of his pet. Everybody loves somebody.

It is that extra level of detail that makes the Star Wars pictures much more than just space operas. Other movies might approach the special effects. Other action pictures might approximate the sense of swashbuckling adventure. But in *Return of the Jedi*, as in *Star Wars* and *The Empire Strikes Back*, there's such a wonderful density to the canvas. Things are happening all over. They're pouring forth from imaginations so fertile that, yes, we do halfway believe in this crazy Galactic Empire long ago and far, far away.

Return of the Jedi is both a familiar movie and a new one. It concludes the stories of the major human characters in the saga, particularly Skywalker, Han Solo, Princess Leia, and Darth Vader. It revisits other characters who seem either more or less than human, including Ben (Obi-Wan Kenobi), Yoda, Chewbacca, and the beloved robots C-3PO and R2-D2. If George Lucas persists in his plan to make nine Star Wars movies, this will nevertheless be the last we'll see of Luke, Han, and Leia, although the robots will be present in all the films.

The story in the Star Wars movies is, however, only part of the film—and a less crucial element as time goes by. What *Jedi* is really giving us is a picaresque journey through the imagination, and an introduction to forms of life less mundane than our own. In *Jedi*, we encounter several unforgettable characters, including the evil Jabba the Hutt, who is a cross between a toad and the Cheshire cat; the lovable, cuddly Ewoks, the furry inhabitants of the "forest moon of Endor"; a fearsome desert monster made of sand and teeth, and hateful little ratlike creatures that scurry about the corners of the frame. And there is an admiral for the Alliance who looks like the missing link between Tyrannosaurus Rex and Charles de Gaulle.

One thing the Star Wars movies never do is waste a lot of time on introductions. Unlike a lot of special effects and monster movies, where new creatures are introduced with laborious setups, *Jedi* immediately plunges its alien beasts into the thick of the action. Maybe that's why the film has such a sense of visual richness. Jabba's throne room, for example, is populated with several weird creatures, some of them only half-glimpsed in the corner of the frame. The camera in *Jedi* slides casually past forms of life that would provide the centerpiece for lesser movies.

The movie also has, of course, more of the amazing battles in outer space—the intergalactic video games that have been a trademark since *Star Wars*. And *Jedi* finds an interesting variation on that chase sequence in *Star Wars* where the space cruisers hurtled through the narrow canyons on the surface of the Death Star. This time, there's a breakneck chase through a forest, aboard airborne motorcycles. After several of the bad guys have run into trees and gotten creamed, you pause to ask yourself why they couldn't have simply flown *above* the treetops . . . but never mind, it wouldn't have been as much fun that way.

And *Return of the Jedi* is fun, magnificent fun. The movie is a complete entertainment, a feast for the eyes and a delight for the fancy. It's a little amazing how Lucas and his associates keep topping themselves. From the point of view of simple moviemaking logistics, there is an awesome amount of work on the screen in *Jedi* (twice as many visual effects as *Star Wars* in the space battles, Lucas claims). The fact that the makers of *Jedi* are able to emerge intact from their task, having created a very special work of the imagination, is the sort of miracle that perhaps Obi-Wan would know something about.

Return of the Secaucus Seven ★ ★ ★

NO MPAA RATING, 110 m., 1981

Mark Arnott (Jeff), Gordon Clapp (Chip), Maggie Cousineau-Arndt (Frances), Adam Le Fevre (J.T.), Bruce MacDonald (Mike), Jean Passanante (Irene), John Sayles (Howie), Maggie Renzi (Katie). Directed and written by John Sayles. Produced by William Aydelott and Jeffrey Nelson.

A friend asked me what *Return of the Secaucus Seven* was about. "It's the story of your life," I said.

"*My* life?"

Well, and my life, too. Everybody's life who was younger once and demonstrated against one thing or another, and is older now and stumped for the moment by the curiosity that the most outspoken advocate of change in our society is Ronald Reagan. The movie tells the story of a group of friends who set out during the late 1960s to join the March on the Pentagon, and were arrested in Secaucus, New Jersey, on charges they still do not fully understand. So they didn't make it to the Pentagon, where their brain power might have made the difference in Abbie Hoffman's plan to levitate that building.

Those were strange times. Even Norman Mailer, in his *Armies of the Night*, reported that when the Yippies started to chant and meditate and try to levitate the Pentagon, he looked to see if it had started to rise: An unlikely event, of course, but one that a reporter would always kick himself for if he had missed it. Years have passed since those days. The original members of the Secaucus Seven have grown older now, can taste their thirtieth birthdays, and as the movie opens have gathered for a weekend reunion in the country. The film tells the story of their weekend, as they take their measure and remember the 1960s.

The Sixties. A director once told me that he had been interviewed by a group of college editors, one of whom asked him, "Was drug usage really prevalent back in the 1960s?" He didn't know whether to laugh or cry. The Secaucus Seven has the same choice. They are never again going to be as young as they were, but they still remember their days of activism so sharply that they refuse to cut loose from them. These days, people still go through their thirtieth birthday crisis, all right, but they seem to hold it on their fortieth birthday.

The Secaucus Seven has grown slightly, with the addition of spouses, lovers, and even children. They gather to play basketball, sing songs, get drunk, fight, break up, and sleep together—or apart. In mood, the film resembles Alain Tanner's wonderful *Jonah Who Will Be 25 in the Year 2000*. Some of the Seven have become fairly successful: There are a congressional aide and a medical student. There is also a kid who is still trying to make it as a folk singer, an occupation that no longer pays very well even if he had the talent, which he does not. And another who has chosen to stay in the old hometown and pump gas.

John Sayles, who wrote and directed the movie, made it as a labor of love (and financed it by writing the screenplays for

Piranha and *Alligator,* so he may still not quite have evened the scales). He alternates among the various couples and groupings and intrigues, and at first the movie is frankly confusing. We can't keep everybody straight, and there's too much explanation of who they all are and what they've all done. Before long, though, we have everyone sorted out. We know the relationships. And we grow quietly grateful that Sayles has chosen not to pack his weekend reunion with a series of dramatic confrontations and crises. There are no overdoses, suicides, or murders. Only the adjustments such a weekend would be expected to bring, and the inevitable bitterness when one couple has broken up, and the old and new lovers have to confront one another.

This is not a perfect film. Odds and ends stick out, and some scenes have a certain gracelessness. But it is an absorbing film that contains shrewd observations about human nature, and more than its share of humor. We leave with mixed feelings: We feel like we've attended that reunion, and at the same time we're relieved that we did not. It is easier to be young if your friends don't age on you.

Revenge of the Nerds II ★ 1/2
PG-13, 89 m., 1987

Robert Carradine (Skolnick), Timothy Busfield (Poindexter), Andrew Cassese (Wormser), Curtis Armstrong (Booger), Larry B. Scott (Lamar), Donald Gibb (Ogre), Courtney Thorne-Smith (Sunny), Ed Lauter (Buzz). Directed by Joe Roth and produced by Ted Field, Robert Cort, and Peter Bart. Screenplay by Dan Guntzelman and Steve Marshall.

These aren't nerds. They're a bunch of interesting guys, and that's the problem with *Revenge of the Nerds II.* The movie doesn't have the nerve to be about real nerds. It hedges its bets. A nerd is not a nerd because he understands computers and wears a plastic pen protector in his shirt pocket. A nerd is a nerd because he brings a special lack of elegance to life. An absence of style. An inability to notice the feelings of other people. A nerd is a nerd from the inside out, which is something the nerds who made this movie will never understand.

The film is subtitled *Nerds in Paradise,* and it continues the saga of the Tri Lambda fraternity and their arch-enemies, the Alpha Betas. The A-Bs are all slick and handsome and cruel, and detest the Tri Lambs because they don't look as if they were cloned from a *GQ* cover. When both houses go to Fort Lauderdale for a fraternity convention, the A-Bs cancel the Tri Lambs hotel reservation and try to get them thrown out of the interfraternity council.

As screenplays go, this is as idiotic as it gets. And yet the story means nothing in these enterprises. What matters is whether an effort, however small, is made to invest the characters with even the most marginal speck of humanity. *National Lampoon's Animal House* succeeded in creating unforgettable characters. *Nerds II* just has a bunch of guys shlepping around wishing somebody had written some dialogue for them.

The true nerds in the movie are, of course, the Alpha Betas, and they get defeated and humiliated at the end, but not in a funny way. The true heroes are the Tri Lambs, but so what? We know that from the first shot. If the filmmakers had possessed an ounce of imagination, they would have invested the Tri Lambs with true nerd-dom, and then watched them try to overcome their nerdy tendencies. It's not enough to say you blow your nose on your shirt. You have to actually be seen doing it.

There is also the problem of The Girl. In all movies like this, there has to be a girl who is a complete dreamboat, perfect, tantalizing, inaccessible. At least one of the nerds has to love her with an intensity beyond words. He has to be rejected. He has to have a broken heart. She has to be a snob. The Girl in this movie is played by Courtney Thorne-Smith, but the role is written all wrong. She's not a bitch, she's a sensitive kid with a good heart, and right away she sees that the Tri Lambs are really the good guys. This is missing the whole point.

There are a couple of marginally funny moments in the movie, like the belching contest, but they don't go anywhere. First one guy belches and then another guy belches louder. Two belches do not a belching contest make, and with that thought I think we have wasted enough time and space on this movie.

Revenge of the Pink Panther ★ ★ ★
PG, 99 m., 1978

Peter Sellers (Clouseau), Herbert Lom (Dreyfus), Dyan Cannon (Simone), Robert Webber (Douvier), Burt Kwouk (Cato). Directed by Blake Edwards and produced by Tony Adams. Screenplay by Frank Walsman, Ron Clark, and Edwards.

In an uncertain world, Inspector Clouseau survives as an island of certainty. He is certain, first of all, of his genius as the greatest chief of detectives in all of history. He is just as certain of his skill as a deadly karate expert (although, in all their practice encounters, his faithful servant Cato reduces him to a trembling heap). Most poignant of all, he has absolute confidence in the disguises supplied to him by the trusted old family costume firm of Balls & Co.

But Clouseau's charm is in the absolute calm he maintains as his world crumbles about him. When everything has gone wrong, when the homes of innocent bystanders have been turned into smoking ruins, when Hong Kong has, alas, been blown off the map . . . Clouseau turns sharply to his colleagues and snaps, "What did you say?" Because, of course, criticism of his methods is unthinkable.

Clouseau's character was lovingly developed during the course of five movies in fifteen years by Peter Sellers, who played him, and Blake Edwards, who wrote and directed him. The inspector was not always quite the man he eventually became. (Which of us was?) He began, in the original *Pink Panther*, as a more-or-less standard comic Frenchman. It was only in the later films that he emerges as an absolute original, a crazed spirit set aside from mundane humanity, a nut without a country.

Revenge of the Pink Panther, which Sellers said was to be the inspector's last adventure (Edwards was not so sure), is quintessential Clouseau. He occupies the center of a maelstrom, confident that no one will notice him in his bizarre disguises, certain that no one could possibly suspect that the dwarfish figure in the corner, the one with the Toulouse-Lautrec costume and the Adidas running shoes, could possibly be Jacques Clouseau. He has reason for his confidence: The film opens with his funeral and burial, at which all France heaves a sigh of relief.

But Clouseau is not dead, merely sidetracked for a moment in his latest case in a showdown with the French Connection. Someone is bringing contraband drugs into France from Hong Kong, and Clouseau, as he is the first to admit, is the man to stop them. He warms up in one of Edwards's most elaborate sight gags, an impossible series of misadventures that ends with the collapse of three floors of a house.

The movie is strongest in its sight gags. Edwards and Sellers seem to be returning to silent slapstick for their inspiration (although sound is, of course, useful when Clouseau mangles the language, speaking English as if it were very, very bad French). There are chases involving an ice cream wagon and bizarre miscalculations in the Chinese bordello that Cato has established in Clouseau's apartment. And then there are all of those disguises—especially the one in which Sellers appears as a sailor and a stuffed parrot is attached horizontally to the old salt's shoulder.

There is, alas, a plot here somewhere, although Edwards and Sellers take it with no more seriousness than in the preceding two Clouseau films (*Return of the Pink Panther* and *The Pink Panther Strikes Again*). Robert Webber plays a mafioso in charge of smuggling drugs into France, and Herbert Lom is, once again, the chief inspector who always winds up discovering Clouseau mangling the case.

Movies like this exist in the moment; like all true slapstick, they're cheerfully willing to do anything to make us laugh, and Edwards is not afraid of throwing in pratfalls, explosions, and people hurtling through the air, if that'll keep things moving. I like his spirit. And Sellers, of course, remains the essence of Clouseaudom. As he struggles with his unique pronunciation of "bomb" (it approximates "beaumbe"), we gradually realize, with him, that he would be incapable of making a bomb threat except by mail.

Richard Pryor Here and Now
★ ★ ★ ★
R, 94 m., 1983

A documentary written and directed by Richard Pryor and produced by Bob Parkinson and Andy Friendly.

Is there anyone else in America who could have pulled off this film? *Richard Pryor Here and Now* is a documentary of one man talking. Pryor walks onto the stage of the Saenger Theater in New Orleans, establishes an immediate rapport with the audience, and away he goes. At the end of the movie we have been wrung out with laughter—and with a few other things, too, because Pryor is more than a comedian in this film: He's a social commentator and a man talking honestly about himself.

This is Pryor's third concert film. The first one, *Richard Pryor Live in Concert*, was made before he set himself on fire while free-basing cocaine. The second, *Richard Pryor Live on the Sunset Strip* (1982), recorded his first filmed concert after the accident, and included his description of Jim Brown's attempts to talk him out of drug use, and Pryor's own now-famous dialogue with cocaine. In *Here and Now*, filmed in August 1983 with Brown as executive producer, Pryor firmly says he hasn't used drugs or alcohol for seven months. The arithmetic would seem to suggest that he hadn't stopped using everything when he made the second film, or that he had a relapse after his initial hospitalization. I mention that only because the Richard Pryor we see on screen in *Here and Now* has obviously found some kind of peace with himself that was lacking in the *Sunset Strip* film.

He can smile more easily. He doesn't have to reach for effects. He handles audience interruptions with grace and cool. He is the master of his instrument. And he takes bigger chances. Some of his material covers familiar ground—sex, booze, race, marriages. But all along he's showing his gift for populating the stage with a lot of different characters. He goes in and out of accents, body language, and characters, giving us confused drunks, defensive husbands, shrill wives, uptight WASPs, impenetrable Africans ("Everybody speaks English," one tells him in Zimbabwe, "but what language do you speak at *home?*"). And then at the end of his act, he goes into an extended characterization of a street black shooting heroin. In this character are humor and pain, self-deception and touching honesty, and the end of the sketch comes closer to tragedy than it does to comedy.

Pryor is a spokesman for our dreams and fears, the things we find funny and the things we're frightened of. He has assumed a role that has previously been filled by such comedians as Will Rogers, Lenny Bruce, Mort Sahl, and Woody Allen—all men who, as Rogers put it, talked about what they'd just seen in the papers. Pryor works off issues and subjects that are absolutely current, and he addresses them with a humor that is aimed so well, we duck. His story could have gone either way. He could have been killed in that wasteful accident. But he was not, and now, given a second chance, he is paying his dues.

Richard Pryor Live on the Sunset Strip

★ ★ ★ ★

R, 82 m., 1982

Directed by Joe Layton and produced by Richard Pryor.

At the beginning of this film, Richard Pryor is clearly nervous. He is back on a stage for the first time since he set himself on fire. That means he is working with the stand-up comedian's greatest handicap, the audience's awareness of his vulnerability. Whatever else they do, comics must project utter confidence in their material, and when Pryor had his accident, he also had his whole hip image blown out from under him. So it's a shaky start. He begins by almost defiantly using the word "fuck" as an incantation, employing it not so much for shock value (does it still have any?) as for punctuation. His timing is a little off. He is not, at first, the supremely confident, cocky Richard Pryor of his earlier films. But as he gets rolling, as he populates the stage with a whole series of characters, we watch the emergence of a Richard Pryor who is older, wiser, and funnier than before. And the last fifty or sixty minutes of this film are extraordinary.

Richard Pryor Live on the Sunset Strip was filmed at the Hollywood Palladium, down at the unfashionable east end of that legendary street of rock clubs, restaurants, hookers and heroes, hot-pillow motels, and some of the most expensive real estate in the world. The movie opens with a montage of the strip's neon signs (including the Chateau Marmont, where John Belushi died). Then it cuts inside to the Palladium auditorium, and Pryor walks onstage and lays claim to being the most talented one-man stage show in existence right now.

His gift is to be funny and painfully self-analytical at the same time. Like Bill Cosby, he gets a lot of his material out of memories of growing up black in America. But he sees deeper than Cosby, and his vignettes capture small truths and build them into an attitude. In the brilliant middle sections of this film, he uses just his own voice and body to create little one-act plays, such as the one where he recalls working in a Mafia-owned nightclub in Ohio. In that one, his Italian-American-gangster accent is perfectly heard; in another skit, about the animals in Africa, he turns into a gifted physical comedian, getting laughs out of his impressions of the movements of gazelles, water buffaloes, and lions—and ending with a hilarious observation of the body language of two whites passing each other on the street in black Africa.

The whole middle passage of the film is that good. The last twenty minutes is one of the most remarkable marriages of comedy and truth I have ever seen. He talks with great honesty about his drug addiction, his accident, and how his life has changed since he stopped using drugs. He confesses that in the three weeks before his accident, he holed up alone in his room with his cocaine pipe, which talked to him in reassuring, seductive tones uncannily like Richard Nixon's. Then a friend, the actor Jim Brown, came to see him, and asked him flat-out, "Whatcha gonna do?" There was nothing he wanted to do but hide in drugs. What he finally did was set himself on fire.

I saw the film the same day that actor Shay Duffin opened his one-man evening with Brendan Behan at the Apollo Theater Center in Chicago. The papers that day carried the news that Belushi had overdosed. Behan, of course, killed himself with alcohol. Some day, inevitably, an actor will give us an evening with John Belushi. The dramatic structure is all there, for the Behans and Belushis: The genius, the laughter, and the doomed drive to self-destruction. Watching *Richard Pryor Live on the Sunset Strip,* a breathtaking performance by a man who came within a hair of killing himself with drugs, was like a gift, as if Pryor had come back from the dead to perform in his own one-man memory of himself. It is good we still have him. He is better than ever.

The Right Stuff ★ ★ ★ ★

PG, 193 m., 1983

Sam Shepard (Chuck Yeager), Ed Harris (John Glenn), Fred Ward (Gus Grissom), Dennis Quaid (Gordon Cooper), Scott Glenn (Alan Shepard), Barbara Hershey (Glennis Yeager), Mary Jo Deschanel (Annie Glenn), Pamela Reed (Trudy Cooper). Directed by Philip Kaufman and produced by Irwin Winkler and Robert Chartoff. Screenplay by Kaufman.

At the beginning of *The Right Stuff,* a cowboy reins in his horse and regards a strange sight in the middle of the desert: the X-1 rocket plane, built to break the sound barrier. At the end of the film, the seven Mercury astronauts are cheered in the Houston Astrodome at a Texas barbecue thrown by Lyndon B. Johnson. The contrast between those two images contains the message of *The Right Stuff,* I think, and the message is that Americans still have the right stuff, but we've changed our idea of what it is.

The original American heroes were loners. The cowboy is the perfect example. He was silhouetted against the horizon and he rode into town by himself and if he had a sidekick, the sidekick's job was to admire him. The new American heroes are team players. No wonder Westerns aren't made much anymore; cowboys don't play on teams. The cowboy at the beginning of *The Right Stuff* is Chuck Yeager, the legendary lone-wolf test pilot who survived the horrifying death rate among early test pilots (more than sixty were killed in a single month) and did fly the X-1 faster than the speed of sound. The movie begins with that victory, and then moves on another ten years to the day when the Russians sent up Sputnik, and the Eisenhower administration hustled to get back into the space race.

The astronauts who eventually rode the first Mercury capsules into space may not have been that much different from Chuck Yeager. As they're portrayed in the movie, anyway, Gus Grissom, Scott Carpenter, and Gordon Cooper seem to have some of the same stuff as Yeager. But the astronauts were more than pilots; they were a public-relations image, and the movie shows sincere, smooth-talking John Glenn becoming their unofficial spokesman. The X-1 flew in secrecy, but the Mercury flights were telecast, and we were entering a whole new era, the selling of space. There was a lot going on, and there's a lot going on in the movie, too. *The Right Stuff* is an adventure film, a special effects film, a social commentary, and a satire. That the writer-director, Philip Kaufman, is able to get so much into a little more than three hours is impressive. That he also has organized this material into one of the best recent American movies is astonishing. *The Right Stuff* gives itself the freedom to move around in moods and styles, from a broadly based lampoon of government functionaries to Yeager's spare, taciturn manner and Glenn's wonderment at the sights outside his capsule window.

The Right Stuff has been a landmark movie in a lot of careers. It announces Kaufman's arrival in the ranks of major directors. It contains uniformly interesting performances by a whole list of unknown or little-known actors, including Ed Harris (Glenn), Scott Glenn (Alan Shepard), Fred Ward (Grissom), and Dennis Quaid (Cooper). It confirms the strong and sometimes almost mystical screen presence of playwright Sam Shepard, who played Yeager. And it joins a short list of recent American movies that might be called experimental epics: movies that have an ambitious reach through time and subject matter, that spend freely for locations or special effects, but that consider each scene as intently as an art film. *The Right Stuff* goes on that list with *The Godfather, Nashville, Apocalypse Now,* and maybe *Patton* and *Close Encounters.* It's a great film.

Risky Business ★ ★ ★ ★

R, 96 m., 1983

Tom Cruise (Joel), Rebecca De Mornay (Lana), Curtis Armstrong (Miles), Bronson Pinchot (Barry), Joe Pantoliano (Guido). Directed by Paul Brickman and produced by Joe Avnet and Steve Tisch. Screenplay by Brickman.

Risky Business is a movie about male adolescent guilt. In other words, it's a comedy. It's funny because it deals with subjects that are so touchy, so fraught with emotional pain, that unless we laugh there's hardly any way we can deal with them—especially if we are now, or ever were, a teen-age boy. The teenager in the movie is named Joel. His family lives in a suburb on Chicago's North Shore. It's the sort of family that has three cars: the family station wagon, Mom's car, and Dad's Porsche. As the movie opens, Mom and Dad are going off on vacation to a sun-drenched consumer paradise and their only son, Joel, is being left alone at home. It's a busy time in Joel's life. He's got college board exams, an interview with a Princeton admissions officer, and finals at high school.

It gets to be an even busier time after his parents leave. Joel gets involved in an ascending pyramid of trouble. He calls a number in one of those sex-contact magazines and meets a young hooker who moves into the house. He runs afoul of the girl's pimp. His mother's expensive Steuben egg is stolen. His dad's Porsche ends up in Lake Michigan. The family home turns into a brothel. He blows two finals. And so on. This description may make *Risky Business* sound like a predictable sitcom. It is not. It is one of the smartest, funniest, most perceptive satires in a long time. It not only invites comparison with *The Graduate,* it earns it. Here is a great comedy about teen-age sex.

The very best thing about the movie is its dialogue. Paul Brickman, who wrote and directed, has an ear so good that he knows what to leave out. This is one of those movies where a few words or a single line says everything that needs to be said, implies everything that needs to be implied, *and* gets a laugh. When the hooker tells the kid, "Oh, Joel, go to school. Learn something," the precise inflection of those words defines their relationship for the next three scenes.

The next best thing about the movie is the casting. Rebecca De Mornay somehow manages to take that thankless role, the hooker with a heart of gold, and turn it into a very specific character. She isn't all good and she isn't all clichés: she's a very complicated young woman with quirks and insecurities and a wayward ability to love. I became quietly astounded when I realized that this movie was going to create an original, *interesting* relationship involving a teen-ager and a hooker. The teen-age kid, in what will be called the Dustin Hoffman role, is played by Tom Cruise, who also knows how to imply a whole world by what he won't say, can't feel, and doesn't understand.

This is a movie of new faces and inspired insights and genuine laughs. It's hard to make a good movie and harder to make a good comedy and almost impossible to make a satire of such popular but mysterious obsessions as guilt, greed, lust, and secrecy. This movie knows what goes on behind the closed bathroom doors of the American dream.

Rita, Sue and Bob Too ★ ★ ★

R, 95 m., 1987

George Costigan (Bob), Siobhan Finneran (Rita), Michelle Holmes (Sue), Lesley Sharp (Michelle), Kulvinder Ghir (Aslam), Willie Ross (Sue's Father), Patti Nicholls (Sue's Mother), Paul Oldham (Lee). Directed by Alan Clarke and produced by Sandy Lieberson. Screenplay by Andrea Dunbar.

I've seen *Rita, Sue and Bob Too* twice, and the audiences were uneasy both times. They didn't seem sure exactly what to feel about this film. I'm not sure, either. The movie is a bleak, sardonic British comedy about the violation of a taboo: A married man in his thirties has affairs with two teen-age girls who are his baby-sitters. If this were a solemn TV docudrama with a psychiatrist to explain everything, we could relax. But it's an angry comedy, further complicated because both of the girls are so sassy and irreverent that it's hard to see them as victims.

The movie opens in a grim housing estate on the barren outskirts of a nondescript midlands city. One long shot establishes the scene: A drunk lurches into view, totters down the sidewalk, and disappears into a depressing brick building, and then a girl comes scurrying out, dressed for school, and runs down the street to meet her friend, whose front yard is occupied by a motorcycle gang.

The two girls are Rita and Sue. They are in their mid-teens but they already look worn by life, and yet they're filled with spirit. Rita (Siobhan Finneran) is more conventional, Sue (Michelle Holmes) is more likely to say things for shock effect, but they're peas in a pod. Like a lot of adolescent best friends, they can finish each other's sentences, and sometimes when the vibes are right they can even speak in unison.

That night they go to baby-sit at Bob and Michelle's home in a nearby suburb that is cosmetically more attractive than where Rita and Sue live, although perhaps there is just as much desperation behind the picture windows. There's a great scene of the two girls sitting side by side on a sofa, bouncing in time to a music video; we can see how young they really are, something that's not always very obvious.

Late at night, Bob brings his wife home and offers to drive the two girls home. Instead, they drive into the country, park overlooking the town, and have sex. Bob proposes the idea, they giggle, and then they get right to it, right there in the car. This is the scene that's hard to read. It is sordid, and Bob's behavior is certainly immoral, and yet the sex itself has a sort of low, bawdy humor to it, and the girls seem surprisingly casual about it.

To fortunate people with middle-class opportunities, the whole episode is likely to seem shocking. But the film means to shock, and the statement it makes is a political one. Rita and Sue come from utterly deprived homes, from the culture of poverty. Nothing is happening in their lives. Bob provides variety, someone to gossip and speculate about, and his demands are no more inconvenient for them than the casual, brutal promiscuity they see at home. The movie challenges us to disapprove of the conditions that produced Rita and Sue, rather than to take a safe, superficial stand against that rascal Bob.

But here I am lecturing, and the curious thing about *Rita, Sue and Bob Too* is that it does not lecture and contains no speeches. It is a comedy, if a sometimes depressing one, and the best thing in it is the irrepressible sauciness of the two girls. If this were an American film, it would be an R-rated sex romp without a brain in its head, another soft-core baby-sitter saga. But *Rita, Sue and Bob Too* is one of those recent small-scale British films that are more interested in human nature than in selling lots of tickets with lots of sex.

This is a movie about two tough, deprived girls from the worst part of town, and an irresponsible, feather-brained adult who thinks he's taking advantage of them when in fact they're a whole lot more worldly and cynical than he is. These aren't bad girls. They're totally without standards—after all, they haven't been taught any—but they have a sense of humor and high spirits, and this is one of those movies you talk about a lot afterward, because the motives of all the characters are so complicated that you're not absolutely sure just who came out ahead.

The River ★ ★
PG-13, 122 m., 1985

Mel Gibson (Tom Garvey), Sissy Spacek (Mae Garvey), Scott Glenn (Joe Wade), Shane Bailey (Lewis Garvey), Becky Jo Lynch (Beth Garvey), Don Hood (Senator Neiswinder). Directed by Mark Rydell and produced by Edward Lewis and Robert Cortes. Screenplay by Robert Dillon and Julian Barry.

The River has some basic problems anyway, but it might have seemed like a much fresher film if it had not been the third of Hollywood's "save the farm" movies released between September 1984 and January 1985. Like *Places in the Heart* and *Country,* it tells the story of brave, stubborn farmers who are determined not to lose their family land to the bankers. The farmers in this film have their own unique challenge—the farm is next to a river that tends to overflow—but *The River* also has a lot in common with the earlier films, including two crucial scenes that are astonishingly similar to ones in *Country.* It is some kind of cosmic bad joke on the makers of *The River,* who worked hard and earnestly on what is essentially a good film, that it came third in the parade.

The movie contains a heartfelt performance by Sissy Spacek as the Tennessee farm wife; an adequate performance by Mel Gibson as her husband; and a scene-stealing performance by Scott Glenn as the local financier who wants to buy up all the land in the valley, dam the river, and generate some jobs with cheap hydroelectric power. (The crucial flaw in the movie's plot is that Glenn's ideas, which are supposed to make him the bad guy, sound like simple common sense.) As the movie opens, Gibson is fighting the river and almost is trapped and drowned beneath a bulldozer. We remember the opening scene in *Country,* where the son of the family is almost suffocated in an overturned load of grain, and *The River* suffers in comparison: A secondary character might be killed in an opening scene, but hardly the male lead.

Then life settles down on the farm, and we get to know the Spacek and Gibson characters and their small children. These scenes of simple domestic life are good ones; a kitchen love scene between Gibson and Spacek is warm, true, and electrifying. But then the farm gets caught in a credit crunch, and Gibson goes off to work as a scab at a struck steel mill in Birmingham, Alabama. It's here that we begin to notice a fairly heavy touch in the screenplay. After a frightened deer wanders into the mill, the strike-breakers take pity on the animal, surround it, and lead it to safety. A memorable image, which is ruined because in the very next scene, the striking workers do exactly the same favor for the scabs.

Meanwhile, back on the farm, an auction is broken up by the chants of fellow farmers, expressing solidarity: "No sale! No sale!" This scene is just like the one in *Country.* Feeling a certain amount of *déjà vu,* we listen to Scott Glenn's reasons that Gibson and Spacek should sell their farm: "Sooner or later, you'll have to. The river will flood again, or there'll be a drought, or a surplus."

I don't think the movie wants us to believe him, but he has logic on his side. You know a movie's got problems when you find yourself wishing the heroes would agree with the villain.

Of the three "save the farm" movies, which one wins the sweepstakes? My vote goes to *Country,* which is the most concerned with actual farm problems, with the credit crunch brought on by low-priced farm loans in the 1970s and falling market prices in the 1980s—and which contains the best performance, Jessica Lange's. *Places in the Heart* is more of a human fable, more concerned with its characters than with actual farm problems, but it placed second. *The River* feels too contrived in comparison with the genuine emotion of *Places* and the authentic politics of *Country.*

River's Edge ★ ★ ★ ½
R, 100 m., 1987

Crispin Glover (Layne), Dennis Hopper (Feck), Keanu Reeves (Matt), Ione Skye (Clarissa), Daniel Roebuck (Leitch Sampson), Joshua Miller (Tim), Roxana Zal (Maggie). Directed by Tim Hunter and produced by Sarah Pillsbury and Midge Sanford. Screenplay by Neal Jimenez.

I remember reading about the case at the time. A high school kid killed his girlfriend and left her body lying on the ground. Over the next few days, he brought some of his friends out to look at her body, and gradually word of the crime spread through his circle of friends. But for a long time, nobody called the cops.

A lot of op-ed articles were written to analyze this event, which was seen as symptomatic of a wider moral breakdown in our society. *River's Edge,* which is a horrifying fiction inspired by the case, offers no explanation and no message; it regards the crime in much the same way the kid's friends stood around looking at the body. The difference is that the film feels a horror that the teen-agers apparently did not.

This is the best analytical film about a crime since *The Onion Field* and *In Cold Blood.* Like those films, it poses these questions: Why do we need to be told this story? How is it useful to see limited and brutish people doing cruel and stupid things? I suppose there are two answers. One, because such things exist in the world and some of us are curious about them as we are curious in general about human nature. Two, because an artist is never merely a reporter and by seeing the tragedy through his eyes, he helps us to see it through ours.

River's Edge was directed by Tim Hunter, who made *Tex,* about ordinary teen-agers who found themselves faced with the choice of dealing drugs. In *River's Edge*—that choice has long since been made. These teen-agers are alcoholics and drug abusers, including one whose mother is afraid he is stealing her marijuana and a twelve-year-old who blackmails the older kids for six-packs.

The central figure in the film is not the murderer, Sampson (Daniel Roebuck), a large, stolid youth who seems perpetually puzzled about why he does anything. It is Layne (Crispin Glover), a strung-out, mercurial rebel who always seems to be on speed and who takes it upon himself to help conceal the crime. When his girlfriend asks him, like, well, gee, she was our friend and all, so shouldn't we feel bad, or something, his answer is that the murderer "had his reasons." What were they? The victim was talking back.

Glover's performance is electric. He's like a young Eric Roberts, and he carries around a constant sense of danger. Eventually, we realize the danger is born of paranoia; he is reflecting it at us with his fear.

These kids form a clique that exists outside the mainstream in their high school. They hang around outside, smoking and sneering. In town, they have a friend named Feck (Dennis Hopper), a drug dealer who lives inside a locked house and once killed a woman himself, so he has something in common with the kid, you see? It is another of Hopper's possessed performances, done with sweat and the whites of his eyes.

River's Edge is not a film I will forget very soon. Its portrait of these adolescents is an exercise in despair. Not even old enough to legally order a beer, they already are destroyed by alcohol and drugs, abandoned by parents who also have lost hope. When the story of the dead girl first appeared in the papers, it seemed like a freak show, an aberration. *River's Edge* sets it in an ordinary town and makes it seem like just what the op-ed philosophers said: an emblem of breakdown. The girl's body eventually was discovered and buried. If you seek her monument, look around you.

The Road Warrior ★ ★ ★ ½
R, 97 m., 1982

Mel Gibson (Max), Bruce Spence (Gyro Captain), Vernon Wells (Wez), Emil Minty (Feral Kid), Virginia Hey (Warrior Woman). Directed by George Miller and produced by Byron Kennedy. Screenplay by Terry Hayes, Miller, and Brian Hannant.

The Road Warrior is a film of pure action, of kinetic energy organized around the barest possible bones of a plot. It has a vision of a violent future world, but it doesn't develop that vision with characters and dialogue. It would rather plunge headlong into one of the most relentlessly aggressive movies ever made. I walked out of *The Road Warrior* a little dizzy and with my ears still ringing from the roar of the sound track; I can't say I "enjoyed" the film, but I'll hardly forget it. The movie takes place at a point in the future when civilization has collapsed, anarchy and violence reign in the world, and roaming bands of marauders kill each other for the few remaining stores of gasoline. The vehicles of these future warriors are leftovers from the world we live in now. There are motorcycles and semi-trailer trucks and oil tankers that are familiar from the highways of 1982, but there are also bizarre customized racing cars, of which the most fearsome has two steel posts on its front to which enemies can be strapped (if the car crashes, the enemies are the first to die).

The road warriors of the title take their costumes and codes of conduct from a rummage sale of legends, myths, and genres: They look and act like Hell's Angels, samurai warriors, kamikaze pilots, street-gang members, cowboys, cops, and race drivers. They speak hardly at all; the movie's hero, Max, has perhaps two hundred words. Max is played by Mel Gibson, an Australian actor who starred in *Gallipoli.* Before that, he made *Mad Max* for the makers of *The Road Warrior,* and that film was a low-budget forerunner to this extravaganza of action and violence. Max's role in *The Road Warrior* is to behave something like a heroic cowboy might have in a classic Western. He happens upon a small band of people who are trying to protect their supplies of gasoline from the attacks of warriors who have them surrounded. Max volunteers to drive a tanker full of gasoline through the surrounding warriors and take it a few hundred miles to the coast, where they all hope to find safety. After this premise is established with a great deal of symbolism, ritual, and violence (and so few words that sometimes we have to guess what's happening), the movie arrives at its true guts. The set piece in *The Road Warrior* is an unbelievably well-sustained chase sequence that lasts for the last third of the film, as Max and his semi-trailer run a gauntlet of everything the savages can throw at them.

The director of *The Road Warrior,* George Miller, compares this chase sequence to Buster Keaton's *The General,* and I can see what he means. Although *The General* is comedic, it's also very exciting, as Keaton, playing the engineer of a speeding locomotive, runs an endless series of variations on the basic possibilities of two trains and several sets of railroad tracks. In *The Road Warrior,* there is basically a truck and a road. The pursuers and defenders have various kinds of cars and trucks to chase or defend the main truck, and the whole chase proceeds at breakneck speed as quasi-gladiators leap through the air from one racing truck to another, more often than not being crushed beneath the wheels. The special effects and stunts in this movie are spectacular; *The Road Warrior* goes on a short list with *Bullitt, The French Connection,* and the truck chase in *Raiders of the Lost Ark* as among the great chase films of modern years.

What is the point of the movie? Everyone is free to interpret the action, I suppose, but I prefer to avoid thinking about the implications of gasoline shortages and the collapse of Western civilization, and to experience the movie instead as pure sensation. The filmmakers have imagined a fictional world. It operates according to its special rules and values, and we experience it. The experience is frightening, sometimes disgusting, and (if the truth be told) exhilarating. This is very skillful filmmaking, and *The Road Warrior* is a movie like no other.

RoboCop ★ ★ ★

R, 103 m., 1987

(See related Film Clip, p. 779.)

Peter Weller (Murphy/RoboCop), Nancy Allen (Lewis), Daniel O'Herlihy (The Old Man), Ronny Cox (Jones), Kurtwood Smith (Clarence), Miguel Ferrer (Morton), Robert DoQui (Sergeant Reed). Directed by Paul Verhoeven and produced by Arne Schmidt. Screenplay by Edward Neumeier and Michael Miner.

There is a moment early in *RoboCop* when a robot runs amok. It has been programmed to warn a criminal to drop his gun, and then to shoot him if he does not comply. The robot, an ugly and ungainly machine, is wheeled into a board meeting of the company that hopes to make millions by retailing it. A junior executive is chosen to pull a gun on the machine. The warning is issued. The exec drops his gun. The robot repeats the warning, counts to five, and shoots the guy dead.

This is a very funny scene. (Whether it was even funnier before the MPAA Code and Ratings Administration requested trims in it is, I suppose, a moot point.) It is funny in the same way that the assembly line in Chaplin's *Modern Times* is funny—because there is something hilarious about logic applied to a situation where it is not relevant.

Because the scene surprises us in a movie that seemed to be developing into a serious thriller, it puts us off guard. We're no longer quite sure where *RoboCop* is going, and that's one of the movie's best qualities.

The film takes place at an unspecified time in the future, in Detroit, a city where gang terror rules. There has been a series of brutal cop killings. A big corporation wants to market the robot cops to stamp out crime, but the demonstrator model is obviously not up to the job.

A junior scientist thinks he knows a better way to make a policeman, by combining robotics with a human brain. And he gets his chance when a hero cop (Peter Weller) is killed in the line of duty. Well, not quite killed. Something remains, and around that human core the first "robocop" is constructed—a half-man, half-machine that operates with perfect logic except for the shreds of human spontaneity and intuition that may be lurking somewhere in the background of its memory.

Nancy Allen co-stars in the movie as a woman cop who was Weller's partner before he was shot. She recognizes something familiar about the robocop, and eventually realizes what it is: Inside that suit of steel, it's her old partner, Weller. It actually shouldn't have taken her long to figure it out, since Weller's original nose, mouth, chin, and jaw are visible. His inventor apparently agrees with Batman and Robin that if you can't see the eyes of someone you know, you'll never recognize them.

The broad outline of the plot develops along more or less standard thriller lines. But this is not a standard thriller. The director is Paul Verhoeven, the gifted Dutch filmmaker whose earlier credits include *Soldier of Orange* and *The Fourth Man.* His movies are not easily categorized. There is comedy in this movie, even slapstick comedy. There is romance. There is a certain amount of philosophy, centering on the question, What is a man? And there is pointed social satire, too, as RoboCop takes on some of the attributes and some of the popular following of a Bernard Goetz.

Oddly enough, a lot of RoboCop's personality is expressed by his voice, which is a mechanical monotone. Machines and robots have spoken like this for years in the movies, and now life is beginning to copy them; I was in the Atlanta airport, boarding the shuttle train to the terminal, and the train started talking to me just like RoboCop, in an uninflected monotone. ("Your-attention-please-the-doors-are-about-to-close.")

I laughed. No one else did. Since the recorded message could obviously have been recorded in a normal human voice, the purpose of the robotic audio style was clear: to make the commands seem to emanate from a pre-programmed authority that could not be appealed to. In *RoboCop,* Verhoeven and Weller get a lot of mileage out of the conflict between that utterly assured voice and the increasingly confused being behind it.

Considering that he spends much of the movie hidden behind one kind of makeup device or another, Weller does an impressive job of creating sympathy for his character. He is more "human," indeed, when he is RoboCop than earlier in the movie, when he's an ordinary human being. His plight is appealing, and Nancy Allen is effective as the determined partner who wants to find out what really happened to him.

Most thriller and special effects movies come right off the assembly line. You can call out every development in advance, and usually be right. *RoboCop* is a thriller with a difference.

Rocky ★ ★ ★ ★
PG, 119 m., 1976

Sylvester Stallone (Rocky), Talia Shire (Adrian), Burt Young (Paulie), Carl Weathers (Apollo Creed), Burgess Meredith (Mickey), Frank Stallone (Timekeeper). Directed by John Avildsen and produced by Robert Chartoff and Irwin Winkler. Screenplay by Sylvester Stallone.

She sits, tearful and crumpled, in a corner of her little bedroom. Her brother has torn apart the living room with a baseball bat. Rocky, the guy she has fallen in love with, comes into the room.

"Do you want a roommate?" she asks shyly, almost whispering.

"Absolutely," says Rocky.

Which is exactly what he should say, and how he should say it, and why *Rocky* is such an immensely involving movie. Its story, about a punk club fighter from the back streets of Philly who gets a crack at the world championship, has been told a hundred times before. A description of it would sound like a cliché from beginning to end. But *Rocky* isn't about a story, it's about a hero. And it's inhabited with supreme confidence by a star.

His name is Sylvester Stallone, and, yes, in 1976 he did remind me of the young Marlon Brando. How many actors have come and gone and been forgotten who were supposed to be the "new Brando," while Brando endured? And yet in *Rocky* he provides shivers of recognition reaching back to *A Streetcar Named Desire*. He's tough, he's tender, he talks in a growl, and hides behind cruelty and is a champion at heart. "I coulda been a contender," Brando says in *On the Waterfront*. This movie takes up from there.

It inhabits a curiously deserted Philadelphia: There aren't any cars parked on the slum street where Rocky lives or the slightest sign that anyone else lives there. His world is a small one. By day, he works as an enforcer for a small-time juice man, offering to break a man's thumbs over a matter of $70 ("I'll bandage it!" cries the guy. "It'll *look* broke"). In his spare time, he works out at Mickey's gym. He coulda been good, but he smokes and drinks beer and screws around. And yet there's a secret life behind his facade. He is awkwardly in love with a painfully shy girl (Talia Shire) who works in the corner pet shop. He has a couple of turtles at home, named Cuff and Link, and a goldfish named Moby Dick. After he wins forty bucks one night for taking a terrible battering in the ring, he comes home and tells the turtles: "If you guys could sing and dance, I wouldn't have to go through this crap." When the girl asks him why he boxes, he explains: "Because I can't sing and dance."

The movie ventures into fantasy when the world heavyweight champion (Carl Weathers, as a character with a certain similarity to Muhammad Ali) decides to schedule a New Year's Eve bout with a total unknown—to prove that America is still a land of opportunity. Rocky gets picked because of his nickname, the Italian Stallion; the champ likes the racial contrast. And even *here* the movie looks like a genre fight picture from the 1940s, right down to the plucky little gymnasium manager (Burgess Meredith) who puts Rocky through training, and right down to the lonely morning ritual of rising at four, drinking six raw eggs, and going out to do roadwork. What makes the movie extraordinary is that it doesn't try to surprise us with an original plot, with twists and complications; it wants to involve us on an elemental, a sometimes savage, level. It's about heroism and realizing your potential, about taking your best shot and sticking by your girl. It sounds not only clichéd but corny—and yet it's not, not a bit, because it really does work on those levels. It involves us emotionally, it makes us commit ourselves: We find, maybe to our surprise after remaining detached during so many movies, that this time we *care*.

The credit for that has to be passed around. A lot of it goes to Stallone when he wrote this story and then peddled it around Hollywood for years before he could sell it. He must have known it would work because he could see himself in the role, could imagine the conviction he's bringing to it, and I can't think of another actor who could quite have pulled off this performance. There's that exhilarating moment when Stallone, in training, runs up the steps of Philadelphia's art museum, leaps into the air, shakes his fist at the city, and you know he's sending a message to the whole movie industry.

The director is John Avildsen, who made *Joe* and then another movie about a loser who tried to find the resources to start again, *Save the Tiger.* Avildsen correctly isolates Rocky in his urban environment, because this movie shouldn't have a documentary feel, with people hanging out of every window: It's a legend, it's about little people, but it's bigger than life, and you have to set them apart visually so you can isolate them morally.

And then there's Talia Shire, as the girl (she was the hapless sister of the Corleone boys in *The Godfather)*. When she hesitates before kissing Rocky for the first time, it's a moment so poignant it's like no other. And Burt Young as her brother—defeated and resentful, loyal and bitter, caring about people enough to hurt them just to draw attention to his grief. There's all that, and then there's the fight that ends the film. By now, everyone knows who wins, but the scenes before the fight set us up for it so completely, so emotionally, that when it's over we've it. We're drained.

Rocky II ★ ★ ★
PG, 119 m., 1979

Sylvester Stallone (Rocky Balboa), Talia Shire (Adrian), Burt Young (Paulie), Carl Weathers (Apollo Creed), Burgess Meryyededith (Mickey), Tony Burton (Apollo's Trainer). Directed by Sylvester Stallone and produced by Irwin Winkler and Robert Chartoff. Screenplay by Stallone.

Rocky II isn't the movie the first *Rocky* was—what could equal that original burst of vitality?—but it's a well-crafted sequel with a lot of the same appeal, and with a climactic fight scene that's sensationally effective. 1979 was a year of sequels and prequels and remakes, and, as they go, this is one of the best.

That's because it's legitimately a sequel: It continues the story and further develops the characters, instead of just ripping off a successful formula. At the end of *Rocky* we wanted to know what came next, and now we do. That's a lot different from something like *Beyond the Poseidon Adventure*, which essentially just repeats the original movie.

Rocky II begins exactly where the first movie ended, with Rocky Balboa's once-in-a-million shot at the heavyweight title. Sylvester Stallone, who directed this time as well as writing and starring, is wise to quote from that fight footage. It's a reminder of the extraordinary impact of *Rocky*, which took a tired old Hollywood genre and brilliantly rediscovered its strength.

Stallone then gives us a scene that speaks directly to our memories of the first movie. After their mutual battering, both Rocky and heavyweight champ Apollo Creed are hospitalized. And in the middle of the night Rocky opens Apollo's door and says, "Apollo? You awake?" Yeah. "Can I ask you somethin'?" Yeah. "Did you give me your best shot?" Yeah, I did. "Thank you."

Rocky's life changes dramatically, of course, after his moral victory in the fight. He's badgered by agents who want him to endorse products and do TV commercials (and he does at least one, holding a club and wearing a leopard skin and standing in a cage to endorse a men's after-shave). One of the first things he does, of course, is to marry his girl friend Adrian (Talia Shire). They buy a car and a house. And Rocky looks around for a job.

His problem is that he can't fight again. Doctor's orders: He suffered damage to his eyes, and another fight could lead to blindness. But Rocky Balboa can't really *do* anything but fight. After a couple of menial jobs, he goes back to the gym run by his trainer, Mickey (played by Burgess Meredith in a jolly, scenery-chewing performance). These scenes—interlaced with Adrian's pregnancy and the birth of their son, Rocky, Jr. (with an astonishing head of hair)—head up to a sustained stretch of soap opera. Adrian goes into a coma. Rocky goes into a depression. Apollo Creed, driven by the need to clear his reputation, taunts Rocky for another fight in newspaper ads.

This is all pretty obvious stuff, and if it were handled with less care we might be tempted to laugh at the clichés. But Stallone as a writer has a way of getting away with things. He tells stories that are simple, basic, and human; he doesn't apologize for them, and he plays them with a conviction that makes them work.

He is also interesting as a director. The first *Rocky* was directed by John Avildsen, who placed it in a Philadelphia landscape deliberately kept barren of people who didn't figure in the story. The streets were empty, and the result was curiously effective: The characters gained a mythic stature because they were kept in relief and not marched through crowds of extras.

Stallone uses that same approach in *Rocky II*. But he also introduces an element of highly personal humor that first surfaced in *Paradise Alley* (1978), which he also wrote and directed. He likes characters who are offbeat and cheerfully grotesque. He likes scenes that are allowed to drift from realism into comic exaggeration. He likes to view life at an angle.

Paradise Alley gave us three heroic, crazy, goofy brothers, and scenes like the one in which the organ grinder's monkey is kept captive in the bathroom. *Rocky II* has fun with the wedding scene, with the absurd TV commercials, and especially with the night of the big fight. Instead of going for conventional devices to build the tension, Stallone cuts between drama and comedy, between the mounting excitement inside the fight arena and Rocky's leisurely progress through the city. Apollo Creed is sweating it out in his dressing room, but Rocky Balboa's stopping off at a parish hall for a quick blessing from the priest.

Then comes the fight scene. I wouldn't dream, of course, of telling you who wins. But the scene itself is terrific action footage, and Stallone's occasional use of slow motion seems to work here; in *Paradise Alley*'s closing fight, it was distracting and excessive. *Rocky II* tells the story crisply and with style, and keeps us hooked even during the soap opera stuff.

But almost any sequel to an enormous hit movie has this problem: We are already familiar with the qualities that made the original extraordinary. *Rocky* introduced us to this strange, eccentric, funny-talking, big lug from Philly who had turtles named Cuff and Link and a dog named Butkus, and was in love with the shy girl who worked at the pet store. It showed us Rocky's one-time shot at the big time. It established a fictional world that was fresh.

Rocky II can't do those things. It doesn't have the advantage of novelty. If you liked *Rocky*, you'll certainly want to see *Rocky II*. But the impact just can't be quite the same. Maybe that's why it's so good to have the fight scene at the end: It has such sheer animal intensity that it's got us cheering, just like the first time around.

Rocky IV ★ ★

PG, 90 m., 1986

Sylvester Stallone (Rocky Balboa), Talia Shire (Adrian), Burt Young (Paulie), Carl Weathers (Apollo Creed), Brigitte Nielsen (Ludmilla), Dolph Lundgren (Drago), Tony Burton (Duke), James Brown (Godfather of Soul). Directed by Sylvester Stallone and produced by Irwin Winkler and Robert Chartoff. Screenplay by Stallone.

The *Rocky* series is finally losing its legs. It's been a long run, one hit movie after another, but *Rocky IV* is a last gasp, a film so predictable that viewing it is like watching one of those old sitcoms where the characters never change and the same situations turn up again and again. Even Sylvester Stallone seems to be getting tired of the series; as the writer and director, as well as the star, he puts himself through the same old paces.

The movie begins with footage from Rocky's big fight with Mr. T. Then we meet Drago (Dolph Lundgren), a six-foot-four, 261-pound Russian fighting machine. Then it's time for a quick roll call of all the regular characters who pop up in every installment.

There's a bizzare birthday party for Paulie (Burt Young), Rocky's brother-in-law, who gets a robot for his present (the robot, by the way, can understand statements and respond spontaneously, suggesting that Rocky's suppliers have licked the problem of artificial intelligence). Maybe Paulie needs the robot for company; he has apparently made no friends during nine years as the champ's in-law, and only three people attend his party.

There's the obligatory romantic scene between Rocky and his wife Adrian (Talia Shire), who seem to have lost all passion during nine years of marriage, and are content to be worshippers at the shrine of their ideal love. There's a walk-on for Rocky, Jr., a couple of scenes with old pal Apollo Creed, and then it's time for the big fight scenes and the final freeze-frame.

It's tempting to forget how good the original *Rocky* was, back in 1976. It was a fresh, wonderful film, and we met some real people—quirky, lovable characters—on the way to the final fight scene. Rocky Balboa had a distinctive way of expressing himself, a love of colorful language that set him apart from the clichés of his characters. The people around him were genuine originals.

The next two Rocky pictures lost some of those qualities, but were still superior entertainments. Maybe it was inevitable that Rocky himself came to dominate his movies, while the others were reduced to perfunctory walk-ons. Maybe Rocky's opponents had to grow more and more bizarre, as the human and vulnerable Apollo Creed gave way to Mr. T's antics. But now, with *Rocky IV*, almost all of the human emotions have been drained out of the series, and what's left is technology. Stallone assembles and photographs two fight scenes (the first always a loss, the second always a victory), and links them together with perfunctory drama. Even the colorful dialogue is missing this time, replaced with endless, unnecessary songs on the sound track; half the time, we seem to be watching MTV.

Rocky IV has many moments that are not believable. My favorite is the moment when Rocky faces Drago in the ring in Moscow, and the all-Russian crowd starts chanting "Rocky! Rocky!" Sure. Uh-huh. You bet.

My next favorite moment is when Drago demonstrates that he has four times the punching strength and glove velocity of any other fighter who has ever lived. By my reckoning, and considering how violent a heavyweight punch is anyway, that should be enough to decapitate Rocky. The third most awkward moment is a grotesque exhibition match between Drago and Apollo Creed, who meet on a Las Vegas stage where Creed's warm-up consists of an appearance with soul singer James Brown. This single scene sets some kind of a record: It represents almost everything that the original 1976 Rocky Balboa would have found repellent.

Drago makes more of a James Bond villain than a Rocky-style character. He's tall, blond, taciturn, and hateful. He lets his wife (Brigitte Nielsen) do almost all of the talking on his behalf, and yet, interestingly, he and his wife do not have a single intimate scene together. Their most personal moments seem to occur at press conferences. Why couldn't (a) Drago do his own talking, or (b) Drago not require a wife in the movie? Could the answer be that Brigitte Nielsen was Stallone's wife?

Rocky IV is movie-making by the numbers. Even the climactic fight scene isn't as exciting as it should be, maybe because we know with a certainty born of long experience how it will turn out. Stallone says this will be the last Rocky movie. He should have taken Rocky Marciano as an example, and retired undefeated.

Romancing the Stone ★ ★ ★

PG, 106 m., 1984

Michael Douglas (Jack Colton), Kathleen Turner (Joan Wilder), Danny DeVito (Thug), Alfonso Arau (Juan), Manuel Ojeda (Zolo). Directed by Robert Zemeckis and produced by Michael Douglas. Screenplay by Diane Thomas.

It may have an awkward title, but *Romancing the Stone* is a silly, high-spirited chase picture that takes us, as they say, from the canyons of Manhattan to the steaming jungles of South America. The movie's about a New York woman who writes romantic thrillers in which the hungry lips of lovers devour each other as the sun sinks over the dead bodies of their enemies. Then she gets involved in a real-life thriller, which is filled with cliff-hanging predicaments just like the ones she writes about. The writer, played by Kathleen Turner, uses her novels as a form of escape. Throbbing loins may melt together on her pages, but not in her life. Then she gets a desperate message from her sister in South America: Unless she flies to Cartagena with a treasure map showing the location of a priceless green jewel, her sister will be killed.

What follows is an adventure that will remind a lot of people of *Raiders of the Lost Ark,* but it will be a pleasant memory. After all the *Raiders* rip-offs, it's fun to find an adventure film that deserves the comparison, that has the same spirit and sense of humor. Turner lands in Colombia, and almost instantly becomes part of the plans of a whole lineup of desperadoes. There are the local police, the local thugs, the local mountain bandits, and the local hero, a guy named Jack Colton, who is played by Michael Douglas.

Movies like this work best if they have original inspirations about the ways in which the heroes can die. I rather liked the pit full of snarling alligators, for example. They also work well if the villains are colorful, desperate, and easy to tell apart. They are. Danny DeVito, from TV's "Taxi," plays a Peter Lorre type, complete with a white tropical suit and a hat that keeps getting trampled in the mud. He's a gangster from up north, determined to follow Turner to the jewel. There's also a suave local paramilitary hero named Zolo (Manuel Ojeda), who wears a French Foreign Legion cap and lusts after not only Turner's treasure map but all of her other treasures. And Alfonso Arau plays a rural bandito who turns out to have memorized all of Turner's thrillers.

Movies like this have a tendency to turn into a long series of scenes where the man grabs the woman by the hand and leads her away from danger at a desperate run. I always hate scenes like that. Why can't the woman run by herself? Don't they both have a better chance if the guy doesn't have to always be dragging her? What we're really seeing is leftover sexism from the days when women were portrayed as hapless victims. *Romancing the Stone* doesn't have too many scenes like that. It begins by being entirely about the woman, and although Douglas takes charge after they meet, that's basically because he knows the local territory. Their relationship is on an equal footing, and so is their love affair. We get the feeling they really care about each other, and so the romance isn't just a distraction from the action.

A Room with a View ★ ★ ★ ★

PG-13, 110 m., 1985

Maggie Smith (Charlotte Bartlett), Helena Bonham-Carter (Lucy Honeychurch), Denholm Elliott (Mr. Emerson), Julian Sands (George Emerson), Daniel Day Lewis (Cecil Vyse), Simon Callow (Reverend Beebe), Judi Dench (Miss Lavish), Rosemary Leach (Mrs. Honeychurch). Directed by James Ivory and produced by Ismail Merchant. Screenplay by Ruth Prawer Jhabvala.

My favorite character in *A Room with a View* is George Emerson, the earnest, passionate young man whose heart beats fiercely with love for Lucy Honeychurch. She is a most respectable young woman from a good family, who has been taken to Italy on the grand tour, with a lady companion, Miss Bartlett. Lucy meets George and his father in their *pensione*. A few days later, while standing in the middle of a waving field of grass, the sun bathing the landscape in a yellow joy, she is kissed by George Emerson, most unexpectedly. He does not ask her permission. He does not begin with small talk. He takes her and kisses her, and for him, something "great and important" has happened between them.

Lucy Honeychurch is not so sure. She catches her breath, and Miss Bartlett appears on top of a hill and summons her back to tea, and a few months later, in England, Lucy announces her engagement to Cecil Vyse, who is a prig. Cecil is the sort of man who would never play tennis, who wears a *pince-nez*, who oils his hair, and who thinks that girls are nice because they like to listen to him read aloud. Cecil does not have many clues as to what else girls might be nice for.

Meanwhile, George Emerson and his father—who is an idealist, a dreamer, and a follower of Thoreau—take a cottage in the neighborhood. And one day George kisses Lucy again. He then delivers himself of an astonishing speech, in which he explains that love exists between them. (Not love but Love—you can hear the capital letter in his voice.) Lucy must not marry Cecil, he explains, for Cecil does not understand women and will never understand Lucy, and wants her only for an ornament. George, on the other hand, wants her as his partner in the great adventure of life.

George does not have many big scenes, other than those two. The rest of the time, he keeps a low profile and says little. But his function is clear: He is the source of passion in a society that is otherwise tightly bound up in convention, timidity, and dryness. He is the man to break the chains, to say what he thinks, to free Lucy's spirit. And that he does, with great energy and efficiency. George is my favorite character because he is such a strange bird, so intense, so filled with conviction, so convinced of Lucy's worth.

A Room with a View is the story of George and Lucy, but it is also an attack on the British class system. In the opening scenes of the movie, Lucy and Miss Bartlett have been given a room in the Italian *pensione* that does not have a view. Dear old Mr. Emerson insists that the women take his rooms, which have a view. By the end of the film, George will have offered Lucy a view out of the room of her own life. She has been living a suffocating, proper existence—and he will open the window for her. That's what's exhilarating about the film, that it is not only about perplexing and eccentric characters, it's about how they can change their lives.

The movie has been adapted from the E.M. Forster novel by three filmmakers who have specialized recently in film adaptations of literary works: Director James Ivory, producer Ismail Merchant, and screenwriter Ruth Prawer Jhabvala. Their other recent credits include *The Bostonians*, *The Europeans*, and *Heat and Dust*. This is the best film they have ever made.

It is an intellectual film, but intellectual about emotions: it encourages us to think about how we feel, instead of simply acting on our feelings. It shows us a young woman, Lucy Honeychurch, who is about to marry the wrong man—not because of her passion, but because of her lack of thought. Only think about your passion, the movie argues, and you will throw over Cecil and marry George. Usually thought and passion are opposed in the movies; this time it's entertaining to find them on the same side.

The story moves at a deliberate pace, with occasionally dramatic interruptions for great passion. The dialogue is stately and abstract, except when all of a sudden it turns direct and honest. The performances are perfectly balanced between the heart and the mind. At the center of everything stands Lucy, who is played by Helena Bonham-Carter, that dark-browed, stubborn little girl from *Lady Jane*. Maggie Smith is wonderfully dotty as her companion. Denholm Elliott, the most dependable of all British character actors, steals scene after scene as George's free-thinking father ("Leave me my portrait of Thoreau," he insists, as they are moving from their cottage). Julian Sands is the intense young George and Daniel Day Lewis creates a foppish masterpiece in his performance as Cecil; give him a monocle and a butterfly, and he could be on the cover of the *New Yorker.*

A Room with a View enjoys its storytelling so much that I enjoyed the very process of it; the story moved slowly, it seemed, for the same reason you try to make ice cream last—because it's so good.

The Rose ★ ★ ★

R, 134 m., 1979

Bette Midler (Rose), Alan Bates (Rudge), Frederic Forrest (Dyer), Harry Dean Stanton (Billy Ray), Barry Primus (Dennis), David Keith (Mal). Directed by Mark Rydell and produced by Martin Worth and Aaron Russo. Screenplay by Bill Kerby and Bo Goldman.

If *The Rose* accomplished nothing else, it would deserve praise for frustrating our national desire to turn the deaths of celebrities into entertainment events. It has gotten to the point in recent years where a popular singer can hardly hope to make it without being dead, and the hot thing for Hollywood lawyers is to put together a portfolio of superstar estates.

The Elvis Industry, balanced precariously between idolatry and necrophilia, is particularly depressing, but count our dead heroes: Jim Croce, Jimi Hendrix, Jim Morrison, Buddy Holly, Otis Redding, Janis Joplin . . . and there was that stir several years ago when yearning Beatles fans tried to bury Paul McCartney the better to praise him.

The girl rock-and-roll singer portrayed by Bette Midler in *The Rose* is officially not Janis Joplin, of course; Midler and director Mark Rydell say they drew from lots of sources, and the movie shows that they did. But the popular conception is that Bette's playing Janis, and audiences are going to *The Rose* to get the lowdown on she and Bobby McGee. The reaction after the movie is over is fascinating: It's a downer, some people complain. Too depressing. You see how fickle we are with our fads. We want movies celebrating the early deaths of our heroes—but they shouldn't be too glum. It's on record that Joplin went to her doom speeded by drugs and Southern Comfort, but maybe what the fans want now is a remake of *Heaven Can Wait*, with Warren Beatty greeting her in heaven.

The Rose is not that movie, and fans hoping to chuckle along at good ol' Rose as she self-destructs will be disappointed. This movie about the pressures of rock stardom and its road tours is told from the inside in two ways: Midler and the filmmakers know what it's like because they've been there, and the movie also concentrates on staying mostly inside the Rose character's head.

Rose, in the movie, is a junkie, a drunk, dependent on uppers, downers, and levelers (she is also, I should probably add, capable of having a good time, able to belt out some terrific performances, and not totally wasted until the end). The movie suggests some of the reasons for her shotgun addictions, but most people use drugs and booze, of course, not because of the personality and behavioral "reasons" so beloved by the social help experts but—quite simply—because they got addicted, and now can't stop. Telling someone he can beat a habit once he understands "why" he's using something is as cruel as telling a man with a broken leg that he can walk if he understands his bone structure.

The Rose seems to understand this. It is intelligent on the subject of addictions, and its insights are reflected in an interesting stylistic strategy. People on booze or certain drugs develop a tunnel vision in dealing with their environment: They focus on what's important to them at a given moment, and screen out the distractions.

The Rose handles its locations and supporting characters in that way, from Rose's point of view, so that cast members swim in and out of focus and we're seduced into Rose's state of mind. That makes the movie's gradual descent from good times into disquiet, pity, doom, and silence an especially effective one.

But some people say they don't like it, it's depressing. One is tempted to wonder what they expected (how do you base a comedy on Janis Joplin?), but maybe it's not their fault. We've been so brainwashed by the Elvis Industry and its lesser clones that we expect dead stars to come in a nice-smelling package. Used to be fans just identified with their heroes. Now they want the final word.

'Round Midnight ★ ★ ★ ★

R, 130 m., 1986

Dexter Gordon (Dale Turner), Francois Cluzet (Francis Borier), Gabrielle Haker (Berangere), Sandra Reaves-Phillips (Buttercup), Lonette McKee (Darcey Leigh), Christine Pascal (Sylvie), Herbie Hancock (Eddie Wayne), Martin Scorsese (Goodley). Directed by Bertrand Tavernier and produced by Irwin Winkler. Screenplay by David Rayfiel and Tavernier.

In Dexter Gordon's voice in this movie there is a quality that at first sounds like a great weariness. As I listened more carefully, however, I realized that there were other notes also present.

Here is a man (I speak of the character, not the actor) who has gone too far and seen too much, and who knows that in one way or another his death is near. Yet he is not impatient with those who still have long to live; he takes what remains of his precious time to speak carefully with them. And when he speaks of the world around him, it is with a quiet amazement that he is still there to see it.

I mention Gordon's voice because it plays the same notes as the music in this film. As with all great musicians, the notes that come from within are the same as the feelings that come from within. I believe that musicians who use breath to play their instruments—those who play the various horns—arrive sooner or later at a point where they play and speak in the same voice. Dexter Gordon makes it easy to hear that; the music that comes from his saxophone is sad and tender, and so are his words.

In *'Round Midnight,* he plays a man named Dale Turner, an American jazzman who goes to Paris in 1959 to play at a club called the Blue Note. Turner is about sixty, an alcoholic and drug abuser whose pattern has been to pull things together for awhile, and then let them slide. Each slide is closer to death. He is on the wagon in Paris, watched over by a ferocious landlady and a vigilant club owner, who want him sober so he can get his job done. In the smoky little club every night, he plays the new music of Monk and Bird, the standards of Gershwin and Porter, and songs that come up spontaneously while they are being played.

Outside in the rain one night, a young Frenchman stands by a window, listening to the music, not caring if he gets wet. He believes Dale Turner is the greatest sax player in the world, but he doesn't have enough money to go inside to hear him. One night he follows the old man out of the club, and is able to see without very much trouble that Dale needs help. So he offers it.

Dale Turner is the most hopeless kind of alcoholic, the kind who tries to stay dry by depending on his own willpower and the enforcement of others. Sooner or later his willpower will advise him to drink, and sooner or later the others will not be there, so sooner or later he will be drunk. The young Frenchman senses this, and also senses the overwhelming loneliness of Dale's life, and invites him home for food and talk.

That seemingly very slight gesture—a fan trying to help the man he admires—is the heart of *'Round Midnight.* This is not a heavily plotted movie, one of these musical biographies that are weighted down with omens and light on music. It is about a few months in a man's life, and about his music. It has more jazz in it than any other fiction film ever made, and it is probably better jazz; it makes its best points with music, not words.

Dexter Gordon plays the central role with an eerie magnetism. He is a musician, not an actor, and yet no actor could have given this performance, with its dignity, its wisdom, and its pain. He speaks slowly, carefully considering, really making his words mean something, and so even commonplace sentences ("Francois, this is a lovely town you have here") are really meant. He calls everyone "Lady" in the movie, and doesn't explain it, and doesn't need to.

The music was recorded live. The director, Bertrand Tavernier, believes that in earlier jazz films, the audience could sense that the actors were not really playing; that you could see in their eyes that they were not listening to the other musicians onstage with them. In *'Round Midnight,* the music happens as we hear it, played by Gordon, Herbie Hancock on piano, and such others as Freddie Hubbard, Bobby Hutcherson, Ron Carter, and Billy Higgins, with Lonette McKee on vocals. You do not need to know a lot about jazz to appreciate what is going on, because in a certain sense this movie teaches you everything about jazz that you really need to know.

There are side-stories: Dale's old loves, new possibilities, painful memories, battle with drink, and his suicidal decision to return to New York (where he is awaited by a slick agent and a patient, fatalistic heroin dealer). They all add up to the story of the end of a life. The story needs a song, and the movie has the song, *'Round Midnight.*

Roxanne ★ ★ ★ ½

PG, 107 m., 1987

Steve Martin (C.D. Bates), Daryl Hannah (Roxanne), Rick Rossovich (Chris), Shelley Duvall (Dixie), John Kapelos (Chuck), Fred Willard (Mayor Deebs), Michael J. Pollard (Andy). Directed by Fred Shepisi and produced by Michael Rachmil and Daniel Melnick. Screenplay by Steve Martin.

Roxanne is a gentle, whimsical comedy starring Steve Martin as a man who knows he has the love of the whole town, because he is such a nice guy, but fears he will never have the love of a woman, because his nose is too big. His nose is pretty big, all right; he doesn't sniff wine, he inhales it.

The movie is based on *Cyrano de Bergerac,* a play that was written in 1890 but still strikes some kind of universal note, maybe because for all of us there is some attribute or appendage we secretly fear people will ridicule. Inside every adult is a second-grader still terrified of being laughed at.

In *Roxanne,* the famous nose belongs to C.D. Bates, a small-town fire chief, who daydreams of a time when the local citizens will have enough confidence in his department to actually call it when there's a fire.

In despair at the incompetence of his firemen, he hires a firefighting expert (Rick Rossovich) to train them. The expert arrives in town almost simultaneously with a tall, beautiful blond (Daryl Hannah), who is an astronomer in search of an elusive comet.

Both men fall instantly in love with the woman. At first she has eyes for Rossovich, who is tall, dark, and handsome. But he is totally incapable of talking to a woman about anything but her body, and after he grosses her out, who can she turn to except Martin, the gentle, intelligent, poetic fire chief?

Martin is afraid to declare his love. He thinks she'll laugh at his nose. He assumes the role of a coach, prompting Rossovich, writing love letters for him, giving him advice. In the movie's funniest scene, Martin radios dialogue to Rossovich, who wears a hat with earflaps to conceal the earphone.

What makes *Roxanne* so wonderful is not this fairly straightforward comedy, however, but the way the movie creates a certain ineffable spirit. Martin plays a man with a smile on his face and a broken heart inside—a man who laughs that he may not cry. He has learned to turn his handicap into comedy, and when a man insults him in a bar, he counterattacks with twenty more insults, all of them funnier than the original. He knows how to deal with his nose, but he has never learned how to feel about it.

Hannah provides a sweet, gentle foil to the romantic fantasies of Martin and Rossovich. She has come to their small town because the air is clear and she can get a good view of the comet with her telescope. She isn't really looking for romance, and although she thinks Rossovich is cute, she's turned off by lines about her body. She likes his letters, though, and when she finds out the letters are really from Martin, she is able to accept him for his heart and not for his nose, which is the whole point, so to speak, of *Cyrano.*

All of the corners of this movie have been filled with small, funny moments. Michael J. Pollard, the getaway driver in *Bonnie and Clyde* twenty years ago, is back as a weird little fireman. Fred Willard is the pompous local mayor. Shelley Duvall, as the owner of the local cafe, does double-takes at the strangeness of ordinary life. And Martin proceeds manfully ahead, rescuing cats from trees, helping strangers, fighting fires, and trying to still the beating of his heart.

Runaway Train ★ ★ ★ ★
R, 111 m., 1985

Jon Voight (Manny), Eric Roberts (Buck), Rebecca De Mornay (Sara), Kyle T. Heffner (Frank Barstow), John P. Ryan (Ranken), Kenneth McMillan (Eddie). Directed by Andrei Konchalovsky and produced by Menahem Golan and Yoram Globus. Screenplay by Djordje Milicevic, Paul Zindel, and Edward Bunker.

The great adventure movies have all been stories of character, not just tales of action. One of the great losses in the movies of recent years has been that sense of real character: One-dimensional people insert themselves into chases and explosions, and the mindless spectacle on the screen is supposed to replace the presence of plausible human beings.

Runaway Train is a reminder that the great adventures are great because they happen to people we care about. That was true of *The African Queen,* and of *Stagecoach,* and of *The Seven Samurai,* three movies that would otherwise seem to have little in common. And it is also true of this tale of two desperate convicts on board a train that is hurtling through the snows of Alaska.

The movie stars Jon Voight and Eric Roberts, who were both nominated for Oscars. They are two actors with dramatically different styles. Voight is always internalized and moody; Roberts has a collection of verbal and physical tics that are usually irritating, and are sometimes meant to be. Here they are both correctly cast, as two convicts in a maximum-security prison in Alaska, who escape through a drain tunnel and then blunder onto the train that takes them on their hellbound mission.

Voight plays Manny, a convict who is so distrusted by the warden that his cell doors have been welded shut for three years. "He's not a human being—he's an animal," the warden says, and this is not just stock dialogue, but the thesis on which the whole movie will rest. Roberts is Buck, a trusty who works for the prison laundry. The warden is Barstow (Kyle T. Heffner), and he has a personal grudge against Manny. In fact, he releases him from solitary in the wicked hope that Manny will try to escape—he's done it before—and that will give Barstow license to kill him.

The opening passages are intense, but somewhat routine; they're out of the basic kit of prison movie clichés. Then the two convicts escape, and stumble by luck into one of the back cabs of a train that consists of four locomotives linked together. The train starts, the engineer suddenly collapses with a heart attack, and the movie's epic journey has begun.

Runaway Train is based on an original screenplay by the Japanese master Akira Kurosawa, whose best movies use the actors as a means of studying character. After some rewriting, *Runaway Train* was directed by Andrei Konchalovsky, the emigré Russian who figures so memorably (under a pseudonym) as Shirley MacLaine's lover in her bestseller *Dancing in the Light.* He has given the story the kind of wildness and passion it requires; this isn't a high-tech Hollywood adventure movie, but a raw saga that works close to the floor.

Once the train has started to move, the movie follows three threads. One involves the three people on the train (the two men discover after a while that a woman crew member, played by Rebecca De Mornay, is also on board, and also powerless to stop the engines). The second thread involves the railway dispatchers, who quarrel over a computer system that may possibly have the ability to clear the tracks ahead of the runaway. The third involves the ferocious determination of Barstow, the warden, to track the train by helicopter, and kill the men inside. Those elements might be enough to make *Runaway Train* a superior action movie. What makes it more than that is the dynamic inside the cab of the train. Voight is seen as a man who is intelligent enough to realize how desperate the situation is—because he has been caught not just in a physical trap, but also in a psychological one. In an impassioned speech that may be the best single scene he has ever played, he tries to explain to Roberts how limited their choices are in life. He uses a story of a man with a broom to create a parable about the impossibility of living as a free man.

The Roberts character does not quite understand the story. He is a wild man of limited intelligence, and prison life has made him dangerous—he acts without regard for the consequences. When these two men are joined by a woman, it is not just a plot gimmick; her role as an outsider gives them an audience and a mirror.

The action sequences in the movie are stunning. Frequently, in recent movies, I've seen truly spectacular stunts and not been much excited, because I knew they were stunts. All I could appreciate was their smoothness of execution. In *Runaway Train,* as the characters try to climb along the sides of the ice-covered locomotive, as the train crashes through barriers and other trains, as men dangle from helicopters and try to kill the convicts, there is such a raw, uncluttered desperation in the feats that they put slick Hollywood stunts to shame.

The ending of the movie is astonishing in its emotional impact. I will not describe it. All I will say is that Konchalovsky has found the perfect visual image to express the ideas in his film. Instead of a speech, we get a picture, and the picture says everything that needs to be said. Afterwards, just as the screen goes dark, there are a couple of lines from Shakespeare that may resonate more deeply the more you think about the Voight character. This was one of the year's best.

Running Scared ★ ★ ★

R, 107 m., 1986

Gregory Hines (Ray), Billy Crystal (Danny), Darlanne Fluegel (Anna), Tracy Reed (Maryann), Joe Pantoliano (Snake), Steven Bauer (Frank), Jonathan Gries (Tony), Dan Hedaya (Captain Logan). Directed by Peter Hyams and produced by David Foster and Lawrence Turman. Screenplay by Gary Devore and Jimmy Huston.

Running Scared is yet another movie about street-smart cops who are best buddies, wisecracking their way through one hair-raising situation after another. This genre is so overpopulated that it hardly seems like we need one more example, and yet *Running Scared* transcends its dreary roots and turns out to be a lot of fun. Most of the fun comes from the relationship between the two cops, who are played by Gregory Hines and Billy Crystal as if they were both successfully stealing the picture.

The movie takes place in the middle of a cold, gray Chicago winter, which is made all the colder and grayer by the hilariously inept use of fake movie snow. Considering how many vertical surfaces are plastered with "snow" in this movie, while the ground remains clear, Chicago must be the only city in which the snow falls from Oak Park instead of from the sky.

Slogging through the grim, mean alleyways, Hines and Crystal stumble across a major drug ring. Their good luck starts with an encounter with Snake (Joe Pantoliano), a two-bit hood who has $50,000 in his briefcase. They want to arrest Pantoliano but don't have anything to charge him with. So, in a brilliant scene, they convince Pantoliano to request arrest: Crystal loudly tells the neighborhood hoods that Pantoliano is carrying fifty grand and requests them to keep an eye out for suspicious perpetrators.

The movie unfolds in the usual ways. A criminal mastermind vows to kill the two cops, a commanding officer bawls them out and orders them to go on vacation, and a couple of friendly women warm the winter nights. As stories go, nothing in *Running Scared* is very original.

But Crystal and Hines (and the screenplay by Gary Devore and Jimmy Huston) don't need a plot because they have so much good dialogue and such a great screen relationship. The intelligence and wit flowing between them are so palpable you can almost see them, and there are so many throw-away lines that even the bit players get some good ones.

The movie was directed by Peter Hyams, who can claim the distinction of using two spectacular locations: There is a chase on the El tracks and an acrobatic shoot-out inside the State of Illinois Center. The original twist with the El chase is that the chase vehicles are cars, not trains. Crystal and Hines pursue a Cadillac limo in their Yellow Cab.

It sounds like a great chase, but it's curiously anticlimactic, maybe because we get mostly point-of-view shots from the two cars. I kept waiting for at least one shot from ground level, showing bystanders doing double-takes as a Yellow Cab zooms past on the El. But the shot is missing—an oversight for which the chase coordinator should be punished by being made to work on the next three *Cannonball Run* movies.

The State of Illinois Center sequence is something else. Hines lowers himself on a cable down through the vast rotunda from the ceiling while firing a machine gun and we reflect that the true test of architecture is its versatility. But even here, oddly enough, the action pales just a little because it is so conventional to end a movie like this with a spectacular shoot-out. I liked the smaller-scale scenes the best, the ones where Hines and Crystal were doing their stuff.

Ruthless People ★ ★ ★ ½

R, 93 m., 1986

Danny DeVito (Sam Stone), Bette Midler (Barbara Stone), Judge Reinhold (Ken Kessler), Helen Slater (Sandy Kessler), Anita Morris (Carol). Directed by Jim Abrahams, David Zucker, and Jerry Zucker and produced by Michael Peyser. Screenplay by Dale Launer.

It is hard to play a lovable villain, and Danny DeVito does it so easily. His eyes narrow, his voice deepens, and he speaks with great earnestness and sincerity about his selfish schemes and vile designs. *Ruthless People* opens as DeVito is having lunch with his mistress, and we can see that this is a man filled with passion. In this case, the passion is hatred for his wife and for all that she stands for, and for all that her rich father stands for, and even for all that her poodle stands for.

DeVito is the mainspring of *Ruthless People*, the engine of murderous intensity right at the center. His passion is so palpable that it adds weight to all the other performances in the movie. If we can believe he really wants to kill his wife, then we can believe he would not pay the ransom if she were kidnapped, which is the movie's comic premise.

It is, indeed, a pleasure to watch his face as he receives the first call from the kidnappers and they threaten to kill his wife if he doesn't follow every single one of their instructions to the letter. As he agrees to their stipulations, one after another, a wondrous calm spreads over his face, and the scene builds to a perfect climax.

The wife is played by Bette Midler, who makes her first entrance kicking and screaming inside a burlap bag. She has been kidnapped by Judge Reinhold and Helen Slater, who want to get even with DeVito, a clothing manufacturer who has ripped off their designs. It's a juicy role for Midler, a first cousin to the airhead housewife she played in *Down and Out in Beverly Hills*, and she milks it for all it's worth, turning into an exercise freak while being held captive in a basement.

The movie doesn't depend on just the one inspiration—the husband who doesn't want to ransom his wife. It has lots of other ideas and characters that fit together like a clockwork mechanism. We have the mistress (Anita Morris) and her boyfriend (Bill Pullman), who is not playing with a full deck. And then there are the police chief (William G. Schilling), who backs himself into an embarrassing situation, and a mad slasher (J.E. Freeman), who picks the wrong victim when he comes after Midler.

The movie is slapstick with a deft character touch here and there. It's hard to keep all the characters and plot lines alive at once, but *Ruthless People* does it, and at the end I felt grateful for its goofiness.

The discovery in the movie is DeVito. After seeing him on television's "Taxi" and here and there in character roles, I began to notice how good he was in *Romancing the Stone*. Then came his great performance in *Wise Guys*, opposite Joe Piscopo, and now this second virtuoso performance in a row.

He is, of course, very short, but there's a funny thing about his stature: It seems to be a fact of his body, not his mind or personality. In close-ups and whenever he speaks, he has so much force that he can easily command his scenes. He never seems to be compensating; he seems to be holding back. Like British actor Bob Hoskins, who is also shorter than most of the people in most of his scenes, he has a way of making the taller people around him seem unsure of what to do with their legs.

DeVito is a great joy to watch in this movie, as the turns of the plot catch him in one dilemma and then another. First he wants the kidnappers to kill his wife. Then, when he is charged with faking her kidnapping, he wants to ransom her. All along, there's a running gag as he negotiates the ransom price, and Midler has a great moment when she learns that her husband is trying to buy her back—at a discount. *Ruthless People* is made out of good performances, a script of diabolical ingenuity, and a whole lot of silliness.

S

Saint Jack ★ ★ ★ ★
R, 112 m., 1979

Ben Gazzara (Jack Flowers), Denholm Elliott (William Leigh), James Villiers (Frogget), Joss Ackland (Yardley), Rodney Bewes (Smale), Peter Bogdanovich (Schuman), Monika Subramaniam (Monika), George Lazenby (Senator). Directed by Peter Bogdanovich and produced by Roger Corman. Screenplay by Howard Sackler, Paul Theroux, and Bogdanovich.

Sometimes a character in a movie inhabits his world so freely, so easily, that he creates it for us as well. Ben Gazzara does that in *Saint Jack,* as an American exile in Singapore who finds himself employed at the trade of pimp. He sticks his cigar in his mouth and walks through the crowded streets in his flowered sport shirts, he knows everyone, he knows all the angles—but this isn't a smart aleck performance, something borrowed from Damon Runyon. It's a performance that paints the character with a surprising tenderness and sadness, with a wisdom that does not blame people for what they do, and thus is cheerfully willing to charge them for doing it.

The character, Jack Flowers, is out of a book by Paul Theroux, who took a nonfiction look at this same territory in *The Great Railway Bazaar,* one of the best modern books of travel. The film is by Peter Bogdanovich, and what a revelation it is, coming after three expensive flops.

Bogdanovich, who began so surely in *The Last Picture Show,* seemed to lose feeling and tone as his projects became more bloated. But here everything is right again, even his decision to organize the narrative into an hour of atmosphere and then an hour of payoff.

Everything. Not many films are this good at taking an exotic location like Singapore and a life with the peculiarities of Jack Flowers's, and treating them with such casual familiarity that we really feel Jack lives there—knows it inside out. The movie's complex without being complicated. Its story line is a narrative as straight as *Casablanca*'s (with which it has some kinship), but its details teem with life.

We meet the scheming Chinese traders Jack sometimes works for; the forlorn and drunken British exiles who inhabit "clubs" of small hopes and old jokes; the whores who do not have hearts of gold or minds at all; the odd Ceylonese girl who is Jack's match in cynicism, but not his better.

And we meet William Leigh, another remarkable fictional creation. Leigh is a British citizen out from Hong Kong on business, who looks up Jack Flowers because Jack can arrange things. To Jack's well-concealed surprise, William Leigh doesn't want a prostitute. He wants some talk, a drink, some advice about a hotel room. Jack never really gets to know Leigh, but a bond forms between them because Leigh is *decent,* is that rare thing, a good man.

Denholm Elliott, usually seen here in third-rate British horror films, has the role, and triumphs in it. It is a subtle triumph; the movie doesn't give Leigh noble speeches or indeed much of anything revealing to say, but Elliott exudes a kind of cheery British self-pride, mixed with fears of death, that communicates as clearly as a bell.

Jack Flowers, meanwhile, runs into trouble. Singapore hoodlums are jealous of the success of his brothel, so they kidnap him and tattoo insulting names on his arms (altogether a more diabolical and satisfactory form of gangland revenge than the concrete overcoat). Jack has the tattoos redecorated into flowers, as William Leigh gets drunk with him. Then, his Singapore business opportunities at an end, he signs up with an American CIA type (Bogdanovich) to run an Army brothel near a rest and recreation center.

One of the joys of this movie is seeing how cleanly and surely Bogdanovich employs the two levels of his plot. One level is Jack's story, and leads up to an attempted blackmailing scene that's beautifully sustained. The other level is the level of William Leigh, whose life is so different from Jack's, and yet whose soul makes sense to him. The levels come together in a conclusion that is inevitable, quietly noble, wonderfully satisfactory.

All of this works so well because Bogdanovich, assisted by a superb script and art direction, shows us Jack Flowers's world so confidently—and because Ben Gazzara makes Jack so special. It's not just a surprise that Gazzara could find the notes and tones to make *Saint Jack* live. He has been a good actor for a long time. What's surprising, given the difficulties of this character, is that anyone could.

Salvador ★ ★ ★

R, 125 m., 1986

James Woods (Richard Boyle), James Belushi (Dr. Rock), Michael Murphy (Ambassador Kelly), John Savage (John Cassady), Elepedia Carrillo (Maria), Tony Plana (Major Max), Colby Chester (Jack Morgan), Cynthia Gibb (Cathy Moore). Directed by Oliver Stone and produced by Gerald Green and Stone. Screenplay by Stone and Richard Boyle.

Given the headlines, you might perhaps think *Salvador* was a controversial movie about America's role in Central America, but actually it's a throwback to a different kind of picture, to the Hunter Thompson story *Where the Buffalo Roam*, where hard-living journalists hit the road in a showdown between a scoop and an overdose. The movie has an undercurrent of seriousness, and it is not happy about the chaos which we are helping to subsidize, but basically it's a character study—a portrait of a couple of burnt-out free-lancers trying to keep their heads above the water.

The movie stars James Woods, that master of nervous paranoia, as a foreign correspondent who has hit bottom. He's drinking, drugging, unemployed, living off past glories. When all hell breaks loose in Central America, he figures it's a good story, since he still has some contacts down there. So he enlists his best friend, a spaced-out disc jockey (James Belushi), and they load up with beer and drive their jalopy down through Mexico to where the action is.

The heart of the movie is in their relationship, and I kept being reminded of another Hunter Thompson saga, his book *Fear and Loathing in Las Vegas*, where the journalist and his lawyer drove their car through the desert, where drug-induced dragons seemed to swoop at them out of the sky. *Salvador* is a movie about real events as seen through the eyes of characters who have set themselves adrift from reality. That's what makes it so interesting.

Once they're at their destination, Woods and Belushi start looking up Woods's old contacts, who include a neofascist general, several bartenders, and an old girlfriend. Woods makes a stab at being a correspondent—he's always on long distance to New York, trying to get credentials from a reputable news-gathering agency—while Belushi settles into the local routine of bars and loose women.

A plot of sorts emerges, along with the usual characters we expect in a story like this—the American generals and embassy spokesmen and CIA types. Woods and Belushi hurry off recklessly in all directions, keep finding themselves surrounded by the wrong people, and escape with their lives only because Woods is such a con artist.

And he is. This is the sort of role James Woods was born to play, with his glibness, his wary eyes, and the endless cigarettes. There is an utter cynicism just beneath the surface of his character, the cynicism of a journalist who has traveled so far, seen so much, and used so many chemicals that every story is just a new version of how everybody gets screwed. That's why there is a special interest in the love affair in this movie, between Woods and Elepedia Carrillo, as the local woman Maria, the woman he truly loves but who lives by a code of Catholicism and respectability—a code that seems constantly in danger of being overwhelmed by events.

The central scene in the movie is possibly the one where Woods goes to confession. He has decided to marry the woman, in order to get her out of the country before all hell breaks loose. She insists on a church wedding. And so we get an extraordinary close-up of Woods's face as he talks with the priest, and tries to make some sort of a bargain between Catholic requirements and his own total ignorance of conventional morality.

Meanwhile, we meet some of the other people on the scene, including John Savage, as a great war photographer, and Michael Murphy, as the American ambassador, a tortured liberal who speaks of peace and freedom while the CIA goes about its usual business right under his nose. The subplot involving the Savage character is not very successful. I can see what they're doing, trying to set him up as a dedicated photojournalist who will risk his life for a great picture, but when he finally does come to his personal turning point, it's for a photo even the audience knows isn't great: A shot of an airplane swooping out of the sky. Without context, it could be any airplane, flying out of any sky.

Salvador is long and disjointed, and tries to tell too many stories for its length. A scene where Woods debates policy with the American officials sounds tacked-on, as if the director and co-writer, Oliver Stone, was afraid of not making his point. But the heart of the movie is fascinating. And the heart consists of Woods and Belushi, two losers set adrift in a world they never made, trying to play games by everybody else's rules.

Sammy and Rosie Get Laid ★ ★ ★ 1/2
R, 97 m., 1987

Shashi Kapoor (Rafi), Frances Barber (Rosie), Claire Bloom (Alice), Ayub Khan Din (Sammy), Roland Gift (Danny), Wendy Gazelle (Anna), Suzette Llewellyn (Vivia), Meera Syal (Rani). Directed by Stephen Frears and produced by Tim Bevan and Sarah Radclyffe. Screenplay by Hanif Kureishi.

London is not entirely made up of Westminster Abbey, the Tower, the Zoo, and bobbies on bicycles, two by two. It is also made up of the homeless in a cardboard city, under Royal Festival Hall. And of squatters living in rows of houses that seem to belong to nobody. And of people like Sammy and Rosie, living unconventional lives that they seem to improvise day by day.

Rosie is British. Sammy is from India or Pakistan—it's deliberately never made quite clear—where his father is a controversial political leader. Sammy and Rosie live in a comfortable house on a nice street that seems to be on the edge of a war zone. Anarchic mobs seem to hover just out of view. Sammy and Rosie have conventional left-wing political views, and a circle of friends that spans several races and sexes. To some degree, they are upwardly mobile. Then one day, Sammy's father (played by the famous Indian actor Shashi Kapoor) comes to visit.

He is a large, genial man who seems to genuinely love people. But as the taxi brings him from the airport, we cannot fail to notice that the driver wears a bloody headband and has an empty eye socket. The father fails to notice, however, perhaps because in his country the unfortunate are less visible, or perhaps because the cabbie is a ghostly vision that will return to haunt him throughout the movie.

We meet other people in this strange new London. A black, for example, who seems to move freely among several groups as a spokesman for the homeless and a prophet of doom. He helps guide the bewildered father home through the dangerous streets, and then seems to casually move in as a member of the family circle. There are other friends, sexually and politically liberated, who seem to have more freedom than they are happy with. And occasionally that bloody and bandaged figure that seems to haunt the edges of the frame.

Sammy and Rosie Get Laid tells the story of all of these people in a film that is far from hopeful about the future of London. It sees the city as a bulwark of privilege against the homeless, a city in which racism is bad, but class divisions are worse and more harmful, and in which real estate values are routinely considered more important than human lives and plans. In this world, Sammy and Rosie do get laid—by each other, by various friends, and (the movie implies) by the system itself. In one scene that many critics have not applauded, the screen splits in three, horizontally, to show the outcome of a wild party. The sex is desperately cheerless, a metaphor for their lives.

The film was directed by Stephen Frears, whose last film, *My Beautiful Laundrette*, was an international success. It told the story of outsiders who banded together in an unlikely cause: Two gays—an Asian and a white neo-Nazi—became lovers and then partners in running a launderette that was financed by the Asian's rich, property-owning uncle.

In *Sammy and Rosie Get Laid*, there is also the sense that interracial love, once considered some kind of social breakthrough, is not going to change anything fundamental when all races are oppressed by the same economic system (the movie begins with the voice of Margaret Thatcher, praising prosperity while we see people living rough in an urban wasteland).

We learn that Kapoor, the father, was a great admirer of London when he studied there, before returning home to preside over a totalitarian regime. He has fond memories of the parks, walking by the Thames, going to plays at the Royal Court, and falling in love with an elegant British woman (Claire Bloom). Now, during his visit, he tries to re-create some of the magic he remembers. While gangs roam the streets, he revisits some of his favorite places, and spends some heartbreaking time with Bloom, who has never married and who still, in some ways, loves him. The conversations they have are the emotional heart of the film, for what Kapoor is trying to believe is that his romanticism and sentimentality can exist completely apart from his politics.

It doesn't work that way, and that seems to be Frears's argument throughout the film. *Sammy and Rosie Get Laid* is a frontal attack on the favorite fantasies of anglophiles and the British themselves, who see the magical facade of London and ignore the inequalities and social crimes that are right underneath their noses. This will be a difficult film for anyone not fairly familiar with the city and its people; it doesn't have the universal comic undertones of *My Beautiful Laundrette.* It is about specific people and the specific hell they inhabit—a hell that is probably meant to be somewhat prophetic, since not all of the horrors in this film exist (yet) in London. For people who love London and yet are thoughtful about it, this film is indispensable.

Saturday Night Fever ★ ★ ★ ½

R, 118 m., 1977

John Travolta (Tony Manero), Karen Gorney (Stephanie), Barry Miller (Bobby C), Joseph Cail (Joey), Paul Paps (Double J), Donna Pescow (Annette). Directed by John Badham and produced by Robert Stigwood. Screenplay by Norman Wexler.

Each night I ask the stars up above:
Why must I be a teen-ager in love?
—Dion and the Belmonts

Saturday Night Fever is an especially hard-edged case and a very good movie. It's about a bunch of Brooklyn kids who aren't exactly delinquents but are fearsomely tough and cynical and raise a lot of hell on Saturday nights. They live for Saturday night, in fact: They hang their gold chains around their necks and put on the new shirts they bought with their Friday paychecks, and they head for a place called Disco 2001, and they take pills and drink and, as Leo Sayer put it, dance the night away. Occasionally they go out to the parking lot for a session in the back seat with a girl.

John Travolta is the center of the crowd: He's Tony Manero, the best dancer, the best looker, the guy with the most confidence. His life is just as screwed up as everyone else's, but they don't know that, and they tell him: "You know somethin', Tony? You always seem to be in control."

He is not. He works all week at a paint and hardware store and comes home to a family that worships his older brother, who is a priest. The family's sketched briefly right at the beginning in a dinner scene which, like the whole movie, is able to walk the tightrope between what's funny and what's pathetic.

We meet Tony's friends and the girls that hang around them, and we are reminded that feminism has not yet conquered Brooklyn. Some of the girls, especially a spunky little number named Annette (Donna Pescow), worship Tony. He dances with Annette because she's a good dancer, but he tries to keep her at arm's length otherwise. He's caught in a sexist vise: Because he likes her, he doesn't want to sleep with her, because then how could he respect her? The female world is divided, he explains, between nice girls and tramps. She accepts his reasoning and makes her choice.

The Brooklyn we see in *Saturday Night Fever* reminds us a lot of New York's Little Italy as Martin Scorsese saw it in *Who's That Knocking at My Door?* and *Mean Streets*. The characters are similar: They have few aims or ambitions and little hope of breaking out to the larger world of success—a world symbolized for them by Manhattan, and the Brooklyn Bridge reaching out powerfully toward it. But *Saturday Night Fever* isn't as serious as the Scorsese films. It does, after all, have almost wall-to-wall music in it (mostly by the Bee Gees, but including even "Disco Duck"). And there are the funny scenes (like the one where Travolta shouts at his father: "You hit my hair!") to balance the tragic and self-destructive ones.

There's also a hint of *Rocky*, whose poster Travolta's character has on his bedroom wall. Travolta meets a Brooklyn girl (Karen Gorney) who's made it in Manhattan, sort of, as a secretary. She comes back to Brooklyn to dance, and they team up to enter a $500 disco contest. They win it, too, but not before winning has become meaningless to Travolta. Their relationship is interesting because Travolta sees Miss Gorney not so much as a girl (although he thinks she's beautiful) but as an example of how *he* might escape Brooklyn.

The movie's musical and dancing sequences are dazzling. Travolta and Miss Gorney are great together, and Travolta does one solo (in an unbroken shot) that the audiences cheered for. The movie was directed by John Badham (*The Bingo Long Traveling All-Stars*), and his camera occupies the dance floor so well that we really do understand the lure of the disco world, for all of the emptiness and cruelty the characters find there.

Say Amen, Somebody ★ ★ ★ ★

G, 100 m., 1983

Featuring Willie May Ford Smith, Thomas A. Dorsey, Sallie Martin, the Barrett Sisters, Edward and Edgar O'Neal, and Zella Jackson Price. Directed by George Nierenberg and produced by George and Karen Nierenberg.

Say Amen, Somebody is one of the most joyful movies I've ever seen. It is also one of the best musicals and one of the most interesting documentaries. And it's a terrific good time. The movie is about gospel music, and it's filled with gospel music. It's sung by some of the pioneers of modern gospel, who are now in their seventies and eighties, and it's sung by some of the rising younger stars, and it's sung by choirs of kids. It's sung in churches and around the dining room table; with orchestras and a capella; by an old man named Thomas A. Dorsey in front of thousands of people, and by Dorsey standing all by himself in his own backyard. The music in *Say Amen, Somebody* is as exciting and uplifting as any music I've ever heard on film.

The people in this movie are something, too. The filmmaker, a young New Yorker named George T. Nierenberg, starts by introducing us to two pioneers of modern gospel: Mother Willie May Ford Smith, who is seventy-nine, and Professor Dorsey, who is eighty-three. She was one of the first gospel soloists; he is known as the Father of Gospel Music. The film opens at tributes to the two of them—Mother Smith in a St. Louis church, Dorsey at a Houston convention—and then Nierenberg cuts back and forth between their memories, their families, their music, and the music sung in tribute to them by younger performers.

That keeps the movie from seeming too much like the wrong kind of documentary—the kind that feels like an educational film and is filled with boring lists of dates and places. *Say Amen, Somebody* never stops moving, and even the dates and places are open to controversy (there's a hilarious sequence in which Dorsey and Mother Smith disagree very pointedly over exactly which of them convened the first gospel convention).

What's amazing in all of the musical sequences is the quality of the sound. A lot of documentaries use "available sound," picked up by microphones more appropriate for the television news. This movie's concerts are miked by up to eight microphones, and the Dolby system is used to produce full stereo sound that really rocks. Run it through your stereo speakers, and play it loud.

Willie May Ford Smith comes across in this movie as an extraordinary woman, spiritual, filled with love and power. Dorsey and his longtime business manager, Sallie Martin, come across at first as a little crusty, but then there's a remarkable scene where they sing along, softly, with one of Dorsey's old records. By the end of the film, when the ailing Dorsey insists on walking under his own steam to the front of the gospel convention in Houston, and leading the delegates in a hymn, we have come to see his strength and humanity. Just in case Smith and Dorsey seem too noble, the film uses a lot of mighty soul music as a counterpoint, particularly in the scenes shot during a tribute to Mother Smith at a St. Louis Baptist church. We see Delois Barrett Campbell and the Barrett Sisters, a Chicago-based trio who have enormous musical energy; the O'Neal Twins, Edward and Edgar, whose "Jesus Dropped the Charges" is a show-stopper; Zella Jackson Price, a younger singer who turns to Mother Smith for advice; the Interfaith Choir, and lots of other singers.

Say Amen, Somebody is the kind of movie that isn't made very often, because it takes an unusual combination of skills. The filmmaker has to be able to identify and find his subjects, win their confidence, follow them around, and then also find the technical skill to really capture what makes them special. Nierenberg's achievement here is a masterpiece of research, diligence, and direction. But his work would be meaningless if the movie didn't convey the spirit of the people in it, and *Say Amen, Somebody* does that with great and mighty joy. This is a great experience.

Scarecrow ★ ★ ★

R, 112 m., 1973

Gene Hackman (Max), Al Pacino (Lion), Dorothy Tristan (Coley), Ann Wedgeworth (Frenchy). Directed by Jerry Schatzberg and produced by Robert M. Sherman. Screenplay by Garry Michael White.

Max has been in the slammer and Lionel has been away at sea. Max has been sending his prison wages back to a savings and loan in Pittsburgh, and Lionel has been sending his to a wife in Detroit and a child he's never seen. They hitch up on the Coast and hit the road with a dream of their own car wash with real nylon brushes.

It's a trip we've taken before. We took it in *Of Mice and Men*, when there was a nice little farm at the end of the rainbow; we took it in *Easy Rider*, with the drug dealers who wanted to retire in Florida; we took it, most recognizably, in *Midnight Cowboy*, where the goal was those Florida orange groves.

Movies like *Scarecrow* (which shared the 1973 grand prize at Cannes) depend upon a couple of conventions. One is that we know more about the lower-middle-class characters than they know about themselves. The other is that we accept the easy rhythm of a picaresque journey without depending too much on plot. *Scarecrow* doesn't quite make it on either count, but it is a well-acted movie and for long stretches we're hoping it will work.

The performers are Gene Hackman and Al Pacino, two of the most gifted of contemporary actors, and the dialogue and locations (on the road, in taverns, at lunch counters, on a prison farm) strike a nicely realistic low key. But then director Jerry Schatzberg and his writer, Garry Michael White, commit the first of several mistakes: They tell us what the title means. The moment we hear the philosophy behind the scarecrow (he doesn't scare the crows; he makes them laugh) we begin to suspect these characters are too conscious of their symbolic roles, and we're right.

There's another problem, too. Schatzberg, a celebrated photographer, has teamed up with Vilmos Zsigmond (*McCabe and Mrs. Miller*) to produce a movie so obsessed with its visual look that it suffers dramatically. The movie is annoyingly lighted; we constantly seem to be peering through fog at the characters. In a scene or two, this could be nice. At almost two hours, it's an affectation. So is Schatzberg's willingness to allow shots to continue at length; an opening conversation at a lunch counter runs maybe three or four minutes. It's a virtuoso piece of acting by Hackman and Pacino, but after a while the shot calls attention to itself and away from them.

Still, there are fine moments, as there would have to be with Hackman and Pacino. There's a scene in a bar when a would-be fight turns into a comic striptease by Hackman. There's a bittersweet interlude with Max's sister and her girl friend. And there are times of just rambling, as the two friends depend on each other in a big and lonely world. It's too bad everything is brought together to a big, smashing, dramatic crisis at the end; *Scarecrow* somehow should have drifted out on a lower key.

Scarface ★ ★ ★ ★
R, 170 m., 1983

Al Pacino (Tony Montana), Steven Bauer (Manny Ray), Michelle Pfeiffer (Elvira), Mary Elizabeth Mastrantonio (Gina), Robert Loggia (Frank Lopez). Directed by Brian De Palma and produced by Martin Bregman. Screenplay by Oliver Stone.

The interesting thing is the way Tony Montana stays in the memory, taking on the dimensions of a real, tortured person. Most thrillers use interchangeable characters, and most gangster movies are more interested in action than personality, but *Scarface* is one of those special movies, like *The Godfather*, that is willing to take a flawed, evil man and allow him to be human. Maybe it's no coincidence that Montana is played by Al Pacino, the same actor who played Michael Corleone. Montana is a punk from Cuba. The opening scene of the movie informs us that when Cuban refugees were allowed to come to America in 1981, Fidel Castro had his own little private revenge and cleaned out his prison cells, sending us criminals along with his weary and huddled masses. We see Montana trying to bluff his way through an interrogation by U.S. federal agents, and that's basically what he'll do for the whole movie: bluff. He has no real character and no real courage, although for a short time cocaine gives him the illusion of both.

Scarface takes its title from the 1932 Howard Hawks movie, which was inspired by the career of Al Capone. That Hawks film was the most violent gangster film of its time, and this 1983 film by Brian De Palma also has been surrounded by a controversy over its violence, but in both movies the violence grows out of the lives of the characters; it isn't used for thrills but for a sort of harrowing lesson about self-destruction. Both movies are about the rise and fall of a gangster, and they both make much of the hero's neurotic obsession with his sister, but the 1983 *Scarface* isn't a remake, and it owes more to *The Godfather* than to Hawks.

That's because it sees its criminal so clearly as a person with a popular product to sell, working in a society that wants to buy. In the old days it was booze. For the Corleones, it was gambling and prostitution. Now it's cocaine. The message for the dealer remains the same: Only a fool gets hooked on his own goods. For Tony Montana, the choices seem simple at first. He can work hard, be honest, and make a humble wage as a dishwasher. Or he can work for organized crime, make himself more vicious than his competitors and get the big cars, the beautiful women, and the boot-licking attention from nightclub doormen. He doesn't wash many dishes.

As Montana works his way into the south Florida illegal drug trade, the movie observes him with almost anthropological detachment. This isn't one of those movies where the characters all come with labels attached ("boss," "lieutenant," "hit man") and behave exactly as we expect them to. De Palma and his writer, Oliver Stone, have created a gallery of specific individuals and one of the fascinations of the movie is that we aren't watching crime-movie clichés, we're watching people who are criminals.

Al Pacino does not make Montana into a sympathetic character, but he does make him into somebody we can identify with, in a horrified way, if only because of his perfectly understandable motivations. Wouldn't we all like to be rich and powerful, have desirable sex partners, live in a mansion, be catered to by faithful servants—and hardly have to work? Well, yeah, now that you mention it. Dealing drugs offers the possibility of such a life-style, but it also involves selling your soul. Montana gets it all and he loses it all. That's predictable. What is original about this movie is the attention it gives to how little Montana enjoys it while he has it. Two scenes are truly pathetic; in one of them, he sits in a nightclub with his blonde mistress and his faithful sidekick, and he's so wiped out on cocaine that the only emotions he can really feel are impatience and boredom. In the other one, trying for a desperate transfusion of energy, he plunges his face into a pile of cocaine and inhales as if he were a drowning man.

Scarface understands this criminal personality, with its links between laziness and ruthlessness, grandiosity and low self-esteem, pipe dreams and a chronic inability to be happy. It's also an exciting crime picture, in the tradition of the 1932 movie. And, like the Godfather movies, it's a gallery of wonderful supporting performances: Steven Bauer as a sidekick, Michelle Pfeiffer as a woman whose need for drugs leads her from one wrong lover to another, Robert Loggia as a mob boss who isn't quite vicious enough, and Mary Elizabeth Mastrantonio, as Pacino's kid sister who wants the right to self-destruct in the manner of her own choosing. These are the people Tony Montana deserves in his life, and *Scarface* is a wonderful portrait of a real louse.

Scenes from a Marriage ★ ★ ★ ★

PG, 168 m., 1974

Liv Ullmann (Marianne), Erland Josephson (Johan), Bibi Andersson (Katarina), Jan Malmslo (Peter). Directed and written by Ingmar Bergman.

They have reached a truce which they call happiness. When we first meet them, they're being interviewed for some sort of newspaper article, and they agree that after ten years of marriage, they're a truly happy couple. The husband, Johan, is most sure: He is successful in his work, in love with his wife, the father of two daughters, liked by his friends, considered on all sides to be a decent chap. His wife, Marianne, listens more tentatively. When it is her turn, she says she is happy, too, although in her work she would like to move in the direction of—but then she's interrupted for a photograph. We are never quite sure what she might have said, had she been allowed to speak as long as her husband. And, truth to tell, he doesn't seem to care much himself. Although theirs is, of course, a perfect marriage.

And so begins one of the truest, most luminous love stories ever made, Ingmar Bergman's *Scenes from a Marriage*. The marriage of Johan and Marianne will disintegrate soon after the film begins, but their love will not. They will fight and curse each other, and it will be a wicked divorce, but in some fundamental way they have touched, really touched, and the memory of that touching will be something to hold to all of their days.

Bergman has been working for years with the theme of communication between two people. At one time, he referred to it as "the agony of the couple." And who can forget the terrible recriminations and psychic bloodshed of the couples in *Winter Light* or *The Passion of Anna*? And here he seems finally to have resolved his crisis.

The years that preceded the making of this film saw a remarkable conciliation going on within the work of this great artist. In *Cries and Whispers*, he was at last able to face the fact of death in a world where God seemed silent. And now, in this almost heartbreaking masterpiece, he has dealt with his fear that all men are, indeed, islands. The film (168 minutes, skillfully and without distraction edited down from six, fifty-minute Swedish television programs) took him four months to make, he has said, but a lifetime to experience.

His married couple are Swedish upper-middle-class. He is a professor, she is a lawyer specializing in family problems (for which, read divorce). They have two daughters, who remain offscreen. They are intelligent, independent. She truly believes their marriage is a happy one (although she doesn't much enjoy sex). One evening, he comes to their summer cottage and confesses that he has gone and fallen in love with someone else. There is nothing to be done about it. He must leave her.

The way in which his wife reacts to this information displays the almost infinite range of Liv Ullmann, who is a beautiful soul and a gifted performer. Her husband (Erland Josephson) has left her literally without an alternative ("You have shut me out. How can I help us?") and still she loves him. She fears that he will bring unhappiness upon himself.

But he does leave, and the film's form is a sometimes harsh, sometimes gentle, ultimately romantic (in an adult and realistic way) view of the stages of this relationship. At first, their sexual attraction for each other remains, even though they bitterly resent each other because of mutual hurts and recriminations. The frustrations they feel about themselves are taken out on each other. At one point, he beats her and weeps for himself, and we've never seen such despair on the screen. But the passage of time dulls the immediate hurt and the feeling of betrayal. And at last, they are able to meet as fond friends and even to make love, as if visiting an old home they'd once been cozy in.

They drift apart, they marry other people (who also remain offscreen), they meet from time to time.

Ten years after the film has opened, they find themselves in Stockholm while both their spouses are out of the country, and, as a nostalgic lark, decide to spend a weekend in their old summer cottage. But it's haunted with memories, and they go to a cottage nearby.

In the last section of the film (subtitled "In the Middle of the Night in a Dark House"), Marianne awakens screaming with a nightmare, and Johan holds her.

And this is twenty years after they were married, and ten years after they were divorced, and they are in middle age now but in the night still fond and frightened lovers holding on for reassurance.

And that is what Bergman has been able to accept, the source of his reconciliation: Beyond love, beyond marriage, beyond the selfishness that destroys love, beyond the centrifugal force that sends egos whirling away from each other and prevents enduring relationships—beyond all these things, there still remains what we know of each other, that we care about each other, that in twenty years these people have touched and known so deeply that they still remember, and still need.

Marianne and Johan are only married for the first part of this film, but the rest of it is also scenes from their marriage.

School Daze ★ ★ ★ ½

R, 114 m., 1988 ✓

(See related Film Clip, p. 763.)

Larry Fishburne (Dap Dunlap), Giancarlo Esposito (Julian Eaves), Tisha Campbell (Jane Toussaint), Kyme (Rachel Meadows), Joe Seneca (President McPherson), Branford Marsalis (Jordan), Spike Lee (Half-Pint). Directed, produced, and written by Spike Lee.

Spike Lee's *School Daze* is the first movie in a long time where the black characters seem to be relating to one another, instead of to a hypothetical white audience. His *She's Gotta Have It* was another, and then you have to go back to films like *Sweet Sweetback's Badass Song* in 1970. Although the film has big structural problems and leaves a lot of loose ends, there was never a moment when it didn't absorb me, because I felt as if I was watching the characters talk to one another instead of to me.

Most good movies are voyeuristic—we feel as if we're getting a glimpse of other people's lives—but most movies about blacks have lacked that quality. They seem acutely aware of white audiences, white value systems, and the white Hollywood establishment. They interpret rather than reveal, and even in attacking mainstream white society (as Eddie Murphy does in the *Beverly Hills Cop* movies), they pay homage to it in a backhanded way. *School Daze* couldn't care less.

What's surprising is that its revolutionary approach is found in a daffy story about undergraduates at an all-black university. The movie is basically a comedy, with some serious scenes that don't always quite seem to fit. (It begins with a demonstration against the school's investments in South Africa, but doesn't remember to resolve that subject.) It deals with divisions within the student body—between Greeks and independents, and between political activists and kids who just want to get good grades.

And with utter frankness it addresses two subjects that are taboo in most "black movies"—complexion and hair. Lee divides the women on his campus into two groups, the lighter-skinned girls of the Gamma Ray sorority, with their straightened and longer hair, and the darker-skinned independents, with shorter hair or Afros. These two groups call each other the "Wannabes" and the "Jigaboos," and in a brilliant and startling song-and-dance sequence called "Straight and Nappy," they express their feelings for each other. Lee's choice of a musical production number to consider these emotionally charged subjects is an inspiration; there is possibly no way the same feelings could be expressed in spoken dialogue without great awkwardness and pain.

The division within the movie is dramatized by two characters—Dap Dunlap (Larry Fishburne), the intellectual activist and leader of demonstrations against the conservative administration; and Half-Pint (Spike Lee), the undersized kid who dreams of being initiated into the school's most popular fraternity. The two characters play cousins, and it is a sign of the movie's subtle appreciation of campus values that Fishburne, the revolutionary who rejects fraternities, quietly goes to the president of the chapter to put in a good word for his cousin.

In its own way, *School Daze* confronts a lot of issues that aren't talked about in the movies these days, not only issues of skin color and hair, but also the emergence of a black middle class, the purpose of all-black universities in an integrated society, and the sometimes sexist treatment of black women by black men. In one of the movie's most uncompromising sequences, a black fraternity pledge-master expresses concern that Half-Pint is still a virgin (none of the brothers in this house should be virgins), and he supplies his own girlfriend (Tisha Campbell) to initiate the freshman. She actually goes through with it, tearfully, and although the scene was so painful it was difficult to watch, I later reflected that Lee played it for the pain, not for the kind of smutty comedy we might expect in a movie about undergraduates.

Although there was a brief age of "black exploitation movies" in the 1970s, there have never been very many good American movies about the varieties of the black experience. Black superstars like Eddie Murphy and Richard Pryor are essentially playing to (and with) white audiences, and serious dramas about blacks, even strong ones like *The Color Purple,* are so loaded with nobility and message that they feel like secular sermons. Now here is Spike Lee with a slight, disorganized comedy named *School Daze,* and he just sort of assumes a completely black orientation for his film. There is not a single white person in it. All of the characters, good and bad, are black, and all of the characters' references are to each other.

In *Shoot to Kill,* a 1988 Sidney Poitier film, no mention at all is made of his race until a scene where he jumps up and down and scares away a bear. Then he says, "People here act like they've never seen a black man before." The line got a big laugh from the sneak preview audience I saw it with, but when you analyze it, it was an aside pitched straight at the audience. There are no asides in *School Daze,* and no self-conscious references to blackness. The result is an entertaining comedy, but also much more than that. There is no doubt in my mind but that *School Daze,* in its own way, is one of the most honest and revealing movies I've ever seen about modern middle-class black life in America.

Secret Honor ★ ★ ★ ★

NO MPAA RATING, 90 m., 1984

Philip Baker Hall (Nixon). Directed and produced by Robert Altman. Screenplay by Donald Freed and Arnold M. Stone.

The most tantalizing images in Woodward and Bernstein's *The Final Days* were those stories of a drunken Richard M. Nixon, falling to his knees in the White House, embarrassing Henry Kissinger with a display of self-pity and pathos. Was the book accurate? Even Kissinger said he had no idea who the authors' sources were (heh, heh). But as Watergate fades into history, and as revisionist historians begin to suggest that Nixon might after all have been a great president—apart from the scandals, of course—our curiosity remains. What were the real secrets of this most complex president? Robert Altman's *Secret Honor,* which is one of the most scathing, lacerating and brilliant movies of 1984, attempts to answer our questions. The film is a work of fiction. An actor is employed to impersonate Nixon. But all of the names and many of the facts are real, and the film gives us the uncanny sensation that we are watching a man in the act of exposing his soul.

The action takes place in Nixon's private office, at some point after his resignation. The shelves are lined with books, and with a four-screen video monitor for the security system. The desk top is weighted down with brass and gold. From the walls, portraits peer down. Eisenhower, Lincoln, Washington, Woodrow Wilson, Kissinger. Nixon begins by fiddling with his tape recorder; there is a little joke in the fact that he doesn't know quite how to run it. Then he begins to talk. He talks for ninety minutes. That bare description may make *Secret Honor* sound like *My Dinner with André,* but rarely have I seen ninety more compelling minutes on the screen. Nixon is portrayed by Philip Baker Hall, an actor previously unknown to me, with such savage intensity, such passion, such venom, such scandal, that we cannot turn away. Hall looks a little like the real Nixon; he could be a cousin, and he sounds a little like him. That's close enough. This is not an impersonation, it's a performance.

What Nixon the character has to say may or may not be true. He makes shocking revelations. Watergate was staged to draw attention away from more serious, even treasonous, activities. Kissinger was on the payroll of the Shah of Iran, and supplied the Shah with young boys during his visits to New York. Marilyn Monroe was indeed murdered by the CIA, and so on. These speculations are interwoven with stories we recognize as part of the official Nixon biography: the letter to his mother, signed "Your faithful dog, Richard"; the feeling about his family and his humble beginnings; his hatred for the Eastern Establishment, which he feels has scorned him.

Truth and fiction mix together into a tapestry of life. We get the sensation of a man pouring out all of his secrets after a lifetime of repression. His sentences rush out, disorganized, disconnected, under tremendous pressure, interrupted by four-letter words that serve almost as punctuation. After a while the specific details don't matter so much; what we are hearing is a scream of a brilliant, gifted man who is tortured by the notion that fate might have made him a loser.

A strange thing happened to me as I watched this film. I knew it was fiction. I didn't approach it in the spirit of learning the "truth about Nixon." But as a movie, it created a deeper truth, an artistic truth, and after *Secret Honor* was over, you know what? I had a deeper sympathy for Richard Nixon than I have ever had before.

The Secret of My Success ★ ½
PG-13, 117 m., 1987

Michael J. Fox (Brantley), Helen Slater (Christy), Richard Jordan (Howard), Margaret Whitton (Vera). Directed and produced by Herbert Ross. Screenplay by Jim Cash and Jack Epps, Jr.

The Secret of My Success seems trapped in some kind of time warp, as if the screenplay had been in a drawer since the 1950s and nobody bothered to update it. This is the kind of movie that should star Tony Randall or Gig Young opposite Judy Holliday or Doris Day, and, in fact, they were wonderful in the 1950s classics that *Secret* recycles.

Those old high-rise office comedies came out of a specific time and place however, and when an eighties star such as Michael J. Fox turns up in one, it's almost like his personal version of *Back to the Future*. He seems to have traveled back through time on a visit to the clichés of yesteryear.

Fox plays a Kansas farm boy who dreams of making it in New York City. He leaves home, arrives in the Big Apple, loses the job he had lined up, and talks his rich uncle (Richard Jordan) into hiring him for the mail room of Jordan's big corporation. Then Fox falls in love with a beautiful junior executive (Helen Slater), who isn't interested in meeting anyone from the mail room.

That inspires him to pull off a risky stunt: He finds an empty office, puts a fictitious name on the door and masquerades as a new executive. At the same time, he keeps his mail room job. He has to keep changing clothes all day long, with all of the obvious and unfunny jokes that implies.

There's really nothing wrong with the premise, but the screenplay could have been a lot more clever. The writers, Jim Cash and Jack Epps, Jr., are experts at recycling old script ideas (their credits include *Top Gun* and *Legal Eagles*), and here they settle for all of the basic gags they can milk out of a mistaken identity.

That includes their decision to provide Fox with an affair with the boss's wife (Margaret Whitton), who is, of course, his aunt. Their carefree coupling is a little startling in the age of AIDS, and so is the movie's amorality. None of the characters has any morals—personal or professional—and the movie doesn't have any satirical fun with that because, I suspect, it actually never occurred to the filmmakers that the behavior was amoral. This is a movie made with expedience, about expedient people, and expecting them to notice their compromises would be like asking a fish to notice water.

Fox provides a fairly desperate center for the film. It could not have been much fun for him to follow the movie's arbitrary shifts of mood, from sitcom to slapstick, from sex farce to boardroom brawls. There is even a chase scene up and down the stairs at corporate headquarters and a scene where Jordan catches Fox and Whitton horizontal on the office couch. Like most movies about mistaken identities, this one relies heavily on the Idiot Plot: Everyone in the movie is an idiot or the mystery would be solved in five minutes. Does the movie really believe anyone is as stupid as these characters? Does it care?

September ★ ★ ★ ½
PG, 82 m., 1987
(See related Film Clip, p. 741.)

Denholm Elliott (Howard), Dianne Wiest (Stephanie), Mia Farrow (Lane), Elaine Stritch (Diane), Sam Waterston (Peter), Jack Warden (Lloyd), Ira Wheeler (Mr. Raines), Jane Cecil (Mrs. Raines), Rosemary Murphy (Mrs. Mason). Directed by Woody Allen and produced by Robert Greenhut. Screenplay by Allen.

If you could take all of the different combinations of love won and love lost from many different periods in your life and join them all together for a weekend in the country, the weekend might turn out a little like *September.* Some of the guests at your party might be older or younger than you are, or smarter or more vulnerable, or of a different sex. But when you looked closely at their romantic strivings, you would recognize yourself, because there are, after all, only so many ways to be in love with the wrong person at the wrong time.

There are six major characters in the movie, each and every one of them hungry to be loved and taken care of. And everyone in the movie loves somebody—but usually not the person who loves him. The entire weekend comes down to a series of little emotional tangos, in which the characters move restlessly from room to room, trying to arrange to be alone with the object of their love—and away from the person obsessed with them.

The dominant person in the household is Diane, the middle-aged but still charismatic movie star. Played by Elaine Stritch, she is a woman who has lived a great deal, compromised too often, and become what is known as a "survivor," which is to say, a person you are surprised is still functioning. She has been married several times, currently to Lloyd (Jack Warden), an industrialist who is no doubt proud to have won this woman who was a sex symbol when they were both much younger. (By the same token, if Marilyn Monroe were still alive today, how many men over forty would not still feel some nostalgic erotic stirring if they found themselves alone in the room with her?)

Diane has come out to the family's country place to join her fortyish daughter, Lane (Mia Farrow), who has been living there for some time, recovering from a breakdown. For several months, Lane's close companion has been Howard (Denholm Elliott), the quiet, self-effacing neighbor. Lane has allowed Howard to grow close to her, but actually she feels passion only for Peter (Sam Waterston), the writer who has taken a place nearby for the summer. Peter has rather encouraged her. But this weekend, Lane has invited Stephanie (Dianne Wiest), her closest friend, to the country. And now Peter has conceived an enormous passion for Stephanie.

So, Howard loves Lane, who loves Peter, who loves Stephanie, who is thinking of breaking up with her husband. And Lloyd loves his memories of Diane, who looks in the mirror and still finds much to love in herself. And meanwhile there is a horrible family secret lurking beneath the pleasant conversations of the mother and the daughter—a secret that will burst out later in the film, in a moment of anger.

What is Allen up to here? The structure of his story is all too neat to make a messy, psychologically complicated modern movie. In the neat pairings of couples and non-couples, Allen almost seems to be making a modern-dress Elizabethan comedy. And that may be his point. When we fall in love, we are always so wound up in the absolute uniqueness of ourselves and our loved one, in the feeling that nothing like this has ever happened before, that we cannot see how the same old patterns repeat themselves. To turn toward one person, we must turn away from another. If the person we turn to is not interested, we are left stranded, which is the way all but the luckiest of us probably feel most of the time.

Allen has made so many comedies that it is easy to insist that he make nothing else. Actually, he is as acute an author of serious dialogue as anyone now making movies, and in *September,* most of the real action goes on in the word choices. By the precise words that they do or don't use, his characters are able to convey exactly how much of what they say is sincere, and how much is polite. Listening to Farrow gently speak to Elliott, for example, anyone but Elliott would know instantly that she does not and never will love him. Listening to Waterston talk to Farrow, anyone but Farrow would know that he does not and never will love her.

How is it that the Farrow character is perceptive enough to know what words to say to Elliott, but not sensitive enough to hear the same words when they are being said to her? That is the whole mystery of this film. We can clearly see the people we are not in love with, but when we look at the people we love, we see only what we choose to see, and hear only what we can stand to hear. *September* is the first movie in a long time that has been able to listen that closely.

The Serpent and the Rainbow ★ ★ ★
R, 98 m., 1988 ✓

Bill Pullman (Dennis Alan), Cathy Tyson (Marielle Celine), Zakes Mokae (Dargent Peytraud), Paul Winfield (Lucien Celine), Brent Jennings (Mozart), Conrad Roberts (Christophe), Badja Djola (Gaston). Directed by Wes Craven and produced by David Ladd and Doug Claybourne. Screenplay by Richard Maxwell and A.R. Simoun.

The Serpent and the Rainbow was inspired by a book by Wade Davis, a Harvard scientist who investigated the voodoo society of Haiti and identified two of the drugs used for "zombification"—drugs that lower the metabolic rate of their victims so much that they appear dead and are buried, only to be dug up later and revived.

Resurrected zombies apparently appear somewhat lobotomized, a not unreasonable result of being turned into the living dead and buried alive. Although Davis himself did not become a zombie—at least not more so than any other doctoral candidate—his adventures inspired this thriller in which a Harvard researcher, played by Bill Pullman, ventures into the heart of voodoo and witnesses strange and gruesome realities.

In the movie, Pullman plays a cross between William Hurt and Indiana Jones: he's a tall, good-looking, sensitive intellectual who is called upon to wrestle leopards, battle corpses, confront an evil voodoo leader, and eventually be buried alive along with a deadly spider that makes itself cozy on his paralyzed eyeball.

Pullman's mission in going to Haiti is to isolate the active ingredient in secret voodoo powder, so that it can perhaps be used as an anesthetic. His contact in Haiti is the beautiful Marielle Celine, played by Cathy Tyson in her first role since *Mona Lisa*. She runs a people's clinic, as the sexy heroines in these movies always do. Other local experts include Paul Winfield, as a well-connected local leader, and Brent Jennings, as a man named Mozart who knows all of the secrets in the secret ingredients.

In most voodoo movies, voodoo itself is taken only as a backdrop, a gimmick. This movie seems to know something about voodoo (it knows more than I do, anyway), and treats it seriously as a religion, a way of life, and an occult circle that does possess secrets unexplored by modern medicine. One of the most convincing elements in the movie is the way the more "modern" Haitians nevertheless regard voodoo as something not to be taken lightly. As Pullman slowly enters the voodoo society, penetrating first one level of concealment and then another, we get the sensation—unusual in a horror film—that his discoveries are genuine.

The movie was shot on location in Haiti and the Dominican Republic, and unlike most voodoo movies, it attempts to look and sound realistic—even including TV clips of the overthrow and flight of the dictator "Baby Doc" Duvalier. The visual look of the movie is stunning; there's never the sense of sets, of costumes, of hired extras, but more of a feeling of a camera moving past real people in real places. Even the obviously contrived scenes, including some of the hallucinations and voodoo fantasies, have an air of solid plausibility to them.

The film was directed by Wes Craven, a master of horror, whose credits include *Last House on the Left*, *Swamp Thing*, and the original *A Nightmare on Elm Street*. Craven will never advance in the Hollywood establishment until he embraces more respectable projects, and yet he has a sure touch for horror and the macabre, and *The Serpent and the Rainbow* is uncanny in the way it takes the most lurid images and makes them plausible.

The Seventh Sign ★ ★
R, 94 m., 1988
(See related Film Clip, p. 765.)

Demi Moore (Abby Quinn), Michael Biehn (Russell Quinn), Jurgen Prochnow (The Boarder), Peter Friedman (Lucci), Manny Jacobs (Avi), John Taylor (Jimmy). Directed by Carl Schultz and produced by Ted Field and Robert W. Cort. Screenplay by W.W. Wicket and George Kaplan.

The Seventh Sign begins with portents of the Apocalypse. The rivers run with blood, the sea boils, the desert freezes, the birds fall from the sky, the earth shakes, and things are not so hot out on the beach in California either. A strange man with burning eyes has just rented the little apartment upstairs over the garage in the backyard of Demi Moore's house, and she finds ancient Hebrew manuscripts in his desk—in a secret code.

This is the kind of movie where I tend to settle back and relax. I actually enjoy thrillers about biblical prophecies and the second coming and the Antichrist. After the sheer anarchy unleashed upon Hollywood by the slice-and-dice movies, it's actually comforting to know that these characters play by the rules. They believe in good and evil, and they act as if individual human beings can have an influence on the outcome of events. Compared to the *Friday the 13th* world view, *The Seventh Sign* is positively sanguine.

Like *Rosemary's Baby, The Exorcist,* and the *Omen* movies, this one places its supernatural events within a framework that at first seems everyday and sane. There is an art to this process. You show characters going about the mundane events of their routine daily lives, but on the sound track you play far-off Gregorian chants, so it's clear that the forces of evil are marshaling their troops offscreen.

Demi Moore has the central role, as a woman who has lost one child during pregnancy and is now fearful of losing another. The story begins in the last two months of her pregnancy, with her husband (Michael Biehn) lending moral support while her doctor shows her the fetus on a television screen. There's a lot of talk, of course, about the quantity of her amniotic fluid. Why is it that movies about the forces of darkness always place such an emphasis on details of the female reproductive process? Ever since Charles Grodin played the gynecologist in *Rosemary's Baby,* you can't see one of these movies without learning something about pregnancy.

But I digress. Moore is strong and clear in the movie's central role, and proves once again (after *About Last Night . . .*) that she has a genuine charisma, an aura of intelligence and resolve, reinforced by her throaty voice. I was not sure at first, however, that she was the correct choice for this movie. I thought she was perhaps too strong, and that the role required more of a screamer. Not so. By the end of the film, she is called upon to save the planet and all living things upon it, and so she needs that strength.

She provides a strong center to the film, but the rest of it, alas, is all over the map. I am not even sure I completely understood all of the details. What connection was there, for example, between the Hebrew code letters with their wax seals, and the dread events that followed every time one was opened? What were those flashbacks to Roman times? Who was that strange priest that traveled around the globe checking out the frozen deserts and bloody rivers? And on whose side was the boarder over the garage?

By the end of the movie, I was fairly certain of the answers to most of those questions, but the body of the film seemed almost deliberately confused and obscure, to no purpose. Why not explain the priest's actual mission, instead of saving it for a denouement at the last minute? Wouldn't that have been more interesting? And why is it that only the characters in the movie seem to be aware that things are going to hell and the Apocalypse is at hand? To be sure, CNN has nonstop bulletins about the weird events taking place in the world, but nobody in the street seems much affected. In fact, the movie's two earthquakes are not commented on by anyone—not even the leading characters.

And then there is the problem of the ending of the movie. I have to go at this very delicately, so as not to give too much away. But if you see the film, ask yourself this: When the baby reaches out his hand toward the mother's face, why doesn't he simply touch it? If you see what I mean.

Shaft ★ ★ ½
R, 98 m., 1971

Richard Roundtree (Shaft), Moses Gunn (Boss), Gwenn Mitchell (Ellie), Christopher St. John (Militant). Directed by Gordon Parks and produced by Joel Freeman. Screenplay by Ernest Tidyman and John D.F. Black.

Gordon Parks's *Shaft* gave us the first really convincing black private eye. Movies about private detectives have always been among my favorites—they seem to be better than most other formula movies—and John Shaft, as played by Richard Roundtree, belongs in the honorable tradition of Philip Marlowe, Sam Spade, Lew Archer, and company. He belongs because, like them, he keeps no regular company. Private eyes (in the movies, anyway) are loners in a way that defines the word. They live in dingy walk-up offices, sipping bourbon from the office bottles and waiting for the phone to ring.

These may all be clichés, but, hell, a private-eye movie without clichés wouldn't be worth the price of admission. We don't go to Westerns to see cowboys riding ostriches. The strength of Parks's movie is his willingness to let his hero fully inhabit the private-eye genre, with all of its obligatory violence, blood, obscenity, and plot gimmicks. The weakness of *Shaft,* I suspect, is that Parks is not very eager to inhabit that world along with his hero.

Gordon Parks was the first black director to make a major studio film, and his *The Learning Tree* (1969) was a deeply felt, lyrically beautiful film that was, maybe, just too simple and honest to be commercial. It didn't find a large audience, and I suspect that Parks turned next to *Shaft* for commercial survival.

The nice thing about *Shaft* is that it savors the private-eye genre, and takes special delight in wringing new twists out of the traditional relationship between the private eye and the boys down at homicide. The story covers some of the same ground as *Cotton Comes to Harlem,* but in a different way. Shaft is brought in by a Harlem rackets boss (Moses Gunn) whose traditional slice of power is being threatened by the Mafia. They don't want a partnership anymore, so they kidnap the boss's daughter. Shaft's job is to get her back.

His adventures along the way include a thoroughly unpleasant encounter with a white pick-up, who is insulted because all black exploitation movies have to insult at least one white pick-up (and why not? Fair is fair). The climax involves a complicated plan with Shaft and his allies swinging from ropes and using firehoses to accomplish with five people in five minutes what could have been done with one, in one. Parks isn't especially good at action direction, but the heart of a private-eye movie is in the mood scenes, anyway, and he supplies a scene in a bar and another one with the Harlem rackets boss that are very nice.

Sharky's Machine ★ ★ ★

R, 119 m., 1981

Burt Reynolds (Sharky), Rachel Ward (Dominoe), Vittorio Gassman (Victor), Brian Keith (Papa), Charles Durning (Frisco). Directed by Burt Reynolds and produced by Hank Moonjean. Screenplay by Gerald Di Pago.

Sharky's Machine contains all of the ingredients of a tough, violent, cynical big-city cop movie, but what makes it intriguing is the way the Burt Reynolds character plays against those conventions. His name is Sharky. As the movie opens, he's an undercover narcotics cop. He blows a big case and is demoted to the vice squad—which is a bawdy, brawling, vocal gang of misfits who act like a cross between "Hill Street Blues" and a Joseph Wambaugh nightmare.

Sharky is not happy in vice. He is, in fact, not happy anywhere, not until a young woman named Dominoe enters his life. She is a hooker. She also seems to be involved with some snaky big-money characters, and so Sharky places her under twenty-four hour surveillance. That involves moving several cops, telescopes, cameras, and bugging devices into the high-rise opposite her apartment. The cops set up housekeeping and settle down for a long wait. And it's here that the movie begins to really involve us. Reynolds, as Sharky, falls in love with the woman. It is a voyeuristic love, involving spying and eavesdropping, and Sharky is not a voyeur—so it is particularly painful for him to witness the woman's sexual involvement with others.

The central scenes of the movie, involving the call girl's private life and the probing eyes of Sharky, could easily have become tawdry—could have disintegrated into a peep show. That doesn't happen, partly because Reynolds (who also directed the film) doesn't provide cheap displays of flesh, but also because the call girl is played by British actress Rachel Ward, who brings poignancy and restraint to the role. She plays a hooker who's not a tramp. She has a husky voice and an astonishing body, but there's an innocence in her manner. Later, we discover that she has been in virtual bondage to her pimp since she was an infant. She knows no other life. This is a setup of sorts, a device in the plot to allow the female lead to be both prostitute and victim, but it clarifies the relationship between Reynolds and Ward. And when they fall in love, as they inevitably do, it provides some leftover innocence to be celebrated.

Reynolds surrounds this central relationship with a lot of cops, known as Sharky's Machine. They are played by actors who have played a lot of other cops in a lot of other movies—Brian Keith, Charles Durning—and by Bernie Casey, who is playing his first cop but does it with special grace. There's a long scene in the film, reportedly improvised, in which Casey tells Reynolds what it felt like, the first time he was shot. We are reminded that cops in the movies hardly ever talk about being shot.

Sharky's Machine has a lot of plot, most of it inspired by the original novel by William Diehl. Maybe it has too much plot for a movie that Reynolds has referred to as *Dirty Harry Goes to Atlanta.* But this is an ambitious film; it's as if something inside Reynolds was chafing at the insipid roles he was playing in one car-chase movie after another. He doesn't walk through this movie, and he doesn't allow himself the cozy little touches that break the mood while they're letting the audience know how much fun Burt is having.

The result of his ambition and restraint is a movie much more interesting than most cop thrillers. *Sharky's Machine* does have a lot of action, including an extended, exhausting, brutal shoot-out at the end. But it also has the special qualities of the relationship between Reynolds and Ward (more fully developed than the camaraderie between Reynolds and Catherine Deneuve, as another hooker in another thriller, *Hustle,* in 1974). As a director, Reynolds allows himself a few excesses (one howler is the dramatic cut from a sex scene to the phallic glory of the Peachtree Plaza Hotel). But he's put a lot of his ambition in this movie, and it reminds us that there is a fine actor within the star of *Cannonball Run.*

Sheena, Queen of the Jungle ★

PG, 117 m., 1984

Tanya Roberts (Sheena), Ted Wass (Vic Casey), Donovan Scott (Fletcher), Elizabeth of Toro (Shaman), Trevor Thomas (Prince Otwani). Directed by John Guillermin and produced by Paul Aratow. Screenplay by David Newman and Lorenzo Semple, Jr.

How can this be? I casually reached over to the old reference shelf, to find some old references to *Sheena, Queen of the Jungle,* the jungle heroine who inflamed the pubescent fantasies of lads in the early 1950s. And not only wasn't there an entry in Halliwell's *Filmgoer's Companion,* but neither the *Oxford Companion of Film* nor *The Film Encyclopedia* had ever heard of Sheena. Could this be because Sheena spent most of her time on television, where she was once played by the one, the only, Irish McCallum? I dunno, but I think they're missing a bet in Oxford if they don't have a Sheena festival right away.

I mention my old memories because the movie *Sheena* seems likely to provide me with few new memories. The movie stars Tanya Roberts as the legendary blonde jungle girl. After Sheena's parents are killed in a cave-in, she is adopted by the beautiful Shaman (played by the fashion model Elizabeth of Toro, who undoubtedly taught Sheena all about makeup, explaining Sheena's plucked eyebrows and purple eye shadow, there in the midst of the trees). Shaman's tribe considers Sheena a god, and she learns to talk to the animals, ride a zebra bareback, and fashion crude jungle bikinis out of only those simple materials one finds in a boutique. Then an American TV crew comes to the jungle to film an interview with an African prince, who is also a place kicker for a U.S. pro football team. The prince is behind a plot to assassinate his brother, the king, and the TV crew stumbles over the story and over Sheena, who the prince's jealous girlfriend has vowed to kill.

Are you following all this? Anyway, Sheena and the anchorman (Ted Wass) disappear into the jungle, where the clichés of male superiority *instantly* take hold. Get this. The clod of an anchorman, faced with a woman who can tame zebras and talk to the elephants, tells this magnificent wild creature that, and I quote, what he'd like to do is take her to Wall Street and show her the World Trade Center while they both eat peanuts.

Anyway, *Sheena* contains all too little of Sheena at some times, and all too much at others. Let me explain. The whole dumb plot about the palace coup, the evil prince, etc., is given a lot of screen time, even though it is awesomely uninteresting. Sheena, who might have been presented as sort of a female Greystoke, a real jungle creature, meanwhile takes nude baths in waterfalls and learns that American men do rude things like pressing their lips against hers. The nudity in the movie is extensive enough to raise eyebrows over its PG rating.

Is there anything good about *Sheena?* Yeah, the animals are fun to watch, especially the lions. But Tanya Roberts is about as convincing, swinging from those vines, as Carol Burnett would have been. And come to think of it, Sheena, Queen of the Jungle, is the kind of character that, in our time, perhaps only Carol Burnett could play.

She's Having a Baby ★ ★
PG-13, 106 m., 1988

Kevin Bacon (Jake Briggs), Elizabeth McGovern (Kristy), Alec Baldwin (Davis), William Windom (Kristy's Father), Cathryn Damon (Kristy's Mother), James Ray (Jake's Father), Holland Taylor (Jake's Mother), Isabel Lorca (The Girl). Directed, produced, and written by John Hughes.

She's Having a Baby begins with the simplest and most moving of stories, and interrupts it with an amazing assortment of gimmicks. It is some kind of tribute to the strength of the story, and the warmth of the performances by Kevin Bacon and Elizabeth McGovern, that the movie somehow manages almost to work, in spite of the adornments.

The story begins on their wedding day, which Bacon faces with deep misgivings. Although he fell in love with McGovern literally at first sight, he is reluctant to surrender his freedom and take up the responsibilities of adulthood. But it's too late to back out, and before long the young couple have settled into a shoebox condo, and Bacon has conned his way into a low-level job with a Chicago advertising agency.

Years pass. The couple moves into what Bacon describes as "a mortgage with three bedrooms." They settle into a version of suburban conformity, although Bacon still grows restless with his neighbor's endless debates on rival brands of lawn mowers. The parents on both sides of the family begin to drop loud hints that they would appreciate a grandchild. Bacon is not ready for the awesome responsibilities of parenthood. But then it develops that he has a deficient sperm count (caused, we learn, by tight underwear raising the temperature of his groin above ideal sperm weather), and he joins McGovern in a determined effort to conceive a child. (Their resulting love scene must be the first copulation on film that is accompanied by the song "Workin' on the Chain Gang.")

Other aspects of their lives drift in and out of view. Adam Baldwin, the best friend, visits Chicago from time to time, makes a pass at McGovern, is rejected ("It's not happening in this lifetime," she explains), remains a friend. The routine at the ad agency begins to tell on Bacon, who has, of course, aspirations of becoming a novelist. And there are the erotic temptations of a strange, beautiful girl, who appears to Bacon in a disco, in the ad agency, and in his dreams, offering an alternative to his quiet yuppie lifestyle. But then come pregnancy, childbirth, and fatherhood, and he realizes that the age-old values are the best ones.

All of this sounds completely straightforward, and a logical development for the filmmaker, John Hughes, who has been charting the progress of teen-agers in a series of good films, including *Sixteen Candles, The Breakfast Club,* and *Ferris Bueller's Day Off.* But something strange got into Hughes this time.

The progression of his ordinary story is interrupted by some extraordinary flights of fancy. There are fantasy sequences, imaginary conversations, and a ballet for suburban husbands and their lawn mowers. Bacon narrates the film, and other characters also get into the act, including the preacher who marries them and incorporates all the duties of the perfect yuppie husband into the wedding vows. On their own, these bizarre touches are sometimes amusing (the choreography of the suite for lawn mowers would make a good TV commercial). But why are they in this story? What additional dimension do they contribute? Mostly they seem merely cute and clever distractions, not part of the story, not adding to it, not necessary.

The last sequence in the movie, where Bacon waits and worries while his wife undergoes a difficult labor, is the most effective. It is honest and strong and has genuine emotional strength. It suggests what a better movie this might have been if the whole story had been told in the same straightforward style, freed of Hughes's flourishes and gimmicks. The good parts of *She's Having a Baby* make the rest of it feel like a missed opportunity.

Shoah ★ ★ ★ ★

NO MPAA RATING, 563 m. on five cassettes, 1986

A documentary directed and produced by Claude Lanzmann.

For more than nine hours I sat and watched a film named *Shoah,* and when it was over, I sat for a while longer and simply stared into space, trying to understand my emotions. I had seen a memory of the most debased chapter in human history. But I had also seen a film that affirmed life so passionately that I did not know where to turn with my confused feelings. There is no proper response to this film. It is an enormous fact, a 563-minute howl of pain and anger in the face of genocide. It is one of the noblest films ever made.

The film's title is a Hebrew word for chaos or annihilation—for the Holocaust. The film is a documentary, but it does not contain images from the 1940s. There are no old newsreel shots, no interviews with the survivors of the death camps, no coverage of the war crimes trials. All of the movie was photographed in the last five or six years by a man named Claude Lanzmann, who went looking for eyewitnesses to Hitler's "Final Solution." He is surprisingly successful in finding people who were there, who saw and heard what went on. Some of them, a tiny handful, are Jewish survivors of the camps. The rest are mostly old people, German and Polish, some who worked in the camps, others who were in a position to observe what happened.

They talk and talk. *Shoah* is a torrent of words, and yet the overwhelming impression, when it is over, is one of silence. Lanzmann intercuts two kinds of images. He shows the faces of his witnesses. And then he uses quiet pastoral scenes of the places where the deaths took place. Steam engines move massively through the Polish countryside, down the same tracks where trains took countless Jews, gypsies, Poles, homosexuals, and other so-called undesirables to their deaths. Cameras pan silently across pastures, while we learn that underneath the tranquility are mass graves. Sometimes the image is of a group of people, gathered in a doorway, or in front of a church, or in a restaurant kitchen.

Lanzmann is a patient interrogator. We see him in the corners of some of his shots, a tall, lanky man, informally dressed, chain-smoking. He wants to know the details. He doesn't ask large, profound questions about the meaning of the extermination of millions of people. He asks little questions. In one of the most chilling sequences in the film, he talks to Abraham Bomba, today a barber in Tel Aviv. Bomba was one of the Jewish barbers ordered to cut off the hair of Jewish women before they were killed in Treblinka. His assignment suggests the shattering question: How can a woman's hair be worth more than her life? But Lanzmann does not ask overwhelming and unanswerable questions like this. These are the sorts of questions he asks:

You cut with what? With scissors?

There were no mirrors?

You said there were about sixteen barbers? You cut the hair of how many women in one batch?

The barber tries to answer. As he talks, he has a customer in his chair, and he snips at the customer's hair almost obsessively, making tiny movements with his scissors, as if trying to use the haircut as a way to avoid the questions. Their conversation finally arrives at this exchange, after he says he cannot talk any more:

A. I can't. It's too horrible. Please.

Q. *We have to do it. You know it.*

A. I won't be able to do it.

Q. *You have to do it. I know it's very hard. I know and I apologize.*

A. Don't make me go on, please.

Q. *Please. We must go on.*

Lanzmann is cruel, but he is correct. He must go on. It is necessary to make this record before all of those who were witnesses to the Holocaust have died.

His methods in obtaining the interviews were sometimes underhanded. He uses a concealed television camera to record the faces of some of the old Nazi officials whom he interviews, and we look over the shoulders of the TV technicians in a van parked outside the buildings where they live. We see the old men nonchalantly pulling down charts from the wall to explain the layout of a death camp, and we hear their voices, and at one point when a Nazi asks for reassurance that the conversation is private, Lanzmann provides it. He will go to any length to obtain this testimony.

He does not, however, make any attempt to arrange his material into a chronology, an objective, factual record of how the "Final Solution" began, continued, and was finally terminated by the end of the war. He uses a more poetic, mosaic approach, moving according to rhythms only he understands among the only three kinds of faces we see in this film: survivors, murderers, and bystanders. As their testimony is intercut with the scenes of train tracks, steam engines, abandoned buildings, and empty fields, we are left with enough time to think our own thoughts, to meditate, to wonder.

This is a long movie but not a slow one, and in its words it creates something of the same phenomenon I experienced while watching *My Dinner with André*. The words themselves create images in the imagination, as they might in a radio play. Consider the images summoned by these words, spoken by Filip Muller, a Czech Jew assigned to work at the doors of the gas chambers, a man who survived five waves of liquidations at Auschwitz:

A. You see, once the gas was poured in, it worked like this: It rose from the ground upwards. And in the terrible struggle that followed—because it was a struggle—the lights were switched off in the gas chambers. It was dark, no one could see, so the strongest people tried to climb higher. Because they probably realized that the higher they got, the more air there was. They could breathe better. That caused the struggle. Secondly, most people tried to push their way to the door. It was psychological; they knew where the door was; maybe they could force their way out. It was instinctive, a death struggle. Which is why children and weaker people and the aged always wound up at the bottom. The strongest were on top. Because in the death struggle, a father didn't realize his son lay beneath him.

Q. *And when the doors were opened?*

A. They fell out. People fell out like blocks of stone, like rocks falling out of a truck.

The images evoked by his words are inutterably painful. What is remarkable, on reflection, is that Muller is describing a struggle that neither he nor anyone else now alive ever saw. I realized, at the end of his words, that a fundamental change had taken place in the way I personally visualized the gas chambers. Always before, in reading about them or hearing about them, my point of view was outside, looking in. Muller put me inside.

That is what this whole movie does, and it is probably the most important thing it does. It changes our point of view about the Holocaust. After nine hours of *Shoah,* the Holocaust is no longer a subject, a chapter of history, a phenomenon. It is an environment. It is around us. Ordinary people speak in ordinary voices of days that had become ordinary to them. A railroad engineer who drove the trains to Treblinka is asked if he could hear the screams of the people in the cars behind his locomotive:

A. Obviously, since the locomotive was next to the cars. They screamed, asked for water. The screams from the cars closest to the locomotives could be heard very well.

Q. *Can one get used to that?*

A. No, it was extremely distressing. He knew the people behind him were human, like him. The Germans gave him and the other workers vodka to drink. Without drinking, they couldn't have done it.

Some of the strangest passages in the film are the interviews with the officials who were running the camps and making the "Final Solution" work smoothly and efficiently. None of them, at least by their testimony, seem to have witnessed the whole picture. They only participated in a small part of it, doing their little jobs in their little corners. If they are to be believed, they didn't personally kill anybody, they just did small portions of larger tasks, and somehow all of the tasks, when added up and completed, resulted in people dying. Here is the man who scheduled the trains that took the Jews to die:

Q. *You never saw a train?*

A. No, never. We had so much work, I never left my desk. We worked day and night.

And here is a man who lived 150 feet from a church where Jews were rounded up, held, and then marched into gas vans for the trip to the crematoriums:

Q. *Did you see the gas vans?*

A. No—yes, from the outside. They shuttled back and forth. I never looked inside; I didn't see Jews.

What is so important about *Shoah* is that the voices are heard of people who did see, who did understand, who did comprehend, who were there, who know that the Holocaust happened, who tell us with their voices and with their eyes that genocide occurred in our time, in our civilization.

There is a tendency while watching *Shoah* to try to put a distance between yourself and the events on the screen. These things happened, after all, forty or forty-five years ago. Most of those now alive have been born since the events happened. Then, while I was watching the film, came a chilling moment. A name flashed on the screen in the subtitles, the name of one of the commandants at Treblinka death camp. At first I thought the name was "Ebert"—my name. Then I realized it was "Eberl." I felt a moment of relief, and then a moment of intense introspection as I realized that it made no difference what the subtitle said. The message of this film (if we believe in the brotherhood of man) is that these crimes were committed by people like us, against people like us.

But there is an even deeper message as well, and it is contained in the testimony of Filip Muller, the Jew who stood at the door of a crematorium and watched as the victims walked in to die. One day some of the victims, Czech Jews, began to sing. They sang two songs: "The Hatikvah," and the Czech national anthem. They affirmed that they were Jews and that they were Czechs. They denied Hitler, who would have them be one but not the other. Muller speaks:

That was happening to my countrymen, and I realized that my life had become meaningless. (His eyes fill with tears.) Why go on living? For what? So I went into the gas chamber with them, resolved to die. With them. Suddenly, some who recognized me came up to me. . . . A small group of women approached. They looked at me and said, right there in the gas chamber . . .

Q. *You were inside the gas chamber?*

A. Yes. One of them said: "So you want to die. But that's senseless. Your death won't give us back our lives. That's no way. You must get out of here alive, you must bear witness to our suffering and to the injustice done to us."

And that is the final message of this extraordinary film. It is not a documentary, not journalism, not propaganda, not political. It is an act of witness. In it, Claude Lanzmann celebrates the priceless gift that sets man apart from animals and makes us human, and gives us hope: the ability for one generation to tell the next what it has learned.

Shoot the Moon ★ ★ ★ ½
R, 124 m., 1982

Albert Finney (George Dunlap), Diane Keaton (Faith Dunlap), Karen Allen (Sandy), Peter Weller (Frank), Dana Hill (Sherry). Directed by Alan Parker and produced by Alan Marshall. Screenplay by Bo Goldman.

Alan Parker's *Shoot the Moon* is a film that sometimes keeps its painful secrets even from itself. It opens with a shot of a man in agony. In another room, his wife, surrounded by four noisy daughters, dresses for a dinner that evening at which the man will be honored. The man has to pull himself together. His voice is choking with tears, he telephones the woman he loves and tells her how hard it will be to get through the evening without her. Then he puts on his rumpled tuxedo and marches out to do battle. As we watch this scene, we assume that the movie will answer several of the questions it raises, such as: What went wrong in the marriage? Why is the man in such agony? What is the nature of his love for the other woman? One of the surprises in *Shoot the Moon* is that none of these questions is ever quite answered, and we are asked to fill in the gaps ourselves.

That is not necessarily a flaw in the film. *Shoot the Moon* is not the historical record of this marriage, but the emotional history. It starts with what should be a happy marriage. A writer of books (Albert Finney) lives with his beautiful, funky wife (Diane Keaton) and their four rambunctious daughters in a converted farmhouse somewhere in Marin County, California. Their house is one of those warm battle zones filled with books, miscellaneous furniture, and the paraphernalia for vast projects half-completed. We learn that the marriage has gone disastrously wrong. That the man is determined to stalk out and be with his new woman. That the wife, after a period of anger and mourning, is prepared to react to this decision by almost deliberately having an affair with the loutish but well-meaning young man who comes to build a tennis court. That the husband and wife still harbor fugitive feelings of love and passion for another.

We never really learn how the marriage went wrong. There is the usual talk about how one partner was not given the room to grow, or the other did not have enough "space"—concepts that love would render meaningless, but that divorce makes into savagely defended positions. We also learn just a tantalizing little about the two new lovers. Albert Finney's new woman (Karen Allen) is so cynical about their relationship in one scene that we wonder if their affair will soon end (we never learn). Diane Keaton's new man (Peter Weller) is so emotionally stiff, closed-off, that we don't know for a long time whether Keaton really likes him, or simply desires him sexually and wants to use him to spite her husband.

Does it matter that the movie doesn't want to provide insights in these areas? I think it does. When Ingmar Bergman covered similar grounds in his *Scenes from a Marriage,* he provided us with enough concrete information about the issues in the marriage that it was possible for us to discuss the relationship afterward, taking sides, seeing both points of view. After *Shoot the Moon,* we don't discuss the relationship, we discuss our questions about it. And yet this is sometimes an extraordinary movie. Despite its flaws, despite its gaps, despite two key scenes that are dreadfully wrong, *Shoot the Moon* contains a raw emotional power of the sort we rarely see in domestic dramas.

The film's basic conflict is within Albert Finney's mind. He can no longer stay with his wife, he must leave and be with the other woman, and yet he still wants to own the family and possessions he has left behind. He doesn't want his ex-wife dating other men. He wants to observe the birthday of an eldest daughter (Dana Hill) who hates him and resents his behavior. He remodeled the house with his own hands, and cannot bear to see another man working on it. In one scene of heartbreaking power, he breaks into his own house and finds himself beating his daughter because he loves her so much and she will not love him.

In scenes like that (and in the quiet scenes where Hill asks, "Why did Daddy leave us?" and Keaton answers, "I don't think he left you; I think he left me"), *Shoot the Moon* is a great film. In scenes like the one where they fight in a restaurant, or argue in court, it ranges from the miscalculated to the disastrous. *Shoot the Moon* is a rare, good film, and yet, afterward, most of my thoughts were about how it might have been better. It is frustrating to feel that the filmmakers knew their characters intimately, but chose to reveal them only in part.

Shoot to Kill ★ ★ ★

R, 100 m., 1988 ✓

Sidney Poitier (Warren Stantin), Tom Berenger (Jonathan Knox), Kirstie Alley (Sarah), Clancy Brown (Steve), Richard Masur (Norman), Andrew Robinson (Harvey), Kevin Scannell (Ben). Directed by Roger Spottiswoode and produced by Ron Silverman and Daniel Petrie, Jr. Screenplay by Harv Zimmel, Michael Burton, and Petrie.

Shoot to Kill is yet another example, rather late in the day, of the buddy movie, that most dependable genre from the early 1970s. The formula still works. Two characters who have nothing in common are linked together on a dangerous mission, and after a lot of close calls they survive, prevail, and become buddies. The movie got more than the usual amount of attention because it marked Sidney Poitier's return to acting after ten years behind the camera. He didn't win any awards for this performance, but it was nice to have him back.

Poitier plays Warren Stantin, an FBI agent who holds himself personally responsible after a kidnapper kills two hostages and escapes into the Pacific Northwest. The killer (Clancy Brown) is a sneering sadist who joins up with a group of sportsmen who plan to trek into the wilderness on a fishing trip. His plan: Kill them and force their guide to lead him through the wilderness to the Canadian border.

The guide is played by Kirstie Alley from the TV show "Cheers," in a robust display of pink cheeks and deep breathing. She leads her charges into the woods. Her boyfriend (Tom Berenger, last seen in *Platoon*) is left behind at a base station, and Poitier tries to convince Berenger to lead him after the fugitive. Of course, the mountain man doesn't believe the city slicker can keep up on a tough cross-country hike that includes some rock climbing, and, of course, Poitier is determined to prove himself.

Have we seen this before? I think so. The route passes along a standard wilderness obstacle course, including a terrifying rope bridge over a chasm far below. Alley leads her group across, but then Brown sabotages the bridge, and Berenger nearly falls to his death before Poitier comes to his rescue. Later, it's Berenger's turn to save Poitier's life, and gradually the two men come to respect one another.

There are just a few teeny-weeny holes in this plot. For example: Why does the FBI assign only one man to this pursuit? Why isn't there any aerial search for the group? Why isn't there a posse at the other end of the trail? Why does the local sheriff spill the beans into the radio without being sure who is listening? Why walk for arduous miles across a grueling landscape when it might be easier to hitch a ride? Why put us through the whole cross-country trek when, at the end, the payoff comes not in the mountains but at sea?

Only a churl would ask such questions. *Shoot to Kill* is a genre movie in which the specifics hardly matter. Only the formula is important: Two guys team up, conquer great difficulties, and become friends. And at that level, *Shoot to Kill* works like an efficient machine. Poitier and Berenger create a nice give-and-take chemistry, and there are some funny gags, mostly involving the city slicker's uneasiness around horses. The device of cutting back and forth between Kirstie Alley's group and their pursuers keeps the buddy formula from growing too oppressive. And the action scene at the end is effective, although I question whether a gun can fire underwater. *Shoot to Kill* is fast-food moviemaking: quick, satisfying, and transient. Now let's see Poitier in something more challenging.

The Shootist ★ ★ ★ 1/2

PG, 100 m., 1976

John Wayne (The Shootist), Lauren Bacall (The Widow), James Stewart (The Doctor), Ron Howard (The Son), Harry Morgan (The Sheriff), John Carradine (The Undertaker), Hugh O'Brien (The Gambler), Richard Boone (The Gunman). Directed by Don Siegel and produced by M.J. Frankovich and William Seif. Screenplay by Miles Hood.

The old man was around for a long time. When he played the fresh-faced Ringo Kid in *Stagecoach,* back in 1939, he was already thirty-two years old. And I didn't believe it either until I'd counted the credits twice—but *Stagecoach* was his sixtieth film. John Wayne grew, role by role, into the most mythic presence in American movies. Some of the roles were pretty bad ones, but maybe at the time we didn't know that. Maybe at the time we were ten or twelve years old, and it was a Saturday afternoon, and what we registered was that Wayne was up there on the screen, squinting into the sun, making decisions, ready for action. For my generation, while presidents came and went, John Wayne merely grew a little more thoughtful.

He rides onscreen in *The Shootist* afraid that he is dying. Not afraid he'll be killed, but afraid he's dying, which is the last thing we anticipated a John Wayne character would do of his own accord. It is 1901: He has outlived his century. A sawbones in the next state has given him the bad news and now he wants to hear it from the lips of Doc Hostetler, who nursed him back to health after a violent afternoon twenty years ago. And so he rides, the Shootist, into a Carson City to which the Old West has become an embarrassment. The streets are still wide enough to turn a mule train in, but now an abashed little horse trolley runs down the middle of them, and electricity's going to put the horse out of business next year. The pain is way down deep in his back, and he rides on a red velvet cushion he stole out of a whorehouse. It doesn't do a damn bit of good. Hostetler hems and haws and comes out with it: cancer. Two months to live, six weeks, maybe less. In the meantime he can do what he wants. After a while he won't feel like doing much.

In his time, the Shootist shot a lot of men dead. Out at the livery stable, burnt into the leather of his saddle, they find his name: J.B. Books. His arrival in Carson City immediately becomes news. Hostetler steers him over to a boarding house run by the Widow Rogers, who shows him a two dollar room. It'll do fine. Books settles down to die. But all these gunfighters had the same problem: People weren't content to let them die in bed, because they made too good a trophy.

So there is a tricky dilemma: To die with some measure of dignity, and to avoid being shot in the meantime. As the film opens, Books has eight days. You will be surprised with what gentleness and humanity he lives them, before the inevitable gunfire at the end. And unless you have already discovered that John Wayne is an actor as well as a movie star, you will be surprised by the dimensions he provides for J.B. Books.

The movie isn't a bit sentimental. Everybody in town wants the bastard dead, except for the Widow Rogers and her son, Gillom. Even Doc Hostetler, who knows what people can go through toward the end of these illnesses, stops Books at the door and advises him point-blank not to wait around and see how things will eventually feel. The Sheriff is almost cheerful at the prospect of Books's approaching end. The Undertaker offers a free funeral, free tombstone, free casket, free flowers, even two mourners thrown in at no extra charge. "You son of a bitch," Books says, "you aim to do to me what they did with John Wesley Hardin. Lay me out and parade every damn fool in the state past me at a dollar a head, half price for children, and then stuff me in a gunny sack and shovel me under." He is correct.

Still, eight days are enough to establish the beginnings of human contact. The Widow Rogers is appalled at first to have a killer as her paying guest, but an affection and respect grows up between them. Her kid, Gillom, contracts a case of hero worship even while trying to swindle the Shootist out of his horse. And Wayne, as Books, occupies the substantial center of the film. He vows to read a newspaper through from front to back before he dies. He sends his Sunday-go-to-meeting clothes out to the cleaners. And he challenges three old Carson City enemies to meet him in the saloon at eleven o'clock Monday morning.

It's here that the movie doesn't quite work. We hardly know the three enemies. We don't know why they'd oblige the Shootist's wish to die in a gunfight. We understand his reasoning, but not theirs. And the movie's final scene, in which Gillom Rogers symbolically steps into the Shootist's boots, is just a little too neat to be real. Westerns probably have to end along these lines with confrontations and gunfire and heroism, but *The Shootist* will be remembered for the quieter scenes that came before.

The cast is excellent because it understands the material, and sympathizes with it: James Stewart, as the doctor, and Lauren Bacall, as the widow, play scenes with Wayne that absolutely make us forget we're watching a movie. Gaunt old John Carradine has been an undertaker all his life; finally they cast him as one. Don Siegel's direction reveals a sensitivity we didn't suspect after films like *Dirty Harry.* And observe the way John Wayne says "Good day, Mrs. Rogers" to Lauren Bacall for the last time.

Shy People ★ ★ ★ ★

R, 120 m., 1988 ✓

(See related Film Clip, p. 000)

Jill Clayburgh (Diana), Barbara Hershey (Ruth), Martha Plimpton (Grace), Merritt Butrick (Mike), John Philbin (Tommy), Don Swayze (Mark), Pruitt Taylor Vince (Paul), Mare Winningham (Candy). Directed by Andrei Konchalovsky and produced by Menahem Golan and Yoram Globus. Screenplay by Gerard Brach, Konchalovsky, and Marjorie David.

Two great early shots define the two worlds of *Shy People.* The first is circular, the second straight ahead.

The film's opening shot circles at a vertiginous height above Manhattan, showing the canyons of skyscrapers with people scurrying below like ants. The camera moves through a complete circle, finally coming to rest inside a high-rise apartment where a restless teen-ager and her distracted mother have no idea what to do about each other.

The second shot, a few minutes later in the film, is also taken from a height; we are above a speedboat that drones relentlessly into the heart of the Louisiana bayou country. This shot, inexplicably thrilling, is like scenes from adventure books we read when we were kids. We feel a quickening of excitement as the boat penetrates the unknown.

The two shots define the two women who are at the heart of the film. Jill Clayburgh plays a shallow, sophisticated Manhattan magazine writer, who convinces her bosses at *Cosmopolitan* to let her write about her family roots. And Barbara Hershey plays Clayburgh's long-lost distant cousin, who lives in isolation in a crumbling, mossy home in the heart of the bayou. The movie is essentially about the differences between these women, about family blood ties, and about the transparent membrane between life and death.

Shy People is one of the great visionary films of recent years, a film that shakes off the petty distractions of safe Hollywood entertainments and develops a large vision. It is about revenge and hatred, about mothers and sons, about loneliness. It suggests that family ties are the most important bonds in the world, and by the end of the film, Clayburgh will discover that Hershey is closer to her "dead" husband than most city-dwellers are to anybody.

Yet the film is not without a wicked streak of humor. Clayburgh invites her precocious daughter (Martha Plimpton) to accompany her into the Louisiana backwaters, where the adolescent girl meets Hershey's ill-assorted sons. One is literally locked in an out-building when the New Yorkers arrive, another is light in the head, and still another is disowned and never mentioned, because he dared to move out of the bayou and open a nightclub in town. As the girl flirts with her cousins, and the women warily spar with each other, the darkness of the swamp closes in.

Shy People was directed by Andrei Konchalovsky, the Russian emigre whose other English-language movies include *Runaway Train* and *Duet for One*. Because he is an outsider, he is not so self-conscious about using American images that an American director might be frightened away from. The world of *Shy People* is the world of Erskine Caldwell's *Tobacco Road*, or Faulkner's Snopes family, of Al Capp and Russ Meyer. Hershey and her family are not small, timid people, but caricatures, and it's to Hershey's credit that she is able to play the role to the hilt and yet still make it real.

There are great sequences in the film, including one extraordinary night in which Clayburgh is lost in the swamp, is up to her neck in the fetid waters, and sees, or thinks she sees, the ghost of Hershey's dead husband.

There is a barroom fight in which the wrathful Hershey wades into her son's nightclub with a gun. Most extraordinary of all, there are spooky, quiet moments in which the mosquitoes drone in the sleepy heat of midday, while the two women pore over old photograph albums.

Sid & Nancy ★ ★ ★ ★

R, 111 m., 1986

Gary Oldman (Sid Vicious), Chloe Webb (Nancy Spungen), Drew Schofield (Johnny Rotten), David Hayman (Malcolm McLaren), Debby Bishop (Phoebe), Jude Alderson (Ma Vicious). Directed by Alex Cox and produced by Eric Fellner. Screenplay by Cox and Abbe Wool.

His real name was John Simon Ritchie, and his father was a trombone player who left before he was born. His mother wore her hair long and went to all the hippie festivals with the little boy at her side. They lived in London's East End, within the culture of poverty and drugs. When he was fifteen, Ritchie dropped out of school. When he was seventeen, he was one of the most famous people in England, although by then he was known as Sid Vicious of the notorious Sex Pistols.

What did he respond to when the American girl, Nancy Spungen, came into his life? She was a groupie from New York, but she was also an authority figure who pushed him to try harder, complained when he was not given his due, and plotted to get him better deals and wider exposure. If she had not bled to death that night in New York, she might have made Vicious really amount to something, someday.

The astonishing thing about *Sid & Nancy* is the amount of subtle information it gives us about their relationship, given the fact that the surface of the movie is all tumult and violence, pain and confusion. This movie doesn't take the easy way out and cast these two lovers as Romeo and Juliet, misunderstood waifs. It sees beneath their leather and chains, their torn T-shirts and steel-toed boots, to a basically conventional relationship between an ambitious woman and a man who was still a boy.

They needed each other. Spungen needed someone to mother, and Vicious, according to his friends, needed self-esteem and was immensely proud that he had an American girlfriend. They were meant for each other, but by the end it was all just ashes and bewilderment, because they were so strung out on drugs that whole days would slip by unnoticed. In their fantasies of doomed romance, they planned to go out together in a suicide pact, but by the end they were too sick to even go out together for a pizza.

By now, everybody knows that Vicious woke up one morning in New York's Chelsea Hotel to find Spungen's dead body. He was booked on suspicion of murder, released on bail, and two months later was dead of a drug overdose. The available evidence strongly suggests that he did not stab Spungen to death, but that she died of one of those untidy accidents that befall drug abusers. A human being is a dangerous thing to let loose in a room with itself, when it cannot think.

There were some good times earlier in their story, but on the evidence of this movie there were not many. By the time Spungen met Vicious in London in the mid-1970s, the Sex Pistols were the most infamous punk rock band in the world. But they were in the position of Gandhi in that apocryphal story where he sees the mob run past and races to get in front of his followers. The punk conceit was a total rejection of conventional society; their credo was the line by Johnny Rotten, the Pistols' lead singer: "Got a problem and the problem is you." For the Pistols to stay in front of that mob, they had to be meaner, more violent, more negative than their followers. How did it feel to stand on a bandstand and make angry music while your fans stood face to face, banging heads until unconsciousness came?

Sid & Nancy suggests that Vicious never lived long enough to really get his feet on the ground, to figure out where he stood and where his center was. He was handed great fame and a certain amount of power and money, and indirectly told that his success depended on staying fucked up. This is a big assignment for a kid who would otherwise be unemployable. Vicious did his best, fighting and vomiting and kicking his way through his brief days and long nights, until Spungen brought him a measure of relief. Some nights she was someone to hold, and other nights she was someone to hold onto. What difference did it make?

Sid & Nancy makes these observations with such complexity, such vividness, and such tenderness that at the end of the film a curious thing happens. You do not weep for Vicious, or Spungen, but maybe you weep for all of us, that we have been placed in a world where it is possible for people to make themselves so unhappy. Vicious was not a hero, just a guy who got himself into a situation he couldn't handle. But to thousands of London kids, he represented an affront to a society that offered no jobs, no training, no education, and no entry into the world of opportunity. If life offers you nothing, the least you can offer it is the finger.

Performances like the ones in this film go beyond movie acting and into some kind of evocation of real lives. Vicious is played by Gary Oldman and Spungen is played by Chloe Webb, and there isn't even a brief period at the top of the movie where we have to get used to them. They are these people, driven and relentless.

The movie was directed by Alex Cox, who made *Repo Man* a couple of years ago, and here he announces himself as a great director. He and his actors pull off the neat trick of creating a movie full of noise and fury, and telling a meticulous story right in the middle of it.

But why should anyone care about a movie about two scabrous vulgarians? Because the subject of a really good movie is sometimes not that important. It's the acting, writing, and direction that count. If a movie can illuminate the lives of other people who share this planet with us and show us not only how different they are but, how even so, they share the same dreams and hurts, then it deserves to be called great. If you have an open mind, it is possibly true that the less you care about Sid Vicious, the more you will admire this movie.

Silent Movie ★ ★ ★ ★

PG, 88 m., 1976

Mel Brooks (Mel Funn), Marty Feldman (Marty Eggs), Dom DeLuise (Dom Bell), Bernadette Peters (Vilma Kaplan), Sid Caesar (Studio Chief), Harold Gould (Engulf), Ron Carey (Devour), Henny Youngman (Fly-in-Soup Man). Directed by Mel Brooks and produced by Michael Hertzorg. Screenplay by Brooks, Ron Clark, Rudy DeLuca, and Barry Levinson.

There's a moment very early in *Silent Movie* (before the opening credits, in fact) when Mel Brooks, Marty Feldman, and Dom DeLuise are tooling through Los Angeles in a tiny sports car. They pass a pregnant lady at a bus stop. "That's a very pregnant lady!" Brooks says (on a title card, of course, since this is a silent movie). "Let's give her a lift!" The lady gets into the back of the car, which tilts back onto its rear wheels. Mel drives off with the front wheels in the air.

This is far from being the funniest scene in a very funny movie, but it helps to illustrate my point, which is that Mel Brooks will do anything for a laugh. Anything. He has no shame. He's an anarchist; his movies inhabit a universe in which everything is possible and the outrageous is probable, and *Silent Movie,* where Brooks has taken a considerably stylistic risk and pulled it off triumphantly, made me laugh a lot. On the Brooks-Laff-O-Meter, I laughed more than in *Young Frankenstein* and about as much as in *Blazing Saddles,* although not, I confess, as much as in *The Producers.*

Silent Movie is not only funny, it's fun. It's clear at almost every moment that the filmmakers had a ball making it. It's set in contemporary Hollywood, where Big Pictures Studio ("If it's a big picture, we've made it") teeters on the edge of bankruptcy and a takeover from the giant Engulf and Devour conglomerate. Enter Mel Funn (Brooks), a once-talented director whose career was cut short by drunkenness, who vows to save the studio by convincing Hollywood's biggest stars to make a silent movie. This is a situation that gives rise to a lot of inside jokes (I wonder whether executives at Gulf and Western, which took over Paramount, will notice any parallels), but the thing about Brooks's inside jokes is that their outsides are funny, too.

The intrepid gang of Mel, Dom, and Marty set out to woo the superstars, materializing in the shower of one (who counts his hands, puzzled, and finds he has eight) and plucking another out of a nightclub audience. (There are several "actual" stars in the movie, but it would be spoiling the fun to name them.) Everything's done amid an encyclopedia of sight gags, old and new, borrowed and with a fly in their soup. There are gags that don't work and stretches of up to a minute, I suppose, when we don't laugh—but even then we're smiling because of Brooks's manic desire to entertain. There's a story about the days, years ago, when Brooks was a writer for Sid Caesar and Caesar would march into the writers' office, pick up their desks, brandish them and shout *"funnier!"* I think the lesson rubbed off.

In a movie filled with great scenes, these moments are classics: The battle with the Coke machine. The behavior with the horse on the merry-go-round. The nightclub scene. The dramatic reaction of Engulf and Devour's board of directors to the photo of sexpot Vilma Kaplan. The fly in the soup. The Pong game in the intensive-care unit. The . . . but space is limited: Perhaps I should mention, though,that the movie isn't really silent. It's filled with wall-to-wall music, sound effects, explosions, whistles, and crashes and, yes, one word.

Silent Running ★ ★ ★ ★

G, 90 m., 1972

Bruce Dern (Lowell), Cliff Potts (Wolf), Ron Rivkin (Barker), Jesse Vint (Keenan), Mark Persons, Steven Brown, Cheryl Sparks, Larry Wisenhunt (Drones). Directed by Douglas Trumbull and produced by Michael Gruskoff. Screenplay by Deric Washburn, Mike Cimino, and Steve Bochco.

In the not very distant future, man has at last finished with Earth. The mountains are leveled and the valleys filled in, and there are no growing plants left to mess things up. Everything is nice and sterile, and man's global housekeeping has achieved total defoliation. Out around the rings of Saturn, a few lonely spaceships keep their vigil. They're interplanetary greenhouses, pointed always toward the sun. Inside their acres and acres of forests, protected by geodesic domes that gather the sunlight, the surviving plants and small animals of Earth grow. There are squirrels and rabbits and moonlit nights when the wind does actually seem to breathe in the trees: a ghostly reminder of the dead forests of Earth.

The keeper of one of these greenhouses, Freeman Lowell, loves the plants and animals with a not terribly acute intelligence. *Silent Running* is his story. In an earlier day, he might have been a forest ranger and happily spent the winter all alone in a tower, spotting forest fires. Now he is millions of miles from Earth, but his thoughts are filled with weedings and prunings, fertilizer and the artificial rainfall.

One day the word comes from Earth: Destroy the greenhouses and return. Lowell cannot bring himself to do this, and so he destroys his fellow crew members instead. Then he hijacks his spaceship and directs it out into the deep galactic night. All of this is told with simplicity and a quiet ecological concern, and it makes *Silent Running* a movie out of the ordinary—especially if you like science fiction.

The director is Douglas Trumbull, a Canadian who designed many of the special effects for Stanley Kubrick's *2001.* Trumbull also did the computers and the underground laboratory for *The Andromeda Strain,* and is one of the best science fiction special effects men. *Silent Running,* which has deep space effects every bit the equal of those in *2001,* also introduces him as an intelligent, if not sensational, director.

The weight of the movie falls on the shoulders of Bruce Dern, who plays the only man in sight during most of the picture. His only companions are Huey, Louie, and Dewey, who are small and uncannily human robots who help with the gardening. They're OK with a trowel but no good at playing poker, as their human boss discovers during a period of boredom.

Dern is a very good, subtle actor, who was about the best thing in Jack Nicholson's directing debut, *Drive, He Said.* Dern played a basketball coach as a man obsessed with the notion of winning—and the deep-space ecologist this time is a quieter variation on the theme.

Silent Running isn't, in the last analysis, a very profound movie, nor does it try to be. (If it had, it could have been a pretentious disaster.) It is about a basically uncomplicated man faced with an awesome, but uncomplicated, situation. Given a choice between the lives of his companions and the lives of Earth's last surviving firs and pines, oaks and elms, and creepers and cantaloupes, he decides for the growing things. After all, there are plenty of men. His problem is that, after a while, he begins to miss them.

Silkwood ★ ★ ★ ★

R, 128 m., 1983

Meryl Streep (Karen Silkwood), Kurt Russell (Drew Stephens), Cher (Dolly Pelliker), Craig T. Nelson (Winston). Directed by Mike Nichols and produced by Nichols and Michael Hausman. Screenplay by Nora Ephron and Alice Arlen.

When the Karen Silkwood story was first being talked about as a movie project, I pictured it as an angry political exposé, maybe *The China Syndrome, Part 2.* There'd be the noble, young nuclear worker, the evil conglomerate, and, looming overhead, the death's-head of a mushroom cloud. That could have been a good movie, but predictable. Mike Nichols's *Silkwood* is not predictable. That's because he's not telling the story of a conspiracy, he's telling the story of a human life. There are villains in his story, but none with motives we can't understand. After Karen is dead and the movie is over, we realize this is a lot more movie than perhaps we were expecting.

Silkwood is the story of some American workers. They happen to work in a Kerr-McGee nuclear plant in Oklahoma, making plutonium fuel rods for nuclear reactors. But they could just as easily be working in a Southern textile mill (there are echoes of *Norma Rae*), or on an assembly line, or for a metropolitan public school district. The movie isn't about plutonium, it's about the American working class. Its villains aren't monsters; they're organization men, labor union hotshots, and people afraid of losing their jobs. As the movie opens, Karen Silkwood fits naturally into this world, and the movie is the story of how she begins to stand out, how she becomes an individual, thinks for herself, and is punished for her freedom. Silkwood is played by Meryl Streep, in another of her great performances, and there's a tiny detail in the first moments of the movie that reveals how completely Streep has thought through the role. Silkwood walks into the factory, punches her time card, automatically looks at her own wristwatch, and then shakes her wrist: It's a self-winding watch, I guess. That little shake of the wrist is an actor's choice. There are a lot of them in this movie, all almost as invisible as the first one; little by little, Streep and her coactors build characters so convincing that we become witnesses instead of merely viewers.

The nuclear plant in the film is behind on an important contract. People are working overtime and corners are being cut. A series of small incidents convinces Karen Silkwood that the compromises are dangerous, that the health of the workers is being needlessly risked, and that the company is turning its back on the falsification of safety and workmanship tests. She approaches the union. The union sees some publicity in her complaints. She gets a free trip to Washington—her first airplane ride. She meets with some union officials who are much more concerned with publicity than with working conditions, and she has a little affair with one of them. She's no angel. At home in Oklahoma, domestic life resembles a revolving door, with her boyfriend (Kurt Russell) packing up and leaving, and her friend (Cher), a lesbian, inviting a beautician to move in. It's a little amazing that established movie stars like Streep, Russell, and Cher could disappear so completely into the everyday lives of these characters.

The real Karen Silkwood died in a mysterious automobile accident. She was on her way to deliver some documents to a *New York Times* reporter when her car left the road. Was the accident caused in some way? Was she murdered? The movie doesn't say. Nor does it point suspicion only toward the company. At the end there were a lot of people mad at Karen Silkwood. *Silkwood* is the story of an ordinary woman, hard-working and passionate, funny and screwed-up, who made those people mad simply because she told the truth as she saw it and did what she thought was right.

Silverado ★ ★ ★ ½

PG-13, 132 m., 1985

Kevin Kline (Paden), Scott Glenn (Emmett), Kevin Costner (Jake), Danny Glover (Mal), Linda Hunt (Stella), Jeff Goldblum (Slick), Brian Dennehy (Sheriff Cobb), Rosanna Arquette (Hannah), John Cleese (Sheriff Langston). Directed and produced by Lawrence Kasdan. Screenplay by Lawrence Kasdan and Mark Kasdan.

Walking home after the second Western was over at the Princess Theater, we'd play the roles we had seen on the screen. We were seven or eight years old at the time, but we didn't have the slightest difficulty in identifying with the cowboys in the movies. All of their motives were transparently clear to us—except, possibly, why anyone would want to kiss a girl when he could be practicing his lasso tricks instead.

The Westerns I remember from those days have been filtered through a golden haze of time, but the one thing I am sure I remember correctly is that they were fun. They were high-spirited, joyous, anarchic movies in which overgrown adolescents jumped on their horses and whooped and waved their hats in the air, and rode as fast as the wind to the next town and to the next adventure.

Silverado is a Western like that. I mean the comparison to be praise. This movie is more sophisticated and complicated than the Westerns of my childhood, and it is certainly better looking and better acted. But it has the same spirit; it awards itself the carefree freedom of the Western myth itself—the myth of a nation "endlessly realizing Westward," as Robert Frost had it, with limitless miles of prairie and desert and mountain, interrupted only occasionally enough for a dozen men to shoot at each other without all of them necessarily getting hit.

Silverado is the work of Lawrence Kasdan, the man who wrote *Raiders of the Lost Ark*, and it has some of the same reckless brilliance about it. It's the story of four cowboys who join up together, ride into town, refuse to knuckle under to the corrupt sheriff, and end up fighting for justice. This is a story, you will agree, that has been told before. What distinguishes Kasdan's telling of it is the style and energy he brings to the project.

The cowboys include a sweet-faced young man who hopes to make his fortune (Kevin

Kline), his goofy brother (Kevin Costner), a black man who vows to avenge his father's murder (Danny Glover), and a taciturn loner (Scott Glenn) who gets restless when he's not a long way from civilization. They meet along the way, after Glenn saves Kline from death in the desert, and together they help Costner escape from jail. Joining up with Glover, they ride on into the next town, Silverado, which is dominated by a slick sheriff (Brian Dennehy) and a gambling saloon run by a formidably competent little woman named Stella (Linda Hunt, in a scene-stealing performance).

I will not tell you too much of what happens next, but then perhaps I do not need to. If you are familiar with the Western, you will be familiar with this one. What may seem a little strange is that, if there is any nostalgia connected to this film, it will be found in our hearts and not in the characters on the screen. Too many Westerns in the last fifteen years have been elegies to a dead past, played out by actors remembering the cowboy roles of their youth (remember, if you can, the last Westerns of Robert Mitchum, William Holden, Randolph Scott, John Wayne, Joel McCrea, Kirk Douglas). *Silverado* contains a group of talented young actors (Scott Glenn, the oldest, is in his forties), and this is not their last Western but, in many cases, their first. The movie is set at the time when the West was still being opened up, when there was still opportunity there, and when the bad guys were still so unsophisticated they could fall for a dumb trick like getting trapped in a box canyon.

What does it prove, this movie about a bunch of cowboys held together by honor, this movie about bartender philosophers, evil sheriffs, and young pioneer women with lines like "My beauty will pass someday, but the land will only grow more beautiful." What does it prove? That the Western myth is most at home in a setting of innocence, that *Silverado* understands that, and that somewhere in our hearts there may still be memories of little boys and girls who chose up sides for who got to be the good guys on the long walk home.

Sisters ★ ★ ★

R, 93 m., 1973

Margot Kidder (Danielle Breton), Jennifer Salt (Grace Collier), Charles Durning (Joseph Larch), Bill Finley (Emil Breton), Lisle Wilson (Philip Woode). Directed by Brian De Palma and produced by Edward R. Pressman. Screenplay by De Palma and Louisa Rose.

Brian De Palma's *Sisters* was made more or less consciously as an homage to Alfred Hitchcock, but it has a life of its own and it's a neat little mystery picture. The opening is pure Hitchcock. The movie begins with events so commonplace they're almost trivial, and the horror of the situation is revealed only gradually. A lithe fashion model and a young newspaperman meet on a quiz show (it's called "Peeping Tom" and asks the question, what would *you* do if you were inadvertently made voyeur-for-a-day?). She wins a set of stainless steel cutlery, he wins dinner for two at a supper club, and they decide they like each other.

After a few brushes with a mysterious stranger who may or may not be her former husband, the young couple spend the night together and in the morning he is brutally knifed to death. And, no, I haven't given away too much of the plot. Because there are a few complications. For example, the girl is half of a famous set of Siamese twins. She's the nice one, but her sister isn't—not at all.

Then there's the crusading young girl newspaper reporter, kind of a women's lib Lois Lane, who lives across the courtyard and witnesses the crime (à la *Rear Window*). She calls the police, but they resent a recent series of exposés she's written. And when they visit the so-called murder apartment they find no blood, no body, no signs of a crime; only the sweet young fashion model.

I don't suppose I can reveal another line of the plot without spoiling some of De Palma's nice surprises. But the movie works not so much because of the twists and turns and complications as because of the performances. In a movie industry filled with young actresses who look great but can't act so well (especially when they've got to play intelligent characters), De Palma has cast two of the exceptions: Margot Kidder and Jennifer Salt.

Both of them are really fine, but Jennifer Salt is the bigger surprise because she's so convincing as the tough, stubborn, doggedly persistent outsider. It's a classic Hitchcock role. She's totally uninvolved and innocent, and in possession of information no one will believe. She can't doubt the evidence of her own eyes, but the cops mistrust her, the body's gone—and the killer knows who and where she is.

De Palma directs with a nice feeling for the incongruous. There is, for example, Ms. Salt's delightful suburban mother (Mary Davenport), who wishes sometimes her daughter would stop writing those newspaper columns and settle down in a nice, comfortable marriage. There's the mysterious stranger (Bill Finley), who looks like an extraterrestrial crossed with a Cold War spy. And there is even the other sister, the other Siamese twin, about whom perhaps the less said the better.

Sixteen Candles ★ ★ ★
PG, 93 m., 1984

Molly Ringwald (Samantha Baker), Anthony Michael Hall (The Geek), Michael Schoeffling (Jake Ryan), Gedde Watanabe (Long Duk Dong), Paul Dooley (Jim Baker). Directed by John Hughes and produced by Hilton A. Green. Screenplay by Hughes.

Sixteen Candles is a sweet and funny movie about two of the worst things that can happen to a girl on her sixteenth birthday: (1) Her grandparents shrieking "Look! She's finally got her boobies!" and (2) her entire family completely and totally forgetting that it's even her birthday. The day goes downhill from there, because of (3) her sister's wedding to a stupid lunkhead, (4) her crush on the best-looking guy in the senior class, and (5) the long, involved story about how a freshman boy named the Geek managed to get possession of a pair of her panties and sell looks at them for a dollar each to all the guys in the locker room.

If *Sixteen Candles* begins to sound a little like an adolescent raunch movie, maybe it's because I haven't suggested the style in which it's acted and directed. This is a fresh and cheerful movie with a goofy sense of humor and a good ear for how teen-agers talk. It doesn't hate its characters or condescend to them, the way a lot of teen-age movies do; instead, it goes for human comedy and finds it in the everyday lives of the kids in its story.

The movie stars Molly Ringwald as Samantha, a bright-eyed brunette who pulls off the difficult trick of playing a character who takes everything too seriously—without ever taking herself too seriously. The movie's told mostly from her point of view, and it's like *Valley Girl*—it's about young kids who think a lot about sex, but who are shy and inexperienced and unsure and touchingly committed to concepts like True Love. She has a crush on a senior boy named Jake (Michael Schoeffling), who looks like Matt Dillon, of course, and doesn't even know she's alive. Meanwhile, the Geek (Anthony Michael Hall) is in love with her. Also, there are complications involving Jake's stuck-up girlfriend, Samantha's impossible grandparents, various older and younger brothers and sisters, and a foreign exchange student named Long Duk Dong, who apparently has come to this country to major in partying.

Sixteen Candles contains most of the scenes that are obligatory in teen-age movies: The dance, the makeout session, the party that turns into a free-for-all. But writer and director John Hughes doesn't treat them as subjects for exploitation; he *listens* to these kids. For example, on the night of the dance, Samamtha ends up in the shop room with the Geek. They're sitting in the front seat of an old car. The Geek acts as if he's sex-mad. Samantha tells him to get lost. Then, in a real departure for this kind of movie, they really start to talk, and it turns out they're both lonely, insecure, and in need of a good friend.

There are a lot of effective performances in this movie, including Paul Dooley as Samantha's harried father, Blanche Baker as the zonked-out older sister, Hall as the Geek, and Gedde Watanabe as the exchange student (he elevates his role from a potentially offensive stereotype to high comedy). Ringwald provides a perfect center for the story, and her reaction in the first scene with her grandmother is just about worth the price of admission.

Sleeper ★ ★ ★ ½
PG, 88 m., 1973

Woody Allen (Miles Monroe), Diane Keaton (Luna), John Beck (Erno), Marya Small (Dr. Nero). Directed by Woody Allen and produced by Jack Grossberg. Screenplay by Allen and Marshall Brickman.

So how would you feel if your name was Miles Monroe and you ran the Happy Carrot

Health Food Store in Greenwich Village and you went into St. Vincent's Hospital for a minor operation one morning and woke up 200 years in the future? And America had become a police state? And the underground wanted to use you because you were the only person alive without an identification number?

What Woody Allen does is scream bloody murder and claim to be a coward: "I'm even beaten up by Quakers." But life becomes a grim struggle, etc., and Woody finds himself at battle with the thought police.

If the plot sounds slightly insane, recollect that one Allen movie began with Howard Cosell doing a play-by-play of an assassination, and another had Woody slapping Listerine under his arms and squirting Right Guard into his mouth before a big date.

Sleeper established Woody Allen as the best comic director and actor in America, a distinction that would mean more if there were more comedies being made. Without making a count, I'd guess that a dozen action movies get made for every comedy, which says more about our taste than our comedians. Mel Brooks only seems to get geared up every three years or so, but Allen is prolific as well as funny.

He gives us moments in *Sleeper* that are as good as anything since the silent films of Buster Keaton. There is, for example, a scene where a futuristic instant pudding erupts from a mixing bowl and threatens to fill the kitchen; Woody beats it down with a broom. The scene is part of a long sequence in which he has to pretend to be a robot house servant; he lurches about and buzzes and finally tears up the robot assembly line (in a scene like something from *Modern Times)*. Protesting all the way, Allen eventually penetrates into the inner circles of the underground and the government, and discovers the terrible truth about the nation's dictator, known as The Leader.

Nine months earlier, The Leader's home had burned down leaving nothing of The Leader but his nose. Through great medical innovation, the nose has been kept alive ever since, and the plan is to use genetic engineering to grow, or clone, The Leader's body back onto the nose. Inevitably, Allen is mistaken as the chief surgeon.

Whether the movie's Leader bears any relationship to the nation's current chief executive is a secret that only Woody Allen knows; he does not, however, go to many pains to keep it.

There's also a funny satirical scene in which Allen, as a genuine relic of 1973, is asked to identify such artifacts as General de Gaulle, a *Playboy* centerfold, and a Howard Cosell broadcast ("When people committed great crimes, they were forced to watch that.")

Sleeper is the closest Allen has come to classic slapstick-and-chase comedy, and he's good at it. His earlier films depended more on plot (except for *Everything You Always Wanted to Know about Sex*).

And sometimes he had a tendency to get a little sentimental as in *Take the Money and Run,* which opened with a hilarious documentary style biography of its hero, but then got bogged down in a love story that Allen apparently took seriously. (There was even a slow-motion Semi-Obligatory Lyrical Interlude in which Allen and his girl ran through the park and he didn't even seize the opportunity to satirize a Salem commercial.)

This time, though, he moves at breakneck speed and will risk anything, especially the plot, for a gag. Things move so fast we don't even get around to wondering how, in the middle of the movie, Allen got into the Miss America contest . . . and won.

Sleuth ★ ★ ★ ★

PG, 138 m., 1972

Laurence Olivier (Andrew Wyke), Michael Caine (Milo Tindle), Alec Cawthorne (Inspector Doppler), Eve Channing (Marguerite), John Matthews (Sergeant Talvant), Teddy Martin (Constable Higgs). Directed by Joseph L. Mankiewicz and produced by Morton Gottleib. Screenplay by Anthony Shaffer.

We come upon Andrew Wyke, the mystery writer, in an appropriate setting. He's in the middle of his vast garden, which is filled with shrubbery planted to form a maze. There is no way into, or out of, the maze—unless you know the secret. The better we come to know Andrew Wyke, the more this seems like the kind of garden he would have.

Wyke is a game-player. His enormous Tudor country manor is filled with games, robots, performing dolls, dart boards, and chess tables. He also plays games with people. One day poor Milo Tindle comes for a meeting with him. Milo is everything Wyke detests: only half-British, with the wrong accent, and "brand-new country gentleman clothes."

But Milo and Andrew's wife have fallen in love, and they plan to marry. So Andrew has a little scheme he wants to float. He is willing—indeed, happy—to give up his wife, but only if he can be sure she'll stay gone. He wants to be sure Milo can support her, and he suggests that Milo steal the Wyke family jewels and pawn them in Amsterdam. Then Milo will have a small fortune, and Andrew can collect the insurance.

Up to this point, everything in *Sleuth* seems so matter-of-fact that there's no hint how complicated things will get later on. But they do get complicated, and deadly, and reality begins to seem like a terribly fragile commodity. Andrew and Milo play games of such labyrinthine ferociousness that they eventually seem to forget all about Andrew's wife (and his mistress) and to be totally absorbed with stalking each other in a macabre game of cat and mouse.

Sleuth, a totally engrossing entertainment, is funny and scary by turns, and always superbly theatrical. It's the kind of mystery we keep saying they don't make anymore, but sometimes they do, and the British seem to write them better than anyone. The movie is based on the long-running play by Anthony Shaffer, who also wrote Alfred Hitchcock's *Frenzy.* Both films have in common a nice flair for dialogue and a delicate counterpoint between the ironic and the gruesome.

What really makes the movie come alive—what makes it work better than the play, really—are the lead performances by Sir Laurence Olivier, Michael Caine, and Alec Cawthorne. Olivier plays the wealthy mystery writer Andrew Wyke as a true-blue British eccentric: His head, like his house, is cluttered with ornate artifacts largely without function. The hero of his detective stories, the wonderfully named St. John Lord Merridewe, is equally dotty. Olivier is clearly having fun in the role, and he throws in all kinds of accents, asides, and nutty pieces of business. Michael Caine, who might seem an unlikely candidate to play Milo Tindle, turns out to be a very good one. He manages somehow to seem smaller and less assured than Olivier (even while he towers over Sir Laurence). And he is strangely touching as he dresses up in an absurd clown's costume to steal the jewels. Inspector Doppler, the kindly old investigator who suspects that Andrew has murdered Milo, is played by Alec Cawthorne, a veteran stage actor making his movie debut.

It's difficult to say more about *Sleuth* without giving away its plot—which in this case would be a capital offense. Let me just mention that the play makes a remarkably easy transition to the screen because of director Joseph L. Mankiewicz's willingness to respect its timing and dialogue, instead of trying to jazz it up cinematically. And, despite the fact that most of the movie takes place indoors, we never get the sense of visual limitations because Ken Adams's set designs give us such an incredible multitude of things to look at (and through) in the mansion.

Small Change ★ ★ ★ ★

PG, 104 m., 1976

Geory Desmouceaux (Patrick), Philippe Goldman (Julien), Christine Pelle (Madame), Jean-François Stevenin and Chantal Mercier (The Teachers). Directed by François Truffaut. Screenplay by Truffaut and Suzanne Schiffman.

There's a moment in François Truffaut's *Small Change* that remembers childhood so well we don't know whether to laugh or cry. It takes place in a classroom a few minutes before the bell at the end of the school day. The class cutup is called on. He doesn't have the answer (he never does), but as he stands up his eyes stray to a large clock outside the window. The hand stands at twenty-eight minutes past the hour. Click: twenty-nine minutes. He stalls, he grins, the teacher repeats the question. Click: thirty past, and the class bell rings. The kid breaks out in a triumphant grin as he joins the stampede from the room.

This moment, like so many in Truffaut's magical film, has to be seen to be appreciated. He re-creates childhood, and yet he sees it objectively, too: He remembers not only the funny moments but the painful ones. The agony of a first crush. The ordeal of being the only kid in class so poor he has to wear the same sweater every day. The painful earnestness that goes into the recitation of a dirty joke that neither the teller nor the listeners quite understand.

Truffaut has been over some of this ground before. His first feature, *The 400 Blows*, told the painful story of a Paris adolescent caught between his warring parents and his own better nature. In *Small Change* he returns to similar material in a sunnier mood. He tells the stories of several kids in a French provincial town, and of their parents and teachers. His method is episodic; only gradually do we begin to recognize faces, to pick the central characters out from the rest. He correctly remembers that childhood itself is episodic: Each day seems separate from any other, each new experience is sharply etched, and important discoveries and revelations become great events surrounded by a void. It's the accumulation of all those separate moments that create, at last, a person.

"Children exist in a state of grace," he has a character say at one point. "They pass untouched through dangers that would destroy an adult." There are several such hazards in *Small Change*. The most audacious—Truffaut at his best—involves a two-year-old child, a kitten, and an open window on the tenth floor. Truffaut milks this situation almost shamelessly before finally giving us the happiest of denouements. And he exhibits at the same time his mastery of film; the scene is timed and played to exist exactly at the border between comedy and tragedy, and from one moment to the next we don't know how we should feel. He's got the audience in his hand.

That's true, too, in a scene involving a little girl who has been made to stay at home as a punishment. She takes her father's battery-powered megaphone and announces indignantly to the neighbors around the courtyard that she is hungry, that her parents have gone out to a restaurant without her, and that she has been abandoned. The neighbors lower her food in a basket: Chicken and fruit but not, after all, a bottle of red wine one of the neighborhood kids wanted to put in.

In the midst of these comic episodes, a more serious story is developed. It's about the kid who lives in a shack outside of town. He's abused by his parents, he lives by his wits, he steals to eat. His mistreatment is finally found out by his teachers, and leads to a concluding speech by one of them that's probably unnecessary but expresses Truffaut's thinking all the same: "If kids had the vote," the teacher declares, "the world would be a better and safer place."

Smash Palace ★ ★ ★ ★

R, 100 m., 1982

Bruno Lawrence (Al Shaw), Anna Jemison (Jacqui Shaw), Greer Robson (Georgie Shaw), Keith Aberdeen (Ray Foley), Des Kelly (Tiny). Directed and produced by Roger Donaldson. Screenplay by Donaldson, Peter Hansard, and Bruno Lawrence.

Step by step, this powerful movie takes a man from perfect happiness into a personal hell. By the end of the film, the man is behaving irrationally, but here's the frightening thing: Because we've followed him every step of the way, we have to admit he's behaving as we ourselves might, in the same circumstances. The man in *Smash Palace* is Al Shaw, a Grand Prix driver who leaves the racing circuit to take over his father's auto garage in New Zealand. Played by Bruno Lawrence, Al is a straight-talking, direct man who enjoys working with his hands and takes a vast delight in the affections of his wife and the love of his small daughter. It's a long way from the Grand Prix to repairing transmissions, but he's happy with his work and content to raise a family in peace and quiet. His wife (Anna Jemison) is not so content. She wanted him to leave the racing circuit before he was killed, but now, in the quiet backwaters of New Zealand, she is going quietly stir-crazy. She begins an affair with a local cop (Keith Aberdeen) and finally tells her husband she's leaving him. She's moving into town.

Her decision starts him on a series of wrong moves that may seem logical, one by one, but which eventually add up in the minds of others to a simple conclusion: He has lost his reason. He is jealous—of course. He holds a great fury against his wife and the cop. But, much more important, he misses his daughter. He wants custody. But because he acts in ways that are violent and frightening to his wife (and because her lover is on the police force, which must respond to the domestic emergencies he creates), he works himself into a Catch-22: The more he does to take back his daughter, the closer he is to losing her. Finally, he kidnaps her. He takes her out into the woods where they live together for a time in isolation and happiness. It's an idyll that can't last. But *Smash Palace* doesn't lead up to the inevitable violent conclusion we might expect. All along the way, this film prefers the unexpected turns of actual human behavior to the predictable plot developments we might have expected, and, at the end, there's another turn, a fascinating one.

Smash Palace is one of 1982's best films, an examination of much the same ground as *Shoot the Moon*, but a better film, because it has the patience to explore the ways in which people can become consumed by anger (*Shoot the Moon* contented itself with the outward symptoms). One of the reasons the movie works so well is the performances, which are all the stronger because they come from actors we have not seen before. Bruno Lawrence, bald-headed, wiry, tough, and surprisingly tender, is just right as the man who loses his family. Anna Jemison has a difficult assignment as his wife: We're on his side, and yet we see the logic of her moves. Keith Aberdeen is properly tentative as the other man; he feels love and lust, and yet is not unaware of the unhappiness he is causing. And there's a guy named Des Kelly who plays Tiny, an employee at the Smash Palace who looks on, and sees all, and wishes he knew what to do.

The movie was directed by a young filmmaker named Roger Donaldson, who, in a sense, *is* the New Zealand film industry. He has produced six features for New Zealand television, and his first feature film, *Sleeping Dogs*, starred Warren Oates in a horrifying and plausible fantasy about the American occupation of New Zealand. Now comes this film, so emotionally wise and observant that we learn from it why people sometimes make the front pages with guns in their hands and try to explain that it's all because of love. Love, yes, but also the terrible frustration of trying to control events, to make people do what you want them to do, what you "know" would make them happy—no matter what they think. The hero of *Smash Palace* does not act wisely, but if we are honest, it's hard to see where we might have acted differently.

Smooth Talk ★ ★ ★ ½

PG-13, 92 m., 1986

Laura Dern (Connie), Treat Williams (Arnold Friend), Mary Kay Place (Katherine), Elizabeth Berridge (June), Levon Helm (Harry), Sarah Inglis (Jill). Directed by Joyce Chopra and produced by Martin Rosen. Music by James Taylor. Screenplay by Tom Cole.

There is a certain kind of teen-ager who always seems to be waiting for something. Others live in the moment, but these waiting ones seem to be the victims of time. It stretches before them in long, empty hours. You can look at them and almost literally see the need in their eyes. It is a need to be someone else, somewhere else.

Connie, the heroine in *Smooth Talk*, is a girl like that. She is about fifteen years old, tall, blonde, unformed. At least that is the vision of her we receive the first time we see her. Then there is a transformation scene. She leaves her house, dressed like a teen-ager on the way to a ballgame, and meets her friends at the mall. They go into the ladies' room and apply makeup and mascara and stuff their jackets into their bags, and when they emerge they look like the runners-up in the Madonna lookalike contest. Sexy beyond their own knowledge, they parade through the mall, attracting attention they do not know how to handle. There is a risky, reckless bounce in their step; they are still waiting, but now they seem to know what they are waiting for.

Appearances deceive. Emotionally, Connie is younger than she looks. At home, she suffers because her mother clearly prefers her older sister. She suffers, too, from the well-meaning idiocy of her father, who talks in vague terms of "finally having a home of our own," as if this were Connie's goal, too, and she would always be fifteen and always coming home to it. She looks at her father as if he were speaking a foreign language. He looks at her as if he were seeing someone else. Connie is played by Laura Dern, an actress who seems perfectly suited to this role; she is a chameleon who looks twelve in one shot, eighteen in the next, and is able to suggest the depth of her unhappiness by the way she tries to seem cheerful.

The first hour of *Smooth Talk* is deceptive. Nothing much seems to happen. Connie and her friends hang out. Connie fights with her parents. Connie waits through the long, endless afternoons of summer. This is the set-up for the second half of the movie, which is an astonishing denouement.

Because *Smooth Talk* depends so completely on surprise, it is hard to know how to write about it. Many will be shocked by the movie's ending, and would want to be warned. Others will see it as a modern morality tale, a Grimm story for the late twentieth century, a time when evil seems more banal and seductive than it should. I will walk lightly around the ending without revealing it.

Smooth Talk is based on a short story by Joyce Carol Oates, who so often finds the materials of classic tragedy in the lives of everyday people. Although the movie is shocking, it is not sensational in the way it might have been—if it had been handled as a horror story, say, instead of as a morality play. Oates's story, adapted by Tom Cole and directed by Joyce Chopra, is about a young girl who is surrounded by sexuality, who is curious about it, who flirts dangerously in the wrong places, and who not only learns her lesson, but grows up, all at once, into a different person than she was.

What happens is that a boy (Treat Williams) sees her at the drive-in. He says his name is Arnold Friend, and that he wants to be *her* friend. Everything about this guy is all wrong. He is nowhere near being as young as he says. There is a bad look in his eye. He pals around with another guy, who doesn't say anything, and doesn't need to, because one look at him and you realize he is missing important parts.

Connie walks around in her shorts and halter top, and Arnold Friend watches her. He makes a pass at her, and she puts him off with the kind of cute flirtation that would work with another kid, but Arnold just looks at her—looks through her—and a chill wind seems to blow. One Sunday when Connie is left at home alone and the family is all hours away, Arnold Friend comes to visit. He does not physically rape her. What he does is much worse than that. He talks to her in a way that forever brings an end to her innocence.

Smooth Talk is not a "teen-age movie." It is not, despite its plot, a horror film. It is a study in deviant psychology, and in the power that one person can have over another, especially if they push in the direction where the other person is already headed. The movie is almost uncanny in its self-assurance, in the way it knows that the first hour, where "nothing" happens, is necessary if the pay-off is to be tragic, instead of merely sensational. The movie is also uncanny in what it does with its last three shots. I watched them, and could not believe so much could be implied so simply. Leave the movie before it's over, and you miss almost everything, because what Connie does at the very end of the film is necessary. It makes *Smooth Talk* the story of the process of life, instead of just a sad episode.

A Soldier's Story ★ ★ ½

PG, 99 m., 1984

Howard E. Rollins, Jr. (Captain Davenport), Adolph Caesar (Sergeant Waters), Art Evans (Private Wilkie), David Alan Grier (Corporal Cobb), David Harris (Private Smalls), Denzel Washington (Private Peterson), Patti LaBelle (Big Mary). Directed by Norman Jewison and produced by Jewison, Ronald L. Schwary, and Patrick Palmer. Screenplay by Charles Fuller.

A Soldier's Story is one of those movies that's about less than you might think. It begins with the murder of a black sergeant, who is shot near an Army base in Louisiana in 1944. Suspicion immediately points to the local whites, who are not too happy about all these blacks stationed in their branch of the deep South. An Army lawyer, a captain, is sent from Washington to handle the investigation, and he turns out to be black, too—the first black officer anyone in the movie has ever seen. As he conducts his investigation, we get to meet some of the important characters on the base, from black privates to the white officers who brag about their experiences at "commanding Negroes." Each time the captain conducts an interview, we get a flashback to another version of the events leading up to the murder. And eventually, we find out who committed the crime.

As a storytelling device, this mechanism is excruciating. The problem is in the time structure. If an investigation begins at the present moment and proceeds, suspense can build. But if the truth is going to emerge from a series of flashbacks, then obviously the movie knows who did it, and is withholding the information from us, using it as a hook to get us to sit through all of its other points. *A Soldier's Story* is not really a murder mystery, then. What is it? I guess it's supposed to be a docudrama. A great deal of the plot revolves around the character of the dead man, Sergeant Waters (Adolph Caesar), who is a scrappy little veteran of World War I, and believes that blacks should always behave so as to favorably impress whites and reflect credit upon their race. He is filled with self-hate, and takes it out on the black men under him who are not acting the way he thinks they should.

This fact is gradually revealed in a series of interviews conducted by the lawyer, Captain Davenport, who is played by Howard E. Rollins, Jr. And what a disappointing performance it is, coming from the same actor who won an Academy Award nomination for *Ragtime*. He invests his character with little humanity; he tries to seem dispassionate, curbed, correct, just a little more noble than anyone else in the picture. The result is such a laid-back performance that the lawyer seems less interested in solving the case than in keeping his cool (the murdered Sergeant Waters would have been proud of him).

The movie ends with a handshake between Davenport and one of the white officers who has made life hard for him. This is a more ironic ending than was perhaps intended, because *A Soldier's Story* was directed by Norman Jewison, the director who ended *In the Heat of the Night* with Sidney Poitier and Rod Steiger shaking hands. The ending worked in 1967, but in 1984 I think we expect a little more. Did this movie have to be so lockstep, so trapped by its mechanical plot, so limited by a murder mystery? What the movie has to say is so pale and limited that, ironically, the most interesting character in the movie is the victim—that black racist sergeant. At least he has fire and life and, misguided as he is, at least he's vital.

Some Kind of Wonderful ★ ★ ★

PG-13, 95 m., 1987

Eric Stoltz (Keith Nelson), Mary Stuart Masterson (Drummer Girl), Craig Sheffer (Hardy Jenns), Lea Thompson (Amanda Jones), John Ashton (Mr. Nelson), Elias Koteas (Skinhead). Directed by Howard Deutch and produced by John Hughes. Screenplay by Hughes.

Most movies are not about people. Most movies are about things, and in the category of things I include those movie stars who have become such icons that "they," rather than their characters, perform the adventures in movies.

Hardly ever do we get an American movie about adults who are attempting to know themselves better, live better lives, get along more happily with the people around them. Most American movies are about the giving and receiving of violent pain. That's why I look forward to John Hughes's films about American teen-agers. His films are almost always about the problems of growing up and becoming a more complete person.

Some Kind of Wonderful, which Hughes wrote and produced, and which Howard Deutch directed, is a movie like that. It's not a great movie. It progresses slowly at times and it uses some fairly standard characters. But it is not about whether the hero will get the girl. It is about whether the hero *should* get the girl, and when was the last time you saw a movie that even knew that could be the question?

The film stars Eric Stoltz as Keith, a pleasantly shaggy young man who is an outsider at his high school. He would rather be an artist than fit in with the crowd, and his best friend is another outsider, a tomboy (Mary Stuart Masterson). Keith has a crush on Amanda Jones (Lea Thompson), who is the school sexpot. He even writes a song about her, which is performed about three times on the sound track. She goes steady with a stuck-up rich kid.

Here we have all the ingredients, I suppose, for another standard John Hughes teen-ager film. But Hughes always gives his characters the right to be real, and by the end of *Some Kind of Wonderful*, I felt a lot of empathy for these kids.

The Thompson character, for example, is not just a distant, unattainable symbol, but a young woman with feelings. The tomboy doesn't just pine from afar, but helps Keith in his campaign to win a date with this girl of his dreams. And in the final sequence, in which the tomboy acts as chauffeur on the dream date, the dialogue isn't about sex; it's about learning to be true to yourself and not fall for the way people are packaged. By the movie's end, everybody has learned something about themselves.

I guess I'm making this sound like a film

they should show in sociology class. *Some Kind of Wonderful* is a worthwhile film, all right, but it's also entertaining—especially in the scenes between Stoltz and John Ashton, who plays his father. Ashton wants his kid to go to college; the kid would rather devote the energy to his artwork. This disagreement doesn't quite degenerate into a shouting match, and by the end of the film the two are able to have a surprisingly civilized fight about it.

All of the actors in this story are appealing, but my favorite was Masterson as the tomboy whose love is totally overlooked by this guy who thinks he knows all about her. There's something a little masochistic about the way she volunteers to chauffeur him on his big date, but something sweet, too, in the way she cares for him. She has a lot of tricky scenes in which she has to look one way and feel another way, and she's good at them.

Some Kind of Wonderful is yet another film in which Hughes and his team show a special ability to make an entertaining movie about teen-agers which is also about life, about insecurity, about rejection, about learning to grow. As somebody who sees almost all the new movies, I sometimes have the peculiar feeling that the kids in Hughes's movies are more grown up than the adults in most of the other ones.

Someone to Watch Over Me ★ ★
R, 106 m., 1987

Tom Berenger (Mike Keegan), Mimi Rogers (Claire Gregory), Lorraine Bracco (Ellie Keegan), Jerry Orbach (Lieutenant Garber), John Rubinstein (Neil Steinhart), Andreas Katsulas (Joey Venza). Directed by Ridley Scott and produced by Thierry de Ganay and Harold Schneider. Screenplay by Howard Franklin.

"High Concept" is a Hollywood expression for a movie story idea that can be summarized in one sentence, such as, "Detroit street cop goes to Beverly Hills." The phrase is a little misleading, since such movies are almost always low in the ambition of their conception, and sometimes so short-sighted that they cannot see the flaws in their own formulas.

Take *Someone to Watch Over Me* as an example. The story of this movie can be summarized in this sentence: "Detective from working-class background falls in love with society beauty." If you have read that sentence and are a reasonably experienced moviegoer, is there anything I can add that would surprise you?

Would you, for example, be surprised to find that the beauty needs a police bodyguard because her life is in danger after she has witnessed a murder? Would you be amazed to learn that the cop assigned to the night shift is young and handsome? That the murderer is vile and sadistic? That the beauty's husband is rich but distant? That the cop's wife is feisty and determined? That the cop's boss threatens to fire him for screwing around with this dame? That the movie's set decorator has supplied the society woman with a Manhattan apartment so lavish that even Donald Trump would need roller skates?

You would not, I suspect, be very surprised. That's the problem with High Concept movies. Once you master the concept, there's nothing left for the movie—except, of course, for the obligatory sequence of the cop tracking the killer through the darkened apartment, which is the high-rise equivalent of the chase scene. Movies like this are on automatic pilot. Unless we are very young, very naive, or hopelessly lusting after one of the stars, there is little to interest us aside from interior decorating hints. And yet, *Someone to Watch Over Me* does contain one element of extraordinary interest. That is the character of the cop's wife, played by Lorraine Bracco with great force and imagination. The character is a cliché: the good-looking but not glamorous woman who has spent the last ten years being married to this guy, cooking his breakfast, and bearing his child. At first she trusts her husband with this beautiful society woman. Then she gets suspicious. The movie's best scene has her playing tough, asking him to level with her.

In an earlier, more literate and inventive age, Hollywood would have known that *this* was the heart of the story. The society woman would have been cast as the brazen hussy—Joan Crawford, maybe—and the wife would have been cast as the heroine. Audiences would have been titillated by the seductive aura of the other woman, and there would have been a scene in which the cop skated dangerously close to the edge. But then there would have been one of those delicious scenes where the rich bitch gets her comeuppance.

In today's Hollywood, money and status are so much a religion that it is obligatory, I guess, for the cop to fall for the rich woman. He does in this movie. The cop is played by Tom Berenger, the socialite is played by Mimi Rogers, and their coupling has all the excitement of an arranged marriage. The movie's high-tech sex scenes are done with all the cinematic technical support the director, Ridley Scott, can muster, but they're dead, because they contain only sex, not passion.

Needless to say, there are no sex scenes in the film between Berenger and Bracco—between the man and wife. They get a tearful reconciliation, and that's that. There is something fundamentally wrong about a script in which the hero sleeps with the wrong woman. I am not talking here in moral terms, but in story terms. The makers of this film got so carried away by their High Concept that they missed the point of the whole story. That rich broad really does have a great kitchen, though.

Something Wild ★ ★ ★ 1/2

R, 106 m., 1986

Jeff Daniels (Charlie Driggs), Melanie Griffith (Lulu Hankel), Ray Liotta (Ray Sinclair), Margaret Colin (Irene), Jack Gilpin (Larry Dillman), Su Tissue (Peggy Dillman). Directed and produced by Jonathan Demme. Screenplay by E. Max Frye.

She has his number. She looks him straight in the eye and tells him he's the kind of guy who sometimes walks out on a check in a restaurant, just for the secret little sexual charge he gets out of it. He squirms and tries to deny it, but she knows. He's supposed to get right back to the office, but she suggests a little ride around town, and the next thing he knows, he's handcuffed to the bed in a sleazy motel and she's holding the phone up to his mouth so he can lie to his boss.

The opening sequence of Jonathan Demme's *Something Wild* is filled with such a headlong erotic charge that it's hard to see how he can sustain it, and, in fact, he can't. After an hour or so of exuberant sexual comedy, the movie settles down into a slightly more conventional groove, and we can begin to guess what's coming next. It's still a good movie; it's just not as inspired as those risky opening scenes where Demme closes his eyes and steps on the gas.

The movie stars Jeff Daniels as Charlie, a superficially conventional businessman whose heart is easily stirred by boldness in women, and Melanie Griffith as Lulu, an alcoholic sex machine with a very creative imagination. Daniels plays some of the same notes here that he used in *Terms of Endearment,* where he was the sound, dependable, serious husband and father who liked to fool around with cute coeds. He looks like he was born to wear a suit and a tie, but he has that naughty look in his eye. Griffith's performance is based not so much on eroticism as on recklessness: She is able to convince us (and Daniels) that she is capable of doing almost anything, especially if she thinks it might frighten him.

Even while they're standing on the sidewalk in front of that restaurant and she's pretending to accuse him of theft, there's a charge between them. The casting is crucial in a movie like this; there has to be some kind of animal compatibility between the man and the woman or it doesn't matter how good the dialogue is.

Once they've made their connection, Daniels willingly goes along for the ride. After a while she even takes his handcuffs off, although he sort of liked the idea of having lunch in a restaurant with the cuffs dangling from one of his wrists. They drive down the East Coast from New York to Tallahassee, while she steals money from cash registers and he sinks into the waking reverie of the sexually drained.

There's a wonderful scene where she takes him home to meet her mother, introducing him as her husband: "See, Mama? Just the kind of man you said I should marry." Her mother greets them, feeds them, welcomes them and then lets Daniels learn that she knows exactly what's going on: "You look out for that girl." I was reminded of Bonnie's mother in *Bonnie and Clyde,* who saw so clearly through the romance to the death that was approaching.

At Griffith's high school reunion, Daniels runs into the last person he wants to see, the accountant from his office. And Griffith runs into the last person she wants to see, her husband, who is fresh out of prison. He follows them, takes them captive, and forces them to join him on a crime spree. And Daniels realizes that he must fight, not only for the woman he has started to love, but for his life. It's here that the movie begins to feel more conventional, even though a newcomer named Ray Liotta is mesmerizing as the evil husband with vengeance on his mind. We have seen stories before that are more or less like this one, and it becomes easier to foresee the movie's ending. After the freedom and anarchy of the opening and middle scenes, the closing passages feel like a reduction of tension.

But *Something Wild* is quite a movie. Demme is a master of finding the bizarre in the ordinary. Remember his *Melvin and Howard* and the topless dancer who had a cast on her arm? If he had conceived this movie as a "madcap comedy," it probably wouldn't have worked. The accomplishment of Demme and the writer, E. Max Frye, is to think their characters through before the very first scene. They know all about Charlie and Lulu, and so what happens after the meeting outside that restaurant is almost inevitable, given who they are and how they look at each other. This is one of those rare movies where the plot seems surprised at what the characters do.

Sometimes a Great Notion ★ ★ ★

PG, 114 m., 1971

Paul Newman (Hank), Henry Fonda (Henry), Michael Sarrazin (Dan), Lee Remick (Henry's Wife). Directed by Paul Newman and produced by John Foreman. Screenplay by John Gay.

Paul Newman's *Sometimes a Great Notion* tells sort of an old-fashioned story about prideful clans carving empires out of the wilderness. The characters seem a little familiar, too. Take the three most important. Henry Fonda is the proud old patriarch, Paul Newman is the son who stays at home but makes up his own mind, and Michael Sarrazin is the kid brother who comes back to the land with all sorts of half-baked notions and scores to settle. So far, the relationships remind us of *Hud*.

But then Newman starts tunneling under the material, coming up with all sorts of things we didn't quite expect, and along the way he proves himself (as he did with *Rachel, Rachel*) as a director of sympathy and a sort of lyrical restraint. He rarely pushes scenes to their obvious conclusions, he avoids melodrama, and by the end of *Sometimes a Great Notion*, we somehow come to know the Stamper family better than we expected to.

The story takes place during a timber strike in the Northwest. The local merchants (especially the neurotic fellow who runs the movie theater and the dry cleaners) are going broke because money has dried up. The striking timber workers idly hang around the union office. But the Stamper family continues to work in defiance of the strike, and despite the fact that Fonda has broken half the bones on his left side in an accident.

Sarrazin, Newman's half-brother by Fonda's second wife, comes home to help—and also to mope, to get over a bummer of a year, and to suggest to Newman's wife (Lee Remick) that maybe she should clear out from the obsessed Stamper clan. There are a lot of things left fairly unclear, though; I'm not quite sure what was on Remick's mind during most of the movie. The character is left wavering, and we don't fully understand her relationship to her husband. Newman shortchanges what you might call the indoor scenes in order to give us the lumber business.

The best scene in the film takes place during a day of work. The Stamper men seem terribly small as they bring enormous trees crashing to the ground, wrap chains around them, and load them on trucks with big, musclebound machines. The direction of this scene is superb; the reality and the danger of the huge logs are caught in a way that defines the men and their job better than any dialogue could.

Another scene that reveals Newman's insight as a director takes place at a lumbermen's picnic. Some of the strikers invite some of the Stampers to a game of touch football. The game develops into a brawl, of course, but in an interesting way; instead of going for a hard-action approach to the scene, Newman shoots it in a sort of twilight, bittersweet style. All through the film, he avoids making the strikers into heavies and their hatred for the Stampers seem melodramatic. Instead, they're clumsy, resentful enemies, and when they try to sabotage a

Stamper lumber raft, they only wind up drifting out to sea—and having to be rescued by the Stampers.

The movie doesn't seem very sure of what it thinks about the Fonda character's fierce and stubborn pride. The character himself believes all that matters is getting up for another day, and working, and eating, and sleeeping, and getting on with life. Another character, a brother-in-law, has been "saved" at the local fundamentalist church and has a sort of sweet simplicity that seems out of place—until the scene where he dies. He dies in a way that is truly filled with grace and humor, and the scene is one of the several things in *Sometimes a Great Notion* that make it worth seeing, even if its overall design is murky.

Songwriter ★ ★ ★ ½

R, 94 m., 1985

Willie Nelson (Doc Jenkins), Kris Kristofferson (Blackie Buck), Melinda Dillon (Honey Carder), Rip Torn (Dino McLeish), Lesley Ann Warren (Gilda), Richard Sarafian (Rocky Rodeo). Directed by Alan Rudolph and produced by Sydney Pollack. Screenplay by Matthew Leonetti.

Songwriter is one of those movies that grows on you. It doesn't have a big point to prove, and it isn't all locked into the requirements of its plot. It's about spending some time with some country musicians who are not much crazier than most country musicians, and are probably nicer than some. It also has a lot of good music.

The movie stars Willie Nelson as a country songwriter named Doc Jenkins, who has a real bad head for business. One day he gets fast-talked into selling control of his company to a slick operator named Rocky Rodeo (Richard Sarafian). Homeless and betrayed, he turns for support to his best friend, a country music star named Blackie (Kris Kristofferson). Blackie, meanwhile, is being promoted by a sleazy manager named Dino (Rip Torn), who has somewhere found a neurotic young singer named Gilda (Lesley Ann Warren). In an early scene that lets us know this movie is not going to be routine, Blackie tries to foist Gilda off on an audience that has paid to see Blackie, and when the audience rebels, Blackie grabs the mike and starts advising them to commit anatomical impossibilities upon themselves.

During the course of some days and nights on the road and back home in Austin, Doc comes up with a clever scheme. Instead of writing any more songs for the despised Dino, he'll write his songs under a pseudonym, and give them to Gilda to record. Blackie will include Gilda on his next tour, and Dino will get screwed. This seems like a good idea to everybody, especially Gilda, who has a tricky drinking problem and thinks she might be falling in love with Doc.

The movie unwinds casually, introducing us to the other people in the lives of these characters. The most important is Doc's former wife (Melinda Dillon), and the best scene in the movie is where Doc visits her and the kids, and is shy and sweet and tremendously moving. Another good scene is one where Gilda invites Doc into her bed, and he tries to be gentle and tactful in explaining that he doesn't think that's a good idea. Willie Nelson is the key to both of those scenes, and it's interesting how subtle his acting is. Unlike a lot of concert stars whose moves tend to be too large for the intimacy of a movie, Nelson is a gifted, understated actor. Watch the expression on his face as he turns down Gilda; not many actors can say as much with their eyes.

Songwriter was directed by Alan Rudolph, who also made *Choose Me*. Rudolph's teacher was Robert Altman, and, like Altman, he specializes in offbeat rhythms of a group of characters in an unpredictable situation. We never have a clear idea of where *Songwriter* is headed; is it about Doc's love for his first wife, or Gilda's self-destruction, or Rocky Rodeo's con games? It's good that we don't know, because then we don't know what to expect next, and the movie can surprise us.

Both Rudolph and Altman also specialize in unlikely combinations of actors; Kris Kristofferson and Nelson don't, at first, seem to belong in the same movie with Warren, Torn, and Dillon, but watch them work together. One of Torn's great unsung roles was in *Payday*, the movie based on the last days of Hank Williams, Sr. This time, he's like the same character a little further down the road, a little more spaced out. Kristofferson is basically the straight man, the hero's best friend. Nelson sings less and acts more than we expected. And Lesley Ann Warren's performance is endlessly inventive: She takes the fairly standard character of a kooky would-be singer, and makes her into a touching, unforgettable creation.

Sophie's Choice ★ ★ ★ ★

R, 157 m., 1982

Meryl Streep (Sophie), Kevin Kline (Nathan), Peter MacNicol (Stingo), Greta Turken (Leslie Lapidus), Gunther Maria Halmer (Rudolf Hoess). Directed by Alan J. Pakula and produced by Pakula and Keith Barish. Screenplay by Pakula.

Sometimes when you've read the novel, it gets in the way of the images on the screen. You keep remembering how you imagined things. That didn't happen with me during *Sophie's Choice*, because the movie is so perfectly cast and well-imagined that it just takes over and happens to you. It's quite an experience.

The movie stars Meryl Streep as Sophie, a Polish-Catholic woman, who was caught by the Nazis with a contraband ham, was sentenced to a concentration camp, lost her two children there, and then was somehow spared to immigrate to Brooklyn, U.S.A., and to the arms of an eccentric charmer named Nathan. Sophie and Nathan move into an old boardinghouse, and the rooms just below them are taken by Stingo, a jug-eared kid from the South who wants to be a great novelist. As the two lovers play out their doomed, romantic destiny, Stingo falls in love with several things: with his image of himself as a writer, with his idealized vision of Sophie and Nathan's romance, and, inevitably, with Sophie herself.

The movie, like the book, is told with two narrators. One is Stingo, who remembers these people from that summer in Brooklyn, and who also remembers himself at that much earlier age. The other narrator, contained within Stingo's story, is Sophie herself, who remembers what happened to her during World War II, and shares her memories with Stingo in a long confessional. Both the book and the movie have long central flashbacks, and neither the book nor the movie is damaged by those diversions, because Sophie's story is so indispensable to Stingo's own growth, from an adolescent dreamer to an artist who can begin to understand human suffering. The book and movie have something else in common. Despite the fact that Sophie's story, her choices, and her fate are all sad, sad stories, there is a lot of exuberance and joy in the telling of them. *Sophie's Choice* begins as a young Southerner's odyssey to the unimaginable North—to that strange land celebrated by his hero, Thomas Wolfe, who took the all-night train to New York with its riches, its women, and its romance. Stingo is absolutely entranced by this plump blonde Polish woman who moves so winningly into his life, and by her intense, brilliant, mad lover.

We almost don't notice, at first, as Stingo's odyssey into adulthood is replaced, in the film, by Sophie's journey back into the painful memories of her past. The movie becomes an act of discovery, as the naive young American, his mind filled with notions of love, death, and honor, becomes the friend of a woman who has seen so much hate, death, and dishonor that the only way she can continue is by blotting out the past, and drinking and loving her way into temporary oblivion. It's basically a three-character movie, and the casting, as I suggested, is just right. Meryl Streep is a wonder as Sophie. She does not quite look or sound or feel like the Meryl Streep we have seen before in *The Deer Hunter* or *Manhattan* or *The French Lieutenant's Woman.* There is something juicier about her this time; she is merrier and sexier, more playful and cheerful in the scenes before she begins to tell Stingo the truth about her past. Streep plays the Brooklyn scenes with an enchanting Polish-American accent (she has the first accent I've ever wanted to hug), and she plays the flashbacks in subtitled German and Polish. There is hardly an emotion that Streep doesn't touch in this movie, and yet we're never aware of her straining. This is one of the most astonishing and yet one of the most unaffected and natural performances I can imagine.

Kevin Kline plays Nathan, the crazy romantic who convinces everyone he's on the brink of finding the cure for polio and who wavers uncertainly between anger and manic exhilaration. Peter MacNicol is Stingo, the kid who is left at the end to tell the story. Kline, MacNicol, and Streep make such good friends in this movie—despite all the suffering they go through—that we really do believe the kid when he refuses to act on an unhappy revelation, insisting, "These are my *friends*. I love them!"

Sophie's Choice is a fine, absorbing, wonderfully acted, heartbreaking movie. It is about three people who are faced with a series of choices, some frivolous, some tragic. As they flounder in the bewilderment of being human in an age of madness, they become our friends, and we love them.

Soul Man ★

PG-13, 101 m., 1986

C. Thomas Howell (Mark Watson), Arye Gross (Gordon Bloomfield), Rae Dawn Chong (Sarah Walker), James Earl Jones (Professor Banks). Directed by Steve Miner and produced by Steve Tisch. Screenplay by Carol Black.

Although the premise of *Soul Man* was greeted with widespread derision, it actually had a lot of potential—even if it was made into a lamebrained movie. The film's hero is a U.C.L.A. graduate who poses as a black in order to qualify for a scholarship to Harvard Law School, and the movie follows him through his first semester, as he spars with a black professor, falls in love with a black woman, and experiences racism at first hand.

This is a genuinely interesting idea, and filled with dramatic possibilities, but the movie approaches it on the level of a dim-witted sitcom. Thoughtful scenes are followed by slapstick, emotional moments lead right into farce, and the movie doesn't have an ounce of true moral courage; it sidesteps every single big issue that it raises. *Soul Man* hardly even seems to realize, for example, that the real subject of the film is not race but ethics—the ethics of pretending to be someone you are not, and lying to others about it.

In the movie, a rich Southern California kid (C. Thomas Howell) is admitted to Harvard, but his millionaire father won't pay the tuition. Howell is distraught, until he finds out about a full scholarship available to a black applicant in the L.A. area. He applies, wins the scholarship, and makes himself look black by getting a curly permanent and overdosing on suntan tablets. Is he convincing as a black? No, but in this movie, who cares?

As a "black" at Harvard, Howell encounters a landlord who doesn't want to rent to him, a father who doesn't want him dating his daughter, and a lot of ethnic jokes. He also encounters a black professor (James Earl Jones) who holds him to the highest standards, and a fellow student (Rae Dawn Chong) who he falls in love with. During these early passages in the movie, I kept urging it to work, because I felt the situation was so interesting. But this movie doesn't have the wit to work; it doesn't grapple sincerely with any of its issues, but just uses them as set-ups for predictable punchlines.

If the movie's first half is filled with unrealized potential, the second half is absolutely dreadful. Consider, for example, the scene where Howell has his parents (who do not know he is "black") in the kitchen, a sex-mad white girl in his bedroom, and Rae Dawn Chong in the living room. He races back and forth like a Marx Brother, pulling on a ski cap so his parents can't see his face, and we realize that all of this idiotic farce is an excuse for avoiding the tough dialogue that would have to be written for realistic scenes involving these people.

Then there's the matter of the student's deception. Are we all agreed that it is not only a moral but a criminal offense to fraudulently accept that scholarship? And what about Howell's lies to Chong, who believes he is really black? At the end of the movie, the big scene has Howell apologizing to Jones, who announces the school will not press charges. That scene is absolutely impossible—he would have been thrown out of Harvard in a second, his reputation ruined. But what's worse is that, in a movie filled with useless scenes, there is no scene at all in which Howell and Chong really discuss what he did, and why.

There are two good performances in this movie, by Chong and Jones. C. Thomas Howell seems to have wandered in from a superficial teen-age comedy; there is never a moment when I felt he was really experiencing any of the feelings in this movie. No, not even the moment when he gets to feeling so black that he tosses around a symbolic basketball and confesses that he doesn't like the Beach Boys so much anymore.

Sounder ★ ★ ★ ★
G, 105 m., 1972

Cicely Tyson (Rebecca Morgan), Paul Winfield (Nathan Lee Morgan), Kevin Hooks (David Lee Morgan), Carmen Mathews (Mrs. Boatwright), Taj Mahal (Ike), James Best (Sheriff Young), Janet MacLachlan (Camille, the Teacher), Sylvia (Kuumba), Williams (Harriet). Directed by Martin Ritt and produced by Robert B. Radnitz. Screenplay by John Alonzo.

Sounder is a story simply told and universally moving. It is one of the most compassionate and truthful of movies, and there's not a level where it doesn't succeed completely. It's one of those rare films that can communicate fully to a child of nine or ten, and yet contains depths and subtleties to engross any adult. The story is so simple because it involves, not so much what people do, but how they change and grow. Not a lot happens on the action level, but there's tremendous psychological movement in *Sounder,* and hardly ever do movies create characters who are so full and real, and relationships that are so loving.

The movie is set in rural Louisiana in about 1933, and involves a black sharecropper family. The boy, David Lee, is twelve or thirteen years old, just the right age to delight in the night-time raccoon hunts he goes on with his father and their hound, Sounder. The hunts are not recreation but necessity. There is no food and no money, and at last, the father steals a ham in desperation. He's sentenced to a year at hard labor, and it's up to the mother and the children (two of them too small to be much help) to get the crop in. They do. "We'll do it, because we have to do it," the mother says.

The boy sets out to find the labor camp where his father is being held. He never does, but he comes across a black school where the teacher talks to him of some of the accomplishments of blacks in America. He decides that he would like to attend her school; by special dispensation, he had been attending a segregated school near his home as sort of a back-row, second-class student.

He returns home, the father returns home, and there is a heartbreaking moment when, for the boy, no school in the world could take him away from this family that loves him. He runs away, filled with angry tears, but his father comes after him and talks to him simply and bluntly: "You lose some of the time what you go after, but you lose all of the time what you don't go after."

The father has a totally realistic understanding of the trap that Southern society set for black sharecroppers, and he is determined to see his son break out of that trap, or else. The scene between the father (Paul Winfield) and the son (Kevin Hooks) is one of the greatest celebrations of the bond between parents and children that I have ever seen in a movie. But it is only one of the scenes like that in *Sounder.*

The mother is played by Cicely Tyson, and it is a wonder to see the subtleties in her performance. We have seen her with her family, and we know her strength and intelligence. Then we see her dealing with the white power structure, and her behavior toward it is in a style born of cynicism and necessity. She will say what they want to hear in order to get what she wants to get.

The story is about love, loss, anger, and hope. That's all, and it's enough; not many movies deal with even one of those subjects with any honesty or power. Hope is probably the emotion evoked most by *Sounder*—the hope of the parents that the school will free their bright and capable son from the dead end of sharecropping; the hope of the teacher, who is representative of the Southern growth of black pride and black studies; and, of course, the boy's hope.

The movie was attacked in a few quarters because of this orientation. It is merely "liberal," some of its critics say. It isn't realistic, it's deceiving. I don't think so. I think it has to be taken as a story about one black family and its struggle. It is, I suppose, a "liberal" film, and that has come to be a bad word in these times when liberalism is supposed to stand for compromise—for good intentions but no action. This movie stands for a lot more than that, and we live in such illiberal times that *Sounder* comes as a reminder of former dreams. It's not surprising that the boy in the movie reminded Mrs. Coretta Scott King of her husband.

This is a film for the family to see. That doesn't mean it's a children's film. The producer, Robert B. Radnitz, has specialized in authentic and serious family films (*A Dog of Flanders, The Other Side of the Mountain*). The director, Martin Ritt, is one of the best

American filmmakers (his credits include *Hud*, *The Molly Maguires*, and *The Great White Hope*), and he has made *Sounder* as a serious and ambitious undertaking. There is no condescension in it, no simplification. The relationship between the man and wife is so completely realized on a mature level that it comes as a shock; we'd forgotten that authentic grown-ups can be portrayed in films. We'd thought, for a moment, that to be a movie adult you had to drive a fast car, be surrounded by sexy dames, and pack an arsenal. *Sounder* proves it isn't so.

Southern Comfort ★ ★ ★
R, 106 m., 1981

Keith Carradine (Spencer), Powers Boothe (Hardin), Fred Ward (Reece), Franklyn Seales (Simms), T.K. Carter (Cribbs), Lewis Smith (Stuckey). Directed by Walter Hill and produced by David Filer. Screenplay by Michael Kane, Hill, and Giler.

Southern Comfort is a well-made film, but it suffers from a certain predictability. I suspect the predictability is part of the movie's point. The film is set in the Cajun country of Louisiana, in 1973, and it follows the fortunes of a National Guard unit that gets lost in the bayous and stumbles into a metaphor for America's involvement in Vietnam.

The movie's approach is direct, and its symbolism is all right there on the surface. From the moment we discover that the guardsmen are firing blanks in their rifles, we somehow know that the movie's going to be about their impotence in a land where they do not belong. And as the weekend soldiers are relentlessly hunted down and massacred by the local Cajuns (who are intimately familiar with the bayou), we think of the uselessness of American technology against the Viet Cong.

The guardsmen are clearly strangers in a strange land, and they make fatal blunders right at the outset. They cut the nets of a Cajun fisherman, they "borrow" three Cajun boats, and they mock the Cajuns by firing blank machine-gun rounds at them. The Cajuns are not amused. By the film's end, guardsmen will have been shot dead, impaled, hung, drowned in quicksand, and attacked by savage dogs. And all the time they try to protect themselves with a parody of military discipline, while they splash in circles and rescue helicopters roar uselessly overhead. All this action is shown with great effect in *Southern Comfort*. The movie portrays the bayous as a world of dangerous beauty. Greens and yellows and browns shimmer in the sunlight, and rare birds call to one another, and the Cajuns slip noiselessly behind trees while the guardsmen wander about making fools and targets of themselves. *Southern Comfort* is a film of drum-tight professionalism.

It is also, unfortunately, so committed to its allegorical vision that it never really comes alive as a story about people. That is the major weakness of its director, the talented young Walter Hill, whose credits include *The Warriors*, *The Driver*, and *The Long Riders*. He knows how to make a movie look great, and how to fill it with energy and style. But I suspect he is uncertain about the human dimensions of his characters. And to cover that up, he makes them into larger-than-life stick figures, into symbolic units who stand for everything except themselves. That tendency was carried to its extreme in *The Driver*, a thriller in which the characters were given titles (the Driver, the Girl) rather than names. It was also Hill's approach in *The Warriors*, which translated New York gang warfare into the terms of Greek myth. His approach bothered me so much in *The Warriors* that I overlooked, I now believe, some of the real qualities of that film. It bothers me again in *Southern Comfort*.

Who *are* these men? Of the Cajuns we learn nothing: They are invisible assassins. Of the guardsmen, however, we learn little more. One is swollen with authority. One intends to look out for himself. One is weak, one is strong, and only the man played by Keith Carradine seems somewhat balanced and sane. Once we get the psychological labels straight, there are no further surprises. And once we understand the structure of the movie (guardsmen slog through bayous, get picked off one by one), the only remaining question is whether any of them will finally survive.

That's the weakness of the storytelling. The strength of the movie is in its look, in its superb use of its locations, and in Hill's mastery of action sequences that could have been repetitive. The action is also good: The actors are given little scope to play with in their characters, but they do succeed in creating plausible weekend soldiers. "We are the Guard!" they chant, and we believe them. And there is one moment of inspired irony, when they are lost, cold, wet, hungry, and in mortal fear of their lives, and one guy asks, "Why don't we call in the National Guard?"

Spaceballs ★ ★ ½
PG, 100 m., 1987

Mel Brooks (Skroob/Yogurt), John Candy (Barf), Rick Moranis (Dark Helmet), Bill Pullman (Lone Starr), Daphne Zuniga (Princess Vespa), Dick Van Patten (King Roland), Joan Rivers (Voice of Dot). Directed and produced by Mel Brooks. Screenplay by Brooks.

Did Mel Brooks make *Spaceballs* to celebrate the tenth anniversary of the *Star Wars* saga? 1987 celebrates the first decade of George Lucas's great entertainment, and now here is Brooks's satire, complete with Dark Helmet and Pizza the Hutt.

I enjoyed a lot of the movie, but I kept thinking I was at a revival. The strangest thing about *Spaceballs* is that it should have been made several years ago, before our appetite for *Star Wars* satires had been completely exhausted.

Brooks's first features, *The Producers* and *The Twelve Chairs,* told original stories. Since then, he has specialized in movie satires; his targets include Frankenstein, Hitchcock, Westerns, silent movies, and historical epics. I usually find a few very big laughs and a lot of smaller ones in his movies, but the earlier ones are stronger than the more recent films, and I keep wishing Brooks would satirize something current and tricky, like the John Hughes teen-age films, instead of picking on old targets. With *Spaceballs,* he has made the kind of movie that didn't really need a Mel Brooks. In bits and pieces, one way or another, this movie already has been made over the last ten years by countless other satirists.

After a fabulous and increasingly funny opening shot of one of those massive George Lucas space cruisers, he launches into a cheerfully silly story about the planet Spaceball and its attempt to steal the atmosphere of its peaceful neighbor, Druidia.

The heroes and villains are all clones of *Star Wars* regulars. Bill Pullman is Lone Starr, a free-lance space jockey. John Candy is Barf, a "mog" (half man, half dog). Rick Moranis is Dark Helmet, always complaining about something. Daphne Zuniga plays Princess Vespa, and so on. Brooks himself gives two of the movie's best performances: as Skroob, the president of Spaceball, and as Yogurt, the wise old man who keeps saying "May the Schwartz be with you" as if he's sure it will eventually get a laugh.

The movie's dialogue is constructed out of funny names, puns, and old jokes. Sometimes it's painfully juvenile. But there are some great visual gags in the movie, and the best is Pizza the Hutt, a creature who roars and cajoles while cheese melts off its forehead and big hunks of pepperoni slide down its jowls.

I dunno. How do you review a movie like this, anyway? I guess by saying whether you laughed or not. I did laugh, but not enough to recommend the film. I keep waiting for Mel Brooks to do something really great, instead of these machine-made satires, where three-quarters of the invention goes into the special-effects technology.

As a producer of other people's movies, Brooks has an amazing track record; his company made *The Elephant Man, My Favorite Year, Frances,* and *The Fly.* But Brook's intelligence and taste seem to switch off when he makes his own films, and he aims for broad, dumb comedy: Jokes about names with dirty double meanings are his big specialty. Maybe the reason *Spaceballs* isn't better is that he was deliberately aiming low, going for the no-brainer satire. What does he *really* think about *Star Wars,* or anything else, for that matter?

Brooks got his start as a writer for Sid Caesar, and sometimes he still seems to be writing for early 1950s television. He is smarter than his films, and sometimes that translates into a feeling that he underestimates his audiences. He is potentially a great comedy director. In 1987, he shouldn't be making *Star Wars* satires. May the Schwartz help him to realize his potential, already.

The Spider's Stratagem ★ ★ ★
PG, 100 m., 1973

Giulio Brogi (Athos Magnani), Alida Valli (Draifa), Tino Scotti (Costa), Pippo Campanini (Gaibazzi). Directed by Bernardo

Bertolucci and produced by Giovani Bertolucci. Screenplay by Bernardo Bertolucci.

Thirty years before, Athos Magnani was a great man, a popular hero, and the leading anti-fascist in the district. But then he was killed, and time has stood still for his little town ever since. It is filled with "old men, madmen, and mad old men," and even though Athos is thirty years dead, he is still the most vital presence in the community.

One day a young man gets off the train for a visit in the village. He is Athos Magnani, Jr., and he looks exactly like his father—so much so, indeed, that his father's mistress attempts to substitute him and begin life all over again in the late 1930s. The son wants to find the killer of his father, in a way. In another way, *The Spider's Stratagem* isn't about a search for a killer, or the truth from the past, or anything else, except a question of human identity: What's more important, who we are, or who people think we are?

The movie is by Bernardo Bertolucci, who later made *Last Tango in Paris.* It's a movie with a beautiful cinematic grace, a way of establishing atmosphere and furthering plot without a lot of talking. We learn all we need to know about the relationship between the father, the son, and the town, in one group of opening shots. The boy stops on "Via Athos Magnani"—a street named for his father—and then approaches the square where his father's statue stands. Bertolucci lines up the deep-focus shot so that it begins with the son completely blocking out the statue. Then, as he walks through the square, the statue completely obscures the son.

He's on a strange sort of quest. He doesn't seem to really care much who killed his father (if you'll forgive me for not taking the plot at quite face value). In a way, he is his own father, or his father's alter-ego. Magnani was the only vital life force in the district, and the district defined itself by his energy. Even the fascist brownshirts gained stature and dignity because Magnani opposed them, and Bertolucci demonstrates this with a great scene at an outdoor dance. The brownshirts order the band leader to play the fascist anthem. All dancing stops, and everyone looks at Magnani to see what he'll do. Coolly, elegantly, he selects the most beautiful girl and begins to dance with her.

But this is, alas, the last waltz in town, because before long Magnani is shot during a concert. The events leading up to his death, and the identity of his killers, remain very murky. Three fellow anti-fascists claim to have done it, in order to (a) punish Magnani for squealing to the police, and (b) provide the district with a genuine martyr. But did they really? It's hard to say.

The Spider's Stratagem is not, as you've probably gathered, a mass-audience movie. It will have most appeal to people sensitive to Bertolucci's audacious use of camera movements and colors; Pauline Kael said a long time ago that, of all directors influenced by Godard, Bertolucci has been the only one to extend Godard's way of looking, instead of just copying. *The Spider's Stratagem* documents that, and is better to look at than analyze.

Splash ★ ½

PG, 111 m., 1984

Tom Hanks (Allen), Daryl Hannah (Madison), Eugene Levy (Walter), John Candy (Freddie). Directed by Ron Howard and produced by Brian Grazer. Screenplay by Lowell Ganz, Babaloo Mandel, and Bruce Jay Friedman.

There is a funny movie lurking at the edges of *Splash,* and sometimes it even sneaks on screen and makes us smile. It's too bad the relentlessly conventional minds that made this movie couldn't have made the leap from sitcom to comedy. They must have thought they had such a great idea (Manhattan bachelor falls in love with mermaid) that they couldn't fail. But great ideas are a dime a dozen. *Splash* tells the story of a young man who is twice saved from drowning by a beautiful young mermaid. She falls in love with him and follows him to Manhattan, where he is a fruit and vegetable wholesaler. He falls in love with her. She can, it appears, metamorphose at will, turning her tail into legs. There are a lot of jokes about her total ignorance about all the ways of civilization. She walks naked onto Ellis Island, for example, and eats lobsters—shell and all.

All right. Now that's the situation. But the situation isn't going to be enough. We need some characters here. The mermaid is just fine. As played by the lovely Daryl Hannah, she is young and healthy and touchingly naive. But what about the guy who falls in love with her? It's here that the movie makes its catastrophic casting mistake. You see, they figured they have a comedy as long as the girl has a tail, and a romance whenever she has legs. So they gave her a romantic leading man when they should have given her a lonely guy who could swim. The leading man is Tom Hanks. He is conventionally handsome and passably appealing, and he would do in a secondary role. He'd be great, for example, as the straight-arrow brother. Instead, they make him the mermaid's lover, and they cast John Candy as the brother.

You remember Candy from SCTV. He is the large, shambling, Charles Laughton-type who has such a natural chrisma that he's funny just standing there. They should have made Candy the lover, and Hanks the brother. Then we'd be on the side of this big lunk who suddenly has a mermaid drop into his life and has to explain her to his creepy, swinging-singles brother. Plus, there's the sweet touch that this transcendently sexy mermaid has fallen for the tubby loser with the heart of lust, and not for his slick brother. See what I mean? Instead, they go the other way. John Candy is not used much in the movie, Tom Hanks comes across as a standard young male lead, and they have to concoct a meaningless and boring subplot in order to make the movie long enough. Don't they know in Hollywood that once all the geniuses think they've finished with the screenplay, you just gotta rotate everything 180 degrees and you got a movie?

The Spy Who Loved Me ★ ★ ★ ½

PG, 125 m., 1977

Roger Moore (James Bond), Barbara Bach (Anya Amasova), Curt Jurgens (Stromberg), Richard Kiel (Jaws), Caroline Munro (Naomi), Bernard Lee (M), Desmond Llewelyn (Q), Lois Maxwell (Miss Moneypenny). Directed by Lewis Gilbert and produced by Albert R. Broccoli. Screenplay by Christopher Wood and Richard Maibaum.

The best of the James Bond adventures have always depended on cheerfully silly violence, and *The Spy Who Loved Me* is one of the best. It's heartening to see there's life in the old series yet. The first 007 caper was released twenty-four years ago, and here's Bond back once again with his beautiful girls, his lethal gadgets, and that tuxedo that never seems to wear out no matter how many mountains he climbs or deserts he treks in it.

There have been a lot of obituaries for the 1960s recently, but, no, Virginia, the sixties will never die, not so long as there is another twenty million dollars somewhere in the world to film another James Bond thriller. Bond lives in that yesterday we can vaguely remember: in a world of conspicuous consumption, fast cars, unliberated women, bizarre weapons, man-eating creatures of land, air, and sea, archvillains with German accents, and a British Empire upon which the sun has not yet set, although it's getting rather dusky out. The Bond universe is an anachronism, but one we've grown fond of, and *The Spy Who Loved Me* celebrates it with abundant energy. There was a time there, during some of the middle Bonds, when the series seemed to be losing its nerve, to be apologizing for its excesses. But not this time: *The Spy Who Loved Me* is gloriously ridiculous from beginning to end, and that's as it should be.

The stories in a lot of the Bond movies bear only the most tenuous relationship to the original fantasies of Ian Fleming, and that's especially true here. The plot involves a villain named Stromberg, who has a plan to capture nuclear submarines and use them to start World War III, after which he will rule the Earth from his undersea headquarters. British Agent 007 (Roger Moore) is assigned to trace the missing British sub, and Soviet Agent XXX (Barbara Bach) is after the Russian sub.

The chase leads to all sorts of places: Cairo, the pyramids, the desert, Sardinia. And it features the best would-be Bond-killer since the immortal Odd Job in *Goldfinger*; Stromberg's hired assassin, named Jaws (Richard Kiel) stands seven-feet-two inches tall, has hands about the size of the Sears catalog, and sharp steel teeth that can chomp through wood and steel, attacking sharks and foreign agents.

It's in the showdowns with Jaws that the movie has a lot of its fun. Jaws can tear apart vans, kill a shark one-on-one, hurl Bond through the air with ease, but he keeps getting almost killed—and one of the movie's standing jokes is his incredible power of survival. Agents 007 and XXX, meanwhile, make their way through incredible difficulties to the one obligatory scene in every Bond movie—the scene involving a gigantic indoor set where the destruction of the world is being plotted and enemy troops dressed in matching jumpsuits scurry about on catwalks high up under the ceiling.

The movie is jammed with special effects. It contains, in fact, almost as many spectacular stunts and effects as *Star Wars,* although their terrestrial locale may make them seem more routine. There's a car that turns into a submarine, and a tanker that turns into a sub-snatcher, and all sorts of guided missiles and instruments of oceanic warfare and spectacular explosions, and of course the underwater headquarters of the evil Stromberg, with its hungry sharks lurking at the bottom of the elevator shaft. *The Spy Who Loved Me* is in the tradition of the best Bonds: thrilling, sexy, ridiculous, gimmicky, violent, and, what all the Bonds are supposed to be, preposterous escapist fun.

Stakeout ★ ★ ★

R, 115 m., 1987

(See related Film Clip, p. 784.)

Richard Dreyfuss (Chris Lecce), Emilio Estevez (Bill Reimers), Madeleine Stowe (Maria McGuire), Aidan Quinn (Stick), Dan Lauria (Phil Coldshank), Forest Whitaker (Jack Pismo), Ian Tracey (Caylor Reese). Directed by John Badham and produced by Jim Kouf and Cathleen Summers. Screenplay by Kouf.

Richard Dreyfuss has always had a certain cockiness about him. He carries himself like a high-school basketball guard, ready to fake you out and go for the basket. And he talks the same way, often with a little smile to let you know there's an edge to his thinking, an angle. He had that way about him in *The Apprenticeship of Duddy Kravitz,* and he has it still. It keeps me watching him even during the slow passages of his movies; there's always the feeling that what you see is not necessarily all you get.

Dreyfuss and his style are the two best things in *Stakeout,* a movie that consists of a good idea surrounded by a bad one. The good idea is the film's basic premise: Two cops stake out a good-looking woman whose ex-boyfriend is a dangerous escaped convict. During the long, weary hours while they're watching her, one of the cops falls in love. He finds a way to move into her life, leaving his partner stuck across the street with the binoculars.

That's the good idea, further fleshed out with the notion that Dreyfuss and his partner (Emilio Estevez) alternate shifts with two other cops who don't much like them. What would happen if the other cops saw Dreyfuss waking up in bed with the suspect?

The movie's bad idea is that this comic notion needs to be surrounded by a violent thriller. The opening scenes of the film are abrupt and bloody, as the dangerous convict (Aidan Quinn) escapes from prison and heads toward a showdown with Dreyfuss and Estevez. The closing scenes are another bad idea, still one more of those routine Hollywood chases and shootouts, with a fight on a boat for good measure.

The two parts of the movie don't go together. The violence is out of keeping with the humor. The humor can't develop in a context of brutality. And yet there's a long central stretch in the movie when things do work, when the courtship between Dreyfuss and the suspect (Madeleine Stowe) gets interesting. Dreyfuss poses as a telephone repairman, bugs her phones, falls in love with her, and eventually begins conducting his investigation from her bedroom. Estevez is stuck with the essentially thankless role of the guy who has to wait across the street and react to everything, but his reactions provide a lot of the movie's humor.

I liked the relationship between Dreyfuss and Stowe, who plays a headstrong Latino, but I might have liked it more if they had cast a funnier actress in the role—maybe Maria Conchita Alonzo. Since it's likely that the director, John Badham, tested Alonzo for this role, I wonder why he didn't cast her. Perhaps because she has an irrepressible good humor about her, and always seems to be amused by everything; she has the same sort of extra angle that Dreyfuss delivers. Maybe Badham was afraid that good humor would work against the violence of his opening and closing scenes.

But all that's speculation. All I can say is *Stakeout* is an example of a movie that would have been a lot better if the filmmakers had been prepared to trust the human dimensions of their characters—to follow these people where their personalities led. Instead, Badham takes out an insurance policy by adding the assembly-line violence.

What is it? Has mainstream Hollywood so lost touch with simple human nature that you can't have a cop movie without everyone being blown away?

Stand and Deliver ★ ★ 1/2
PG-13, 106 m., 1988 ✓

Edward James Olmos (Jaime Escalante), Lou Diamond Phillips (Angel), Rosana De Soto (Fabiola Escalante), Andy Garcia (Ramirez), Virginia Paris (Chairwoman Ortega), Carmen Argenziano (Principal Molina). Directed by Ramon Menendez and produced by Tom Musca. Screenplay by Menendez and Musca.

There were moments in *Stand and Deliver* that moved me very deeply, and other moments so artificial and contrived that I wanted to edit them out, right then and there. The result is a film that makes a brave, bold statement about an unexpected subject—but that lacks the full emotional power it really should have.

Stand and Deliver tells the story of a high school mathematics teacher who takes a class of losers and potential drop-outs and transforms them, in the course of one school year, into kids who have learned so much that eighteen of them are able to pass a tough college credit calculus exam at the end of the year—an exam so hard that only two percent of students nationwide can pass it, although everyone in this class does.

The story is based on fact, on the life of Jaime Escalante, an actual East Los Angeles man who left a higher-paying job in business to return to education and prove something. What he proved is that motivation and hard work can rewrite the destinies of kids that society might be willing to write off.

Escalante, played in the film by Edward James Olmos, faces a disheartening challenge on the first day of school. His class is undisciplined, unmotivated, and rebellious. He doesn't confront them; he outflanks them. Adopting a weird sideways shuffle and a strange habit of talking to himself, he strikes them at first as simply bizarre; they stop making noise because they want to hear what foolish thing he'll say next.

Then he starts teaching, using examples out of the everyday lives of his students, making them think things out for themselves, announcing that the "punishment" for not working hard in class is to be banished from the class—a class most of the kids would rather be out of, anyway. The kids themselves are amazed that this strategy works, and more amazed still to find that they're expected to do thirty hours of homework a week, and come in on Saturday mornings for extra classes.

All of this material is fine and strong. Not so fascinating, however, are the vignettes of student life outside the school. Some of these scenes are important to the story—as when we discover why it is so hard for some of the kids to find time for their homework—but others, including a high school romance, are simply marking time.

I was also disturbed by the cloudiness of the screenplay in the movie's most crucial scene. After the eighteen kids have taken, and passed, the exam, their test scores are questioned by the Educational Testing Service for two reasons: (1) It seems extremely unlikely that all of these kids could pass the exam without cheating, and (2) they all suspiciously made some of the same mistakes.

Because we have been though the movie and the experience with the kids, we know they were not cheating. But the ETS authorities cannot be blamed for their suspicions. What the screenplay needed, I think, was at least one speech in simple, clear dialogue, explaining what I assume to be true: The kids all made the same mistake because their teacher made that mistake in teaching them. There is a scene in the movie that seems to suggest this possibility; the teacher comes up with an assertion that everyone in the classroom tells him is wrong, but he won't back down. However, that scene ends without making it clear whether the teacher was wrong, and the later scene never explains the similar wrong answers. This adds unnecessary cloudiness to no purpose.

Other things in the movie may bother some viewers more than they did me. The Olmos performance takes a lot of chances. He is so mannered in his stooped shuffle and his sideways manner of expressing himself, that perhaps he should have toned it down once he'd made his point. The kids in his class, on the other hand, do a good job of avoiding the usual high school clichés—especially Lou Diamond Phillips, who, in a wonderful scene, explains why he needs two sets of textbooks—one to keep at school and the other to keep at home, since it would never do for his street friends to see him carrying books.

The last shot of *Stand and Deliver* puts some astonishing statistics on the screen, indicating that in every year since 1982 (the year of the story), even more students from this East L.A. high school have passed the difficult ETS exam. That is a dramatic story, and this is a worthy movie for telling it. I only wish I hadn't been reminded, so often, that the movie was making it feel just a little better than life.

STAR 80 ★ ★ ★ ★

R, 102 m., 1983

Mariel Hemingway (Dorothy Stratten), Eric Roberts (Paul Snider), Cliff Robertson (Hugh Hefner), Carroll Baker (Dorothy's Mother), Roger Rees (Aram Nicholas). Directed by Bob Fosse and produced by Wolfgang Glattes and Kenneth Utt. Screenplay by Fosse.

Bob Fosse dresses all in black and makes films about the demonic undercurrents in our lives. Look at his credits: *Cabaret, Lenny, All That Jazz*, and now *STAR 80*. Although his Broadway musicals have been upbeat entertainment, he seems to see the movie camera as a device for peering into our shames and secrets. *STAR 80* is his most despairing film. After the Nazi decadence of *Cabaret*, after the drug abuse and self-destruction in *Lenny*, and the death-obsessed hero of *All That Jazz*, here is a movie that begins with violent death and burrows deeper. There were times when I could hardly keep my eyes on the screen, and a moment near the end when I seriously asked myself if I wanted to continue watching.

And yet I think this is an important movie. Devastating, violent, hopeless, and important, because it holds a mirror up to a part of the world we live in, and helps us see it more clearly. In particular, it examines the connection between fame and obscurity, between those who have a moment of praise and notoriety, and those who see themselves as condemned to stand always at the edge of the spotlight. Like Martin Scorsese's *Taxi Driver*, it is a movie about being an outsider and about going crazy with the pain of rejection.

The movie tells the story of two young people from Vancouver. One of them was Dorothy Stratten, a shy, pretty blonde who thought her hands and feet were too big, who couldn't understand why anyone would value her, and who was close enough to some sort of idealized North American fantasy that she became the 1979 Playmate of the Year. The other was Paul Snider, a Vancouver small-timer who worked as a salesman, con man, and part-time pimp. When Paul saw Dorothy behind the counter of a hamburger stand, he knew she was his ticket to the big time. Dorothy resisted his compliments at first, but he was so relentless in his adoration that she surrendered to his fantasies. Paul masterminded Dorothy's rise. He arranged the photo session that attracted the eye of *Playboy*'s talent scouts. He bought her dresses and flowers. He pushed her into the limelight and then edged into it next to her. But then she went to Los Angeles and found the real stardust, the flattery of the Playboy Mansion, the attentions of young men whose sports cars were bought with their own money, while Paul's was bought with hers.

Paul had a vanity license plate made: STAR 80. But Dorothy had moved out of his world, had been given a taste of a larger world that, frankly, Paul didn't have the class to appreciate. She fell in love with a movie director. She went out of town on location. She and Paul drifted apart, and he went mad with jealousy and resentment. On August 14, 1980, Dorothy went back to the shabby little North Hollywood bungalow they had rented together, and Paul murdered her.

STAR 80 begins with the murder. Everything else is in flashback, and, therefore, the film has no really happy scenes. Dorothy's triumphs are all stained with our knowledge of what will happen. Every time she smiles, it's poignant. We know Paul will go berserk and kill her, and so we can see from the beginning that he's unbalanced. Fosse knows his material is relentlessly depressing, and so he doesn't try for moments of relief. Although we enter the world of *Playboy* and see Dorothy partying in the mansion and posing in nude modeling sessions, although the whole movie is concerned with aspects of sex, there is never an erotic moment. Fosse keeps his distance, regarding Dorothy more as a case study than as a fantasy. That makes Mariel Hemingway's performance as Dorothy all the more powerful. She has been remade into the sleek, glossy Playmate image, but she still has the adolescent directness and naiveté that she used so well in *Manhattan* and *Personal Best.* She's a big kid. Her eyes open wide when she gets to Los Angeles, and she's impressed by the attention she's receiving. The character she plays is simple, uncomplicated, shallow, and so trusting that she never does realize how dangerous Paul is.

The other performances in the movie are equally strong. Eric Roberts as Paul even succeeds in persuading us to accept him as a suffering human being rather than as a hateful killer. Like Robert De Niro as Travis Bickle in *Taxi Driver,* he fills his role with so much reality that we feel horror, but not blame. Carroll Baker, as Dorothy's mother, is heartbreakingly incapable of connecting in any meaningful way with her daughter.

What is the point of *STAR 80?* I'm not sure, just as I wasn't sure of the points of *In Cold Blood* or *Lacombe, Lucien* or "The Executioner's Song." There is no redemption in the movie, no catharsis. It unblinkingly looks at the short life of a simple, pretty girl, and the tortured man who made her into something he couldn't have, and then killed her for it. The movie seems to be saying: These things happen. After it was over, I felt bad for Dorothy Stratten. In fact, for everybody.

A Star Is Born ★ ★ ★ ★

PG, 175 m., 1954 (1983)

Judy Garland, James Mason, Jack Carson, Tommy Noonan, Charles Bickford. Directed by George Cukor.

A Star Is Born hasn't merely been restored. It has been rediscovered. George Cukor's 1954 movie, which starred James Mason and Judy Garland in the story of Hollywood lives destroyed by alcoholism, always has been considered one of the great tear-jerking Hollywood melodramas, populated with bravura performances. But has it ever been praised for its purely cinematic qualities? I don't think so, and yet it showed Cukor's mastery not only of the big effects, but also of subtle lighting and exquisite compositions. It's an irony, but if Warner Brothers hadn't chopped twenty-seven minutes out of the movie in 1954 and tried to throw them away, the whole movie never would have been rereleased in its current form. It is very good to have the missing footage back, of course, but it's even better to have the whole movie back again, a landmark of Hollywood melodrama.

Although this version is exactly as long as Cukor's final cut in 1954, it doesn't have quite all the footage. Two major production numbers and a charming little scene in a drive-in restaurant were rediscovered by film historian Ron Haver (after months of detective work). Haver also found the movie's complete stereo soundtrack, but about seven minutes of the visual footage seem to be gone forever—and so this restoration uses an effective montage of music, dialogue, and production stills to bridge the gaps. Seeing this version of the movie makes it clear what major surgery was performed by Warner Brothers. The studio chopped out an entire Judy Garland musical number, "Here's What I'm Here For," filled with fire and energy. That's wonderful to have back again, but the other major restored sequence is almost indispensable to the film.

It's a scene from fairly early in the film. The alcoholic movie star (Mason) has convinced the young band vocalist (Garland) to risk everything and try for a movie career. With his support, she's on the brink of stardom. She's recording a song with a studio orchestra, and afterward she rests on a staircase with Mason. He proposes marriage. She says he drinks too much. He promises to reform. Neither one realizes that their whole conversation is being recorded by an eavesdropping overhead mike. Then, as a joke by the director, the proposal is played back for all the musicians to hear—and Garland accepts. By taking out that proposal scene, Warner Brothers had a movie that skipped unconvincingly from Garland's movie debut to her elopement with Mason. The earlier missing footage—the scenes represented by the still photos—also represented important bridging material, covering an uncertain period during which Garland thinks Mason has forgotten about her. Without those scenes, the movie skips directly from Garland's early hopes to her first day at the studio, with no period of uncertainty.

The missing scenes are good to have back again. But the movie's central scenes are even better to see again. There is an absolutely brilliantly lit and directed scene in a darkened nightclub, with Garland singing while the camera prowls silently among the musicians' instruments; it's one of the best examples of composition I've ever seen. And near the end of the movie, there's Garland's big, bravura scene, in which she interrupts a big production number for a heart-rending dressing-room conversation with her studio chief (Charles Bickford). And then, of course, there is Mason's sad, lonely walk into the sea, and the movie's unforgettable closing line: "Good evening, everyone. This is Mrs. Norman Maine."

A Star Is Born is one of the rare films that successfully integrate music with drama; it's not exactly a musical, but it has more music than most musicals. It's also not exactly a serious drama—it's too broad and predictable for that—but it's the sort of exaggerated, wide-gauge melodrama that Rainer Werner Fassbinder would experiment with twenty years later; a movie in which larger-than-life characters are used to help us see the melodramatic clichés that we do, indeed, sometimes pattern our own lives after.

I was lucky enough to visit George Cukor at his Hollywood home in December of 1981. He said he had never seen the butchered version of *A Star Is Born* and never would. "If they wanted it shorter," he said, "I could have sweated out twenty-five minutes here and there, and nobody would have missed them. Instead, they took an ax to the movie." George Cukor died on the evening before he was to see a rough version of this restored print. That is sad, but then Cukor, of course, knew what his original movie looked like. Now the rest of us can know, too.

Star Trek: The Motion Picture ★ ★ ★

G, 132 m., 1979

William Shatner (Kirk), Leonard Nimoy (Spock), DeForest Kelley ("Bones" McCoy), James Doohan (Scotty), George Takei (Sulu), Walter Koenig (Chekov). Directed by Robert Wise and produced by Gene Roddenberry. Screenplay by Harold Livingston.

Two things occurred to me as I watched *Star Trek:*

• The producers have succeeded at great expense in creating a toy for the eyes. This movie is fun to watch.

• Epic science fiction stories, with their cosmic themes and fast truths about the nature of mankind, somehow work best when the actors are unknown to us. The presence of the *Star Trek* characters and actors—who have become so familiar to us on television—tends in a strange way to undermine this movie. The audience walks in with a possessive, even patronizing attitude toward Kirk and Spock and Bones, and that interferes with the creation of the "sense of wonder" that science fiction is all about.

Let's begin with the toy for the eyes. The *Star Trek* movie is fairly predictable in its plot. We more or less expected that two of the frequent ingredients in the television episodes would be here, and they are: a confrontation between Starship *Enterprise* and some sort of alien entity, and a conclusion in which basic human values are affirmed in a hostile universe. In *Star Trek: The Motion Picture,* the alien entity is an unimaginably vast alien spaceship from somewhere out at the edge of the galaxy. The movie opens as it's discovered racing directly toward Earth, and it seems to be hostile. Where has it come from, and what does it want?

The Starship *Enterprise,* elaborately rebuilt, is assigned to go out to intercept it, with Admiral Kirk, of course, in charge. And scenes dealing with the *Enterprise* and the other ship will make up most of the movie—if the special effects aren't good, the movie's not going to work. But they are good, as, indeed, they should be: The first special effects team on this movie was fired, and the film's release was delayed a year while these new effects were devised and photographed. (The effects get better, by the way, as the movie progresses. The alien ship looks great but the spaceports and futuristic cities near the film's beginning loom fairly phony.)

The *Enterprise,* perhaps deliberately, looks a lot like other spaceships we've seen in *2001, Silent Running, Star Wars,* and *Alien.* Kubrick's space odyssey set a visual style for the genre that still seems to be serviceable. But the look of the other spaceship in *Star Trek* is more awesome and original. It seems to reach indefinitely in all directions, the *Enterprise* is a mere speck inside of it, and the contents of the alien vessel include images of the stars and planets it has passed en route, as well as enormous rooms or spaces that seem to be states of a computer-mind. This is terrific stuff.

But now we get to the human level (or the half-human level, in the case of Mr. Spock). The characters in this movie are part of our cultural folklore; the *Star Trek* television episodes have been rerun time and time again. Trekkies may be unhappy with me for saying this, but there are ways in which our familiarity with the series works against the effectiveness of this movie. On the one hand we have incomprehensible alien forces and a plot that reaches out to the edge of the galaxy. On the other hand, confronting these vast forces, we have television pop heroes. It's great to enjoy the in-jokes involving the relationships of the *Enterprise* crew members and it's great that Trekkies can pick up references meant for them, but the extreme familiarity of the Star Trek characters somehow tends to break the illusion in the big scenes involving the alien ship.

Such reservations aside, *Star Trek: The Motion Picture* is probably about as good as we could have expected. It lacks the dazzling brilliance and originality of *2001* (which was an extraordinary one-of-a-kind film). But on its own terms it's a very well-made piece of work, with an interesting premise. The alien spaceship turns out to come from a mechanical or computer civilization, one produced by artificial intelligence and yet poignantly "human" in the sense that it has come all this way to seek out the secrets of its own origins, as we might.

There is, I suspect, a sense in which you can be too sophisticated for your own good when you see a movie like this. Some of the early reviews seemed pretty blasé, as if the critics didn't allow themselves to relish the film before racing out to pigeonhole it. My inclination, as I slid down in my seat and the stereo sound surrounded me, was to relax and let the movie give me a good time. I did and it did.

Star Trek II: The Wrath of Khan

★ ★ ★

PG, 113 m., 1982

William Shatner (Kirk), Leonard Nimoy (Spock), Ricardo Montalban (Khan), DeForest Kelley ("Bones" McCoy), Kirstie Alley (Lieutenant Saavik). Directed by Nicholas Meyer and produced by Robert Sallin. Screenplay by Jack B. Sowards.

The peculiar thing about Spock is that, being Vulcan and therefore possessing no human emotions, he consistently, if dispassionately, behaves as if he possessed very heroic human emotions indeed. He makes a choice in *Star Trek II* that would be made only by a hero, a fool, or a Vulcan. And when he makes his decision, the movie rises to one of its best scenes, because the *Star Trek* stories have always been best when they centered around their characters. Although I liked the special effects in the first movie, they were probably not the point; fans of the TV series wanted to see their favorite characters again, and *Trek II* understood that desire and acted on it.

Time has passed since the last episode. Kirk has retired to an administrative post. Spock is commanding the *Enterprise,* with a lot of new faces in the crew. The ship is conducting tests of the Genesis device, a new invention which, if I understand it correctly, is capable of seeding a barren planet with luxuriant life. (Genesis is actually considered to be a weapon, but the logic escaped me.) Scouting for barren planets, *Enterprise* discovers one that seems to be dead, but its instruments pick up a small speck of life. Crew members investigate, and find the planet inhabited by an outlaw named Khan, who was exiled there years ago by Kirk, and has brooded of vengeance ever since.

Khan is played as a cauldron of resentment by Ricardo Montalban, and his performance is so strong that he helps illustrate a general principle involving not only *Star Trek* but *Star Wars* and all the epic serials, especially the James Bond movies: Each film is only as good as its villain. Since the heroes and the gimmicks tend to repeat from film to film, only a great villain can transform a good try into a triumph. In a curious way, Khan captures our sympathy, even though he is an evil man who introduces loathesome creatures into the ear canals of two *Enterprise* crew members. Montalban doesn't overact. He plays the character as a man of deeply wounded pride, whose bond of hatred with Admiral Kirk is stronger even than his traditional villain's desire to rule the universe.

There is a battle in outer space in this movie, a particularly inept one that owes more to "Captain Video" than to state-of-the-art special effects. I always love it when they give us spaceships capable of leaping across the universe, and then arm them with weapons so puny that a direct hit merely blows up a few control boards and knocks people off their feet. Somehow, though, I don't much care if the battles aren't that amazing, because the story doesn't depend on them. It's about a sacrifice made by Spock, and it draws on the sentiment and audience identification developed over the years by the TV series.

Perhaps because of that bond, and the sense that an episode may be over but the *Enterprise* will carry on, the movie doesn't feel that it needs an ending in a conventional sense. The film closes with the usual *Star Trek* end narration, all about the ship's mission and its quest, and we are obviously being set up for a sequel. You could almost argue that the last few minutes of *Trek II* are a trailer for *Trek III*, but, no, that wouldn't be in the spirit of the *Enterprise*, would it?

Star Trek III: The Search for Spock

★ ★ ★

PG, 105 m., 1984

William Shatner (Kirk), DeForest Kelley ("Bones" McCoy), James Doohan (Scotty), Walter Koenig (Chekov), George Takei (Sulu), Nichell Nichols (Uhura), Mark Lenard (Sarek), Leonard Nimoy (Spock). Directed by Leonard Nimoy and produced by Harve Bennett. Screenplay by Bennett.

Read no further if you don't want to know whether Mr. Spock is alive at the end of *Star Trek III: The Search for Spock.* But, if you, like me, somehow had the notion that there was a 100 percent chance that they would find Spock (if only so he would be available for *Star Trek IV*), then you will be relieved to learn that his rediscovery and rebirth pay due homage to the complexities of the Vulcan civilization. By the end of this movie, all Mr. Spock has to do is raise one of those famous eyebrows, and the audience cheers.

This is a good but not great *Star Trek* movie, a sort of compromise between the first two. The first film was a *Star Wars* road company that depended on special effects. The second movie, the best one so far, remembered what made the *Star Trek* TV series so special: not its special effects, not its space opera gimmicks, but its use of science fiction as a platform for programs about human nature and the limitations of intelligence. *Star Trek III* looks for a balance between the first two movies. It has some of the philosophizing and some of the space opera, and there is an extended special effects scene on the exploding planet Genesis that's the latest word in fistfights on the crumbling edges of fiery volcanoes.

There is also a great-looking enemy spaceship that resembles a predatory bird in flight (although why ships in the vacuum of space require wings is still, of course, a question *Star Trek* prefers not to answer).* The ship is commanded by the fairly slow-witted Klingon warrior Kruge (played by Christopher Lloyd of "Taxi"), who falls for a neat little double cross that is audacious in its simplicity. The movie's plot involves a loyal attempt by the Enterprise crew to return to the planet Genesis in an attempt to reunite Spock's body and spirit. The alien spaceship is in the same sector, attempting to steal the secret of Genesis, a weapon from the last movie that begins by bringing life to dead planets and goes on from there. The showdown between the Klingons and the Enterprise crew resembles, at times, one of those Westerns where first Bart had the draw on Hoppy and then Hoppy had the draw on Bart, but the struggle to the death between Kirk and Kruge takes place against such a great apocalyptic background that we forgive all.

The best thing the *Star Trek* movies have going for them is our familiarity with the TV series. That makes for a sort of storytelling shorthand. At no point during this film, for example, is it ever explained that Vulcans are creatures of logic, not emotion—although we have to know that in order to understand most of the ending. It's not necessary. These characters are under our skins. They resonate, and a thin role in a given story is reinforced by stronger roles in a dozen others. That's sort of reassuring, as (a fanfare, please) the adventure continues.

**Leonard Nimoy sent me a helpful explanation: "The Klingon Bird of Prey has wings for the same reason that our own space shuttle does. It can land in an earth-like atmosphere."*

Star Trek IV: The Voyage Home

★ ★ ★ ½
PG, 119 m., 1986

William Shatner (Admiral Kirk), Leonard Nimoy (Mr. Spock), DeForest Kelley (McCoy), Catherine Hicks (Gillian Taylor), Robert Ellenstein (Federation President), Brock Peters (Cartwright), John Schuck (Klingon Ambassador), Jane Wyatt (Spock's Mother). Directed by Leonard Nimoy and produced by Harve Bennett. Screenplay by Steve Meerson, Peter Krikes, Bennett, and Nicholas Meyer.

When they finished writing the script for *Star Trek IV*, they must have had a lot of silly grins on their faces. This is easily the most absurd of the *Star Trek* stories—and yet, oddly enough, it is also the best, the funniest, and the most enjoyable in simple human terms. I'm relieved that nothing like restraint or common sense stood in their way.

The movie opens with some leftover business from the previous movie, including the Klingon ambassador's protests before the Federation Council; these scenes have very little to do with what the rest of the movie is about, and yet they provide a certain reassurance (like James Bond's ritual flirtation with Miss Moneypenny) that the series remembers that it has a history.

Meanwhile, the crew of the Starship *Enterprise* is still marooned on a faraway planet with the Klingon starship* they commandeered in *Star Trek III*. They vote to return home aboard the alien vessel, but on the way they encounter a strange deep-space probe. It is sending out signals in an unknown language which, when deciphered, turns out to be the song of the humpback whale.

It's at about this point that the script conferences must have really taken off. See if you can follow this: The *Enterprise* crew determines that the probe is zeroing in on earth, and that if no humpback songs are picked up in response, the planet may well be destroyed. Therefore, the crew's mission becomes clear: Since humpback whales are extinct in the twenty-third century, they must journey back through time to the twentieth century, obtain some humpback whales, and return with them to the future—thus saving earth. After they thought up this notion, I hope the writers lit up cigars.

No matter how unlikely the story is, it supplies what is probably the best of the *Star Trek* movies so far, directed with calm professionalism by Leonard Nimoy. What happens is that the *Enterprise* crew land their Klingon starship in San Francisco's Golden Gate Park, surround it with an invisibility shield, and fan out through the Bay Area looking for humpback whales and a ready source of cheap nuclear power.

What makes their search entertaining is that we already know the crew members so well. The cast's easy interaction is unique among movies, because it hasn't been learned in a few weeks of rehearsal or shooting; this is the twentieth anniversary year of "Star Trek," and most of these actors have been working together for most of their professional lives. These characters *know* one another.

An example: Admiral Kirk (William Shatner) and Mr. Spock (Leonard Nimoy) visit a Sea World-type operation, where two humpback whales are held in captivity. Catherine Hicks, as the marine biologist in charge, plans to release the whales, and the Trek crew needs to learn her plans so they can recapture the whales and transport them three centuries into the future.

Naturally, this requires the two men to ask Hicks out to dinner. She asks if they like Italian food, and Kirk and Spock do a delightful little verbal ballet based on the running gag that Spock, as a Vulcan, cannot tell a lie. Find another space opera in which verbal counterpoint creates humor.

The plots of the previous Trek movies have centered around dramatic villains, such as Khan, the dreaded genius played by Ricardo Montalban in *Star Trek II*. This time, the villains are faceless: The international whale hunters who continue to pursue and massacre whales despite clear indications that they will drive these noble mammals from the face of the earth. "To hunt a race to extinction is not logical," Spock calmly observes, but we see shocking footage of whalers who are doing just that.

Instead of providing a single human villain as counterpoint, *Star Trek IV* provides a heroine, in Hicks. She is obviously moved by the plight of the whales, and although at first she not unreasonably doubts Kirk's story that he comes from the twenty-third century, eventually she enlists in the cause and even insists on returning to the future with them, since of course, without humpback whales, the twenty-third century also lacks humpback whale experts.

There are some major action sequences in the movie, but they aren't the high points; the *Star Trek* saga has always depended more on human interaction and thoughtful, cause-oriented plots. What happens in San Francisco is much more interesting than what happens in outer space, and this movie, which might seem to have an unlikely and ungainly plot, is actually the most elegant and satisfying *Star Trek* film so far.

**Leonard Nimoy, we've got you now.*

In Star Trek III, *the Klingon starship was in the shape of a vast, evil bird of prey—inspiring me to ask, in my review of that film, why a starship needed wings to operate in interstellar space. After all, the* Enterprise *certainly didn't have wings.*

You wrote me a helpful note, explaining that the Klingon vessel needed wings because it operated in planetary atmospheres.

All right, except in Star Trek IV, *when the* Enterprise *crew commandeers the Klingon ship and uses it to travel through time, there is a scene in Golden Gate Park where the ship levitates vertically from the grass. If it can conquer gravity, then once again, I ask, why does it have wings?*

Your answer, please?

"It doesn't conquer gravity," he told me soon after the movie opened. "It uses vertical take-off technology, like the Harrier jets in the Royal Air Force."

Oh.

Star Wars ★ ★ ★ ★

PG, 121 m., 1977

Mark Hamill (Luke Skywalker), Carrie Fisher (Princess Leia), Harrison Ford (Han Solo), Alec Guinness (Obi-Wan Kenobi), David Prowse (Darth Vader), James Earl Jones (Vader's Voice), Kenny Baker (R2D2), Anthony Daniels (C3PO). Directed by George Lucas and produced by Gary Kurtz. Screenplay by Lucas.

Every once in a while I have what I think of as an out-of-the-body experience at a movie. When the ESP people use a phrase like that, they're referring to the sensation of the mind actually leaving the body and spiriting itself off to China or Peoria or a galaxy far, far away. When I use the phrase, I simply mean that my imagination has forgotten it is actually present in a movie theater and thinks it's up there on the screen. In a curious sense, the events in the movie seem real, and I seem to be a part of them.

Star Wars works like that. My list of other out-of-the-body films is a short and odd one, ranging from the artistry of *Bonnie and Clyde* or *Cries and Whispers* to the slick commercialism of *Jaws* and the brutal strength of *Taxi Driver.* On whatever level (sometimes I'm not at all sure) they engage me so immediately and powerfully that I lose my detachment, my analytical reserve. The movie's *happening,* and it's happening to me.

What makes the *Star Wars* experience unique, though, is that it happens on such an innocent and often funny level. It's usually violence that draws me so deeply into a movie—violence ranging from the psychological torment of a Bergman character to the mindless crunch of a shark's jaws. Maybe movies that scare us find the most direct route to our imaginations. But there's hardly any violence at all in *Star Wars* (and even then it's presented as essentially bloodless swashbuckling). Instead, there's entertainment so direct and simple that all of the complications of the modern movie seem to vaporize.

Star Wars is a fairy tale, a fantasy, a legend, finding its roots in some of our most popular fictions. The golden robot, lion-faced space pilot, and insecure little computer on wheels must have been suggested by the Tin Man, the Cowardly Lion, and the Scarecrow in *The Wizard of Oz.* The journey from one end of the galaxy to another is out of countless thousands of space operas. The hardware is from *Flash Gordon* out of *2001,* the chivalry is from *Robin Hood,* the heroes are from Westerns and the villains are a cross between Nazis and sorcerers. *Star Wars* taps the pulp fantasies buried in our memories, and because it's done so brilliantly, it reactivates old thrills, fears, and exhilarations we thought we'd abandoned when we read our last copy of *Amazing Stories.*

The movie works so well for several reasons, and they don't all have to do with the spectacular special effects. The effects *are* good, yes, but great effects have been used in such movies as *Silent Running* and *Logan's*

Run without setting all-time box-office records. No, I think the key to *Star Wars* is more basic than that.

The movie relies on the strength of pure narrative, in the most basic storytelling form known to man, the Journey. All of the best tales we remember from our childhoods had to do with heroes setting out to travel down roads filled with danger, and hoping to find treasure or heroism at the journey's end. In *Star Wars*, George Lucas takes this simple and powerful framework into outer space, and that is an inspired thing to do, because we no longer have maps on Earth that warn, "Here there be dragons." We can't fall off the edge of the map, as Columbus could, and we can't hope to find new continents of prehistoric monsters or lost tribes ruled by immortal goddesses. Not on Earth, anyway, but anything is possible in space, and Lucas goes right ahead and shows us very nearly everything. We get involved quickly, because the characters in *Star Wars* are so strongly and simply drawn and have so many small foibles and large, futile hopes for us to identify with. And then Lucas does an interesting thing. As he sends his heroes off to cross the universe and do battle with the Forces of Darth Vader, the evil Empire, and the awesome Death Star, he gives us lots of special effects, yes—ships passing into hyperspace, alien planets, an infinity of stars—but we also get a wealth of strange living creatures, and Lucas correctly guesses that they'll be more interesting for us than all the intergalactic hardware.

The most fascinating single scene, for me, was the one set in the bizarre saloon on the planet Alderaan. As that incredible collection of extraterrestrial alcoholics and bug-eyed martini drinkers lined up at the bar, and as Lucas so slyly let them exhibit characteristics that were universally human, I found myself feeling a combination of admiration and delight. *Star Wars* had placed me in the presence of really magical movie invention: Here, all mixed together, were whimsy and fantasy, simple wonderment and quietly sophisticated story-telling.

When Stanley Kubrick was making *2001* twenty years ago, he threw everything he had into the special effects depicting outer space, but he finally decided not to show any aliens at all—because they were impossible to visualize, he thought. But they weren't at all, as *Star Wars* demonstrates, and the movie's delight in the possibilities of alien life forms is at least as much fun as its conflicts between the space cruisers of the Empire and the Rebels.

And perhaps that helps to explain the movie's one weakness, which is that the final assault on the Death Star is allowed to go on too long. Maybe, having invested so much money and sweat in his special effects, Lucas couldn't bear to see them trimmed. But the magic of *Star Wars* is only dramatized by the special effects; the movie's heart is in its endearingly human (and non-human) people.

Stardust Memories ★ ★

PG, 89 m., 1980

Woody Allen (Sandy), Charlotte Rampling (Dori), Jessica Harper (Violinist), Marie-Christine Barrault (Frenchwoman). Directed by Woody Allen and produced by Robert Greenhut. Screenplay by Allen.

Woody Allen's *Stardust Memories* is a deliberate homage to *8½*, the 1963 film in which Federico Fellini chronicled several days in the life of a filmmaker who had no idea where to turn next. The major difference between the two films is that Fellini's movie was *about* a director bankrupt of new ideas, while Allen's is a movie *by* a director with no new ideas. I know that sounds harsh, especially when applied to one of the few American directors who can be counted on for freshness and intelligence, but *Stardust Memories* is an incomplete, unsatisfying film.

The movie begins by acknowledging its sources of visual inspiration. We see a claustrophobic Allen trapped in a railroad car (that's from the opening of *8½*, with Marcello Mastroianni trapped in an auto), and the harsh black and white lighting and the ticking of a clock on the soundtrack give us a cross-reference to the nightmare that opens Ingmar Bergman's *Wild Strawberries*. Are these the exact scenes Allen had in mind? Probably, but no matter; he clearly intends *Stardust Memories* to be his *8½*, and it develops as a portrait of the artist's complaints.

Most of the action of the film centers around two subjects. The first is a weekend film seminar (obviously patterned after Judith Crist's weekends at Tarrytown, N.Y.), to which the Allen character has been invited. The second subject is a very familiar one, Allen's stormy relationships with women. The subjects blend into the basic complaint of the Woody Allen persona we have to come to know and love, and can be summarized briefly: If I'm so famous and brilliant and everybody loves me, then why doesn't anybody *in particular* love me?

At the film seminar, the Allen character is constantly besieged by groupies. They come in all styles: pathetic young girls who want to sleep with him, fans who want his autograph, weekend culture vultures, and people who spend all their time at one event promoting the next one they're attending. Allen makes his point early, by shooting these unfortunate creatures in close-up with a wide-angle lens that makes them all look like Martians with big noses. They add up to a nightmare, a non-stop invasion of privacy, a shrill chorus of people whose praise for the artist is really a call for attention.

Fine, except what *else* does Allen have to say about them? Nothing. In the Fellini film, the director-hero was surrounded by sycophants, business associates, would-be collaborators, wives, mistresses, old friends, all of whom made calls on his humanity. In the Allen picture, there's no depth, no personal context: They're only making calls on his time. What's more, the Fellini character was at least trying to create something, to harass his badgered brain into some feeble act of thought. But the Allen character expresses only impotence, despair, uncertainty, discouragement. All through the film, Allen keeps talking about diseases, catastrophes, bad luck that befalls even the most successful. Yes, but that's what artists are for: to hurl their imagination, joy, and conviction into the silent maw. Sorry if I got a little carried away. *Stardust Memories* inspires that kind of frustration, though, because it's the first Woody Allen film in which impotence has become the situation rather than the problem. This is a movie about a guy who has given up. His relationships with women illustrate that; after the marvelous and complex women in *Annie Hall* and *Manhattan*, in *Stardust Memories* we get a series of enigmas and we never really feel that Allen is connecting with them. These women don't represent failed relationships, they represent walk-throughs.

Woody Allen has always loved jazz and the great mainstream American popular music. There's a lot of it in *Stardust Memories*, but it doesn't amplify or illustrate the scene this time—it steals them. There's a scene where Allen remembers a wonderful spring morning spent with a former love (Charlotte Rampling), and how he looked up in his apartment to see her there, and for a moment felt that life was perfect. As Allen shows that moment, Louis Armstrong sings "Stardust" on the soundtrack, and something happens that should not be allowed to happen. We find our attention almost entirely on Armstrong's wonderfully loose jazz phrasing.

Stardust Memories is a disappointment. It needs some larger idea, some sort of organizing force, to pull together all these scenes of bitching and moaning, and make them lead somewhere.

Starman ★ ★ ★

PG, 112 m., 1984

Jeff Bridges (Starman), Karen Allen (Jenny Hayden), Charles Martin Smith (Mark Shermin), Richard Jaeckel (George Fox). Directed by John Carpenter and produced by Larry J. Franco. Screenplay by Bruce A. Evans and Raynold Gideon.

Starman begins by reminding us of Voyager, that little spacecraft that is even now speeding beyond the solar system. Remember Carl Sagan on the "Tonight" show, explaining to Johnny about all the messages that were on board, in case someday an alien race found this postcard from Earth? Voyager carried greetings in all of the tongues of man, and there is something inevitable about the scene, early in *Starman*, when we get an extraterrestrial visitor who has studied them carefully, and is able to say "hello" a hundred different ways.

The starman of the title is a ball of glowing light. He, or it, has traveled to Earth in response to the invitation from Voyager, but of course the Air Force treats the spacecraft as a possible invader and shoots missiles at it. Knocked off course, the starman lands in rural Wisconsin, where it becomes the identical clone of a dead house painter. The painter's widow (Karen Allen) is stunned when she sees this creature from beyond the grave. It is even more difficult when she realizes this is not her husband, but something infinitely different that just happens to look exactly like her husband. The visitor is very smart, but has a lot to learn, and at first it controls its human host body with a lot of awkward lurching. Meanwhile, government officials led by Richard Jaeckel are seeking the extraterrestrial for "security" reasons, and scientist Charles Martin Smith hopes to get there first and record the historic moment of man's first meeting from a race from another world.

All of this seems like a setup for a science-fiction movie, but what's interesting is the way the director, John Carpenter, makes a U-turn and treats *Starman* as a road movie. The visitor (played by Jeff Bridges) forces Allen to start driving in the direction of the Great Meteor Crater, where he has a rendezvous with his ride home. And as the two characters spend time together as refugees from the search parties, they begin to communicate, and the woman's initial hostility turns into respect and finally into love. This is a wonderfully sweet process, especially as Allen and Bridges go about it. *Starman* contains the potential to be a very silly movie, but the two actors have so much sympathy for their characters that the movie, advertised as space fiction, turns into one of 1984's more touching love stories. Meanwhile, Carpenter provides many of the standard scenes from earlier road movies, including a stop in a roadside diner where the alien's uncertain behavior draws attention. And there's an interlude in Vegas where the extraterrestrial tries to outsmart the slots.

The most interesting thing about *Starman* is probably Bridges's approach to playing a creature from another world. The character grows gradually more human as the film moves along, but he is never completely without glitches: His head movements are birdlike, his step is a little uncertain, he speaks as if there were just a millisecond's delay between brain and tongue. Actors sometimes try to change their appearance; Bridges does something trickier, and tries to convince us that Jeff Bridges is not inhabited by himself. I think he succeeds, and that *Starman* makes Voyager seem like a good investment.

Stay Hungry ★ ★ ★
R, 102 m., 1976

Jeff Bridges (Craig Blake), Sally Field (Mary Tate), Arnold Schwarzenegger (Joe Santo), R.G. Armstrong (Thor Erickson), Robert Englund (Franklin), Helena Kallianiotes (Anita), Roger E. Mosley (Newton), Woodrow Parfrey (Uncle Albert), Scatman Crothers (William). Directed by Bob Rafelson and produced by Harold Schneider and Rafelson. Screenplay by Charles Gaines and Rafelson.

Bob Rafelson's *Stay Hungry* is ungainly and confused at times—it stretches its seams a little too much—but it's a breath of fresh air—a quirky, funny, oddball movie about the most unlikely characters ever to be trapped in the same plot. Jeff Bridges plays the lead, an Alabama blueblood of uncounted generations of aristocracy. He's involved in a real estate deal that involves convincing a gymnasium owner to sell his property so a high-rise can go up. Bridges visits the gym, becomes fascinated by the earnest body-builders and fierce female karate instructors and sort of forgets to do anything about the deal. And one of the body-builders (the former Mr. Universe, Arnold Schwarzenegger, who likes to work out in a rubber Batman suit) introduces him to a sweet young thing he can't help falling in love with.

The girl is played by Sally Field, and she's a simple country type who doesn't exactly fit in with Bridges's genteel cousins; she attends a family party dressed in something that looks mail-ordered from Frederick's of Hollywood. Bridges begins to get letters from his Uncle Albert, who points out that this new found interest in muscle-building and girls without any breeding is going to qualify him as the family's first black sheep since the cousin who moved to Puerto Rico and opened a goat farm. Meanwhile, the would-be real estate investors turn out to be mob types with a penchant for sending guys around to wreck the air conditioning.

The movie doesn't concern itself very much with plot; like Rafelson's *Five Easy Pieces* and the underrated *King of Marvin Gardens*, it introduces us to sharply defined, rather odd characters and then lets them mix it up. The movie is episodic, and some of the episodes are brilliant. Among the best is a scene in which the aged family retainer (Scatman Crothers) announces his resignation and his intention of taking a suit of armor with him, another in which several dozen body-builders race through the startled streets of Birmingham, a harrowing fight scene in a gym in which people throw weights at each other, and a tables-turned situation in which a hooker is forcibly given a massage.

Schwarzenegger, in his first dramatic role, turns in an interesting performance as Bridges's new found buddy. He works out incessantly, speaks in an Austrian accent, and then turns out to be the lead fiddler in a bluegrass band (people in Rafelson movies are always revealing unsuspected musical abilities).

One of the best things about *Stay Hungry* is that we have almost no idea where it's going; it's as free-form as *Nashville* and Rafelson is cheerfully willing to pause here and there for set-pieces like the woman's karate class and the eventual Mr. Universe competition (in which the muscled competitors, back-lit, rise slowly onto a revolving stage in a moment reminiscent of the sunrise in *2001*). When the movie's over, we're still not sure why it was made (maybe it's a subtle comment on Southern class structure—very subtle), but we've had fun and so, it appears, has Rafelson.

Staying Alive ★

PG, 96 m., 1983

John Travolta (Tony Manero), Cynthia Rhodes (Jackie), Finola Hughes (Laura), Julie Bovasso (Mother). Directed by Sylvester Stallone and produced by Robert Stigwood. Screenplay by Stallone and Norman Wexler.

Staying Alive is a big disappointment. This sequel to the gutsy, electric *Saturday Night Fever* is a slick, cinematic jukebox, a series of self-contained song-and-dance sequences that could be cut apart and played forever on MTV. Like *Flashdance,* it isn't really a movie at all, but an endless series of musical interludes between dramatic scenes that aren't there. It's not even as good as *Flashdance,* but it may appeal to the same audience; it's a Walkman for the eyes.

The movie has an extremely simple plot. Extremely. Six years have passed since Tony Manero (John Travolta) gazed longingly at the lights of Manhattan at the end of *Saturday Night Fever.* Now he lives in a fleabag Manhattan hotel, works as a waiter and a dance instructor, and dates a young dancer (Cynthia Rhodes) with the patience of a saint. He's still a woman-chaser. But he meets a long-haired British dancer (Finola Hughes) who's his match. She's a queen bitch who takes him to bed and jilts him. Meanwhile, he gets a job as a dancer in her new show and when her lead dancer falters, Tony gets the job. Does this all sound familiar?

The movie was co-authored and directed by Sylvester Stallone, and is the first bad movie he's made. He remembers all the moves from his Rocky plots, but he leaves out the heart—and, even worse, he leaves out the characters. Everybody in *Staying Alive* is Identikit. The characters are clichés, their lives clichés, and God knows their dialogue is clichés. The big musical climaxes are interrupted only long enough for people to shout prepackaged emotional countercharges at each other. There is little attempt to approximate human speech. Like the Rocky movies, *Staying Alive* ends with a big, visually explosive climax. It is so ludicrous it has to be seen to be believed. It's opening night on Broadway. Tony Manero not only dances like a hero, he survives a production number of fire, ice, smoke, flashing lights, and laser beams, throws in an improvised solo—and ends triumphantly by holding Finola Hughes above his head with one arm, like a quarry he has tracked and killed. The musical he is allegedly starring in is something called *Satan's Alley,* but it's so laughably gauche it should have been called *Springtime for Tony.* Stallone makes little effort to convince us we're watching a real stage presentation; there are camera effects the audience could never see, montages that create impossible physical moves, and—most inexplicably of all—a vocal track, even though nobody on stage is singing. It's a mess. Travolta's big dance number looks like a high-tech TV auto commercial that got sick to its stomach.

What I really missed in *Staying Alive* was the sense of reality in *Saturday Night Fever*—the sense that Tony came from someplace and was somebody particular. There's no old neighborhood, no vulgar showdowns with his family (he *apologizes* to his mother for his "attitude"!), and no Brooklyn eccentricity. Tony's world has been cloned into a backstage musical. And not a good one.

Still, the movie has one great moment. A

victorious Tony says "I want to strut!" and struts across Times Square while the Bee Gees sing "Stayin' Alive." That could have been the first shot of a great movie. It's the last shot of this one.

The Stepfather ★ ★ ½
R, 95 m., 1987

Terry O'Quinn (The Stepfather), Jill Schoelen (Stephanie Maine), Shelley Hack (Susan Blake), Charles Lanyer (Dr. Bondurant), Stephen Shellen (Ogilvie), Robyn Stevan (Karen). Directed by Joseph Ruben and produced by Jay Benson. Screenplay by Donald E. Westlake.

He's one of those guys with a bland smile and a voice so nice and sweet that right away you know he's twisted. He has a knack for convincing women to marry him, but children see him with clearer eyes, and know there's something wrong. There sure is. Battling inside of him are two conflicting obsessions: The desire to be the perfect father of a model family, and a towering rage that turns him into a killer.

The Stepfather tells his story in a blood-soaked thriller that is uneven but haunting. While I was watching the film, I was distracted by elements of the Idiot Plot Syndrome—moments when only an idiot would have made such obvious mistakes. Now, remembering the film, what I recall most clearly is the central performance by Terry O'Quinn.

He is a journeyman actor from TV and many movies, usually in supporting roles, and you may or may not recognize him. What's clear at once is that he is a strong actor, and given this leading role he brings all kinds of creepy dimensions to it. He has the thankless assignment of showing us a completely hateful, repellent character—and he approaches the task as an exercise in cloying middle-class good manners.

The stepfather seems to be such a nice man. So understanding. So accommodating. He always marries into families with children—providing a strong shoulder for a widow to lean on. He's handy around the house. He likes to spend time in his basement workshop, where sometimes the pressure builds up so intensely that he has to smash things.

He's obsessed with a vision of the perfect family. He wants each of his families to be perfect. When they disappoint him, as every family eventually will, he starts shopping around for his next family and his next identity. When he has that lined up, he murders this family.

The Stepfather is very effective in presenting that character. Unfortunately, it places him inside a plot that has too many distracting loose ends and oversights, avoidable errors and Idiot Plot mistakes. Why did the movie have to be a thriller at all? Why not simply a character study?

There were box-office considerations, I suppose, and yet the thriller aspects of the film are the least satisfying. It's distracting to watch a movie and know that a movie character is doing something that makes no sense—and is doing it only so that the plot can move on to its next chapter.

Like many movies that study psychopathic killers (*Badlands, In Cold Blood*, even *Black Widow*), this film seems to have no larger purpose than simply to show us the killer. Because the murderer is mentally ill, because he is not killing out of any motive that we can understand, the film is simply an exercise in despair; a portrait of a tragic man.

Violence itself seems to sell, even when it's divorced from any context. Maybe that's what the filmmakers were thinking. What often happens, though, is that in an otherwise flawed film there are a couple of things that are wonderful. *The Stepfather* has one wonderful element: Terry O'Quinn's performance.

Stevie ★ ★ ★ ★
NO MPAA RATING, 102 m., 1981

Glenda Jackson (Stevie Smith), Mona Washbourne (Her Aunt), Alec McCowen (Freddie), Trevor Howard (The Man). Directed and produced by Robert Enders. Screenplay by Hugh Whitemore.

Stevie Smith came across a newspaper clipping one day that told of a man who drowned within a few hundred yards off the shore. The people on the beach saw him waving, and they waved back. The truth, as Stevie expressed it in a famous poem, was the man's problem was just like her own:

I was much too far out all my life
And not waving, but drowning.

In those lines, Stevie Smith made an image of her own life, and it is an image that Glenda Jackson's film *Stevie* expresses with clarity, wit, and love.

Stevie Smith was a British poet of considerable reputation, who died in 1971 at the age of sixty-nine. She spent almost all of her life living in a small home in the London suburb of Palmers Green, where she moved as a child. She worked every day in an office in the city, until her growing reputation as a poet allowed her to take an early retirement. She lived with an old maid aunt, and eventually she became an old maid herself. We watch this process as it is punctuated by a marriage proposal, by a visit to Buckingham Palace for tea with the queen, by a half-hearted suicide attempt. Every night, there was definitely a glass or two or more of sherry, or sometimes gin.

To the world, she must have appeared to be an exemplary example of a talented English eccentric. Her poems were irreverent, sharply satirical, and laconic. She was capable of writing one day:

The Englishwoman is so refined
She has no bosom and no behind.

And on another day, writing about death:

I have a friend
At the end
of the world.
His name is a breath
Of fresh air.

She was not waving, but drowning. The film *Stevie* captures this laconic despair, but it also does a great deal more. It gives us a very particular portrait of a woman's life. The movie is based on a play by Hugh Whitemore, and it contains one of Glenda Jackson's greatest performances. She knows this character well. She played Stevie on the London stage and on a BBC radio production before making this film. She does what great actors can do: She takes a character who might seem uninteresting, and makes us care deeply about the uneventful days of her life.

Although *Stevie* is totally dominated by Jackson's performance, it is not a one-character film by any means. The veteran British actress Mona Washbourne provides a magnificent performance as Stevie's maiden aunt, who is a little dotty and a little giggly and very loving, who likes her glass of sherry and wears flowered print dresses that Stevie says look like a seed catalog illustration titled "They All Came Up." Alec McCowen plays Freddie, the not-so-young man who comes calling, and whose proposal Stevie rejects. And the wonderful Trevor Howard has an ambiguous part as "the man." On one level, "the man" is just someone she met at a literary party and conned into giving her rides to poetry readings. At another level, especially when he is seen by himself, telling us about Stevie and reading some of her lines, he is the understanding, forgiving father figure Stevie never had.

Movies like *Stevie* run the risk of looking like photographs of stage plays, but *Stevie* somehow never feels that way. Even though it uses the artifices of the stage (including remarks addressed by Glenda Jackson directly to the audience), and even though a lot of its dialogue is poetry, *Stevie* always feels as if it occupies this woman's life. She is the poet, we are her confidantes, and it is a privilege to get to know her. I have perhaps given the impression that *Stevie* is grim and depressing. It is not at all. It is very sad at times, of course, but there are other times of good humor and barbed wit, when she's not drowning, but waving.

Stop Making Sense ★ ★ ★ 1/2

NO MPAA RATING, 88 m., 1984

With the Talking Heads: David Byrne, Chris Frantz, Jerry Harrison, and Tina Weymouth. Guest musicians: Edna Holt, Lynn Mabry, Steve Scales, Alex Weir, and Bernie Worrell. Directed by Jonathan Demme and produced by Gary Goetzman.

The overwelming impression throughout *Stop Making Sense* is of enormous energy, of life being lived at a joyous high. And it's not the frenetic, jangled-nerves energy of a rock band that's wired; it's the high spirits and good health we associate with artists like Bruce Springsteen. There are a lot of reasons to see concert films, but the only ones that usually get mentioned are the music and the cinematography. This time the actual physical impact of the film is just as exhilarating: Watching the Talking Heads in concert is a little like rock 'n' roll crossed with "Jane Fonda's Workout." The movie was shot during two live performances of the Talking

Heads, a New York rock band that centers on the remarkable talent of its lead singer, David Byrne. Like David Bowie, his stage presence shows the influence of mime, and some of his best effects in *Stop Making Sense* are achieved with outsize costumes and hand-held lights that create shadow plays on the screen behind him.

Given all the showmanship that will develop later during the film, the opening sequences are a low-key, almost anticoncert throwaway. Byrne walks on a bare stage with a ghetto-blaster in his hand, puts it down on the stage, turns it on and sings along with "Psycho Killer." Eventually he is joined onstage by Tina Weymouth on bass. Then stagehands wander out from the wings and being to assemble a platform for drummer Chris Frantz. Gear is moved into place. Electical cables are attached. The backup singers, Edna Holt and Lynn Mabry, appear. And the concert inexorably picks up tempo.

The music of the Talking Heads draws from many sources, in addition to traditional rock 'n' roll. You can hear the echoes, in Byrne's voice, of one of his heroes, country singer Hank Williams. In the music itself, there are elements of reggae and of gospel, especially in the driving repetitions of single phrases that end some of the songs. What is particularly delightful is that the Talking Heads *are* musical: For people who have passed over that invisible divide into the age group when rock sounds like noise, the Heads will sound like music.

The film is good to look at. The director is Jonathan Demme *(Melvin and Howard)*, making his first concert film, and essentially using the visuals of the Talking Heads rather than creating his own. Instead of the standard phony cutaways to the audience (phony because, nine times out of ten, the audience members are not actually reacting to the moment in the music that we're hearing), Demme keeps his cameras trained on the stage. And when Byrne and company use the stage-level lights to create a shadow play behind them, the result is surprisingly more effective than you might imagine: It's a live show with elements of *Metropolis*.

But the film's peak moments come through Byrne's simple physical presence. He jogs in place with his sidemen; he runs around the stage; he seems so happy to be alive and making music. Like Springsteen and Prince, he serves as a reminder of how sour and weary and strung-out many rock bands have become. Starting with Mick Jagger, rock concerts have become, for the performers, as much sporting events as musical and theatrical performances. *Stop Making Sense* understands that with great exuberance.

Stormy Monday ★ ★ ★ 1/2

R, 93 m., 1988 ✓

(See related Film Clip, p. 775.)

Melanie Griffith (Kate), Tommy Lee Jones (Cosmo), Sting (Finney), Sean Bean (Brendan). Directed by Mike Figgis and produced by Nigel Stafford-Clark. Screenplay by Figgis.

"Why is it," someone was asking the other day, "that you movie critics spend all of your time talking about the story, and never talk about the visual qualities of a film—which are, after all, what *make* it a film?" Good question. Maybe it's because we work in words, and stories are told in words, and it's harder to use words to paint pictures. But it might be worth a try.

Stormy Monday is about the way light falls on wet pavement stones, and about how a neon sign glows in a darkened doorway. It is about the attitudes that men strike when they feel in control of a situation, and the way their shoulders slump when someone else takes power. It is about smoking. It is about cleavage. It is about the look on a man's face when someone is about to deliberately break his arm, and he knows it. And about the look on a woman's face when she is waiting for a man she thinks she loves; he is late, and she fears it is because he is dead.

Stormy Monday is also about symbols. It takes place mostly near the seedy waterfront of Newcastle, where a crooked Texas millionaire is trying to run a nightclub owner out of business, so he can redevelop the area with laundered money. But now we're back to the story again. You see how easy it is to slip. The movie uses a lot of symbols of America: The flag, stretched large and bold behind a podium. Baton-twirlers. A curiously frightening old man with a sinister smile, who struts in front of the baton twirlers, his shoulders thrown back, tipping his hat to the crowd. A car—big, fast, and red. Bourbon whiskey. Marlboros and cigars.

It is also about lonely furnished rooms,

and rain, and standing in the window at night looking out into the street, and signaling for someone across a crowded nightclub floor, and about saxophones, which are the instrument of the night. It is about the flat, masked expressions on the faces of bodyguards, and about the face of a man who is consumed by anger. And it is about kissing, and about the look in a woman's eyes when she is about to kiss a man for the first time. And it is about high heels, and cleavage. I believe I already mentioned cleavage. Some images reoccur more naturally than others.

The movie is not all images. It is also about sounds. About the breathy, rich, and yet uncertain tone of Melanie Griffith's voice, which makes her sound as if she's been around the track too many times, and yet is still able to believe in love. And the flat, angry voice of Tommy Lee Jones, who never seems to raise his voice, or need to. And about the innocence in the voice of Sean Bean, an earnest young man who only wants a job, and gets trapped in a bloodbath. And about the voice of Sting, who looks Jones in the eye and talks as flat and angry as he does, until Jones's shoulders slump. And about saxophones, the sound of the night.

It is also about the sound of a deliberately discordant performance of "The Star Spangled Banner," and about explosions and gunfire and squealing tires, and about modern jazz from Krakow. It is about the sound of ice cubes in a glass, and smoke being exhaled, and bones being broken. It is about the sound of a marching band, and about the voice of a disc jockey who wants to sound American and doesn't know when to stop. And about how a woman tells a man, "I get off work at midnight." And how she looks when she says that. And how he looks.

So there's your review.

Straight Time ★ ★ ★ 1/2

R, 114 m., 1978

Dustin Hoffman (Max Dembo), Theresa Russell (Jenny Mercer), Harry Dean Stanton (Jerry Schue), Gary Busey (Willy Darin), M. Emmet Walsh (Earl Frank), Sandy Baron (Manny). Directed by Ulu Grosbard and produced by Stanley Beck and Tim Zinnemann. Screenplay by Alvin Sargent, Edward Bunker, and Jeffrey Boam.

Straight Time is a great sleeper, a film good enough that we wonder why we didn't hear more about it. So does Dustin Hoffman, who sued Warner Brothers for what he considered the mishandling of the picture. He may have had a point; his performance here as Max Dembo, ex-con turned thief, is one of his very best.

Max gets out of prison determined to go straight. It's not easy. Under the conditions of his parole, for example, he can't take a job that involves the handling of money. But a girl in an employment office does find him a job, at a can company. And when he asks her out to dinner, she accepts. He also finds a room he can afford to rent, and so he's doing fairly well. He's on the road to personal rehabilitation, as his parole officer might put it. The parole officer (M. Emmet Walsh) is not, however, very good at the rehabilitation game. He's mean-spirited, suspicious and sadistic, all behind a large, cynical smile. He busts Max on suspicion of drug use, causing him to lose his job—and that's enough for Max, who returns to the trade he knows best, theft.

Straight Time is based on a novel by an ex-con, and it feels authentic. What especially absorbs us is the way the movie projects the feeling of being a thief—the compulsion, the addiction, the rush of adrenaline, the fear. It's also good at explaining why this guy would be attractive to a girl, and especially the girl at the employment office.

She's played by Theresa Russell, who does a good job of projecting her feelings. She doesn't talk a lot, but she listens well, and she's drawn to the mysteries in Max's character. He wants to keep her out of his jobs but not out of his life, and she is eventually willing to settle for his terms.

Max pulls several jobs. He sticks up a grocery, for example, and then a pawnshop, where he gets the shotgun that will be useful in his stick-ups of a bank and a jewelry store. He enlists old buddies as his accomplices, and Harry Dean Stanton is especially good as an ex-con who almost succeeds in going straight. Stanton's got it all together: A house, a swimming pool, hamburgers grilled on the patio . . . but he can't resist the urgency of Max Dembo's sales pitch.

The robberies themselves have the same sense of manic desperation we felt in *Dog Day Afternoon*. And they have something else, as well: They project the feeling that

Max Dembo, without admitting it even to himself, *wants* to get caught again. He lingers. He dawdles. His partner is calling out the number of seconds that have elapsed, as part of their plan to get out before the cops arrive. But Max Dembo isn't listening. Maybe that's part of the emotional payoff he needs, stretching a job to its last second, walking out the back door as the cops come in the front, taunting society while at the same time almost begging for punishment.

Hoffman's performance reminds me of his Ratso Rizzo in *Midnight Cowboy*, especially in his ways of telling the world to go to hell. Ratso was far gone on his own personal death trip, of course, and Max Dembo has whole moments when he rathers enjoys life. But they're similar in their moves, their choices. They belong outside society because it doesn't dare have places for them. Maybe *that's* what turns the girl on; maybe she has a sheltering instinct.

Straight Time exists so close to the drabness and desperation of its story that it might turn some people off. Hoffman must have known that; this is such a personal project that after he bought the original novel he planned to direct it himself before deciding, instead, on the Broadway and sometime movie director Ulu Grosbard. But Hoffman and Grosbard don't change details just to make their movie more palatable. Instead, they stick with Max Dembo, figuring him out, following his impulses, until those oddly disturbing final photographs—his mug shots—with the eyes suggesting that somehow this particular human being was *always* doomed.

Stranger than Paradise ★ ★ ★ ★

R, 90 m., 1984

John Lurie (Willie), Eszter Balint (Eva), Richard Edson (Eddie), Cecillia Stark (Aunt Lottie), Danny Rosen (Billy), Rammellzee (Man with Money), Tom Decillo (Airline Agent). Directed by Jim Jarmusch and produced by Sara Driver. Screenplay by Jarmusch.

Stranger than Paradise is filmed in a series of uninterrupted shots; the picture fades in, we watch the scene, and when the scene is over, there's a fade to black. Then comes the next fade-in. This is not a gimmick, but a visual equivalent of the film's deadpan characters, who take a lot to get excited.

The movie's hero is Willie (John Lurie), who arrived on these shores from Hungary about ten years ago, and has spent the intervening decade perfecting his New York accent and trying to make nothing out of himself. He lives in an apartment where the linoleum is the highlight. On a good day, he'll sleep late, hang out, play a little poker. His cousin Eva arrives from Budapest. This is the last thing he needs, a 16-year-old girl who needs a place to stay. She hates him, too. But she has to kill some time before she goes to Cleveland to live with her aunt Lottie. She has good taste in American music, but not according to him. Willie's friend, Eddie, comes over occasionally and eyeballs Eva. Nothing much happens. She leaves for Cleveland.

The screen is filled with large letters: ONE YEAR LATER. This in itself is funny, that we'd get such a momentous time cue in a movie where who even knows what day it is. Eddie and Willie get in some trouble over a poker game and Eddie suddenly remembers Willie's cousin in Cleveland. They go to see her. It is cold in Cleveland. Eva has bought the American Dream and is working in a fast-food outlet. They all go to look at the lake, which is frozen. Aunt Lottie turns out to make Clara Peller look like Dame Peggy Ashcroft. The guys say to hell with it and head for Florida. Then they come back and get Eva and take her along with them. They have a postcard that makes Florida look like paradise, but they wind up living at one of those hotels where the permanent guests live in the woodwork. Everything goes sour. Eva wants to go back to Hungary. The guys lose all their money at the dog races. Creeps start hanging around. It will take a miracle to give this movie an upbeat ending. There is a miracle.

Stranger than Paradise is a treasure from one end to the other. I saw it for the first time at the 1984 Cannes Film Festival, where it was having its first public showing. Half the people in the theater probably didn't speak English, but that didn't stop them from giving the movie a standing ovation, and it eventually won the Camera d'Or prize for the best first film. It is like no other film you've seen, and yet you feel right at home in it. It seems to be going nowhere, and knows every step it wants to make. It is a constant, almost kaleidoscopic experience of discovery, and we try to figure out what the film is up to and it just keeps moving steadfastly ahead, fade in, fade out, fade in, fade out, making a mountain out of a molehill.

Streamers ★ ★ ★ ★
R, 118 m., 1984

Matthew Modine (Billy), Michael Wright (Carlyle), Mitchell Lichtenstein (Richie), David Alan Grier (Roger), Guy Boyd (Rooney), George Dzundza (Cokes). Directed by Robert Altman and produced by Altman and Nick H. Mileti. Screenplay by David Rabe.

Robert Altman's *Streamers* is one of the most intense and intimate dramas I've ever seen on film. It's based on the play by David Rabe, about young soldiers waiting around a barracks for their orders to go to Vietnam. Most directors, faced with a play that takes place on one set, find ways to "open it up" and add new locations. Altman has moved in the opposite direction, taking advantage of the one-room set to tighten the play until it squeezes like a vise. Watching this film is such a demanding experience that both times I've seen it, it has been too much for some viewers, and they've left. Those who stay, who survive the difficult passages of violence, will find at the end of the film a conclusion that is so poetic and moving it succeeds in placing the tragedy in perspective.

It is the era of Vietnam. In a barracks somewhere, three young men wait for their orders. They are Billy, who is white and middle-class; Roger, who is black and middle-class; and Richie, a dreamy young man who likes to tease the others with hints that he is a homosexual. The only other occupants of the barracks are two drunken master sergeants, Rooney and Cokes, who are best friends and who are stumbling through idiotic revelry in an attempt to drown the realization that Cokes has leukemia. Into this little world comes Carlyle, an angry young black man who is gay, and whose conversations with Richie will lead the others into anger and denial before the situation finally explodes.

There are some surprises, but the developments in *Streamers* flow so naturally out of the material that its surprises should be left intact. A lot can be said, however, about the acting, Altman's direction, and Rabe's writing. I didn't see this play on stage and don't know how it worked there, but Altman is so completely the visual master of this material that we're drawn into that barracks room and into its rhythms of boredom, drunkenness, and passion.

The actors are all unknown to me, except for George Dzundza, who plays Cokes. They are all so natural that the dialogue has an eerie double quality: We know it's written dialogue because it has a poetry and a drama unlikely in life, but Rabe's ear is so accurate it sounds real, and the performers make it so convincing there's never a false note. The two key performances are by Mitchell Lichtenstein, as Richie, and Michael Wright, as Carlyle. Richie is indeed homosexual, as we realize long before his barracks mates are willing to acknowledge it. He likes to tease the others with insinuations that they may be gay, too. Billy boasts that he is straight, but he protests too much. Roger tries to be a peacekeeper. Then Carlyle wanders in from another unit. He is drunk and angry, collapses, sleeps it off, blearily looks around, figures out Richie, and tries to make a connection.

But there is a lot more going on here than sexual competition. *Streamers* uses both sex and race as foreground subjects while the movie's real subject, war, hovers in the background and in several extraordinary monologues—one about snakes, one about a battle, and one about the realities of parachuting. As the veteran master sergeants make their drunken way through the movie, they drop these hard realities into the lives of the unseasoned kids. And when anger turns to violence and a tragedy occurs, it is up to one of the fat old guys (Dzundza) to deliver a monologue that is one of the most revealing, intimate, honest, and moving speeches I've ever heard.

Street Smart ★ ★ ★
R, 97 m., 1987

Christopher Reeve (Jonathan Fisher), Mimi Rogers (Alison Parker), Morgan Freeman (Fast Black), Kathy Baker (Punchy). Directed by Jerry Schatzberg and produced by Menahem Golan and Yoram Globus. Screenplay by David Freeman.

Sometimes you run across a movie that's far from perfect and yet it contains things that are so good they take your breath away. *Street Smart* is a movie like that—a clever thriller with a lot of unbelievable scenes and a sappy ending, but two wonderful performances.

The performances are by Morgan Freeman, as a Times Square pimp, and by Kathy Baker, as one of the hookers he controls. They play their characters as well as I can imagine them being played. Freeman has the flashier role, as a smart, very tough man who can be charming or intimidating—whatever's needed. Baker is a small-town girl who has been a hooker for years, who lives by the rules of the street but still has feelings.

Surrounding their performances is a plot that would have been interesting if it had been handled more realistically. Christopher Reeve plays a magazine reporter who concocts a completely fictional story about a colorful pimp. After the story is published and creates a sensation, the district attorney becomes convinced that the subject of the story is really the Freeman character—who is on trial for murder. He subpoenas Reeve's notes, but of course there aren't any.

From this promising beginning, *Street Smart* takes its story in two different directions. On one hand, we get a satirical view of the New York publishing and television industries, with Andre Gregory as the cynical magazine publisher and Reeve as an overnight journalism star who is instantly hired as a TV street reporter. On the other hand, we get Reeve trying to cover his tracks by going back and doing the reporting he should have done in the first place.

This second story—which involves Freeman and Baker—is much more interesting than the first. The pimp quickly figures out Reeve's problem and offers him a deal: He'll agree that he was the subject of the fictional story if Reeve provides him with an alibi. Reeve refuses. Freeman turns dangerous and violent: He's facing a life sentence and, for him, this isn't a matter of ethics but of his life.

The second hour of *Street Smart* almost seems to be scenes from two different movies. Freeman's dialogue is particularly good, as he analyzes Reeve's motives, talks about people who condescend to him, and terrorizes Baker for becoming Reeve's friend. There is one powerful, frightening scene where he threatens her with scissors; the power on the screen reminded me of vintage De Niro or Pacino.

Many of the street scenes have the uncanny feeling of real life, closely observed. For example, look at the scene where Freeman and his sidekick take Reeve for a tour of the streets in their Cadillac. When Freeman decides to discipline one of his girls, he squeezes her into the front seat, too, so Reeve is forced to confront reality up close, and maybe get blood on his suit. The staging of this scene—four people all in the front seat—is what makes it work.

The movie's other story, the one involving the magazine and TV news, is sort of silly. It's impossible to believe Reeve would so quickly become a TV newsman, difficult to believe most of the stories he reports, and incredible that Baker somehow always knows exactly where, in all of Manhattan, Reeve is going to be doing his next remote TV report.

The end of the movie is also a disappointment. It's yet another shoot-out. Screenwriters have grown so lazy in recent years that it's almost too much to ask them to resolve a plot on human terms. The last reel of most thrillers now involves the obligatory death of the villain, as if death were a solution. Since we know that's how the movie will end, the last reel is a loss—a waste of the movie's own time. And in *Street Smart* where Freeman creates such an unforgettable villain, I really resented it when he wasn't given the chance to participate in his own fate.

As a film school exercise, would-be screenwriters should be required to rewrite thrillers like this, with real human endings instead of the out of the standard sequence: chase, shoot-out, death, fade out. When an actor like Freeman goes to the trouble of creating a great character, the film should go to the trouble of providing him with a final scene.

Streetwise ★ ★ ★ ★
R, 92 m., 1985

Directed by Martin Bell and produced by Cheryl McCall. Reported by Mary Ellen Mark.

The mother is being frank about her daughter. She says she knows the girl is working as a prostitute, but she figures "it's just a phase she's going through." Her daughter is about fifteen years old. That is not the most harrowing moment in *Streetwise*, a heartbreaking documentary about the street children of Seattle. There are worse moments, for example the one where a street kid tries to talk to her mother about the fact that her stepfather "was fooling around . . . doing perverted things with me" when she was a baby. "Yes," says the mother philosophically, "but now he's stopped."

The subject of runaway, abducted, and abandoned children has received a lot of attention in the news, but never anything remotely like *Streetwise*, which enters into the lives of these under-age survivors as they fight for life and love on the streets of Seattle. The movie was inspired by a *Life* magazine article on a group of the kids, who, at an age when other kids are in school, are learning to be hookers, thieves, con men, pushers, and junkies. Now comes this movie, which contains extraordinary everyday footage, which the filmmakers obtained by spending months hanging out with the kids, until they gained their trust and their cameras became accepted.

The street kids lead horrifying lives, but sometimes there are moments of acceptance and happiness. They cling to each other. They relate uneasily with a social worker who seems philosophically resigned to the facts of street life. They try to dodge the cops. They live in an abandoned hotel, get money by begging and prostitution, eat by raiding the dumpsters behind restaurants. They even have a system for marking garbage so they don't eat food that's too old.

What is amazing is that some of these kids are still in touch with their parents. One girl shrugs that her mother is off to the woods for a weekend: "I've always known she don't love me or shit. So OK." She hugs herself. Another girl tries to talk to her mother, who says, "Be quiet. I'm drinking." A kid named DeWayne goes to visit his father in prison and gets a long lecture about smoking, drinking, and taking drugs, and a pie-in-the-sky speech about how they're going to open a thrift shop when the old man gets out of prison. The next time we see DeWayne, it is at his funeral; he hanged himself in a jail cell.

You walk out of *Streetwise* realizing that these aren't bad kids. They are resourceful, tough, and true to their own standards. They break the law, but then how many legal ways are there for fourteen-year-olds to support themselves? They talk about their parents in a matter-of-fact way that, we suspect, covers up great wounds, as when one girl says she's never met her natural father—"unless maybe I dated him once."

Streetwise is surprising for the frankness of the material it contains. How did the filmmakers get these people to say these things, to allow the cameras into their lives? We see moments of intimacy, of violence, of pain. The answer, I suspect, is that a lot of these kids were so starving for attention and affection that by offering both, the filmmakers were able to get whatever they wanted. Some of the scenes are possibly staged, in the sense that the characters are aware they are in a movie, but none of the scenes are false or contrived. These are children living rough in an American city, and you would blame their parents if you didn't see that the parents are just as alienated and hopeless, and that before long these kids will be damaged parents, too.

Stripes ★ ★ ★ ½

R, 105 m., 1981

Bill Murray (John), Harold Ramis (Russell), Warren Oates (Sergeant Hulka), P.J. Soles (Stella), Sean Young (Louise), John Candy (Ox). Directed by Ivan Reitman and produced by Reitman and Dan Goldberg. Screenplay by Goldberg, Len Blum, and Harold Ramis.

Stripes is an anarchic slob movie, a celebration of all that is irreverent, reckless, foolhardy, undisciplined, and occasionally scatalogical. It's a lot of fun. It comes from some of the same people involved in *National Lampoon's Animal House*, and could have been titled *National Lampoon's Animal Army* with little loss of accuracy. As a comedy about a couple of misfits who find themselves in the U.S. Army's basic training program, it obviously resembles Goldie Hawn's *Private Benjamin*. But it doesn't duplicate that wonderful movie; they could play on the same double feature. *Stripes* has the added advantage of being a whole movie about the Army, rather than half a movie (*Private Benjamin* got sidetracked with Hawn's love affair).

The movie is not only a triumph for its stars (Bill Murray and Harold Ramis) and its director (Ivan Reitman), but a sort of vindication. To explain: Reitman directed, and Murray starred in, the enormously successful *Meatballs*, which was an entertaining enough comedy but awfully ragged. No wonder. It was shot on a shoestring with Canadian tax shelter money. What Murray and Reitman prove this time is that, given a decent budget, they can do superior work—certainly superior to *Meatballs*, for starters. For Harold Ramis, who plays Murray's grave-eyed, flat-voiced, terminally detached partner in *Stripes*, this is a chance, at last, to come out from behind the camera. Ramis and Murray are both former Second City actors, but in Hollywood, Ramis has been typecast as a writer *(Animal House, Meatballs, Caddyshack)*, maybe because he sometimes looks too goofy for Hollywood's unimaginative tastes.

In *Stripes*, Murray and Ramis make a wonderful team. Their big strength is restraint. Given the tendency of movies like this to degenerate into undisciplined slapstick, they wisely choose to play their characters as understated, laid-back anarchists. Murray enlists in the Army in a what-the-hell mood after his girlfriend throws him out, and Ramis enlists because one stupid gesture deserves another. They're older than the usual Army recruit, less easily impressed with gung-ho propaganda, and quietly amazed at their drill instructor, Sergeant Hulka, who is played by Warren Oates with tough-as-nails insanity.

The movie has especially good writing in several scenes. My favorite comes near the beginning, during a session when recruits in the new platoon get to know one another. One obviously psycho draftee, who looks like Robert De Niro, quietly announces that if his fellow soldiers touch him, touch his stuff, or interfere in any way with his person or his privacy, he will quite simply be forced to kill them. Sergeant Hulka replies: "Lighten up!"

The movie's plot follows basic training, more or less, during its first hour. Then a romance enters. Murray and Ramis meet a couple of cute young military policewomen (P.J. Soles and Sean Young), and they happily violate every rule in the book. One funny scene: Murray and Soles sneak into the kitchen of the base commander's house and do unprecedented things with kitchen utensils.

It's an unwritten law of these movies that the last half hour has to involve some kind of spectacular development. In *Animal House*, it was the homecoming parade. In *Stripes*, the climax involves the Army's latest secret weapon, which is a computerized, armored, nuclear weapons carrier disguised as a recreational vehicle. Murray's platoon is assigned to go to Europe and test it. Murray, Ramis, and their girls decide to test it during a weekend holiday swing through the Alps. After they inadvertently cross the Iron Curtain, all hell breaks loose.

Stripes is a complete success on its intended level—it's great, irreverent entertainment—but it was successful, too, as a breakthrough for Ramis, Reitman, and Murray, on their way to *Ghostbusters*. Comedy is one of the hardest film genres to work in. Nobody knows all its secrets, not even Woody Allen and Mel Brooks. Here's a comedy from people who know some of the secrets most of the time.

Stroszek ★ ★ ★ ★

NO MPAA RATING, 108 m., 1978

Bruno S. (Stroszek), Eva Mattes (Eva), Clement Scheitz (Scheitz), Wilhelm von Homburg (Pimp), Burkhard Dreist (Pimp), Clayton Szlapinski (Scheitz's Nephew), Ely Rodriguez (Indian). Directed, produced, and written by Werner Herzog.

Werner Herzog has subtitled *Stroszek* as "a ballad," and so it is: It's like one of those bluegrass nonsense ballads in which impossible adventures are described in every verse, and the chorus reminds us that life gets teed-jus, don't it? But because Herzog has one of the most original imaginations of anyone now making movies, *Stroszek* is a haunting and hilarious ballad at the same time, an almost unbelievable mixture of lunacy, comedy, tragedy, and the simply human.

Consider. He gives us three main characters who are best friends, despite the fact that they're improbable as people and impossible as friends. There's Stroszek himself, just released from prison in Germany. He's a simple soul who plays the piano and the accordion and never quite understands why people behave as they do. There's Eva, a dim but pleasant Berlin prostitute. And there's old Scheitz, a goofy soul in his seventies who has been invited to live with his nephew in upstate Wisconsin.

This mixture is further complicated by the fact that Stroszek is played by Bruno S., the same actor Herzog used in *Kaspar Hauser.* Bruno S. is a mental patient, described by Herzog as schizophrenic, and it's a good question whether he's "acting" in this movie or simply exercising a crafty survival instinct. No matter: He comes across as saintly, sensitive, and very strange.

The three friends meet when Eva's two pimps beat her up and throw her out. She comes to live with Stroszek. The pimps (evil hoods right out of a Fassbinder gangster movie) later visit Stroszek and Eva and beat them both up, leaving Stroszek kneeling on his beloved piano with a school bell balanced on his derriere.

It is clearly time to leave Berlin, and old Scheitz has the answer: Visit his relatives in America. The nephew lives on a Wisconsin farm in an incredibly barren landscape, but to the Germans it's the American Dream. They buy an enormous mobile home, seventy feet long and fully furnished, and install a color TV in it. Eva gets a job as a waitress, and turns some tricks on the side at the truck stop. Stroszek works as a mechanic, sort of. Old Scheitz wanders about testing the "animal magnetism" of fence posts.

The Wisconsin scenes are among the weirdest I've ever seen in a movie: Notice, for example, the visit Stroszek and Eva get from that supercilious little twerp from the bank, who wants to repossess their TV set and who never seems to understand that nothing he says is understood. Or notice the brisk precision with which an auctioneer disposes of the mobile home, which is then carted away, all seventy feet of it, leaving the bewildered Stroszek looking at the empty landscape it has left behind.

Stroszek gets most hypnotically bizarre as it goes along, because we understand more of the assumptions of the movie. One of them is possibly that Kaspar Hauser might have become Stroszek, had he lived for another century and studied diligently. (Hauser, you might remember, was the "wild child" kept imprisoned in the dark for nineteen years, never taught to speak, and then dumped in a village square.)

The film's closing scenes are wonderfully funny and sad, at once. Stroszek and Scheitz rob a barber shop, and then Stroszek buys a frozen turkey, and then there is an amusement park with a chicken that will not stop dancing (and a policeman reporting "The dancing chicken won't stop"), and a wrecker driving in a circle with no one at the wheel, and an Indian chief looking on impassively, and somehow Herzog has made a statement about America here that is as loony and utterly original as any ever made.

Sudden Impact ★ ★ ★

R, 117 m., 1983

Clint Eastwood (Harry Callahan), Sondra Locke (Jennifer Spencer), Pat Hingle (Chief Jannings), Bradford Dillman (Captain Briggs). Directed and produced by Clint Eastwood. Screenplay by Joseph C. Stinson.

Most of what you hear about pop art and pop culture is pure hype. But there comes a moment about halfway through *Sudden Impact,* a Dirty Harry movie, when you realize that Harry has achieved some kind of legitimate pop status, as the purest distillation in the movies of the spirit of vengeance. To all those cowboy movies we saw in our youth, all those TV westerns and cop dramas and war movies, Dirty Harry has brought a great simplification: A big man, a big gun, a bad guy, and instant justice.

We learned early to cheer when John Wayne shot the bad guys. We cheered when the cavalry turned up, or the Yanks, or the SWAT team. What Eastwood's Dirty Harry movies do is very simple. They reduce the screen time between those cheers to the absolute minimum. *Sudden Impact* is a Dirty Harry movie with only the good parts left in. All the slow stuff, such as character, motivation, atmosphere, and plot, has been pared to exactly the minimum necessary to hold together the violence. This movie has been edited with the economy of a thirty-second commercial. As a result, it's a great audience picture. It's not plausible, it doesn't make much sense, it has a cardboard villain and, for that matter, a hero who exists more as a set of functions (grin, fight, chase, kill) than as a human being. But none of those are valid objections. *Sudden Impact* is more like a music video; it consists only of setups and payoffs, its big scenes are self-contained, it's filled with kinetic energy, and it has a short attention span. That last is very important, because if anyone were really keeping track of what Callahan does in this movie, Harry would be removed from the streets after his third or fourth killing. Dirty Harry movies are like Roadrunner cartoons; the moment a body is dead, it is forgotten, and nobody stands around to dispose of the corpses.

The movie's basically a revenge tragedy. A young woman (Sondra Locke) and her sister are sexually attacked at a carnival by a group of quasi-human bullies. The sister goes nuts, and Locke vows vengeance. One by one, she tracks down the rapists, and murders them by shooting them in the genitals and forehead. Dirty Harry gets assigned to the case, and the rest is a series of violent confrontations. Occasionally there's comic relief, in the form of Harry's meetings with his superiors, and his grim-jawed putdowns of anyone who crosses his path. ("Suck fish heads," he helpfully advises one man.)

If the movie has a weakness, it's the plot. Because I'm not sure the plot is relevant to the success of the film, I'm not sure that's a weakness. The whole business of Locke's revenge is so mechanically established and carried out that it's automatic, and because she has a "good" motive for her murders, she doesn't make an interesting villain. If Eastwood could create a villain as single-minded, violent, economically chiseled, and unremittingly efficient as Dirty Harry Callahan, then we'd be onto something.

Sunday Bloody Sunday ★ ★ ★ ★

R, 110 m., 1971

Glenda Jackson (Alex Greville), Peter Finch (Dr. Daniel Hirsh), Murray Head (Bob Elkin), Peggy Ashcroft (Mrs. Greville), Tony Britton (Businessman), Maureice Denham (Mr. Greville). Directed by John Schlesinger and produced by Joseph Janni. Screenplay by Penelope Gilliatt.

The official East Coast line on John Schlesinger's *Sunday Bloody Sunday* was that it is civilized. That judgment was enlisted to carry the critical defense of the movie; and, indeed, how can the decent critic be against a civilized movie about civilized people? My notion, all the same, is that *Sunday Bloody Sunday* is about people who suffer from psychic amputation, not civility, and that this film is not an affirmation but a tragedy.

The story involves three people in a rather novel love triangle: A London doctor in his forties, a divorced woman in her thirties, and the young man they are both in love with. The doctor and the woman know about each other (the young man makes no attempt to keep secrets) but don't seem particularly concerned; they have both made an accommodation in order to have some love instead of none at all.

The screenplay by Penelope Gilliatt takes us through eight or nine days in their lives, while the young man prepares to leave for New York. Both of his lovers will miss him—and he will miss *them,* after his fashion—but he has decided to go, and between them, they don't have enough pull on him to make him want to stay. So the two love affairs approach their ends, while the lovers go about a melancholy daily existence in London.

Both the doctor and the woman are involved in helping people, he by a kind and intelligent approach to his patients, she through working in an employment agency. The boy, on the other hand, seems exclusively preoccupied with the commercial prospects in America for his sculpture (he does things with glass tubes, liquids, and electricity). He isn't concerned with whether his stuff is any good, but whether it will sell to Americans. He doesn't seem to feel very deeply about anything, in fact. He is kind enough and open enough, but there is no dimension to him, as there is to his lovers.

It is with the two older characters that we get to the core of the movie. In a world where everyone loses eventually, they are still survivors. They survive by accommodating themselves to life as it must be lived. The doctor, for example, is not at all personally disturbed by his homosexuality, and yet he doesn't reveal it to his close-knit Jewish family; maintaining relations-as-usual with them is another way for him to survive. The woman tells us late in the film, "Some people believe something is better than nothing, but I'm beginning to believe that nothing can be better than something." Well, maybe so, but we get to know her well enough to suspect that she will settle for something, not nothing, again the next time.

The glory of *Sunday Bloody Sunday* is supposed to be the intelligent, sophisticated—civilized!—way in which these two people gracefully accept the loss of a love they had shared. Well, they *are* graceful as hell about it, and there is a positive glut of being philosophical about the inevitable. But that didn't make me feel better for them, or about them, the way it was supposed to; I felt pity for them. I insist that they would *not* have been so bloody civilized if either one had felt really deeply about the boy. The fact that they were willing to share him is perhaps a clue: They shared him not because they were willing to settle for half, but because they were afraid to try for all. The three-sided arrangement was, in part, a guarantee that no one would get in so deep that being "civilized" wouldn't be protection enough against hurt.

The acting is flawless. The late Peter Finch is the doctor, Glenda Jackson the woman, and Murray Head the young man. They are good to begin with and then just right for Gilliatt's screenplay and Schlesinger's direction. They are set down in a very real and sad London (seen mostly in cold twilights), and surrounded by supporting actors who resonate in a way that fills in all the dimensions of the characters. I think *Sunday Bloody Sunday* is a masterpiece, but I don't think it's about what everybody else seems to think it's about. This is not a movie about the loss of love, but about its absence.

Superman ★ ★ ★ ★

PG, 144 m., 1978

Christopher Reeve (Superman/Clark Kent), Marlon Brando (Jor-El), Gene Hackman (Lex Luthor), Margot Kidder (Lois Lane), Ned Beatty (Otis), Jackie Cooper (Perry White), Glenn Ford (Jonathan Kent), Trevor Howard (First Elder), Valerie Perrine (Miss Teschmacher). Directed by Richard Donner and produced by Pierre Spengler. Screenplay by Mario Puzo, David and Leslie Newman, and Robert Benton.

Superman is a pure delight, a wondrous combination of all the old-fashioned things we never really get tired of: adventure and romance, heroes and villains, earthshaking special effects, and—you know what else? Wit. That surprised me more than anything: That this big budget epic, which was half a decade making its way to the screen, would turn out to have an intelligent sense of humor about itself.

The wit, to be sure, is a little slow in revealing itself. The film's opening scenes combine great intergalactic special effects with ponderous acting and dialogue—most of it from Marlon Brando, who, as Superman's father, sends the kid to Earth in a spaceship that barely survives the destruction of the planet Krypton. Brando was allegedly paid $3 million for his role, or, judging by his dialogue, $500,000 a cliché. After Superbaby survives his space flight and lands in a Midwestern wheat field, however, the movie gets down to earth, too. And it has the surprising ability to have *fun* with its special effects. That's surprising because special effects on this vast scale (falling airliners, derailing passenger trains, subterranean dungeons, cracks in the earth, volcanic eruptions, dams bursting) are so expensive and difficult that it takes a special kind of courage to kid them a little—instead of regarding them with awe, as in the witless *Earthquake*.

The audience finds itself pleasantly surprised, and taken a little off guard; the movie's tremendously exciting in a comic book sort of way (kids will go ape for it), but at the same time it has a sly sophistication, a kidding insight into the material, that makes it, amazingly, a refreshingly offbeat comedy.

Most of the humor centers, of course, around one of the central icons of American popular culture, Superman (who, and I quote from our common memory of hundreds of comic books and radio and TV shows, in his dual identity as Clark Kent is a mild-mannered reporter for the *Daily Planet*). The producers held a worldwide talent search for an actor to play Superman, and although "talent searches" are usually 100 percent horsefeathers, this time, for once, they actually found the right guy.

He is Christopher Reeve. He *looks* like the Superman in the comic books (a fate I would not wish on anybody), but he's also an engaging actor, open and funny in his big love scene with Lois Lane, and then correctly awesome in his showdown with the archvillain Lex Luthor. Reeve sells the role; wrong casting here would have sunk everything.

And there would have been a lot to sink. *Superman* may have been expensive, all right, but the money's there on the screen. The screenplay was obviously written without the slightest concern for how much it might cost. After Clark Kent goes to work for the *Daily Planet* (and we meet old favorites Perry White, Lois Lane, and Jimmy Olsen), there's a nonstop series of disasters just for openers: Poor Lois finds herself dangling from one seatbelt after her helicopter crashes high atop the Daily Planet Building; Air Force One is struck by lightning and loses an engine; a thief climbs up a building using suction cups, and so on. Superman resolves his emergencies with, well, tact and good manners. He's modest about his abilities. Snaps a salute to the president. Says he's for "truth, justice, and the American Way." And, of course, falls in love with Lois Lane.

She's played by Margot Kidder, and their relationship is subtly, funnily wicked. She lives in a typical girl reporter's apartment (you know, a penthouse high atop a Metropolis skyscraper), and Superman zooms down to offer an exclusive interview and a free flight over Metropolis. Supposing *you're* a girl reporter, and Superman turns up. What would you ask him? So does she.

Meanwhile, the evil Lex Luthor (Gene Hackman) is planning an apocalyptic scheme to destroy the entire West Coast, plus Hackensack, New Jersey. He knows Superman's weak point: the deadly substance Kryptonite. He also knows that Superman cannot see through lead (Lois Lane, alas, forgets). Luthor lives in a subterranean pad that's a comic inspiration: A half-flooded, subterranean train station. Superman drills through the earth for a visit.

But enough of the plot. The movie works so well because of its wit and its special effects. A word more about each. The movie begins with the tremendous advantage that almost everyone in the audience knows the Superman saga from youth. There aren't a lot of explanations needed; that's brilliantly demonstrated in the first scene where Superman tries to change in a phone booth. Christopher Reeve can be allowed to smile, to permit himself a double entendre, to kid himself.

And then the special effects. They're as good in their way as any you've seen, and they come thick and fast. When the screenplay calls for Luthor to create an earthquake and for Superman to try to stop it, the movie doesn't give us a falling bridge or two, it gives us the San Andreas Fault cracking open. No half measures for Superman. The movie is, in fact, a triumph of imagination over both the difficulties of technology and the inhibitions of money. *Superman* wasn't easy to bring to the screen, but the filmmakers kept at it until they had it right.

Superman II ★ ★ ★ ★
PG, 127 m., 1981

Christopher Reeve (Superman/Clark Kent), Gene Hackman (Lex Luthor), Ned Beatty (Otis), Margot Kidder (Lois Lane), Jackie Cooper (Perry White), Sarah Douglas (Ursa), Jack O'Halloran (Non), Valerie Perrine (Eve). Directed by Richard Lester and produced by Alexander and Ilya Salkind and Pierre Spengler. Screenplay by Mario Puzo, David Newman, and Leslie Newman.

I thought the original *Superman* was terrific entertainment—and so I was a little startled to discover that I liked *Superman II* even more. Perhaps the secret of the sequel is that it has more faith in Superman. Before the original *Superman* was released in 1978, the producers knew he could carry a speeding locomotive, all right—but could he carry a movie? They weren't sure, and since they were investing millions of dollars in the project, they didn't want to rest a whole movie on the broad shoulders of their unknown star, Christopher Reeve. So they began *Superman* ponderously, on the planet Krypton, with the presence of Marlon Brando as a sort of totem to convince audiences that this movie was big league. They told us of Superman's origins with a solemnity more befitting a god. They were very serious and very symbolic, and it wasn't until Superman came to Earth that the movie really caught fire. *Then*, half an hour or more into its length, it started giving us what we came for: Superman flying around with his red cape, saving mankind.

Superman II begins in midstream, and never looks back (aside from a brief recap of the first movie). In many ways, it's a repeat of the last ninety minutes of the first film. It has the same key characters, including archvillain Lex Luthor. It continues the love story of Lois Lane and Superman, not to mention the strange relationship of Lois and Clark Kent. It features the return of three villains from Krypton, who when last seen were trapped in a one-dimensional plane of light and cast adrift in space. And it continues those remarkable special effects.

From his earliest days in a comic book, Superman always has been an urban hero. He lived in a universe that was defined by screaming banner headlines and vast symbolic acts, and *Superman II* catches that flavor perfectly with its use of famous landmarks like the Eiffel Tower, the Empire State Building, Niagara Falls, and the Coca-Cola sign in Times Square. He was a pop hero in a pop world, and like Mickey Mouse and the original Coke trademark, he became an instantly recognizable trademark.

That's why the special effects in both *Superman* movies are so crucial. It is a great deal simpler to show a rocket ship against the backdrop of outer space than to show Kryptonian villains hurling a city bus through the air in midtown Manhattan. But the feeling of actuality makes Superman's exploits more fun. It brings the fantastic into our everyday lives; it delights in showing us the reaction of the man on the street to Superman's latest stunt. In the movie, as in the comic book, ordinary citizens seems to spend their days glued to the sidewalk, gazing skyward, and shouting things like "Superman is dead!" or "Superman has saved the world!"

In *Superman II* he saves large portions of the world, all right, but what he preserves most of all is the element of humanity within him. The Superman movies made a basic decision to give Superman and his alter ego, Clark Kent, more human feelings than the character originally possessed. So *Superman II* has a lot of fun developing his odd dual relationship with Lois Lane. At long, long last, Lois and Superman make love in this movie (after champagne, but discreetly offscreen in Superman's ice palace). But Lois and Clark Kent also spend the night together in highly compromised circumstances, in a Niagara Falls honeymoon haven. And the movie has fun with another one of those ultimate tests that Lois was always throwing at Clark to make him admit he was really Superman. Lois bets her life on it this time, hurling herself into the rapids below Niagara Falls. Either Clark can turn into Superman and save her—or she'll drown. And what then? All I can say is, Clark does *not* turn into Superman.

This scene has a lot of humor in it, and the whole film has more smiles and laughs than the first one. Maybe that's because of a change in directors. Richard Donner, who made the first *Superman* film and did a brilliant job of establishing a basic look for the series, was followed this time by Richard Lester *(A Hard Day's Night, The Three Musketeers),* and this is some of Lester's best work. He permits satire to make its way into the film more easily. He has a lot of fun with Gene Hackman, as the still-scheming, thin-skinned, egomaniacal Lex Luthor. And he draws out Christopher Reeve, whose performance in the title role is sly, knowing, and yet still appropriately square. This movie's most intriguing insight is that Superman's disguise as Clark Kent isn't a matter of looks as much as of mental attitude: Clark is disguised not by his glasses but by his ordinariness. Beneath his meek exterior, of course, is concealed a superhero. And, the movie subtly hints, isn't that the case with us all?

Superman III ★ ★ 1/2

PG, 125 m., 1983

Christopher Reeve (Superman/Clark Kent), Richard Pryor (Gus Gorman), Annette O'Toole (Lana Lang), Robert Vaughn (Ross Webster). Directed by Richard Lester and produced by Alexander Salkind. Screenplay by David and Leslie Newman.

Superman III is the kind of movie I feared the original *Superman* would be. It's a cinematic comic book, shallow, silly, filled with stunts and action, without much human interest. What's amazing is that the first two Superman movies avoided that description, creating a fantasy with a certain charm. They could have been manipulative special effects movies, but they were a great deal more. With this third one, maybe they've finally run out of inspiration.

The big news about *Superman III* is, of course, the presence of Richard Pryor in the cast. But Pryor isn't used very well here. He never really emerges as a person we care about. His character and the whole movie seem assembled out of prefabricated pieces. The first two films were too, in a way, but real care was taken with the dialogue, and we could occasionally halfway believe that real people had gotten themselves into this world of fantasy. Not this time. *Superman III* drops most of the threads of the first two movies—including Lois Lane's increasingly complex love affair with Clark Kent and Superman—and goes for the action. There's no real sense of what Superman, or Clark, ever really feels. The running gag about the hero's double identity isn't really exploited this time. The sheer amazingness of Superman isn't explored; the movie and the people in it take this incredible creature for granted. After the bird and the plane, it's "Superman" when it should be SUPERMAN!

The plot involves the usual scheme to control the Earth. The villain this time is Robert Vaughn, as a mad billionaire who wants to use satellites to control the Earth's crops and become even richer. He directs his satellites and weapons systems by computer, and that's how he hooks up with Pryor, as a brilliant, but befuddled, computer programmer. Superman, meanwhile, has a couple of things on his mind. After Lois Lane leaves to go on vacation at the beginning of the movie (in a particularly awkward scene), Clark goes home to his Smallville High School reunion, and has a love affair with Lana Lang (Annette O'Toole). It's sweet, but it's not half as interesting as the Ice Castle footage with Lois Lane in *Superman II.* Then Superman gets zapped with some ersatz Kryptonite and turns into a meanie, which is good for some laughs (as a practical joke, he straightens the Leaning Tower of Pisa).

All of this is sort of fun, and the special effects are sometimes very good, but there's no real sense of wonder in this film—no moments like the scene in *Superman* where California threatened to fall into the sea and Superman turned back time to save humanity. After that, who cares about Robert Vaughn's satellites? Or Richard Pryor's dilemma? Pryor can be a wicked, anarchic comic actor, and that presence would have been welcome here. Instead, like the rest of *Superman III*, he's kind of innocuous.

The Sure Thing ★ ★ ★ ½

PG-13, 94 m., 1985

John Cusack (Walter Gibson), Daphne Zuniga (Alison Bradbury), Anthony Edwards (Lance), Boyd Gaines (Jason), Tim Robbins (Gary Cooper), Lisa Jane Persky (Mary Ann Webster), Vivica Lindfors (Professor), Nicolette Sheridan (Sure Thing). Directed by Rob Reiner and produced by Roger Birnbaum. Screenplay by Steven Bloom and Jonathan Roberts.

The love story is one of Hollywood's missing genres. The movie industry seems better at teen-age movies like *Porky's*, with its sleazy shower scenes, than with screenplays that involve any sort of thought about the love lives of its characters. That's why *The Sure Thing* is a small miracle. Although the hero of this movie is promised by his buddy that he'll be fixed up with a "guaranteed sure thing," the film is not about the sure thing but about how this kid falls genuinely and touchingly into love.

The movie's love story begins in an Eastern college classroom. Walter Gibson (John Cusack) walks into his English class and falls immediately into love with Alison Bradbury (Daphne Zuniga), who is smart and good-looking and not one of your brainless movie broads. He asks her out, but succeeds, of course, in acting like a total nerd, and she invites him to get out of her life. End of act one. In act two, Walter plans to spend his Christmas vacation in Los Angeles, where his buddy says the Sure Thing is eagerly awaiting his arrival. Alison also plans to go to L.A., to visit her fiancé, who is studying to be a boring middle-class vegetable. They both sign up for rides, and, of course, they both wind up in the back seat of the same car. At first they don't talk. They they start to fight. Then they are ditched at the side of the road and have to hitchhike to L.A. together.

I know this is an obvious movie ploy. I know, in fact, that what will happen next is completely predictable: They'll fight, they'll share experiences, they'll suffer together, and eventually they'll fall in love. I know all of these things, and yet I don't care. I don't care because love is always a cliché anyway, and the only thing that makes it endlessly fascinating is that the players are always changing. These two particular characters, Walter and Alison, played by these two gifted young actors, Cusack and Zuniga, make *The Sure Thing* into a special love story.

One of the unique things about the movie is that the characters show a normal shyness about sex. Most movie teen-agers seem to be valedictorians from the Masters & Johnson Institute. They're born knowing more about sex than Rhett Butler would have been able to teach Scarlett O'Hara. They are also, of course, not shy, not insecure, not modest, and occasionally not human. Walter and Alison are closer to real teen-agers, with real doubts and hesitations and uncertainties. The other surprising thing about the film is that it successfully avoids an obligatory sex scene with the Sure Thing (Nicollette Sheridan, in a thankless role). This film is so revolutionary, it believes sex should be accompanied by respect and love! By the end of the movie, when Walter and Alison finally do kiss, it means something. It means more, in fact, than any movie kiss in a long time, because it takes place between two people we've gotten to know and who have gotten to know each other.

Surrender ★ ★

PG, 96 m., 1987

Michael Caine (Sean Stein), Sally Field (Daisy Morgan), Steve Guttenberg (Marty Caesar), Peter Boyle (Lawyer). Directed by Jerry Belson and produced by Aaron Spelling and Alan Greisman. Screenplay by Belson.

In my mind, I visualize a Hollywood story conference where everybody is laughing. Here's the story being told: Michael Caine is a rich author who has been taken to the cleaners in two divorces and a palimony suit. He hates women so much he wants to move to a country where they are flogged. Then he finds true love.

At a charity benefit, robbers break in, force everyone to strip, and abscond with the jewelry after tying Caine and Sally Field together, naked. In such close quarters Caine finds his interest in Field rising, and after they are freed, he pursues her and they fall in love. But he keeps it a secret that he is a wealthy writer, because he wants to be sure she loves him for himself and not for his money.

Great story idea? You bet. I'd make the movie in a second. So did Cannon. But did anyone ask Jerry Belson, the writer and director, what happened then? *Surrender* is an astonishing case of a movie that can do no wrong for its first half, and little right thereafter. The story has no place to go, and Belson's contrivances in keeping it floating are desperate.

The chemistry, of course, is a lot of fun. Caine has developed into one of the most sure-footed and unfailingly entertaining leading men in modern Hollywood, and Field is delightful as Daisy Morgan, who works all day in an art factory, producing "genuine oils" on an assembly line. She wants to work on her own paintings, but never finds the time, and when Caine meets her, she has just about given up on her rich, boring boyfriend (Steve Guttenberg).

The early scenes of their courtship are charming. Caine is good at playing shy and uncertain, which he can manage even while proposing sex almost as soon as he walks into Field's house for the first time. "I make it a policy never to have sex before the first date," she explains.

Caine carries on an interior struggle between his romantic inclinations and his financial fears, and is counseled by his lawyer (Peter Boyle), who foresees the day when his client will be mailing *all* his money to former wives. But at last, trust and romance win out, and Caine and Field are able to acknowledge that they love one another.

It's about there that the movie runs out of gas. Instead of continuing to develop their relationship, Belson starts throwing unnecessary plot developments at his story, involving prenuptial agreements, Reno jackpots, terrorist kidnappings, personality tranformations, and fatal misunderstandings. The movie loses track of its simple human feelings, and gets bogged down in plot gimmicks. The fragile relationship between Caine and Field is one of the casualties.

Too bad. There are so many good things in the first part of *Surrender* (including one big, *big* laugh), that I thought we were home free. Then the movie lost its confidence and its grasp. When I picture that imaginary Hollywood story conference, the thing that bothers me the most is that maybe everyone liked the second half of Belson's story better than the first. In so many movies these days, something always has to be happening—no matter what. And it's easy to lose a character in the confusion.

The Survivors ★ ½

R, 102 m., 1983

Walter Matthau (Sonny Paluso), Robin Williams (Donald Quinelle), Jerry Reed (Jack Locke), James Wainwright (Wes Huntley). Directed by Michael Ritchie and produced by

William Sackheim. Screenplay by Michael Leeson.

Survivalists are very cautious people who have secret hideaways somewhere in the woods, which they've stocked with food, weapons, ammunition, and survival gear. In case of a nuclear attack, they alert each other by CB radio and light out for the trees. *The Survivors*, which attempts to have fun with their prudence, is an aimless, self-indulgent, confusing comedy that never comes to grips with its material. And it allows Robin Williams to run wild, destroying any marginal credibility the story might have had.

It's a mess. One of the reasons it's a mess is that it doesn't know whether to be a human comedy or a slapstick, satirical comedy. The first approach would have involved creating plausible characters and plugging them into a comic situation. The second approach allows anything to be funny in any way possible. *The Survivors* goes for both approaches simultaneously, which is confusing. For example, after a slapstick opening in which Williams is fired by a trained parrot, there's a scene of social satire set in an unemployment office. Even within scenes, the styles of the actors suggest they think they're in different movies. Walter Matthau manfully acts as if he's in a plausible movie, while Williams mugs, improvises, and randomly alters his accent. See the problem? If it's a "real" world, then Matthau should observe that Williams isn't playing with a full deck. If it's an anarchic satire, then the joke's on Matthau, who does not seem to realize it.

The story involves two newly unemployed men. Williams has been fired by the parrot and Matthau's gas station has been blown up. After they get discouraged by the lines at the unemployment office, they happen to go to the same diner, which is stuck up by a fierce criminal (Jerry Reed). They snatch off his ski mask and see him, and so Reed believes he has to kill these two witnesses. What happens next is very long and involved. Williams signs up for a wilderness survival training course. He hopes to become tough enough to protect himself. Reed and Matthau both find themselves at the same isolated survivalist area. The head survivalist is a reactionary paramilitary nut who believes American society is doomed to collapse. And so on.

This material is the stuff of promising satire, but the movie's director, Michael Ritchie, goes nowhere with it. His parts don't seem to fit together. One moment we'll be getting a heartfelt talk, and the next moment there's a wilderness shoot-out straight out of *The Road Runner.* The story gets so confused that the movie can't even account for why its characters happen to be in the same place at the same time; in desperation, it gives us a scene where Williams actually calls Reed and tells him where he can be found. Uh-huh.

The Survivors wouldn't be such a disappointment if it didn't employ such talented people, and if it weren't directed by Michael Ritchie, whose gift for satirizing American institutions has given us good movies like *Smile, The Bad News Bears, The Candidate,* and *Semi-Tough.* This time he seems so fast off the starting line he left his screenplay behind.

Suspect ★ ★ ½
R, 118 m., 1987
(See related Film Clips, pp. 744 and 747.)

Cher (Kathleen Riley), Dennis Quaid (Eddie Sanger), Liam Neeson (Carl Wayne Anderson), John Mahoney (Judge Helms), Joe Mantegna (Charlie Stella), Philip Bosco (Paul Gray). Directed by Peter Yates and produced by Daniel A. Sherkow. Screenplay by Eric Roth.

Art films can play all the games they want. But if you're going to make a film in a commercial genre, then I think you have to play by the rules of that genre. In the case of a courtroom whodunit, that means you can't produce the guilty man out of left field, with no clues and no preparation. The audience has to have a fair chance to figure things out. *Suspect* is a well-made thriller, but it was spoiled for me by an extraordinary closing scene where Cher, as the defense attorney, solves the case with all the logic of a magician pulling a rabbit out of a hat.

The plot involves the murder of a Washington legal secretary. A Skid Row bum is arrested for the murder, and Cher is the public defender assigned to his case. He is a deaf-mute who has lost all trust in society, but Cher penetrates his defenses and becomes convinced he is innocent. In that case, who committed the murder?

A key clue is provided in the first scene of

the movie, which shows a Supreme Court justice committing suicide. Other clues appear from time to time, especially after one of the jurors on the case decides to take things into his own hands. He's played by Dennis Quaid, as a lobbyist who is summoned for jury duty and becomes convinced the defendant didn't commit the crime. He conducts his own private investigation, and feeds clues to Cher.

She's afraid of jury-tampering charges (although this seems more like a case of lawyer-tampering). But things get really sticky when Cher and Quaid fall in love. I liked their scenes together, and I admired their performances. Indeed, I found a lot to like in this movie, which was directed by Peter Yates with particular attention to the texture of the lives of his characters.

One of the movie's themes is that all the characters are homeless—not just the bum, but also the lobbyist, the public defender, and everyone else we meet. They have places that they live in, that they use to sleep at night, but they do not have a "home" and they do not have loved ones around them. Their loneliness is underlined in one of the movie's most quietly effective scenes, where Quaid sleeps with a congresswoman, and it's a toss-up whether he's doing it out of ambition, politics, or need.

The movie develops its case with the kind of logic I enjoy in a whodunit. We meet the suspects, we evaluate the clues, and then (after the obligatory woman-in-danger sequence with a knife-wielding assailant chasing Cher through shadowy corridors) there's the big showdown in court. That's where the movie goes wrong. Cher stands up and rattles off a long, complicated speech in which the real murderer is revealed—and I began to develop a real case of resentment, because the murderer is a complete dark horse. That's not fair. It's as if an Agatha Christie novel evaluated six suspects in a British country house, and then in the last chapter we discover that the killer was a guy from next door.

Swamp Thing ★ ★ ★

R, 102 m., 1982

Louis Jourdan (Arcane), Adrienne Barbeau (Alice), Ray Wise (Dr. Holland), Dick Durock (Swamp Thing), David Hess (Ferret), Nicholas Worth (Brung). Directed by Wes Craven and produced by Benjamin Melniker and Michael Uslan. Screenplay by Craven.

Swamp Thing had already won my heart *before* its moment of greatness, but when that moment came, I knew I'd discovered another one of those movies that fall somewhere between buried treasures and guilty pleasures. The moment comes after Dr. Alec Holland, brilliant scientist, is attacked by thugs, is splashed with his own secret formula, catches on fire, leaps into the swamp, and turns into Swamp Thing when the formula interacts with his body and the vegetation in the swamp. Crawling back onto dry land, Swamp Thing is not recognized by his former girlfriend, the beautiful Alice Cable (Adrienne Barbeau). But after the thugs fill him with machine gun bullets and hack off his left arm, Alice asks, "Does it hurt?" and Swamp Thing replies, "Only when I laugh."

That was the movie's moment of greatness. There are others that come close, as when Swamp Thing, dripping with moss and looking like a bug-eyed spinach soufflé, says "There is great beauty in the swamp . . . if you know where to look." And when the evil villain (Louis Jourdan) drinks the secret formula and confidently waits for it to transform him into a powerful genius, he discovers that the formula doesn't so much *change* you, as develop what is already latent within you. Therefore, once a horse's ass, *always* a horse's ass.

This is one of those movies like *Infra-Man* or *Invasion of the Bee Girls:* an off-the-wall, eccentric, peculiar movie fueled by the demented obsessions of its makers. *Swamp Thing* first saw the light of day, so to speak, as a hero in a celebrated series of DC Comics. The movie version was written and directed by Wes Craven, who made *Last House on the Left,* a movie I persist in admiring even in the face of universal repugnance. Craven also made *The Hills Have Eyes,* which even I found decadent, and the made-for-NBC movie *Stranger in Our House,* with Linda Blair. This time, with *Swamp Thing,* he betrays a certain gentleness and poetry along with the gore; in fact, this movie is a lot less violent than many others in the same genre. Craven's inspiration seems to come from James Whale's classic *Bride of Frankenstein* (1935), and he pays tribute in scenes where his swamp monster sniffs a flower, admires a young girl's beauty from afar, and looks sadly at a photograph in a locket. *Swamp Thing* doesn't stop there; it also contains an exact visual quote from Russ Meyer's *Lorna,* and a scene in which the jailer in a dungeon cheerfully quotes the title of a Werner Herzog film: "It's every man for himself, and God against all!"

Will you like this film? Yes, probably, if you like monster and horror movies. The movie occupies familiar ground, but it has a freshness and winsome humor to fit it, and Craven moves confidently through the three related genres he's stealing from (monster movies, mad scientist movies and transformation movies—in which people turn into strange beings). There's beauty in this movie, if you know where to look for it.

Swann in Love ★ ★ ★
R, 110 m., 1984

Jeremy Irons (Charles Swann), Ornella Muti (Odette de Crecy), Alain Delon (Baron de Charlus), Fanny Ardant (Duchesse de Guermantes), Marie-Christine Barrault (Madame Verdurin). Directed by Volker Schlondorff and produced by Nicole Stephane. Written by Peter Brook, Jean-Claude Carriere, and Marie-Helene Estienne.

All of the reviews I've read of Volker Schlondorff's *Swann in Love* treat it like a classroom assignment. The movie is described as a version of one of the stories that make up *Remembrance of Things Past,* the epic novel by Marcel Proust, and then the exercise becomes almost academic: "Compare and contrast Proust and Schlondorff, with particular attention to the difference between fiction and the film." Imagine instead, that this is not a film based on a novel, but a new film from an original screenplay. It will immediately seem more lively and accessible. Because not one person in a hundred who sees the film will have read Proust, this is a sensible approach; it does away with the nagging feeling that one should really curl up with those twelve volumes before going to the theater.

Schlondorff's *Swann in Love*—as opposed to Proust's—is the story of a pale young man who goes one day to visit a prostitute, and is actually indifferent to her until she stands him up. Then he becomes obsessed. She is not the right woman for him, but her very wrongness becomes fascinating. Because she is vulgar, because she lies, because she toys with his affection, and most particularly because she lets him smell the orchid in her bodice, she becomes the most important person in the world to him, and he throws his life and reputation at her feet. Proper society, of course, disapproves of his affair—and talks of nothing else. In the elegant salons where ladies and gentlemen gather, Swann is not welcome if he brings along his Odette, but because he cannot be happy without her, this is no punishment. In the most humiliating scenes in the movie, he abjectly follows her through the night, knocks on a door he hopes is hers, and stands in her boudoir while she nonchalantly disrobes and dresses for an appointment with another man.

Casting is everything in a film like this. Jeremy Irons is perfect as Charles Swann, pale, deep-eyed, feverish with passion. This was his third movie (after *The French Lieutenant's Woman* and *Betrayal*) in which love seemed necessary to his nature. We can believe his passion. As Odette, Schlondorff has cast Ornella Muti, who has a sort of languorous bemusement that is maddening: We wonder if she is even capable of understanding that the man before her is mad with love and desire, and then we realize, of course, that her very *inability* to care is what creates her fatal attraction. *Swann in Love* is a stylish, period love story, surrounding its central characters with still other pathetic seekers of perfection (Alain Delon is wonderful as a gloomy homosexual who pursues an idealized form of misery). Yet at the film's end, we've probably learned nothing except that lovers were as silly in 1875 as they are now. Sillier, perhaps; they had more time.

Sweet Liberty ★ ★ ½
PG, 107 m., 1986

Alan Alda (Michael Burgess), Michael Caine (Elliott James), Michelle Pfeiffer (Faith Healy), Bob Hoskins (Stanley Gould), Lise Hilboldt (Gretchen Carlsen), Lillian Gish (Cecelia Burgess), Saul Rubinek (Bo Hodges). Directed by Alan Alda and produced by Martin Bregman. Screenplay by Alda.

Sweet Liberty tells the story of a Hollywood movie company that arrives in a small South-eastern college town to shoot a film about the Revolutionary War. It also tells three or four other stories, and that is the problem: The movie wants to juggle a lot of characters all at once, but it keeps dropping the most interesting ones.

The movie stars Alan Alda as the local history professor who sold his book to the movies. He didn't exactly expect them to turn it into a scholarly documentary, but he is shocked to see it rewritten into a seamy tale of lust, betrayal, intrigue, and violence. He makes a liaison with the screenwriter (Bob Hoskins), who tutors him in cynicism, and together they try to change some of the worst parts.

Meanwhile, the small town itself is turning into a seamy hotbed of lust, betrayal, and intrigue. Alda has been dating another faculty member (Lise Hilboldt), but then he falls instantly in love with the movie's sexy leading lady (Michelle Pfeiffer). That's sort of all right, because Hilboldt has a fling with the leading man (Michael Caine). And there are subplots involving the director, the local extras, and even Alda's ancient mother (portrayed by the legendary Lillian Gish, who, old as the character is, still plays below her age).

These are a lot of story strands to keep straight, and *Sweet Liberty* doesn't always succeed. I was left with the impression there was more material than the time to deal with it, and I especially wanted to see more of that excellent comic actor, Michael Caine. His character, a shameless philanderer with a streak of poetry in his soul, is so promising that it's a shame he's on screen so infrequently.

Alda wrote and directed the movie, as well as starred in it, and he has some nice touches. I liked the scene in which Caine covered up the unexpected arrival of his wife by taking everybody on a rollercoaster ride. And I liked the next scene, too, where they walk drunkenly through the town late at night, talking about those great romantic truths which always seem so elusive in the morning.

Alda's best-written character in the movie is probably Faith Healy, the sexy actress played by Michelle Pfeiffer—and her performance uses some wonderfully subtle touches, as she moves back and forth between her historical character and her distinctly more cynical modern one. It's here that the movie comes closest to its theme, which is (I think) the ways that adults can deceive themselves even while thinking they are perfectly aware of all their motives.

The Lillian Gish character is a distraction. Her obsession with an old boyfriend is intriguing enough, however, that maybe this particular story should have been lifted completely out of *Sweet Liberty* and made into a movie of its own. There's a great scene where Alda and Hilboldt go to visit the old boyfriend, whose wife complains that the old lady has made their life miserable. It's such a strong scene that, paradoxically, it doesn't belong in this movie; its tone is wrong for the other stuff.

Sweet Liberty will probably play better on TV and video than it did at the theatre, where its episodic structure will be more at home, and it won't be so obvious how all of the little set-pieces don't hang together. Like most movies about movies, it is not very realistic. It's unlikely a big-budget historical movie would use such shabby painted backdrops, and completely impossible for the climactic scene (a sabotaged battle) to unfold the way it does. Few movies have had the patience to show moviemaking the way it really is (Truffaut's *Day for Night* came fairly close), but there are times here when the onscreen director (Saul Rubinek) doesn't even seem convinced of his own authenticity.

Swimming to Cambodia ★ ★ ★

NO MPAA RATING, 87 m., 1987

Written by and starring Spalding Gray.
Directed and produced by Jonathan Demme.

Spalding Gray is an actor who had a small role in *The Killing Fields* (the assistant to the American ambassador), and in this movie he talks about that performance and other matters. He sits at a table—a glass of water and a microphone before him, a couple of maps behind him—and talks and talks. Because he is a good talker, and because he has something to say, this curious idea for a movie actually works.

Swimming to Cambodia is based on a one-man, two-evening stage performance that Gray polished and took on tour a couple of years ago. It has been edited down to less than two hours and directed by Jonathan Demme with an unobtrusive authority.

There are subtle light and music cues, a few sound effects such as fluttering helicopter blades, and, for the rest, there is Gray's face and his voice.

His monologue begins with his auditions for the role in *The Killing Fields,* the film that told the story of a friendship between a *New York Times* correspondent and his Cambodian assistant. The assistant, Dith Pran, was played by Haing S. Ngor, who won an Academy Award for his performance. Gray won no awards for his work in the movie and indeed is a minor character whose few scenes are shown in the course of his monologue.

What he had, during the course of the shooting in Thailand, was a great deal of spare time. He seems to have used this time to investigate not only the fleshpots of Bangkok, but also the untold story of the genocide that was practiced by the fanatic Khmer Rouge on their Cambodian countrymen. He recounts in great and gory detail all of his findings, from the infamous "banana show" in a local nightclub to the disappearance of millions of Cambodians in the greatest mass murder of modern history.

He is a spellbinding storyteller, and as he speaks, something occurs that might be called the "radio phenomenon." This is the same effect that was created in *My Dinner with André* (1981), another movie in which the characters simply sit and talk. Although we are essentially only seeing a face on a screen, we are picturing the story's events in our minds; it's like listening to a radio play.

Gray is not afraid to be dramatic. His voice races quickly through a litany of images, his arms wave, his eyes flash. Then sometimes he is quiet, contemplative. This is a monologue that has been polished during many hundreds of hours on the stage, and although he makes it sound fresh, he is so familiar with it that he can gallop through a tricky passage with the confidence of an auctioneer. Like a good preacher, some of his power comes from the sheer virtuosity of his speech.

Gray's theater performance, and now this film, have been praised in many quarters, but in the *New Yorker* review, Pauline Kael was not amused. She admired Demme's direction and even Gray's presence, but asked aloud if it had occurred to him that he was exploiting the genocide in Cambodia for his own aggrandizement. This is a serious charge, particularly since Gray did not, of course, personally witness anything at all in Southeast Asia except some strip shows, some local scenery, and the filming of part of *The Killing Fields.* His material about the war is all hearsay.

I respect what Kael is getting at, but I ask myself this question: Would it have been more worthy for Gray to talk about the strippers and the moviemaking while ignoring the fact that *The Killing Fields* was inspired, indirectly, by the deaths of those millions of people? There is a fine line to be drawn here, and I am not sure where it falls.

Of course, *Swimming to Cambodia* is, on some level, self-aggrandizement. All actors might enjoy the thought of a feature film devoted entirely to their face and their voice, but few would have the nerve to go ahead with one. On the other hand, literally all possible subjects are exploited whenever they are turned into fiction. All war movies, for example, take the suffering and deaths of untold victims and use them as the setting for a fictional story about a few idealized characters. Is *Swimming to Cambodia* any more exploitive than *The Deer Hunter,* Platoon, or for that matter, *Paths of Glory* or *All Quiet on the Western Front?*

None of us can directly experience more than we actually see and hear. Everything else is hearsay. All we really know, for sure, is what happened to us. There's that story about the actor hired to play the gravedigger in *Hamlet.* Asked what the play was about, he replied, "It's about this gravedigger, who meets a prince. . . ."

Swimming to Cambodia is about this actor, who meets a war.

Switching Channels ★ ★ ★

PG-13, 105 m., 1988 ✓

Kathleen Turner (Christy Colleran), Burt Reynolds (John L. Sullivan IV), Christopher Reeve (Blaine Bingham), Ned Beatty (Roy Ridnitz), Henry Gibson (Ike Roscoe), George Newbern (Siegenthaler), Al Waxman (Berger), Ken James (Warden Terwillinger), Barry Flatman (Zaks), Ted Simonett (Tillinger). Directed by Ted Kotcheff and produced by Martin Ransohoff. Screenplay by Jonathan Reynolds.

Newspapers once had editions all day long,

and reporters were forever feeding rewritemen a new angle for the replate. The front-page headlines changed from edition to edition, to make the news seem forever breathlessly new. Now that kind of continuing update is left to television; ever notice how Headline News updates the breaking stories while repeating the feature stuff over and over again?

The Front Page is, of course, a comedy about newspapers—the most famous newspaper comedy ever written. It was conceived in the hothouse of the Chicago newspaper world in the 1920s, when a dozen reporters were chasing every story, and there were new editions all day long. Those were the days when a "scoop" meant you stole a story right out from under the other guy's nose. These days, an "exclusive" is more likely to mean you outbid the opposition for the serial rights to a TV star's steamy confessions.

So maybe it's only appropriate that the latest remake of *The Front Page* involves, not newspapers, but a TV cable news operation. Ben Hecht and Charles MacArthur, who wrote the classic play, might even approve; they abandoned Chicago for Hollywood, where remakes were routine and the 1931 screen version of *The Front Page* was updated nine years later in *His Girl Friday* by simply making one of the boys in the press room into a girl.

The Front Page was filmed again by Billy Wilder in 1974, with Jack Lemmon and Walter Matthau, and now here is Ted Kotcheff's 1988 version, titled *Switching Channels* and starring Burt Reynolds, Kathleen Turner, and Christopher Reeve. It's not as good as *His Girl Friday*, but it's comparable with the others.

Turner plays a hard-driving TV news reporter who seems willing, in the opening credits, to go anywhere and do anything as long as the videotape is rolling. Reynolds is her ex-husband and current boss, the managing editor of the cable news operation. And on a long-overdue vacation, Turner falls in love with Christopher Reeve, a New York millionaire. She decides to quit TV, marry Reeve, and move to New York, but hold on a minute—a famous criminal is scheduled to be executed at midnight, and Reynolds will do anything to keep his star reporter on the story.

This is more or less the same premise as the first three versions, allowing for the adjustments that have to be made when the star reporter is a woman (as Rosalind Russell was in the 1940 edition). Christopher Reeve's role has been greatly expanded (the fiancé was mostly offstage in the earlier versions), and I'm not sure that's a good thing; too much time is wasted while Reynolds and Reeve insult each other while the news is put on hold.

But Kathleen Turner has perfect timing as the long-suffering anchor, and she and Reynolds work up a nice sweat and some good chemistry in their relationship, which seems to be based on a few good memories and a whole lot of one-liners. The Reeve character is unnecessary much of the time, but Reeve has fun with it anyway, with his floppy tailored suits, his newly blond hair, and his willingness to accommodate the obviously derailed Turner.

The details of the update don't much matter, either. This time the convicted man is hidden inside a Xerox machine instead of a roll-top desk, but the basic mechanics of the original Hecht-MacArthur story are still sound, and *Switching Channels* is true to the obsessive-compulsive hostility that is the fuel for all good reporters.

There is, however, one major lapse that should not go unreported. As everyone who has ever seen the play knows, it ends with the most famous closing line in American theatrical history: "The son of a bitch stole my watch!" The first two movie versions couldn't get away with that language, but the 1974 version did, and now here it is 1988, and *Switching Channels* has the temerity to leave the line out altogether (even though Reynolds steals Reeve's expensive pen, in what looks like a set-up). If the ghosts of Hecht and MacArthur see this movie, may they haunt the filmmakers, their spectral voices complaining, "The sons of bitches didn't steal our greatest line!"

T

Tampopo ★ ★ ★ ★
NO MPAA RATING, 117 m., 1987

Tsutomu Yamazaki (Ooro), Nobuko Miyamoto (Tampopo [Dandelion]), Koji Miyamoto (Man in White Suit), Ken Watanabe (Gun), Rikiya Yasuoka (Pisken), Kinzo Sakura (Shohei). Directed by Juzo Itami and produced by Juzo Itami, Yasushi Tamaoki, and Seigo Hosogoe. Screenplay by Itami.

Tampopo is one of those utterly original movies that seems to exist in no known category. Like the French comedies of Jacques Tati, it's a bemused meditation on human nature, in which one humorous situation flows into another off-handedly, as if life were a series of smiles.

As it opens, the film looks like some sort of Japanese satire of Clint Eastwood's spaghetti Westerns. The hero is Ooro (Tsutomu Yamazaki), a lone rider with a quizzical smile on his face, who rides a semi instead of a horse. Along with some friends, he stages a search for the perfect noodle restaurant, and cannot find it. Then he meets Tampopo (Nobuko Miyamoto), a sweet young woman who has her heart in the right place, but not her noodles.

The movie then turns into the fairly free-style story of the efforts by Tampopo and her protector to research the perfect noodle and open the perfect noodle restaurant. Like most movies about single-minded obsessions, this one quickly becomes very funny. It might seem that American audiences would know little and care less about the search for the perfect Japanese noodle, but because the movie is so consumed and detailed, so completely submerged in "noodleology," it takes on a kind of weird logic of its own.

Consider, for example, the *tour de force* of a scene near the beginning of the movie, where a noodle master explains the correct ritual for eating a bowl of noodle soup. He explains every ingredient. How to cut it, how to cook it, how to address it, how to think of it, how to regard it, how to approach it, how to smell it, how to eat it, how to thank it, how to remember it. It's a kind of gastronomic religion, and director Juzo Itami languishes in creating a scene that makes noodles in this movie more interesting than sex and violence in many another.

The movie is constructed as a series of episodes along the route to the perfect noodle restaurant. Some of the scenes hardly even seem to apply, but are hilarious anyway—the treatment, for example, of a man who dies in the pursuit of the perfect bowl of noodles. *Tampopo* doesn't limit itself to satirizing one genre of Hollywood film, either; although the central image is of an Eastwood-style hero on an ultimate quest, there are all sorts of other sly little satirical asides, including one so perfectly aimed that even to describe it would take away some of the fun.

Humor, it is said, is universal. Most times it is not. The humor that travels best, I sometimes think, is not "universal" humor at all, but humor that grows so specifically out of one culture that it reaches other cultures almost by seeming to ignore them. The best British comedies were the very specifically British films like *The Lavender Hill Mob* and *School for Scoundrels*. The best Italian comedies were local products like *Seduced and Abandoned*. The funniest French films were by Tati, who seemed totally absorbed in himself. And this very, very Japanese movie, which seems to make no effort to communicate to other cultures, is universally funny almost for that reason. Who cannot identify with the search for the perfect noodle? Certainly any American can, in the land of sweet corn festivals, bake-offs, and contests for the world's best chili.

Taps ★ ★ ★

PG, 126 m., 1981

George C. Scott (General Bache), Timothy Hutton (Brian Moreland), Ronny Cox (Colonel Kerby), Sean Penn (Alex), Tom Cruise (David). Directed by Harold Becker and produced by Stanley R. Jaffe and Howard B. Jaffe. Screenplay by Darryl Ponicsan and Robert Mark Kamen.

Taps is a meditation on two subjects for which some adolescents have a great capacity: idealism and authoritarianism. It takes place in a realistic setting (it was shot on location at Valley Forge Military Academy), but it is not intended as a realistic film. There are all sorts of clues, including the pointed absence of all but one of the academy's adult faculty members, to indicate that *Taps*, like the emotionally similar *Lord of the Flies*, is using its realistic texture as a setting for a fantasy about human nature.

The film begins with an emotionally stirring commencement exercise at Bunker Hill Military Academy (as the school is called in the film). Sousa marches fill the air, the cadets march around the parade ground looking gloriously proud of themselves, and the reviewing stand is dominated by the legendary old General Harlan Bache, the academy's commander. Bache is played by George C. Scott, and it is probably no accident that his performance in this movie echoes his title role in *Patton* (1970): He is an iron-willed and yet incurably romantic professional soldier.

We soon meet the leading upperclassman, Brian Moreland (Timothy Hutton). He has been selected to lead the cadet corps next year. In one of the most important evenings of his life, he is granted the great privilege of having dinner with old General Bache and sipping some of the old man's brandy. Soon after, however, this whole network of discipline, glory, and tradition is destroyed when it's revealed that the school's pigheaded trustees intend to sell the school and its land to some condominium developers (it is almost worth the price of admission to hear Scott pronouce "condominiums"). Bache is removed from the scene, in a dramatic development I will not reveal. And then Moreland, the cadet commander, takes inventory of the school's supplies of weapons and decides to lead the student body in making a stand for it. They'll take over the school in a military occupation, bar the gates, mount machine guns, and guard posts, and issue a set of demands designed to save the school.

The central passages of *Taps* are devoted to this scheme. The students barricade themselves in the school grounds, the police and National Guard surround the school, and a standoff develops. Meanwhile, within the student body, tensions develop between those kids who are unstable and a little too violent, and those who would secretly rather be on the outside looking in. Hutton, as Moreland, does a lot of learning and soul-searching as he tries to hold his mad scheme together.

There are obviously various problems of plot (such as: Where are the other faculty members? Why are the outside authorities both so stupid and so uncompromising? Why would the trustees have no appreciation of the school's tradition? Why would the grade-school-age cadets be issued live ammunition?, etc.). These questions do not really matter. *Taps* is basically a character study, a portrait of the personalities engaged in the showdown. And, like *Lord of the Flies*, it observes that adolescent males can easily translate the idealistic lessons they have been taught into a rationale for acting in ways that are rigid, dogmatic, and self-justifying.

Taps works as an uncommonly engrossing story, primarily because the performances are so well done. All of the cadet roles are well-acted, not only by seasoned actors like Hutton (who won an Academy Award for *Ordinary People*) but even by the very young kids who struggle with guns and realities much too large for them. By the film's end, we share their love for their school, we despair at the situation they have gotten themselves into, and we are emotionally involved in the outcome. After the film, there are some ideas to think about, involving the implications when might and right are on the same side—and when they are not.

Tarzan, the Ape Man ★ ★ ½

R, 112 m., 1981

Bo Derek (Jane), Richard Harris (Parker), John Phillip Law (Holt), Miles O'Keefe (Tarzan), Akushula Seleyah (Africa), Steven Strong (Ivory King). Directed and photographed by John Derek and produced by Bo Derek. Screenplay by Tom Rowe and Gary Goddard.

Tarzan, the Ape Man is *The Blue Lagoon* with elephants. Of course it's completely ridiculous, but at the same time it has a certain disarming charm. Sure, it's easy to groan at the secondhand "plot." It's easy to laugh at the clichés and mourn the demotion of Tarzan, who started out in the movies as king of the jungle and now gets fourth billing behind a schoolgirl, an anthropologist, and a wimp. And yet when Tarzan beats his chest and screams and swings to the rescue on a vine, there is something primal happening on the screen. And when Jane and three loyal chimpanzees tenderly bathe the body of the unconscious ape-man, we're getting very close to the reasons why we watch movies, and why there will always be a few movies to reawaken the child within us.

This Bo Derek version of the "Tarzan" legend is allegedly a remake of the MGM version of 1932, starring Johnnie Weissmuller and Maureen O'Sullivan. Not in that version or in any of the others, however, did Hollywood honestly address the central mystery of the Tarzan story, which is—what, exactly, *was* the intimate relationship between Tarzan and Jane? Were they lovers? Friends? Neighbors? Business partners? They presumably made love in order to produce Boy, but the reproduction took place far, far offscreen. I always thought there was something just a little peculiar about the behavior of Weissmuller, Lex Barker, Gordon Scott, and other movie Tarzans. There they were, all alone in the jungle with the beautiful Jane, and what did they do? Swing around on vines and talk to the animals. If I'd wanted *Dr. Doolittle*, I would have seen *Dr. Doolittle*.

This 1981 version is nothing if not willing to satisfy our curiosity about sex life in the rain forest. Bo Derek (who stars and produced) and her husband John (who directed and photographed) are frankly interested only in the relationship between Tarzan and Jane. The whole movie is a setup for several steamy scenes of confrontation between the savage, muscular jungle man and the petite young girl with eyes as wide as her shoulders. When Tarzan and Jane first meet, the movie all but abandons its plot in favor of foreplay. This is not a movie to waste time on ivory-smuggling, Nazis, cities of gold, ant-men, slave girls, lost safaris, or any of the countless other plot devices Edgar Rice Burroughs used as substitutes for interpersonal relationships. It gets right down to business.

The movie opens with a vow by Bo Derek's scientist father (Richard Harris) to lead an expedition to plunder the jungle of its secrets. His real mission: To capture the legendary ape-man Tarzan and bring him back to his club—stuffed and mounted, if possible. Harris takes Bo along on his expedition, which also includes John Phillip Law in the role of the wimp assistant. Law has hardly anything to say, and is always the guy who's looking the other way when Tarzan kidnaps Jane. After a series of routine shots of the jungle march, Tarzan *does* meet Jane and finds himself powerfully attracted to her. Harris is of course insane with jealousy: "Do you know what he *really* wants?" he asks Jane. She hopes so.

Tarzan kidnaps Jane, and then the movie boringly intercuts the jealous father searching for the curious girl. Harris's role in this movie is as hapless as Jason Robards's role in *The Lone Ranger.* Nobody cares about him, his dialogue is overwrought and underwritten, and every time Tarzan and Jane are poised to jump into the bullrushes, the movie cuts back to Harris, slogging through the jungle and cursing the ape-man.

The story line was ridiculous to begin with, but it goes berserk by the time of the movie's incomprehensible climax in a village of mud worshippers. They capture Derek, smear her with paint, and prepare her for some sort of unspeakable sacrifice before Tarzan gallops to the rescue with a herd of elephants. Those friendly elephants are, of course, part of the Tarzan legend. Tarzan speaks Elephant, and there's always that great moment when he needs help, and the elephants hear his screams and perk up their ears. I've always thought it would be dangerous to ask Tarzan for help unless you really wanted it. Say you had a small problem like a missing gourd or a stolen spear, and Tarzan arrived at your village with a herd of elephants to fix things. You'd get your gourd back, maybe, but you'd be cleaning up for weeks.

But never mind. This movie's scenes between Bo Derek, as Jane, and Miles O'Keefe, as a Tarzan who never speaks a word, show them as complete sexual innocents, fascinated by the wonderment of each other's bodies. Jane's expression as she looks at the unconscious Tarzan is entrancing. Her unabashed curiosity about him is sexier than any number of steamy sex scenes would have been. Although some of Bo Derek's nude scenes have reportedly been cut from the movie at the insistence of the spoilsport Edgar Rice Burroughs estate, the remaining nude footage is remarkably free of purience. The Tarzan-Jane scenes strike a blow for noble savages, for innocent lust, for animal magnetism, and, indeed, for soft-core porn, which is ever so much sexier than the hard-core variety. If you do not agree with me, you will probably think Bo's banana scene is ridiculous. I prefer to think it was inevitable.

Taxi Driver ★ ★ ★ ★

R, 112 m., 1976

Robert De Niro (Travis Bickle), Jodie Foster (Iris), Albert Brooks (Tom), Harvey Keitel (Sport), Leonard Harris (Palantine), Peter Boyle (Wizard), Cybill Shepherd (Betsy). Directed by Martin Scorsese and produced by Michael Phillips and Julia Phillips. Screenplay by Paul Schrader.

Taxi Driver shouldn't be taken as a New York film; it's not about a city but about the weathers of a man's soul, and out of all New York he selects just those elements that feed and reinforce his obsessions. The man is Travis Bickle, ex-Marine, veteran of Vietnam, composer of dutiful anniversary notes to his parents, taxi driver, killer. The movie rarely strays very far from the personal, highly subjective way in which he sees the city and lets it wound him.

It's a place, first of all, populated with women he cannot have: Unobtainable blonde women who might find him attractive for a moment, who might join him for a cup of coffee, but who eventually will have to shake their heads and sigh, "Oh, Travis!" because they find him . . . well, he's going crazy, but the word they use is "strange." And then, even more cruelly, the city seems filled with men who *can* have these women—men ranging from cloddish political hacks to street-corner pimps who, nevertheless, have in common the mysterious ability to approach a woman without getting everything wrong.

Travis could in theory look for fares anywhere in the city, but he's constantly drawn back to 42nd Street, to Times Square and the whores, street freaks, and porno houses. It's here that an ugly kind of sex comes closest to the surface—the sex of buying, selling, and using people. Travis isn't into that, he hates it, but Times Square feeds his anger. His sexual frustration is channeled into a hatred for the creeps he obsessively observes. He tries to break the cycle—or maybe he just sets himself up to fail again. He sees a beautiful blonde working in the storefront office of a presidential candidate. She goes out with him a couple of times, but the second time he takes her to a hard-core film and she walks out in disgust and won't have any more to do with him. All the same, he calls her for another date, and it's here that we get close to the heart of the movie. The director, Martin Scorsese, gives us a shot of Travis on a pay telephone—and then, as the girl is turning him down, the camera slowly dollies to the right and looks down a long, empty hallway. Pauline Kael's review called this shot—which calls attention to itself—a lapse during which Scorsese was maybe borrowing from Antonioni. Scorsese calls this shot the most important one in the film.

Why? Because, he says, it's as if we can't bear to watch Travis feel the pain of being rejected. This is interesting, because later, when Travis goes on a killing rampage, the camera goes so far as to adopt slow motion so we can see the horror in greater detail. That Scorsese finds the rejection more painful than the murders is fascinating, because it helps to explain Travis Bickle, and perhaps it goes some way toward explaining one kind of urban violence. Travis has been shut out so systematically, so often, from a piece of the action that eventually he has to hit back somehow.

Taxi Driver is a brilliant nightmare and like all nightmares it doesn't tell us half of what we want to know. We're not told where Travis comes from, what his specific problems are, whether his ugly scar came from Vietnam—because this isn't a case study, but a portrait of some days in his life. There's a moment at a political rally when Travis, in dark glasses, smiles in a strange way that reminds us of those photos of Bremer just before he shot Wallace. The moment tells us nothing, and everything: We don't know the specifics of Travis's complaint, but in a chilling way we know what we need to know of him. The film's a masterpiece of suggestive characterization; Scorsese's style selects details that evoke emotions, and that's the effect he wants. The performances are odd and compelling: He goes for moments from his actors, rather than slowly developed characters. It's as if the required emotions were written in the margins of their scripts: Give me anger—fear—dread. Robert De Niro, as Travis Bickle, is as good as Brando at suggesting emotions even while veiling them from us (and in many of his close-ups, Scorsese uses almost subliminal slow motion to draw out the revelations). Cybill Shepherd, as the blonde goddess, is correctly cast, for once, as a glacier slowly receding toward humanity. And there's Jodie Foster, chillingly cast as a twelve-year-old prostitute whom Travis wants to "save." Harvey Keitel, a veteran of all of Scorsese's films (he was the violent maniac in *Alice Doesn't Live Here Anymore)* is the pimp who controls her, and he's got the right kind of toughness that's all bluff.

These people are seen almost in flashes, as if darkness threatens to close over them altogether. *Taxi Driver* is a hell, from the opening shot of a cab emerging from stygian clouds of steam to the climactic killing scene in which the camera finally looks straight down. Scorsese wanted to look away from Travis's rejection; we almost want to look away from his life. But he's there, all right, and he's suffering.

Teen Wolf Too ½★

PG, 95 m., 1987

Jason Bateman (Todd Howard), Kim Darby (Professor Brooks), John Astin (Dean Dunn), Paul Sand (Coach Finstock), James Hampton (Uncle Harold), Mark Holton (Chubby), Estee Chandler (Nicki). Directed by Christopher Leitch and produced by Kent Bateman. Screenplay by R. Timothy Kring.

What we have here is a failure of imagination. Here's a movie about a teen-ager who can change himself into a werewolf, and all the filmmakers come up with is a plot where the werewolf is a champion boxer. Oh, and I forgot that when he becomes a werewolf he grows insensitive, which means his girlfriend gets mad at him. Were teen-age werewolf movies always this dumb? They were?

Teen Wolf Too stars Jason Bateman as the cousin of the original teen wolf, who was played by Michael J. Fox in a box office hit I did not see. The family trait is apparently passed along with the genes. Bateman looks like a normal, average teen-age kid, but when he gets mad, his eyes start to glow like red-hot coals, and when he gets real mad, he grows hair all over his body.

We meet Jason at the beginning of his freshman year at Hamilton College, where the dean (John Astin) is aghast because the school has no winning teams. He offers to fire the boxing coach (Paul Sand) unless the coach comes up with a winner. Sand has a surprise up his sleeve: Having heard about the supernormal strength of the Michael J. Fox character, he has recruited Jason Bateman on a full athletic scholarship. He has a hunch Bateman will turn out to be a werewolf, too.

Is this something new, giving scholarships to monsters? Not at the big football schools. The twist is that Bateman gets a *boxing* scholarship, even though boxing is hardly a major intercollegiate sport. Why boxing? Probably because it's a cheap sport to photograph, requiring only gloves, shorts, a ring, and a small crowd (nineteen people witness Bateman's first fight).

There is a little pathos here and there in the story. When he is not being a werewolf, Bateman is a serious science student, who captures the attention of his professor (Kim Darby, looking great). She believes he has academic potential. But when he turns into the wolf that makes him an instant campus hero, he starts cutting class and acting rude to people, including his girlfriend (Estee Chandler).

The movie makes a feeble attempt to rip off its betters, including *Animal House,* with dumb jokes about the dean, the coach, and the campus animals. I did not laugh. What is most amazing about the Hamilton campus is that no one on it seems much surprised that one of the students should be a werewolf.

Isn't this some kind of a sensational anthropological breakthrough? Shouldn't the *National Geographic* be following Bateman around filming a special?

Somebody financed this movie. Somebody produced it, directed it, wrote it, and distributed it. As I sat in stunned silence regarding the film, with its complete lack of wit and imagination, I reflected that anyone in the audience could probably come up with three funnier notions about teen-age werewolves than all of those people put together. How did they manage to find the only people in America with no interesting thoughts on werewolves, and assign them all to the same movie? Uncanny.

Tell Them Willie Boy Is Here ★ ★ ★ ½
PG, 96 m., 1970

Robert Redford (Cooper), Katharine Ross (Lola), Robert Blake (Willie Boy), Susan Clark (Liz). Directed by Abraham Polonsky and produced by Philip A. Waxman. Screenplay by Polonsky.

Abraham Polonsky's *Tell Them Willie Boy Is Here* is a simple, direct, almost stark retelling of an event that took place in 1909. It's about Willie Boy, a Paiute Indian whose personal fight for freedom was elevated by the press into an Indian uprising against President William Howard Taft. It is also about white racism and Indian pride, and it is no ordinary Western. It marked the resumption of the directorial career of Polonsky, interrupted twenty years earlier by the House Committee on Un-American Activities during the Hollywood witchhunt. Before he was blacklisted in 1950, Polonsky had written Robert Rossen's *Body and Soul* and directed John Garfield in the classic *Force of Evil*.

Polonsky, who also wrote *Willie Boy*, is at pains to tell his story without gimmicks. It's about how Willie Boy (Robert Blake) comes back to the reservation to marry the girl he loves, Lola (Katharine Ross). But her father forbids them to see each other. In a confrontation, Willie Boy kills the father in self-defense and then goes on the run with Lola. The Indians accept the event as "marriage by capture," forced upon Willie Boy because, as he tells Lola, "I've asked for you the white man's way, and I'm through asking." But Lola, it turns out, was a favorite of the reservation superintendent (Susan Clark), a proper Bostonian who wanted her to be a teacher. At the superintendent's insistence, the sheriff (Robert Redford) gets up a posse and goes after the couple.

Almost all the movie is concerned with the chase, which takes place at a time when President Taft is visiting the area. The president's visit has drawn dozens of newspaper reporters to town, and they sensationalize Willie Boy's case. When Willie Boy accidentally kills one of the members of the posse, an instant "uprising" is born in the papers. Redford wants to forget the whole thing: "It's Indian business, and besides, this posse couldn't catch a dog in the street." But the publicity forces him to keep after Willie Boy, until a final personal confrontation.

Redford gets top billing, and is very good as the sheriff. He has a natural feel for acting in movies; he makes small gestures do the work of large ones, and he can convey a lot of meaning without spelling it out in dialogue. But the film's real star is Robert Blake, who played one of the killers in *In Cold Blood*. Blake is all gristle and nerve and pride, and gained his greatest fame as TV's Barretta.

The movie is paced more slowly than we'd expect for a Western, but then it's not really a Western at all, but a study of personality. There aren't a lot of action scenes and shootouts; this is essentially an essay on the stereotypes by which white men have attempted to justify their theft of the Indian lands and independence. *Tell Them Willie Boy Is Here* works powerfully on that level, and it is impossible to see it without thinking that the same sort of exploitation still goes on today.

10 ★ ★ ★ ★
R, 123 m., 1979

Dudley Moore (George), Julie Andrews (Sam), Bo Derek (Jenny), Robert Webber (Hugh), Dee Wallace (Mary Lewis), Sam Jones (David), Brian Dennehy (Bartender). Directed by Blake Edwards and produced by Edwards and Tony Adams. Screenplay by Edwards.

Blake Edwards's *10* is perhaps the first comedy about terminal yearning. Like all great comedies, it deals with emotions very close to our hearts: In this case, the unutterable poignance of a man's desire for a woman he cannot have. The woman, of course, must be unbelievably desirable (and the hero of *10*, on a scale of 1 to 10, gives this particular woman an 11). It helps, too, if the man is short, forty-two years old, and filled with inchoate longings.

You remember inchoate longings. They used to stalk the pages of novels by Thomas Wolfe, back in the years before the Me Generation and the cult of instant gratification. There used to be a time, incredibly, when you couldn't have something *just because you wanted it*—*10* remembers that time. Its hero, Dudley Moore, begins *10* as a man who seems to have more or less what any man could desire. He is a successful composer. His girl friend is Julie Andrews. He has a great house up in the hills, he drives a Rolls-Royce, he has cable TV with remote tuning.

But then one day, driving his Rolls down Santa Monica Boulevard, he is visited by a vision. She is a preternaturally beautiful young woman in the next car. She turns to regard him, and he is instantly, helplessly, in love. She turns away. She must be about her business. She is dressed in a bridal gown and is on her way to the church to be married.

He follows her. He is stung by a bee in the church. He has six cavities painfully filled by her father, who is a dentist. Groggy from pain pills and brandy, he finds himself aboard an airplane flying to Mexico—where, amazingly, he winds up at the same resort as his ideal woman (and, of course, her husband—one of the vacuous beach-boy types with a smile fit for a Jockey T-shirts model).

Blake Edwards's screenplay now plunges into some slightly more serious waters, where we will not follow. What we're struck with, in *10*, is the uncanny way its humor gets laughs by touching on emotions and yearnings that are very real for us. We identify with the characters in this movie: Their predicaments are funny, yes—but then ours would be, too, if they weren't our own.

The central treasure in the film is the performance by Dudley Moore. There must have been times when Moore wondered if he'd *ever* get the girl. In *10*, he does. He also brings his character such life and dimension that *10* is a lot more than a comedy: It's a study in the follies of human nature.

The girl (the one who scores 11) is played by Bo Derek. She is so desirable, such a pure and cheerful embodiment of carnal perfection, that we're in there with Dudley Moore every step of the way, even when he's slogging it out to Ravel's interminable "Bolero." Julie Andrews has a small but delightful role as the sensible mistress, and the movie also has warm performances by Robert Webber, as Moore's vulnerable gay friend, and by Brian Dennehy, as a particularly understanding bartender in Mexico.

10 is not only one of the best films Blake Edwards has ever made, but was something of a turning point in his career: The previous decade he had alternated between successful Pink Panther movies and non-Panther flops like *The Tamarind Seed, The Wild Rovers,* and *The Carey Treatment.* Did he have another good straight movie in him? Yes, as a matter of fact, he did.

Tender Mercies ★ ★ ★

PG, 93 m., 1983

Robert Duvall (Mac Sledge), Tess Harper (Rosa Lee), Betty Buckley (Dixie), Wilford Brimley (Harry), Ellen Barkin (Sue Anne), Allan Hubbard (Sonny). Directed by Bruce Beresford and produced by Philip S. Hobel. Screenplay by Horton Foote.

Tender Mercies visits some fairly familiar movie territory, and achieves some quietly touching effects. The movie's about the rhythms of a small Texas town, and about the struggle of a has-been country singer to regain his self-respect. It might remind you of parts of *The Last Picture Show* and *Honkytonk Man,* with a little bit of *Payday* thrown in (that was the movie starring Rip Torn, based on the last days of the dying Hank Williams, Sr.). This time, the broken-down country singer is named Mac Sledge. He's at the end of his personal road. He was once a big star and a hero to young musicians around the Southwest, but as his final act opens he's sitting in a fleabag motel outside a small Texas town, drinking himself to death, and fighting for the bottle with another guy he hardly even knows.

When he wakes up on the floor the next morning, the other guy is gone and Sledge is hung over, broke, and without prospects. He throws himself on the mercy of the young widow who runs the motel: He'll work for his room and board. She agrees to that, and throws in $2 an hour, but says he can't drink while he's at the motel. He agrees, and that is the day his life turns around and he begins the rebuilding process.

Tender Mercies tells the story of the relationship between the singer and the young widow in a quiet, subtle way; this isn't one of those movies that spells everything out. The key to the movie's tone is in the performance by Robert Duvall as Sledge. Duvall plays him as a bone-weary, seedy, essentially very simple man who needs some values to hold onto. The widow can provide those, and can also provide the stability of a home and family (she has a young son, whose father was killed in Vietnam). What the Duvall character wants to do, essentially, is keep a low profile, work hard, not drink, and forget about the glories of country singing. It's hard for him to remain invisible, though, after the local paper prints a story and the members of a local band start dropping around for advice. There are more complications: Sledge's ex-wife is still touring as a country singer, and would like to turn his eighteen-year-old daughter against him.

What's interesting about *Tender Mercies* is the way it refuses to approach this material as soap opera *or* as drama. The movie's told more like one of those quiet, sly *New Yorker* stories where the big emotional moments sneak up on you, and the effects are achieved indirectly. Sometimes this movie smiles (as in a scene of a double baptism). Sometimes it simply sits there and talks straight (as in a touching speech by Sledge on the meaning of life). Sometimes its low budget allows the seams to show (as in the unconvincing concert scene involving Sledge's wife). But mostly it just lets these stories happen, lets them get to know these people, and see them dealing with life. Some of them get better, and some of them get worse. It's like a country song.

Terms of Endearment ★ ★ ★ ★

PG, 129 m., 1983

Debra Winger (Emma Horton), Shirley MacLaine (Aurora Greenway), Jack Nicholson (Breedlove), Jeff Daniels (Flap Horton), Danny DeVito (Vernon), John Lithgow (Sam Burns). Directed, produced, and written by James L. Brooks.

When families get together to remember their times together, the conversation has a way of moving easily from the tragedies to the funny things. You'll mention someone who has passed away, and there'll be a moment of silence, and then somebody will grin and be reminded of some goofy story. Life always has an unhappy ending, but you can have a lot of fun along the way, and everything doesn't have to be dripping in deep significance.

The most remarkable achievement of *Terms of Endearment,* which is filled with great achievements, is its ability to find the balance between the funny and the sad, between moments of deep truth and other moments of high ridiculousness. A lesser movie would have had trouble moving between the extremes that are visited by this film, but because *Terms of Endearment* understands its characters and loves them, we never have a moment's doubt: What happens next is supposed to happen, because life's like that. *Terms of Endearment* feels as much like life as any movie I can think of. At the same time, it's a triumph of show business, with its high comic style, its flair for bittersweet melodrama, and its star turns for the actors. Maybe the best thing about this movie is the way it combines those two different kinds of filmmaking. This is a movie with bold emotional scenes and big laughs, and at the same time it's so firmly in control of its tone that we believe we are seeing real people.

The movie's about two remarkable women, and their relationships with each other and with the men in their lives. The mother is played by Shirley MacLaine. She's a widow who lives in Houston and hasn't dated a man since her husband died. Maybe she's redirected her sexual desires into the backyard, where her garden has grown so large and elaborate that she either will have to find a man pretty quickly or move to a house with a bigger yard. Her daughter, played by Debra Winger, is one of those people who seems to have been blessed with a sense of life and joy. She marries a guy named Flap who teaches English in a series of Midwestern colleges; she rears three kids and puts up with Flap, who has an eye for coeds.

Back in Houston, her mother finally goes out on a date with the swinging bachelor (Jack Nicholson) who has lived next door for years. He's a hard-drinking, girl-chasing former astronaut with a grin that hints of unspeakable lusts. MacLaine, a lady who surrounds herself with frills and flowers, is appalled by this animalistic man and then touched by him.

There are a couple of other bittersweet relationships in the film. Both mother and daughter have timid, mild-mannered male admirers: MacLaine is followed everywhere by Vernon (Danny DeVito), who asks only to be allowed to gaze upon her, and Winger has a tender, little affair with a banker.

The years pass. Children grow up into adolescence, Flap gets a job as head of the department in Nebraska, the astronaut turns out to have genuine human possibilities of becoming quasi-civilized, and mother and daughter grow into a warmer and deeper relationship. All of this is told in a series of perfectly written, acted, and directed scenes that flow as effortlessly as a perfect day, and then something happens that is totally unexpected, and changes everything. I don't want to suggest what happens. It flows so naturally that it should be allowed to take place.

This is a wonderful film. There isn't a thing that I would change, and I was exhilarated by the freedom it gives itself to move from the high comedy of Nicholson's best moments to the acting of Debra Winger in the closing scenes. She outdoes herself. It's a great performance. And yet it's not a "performance." There are scenes that have such a casual gaiety that acting seems to have nothing to do with it. She doesn't reach for effects, and neither does the film, because it's all right there.

Tess ★ ★ ★ ★

PG, 180 m., 1980

Nastassja Kinski (Tess), Peter Firth (Angel Clare), Leigh Lawson (Alec d'Urberville), Rosemary Martin (Mrs. Durbeyfield), Sylvia Coleridge (Mrs. d'Urberville), John Collin (John Durbeyfield), Tony Church (Parson), Brigid Erin Bates (Girl in Meadow). Directed by Roman Polanski and produced by Claude Berri. Screenplay by Gerard Brach, Polanski, and John Brownjohn.

Roman Polanski's *Tess* is a love song with a tragic ending—the best kind of love song of all, just so long as it's not about ourselves. He tells the story of a beautiful young girl, innocent but not without intelligence, and the way she is gradually destroyed by the exercise of the male ego. The story is all the more touching because it is not an unrelenting descent into gloom, as it might have been in other hands, but a life lived in occasional sight of love and happiness. Tess is forever just on the brink of getting the peace she deserves.

The movie is based on a novel by Thomas Hardy, but Polanski never permits his film to become a Classics Illustrated; this isn't a devout rendering of a literary masterpiece, but a film that lives and breathes and has a quick sympathy for its heroine. Nastassja Kinski is just right for the title role. She has the youth, the freshness, and the naiveté of a Tess, and none of the practiced mannerisms of an actress engaged to "interpret" the role. That's good because Tess is a character who should stick out like a sore thumb in many scenes, and Kinski's occasional shy awkwardness is just right for the story of a girl who attempts to move up in social class on sheer bravado.

The story involves a young girl who will be the victim, the prey, and sometimes the lover of many men, without ever quite understanding what it is that those men want of her. The first man in her life is her father, a drunken farmer named John Durbeyfield, who discovers from the local parson that he is related to the noble local family of d'Urbervilles. The farmer and his wife immediately send their beautiful daughter, Tess, off to confront the d'Urbervilles and perhaps win a position in their household.

Tess is almost immediately seduced by a rakish cousin. She becomes pregnant, and her child dies soon after it is born. She never tells the cousin. But later, after she falls in love with the son of a local minister and marries him, she confesses her past. This is too much for her new husband to bear; he "married down" because he was attracted to Tess's humble origins. But he is not prepared to accept the reality of her past. He leaves on a bizarre mission to South America. Tess, meanwhile, descends to rough manual labor for a few pennies an hour. She is eventually reunited with her cousin (who is not a complete bastard, and complains that he should have been informed of her pregnancy). She becomes his lover. Then the wayward husband returns, and the physical and psychic contest for Tess ends in tragedy.

As a plot, these events would be right at home in any soap opera. But what happens in Polanski's *Tess* is less important than how Tess feels about it, how we feel about it, and how successfully Polanski is able to locate those events in a specific place and time. His movie is set in England, but was actually photographed in France. It is a beautifully visualized period piece that surrounds Tess with the attitudes of her time—attitudes that explain how restricted her behavior must be, and how society views her genuine human emotions as inappropriate. This is a wonderful film; the kind of exploration of doomed young sexuality that, like *Elvira Madigan*, makes us agree that the lovers should never grow old.

Testament ★ ★ ★ ★
PG, 90 m., 1983

Jane Alexander (Carol Wetherly), William Devane (Tom Wetherly), Ross Harris (Brad), Roxana Zal (Mary Liz), Lukas Haas (Scottie), Philip Anglim (Hollis), Leon Ames (Henry Abhart), Rebecca De Mornay (Mother with Baby). Directed by Lynne Littman and produced by Jonathan Bernstein and Littman. Screenplay by John Sacret Young.

Testament may be the first movie in a long time that will make you cry. It made me cry. And seeing it again for a second time, knowing everything that would happen, anticipating each scene before it came, I was affected just as deeply. But the second time I was able to see more clearly that the movie is more than just a devastating experience, that it has a message with a certain hope.

The film is about a suburban American family, and what happens to that family after a nuclear war. It is not a science fiction movie, and it doesn't have any special effects, and there are no big scenes of buildings blowing over or people disintegrating. We never see a mushroom cloud. We never even know who started the war. Instead, *Testament* is a tragedy about manners: It asks how we might act toward one another, how our values might stand up in the face of an overwhelming catastrophe.

The movie begins with one of those typical families right out of TV commercials. The father (William Devane) is a physical-fitness nut. The mother (Jane Alexander) is loving, funny, and a little harried. The kids include a daughter who practices the piano, a son who races his dad up hills on their ten-speed bikes, and a little boy who guards the "treasure" in the bottom drawer of his chest. The movie follows these people long enough for us to know them, to appreciate their personalities, their good and weak points, and then one sunny afternoon the war starts.

Most of the film is about what happens then. Anarchy does not break out. There is some looting, but it is limited. For the most part, the people in the small northern California town stick together and try to do the best that they can. There are meetings in the church. There are public-health measures. A beloved community leader (Leon Ames, of TV's "Life with Father" many years ago) is a ham-radio operator, and makes contact with a few other places. A decision is made to go ahead with the grade-school play. Life goes on . . . but death invades it, as radiation poisoning begins to take a toll, first on the babies, then on the children, until finally the cemetery is filled and the bodies have to be burned on a pyre.

The movie finds dozens of small details to suggest existence after the bomb. All the kids, for example, take the batteries out of their toys and computer games, and turn them in for emergency use. Gasoline is rationed, and then runs out. The survivors have no garbage collection, no electricity, and, worst of all, no word from elsewhere. The sky gradually grows darker, suggesting realistically that a nuclear war would finally kill us all by raising great clouds of dust that would choke the Earth's vegetation.

In the midst of this devastation, Jane Alexander, as the mother, tries to preserve love and decency. She stands by her children, watches as they grow in response to the challenges, cherishes them as she sees all her dreams for them disappear. It is a great performance, the heart of the film. In fact, Alexander's performance makes the film possible to watch without unbearable heartbreak, because she is brave and decent in the face of horror. And the last scene, in which she expresses such small optimism as is still possible, is one of the most powerful movie scenes I've ever seen.

Tex ★ ★ ★ ★
PG, 103 m., 1982

Matt Dillon (Tex), Jim Metzler (Mason), Meg Tilly (Jamie), Bill McKinney (Pop), Frances Lee McCain (Mrs. Johnson), Ben Johnson (Cole Collins). Directed by Tim Hunter and produced by Ron Miller. Screenplay by Charlie Haas and Hunter.

There is a shock of recognition almost from the beginning of *Tex*, because we're listening to the sound of American voices in an authentically American world, the world of teen-age boys trying to figure things out and make the right decisions. The voices sound right but may be a little unfamiliar, because adolescents on television are often made to talk in pseudo-hip sitcom nonspeak. Here in *Tex* are the clear voices of two young men who are worthy of attention. Their names are Tex and Mason. They're brothers, one about eighteen, the other fourteen and a half. They live by themselves in a rundown house on some land outside a rural suburb of Tulsa. Their father is a rodeo cowboy who hardly ever stops in at home and forgets to send money for weeks at a time. These two kids are raising themselves and doing a pretty good job of it.

The movie tells the story of a couple of weeks in their lives. These are the kinds of weeks when things can go either well or badly—and if they go badly, we sense, Tex could get his whole life off to the wrong start. The brothers are broke. Mason sells their horses to raise money to buy food and get the gas turned back on. That makes Tex angry and sad; he's a kid looking for trouble.

We meet the other people in their world. There's the rich family down the road, dominated by a stern father who makes his teenagers toe a strict line. His kids are just as unpredictable as anyone else's, but he doesn't believe that. He believes their two undisciplined friends, Tex and Mason, are leading them into trouble and practically dragging them to late-night beer parties. There's another complication. His daughter and Tex are beginning to fall in love.

There's another friend, a local kid who got a girl pregnant, married her, and moved to Tulsa to start a family. He's dealing drugs. Mason knows this intuitively and surely, and knows the kid is heading for trouble. Tex knows it, too, but there comes a time in this story when Tex just doesn't give a damn, and when the drug dealer happens to be there, Tex accepts a ride into Tulsa with him. Tex doesn't do drugs himself, but he gets into a very scary situation with another dealer, and there's a harrowing scene in which Tex wavers just at the brink of getting into serious trouble.

There is more to this movie's story, but the important thing about it isn't what happens, but how it happens. The movie is so accurately acted, especially by Jim Metzler as Mason and Matt Dillon as Tex, that we care more about the characters than about the plot. We can see them learning and growing, and when they have a heart-to-heart talk about "going all the way," we hear authentic teen-agers speaking, not kids who seem to have been raised at Beverly Hills cocktail parties.

Tex is based on a famous novel by S.E. Hinton, who has had two of her other novels filmed by Francis Ford Coppola. She knows a great deal about adolescents, and her work is unaffected by sentimentality and easy romance. It's authentic. But the backgrounds of the two filmmakers are also interesting. Tim Hunter and Charles Haas bought the book and wrote the screenplay, and Hunter directed. Their previous collaboration was a little movie named *Over the Edge*, about teen-agers who feel cornered and persecuted by the rigid middle-class rules of a cardboard Denver suburb. That movie, a small masterpiece containing Matt Dillon's first movie appearance, never got a fair chance in theaters. Now here are Hunter and Haas again, still remembering what it's like to be young, still getting the dialogue and the attitudes, the hang-ups and the dreams, exactly right.

The Texas Chain Saw Massacre ★ ★
R, 87 m., 1974

Paul A. Partain (Frankle), Marilyn Burns (Debbie), Teri McMinn (Other Girl). Directed and produced by Tobe Hooper. Screenplay by Kim Henkel and Hooper.

Now here's a grisly little item. *The Texas Chain Saw Massacre* is as violent and gruesome and blood-soaked as the title promises—a real Grand Guignol of a movie. It's also without any apparent purpose, unless the creation of disgust and fright is a purpose. And yet in its own way, the movie is some kind of weird, off-the-wall achievement. I can't imagine why anyone would want to make a movie like this, and yet it's well-made, well-acted, and all too effective.

The movie's based on factual material, according to the narration that opens it. For all I know, that's true, although I can't recall having heard of these particular crimes, and the distributor provides no documentation. Not that it matters. A true crime movie like Richard Brooks's *In Cold Blood,* which studies the personalities and compulsions of two killers, dealt directly with documented material and was all the more effective for that. But *The Texas Chain Saw Massacre* could have been made up from whole cloth without any apparent difference. No motivation, no background, no speculation on causes is evident anywhere in the film. It's simply an exercise in terror.

It takes place in an isolated area of Texas, which five young people (one of them in a wheelchair) are driving through in their camper van. They pick up a weirdo hitchhiker who carries his charms and magic potions around his neck and who giggles insanely while he cuts himself on the hand and then slices at the paraplegic. They get rid of him, so they think.

But then they take a side trip to a haunted-looking old house, which some of them had been raised in. The two girls laugh as they clamber through the litter on the floor, but one of the guys notices some strange totems and charms which should give him warning. They don't. He and his girlfriend set off for the old swimming hole, find it dried up, and then see a farmhouse nearby. The guy goes to ask about borrowing some gasoline and disappears inside.

His girl gets tired of waiting for him, knocks on the door, and disappears inside, too. A lot of people are going to be disappearing into this house, and its insides are a masterpiece of set decoration and the creation of mood. We see the innocent victims being clubbed on the hand, hung from meat hooks, and gone after with the chain saw.

We see rooms full of strange altars made from human bones, and rooms filled with chicken feathers and charms and weird relics. And gradually we realize that the house is inhabited by a demented family of retarded murderers and grave robbers. When they get fresh victims, they carve them up with great delight. What they do with the bodies is a little obscure, but, uh, they run a barbecue stand down by the road.

One way or another, all the kids get killed by the maniac waving the chain saw—except one girl, who undergoes a night of panic and torture, who escapes not once but twice, who leaps through no fewer than two windows, and who screams endlessly. All of this material, as you can imagine, is scary and unpalatable. But the movie is good technically and with its special effects, and we have to give it grudging admiration on that level, despite all the waving of the chain saw.

There is, for example, an effective montage of quick cuts of the last girl's screaming face and popping eyeballs. There are bizarrely effective performances by the demented family (one of them, of course, turns out to be the hitchhiker, and Grandfather looks like Dustin Hoffman in *Little Big Man*). What we're left with, though, is an effective production in the service of an unnecessary movie.

Horror and exploitation films almost always turn a profit if they're brought in at the right price. So they provide a good starting place for ambitious would-be filmmakers who can't get more conventional projects off the ground. *The Texas Chain Saw Massacre* belongs in a select company (with *Night of the Living Dead* and *Last House on the Left*) of films that are really a lot better than the genre requires. Not, however, that you'd necessarily enjoy seeing it.

That's Dancing! ★ ★ ★

PG, 105 m., 1985

With hosts Mikhail Baryshnikov, Ray Bolger, Sammy Davis, Jr., Gene Kelly, and Liza Minnelli. Directed by Jack Haley, Jr., and produced by David Niven, Jr., and Haley. Screenplay by Haley.

There is a sense in which it is impossible to dislike *That's Dancing!* and another sense in which movies like this—made by splicing together all the "good parts" —are irritating and sort of unfair to the original films. Given the choice of seeing *Singin' in the Rain* again or spending the same amount of time looking at scenes from *Singin'* and maybe sixty other films, I'd rather see the real movie all the way through. But *That's Dancing!* is not setting an either-or test for us; what it basically wants to do is entertain us with a lot of good dance scenes from a lot of good, and bad, movies, and that is such a harmless ambition that I guess we can accept it.

The movie has been put together by Jack Haley, Jr., and David Niven, Jr., and it recycles Haley's formula in *That's Entertainment!* (1973), the original slice-and-dice anthology from Hollywood's golden ages. There also has been a *That's Entertainment II* (or "too," I seem to recall), and the law of diminishing returns is beginning to apply. Sooner or later, we'll get *That's All, Folks!* In the first movie, for example, we got Gene Kelly's immortal title dance number from *Singin' in the Rain;* in the second movie, we got Donald O'Conner's equally immortal "Make 'em Laugh" sequence; and that leaves Kelly and O'Conner's only somewhat immortal "Moses Supposes" number for this film. Pretty soon we're going to be getting *That's What's Left of Entertainment!*

That's Dancing! shares with the earlier movies an irritating compulsion to masquerade as a documentary, which it isn't. The tone is set by Kelly's opening generalizations about the universality of dance, etc., while we see *National Geographic* outtakes of dancing around the world: tribes in Africa, hula skirts in Hawaii, polkas, geisha girls and so on. Kelly is later spelled by such other dance analysts as Liza Minnelli, Ray Bolger, Mikhail Baryshnikov, and Sammy Davis, Jr., all of whom can dance with a great deal more ease than they can recite pseudo-profundities.

There is, however, a lot of good dancing in this movie, including rare silent footage of Isadora Duncan. We see Busby Berkeley's meticulously choreographed dance geometries, the infinite style of Fred Astaire, the brassy joy of Ginger Rogers, the pizazz of Cyd Charisse and Eleanor Powell, a charming duet between Bill "Bojangles" Robinson and Shirley Temple, and a dazzling display by the Nicholas Brothers, who were the inspiration for the dance team played by the Hines brothers in *Cotton Club.* The movie is up-to-date, with John Travolta from *Saturday Night Fever* and footage from break-dance movies, *Flashdance,* and Michael Jackson's *Thriller.* But perhaps its most pleasing single moment is a little soft-shoe by Jimmy Cagney, who was perhaps not the technical equal of Astaire, but was certainly on the same sublime plane when it came to communicating sheer joy.

One of the insights offered in the narration of *That's Dancing!* is that Astaire was responsible for the theory that you should see the entire body of the dancer in most of the shots in a dance scene, and that the scene should be shown in unbroken shots, as much as possible, to preserve the continuity of the dancer's relationship with space and time. That's the kind of seemingly obvious statement that contains a lot of half-baked conclusions. True, you have to see the dancer's whole body to appreciate what he's doing (look at the disastrous choreography in Travolta's *Stayin' Alive,* which inspired Ginger Rogers to call it a dance film—"from the waist up"). But you also need the cutaways to show the faces of the dancers, and the chemistry between them, as when Astaire and Rogers have their enchanted dancing lesson in *Swing Time.* True, shooting the whole thing in one unbroken take preserves the integrity of the visual record—but what about the sensational dance sequences in *Flashdance* that were achieved by literally cutting between different dancers, all doing their own specialty? All that really matters is the end result.

What conclusions can be drawn from the movie's survey of sixty years of dancing on screen? I can think of one, sort of obvious and sort of depressing: Style has gone out of style. New dancers in recent dance movies are in superb physical shape and do amazing things on the screen, but they do not have the magical personal style of an Astaire or a Kelly. They're technicians. And there's another thing: They don't really dance together. A lot of them are soloists, or two soloists sharing the same floor. When Astaire and Rogers danced together, they danced *together.* And that is maybe what dancing is finally all about.

That's Entertainment! ★ ★ ★ ★
G, 132 m., 1974

Selected scenes from MGM musicals between 1929 and 1958, introduced by Frank Sinatra, Fred Astaire, Gene Kelly, Mickey Rooney, Liza Minnelli, Elizabeth Taylor, James Stewart, Donald O'Connor, and others. Written, produced, and directed by Jack Haley, Jr.

It used to be said that the trickiest thing about a musical was to figure out a way for the characters to break gracefully into song. Maybe that was all wrong. Maybe the hardest thing was for them to stop, once the singing had started. That's my notion after seeing *That's Entertainment!*, a magical tour through the greatest musicals produced by the king of Hollywood studios, Metro-Goldwyn-Mayer.

This isn't just a compilation film, with lots of highlights strung together. Those kinds of movies quickly repeat themselves. *That's Entertainment!* is more of a documentary and a eulogy. A documentary of a time that began in 1929 and seemed to end only yesterday, and a eulogy for an art form that will never be again.

Hollywood will continue to make musicals, of course (although, curiously enough, the form never has been very popular overseas). But there will never be musicals like this again, because there won't be the budgets, there won't be the sense of joyous abandon, there won't be so many stars in the same place all at once and—most of all—there won't be the notion that a musical has to be "important."

The various segments of the film are introduced and narrated by MGM stars of the past (Fred Astaire, Gene Kelly), superstars like Frank Sinatra and Elizabeth Taylor, offspring like Liza Minnelli, and even a ringer like Bing Crosby (he was a Paramount star, but never mind). They seem to share a real feeling of nostalgia for MGM, which, in its heyday, was not only a studio, but also a benevolent and protective organization ruled by the paternal Louis B. Mayer. Liza Minnelli sounds at times as if she's narrating a visit to her mother's old high school. The movie avoids the trap of being too worshipful in the face of all this greatness. It's not afraid to kid; we see Clark Gable looking ill at ease as he pretends to enjoy singing and dancing, and we see a hilarious montage of Judy Garland and Mickey Rooney ringing endless changes to the theme, "I know—we'll fix up the old barn and put on a show!"

And then there are the glorious, unforgettable moments from the great musicals. My favorite musical has always been *Singin' in the Rain,* the 1952 comedy about Hollywood's traumatic switch to talkies. *That's Entertainment!* opens with a montage of musicals (neatly surveying three decades of film progress), and later returns to the two most unforgettable numbers in the film: Gene Kelly sloshing through puddles while singing the title song, and Donald O'Connor in his amazing "Make 'em Laugh," in which he leaps up walls, takes pratfalls, and dives through a set.

There are other great moments: The closing ballet from *An American in Paris;* Nelson Eddy and Jeanette MacDonald being hilariously serious in *Rose Marie;* Astaire and Ginger Rogers, so light-footed they seem to float; Gene Kelly's incredible acrobatics as he does his own stunts, swinging from rooftop to rooftop; William Warfield singing "Old Man River" in *Showboat*; Judy Garland singing "You Made Me Love You" to a montage of stills of Clark Gable; Garland, again, with "Get Happy" (and a vignette of little Liza's first movie appearance, aged about three); the acrobatic woodchopper's scene from *Seven Brides for Seven Brothers,* and even Esther Williams rising from the deep.

The movie's fun from beginning to end. It's not camp, and it's not nostalgia: It's a celebration of a time and place in American movie history when everything came together to make a new art form.

Therese ★ ★ ★ ½

NO MPAA RATING, 90 m., 1987 ✓

Catherine Mouchet (Therese), Aurore Prieto (Celine), Silvie Habault (Pauline), Ghislane Mona (Marie), Helene Alexandridis (Lucie), Jean Pelegri (Father), Armand Meppiel (The Pope). Directed by Alain Cavalier and produced by Maurice Bernart. Screenplay by Cavalier and Camille De Casabianca.

Therese is such a strong, pure, apparently simple movie that there's a temptation to let it carry us along. We don't want to ask questions. And yet at the end of this movie there are so many unanswered questions that we realize the movie is one long question: What was the secret of Therese Martin's joy?

She was known as the "Little Flower of Jesus." As a girl, she wanted to enter the strict cloisters of the Carmelite nuns, and when she was refused permission she went all the way to the Pope to finally obtain it. Inside the walls, she struck everyone with the openness and sweetness of her disposition, and after she died in 1897 she became famous through the publication of her journal. She was canonized in 1925.

The movie centers itself around the depth of her passionate love affair with Jesus. The nuns are figuratively wed to Christ in the ceremony which admits them to the order, and in Therese's case she seems to have taken the wedding not only seriously but literally. In a way, *Therese* is the story of a girl who dies on her honeymoon.

The story is told with stark visual simplicity by Alain Cavalier, who shoots against plain backdrops and includes only those costumes or props that are needed to make sense of a scene. His real visual subject is the human face. And after Therese is admitted to the closed convent, where a vow of silence is usually enforced, the faces themselves seem to speak.

We become familiar with the other nuns. With an old, old woman of great saintliness. With a wise mother superior. With a young nun who has a crush on Therese. And with Therese herself, who is played by Catherine Mouchet with a kind of transparent, low-key ecstasy. There is a real sense of the community of the convent. In one of the movie's best scenes, a man comes from outside to bring gifts of food to the nuns, who cover their faces and flutter around him like blinded birds.

Therese is not like any other biographical film of a saint—or of anyone else. It makes a bold attempt to penetrate to the mystery of Therese's sainthood, and yet it isn't propaganda for the church and it doesn't necessarily even approve of her choice of a vocation. Perhaps the local bishop was right, in saying Therese was too young for the strenuous life of the convent. Perhaps her devotion to Jesus was indeed, as Andrew Sarris wrote in his review of the film, "displaced sexuality and transsubstantiated fetishism."

This movie is so deep and so subtle that we cannot ever be sure just what the filmmaker thinks about Therese. That's one of the reasons I found it so disturbing and provoking. What Cavalier gives us is a portrait of the externals of sainthood, and just those internals that can be glimpsed and guessed through the eyes of a gifted actress. He makes no statement about his material. After we've seen the movie, we ask ourselves what it was that motivated Therese, and whether perhaps it was good even though it violates modern notions, and we also ask ourselves why she was so happy. We would not be happy living her life. But then we are not saints.

They Shoot Horses, Don't They?

★ ★ ★ ★

PG, 123 m., 1970

Jane Fonda (Gloria), Michael Sarrazin (Robert), Susannah York (Alice), Gig Young (Rocky), Red Buttons (Sailor), Bonnie Bedelia (Ruby), Severn Darden (Cecil). Directed by Sydney Pollack and produced by Irwin Winkler and Robert Chartoff. Screenplay by James Poe and Robert E. Thompson.

Erase the forced smiles from the desperate faces, and what the dance marathons of the 1930s came down to was fairly simple. A roomful of human beings went around and around within four walls for weeks at a time without sleep, populating a circus for others who paid to see them. At the end, those who didn't collapse or drop dead won cash prizes that were good money during the Depression. And the Depression, in an oblique sort of way, was the reason for it all. The marathons offered money to the winners and distraction to everyone else. To be sure, some of the marathons got pretty grim. Contestants tried to dance their way through illnesses and pregnancies, through lice and hallucinations, and the sight of them doing it was part of the show. Beyond the hit tunes and the crepe paper and the free pig as a door prize, there was an elementary sadism in the appeal of the marathons.

Among American spectator sports, they rank with stock car racing. There was always that delicious possibility, you see, that somebody would die. Or freak out. Or stand helplessly while his partner collapsed and he lost the investment of thousands of hours of his life.

They Shoot Horses, Don't They? is a masterful re-creation of the marathon era for audiences that are mostly unfamiliar with it. In addition to everything else it does, *Horses* holds our attention because it tells us something we didn't know about human nature and American society. It tells us a lot more than that, of course, but because it works on this fundamental level as well it is one of the best American movies of the 1970s. It is so good as a movie, indeed, that it doesn't have to bother with explaining the things in my first two paragraphs; they are all there (and that's where I found them), but they are completely incorporated into the structure of the film.

Director Sydney Pollack has built a ballroom and filled it with characters. They come from nowhere, really; Michael Sarrazin is photographed as if he has walked into the ballroom directly from the sea. The characters seem to have no histories, no alternate lives; they exist only within the walls of the ballroom and during the ticking of the official clock. Pollack has simplified the universe. He has got everything in life boiled down to this silly contest; and what he tells us has more to do with lives than contests.

Sarrazin meets Jane Fonda, and they became partners almost absentmindedly; he wasn't even planning on entering a marathon. There are other contestants, particularly Red Buttons and Bonnie Bedelia in splendid supporting performances, and they are whipped around the floor by the false enthusiasm of Gig Young, the master of ceremonies. "Yowzza! Yowzza!" he chants, and all the while he regards the contestants with the peculiarly disinterested curiosity of an exhausted god.

There are not a lot of laughs in *Horses*, because Pollack has directed from the point of view of the contestants. They are bitter beyond any hope of release. The movie's delicately timed pacing and Pollack's visual style work almost stealthily to involve us; we begin to feel the physical weariness and spiritual desperation of the characters.

The movie begins on a note of alienation and spirals down from there. *Horses* provides us no cheap release at the end; and the ending, precisely because it is so obvious, is all the more effective. We knew it was coming. Even the title gave it away. And when it comes, it is effective not because it is a surprise but because it is inevitable. As inevitable as death.

The performances are perfectly matched to Pollack's grim vision. Jane Fonda is hard, unbreakable, filled with hate and fear. Sarrazin can do nothing, really, but stand there and pity her; no one, not even during the Depression, should have to feel so without hope. Red Buttons, as the sailor who's a veteran of other marathons and cheerfully teaches everybody the ropes, reminds us that the great character actor from *Sayonara* still exists, and that comedians are somehow the best in certain tragic roles.

And that's what the movie comes down to, maybe. The characters are comedians trapped in tragic roles. They signed up for the three square meals a day and the crack at the $1,500 prize, and they can stop (after all) whenever they want to. But somehow they can't stop, and as the hundreds and thousands of hours of weariness and futility begin to accumulate, the great dance marathon begins to look more and more like life.

Thief ★ ★ ★ ½

R, 126 m., 1981

James Caan (Frank), Tuesday Weld (Jessie), Willie Nelson (Okla), James Belushi (Barry), Robert Prosky (Leo), Tom Signorelli (Attaglia), John Santucci (Urizzi), Tom Erhart (Judge). Directed by Michael Mann and produced by Jerry Bruckheimer and Ronnie Caan. Screenplay by Mann.

Michael Mann's *Thief* is a film of style, substance, and violently felt emotion, all wrapped up in one of the most intelligent thrillers I've seen. It's one of those films where you feel the authority right away: This movie knows its characters, knows its story, and knows exactly how it wants to tell us about them. At a time when thrillers have been devalued by the routine repetition of the same dumb chases, sex scenes, and gunfights, *Thief* is completely out of the ordinary.

The movie stars James Caan as a man who says he was "raised by the state" and spent eleven years in prison. As the movie opens, he's been free four years, and lives in Chicago. He is a highly skilled professional thief—a trade he learned behind bars from Okla (Willie Nelson), a master thief. The film's opening sequence establishes Caan's expertise as he cracks a safe with a portable drill. Caan sees himself as a completely independent loner. But we see him differently, as a lonely, unloved kid who is hiding out inside an adult body. He's a loner who desperately needs to belong to somebody. He trusts his partner (James Belushi), but that's not enough. He decides, on an almost abstract intellectual level, to fall in love with a cashier (Tuesday Weld), and in one of the movie's best scenes he tells this woman, who is essentially a stranger, all about his life in prison and his plans for the future. She takes his hand and accepts him.

But there is another person who comes into his life: Leo, the master criminal, the fence who sets up heists and hires people to pull them. Leo, in a wonderfully complex performance by the sad-faced Robert Prosky, knows how to enlist Caan: "Let me be your father," he says. "I'll take care of everything." He does. He even supplies Caan and Weld with an illegally obtained baby boy when they're turned down at the adoption agency. But once the thief goes with Leo, his life gets complicated. The cops seem to be on his case. His phone is bugged. Everybody knows his business. The movie leads up to one final caper, a $4 million diamond heist in Los Angeles, and then it ends in a series of double crosses and a rain of violence.

This movie works so well for several reasons. One is that *Thief* is able to convince us that it knows its subject, knows about the methods and criminal personalities of its characters. Another is that it's well cast: Every important performance in this movie successfully creates a plausible person, instead of the stock-company supporting characters we might have expected. And the film moves at a taut pace, creating tension and anxiety through very effective photography and a wound-up, pulsing score by Tangerine Dream.

If *Thief* has a weak point, it is probably in the handling of the Willie Nelson character. Nelson is set up well: He became Caan's father-figure in prison, Caan loves him more than anybody, and when he goes to visit him in prison they have a conversation that is subtly written to lead by an indirect route to Nelson's understated revelation that he is dying and does not want to die behind bars. This scene is so strong that it sets us up for big things: We expect Willie to get out, get involved in the plot, and be instrumental in the climax. That doesn't happen. There is a very nice courtroom scene, during which you'll have to pay close attention to catch on to the subverbal and illegal conversation conducted between the judge and the lawyer. But then the Nelson character quickly disappears from the movie, and we're surprised and a little disappointed. Willie has played the character so well that we wanted more. But, then, I suppose it is a good thing when a movie creates characters we feel that strongly about, and *Thief* is populated with them. It's a thriller with plausible people in it. How rare.

Thieves Like Us ★ ★ ★ ½

R, 123 m., 1974

Keith Carradine (Bowie), Shelley Duvall (Keechie), John Schuck (Chicamaw), Bert Remsen (T-Dub), Louise Fletcher (Mattie), Ann Latham (Luie). Directed by Robert Altman and produced by Jerry Bick. Screenplay by Calder Willingham, Joan Tewksbury, and Altman.

Like so much of his work, Robert Altman's *Thieves Like Us* has to be approached with a certain amount of imagination. Some movies are content to offer us escapist experiences and hope we'll be satisfied. But you can't sink back and simply absorb an Altman film; he's as concerned with style as subject, and his preoccupation isn't with story or character, but with how he's showing us his tale. That's the case with *Thieves Like Us*, which no doubt has all sorts of weaknesses in character and plot, but which manages a visual strategy so perfectly controlled that we get an uncanny feel for this time and this place. The movie is about a gang of fairly dumb bank robbers, and about how the youngest of them falls in love with a girl, and about how they stick up some banks and listen to the radio and drink Coke and eventually get shot at.

The outline suggests *Bonnie and Clyde*, but *Thieves Like Us* resembles it only in the most general terms of period and setting. The characters are totally different; Bonnie and Clyde were anti-heroes, but this gang of Altman's has no heroism at all. Just a kind of plodding simplicity, punctuated by some of them with violence, and by the boy with a kind of wondering love. They play out their sad little destinies against two backdrops: One is the pastoral feeling of the Southern countryside, and the other is an exactly observed series of interior scenes that recapture just what it was like to drowse through a slow, hot summer Sunday afternoon, with the radio in the background and the kids playing at pretending to do Daddy's job. If Daddy is a bank robber, so what?

The radio is constantly on in the background of *Thieves Like Us*, but it's not used as a source of music as it was in *American Graffiti* or *Mean Streets*. The old shows we hear are not supposed to be heard by Altman's characters; they're like theme music, to be repeated in the film when the same situations occur. "Gangbusters" plays when they rob a bank, for example, even though the bank would have been closed before "Gangbusters" came on. That's OK, because the radio isn't supposed to be realistic; it's Altman's wry, elegiac comment on the distance between radio fantasy and this dusty, slow-witted reality.

At the heart of the movie is a lovely relationship between the young couple, played by Keith Carradine and Shelley Duvall. They've both been in Altman movies before (just about everybody in view here is in his stock company), and it's easy to see why he likes them so. They don't look like movie stars. They share a kind of rangy grace, an ability to project shyness and uncertainty. There's a scene in bed that captures this; it's a two-shot with Keith in the foreground and Shelley, on her back, eyes to the ceiling, slowly exhaling little plumes of smoke. Nothing is said. The radio plays. Somehow we know just how this quiet, warm moment feels.

The movie's fault is that Altman, having found the perfect means for realizing his story visually, did not spend enough thought, perhaps, on the story itself. *Thieves Like Us* is not another *Bonnie and Clyde*, and yet it does end in a similar way, with a shoot-out. And by this time, we've seen too many movies that have borrowed that structure; that have counted on the bloody conclusion to lend significance to what went before. In *Thieves Like Us*, there just wasn't that much significance, and I don't think there's meant to be. These are small people in a weary time, robbing banks because that's their occupation, getting shot because that's the law's occupation.

Altman's comment on the people and time is carried out through the way he observes them; if you try to understand his intention by analyzing the story, you won't get far. Audiences have always been so plot-oriented that it's possible they'll just go ahead and think this is a bad movie, without pausing to reflect on its scene after scene of poignant observation. Altman may not tell a story better than any one, but he sees one with great clarity and tenderness.

The Thing ★ ★ ½

R, 108 m., 1982

Kurt Russell (MacReady), Wilford Brimley (Blair), T.K. Carter (Nauls), David Clennon (Palmer), Keith David (Childs), Richard Dysart (Dr. Copper). Directed by John Carpenter and produced by David Foster and Lawrence Turman. Screenplay by Bill Lancaster.

A spaceship crash-lands on Earth countless years ago and is buried under Antarctic ice. It has a creature on board. Modern scientists dig up the creature, thaw it out, and discover too late that it still lives—and has the power to imitate all life-forms. Its desire to live and expand is insatiable. It begins to assume the identities of the scientists at an isolated Antarctic research station. The crucial question becomes: Who is real, and who is the Thing? The original story was called *Who Goes There?* It was written by John W. Campbell, Jr., in the late 1930s, and it provided such a strong and scary story that it inspired at least four movie versions before this one: The original *The Thing* in 1952, *Invasion of the Body Snatchers* in 1956 and 1978, *Alien* in 1979, and now John Carpenter's 1982 remake, again called *The Thing*.

I mention the previous incarnations of *The Thing* not to demonstrate my mastery of *The Filmgoer's Companion*, but to suggest the many possible approaches to this material. The two 1950s versions, especially *Body Snatchers*, were seen at the time as fables based on McCarthyism; communists, like victims of the Thing, looked, sounded, and acted like your best friend, but they were infected with a deadly secret. *Alien*, set on a spaceship but using the same premise, paid less attention to the "Who Goes There?" idea and more to the special effects: Remember that wicked little creature that tore its way out of the astronaut's stomach? Now comes this elaborate version by John Carpenter, a master of suspense *(Halloween)*.

His *Thing* depends on its special effects, which are among the most elaborate, nauseating, and horrifying sights yet achieved by Hollywood's new generation of visual magicians. There are times when we seem to be sticking our heads right down into the bloody, stinking maw of the unknown, as the Thing transforms itself into creatures with the body parts of dogs, men, lobsters, and spiders, all wrapped up in gooey intestines.

The Thing is a great barf-bag movie, all right, but is it any good? I found it disappointing, for two reasons: the superficial characterizations and the implausible behavior of the scientists on that icy outpost. Characters have never been Carpenter's strong point; he says he likes his movies to create emotions in his audiences, and I guess he'd rather see us jump six inches than get involved in the personalities of his characters. This time, though, despite some roughed-out typecasting and a few reliable stereotypes (the drunk, the psycho, the hero), he has populated his ice station with people whose primary purpose in life is to get jumped on from behind. The few scenes that develop characterizations are overwhelmed by the scenes in which the men are just setups for an attack by the Thing.

That leads us to the second problem, plausibility. We know that the Thing likes to wait until a character is alone, and then pounce, digest, and imitate him—by the time you see Doc again, is he still Doc, or is he the Thing? Well, the obvious defense against this problem is a watertight buddy system, but, time and time again, Carpenter allows his characters to wander off alone and come back with silly grins on their faces, until we've lost count of who may have been infected, and who hasn't. That takes the fun away.

The Thing is basically, then, just a geek show, a grossout movie in which teenagers can dare one another to watch the screen. There's nothing wrong with that; I like being scared and I *was* scared by many scenes in *The Thing*. But it seems clear that Carpenter made his choice early on to concentrate on the special effects and the technology and to allow the story and people to become secondary. Because this material has been done before, and better, especially in the original *The Thing* and in *Alien*, there's no need to see this version unless you are interested in what the Thing might look like while starting from anonymous greasy organs extruding giant crab legs and transmuting itself into a dog. Amazingly, I'll bet that thousands, if not millions, of moviegoers *are* interested in seeing just that.

This Is Elvis ★ ★ ★ ½

PG, 88 m., 1981

Voices: Elvis (Ral Donner), Joe Esposito (Joe Esposito), Linda Thompson (Linda Thompson), Priscilla Presley (Lisha Sweetnam). Directed, produced, and written by Malcolm Leo and Andrew Solt. Featuring documentary footage of Elvis Presley.

This Is Elvis is the extraordinary record of a man who simultaneously became a great star and was destroyed by alcohol and drug addiction. What is most striking about its documentary footage is that we can almost always see both things happening at once. There is hardly a time when Elvis doesn't appear to be under the influence of mind-altering chemicals, and never a time, not even when he is only weeks from death, when he doesn't possess his special charisma. The movie's lesson is brutal, sad, and inescapable: Elvis Presley was a man who gave joy to a great many people but felt very little of his own, because he became addicted and stayed addicted until the day it killed him.

This movie does not, however, intend to be a documentary about Presley's drug usage. It just turns out that way, because Presley's life turned out that way. The film is a re-creation of his life and image, and uses documentary footage from a wide variety of sources, including Presley's own professionally made home movies. Not all the footage is even really of Presley. Some early childhood scenes are fiction, with a young actor playing Elvis. They don't work, but they're soon over. A few other scenes are also faked, including one shot following Presley into his home on the night he died, and another showing him rushing to his mother's sickbed (the double is an Elvis imitator named Johnny Harra). But the faked footage adds up to only about 10 percent of the movie, and is helpful in maintaining continuity.

The rest of the film's footage is extraordinary, and about half of it has never been seen anywhere. This film isn't just a compilation of old Elvis documentaries. The filmmakers got permission from Presley's manager, Colonel Tom Parker, to use Presley's own private film archives and to shoot inside Graceland, his mansion. They include footage that was not even suspected to exist, including scenes from a birthday party Elvis had in Germany when he was still in the Army (we see a very young Priscilla at the party), scenes of Elvis's parents moving into Graceland, scenes with Elvis clowning around with buddies, and shots taken inside his limousine very near the end, when he was drunk and drugged and obviously very ill. There are also sequences during which we frankly wonder if he will be able to make it onto the stage.

The documentary also includes some of Presley's key television appearances, including his first guest appearances on the old "Dorsey Brothers Bandstand" and the "Ed Sullivan Show" (with Ed assuring America that Elvis was "a real decent, fine boy . . . Elvis, you're thoroughly all right"). There is newsreel footage of Elvis getting out of the Army (and, significantly, observing "it was so cold some nights we had to take bennies to stay awake"). There is an old kinescope, long thought to be lost, of a TV special hosted by Frank Sinatra to welcome Elvis back to civilian life (and in his duet with Sinatra, Presley is confused and apparently under the influence of tranquilizers).

The young Elvis in this movie is an entertainer of incredible energy and charisma. The charisma stays, but somewhere along the way we notice a change in his behavior, a draining away of cheerfulness, a dreadful secret scourge. And in the film's final scenes, Presley is shockingly ill: He's bloated, his skin is splotchy, he's shaking and dripping with sweat, and, in one very painful sequence shot during a concert, he cannot remember the words to his songs. But he pushes through anyway, and his final renditions of "My Way" and "Are You Lonesome Tonight?" are beautiful and absolutely heartbreaking. He may have lost his mind, but he never lost his voice or his heart.

Elvis Presley should, of course, still be alive. The film interviews his former bodyguards about his drinking and drug usage, and they argue convincingly that they could not stop him from doing what he was determined to do. But an addict, of course, has only two choices, no matter how he might deceive himself that he has many. He can either continue to use, or he can ask for help.

The irony in Presley's case is that his own doctor was apparently the source of most of his drugs. Could Elvis have stopped? Sure. Would he have been alive today? Probably. But he was never able to admit his addiction and find the will to seek help. And he was surrounded by foot-kissers and yes-men. This movie shows the disintegration and death of a talented man who backed himself into a corner. He did it his way.

This Is Spinal Tap ★ ★ ★ ★

R, 87 m., 1984

Rob Reiner (Marty DiBergi), Michael McKean (David St. Huggins), Christopher Guest (Nigel Tufnel), Harry Shearer (Derek Smalls). Directed by Rob Reiner and produced by Karen Murphy. Screenplay by Christopher Guest, Michael McKean, Harry Shearer, and Reiner.

The children born at Woodstock are preparing for the junior prom, and rock 'n' roll is still here to stay. Rock musicians never die, they just fade away, and *This Is Spinal Tap* is a movie about a British rock group that is rocketing to the bottom of the charts.

The movie looks like a documentary filmed during the death throes of a British rock band named Spinal Tap. It is, in fact, a satire. The rock group does not really exist, but the best thing about this film is that it could. The music, the staging, the special effects, the backstage feuding, and the pseudo-profound philosophizing are right out of a hundred other rock groups and a dozen other documentaries about rock.

The group is in the middle of an American tour. The tour is not going well. Spinal Tap was once able to fill giant arenas, but its audiences have grown smaller and smaller, and concert dates are evaporating as the bad news gets around. No wonder. Spinal Tap is a bad rock 'n' roll band. It is derivative, obvious, phony, and pretentious, and it surrounds itself with whatever images seem commercial at the moment (a giant death's-head on stage, for one). The movie is absolutely inspired in the subtle way it establishes Spinal Tap's badness. The satire has a deft, wicked touch. Spinal Tap is not that much worse than, not that much different from, some successful rock bands. A few breaks here or there, a successful album, and they could be back in business. (Proof of that: A sound track album, "Smell the Glove," is getting lots of air play with cuts like "Sex Farm".)

The documentary is narrated by its director, Marty DiBergi, played by Rob Reiner, the director of the real movie. He explains that he was first attracted to the band by its unusual loudness. He follows them on tour, asking profound questions that inspire deep, meaningless answers, and his cameras watch as the group comes unglued. One of the band members brings in a girlfriend from England. She feuds with the group's manager. Bookings are canceled. The record company doesn't like the cover for the group's new album. One disastrous booking takes Spinal Tap to a dance in a hangar on a military base. The movie is brilliant at telling its story through things that happen in the background and at the edges of the picture: By the end of the film, we know as much about the personalities and conflicts of the band members as if the movie had been straightforward narrative.

There are a lot of great visual jokes, which I don't want to spoil—especially the climax of the band's Stonehenge production number, or another number that involves them being reborn from womblike stage props. There also are moments of inspired satire aimed at previous styles in rock films, as when we get glimpses of Spinal Tap in its earlier incarnations (the band started as sort of a folk group, plunged into the flower-people generation, and was a little late getting into heavy metal, satanism, and punk).

This Is Spinal Tap assumes that audiences will get most of the jokes. I think that's right. "Entertainment Tonight" and music TV and Barbara Walters specials have made show-business trade talk into national gossip, and one of the greatest pleasures of the movie is that it doesn't explain everything. It simply, slyly, destroys one level of rock pomposity after another.

Three Men and a Baby ★ ★ ★
PG, 99 m., 1987 ✓
(See related Film Clip, p. 767.)

Tom Selleck (Peter), Steve Guttenberg (Michael), Ted Danson (Jack), Nancy Travis (Sylvia), Margaret Colin (Rebecca). Directed by Leonard Nimoy and produced by Ted Field and Robert W. Cort. Screenplay by James Orr and Jim Cruickshank.

Three Men and a Baby begins with too many characters and too much plot, and fifteen minutes into the film, I was growing restless. It spends a lot of time describing the lifestyles of three bachelors—Tom Selleck, Steve Guttenberg, and Ted Danson—who share a luxury apartment and play host to a never-ending stream of girlfriends. We meet too many of the girlfriends and too many of their friends, and then it's the morning after Selleck's big birthday bash, and on the doorstep outside their apartment is a bassinette containing a little baby named Mary. From that point on, the movie finds its rhythm, and it works.

The baby was apparently fathered by Danson, an actor who has just left to spend ten weeks shooting a film in Turkey. Selleck and Guttenberg contemplate the little bundle with dread, and Selleck's confusion is not helped when he goes to the market to buy baby food and gets a lot of advice about babies from a helpful clerk. ("You mean you don't even know how *old* your baby is?" she asks incredulously.)

Shortly after comes one of the funniest scenes in a long time, as Selleck and Guttenberg, an architect and a cartoonist, try to change Mary's diapers. The basic situation may sound familiar and even overworked, but the way they act it and the way Leonard Nimoy directs it, it builds from one big laugh to another.

The movie never steps wrong as long as it focuses on the developing love between the two big men and the tiny baby. At first they're baffled by this little bundle that only eats, sleeps, cries, and makes poo-poo—lots and lots of poo-poo. "The book says to feed the baby every two hours," Selleck complains, "but do you count from when you start, or when you finish? It takes me two hours to get her to eat, and by the time she's done, it's time to start again, so that I'm feeding her all of the time."

Those scenes are the heart of the movie. Unfortunately, there is also a completely unnecessary subplot to distract from the good stuff. *Three Men and a Baby* is a faithful reworking of a French film from a few years ago, in which the basic plot device was that two "packages" were left with the bachelors on the same day—a baby and a fortune in heroin—along with the message that "the package" would be picked up a few days later.

The plot allows them to know nothing about the heroin, so they think the "package" is the baby, and that leads to a misunderstanding with some vicious drug dealers. Learning that an American remake of the French movie was being planned, I assumed that the drug angle would be the first thing written out of the script. To begin with, it's completely unnecessary; the fact that the baby is left on the doorstep is all the story needs to get under way, and the central story is so funny and heartwarming that drugs are a downer.

But, no, Leonard Nimoy and writers James Orr and Jim Cruickshank have remade the entire French movie, drugs and all, leading to a badly staged and distracting confrontation betweeen the heroes and the dealers in a mid-town construction site. Why bother with all the exhausted apparatus of crime and violence, recycled out of TV crime shows, when the story of the men and the baby is so compelling?

Luckily, there's enough of the domestic comedy to make the movie work despite its crasser instincts. And one of the big surprises in the movie is Tom Selleck's wonderful performance as the bachelor architect. After playing action heroes on TV and in the movies, he now reveals himself to be a light comedian in the Cary Grant tradition—a big, handsome guy with tenderness and vulnerability. When he looks at baby Mary with love in his eyes, you can see it there, and it doesn't feel like acting.

Because of Selleck and his co-stars (including twin baby girls Lisa and Michelle Blair), the movie becomes a heartwarming entertainment. There are, however, a couple of glitches at the end. When Mary's mother turns up, the men allow her to leave with the baby without even asking the obvious question on the mind of everyone in the audience: How could she have abandoned the baby in the first place? Another problem is that Selleck isn't the only one who doesn't know how old Mary is. If you follow the various dates mentioned in the script, the filmmakers also haven't a clue. But by the time the movie reaches its predictable but comfortable ending, who cares?

3 Women ★ ★ ★ ★

PG, 125 m., 1977

Sissy Spacek (Pinky), Shelley Duvall (Millie), Janice Rule (Willie), Robert Fortier (Edgar), Ruth Nelson (Mrs. Rose), John Cromwell (Mr. Rose), Craig Richard Nelson (Dr. Maas), Maysie Hoy (Doris). Directed, produced, and written by Robert Altman.

Robert Altman's *3 Women* is, on the one hand, a straightforward portrait of life in a godforsaken California desert community, and, on the other, a mysterious exploration of human personalities. Its specifics are so real you can almost touch them, and its conclusion so surreal we can supply our own.

The community exists somewhere in Southern California, that uncharted continent of discontent and restlessness. Some of its people have put themselves down in a place that contains, so far as we can see, a spa where old people take an arthritis cure, a Western-style bar with a shooting range out back, and a singles residential motel with a swimming pool that has the most unsettling murals on its bottom.

Into this outpost one day comes Pinky (Sissy Spacek), a child-woman so naive, so open, so willing to have enthusiasm, that in another century she might have been a saint, a strange one. She takes a job at the spa and is instructed in her duties by Millie (Shelley Duvall), who is fascinated by the incorrect belief that the men in town are hot for her. Millie recruits Pinky as a roommate in the motel.

This whole stretch of the film—the first hour—is a funny, satirical, and sometimes sad study of the community and its people, who have almost all failed at something else, somewhere else. The dominant male is Edgar (Robert Fortier), a onetime stuntman, now a boozer with a beer bottle permanently in his hand. He's married to Willie (Janice Rule), who never speaks, and is pregnant, and is painting the murals. It's all terrifically new to Pinky: Drinking a beer (which she does as if just discovering the principle of a glass), or moving into Millie's apartment (which she solemnly declares to be the most beautiful place she's ever seen).

Then the film arrives at its center point, one of masked sexual horror. Millie comes home with Edgar and throws Pinky out of their bedroom, and Pinky tries to commit suicide by jumping into the pool. She survives, but as she recovers the film moves from realism to a strange, haunted psychological landscape in which, somehow, Pinky and Millie exchange personalities. *3 Women* isn't Altman out of Freud via *Psychology Today,* and so the movie mercifully doesn't attempt to explain what's happened in logical terms (*any* explanation would be disappointing, I think, compared to the continuing mystery). Somehow we *feel* what's happened, though, even if we can't explain it in so many words.

The movie's been compared to Bergman's *Persona,* another film in which women seem to share personalities, and maybe *Persona,* also so mysterious when we first see it, helps point the way. But I believe Altman has provided his own signposts, in two important scenes, one at the beginning, one at the end, that mirror one another. Millie, teaching Pinky how to exercise the old folks' legs in the hot baths, places Pinky's feet on her stomach and moves them back and forth, just as Pinky sees the apparition of two twins on the other side of the pool.

Later, when the older woman, Willie, is in labor, Millie places her legs in the same way and moves them in the same way, trying to assist the delivery. But the baby is stillborn, and so are the male-female connections in this small society. And so the women symbolically give birth to each other, around and around in a circle, just as (Altman himself suggests) the end of the picture could be seen as the moment just before its beginning.

The movie's story came to Altman during a dream, he's said, and he provides it with a dreamlike tone. The plot connections, which sometimes make little literal sense, do seem to connect emotionally, viscerally, as all things do in dreams. To act in a story like this must be a great deal more difficult than performing straightforward narrative, but Spacek and Duvall go through their changes so well that it's eerie, and unforgettable. So is the film.

Throw Momma from the Train ★ ★
PG-13, 87 m., 1987

Danny DeVito (Owen), Billy Crystal (Larry), Kim Greist (Beth), Anne Ramsey (Momma), Kate Mulgrew (Margaret), Branford Marsalis (Lester). Directed by Danny DeVito and produced by Larry Brezner. Screenplay by Stu Silver.

Movies borrow from other movies all the time, but few have the honesty to admit it. Danny DeVito is nothing if not an honest man. He not only borrows the plot device from Alfred Hitchcock's *Strangers on a Train* for his comedy *Throw Momma From the Train,* but he even has one of his characters actually go to the movies and study the relevant scene from Hitchcock's 1951 classic.

The character (played by DeVito himself) sits in the dark of a revival house and gazes moonily up at the screen, where Robert Walker is smoothly explaining to Farley Granger how two strangers can commit two perfect murders. Each one commits the *other* man's murder, while preparing an airtight alibi for his "own." Since the prime suspect will have an unshakable alibi and the killer cannot be linked to the crime by any possible motive, the police will be stymied.

This seems like a wonderful idea to DeVito, whose character is a little light in the head. He wants to murder his mother, who is a cross between a bag lady and a boxing instructor, and he has the ideal partner in crime: Billy Crystal, his creative writing instructor at the local community college. Crystal is angry because his ex-wife has ripped off a book he wrote, and turned it into a bestseller. "I wish she was dead!" he cries one day at the school cafeteria, and DeVito takes him at his word.

Most of the movie centers on the relationship between DeVito and Crystal, who are complete opposites—the genial, smiling, round little man, and the distracted intellectual. DeVito is the kind of man who (in one of the movie's best moments) can calmly discuss murder and then interrupt himself to exclaim, "Look! Cows!" as they pass a billboard advertising a dairy.

This relationship produces a fair number of laughs, but *Throw Momma from the Train* is not as funny as it might have been, maybe because the script lacks the maniacal tension that the material requires. For a relatively short movie (eighty-seven minutes) it seems too heavy on plot, with all sorts of comings and goings and explanations and misunderstandings, all of which are not really necessary. In his study of Hitchcock, DeVito should have absorbed the Master's theory of the MacGuffin, defined as whatever it is that everybody is concerned about. Hitchcock believed that most movies spent too much time on the MacGuffin, and not enough time on how the characters felt about the MacGuffin. The plot in *Throw Momma from the Train* is top-heavy, but the movie doesn't make as much as it could from its weird characters.

What about Momma, for example? As played by Anne Ramsey in one of the most thankless portrayals since Dick Durdock played Swamp Thing, she is a true monster: A shambling wreck of a woman who talks as if her mouth is full of marbles, and bitterly castigates her son for minor infractions. In fantasies perhaps inspired by *Where's Poppa?* DeVito imagines himself slipping lye into his mother's soft drink, or driving a scissors into her ear. But where did this woman come from, and what makes her tick? If her relationship with her son is exclusively barbaric, how did it get that way? By leaving out complexities and guilt, DeVito probably missed some good comic opportunities.

Billy Crystal, a good actor, is also underutilized by Stu Silver's thin screenplay. An early writer's block scene goes on forever; he's stuck on the words "The night was . . ." and tries countless combinations (wet, dry, humid) without ever (a) stumbling on the old dependable "It was a dark and stormy night . . ." or (b) finding any business funnier than throwing crumpled sheets of typing paper into the wastebasket. Blocked writers don't do that anymore. They work on computers, not typewriters, and when they're blocked, they play computer games like "Leather Goddesses of Phobos."

No matter. *Throw Momma from the Train* is a series of missed opportunities and unexploited situations, a movie that wants to have genuine nastiness at its heart, but never quite works up the energy or the nerve to be truly heartless. Paradoxically, its best scenes are the ones of gentle whimsy. The scene, for example, in which DeVito shows Crystal his coin collection, which is made up, not of valuable coins, but of "important" ones, like the penny he got in change the day his dad took him to the zoo. Maybe at some point during the rewrites, they should have just forgotten about Momma and Hitchcock, and started all over again with that scene.

THX 1138 ★ ★ ★

PG, 88 m., 1971

Robert Duvall (THX 1138), Donald Pleasence (SEN 5241), Don Pedro Colley (SRT), Maggie McOmie (LUH 3417). Directed by George Lucas and produced by Lawrence Sturhahn. Screenplay by Lucas and Walter Murch.

The brave new world of the American Zoetrope studio began in the late 1960s in San Francisco. Francis Ford Coppola, a young director of promise, persuaded Warner Bros. to help finance and distribute a group of features by the bright new filmmakers he'd gathered around him. Coppola had just finished a successful mainstream production for Warners', *Finian's Rainbow*, and his proposal sounded good in that era of youth films, bike films, trip films, and other high hopes.

The youth film and the others turned out to be lost causes, however, and as the American film industry moved back to traditional narrative pictures, not many of the proposed American Zoetrope films were made, and even fewer ever opened. Warner Bros., having decided to drop the San Francisco experiment, didn't back the surviving features very enthusiastically. The greatest casualty was George Lucas's *THX 1138*, a science fiction parable set in the twenty-fifth century and displaying remarkable visual mastery.

The movie's strength is not in its story but in its unsettling and weirdly effective visual and sound style. The story is standard sci-fi stuff: Five centuries in the future, mankind inhabits vast underground cities which are programmed by computers and policed by robots. The citizens are force-fed drugs to inhibit their passions, but THX 1138 (Robert Duvall) and his mate LUH 3417 (Maggie McOmie) cut down on their drug rations and discover that they have sexual appetites. Worse still, they are in love.

What follows is a battle against the centralized computer system, a few episodes of outsmarting the dumb robot policemen, and a chase scene. None of this is very original, and the whole business of Love versus State is out of Orwell and countless lesser writers. But Lucas doesn't seem to have been very concerned with his plot, anyway. His film was inspired by a student film he did at UCLA, which won the National Student

Film Festival in 1968. The student work was sort of a dry run for this one, exploring ways of creating inexpensive but totally convincing special effects for a futuristic society. The experiment was a success; the subterranean laboratories, apartments, and corridors in *THX 1138* have a blinding, white porcelain sameness, and the characters seem to inhabit the future's most spectacular and sanitary bathroom fixtures.

The sound effects add to the illusion of a distant and different society. The dialogue seems half-heard, half-forgotten; people talk in a bemused way, as if the drugs had made them indifferent. Their words are suspended in a muted, echoing atmosphere in which only the computer-programmed recorded announcements seem confident. And the featureless whiteness of this universe stretches away into infinity (especially in the effective scene involving a prison with no walls—how can you escape from a prison that is simply an empty void?). *THX 1138* suffers somewhat from its simple story line, but as a work of visual imagination it's special, and as haunting as parts of *2001*, *Silent Running*, and *The Andromeda Strain*.

Ticket to Heaven ★ ★ ★ ½

R, 107 m., 1981

Nick Mancuso (David), Saul Rubinek (Larry), Meg Foster (Ingrid), Kim Cattrall (Ruthie), R.H. Thomson (Linc Strunk), Jennifer Dale (Lisa). Directed by Ralph L. Thomas and produced by Vivienne Lebosh.

Ticket to Heaven is about a young man who enters the all-encompassing world of a religious cult. What makes the movie absolutely spellbinding is that it shows us not only how he is recruited into the group, but how *anyone* could be indoctrinated into one of the many cults in America today. This is a movie that has done its research, and it is made with such artistry that we share the experience of the young man.

His name is David. He is played by Nick Mancuso, a powerful young actor, as an independent type who flies from Toronto to San Francisco to discover what has happened to a friend who joined up with the cult. He is welcomed to their communal residence, joins in a meal and some singing, and is asked if he'd like to spend the weekend at a retreat on the group's farm. He would. By the end of the weekend, he is a cult member. Can it happen that fast? I've read stories claiming that some cults need only seventy-two hours to convert almost anyone to their way. The best and the brightest make the best recruits, they say. The movie shows the three techniques used to indoctrinate new members: (1) low-calorie, low-protein diets; (2) sleep deprivation; (3) "love-bombing," which involves constant positive reinforcement, the chanting of slogans and great care *never* to allow the recruit to be alone for a moment.

Although *Ticket to Heaven* does not mention any existing cult by name, it is based on a series of newspaper articles about a former Moonie. The techniques in the film could, I suppose, be used by anybody. What makes the film so interesting is that it's not just a docudrama, not just a sensationalist exposé, but a fully realized drama that involves us on the human level as well as with its documentary material. There are scenes that are absolutely harrowing: an overhead shot of David trying to take a walk by himself and being "joined" by jolly friends; a scene where he guiltily bolts down a forbidden hamburger; a scene where another cult member whispers one sentence that sounds to us, as much as to David, like shocking heresy. By that point in the film, we actually understand why David has become so zombie-like and unquestioning. We have shared his experience.

The final scenes in the film involve a deprogramming attempt. They are not as absorbing as what went before, if only because they involve an effort of the intellect, instead of an assault on the very personality itself. I've seen *Ticket to Heaven* three times, and at first I thought the film's ending was "weaker" than the rest. Now I wonder. What cults offer is freedom from the personality. They remove from your shoulders the burden of being you. That is a very seductive offer: why else do people also seek freedom from self through drugs, alcohol, and even jogging? As David is seduced into the cult's womb, we also submit vicariously to the experience. We understand its appeal. At the end, as David's reason is appealed to, as his intellect is reawakened, as he is asked to once again take up the burden of being himself, he resists—and maybe we do, too.

A Tiger's Tale ★ ★
R, 97 m., 1988

Ann-Margret (Rose), C. Thomas Howell (Bubber), Charles Durning (Charlie), Kelly Preston (Shirley), Ann Wedgeworth (Claudine), William Zabka (Randy). Directed and produced by Peter Douglas. Screenplay by Douglas.

Some movies don't seem to know what they're really about, and *A Tiger's Tale* is one of them. It only seems to be about cornpone weirdos on a snake-and-tiger ranch. It only thinks it's about good ol' boys and girls who go to the square dance on Saturday night and spend the rest of the week trading philosophies and partners. Actually, it's an erotic movie that just doesn't have the nerve to declare itself.

The movie takes place in a Texas backwater where the people have names like Bubber and the tigers have names like Valentino. Bubber, played by C. Thomas Howell, is an eighteen-year-old who has a problem. His girlfriend likes to park and neck only in the front yard of her home, where she'll get caught by her mother. Maybe she gets some kind of thrill that way.

The mother is played by Ann-Margret. She's a little strange. One night a week, she likes to dress up like a geisha and eat Chinese food by candlelight. Bubber observes that she sure looks good in a kimono, and the next thing you know, he has abandoned his girlfriend and developed a passion for her mother. No wonder. Ann-Margret in this movie, as in most of her movies, looks disturbingly ravishing.

Problem is, Bubber is at least twenty-five years younger than the woman of his dreams. One thing leads to another, however, and they find themselves in the midst of a relatively serious affair. Ann-Margret begins by saying the affair is insane, then agrees to only one more night, then says the whole thing has to end at the end of the summer, and finally finds herself a great deal more involved than she could ever have imagined.

Meanwhile, we meet the local citizens, including Bubber's father (Charles Durning), who runs a menagerie out behind his gas station. All of the people in the movie talk just like Ma and Pa Kettle and act like refugees from "L'il Abner," and it is the movie's conceit that this is funny when it is actually only annoying.

What does work in the film, however, is the unlikely relationship between Howell and Ann-Margret, who, if she had played Mrs. Robinson, would have made Benjamin a happy man. Ann-Margret glows with health and good humor in the role, and is so splendidly sexy that, in a way, she undermines the whole problem of the generation gap. She may be twenty-five years older than Howell, but she sure doesn't seem twenty-five years older, and not even the local gossips seem seriously surprised that she could be attractive to a teen-ager.

The relationship between Ann-Margret and Howell is not only at the heart of the movie, it is the movie. All the rest is simply overdone window dressing. A few of the other scenes are intrinsically interesting (there is an amazing sequence in which Howell wrestles with his pet tiger), but basically the movie isn't alive except when Howell and Ann-Margret are on the screen.

There's one moment of pure magic, when the two of them and the tiger sit on a hilltop behind the local drive-in theater. And to give the movie its due, it does deal with the consequences of the affair, when Ann-Margret gets most unexpectedly pregnant. But there are many moments of aimless wheel-spinning, particularly during the entire plot involving Kelly Preston as Ann-Margret's daffy daughter. The movie is top-heavy with plot, and what's good in it gets lost in the confusion.

Tightrope ★ ★ ★ ½
R, 114 m., 1984

Clint Eastwood (Wes Block), Genevieve Bujold (Beryl Thibodeaux), Dan Hedaya (Detective Molinari), Alison Eastwood (Amanda Block), Jennifer Beck (Penny Block). Directed by Richard Tuggle and produced by Clint Eastwood and Fritz Manes. Screenplay by Tuggle.

Most modern police thrillers are simple-minded manipulations of chases, violence, pop psychology, and characters painted in broad stereotypes. *Tightrope* contains all four of those ingredients, to be sure, but it also contains so much more that it's a throwback to the great cop movies of the 1940s—when the hero wrestled with his conscience as much as with the killer.

The movie stars Clint Eastwood as a New Orleans homicide detective who is as different as possible from Dirty Harry Callahan. The guy's name is Wes Block. His wife has recently left him, and he lives at home with his two young daughters and several dogs. He is a good but flawed cop, with a peculiar hang-up: He likes to make love to women while they are handcuffed. The movie suggests this is because he feels deeply threatened by women (a good guess, I'd say). Detective Block is well-known to most of the kinkier prostitutes in the French Quarter, but his superiors don't know that when they assign him to a big case: A mad slasher, apparently an ex-cop, is killing hookers in the Quarter. Block's problem is that he cannot easily enter this world as a policeman after having entered it often as a client. His other problem is that when he walks into that world, all of his old urges return.

The police work in *Tightrope* is more or less standard: The interviews of suspects, the paperwork, the scenes where his superiors chew him out for not making more progress on the case. What makes *Tightrope* better than just another police movie are the scenes between Eastwood and the women he encounters. Some of them are hookers. Some are victims. One of them, played by Genevieve Bujold, is a feminist who teaches women's self-defense classes. Block has always been attracted to flashy, gaudy women, like the Quarter's more bizarre prostitutes. We do not know why his wife left him, and we are given no notions of what she was like, but right away we figure that Bujold isn't his type. She's in her mid-thirties, uses no makeup, wears sweat shirts a lot, and isn't easily impressed by cops. But somehow a friendship does begin. And it becomes the counterpoint for the cop's investigation, as he goes deeper into the messy underworld of the crimes—and as more of the evidence seems to suggest that he should be one of the suspects. It's interesting that the movie gives Eastwood two challenges: To solve the murders, and to find a way out of his own hang-ups and back into an emotional state where he can trust a strong woman.

Tightrope may appeal to the Dirty Harry fans, with its sex and violence. But it's a lot more ambitious than the Harry movies, and the relationship between Eastwood and Bujold is more interesting than most recent male-female relationships in the movies, for three reasons: (1) There is something at risk in it, on both sides; (2) it's a learning process, in which Eastwood is the one who must change; (3) it pays off dramatically at the end, when their developing relationship fits into the climax of the investigation. Think how unusual it is for a major male star to appear in a commercial cop picture in which the plot hinges on his ability to accept and respect a woman. Apart from the other good things in *Tightrope*, I admire it for taking chances; Clint Eastwood can get rich making Dirty Harry movies, but he continues to change and experiment, and that makes him the most interesting of the box office megastars.

Time Bandits ★ ★ ★

PG, 98 m., 1981

Craig Warnock (Kevin), John Cleese (Robin Hood), Sean Connery (Agamemnon), Shelley Duvall (Pansy), Ian Holm (Napoleon), Ralph Richardson (Supreme Being). The Dwarfs: David Rappaport (Randall), Kenny Baker (Fidget), Jack Purvis (Wally), Mike Edmonds (Og), Malcolm Dixon (Strutter), Tiny Ross (Vermin). Directed and produced by Terry Gilliam. Screenplay by Michael Palin and Gilliam.

First reactions while viewing *Time Bandits:* It's amazingly well-produced. The historic locations are jammed with character and detail. This is the only live-action movie I've seen that literally looks like pages out of *Heavy Metal* magazine, with kings and swordsmen and wide-eyed little boys and fearsome beasts. *But* the movie's repetitive, monotonous in the midst of all this activity. Basically, it's just a kid and six dwarfs racing breathlessly through one set-piece after another, shouting at one another. I walked out of the screening in an unsettled state of mind. When the lights go up, I'm usually fairly certain whether or not I've seen a good movie. But my reaction to *Time Bandits* was ambiguous. I had great admiration for what was physically placed on the screen; this movie is worth seeing just to *watch.* But I was disappointed by the breathless way the dramatic scenes were handled and by a breakneck pace that undermined the most important element of comedy, which is timing.

Time Bandits is the expensive fantasy by Terry Gilliam, one of the resident geniuses of Monty Python's Flying Circus. It is *not* a Monty Python film. It begins with a little boy who goes up to bed one night and is astonished, as we all would be, when a horseman gallops through his bedroom wall and he is in the middle of a pitched battle. Before long, the little kid has joined up with a band of six intrepid dwarfs, and they've embarked on an odyssey through history. The dwarfs, it appears, have gained possession of a map that gives the location of several holes in time—holes they can pop through in order to drop in on the adventures of Robin Hood, Napoleon, and King Agamemnon, and to sail on the *Titanic*'s maiden voyage.

As a plot gimmick, this sets up *Time Bandits* for a series of comic set-pieces as in Mel Brooks's *History of the World—Part I.* But *Time Bandits* isn't revue-style comedy. It's more of a whimsical, fantastic excursion through all those times and places, and all of its events are seen through the wondering eyes of a child. That's where the superb art direction comes in—inspired work by production designer Milly Burns and costume designer Jim Acheson. I've rarely, if ever, seen a live-action movie that looks more like an artist's conception. And yet, admiring all of these good things (and I might also mention several of the performances), I nevertheless left the screening with muted enthusiasm. The movie was somehow all on the same breathless, nonstop emotional level, like an overlong Keystone Kops chase. It didn't pause to savor its delights, except right near the end, when Sir Ralph Richardson lingered lovingly over a walk-on as the Supreme Being. I had to sort things out. And I was helped enormously in that process by the review of *Time Bandits* by Stanley Kauffmann in *The New Republic.* He describes the film, unblinkingly, as a "children's movie." Of course.

There have been so many elaborate big-budget fantasies in recent years, from *Raiders* to *Superman* to *Clash of the Titans,* that we've come to assume that elaborate costume fantasies are aimed at the average eighteen-year-old filmgoer who is trying to recapture his adolescence. These movies have a level of (limited) sophistication and wickedness that is missing in *Time Bandits.* But perhaps *Time Bandits* does work best as just simply a movie for kids. I ran it through my mind that way, wondering how a kid would respond to the costumes, the panoply, the explosions, the horses and heroic figures and, of course, the breathless, nonstop pacing. And I decided that a kid would like it just fine. I'm not sure that's what Gilliam had in mind, but it allows me to recommend the movie—with reservations, but also with admiration.

A Time of Destiny ★ ★ ★ ½
PG-13, 118 m., 1988 ✓

William Hurt (Martin), Timothy Hutton (Jack), Melissa Leo (Josie), Stockard Channing (Margaret), Megan Follows (Irene), Francisco Rabal (Jorge). Directed by Gregory Nava and produced by Anna Thomas. Screenplay by Nava and Thomas.

A Time of Destiny is a film of strong, pure emotions, of which the most powerful are love, hate, and jealousy. It is not a film about timid little people peeking out of their small lives, but about characters whose motives are so large they are operatic, and whose faults are so ancient they are biblical. Any criticism of this film on the basis of implausibility completely misses the point.

The movie tells the story of a proud, flawed family, and the outsider who marries into it. The sickness of the family flows from the father, a proud Basque immigrant who has found success in California in the years before World War II, but still rules his life and family by old-world paternalism. As the movie opens, one of his sons is dead, another son is all but disowned, and all of his love and possessiveness are focused on his youngest child, a daughter. When she elopes to get married, his rage and jealousy are towering.

The old man is played by Francisco Rabal as a survivor with a fierce stubbornness. He knows he is right, and one of the things he is right about is this—few men, if any, are good enough for his daughter. She is played by Melissa Leo as a girl caught halfway between modern America and the values of her childhood. And the man she elopes with, one rainy night, is played by Timothy Hutton as the kind of straight-arrow American who seems commonplace against this convoluted family's deep passions.

If jealousy is a family disease, the old man

is the carrier, but his son is the victim. He is also an enigma. Played by William Hurt as a man who seems, at first glance, confident and competent, he is actually on the edge of emotional collapse. His father has no use for him because of his history of failure—failure, we suspect, inspired by the father's inability to make room inside the family for more than one strong man. The Hurt character has grown up into a man filled with grandiose notions of family tradition and pride, and they are all a fantasy, because his father considers him worthless and has written him out of the will.

This convoluted family situation sets the stage for *A Time of Destiny,* which is a melodramatic romance in which the images all seem a little larger and clearer than life. The movie was directed by Gregory Nava and produced and written by Anna Thomas; they are the team who made *El Norte* five years earlier, and their gift is for passionate, headlong narrative. In this film, the opening scenes are literally explosive; there is a spectacular point-of-view shot of a shell flying through a cannon barrel and down upon a straggling line of Yankee soldiers in Italy, and then we see two of the soldiers, tired beyond exhaustion, pledge to each other to somehow survive the madness.

The soldiers are Hutton and Hurt, and in a flashback we find that this pledge is not as simple as it seems. Hutton and Leo conduct a courtship in the face of her father's disapproval, and everything leads up to a rain-swept night when they elope, are married, and then are tracked down to their hotel by the father, in a towering rage. He demands that she return with him or lose his love. She agrees, promising Hutton that they will eventually be together. The old man and his daughter drive out into the dangerous night, Hutton pursues in his car, there is an accident, and the old man dies.

For William Hurt, this is a long-awaited moment. He is simultaneously freed of his father's persecution and given a stage on which to pretend to inherit his father's crown. Hutton (who has never met Hurt and does not know what he looks like) goes off to fight the war; Hurt arranges to join the same Army group, and he vows to murder Hutton to avenge the death of his father. But during a dark and confused night of hand-to-hand fighting, the two men instead save each other's lives. That should set the stage for a reconciliation, but instead, Hurt gradually reveals the true depths of the wound inside his soul.

You see what I mean when I call the movie operatic. It glories in brooding vengeance, fatal flaws of character, coincidence, and deep morality. Its plot is so labyrinthine that it constitutes the movie's major weakness; can we follow this convoluted emotional journey? Its passions are so large that they are a challenge to actors trained in a realistic tradition, but Hurt, who has the most difficult passages, rises to the occasion with one of the strangest and most effective performances he has given. A great deal hinges on one scene that he plays before a mirror, as various aspects of his personality fight for control, and the way he plays this scene is further evidence of his power as an actor. He does not overact, and yet he is not afraid of pulling out all the stops, of taking the risk of making himself look silly. Many actors would have protected themselves by pulling back during this scene. Not William Hurt.

Even the title of *A Time of Destiny* reflects the film's vision. It is a movie about fate in an age that does not believe in fate; its plot is nineteenth-century, without apology, and it is not timid or compromised. As I watched the film, I grew increasingly grateful for the chances it was taking. This same story could have been ground in the mill of psychological realism and come out as oatmeal. But Nava and Thomas have chosen a more difficult and risky approach, and the result is muscular and brave.

The Times of Harvey Milk ★ ★ ★ ½

NO MPAA RATING, 87 m., 1985

A documentary by Robert Epstein and Richard Schmiechen, narrated by Harvey Fierstein.

Harvey Milk must have been a great guy. You get the sense watching this documentary about his brief public career that he could appreciate the absurdities of life and enjoy a good laugh at his own expense. He was also serious enough and angry enough about the political issues in his life that he eventually ran for the San Francisco Board of Supervisors and became California's first openly homosexual public official. That victory may have cost him his life.

The Times of Harvey Milk describes the

lives and deaths of Milk and Mayor George Moscone, who both were shot dead in 1978 by Dan White, one of Milk's fellow supervisors. It also describes the political and social climate in San Francisco, which during the 1960s and 1970s began to attract growing numbers of gays because of its traditionally permissive attitude. Milk was one of those gays, and in old photographs we see him in his long-haired beatnik and hippie days before he eventually shaved off the beard and opened a camera store in the Castro District. It was from the Castro that Milk ran for office and was defeated three times before finally winning in the same election that placed the first Chinese-American, the first black woman, and the first avowed feminist on the board. Milk was a master at self-promotion, and the movie includes vintage TV news footage showing him campaigning on such issues as "doggy-do," and stepping, with perfect timing, into a strategically placed pile of same at the climax of the interview.

There is a lot of footage of Milk, Moscone, and White (who disapproved of homosexuals but was naive enough to once suggest that the issue be settled by a softball game between his ward and Milk's ward). It is intercut with later interviews with many of Milk's friends, including a veteran leftist who admits that he was prejudiced against gays for a long time, until he met Milk and began to understand the political issues involved. There is a Chinese-American who parallels his own radicalization with Milk's. And there is immensely moving, emotional footage of the two demonstrations inspired by the deaths of Milk and Moscone: a silent, candlelight parade of forty-five-thousand people on the night of their deaths, and an angry night of rioting when White got what was perceived as a lenient sentence.

"If Dan White had only killed George Moscone, he would have gone up for life," one person says in the film. "But he killed a gay, and so they let him off easy." This is not necessarily the case, and the weakest element in *The Times of Harvey Milk* is its willingness to let Milk's friends second-guess the jury, and impugn the jurors' motives.

Many people who observed White's trial believe that White got a light sentence, not because of antigay sentiment, but because of incompetent prosecution. Some of the jurors were presumably available to the filmmakers, and the decision not to let them speak for themselves—to depend instead on the interpretation of Milk's friends and associates—is a serious bias. That objection aside, this is an enormously absorbing film, for the light it sheds on a decade in the life of a great American city and on the lives of Milk and Moscone, who made it a better, and certainly a more interesting, place to live.

Tin Men ★ ★ ★

R, 109 m., 1987

Richard Dreyfuss (BB), Danny DeVito (Tilley), Barbara Hershey (Nora), John Mahoney (Moe), Jackie Gayle (Sam), Stanley Brock (Gil), Seymour Cassell (Cheese), Bruno Kirby (Mouse). Directed by Barry Levinson and produced by Mark Johnson. Screenplay by Levinson.

They tool up to work in those bloated '50s Cadillacs from back in the days when you knew a Cadillac was the best car on the road because it was the biggest car on the road. They park their Caddys and hang around the diner, drinking coffee and killing time, talking about the citizens they've defrauded and the TV shows they're gonna watch tonight. They're tin men. They sell aluminum siding. One day, BB (Richard Dreyfuss) takes delivery on his new Caddy, and backs it out of the showroom and into the path of a Caddy owned by Tilley (Danny DeVito). Sheet metal is crunched and words are exchanged. They become mortal enemies. They hurl insults and threats at one another, and for weeks afterward they plot and scheme to wreak vengeance for the dents in the fenders of their phallic symbols.

The feud between BB and Tilley is the centerpiece of *Tin Men*, a loosely organized series of events in the lives of some middle-aged and fairly desperate Baltimore salesmen, circa 1958. These guys are worried because the law is closing in, a commission is holding hearings on their high-pressure sales techniques, and they're afraid they'll lose their jobs.

Meanwhile, they carry on in the only ways they know. They use the "loss leader" scam ("After your house becomes the neighborhood showplace, we'll give you a cut when your neighbors sign up for siding"), the *Life* magazine scam ("We need a picture of your house for a layout on how ugly houses are before the aluminum siding is added"), and the sudden breakdown scam'My buddy didn't mean to make you that offer. He hasn't been quite right lately. But I'll tell you what I will do"). And then they meet after work to trade lies and philosophies.

BB figures out a way to really get even with Tilley. He'll seduce his wife (Barbara Hershey). Two things go wrong with this plan. First, Tilley hates his wife and is happy to get rid of her. Second, BB falls in love. That is a high price to pay for a dented fender.

Tin Men was written and directed by Barry Levinson in a style similar to his inspired 1982 comedy, *Diner.* That was a movie about a crowd of teen-age buddies who were mystified by sex, life, ambition, and especially women. They were trying to grow up at an age when they were already supposed to be grown-up. The median age of the characters in *Tin Men* is probably forty-five, but they're still growing up too, and they're still mystified by sex, life, ambition, and women—by everything but Cadillacs.

Like *Diner,* Levinson's new movie uses a series of scenes strung together with the diner as home base. There, in a window booth, pouring sugar into their coffee, the salesmen discuss the bafflements of life. "This show 'Bonanza' is about a fifty-year-old father and his three forty-seven-year-old sons," one of the guys says. "What kind of a show is that?" That line is delivered by Jackie Gayle, who has a lot of the movie's funniest moments, maybe because the Dreyfuss and DeVito characters have serious undertones.

Why do BB and Tilley hate each other so much? Because they hate themselves so much. Why's that? Because they're secretly ashamed to be con men, and their Cadillacs impart a respectability they don't really feel. So if you dent their fenders, you question the very depths of their identities.

Because *Tin Men* is based on fundamental truth, it is able to be funny even in some of its quieter moments. The good jokes always hurt a little. This movie isn't slapstick and it's not a farce; it's the kind of comedy the guy was thinking about when he wrote, "We laugh, that we may not cry."

To Be or Not To Be ★ ★ ★

R, 108 m., 1983

Mel Brooks (Bronski), Anne Bancroft (Anna Bronski), Tim Matheson (Lieutenant Sobinski), Charles Durning (Colonel Erhardt), Jose Ferrer (Professor Siletski). Directed by Alan Johnson and produced by Mel Brooks. Screenplay by Thomas Meehan and Ronny Graham.

It's an old gag, the one about the actor who is always interrupted in the middle of Hamlet's soliloquy by a guy in the third row who has to go to the john and loudly excuses himself all the way to the end of the row. But I can't think of a better Hamlet for this particular gag than Mel Brooks. "That is the QUESTION!" he bellows, as the guy screws up his timing, his delivery, his concentration. And the punch line is that the guy is actually going backstage to have a quick assignation with the actor's wife.

Mel Brooks loves show business and has worked it into a lot of his movies, most unforgettably in *The Producers.* He also loves musicals and has worked musical numbers into the most unlikely moments in his movies. (Remember Frankenstein's monster doing the soft-shoe?) In *To Be or Not To Be,* Brooks combines a backstage musical with a wartime romance and comes up with an eclectic comedy that races off into several directions, sometimes successfully.

The movie costars Brooks and his wife, Anne Bancroft, working together for the first time on screen as Frederick and (Anna) Bronski, the impresarios of a brave little theatrical troupe in Warsaw on the brink of war. (Anna) Bronski, whose name is in parentheses because her husband has such a big ego, is a femme fatale with an eye for the handsome young servicemen that worship her nightly in the theater. Bronski is an all-over-the-map guy who does Hamlet's soliloquy and stars in a revue called *Naughty Nazis* in the same night and on the same stage. Then the Nazis march into Poland. What can a humble troupe of actors do to stop them? "Nothing!" Bronski declares—but then the troupe gets involved in an elaborate masquerade, pretending to be real Nazis in order to throw Hitler's men off-course and prevent the success of the German plans.

When *To Be or Not To Be* was originally made, by Ernst Lubitsch in 1942, the Nazis *were* in Poland, which gave a certain poignancy to every funny line. Lubitsch's stars were Jack Benny and Carole Lombard, both specialists in underplaying. Brooks and Bancroft go in the opposite direction, cheerfully allowing farce, slapstick, pratfalls, and puns into the story, until the whole movie seems strung together like one of the revues in Bronski's theater.

The supporting players, given license to overact, have fun. Charles Durning plays a rigid but peculiarly confused Nazi colonel, and Tim Matheson is the young aviator who excuses himself loudly and sneaks backstage to meet Bancroft. The veteran actor Jose Ferrer plays Professor Siletski, a two-faced collaborator.

It will probably always be impossible for Brooks to remain entirely within the dramatic logic of any story, and here he gives himself a lot of freedom with lines like "Sondheim! Send in the clowns!" But *To Be or Not To Be* works as well as a story as any Brooks film since *Young Frankenstein*, and darned if there isn't a little sentiment involved as the impresario and his wife, after years of marriage, surprise each other by actually falling in love.

To Live and Die in L.A. ★ ★ ★ ★

R, 110 m., 1985

William L. Petersen (Richard Chance), Willem Dafoe (Eric Masters), John Pankow (John Vukovich), Debra Feuer (Bianca Torres), John Turturro (Carl Cody), Darlanne Fluegel (Ruth Lanier), Dean Stockwell (Bob Grimes), Robert Downey (Thomas Bateman). Directed by William Friedkin and produced by Irving H. Levin. Screenplay by Gerald Petievich and Friedkin.

In the hierarchy of great movie chase sequences, the recent landmarks include the chases under the Brooklyn elevated tracks in *The French Connection*, down the hills of San Francisco in *Bullitt*, and through the Paris Metro in *Diva*. Those chases were not only thrilling in their own right, but they reflected the essence of the cities where they took place. Now comes William Friedkin, director of *The French Connection*, with a movie that contains a second chase that belongs on that short list. The movie is set in Los Angeles, and so of course the chase centers around the freeway system.

To Live and Die in L.A. is a law enforcement movie, sort of. It's about Secret Service agents who are on the trail of a counterfeiter who has eluded the law for years, and who flaunts his success. At one point, when undercover agents are negotiating a deal with the counterfeiter in his expensive health club, he boasts, "I've been coming to this gym three times a week for five years. I'm an easy guy to find. People know they can trust me."

Meanwhile, he's asking for a down payment on a sale of bogus bills, and the down payment is larger than the Secret Service can authorize. So, Richard Chance (William L. Peterson), the hot-dog special agent who's the hero of the movie, sets up a dangerous plan to steal the advance money from another crook, and uses it to buy the bogus paper and bust the counterfeiter.

Neat. The whole plot is neat, revolving around a few central emotions—friendship, loyalty, arrogance, anger. By the time the great chase sequence arrives, it isn't just a novelty, tacked onto a movie where it doesn't fit. It's part of the plot. The Secret Service agents bungle *their* crime, the cops come in pursuit, and the chase unfolds in a long, dazzling ballet of timing, speed, and imagination.

The great chases are rarely just chases. They involve some kind of additional element—an unexpected vehicle, an unusual challenge, a strange setting. The car-train chase in *The French Connection* was a masterstroke. In *Diva*, the courier rode his motor scooter into one subway station and out another, bouncing up and down the stairs. Or think of John Ford's sustained stagecoach chase in *Stagecoach*, or the way Buster Keaton orchestrated *The General* so that trains chased each other through a railway system.

The masterstroke in *To Live and Die in L.A.* is that the chase isn't just on a freeway. It goes *the wrong way* down the freeway. I don't know how Friedkin choreographed this scene and I don't want to know. It probably took a lot of money and a lot of drivers. All I know is that there are high-angle shots during the chase during which you can look a long way ahead and see hundreds of cars across four lanes, all heading for the escape car which is aimed at them, full-speed. It is an amazing sequence.

The rest of the movie is also first-rate. The direction is the key. Friedkin has made some good movies (*The French Connection*, *The Exorcist*, *Sorcerer*) and some bad ones (*Cruising*, *Deal of the Century*). This is his comeback, showing the depth and skill of the early pictures. The central performance is by William L. Petersen, a Chicago stage actor who comes across as tough, wiry, and smart. He has some of the qualities of a Steve McQueen, with more complexity. Another strong performance in the movie is by Willem Dafoe, as the counterfeiter, cool and professional as he discusses the realities of his business.

I like movies which teach me about something, movies which have researched their subject and contain a lot of information, casually contained in between the big dramatic scenes. *To Live and Die in L.A.* seems to know a lot about counterfeiting, and also about the interior policies of the Secret Service. The film isn't just about cops and robbers, but about two systems of doing business, and how one of the systems finds a way to change itself in order to defeat the other. That's interesting. So is the chase.

Tommy ★ ★ ★

PG, 108 m., 1975

Ann-Margret (Nora Walker), Oliver Reed (Frank Hobbs), Roger Daltrey (Tommy), Elton John (Pinball Wizard), Eric Clapton (Preacher), Keith Moon (Uncle Ernie), Jack Nicholson (Specialist), Tina Turner (Acid Queen). The Who: Pete Townshend, John Entwhistle, Daltrey, and Moon. Directed by Ken Russell and produced by Robert Stigwood and Russell. Screenplay by Russell.

Ken Russell's *Tommy* is a case of glorious overkill—a big, brassy, vulgar overproduction that works because it never stops for a breath or a second thought. It's got confidence. It's a blast of wall-to-wall music for almost two hours, and its quietest moment is a Moog-synthesized belch from Oliver Reed that sounds like the Carlsbad Caverns throwing up. There's not the slightest hint of moderation or restraint in the movie,and there shouldn't be. This is Ken Russell giving a Bronx cheer to the most pretentious of the late 1960s rock operas, turning it into a clothesline on which he strings a series of bizarre, manic production numbers. Sit down in front, slide back in your seat, and let it assault you.

The movie's purpose and achievement would be hard to figure out on the basis of what its makers say about it. Pete Townshend, who wrote the original album for the Who, says *Tommy* is an attack on the hypocrisy of organized religion. Ken Russell, who's made a specialty of films about musicians (Tchaikovsky, Mahler, and Liszt), says *Tommy* is the greatest work of art the twentieth century has produced. He was almost certainly misquoted. What he meant to say was that it was a heaven-sent opportunity for him to exercise his gift for going too far, for creating three-ring cinematic circuses with kinky sideshows.

The message of *Tommy*, if any, is contained mostly in the last thirty minutes (of which we could have done without about fifteen). By then the hero (who started out in life as a blind deaf-mute) has become the pinball superstar of all time, even though he can't see the machine. Stardom brings him a fortune, he becomes the leader of a quasireligious cult, regains his senses, and gets his own Tommy T-shirt. But then things get out of hand. Tommy is on the level, but the people around him begin to commercialize on his fame in order to peddle T-shirts, record albums, and other artifacts. Tommy's enraged fans turn on him and what they perceive as his hypocrisy. How the makers of the film feel about this commercialization can be gauged by the prominence with which the end titles inform us that the sound track album is available on Polydor Records. To make money on a rock opera attacking those who would make money on a rock opera: that was the brave moral stand taken by *Tommy*.

But none of this matters, because Russell correctly doesn't give a damn about the material he started with, greatest art work of the century or not, and he just goes ahead and gives us one glorious excess after another. He is aided by his performers, especially Ann-Margret, who is simply great as Tommy's mother. She has one number that begins in an all-white bedroom with her sexy red dress slit up the side to about the collarbone, and ends with her slithering through several hundred pounds of baked beans. It's that kind of movie.

Tommy's odyssey through life is punctuated by encounters with all sorts of weird folks, of whom the most seductive is Tina Turner as the Acid Queen. The scene begins with Tina as the hooker upstairs from the strip parlor operated by Tommy's wicked stepfather, and ends with a psychedelic stainless steel mummy with acid in its veins. This scene is the occasion for Tommy's first smile, as well it might be.

Then there's the great pinball tournament, which is the movie's best single scene: a pulsating, orgiastic turn-on edited with the precision of a machine gun burst. Elton John, wearing skyscraper shoes, is the defending pinball champion. Tommy is the challenger. Russell cuts between the crowds, the arena, and a dizzying series of close-ups of the games (at times, we almost seem to be inside the pinball machines), and the effect is exhilarating and exhausting.

Tootsie ★ ★ ★ ★

PG, 116 m., 1982

Dustin Hoffman (Michael), Jessica Lange (Julie), Charles Durning (Les Nichols), Teri Garr (Sandy), Bill Murray (Roommate), Dabney Coleman (Ron), Doris Belack (Rita), Sydney Pollack (Agent). Directed by Sydney Pollack and produced by Dick Richards. Screenplay by Larry Gelbart.

One of the most endearing things about *Tootsie*, a movie in which Dustin Hoffman plays a middle-aged actress, is that the actress is able to carry most of her own scenes as herself—even if she weren't being played by Hoffman. *Tootsie* works as a story, not as a gimmick. It also works as a lot of other things. *Tootsie* is the kind of Movie with a capital M that they used to make in the 1940s, when they weren't afraid to mix up absurdity with seriousness, social comment with farce, and a little heartfelt tenderness right in there with the laughs. This movie gets you coming and going.

Hoffman stars as Michael Dorsey, a character maybe not unlike Hoffman himself in his younger days. Michael is a New York actor: bright, aggressive, talented—and unemployable. "You mean *nobody in New York* wants to hire me?" he asks his agent, incredulously. "I'd go farther than that, Michael," his agent says. "Nobody in Hollywood wants to hire you, either." Michael has a bad reputation for taking stands, throwing tantrums, and interpreting roles differently than the director. How to get work? He goes with a friend (Teri Garr) to an audition for a soap opera. The character is a middle-age woman hospital administrator. When his friend doesn't get the job, Michael goes home, thinks, decides to dare, and dresses himself as a woman. And, improvising brilliantly, he gets the role.

That leads to *Tootsie's* central question: Can a fortyish New York actor find health, happiness, and romance as a fortyish New York actress? Dustin Hoffman is actually fairly plausible as "Dorothy," the actress. If his voice isn't quite right, a Southern accent allows it to squeak by. The wig and the glasses are a little too much, true, but in an uncanny way the woman played by Hoffman looks like certain actual women who look like drag queens. Dorothy might have trouble passing in Evanston, but in Manhattan, nobody gives her a second look.

Tootsie might have been content to limit itself to the complications of New York life in drag; it could have been *Victor/Victoria Visits Elaine's*. But the movie's a little more ambitious than that. Michael Dorsey finds to his interest and amusement that Dorothy begins to take on a life of her own. She's a liberated eccentric, a woman who seems sort of odd and funny at first, but grows on you and wins your admiration by standing up for what's right. One of the things that bothers Dorothy is the way the soap opera's chauvinist director (Dabney Coleman) mistreats and insults the attractive young actress (Jessica Lange) who plays Julie, a nurse on the show. Dorothy and Julie become friends and finally close confidantes. Dorothy's problem, however, is that the man inside her is gradually growing uncontrollably in love with Julie. There are other complications. Julie's father (Charles Durning), a gruff, friendly, no-nonsense sort, lonely but sweet, falls in love with Dorothy. Michael hardly knows how to deal with all of this, and his roommate (Bill Murray) isn't much help. Surveying Dorothy in one of her new outfits, he observes dryly, "Don't play hard to get."

Tootsie has a lot of fun with its plot complications; we get almost every possible variation on the theme of mistaken sexual identities. The movie also manages to make some lighthearted but well-aimed observations about sexism. It *also* pokes satirical fun at soap operas, New York show business agents, and the Manhattan social pecking-order. *And* it turns out to be a touching love story, after all—so touching that you may be surprised how moved you are at the conclusion of this comedy.

Top Gun ★ ★ ½
PG, 109 m., 1986

Tom Cruise (Maverick), Kelly McGillis (Charlie), Val Kilmer (Iceman), Tom Skeritt (Viper), Anthony Edwards (Goose). Directed by Tony Scott and produced by Don Simpson and Jerry Bruckheimer. Screenplay by Jim Cash and Jack Epps, Jr.

In the opening moments of *Top Gun*, an ace Navy pilot flies upside down about eighteen inches above a Russian-built MiG and snaps a Polaroid picture of the enemy pilot. Then he flips him the finger and peels off.

It's a hog-dog stunt, but it makes the pilot (Tom Cruise) famous within the small circle of Navy personnel who are cleared to receive information about close encounters with enemy aircraft. And the pilot, whose code name is Maverick, is selected for the Navy's elite flying school, which is dedicated to the dying art of aerial dogfights. The best graduate from each class at the school is known as "Top Gun."

And there, I think, you have the basic materials of this movie, except, of course, for three more obligatory ingredients in all movies about brave young pilots: (1) the girl, (2) the mystery of the heroic father, and (3) the rivalry with another pilot. It turns out that Maverick's dad was a brilliant Navy jet pilot during the Vietnam era, until he and his plane disappeared in unexplained circumstances. And it also turns out that one of the instructors at the flying school is a pretty young blonde (Kelly McGillis) who wants to know a lot more about how Maverick snapped that other pilot's picture.

Top Gun settles fairly quickly into alternating ground and air scenes, and the simplest way to sum it up is to declare the air scenes brilliant and the earthbound scenes grimly predictable. This movie comes in two parts: It knows exactly what to do with special effects, but doesn't have a clue as to how two people in love might act and talk and think.

Aerial scenes always present a special challenge in a movie. There's the danger that the audience will become spatially disoriented. We're used to seeing things within a frame that respects left and right, up and down, but the fighter pilot lives in a world of 360-degree turns. The remarkable achievement in *Top Gun* is that it presents seven or eight aerial encounters that are so well choreographed that we can actually follow them most of the time, and the movie gives us a good secondhand sense of what it might be like to be in a dogfight.

The movie's first and last sequences involve encounters with enemy planes. Although the planes are MiGs, the movie provides no nationalities for their pilots. We're told the battles take place over the Indian Ocean, and that's it. All of the sequences in between take place at Top Gun school, where Maverick quickly gets locked into a personal duel with another brilliant pilot, Iceman (Val Kilmer). In one sequence after another, the sound track trembles as the sleek planes pursue each other through the clouds, and, yeah, it's exciting. But the love story between Cruise and McGillis is a washout.

It's pale and unconvincing compared with the chemistry between Cruise and Rebecca De Mornay in *Risky Business*, and between McGillis and Harrison Ford in *Witness*—not to mention between Richard Gere and Debra Winger in *An Officer and a Gentleman*, which obviously inspired *Top Gun*. Cruise and McGillis spend a lot of time squinting uneasily at each other and exchanging words as if they were weapons, and when they finally get physical, they look like the stars of one of those sexy perfume ads. There's no flesh and blood here, which is remarkable, given the almost palpable physical presence McGillis had in *Witness*.

In its other ground scenes, the movie seems content to recycle clichés and conventions out of countless other war movies. Wouldn't you know, for example, that Maverick's commanding officer is the only man who knows what happened to the kid's father in Vietnam? And are we surprised when Maverick's best friend dies in his arms? Is there any suspense as Maverick undergoes his obligatory crisis of conscience, wondering whether he can ever fly again?

Movies like *Top Gun* are hard to review

because the good parts are so good and the bad parts are so relentless. The dogfights are absolutely the best since Clint Eastwood's electrifying aerial scenes in *Firefox*. But look out for the scenes where the people talk to one another.

Top Secret! ★ ★ ★ ½
R, 90 m., 1984

Val Kilmer (Nick Rivers), Lucy Gutteridge (Hillary), Omar Sharif (Cedric), Peter Cushing (Bookseller). Directed by Jim Abrahams, David Zucker, and Jerry Zucker and produced by Jon Davison and Hunt Lowry. Written by Abrahams, Zucker and Zucker, with Martyn Burke.

I have a friend who claims he only laughed real loud on five occasions during *Top Secret!* I laughed that much in the first ten minutes. It all depends on your sense of humor. My friend claims that I have a cornpone sense of humor, because of my origins deep in central Illinois. I admit that is true. As a Gemini, however, I contain multitudes, and I also have a highly sophisticated, sharply intellectual sense of humor. Get me in the right mood, and I can laugh all over the map. That's why I liked *Top Secret!* This movie will cheerfully go for a laugh wherever one is even remotely likely to be found. It has political jokes and boob jokes, dog poop jokes, and ballet jokes. It makes fun of two completely different Hollywood genres: the spy movie and the Elvis Presley musical. It contains a political refugee who fled America by balloon during the Carter administration, a member of the French underground named Escargot, and Omar Sharif inside a compacted automobile.

To describe the plot would be an exercise in futility. This movie has no plot. It does not need a plot. One does not attend movies like *Top Secret!* in order to follow the story line. I think you can figure that out right away, in the opening sequence, which is devoted to the sport of "skeet surfin'" and has beach boys on surfboards firing at clay targets. Instead of a plot, it has a funny young actor named Val Kilmer as the hero, a 1950s-style American rock 'n' roller who is sent on a concert tour behind the Iron Curtain, and manages to reduce East Germany to a shambles while never missing a word of "Tutti Frutti" (he never even stumbles during *a-wop-bop-a-doo bop, a bop-bam-boom*).

The movie is physical humor, sight gags, puns, double meanings, satire, weird choreography, scatalogical outrages, and inanity. One particular sequence, however, is such an original example of specifically cinematic humor that I'd like to discuss it at length. (Do not read further if you don't like to understand jokes before laughing at them.) The sequence involves a visit by the hero to a Swedish bookshop. Never mind why he goes there. The scene depends for its inspiration on this observation: People who run tape recorders backward often say that English, played backward, sounds like Swedish (especially, of course, to people who do not speak Swedish). What *Top Secret!* does is to film an entire scene and play it backward, so that the dialogue sounds Swedish, and then translate it into English subtitles. This is funny enough at the beginning, but it becomes inspired at the end, when the scene finally gives itself away.

There are other wonderful moments. The dance sequence in the East Berlin nightclub develops into something Groucho Marx would have been proud of. The malt shop musical number demolishes a whole tradition of Elvis Presley numbers. And how the ballerina makes her exit in *Swan Lake* will, I feel confident, be discussed for years wherever codpieces are sold.

Topaz ★ ★ ★ ½
PG, 124 m., 1970

Frederick Stafford (Andre Deverauz), Dany Robin (Nicole, His Wife), John Vernon (Rico Parra), Karin Dor (Juanita), Michel Piccoli (Jacques Granville), Philippe Noiret (Henri Jarre), John Forsythe (Nordstrom). Directed by Alfred Hitchcock. Screenplay by Samuel Taylor.

In some ways *Topaz* is a perfectly typical Alfred Hitchcock movie, but in other ways it's something new and rather unexpected from the master. The Hitchcock style is still there, all right: The action in incongruous places, the montages showing cause and effect, the sinister qualities of everyday objects, the tightly programmed editing style. That's all there and, even if you don't notice it, it works the old Hitchcock tricks on you and you're scared when he wants you to be. But what's new in *Topaz* is Hitchcock's choice of a field of action. He goes much wider this time, using three groups of protagonists instead of one or two central characters, and his subject is nothing less than the spy systems of the Cold War.

Hitchcock claimed, and he was probably telling the truth, that he really didn't care what his movies were about. He approached them scientifically, manipulating his actors to produce the desired effects in the audience. He liked to get suspense when he wanted it; he liked to play an audience like a piano. In most of his movies, then, he ignored the "real" world and made no attempt to show things as they might really happen. He shut everybody into a Hitchcock universe and tried to trap you in it, too.

So his basic theme was usually the same: An innocent man, wrongly accused, is placed in a position where he must clear himself before he is overtaken by either the bad guys or the law. This theme is terribly useful for getting viewers involved and perhaps (psychology aside) that's why Hitchcock likes it. But in *Topaz,* he made one of his occasional excursions into other areas, and this time he went farther afield than he ever did in *Foreign Correspondent* or *The 39 Steps* or *The Birds.*

Properly speaking, *Topaz* doesn't have a hero, although it has two or three characters who function that way occasionally. It doesn't have a hero because it doesn't have a moral point of view; Hitchcock deals with an American-French-Cuban spy network at the time of the Cuban missile crisis, and yet his focus is so firmly on the spies as professionals that we hardly get the feeling we should be for the French or against the Cubans. The plot is complex, with a lot of characters left over from the mediocre Leon Uris novel. The action moves from Washington to New York to Havana to Paris as two spy networks conspire to get information on the missile crisis to either Washington or Moscow. The movie begins with a good chase scene in Denmark, where a high-ranking Russian has defected. It's not a *Bullitt*-type chase with lots of speed and fast cutting, but one of those Hitchcock chases where everyone's forced to walk slowly and act naturally and smile a lot, nervously. The Americans finally get the Russian back to Washington where he reveals information about the Cuban missiles and also about a security leak in Paris.

Hitchcock does a good job of re-creating that far-off time, 1963. There is a fascinating sequence in Harlem where the Cuban UN delegation (remember?) had taken over the Theresa Hotel. The idea is to get some papers to photograph them. Hitchcock uses a remarkable actor, Roscoe Lee Brown, as a black journalist who saunters in and breezes out again with the secrets. Brown's scenes are the most delightful in the movie; for the most part, Hitchcock allowed his actors to remain so wooden they all look alike.

There is then some hanky-panky in Cuba, including the most protracted tearful-death scene in years (the beautiful Karin Dor done in by blue-eyed, sinister John Vernon). And then the action switches to Paris for the complicated conclusion. The interesting thing about that conclusion, by the way, is that Hitchcock goes out on a downbeat. There's no climax, no chase; just the sordid working-out of a messy game of spying. It's a nice, quiet ending, very much in keeping with the film, and *Topaz* is good Hitchcock. When you see it, wait for that scene where Michel Piccoli urges Philippe Noiret to hurry up and drink his cognac, and you tell me if you believe Piccoli expects a visitor.

Tough Guys Don't Dance ★ ★ ½

R, 109 m., 1987

Ryan O'Neal (Tim Madden), Isabella Rossellini (Madeleine), Debra Sandlund (Patty Lareine), Wings Hauser (Regency), John Bedford Lloyd (Wardley Meeks III), Lawrence Tierney (Dougy Madden), Frances Fisher (Jessica Pond), Penn Jillette (Big Stoop). Directed by Norman Mailer and produced by Tom Luddy. Screenplay by Mailer.

Norman Mailer's *Tough Guys Don't Dance* has the form of a thriller, and an impressive content of sex and violence, but beneath that is a strange nostalgia that seems to have nothing to do with anything else. The nostalgia is for Provincetown, seen in a cold winter season with the weathered gray houses against a pink and purple sky, the gulls' cries lonely in the twilight. This place is so deeply seen that the people in the movie sometimes seem like ghosts, occupying it for a time.

That is the deepest level. Above it is the practical plot level of severed heads, missing persons, alcoholic blackouts, and dirty business to be done. The film's hero is Tim Madden (Ryan O'Neal), a writer in a slow season, whose past begins to catch up with him. He has spent a good many years drinking too much, smoking too much pot, sleeping with the wrong women, and not sleeping with the right ones. Now he has made some people mad at him, and one day he discovers a severed head in the place where he hides his stash.

I will not reveal the owner of the head for two reasons: First, because it would be unfair to reveal the plot, and second, because although I have read the novel and seen the movie and even visited the location while the filming was under way, I cannot remember whose head it was. There is a press release here from the distributors that I could easily consult for the name, but that would be cheating: It says something about this film that the women, played by such memorable actresses as Isabella Rossellini, the blonde newcomer Debra Sandlund, and the intriguing Frances Fisher, play characters not nearly as memorable as themselves.

Something comes back to me now. The Sandlund character, Patty Lareine, is a hillbilly once married to a preacher. The O'Neal character and his then-girlfriend met them through a singles ad and engaged in a weekend of sexual abandon, which led in a complicated way to the more recent events, after Patty Lareine left the preacher to marry the hero's rich friend from prep school, Wardley Meeks III, who now appears on the scene after a crisis of identity.

This is as confusing as *The Big Sleep.* The characters come and go, in the past and the present, and their severed heads appear and disappear, and it is almost as if Mailer himself does not much care to take inventory. The film's center of gravity is in Tim Madden's befuddled and paranoid head, and much depends on a night he cannot remember, a night when he gained a tattoo and perhaps committed a murder.

He drinks, and makes cautious inquiries, and tries to determine from people's actions what they think he did. The local police chief calls him in, for reasons not entirely clear. The inventory of heads in his stash changes from one, to two, to none. He can hardly bear to look to see whose heads they are. He cannot understand who knows the location of his stash, and the identities of women from his past, and even more so, who would want to kill them. Then there is the question of the strange couple from California, who turned up in the local inn shopping for real estate, and drank with him, and who disappeared, their car abandoned, after the night he cannot remember.

In the middle of this morass, the film's best character appears: Dougy Madden (Lawrence Tierney), father of the O'Neal character, a tough old bartender and fighter who always seemed to the son more authentic and courageous than he could ever possibly be. Now Dougy is dying of cancer, but is still man enough to put the bodies—there are more of them by this point—into a boat and row them out to sea and sink them beyond the reach of gulls and police. The relationship between the father and son is the best thing in the movie.

I wonder if Mailer even cared about the details of his thriller. Few people who see the film only once will be able to accurately describe just what happens in it at a plot level. I suspect he used his thriller, with its lurid sex and blood-soaked bodies, as a lure to convince his backers to let him direct the movie, and that his attention was really on the father-son relationship and on Provincetown itself, which becomes as important as what happens in it. The photography, under the "supervision" of John Bailey, is stunning and evocative of a time and place, and O'Neal occupies it like a man on a last, sad visit.

What is strange is that *Tough Guys Don't Dance* leaves me with such vivid memories of its times and places, its feelings and weathers, and yet leaves me so completely indifferent to its plot. Watching the film, I laughed a good deal; many of the situations play like comedy. Remembering it, it seems elegiac, but in a way that has nothing to do with the deaths in the plot. Something else seems to die and be mourned, something to do with Dougy and the cold flats of the sand at twilight.

Trading Places ★ ★ ★ ½

R, 106 m., 1983

Dan Aykroyd (Louis Winthorpe III), Eddie Murphy (Billy Ray Valentine), Ralph Bellamy (Randolph Duke), Don Ameche (Mortimer Duke), Denholm Elliott (Coleman), Jamie Lee Curtis (Ophelia), Jim Belushi (King Kong). Directed by John Landis and produced by Aaron Russo. Screenplay by Timothy Harris and Herschel Weingrod.

Trading Places resembles *Tootsie* and, for that matter, some of the classic Frank Capra and Preston Sturges comedies: It wants to be funny, but it also wants to tell us something about human nature and there are whole stretches when we forget it's a comedy and get involved in the story. And it's a great idea for a story: A white preppy snot and a black street hustler trade places, and learn new skills they never dreamed existed.

This isn't exactly a new idea for a story (Mark Twain's *The Prince and the Pauper* comes to mind). But like a lot of stories, it depends less on plot than on character, and the characters in *Trading Places* are wonderful comic inventions. Eddie Murphy plays Billy Ray Valentine, the con man who makes his first appearance as a blind, legless veteran. Dan Aykroyd is Louis Winthorpe III, the stuck-up commodities broker. And, in a masterstroke of casting, those aging veterans Ralph Bellamy and Don Ameche are cast as the Duke brothers, incalculably rich men who compete by making little wagers involving human lives.

One day a particularly tempting wager occurs to them. Aykroyd has had Murphy arrested for stealing his briefcase. It's an unfair charge and Murphy is innocent, but Murphy is black and had the misfortune to bump into Aykroyd in front of a snobby club. To Mortimer Duke (Ameche), a believer that enviroment counts for more than heredity, this is a golden opportunity to test his theory. He bets his brother that if Aykroyd and Murphy were to change places, the black street kid would soon be just as good at calling the shots in the commodity markets as the white Ivy Leaguer ever was. Because the Dukes are rich, they can make almost anything happen. They strip Aykroyd of everything—his job, his home, his butler, his fiancée, his limousine, his self-respect. They give Murphy what they've taken from Aykroyd. And the rest of the movie follows the fortunes of the two changelings as they painfully adjust to their new lives, and get involved in a commodities scam the Duke brothers are trying to pull off.

This is good comedy. It's especially good because it doesn't stop with sitcom manipulations of its idea, and it doesn't go only for the obvious points about racial prejudice in America. Instead, it develops the quirks and peculiarities of its characters, so that they're funny because of who they are. This takes a whole additional level of writing on top of the plot-manipulation we usually get in popular comedies, and it takes good direction, too.

But what's most visible in the movie is the engaging acting. Murphy and Aykroyd are perfect foils for each other in *Trading Places*, because they're both capable of being so specifically eccentric that we're never just looking at a "black" and a "white" (that would make the comedy unworkable). They both play characters with a lot of native intelligence to go along with their prejudices, peculiarities, and personal styles. It's fun to watch them thinking. The supporting cast has also been given detailed attention, instead of being assigned to stand around as stereotypes. Jamie Lee Curtis plays a hooker with a heart of gold and a lot of T-bills; Ameche and Bellamy have a lot of fun with the Duke brothers; and Denholm Elliott successfully plays butler to both Aykroyd and Murphy, which is a stretch. The movie's invention extends all the way to the climactic scenes, which involve, not the usual manic chase, but a commodities scam, a New Year's Eve party on a train, and a gay gorilla.

Tribute ★ ★ ★

PG, 123 m., 1981

Jack Lemmon (Scottie Templeton), Robby Benson (Jud Templeton), Lee Remick (Maggie Stratton), Colleen Dewhurst (Gladys Petrelli), John Marley (Lou Daniels), Kim Cattrall (Sally Haines). Directed by Bob Clark and produced by Joel B. Michaels and Garth H. Drabinski. Screenplay by Bernard Slade.

I am aware that *Tribute* hauls out some of the oldest Broadway clichés in the book, that it shamelessly exploits its melodramatic elements, and that it is not a movie so much as a filmed stage play. And yet if I were to review it just on those grounds, I would be less than honest. In the abstract, *Tribute* may not be a very good film at all. But in its particulars, and in the way they affected me, it is a touching experience.

It's supposed to be cheating to make an admission like that. I myself believe that it is a film's form, more than its message, that makes it great. And yet *Tribute* is not a visually distinguished film. It has been directed, by Bob Clark, as a straightforward job of work. There are long sequences that are obviously just filmed scenes from Bernard Slade's original stage play. Yet the characters transcend these limitations and become people that we care about.

The film is mostly Jack Lemmon's, and he deserved his seventh Academy Award nomination for his performance as Scottie Templeton, the movie's hero. We all know somebody like Scottie—if we are not, God forbid, a little like Scottie ourselves. He's a wisecracking, popular guy with hundreds of deeply intimate passing acquaintances. He also has a few friends. One of them is his business partner (John Marley) and another is his ex-wife (Lee Remick). They love him and stand by him, but he can't allow himself to reveal how much that means to him. He is also hurt by his relationship with his son (Robby Benson), who has the usual collection of post-adolescent grudges against his father. All of these relationships suddenly become much more important when Scottie discovers he is dying. The movie begins at about that point in Scottie's life, and examines how the fact of approaching death changes all of Scottie's ways of dealing with the living.

His son comes home to visit for a few weeks. His wife returns to New York for a college reunion and stays to become involved in the crisis. The friend, Marley, acts as counsel and adjudicator. Other characters pass through, including a young woman (Kim Cattrall) who Scottie thinks would be ideal for his son (after all, she'd previously been ideal for Scottie himself). Veteran playgoers can already predict the obligatory scenes growing out of this situation. Scottie will be brave at first, then angry, then depressed, then willing to reach out to his son, and finally reconciled to his fate. Scottie's friends will rally around. His son will learn to love the old man. Everybody will become more human and sensitive, and the possibility of death will provide an occasion for a celebration of life. Et cetera.

What's amazing is that when these predictable situations appear, the movie makes them work. A great deal of the credit for that belongs to Lemmon and Benson. They are both actors with a familiar schtick by now: Benson trembling with emotions, Lemmon fast-talking his way into sincerity. In *Tribute*, though, the movie's characters are so close to the basic strengths of Lemmon and Benson that everything seems to work.

Take Lemmon, for example. Another actor, playing Scottie Templeton, might simply seem to be saying funny lines, alternating with bittersweet insights. Lemmon makes us believe that they're not lines; they're the way this guy talks. The big emotional changes take place underneath the surface wisecracks, making them all the more poignant. Robby Benson sometimes comes across as too vulnerable, almost affected in his sensitivity. Here, he's good, too: Examine the early scene where his father asks what the hell's going on, and Benson begins, "Let me try to explain about that . . ." with touching formality.

Maybe your reaction to *Tribute* will depend on your state of mind. I know people who say they "saw through it," dismissing it as merely a well-made play. I know others, myself included, who were really touched by it. Perhaps the film works better because it's *willing* to be a bittersweet soap opera. Life itself, after all, is rarely a great directorial achievement, but almost always seems to work on the melodramatic level.

The Trip to Bountiful ★ ★ ★ ½

PG, 106 m., 1985

Geraldine Page (Mrs. Watts), John Heard (Ludie Watts), Carlin Glynn (Jessie Mae), Richard Bradford (Sheriff), Rebecca De Mornay (Thelma). Directed by Peter Masterson and produced by Sterling Van Wagenen and Horton Foote. Screenplay by Foote.

The thing that saves this movie from sentimentality is that the heroine is a little ornery. She's not just a sweet and gentle little old lady. She's a big old lady, with a streak of stubborness. And just because she's right doesn't mean she's always all that nice.

When *The Trip to Bountiful* tells us that she wants to leave her miserable life in the city and pay one last visit to her childhood country home, somehow we know that the movie won't be over when she hears the birds singing in the trees.

The movie stars the redoubtable Geraldine Page in her Academy Award-winning role as Mrs. Watts, a country woman who has come to live in a cramped city apartment with her son and daughter-in-law. The apartment isn't big enough for two women. They're always on each other's nerves.

The wife, Jessie Mae (Carlin Glynn), doesn't like Mrs. Watts singing her hymns around the house. Mrs. Watts's strategy is more subtle: She tries to appear long-suffering, a martyr, and she is much given to throwing herself on the couch and pulling a comforter over her head to muffle her sobs.

Both of these women have a pretty good case against each other, but it's Mrs. Watts we sympathize with. She hates life in the city, she knows it's choking her to death, and she wants to pay one final visit to Bountiful, the little town where she was born. So she goes to the train station, but the milk train doesn't stop in Bountiful anymore. So she goes to the bus station and buys a ticket to the nearest large town. This is in Texas in 1947. Because her son and daughter-in-law have gone to the train station to head her off (she's tried to escape before), she makes her getaway.

The whole middle section of the movie is the best, as she meets another traveler on the bus, a young woman named Thelma (Rebecca De Mornay). They sit next to each other during the long, drowsy trip, and they exchange memories and confidences. Thelma is, in a way, only an excuse to give Mrs. Watts someone to talk to, so that we can eavesdrop. Yet De Mornay makes the character so interesting, so young and open-faced, that the relationship between these two women becomes the heart of the movie. Even the ending itself doesn't quite live up to it.

The Trip to Bountiful has a quiet, understated feel for the small towns of its time. The little rural bus station, with its clerk drowsing under a lonely lamp bulb, looks just right, and so do the midnight streets outside. And when the sheriff arrives, alerted to look for a runaway old lady, it's perfect the way he and the ticket agent size up the situation and let Mrs. Watts have her last look at her childhood home.

Then her family arrives: her son Ludie (John Heard) and his wife Jessie Mae. Ludie really has his work cut out with these two women. Both of them live at a time when many women lived their lives through their men, and there is not enough room inside Ludie's simple, desperate soul for both of these women. Yet there is a moment of poetry as she sits on the porch of the old farmhouse and talks about how she almost expected to see her own parents come walking through the door, just as if all those years had never passed, just as if her own lifetime was a dream, and she was still a young girl again.

The Trip to Bountiful was written by Horton Foote, who based it on his own stage play. This is Foote's second recent slice of life from Texas: *Tender Mercies*, the wonderful movie starring Robert Duvall as an alcoholic country singer, was also written by him. You can see that *Bountiful* was based on a play—it falls fairly obviously into three acts—but the rhythms and dialogue come out of unstudied real life. And Geraldine Page inhabits the central role with authority and vinegar. The movie surprises us: It's not really about conflict between the generations, but about the impossibility of really understanding that you are even a member of an older generation, that decades have gone by.

Geraldine Page, who somehow always manages to have a hint of girlishness in her performances, who always seems to be up to something roguish and not ever quite ready to cave in to age, finds just the right notes in the final scenes to tell her son something he might never be able to understand: Someday he will be old, too, and he won't be able to believe it either.

Tron ★ ★ ★ ★

PG, 96 m., 1982

Jeff Bridges (Flynn/Clu), Bruce Boxleitner (Alan/Tron), David Warner (Dillinger/Sark), Cindy Morgan (Lora/Yori), Barnard Hughes (Gibbs/Dumont), Dan Shor (Ram). Directed by Steven Lisberger and produced by Donald Kushner. Screenplay by Lisberger.

The interior of a computer is a fine and private place, but none, I fear, do there embrace, except in *Tron*, a dazzling movie from

Walt Disney in which computers have been used to make themselves romantic and glamorous. Here's a technological sound-and-light show that is sensational and brainy, stylish and fun.

The movie addresses itself without apology to the computer generation, embracing the imagery of those arcade video games that parents fear are rotting the minds of their children. If you've never played Pac-Man or Space Invaders or the Tron game itself, you probably are not quite ready to see this movie, which begins with an evil bureaucrat stealing computer programs to make himself look good, and then enters the very mind of a computer itself to engage the villain, the hero, and several highly programmable bystanders in a war of the wills that is governed by the rules of both video games and computer programs.

The villain is a man named Dillinger (David Warner). The hero is a bright kid named Flynn (Jeff Bridges) who created the original programs for five great new video games, including the wonderfully named "Space Paranoia." Dillinger stole Flynn's plans and covered his tracks in the computer. Flynn believes that if he can track down the original program, he can prove Dillinger is a thief. To prevent that, Dillinger uses the very latest computer technology to break Flynn down into a matrix of logical points and insert him *into* the computer, and at that point *Tron* leaves any narrative or visual universe we have ever seen before in a movie and charts its own rather wonderful path.

In an age of amazing special effects, *Tron* is a state-of-the-art movie. It generates not just one imaginary computer universe, but a multitude of them. Using computers as their tools, the Disney filmmakers literally have been able to imagine any fictional landscape, and then have it, through an animated computer program. And they integrate their human actors and the wholly imaginary worlds of Tron so cleverly that I never, ever, got the sensation that I was watching some actor standing in front of, or in the middle of, special effects. The characters *inhabit* this world. And what a world it is! Video gamesmen race each other at blinding speed, hurtling up and down computer grids while the movie shakes with the overkill of Dolby stereo (justified, for once). The characters sneak around the computer's logic guardian terminals, clamber up the sides of memory displays, talk their way past the guardians of forbidden programs, hitch a ride on a power beam, and succeed in entering the mind of the very Master Control Program itself, disabling it with an electronic Frisbee. This is all a whole lot of fun. *Tron* has been conceived and written with a knowledge of computers that it mercifully assumes the audience shares. That doesn't mean we *do* share it, but that we're bright enough to pick it up, and don't have to sit through long, boring explanations of it.

There is one additional observation I have to make about *Tron*, and I don't really want it to sound like a criticism: This is an almost wholly technological movie. Although it's populated by actors who are engaging (Bridges, Cindy Morgan) or sinister (Warner), it is not really a movie about human nature. Like *Star Wars* or *The Empire Strikes Back*, but much more so, this movie is a machine to dazzle and delight us. It is not a human-interest adventure in any generally accepted way. That's all right, of course. It's brilliant at what it does, and in a technical way maybe it's breaking ground for a generation of movies in which computer-generated universes will be the background for mind-generated stories about emotion-generated personalities. All things are possible.

Trouble in Mind ★ ★ ★ ★

R, 111 m., 1985

Kris Kristofferson (Hawk), Keith Carradine (Coop), Lori Singer (Georgia), Genevieve Bujold (Wanda), Joe Morton (Solo), Divine (Hilly Blue), George Kirby (Detective). Directed by Alan Rudolph and produced by Carolyn Pfeiffer and David Blocker. Screenplay by Rudolph.

Here is a movie that takes place within our memories of the movies. The characters and the mysteries and especially the doomed romances are all generated by old films, by remembered worlds of lurid neon signs and deserted areas down by the docks, of sad cafes where losers linger over a cup of coffee, and lonely rooms where the lightbulb is a man's only friend. This is a world for which the saxophone was invented, a world in which the American Motors Javelin was a popular car.

The movie begins with a man being

released from prison, of course, and he is dressed in black and has a beard and wears a hat, of course, and is named Hawk, of course, and the first place he goes when he arrives in town is Wanda's Cafe, where Wanda keeps a few rooms upstairs for her old lovers to mend their broken dreams.

The cafe is on a worn-out old brick street down at the wrong end of Rain City. It's the kind of place that doesn't need to advertise, because its customers are drawn there by their fates. One day a young couple turn up in a broken-down camper. The kid is named Coop, and he knows he always gets into trouble when he comes to the city, but he needs to make some money to support his little family. His girlfriend is named Georgia, and she looks way young to have a baby, but there it is, bawling in her arms. She's a blonde with a look in her eyes that makes the Hawk's heart soar.

Coop falls into partnership with the wrong man, a black man named Solo who sits in a back booth at Wanda's Cafe and recites poems about anger and hopelessness. Before long, Coop and Solo are involved in a life of crime, and Hawk is telling Georgia she's living with a loser.

Wanda stands behind the counter and watches all this happen with eyes that have seen a thousand plans go wrong. She hires Georgia as a waitress. That turns Hawk into a regular customer. Wanda knows Hawk is in love with Georgia, because Wanda and Hawk used to be in love with each other, and once you learn to hear that note in a man's voice, you hear it even when he's not singing to you.

Coop and Solo are trying to sell some hot wristwatches. Hilly Blue doesn't like that. Hilly is the boss of the local rackets, and lives in a house that is furnished like the Museum of Modern Art. The best way to describe Hilly Blue is to say that if Sydney Greenstreet could have reproduced by parthenogenesis after radioactive damage to his chromosomes, Hilly would have been the issue.

Trouble in Mind is not a comedy, but it knows that it is funny. It is not a fantasy, and yet strange troops patrol the streets of Rain City, and as many people speak Korean as English. It does not take place in the 1940s, but its characters dress and talk and live as if it did. Could this movie have been made if there had never been any movies starring Richard Widmark, Jack Palance, or Robert Mitchum? Yes, but it wouldn't have had any style.

To really get inside the spirit of *Trouble in Mind,* it would probably help to see *Choose Me* first. Both films are the work of Alan Rudolph, who is creating a visual world as distinctive as Fellini's and as cheerful as Edward Hopper's. He does an interesting thing. He combines his stylistic excesses with a lot of emotional sincerity, so that we believe these characters are really serious about their hopes, and dreams, even if they do seem to inhabit a world of imagination. Look at it this way. In Woody Allen's *The Purple Rose of Cairo,* a character stepped out of a movie and off the screen and into the life of a woman in the audience. If that had happened in *Trouble in Mind,* the woman would have asked the character why he even bothered.

Sometimes the names of movie actors evoke so many associations that further description is not necessary. Let's see. Hawk is played by Kris Kristofferson. Coop is Keith Carradine. Wanda is Genevieve Bujold. Hilly Blue is the transvestite Divine, but he is not in drag this time, allegedly. Mix them together, light them with neon reds and greens, and add a blonde child-woman (Lori Singer) and a black gangster (Joe Morton) whose shades are his warmest feature, and perhaps you can begin to understand why they call it Rain City.

True Confessions ★ ★ ★

R, 110 m., 1981

Robert De Niro (Des Spellacy), Robert Duvall (Tom Spellacy), Charles Durning (Jack Amsterdam), Ed Flanders (Dan T. Campion), Burgess Meredith (Seamus Fargo). Directed by Ulu Grosbard and produced by Irwin Winkler and Robert Chartoff. Screenplay by John Gregory Dunne and Joan Didion.

True Confessions contains scenes that are just about as good as scenes can be. Then why does the movie leave us disoriented and disappointed, and why does the ending fail dismally? Perhaps because the attentions of the filmmakers were concentrated so fiercely on individual moments that nobody ever stood back to ask what the story was about. It's frustrating to sit through a movie filled with clues and leads and motivations, only to discover at the end that the filmmakers can't be bothered with finishing the story.

The film is about two brothers, one a priest, the other a cop. In a nice insight in casting, Robert De Niro plays the priest and Robert Duvall plays the cop; offhand, we'd expect it to be the other way around, but Duvall is just right, seedy and wall-faced, as the cop, and after a scene or two we begin to accept De Niro as a priest (although he seems too young for a monsignor).

The brothers live in Los Angeles in 1948. It is a Los Angeles more or less familiar from dozens of other movies, especially *Chinatown* and the Robert Mitchum *Farewell, My Lovely*—a small town, really, where the grafters and the power brokers know each other (and in some cases are each other). The movie's plot is complicated on the surface but simple underneath. It centers around a creep named Amsterdam (Charles Durning), a construction tycoon who got his start as a pimp. Both brothers have had dealings with the man. When Duvall was a vice cop, he helped handle the protection for Amsterdam's whorehouses. Now De Niro, the cardinal's right-hand man, oversees the building projects of the Los Angeles archdiocese. And Amsterdam gets most of the contracts for new schools and hospitals, even though his operation is tainted with scandal.

It's tainted with more than that after the dead body of a young woman is found in a field, cut in two. Duvall's investigation leads to a madam who once took a rap for him, long ago, and to a sleazy L.A. porno filmmaker. Eventually, certain clues point all the way back to Amsterdam. Try to follow this closely: Amsterdam met the girl through a business associate, who met her as a hitchhiker. When he first gave her a lift in his car, De Niro was another passenger. The movie makes a great deal of the fact that the monsignor once shared a car with the "virgin tramp," as the newspapers label the victim. But so what? One of the maddening things about *True Confessions* is that it's shot through with such paranoia that innocent coincidences take on the same weight as evil conspiracies.

The movie's emotional center is in the cop character. He's painted as a man who's not above taking a bribe. But at the same time he has a moral code that's stiffer than his brother's. (The monsignor, for example, isn't above rigging a church raffle so that a city councilman's daughter will win the new car.) What begins to eat away at Duvall is that this Amsterdam, honored as the Catholic Layman of the Year, is a grafter and former pimp. Did he also murder the girl? Duvall frankly doesn't care: The guy is such slime he should be arrested for the crime just on general principles.

True Confessions spends a lot of effort in laying the groundwork for its complex plot, but then it refuses to ever settle things. Instead, there are inane prologues and epilogues showing the two brothers years later, their hair gray, as they sigh philosophically over impending death and shake their heads at the irony and tragedy of it all—whatever it all was.

Since this isn't a thriller, we are invited, I guess, to take it as a cynical meditation on the corruptibility of man. Joan Didion and John Gregory Dunne, who based the screenplay on his novel, see the social institutions in their story as just hiding places for hypocrites and weary, defeated men. But they never follow through on their insights. The movie has, for example, a major subplot involving an old priest (Burgess Meredith) who is being put out to pasture. The priest is evidently a symbol of something, especially since the young De Niro gets the dirty job of firing him. But the movie never comes to terms with this story; it just leaves it sitting there.

At the end of *True Confessions*, we're just sitting there, too. We have been introduced to clearly drawn and well-acted characters, we've entered a period in time that is carefully reconstructed, we've seen moments between men and women that are wonderfully well-observed. But we haven't seen a film that cares to be about anything in particular, to state its case or draw its lines, or be much more than a skilled exercise in style.

True Stories ★ ★ ★ ½

PG-13, 88 m., 1986

John Goodman (Louis Fyne), Swoosie Kurtz (Laziest Woman), Spaldinntg Gray (Earl Culver), Alix Elias (Cute Woman), Annie McEnroe (Kay Culver), Pops Staples (Mr. Tucker), Jo Harvey Allen (Lying Woman), David Byrne (Narrator). Directed by David Byrne and produced by Gary Kurfirst.

Screenplay by Stephen Tobolowsky, Beth Henley, and Byrne.

There are more than fifty sets of twins in David Byrne's *True Stories,* I learned by studying the press notes, and perhaps we should pause here for a moment to meditate upon that fact. A hundred twins are not going to make or break a movie, and the average audience is not going to notice more than a fraction of them.

But, consider the state of mind of the person who decided the film should *have* fifty sets of twins.

That person undoubtedly is Byrne. What was he thinking of? My hunch is that he was thinking about the movie's voodoo: the magical things that go on beneath the surface of the work of art, lending it an aura that seeps up into the visible parts. Any movie made by actors and technicians who know that the director has hired fifty sets of twins is going to be a movie made by people who think the director is a very strange man. And that will affect their work. Even the ordinary moments in *True Stories* seem a little odd, as if the actors are trying to humor the weirdo they're working for.

Byrne says the movie was influenced by true stories he read in the papers, and he has published a book of some of those stories he has collected. They range from the mundane (the happily married couple who have not spoken to one another for fifteen years) to the cosmic (the Universal Product Code on grocery items is the advance sign of the coming of the Antichrist).

In *True Stories,* Byrne visits a mythical Texas town named Virgil in which everyone is a little strange and some people are downright unique. Try to imagine Virgil as being populated by everyone who went stir-crazy in Lake Wobegon.

Byrne narrates his film and is the host for the tour of Virgil. He is a thin, quiet, withdrawn figure with a voice so flat that you have to listen to the pauses to figure out when the sentences end. He drives a new red convertible and wears Saturday night cowboy clothes. He takes us to Virgil just as it's about to celebrate "150 Years of Specialness."

There is no real plot here, just wonderment. We meet a woman too lazy to get out of bed, and a man who advertises for a wife but says she must be prepared to accept his teddy-bear figure. We meet the lying woman, who confides shocking inside scandal on many of the most important events of the last twenty-five years. She knows because she was there. We meet civic leaders and marching bands, we visit an old man who casts spells and foretells the future, and we meet a preacher who in one unbroken sentence leaps from the death of Elvis Presley to the fact that we always run out of Kleenex and toilet paper at the same time. The studio went nuts trying to figure out how to sell this film. They came down hard on the angle that it had a lot of music by the Talking Heads, the avant-garde rock group that Byrne founded and leads. It does have a lot of music in it, and that will appeal to the viewers who have made *Stop Making Sense,* the Talking Heads concert film, a hit.

But this is not a musical. It's a bold attempt to paint a bizarre American landscape. This movie does what some painters try to do: It recasts ordinary images into strange new shapes. There is hardly a moment in *True Stories* that doesn't seem everyday to anyone who has grown up in Middle America, and not a moment that doesn't seem haunted with secrets, evasions, loneliness, depravity, or hidden joy—sometimes all at once. This is almost like a science-fiction movie: Everyone on screen looks so normal and behaves so oddly, they could be pod people.

The photography is an important element of the film. The movie was shot by Ed Lachman, who has become a brand name for people interested in offbeat directors. He was the guy who followed Werner Herzog to the slopes of a volcano that was about to erupt to film *La Soufriere,* and he has worked for Wim Wenders, Shirley Clarke, Bernardo Bertolucci, Jean-Luc Godard, and Tina Turner.

This time, he finds a new look: His landscapes and city scenes are like those old postcards in which everything seems slightly skewed. His buildings look like parodies of buildings. His people are seen against indoor landscapes of the objects they own—so many objects they seem about to be buried.

And then Byrne orchestrates all of this in the most deadpan way. If you walk in looking for payoffs, you're going to be disappointed. This movie doesn't start here and go there, and the closest thing it has to a story is the quest of the shy bachelor (John Goodman) for a wife. Will he marry the woman who never leaves her bed? If he does, where will the ceremony take place? It's the kind of courtship where, when you know the woman well enough, you ask her if she'd like to get *out* of bed. You see how one thing leads to another?

The Turning Point ★ ★ ★ ½
PG, 119 m., 1977

Anne Bancroft (Emma), Shirley MacLaine (Deedee), Mikhail Baryshnikov (Yuri), Leslie Browne (Emilia), Tom Skerritt (Wayne), Martha Scott (Adelaide). Directed by Herbert Ross and produced by Ross and Arthur Laurents. Screenplay by Laurents.

Perfect movies are very rare, and very easy to write about. Imperfect movies are harder to write about, and the hardest reviews of all are of movies like *The Turning Point* that are touched with greatness and yet keep losing their way. The good things in it are *so* good that you cherish them, and there's the temptation to forgive the lapses.

So let's start with the good. The movie's the story of an old friendship between a great ballerina (Anne Bancroft) and a ballerina (Shirley MacLaine) who might have been great but will never really know for sure. Twenty years have passed since they were both young dancers, and now Miss Bancroft performs in Miss MacLaine's hometown and their friendship reasserts itself. Miss MacLaine's daughter is a promising young ballerina—she already has professional experience—and Miss Bancroft arranges for her to join her company.

As Miss MacLaine accompanies her daughter to New York, three themes assert themselves: Miss MacLaine's jealousy, smoldering for twenty years; Miss Bancroft's fear of approaching age and yet her desire to see the young girl succeed; the self-doubt both women have about the choices they made of careers or marriage. These are adult themes, and *The Turning Point* handles them thoughtfully.

It also gives us a love story or two. Miss MacLaine's daughter falls in love with the ballet company's superstar (Mikhail Baryshnikov, typecast). And during the long summer of the movie's action, Miss MacLaine has to deal not only with her own feelings but with her daughter's. We're dealing here with soap opera stuff, but never in a soap opera way. *The Turning Point* confronts its big emotional moments directly and simply, and maybe that's why they affect us so much.

The straightforward dramatic sections of the movie, then, are very well written and acted; Miss Bancroft and Miss MacLaine are particularly good, and then there are sensitive supporting performances by Tom Skerritt, as Miss MacLaine's husband, and by Leslie Browne, the talented young dancer who plays their daughter. When people say they loved *The Turning Point*, they're probably thinking about moments like the one when Miss Bancroft pushes the reluctant and sick young girl back onto the stage, or when the two older women go aside at a party and finally say all the things they've bottled up, or when Miss MacLaine is so touchingly mystified by how she should react to the news of her daughter's first affair.

Those moments are good enough to make the movie. And, of course, there's also a lot of dancing in the film; Baryshnikov is a wonder, and the film's director, Herbert Ross, is a choreographer who knows how to see dance through his camera. But it's during the ballet sequences that the film breaks down, because Ross can photograph the dances so much better than he can work them into his film.

This has been a juicy, realistic, achingly human movie for most of its length, dealing with age and jealousy, love and the cruel demands of great art. So we feel real disappointment when Ross breaks the mood and the flow. He does that most unforgivingly in a sequence where Miss Browne has a triumph onstage, and Ross cuts away to closeups of Miss MacLaine and Miss Bancroft watching her—while prophetic dialogue from earlier in the film is repeated in flashback on the sound track. Unforgivable. And the movie's climactic dance scenes—the evening at ballet, punctuated by the hoary old gimmick of a hand turning the pages of a program —are fun for ballet fans, yes, but they land with a thud in the middle of the movie's emotional drama.

To sort out my feelings: *The Turning Point*'s story is handled with real care and touches us. The movie's dance sequences are vurtuoso in themselves. But the pieces don't match, and Ross doesn't help by encumbering the dance material with ungainly story devices from the 1930s. You watch this film about a woman wondering if she could have been a great dancer, and you find yourself wondering if it could have been a great film.

Turtle Diary ★ ★ ★ ½
PG-13, 97 m., 1985

Ben Kingsley (William Snow), Glenda Jackson (Neaera Duncan), Michael Gambon (George Fairbairn), Eleanor Bron (Miss Neap), Harriet Walter (Harriet). Directed by John Irvin and produced by Peter Snell. Screenplay by Harold Pinter.

I saw this scene once in the London Zoo. It happened in the gloom of an insect house. Two men stood stooped over, side by side, their hands clasped behind their backs, peering through a glass into the chamber where a rare spider lived. Their faces were bathed in the low red light coming from the enclosure.

As they watched the spider, I watched them, until at last the spider did whatever it was they had been waiting for it to do. Then they stood up, looked briefly at each other, exchanged a matter-of-fact nod, and went their separate ways. London has always seemed to me to be a city of hobbyists and fanatics, experts in obscure specialities. But this moment stands out in particular, as a spider and two voyeurs shared one of the spider's most intimate moments.

Turtle Diary, the quiet, sly, and immensely amusing film from a screenplay by Harold Pinter, begins with two more such devotees. They are obsessed by giant sea turtles. They peek through the glass as the turtles lazily wheel around and around their cramped space in a tank at the London Zoo. They meet again, by chance, in a bookshop way over on the other side of the city, where the man (Ben Kingsley) is a clerk, and the woman (Glenda Jackson) has come to buy a book on turtles. They gradually become aware that they are seeing each other frequently at the turtle house, and then they discover that each has approached the turtles' keeper with the same question: What would it take to steal those giant turtles and set them free in the sea?

Turtle Diary is about a scheme by Kingsley, Jackson, and the zoo curator to do just that. But it is about a great many other things, as well. It is about the strange boarding house where Kingsley lives in company with a jolly landlady, a moody spinster, and a Turk who never cleans up the kitchen after himself. It is about the flat where Jackson lives, alone with her pet water beetle and about the man across the landing who knows a great deal about snails. And it is about the young woman who works with Kingsley in the bookshop, and lusts after him.

In a movie filled with wonderful, small sequences, I think my favorite begins when Kingsley suddenly turns to the young woman and says, out of the clear sky, "That's a pretty dress." In the next scene they are in a pub, in the next scene a restaurant. And if you want to observe the mastery of screen acting, watch the way Kingsley keeps a poker face while discussing his sex life with the woman, and then watch the way he allows himself to smile.

Ben Kingsley's smile, so warm and mysterious, is the sun that shines all through *Turtle Diary*. This is not a predictable movie, and it does not have a predictable structure (it does not even begin to end with the climax of the turtle caper). It is about peculiar people who somewhere find the impulses to do things that make them very happy.

If this movie had been made in America, I fear, it would have turned into a burlesque, with highway cops chasing turtles down the Santa Monica Freeway. *Turtle Diary* could only have been written, directed, and acted in the country where I saw those two strangers wait with such infinite patience for the spider to do its thing.

28 Up ★ ★ ★ ★
NO MPAA RATING, 136 m., 1985

Featuring Tony Walker, Bruce Balden, Suzanne Dewey, Nicholas Hitchon, Peter Davies, Paul Kligerman, John Brisby, Andrew Brackfield, Charles Furneaux, Neil Hughes, Jackie Bassett, Lynn Johnson, Susan Sullivan, and Simon Basterfield. Directed by Michael Apted and produced by Margaret Bottomley and Apted.

The child is father of the man.
—William Wordsworth

Somewhere at home are photographs taken when I was a child. A solemn, round-faced little boy gazes out at the camera, and as I look at him I know in my mind that he is me and I am him, but the idea has no reality. I cannot understand the connection, and as I think more deeply about the mystery of the passage of time, I feel a sense of awe.

Watching Michael Apted's documentary *28 Up*, I had that feeling again and again, the awe that time does pass, and that the same individual does pass through it, grows from a child to an adult, becoming someone new over the passage of years, but still containing some of the same atoms and molecules and fears and gifts that were stored in the child.

This film began twenty-eight years ago as a documentary for British television. The assignment for Michael Apted was to interview several seven-year-olds from different British social classes, races, backgrounds, and parts of the country, simply talking with them about what they found important or interesting about their lives. Seven years later, when the subjects were fourteen, Apted tracked them down and interviewed them again. He repeated the process when they were twenty-one, and again when they were twenty-eight, and this film moves back and forth within that material, looking at the same people when they were children, teenagers, young adults and now warily approaching their thirties.

We have always known that the motion picture is a time machine. John Wayne is dead, but the angle of his smile and the squint in his eye will be as familiar to our children as it is to us. Orson Welles is dead, but a hundred years from now the moment will still live when the cat rubs against his shoe in *The Third Man*, and then the light from the window catches his sardonic grin. What is remarkable about *28 Up* is not, however, that the same individuals have been captured at four different moments in their lives. We quickly grow accustomed to that. What is awesome is that we can see so clearly how the seven-year-old became the adolescent, how the teen-ager became the young man or woman, how the adult still contains the seeds of the child.

One sequence follows the lives of three upper-class boys who come from the right families and go to all the right schools. One of the boys is a snot, right from the beginning, and by the time he is twenty-one he is a bit of a reactionary prig. We are not surprised when he declines to be interviewed at twenty-eight; we could see it coming. We are curious, though, about whether he will check back in at thirty-five, perhaps having outlived some of his self-importance.

Another little boy is a winsome loner at seven. At fourteen, he is a dreamy idealist, at twenty-one he is defiant but discontented, and at twenty-eight—in the most unforgettable passage in the film—he is an outcast, a drifter who moves around Great Britain from place to place, sometimes living in a shabby house trailer, still a little puzzled by how he seems to have missed the boat, to never have connected with his society.

There is another little boy who dreams of growing up to be a jockey, and who is a stable boy at fourteen, and does get to be a jockey, briefly, and now drives a cab and finds in his job some of the same personal independence and freedom of movement that he once thought jockeys had. There is a determined young Cockney who is found, years later, happily married and living in Australia and doing well in the building trades. There is a young woman who at twenty-one was clearly an emotional mess, a vague, defiant, bitter, and unhappy person. At twenty-eight, married and with a family, she is a happy and self-assured young woman; the transformation is almost unbelievable.

As the film follows its subjects through the first halves of their lives, our thoughts are divided. We are fascinated by the personal progressions we see on the screen. We are distracted by wonderment about the mystery of the human personality. If we can see so clearly how these children become these adults—was it just as obvious in our own cases? Do we, even now, contain within us our own personal destinies for the next seven years? Is change possible? Is the scenario already written?

I was intending to write that certain groups would be particularly interested in this movie. Teachers, for example, would hardly be able to see *28 Up* without looking at their students in a different, more curious light. Poets and playwrights would learn from this film. So would psychiatrists. But then I realized that *28 Up* is not a film by or for experts. It is superb journalism, showing us these people passing through stages of their lives in such a way that we are challenged to look at our own lives. It is as thought-provoking as any documentary I've ever seen.

I look forward to the next edition of this film, when its subjects are thirty-five. I have hope for some, fear for others. It is almost scary to realize this film has given me a fair chance of predicting what lies ahead for these strangers. I almost understand the motives of those who chose to drop out of the experiment.

Twice in a Lifetime ★ ★ ★ ½
R, 117 m., 1985

Gene Hackman (Harry), Ann-Margret (Audrey), Ellen Burstyn (Kate), Amy Madigan (Sonny), Ally Sheedy (Helen), Stephen Lang (Keith), Darrell Larson (Jerry), Brian Dennehy (Nick). Directed and produced by Bud Yorkin. Screenplay by Colin Welland.

Everyday American life is so rare in the movies these days that some of the pleasures of *Twice in a Lifetime* are very simple ones, like seeing a family around a dinner table, or watching a kid sister prepare for her wedding day. The rhythms of life and the normal patterns of speech seemed almost unfamiliar, after all the high-tech thrillers and teenage idiot films I've seen. This film was so sensible, perceptive, and grown-up that I almost looked for the subtitles.

The film stars Gene Hackman as a working man whose marriage is happy in all the official ways, and dead in the personal ways. His wife (Ellen Burstyn) has centered her life entirely around her home and her family to such an extent that on Hackman's birthday she doesn't even want to go out with him. She tells him to go down to the corner tavern and enjoy himself. And she means it. There is a lot missing in this marriage.

At the saloon, Hackman meets the new barmaid (Ann-Margret) and begins a wary process of falling in love with her. He eventually decides to leave his wife and move in with this woman, and this decision causes upheaval throughout his family. His wife is devastated. But the angriest family member is his oldest daughter (Amy Madigan), who bitterly resents the way he's dumping them—especially when her kid sister (Ally Sheedy) is about to get married.

Twice in a Lifetime stacks its cards very carefully. One of the strengths of the movie is that it allows us to see so many points of view. Hackman has not simply dumped his wife for a sex bomb: the Ann-Margret character has been around the block a few times and operates from a center of quiet realism. It is possibly true that the life and growth has gone out of his marriage. Perhaps he deserves another chance—although the movie is too hasty to assume that his wife does, too, if only she knew it.

The most complicated and interesting character in the movie is Amy Madigan's angry daughter. She's mad about more than the broken marriage. Her husband is out of work, and in her late twenties she feels somewhat trapped by her marriage and children. A lot of her hopes have gone into her kid sister. She wants her to go to college and make a future for herself, but Ally Sheedy is rushing into her own early marriage, blinded by young love.

Madigan acts as the contact point between the various parts of the story: loving her sister, exasperated by her, standing by her mom, resentfully excluding her father. It's quite an assignment, and as she tries to balance all those demands we see one of the most complex movie characters in a long time (have you noticed how many recent movies assign their characters one mood and think that's enough?).

The Gene Hackman and Ann-Margret characters are complex, too. They are attracted not by lust but by the promise of a new life. They both feel that when they get up in the morning there's nothing to look forward to all day. This movie knows one of the differences between young love and middle-aged love: Kids often are motivated by romance, but people in their forties and fifties sometimes are inspired by the most romantic notion of all—idealism, and the notion that they have found a mate for their minds.

The least-defined character in *Twice in a Lifetime* is the wife, played by Burstyn. Her husband has made his decision and left her to make hers. At first she is simply lost. Eventually she starts picking up the pieces, and she gets a job in the local beauty parlor. She even gets a new hairdo (in one of the movie's most durable clichés). By the end of the film she has started to realize that she, too, was trapped by the marriage. But there is the slightest feeling that her realization owes more to the convenience of the screenplay than to her own growth.

The movie does not have a conventional happy ending. Life will go on, and people will strive, and new routines will replace old ones. The movie has no villains and few heroes. But it has given us several remarkable scenes, especially two confrontations between Madigan and Hackman, one in a bar, the other at a wedding rehearsal, in which the movie shows how much children expect from their parents, and how little the parents often have to give. Growing up is learning that parents are fallible. The people who find that hardest to learn are parents.

Twilight Zone—the Movie

Prologue and Segment 1. Written and directed by John Landis. Starring Dan Aykroyd, Albert Brooks, Vic Morrow, and Doug McGrath. ★ ★

Segment 2. Directed by Steven Spielberg. Written by George Johnson. Starring Scatman Crothers. ★ ½

Segment 3. Directed by Joe Dante. Written by Richard Matheson. Starring Kathleen Quinlan, Jeremy Light, and Kevin McCarthy. ★ ★ ★ ½

Segment 4. Directed by George Miller. Written by Richard Marheson. Starring John Lithgow and Abbe Lane. ★ ★ ★ ½

PG, 101 m., 1983

Produced by Steven Spielberg and inspired by the television series created by Rod Serling.

Every year at Oscar time, somebody comes up with the bright idea of making the Academy Awards into a fair fight. Instead of making the voters choose among five widely different performances, they say, they ought to have five actors playing the same scene. That way you'd really be able to see who was best. It's an impractical idea, but *Twilight Zone—the Movie* does almost the same thing. It takes four stories that are typical of the basic approach of the great "Twilight Zone" TV series, and has four different directors try their hand at recapturing Rod Serling's "wondrous land whose boundaries are that of imagination." And the surprising thing is, the two superstar directors are thoroughly routed by two less-known directors whose previous credits have been horror and action pictures.

The superstars are John *(Blues Brothers)* Landis and Steven *(E. T.)* Spielberg. The relative newcomers are Joe Dante, whose *The Howling* was not my favorite werewolf movie, and George Miller, whose *The Road Warrior* is some kind of a manic classic. Spielberg, who produced the whole project, perhaps sensed that he and Landis had the weakest results, since he assembled the stories in an ascending order of excitement. *Twilight Zone* starts slow, almost grinds to a halt, and then has a fast comeback.

Landis directed the first episode, which stars Vic Morrow in the story of a bigot who is transported back in time to Nazi Germany and Vietnam and forced to swallow his own racist medicine. This segment is predictable, once we know the premise, and Landis does nothing to surprise us. Because we know that Morrow was killed in a helicopter accident during the filming of the segment, an additional pall hangs over the whole story.

Spielberg's segment is next. It stars Scatman Crothers as a mysterious old man who turns up at an old folks' home one day and literally gives the residents what they think they want; to be young again. The easily anticipated lesson is that one lifetime is enough. Spielberg's visual style in this segment is so convoluted and shadowy that the action is hard to follow; the master of clear-cut, sharp-edged visuals is trying something that doesn't work.

But then comes Joe Dante's weird, offbeat segment about a traveler (Kathleen Quinlan) who strays off the beaten path and accepts an offer of hospitality from a fresh-faced young kid who looks healthy and harmless. Once Quinlan is inside the roadside farmhouse where the kid lives, however, she's in another dimension—a bizarre world telepathically projected by the boy's imagination. The kid loves video games and TV cartoons, and he's trapped a whole group of adults in his private fantasies. The art direction in this segment is especially good at giving the house interior a wonderland quality.

George Miller's fourth segment stars John Lithgow in a remake of a famous "Twilight Zone" TV story in which a nervous air traveler sees (or imagines that he sees) a little green man hacking away at the engine of his airplane. But there *couldn't* be a little green man out there—could there? The beauty of *Twilight Zone—the Movie* is the same as the secret of the TV series: It takes ordinary people in ordinary situations and then zaps them with "next stop—the Twilight Zone!"

Two English Girls ★ ★ ★ ★
R, 108 m., 1972

Jean-Pierre Leaud (Claude), Kika Markham (Anne Brown), Stacey Tendeter (Muriel Brown), Sylvia Marriott (Mrs. Brown), Marie Mansart (Madame Roc), Phillipe Leotard (Diurka), Mark Peterson (Mr. Flint), Irene Tunc (Ruta). Directed by François Truffaut and produced by Claude Miler. Screenplay by Truffaut and Jean Gruault.

It's wonderful how offhand François Truffaut's best films fall. There doesn't seem to be any great effort being made; he doesn't push for his effects, but lets them flower naturally from the simplicities of his stories. His film, *Two English Girls*, is very much like that. Because he doesn't strain for an emotional tone, he can cover a larger range than the one-note movies. Here he is discrete, even while filming the most explicit scenes he's ever done; he handles sadness gently; he is charming and funny even while he tells us a story that is finally tragic.

The story is from the second novel by Henri-Pierre Roche, who began writing at the age of seventy-four and whose first novel, *Jules and Jim*, provided the inspiration for nearly everyone's favorite Truffaut film. The two novels (and the two films) are variations on the same theme: What a terrible complex emotional experience it is to have to share love.

We would say that both stories involve romantic triangles, but Roche seems to see them more simply (and poignantly) as the shared dilemmas of people caught helplessly in their situations. Nobody sets out deliberately to involve himself in a triangular relationship—not when the love involved is real. It hurts too much.

Truffaut introduces us to Claude, a young French art critic, and then introduces him to Anne Brown, an English girl visiting in Paris. They form a friendship, and the girl invites him to come and visit her mother and sister in Wales. During the visit, he falls in love (or thinks he does) with the sister, Muriel. They want to marry, but they both have poor health, and it is decided to put off the marriage for a year. Claude returns to Paris, where Anne follows after a while, and then they fall into a sexual relationship that passes for a time as love. The virgin Muriel, meanwhile, remains passionately in love with Claude and nearly has an emotional breakdown when she learns that he no longer plans to marry her.

The story, as it unfolds, is involved but never untrue. Love itself is an elusive prize that passes among them; it is their doom that whenever two of them are together, it is the third who possesses love. The film relates love and loss so closely that we almost forgive Claude for his infidelities and stubbornness. Perversely, he wants to be apart from Muriel (and later Anne) so that he can desire all the more.

If *Two English Girls* resembles *Jules and Jim* in theme, it has an unmistakable stylistic relationship to Truffaut's little-seen masterpiece of 1970, *The Wild Child.* Both films used diaries, journals, and a spoken narration in order to separate us from the immediate experience of the stories. Truffaut wants us to feel that we're being told a fable, a sad winter's tale, that is all the more touching because these events happened long ago and love is trapped irretrievably in the past.

His visual strategy for creating this feeling is another favorite device from *The Wild Child*: the iris shot. (Put simply, this is the use of a slowly contracting circle to bring a shot to an end, instead of a fade or a cut). The iris isolates one element in the picture, somehow making it feel alone and vulnerable—and past. The film is photographed in a low-keyed color, and the sound recording is also a little muted; this isn't a film for emotional highs, we sense, because it's far and away too late for these lost love opportunities to be regained.

The one scene that violates this tone is as necessary as it is effective; when Muriel finally makes love with Claude we feel the terrible force of her passion, pent up for so many years, and then the camera pans to the blood-stained sheet and goes out of focus. Put in so many words, this probably sounds crude and obvious; in fact, this is almost the only red in the film, and is Truffaut's perfect visual metaphor for the fact that these three people have created a lot of their own unhappiness by avoiding or deflecting the consequences of their emotional feelings.

Jules and Jim was a young man's film

(Truffaut was twenty-eight when he made it). *Two English Girls* is the film of a man some ten or twelve years down the road; it is still playful and winsome, but it realizes more fully the consequences of an opportunity lost. The final scene shows Claude, fifteen years later, wandering in the garden where he used to walk with Anne and Muriel. There are English children playing there, and he thinks to ask one of them, "Are you Muriel Brown's daughter?" But he doesn't, because . . . well, because.

2001: A Space Odyssey ★ ★ ★ ★

G, 141 m., 1968

Keir Dullea (Bowman), Gary Lockwood (Poole), William Sylvester (Dr. Heywood Floyd), Daniel Richter (Moonwatcher), Douglas Rain (HAL 9000 [Voice]), Leonard Rossiter (Smyslov), Margaret Tyzack (Elena), Robert Beatty (Halvorsen), Sean Sullivan (Michaels), Frank Miller (Mission Controller). Directed and produced by Stanley Kubrick. Screenplay by Kubrick and Arthur C. Clarke.

It was e.e. cummings, the poet, who said he'd rather learn from one bird how to sing than teach ten thousand stars how not to dance. I imagine cummings would not have enjoyed Stanley Kubrick's *2001: A Space Odyssey*, in which stars dance but birds do not sing. The fascinating thing about this film is that it fails on the human level but succeeds magnificently on a cosmic scale.

Kubrick's universe, and the spaceships he constructed to explore it, are simply out of scale with human concerns. The ships are perfect, impersonal machines which venture from one planet to another, and if men are tucked away somewhere inside them, then they get there, too. But the achievement belongs to the machine. And Kubrick's actors seem to sense this; they are lifelike but without emotion, like figures in a wax museum. Yet the machines are necessary because man himself is so helpless in the face of the universe.

Kubrick begins his film with a sequence in which one tribe of apes discovers how splendid it is to be able to hit the members of another tribe over the head. Thus do man's ancestors become tool-using animals. At the same time, a strange monolith appears on Earth. Until this moment in the film, we have seen only natural shapes: earth and sky and arms and legs. The shock of the monolith's straight edges and square corners among the weathered rocks is one of the most effective moments in the film. Here, you see, is perfection. The apes circle it warily, reaching out to touch, then jerking away. In a million years, man will reach for the stars with the same tentative motion.

Who put the monolith there? Kubrick never answers, for which I suppose we must be thankful. The action advances to the year 2001, when explorers on the moon find another of the monoliths. This one beams signals toward Jupiter. And man, confident of his machines, brashly follows the trail.

Only at this point does a plot develop. The ship is manned by two pilots, Keir Dullea and Gary Lockwood. Three scientists are put on board in suspended animation to conserve supplies. The pilots grow suspicious of the computer, "HAL," which runs the ship. But they behave so strangely—talking in monotones like characters from "Dragnet"—that we're hardly interested.

There is hardly any character development in the plot, then, and as a result little suspense. What remains fascinating is the fanatic care with which Kubrick has built his machines and achieved his special effects. There is not a single moment, in this long film, when the audience can see through the props. The stars look like stars and outer space is bold and bleak.

Some of Kubrick's effects have been criticized as tedious. Perhaps they are, but I can understand his motives. If his space vehicles move with agonizing precision, wouldn't we have laughed if they'd zipped around like props on *Captain Video*? This is how it would really be, you find yourself believing.

In any event, all the machines and computers are forgotten in the astonishing last half-hour of this film, and man somehow comes back into his own. Another monolith is found beyond Jupiter, pointing to the stars. It apparently draws the spaceship into a universe where time and space are twisted.

What Kubrick is saying, in the final sequence, apparently, is that man will eventually outgrow his machines, or be drawn beyond them by some cosmic awareness. He will then become a child again, but a child of an infinitely more advanced, more ancient race, just as apes once became, to their own dismay, the infant stage of man.

And the monoliths? Just road markers, I suppose, each one pointing to a destination so awesome that the traveler cannot imagine it without being transfigured. Or as cummings wrote on another occasion, "Listen—there's a hell of a good universe next door; let's go."

NOTE: This movie is best viewed in the letterboxed version, which preserves the widescreen compositions.

2010 ★ ★ ★

PG, 157 m., 1984

Roy Scheider (Heywood Floyd), John Lithgow (Curnow), Helen Mirren (Kirbuk), Bob Balaban (Chandra), Keir Dullea (Bowman), Douglas Rain (HAL 9000). Directed and produced by Peter Hyams. Screenplay by Hyams.

All those years ago, when *2001: A Space Odyssey* was first released, I began my review with a few lines from a poem by e.e. cummings:

I'd rather learn from one bird how to sing
than teach ten thousand stars how not to dance.

That was my response to the people who said they couldn't understand *2001,* that it made no sense and that it was one long exercise in self-indulgence by Stanley Kubrick, who had sent a man to the stars, only to abandon him inside some sort of extraterrestrial hotel room. I felt that the poetry of *2001* was precisely in its mystery, and that to explain everything was to ruin everything—like the little boy who cut open his drum to see what made it bang.

2001 came out in the late 1960s, that legendary time when yuppies were still hippies, and they went to see the movie a dozen times and slipped up to the front of the theater and lay flat on their backs on the floor, so that the sound-and-light trip in the second half of the movie could wash over them and they could stagger to the exits and whisper "far out" to one another in quiet ecstasy. Now comes *2010,* a continuation of the Kubrick film, directed by Peter Hyams, whose background is in more pragmatic projects such as *Outland,* the Sean Connery space station thriller. The screenplay is by Arthur C. Clarke (who, truth to tell, I always have suspected was a little bewildered by what Kubrick did to his original ideas). *2010* is very much a 1980s movie. It doesn't match the poetry and the mystery of the original film, but it does continue the story, and it offers sound, pragmatic explanations for many of the strange and visionary things in *2001* that had us arguing endlessly through the nights of 1968.

This is, in short, a movie that tries to teach 10,000 stars how not to dance. There were times when I almost wanted to cover my ears. Did I really want to know (a) why HAL 9000 disobeyed Dave's orders? or (b) the real reason for the Discovery's original mission? or (c) what the monoliths were trying to tell us? Not exactly. And yet we live in a most practical time, and they say every decade gets the movies it deserves. What we get in *2010* is not an artistic triumph, but it is a triumph of hardware, of special effects, of slick, exciting filmmaking. This is a movie that owes more to George Lucas than to Stanley Kubrick, more to *Star Wars* than to *Also Sprach Zarathustra.* It has an ending that is infuriating, not only in its simplicity, but in its inadequacy to fulfill the sense of anticipation, the sense of wonder we felt at the end of *2001.*

And yet the truth must be told: This is a good movie. Once we've drawn our lines, once we've made it absolutely clear that *2001* continues to stand absolutely alone as one of the greatest movies ever made, once we have freed *2010* of the comparisons with Kubrick's masterpiece, what we are left with is a good-looking, sharp-edged, entertaining, exciting space opera—a superior film of the *Star Trek* genre.

Because *2010* depends so much upon its story, it would be unfair to describe more than the essentials: A joint Soviet-American expedition sets out for the moons of Jupiter to investigate the fate of the Discovery, its crew, and its on-board computer HAL 9000. There is tension on board between the American leader (Roy Scheider) and the Soviet captain (Helen Mirren), and it's made worse because back on Earth, the superpowers are on the brink of nuclear war over Central America. If Kubrick sometimes seemed to be making a bloodless movie with faceless characters, Hyams pays a great deal of attention to story and personality. But only one of the best moments in his movie grows out of character (the touching scene where a Soviet and an American hold onto each other for dear life during a terrifying crisis). The other great moments are special effects achievements: a space walk threatened by vertigo, the awesome presence of Jupiter, and a spectacular flight through the planet's upper atmosphere.

It is possible that *no* conclusion to *2010* could be altogether satisfying, especially to anyone who still remembers the puzzling, awesome simplicity of the Star Child turning to regard us at the end of *2001.* This sequel has its work cut out for it. And the screenplay compounds the difficulty by repeatedly informing us that "something wonderful" is about to happen. After we've been told several times about that wonderful prospect, we're ready for something *really* wonderful, and we don't get it. We get a disappointly mundane conclusion worthy of a 1950s sci-fi movie, not a sequel to *2001.* I, for one, was disappointed that the monoliths would deign to communicate with men at all—let alone that they would use English, or send their messages via a video screen, like the latest generation of cable news.

So. You have to make some distinctions in your mind. In one category, *2001: A Space Odyssey* remains inviolate, one of the handful of true film masterpieces. In a more temporal sphere, *2010* qualifies as superior entertainment, a movie more at home with technique than poetry, with character than with mystery, a movie that explains too much and leaves too little to our sense of wonderment, but a good movie all the same. If I nevertheless sound less than ecstatic, maybe it's because the grave eyes of the *2001* Star Child still haunt me, with their promise that perhaps someday man would learn to teach 10,000 stars how to sing.

U

Uforia ★ ★ ★ ★
PG, 100 m., 1985

Cindy Williams (Arlene), Harry Dean Stanton (Brother Bud), Fred Ward (Sheldon), Alan Beckwith (Brother Roy), Beverly Hope Atkinson (Naomi), Harry Carey, Jr. (George Martin), Diane Diefendorf (Delores), Robert Gray (Emile). Directed by John Binder and produced by Gordon Wolf. Screenplay by Binder.

I've always wanted to know one of those women you read about in the *National Enquirer,* those intense Midwestern housewives who are sucked up into flying saucers and flown to Mars, where they have their measurements taken, and are told they will be contacted again real soon. It's not that I want to hear about the trip to Mars. I'd just enjoy having her around the house, all filled with a sense of mystery and purpose.

Uforia is a great and goofy comedy about a woman just like that. Her name is Arlene, and she works as a supermarket checker in a backwater town in the Southwest. She reads all the UFO publications and believes every word, and knows in her heart that They are coming. But the movie is not really about whether They come or not. It's about how waiting for Them can give you something wonderful to think about, to pass the time of those dreary, dusty days.

The movie has two other characters who get involved in Arlene's dream. One of them is named Sheldon, and he is the kind of good ol' boy who drives through the desert in a big ol' convertible, with the car on cruise control and his feet propped up on the dashboard and a can of beer in his hand.

The other one is named Brother Bud, a phony faith-healer who conducts revival services in a tent outside of town. When Sheldon sees Arlene at the supermarket, he falls in love, and before long he has settled down, sort of, in her mobile home. Sheldon and Brother Bud are brothers, and Sheldon hires on with Bud to portray a guy whose sick leg gets healed every night. Meanwhile, Arlene's faith grows that the UFO will arrive at any moment.

This is one of those movies where you walk in not expecting much, and then something great happens, and you laugh, and you start paying more attention, and then you realize that a lot of great things are happening, that this is one of those rare movies that really has it. *Uforia* is not just another witless Hollywood laugh machine, but a movie with intelligence and a sly, sardonic style of humor. You don't have to shut down half of your brain in order to endure it.

The casting is just perfect. Cindy Williams is the cornerstone, as Arlene, a woman whose hopes and dreams are too big for the small corner of the Earth she has been given to occupy. She doesn't know what to do when she meets Sheldon (played by Fred Ward, from *Remo Williams* and *The Right Stuff*). She likes this guy and she hasn't had a man in a long time. But, then again, she always gets her heart "broke" when she falls for a guy, and so she prays for guidance and starts on the tequila.

Ward gives a wicked performance as the good ol' boy Sheldon. He's Smokey and the Bandit with brains. He has a couple of double takes in this movie that are worth the price of a ticket. And he's not a male chauvinist pig, although everything in his background probably points him in that direction. He doesn't see Arlene as a conquest, but as just the lady he's been looking for. He gets a little tired of the flying saucer stuff, however.

Harry Dean Stanton plays Brother Bud. This is exactly the kind of role Stanton has been complaining that he's tired of: the weary, alcoholic con man with the jolly cynicism. Yet they keep casting him in these roles, and in *Uforia* you can see why: Nobody does a better job. He has an assistant in the movie, a junior evangelist named Brother Roy (Alan Beckwith), whose face shines with conviction and who is always bathed in wonderment and glory. The quiet, offhand way Stanton deals with him is one of the movie's many treasures.

Uforia didn't have a lot of money and a big ad campaign behind it. It doesn't have big stars, unless you are the kind of movie lover for whom the names Cindy Williams, Harry Dean Stanton, and Fred Ward guarantee a movie will at least be interesting.

Like *Repo Man* and *Turtle Diary* and *Hannah and Her Sisters*, it is willing to go for originality in a world that prizes the entertainment assembly line. I was hugging myself during this movie, because it had so many moments that were just right.

The Unbearable Lightness of Being

★ ★ ★ ★

R, 172 m., 1988 ✔

Daniel Day Lewis (Tomas), Juliette Binoche (Tereza), Lena Olin (Sabina), Derek de Lint (Franz), Erland Josephson (The Ambassador), Pavel Landovsky (Pavel), Donald Moffat (Chief Surgeon), Daniel Olbrychski (Interior Ministry Official), Stellan Skarsgard (The Engineer), Tomek Bork (Jiri). Directed by Philip Kaufman and produced by Saul Zaentz. Screenplay by Jean-Claude Carriere.

In the title of Philip Kaufman's *The Unbearable Lightness of Being*, the crucial word is "unbearable." The film tells the story of a young surgeon who attempts to float above the mundane world of personal responsibility and commitment, to practice a sex life that has no traffic with the heart, to escape untouched from the world of sensual pleasure while retaining his privacy and his loneliness. By the end of the story, this freedom has become too great a load for him to bear.

The surgeon's name is Tomas, and he lives in Prague; we meet him in the blessed days before the Russian invasion of 1968. He has an understanding with a woman named Sabina, a painter whose goal is the same as his own—to have a physical relationship without an emotional one. The two lovers believe they have much in common, since they share the same attitude toward their couplings, but actually their genitals have more in common than they do. That is not to say they don't enjoy great sex; they do, and in great detail, in this most erotic serious film since *Last Tango in Paris*.

One day the doctor goes to the country, and while waiting in a provincial train station, his eyes fall upon the young waitress Tereza. He orders a brandy. Their eyes meet. They go for a little walk after she gets off of work, and it is clear there is something special between them. He returns to Prague. One day she appears in the city and knocks at his door. She has come to be with him. Against all of his principles, he allows her to spend the night, and then to move in. He has betrayed his own code of lightness, or freedom.

The film tells the love story of Tomas and Tereza in the context of the events of 1968, and there are shots that place the characters in the middle of the riots against the Russian invaders. Tereza becomes a photographer, and tries to smuggle pictures of the uprising out of the country. Finally, the two lovers leave Prague for Geneva, where Sabina has already gone—and then Tomas resumes his sexual relationship with Sabina because his philosophy, of course, is that sex has nothing to do with love.

Crushed by his decision, Tereza attempts her own experiment with free love, but it does not work because her heart is not built that way. Sabina, meanwhile, meets a professor named Franz who falls in love with her so urgently that he decides to leave his wife. Can she accept this love? Or is she even more committed to "lightness of being" than Tomas, who tutored her in the philosophy? In the middle of Sabina's indecision, Tereza appears at her door with a camera. She has been asked to take some shots for a fashion magazine and needs someone to pose nude. Sabina agrees, and the two women photograph each other in a scene so carefully choreographed that it becomes a ballet of eroticism.

By this point in the movie, a curious thing

had happened to me as a viewer. I had begun to appreciate some of the life rhythms of the characters. Most films move so quickly and are so dependent on plot that they are about events, not lives. *The Unbearable Lightness of Being* carries the feeling of deep nostalgia, of a time no longer present, when these people did these things and hoped for happiness, and were caught up in events beyond their control.

Kaufman achieves this effect almost without seeming to try. At first his film seems to be almost exclusively about sex, but then we notice in countless individual shots and camera decisions that he does not allow his camera to become a voyeur. There is a lot of nudity in the film, but no pornographic documentary quality; the camera does not linger, or move for the best view, or relish the spectacle of nudity. The result is some of the most poignant, almost sad, sex scenes I have ever seen—sensuous, yes, but bittersweet.

The casting has a lot to do with this haunting quality. Daniel Day Lewis plays Tomas with a sort of detachment that is supposed to come from the character's distaste for commitment. He has a lean, intellectual look, and is not a voluptuary. For him, sex seems like a form of physical meditation, rather than an activity with another person. Lena Olin, as Sabina, has a lush, voluptuous body, big-breasted and tactile, but she inhabits it so comfortably that the movie never seems to dwell on it or exploit it. It is a fact of nature. Juliette Binoche, as Tereza, is almost ethereal in her beauty and innocence, and her attempt to reconcile her love with her lover's detachment is probably the heart of the movie.

The film is based on the novel by the Czech novelist Milan Kundera, whose works all seem to consider eroticism with a certain wistfulness, as if to say that while his characters were making love, they were sometimes distracted from the essentially tragic nature of their existence. That is the case here. Kaufman, whose previous films have included *The Right Stuff* and a remake of *Invasion of the Body Snatchers*, has never done anything remotely like this before, but his experiment is a success in tone; he has made a movie in which reality is asked to coexist with a world of pure sensuality, and almost, for a moment, seems to agree.

The film will be noticed primarily for its eroticism. Although major films and filmmakers considered sex with great frankness and freedom in the early and mid-seventies, films in the last decade have been more adolescent, more plot- and action-oriented. Catering to audiences of adolescents, who are comfortable with sex only when it is seen in cartoon form, Hollywood has also not been comfortable with the complications of adult sexuality—the good and the bad. What is remarkable about *The Unbearable Lightness of Being*, however, is not the sexual content itself, but the way Kaufman has been able to use it as an avenue for a complex story, one of nostalgia, loss, idealism, and romance.

Under Fire ★ ★ ★ ½

R, 128 m., 1983

Nick Nolte (Russell Price), Gene Hackman (Alex Grazier), Joanne Cassidy (Claire), Ed Harris (Oates). Directed by Roger Spottiswoode and produced by Jonathan Taplin. Screenplay by Ron Shelton and Clayton Frohman.

This is the kind of movie that almost always feels phony, but *Under Fire* feels real. It's about American journalists covering guerrilla warfare in Central America, and so right away we expect to see Hollywood stars transplanted to the phony jungles of one of those movie nations with madeup names. Instead, we see Hollywood stars who create characters so convincing we forget they're stars. And the movie names names: It's set in Nicaragua, in 1979, during the fall of the Somoza regime, period.

We meet three journalists who are there to get the story. This is not the first small war they've covered, and indeed we've already seen them packing up and leaving Africa. Now they've got a new story. Nick Nolte is Price, a photographer. Gene Hackman is Grazier, a TV reporter who dreams of becoming an anchorman. Joanna Cassidy is a radio reporter. During the course of the story, Cassidy will fall out of love with Hackman and into love with Nolte. These things happen under deadline pressure. Hackman cares, but not enough to affect his friendship with both of them.

The story is simply told, since *Under Fire* depends more upon moments and atmosphere than on a manufactured plot. During a lull in the action, Hackman heads back for

New York and Nolte determines to get an interview with the elusive leader of the guerrillas. He doesn't get an interview, but he begins to develop a sympathy for the rebel cause. He commits the journalistic sin of taking sides, and it leads him, eventually, to a much greater sin: faking a photograph to help the guerrilla forces. That is, of course, wrong. But *Under Fire* shows us a war in which morality is hard to define and harder to practice. One of the key supporting characters in the movie is a mysterious American named Oates (played by Ed Harris). Is he CIA? Apparently. He's always in the thick of the dirty work, however, and if his conscience doesn't bother him, Nolte excuses himself for not taking an ethical stand. There are, in fact, a lot of ethical stands not taken in this movie. It could almost have been written by Graham Greene; it exists in that half-world between exhaustion and exhilaration, between love and cynicism, between covering the war and getting yourself killed. This is tricky ground, and the wrong performances could have made it ridiculous (cf. Richard Gere's sleek sexual athlete in *Beyond the Limit*). The actors in *Under Fire* never step wrong.

Nolte is great to watch as the seedy photographer with the beer gut. Hackman never really convinced me that he could be an anchorman, but he did a better thing. He convinced me that he thought he could be one. Joanna Cassidy takes a role that could have been dismissed as "the girl" and fills it out as a fascinating, textured adult. *Under Fire* surrounds these performances with a vivid sense of place and becomes, somewhat surprisingly, a serious and moving film.

Under the Volcano ★ ★ ★ ★
R, 109 m., 1984

Albert Finney (Geoffrey Firmin), Jacqueline Bisset (Yvonne Firmin), Anthony Andrews (Hugh Firmin), Ignacio Lopez Tarso (Dr. Vigil), Kathy Jurado (Senora Gregoria). Directed by John Huston and produced by Michael Fitzgerald. Screenplay by Guy Gallo.

The consul drinks. He has been drinking for so many years that he has arrived at that peculiar stage in alcoholism where he no longer drinks to get high or to get drunk. He drinks simply to hold himself together and continue to function. He has a muddled theory that he can even "drink himself sober," by which he means that he can sometimes find a lucid window through the fog of his life. *Under the Volcano* is the story of the last day in his drinking.

He lives in Cuernavaca, Mexico, in the years just before World War II. He is not really the British consul anymore: he was only a vice consul, anyway, and now that has been stripped from him, and he simply drinks. He has a few friends and a few acquaintances, and his long days are spent in a drunk's neverending occupation, monitoring his own condition. On this morning, for example, he had a bit too much and passed out in the road. One of those things. Earlier, or later, sometime in there, he had stumbled into a church and prayed for the return of his wife, who had left him. Now he sits on his veranda talking with his half-brother. He turns his head. His wife is standing in the doorway. He turns back. It cannot be her. He looks again. She is still there. Turns away. It cannot be. Looks again. A hallucination. But it persists, and eventually he is forced to admit that his wife has indeed returned, in answer to his prayers.

He drinks. He passes out. He wakes. The three of them set off on a bus journey. A peasant is found dead on a roadside. Later, in a bar, there is an unpleasantness with a whore. Still later, the day ends in a ditch. The consul's day is seen largely through his point of view, and the remarkable thing about *Under the Volcano* is that it doesn't resort to any of the usual tricks that movies use when they portray drunks. There are no trick shots to show hallucinations. No spinning cameras. No games with focus. Instead, the drunkenness in this film is supplied by the remarkably controlled performance of Albert Finney as the consul. He gives the best drunk performance I've ever seen in a film. He doesn't overact, or go for pathos, or pretend to be a character. His focus is on communication. He wants, he desperately desires, to penetrate the alcoholic fog and speak clearly from his heart to those around him. His words come out with a peculiar intensity of focus, as if every one had to be pulled out of the small hidden core of sobriety deep inside his confusion.

The movie is based on the great novel by Malcolm Lowry, who used this day in the life of a drunk as a clothesline on which to hang several themes, including the political disintegration of Mexico in the face of the rising tide of Nazism. John Huston, the surefooted old veteran who directed the film, wisely leaves out the symbols and implications and subtexts and just gives us the man. Lowry's novel was really about alcoholism, anyway; the other materials were not so much subjects as they were attempts by the hero to focus on something between his ears.

The movie belongs to Finney, but mention must be made of Jacqueline Bisset as his wife and Anthony Andrews as his half-brother. Their treatment of the consul is interesting. They understand him well. They love him (and, we gather, each other). They realize nothing can be done for him. Why do they stay with him? For love, maybe, or loyalty, but also perhaps because they respect the great effort he makes to continue to function, to "carry on," in the face of his disabling illness. Huston, I think, is interested in the same aspect of the story, that within every drunk is a man with self-respect trying to get free.

An Unmarried Woman ★ ★ ★ ★

R, 124 m., 1978

Jill Clayburgh (Erica), Alan Bates (Saul), Michael Murphy (Martin), Lisa Lucas (Patti), Cliff Gorman (Charlie), Pat Quinn (Sue), Kelly Bishop (Elaine), Linda Miller (Jeannette), Andrew Duncan (Bob), Penelope Russianoff (Tanya). Directed by Paul Mazursky and produced by Mazursky and Tony Ray. Screenplay by Mazursky.

It is, Erica thinks, a happy marriage, although perhaps she doesn't think about it much. It's *there.* Her husband is a stockbroker, she works in an art gallery, their daughter is in a private high school, they live in a high-rise and jog along the East River. In the morning there is "Swan Lake" on the FM radio, and the last sight at night is of the closing stock prices on the TV screen. Had she bargained for more?

One day, though, swiftly and cruelly, it all comes to an end: Her husband breaks down in phony tears on the street and confesses he's in love with another woman. A younger woman. And so her happy marriage is over. At home, consumed by anger, grief, and uncertainty, she studies her face in the mirror. It is a good face in its middle thirties, and right now it looks plain scared.

So end the first, crucial passages of Paul Mazursky's *An Unmarried Woman.* They are crucial because we have to understand how *completely* Erica was a married woman if we're to join her on the journey back to being single again. It's a journey that Mazursky makes into one of the funniest, truest, sometimes most heartbreaking movies I've ever seen. And so much of what's best is because of Jill Clayburgh, whose performance is, quite simply, luminous.

We know that almost from the beginning. There's a moment of silence in the morning, right after Erica's husband and daughter have left the house. "Swan Lake" is playing. She's still in bed. She's just made love. She speaks from her imagination: "The ballet world was thrilled last night. . . ." And then she slips out of bed and dances around the living room in her T-shirt and panties, because she's so happy, so alive . . . and at that moment the movie's got us. We're in this thing with Erica to the end.

The going is sometimes pretty rough, especially when she's trying to make sense out of things after her husband (Michael Murphy) leaves her. She gets a lot of support and encouragement from her three best girl friends, and some of the movie's very best scenes take place when they meet for long lunches with lots of white wine, or lie around on long Sunday mornings paging through the *Times* and idly wondering why *their* lives don't seem to contain the style of a Bette Davis or a Katharine Hepburn. And then there are the scenes when she talks things over with her daughter (Lisa Lucas), who's one of those bright, precocious teen-agers who uses understatement and cynicism to conceal how easily she can still be hurt.

After Erica gets over the period where she drinks too much and cries too much and screams at her daughter when she doesn't mean to, she goes to a woman psychiatrist, who explains that men are the problem, yes, but they are not quite yet the enemy. And so Erica, who hasn't slept with any man but her husband for seventeen years, finds herself having lunch in Chinese restaurants with boors who shout orders at waiters and try to kiss her in the back seat of a cab. There's also the self-styled stud (Cliff Gorman) who's been hanging around the art gallery, and she finally does go up to his place—warily, gingerly, but she has to find a way sometime of beginning her life again.

And then one day a British artist is hanging a show at the gallery, and he asks her if she doesn't think one side of the painting is a little low, and she says she thinks the *whole* painting is too low, and he doesn't even seem to have noticed her as he says, "Let's discuss it over lunch." They fall in love. Oh, yes, gloriously, in that kind of love that involves not only great sex but walking down empty streets at dawn, and talking about each other's childhood. The painter is played by Alan Bates, who is cast, well and true, as a man who is perfectly right for her and perfectly wrong for her, both at the same time.

An Unmarried Woman plays true with all three of its major movements: The marriage, the being single, the falling in love. Mazursky's films have considered the grave and funny business of sex before (most memorably in *Bob & Carol & Ted & Alice* and *Blume in Love*). But he's never before been this successful at really dealing with the complexities and following them through. I wouldn't want to tell you too much about the movie's conclusion, but believe this much: It's honest and it's *right*, because Mazursky and Jill Clayburgh care too much about Erica to dismiss her with a conventional happy ending.

Clayburgh takes chances in this movie. She's out on an emotional limb. She's letting us see and experience things that many actresses simply couldn't reveal. Mazursky takes chances, too. He wants *An Unmarried Woman* to be true, for starters: We have to believe at every moment that life itself is being considered here. But the movie has to be funny, too. He won't settle for less than the truth *and* the humor, and the wonder of *An Unmarried Woman* is that he gets it. I've been reviewing movies for a long time now without ever feeling the need to use dumb lines like "You'll laugh—you'll cry." But I did cry, and I did laugh.

The Untouchables ★ ★ ½

R, 127 m., 1987

Kevin Costner (Eliot Ness), Robert De Niro (Al Capone), Sean Connery (Jimmy Malone), Andy Garcia (George Stone), Charles Martin Smith (Oscar Wallace). Directed by Brian De Palma and produced by Art Linson. Screenplay by David Mamet.

There is a moment in *The Untouchables* when a mobster doesn't want to talk to the law. He's just been captured by federal agents up at the Canadian border, while trying to run some booze down to Chicago for Capone. One of the guy's pals has been shot dead, out on the porch. He doesn't know his partner is dead.

Sean Connery walks outside, grabs the corpse, props it up against a wall, says he's gonna shoot the guy if he doesn't talk—and then puts a bullet into him and drops him. Inside the cabin, the other mobster decides to talk.

It's a moment of quick, brutal improvisation, and it has an energy that's lacking during most of *The Untouchables*. Here is a movie about an era when law enforcement resembled gang warfare, but the movie seems more interested in the era than in the war. *The Untouchables* has great costumes, great sets, great cars, great guns, great locations, and a few shots that absolutely capture the Prohibition Era. But it does not have a great script, great performances, or great direction.

The script is by David Mamet, the playwright, but it could have been by anybody. It doesn't have the Mamet touch, the conversational rhythms that carry a meaning beyond words. It also lacks any particular point of view about the material, and, in fact, lacks the dynamic tension of many gangster movies written by less talented writers. Everything seems cut and dried, twice-told, preordained.

The performances are another disappointment. The star of the movie is Kevin Costner, as Eliot Ness, the straight-arrow federal agent who vows a personal struggle against the Capone mob. Costner is fine for the role, but it's a thankless one, giving him little to do other than act grim and incorrigible. The script doesn't give him, and he doesn't provide, any of the little twists and turns of character that might have made Ness into an individual.

But the big disappointment is Robert De Niro's Al Capone. All of the movie's Capone segments seem cut off from the rest of the story; they're like regal set-pieces, dropped in from time to time. De Niro comes on screen with great dramatic and musical flourish, strikes an attitude, says a line, and that's basically the whole idea. There isn't a glimmer of a notion of what made this man tick, this Al Capone who was such an organizational genius that he founded an industry and became a millionaire while he was still a young man.

The best performance in the movie is by Sean Connery, as a Scottish-American cop who signs on as Ness's right-hand man and seems, inexplicably, to know everything about the mob and its liquor business. Connery brings a human element to his character; he seems to have had an existence apart from the legend of the Untouchables, and when he's on screen we can believe, briefly, that the 1920s were inhabited by people, not caricatures.

What's good about the movie is the physical production itself. There's a shot of the canyon of LaSalle Street, all decked out with 1920s cars and extras, that's sensational. And a lot of other nice touches, like Capone's hotel headquarters, or the courtroom where his trial is held. But even the good use of sets and locations is undermined by Brian De Palma's curiously lead-footed direction—curious, because he is usually the most nimble and energetic of directors.

Look, for example, at an early scene where Ness and his men are staking out a gang headquarters, and Ness spots a nosy photographer snooping around. The editing is so clumsy we can't understand why the mob doesn't see Ness and the photographer. (And the photographer himself stays around for the whole picture as an implausible distraction, who is somehow always able to turn up whenever he's needed.)

The 1920s were already a legend by the 1930s, when Warner Brothers turned them into the gangster movie industry. Directors have been struggling ever since to invest them with life, and free them from clichés. The best film about the era remains the uncut original version of Sergio Leone's *Once Upon a Time In America*. De Palma's *Untouchables*, like the TV series that inspired it, depends more on clichés than on artistic invention.

Up the Creek ★ ★ ★

R, 95 m., 1984

Tim Matheson (Bob McGraw), Jennifer Runyon (Heather Merriweather), Stephen Furst (Gonzer), Dan Monahan (Max), Sandy Helberg (Irwin), John Hillerman (Dean Burch). Directed by Robert Butler and produced by Michael L. Meltzer. Screenplay by Jim Kouf.

Up the Creek is in the great tradition of the Undergraduate Slob Movie, a genre that was created by *Animal House*, perfected by Bill Murray, and defiled by the 1984 *Where the Boys Are*. We know where we stand right in the first few minutes, when a fat kid throws his sandwich out the car window, it hits a motorcyclist in the face, and the motorcyclist hurtles over a cliff. This is not what you call subtle, but Undergraduate Slob Movies do not quibble.

The movie is about an intercollegiate white-water raft race. The defending champions are from a hard-ass military academy. The favorites are from the Ivy League. Our team is from Lepetoname University, described by its dean as the worst university in the world. (In French, by the way, le petoname is the kind of guy who was sitting around the campfire in *Blazing Saddles*.) This university has never won anything. Its students have transferred to it from dozens of other universities—each. The dean makes them a deal. If they win the race, he will give them the diplomas of their choice.

The Lepetoname team is made up of an all-star Undergraduate Slob Movie cast: Tim Matheson and Stephen Furst are from *Animal House*, Dan Monahan is from *Porky's*, and Sandy Helberg was in *History of the World—Part One*, which was a Historical Slob Movie. They pile into a car and head for the race, accompanied by Chuck the Wonder Dog, a dog who is so instrumental to the success of this movie that I will even give you its real name, which is Jake.

One of the joys of this kind of movie comes during the scenes where we meet the competitors. The guys from the military school are led by an uptight, future general. The guys from the Ivy League are all blond, rich, good-looking, and unscrupulous: They plan to use bombs, torpedoes, and even radio-controlled model airplanes to shoot their enemies out of the water. There is, of course, a big beer blast before the race gets underway. The party scene has been an obligatory element of Undergraduate Slob Movies ever since the toga party in *Animal House.* But there are good parties and bad ones. In *Where the Boys Are,* the party is a shapeless confusion. In *Up the Creek,* it's a funny, sustained sequence that establishes all the important characters and sets up the tension.

There's one other scene in the movie that has to be singled out. That's when one of the Lepetoname team members is kidnapped, and Chuck the Wonder Dog uses charades to explain where he is. That's a great scene—and so, by the way, are the scenes of the actual race itself, where some skillful and difficult photography makes the river and its rapids seem convincingly dangerous. *Up the Creek* belongs to an honorable movie tradition, the slapstick comedy. It is superficial, obvious, vulgar, idiotic, goofy, sexy, and predictable. Those are all, by the way, positive qualities—at least, in an Undergraduate Slob Movie.

Up the Sandbox ★ ★ ★

R, 98 m., 1973

Barbra Streisand (Marjorie), David Selby (Paul), Ariana Heller (Elizabeth), Jacobo Morales (Fidel Castro), Carol White (Miss Spittlemeister). Directed by Irvin Kershner and produced by Robert Chartoff and Irwin Winkler. Screenplay by Paul Zindel.

It's a little hard to make a movie about a woman's liberation when the woman in question is happy with her life, in love with her husband, and looking forward to having her third child. Such a woman somehow doesn't seem to be your typical *MS* subscriber.

I'm dealing in stereotypes, of course, but so does *Up the Sandbox*—sometimes. This is a Barbra Streisand movie, and so we know the central character won't (can't) be stereotyped; nothing even remotely like Streisand has existed in movies before. But the movie's other characters stray dangerously close to becoming case histories for Gloria Steinem.

Streisand plays Marjorie, a woman who once wrote a term paper so brilliant that her old professor still remembers it. She doesn't; she's set aside plans for an academic career and devotes herself to loving her husband, raising her children, and maintaining a New York apartment that even Erma Bombeck would describe as a mess.

Marjorie's husband is a professor at Columbia, and of course he's brilliant and engaged in "important" work and is fascinating to young women at cocktail parties—particularly, Marjorie observes, young women with low-cut dresses. This causes her some concern, and so do the erratic guerrilla raids staged on her apartment by her mother. Marjorie's mother is a spokesman for all that women's lib is against: She wants Marjorie to move to the suburbs, play cards, engage in housekeeping competition with the other women in the block, and, in general, degenerate gracefully into the zombie-like state of housewives who are attracted to detergents (but nothing else) by sex appeal.

Marjorie retaliates with a series of fantasies which sometimes work, in terms of the movie, and sometimes fail terribly. The best ones are inspired. Director Irvin Kershner (who directed the best party scene of 1971 in his comedy masterpiece *Loving*), gives us another party that is horrifying in its realism.

It's the thirty-third anniversary for Marjorie's mom and dad, and Mom seizes on her after-dinner speech as the proper occasion to (1) urge Marjorie to surrender to the suburbs and (2) announce that Marjorie is preggers. Marjorie's fantasy is to the point. She mashes her mother's face into the anniversary cake and then they wrestle under the table while a tipsy cousin shoots the action for a home movie.

Scenes like this work as fierce, funny satire; but some of the other fantasies (particularly a visit to an African tribe where the women carry the spears and the men wash the dishes) are a waste of effort. Considerable effort; the cast went to Africa to film them, and perhaps they cost so much money Kershner was reluctant to cut them out.

No matter; Streisand herself is really fine in *Up the Sandbox,* which was more or less her first straight role (depending on how you took *On a Clear Day You Can See Forever*). She does not give us a liberated woman, or even a woman working in some organized way toward liberation. Instead, she gives us a woman who feels free to be herself, no matter what anyone thinks. This is a kind of woman, come to think of it, who is rare in American movies; female intelligence on the screen still actually seems quietly revolutionary, which is a sad truth but one *Up the Sandbox* does nothing to further.

Used Cars ★ ★
R, 113 m., 1980

Kurt Russell (Rudy Russo), Jack Warden (The Fuchs Brothers), Gerrit Graham (Jeff), Frank McRae (Jim), Deborah Harmon (Barbara Fuchs). Directed by Robert Zemekis and produced by Bob Gale. Screenplay by Zemekis and Gale.

I wonder where the idea got started that it's intrinsically funny to see cars crashing into each other. It's not. It is also not *more* funny when there are dozens or hundreds of cars; the delicate timing you need for comedy is lost when a scene becomes a logistical demonstration. When it comes to cars in movies, more is less—a lesson *Used Cars* does not demonstrate.

When the movie isn't manipulating cars, it does have its good moments. It involves an ancient family feud between two brothers who own competing used car lots across the street from each other. The brothers, both played by Jack Warden, have been treated differently by fate: One is rich and successful; the other is on his last legs, like the cars on his lot. Warden does a good enough job in the dual role, but I always wonder why dual roles seem like a good idea in the first place. If you want two brothers, why not cast two brothers, and accentuate their differences? Why cast one actor and settle for one tour de force instead of two undistracting performances?

Anyway, the movie's plot thickens when it appears that the rich brother will run the poor brother out of business. The plot, in fact, does more than thicken, it congeals. There are so many different characters and story lines in the movie that it's hard to keep everything straight, and harder still to care.

The great comedies almost always have very simple story structures, upon which complex gags can be elaborated. Remember, for example, Buster Keaton's *The General,* in which magnificent complexities were developed out of a story that essentially amounted to Keaton driving a locomotive from point A to point B and back again. *Used Cars* makes the fatal error of achieving the reverse effect: Simple gags are generated out of bafflingly complex situations.

Meanwhile, back at the used car lot . . . Kurt Russell plays a used car salesman who hopes to save the failing business in order to raise money for his political campaign. Gerrit Graham has some funny moments as a superstitious, sex-mad salesman. Deborah Harmon is the long-lost daughter of the less successful brother; her surprise reappearance gives him an heir just when he needs one the most.

Used Cars was written, directed, and produced by the team of Bob Zemekis and Bob Gale, two young filmmakers who seem to be higher on kinetic energy than on structure and comedic instinct. Their first collaboration, which I really enjoyed, was *I Wanna Hold Your Hand,* a fantasy about the Beatles' first concert in New York. Their next collaboration was the screenplay for Steven Spielberg's unsuccessful *1941.* Next came *Used Cars.* The second and third projects, in particular, are filled with too many ideas, relationships and situations—with plot overkill. And they seem to share the notion that if something is big enough and expensive enough, it will also be funny enough.

V

Vagabond ★ ★ ★ ★
NO MPAA RATING, 105 m., 1986

Sandrine Bonnaire (Mona), Macha Meril (Madame Lanier), Stephane Friess (Jean-Pierre), Laurence Cortadellas (Elaine), Marthe Jarnias (Tante Lydie), Yolande Moreau (Yolande), Joel Fosse (Paulo). Directed by Agnes Varda. Screenplay by Varda.

The opening shot moves in ever so slowly across the bleak fields of a French winter landscape. Two trees stand starkly outlined at the top of a hill. There is no joy here. As the camera moves closer, we see in the bottom of a ditch the blue and frozen body of a young woman. A field hand discovers her and sets up a cry. Soon the authorities are there with their clipboards, recording those things which can be known, such as the height and weight and eye color of the corpse, and wondering about all the things which cannot be known, such as her name and why she came to be dead in the bottom of a ditch.

Then we hear Agnes Varda's voice on the sound track, telling us that she became absorbed by the mystery of this young stranger's last months on earth and sought the testimony of those people who had known her. *Vagabond*, however, is the story of a woman who could not be known. And although there are many people who can step forward and say they spoke with the young woman, sheltered her, gave her food and drink, shared cigarettes and even sex with her, there is no one to say that they knew her.

Vagabond tries to feel like a documentary, a series of flashbacks to certain days in the last months of the girl's life. Actually, it is all fiction. And, like all good fiction, it is able to imply much more than it knows. From bits and pieces of information that the girl spreads out among the people that she meets, we learn that she was born of middle-class parents, that she took secretarial training, that she worked in an office but hated it, that eventually she went on the road, carrying her possessions and a tent in a knapsack on her back, begging food and shelter, sometimes doing a little work for a little money.

She looks ordinary enough, with her wide, pleasant face and her quiet smile. People talk about how bad she smells, but we cannot know about that. She rolls her own cigarettes and sometimes prefers them to food. Sometimes in a cafe, when she is given a few francs, she spends them on the jukebox instead of on bread.

Only gradually do we realize that she contains a great passivity. When a goat herder and his wife take her in, feed her and give her a small trailer to spend the winter in, she does not embrace the opportunity to help them in their work. She sits inside the trailer, staring blankly ahead. She is utterly devoid of ambition. She has gone on the road, not to make her fortune, but to drop out completely from all striving.

It is hard to read her signals. Sometimes she seems to be content, opening the flap of her tent and staring out, half-blinded, at the brightness of the morning sun. She stops for a few days in a chateau and laughs with the old countess who lives there as they get drunk on the countess's brandy and the old lady complains that her son is only waiting for her to die. She seems to respond briefly to a woman professor, an agronomist who takes her along in the car as she inspects a plague among the plane trees. But is she really warming up to these people, or only providing them with a mirror that reflects their own need to touch somebody?

One of the most painful subtleties of this film is the way we see the girl's defenses finally fall. One day after another, almost without seeming to, she sinks lower and lower. The life of the vagabond becomes the life of the outcast, and then the outcast becomes the abandoned. Finally, the abandoned becomes an animal, muddy and unkempt, disoriented, at the bottom, no longer bewildered, frightened, amazed at how low she has fallen. Finally she cries, and we remember how young and defenseless she is, under that tough skin.

What a film this is. Like so many of the greatest films, it tells us a very specific story, strong and unadorned, about a very particular person. Because it is so much her own story and does not seem to symbolize anything—because the director has no parables, only information—it is only many days after the end of the film that we reflect that the story of the vagabond could also be the story of our lives. For how many have truly known us, although many have shared our time.

Valley Girl ★ ★ ★
R, 95 m., 1983

Nicholas Cage (Randy), Deborah Foreman (Julie), Elizabeth Dailey (Loryn), Michael Bowen (Tommy), Colleen Camp (Mom), Frederic Forrest (Dad). Directed by Martha Coolidge and produced by Wayne Crawford and Andrew Lane. Screenplay by Crawford and Lane.

Disgruntled and weary after slogging through Sex-Mad Teen-ager Movies, I came upon *Valley Girl* with low expectations. What can you expect from a genre inspired by *Porky's?* But this movie is a little treasure, a funny, sexy, appealing story of a Valley Girl's heartbreaking decision: Should she stick with her boring jock boyfriend, or take a chance on a punk from Hollywood? Having seen many Sex-Mad Teen-ager Movies in which a typical slice of teen-ager life consisted of seducing your teacher, being seduced by your best friend's mom, or driving off to Tijuana in search of hookers, I found *Valley Girl* to be surprisingly convincing in its portrait of kids in love. These *are* kids. They're uncertain about sex, their hearts send out confusing signals, and they're slaves to peer pressure.

The movie stars Deborah Foreman as Julie, a bright, cute high school girl who is in the process of breaking up with her blond jock boyfriend (Michael Gowen). He's gorgeous to look at, but he's boring and conceited and he does the one thing that drives all teen-age girls mad: He sits down next to them in a burger joint and casually helps himself to their lunch. One night at a party, Julie meets Randy (Nicholas Cage). He's a lanky, kind of goofy-looking kid with an appealing, crooked smile. He's also a punk from across the hills in Hollywood. Julie likes him. He makes her laugh. He's tender. It's awesome. She falls in love. And then her friends start working her over with all sorts of dire predictions, such as that she'll be "totally dropped" if she goes out with this grotty punk. Caving in to peer pressure, Julie agrees to go to the prom with the jock. And then there's the big climax where the punk gets his girl.

One of the nicest things about this movie is that it allows its kids to be intelligent, thoughtful, and self-analytical. Another thing is that it allows the *parents* to be modern parents. Have you ever stopped to think how *dated* all the parents in teen-ager movies are? They seem to have been caught in a time warp with Dagwood and Blondie. In *Valley Girl,* the parents (Frederic Forrest and Colleen Camp) are former hippies from the Woodstock generation, now running a health food restaurant and a little puzzled by their daughter's preppy friends. It's a perfect touch.

And here's one more nice thing about *Valley Girl.* Maybe because it was directed by a woman, Martha Coolidge, this is one of the rare teen-ager movies that doesn't try to get laughs by insulting and embarrassing teenage girls. Everybody's in the same boat in this movie—boys and girls—and they're all trying to do the right thing and still have a good time. It may be the last thing you'd expect from a movie named *Valley Girl,* but the kids in this movie are human.

The Verdict ★ ★ ★ ★
R, 122 m., 1982

Paul Newman (Frank Galvin), Charlotte Rampling (Laura Fischer), Jack Warden

(Mickey Morrissey), James Mason (Ed Concannon), Milo O'Shea (Judge Hoyle), Edward Binns (Bishop Brophy), Julie Bovasso (Maureen Rooney), Lindsay Crouse (Kaitlin Costello). Directed by Sidney Lumet and produced by Richard Zanuck and David Brown. Screenplay by David Mamet.

There is a moment in *The Verdict* when Paul Newman walks into a room and shuts the door and trembles with anxiety and with the inner scream that people should *get off his back.* No one who has ever been seriously hung over or needed a drink will fail to recognize the moment. It is the key to his character in *The Verdict*, a movie about a drinking alcoholic who tries to pull himself together for one last step at salvaging his self-esteem.

Newman plays Frank Galvin, a Boston lawyer who has had his problems over the years—a lost job, a messy divorce, a disbarment hearing, all of them traceable in one way or another to his alcoholism. He has a "drinking problem," as an attorney for the archdiocese delicately phrases it. That means that he makes an occasional guest appearance at his office and spends the rest of his day playing pinball and drinking beer, and his evening drinking Irish whiskey and looking to see if there isn't at least one last lonely woman in the world who will buy his version of himself in preference to the facts. Galvin's pal, a lawyer named Mickey Morrissey (Jack Warden) has drummed up a little work for him: An open-and-shut malpractice suit against a Catholic hospital in Boston where a young woman was carelessly turned into a vegetable because of a medical oversight. The deal is pretty simple. Galvin can expect to settle out-of-court and pocket a third of the settlement—enough to drink on for what little future he is likely to enjoy.

But Galvin makes the mistake of going to see the young victim in a hospital, where she is alive but in a coma. And something snaps inside of him. He determines to try this case, by God, and to prove that the doctors who took her mind away from her were guilty of incompetence and dishonesty. In Galvin's mind, bringing this case to court is one and the same thing with regaining his self-respect—with emerging from his own alcoholic coma. Galvin's redemption takes place within the framework of a courtroom thriller. The screenplay by David Mamet is a wonder of good dialogue, strongly seen characters, and a structure that pays off in the big courtroom scene—as the genre requires. As a courtroom drama, *The Verdict* is superior work. But the director and the star of this film, Sidney Lumet and Paul Newman, seem to be going for something more; *The Verdict* is more a character study than a thriller, and the buried suspense in this movie is more about Galvin's own life than about his latest case.

Frank Galvin provides Newman with the occasion for one of his great performances. This is the first movie in which Newman has looked a little old, a little tired. There are moments when his face sags and his eyes seem terribly weary, and we can look ahead clearly to the old men he will be playing in ten years' time. Newman always has been an interesting actor, but sometimes his resiliency, his youthful vitality, have obscured his performances; he has a tendency to always look great, and that is not always what the role calls for. This time, he gives us old, bone-tired, hung over, trembling (and heroic) Frank Galvin, and we buy it lock, stock, and shot glass.

The movie is populated with finely tuned supporting performances (many of them by British or Irish actors, playing Bostonians not at all badly). Jack Warden is the old law partner; Charlotte Rampling is the woman, also an alcoholic, with whom Galvin unwisely falls in love; James Mason is the ace lawyer for the archdiocese; Milo O'Shea is the politically connected judge; Wesley Addy provides just the right presence as one of the accused doctors. The performances, the dialogue, and the plot all work together like a rare machine.

But it's that Newman performance that stays in the mind. Some reviewers have found *The Verdict* a little slow-moving, maybe because it doesn't always hum along on the thriller level. But if you bring empathy to the movie, if you allow yourself to think about what Frank Galvin is going through, there's not a moment of this movie that's not absorbing. *The Verdict* has a lot of truth in it, right down to a great final scene in which Newman, still drinking, finds that if you wash it down with booze, victory tastes just like defeat.

Vice Versa ★ ★ ★ ½
PG, 97 m., 1988

Judge Reinhold (Marshall), Fred Savage (Charlie), Corinne Bohrer (Sam), Swoosie Kurtz (Tina), Jane Kaczmarek (Robyn), David Proval (Turk), William Prince (Avery), Gloria Gifford (Marcie), Beverly Archer (Mrs. Luttrell), Harry Murphy (Larry). Directed by Brian Gilbert and produced by Dick Clement and Ian La Frenais. Screenplay by Clement and La Frenais.

Who would have guessed it? Who would have been able to predict that the plot of one of 1987's worst movies could produce one of 1988's most endearing comedies? Here at last is proof that the right actors can make anything funny, or perhaps it is proof that the wrong actors cannot. The name of the movie is *Vice Versa,* and when they made it in 1987 it was called *Like Father, Like Son.* The screenplays for the two movies are amazingly similar, through a rare Hollywood coincidence. But what a difference there is in the movies.

It was, I must admit, with lagging step and a heavy heart that I made my way to see *Vice Versa.* I had sincerely disliked *Like Father, Like Son,* which starred Dudley Moore and Kirk Cameron in the story of a father and son whose minds magically enter each other's bodies, forcing them to trade identities. Now here was *Vice Versa*, which stars Judge Reinhold and Fred Savage in the story of a father and son whose minds magically enter each other's bodies, forcing them to trade identities. If the material was bad when it was fresh, how could it be good when it was familiar?

My state of mind lasted for perhaps the first five minutes of the movie. Then I was laughing too hard to care. I suppose film students of the future will want to analyze the differences between the two treatments of similar material, to see how Reinhold and Savage and director Brian Gilbert and writers Dick Clement and Ian La Frenais got it right when the 1987 team got it all wrong. I would prefer to think maybe it was a matter of style.

Reinhold plays a Chicago department store executive, divorced, hard-working, upward-bound in his organization. Savage plays his eleven-year-old son, who comes to stay for a few weeks while his mother is on vacation. At one point, while they are both touching an ancient gold-trimmed Tibetan skull, they are unwise enough to wish that they could be each other. Through a mysterious, magical process that need not concern us, Reinhold and Savage are suddenly consumed in a searing bolt of light, and their personalities are transferred. That puts a little boy into a man's body and, as the title suggests, vice versa.

The movie's plot situations are fairly predictable. The kid goes to the department store in his dad's body, plays with the drums in the musical instrument section, acts like a kid with his secretary, and behaves strangely at a board meeting. Meanwhile, his dad, in a kid's body, goes to school in a limousine, barks orders into the phone, finishes exams in three minutes, and talks back to the teachers. In a couple of the best scenes, the kid (as his dad) visits his grade school teacher, and gets even with the bullies who have been tormenting him. And the dad (as his son) tells his girlfriend things he lacked the courage to say when he was an adult.

All of this is fun and well-done, but it is simply plotting. What makes *Vice Versa* so wonderful is the way Reinhold and Savage are able to convince us that each body is inhabited by the other character. They are masters of body language. Notice, for example, the scene where Reinhold demolishes the fifth-grade bullies and then, when he thinks no one is watching him, swings his arm through the air in a joyous boilermaker. Look, too, at the restless and immature way he suggests that a child would inhabit an adult body; children haven't yet had their spirits broken to make them sit still all the time.

Savage, as the adult inside the kid, is equally good at moving with quiet confidence, even impatience, and ordering people around, and expecting to be obeyed. After he calls a limousine and it lets him out in front of the department store, he strides inside and a doorman asks the chauffeur, "Is he famous?" "He's about to be," the chauffeur says, "because I'm gonna kill him."

Vice Versa is a treasure of a movie, in which the performances hold the key. It's a movie that finds its humor in many small moments of truth and accurate observation, and if there is even a certain gentle knowledge of human nature in this film, you know what? That is not necessarily wrong for a comedy, not even in the cynical weathers that surround us.

Victor/Victoria ★ ★ ★

R, 133 m., 1982

Julie Andrews (Victor/Victoria), James Garner (King), Robert Preston (Toddy), Lesley Ann Warren (Norma), Alex Karras (Squash), John Rhys-Davis (Cassell). Directed by Blake Edwards and produced by Edwards and Tony Adams.

I've always felt this way about female impersonators: They may not be as pretty as women, or sing as well, or wear a dress as well, but you've got to hand it to them; they sure look great and sing pretty—for men. There are no doubt, of course, female impersonators who practice their art so skillfully that they cannot be told apart from real women—but that, of course, misses the point. A drag queen should be maybe 90 percent convincing as a woman, tops, so you can applaud while still knowing it's an act.

Insights like these are crucial to Blake Edwards's *Victor/Victoria,* in which Julie Andrews plays a woman playing a man playing a woman. It's a complicated challenge. If she just comes out as Julie Andrews, then of course she looks just like a woman, because she is one. So when she comes onstage as "Victoria," said to be "Victor" but really (we know) actually Victoria, she has to be an ever-so-slightly imperfect woman, to sell the premise that she's a man. Whether she succeeds is the source of a lot of comedy in this movie, which is a lighthearted meditation on how ridiculous we can sometimes become when we take sex too seriously.

The movie is made in the spirit of classic movie sex farces, and is in fact based on one (a 1933 German film named *Viktor und Viktoria,* which I haven't seen). Its more recent inspiration is probably *La Cage Aux Folles,* an enormous success that gave Hollywood courage to try this offbeat material. In the movie, Andrews is a starving singer, out of work, down to her last franc, when she meets a charming old fraud named Toddy, who is gay, and who is played by Robert Preston in the spirit of Ethel Mertz on "I Love Lucy." Preston is kind, friendly, plucky, and comes up with the most outrageous schemes to solve problems that wouldn't be half so complicated if he weren't on the case. In this case, he has a brainstorm: Since there's no market for girl singers, but a constant demand for female impersonators, why shouldn't Andrews assume a false identity and pretend to be a drag queen? "But they'll *know* I'm not a man!" she wails. "Of course!" Preston says triumphantly.

The plot thickens when James Garner, as a Chicago nightclub operator, wanders into Victor/Victoria's nightclub act and falls in love with him/her. Garner refuses to believe that lovely creature is a man. He's right, but if Andrews admits it, she's out of work. Meanwhile, Garner's blonde girlfriend (Lesley Ann Warren) is consumed by jealousy, and intrigue grows between Preston and Alex Karras, who plays Garner's bodyguard. Edwards develops this situation as farce, with lots of gags depending on split-second timing and characters being in the wrong hotel rooms at the right time. He also throws in several nightclub brawls, which aren't very funny, but which don't much matter. What makes the material work is not only the fact that it is funny (which it is), but that it's about likable people.

The three most difficult roles belong to Preston, Garner, and Karras, who must walk a tightrope of uncertain sexual identity without even appearing to condescend to their material. They never do. Because they all seem to be people first and genders second, they see the humor in their bewildering situation as quickly as anyone, and their cheerful ability to rise to a series of implausible occasions makes *Victor/Victoria* not only a funny movie, but, unexpectedly, a warm and friendly one.

Vision Quest ★ ★ ★ ½

R, 108 m., 1985

Matthew Modine (Louden Swain), Linda Fiorentino (Carla), Michael Schoeffling (Kuch), Ronny Cox (Louden's Dad), Harold Sylvester (Tanneran), Charles Hallahan (Coach), R.H. Thomson (Kevin), J.C. Quinn (Elmo), Frank Jasper (Shute). Directed by Harold Becker and produced by Jon Peters and Peter Guber. Screenplay by Darryl Poniscan.

We think we know the story pretty well already: Young wrestler has two dreams: (a) to win the state championship, and (b) to win the love of a girl. The defending state champion is a man-mountain who carries telephone poles to the top of stadiums. The girl is an independent drifter who is twenty years old and doesn't take the hero seriously. By the end of the movie, the only suspense is whether it will end with a victory in bed or in the ring. Although *Vision Quest* sticks pretty close to that outline, it is nevertheless a movie with some nice surprises, mostly because it takes the time to create some interesting characters. The movie's hero, Louden Swain, is probably the closest thing to a standard movie character, but Matthew Modine plays him with such an ingratiating freshness that he makes the character quirky and interesting, almost in spite of the script.

The other people in the movie are all real originals. They include Louden's father (Ronny Cox), who has lost the family farm and his wife, but still retains the respect of his son; Louden's best pal (Michael Schoeffling), who bills himself as a "half-Indian spiritual adviser"; a black history teacher (Harold Sylvester) who cares about Louden and listens to him; an alcoholic short-order cook (J.C. Quinn) who works in the kitchen of the hotel where Louden's a bellboy, and a wrestling coach (Charles Hallahan) who has mixed feelings about Louden's drive to get down to the 168-pound class so he can wrestle the toughest wrestler in the state. All of those characters are written, directed, and acted just a little differently than we might expect; they have small roles, but they don't think small thoughts.

And then there is the movie's most original creation, the twenty-year-old drifter, Carla (Linda Fiorentino). Without having met the actress, it's impossible for me to speculate on how much of Carla is original work and how much is Fiorentino's personality. What comes across, though, is a woman who is enigmatic without being egotistical, detached without being cold, self-reliant without being suspicious. She has a way of talking—kind of deliberately objective—that makes you listen to everything she says.

All of these people live in Spokane, which looks sort of wet and dark in many scenes, and feels like a place that prizes individuality. Instead of silhouetting the Modine character against the city and a lot of humble supporting roles, and turning him into a Rocky of wrestlers, the movie takes time to place the character in the city and in the lives of the other people. We begin to value his relationships, and it really means something when the short-order cook puts on a clean shirt and goes to the big wrestling meet.

The movie's plot doesn't really equal its characters. After the Rocky movies and *Breaking Away* and *The Karate Kid* and a dozen other movies with essentially the same last scene, it's hard to care about the outcome of the big fight, or race, or match, because, let's face it, we know the hero's going to win. Just once, why couldn't they give us characters as interesting as the ones in *Vision Quest*, in a movie where they'd be set free from the same tired old plot and allowed to live?

Visions of Eight ★ ★ ★

NO MPAA RATING, 110 m., 1973

Segments directed by Milos Forman, Arthur Penn, Kon Ichikawa, Claude Lelouch, John Schlesinger, Mai Zetterling, Juri Ozerov, and Michael Pfleghar. Produced by Stan Marguiles.

The idea sounded like a great one at the time: Eight important directors would be given their own budgets and camera crews and dispatched to Munich to record their personal visions of the 1972 Olympics. What nobody could have anticipated, perhaps, is how similar many of those visions would be. Too often during *Visions of Eight* the Olympic events are reduced to slow-motion ballets that finally just repeat themselves.

There is, I suppose, some interest in Kon Ichikawa's slow-motion replay of the 100-meter dash; the world's fastest men are slowed down to grotesque life-sized robots with pumping cheeks and contorted faces, and we get a feeling for the event's special agony. But the sequence is held too long; and so is Arthur Penn's segment on pole vaulting. We get jump after jump in slow motion, but all of that footage doesn't tell us as much about the vaulters as one single shot, near the end, where Penn shows us a competitor meticulously removing an invisible piece of lint from his hand grip.

There are other small touches that make the film worth seeing. In Claude Lelouch's segment on the losers, for example, there's an astonishing display of bad sportsmanship from a defeated boxer who refuses to leave the ring. For three or four minutes caught in a single take, he expresses his contempt for the decision and his outrage at the crowd (which generously boos him).

There's another kind of losing, too. In Mai Zetterling's segment, we see a massive weightlifter as he nervously circles the weights, and we can almost taste his apprehension. We've seen other competitors lift this bar (which takes five men to carry from the stage), and we know how heavy it is. So does he. He circles the stage, breathing deeply, trying to psych himself into the lift. He approaches the bar, grabs it, backs away. Circles some more. Just looking at him, we sense he can't lift it. He approaches the bar again, heaves, gets it a foot off the ground, then throws it back down again with disgust and walks off the stage. In a moment like that, we begin to understand something of the difficulties of the weightlifter.

The movie's still, beautiful center is occupied by the fawnlike Soviet gymnast Ludmilla Tourischeva. She's in Michael Pfleghar's segment on the women in the Olympics, and he shows us her entire routine on the uneven parallel bars. It is an exercise of grace made possible through superb athletic skill, and he wisely refuses to gimmick it up with cuts or slow motion. (Surely, as a general rule, the beauty of the Olympic events is that they take place in real time; slowing down Tourischeva's gymnastics would have missed the point.)

The most successful segment was directed by John Schlesinger, who considers the twenty-six-mile marathon race from the points of view of one of the British competitors. We see the runner in his home in the north of England, getting up every morning to run ten miles to and from work. Some days he runs home for lunch. On Saturdays he does a complete marathon course. We get a real feel for the loneliness of the long-distance runner as we see him running on dreary country roads during an overcast morning.

Then Schlesinger shows the runner at the Olympics, and in a stunning use of imagination, he gives us dream-like sequences designed to suggest what goes through the mind of the marathon runner: Memories of the long morning runs, thoughts of his family, wordless awareness of his surroundings. Schlesinger intercuts this footage with rather superficial coverage of the murdered Israelis.

His is the only segment to refer to the tragedy, and at first he doesn't really seem to have anything coherent to say. But then he pulls his images together in his last few minutes; as Avery Brundage is making his closing speech as if the whole Olympic pageantry hadn't already turned to ashes with the murders, a final dogged marathon runner, hours behind the rest, stubbornly runs into the stadium and crosses the finish line. That's it, Schlesinger seems to be saying: The dignity of this loser, still loyal to his sport, eclipses the electric scoreboards and the official blazers.

Vixen ★ ★ ★

x, 68 m., 1969

Erica Gavin (Vixen), Harrison Page (Niles), Garth Pillsbury (Tom), Michael O'Donnell (O'Banlon), Vincent Wallace (Janet), Robert Aiken (Dave), Jon Evans (Jud). Directed and produced by Russ Meyer. Screenplay by Robert Rudelson.

Some time ago it might have been necessary to devise all sorts of defenses for Russ Meyer's *Vixen*, finding hidden symbolism and all that. But I see no reason why we can't be honest: *Vixen* was the best film of its day in that uniquely American genre, the skin-flick.

It is also a celebration of zestful direction and photography, and a lot of the time it's very funny. In a field filled with cheap, dreary productions, Meyer is the best craftsman and the only artist. He has developed a directing style so open, direct, and good-humored that it dominates his material; what a relief it was to hear laughter during a skin-flick, instead of the dead silence that usually envelops their cheerless audiences.

Vixen is not only a good skin-flick, but a merciless put-on of the whole genre. As Terry Southern demonstrated with his novel *Candy*, you can't satirize pornography without writing it. The movie version of *Candy* failed because it lacked the courage to find itself ridiculous; how can a put-on take itself seriously? *Vixen*, on the other hand, catalogs the basic variations in skin-flick plots and ticks them off one after another.

It's done with such droll dialogue and high humor that even the most torrid scenes somehow manage to get outside themselves; instead of placing his hero and heroine in the shower and grinding away in the panting style of his imitators, Meyer takes the basic shower scene, writes it with hilariously malaprop dialogue ("We decided to stop doing this when we were twelve," Vixen's brother protests), and intercuts it with a scene outside in which a red-bearded Irish Communist makes a speech to a black draft dodger.

Meyer is also heavy on the redeeming social value department. His characters debate communism, Cuban Marxism, Vietnam, draft-dodging, civil rights, and airplane hijacking, deciding in favor of civil rights and against the others.

The story line is barely strong enough to hold the scenes together; it involves a bush pilot and his wife (Vixen, portrayed admirably by Erica Gavin) who take another couple on a fishing weekend in Canada. Also present are Vixen's brother and his black friend, a draft evader protesting what he believes is a racist war. The Irish Marxist wanders in later from somewhere. There is also a Royal Canadian Mounted Policeman who wanders off somewhere.

At the time the movie was released, "redeeming social value" was a key line of defense against charges that a movie was pornographic. Meyer's inspiration was to put all of the redeeming speeches at the end. "The audience will know," he once said, "that when the characters get on the airplane, the good parts are over." Sound advice.

W

Walkabout ★ ★ ★ ★
PG, 95 m., 1971

Jenny Agutter (The Girl), Lucien John (Brother), David Gumpilil (Aborigine), John Mellon (Father). Directed by Nicholas Roeg and produced by Si Litvinoff. Screenplay by Edward Bond.

It is possible to consider *Walkabout* entirely as the story it seems to be: The story of a fourteen-year-old girl and her little brother, who are abandoned in the Australian outback and then saved through the natural skills of a young aborigine boy. It is simpler and easier to consider it on that level, too, because *Walkabout* is a superb work of storytelling and its material is effortlessly fascinating. There's also a tendency (unfortunate, probably) to read *Walkabout* as a catch-all of symbols and metaphors, in which the Noble Savage and his natural life are tested and found superior to civilization and cities. The movie does, indeed, make this comparison several times. Hundreds of miles from help, the girl turns on her portable radio to hear a philosopher observe: "It is now possible to state that 'that is' is." Well, this isn't exactly helpful, and so we laugh. And more adolescent viewers may have to stifle a sigh and a tear when the girl is seen, at the movie's end, married to a cloddish office clerk and nostalgically remembering her idyllic days in the desert.

The contrast between civilization and man's more natural states is well-drawn in the movie, and will interest serious-minded younger people (just as, at the level of pure story, *Walkabout* will probably fascinate kids). But I don't think it's fruitful to draw all the parallels and then piously conclude that we would all be better off far from the city, sipping water from the ground, and spearing kangaroos for lunch. That sort of comparison doesn't really get you anywhere and leaves you with a movie that doesn't tell you more than you already knew. I think there's more than that to *Walkabout.* And I'm going to have a hard time expressing that additional dimension for you, because it doesn't quite exist in the universe of words. Even in these days of film experiments, most movies have their centers in the worlds of plots and characters. But *Walkabout* . . .

Well, to begin with, the film was directed and photographed by Nicholas Roeg, the cinematographer of *Petulia* and many other British films. Roeg's first stab at direction was as co-director of *Performance.* This was his first work as an individual. I persisted in seeing *Performance* on the level of its perfectly silly plot, and on that level it was a wretched movie indeed. People told me I should forget the plot and simply enjoy the movie itself, but I have a built-in resistance to that notion, usually. Perhaps I should have listened. Because Roeg's *Walkabout* is a very rare example of that kind of movie, in which the "civilized" characters and the aborigine exist in a wilderness that isn't really a wilderness but more of an indefinite place for the story to be told. Roeg's desert in *Walkabout* is like Beckett's stage for *Waiting for Godot.* That is, it's nowhere in particular, and everywhere.

Roeg's photography reinforces this notion. He is careful to keep us at a distance from the physical sufferings of his characters. To be sure, they have blisters and parched lips, but he pulls up well short of the usual clichés of suffering in the desert. And his cinematography (and John Barry's otherworldly music) make the desert seem a mystical place, a place for visions. So that the whole film becomes mystical, a dream, and the suicides which frame it set the boundaries of reality. Within them, what happens between the boy and the girl, and the boy and the little brother, is not merely "communication" or "survival" or "cooperation," but the same kind of life-enhancement that you imagine people feel when they go into the woods and eat berries and bring the full focus of their intelligence to bear on the problem of co-existing with nature.

Wall Street ★ ★ ★ ½

R, 125 m., 1987

Charlie Sheen (Bud Fox), Michael Douglas (Gordon Gekko), Daryl Hannah (Darien Taylor), Martin Sheen (Carl Fox), Terence Stamp (Sir Larry), Hal Holbrook (Lou Mannheim), Sean Young (Kate Gekko), James Spader (Roger Barnes), Saul Rubinek (Harold Salt), Sylvia Miles (Realtor). Directed by Oliver Stone and produced by Edward R. Pressman. Screenplay by Stanley Weiser and Stone.

How much is enough? the kid keeps asking the millionaire stock trader. How much money do you want? How much would you be satisfied with? The trader seems to be thinking hard, but the answer is, he just doesn't know. He's not even sure how to think about the question. He spends all day trying to make as much money as he possibly can, and he cheerfully bends and breaks the law to make even more millions, but somehow the concept of "enough" eludes him. Like all gamblers, he is perhaps not even really interested in money, but in the action. Money is just the way to keep score.

The millionaire is a predator, a corporate raider, a Wall Street shark. His name is Gordon Gekko, the name no doubt inspired by the lizard that feeds on insects and sheds its tail when trapped. Played by Michael Douglas in Oliver Stone's *Wall Street,* he paces relentlessly behind the desk in his skyscraper office, lighting cigarettes, stabbing them out, checking stock prices on a bank of computers, barking buy and sell orders into a speaker phone. In his personal life, he has everything he could possibly want—wife, family, estate, pool, limousine, priceless art objects—and they are all just additional entries on the scoreboard. He likes to win.

The kid is a broker for a big Wall Street firm. He works the phones, soliciting new clients, offering second-hand advice, buying and selling and dreaming. "Just once I'd like to be on *that* side," he says, fiercely looking at the telephone a client has just used to stick him with a $7,000 loss. Gekko is his hero. He wants to sell him stock, get into his circle, be like he is. Every day for thirty-nine days, he calls Gekko's office for an appointment. On the fortieth day, Gekko's birthday, he appears with a box of Havana cigars from Davidoff's in London, and Gekko grants him an audience.

Maybe Gekko sees something he recognizes. The kid, named Bud Fox (Charlie Sheen), comes from a working-class family. His father (Martin Sheen) is an aircraft mechanic and union leader. Gekko went to a cheap university himself. Desperate to impress Gekko, young Fox passes along some inside information he got from his father. Gekko makes some money on the deal and opens an account with Fox. He also asks him to obtain more insider information, and to spy on a competitor. Fox protests that he is being asked to do something illegal. Perhaps "protests" is too strong a word—he "observes."

Gekko knows his man. Fox is so hungry to make a killing, he will do anything. Gekko promises him perks—*big* perks—and they arrive on schedule. One of them is a tall blonde interior designer (Daryl Hannah), who decorates Fox's expensive new high-rise apartment. The movie's stylistic approach is rigorous: We are never allowed to luxuriate in the splendor of these new surroundings. The apartment is never quite seen, never relaxed in. When the girl comes to share Fox's bed, they are seen momentarily, in silhouette. Sex and possessions are secondary to trading, to the action. Ask any gambler.

Stone's *Wall Street* is a radical critique of the capitalist trading mentality, and it obviously comes at a time when the financial community is especially vulnerable. The movie argues that most small investors are dupes, and that the big market killings are made by men like Gekko, who swoop in and snap whole companies out from under the noses of their stockholders. What the Gekkos do is immoral and illegal, but they use a little litany to excuse themselves: "Nobody gets hurt." "Everybody's doing it." "There's something in this deal for everybody." "Who knows except us?"

The movie has a traditional plot structure: The hungry kid is impressed by the successful older man, seduced by him, betrayed by him, and then tries to turn the tables. The actual details of the plot are not so important as the changes we see in the characters. Few men in recent movies have been colder and more ruthless than Gekko, or more convincing. Charlie Sheen is, by comparison, a babe in the woods; I would have preferred a young actor who seemed more rapacious, like James Spader, who has a supporting role in the movie. If the film has a flaw, it is that Sheen never seems quite relentless enough to move in Gekko's circle.

Stone's most impressive achievement in this film is to allow all the financial wheeling and dealing to seem complicated and convincing, and yet always have it make sense. The movie can be followed by anybody, because the details of stock manipulation are all filtered through transparent layers of greed. Most of the time we know what's going on. All of the time, we know why.

Although Gekko's law-breaking would of course be opposed by most people on Wall Street, his larger value system would be applauded. The trick is to make his kind of money without breaking the law. Financiers who can do that, like Donald Trump, are mentioned as possible presidential candidates, and in his autobiography Trump states, quite simply, that money no longer interests him very much. He is more motivated by the challenge of a deal, and by the desire to win. His frankness is refreshing, but the key to reading that statement is to see that it considers only money, on the one hand, and winning, on the other. No mention is made about creating goods and services, or manufacturing things, or investing in a physical plant, or contributing to the infrastructure.

What's intriguing about *Wall Street*—what may cause the most discussion—is that the movie's real target isn't Wall Street criminals who break the law. Stone's target is the value system that places profits and wealth and the Deal above any other consideration. His film is an attack on an atmosphere of financial competitiveness so ferocious that ethics are simply irrelevant, and the laws are sort of like the referee in pro wrestling, part of the show.

WarGames ★ ★ ★ ★

PG, 110 m., 1983

Matthew Broderick (David), Dabney Coleman (McKittrick), John Wood (Falken), Ally Sheedy (Jennifer), Barry Corbin (General Beringer). Directed by John Badham and produced by Harold Schneider. Screenplay by Lawrence Lasker and Walter F. Parkes.

Sooner or later, a self-satisfied, sublimely confident computer is going to blow us all off the face of the planet. That is the message of *WarGames*, a scary and intelligent thriller that is one of the best films of 1983. The movie stars Matthew Broderick as a bright high school senior who spends a lot of time locked in his bedroom with his home computer. He speaks computerese well enough to dial by telephone into the computer at his school and change grades. But he's ready for bigger game. He reads about a toy company that's introducing a new computer game. He programs his computer for a random search of telephone numbers in the company's area code, looking for a number that answers with a computer tone. Eventually, he connects with a computer. Unfortunately, the computer he connects with does not belong to a toy company. It belongs to the Defense Department, and its mission is to coordinate early warning systems and nuclear deterrents in the case of World War III. The kid challenges the computer to play a game called "Global Thermonuclear Warfare," and it cheerfully agrees.

As a premise for a thriller, this is a masterstroke. The movie, however, could easily go wrong by bogging us down in impenetrable computerese, or by ignoring the technical details altogether and giving us a *Fail Safe* retread. *WarGames* makes neither mistake. It convinces us that it knows computers, and it makes its knowledge into an amazingly entertaining thriller. (Note: I do not claim the movie is *accurate* about computers—only convincing.) I've described only the opening gambits of the plot, and I will reveal no more. It's too much fun watching the story unwind. Another one of the pleasures of the movie is the way it takes cardboard characters and fleshes them out. Two in particular: the civilian chief of the U.S. computer operation, played by Dabney Coleman as a man who has his own little weakness for simple logic, and the Air Force general in charge of the war room, played by Barry Corbin as a military man who argues that men, not computers, should make the final nuclear decisions.

WarGames was directed by John Badham, best known for *Saturday Night Fever* and *Blue Thunder*, a thriller that I found considerably less convincing on the technical level. There's not a scene here where Badham doesn't seem to know what he's doing, weaving a complex web of computerese, personalities, and puzzles; the movie absorbs us on emotional and intellectual levels at the same time. And the ending, a moment of blinding and yet utterly elementary insight, is wonderful.

The Weavers: Wasn't That a Time!

★ ★ ★ ★

PG, 78 m., 1982

Featuring Lee Hays, Ronnie Gilbert, Fred Hellerman, and Pete Seeger. Directed by Jim Brown and produced by Brown, George Stoney, and Harold Leventhal.

Here is one of the most joyous musical documentaries in a long time, a celebration of the music and the singers that made up the Weavers. There are, I suppose, a lot of people who don't know who the Weavers were, but for a time in the fifties they were the top pop quartet in America, and for twenty years their recordings were a key influence on modern American folk music.

The owners of old Weavers record albums treasure them. I have four or five, and when things get depressing and the sky turns overcast and grim, I like to play one of them. There's just something magical about the joy with which the Weavers sing "Goodnight, Irene" or "Kisses Sweeter than Wine" or "The Sloop John B." or "This Land is Your Land."

The Weavers reached their popular peak in the fifties, with a string of Top Ten hits, which also included "On Top of Old Smokey," "Tzena, Tzena," and "If I Had a Hammer" (which was written by the Weavers, and not, as many people believe, by Bob Dylan). The height of their popularity unfortunately coincided with the height of McCarthyism, and the Weavers, all of them longtime left-wing activists, were blacklisted. They couldn't get jobs on television or in nightclubs, and their records were banned.

For several years in the late fifties, the group existed primarily on records. And the artists went their separate ways: Ronnie Gilbert into theater, Fred Hellerman into San Franciso-area media projects, Pete Seeger into a successful solo concert career, and Lee Hays into semi-retirement on his New England farm.

There were many calls for a Weavers reunion (in some circles, an event more fervently desired than the Beatles reunion). And in May of 1980, Lee Hays himself convened such a reunion, inviting the other Weavers and their families and friends to a picnic on his farm. As they sat around and sang and played, the idea of a public reunion began to take shape, and on November 28 and 29 of 1980, they held one last historic concert at Carnegie Hall.

The Weavers: Wasn't That a Time! is not simply a concert film, however, but a documentary about the Weavers. The director, Jim Brown, was a neighbor of Hays, and grew to admire the old man who kept on singing after his legs were amputated for diabetes and his heart needed a pacemaker.

Brown's film begins with the picnic at Hays's farm, flashes back to newsreel and archive footage of the Weavers in their prime, and then concludes with the concert in Carnegie Hall. It is impossible not to feel a lump in your throat as the Weavers gather once again on stage, and it's hard not to tap your feet when they start to sing.

Seeing this film is a wonderful experience. I'd recommend it wholeheartedly to those who don't know about the Weavers. I imagine that Weavers fans won't need any encouragement.

A Wedding ★ ★ ★ ½

PG, 125 m., 1978

Desi Arnaz, Jr. (Dino Corelli), Carol Burnett (Tulip Brenner), Geraldine Chaplin (Rita Billingsley), Howard Duff (Dr. Meecham), Mia Farrow (Buffy Brenner), Vittorio Gassman (Luigi Corelli), Lillian Gish (Nettie Sloan), Lauren Hutton (Photographer), Viveca Lindfors (Ingrid Hellstrom), Pat McCormick (MacKenzie Goddard), Dina Merrill (Antoinette Goddard), Nina Van Pallandt (Regina Corelli). Directed and produced by Robert Altman. Screenplay by John Considine, Patricia Resnick, Allan Nicholls, and Altman.

The two families in Robert Altman's *A Wedding* live right there in the closets with their skeletons. They present a cheerful facade to the outer world, of old Lake Forest money on the one hand and new Southern money on the other. But just beneath the surface there are jealousies and greeds and hates, and the random dirty tricks of fate.

Altman plunges gleefully into this wealth of material; there are forty-eight characters in his movie, give or take a few, and by the film's end we know them all. We may not know them *well*—at weddings there are always unidentified cousins over in the corner—but we can place them, and chart the lines of power and passion that run among them. And some of them are drawn as well as Altman has drawn anyone.

That's because *A Wedding* is a lot deeper and more ambitious than we might at first expect. It begins in comedy, it moves into realms of social observation, it descends into personal revelations that are sometimes tragic, sometimes comic . . . and then it ends in a way that turns everything back upon itself. The more you think about what Altman's done, the more impressive his accomplishment becomes.

A Wedding aims to upset our expectations. It takes our society's most fertile source of cliches and stereotypes—a society wedding—and then chisels away at it with maniacal and sometimes savage satire. Nobody gets away: not the bride and groom, so seemingly "ideal;" not the loving parents on either side; not the relatives, with their little dramas that are no doubt played out on every family occasion, and not even the staff of wedding coordinators, chefs, photographers, musicians, and other accomplices.

Altman begins in solemnity and ceremony, with the high Episcopalian wedding. Desi Arnaz, Jr., and Amy Stryker, as the wedding couple, are all but lost in the chaos: The bishop fumbles his lines, a camera crew maneuvers awkwardly behind the palms and, meanwhile, back at the mansion, the groom's grandmother (Lillian Gish) drops dead of anticipated mortification.

Her death is concealed when the wedding party returns to the mansion: Concealed from the family and from the single guest who turns up for the magnificently catered affair. Altman introduces us almost effortlessly to the house jammed with people; his compositions allow characters to be established in the backgrounds while the plot is being pushed ahead in the foreground, so it's as if we're wandering around the house like everyone else.

There are any number of subplots. The parents of the groom are Nina Van Pallandt, whose drug habit is ministered to by the family doctor, and Vittorio Gassman, an Italian who seems to have sinister associations in his past. The bride's parents are Carol Burnett, all sweetness and convention until—gasp!—she's wooed by one of the guests, and Paul Dooley, vulgar, hard-drinking, with a tad too much affection for his youngest daughter (Mia Farrow).

Farrow, it develops, is pregnant—by her sister's new husband, perhaps, or (it develops) by any other member of his class at military school. Other characters reveal themselves as drunks, unreconstructed Communists, secret weepers, fountains of jealousy, reservoirs of lust, or advocates of diverse sexual proclivities.

This is the sort of material that easily lends itself to farce, and, when it does, Altman cheerfully follows. But he leads in other directions, as well. He moves so slyly from one note to another that when Pat McCormick attempts a clumsy seduction of Carol Burnett, we're moved simultaneously by comedy and pathos. And there are scenes of extraordinary emotional complexity, as when a singalong is organized in the basement dining room, or when Nina Van Pallandt tearfully and defiantly reviews the terms under which she's lived her marriage.

Like Altman's other movies with lots of characters (*M*A*S*H, McCabe and Mrs. Miller,* the incomparable *Nashville*), *A Wedding* doesn't fit easily into established feature film categories. For some viewers, it won't satisfy; it doesn't set up situations and then resolve them in standard ways. It's got all the disorganization and contradictions of life—and then Altman almost mystically gives everything a deeper meaning by the catastrophic surprise he springs on us near the end.

Weeds ★ ★ ★

R, 115 m., 1987

Nick Nolte (Lee Umstetter), Lane Smith (Claude), William Forsythe (Burt), John Toles-Bey (Navarro), Joe Mantegna (Carmine), Ernie Hudson (Bagdad), Mark Rolston (Dave), J.J. Johnson (Lazarus), Rita Taggart (Lillian). Directed by John Hancock and produced by Bill Badalato. Screenplay by Dorothy Tristan and Hancock.

Weeds tells a story as old as the movies—the rags-to-riches saga of a troupe of theatrical amateurs who bring their show to Broadway—but it tells it with such a distinctive style, such a curious mixture of pathos and offhand wit, that it works for one more time. There's never a moment when there's much doubt about the outcome, but the movie gets there by a series of small delights and surprises.

The movie opens with the hero trying to kill himself in prison. He throws himself over a railing, but breaks only his arms. Then he tries to hang himself. No luck. He's in for life, with no possibility of parole, and so in desperation he does something that's even harder for him than suicide: He checks a book out of the prison library.

The prisoner's name is Lee Umstetter, played by Nick Nolte with a certain weathered weariness and a way of hanging his head to one side and walking crooked. He's a lifer with a broken spirit, until the books put ideas in his head and he writes a play in prison. He decides to produce it, and the auditions provide a scene that's a small masterpiece, as one convict sings "The Impossible Dream" and another one recites "Eeny Meeny Miney Moe," which is the only poem he knows, and not a good one for prison recitals.

The play is a success, and a warmhearted middle-aged drama critic (Rita Taggart) falls in love with Nolte and tries to convince the governor to commute his sentence. The rest of the movie involves Nolte's attempts to round up his old prison friends, reassemble the troupe on the outside, and take the show on the road. First stop, San Francisco. Then Iowa, Illinois, and Broadway. The opening night off-Broadway supplies an example of how the movie finds surprises in familiar themes. We see a famed drama critic, drenched by a rainstorm, arriving late and trying to compose himself for the opening curtain. Will he be able to be objective? The movie gets such a big laugh with his arrival that we hardly care. The opening night party at Sardi's has more surprises, and the scene is stolen by Anne Ramsey, as Nolte's ramshackle but lovable mother. And there's another great moment, done with body language and a perfect double-take, when Nolte is so overjoyed he tries to kiss Ernie Hudson, one of his fellow actors, on the lips.

The troupe develops into a tight-knit band, played by Nolte, Hudson, Lane Smith, William Forsythe, John Toles-Bey, Mark Rolston, and J.J. Johnson, with Joe Mantegna as a professional New York actor who joins them midstream and seems baffled by what kind of situation he's walked into. There is a real sense of community in their little group, which communicates itself even if the play they are performing does not. It's usually the case with plays-within-movies that the plays seem less than convincing, although in this movie there's a reason for that.

Unfortunately, the whole prison sequence at the end of the film is also less than convincing, and so are the recycled '60s leftist panaceas that pass, in that sequence, as electrifying truth-telling. It's all a little too pat. *Weeds* is a movie that is best when it observes small moments of human truth, and at its worst when it tries to inflate them into large moments.

A Week's Vacation ★ ★ ★ ½

NO MPAA RATING, 102 m., 1980

Nathalie Baye (Laurence Cuers), Gerard Lanvin (Pierre). Directed by Bertrand Tavernier. Screenplay by Tavernier, Colo Tavernier, and Marie-Francoise Hans.

It's nothing special, just an overcast day in Lyons when everybody's going to work just as usual. A car pulls out of the stream of traffic, and a young woman gets out. Her name is Laurence, she is a schoolteacher, and this day she does not feel like teaching school. It is more than that: She cannot. There is no particular crisis. A great tragedy has not descended on her life. In fact, things are going fairly well. She is thirty-one years old, she lives with her boyfriend, she has been teaching at the same school for ten years. It is simply that large and inarticulate emotions are welling up inside her, and she is desperately unhappy. She goes to see her doctor, and he prescribes a week's vacation.

A Week's Vacation is as simple, and as complicated, as that. It was directed by Bertrand Tavernier, the gifted French filmmaker who has made his hometown of Lyons the locale for some of his best work, including *The Clockmaker* (1974). That movie was based on a novel by Georges Simenon, and *A Week's Vacation* could well have been; it has the same matter-of-fact fascination with the great depths and unexpected secrets in the lives of people who outwardly seem ordinary. *A Week's Vacation* follows the schoolteacher, played by Nathalie Baye, as she spends her week of freedom wandering without a plan through her city, her past, and her sexuality. She meets a friendly café owner and talks to him. She goes out to the country to visit her father, who is so old he has surely discovered the answer to the puzzle of life, but it has made him speechless. Returning to the city, she has an embarrassing encounter. The café owner, mistaking her friendliness for sexual interest, tries to kiss her. She was not thinking along those lines. As they both try to free themselves from the awkward situation, as he damns himself for being such a fool, there comes a turning point in her week's vacation: It seems to me that this foolish encounter, this mundane sexual pass based on mistaken assumptions, is the catalyst she needs to get back into life again.

What is best about Tavernier is his feeling for the ordinary currents of everyday life. He creates such empathy between his audiences and his characters that when they fall into a reverie, we have no difficulty imagining their thoughts. In *A Week's Vacation*, he has taken the occasional feeling we all have that we just can't go on any longer, not because of sadness or illness or tragedy, but simply because we have forgotten why we set out in the first place on this journey of life. And he has shown us the answer. The key is in that funny, embarrassing, fumbling little attempt at a kiss: We keep on plugging away because we never know when someone might decide to kiss us, and, better still, because it's so interesting to see how we'll react.

Weird Science ★ ★ ★ 1/2

PG-13, 94 m., 1985

Anthony Michael Hall (Gary), Kelly LeBrock (Lisa), Ilan Mitchell-Smith (Wyatt), Bill Paxton (Chet), Suzanne Snyder (Deb), Judie Aronson (Hilly). Directed by John Hughes and produced by Joel Silver. Screenplay by Hughes.

Weird Science combines two great traditions in popular entertainment: Inflamed male teen-age fantasies and Frankenstein's monster. Then it crosses them with a new myth, of the teen-age computer geniuses who lock themselves in their bedrooms, hunch over their computer keyboards, and write programs that can change the universe.

In the movie's opening scenes, a couple of bright kids write a program with their specifications for a perfect woman. They feed in centerfolds and magazine covers, measurements and parameters. Then, for additional brain power, they tap into a giant government computer. And at exactly that instant, lightning strikes (just as it did in *The Bride of Frankenstein*), and out of the mix of bytes and kilowatts steps . . . a perfect woman.

She is played by Kelly LeBrock in the movie, and she has full, sensuous lips, and a throaty English accent, and a lot of style. She is a little more than the kids had bargained on. For one thing, she isn't an idealized Playmate, all staples and no brains, but an intelligent, sensitive woman who sees right through these teen-age boys and tries to do them some good.

That's why *Weird Science* is funnier, and a little deeper, than the predictable story it might have been. The movie is the third success in a row for John Hughes, a director who specializes in films about how teenagers really talk and think. His two earlier films were *Sixteen Candles* and *The Breakfast Club*, and they both featured a young actor named Anthony Michael Hall, who is the costar of *Weird Science*.

Hall was the geek in *Sixteen Candles* and the intellectual in *Breakfast Club*, and I like John Hughes's definition of a geek: "A geek is a guy who has everything going for him, but he's just too young. By contrast, a nerd will be a nerd all of his life." Hall talks fast, with a sprung rhythm that lets you feel you can hear him thinking. He has the ordinary lusts of a teen-age boy, but once he invents this perfect woman, he is quick to catch on to the advantages: For example, your status in high school is sure to change dramatically if a gorgeous model thinks you're the max.

Hughes's earlier teen-age films depended mostly on character and dialogue (which was fine). This one has a lot of special effects, including some reverse photography that plays tricks with time. But the center of the film is the simple, almost elementary insight that fantasies can be hazardous: You've got to be careful what you ask for, because you might get it. Kelly LeBrock is wonderful as the fantasy woman, because she plays the character, not for sex, but for warmth and an almost motherly affection for these two kids. "All you have to do is command me," she says at one point. "You created me. You are my master." It could be soft porn, but the way she says it, her voice has a wink.

Wetherby ★ ★ ★ ★
R, 118 m., 1985

Vanessa Redgrave (Jean Travers), Ian Holm (Stanley Pilborough), Judi Dench (Marcia Pilborough), Marjorie Yates (Verity Braithwaite), Tim McInnerny (John Morgan), Suzanna Hamilton (Karen Creasy), Joely Richardson (Young Jean). Directed by David Hare and produced by Simon Relph. Screenplay by Hare.

A man kills himself among strangers. They never knew who he was, and they do not know why he chose to die. A man dying among strangers is like a tree falling unobserved in the forest. Death, especially suicide, requires resonance from those who knew the living person before it can be assigned its proper meaning. That is why *Wetherby* is such a haunting film, because it dares to suggest that the death of the stranger is important to everyone it touches—because it forces them to decide how alive they really are.

The movie begins with a woman who is living a sort of dead life. Her name is Jean Travers (played by Vanessa Redgrave); she was once in love with a young man who went off to fight the war and was killed. He was not killed gloriously, but stupidly, while getting involved in someone else's drunken quarrel, but he was dead all the same. As the movie opens, Jean has been teaching school in the small town of Wetherby, where her life is on hold. She doesn't walk around in a state of depression, she does have friends, she is a good teacher, but she is not engaged in life because she put all of her passion into the boy who died so many years ago.

One night she throws a small dinner party. Everyone drinks wine and sits around late, talking. One of the men at the table, John Morgan, sits mute all evening and finally makes a short speech about pain and love and honesty that sounds as if every word were written with his own bitter tears. The next day, John Morgan comes back to Jean's house, sits down for a cup of tea, and kills himself. A funny thing comes out in the investigation: John Morgan was not known to any of the people at the dinner party. Apparently he invited himself.

The film moves from this beginning into an examination of the people who were touched by the death. In addition to Jean, there are the Pilboroughs (Ian Holm and Judi Dench), the local constable (Tom Wilkinson), and a young woman (Suzanna Hamilton) who knew the dead man. Some small suspense develops for a while when it appears that Jean spent some time upstairs with John Morgan during the evening of her party—but that, and many other things, seem to be dead ends.

The movie flashes back into events in Jean's youth, and she is played as a young girl by Joely Richardson, Redgrave's daughter. There is an innocence and tenderness in those early scenes, as young Jean and her boyfriend kiss and neck and make promises, and as Jean gradually realizes that she is looking forward to marriage but he is much more excited by the prospect of putting on a uniform and going overseas. He goes overseas, and in some ways this movie is about the fact that Jean has become a middle-aged woman still waiting for him to come back.

Wetherby was written and directed by David Hare, who also wrote the film *Plenty.* Both films are about women who were never able to fully live their lives after what happened to them during the War. I admire both films, but I found *Wetherby* more moving, because the heroine of *Plenty* was essentially a disturbed woman using her war memories as a crutch, and Jean Travers is a whole and healthy woman who only needs to give herself the permission to live. I left the movie thinking that was the lesson she learned from John Morgan. Hoping so, anyway.

The Whales of August ★ ★ ★

NO MPAA RATING, 90 m., 1987

Bette Davis (Libby Strong), Lillian Gish (Sarah Webber), Vincent Price (Mr. Maranov), Ann Sothern (Tisha Doughty), Harry Carey, Jr. (Joshua), Frank Grimes (Mr. Beckwith), Mary Steenburgen (Young Sarah). Directed by Lindsay Anderson and produced by Carolyn Pfeiffer and Mike Kaplan. Screenplay by David Berry.

The two old women have been at war for years, until they have become beloved enemies. Now death is near for both of them—not today or tomorrow or perhaps even this year, but before long. For decades, since they were children, they have returned to this old cottage on an island off the coast of Maine, where in August it has been their custom to watch at twilight as the whales pass on their journeys to wherever it is that whales go. Although they make plans for the future and argue over whether they should install a new picture window, there is the sense that this will be their last summer in the cottage.

That is the story. As stories go, it is conventional enough, but in *The Whales of August,* as in grand opera, the story is only the occasion for the performances. This film stars Lillian Gish and Bette Davis, and to cast those two actresses as the leads of the same movie is to make their very presences more important than anything else. This is not their fault, nor do they use it as the occasion for self-conscious acting, for any inappropriate drawing of attention to themselves. It is just a fact.

Lillian Gish, who was born in 1896, was the star of D.W. Griffith's *The Birth of a Nation* (1915), the first great narrative film. She appeared in some 150 movies before and since. Bette Davis, who was born in 1908, was one of the great movie queens of Hollywood's golden age. Together they make this movie into the kind of project that filmmakers dream about but are rarely about to arrange. They are supported in the film by two other actors who bring a lot of memories onscreen with them: Vincent Price and Ann Sothern.

The film mostly takes place during the course of one day, which ends in a birthday dinner party and a good deal of truth. It begins with Gish and Davis gingerly talking around many of the issues that have divided them for years—and some of the issues, we feel, are not nearly so important to them as the simple satisfaction of being right, of prevailing in a personality struggle that has continued since childhood. Gish is the older sister, but in slightly better health. Davis, whose character is blind, has the blind person's love of order and continuity, as a way of finding her way around not only a familiar house but a familiar life.

Nothing of great moment happens during the day, but many small moments occur. One of them, the most touching, is Gish's quiet "private time" with the memory of her late husband. She speaks to him in a monologue that is not only moving but surprisingly passionate. Another special moment occurs when the two sisters walk out on the lawn to look for the whales, which only Gish can see. And I liked the subtle verbal gamesmanship that was the real subject of most of their conversations.

Many of the crucial moments in the movie play mostly in closeup, and I could not help meditating on these famous faces as I watched them. At her great age, Gish still sometimes looks girlish, capable of teasing and practical jokes, but the moment when she lets her hair down in front of the portrait of her dead husband is a revelation, because it contains a genuine erotic content, a sense of memory of her character's romance with this man. Davis contains surprises, too. In so many of the roles in the third act of her career, her face was a painted mask of makeup—not out of vanity, but because she was often cast as a painted madwoman or harpy. Here, devoid of much makeup, her features emerge with strength and a kind of peace that is no longer denying age. Both women, in other words, are beautiful.

Against such competition, supporting actors have their work cut out. Ann Sothern is sensible and cheery as a neighbor woman, who has shared the lives of these sisters for many years and accepts them. She is sort of a peacemaker, whose life lacks the complexity that the sisters' long struggle has created. The other major character in the film is the old aristocrat, down on his luck, played by

Vincent Price with a self-deprecating humor that creates dignity out of thin air. Mr. Maranov, his character, was once a "real" member of European nobility, but now has no money and no prospects, and depends on the kindness of strangers. His previous sponsor has died, and now he is searching for someone else to support him. He knows this, and everyone else knows it, and yet he still retains a certain nobility, even as a beggar. It is an interesting character.

The movie was directed by Lindsay Anderson, whose previous films have been nothing at all like this one, to put it mildly. After *This Sporting Life*, *If*, *O Lucky Man*, and *Britannia Hospital*, here is a quiet film of a conventional story, a star vehicle designed to show everyone to advantage. This is not one of Anderson's great films, but he succeeds at the assignment he has set himself. There is a story that during the filming of *The Whales of August*, Anderson told Miss Gish one day that she had just performed wonderfully in a closeup. "She should," Miss Davis declared. "She invented them."

Where the Buffalo Roam ★ ★
R, 98 m., 1980

Peter Boyle (Lazlo), Bill Murray (Hunter S. Thompson), Bruno Kirby (Marty Lewis), Rene Auberjonois (Harris of the Post), R.G. Armstrong (Judge Simpson), Danny Goldman (Porter). Directed and produced by Art Linson. Screenplay by John Kaye.

Dr. Hunter S. Thompson is the high priest of Gonzo journalism, a reporting style in which the reporter throws himself wildly into the event he is reporting, so that in a way he becomes the event. Karl Lazlo (not his real name) was a Mexican-American attorney Thompson met in the late 1960s and immortalized in *Fear and Loathing in Las Vegas*, a book in which, "speaking as your attorney," Lazlo regularly advised his client to ingest large quantities of booze, drugs, and pills. The purpose: to ward off paranoia and insanity as the two engaged on a drunken odyssey through the craziness of the Vegas Strip.

The Vegas book was followed by *Fear and Loathing on the Campaign Trail*, in which Thompson terrorized the 1972 presidential campaign as a correspondent for *Rolling Stone*. His mere presence was enough to cause terror in the hearts of advance men. The last appearance—or rather disappearance—of Lazlo in Thompson's writing is in "The Banshee Screams for Buffalo Meat," a 1976 *Rolling Stone* article in which the doctor speculates that his attorney has disappeared for good and been murdered.

Where the Buffalo Roam is a comedy inspired by the relationship between Thompson (Bill Murray) and Lazlo (Peter Boyle). The credits say it's "based on the twisted legend of Dr. Hunter S. Thompson." The doctor has become an American folk legend not only through his increasingly infrequent and incoherent *Rolling Stone* articles, but also through his frequent walk-ons (as Duke) in the comic strip Doonesbury. We know his uniform: eyeshade, cigarette holder, garish Hawaiian shirt, Bermuda shorts, bottle of Wild Turkey or similar beverage.

In Doonesbury, the character fights crisis with paranoia. In real life, Thompson has proven no more immune to the effects of alcohol and drug addiction than anybody else, and lives in isolation in his cabin in Woody Creek, Colorado, where he has written almost nothing worth reading since his original brilliant books. He seems to be spending these latter days of his fame having almost as much fun as Brendan Behan did.

But *Where the Buffalo Roam* is a celebration of the self-created public legend of Hunter Thompson, with no insights or hints into the dark night of his soul. That's a legitimate approach, and there are times during the movie when it works: There are really funny moments here, as when we learn that Thompson's dog has been trained to go berserk at the mention of the name Nixon, or when Thompson covers the Super Bowl by staging a football game in his hotel suite, or when he pulls a gun on a telephone, or turns a hospital room into an orgy, or attempts to impersonate a correspondent from the *Washington Post.* An amazing number of these scenes are inspired by real life—although it was Senator George McGovern, not Richard Nixon, who found himself being interviewed by Thompson while standing at a urinal.

We laugh at a lot of these moments; this is the kind of bad movie that's almost worth seeing. But there are large things wrong with *Where the Buffalo Roam.* One of them is its depiction of the relationship between

Thompson and Lazlo. That's what the movie is supposed to be about, and yet we never discover why these two characters like one another. What *is* their relationship, aside from the coincidence that they happen to get stoned or drunk together under bizarre circumstances? Are they even really friends? Because the movie's central relationship just isn't there, the events don't matter so much: We get bizarre episodes but no insights.

The other problem is that the Dr. Thompson character never seems to really feel the effects of the chemicals he hurls so recklessly at his system. Murray plays Thompson well, but in a mostly one-level performance: He walks through the most insane situations with a quizzical monotone, a gift for understatement, a drug-induced trance. Any real person drinking and drugging like Thompson would have an occasional high, and a more than occasional disastrous low. Here he has neither.

And so the movie fails to deal convincingly with either Thompson's addictions or with his friendship with Lazlo. It becomes just a series of set-pieces, oft-told tales about the wild and crazy things he's done while he was zonked. We wish him well, but we end up wondering, a little cynically, if Thompson has had as much fun destroying himself as we've had watching him.

Who Framed Roger Rabbit ★ ★ ★ ★

PG, 103 m., 1988

Bob Hoskins (Eddie Valiant), Christopher Lloyd (Judge Doom), Joanna Cassidy (Dolores), Charles Fleischer (Roger's voice), Stubby Kaye (Marvin Acme). Directed by Robert Zemeckis and produced by Robert Watts and Frank Marshall. Screenplay by Jeffrey Price and Peter S. Seaman.

I stopped off at a hot dog stand before the screening of *Who Framed Roger Rabbit*, and ran into a couple of the other local movie critics. They said they were going to the same screening. I asked them what they'd heard about the film. They said they were going to see it for the second time in two days. That's the kind of word of mouth that money can't buy.

And *Who Framed Roger Rabbit* is the kind of movie that gets made once in a blue moon, because it represents an immense challenge to the filmmakers: They have to make a good movie while inventing new technology at the same time. Like *2001*, *Close Encounters*, and *E.T.*, this movie is not only a great entertainment, but a breakthrough in craftsmanship—the first film to convincingly combine real actors and animated cartoon characters in the same space in the same time and make it look real.

I've never seen anything like it before. Roger Rabbit and his cartoon comrades cast real shadows. They shake the hands and grab the coats and rattle the teeth of real actors. They change size and dimension and perspective as they move through a scene, and the camera isn't locked down in one place to make it easy, either—the camera in this movie moves around like it's in a 1940s thriller, and the cartoon characters look three-dimensional and seem to be occupying real space.

In a way, what you feel when you see a movie like this is more than appreciation. It's gratitude. You know how easy it is to make dumb, no-brainer action movies, and how incredibly hard it is to make a movie like this, where every minute of screen time can take days or weeks of work by the animators. You're glad they went to the trouble. The movie is a collaboration between the Disney studio and Steven Spielberg, the direction is by Robert (*Back to the Future*) Zemeckis, and the animation is by Raymond Williams. They made this a labor of love.

How did they do it? First they plotted every scene, shot by shot, so they knew where the live actors would be, and where the animated characters would be. Then they shot the live action, forcing actors like Bob Hoskins, the star, to imagine himself in a world also inhabited by cartoons (or "Toons," as the movie calls them). Then they laboriously went through the movie frame by frame, drawing in the cartoon characters. This is not a computer job. Real, living animators did this by hand, and the effort shows in moments like the zowie zoom shots where the camera hurtles at Roger Rabbit and then careens away, with the rabbit changing size and perspective in every frame.

But I'm making the movie sound like homework for a movie class. *Who Framed Roger Rabbit* is sheer, enchanted entertainment from the first frame to the last—a joyous, giddy, goofy celebration of the kind of fun you can have with a movie camera.

The film takes place in Hollywood in 1947, in a world where humans and Toons exist side by side. The Toons in the movie include not only new characters like Roger Rabbit and his wife, the improbably pneumatic Jessica, but also established cartoon stars like Bugs Bunny, Betty Boop, Dumbo, Mickey Mouse, and both of the great ducks, Donald and Daffy (they do an act together as a piano duo).

The Toons live in Toontown, a completely animated world where the climax of the movie takes place, but most of the time they hang out in a version of Hollywood that looks like it was borrowed from a 1940s private eye movie. The plot revolves around the murder of a movie tycoon, and when Roger Rabbit is framed for the murder, private eye Hoskins gets caught in the middle of the action. As plots go, this one will be familiar to anyone who has ever seen a hard-boiled '40s crime movie—except, of course, for the Toons.

The movie is funny, but it's more than funny, it's exhilarating. It opens with what looks like a standard studio cartoon (Mother goes shopping and leaves Roger Rabbit to baby-sit her little brat, who immediately starts causing trouble). This cartoon itself, seen apart from the movie, is a masterpiece; I can't remember the last time I laughed so hard at an animated short. But then, when a stunt goes wrong and the cartoon "baby" stalks off the set and lights a cigar and tells the human director to go to hell, we know we're in a new and special universe.

The movie is filled with throwaway gags, inside jokes, one-liners, and little pokes at the screen images of its cartoon characters. It is also oddly convincing, not only because of the craft of the filmmakers, but also because Hoskins and the other live actors have found the right note for their interaction with the Toons. Instead of overreacting or playing up their emotions cartoon-style, Hoskins and the others adopt a flat, realistic, matter-of-fact posture toward the Toons. They act as if they've been talking to animated rabbits for years.

One tricky question is raised by a movie like this: Is it for kids, or adults, or both? I think it's intended as a universal entertainment, like *E.T.* or *The Wizard of Oz,* aimed at all audiences. But I have a sneaky hunch that adults will appreciate it even more than kids, because they'll have a better appreciation of how difficult it was to make, and how effortlessly it succeeds. Kids will love it too—but instead of being amazed at how they got the rabbits in with the humans, they'll be wondering what adults are doing walking around inside a cartoon.

The Whistle Blower ★ ★ ★ ½

PG, 100 m., 1987

Michael Caine (Frank Jones), James Fox (Lord), Nigel Havers (Bob Jones), Felicity Dean (Cynthia Goodburn), John Gielgud (Sir Adrian Chappel), Kenneth Colley (Bill Pickett), Gordon Jackson (Bruce). Directed by Simon Langton and produced by Geoffrey Reeve. Screenplay by Julian Bond.

The Whistle Blower is about the British spy establishment, but at first it doesn't feel at all like a spy movie. It begins as the quiet account of the daily life of a middle-aged man who has set up in the office equipment business and who almost welcomes his anonymity. He was once in intelligence, he was once at the center of important matters, but now he has put all that behind him.

The man is played by Michael Caine, with a quiet self-effacement that is very convincing. He is mild and soft-spoken, and it is clear that to some extent he is living his life through the life of his son, whom he loves very much. The son is a likable, disorganized, untidy, very serious young man who is in love with an older woman with children.

Caine is not sure this is the right relationship, but in his performance there are a few quiet, crucial moments when he seems to do nothing—he just sort of stands there in a shot, regarding those around him—and you can feel his hope that his son will be happy.

Caine is such a good actor that he doesn't overplay those moments or indeed seem to play them at all. Yet they underlie the whole film. We begin by understanding that Caine has placed action behind him, we identify with his new emotional calm, we sense his love for his son and that prepares us for everything that follows.

It is important that I not reveal, however, too much of what follows. *The Whistle Blower* is not a conventional spy thriller, but it does depend upon surprises and unexpected revelations of character, and they grow naturally out of the story. In general terms, I can say that Caine's son becomes a pawn in an intelligence game with much higher stakes and that what Caine eventually comes to understand is that little people such as himself and his son are expendable in the view of the entrenched establishment that rules the country.

Like another British thriller, *Defence of the Realm,* this movie uses the British spy apparatus as a way of dramatizing the class distinctions that still exist in Britain. The Caine character is in reaction against the feeling that nothing—not God, not the throne, not patriotism, certainly not security considerations—is as important as defending a network of privilege. The crucial moment in the film comes when Caine accuses a traitor of letting innocent people die, just so that he can continue to have tea with the queen. The steps by which Caine arrives at this speech are what the movie is about.

The Whistle Blower was hardly ahead of the headlines in Britain. The Spycatcher controversy had the country in an uproar against the action of five bewigged Law Lords, solemnly forbidding the press from printing details from a book that was a worldwide bestseller. The book alleges, of course, that a head of British intelligence was a Soviet mole from the start, the same assumption *The Whistle Blower* is founded on.

Despite a few obligatory scenes of threats and violence, most of the action in the movie takes place within the mind of the Caine character. Having taken his leave of Hollywood with the truly dreadful *Jaws the Revenge,* Caine returned to England in three quite different performances: this one, the slimy Soho mob boss in *Mona Lisa,* and the maverick spy who tries to prevent a nuclear explosion in *The Fourth Protocol.* The three performances are completely different, and yet it is hard to see what Caine does differently in them. He has the same dry, flat inflection, the sometimes masked face, the way of seeming to stand completely impassively until action is called for, the sense of enormous reserves of strength and anger banked inside. Yet in *Mona Lisa* he is a villain, in this film he is a decent, angry man, and in *The Fourth Protocol* he is more of an action hero.

It all seems to come from inside. The one thing you will rarely catch Caine doing in a movie is seeming to go for an effect. Maybe that's why he achieves them so consistently; the screen is a magnifying glass that rarely forgives excess.

What's especially nice about *The Whistle Blower* is that it never quite lets plot become more important than character. Like a novel by Graham Greene, it isn't really about what happens, but about how the events feel to the characters and how they change them. There is a scene in this movie, a quiet walk and talk between father and son, that is as touching a portrait of parenthood as any I can remember.

Wildcats ★ ½

R, 107 m., 1985

Goldie Hawn (Molly), Swoosie Kurtz (Verna), Robin Lively (Alice), Brandy Gold (Marian), James Keach (Frank), Jan Hooks (Stephanie), Bruce McGill (Darwell), Nipsy Russell (Edwards), Tab Thacker (Finch), Scott Eng (Lineman). Directed by Michael Ritchie and produced by Anthea Sylbert. Screenplay by Ezra Sacks.

Wildcats is allegedly about Goldie Hawn's attempts to find success as the coach of a boys' high school football team. But most of the big scenes and almost all of the dialogue in the movie are assigned to her grown-up friends, and the team gets lost in the shuffle—it's the gimmick, not the subject of this movie. With the exception of a Refrigerator clone (Tab Thacker) who plays the tallest and fattest member of her team, Goldie's players are sort of a faceless mass that mills around on cue.

The movie was directed by Michael Ritchie, the same man who made *The Bad News Bears* ten years ago. That was a movie where we really cared about the members of the team—a movie that was about a coach and a team. *Wildcats* is about how spunky Goldie Hawn is, and how cute it's supposed to be that this little woman can make all those great big football players do what she says.

See what happened here? The filmmakers, the producers, and Hawn herself bought the premise instead of looking for the plot. The problem with the movie is that they started with a character description instead of with a story. The fact that Goldie plays a boys' football coach is not in itself interesting. Her relationship with the team would have been interesting, if they'd developed one.

But, no, they thought they had everything they needed. They thought they could clone *Rocky* one more time. At the end of *Wildcats,* whaddaya know, Goldie's team beats its cross-town rivals. I've seen that ending before. I saw the winning football game at the end of *The Best of Times,* and the winning hockey match at the end of *Youngblood,* and God knows how many winning bicycle races and wrestling matches—not to mention *Rocky IV,* of course. The formula is becoming an insidious force in the movie industry; it convinces producers that they have a plot when in fact all they have is a boring structure to trap their characters.

I mentioned that the movie doesn't make much of an effort to make the football players into individuals. Instead, it gives us an astonishingly uninteresting subplot, in which Goldie Hawn's ex-husband (James Keach) threatens to win custody of his daughters because of Goldie's alleged misconduct. (Her players drink beer in her house and make out with their girlfriends, etc., which would be ludicrous except that the players are mostly black, and the movie supples a wholly unnecessary streak of implied racism in the Keach character.)

Wildcats is clearly an attempt by Hawn to repeat a formula that was wonderfully successful in *Private Benjamin:* Wide-eyed Goldie copes with the real world. It was less successful in *Protocol,* and now it's worn out altogether.

Willard ★ ★
PG, 95 m., 1971

Bruce Davison (Willard Stiles), Elsa Lanchester (Mrs. Stiles), Ernest Borgnine (Martin), Sondra Locke (Gin). Directed by Daniel Mann and produced by Mort Briskin. Screenplay by Gilbert A. Ralston.

Willard is about rats, and about a young man who likes rats and has a mysterious ability to communicate with rats. I hate rats. I also hate spiders. I hate spiders even more than rats, although rats are more dangerous, because of my anthropomorphic bias. But more of that later.

Willard, as I discovered, isn't actually about rats at all. It is a typical Horatio Alger story ("Jed the Poorhouse Boy," if I recollect correctly, or maybe "Do and Dare, or A Brave Boy's Fight for Fortune"), with rats playing more prominent supporting roles than they customarily did in Horatio Alger (where they were limited to run-ons).

The story concerns the plight of plucky young Willard, whose father was cheated out of the family business by the evil Mr. Martin. Willard had counted on inheriting the family concern, but now finds himself a lowly stockboy, the butt of Mr. Martin's cruel jests. Willard and his mother inhabit the old family home, where his mother is bedridden with a disease brought on by the family reversals, and as he struggles to keep a roof over his dear old mother's head, the heartless Mr. Martin weaves an evil scheme to foreclose on the mortgage, tear down the old homestead, and make a killing in real estate. Bad luck on this scale inevitably makes Willard broody, so imagine his delight when he discovers that he can communicate with rats. He discovers, but we don't. I guess you just tickle them and feed them Dog Chow and they like you.

Anyway, Willard has revenge on the evil Mr. Martin by training a bunch of rats to disrupt a garden party on the occasion of Mr. Martin's wedding anniversary. These days, when there are so few banker's daughters in runaway carriages, direct action seems to be the best policy. Willard's rats bust up the party, and Willard makes special friends of two rats who get upstairs privileges and don't have to stay in the basement. Meanwhile, his mother dies, although not of being eaten alive by rats. I wonder if they missed a bet there.

Willard's rats reproduce and train themselves at such a furious rate that Willard eventually has more rats than he exactly needs, and he gets a little uneasy about the size of his army. One is reminded of Gandhi seeing his troops march past, and running to get at the head of them because he was, after all, their leader. The rats eventually get their opportunity to dine on Mr. Martin (exhibiting the curious ability of being able to fly through the air—almost as if they were being tossed onscreen by a prop man). And then . . .

But I should leave the ending to your imagination. I want to consider, instead, the sociological and psychological implications of Willard. What is it in this film that touches some deep-buried nerve in the public psyche? Why does wholesome family entertainment fade away, while rats make millions? I've thought long and deeply on this subject, believe me, and I've reached a conclusion at last. People have waited a long time to see Ernest Borgnine eaten alive by rats, and now that they have their chance they aren't going to blow it.

Willie and Phil ★ ★ ★
R, 116 m., 1980

Michael Ontkean (Willie), Margot Kidder (Jeannette), Ray Sharkey (Phil), Jan Miner (Mrs. Kaufman), Tom Brennan (Mr. Kaufman), Julie Bovasso (Mrs. D'Amico), Louis Guss (Mr. D'Amico), Kathleen Maguire (Mrs. Sutherland). Directed and written by Paul Mazursky and produced by Mazursky and Tony Ray.

Willie and Phil meet after a screening of Truffaut's *Jules and Jim,* which is a movie about two good friends and how they both fall in love with the same woman, who becomes the third good friend. Shortly after they see the movie, in Greenwich Village in 1970, Willie and Phil meet Jeannette, and then the three of them spend the 1970s working out their own version of a triangle.

If Paul Mazursky's *Willie and Phil* is supposed to be a psychologically plausible telling of this story, then it doesn't work. The movie gives away its own game right at the beginning, with the reference to *Jules and Jim.* These aren't real people in this movie; they're characters. They don't inhabit life, they inhabit Mazursky's screenplay—which takes them on a guided tour of the cults, fads, human potential movements, and alternative life-styles of the decade during which zucchini replaced Faulkner as the most popular subject on campus.

But I don't think *Willie and Phil* was intended to work on a realistic level, or that we're intended to believe that Willie, Phil, and Jeannette are making free choices throughout the movie. In a subtle, understated sort of way, Mazursky is giving us a movie that hovers between a satirical revue and a series of life-style vignettes. The characters in his movie are almost exhausted by the end of the decade (weren't we all?). Not only have they experimented with various combinations of commitments to one another, but they've also tried out most of the popular 1970s belief systems.

Willie (Michael Ontkean) is a high school teacher as the movie opens, but he wants to be more, to feel deeply, to think on more exalted levels, and his journey through the decade takes him into radicalism, back to the earth, and all the way to India for lessons in meditation. Phil (Ray Sharkey) says he wants love and security, but he holds himself at arm's length from Jeannette and other possible sources of love. Unable to communicate, he channels all of his energy into making it in the communications industries. Jeannette (Margot Kidder) . . . well, what does she want? To love, to be loved, to be possessed, to be free, to commit, but not to be trapped, to . . . have kids? A career? Willie? Phil?

I think Mazursky's suggesting something interesting about the 1970s. It was a decade without a consuming passion, without an overall subject or tone. Every decade from the 1920s to the 1960s had an overriding theme, at least in our collective national imagination, but in the 1970s we went on life-style shopping trips, searching for an impossible combination of life choices that would be morally good, politically correct, personally entertaining, and outperform the market—all at once.

And what were we left with in the 1980s? Confusion, vague apprehension, lack of faith in belief systems, EPA mileage estimates, megavitamins as the last blameless conspicuous consumption, and, echoing somewhere in the back of our minds, Peggy Lee singing "Is That All There Is?" How'd we get stuck? Why'd we wind up with a sense of impending doom when we tried every possible superficial substitute for profound change? Mazursky finds this note and strikes it in *Willie and Phil,* and that's what's best about his movie.

But like the decade itself, *Willie and Phil* is not completely substantial or satisfying. What redeems it, curiously, are the scenes involving Willie's Jewish parents, Phil's Italian parents, and Jeannette's Southern mother. Their scenes are reactions to what's happening to their kids in the 1970s, and they work like field trips from other decades. The parents observe, try to understand, are baffled, react with resentment, anger, love, confusion. I loved it when the Italian mother, trying to figure out how Jeannette was going to sleep with her boyfriend in the house of her ex-husband while the ex-husband bunked downstairs and the parents took the guest room, got up, said it was all just too complicated for her, and left for the airport. That's sort of the motif for this movie.

Willie Wonka and the Chocolate Factory ★ ★ ★ ★

G, 98 m., 1971

Gene Wilder (Willie Wonka), Jack Albertson (Grandpa Joe), Peter Ostrum (Charlie), Michael Bollner (Augustus Gloop), Aubrey Wood (Mr. Bill), Gunter Meissner (Mr. Slugwork). Directed by Mel Stuart and produced by Stan Margulies and David L. Wolper. Screenplay by Roald Dahl.

Kids are not stupid. They are among the sharpest, cleverest, most eagle-eyed creatures on God's Earth, and very little escapes their notice. You may not have observed that your neighbor is still using his snow tires in mid-July, but every four-year-old on the block has, and kids pay the same attention to detail when they go to the movies. They don't miss a thing, and they have an instinctive contempt for shoddy and shabby work. I make this observation because nine out of ten children's movies are stupid, witless, and display contempt for their audiences, and that's why kids hate them. Is that all parents want from kids' movies? That they not have anything bad in them? Shouldn't they have something good in them—some life, imagination, fantasy, inventiveness, something to tickle the imagination? If a movie isn't going to do your kids any good, why let them watch it? Just to kill a Saturday afternoon? That shows a subtle kind of contempt for a child's mind, I think.

All of this is preface to a simple statement: *Willie Wonka and the Chocolate Factory* is probably the best film of its sort since *The Wizard of Oz.* It is everything that family movies usually claim to be, but aren't: Delightful, funny, scary, exciting, and, most of all, a genuine work of imagination. *Willie Wonka* is such a surely and wonderfully spun fantasy that it works on all kinds of minds, and it is fascinating because, like all classic fantasy, it is fascinated with itself.

It's based on the well-known Roald Dahl children's book, and it was financed by the Quaker Oats Company as an experiment in providing high-quality family entertainment. It succeeds. It doesn't cut corners and go for cheap shortcuts like Disney. It provides a first-rate cast (Gene Wilder as the compulsively distrustful chocolate manufacturer, Jack Albertson as the game old grandfather), a first-rate production, and—I keep coming back to this—genuine imagination.

The story, like all good fantasies, is about a picaresque journey. Willie Wonka is the world's greatest chocolate manufacturer, and he distributes five golden passes good for a trip through his factory and a lifetime supply of chocolate. Each pass goes to a kid, who may bring an adult along, and our hero Charlie (a poor but honest newsboy who supports four grandparents and his mother) wins the last one.

The other four kids are hateful in one way or another, and come to dreadful ends. One falls into the chocolate lake and is whisked into the bowels of the factory. He shouldn't have been a pig. Another is vain enough to try Wonka's new teleportation invention, and winds up six inches tall—but the taffy-pulling machine will soon have him back to size, right? If these fates seem a little gruesome to you, reflect that all great children's tales are a little gruesome, from the Brothers Grimm to Alice to Snow White, and certainly not excluding Mother Goose. Kids are not sugar and spice, not very often, and they appreciate the poetic justice when a bad kid gets what's coming to him.

Willow ★ ★ ½

PG, 126 m., 1988 ✓

Val Kilmer (Madmartigan), Joanne Whalley (Sorsha), Warwick Davis (Willow), Jean Marsh (Queen Bavmorda), Patricia Hayes (Raziel), Billy Barty (High Aldwin), Pat Roach (Kael), Gavan O'Herlihy (Airk). Directed by Ron Howard and produced by George Lucas. Screenplay by Bob Dolman.

A producer and a pharaoh find a baby on a raft on the Nile. "What an ugly kid," the pharaoh says. "That's funny," says the producer. "He looked great in the rushes."—Old movie joke

Willow is a fearsomely ambitious movie, but it is not fearsome, and it is not wondrous, and it is about a journey too far down a road too well-traveled by other movies. It's a fantasy about the quest of a lovable little person and his heroic newfound friend to return a lost baby to where it belongs, and to outsmart a wicked queen and kill a two-headed dragon in the process. In other words, standard stuff.

What was supposed to make *Willow* special was the quality of the production. This is a sword-and-sorcery epic produced by George Lucas, whose *Star Wars* portrayed the same kind of material in the future, and directed by Ron Howard, whose human touch made *Cocoon* one of the best recent science-fiction movies. The special effects are by Lucas's company, Industrial Light and Magic, which has set the standard in such matters. The budget was umpteen million dollars, and Hollywood was hoping that the Force was definitely with this film.

Alas, even the largest budgets and the most meticulous special effects are only dead weight unless they have a story to make them move. And at the story level, *Willow* is turgid and relentlessly predictable. Not much really happens, and when it does, its pace is slowed by special effects set-pieces that run on too long and seem to be recycled out of earlier movies.

The story. Willow, citizen of the Nelwyns, a race of little people, is chosen by his community to take a baby to a far-off crossroads where it can be found by its people, the Daikinis. The baby was carried to Willow's land on a crude raft that was swept along by river waters, but what Willow does not know is that the baby was placed on the raft by its desperate mother. That was to save it from a decree of death dealt out to all girl-children by Bavmorda, the vicious queen and sorceress, who fears her successor has been born. So already we have the story of Moses, cross-pollinated with *Snow White and the Seven Dwarfs*. Lucas has a reputation as a student of old legends and folklore, but there is a thin line between that and simply being a student of old movies.

One of the crucial problems in *Willow* is that we are going to be seeing so much of this baby. It is dragged from one end of the known world to the other, usually with a plucky smile on its face, and whenever something interesting happens, we get an appropriate reaction shot from the baby. Hey, I like kids, but even Baby Leroy couldn't have saved this character.

Willow (Warwick Davis) sets off with the baby in arms, and at the crossroads he meets Madmartigan (Val Kilmer), a warrior who has been imprisoned in a cage. Madmartigan convinces Willow to free him, using much too much dialogue in the process, and then they team up to continue their quest, which leads eventually to Bavmorda's fortress, guarded by a two-headed, fire-breathing dragon.

So, OK, the dragon is well done. All of the special effects are competent, but they do not breathe with the fire of life because they are not motivated by a strong story we really care about. The characters in *Willow* are shallow and unexciting, the story is a plod through recycled legend, and therefore, even the battle with the dragon is a foregone conclusion. There can be no true suspense in a movie where even the characters seem to be inspired by other movies.

Willow is certainly not a breakthrough film to a mass audience—but is it at least a successful children's picture? I dunno. Its pacing is too deliberate, and it doesn't have a light heart. That's revealed in the handling of some *really* little characters named the Brownies, represented by a couple of men who are about nine inches tall and fight all the time. Maybe Lucas thought these guys would work like R2D2 and C3PO did in *Star Wars*. But they have no depth, no personalities, no dimension; they're simply an irritant at the edge of the frame. Touches like that will only confuse kids, who know that good dreams do not have to be clever, or consistent, or expensive, but that they should never, ever make you want to wake up.

Winter of Our Dreams ★ ★ ★

R, 89 m., 1983

Judy Davis (Lou), Bryan Brown (Rob), Cathy Downes (Gretel), Baz Luhrmann (Pete). Directed by John Duigan and produced by Richard Mason. Screenplay by Duigan.

Rob runs a bookstore and lives in one of those houses where the bedrooms hang under the eaves; one false move and you dash your brains out onto the living room floor below. Lou is a prostitute who lives on the streets. They both once had a friend named Lisa, back in the late 1960s when they were all part of the Australian protest movement. Now Lisa has been murdered, and Lou, searching for a meaning in her life or death, runs into Rob again. She thinks he's a trick. He thinks she's an interesting, complicated person who deserves his attention. I think she's closer to the mark.

This is the setup for *Winter of Our Dreams,* an Australian film starring two popular Australian new wave actors, Judy Davis (of *My Brilliant Career*) and Bryan Brown (of *Breaker Morant* and TV's "A Town Like Alice"). Davis brought a kind of wiry, feisty intelligence to *My Brilliant Career,* playing an Australian farm woman who rather felt she would do things her own way. She's wonderful this time, in a completely different role as an insecure, distrustful, skinny street waif. It's Brown who is the trouble. Maybe it's the performance, maybe it's the character, or maybe it's Brown, but I've rarely seen a more closed-off person on the screen. When the story calls for him to reach out to Davis, we feel he's holding his nose. Sometimes there are movies where the leading actors cannot stand one another (Ken Wahl said he was only able to kiss Bette Midler in *Jinxed!* by thinking of his dog), and maybe Brown just couldn't express the feelings that were in the script. But I was never really convinced that he cared for Davis.

That's less of a handicap later in the movie, however, when the Brown character is *required* to draw back from any involvement with this pathetic street kid. The relationships in *Winter of Our Dreams* are very tangled—maybe too tangled. Brown's character has been married for six years to Gretel (Kathy Downes), a handsome, smart woman who has a lover. They have an open marriage, and there's no objection when Brown brings Davis home for the night. Davis, taking this all in, can't understand it. Trying to learn how to feel again, she can't understand why anyone would deliberately trivialize his feelings. The key passages in the film involve Brown's discovery that Davis is a heroin junkie, and then her tortured period of drug withdrawal. They are both pretending to care for one another, and after Davis gets straight maybe Brown will become her lover, while his wife disappears into the woodwork. That is not, however, even remotely in the cards, and there's a painful scene during a party at Brown's house, where Davis realizes that Brown is *very* married, open marriage or not.

There seem to be two movements in *Winter of Our Dreams.* One is Davis's movement away from the cynicism and despair of prostitution, and back toward an ability to care for another person. The other is Brown's initial concern for this girl, and then his retreat back into his shell. Davis performs her movement magnificently. Brown didn't win my sympathy for a moment. What just barely saves this film is the fact that we're not *supposed* to like the Brown character. As for Davis, she's a wonder.

Wise Guys ★ ★ ★ ½

R, 92 m., 1986

Danny DeVito (Harry Valentini), Joe Piscopo (Moe Dickstein), Harvey Keitel (Bobby DiLea), Ray Sharkey (Marco), Dan Hedaya (Tony Castelo), Captain Lou Albano (Fixer), Julie Bovasso (Lil Dickstein), Patti LuPone (Wanda Valentini). Directed by Brian DePalma and produced by Aaron Russo. Screenplay by George Gallo.

Wise Guys tells the story of Harry and Moe, two low-level hoodlums who become the toys of the Mafia gods. They're just ordinary guys, working stiffs who live next door to each other in houses tucked under a New Jersey expressway. They dream of the day when they'll be assigned to really important jobs, like shaking down widows. But when the godfather holds his morning staff meetings in the back booth of his favorite restaurant, these guys get humiliated: Their job is to pick up the boss's laundry.

The two friends are played by Joe Piscopo, as Moe Dickstein, and Danny DeVito, as Harry Valentini. They move with easy familiarity through the world of the mob; sometimes the little guys get the best view. They all know so much, in fact, that when they screw up, when they do something that is very, very bad, they don't even have to be told they're dead. It goes without saying.

Here's what they do. They go to the track with Fixer, the mob's chief enforcer (played by Captain Lou Albano, the gigantic professional wrestler). Their assignment is to place a bet for Tony, the boss (Dan Hedaya). DeVito gets to thinking, which is always dangerous. The boss has been betting on the wrong horses for weeks. They could be heroes by placing the money on the nose of the horse that DeVito knows will win. Better still, they could get rich by betting on the winning horse and then letting Fixer and the boss believe the money was lost.

This is a great plan, except unfortunately, this is the one day that the boss's horse comes in first, and so DeVito and Piscopo have lost the boss hundreds of thousands of dollars. This is bad. It is so bad that DeVito is plunged into a lobster tank at the restaurant, and Piscopo is suspended over a pit full of attack dogs. Then the boss thinks up their *real* punishment: He will secretly assign each one of them to kill the other one. It's here that the movie really gets rolling. The two wise guys hit the road, looking for safety, looking for a mob elder statesman who can bargain for their safety. And we begin to realize that the movie is filled with an inexhaustible supply of great character actors, that we are going to meet a lot of people in this story, and they are all going to be memorable.

In New Jersey, there was Hedaya as the boss, clean-shaven and slick, and Albano as Fixer, in one of the year's great supporting roles. Then, in Atlantic City, we meet the casino manager Bobby DiLea, played by the great Harvey Keitel. He doesn't want anyone to get killed in his casino, and once Harry and Moe check into the penthouse suite (using Fixer's stolen credit card), he knows he is going to have to be very lucky to keep that from happening. Very lucky, or very weird.

Wise Guys is an abundant movie, filled with ideas and gags and great characters. It never runs dry. It never has the desperation of so many gangster comedies, which seem to be marching over the same tired ground. This movie was made with joy, and you can feel it in the sense of all the actors working at the top of their form.

The movie was directed by Brian DePalma, who specializes in movies about crime and whose credits include *Scarface*, *Body Double*, and *Dressed to Kill*. I admired all those movies—indeed, I think DePalma is one of the best stylists at work right now—but I wouldn't have suspected that he had this comedy in him. His early credits include such problematic comedies as *Hi, Mom!* (which was one of Robert De Niro's first movie jobs), but here's this polished, confident comedy that never seems to step wrong.

A lot of the credit goes to Piscopo and DeVito, who develop an instant, easy camaraderie. I really did feel that they care for each other. I liked the way DeVito waved his arms and demanded attention, and the way Piscopo played his slightly slower, sweeter, dumber pal. DeVito has been good in other recent movies (such as *Romancing the Stone*), but this is the first time he's been at the top of the cast, and really free to show his stuff. He is inspired: This could be a new beginning for his career. Piscopo, from "Saturday Night Live," has worked less in the movies, and has always seemed in search of a character. Here he finds one.

And then there's that gallery of supporting performances. Albano is so fearsome as Fixer that I found myself laughing at a time I don't think was supposed to be funny: There's a reference to "Mrs. Fixer." Keitel is suave and sinister as the casino boss, always staying within character, playing it straight, not going for laughs, and so getting more of them.

Laughter doesn't come out of formula, or stupidity, or the manipulation of things that worked before in other films. It comes out of characters and performances, out of people who have some measure of reality, and whose dilemmas we can share. *Wise Guys* is broad and farcical, but there's not a moment when Moe and Harry stop being lovable, and even sort of believable.

Wish You Were Here ★ ★ ★ ½

R, 92 m., 1987

Emily Lloyd (Lynda), Tom Bell (Eric), Jesse Birdsall (Dave), Geoffrey Durham (Harry Figgis), Pat Heywood (Aunt Millie), Geoffrey Hutchings (Hubert). Directed by David Leland and produced by Sarah Radclyffe. Screenplay by Leland.

Her mother's dead, her father's a drunk, and inside of her beats a spirit that is free and true. But this is a working-class neighborhood of an English provincial town in 1951, when a girl such as Lynda was expected to know her place, to apologize by her very manner for having come from humble origins, and done little to distinguish herself. Lynda isn't made that way. The boys like to look at Betty Grable's legs in the cinema, so Lynda flashes her knickers on the beach. What's to lose?

Wish You Were Here tells the story of an adolescent girl with a spirit that refuses to be crushed, but who has few ways to express herself. Her father absolutely fails to comprehend her. An aunt sees her as a bad girl, a problem girl. The lads of the town see her as a tramp and a possible good time. There is no one in the town to understand her high spirits and good nature, except, perhaps, for the little old lady who plays piano in the tea room and applauds her the day she tells a customer to shove it.

Wish You Were Here is a comedy with an angry undertone, a story of a free-spirited girl who holds a grudge against a time when such girls were a threat to society, to the interlocking forces of sexism and convention that conspired to break their spirits. Because the film sometimes doesn't know whether to laugh or cry, it's always interesting: We see a girl whistling on her way to possible tragedy.

The movie was written and directed by David Leland. You may have seen or heard about *Personal Services*, an earlier movie he wrote. It was based on the story of a notorious British madam named Cynthia Payne, who ran a house of ill repute for old-age pensioners and retired military men with kinky tastes.

Although *Wish You Were Here* never makes the connection, it is based on stories that Payne told Leland about her childhood, when sex was something nobody talked about and sexual initiation was accompanied by ignorance, fear, and psychic trauma. Payne could never quite see what the fuss was about—still can't, if the latest headlines about her are correct. Her approach was completely amoral: If sex is something they want and you can supply, and you can benefit as much as, or more than, they can, then where's the problem?

The answer is, of course, is that there can be endless problems, especially to a girl so essentially innocent and vulnerable as Lynda in this movie. After she gets a job at the bus station, her boss walks in to catch her flashing her legs for the appreciative bus drivers. A young local lad fancies himself a Don Juan, and gets her into bed, only to appear in the bedroom door in a silk dressing gown, smoking a cigarette in a holder, and doing his Ronald Colman imitation (which is, as it turns out, his idea of sex).

"Do you fancy me?" he asks. "Not half as much as you fancy yourself," she says, and the night ends with her still largely ignorant about the facts of life. But her schooling resumes at the hands of a middle-aged projectionist at the local theater, who understands the mechanics of sex and totally lacks any understanding of human nature—hers, or his own.

Under the circumstances, it is hard for Lynda to keep smiling, to think positive in the face of a general conspiracy to treat sex as filthy and herself as worthless. The last shot of the movie will strike some people as hopeless and misleading romanticism; I prefer to see it as optimism in the face of despair.

The key to this movie is the performance by sixteen-year-old Emily Lloyd as Lynda. The screenplay could have gone a dozen different ways, depending on who was cast in the role. Lloyd is so fresh, so filled with fun and rebellion, that she carries us past the tricky parts on the strength of personality alone. It's one of the great debut roles for a young actress. I was reminded of a cross between Julie Christie in *Darling* and Rita Tushingham in *A Taste of Honey*. It'll be interesting to see what the future holds for her. More than it did for Lynda, I imagine, and for Cynthia Payne.

The Witches of Eastwick ★ ★ ★ ½

R, 125 m., 1987

Jack Nicholson (Daryl), Cher (Alexandra), Susan Sarandon (Jane), Michelle Pfeiffer (Sukie), Veronica Cartwright (Felicia), Richard Jenkins (Clyde), Keith Jochim (Walter). Directed by George Miller and produced by Neil Canton, Peter Guber, and Jon Peters. Screenplay by Michael Christofer.

It's all done with the ambidextrous eyebrows. Jack Nicholson can elevate either brow singly to express his intention of getting away with murder, and he can elevate them in unison to reflect his delight when he has done so. In the annals of body language, his may be a small skill, but it's a crucial one, because it makes us conspirators with Nicholson; he's sharing his raffish delight with us.

He does that a lot in *The Witches of Eastwick*, in which he plays the devil: a role he was born to fill. He finds himself in Eastwick, a sedate New England village, after being invoked by three bored housewives who have not found what they are looking for in the local male population. Nicholson is exactly what they are looking for, by definition, because he can be all things to all people.

He buys the big mansion on the edge of town, moves in, and starts cooking. Nobody knows where he came from or what his story is, and he's certainly an oddball: Look at those floppy, ungainly clothes, or remember the time he began to snore, deafeningly, at the village concert. But the three women who summoned him aren't complaining, because he's giving each one of them just what she wants.

The women are played in the movie by Cher, Michelle Pfeiffer, and Susan Sarandon, and they have a delicious good time with their roles. These women need to be good at double takes, because they're always getting into situations that require them. When they're together, talking up a storm, they have the kind of unconscious verbal timing that makes comedy out of ordinary speech. We laugh not only because they say funny things but because they give everyday things just a slight twist of irony.

But it's Nicholson's show. There is a scene where he dresses in satin pajamas and sprawls full length on a bed, twisting and stretching sinuously in full enjoyment of his sensuality. It is one of the funniest moments of physical humor he has ever committed. There is another sequence in which he presides over a diabolical celebration in his mansion, orchestrating unspeakable acts and realizing unconscious fantasies. In the hands of another actor it might look ridiculous, but Nicholson seems perfectly at home with the bizarre.

The Witches of Eastwick is based on the John Updike novel, which must have presented a mine field for George Miller, the director. Fantasies usually play better on the page than on the screen, because in the imagination they don't seem as ridiculous as they sometimes do when they've been reduced to actual images. There are moments in *The Witches of Eastwick* that stretch uncomfortably for effects—the movie's climax is overdone, for example—and yet a lot of the time this movie plays like a plausible story about implausible people. The performances sell it. And the eyebrows.

Withnail & I ★ ★ ★ ★

R, 104 m., 1987 ✓

Richard E. Grant (Withnail), Paul McGann (Marwood), Richard Griffiths (Monty), Ralph Brown (Danny), Michael Elphick (Jake), Daragh O'Malley (Irishman), Michael Wardle (Isaac Parkin), Una Brandon-Jones (Mrs. Parkin). Directed by Bruce Robinson and produced by Paul M. Heller. Screenplay by Robinson.

Withnail & I takes place in England at the end of the Swinging Sixties. Two would-be actors live in squalor and poverty in a mean little flat in a wretched section of London. They are cold, desperate, broke, and hung over. They dream of glory but lurk about in the corners of pubs to keep warm.

One of them is Withnail, who is tall, craggy, and utterly cynical. He affects a kind of weary bitterness. The other is Marwood, younger, more optimistic, more impressionable. Their situation is desperate. "Something has to happen," Withnail says, "or I'm going to crack."

Then he has an inspiration: His rich and eccentric Uncle Monty has some sort of a place in the country. They'll talk him into lending it to them, and perhaps the change of scenery will give them the courage to carry on. The scene that begins when they appear at the door of Monty's London mansion is sly and droll, filled with hazardous currents and undertows as Monty takes a fancy to young Marwood. He agrees to lend them his country place.

The country is bitter, cold, angry, and hostile. Neighbors will not talk to them. Farmers will not sell them firewood. Their wives will not part with eggs or milk. Huddled over a wretched blaze made of Uncle Monty's furniture, Withnail and Marwood contemplate a bleak prospect: They have no food, fuel, money, or (worst of all) drink. Outside the door, the idyllic countryside is roamed by randy bulls.

Then Uncle Monty arrives unexpectedly and sets himself on a determined romantic pursuit of young Marwood, who wants nothing to do with him. Withnail confesses that he told his uncle that Marwood was gay, "because otherwise who would we have gotten the cottage?" Uncle Monty is, however, not only gay but also rich and fat, and the erotic tension in the cottage is interrupted by large and leisurely meals.

The performances make the movie, and Richard Griffiths is wonderful as Uncle Monty: overfed, burbling with second-hand eloquence, yet with a cold intelligence lurking behind his bloodshot eyes. It's the best supporting performance in a British movie since Denholm Elliott in *A Room With a View.* Withnail and Marwood, played by Richard E. Grant and Paul McGann, are like Rosencrantz and Gildenstern: They know all their lines but are uncertain about which direction the play is taking.

Withnail & I is a comedy, but a grimly serious one. Nothing is played for laughs. The humor arises from poverty, desperation, and bone-numbing cold. It is not the portrait of two colorful, lovable characters, but of two comrades in emotional shipwreck. The movie is rigorously dyspeptic, and that's why I liked it: It doesn't go for the easy laughs or sentimentalized poverty, but finds its humor in the unforgiving study of selfish human nature.

Without a Trace ★ ★ ★ 1/2

PG, 119 m., 1983

Kate Nelligan (Susan Selky), Judd Hirsch (Menetti), David Dukes (Graham Selky), Stockard Channing (Jocelyn). Directed and produced by Stanley Jaffe. Screenplay by Beth Gutcheon.

"A woman's bravery and a police detective's relentless search for her missing son provide the elements of suspenseful human drama in Without a Trace."

—Press release

They have it exactly wrong. The press release describes what might have happened to this story if it had been turned into one of those TV docudramas where every emotion is predictably computed. What makes *Without a Trace* interesting is that it's *not* predictable, because it goes with the ebbs and flows of imperfect human beings. It's not about a woman's bravery but about her intelligence and vulnerability. It's not about a detective's relentless search, but about routine police work, made up of realism and hunches.

Without a Trace opens with a sequence that is very painful, since we know from the movie's title what's about to happen. A young mother (Kate Nelligan), who lives alone with her first-grader, gets him up, gets him his breakfast, scolds him for feeding his breakfast to the dog, tells him he's a good boy, and sends him off to school. He's almost seven—sort of young to walk alone to school, but it's only two blocks and there's a crossing guard. Nelligan goes off to school herself. She's an English professor at Columbia University. She comes home and waits for her child. He's late. She makes a call. He never arrived at the school. She calls the police and a search begins at once, but her son has apparently disappeared into thin air. There are door-to-door canvasses, helicopter searches, anonymous phone calls, predictions by psychics, and a neighborhood campaign to put "missing" posters in store windows. But there is no little boy.

One of the unexpected things about *Without a Trace* is that it's not really about the police search for the child. Instead, it's about what happens to people when tragedy turns into open-ended frustration. The mother waits and waits. The detective in charge of the case (Judd Hirsch) follows up leads and does all the things a competent cop is supposed to do. The city lends its resources and pays for an expensive investigation. But everything leads to nothing.

The central passages of the film are the best, as Nelligan plays an intelligent, civilized woman fighting to keep control. She feels rage, yes, but she is a rational person and she tries to behave reasonably. Underneath, she is deeply grieving. It takes her best friend (Stockard Channing) to suggest, after several months, that perhaps it is time to give up and admit that the little boy must be dead. It's time to let go of the past and rebuild her own life. Nelligan rejects that reasoning. And the movie remains neutral. What *is* the right answer: Should she accept what looks like the inevitable, or should she continue to hope? Nelligan's performance grows immensely subtle at this point. We can almost read her mind, and what we are reading is a battle between instinct and intelligence, between common sense and a mother's love.

Then a "suspect" is arrested—a gay sadomasochist. The circumstantial evidence against him is overwhelming. But Nelligan refuses to be bullied into agreement by a police department eager to close its books on the case. She becomes convinced that the man is innocent. And *Without a Trace*, which could so easily have been just another police drama, grows into a thought-provoking movie about how we behave, and why. It asks hard questions. It also has its moments of joy, but it earns every one of them.

Witness ★ ★ ★ ★
R, 120 m., 1985

Harrison Ford (John Book), Kelly McGillis (Rachel), Josef Sommer (Schaeffer), Lukas Haas (Samuel), Alexander Godunov (Daniel Hochleitner). Directed by Peter Weir and produced by Edward S. Feldman. Screenplay by Earl Wallace.

Witness comes billed as a thriller, but it's so much more than a thriller that I wish they hadn't even used the word "murder" in the ads. This is, first of all, an electrifying and poignant love story. Then it is a movie about the choices we make in life and the choices that other people make for us. Only then is it a thriller—one that Alfred Hitchcock would have been proud to make.

The movie's first act sets up the plot, leaving it a lot of time to deal with the characters and learn about them. The film begins on an Amish settlement in Pennsylvania, where for two hundred years a self-sufficient religious community has proudly held onto the ways of their ancestors. The Amish are deeply suspicious of outsiders and stubbornly dedicated to their rural life-style, with its horses and carriages, its communal barn-raisings, its gas lanterns instead of electricity, hooks instead of buttons.

An Amish man dies. His widow and young son leave on a train journey. In the train station in Philadelphia, the little boy witnesses a murder. Harrison Ford plays the tough big-city detective who gets assigned to the case. He stages lineups, hoping the kid can spot the murderer. He shows the kid mug shots. Then it turns out that the police department itself is implicated in the killing. Ford is nearly murdered in an ambush. His life, and the lives of the widow and her son, are in immediate danger. He manages to drive them all back to the Amish lands of Pennsylvania before collapsing from loss of blood.

And it's at this point, really, that the movie begins. Up until the return to Pennsylvania, *Witness* has been a slick, superior thriller. Now it turns into an intelligent and perceptive love story. It's not one of those romances where the man and woman fall into each other's arms because their hormones are programmed that way. It's about two independent, complicated people who begin to love each other because they have shared danger, they work well together, they respect each other—*and* because their physical attraction for each other is so strong it almost becomes another character in the movie.

Witness was directed by Peter Weir, the gifted Australian director of *The Year of Living Dangerously.* He has a strong and sure feeling for places, for the land, for the way that people build their self-regard by the way they do their work.

In the whole middle section of this movie, he shows the man from the city and the simple Amish woman within the context of the Amish community. It is masterful filmmaking. The thriller elements alone would command our attention. The love story by itself would be exciting. The ways of life in the Amish community are so well-observed that they have a documentary feel. But all three elements work together so well that something organic is happening here; we're *inside* this story.

Harrison Ford has never given a better performance in a movie. Kelly McGillis, the young actress who plays the Amish widow, has a kind of luminous simplicity about her; it is refreshing and even subtly erotic to see a woman who doesn't subscribe to all the standard man-woman programmed responses of modern society.

The love that begins to grow between them is not made out of clichés; the cultural gulf that separates them is at least as important to both of them as the feelings they have. When they finally kiss, it is a glorious, sensuous moment, because this kiss is a sharing of trust and passion, not just another plug-in element from your standard kit of movie images.

We have been getting so many pallid, bloodless little movies—mostly recycled teen-age exploitation films made by ambitious young stylists without a thought in their heads—that *Witness* is like a fresh new day. It is a movie about adults, whose lives have dignity and whose choices matter to them. And it is also one hell of a thriller.

The Wiz ★ ★ ★
G, 133 m., 1978

Diana Ross (Dorothy), Michael Jackson (Scarecrow), Nipsey Russell (Tinman), Ted Ross (Lion), Mabel King (Evillene), Theresa Merritt (Aunt Em), Thelma Carpenter (Miss One), Lena Horne (Glinda the Good), Richard Pryor (The Wiz). Directed by Sidney Lumet and produced by Rob Cohen. Screenplay by Joel Schumacher.

Magical tornadoes can strike down anywhere, I guess, and spin you off to the land of Oz. On that wonderfully logical premise, the classic *Wizard of Oz* was transformed into a Broadway musical named *The Wiz,* and then the most expensive movie musical ever made. Is the movie a match for the 1938 Judy Garland version? Well, no, it's not—what movie could be?—but as a new approach to the same material, it's slick and energetic and fun.

The Wiz is set in present-day New York City, and finds its locations in fanciful sets suggesting Harlem, Coney Island, school playgrounds, the subway system, and a sweatshop. Our heroine, Dorothy, has been transformed from a Kansas teen-ager to a twenty-four-year-old black schoolteacher. And Diana Ross wears the same simple white frock for the entire film and projects a wide-eyed innocence that kind of grows on you.

Some churlish souls suggested, however, that *The Wiz* strains our credibility too much. That a twenty-four-year-old schoolteacher should be too sophisticated to consort with cowardly lions and scarecrows and men made out of tin. Pay no attention: Critics like that wouldn't know a yellow brick road if they saw one.

The Wiz asks for our suspension of disbelief and earns it (after a slow start) in that great shot of Dorothy and the Scarecrow dancing across a yellow brick bridge toward the towers of Manhattan. Up until then the going has been a little awkward. We don't really understand why Dorothy's such a mope at her aunt's dinner party—and, after she and her dog Toto are whirled away by a snowstorm, the scene in the playground really drags. Lots of graffiti people, drawn on the walls, come to life and dance about like a Broadway chorus line (which, of course, they are), and then Dorothy finally finds her first yellow brick.

It's good that the Scarecrow is the first traveling companion she meets; Michael Jackson fills the role with humor and warmth. Nipsey Russell is fine as the Tinman, too, but Ted Ross sort of disappears into his lion's costume, done in by the makeup man. We can't see enough of him to get to know him.

There are lots of good scenes in the Emerald City. A dance sequence, for example, where The Wiz calls the shots and everybody instantly changes their clothes to stay in fashion. A run-in with a roller-coaster. The scenes in the subway, where Dorothy and her friends are chased by enormous, menacing trash bins that snap their jaws ferociously. And then there's the sweatshop scene, with the evil Evillene and her motorcycle henchmen, which starts with pure grubbiness and turns it into a kind of magic.

Finally, at the very end of the journey, there's Richard Pryor as The Wiz, coward at heart, filled with doubts, hiding behind the electronic gadgets he uses to enslave the Emerald City and keep Evillene at bay. The songs get a little sticky about here—all sorts of unthrilling messages about how you can achieve anything if only you believe—but Diana Ross knows how to sell them, and she has a virtuoso solo in a totally darkened frame that reminds us of Barbra Streisand's closing number in *Funny Lady*.

The movie has great moments and a lot of life, sensational special effects and costumes—and Ross, Jackson, and Russell. Why *doesn't* it involve us as deeply as *The Wizard of Oz*? Maybe because it hedges its bets by wanting to be sophisticated *and* universal, childlike *and* knowing, appealing to both a mass audience and to media insiders. *The Wizard of Oz* went flat-out for the heart of its story; there are times when *The Wiz* has just a touch too much calculation.

A Woman Under the Influence
★ ★ ★ ★
R, 155 m., 1975

Peter Falk (Nick Longhetti), Gena Rowlands (Mabel Longhetti), Katherine Cassavetes (Mama Longhetti), Lady Rowlands (Martha Mortensen), Fred Draper (George Mortensen). Directed by John Cassavetes and produced by Sam Shaw. Screenplay by Cassavetes.

John Cassavetes's *A Woman Under the Influence* gives us a woman whose influences only gradually reveal themselves. And as they do, they give us insight not only into one specific, brilliantly created, woman, but into some of the problems of surviving in a society where very few people are free to be themselves. The woman is Mabel Longhetti, wife and mother and (in some very small, shy, and faraway corner) herself. Her husband, Nick, is the head of a construction gang and a gregarious type with an expansive nature; he's likely to bring his whole crew home at 7 A.M. for a spaghetti dinner.

Mabel isn't gregarious, but she tries. She tries too hard, and that's her problem. She desperately wants to please her husband, and when they're alone, she does. They get along, and they do love one another. But when people are around, she gets a little wacky. The mannerisms, the strange personal little ways she has of expressing herself, get out of scale. She's not sure how to act, because she's not sure who she is. "I'll be whatever you want me to be," she tells Nick, and he tells her to be herself. But who is that?

The film takes place before and after six months she spends in a mental institution. Her husband has her committed, reluctantly, after she begins to crack up. There have been some indications that she's in trouble. She behaves strangely when some neighbor children are brought over to stay for a while with her own, and the neighbor is afraid to leave his kids because of the way she's acting. But what, exactly, is "strange"? Well she's insecure, hyper, manic. She laughs too much and pushes too hard. She's not good with other people around. So her husband does what he thinks he has to do and commits her. But what about him? What kind of a guy is he? It's here that *A Woman Under the Influence* gets to be complicated, involved, and fascinating—a revelation. Because if Mabel is disturbed, then so is he. He's as crazy as she is, maybe more so. But because he's a man and has channels for his craziness, he stays at home and she gets sent away.

Their ways with kids, for example, are revealing. She feels insecure around them. She's not confident enough to be a mother, and almost wants to be another kid. But the father, when he takes over the responsibility of raising them, yanks them out of school in the middle of the day and drags them, bewildered, to the seashore for the most depressing, compulsory day at the beach we can imagine. And then on the way home, he lets them share a six-pack with him. If Mabel wants to be one of the kids, Nick wants them to be three of the boys.

I don't suppose (although I'm not sure) that real families like this exist, and I don't think Cassavetes wants us to take the film as a literal record. The characters are larger than life (although not less convincing because of that), and their loves and rages, their fights and moments of tenderness, exist at exhausting levels of emotion.

Nick, as played by Peter Falk, shouts and storms and is always on. Mabel (Gena Rowlands, who won an Oscar nomination), seems so touchingly vulnerable to every kind of influence around her that we don't want to tap her, because she might fall apart. Because their personalities are so open, so visible, we see what might be hidden in a quieter, tidier film: that Nick no less than Mabel is trapped in a society where people are assigned roles, duties, and even personalities that have little to do with what they really think and who they really are. This is where Cassavetes is strongest as a writer and filmmaker: at creating specific characters and then sticking with them through long, painful, uncompromising scenes until we know them well enough to read them, to predict what they'll do next, and even to begin to understand why.

Mabel and Nick and their relatives and friends are fully realized, convincing, fictional creations, even though Cassavetes does sometimes deliberately push them into extreme situations. There's a scene, for example, where Nick goes almost berserk in throwing a party for Mabel, who's due home from the institution, then tells all the non-family guests to leave immediately and then berates the family, and Mabel, and himself, in a painful confrontation around the dining room table. The scene's just too extreme to take literally. But as psychodrama, or whatever you want to call it, it abandons any niceties or evasions and deals directly with what the characters are really thinking.

There's also the scenes of great quiet comedy, as when one of Nick's co-workers somehow dumps his entire plate of spaghetti into his lap and the others battle between decorous table manners and their desire to laugh. There's Gena Rowlands's incredible command of her physical acting resources to communicate what Mable feels at times when she's too unsure or intimidated to say. There's Falk, in a performance totally unlike his Columbo, creating this character who's so tender, so much in love, and so screwed up. I have a friend who said, after seeing *A Woman Under the Influence*, that she was so affected, she didn't know whether to cry or throw up. Well, sometimes that's the choice life presents you with—along with the laughs.

Woodstock ★ ★ ★ ★
R, 180 m., 1970

Featuring Richie Havens, Joan Baez, Joe Cocker, Santana, The Who, Sha-Na-Na, Ten Years After, John Sebastian, Crosby, Stills & Nash, Country Joe and The Fish, Arlo Guthrie, Sly and the Family Stone, and Jimi Hendrix. Directed by Michael Wadleigh and produced by Bob Maurice.

Defense Attorney: "Where do you live?"

Abbie Hoffman: "I live in Woodstock nation."

Defense Attorney: "Will you tell the court and the jury where it is?"

Abbie Hoffman: "Yes, it is a nation of alienated young people. We carry it around with us as a state of mind, in the same way the Sioux Indians carry the Sioux nation with them. . . ."

Michael Wadleigh's *Woodstock* is an archaeological study of that nation, which existed for three days in 1969. Because of this movie, the Woodstock state of mind now has its own history, folklore, myth. In terms of evoking the style and feel of a mass historical event, *Woodstock* may be the best documentary ever made in America. But don't see it for that reason; see it because it is so good to see.

It has a lot of music in it, photographed in an incredible intimacy with the performers, but it's not by any means only a rock-music movie. It's a documentary about the highs and lows of a society that formed itself briefly at Woodstock before moving on. It covers that civilization completely, showing how the musicians sang to it and the Hog Farm fed it and the Port-O-San man provided it with toilet facilities.

And it shows how 400,000 young people formed the third largest city in New York State, and ran it for a weekend with no violence, in a spirit of informal cooperation. The spirit survived even though Woodstock was declared a "disaster area," and a thunderstorm soaked everyone to the skin, and the food ran out. The remarkable thing about Wadleigh's film is that it succeeds so completely in making us feel how it must have been to be there. It does that to the limits that a movie can.

Woodstock does what all good documentaries do. It is a bringer of news. It reports, it shows, it records, and it interprets. It gives us maybe sixty percent music and forty percent on the people who were there, and that is a good ratio, I think. The music is very much part of the event, especially since Wadleigh and his editors have allowed each performer's set to grow and build and double back on itself without interference. That is what rock music in concert is all about, as I understand it. Rock on records is another matter, usually, but in the free form of a concert like Woodstock, the whole point is that the performers and their audience are into a back-and-forth thing from which a totally new performance can emerge.

We get that feeling from Jimi Hendrix when he improvises a guitar arrangement of "The Star Spangled Banner," rockets bursting in air and all. We get it from Country Joe, poker-faced, leading the crowd through the anti-Vietnam "I Feel Like I'm Fixin' to Die Rag." We get it in the raunchy 1950s vulgarity of Sha-Na-Na doing a tightly choreographed version of "At the Hop." And we get it so strongly that some kind of strange sensation inhabits our spine, when Joe Cocker and everybody else in the whole Woodstock nation sings "With a Little Help from My Friends."

This sort of participation can happen at a live concert, and often enough it does. But it is hard to get on film, harder than it looks. It is captured in *Woodstock*, maybe because Wadleigh's crew understood the music better and had the resources to shoot 120 miles of film with sixteen cameras. This gave them miles and hours of film to throw away, but it also gave them a choice when they got into the editing room. They weren't stuck with one camera pointed at one performer; they could cut to reaction shots, to multiple images, to simultaneous close-ups when two members of a band did a mutual improvisation.

And of course they always had the option of remaining simple, even shy, when the material called for it. One of the most moving moments of the film, for me, is Joan Baez singing the old Wobbly song "Joe Hill," and then rapping about her husband David, and then putting down the guitar and singing "Swing Low, Sweet Chariot," with that voice which is surely the purest and sweetest of our generation. Wadleigh and company had the integrity to let her just sing it. No tricks. No fancy camera angles. Just Joan Baez all alone on a pitch-black screen.

But then when the occasion warrants it, they let everything hang out. When Santana gets to their intricate rhythm thing, Wadleigh goes to a triple-screen and frames the drummer with two bongo players. All in synchronized sound (which is not anywhere near as easy as it sounds under outdoor concert conditions). And the editing rhythm follows the tense, driving Santana lead. The thing about this movie, somehow, is that the people who made it were right there, right on top of what the performers were doing.

Watch, for example, the way Richie Havens is handled. He is supposed to be more or less a folk singer—a powerful one, but still within the realm of folk and not rock. So you would think maybe he's seem slightly less there than the hard-rock people? Not at all, because Wadleigh's crew went after the power in Havens's performance, and when they got it they stuck so close to it visually that in his second song, "Freedom," we get moved by folk in the way we ordinarily expect to be moved by rock.

We see Havens backstage, tired, even a little down. Then he starts singing, and we don't see his face again, but his thumb on the guitar strings, punishing them. And then (in an unbroken shot) down to his foot in a sandal, pounding with the beat, and then the fingers, and then the foot, and only then the face, and now this is a totally transformed Richie Havens, and we are so close to him, we see he doesn't have any upper teeth. Not that it matters; but we don't usually get that close to anybody in a movie.

Moving along with the music, paralleling it sometimes on a split screen, are the more traditionally documentary aspects of *Woodstock.* There are the townspeople, split between those who are mean and ordinary and closed off, and those like the man who says, "Kids are hungry, you gotta feed 'em. Right?" And the farmer who made his land available. And kids skinny-dipping, and turning on, and eating and sleeping.

Wadleigh never forces this material. His movie is curiously objective, in fact. Not neutral; he's clearly with the kids. But objective; showing what's there without getting himself in the way, so that the experience comes through directly.

With all that film to choose from in the editing room, he was able to give us dozens of tiny unrehearsed moments that sum up the Woodstock feeling. The skinny-dipping, for example, is free and unself-conscious, and we can see that. But how good it is to see that kid sitting on a stump in the water and turning to the camera and saying, "Man, a year ago I never would have believed this was the way to swim. But, man, this *is* the way to swim."

What you're left with finally, though, are the people. I almost said the "kids," but that wouldn't include the friendly chief of police, or the farmer, or Hugh Romney from the Hog Farm ("Folks, we're planning breakfast in bed for 400,000 people"), or the Port-O-San man, or the townspeople who took carloads of food to the park.

Wadleigh and his team have recorded all the levels. The children. The dogs (who were allowed to run loose in this nation). The freaks and the straights. The people of religion (Swami Gi and three nuns giving the peace sing). The cops (eating Popsicles). The Army (dropping blankets, food, and flowers from helicopters). *Woodstock* is a beautiful, complete, moving, ultimately great film, and now that many years have come to pass and the Woodstock generation is attacked for being just as uptight as all the rest of the generations, it's good to have this movie around to show that, just for a weekend anyway, that wasn't altogether the case.

Working Girls ★ ★ ★

NO MPAA RATING, 90 m., 1987

Louise Smith (Molly), Ellen McElduff (Lucy), Amanda Goodwin (Dawn), Marusia Zach (Gina), Janne Peters (April), Helen Nicholas (Mary). Directed by Lizzie Borden and produced by Borden and Andi Gladstone. Screenplay by Borden and Sandra Kay.

There is, I imagine, somewhere in the mind of every man who goes to a prostitute the fantasy that he is somehow unique; that the woman has never met anyone quite like him before, and that, although her other clients may be "johns," he is an individual.

Working Girls both supports and destroys that illusion. The prostitutes in this movie may, indeed, never have met anyone quite like certain clients before, but that is not necessarily a compliment. What makes each man different is the nature of his fantasy life, the specific scenario he is seeking from a prostitute. What makes each man the same is that there are only so many fantasies, and so many ways to fulfill them, and, for the working girls, only so many hours in a day.

Working Girls takes place during one day in a Manhattan bordello. The routine is well-established. The guys call in, the "phone girl" makes an appointment or a sales pitch, the women pass the time with idle small talk and gossip, and occasionally something truly exciting happens—such as when the phones are put on hold and the madam has a temper tantrum.

One by one, the guys come in through the door, each one burdened with the weight of his uniqueness. "How's everything?" one of the hookers asks a client. "Terrific," he says. "We have a new secretary at the office." "Yeah, it's been pretty busy around here," the girl says. "I can imagine," the guy says.

Some of the johns have really wild scenarios going on in their heads. One of them, for example, wants a hooker to enact a situation in which she is blind and only sexual intercourse with the guy can make her see again.

Others are into more kinky situations, but the bottom line is always the same: What goes on in bed between the hooker and the john is simply the occasion for the man to replay old and deep needs that have been in place for years. The woman is relatively unimportant, because she is not the fantasy but more like the supporting cast.

Working Girls has a lot of fascinating stuff in it, but most of it has to do with management and capitalism, not sex. We learn a great deal about clean towels, birth control, disease prevention, and never putting the phones on hold. We also learn a lot of euphemisms: For example, "Make sure the client is completely comfortable before you take any money." In other words, make sure the guy is naked, because then you know he's not a cop.

The movie is told largely through the eyes of Molly (Louise Smith), a lesbian whose lover doesn't know what she does for a living. After Molly arrives at work (on her ten-speed bike), we meet the other girls, some of them naive, some of them middle-age and weary, all of them bereft of illusions about men.

Sometimes, however, something touching happens in the sessions behind the closed doors. There are fugitive moments of tenderness, quiet passages of communication. It is a cliché that prostitutes are really selling companionship, not sex, and *Working Girls* seems to support that notion. What is remarkable is not that the girls are cynical and hardened, but that they have retained as much gentleness and empathy as they have. Like workers in more respectable professions such as psychiatry, medicine, and the ministry, they seem to have the ability to care, if only for a short time, about some of their clients, and to be nice to them. By the end of this movie, you wonder where they find not only the patience, but also the strength.

Working Girls is not a slick and dramatic movie. There are moments that seem forced and amateurish, and the overall structure of the story is fairly predictable. What the movie does have, though, is the feeling of real life being observed accurately. I was moved less by the movie's conscious attempts at artistry than by its unadorned honesty: The director, Lizzie Borden, has created characters who seem close to life, and her movie helps explain why the world's oldest profession is, despite everything, a profession.

The World According to Garp ★ ★ ★
R, 126 m., 1982

Robin Williams (Garp), Mary Beth Hurt (Helen Holm), Glenn Close (Jenny Fields), John Lithgow (Roberta), Hume Cronyn (Mr. Fields), Jessica Tandy (Mrs. Fields), Swoozie Kurtz (Hooker), Amanda Plummer (Ellen James). Directed by George Roy Hill and produced by Hill and Robert L. Crawford. Screenplay by Steve Tesich.

John Irving's best-selling novel, *The World According to Garp,* was cruel, annoying, and smug. I kept wanting to give it to my cats. But it was wonderfully well-written and was probably intended to inspire some of those negative reactions in the reader. The movie version of *Garp,* however, left me entertained but unmoved, and perhaps the movie's basic failing is that it did not inspire me to walk out on it. Something has to be wrong with a film that can take material as intractable as *Garp* and make it palatable.

Like a lot of movie versions of novels, the film of *Garp* has not reinterpreted the material in its own terms. Indeed, it doesn't interpret it at all. It simply reproduces many of the characters and events in the novel, as if the point in bringing *Garp* to the screen was to provide a visual aid for the novel's readers. With the book we at least know how we feel during the saga of Garp's unlikely life; the movie lives entirely within its moments, keeping us entirely inside a series of self-contained scenes.

The story of Garp is by now part of best-selling folklore. We know that Garp's mother was an eccentric nurse, a cross between a saint and a nuisance, and that Garp was fathered in a military hospital atop the unconscious body of a brain-damaged technical sergeant. That's how much use Garp's mother, Jenny Fields, had for men. The movie, like the book, follows Garp from this anticlimactic beginning through a lifetime during which he is constantly overshadowed by his mother, surrounded by other strange women and women-surrogates, and asks for himself, his wife and children only uneventful peace and a small measure of happiness.

A great deal happens, however, to disturb the peace and prevent the happiness. Garp is accident-prone, and sadness and disaster surround him. Assassinations, bizarre airplane crashes, and auto mishaps are part of his daily routine. His universe seems to have been wound backward.

The movie's method in regarding the nihilism of his life is a simple one. It alternates two kinds of scenes: those in which very strange people do very strange things while pretending to be sane, and those in which all of the dreams of those people, and Garp, are shattered in instants of violence and tragedy.

What are we to think of these people and the events in their lives? The novel *The World According to Garp* was (I *think*) a tragicomic counterpoint between the collapse of middle-class family values and the rise of random violence in our society. A protest against that violence provides the most memorable image in the book, the creation of the Ellen James Society, a group of women who cut out their tongues in protest against what happened to Ellen James, who had her tongue cut out by a man. The bizarre behavior of the people in the novel, particularly Garp's mother and the members of the Ellen Jamesians, is a cross between activism and insanity, and there is the clear suggestion that without such behavior to hold them together, all of these people would be unable to cope at all and would sign themselves into the nearest institution. As a vision of modern American life, *Garp* is bleak, but it has something to say.

The movie, however, seems to believe that the book's characters and events are somehow real, or, to put it another way, that the *point* of the book is to describe these colorful characters and their unlikely behavior, just as Melville described the cannibals in *Typee.* Although Robin Williams plays Garp as a relatively plausible, sometimes ordinary person, the movie never seems bothered by the jarring contrast between his cheerful pluckiness and the anarchy around him.

That created the following dilemma for me. While I watched *Garp,* I enjoyed it. I thought the acting was unconventional and absorbing (especially by Williams, by Glenn Close as his mother, and by John Lithgow as a transsexual). I thought the visualization of the events, by director George Roy Hill, was fresh and consistently interesting. But when the movie was over, my immediate response was not at all what it should have been. All I could find to ask myself was: What the hell was *that* all about?

Y,Z

The Year of Living Dangerously

★ ★ ★ ★

PG, 114 m., 1983

Mel Gibson (Guy Hamilton), Linda Hunt (Billy Kwan), Sigourney Weaver (Jill Bryant), Michael Murphy (Pete Curtis), Noel Ferrier (Wally O'Sullivan), Bill Kerr (Colonel Henderson). Directed by Peter Weir and produced by Jim McElroy. Screenplay by David Williamson, Weir, and C.J. Koch.

The Year of Living Dangerously achieves one of the best re-creations of an exotic locale I've ever seen in a movie. It takes us to Indonesia in the middle 1960s, a time when the Sukarno regime was shaky and the war in Vietnam was just heating up. It moves us into the life of a foreign correspondent, a radio reporter from Australia who has just arrived in Jakarta, and who thrives in an atmosphere heady with danger. How is this atmosphere created by Peter Weir, the director? He plunges into it headfirst. He doesn't pause for travelogue shots. He thrusts us immediately into the middle of the action—into a community of expatriates, journalists, and embassy people who hang out in the same bars, restaurants, and clubs, and speculate hungrily on the possibility that Sukarno might be deposed. That would be a really big story, a corrective for their vague feelings of being stuck in a backwater.

Guy Hamilton, the journalist (Mel Gibson), is a lanky, Kennedyesque, chain-smoking young man who has a fix on excitement. He doesn't know the ropes in Indonesia, but he learns them quickly enough, from a dwarfish character named Billy Kwan. Billy is half-Oriental and half-European, and knows everybody and can tell you where all the bodies are buried. He has a warm smile and a way of encouraging you to do your best, and if you sometimes suspect he has unorthodox political connections—well, he hasn't crossed you yet. In all the diplomatic receptions he's a familiar sight in his gaudy tropical shirts. *The Year of Living Dangerously* follows Guy and Billy as they become friends, and something more than friends; they begin to share a common humanity and respect. Billy gets Guy a good interview with the local Communist Party chief. He even introduces Guy to Jill Bryant (Sigourney Weaver), a British attaché with two weeks left on her tour. As the revolution creeps closer, as the stories get bigger, Guy and Jill become lovers and Billy, who once proposed to Jill, begins to feel pushed aside.

This sounds, no doubt, like a foreign correspondent plot from the 1940s. It is not. *The Year of Living Dangerously* is a wonderfully complex film about personalities more than events, and we really share the feeling of living in that place, at that time. It does for Indonesia what Bogdanovich's *Saint Jack* did for Singapore. The direction is masterful; Weir (whose credits include *Picnic at Hanging Rock*) is as good with quiet little scenes (like Billy's visit to a dying child) as big, violent ones (like a thrilling attempt by Guy and Billy to film a riot).

The performances of the movie are a good fit with Weir's direction, and his casting of the Billy Kwan character is a key to how the film works. Billy, so small and mercurial, likable and complicated and exotic, makes Indonesia seem more foreign and intriguing than any number of standard travelogue shots possibly could. That means that when the travelogue shots *do* come (and they do, breathtakingly, when Gibson makes a trip into the countryside), they're not just scenery; they do their work for the film because Weir has so convincingly placed us in Indonesia. Billy Kwan is played, astonishingly, by a woman—Linda Hunt, a New York stage actress who enters the role so fully that it never occurs to us that she is not a man. This is what great acting is, a magical transformation of one person into another. Mel Gibson (of *The Road Warrior*) is just right as a basically conventional guy with an obsessive streak of risk-taking. Sigourney Weaver has a less interesting role but is always an interesting actress. This is a wonderfully absorbing film.

Yentl ★ ★ ★ ½

PG, 134 m., 1983

Yentl (Barbra Streisand), Mandy Patinkin (Avigdor), Amy Irving (Hadass), Nehemiah Persoff (Papa). Directed and produced by Barbra Streisand. Screenplay by Jack Rosenthal and Streisand.

To give you a notion of the special magic of *Yentl*, I'd like to start with the following complicated situation:

Yentl, a young Jewish girl, wants to be a scholar. But girls are not permitted to study books. So she disguises herself as a boy, and is accepted by a community of scholars. She falls in love with one of them. He thinks she is a boy. He is in love with a local girl. The girl's father will not let him marry her. So he convinces Yentl to marry his girlfriend, so that at least he can visit the two people he cares for most deeply. (The girlfriend, remember this, thinks Yentl is a boy.) Yentl and the girl are wed. At first Yentl manages to disguise her true sex. But eventually she realizes that she must reveal the truth. That is the central situation in *Yentl*. And when the critical moment came when Yentl had to decide what to do, I was quietly astonished to realize that I did not have the slightest idea how this situation was going to turn out, and that I really cared about it.

I was astonished because, quite frankly, I expected *Yentl* to be some kind of schmaltzy formula romance in which Yentl's "secret identity" was sort of a running gag. You know, like one of those plot points they use for Broadway musicals where the audience is really there to hear the songs and see the costumes. But *Yentl* takes its masquerade seriously, it treats its romances with the respect due to genuine emotion, and its performances are so good that, yes, I really did care.

Yentl is Barbra Streisand's dream movie. She had been trying to make it for ten years, ever since she bought the rights to the Isaac Bashevis Singer story it's based on. Hollywood told her she was crazy. Hollywood was right—on the irrefutable logical ground that a woman in her forties can hardly be expected to be convincing as a seventeen-year-old boy. Streisand persisted. She worked on this movie four years, as producer, director, cowriter, and star. And she has pulled it off with great style and heart. She doesn't really look like a seventeen-year-old boy in this movie, that's true. We have to sort of suspend our disbelief a little. But she *does* look seventeen, and that's without a lot of trick lighting and funny filters on the lens, too. And she sings like an angel.

Yentl is a movie with a great middle. The beginning is too heavy-handed in establishing the customs against women scholars (an itinerant book salesman actually shouts, "Serious books for men . . . picture books for women"). And the ending, with Yentl sailing off for America, seemed like a cheat; I missed the final scene between Yentl and her "bride." But the middle 100 minutes of the movie are charming and moving and surprisingly interesting. A lot of the charm comes from the cheerful high energy of the actors, not only Streisand (who gives her best performance) but also Mandy Patinkin, as her long-suffering roommate, and Amy Irving, as the girl Patinkin loves and Streisand marries.

There are, obviously, a lot of tricky scenes involving this triangle, but the movie handles them all with taste, tact, and humor. It's pretty obvious what strategy Streisand and her collaborators used in approaching the scenes where Yentl pretends to be a boy. They began by asking what the scene would mean if she *were* a male, and then they simply played it that way, allowing the ironic emotional commentaries to make themselves.

There was speculation from Hollywood that *Yentl* would be "too Jewish" for middle-American audiences. I don't think so. Like all great fables, it grows out of a particular time and place, but it takes its strength from universal sorts of feelings. At one time or another, almost everyone has wanted to do something and been told they couldn't, and almost everyone has loved the wrong person for the right reason. That's the emotional ground that *Yentl* covers, and it always has its heart in the right place.

Young Doctors in Love ★ ★
R, 96 m., 1982

Michael McKean (Dr. August), Sean Young (Dr. Brody), Harry Dean Stanton (Dr. Ludwig), Patrick MacNee (Dr. Jacobs), Hector Elizondo (Angelo), Dabney Coleman (Dr. Prang). Directed by Garry Marshall and produced by Jerry Bruckheimer. Screenplay by Michael Elias and Rich Eustis.

The basic joke in *Young Doctors in Love* was anticipated five years ago, in Mel Brooks's *Silent Movie*. Remember the scene where Brooks and his cohorts stand by Sid Caesar's bedside, watching his heartbeat reflected on a television monitor, when suddenly the heart beep turns into a Pong game? That combination of gallows humor and contemporary cross-references is repeated again and again in *Young Doctors in Love*, and it's finally not very funny. Yet the movie sounds like a good idea. Maybe it was a good idea, lost in the execution. *Young Doctors in Love* has as its modest ambition to be to "General Hospital" what *Airplane!* was to the *Airport* movies and ABC's "Police Squad" was to TV cop shows. Maybe there are two problems here: (1) It is rather hard to outflank "General Hospital," a parody of itself, and (2) If you do, you wind up skirting the edges of very unpleasant comic material about blood and death. Hospitals are just not very funny.

The movie takes place in a loony Los Angeles city hospital, where we meet all the standard types: the monomaniac surgeon, the befuddled chief of staff, and sex-and-dope crazed interns and nurses, and the ambitious young medical students in their first year of residence. There also are several long-running gags, the unfunniest being about a hit man who is turned into the hapless victim of accidents and near-fatal emergency treatments. The movie looks at times like a real-life version of one of those drawings by *Mad* magazine's Jack Davis, in which lunatics chase each other in circles.

Are there funny moments in the middle of the chaos? Yes, there are. There is, in fact, one wonderfully funny moment, starring that superb character actor Harry Dean Stanton, he of the long face, the quivering eyelids, and the perpetual hangover. He attempts to explain the secretion of bodily fluids to the amazed young medical students, and by the time he is finished with his amazing catalog, there is not an orifice left untapped.

That's a great scene, and Dabney Coleman has some nice moments as the egotistical surgeon, obviously modeled on the sorts of Texas super doctors who do most of their operations on the cover of *Life* magazine. Coleman reminds us again here of his versatility; his roles also have included the boss in *9 to 5* and Jane Fonda's fiancé in *On Golden Pond*. But for the rest, *Young Doctors in Love* is not very funny and not very inventive. God knows it tries. Like *Airplane!*, it spends its energy trying to wedge laughs into every crevice of the plot. There are some nice moments, especially a gag about *E.T.* But most of the time I wasn't laughing, and toward the end I wasn't even smiling. When a comedy goes wrong, it goes very wrong. *Young Doctors in Love* goes very wrong.

Young Frankenstein ★ ★ ★ ★
PG, 108 m., 1974

Gene Wilder (Dr. Frankenstein), Peter Boyle (His Monster), Madeline Kahn (Elizabeth), Cloris Leachman (Frau Blucher), Gene Hackman (Blind Man). Directed by Mel Brooks and produced by Michael Gruskoff. Screenplay by Gene Wilder and Brooks.

The moment, when it comes, has the inevitability of comic genius. Young Victor Frankenstein, grandson of the count who started it all, returns by rail to his ancestral home. As the train pulls into the station, he spots a kid on the platform, lowers the window, and asks: "Pardon me, boy; is this the Transylvania station?" It is, and director Mel Brooks is home with *Young Frankenstein*, his most disciplined and visually inventive film (it also happens to be very funny). Victor is a professor in a New York medical school, trying to live down the family name and giving hilarious demonstrations of the difference between voluntary and involuntary reflexes. He stabs himself in the process, dismisses the class, and is visited by an ancient family retainer with his grandfather's will.

Frankenstein quickly returns to Transylvania and the old ancestral castle, where he is awaited by the faithful houseboy Igor, the voluptuous lab assistant Elizabeth, and the mysterious housekeeper Frau Blucher, whose very name causes horses to rear in fright. The young man had always rejected his grandfather's medical experiments as impossible, but he changes his mind after he discovers a book entitled *How I Did It* by Victor Frankenstein. Now all that's involved is a little grave-robbing and a trip to the handy local Brain Depository, and the Frankenstein family is back in business.

In his two best comedies, before this, *The Producers* and *Blazing Saddles*, Brooks revealed a rare comic anarchy. His movies weren't just funny, they were aggressive and subversive, making us laugh even when we really should have been offended. (Explaining this process, Brooks once loftily declared, "My movies rise below vulgarity.") *Young Frankenstein* is as funny as we expect a Mel Brooks comedy to be, but it's more than that: It shows artistic growth and a more sure-handed control of the material by a director who once seemed willing to do literally anything for a laugh. It's more confident and less breathless.

That's partly because the very genre he's satirizing gives him a strong narrative he can play against. Brooks's targets are James Whale's *Frankenstein* (1931) and *Bride of Frankenstein* (1935), the first the most influential and the second probably the best of the 1930s Hollywood horror movies. Brooks uses carefully controlled black-and-white photography that catches the feel of the earlier films. He uses old-fashioned visual devices and obvious special effects (the train ride is a study in manufactured studio scenes). He adjusts the music to the right degree of squeakiness. And he even rented the original *Frankenstein* laboratory, with its zaps of electricity, high-voltage special effects, and elevator platform to intercept lightning bolts.

So the movie is a send-up of a style and not just of the material (as Paul Morrissey's dreadful *Andy Warhol's Frankenstein*). It looks right, which makes it funnier. And then, paradoxically, it works on a couple of levels: first as comedy, and then as a weirdly touching story in its own right. A lot of the credit for that goes to the performances of Gene Wilder, as young Frankenstein, and Peter Boyle as the monster. They act broadly when it's required, but they also contribute tremendous subtlety and control. Boyle somehow manages to be hilarious and pathetic at the same time.

There are set-pieces in the movie that deserve comparison with the most famous scenes in *The Producers*. Demonstrating that he has civilized his monster, for example, Frankenstein and the creature do a soft-shoe number in black tie and tails. Wandering in the woods, the monster comes across a poor, blind monk (Gene Hackman, very good) who offers hospitality and winds up scalding, burning, and frightening the poor creature half to death.

There are also the obligatory town meetings, lynch mobs, police investigations, laboratory experiments, love scenes, and a cheerfully ribald preoccupation with a key area of the monster's stitched-together anatomy. From its opening title (which manages to satirize *Frankenstein* and *Citizen Kane* at the same time) to its closing, uh, refrain, *Young Frankenstein* is not only a Mel Brooks movie but also a loving commentary on our love-hate affairs with monsters. This time, the monster even gets to have a little love-hate affair of his own.

Young Sherlock Holmes ★ ★ ★

PG-13, 109 m., 1985

Nicholas Rowe (Holmes), Alan Cox (Watson), Sophie Ward (Elizabeth), Anthony Higgins (Rathe), Susan Fleetwood (Mrs. Dribb), Freddie Jones (Cragwitch), Nigel Stock (Waxflatter). Directed by Barry Levinson and produced by Mark Johnson. Executive producer, Steven Spielberg. Screenplay by Chris Columbus.

It really does make sense, once you've overcome the novelty of the idea, that Sherlock Holmes and John H. Watson originally met while at school. Their friendship is the sort of immature bond that can best be forged between adolescents, based on Watson's hero worship and Holmes's need for an admiring audience. There has always been something of the eternal teen-ager about Holmes and Watson, especially in their love of gadgets and mysteries and technical intricacies, and their complete bafflement when faced with such complex subjects as human nature, for example, or women.

Young Sherlock Holmes suggests that Holmes and Watson met in their middle teens, at an English public school, and that Holmes solved his first case at about the same time. This theory involves a rewriting of their historic first meeting, but the movie suggests that it set a pattern for many more meetings to come: Watson blunders into the orbit of the supercilious Holmes, who casually inspects him and uses a few elementary clues to tell him everything about himself.

The school they attend is one of those havens of eccentricity that have been celebrated in English fiction since time immemorial. It is run by Rathe (Anthony Higgins), a bright young man, but it is also inhabited by old professor Waxflatter (Nigel Stock), a retired don who hopes to invent the first airplane, and who regularly launches unsuccessful flights from the tops of the school buildings.

Holmes and Watson look, as schoolboys, like younger versions of the men they would someday become. Holmes (Nicholas Rowe) is tall, slender, and taciturn, and Watson (Alan Cox) is short and round and nearsighted. Watson is in every sense the new boy, always available to run an errand for the adored Holmes, to provide a cheering section, and to chronicle the great man's adventures.

The plot of *Young Sherlock Holmes* seems constructed out of odds and ends of several stories by Arthur Conan Doyle. For unknown reasons, several men with no apparent connection to one another die under mysterious circumstances. To Watson's amazement, Holmes finds the missing connection, determines that they have died while hallucinating, identifies the hallucinatory drug and its means of attack, and arrives at a likely suspect.

If these story elements seem typical of Conan Doyle, there is also a lot in this movie that can be traced directly to the work of Steven Spielberg, the executive producer. The teen-age heroes, for example, are not only inspired by Holmes and Watson, but are cousins of the young characters in *The Goonies*. The fascination with lighter-than-air flight leads to a closing scene that reminded me of *E. T.* And the villain's secret temple, with its ritual of human sacrifice, was not unlike scenes in both Indiana Jones movies.

It also doesn't take a Sherlock Holmes to identify the one element of *Young Sherlock Holmes* that definitely doesn't fit; that's the character of Elizabeth, a fetching young girl played by Sophie Ward. She is the granddaughter of the mad inventor, and also lives at the school, and we are asked to believe that young Holmes has had a schoolboy crush on her. I personally do not believe that Sherlock Holmes, the great investigator, ever even began to penetrate the mystery of women, but the movie just barely gets away with the character of Elizabeth by having Holmes swear there will never be another woman for him, for the rest of his life.

The elaborate special effects also seem a little out of place in a Sherlock Holmes movie, although I'm willing to forgive them because they were fun. The traditional world of Holmes (in the movies, anyway) has been limited to fogbound streets, speeding carriages, smoky sitting rooms, and the homes and laboratories of suspects. In this film, we get a series of hallucinations that are represented by fancy special effects, and then there's the pseudo-Egyptian temple of doom at the end.

The effects were supplied by Industrial Light & Magic, the George Lucas brain trust, and the best one is a computer-animated stained-glass window that fights a duel with Holmes. I liked the effect, but I would have liked it more if, at the end of the movie, Holmes had drawn Watson aside, and, using a few elementary observations on the apparent movement of the stained glass, had deduced the eventual invention of computers.

Zabriskie Point ★ ★

R, 111 m., 1970

Mark Frechette (Mark), Daria Halprin (Daria), Paul Fix (Café Owner), Rod Taylor (Lee Allen). Directed by Michelangelo Antonioni and produced by Carlo Ponti. Screenplay by Fred Gardner, Sam Shepard, Tonino Guerra, Clare Peplo, and Antonioni.

One of the most unpleasant conventions of movie shorthand is that when adults are happy they act like children. The hero and heroine fall in love, and lickety-split the camera goes all mushy and they race through the park, fly kites, feed the swans in the cemetery, and (most important of all) giggle as the mustard drips out of their hot dogs. I've yet to see one of these sequences that didn't end with the lovers buying hot dogs from that bushy-haired Italian vendor whose specialty is peddling drippy hot dogs to lovers. Turns out the guy's name is Antonioni, and watch it, you're getting that stuff all over your Berkeley sweatshirt.

Michelangelo Antonioni is a fitfully brilliant director whose best, and basic, insight is that the fashionable cultivation of boredom can break down our ability to feel and love. In the 1950s, it seemed to him, people became so shy of spontaneity that they lost the knack. His characters were so alienated and spiritually exhausted they could hardly even get through breakfast together.

We loved it. *Eclipse* (1962) had us leaving the theater feeling deliciously betrayed and alone. *Blow Up* (1967) was even better. It was set in swinging London and left us feeling betrayed, alone, and with-it. In between, Antonioni gave us *The Red Desert* (1964), possibly the most passive and empty serious movie of the decade. That was Antonioni's thing, anyway, and he knew where he was going with it. But something (the enthusiasm young people had for *Blow Up* maybe) caused him to fall victim to that plague of personal directors, involvement. He had been getting his material out of his own instincts, but now he decided to do a "committed" movie about American society and the radical movement.

I suspect the project itself was exactly counter to his talents. He is not remotely an activist in his personal style, and I have a notion he recoils from people who raise their voices in public disagreement. But he decided to make *Zabriskie Point* anyway and cast his lot with the militants, who cast it right back at him. This is such a silly and stupid movie, all burdened down with ideological luggage it clearly doesn't understand, that our immediate reaction is pity. His earlier films have made us think of Antonioni as vulnerable; he shouldn't have exposed himself like this.

The director who made Monica Vitti seem so incredibly alone is incapable, in *Zabriskie Point*, of making his young characters seem even slightly together. Their voices are empty; they have no resonance as human beings. They don't play to each other, but to vague narcissistic conceptions of themselves. They wouldn't even meet were it not for a preposterous Hollywood coincidence. After the hero rejects radical rhetoric (just like that), he decides to try direct personal action and there's a clumsy sequence during which he maybe kills a policeman (the murder in this one is as iffy as the one in *Blow Up*). Then the hero steals an airplane, flies into the desert, sees the girl's 1952 Buick, buzzes it a couple of times, lands, and they go into the desert and make love. They make love, in fact, at Zabriskie Point, which is the lowest point in the United States. That is just as symbolic as Mount Whitney, which is the highest, but colder.

The love scenes are obnoxiously true to all the corrupt love scenes Antonioni copies them from. There is no feeling of liberation, or delight, or anything else other than a long, ridiculous time when lots of people roll around in the sand. Then, let's see, the hero paints the airplane in psychedelic colors, flies it back to Los Angeles, and is killed by cops. Period. The movie is not this uncomplicated, but it is certainly this simple. Antonioni attempts to flesh it out with thousands of yards of outdoor billboards, which are supposed to show America being corrupted by advertising and capitalism, I guess.

The fact is, Antonioni has no feeling for young people. In his European films, he allowed his characters to behave mostly as adults. But in *Zabriskie Point* we get kids who fall in love and act like kids (running up and down sand dunes, etc.) and the sight is even more depressing than adults doing it. He has tried to make a serious movie and hasn't even achieved a beach-party level of insight.

Zelig ★ ★ ★

PG, 79 m., 1983

Woody Allen (Leonard Zelig), Mia Farrow (Dr. Fletcher). Interviews: Susan Sontag, Irving Howe, Saul Bellow, Bricktop, Bruno Bettelheim, Professor John Morton Blum. Directed by Woody Allen. Produced by Robert Greenhut. Screenplay by Allen.

Woody Allen's *Zelig* represents an intriguing idea for a movie, and it has been made with great ingenuity and technical brilliance. That's almost enough. In fact, if *Zelig* were only about an hour long, it would be enough, but the unwritten code of feature films requires that it be longer, and finally there is just so much Zelig that we say enough, already.

The movie is a fake documentary, a film that claims to tell the story of Leonard Zelig, a once-famous American who suffered from a most curious disease: He was a human chameleon. He was so eager to please, so loath to give offense, so willing to blend right in, that perhaps some change took place at a cellular level, and Zelig began to take on the social, intellectual, and even physical characteristics of people that he spent time with. Put him with a psychiatrist, and he began to discuss complexes. Put him next to a Chinese man, and he began to look Oriental. This ability to fit right in propelled Zelig, we are told, to the heights of fame in the earlier decades of this century. He hobnobbed with presidents, was honored by ticker-tape parades, and his case was debated by learned societies. *Zelig* at first seems to be simply the documentary record of Zelig's case, but then another level begins to sneak in.

We are introduced (always through the documentary means of newsreel film, still photos, old radio broadcasts, and narration) to one Dr. Eudora Fletcher, who is a psychiatrist. She takes Zelig as a patient, and eventually they fall in love (we can see it happening, by implication, in documentary footage that apparently concerns other matters). The best thing about *Zelig*, apart from its technical accomplishment, is the way Woody Allen develops the human story of his hero; we get a portrait of a life and a poignant dilemma, peeking out from behind the documentary façade. The technical approach of *Zelig* has been experimented with before, most memorably in the fictional *March of Time* newsreel that introduced *Citizen Kane*. In that movie, we saw Charles Foster Kane apparently standing on balconies with Hitler and talking with Mussolini. In *Zelig*, the actors (Woody Allen, Mia Farrow, and dozens more) are so successfully integrated into old footage that we give up trying to tell the real from the fictional.

Zelig is a technical success, and it is also a success as a statement: Allen has a lot to say here about the nature of celebrity, science, and the American melting pot. He has also made an essay about film itself; the way that *Zelig*'s documentary material goes at right angles to its human story makes us think about the line between documentary and poetic "truth."

But the problem is, all of those achievements are easily accomplished at less length than the movie takes. The basic visual approach is clear from the first frames, and although it continues to impress us, it ceases after a while to amaze us. The emerging of Zelig's personality is intriguing, but the documentary framework allows it to emerge only so far, and no farther. We're left wanting more of Zelig and less of the movie's method; the movie is a technical masterpiece, but in artistic and comic terms, only pretty good.

Zorro, the Gay Blade ★ ★

PG, 96 m., 1981

George Hamilton (Don Diego/Bunny), Lauren Hutton (Charlotte), Brenda Vaccaro (Florinda), Ron Liebman (Esteban), Donovan Scott (Paco), James Booth (Velasquez). Directed by Peter Medak and produced by George Hamilton and E.O. Erickson. Screenplay by Hal Dresner.

It is hard to reconstruct these fragments from the memories of childhood but as nearly as I can remember, the Zorro craze came after the Davy Crockett craze and before Elvis. Kids made Z-marks everywhere—on walls, fences, blackboards, and with ballpoints on the shirts of the kids sitting in front of them—and my personal notion is that Datsun sells half of their Z-cars to guys harboring sublimated Zorro fantasies.

Here's the curious thing. I remember a lot about Zorro. I even remember that he was once played by Clayton Moore, who got to keep wearing his Lone Ranger mask. But I cannot remember if the Zorro movies were ever supposed to be funny. I assume that the Zorros played by Douglas Fairbanks, Tyrone Power, and John Carroll were more or less serious, within the broad outlines of the adventure genre. But what about all the Zorro movies and TV shows that Guy Williams made for Disney? Were we laughing at him, or with him?

I ask because I am just as confused after seeing *Zorro, the Gay Blade,* which stars George Hamilton in a dual role as Don Diego Vega and his twin brother, Bunny. (The brother was originally a Vega, too, but after enlisting in the British Navy he changed his name to Bunny Wigglesworth.) This movie is, of course, intended as a comedy, and it has some funny moments. But it's just not successful, and I think the reason is that Hamilton never for a second plays Zorro as if he were really playing Zorro. We could laugh at the previous movie Zorros because they were so serious about their ridiculous codes and vows and pledges of loyalty and chivalric passions. They were funny as long as they played it straight. But when a movie sets out a create a funny Zorro, that's bringing coals to Newcastle. By playing every scene for laughs, Hamilton has nothing to play against.

Zorro, the Gay Blade was no doubt inspired by the enormous success of Hamilton's spoof of a durable Hollywood character, when he played Dracula in *Love at First Bite* (1979). Hamilton demonstrated in that movie, and demonstrates again in this one, that he is a gifted comic actor. He can have fun with his improbably handsome appearance, he can poke fun at his character's vanity, and he can look convincing enough as Zorro (or Dracula) to remind us of the quintessential Hollywood leading men whose footsteps he is stalking.

But . . . should Zorro be funny because of his puffed-up self-importance, or because his role in life is inescapably ridiculous any way you look at it? Should he be funny because of what he is (my theory), or what he does (this movie's theory)? A funnier comedy might have been made out of a more genuinely satirical examination of the Zorro character. Instead, this one provides Zorro with a gay brother who's a screamingly limp-wristed stereotype, and then goes for jokes that are disappointingly predictable. It also gives him a leading lady (Lauren Hutton) who has all she can do to play her role at all, much less play it satirically. And it never provides a comprehensive story to hold the jokes together. Too bad. I think I remember now: We laughed more at the old Zorros, because they didn't know they were funny.

Film Clips

Albert Brooks

Chicago, December 15, 1987—The waiter flawlessly recited the specials for the day, and then he asked if there were any questions.

"Yes, I have one," Albert Brooks said. "Do the fish have names?"

This is the same Albert Brooks who once made a movie where he was trying to tell his girlfriend that their relationship was over.

"It's a no-win situation," he explained.

"No win?" she asked.

"Yes, you know, like Vietnam? And us?"

Brooks was on a tour to promote his movie, *Broadcast News*, but then in another sense he wasn't even officially in town. James L. Brooks, the writer and director of the film, was on a press tour, and Albert had come along sort of because he was headed for New York anyway. Why that explained his presence in Chicago seemed to be a mystery to him.

The movie stars Brooks as a smart, aggressive network TV news reporter who has a crush on a bright young woman producer, played by Holly Hunter. Unfortunately, she feels lust for William Hurt, as a dumb blond anchorman whose looks are carrying him straight to the top. It is Brooks's curse in the movie that he is simply not an anchorman "type," despite his superior intelligence—and apparently not quite Hunter's type, either. As the three of them sort out their emotional involvement, the movie goes on to become a pointed and informed comedy about TV news.

"I love TV news," Brooks was explaining to me. "I'm in the *Guinness Book of Records* as the first person to switch on CNN. I keep a TV on all night long, even in hotel rooms. I wake up in the middle of the night hearing all those terrible things. It was the worst in Washington. All they had was the Headline News Service. I heard the same stories over and over. It was like being in a Chinese prison camp. By morning, I was brainwashed. I called room service and when they answered, I ordered an exploding missile launcher."

Maybe, I said, the reason you seem so convincing as a TV reporter in this movie is that you have absorbed all of their cadences in your sleep.

"Now that Reagan and Gorbachev are going to dismantle all these missiles," Brooks said, "the Sharper Image catalog should sell them as executive paperweights, little chunks of history, at about $350 each. People wouldn't buy them if they were priced any cheaper. Each piece should be numbered, and come with a little history of where it was in the missile. The pamphlet should be in English and Russian. It always looks better if you can't read one of the languages. If I were selling Lysol in Cincinnati, I'd put the instructions in seven different languages. Makes it look Japanese."

Were you ever in the news business?

"The first job I ever had in high school was writing sports for the news. Preparing for this role, I did some research, I hung out with a CBS News crew in L.A., I covered a Reagan dinner in Santa Barbara, and a *Voyager* landing in the middle of the night. Kind of fun."

Brooks examined the appetizer that has been brought to him in Jackie's restaurant and declared it was the most beautiful plate of food he had ever seen. "Would you like a taste of my flower?" he asked.

The overriding fact about Albert Brooks is that he is so intelligent. It must also be his special cross to bear in Hollywood, since he writes and directs movies for audiences that he expects to be at least as intelligent as he is. He has made three: *Real Life, Modern Romance,* and *Lost in America.* All have been successful to a certain degree, but he still finds it a struggle to float a project at the big studios, while the oddball reputation of his movies has not exactly made him more desirable as an actor in other people's films. He runs through his credits:

"I was the campaign manager in *Taxi Driver,* the husband who died in *Private Benjamin,* Dudley Moore's manager in *Unfaithfully Yours,* in the prologue of *Twilight Zone* . . . I always wanted to act, and to finally get a big role like this one has been immensely satisfying. I *knew* and have always known that I had the capacity to go opposite from being funny. I never wanted to be a comedian who only did comedy. There is a scene in the movie where they go from laughing as hard as they can to complete silence in about a tenth of a second, and I thank God I had the opportunity as an actor to do that at least once.

"In my movies, people somehow always think the character is me. Here I am definitely playing someone else. I do not live in Washington, D.C., I do not cover the news, I had never met William Hurt, I am not in love with Holly Hunter—hey, this is a performance here!"

You sound, I said, as if it takes some kind of miracle to make a good movie and to supply a good performance in it.

"Nothing will change in this art form," he said, "unless someone in control is willing to take chances. One good movie occasionally won't do it. When a good movie gets through, to many people they think that's good enough. They think the system's working. But I don't think it's working unless we get eleven a month."

How would you define a good picture?

"A movie that dares to possibly bother somebody, that makes somebody think—of pleasant things or not. That challenges their beliefs, and makes them angry, and makes them roar with laughter, and makes them think, and portrays life somewhat like it really is. The movies are turning into a place to see life as it might be on another planet. I am hopeful that someday we will see a movie in which a large, handsome man has a bad day. But it doesn't seem to be happening. Maybe audiences would get to like movies that have the same unpredictable quality as life. Maybe it would be like the first time you taste broccoli."

I want to get back to this Cable News Network thing, I said. You are in a movie that questions all of the basic assumptions of television news, and yet you say you love news on television. Do you share the opinions of the character you play, or do you like TV news more than he does?

"I love Cable News. I love the *Wall Street Journal.* In L.A., they throw me the *Daily News* even when I don't order it. I love the fact that Larry King can talk to Henry Kissinger and Sandy Duncan in the same hour. I'm not a great sleeper, and at 3 A.M. when I'm awake in California, it's daybreak on the East Coast and I can get my day started, I don't have to wait for that delayed "Today" Show.

"Now maybe if I was watching TV with all of the problems of *Broadcast News* in mind, I might not like it as much. But I'm not watching it like that. Maybe I'm watching some small part of a story they're covering, and looking at it not as news, but as some kind of human story. If they're interviewing a man and his wife, and the man is talking, I may stare at the wife's face. TV news allows you an occasional glimpse of lives that are not staged."

Woody Allen

New York, November 24, 1987—It was one of those November days when a movie named *September* sounds like warm weather. Woody Allen was working down around the corner of Broadway and 19th Street, directing a film, and he was under a certain amount of pressure. One of his stars, Mia Farrow, was pregnant with his child and was playing a pregnant woman, and now the doctor was speculating that she might deliver before she was finished with the role. Also, his editor, Sandy Morse, was pregnant, and might deliver at any moment. Woody was like a gynecologist trying to figure out when to schedule a ski weekend.

Allen was filming seven days a week to beat those deadlines on his movie, which, like all of his movies, has no title and is being filmed in secrecy. He was also planning to spend his lunch break talking about *September,* his latest film, which is not a comedy and was up against a lot of big-budget movies that are comedies. So it was with a certain irony that he was reminded of his predicament by Sven Nykvist, who is the cinematographer on the untitled production.

All Nykvist really said, on his way to his own lunch, was "hello." But that was enough to start Woody Allen thinking about his hero Ingmar Bergman, the great Swedish director who employed Nykvist to film many of his masterpieces.

"I was going to visit Bergman last year when we were all in Sweden," Allen said, settling into the front seat of the car that would take him to lunch, "but I thought, you know, with all of Mia's kids, getting all the right travel documents was just too much of an undertaking. I did meet him once. Do you know how he spends his day, now that he's in retirement? He wakes up early in the morning, he sits quietly for a time and listens to the ocean, he has breakfast, he works, he has an early lunch, he screens a different movie for himself each and every day, he has an early dinner, and then he reads the newspaper, which would be too depressing for him to read in the morning."

As Allen wistfully described Bergman's idyll, so different from his own, the car shot down Broadway and went weaving through autumn leaves to bring us up with a bounce before John's Pizza, the celebrated Greenwich Village pizzeria. "I eat here whenever I have the nerve to have a good meal," Allen explained.

In the back room, the manager came to take his order and said they had laid in a supply of the special low-fat cheese Allen prefers on his pizza. Allen ordered a medium cheese. So did I. The manager suggested we could share a large, and we both simultaneously said, no, we'd have the two mediums. You've got to know someone pretty well to share a pizza with him.

Allen was looking slightly harried and rushed, as a director has a right to when he is making a film, even if he is not awaiting the birth of his first baby. I told him that when I read in the paper that he and Mia were expecting, I felt a genuine rush of pleasure for him. This is a man who once told me that not a day goes by when he does not seriously contemplate suicide, and somehow I had the feeling that lately a few days were getting by.

"My feelings about the baby are very complicated," he said. "You know, Mia and I adopted a baby, Dylan, before she got pregnant. And there is absolutely no difference in the love I will feel for the new child, and the love I feel for Dylan. In fact, I love Dylan so much that I would be pleasantly surprised if I love the baby we are having together as much as the one we adopted.

"I've noticed in recent months that a lot of the people I know are having babies. Women friends will say the biological clock is ticking, and I tell them not to bother to get pregnant—just adopt. When I first met Mia and she was telling me about all the children she had adopted, I said, 'What a nice gesture.' And she said, no, I had it all wrong; it's not what she had done for them, it was what they had done for her. Now I know how she felt."

The waiter arrived with our pizza. "Hey, you know what?" he said, "what a coincidence. I was watching cable TV last night, and one of your movies was on, you know, the one you did with Mary Hartman?"

"Right, Louise Lasser," Allen said.

". . . and I was saying to my son's fiancee, wouldn't it be a coincidence if he came in today, and here you are."

"Well, it's great pizza," Allen said. He took a slice and doubled it up lengthwise and started to eat it. John's Pizza is owned by a man named Pete Castellotti, who has had roles in three of Allen's movies, *Broadway Danny Rose*, *The Purple Rose of Cairo*, and *Radio Days*. The pizzeria is emblematic of Allen's whole approach to Manhattan, an island he loves so much that he once spent the Fourth of July watching *Poltergeist* in a midtown movie palace, just to avoid the terrible experience of having to spend the holiday in the country.

That's why the plot of *September* is such a departure from all of his other films, although it shares a country setting with *A Midsummer Night's Sex Comedy*. It's not a comedy and it's not a tragedy; it's more of an irony, a scrutiny of six people who have made a pattern of looking for love in all the wrong places.

The film takes place is an isolated country cottage where several romances are running their separate courses fairly swiftly. Elaine Stritch plays a legendary, much-married actress of a certain age, now wed to Jack Weston, a wealthy manufacturer. Mia Farrow plays her daughter, whose life has never been the same since a day in adolescence when she seized a gun and killed her mother's lover. Some months earlier, Farrow came out to the country to recover from a nervous breakdown, and took many long walks with a neighbor, Denholm Elliott, who is now quietly and hopelessly in love with her.

But Farrow is in love with Sam Waterston, a writer who lives nearby. The writer, however, is just in the process of falling in love with Dianne Wiest, Farrow's best friend, who has left her husband and is spending some time in the country to sort out her thoughts. Wiest does not want to hurt Farrow's feelings, but is swept away by passion and feels this thing may be bigger than either of them. During a long weekend in the country, all of these entanglements sort themselves out, with much pain and some truth, and a good deal of Allen's literate, ironic dialogue.

"This story has a very old provenance," Allen was explaining in the back room of the pizzeria. "You know Mia has this country house, a real Chekovian setting, a little cottage, a little lake, very Russian. For a long time I've wanted to write a little Russian family drama to set there. I finally did it, but by the time the screenplay was ready the weather had changed, and so we had to build the sets in Astoria Studios here in New York."

"Therefore avoiding the need to go out to the country," I observed. Allen's acute discomfort around forests, fields, and mosquitoes is well known.

"I'm actually sort of glad it turned out that way," Allen said. "I knew I wanted to do this movie, but I kept asking myself if I could stand to stay in the country for six weeks, where every fifteen minutes seems like six hours. I knew I would be working all the time, surrounded by friends and associates, and yet still I'd miss the city. Although let me tell you, shooting at Astoria is not all that easy. You ever been out there? My idea of a perfect location for a studio would be on Park Avenue, right where the Armory is.

"When we were shooting *Hannah and Her Sisters*, that was the perfect set-up. We shot a lot of it in Mia's apartment, and all I had to do was cross Central Park every day. Bergman shoots right in his own house, and on his island. I'd shoot in my house, but I live in a co-op apartment, and it's against the rules. I keep thinking, maybe if I had a beach house, I could maybe go out there and shoot . . ."

"But you had a beach house," I said. "You had a beach house, and you never went to it. That's what you told me once."

He folded another piece of pizza and regarded it as if it were a beach house.

"I really bought it for my sister. I went out and looked at it, and bought it, and I thought, gee, this is nice, maybe I could use it for myself some weekends, you know. But I only went out once. I hated it, and my sister hated it, and we sold it."

He performed that characteristic Woody Allen shrug, the one with the quizzical expression that seems to say, you just can't depend on beach houses anymore.

"Shooting in Mia's house led to a very strange experience for Mia the other night," he said. "She told me she was in bed in her bedroom, looking at *Hannah and Her Sisters* on the TV set at the end of the bed. She realized she was looking at a scene in the movie that showed the same bed and the same TV set, in the same room."

I said I had been meaning to ask him about *King Lear,* the Jean-Luc Godard film he agreed to appear in. That was the movie inspired by the famous deal at the Cannes Film Festival three years ago, when the legendary French director and Cannon president Menahem Golan signed a deal on a table napkin. I told Woody I had seen the napkin, on which Golan misspelled Godard's name, but promised him a script by Norman Mailer, and a cast including Orson Welles as Lear and Woody Allen as the Fool.

"Norman Mailer wrote the screenplay?" Allen asked.

"Yeah."

"Well, there was no screenplay at all the day Godard shot me. I worked for half a day. I completely put myself into his hands. He shot over in the Brill Building, working very sparsely, just Godard and a cameraman, and he asked me to do foolish things, which I did because it was Godard. I'd be amazed if I was anything but consummately insipid. What I did seemed foolish and was foolish.

"He was very elusive about the subject of the film. First he said it was going to be about a Lear jet that crashes on an island. Then he said he wanted to interview everyone who had done *King Lear,* from Kurosawa to the Royal Shakespeare. Then he said I could say whatever I wanted to say. He plays the French intellectual very well, with the five o'clock shadow and a certain vagueness. When I got there for the shoot, he was wearing pajamas—tops and bottoms—and a bathrobe and slippers, and smoking a bad cigar. I had the uncanny feeling that I was being directed by Rufus T. Firefly—you know, when Groucho is supposed to be the great genius, and nobody has the nerve to challenge him? But Godard *is* supposed to be a genius, I guess . . ."

He looked uncertain. I asked him about the campaign against colorization, the insidious and immoral practice of taking old black-and-white films and artificially adding color to them. Allen journeyed to Washington in August to testify at Senate hearings on the question.

"I'm telling you," he said, sounding dubious, "we may not win this fight. It's amazing how insensitive people are on the issue. Even well-meaning newspaper editorials, like one in the *Atlanta Constitution,* completely miss the point. They treat it as a free enterprise issue, instead of asking whether anyone has the right to change an artist's work. And when you go to Washington and see what's there . . . I dunno. Most of the senators and congressmen were OK, but some of them were real backwoodsmen. Listening to them at the hearings was like sitting on an airplane trapped next to a guy from the swamps. They kept asking a million questions and never grasped the real issues. One guy asked me if I would be against colorizing *Gone With the Wind.* He didn't know it was made in color."

"Have you ever thought about making a political satire?"

"I've thought about it. Especially now. When Reagan was elected, I knew he was gonna be bad, but I didn't realize how bad. They say we get the president we deserve. Great, but I got the president *they* deserve."

The pizza was mostly gone, and it was time for Allen to get back in his car and return to the set. On the way back, winding through the busy streets, he fell to musing on great movie directors.

"Bergman has apparently definitely retired," he said. "No more Bergman films. Bunuel is dead. Truffaut. You didn't like the new Fellini movie? I haven't seen it yet. Jeez, there are so few of the giants left that when one of them like Fellini makes a movie, you can't wait to see it. But that whole generation is disappearing. No more giants."

"What about American directors?" I asked him.

"Isn't that funny?" he said. "I never even think of Americans as geniuses. We had one. Orson Welles. Gone too."

Dennis Quaid

Los Angeles, October 14, 1987—The weekly personality magazines say Dennis Quaid is Hollywood's hottest new sex symbol, and so I put the big question to him: When are we going to see a condom in a movie love scene?

"See it?"

"Know it's there."

"That's more likely than seeing it. Seeing it might inspire the wrong kind of audience reaction. But, I grant you, today when you go to the movies and the characters jump into bed without a care in their heads, the thought has to pass through your mind that maybe at some point after the kissing, a hand ought to appear in the frame holding a little packet."

"No major star has yet appeared in the same love scene as a condom. Would you be willing?"

"Hmmm. Using a rubber? Well, the first time out, it would have to be portrayed with a little humor, because the audience is likely to laugh. When I was making this film with Cher, we wondered if we should use a condom, because here you have a public defender and a lobbyist and they're both grown-up, smart people, and so they would be most unlikely to just pop into bed without any fears."

"So what did you do?"

"Left out the sex scene. They never go to bed with each other. But that decision may have also been because it was very unlikely, given the ethics of the situation, that a lawyer *would* make love with a member of the jury while the trial was under way. She could lose her case that way."

Quaid grinned and twirled an enormous coil of spaghetti on his fork. This was at lunch the day after the premiere of *Suspect*.

"The problem you would face with a condom," he said, "is, how do you depict the necessary actions without spoiling the romance? In real life, it's one thing. In the movies, the audience wants their romantic illusions. But then there's the other side of the coin: AIDS has actually put the romance back into movie relationships. People are getting to know each other better before they hop into the sack. Maybe it's kinda good for all of us."

Quaid lifted the spaghetti into the air and regarded it with the childlike delight of Gordo Cooper, the astronaut he played in *The Right Stuff.* "Of course," he added, "there's gonna be dancing in the streets when they cure it!"

When he was talking about the new depth in movie romances, Quaid could have been referring to the extraordinary chemistry he generated with Ellen Barkin in *The Big Easy.* In that one, Barkin played a prosecutor and Quaid played the cop she was prosecuting, and that didn't stop them from falling in love. But in their first big love scene, *The Big Easy* made a major break with movie tradition by showing the two would-be lovers ending in tears and confusion, rather than passion and triumph.

"We did a lot of improvisation with the role," he said. "Usually the so-called woman's role is just a backup for the man. Ellen and I worked on the script, and fought very hard to make the woman's role bigger. Because when the woman is a better character, that makes the man more interesting, too. That's true as a general principle: Sometimes you see big stars who get the top billing in their movies, and then there aren't any other interesting characters or good actors anywhere around. I'd rather work with actors who are better than me. I love great character actors. Of course, I *was* a character actor for a long time."

To be precise, Quaid took twelve years in the movies before he hit the big time, and if after *The Big Easy*, *Suspect*, and *Innerspace* he is indeed one of the hottest new stars in Hollywood, success was a long time in coming. He followed his brother Randy into the movies, started by hanging around sets and lending a hand when needed, and got his first big break in *Breaking Away* (1978), the great Peter Yates movie about a big bicycle race in Bloomington, Ind. Yates is also the director of *Suspect*, but had to pay a lot more to hire Quaid this time.

"Twelve years to be an overnight success," Quaid said. "I'm glad it happened this way. If you have a lot of success when you're young, you have no chance to be good. You play it too safe, trying to protect what you've built up. Playing supporting roles for a long time gave me a chance to get my chops up, and a chance to appreciate what I finally achieved when I got it."

"What do you think about being described as a sex symbol?"

He grinned. "I'll take whatever I can get."

Quaid's biggest 1987 film was not supposed to be *The Big Easy* or *Suspect*, however, but *Innerspace*, a summer release in which he played a renegade astronaut who was miniaturized along with his space capsule, and injected by accident into the bloodstream of an ordinary citizen, played by Martin Short.

"That was allegedly supposed to be the biggest hit of the year, but they screwed up the ad campaign," Quaid said. "They made it look like a space hardware adventure instead of a human comedy. They're bringing it out again with a new campaign."

Disappointments over would-be hits are not new for Quaid, who almost saw *The Big Easy* evade success: "I made it two years ago. I thought it was good, but Vestron, which owned it, didn't know. It was on the shelf awhile. It was set to be released in a couple of Southern cities when it was premiered last January (1987) at the U.S. Film Festival in Park City, Utah. David Puttnam, who was then the head of Columbia Pictures, saw it and stood up and said, 'I want it!' and he bought it and gave it the release it deserved."

That kind of reprieve did not come for the role of Quaid's career, in one of the great American films of its time, which foundered at the box office. That was *The Right Stuff*, the brilliant 1983 movie about the early days of the U.S. space program, with Quaid playing astronaut Gordon Cooper.

"What can I say that hasn't already been said? Kids thought it was a history lesson. Or people thought it was a political film about John Glenn's presidential campaign. Who knows? When I was appearing with my brother off-Broadway in Sam Shepard's *True West*, we got a bottle backstage with a note on it: 'From the best pilot in the world.' Gordo was in the audience."

In *True West*, Randy and Dennis Quaid emerged bruised and bloodied every night after performing Shepard's violently physical family drama, with its climactic scene of hot toasters and kitchen appliances flying through the air. It was, Dennis said, a test of his friendship with his brother: "One night we got into a screaming and shouting match backstage, and the audience could hear us and figured it was part of the show. We almost came to blows. Then we started talking, about what we liked about each other, and what we hated, what we envied, and what we loved. We wound up skipping hand-in-hand down Christopher Street."

Quaid grinned and finished his mountainous plate of spaghetti and wondered if he should go for dessert.

"I have to put on thirty pounds for my next role," he said. "I play an ex-football player who is married to Jessica Lange, and the movie is about twenty-five years of marriage. He was the football hero and she was the homecoming queen. What do you do when the greatest moment of your life was when you were twenty-five?"

He considered.

"Not a problem I have had myself," he said.

Albert Finney

Toronto, September 24, 1987—Albert Finney walked into the hotel room and in one smooth, unbroken stride was at the minibar next to the desk.

"Let's take that one," he said, extracting a bottle of champagne from the little refrigerator. "It seems to be the larger one. And order me a gross of them. Yes, this one should do nicely. Ordinary champagne. It's pink champagne I mistrust. Do you know . . . I have just finished doing a dozen or two interviews for television, and anyone crossing the country for the next month or two would think I only own one suit of clothes."

He settled down wearily on a sofa and watched the bubbles subside in his glass.

Somebody had written, in a review of his film *Orphans*, that the years had not been kind to his face, but as he grinned, I thought that they had. It is a large, wide face filled with character, but guarded. When he smiles, the sun comes up and you are reminded of Tom Jones or of Harold, the Chicago gangster he plays in *Orphans*. When the sun goes behind the clouds, you are looking at the face of a man who has felt as much pain as pleasure. It is just the face an actor should prize.

He had shepherded *Orphans* all the way from its origins in Chicago to its run on the London stage and now to its film version, directed by Alan Pakula, and he was at the Toronto Film Festival to premiere the film and grant interviews and attend parties and drink hotel champagne out of minibars. He said he had fallen in love with Harold when he first saw the play performed at the Steppenwolf Theater in Chicago, and although he had brought the play to London, he was surprised to be asked to star in the film. He thought the part would go to an American actor, his voice said, but his face said, "Not bloody likely."

In the movie he is kidnapped by two strange, almost feral, young men who live in a ruined house in the middle of an urban wasteland. He frees himself, and then, instead of escaping, he stays to teach them the ropes—how to be really tough guys, disciplined, and thoughtful. Matthew Modine and Kevin Anderson play the two boys, who run wild through the house like monkeys in a zoo, and at the center of their manic displays, Finney comes on like an old Irish-American charmer, conning them into accepting his total authority.

The role is his third drunk in a row, after Sir, the weathered old trouper in *The Dresser*, and the Consul, who spends all of *Under the Volcano* in an alcoholic hallucination. Harold drinks himself into oblivion early in *Orphans*, but then stays sober and watchful as he gains the upper hand over the two wild youths. When *Under the Volcano* premiered at the Cannes Film Festival, its director, John Huston, was told at a press conference that Finney's acting was so convincing he must have been drunk the whole time. "Albert never drank when we were filming," Huston replied in a grave, judicious tone, "but in the evenings, I believe he did a certain amount of drinking. The performance was based on his understanding of drunkenness, which is profound."

"I don't think Harold in *Orphans* is actually an alcoholic," Finney said. "He just wants to celebrate. Or perhaps to escape. If you want to know what I think about the subject, drunkenness is not a permanent way out. In my youth, I got pissed quite a bit, and at one time flirted with the idea of becoming the next John Barrymore, but that didn't work out because at a certain stage I tended to throw up. I would go off to the Gents, and come back to the table smiling as if I had just taken a leak.

"Many actors have used alcohol as a get-out clause, as if people would say, 'Oh, well, he would have been a great actor, but for the drink.' In *Volcano*, I would have my dresser bring me a tot of tequila, which I would use to wet my lip, to create a memory of that horrible dehydrated feeling when one has drunk much too much, much too long."

Did you discuss drinking with Huston?

"We did not discuss a great many things. That was not John's way. I've been thinking of him a lot since his death. I was upset, of course, but perhaps he was in pain and perhaps it was for the best. His courage was remarkable. We shot that film in Cuernavaca, which is 6,000 feet above sea level. By 1983 he was already on oxygen, not during the filming but at lunchtimes and in the evening. In no way did he let it affect his attention to the film.

"You know, right from the first and up until now, I've been seeing films by John Huston. And he still has another one left for us—*The Dead*. I think he had a tremendous respect for the Consul, who needed the infusion of alcohol to cope with the betrayal of his wife, knowing full well that drinking would kill him. But John didn't discuss the scenes very much. Not at all. When I came to leave, I felt very emotional, and I believe he did, too, but he would not show it. All he said was, 'See you later, kid.' Perhaps John—remember, I only knew him toward the end of his life—perhaps John had a problem with emotion, and displaying it."

Finney leaned forward and drank some of the hotel champagne, and settled back again and sighed. Since he first became a star in the angry British working-class film *Saturday Night and Sunday Morning* (1961), Finney has worked as hard and as visibly as any actor in his generation, and he has never abandoned his dedication to the stage, even while ranking second only to Michael Caine among British actors who have worked frequently in American movies; his recent credits also include *Wolfen* and Oscar-nominated performances in *Shoot the Moon* and Huston's *Annie*.

He was preparing to go back to London for rehearsals for a new play by Ronald Harwood, who wrote *The Dresser*, but he said he sometimes felt like Her Ladyship, the wife of Sir, in *The Dresser*, who despairingly asks her husband, "What difference does one Lear more or less really make?"

"It makes a difference to the man who's done it," Finney said. "Sir and many other actors simply have the smoldering desire to portray life on the stage as something we care about, even if it stops at the footlights. Sir says he is putting himself through his ordeal to win a real knighthood, but actually his requirement to act is a compulsion."

Do you ever go back and review your own films and plays, and try to decide what was really important to you?

"I saw a bit of *Tom Jones* on the telly the other evening, and I thought, oh, there's that young chap who played that role. I'm not yet at the stage of *Sunset Boulevard*, with my butler screening my old movies to make me young and happy again. When I glimpse that person who was me, in those films I made years ago, what I may see is, there a technique that no longer works, there a moment when I was self-conscious, there a moment when I was not really there. I am more interested in now and in the future. I don't live a planned life."

He thought for a moment. "I was astonished, as everyone was, to read in Olivier's autobiography that he left the stage for six or seven years because he was paralyzed by a fear of drying up, of forgetting his lines. Even for Olivier, whatever works on the stage remains elusive. It slips through your fingers at the crucial moment. You never stop looking for it. And that generation of Olivier and Richardson and Gielgud provides a mark we all strive for.

"The next generation was Guinness, and then Scofield and Burton. Then O'Toole and Courtenay and perhaps myself. Then Hoskins and Hopkins, all trying to figure it out. Tom Courtenay told me once, after seeing Richardson and Gielgud on the stage, that there was something there above and beyond their brilliance. It had to do with their combined experience, the unity of a generation. Tom said, 'It will never be like that again. We have divided our time between stage and film. We will never total the stage hours they have.' "

But does it matter?

"It does," Finney repeated, "to the man who's done it."

Cher

Los Angeles, October 14, 1987—Cher's daughter, Chastity, was asking her a question the other day: "Mom, you were alive in the sixties. Did you wear love beads?"

Cher repeated the question and then she looked up, and was silent for a moment, letting the irony sink in. " 'I not only wore them,' I told her, 'I made them.' But she has trouble visualizing that whole time. She said she saw a movie about love-ins and body painting, and she wanted to know if people got together in the park and gave flowers to one another. And I said, 'Well, kinda. Your dad and I protested in some political demonstrations, and they tried to arrest us. There was a feeling of unity, a feeling that something good would come out of all of that.' "

Cher put her feet up on a coffee table and thought about that time. And I thought about the first time I interviewed Sonny and Cher, in a Chicago hotel room nearly twenty years ago, when they were young and I was young and the world was young, and everybody knew what love beads were. Now Cher sat before me, and she looked great, and I knew that her career had never looked better, but there was a gravity about her, a seriousness. She was a grown-up, a thoughtful one, and in the Flower Power summer of 1968, it would never have occurred to me that Cher would ever be a thoughtful grown-up, or that I would, either.

Hollywood calls it career management. Cher has been a master of it. Through all the twists and turns of popular taste, she has remained a star for twenty years, and she has never received more respect than in the four years since she put her music on the back burner and began to work as a serious movie actress.

She was nominated for an Oscar for her work in *Silkwood* (1983). She won the best actress award at Cannes for *Mask* (1985), and in 1987 she appeared in one of the summer's best movies, *The Witches of Eastwick*. Her next movie was *Suspect*; and she still had a great triumph ahead of her in in Norman Jewison's *Moonstruck*.

Cher had a lot to prove when she left rock music to appear in Robert Altman's Broadway and movie versions of *Come Back to the 5 & Dime, Jimmy Dean, Jimmy Dean* (1982), but now in Hollywood it is no longer, "Can Cher handle it?" It is, "Can we get Cher?"

In *Suspect,* she plays a lawyer from the District of Columbia's public defender's office. A lawyer?

"That's what a lot of people have asked me about," she said. "How can Cher play a lawyer? Actually, I spend a lot of my time with lawyers. To create the character, I did the same thing I did to create the lesbian character in *Silkwood.* There wasn't much I could draw on from within myself, but I just figured, the person is a person first, and all the rest is just an additional layer. The lesbian was a woman; her sexuality was just a facet of that. To play the lawyer, I had to learn to say a lot of complicated legal things as if I understood them, but the key to the character wasn't the law, it was that she had no personal life. She's defending a homeless man, but the key to the movie is that everyone in it is homeless."

In the film, she is assigned to the case of a skid row bum who is the prime suspect in the murder of a government legal secretary. Dennis Quaid, one of the hottest actors in Hollywood, co-stars as a Capitol Hill lobbyist who is a member of the jury, and who begins to develop some theories about the case—and a warm interest in Cher's empty private life.

"I went to meet the women in the public defender's office," Cher said, "and I learned a few physical things. Like, I hold myself differently in the movie, and I walk differently. But the key thing I discovered is that none of them have any lives outside the office. The men in the office are married or have girlfriends, but the women are single and say they don't have time for private lives. Their work is their life."

She sighed, and crossed her legs, and looked pensive.

"That's what you had in common with them?" I asked.

"Even with my situation, with all kinds of money and all kinds of help, my life seems crazy and out of proportion right now. I'm worried about my children, maintaining a home, maintaining a relationship. It's hard to balance everything."

She looked tired and a little sad. This was the morning after the world premiere of *Suspect,* and she was supposed to be going through the motions, talking about how great it was to make the movie, et cetera and so forth, and she was making an effort, but there were things on her mind.

"Right now," she said, "is the busiest I have ever been."

"Too busy?"

"Between now and December 4, I have so many things to do, I don't know how I'm going to get it all done—or what I'm doing it for. Yesterday I threw myself flat on my back in my bed and looked up at the ceiling and asked myself why I was driving myself so hard. What it proved. I've committed myself and so I will do it all, because it's my nature to follow through on commitments. But it makes you think about the nature of success."

"You're not happy."

"Oh, I'm happy." A pause. "I'm happy enough. I'm not delirious. The actual work that I do—the actual acting, the actual singing, the actual dancing—that's fun. It's all the other stuff around it that drives me crazy."

I asked her what she had to do between now and Dec. 4.

"Are you serious? Do you really want to know?"

I said I was serious. She took a deep breath.

"OK. I had three days in between *Moon-*

struck and *Suspect,* which was filmed six days a week, up at six, home at eight, in Toronto, Boston, and Washington. Hotel rooms. Work and sleep. I was a dead person. Right now, I am preparing for a video I'm going to star in and direct. I get up at seven, take a dance class, then an exercise class—weight training, to make me strong. Then I practice dancing with my partner. It's hard. I haven't danced in six years. Then I work on the storyboard for the music video. Then next week I rehearse all night, every night. Then on Sunday and Monday of the week after that, we shoot all night.

"Tuesday, I sleep. Tuesday night, we do the film-to-tape transfer. Wednesday, I pose for some ads for health and tennis clubs. Wednesday night, editing on the video. Thursday, I edit. Friday, I get up in the morning and pose for the poster for *Moonstruck.* Friday night, editing. Saturday, editing.

"On Sunday, I fly to New York. On Monday, three episodes of the 'Today' show with Gene Shalit. Then I do interviews with 'Entertainment Tonight,' CNN, and *USA Today*. Tuesday, the New York written press. Wednesday, Concorde to France. Thursday, two TV shows in Paris. No jet lag, of course. Friday, fly to England, two more TV shows. Then to Germany, two more TV shows.

"Then back to New York, prepare for David Letterman and 'Saturday Night Live.' I go to a voice teacher to coach me with my songs. Then up to Toronto to meet Norman Jewison for the premiere of *Moonstruck.* Then to L.A. for the Academy screening of *Moonstruck.* And in between, all of the advance interviews for magazines with a lot of lead time, so they will come out when the movies are in the theaters."

She recited this extraordinary list in a flat voice, her eyes looking at an appointment calendar in her mind.

"I have two movies, a music video, and an album all happening at once," she said. "It never occurred to me. When I get up in the morning, my assistant Debbie gives me a little page of all the things I have to do. I do them. Then the day is over. I love the acting and the singing, but whoever said there was gonna be all this other stuff?

"Plus, I'm trying to remodel an apartment in New York. These guys I have working for me, I don't know where they came from. Nobody ever seems to be doing anything. I saw *The Money Pit* and I laughed a lot. It's exactly true. The electrician is waiting on the carpenter. The carpenter is waiting on the plumber. Everybody's waiting on somebody, and three weeks go by, and nothing has happened, and it's cost you a fortune."

"So," I said, repeating myself, "are you happy?"

"I'm not really happy today," Cher said. "Today I have to feel that if I can get this period of a couple of months out of the way, I can take some time off. I'm too tired. The last vacation we had, I took the kids and my best friends and we went to Italy, backpacking, bumming around, looking at wonderful things. It was a wonderful time. Then back to the rat race again."

She put her feet back up on the coffee table again.

"I guess I must love it," she said, "or I wouldn't do it. Huh?"

Martin Short

Chicago, November 11, 1987—There's a benefit at Chicago's Second City for Comic Relief, the stand-up's favorite charity, and word is all over the room that Martin Short is going to sit in on the 11 p.m. improvisational set. Nobody budges when the lights go up after the early show, and there is a certain buzz in the room. These guest appearances by famous former Second Citians have become a tradition over the years, a promise that if others who once labored in wretched anonymity made it onto "Saturday Night Live," there is hope for us all.

The lights go down, and it is announced to no one's surprise that Short is joining the cast. He sticks his head out from the wings, grins, and wiggles his eyebrows. There is a roar from the crowd. Later he appears as one of his most famous Second City characters, the hairdresser who reads the supermarket tabloid over his customer's shoulder and confides that everyone in the paper "goes both ways, y'know."

Halfway through this sketch, he does a little dance step on the stage, and the crowd roars again, because they recognize the distinctive footwork of Ed Grimley, the most famous character Short created on "SNL." And I remembered what Short had been telling me earlier in the day: "On the stage at Second City, if you come out with a funny look on your face and get a laugh, well, that's one laugh you didn't have to write. The whole idea is, How do I get out of writing?"

But a second later he was telling me about his all-time favorite Second City sketch, which was entirely written, and which he first saw performed on stage at the Toronto branch of Second City, by Brian Doyle-Murray and Joe Flaherty:

"That's the one where the student goes into the professor's office to try to talk him out of doing the take-home exam, and the professor surprises him by agreeing—and then insisting on an oral exam, on the spot. The student is, of course, caught completely off-guard, and has not spent a second studying for the course. The professor asks him to describe the principal provisions of a famous European treaty. "Well," the student says, "in connection with this treaty, France . . . of course . . . had nothing to do with it . . . and Russia . . . which was, of course, on the periphery of Europe . . . did not precisely, I think we could say, see eye-to-eye with England on certain provisions . . . although the Germans were, typically, not uninvolved . . ."

"The whole genius of the sketch," Short had explained, "is that the student is trying to read the right answer in the professor's eyes. Everybody has gone through a situation like that, in which you are desperately trying to say the right thing, and have no idea what the right thing is."

Onstage, Short was in another sketch now, one in which a middle-aged man was trying to live with the consequences of having persuaded two disco bimbos to move in with him. But I was flashing back to a scene in *Cross My Heart*, where Short and Annette O'Toole appear in a scene with the same basic premise as the oral examination.

In the movie, Short plays a district sales manager for a firm that sells designer sunglasses. He has just been fired. He is out on a date with O'Toole, a woman he thinks may be perfect for him. His problem is, he has filled her full of lies. He's told her he just got a promotion, when in fact he has just been fired. He has borrowed a car from his successful friend Bruce, and now he has brought her back to Bruce's apartment, passing it off as his own. His problem is that Bruce's apartment is filled with Bruce's mail, Bruce's family photos, Bruce's model airplanes, Bruce's telephone answering machine with Bruce's voice on it.

As Short desperately tries to explain one inconsistency after another, O'Toole grows more and more suspicious, until finally he confesses one small fib, and she confesses two large ones, and then he turns on her, drawing attention to her falsehoods in order to draw the truth away from himself. It is a fascinating sequence in the film—even if he is rather cruel to her—and what I found myself realizing, as I thought about the scene and watched Short on the stage, was that he approached it in a completely different way than he might have for Second City or "SNL." He played it straight as an actor, with no funny faces and no little Ed Grimley two-step.

That is the secret of Martin Short: That he is a complete actor, who spent ten years in Toronto working at any acting job he could find. His experience does not begin and end with the most visible part of it, his enormously successful time on "Saturday Night Live," nor even with the similar comic acting he did for *SCTV* and at Second City in Toronto.

"My requirements were fairly simple, when it came to acting jobs," he was remembering. "Is it a job? Does it pay? I'll be there." In Toronto, he did all sorts of acting, community, experimental, improvisational, commercial, and by the time he landed his first American network job, on the late TV series "The Associates," he already had four Canadian series under his belt.

"It all started for me in 1972, when they held the famous open auditions for *Godspell* in every city where it played. I stood in line with hundreds or even thousands of other people in Toronto, but somehow I was chosen. That was my first acting job. And in that same cast, from those same auditions, they also picked Gilda Radner, Andrea Martin, and Dave Thomas, and Paul Schafer was the piano player. Within a few months I had met some of the other people who were going to come out of Toronto, like John Candy and Danny Aykroyd, who always smelled of gasoline, because he was always tearing down cars and cycles and rebuilding them."

For some of that crowd, like Radner and Aykroyd, success came quickly. But in 1975, when they were beginning to be successful in New York, Short was having the worst year of his life.

"I went for five straight months completely unemployed," he said, drinking diet pop in his suite at the Ritz-Carlton. "That's why I feel for this guy in the movie, this sunglasses salesman who depends on confidence and poise and luck for everything, and fears that he will never be hired again. I would actually keep tabs of things like subway trains. When I was unemployed, I would go down to the subway station, and the train would just be pulling away. Time after time. Once I finally got a job again, I would go down to the station, and the train would just be pulling in. I don't know. I think it's got to be more than mere coincidence. You start questioning yourself. Your luck is gone. Your magic is gone."

For Short, there were more years when it looked like the train had passed him by, while Aykroyd and Candy became big stars and he was still on the brink. Then came the big rebuilding season at "SNL," with Eddie Murphy and Martin Short as the two hot names on the revitalized show, and Ed Grimley leaping around on the furniture, his pants pulled up under his armpits, his hair marcelled into a fin, making Pee Wee Herman look like a Supreme Court nominee.

For a decade, ever since *National Lampoon's Animal House*, "SNL" has been a launchpad for movie careers. Short's began with *The Three Amigos*, which co-starred Chevy Chase and Steve Martin and opened Christmas, 1986, and closed very soon. Then there was *Innerspace*, with Short playing a wimp who was accidentally injected with a tiny, tiny capsule bearing the miniaturized body and spaceship of a former astronaut played by Dennis Quaid. It opened in August, 1987, and also closed quickly. Next was *Cross My Heart*, with Short and O'Toole onstage for almost the entire movie, including a long and elaborate sex scene during which they become the first reputable Hollywood stars to discuss and employ condoms.

"I wasn't that disturbed about the failure of *Three Amigos*, because it was not necessarily a great movie," Short said. "With *Innerspace*, it was a different story. Everyone thought it had the potential to be a big hit. I was talking all the time with Quaid, who was in *The Right Stuff*, which people thought was going to be the greatest hit of all time, and when it didn't do so well at the box office, he was crushed. So he warned me against getting my hopes up.

"I told him the thing we used to do at Second City, which was to look at one another and say, 'What if we go out there . . . and nobody laughs?' I asked him, 'What if there are *no* laughs in this film?' He said I would get over it: 'In ten or eleven months, you're fine.' But then they started test-marketing the movie, and people loved it. And even Dennis began to cautiously permit himself some hope. And then it didn't do it at the box office, maybe because nobody knew what the movie was about."

He sighed. "Well, I felt good about it," he said. "I saw it, and I felt it was a good movie and I did a good job, and all the rest is just a bonus. It's nice to be in a movie good enough so that, if it comes up in a conversation, you don't have to jump in and say something so your friends won't feel they have to talk about it."

What about *Cross My Heart*, with its sexual frankness and extended bedroom scenes and nonstop game-playing and, of course, its condoms?

"The first thing you have to understand is that I am very happily married and have not gone out on a date for thirteen years. If I had to go out on a date, I have no idea what I would do. Anything would be preferable. In the movies, comedies about dates have a tendency to be about how the guy knocks over the grandfather clock. What we really do on dates is, we do an impersonation of ourselves being relaxed. That was what I was trying to bring to the character. When I first read the script, I asked myself, can I play this guy? And I knew I could. Sometimes the cadences just fall out of your mouth.

"The sex. It was not fun. I am happily married and Annette is happily married and we had to work at those scenes. When I first saw the movie all the way through with my wife, it was in a completely empty theater because we did not want to have to talk to anyone afterwards."

What did she say?

"My wife? She said, 'You were good, honey. And this girl Annette is astounding.' I was not surprised to hear that. Is Annette not sexy? When we were dubbing the movie, I stood there and I saw her filling up the screen with her sexuality."

Just a few weeks ago, I said, Dennis Quaid was saying it would be a long time before a major star in a major movie used a condom. Now here is the first condom movie, so to speak. Was there any discussion about that?

"The movie was written some time ago, and it didn't have any condoms in it. But if you're going to discuss dating in the eighties, how can you logically—or morally—leave out condoms? When we all sat down to read the script with Armyan Bernstein, who wrote and directed the movie, we agreed they had to be in. We came up with a scene that was three or four pages long. Too much. Too awkward. So we approached it more from a wry point of view."

It was time to go. There was time to say one more thing. I told Short that I thought his "SNL" satire of Olympic syncronized swimmers was one of the funniest things I had ever seen on television.

"It was funny," he said, "before we put one word to paper. I saw syncro swimming on TV—real syncro swimming—and I laughed out loud. It is the funniest sport in history."

Fatal Attraction's Fatal Flaw

How should *Fatal Attraction* end? Thoughtfully, or like a slice-and-dice horror movie? That was the choice facing the makers of the film after they held a series of sneak previews in order to test audience reaction.

They knew immediately that they had a potential hit on their hands. But their original ending didn't exactly set audiences on fire. In it, the villain of the film, played by Glenn Close, commits suicide offscreen. But that's not the ending seen by the millions of people who made *Fatal Attraction* a top box-office hit. Instead, the film ends with a protracted and violent sequence that's worthy of one of the *Friday the 13th* movies.

When I saw the film, I felt betrayed and disappointed by that ending—angry that the film's greatness was thrown away with a cheap, compromised conclusion. If you've seen the film, you'll remember the moment that offended me the most—the bathtub scene and its aftermath. After the movie was over, I sat staring at the screen in disbelief, unwilling to believe that the same people who had made such a good film could make such a corrupt ending.

Make no mistake. *Fatal Attraction* is a very good film for most of its length. It tells the story of a happily married man who has a brief fling with a woman who turns out to be a tragically wrong choice. Michael Douglas has been married for nine years to Anne Archer, they have a six-year-old daughter, they are happy—and then, during a weekend when his family is out of town, Douglas has a passionate interlude with Glenn Close.

She's a publishing executive he met through his work. She seems competent and together, but she's not. She is a sick woman who begins to pursue Douglas obsessively—calling him in the middle of the night, visiting his wife, making threats, issuing ultimatums, eventually trying emotional blackmail after she tells him she is pregnant.

Although it is clear fairly quickly that Close is deeply disturbed, much of what she says makes sense. Douglas is appalled when he walks into his apartment and finds Close talking with Archer—ostensibly about buying the place. He screams at her. Her icy answer is irrefutable: "If you won't answer my phone messages, then I have to do something. I am pregnant with your child, and I will not be ignored."

Yes, except that she essentially set up her own rejection. After that first weekend of wild sex, there was little doubt in my mind that Douglas would be back for more. If Close had not been so possessive, trying to keep him in bed, keep him in the room, pin him down on their next date—if she had simply let him go—he would have been on the phone to her in a couple of days, setting up a new date. Her behavior deliberately drove him away. She *wanted* to be rejected.

Douglas's own behavior is not very rational. He is confused by guilt and fear. He tries to confide in his best friend and law partner, but nothing comes of that attempt. He isn't thinking straight. For example, when Close tells him she is pregnant, does Douglas stop to wonder how she could possibly know that, so soon after they had sex? Of course he doesn't think, doesn't do all the things a rational man would do, because her craziness is infectious. He fears her, he dreads his wife's discovery of the affair, he acts irrationally.

All of this emotional turmoil is absolutely spellbinding. *Fatal Attraction* has something complex and tough to say about the emotional warfare between these two people. It demonstrates to Douglas that there are consequences to the "uncomplicated" weekend he envisioned between "two adults who saw their chance, and took it."

The movie is perfectly observed all through the opening and middle passages. Adrian Lyne's direction and James Dearden's screenplay seem incapable of stepping wrong. The words are right, the characters are right, the logic is right. And then it all goes horribly wrong. What happened?

"All sorts of endings had been considered for this film," Lyne told *New York Post* writer Nina Darnton. "We thought of just about everything, apart from the dog doing it. Maybe if we were making a French movie, which, in truth, most of the films I like best tend to be, we wouldn't have taken this route. We had shot it the other way, but when we screened it in the previews, the audience hated her (Close) so much. People were unsatisfied by an off-camera solution."

And so they got an on-camera solution. Boy, did they ever. In a sequence of carnage and violence that literally recalls the bathtub murder at the beginning of Russ Meyer's *Super Vixens* (1975), Close and Douglas have a deadly duel that ends with him drowning her in the bathtub. And then she rises up out of the water like Jason, the unkillable slasher in *Friday the 13th*, and goes after him again—until Anne Archer shoots her through the heart.

Is it true that all audiences "hate" the Glenn Close character? Are people that crude and insensitive? I don't think so. I thought one of the strengths of the movie was the way it played fair with the Close character—making it possible for us to empathize with her reality.

Yes, she is mentally ill. Yes, she is a psychotic. But yes, she is also a suffering human being, and most of her suffering is at her own hands. I felt sorry for her. I knew that Hollywood convention required her to die at the end of the film, but I hoped it would be in a way that preserved some dignity for her character. I felt enraged that the movie caused me to care so deeply for her, and then casually dismissed the entire buildup in order to turn her into a laughable caricature from a routine horror film.

I've talked with several people who have seen *Fatal Attraction* with different audiences in different parts of the country. One person reported that a Chicago audience hissed at the bathtub scene and its aftermath. Most of the reports, however, were that the audience "went crazy" with excitement during the scenes beginning with the roller-coaster ride.

What does this mean? That Adrian Lyne was right to reshoot the ending and kill Glenn Close in a slice-and-dice climax? Yes, that is what it means—if box-office profits justify anything (and in Hollywood, they do). But if you listen carefully to Adrian Lyne, he is confessing that his film's current ending is not even the kind of ending he himself likes.

He prefers "French films," by which I guess he means films told with an adult and thoughtful sensibility. In his system, "American films" are films that aim cheerfully for the lowest common denominator. Lyne boasted to *Chicago Sun-Times* writer Peter Keough that with the current ending, audiences "go nuts! They go potty! . . . They sing along!"

Well, terrific. But I remember one of the movie's best scenes, in which Glenn Close is all alone in her apartment, lonely and isolated, and she compulsively flicks a light on and off. Lyne says that is his own favorite scene in the movie. I have a question. Why couldn't the movie have ended with that scene? Play it through in your head: At the end, but before the bloodshed and carnage, Close achieves some sort of insight into herself—some glimmer of sanity, some brief window in which she can see her madness from the outside. And then she is really alone.

That's one possible ending. Another one would be to replace the "unsatisfactory" off-screen suicide with an on-screen suicide death scene for Close. Early in the film, she and Douglas have a scene where they discuss their love of opera and the plot of *Madame Butterfly*, in which the Japanese heroine commits suicide after her American lover abandons her and goes back to his wife. The conversation is obviously there to set up a suicide. Why not let it happen, poignantly, tragically, and then supply a closing scene in which Douglas surveys the emotional fallout of his one-night stand.

Would such an ending affect the movie's box office? How will we ever know? My notion is that *Fatal Attraction* tells such a compelling story and creates such unforgettable characters that audiences would be *more* moved by an honest ending than by the fraudulent cop-out of the bathtub scene.

What's so bad about French movies, anyway?

And more to the point, why is it assumed that the American audience is so stupid that it should get the weirdo ending it deserves?

Lee Marvin (In Memoriam)

Chicago, September 2, 1987—The first time I saw Lee Marvin, he was holed up in a bar outside the back gate at Paramount, making funny little whistle-and-pop noises while he shot people with his index finger. The last time I saw him, he was getting sort of thoughtful and philosophical, down in his ranch home in Tucson. The time I saw him in between, he had a killer hangover and was nursing it with beer and anchovy pizza at ten in the morning. All three times he was funny, and the last time I saw him, he was happy, too.

Marvin was one of the great off-screen entertainers in Hollywood, a man with a deep, rumbling voice and a cockeyed view of the world that went along with a great irreverence for authority of all kinds, and especially the kind represented by movie directors. That first time I saw him was twenty years ago, when he was starring with Clint Eastwood in *Paint Your Wagon*, and he was spending the afternoon drinking and making libelous remarks about the director, Josh Logan.

The movie was a star-crossed production, which cost untold millions and included such bizarre special effects as a whole village collapsing and Clint Eastwood singing. Marvin had arrived for work at the crack of dawn, and now it was mid-afternoon and the day's first shot had still not been taken. Marvin was running a pool on when Logan would finally get organized, and meanwhile he was getting seriously drunk; if Logan didn't call soon, there wouldn't be much left to summon.

Marvin was at the height of his glory that afternoon. He had won his Academy Award not many years before for *Cat Ballou*, and he was fresh from the box-office triumph of *The Dirty Dozen*. He was holding court like a man for whom there was no tomorrow, and he had attracted the kind of crowd colorful drunks often attract, of people enjoying themselves while waiting to see if there would be any trouble.

As it happened, I had not liked *The Dirty Dozen*, and was at the time a very young film critic who perhaps actually believed that Marvin had read my review, and even cared about it. I was a little hesitant, approaching this large, loud man in the middle of the crowd at the bar, but Marvin was not an actor with a thin skin. He had better things to think about than reviews.

His acting was always strong and confident, and it was usually in action roles. He made some of the best: *The Killers*, *The Professionals*, *Point Blank*, *The Big Red One*. Because he was tall and macho and instantly recognizable with those big, rough-hewn features, he didn't play many subtle roles and wasn't in a lot of seriously artistic films. But when he got the chance, he ran with it. In 1972 John Frankenheimer did a long film version of Eugene O'Neill's *The Iceman Cometh* for the short-lived American Film Theater, and Marvin took the central role of Hickey, the man who appeared in the saloon once a year for his "periodical." It was great, strong, true acting.

Most of the time, though, Marvin was the rumbling professional gunman, or the hard-bitten old soldier, or the cold hired killer. He had a mean look in his eye that could stop a clock. And for a lot of his career, that look was inspired, in one way or another, by hangovers. Marvin was a heavy-duty drinker, and I spent several hours one Saturday in his beach house at Malibu, watching him assault a hangover while engaging in a stream-of-consciousness monologue.

It was a strange but inspired performance. Marvin was being coached through the morning by Michelle Triola, later to figure in the famous "palimony" case, and he sprawled in a chair with his back to the Malibu surf, free-associating about his life, his loves, his travels ("Where were we? Bulgaria? No, Belgravia. I was seriously confused.")

At one point, their dog, LaBoo, walked into the room with a pair of women's panties in its mouth.

"LaBoo," said Triola, "where'd you get those?"

"Hell, Michelle, they're yours," Marvin said.

"They are definitely not mine," said Triola.

"*Bad* dog!" said Marvin.

In 1983, when I visited Marvin at his big, rambling house outside Tucson, the Malibu lifestyle was a thing of the past. He had married his teen-age sweetheart, Pam, and explained that between them they had eight children (four apiece) and nine grandchildren, two of whom were visiting at that very moment.

Marvin had climbed down from the roof, where he was doing some repairs, and now he took me on a tour of the house, which included the 607-pound world record blue marlin he caught off Australia. When we settled down for lunch, he was drinking Diet Coke.

"You're not drinking so much these days?" I asked.

"If I were," he said, "I'd be dead."

He said the move to Tucson was not merely a move out of the mainstream: "I'm as far away as I can get. I hate the Los Angeles scene. Beverly Hills isn't my style anymore, being that I'm not part of the party hierarchy. I don't think I've actually made three films in Los Angeles in fifteen years. Out here, I read, I get involved in a lot of dumb projects, I'm helping this guy fix the roof . . ."

He had just finished shooting what would turn out to be his last feature film, *Gorky Park*, on location in Finland. His co-star was the hot young actor William Hurt, and I asked the old pro what it was like for them, working together.

"He's a pain in the ass," Marvin said. "That's not to say he isn't a good actor. That, I'll give him. But I knew I was in trouble on the first day I met him. I said, 'How about joining us for dinner?' And Bill said, 'How's your soul?' And I thought, 'Oh shit, one of them.' "

One of what?

"One of the profound. Bill is great when he has lines to say. Give him dialogue, and he does just fine. But on his own, you don't know what the hell he's talking about. What he needs in life is a script. Also a director."

Marvin was gentler with another famous co-star, Charles Bronson.

"We did our first film together. It was called *You're in the Navy Now.* That was 1948. We've done five or six films over the years. We look at each other and shake our heads. He's so bad. So mean. He wants to intimidate you, but there's a little gleam way back behind his eyes, if you can see it. We were sitting in London once in a very posh club, wearing black suits, talking to a girl. Charlie says, 'Yeah, sweetheart, it's tough lying on your side in a coal mine.' I say, 'Jesus, Charlie, you ain't been in a coal mine in thirty years.' He drives around in a Rolls-Royce and he's talking about hard times down in the mine."

We talked about movies and about Hollywood. "This was only my third movie in six years," he said. "I don't work as much. I work more than I want to, though. I'd rather just sit around here and do nothing. In my age bracket, I'm not exactly ready for *On*

Golden Pond yet, but I don't see myself making teen-ager pictures."

He stood up and walked over to a window that looked out on a limitless expanse of Arizona.

"I'm happy here. I go to bed early. I get up to greet the dawn. Pam and I have a good time. I met her, you know, back in Woodstock, N.Y., when I got out of the Marines after the war. We went around together for the summer. I was in summer stock. I left to be an actor. She didn't want to go at that time. We met up again years later."

It was time for me to go to the airport, and Marvin wheeled out his pride and joy, a vintage Imperial with 137,900 miles on the odometer, to take me to town. On the way, I asked him what he thought had been his best role.

"I dunno."

What about Hickey in *The Iceman Cometh*?

"Oh, Hickey, yeah. Playing that drunk changed my life in a great way. It taught me the severity of great performances. I'd been lucking my way through for a long time, acting instinctively. *Iceman* forced me to want to be right. I think I went a bit mad playing Hickey. I was stuck for so long in that one night in the gin mill."

We were almost to the airport. I asked him if he had ever thought about writing an autobiography.

"Years ago, there was a book about me," he said. "One of those as-told-to books. I said a lot of astounding things in that book. That was back when I was still in the image-building stage. I wasn't misquoted. I really did say all of those things."

The car came to a stop.

"Well," he said, "they might be true and they might not be true. What do I know?"

John Huston (In Memoriam)

Chicago, September 1, 1987—If I were to make a list of all my favorite movies, and then look at the names of their directors, I would find John Huston's name mentioned more often than any other. No one else made more great films over a longer time, films that stand up today as well as on the day they premiered, films that stand solid and true and have character and strength.

Now that the obituaries are appearing and the tributes are being made, the titles of the films have become a sort of litany, a rosary of names that people recite to give honor to John Huston.

There are the films that everybody knows: *The Maltese Falcon, The Treasure of Sierra Madre, The African Queen, The Night of the Iguana, The Man Who Would Be King.* Then there are *Under the Volcano* and *Prizzi's Honor,* two extraordinary films made at the end of his career, made when he was so ill a lesser man would have taken to his bed, yet made so well they won money and prizes not because they were made by a legend, but because, damn it, they were good movies.

As I sat and thought about John Huston, however, I thought not only of the great and famous films, but of all the others. Here was a man who did not direct films simply so they would be successful, so they would make money. In his long and full career, he made many odd and strange movies, films made simply because he wanted to make them. And on the list are wonderful entertainments like *Beat the Devil*, quirky psychodramas like *Reflections in a Golden Eye*, romantic follies like *A Walk With Love and Death*, strange relationships like the one between an infantryman and a nun in *Heaven Knows, Mr. Allison*, grimy walks on the wild side like *Fat City*, offbeat war stories like *The Red Badge of Courage*, grandiose epics like *The Bible* and *Moby Dick*, and small, bold curiosities like *Wise Blood*, a film so personal and impenetrable you would swear it was directed by a wild-eyed young film school rebel, and not by a man already in his seventies.

For anyone who grew up during John Huston's lifetime, the image of the man came to stand for the fullness of a life of action. He was a tall, joyful, handsome buccaneer who lived life so fully that he had a kind of invincibility about him. He was known not only as a great director, but as a figure of legend, friend of the great, the lord of his castle in Ireland, a man whose famous home in Puerto Vallarta, Mexico, could be reached only from the sea, a lover of racehorses, a formidable drinker, a lover whose five wives only began the list of women who fell for his spell.

Before he became a film director he was a newspaper reporter and a boxer, and when he was hired by Warner Bros. to adapt Dashiell Hammett's *The Maltese Falcon* for the screen, he banged out the script in days and then walked into Jack Warner's office and told him that he, John Huston, was the only man who would ever direct that script. Warner's agreement set in motion one of the most extraordinary careers in movie history.

All his life, Huston was represented by only one agent, Paul Kohner, who was also the agent of his father, actor Walter Huston. Typically, no contract was ever signed; it was a handshake deal. The first time I met Huston it was in Kohner's office in a little white building left over from the earliest days of Sunset Boulevard.

Huston sat on a sofa in front of a wall of photographs. One of them showed John and Walter Huston on the day they both won Academy Awards—John for directing *The Treasure of Sierra Madre*, his father for best supporting actor. Another one of the photos showed Huston and Kohner on location in Mexico for the film, standing on either side of a small, obscure man. The little man was alleged to be B. Traven, author of *Sierra Madre* and the most mysterious literary figure of the twentieth century. Said to be a German refugee to Mexico, his real name was unknown.

I asked Huston if the man were really Traven—a man so reclusive he had hardly been seen, let alone photographed, apart from that one occasion. Huston drew on a long black cigar and thought for a moment. "If you want my opinion," he said, "that is a picture of the man who murdered the man who was B. Traven and sold his manuscripts as his own."

I looked up. Huston was not exactly smiling. But there was something in his eyes, and it was the look of a storyteller with a good yarn to spin. I have since talked with Paul Kohner about that theory of the two Travens, and am not sure if Huston even meant what he said that day. Maybe he was only amusing himself. What I know is that Huston knew his answer provided the best possible story.

And it was that instinct that drove Huston through fifty years of filmmaking. If you look for the common thread in his films, you will find it at the narrative level: He liked to tell good stories about strong, robust characters caught in a tight place. *The African Queen*, *The Treasure of Sierra Madre*, and *Heaven Knows, Mr. Allison* all contain his favorite story construction: Characters who are opposites, forced to share a perilous journey together because they have a common goal. That is the fundamental story line of the oldest stories known to man, and it came naturally to John Huston.

I saw him at work once on the set of a movie, *Victory*, filmed in Hungary in 1980. The story was classic Huston: In a Nazi prison camp, British and American prisoners of war (including Michael Caine and Sylvester Stallone) learn that the commandant is a soccer fanatic. Caine trains Stallone and the rest of a team until the prisoners are so good the commandant challenges a champion Nazi team—and the prisoners use the match to stage an escape.

Huston was seventy-four when he made the film, and already suffering from the emphysema that was his deadly antagonist. But he was the most prepossessing man on the set, handsome, graceful, and courtly, and obviously accustomed to being listened to. When he had an order to give, he gave it quietly, to an assistant. He seemed unperturbed by problems and delays. After a scene had been completed, he thanked his actors with an almost formal graciousness. And they listened to his direction with an attention I had never quite seen before on the sets of other directors. It was as if everyone knew Huston had limitless imagination but limited strength, and the whole company was conspiring to conserve his resources.

John Huston had long been a legend in the movie industry, but in his last years he experienced a kind of renewal of his genius that caused a quiet amazement in the business. Old and weak and, some said, dying, he directed three final films, and the two that had been released at the time of his death were among the best movies that anyone made in those years. They were about three subjects central to his life: drinking, sexual warfare, death.

Under the Volcano starred Albert Finney in a nightmarish screen version of Malcolm Lowry's classic novel about the last day in the life of an alcoholic Englishman in Mexico. *Prizzi's Honor* was a wickedly funny and savagely cynical comedy about two Mafia hitmen (Jack Nicholson and Kathleen Turner) who marry each other and then try to kill each other.

That film won a lot of Oscar nominations, including those for Huston, as best director, and his daughter Anjelica, for best supporting actress (she played a Mafia princess). On Oscar night, they were both favored to win, and history would have repeated itself, with Huston having directed both his father and his daughter to Oscars while winning one himself. Anjelica Huston won her statuette, but Huston was upset by Sydney Pollack (for *Out of Africa*). The camera was on his face when Pollack's name was announced. John Huston did not pretend to be pleased.

The Dead, his final film, not released until after his death, was based on the short story by James Joyce on Irish guilt and redemption. He had always intended it as his last film, and, although he was tethered to an oxygen machine while he made it, it was typical of John Huston that he finished it. It would be surprising if it were not a good film, but even more surprising if it is not exactly the way he wanted it.

Michael J. Fox

Los Angeles, March 16, 1988—Michael J. Fox posed for an *Esquire* cover recently wearing a dark blue pinstripe, a striped shirt, and a power tie. He was using chopsticks to eat sushi, but he wasn't looking at the sushi, he was looking at us. The cover illustrated an article titled "Did the Yuppie Die for Our Sins?" Inside, Fox appeared in another half-dozen photos that symbolized the ultimate yuppie, playing tennis, wearing red suspenders, reading the *Wall Street Journal.*

Michael J. Fox is young, he is urban, and he is certainly professional. In 1987 he made $17 million from activities ranging from the TV series "Family Ties" to the movie *The Secret of My Success* to his commercials for Diet Pepsi. In 1988 he may make even more money, but he will have to work harder for it; he is about to leave for many weeks of location shooting in Thailand for a new Brian De Palma movie. While he is out of the country, his newest movie, *Bright Lights, Big City,* will open. It is based on the huge bestseller about a fact-checker at a New York magazine, whose ambition outruns his talent and his opportunities.

Cut to the back lot at Paramount, late winter, late afternoon. The guard at the gate pointed the way to the long, white building where Michael J. Fox has his offices. There was a chill in the air, and studio messengers on their bicycles pedaled with a certain urgency as they raced from the mail room to the producers' suites. Was there some kind of symbolism here, too?

The Secret of My Success told the story of an ambitious office boy who became successful by pretending to be successful—sneaking out of the mail room to pose as a rising young executive. And now here was Michael J. Fox himself, up these stairs and down this corridor and inside this office door that still didn't have a name on it, and past the secretary at the word processor—Michael J. Fox with his feet up on top of a big, polished executive desk.

"Working in television," he said, "I saw a lot of actors who had some kind of title like associate producer, and they gave them an office the size of a Brillo Pad box, and they got to sit around there and make telephone calls. I never wanted an office until I had a reason for an office. I have deals now with Paramount and NBC, and I have a partner, and we have some really neat plans."

He asked me if I'd like something to drink, and I specified a Diet Pepsi, and he grinned and got a couple out of the office refrigerator. His office was good-sized, and it was in the corner of the building, the power position, but it didn't look lived in yet. The inventory included the desk, a desk calendar, a telephone, a copy of *USA Today*, a wall-to-wall gray carpet, a bookcase bearing the telephone book and a couple of scripts, a sofa, a coffee table, and several golden Emmy statuettes, which were arranged along a shelf behind the desk. No ashtray. Fox has finally stopped smoking.

"I got my shots for Thailand today," he said. "Typhoid, cholera, typhus, diphtheria. It's going to be a hell of an experience. I don't know what to expect. I was talking to a guy who served in Vietnam, and he brought along some of the letters he wrote home. At first they were very thoughtful and poetic, a journal of his experiences. By the end of his tour, he was so crippled by dysentery and everything else, all he could do was scribble. He started writing his mother with the menu of the first meal he wanted on Day One after he got back home: mashed potatoes, a rib eye steak, sour cream coffee cake."

Fox was wearing faded Levi's and a sport shirt, and he looked like a young executive in his mid-twenties who had come into the office on his day off. I mention his apparent age because there was some concern at United Artists (which released *Bright Lights, Big City*) that Fox is still perceived as a kid, as a teen-ager. The *Esquire* cover was part of a campaign to reposition him as an adult.

The irony is that Fox is perceived inside the Hollywood community as owning one of the cannier heads for business of any of the younger stars, to be as involved in his deals and his own financial destiny as anyone since Warren Beatty. "Take the Pepsi thing," he volunteered at one point in our conversation. "Some people will tell you I shouldn't be doing commercial endorsements. But people like Cher, myself, Bruce Willis, we all have affiliations with companies, and we're taken seriously. Or people will get into the question of whether I should continue to do television now that I'm making movies. Years ago, actors had a hard time jumping from TV to movies. But these days, with 'Entertainment Tonight,' CNN, cable movies, you see people all over the place anyway. I've seen Meryl Streep as much as I've seen Michael Landon—probably more."

Listen to him describe his acting career, however, and he will try to create the notion of an impulsive young actor, moving from one project to the next without deep thought.

"After I made *Teen Wolf*, I thought, I'm damned. I've killed myself in the movies before I even started. But I wanted to do a movie, and it looked like fun, so I did it. Then *Back to the Future* came along. It was a change. Spielberg had his name attached to it, and everybody wants to work with Spielberg. And it had a great premise. So I did it. Then *Teen Wolf* surprised everyone by making millions of dollars. So people began to take me seriously, in terms of movies.

"So what should I do then? I'm not a strategist. I'm not a Stallone with a 'let's make as much as we can' attitude. So I was looking around, and along came *Light of Day*, with a script that affected me. Everybody warned me it wasn't commercial, and they were right, and in a sense, I had the supporting role. But I did it, and it wasn't successful at the box office, and I didn't care."

Light of Day, which is the film in the list that you may not have heard of, was written and directed by Paul Schrader, and starred Fox as a dutiful brother to rock singer Joan Jett, whose rebellion against their parents had turned into anger and dangerous irresponsibility involving her child. As Jett grew more disturbed and their mother developed a fatal illness, Fox tried to hold the family together. The movie contained some of his best and most subtle acting, but then came *The Secret of My Success*, essentially a dumb sitcom strung out to feature length and with jokes about Fox changing his clothes in the elevator.

"Well, I had some problems with it, too," Fox said. "But it was a comedy and I wanted to do a comedy, and I wanted to do another one, but along came De Palma with this Vietnam project co-starring Sean Penn, and it sounded too good to turn down. That's where I got this short haircut. Sean and I just got our haircuts for the movie. I think he is one of the best actors around. They talk about his temper, but I saw him do something the other day that was really controlled. I met him in this restaurant in Beverly Hills, and at the next table was sitting Rupert Murdoch. *At the next table*. And you know how Sean feels about the way he and Madonna have been portrayed in the press. I would have expected him to smash a plate of crackers in Murdoch's face, but this is the amazing thing. He did nothing. I have a lot of sympathy for the guy. It's really bad, to have forty people shoving cameras in your face and saying dirty things about your wife . . ."

Sean Penn has gained a reputation for immersing himself in his roles—living the life he is about to play. Fox said he takes a different approach: "I show up for work. I like to work technically, to get the performance to where I want it, and then lock it in. I study the material carefully, understand who the character is and how he fits within me, and then set it, and forget it. Also, you have to remember I've done 175 episodes of network television over the years. I've done enough acting that no matter how serious the role is, there is a certain spirit in my work of just simple enjoyment, enjoying the work. I don't always have to bleed."

But he does bleed, literally, in *Bright Lights, Big City,* which offered one of the most sought-after roles in recent years for a young actor. The novel, by Jay McInerney, was about a young New York magazine staffer, who can't handle the fast lane and retreats into cocaine. It was read by hundreds of thousands of people, although not by me, because I refuse to read any novel written in the second person. You know how it is. It makes your skin crawl.

Fox plays the second-person "you" of the book, who has now mercifully surrendered to an omnipotent point of view and has a name, Jamie Conway.

"A lot of people told me it was so strange to think of me playing a guy with a drug problem," Fox said. "But I dunno. If there's a consistent quality about my acting and the characters I play, it's a guy who's gonna make it. But there is a fine line in this movie between a guy who has unfulfilled potential and is very frustrated, and a guy who starts taking himself out of his mind chemically.

"One of the scenes in the movie that was most important to me was the one with Jason Robards, who takes me out drinking to a den of aging writers and literary people, and gives me his philosophy. I was nervous. This is a serious actor. He knows more about what he's doing than I know about what I'm doing. Am I good enough? But my sense was, this movie was very important to him. He has made no secret that he's a former drinker. In preparing for the movie, I spoke to a lot of people who had cocaine problems, or alcohol problems, or something similar. Jason was very special, very open, in talking to me about the struggles people go through.

"The character I play in this movie is like some of the people I met who had lost their jobs, lost their houses, everything. The movie is about his last couple of days. It really needs a character like the Tracy Pollan character, at the end, someone who is understanding, a life raft, when he has reached the end of his rope."

It will be, Fox suggested, the aura of success that he brings to the character of Jamie Conway that will make his descent into failure more dramatic. Sure, this is a guy who seems to have it together. That's why it makes it harder for everyone, including himself, to understand how it all comes apart.

What, I asked, comes after this movie, and the De Palma project?

"Well . . . someday I would like to direct. All my dreams have been realized, in one way or another, except for that one. I told my agent, and he said, well, OK, write something and shoot it and we'll look at it. So I was sitting around thinking about that and I got a call from the David Letterman show; they were asking some people to make a short film, and they gave me $45,000."

And you made it?

"For $30,000. The rest we spent on a big party after the film was finished."

Kelly McGillis

Chicago, February 24, 1988—After our interview was over and she was saying goodbye, Kelly McGillis mentioned, almost in passing, "I just can't lie. Sometimes I wish I could. It would have saved me a lot of pain." As I was standing in the hotel corridor waiting for the elevator to come, I thought about that. She didn't say she wouldn't lie. She said she couldn't. And as I remembered her movie appearances, I was able to see how that quality of honesty was reflected in her work. If there is a common note in every character she has played, it is the feeling that her character is telling the truth.

Remember the Amish mother in *Witness.* The flight instructor in *Top Gun.* The new soul in *Made in Heaven.* And in *The House on Carroll Street*, where she plays a victim of McCarthyism who stumbles across a cell of Nazi war criminals. Of course the plot is contrived; plots like this are supposed to be filled with contrivance, and the ingenious spirit of Alfred Hitchcock haunts every frame of the movie. But what makes the performance work is the level quality of McGillis's gaze, the straightforward quality of her voice, the conviction.

I am not writing a character reference here. Some of my favorite actors are so shifty you can hardly believe a word they say; James Woods has given me wonderful moments in the movies by always seeming to be playing an angle. No, I am simply observing the special quality that McGillis has, and there is a list of other movie stars who have had it: Bogart, Bergman, Cooper, and among her contemporaries, Harrison Ford. If you have a character who needs to lie, you hire somebody else.

McGillis sometimes seems to have been an instant star. She was unknown when she won her first key role, opposite Tom Conti in *Reuben, Reuben.* Her next performance, as the Amish widow who falls in love with Harrison Ford in *Witness,* has become a classic. Then she was the flight instructor and rather unlikely romantic partner of Tom Cruise in *Top Gun,* an all-time box office winner. *Made in Heaven,* the love affair with Timothy Hutton in heaven and on earth, was not a successful film, but here she is with *Carroll Street,* and since then she has made three more films.

"I am a workaholic," she told me. "I love to act. I am happiest when I'm acting. There can be a moment when everything, absolutely everything, comes together. I love the challenge of losing myself in the movement—that moment of absolute absorption, the movement of the camera, the other actors, all in the same dance. Of course, it only happens for three or four seconds in a movie. But it's what I act for."

She lit a Merit and thought a moment, and said it wasn't even necessarily true that she had chosen acting as a career.

"Why do I act? I have to. It picked me to do it. If I didn't act, I don't know what else I would be able to do. I can look at various philosophical reasons why one might act—displaying emotion, educating people through behavior—but basically I'm compelled to do it, and everything else is an afterthought."

She sounded like a philosopher as she spoke, and she is not slow to point out that her "overnight success" came after she studied acting for eight years, four of them at the prestigious Juilliard School in New York: "I was fully prepared to be a waitress for the rest of my life, if that's what it took. After Juilliard, you don't act just because you're idealistic. You get very realistic about it. You learn how to do things, how to control yourself. If a director wants me to cry on one word instead of another, I can do it. I'm prepared. The fact that I had three great roles right at the start, that was luck. But that I was ready for them, that was work."

I wondered, then, how she felt about the other side of the job, about the fact that Kelly McGillis is a big movie star who recently made the gossip pages after she ended an engagement, and whose romantic involvements, real and fancied, are breathlessly reported.

"The first thing I do after I finish a role is to cut my hair or dye my hair," she said, grinning. She was a blonde today. "I find that people don't recognize me very often in public, maybe because I'm not what they're looking for. I like that. I suppose being recognized is the price you pay for wanting to act in the movies, but I like anonymity. I don't like wearing makeup and dressing up anyway. When I'm around movie stars, I'm awestruck. I feel like I don't belong. I want to be a face in the crowd. I'm very private. When people make a big deal, I get a panicky feeling. People look at movie stars as demigods, and I know that I struggle with everything in my daily life. I wish I had the answer, but I don't."

She is sometimes able to project that privacy in a movie role, as she does in *The House on Carroll Street,* where there is a great deal she keeps to herself. In the movie, she plays a photo researcher for *Life* magazine, who in the early 1950s is called before a congressional witch-hunt after her name is found on the lists and petitions of various left-wing groups. She refuses to name names, is fired by the magazine, and finally finds a low-paying job reading aloud to a rich widow who is partially blind.

One afternoon, standing in the garden of her employer's Manhattan town house, McGillis notices a heated conversation going on in the tall windows of the house at the foot of the garden. She grows curious. Later, on the street, she meets a young man she saw in the window, and her efforts to engage him in conversation lead her, by a roundabout path, to the discovery that the people in the house are operating a ring to smuggle Nazi war criminals into the country. Meanwhile, her life is doubly complicated because the FBI is spying on her—but after she grows friendly with a fair-minded FBI man from the Midwest (Jeff Phillips), they team up to unravel the threads of the mystery.

The movie was directed by Peter (*Breaking Away*) Yates, a British craftsman who must have studied Hitchcock in preparing for this project. McGillis's character is in a classic Hitchcock posture: She's the innocent, uninvolved outsider, who through fate and curiosity gets enmeshed in a plot she only vaguely understands. Yates makes great use of a favorite Hitchcock visual technique, where the hero observes puzzling events at a distance, and tries to figure out their meaning without benefit of dialogue.

"One of the people who saw this movie complained that things were not spelled out very completely," McGillis said. "The audience *does* have to figure things out and supply some of the missing pieces. That's the fun. I hate movies that explain literally everything. When you do that, you're patronizing your audience. People are not stupid. I get so frustrated when I have to sit through a movie while it's spelling everything out. I think maybe that's the heritage of television, where everything . . . is . . . carefully . . . explained."

When she goes through a script, McGillis says, she tries to cut her dialogue. She'd rather act than talk. I said that was fairly uncommon among actors, who often want more dialogue, not less.

"I'll say to the director, 'I know how to convey this without saying anything,'" she said. "You can do so much in a shot, in a look." She does that in two extended sequences in the movie that are essentially without dialogue: the first as she tries to figure out what the neighbors are up to, and a later one in a cemetery. In both scenes, Yates shoots mostly in long shots from the McGillis point of view, so that the audience becomes a co-conspirator, trying to spy right along with her.

When she isn't cutting her dialogue, McGillis said she annotates her scripts with voluminous notes as she goes along, filling the margins and writing between the lines until the original words can scarcely be seen. I asked her if she had kept the scripts, which might be fun for film students to study someday.

"Gee, I dunno. I have *Witness.* I have *Reuben, Reuben.* Not *Top Gun.* I've moved so many times, I don't really know what I have anymore. Nobody could understand them anyway. I have little star marks for key moments, and a lot of shorthand."

But she does, she says, keep a journal, and it was beside her on the hotel couch, along with a newspaper crossword puzzle and a battered Filofax that seemed to be bursting with names. The journal was one of those handmade Venetian books, and it looked like it had been carried by hand through several wars.

"It's not so much a record of the movies I've made," she said, "as a record of what goes on between movies. I watch people and write down what they do. In my reading, sort of the same thing goes on. I read a lot. All fiction. I just finished a wonderful book named *Perfume,* about a man in love with the scents of women. It's a very strange novel. I don't see how it can possibly be filmed. In movies, you can do a lot of things to convey heat, cold, anger, discomfort. But it is almost impossible to deal with the sense of smell."

McGillis said she'd finished three movies since wrapping *The House on Carroll Street*, all very different: *Once We Were Dreamers*, *Accused*, and *Winter People*, and her greatest acting challenge came in *Accused*, where she plays an attorney for rape victim Jodie Foster.

"I always like to prepare for my roles. I do a lot of research. I read books. I want the dialogue to sound natural when I say it, as if I were accustomed to talking that way. But to play a lawyer, I had to learn all of this jargon that I could barely understand. I worked for *days* trying to say, 'sleazy plea bargain.' Try saying it. See what I mean?"

Spike Lee

Chicago, February 10, 1988—Spike Lee is happy to tell you that the studio didn't want to open his movie, *School Daze*, on February 12. Looking over the list of other movies scheduled to be released the same day, the Hollywood strategists spotted *Action Jackson*, a thriller with a black hero. Since Lee's film is a comedy about the students at a black university, the analysts figured it might be wiser to delay it for a few weeks, until *Action Jackson* had finished its run.

When Lee heard of this plan, he says, he advised the studio to go to hell. "What is this?" he asked. "You can't have two pictures about blacks opening on the same day? I made a comedy about college kids. Action Jackson is a Detroit cop. Are these pictures going to appeal to the same audience? No way! Do you think they call up Woody Allen and ask him to postpone his new comedy because Chuck Norris has a movie coming out on the same day?"

Spike Lee had his way, and *School Daze* did indeed open as scheduled—along with *Action Jackson* and also *Shoot to Kill*, another thriller with a black hero, played by Sidney Poitier. And Lee was right. *School Daze* will not appeal to the action audience. It's a movie about black college students, about fraternities and sororities, about social pressure and class warfare on an all-black campus. And he knows from his sneak previews that the movie is likely to stir up controversy even among its primary target audience in the black middle class.

That's because *School Daze* openly discusses a subject that Lee believes many blacks would rather were not mentioned: value systems within the black community based on lighter or darker complexions, straighter or more natural hair. In a scene that in its own way is revolutionary, Lee's film even includes a song-and-dance number, "Straight and Nappy," in which sorority girls with lighter skin tones and straighter hair feud with darker-skinned independent students on the campus.

"People in the black community who have talked to me about this issue seem to be divided into two camps," Lee told me. "A lot of people simply deny the issue even exists. Others say it does exist, but that I shouldn't be putting it out there in a movie for white people to see, to put ideas into their heads. And the issue goes both ways. You have some blacks who value lighter complexions, and others, like the political activist in the movie, who wouldn't be caught dead dating a light-skinned girl. It wouldn't be in sync with his program. There's a scene where his girlfriend gets mad and says she thinks he only dates her because she's got the darkest skin on campus.

"The same goes for hair. This whole class, color, and hair thing goes very deep among black people. We've all been touched by it, exposed to it, sometimes hurt by it. I think this movie may help get it out into the open. You can't get rid of something if you refuse to acknowledge it exists."

Lee's approach to the subject was bold and sometimes painful while he was filming *School Daze*. He divided the women in his large cast into two factions with the nicknames "Wannabees" and "Jigaboos"—the names they use for each other in the movie—

and deliberately created hostility between them.

"While we were shooting in Atlanta," he said, "I put the Wannabees in the Regency Suites, but the Jigaboos and the crew stayed at the downscale Ramada Inn. Sometimes on locations, the whole cast and crew starts to feel like a family, and I didn't want them to get too chummy. The Wannabees, with their straightened hair and weaves and all, naturally required a lot more attention from the makeup people, and the other faction was always complaining that they were being neglected. A lot of tension built up, which I felt was good for the film, although while we were filming the Greek dance scene, the pushing match you see was real—it wasn't staged."

If Lee gets criticism for his portrayal of blacks in *School Daze,* it won't be the first time. His previous film, *She's Gotta Have It,* was attacked in some circles for its portrayal of a black heroine who was sexually independent, knew what she wanted from her men, and got it. That, too, was a new image, according to Lee, after years of films in which black women were subordinate or invisible.

"I don't agree with the concept that a film should have 'universal' appeal," he told me. "Not if that means you put in a Jew, a black, an Italian, and a Chinese so there's something for everyone. I believe the most universal films are the most specific ones, growing out of a particular experience that other people might be able to identify with. I made this film for black audiences. I believe white people will find it interesting, but when the studio came to me and suggested I might want to have some white characters in my film, and maybe get a wider audience, I told them I wasn't that kind of filmmaker.

"I reject the whole process of so-called 'broadening' a film's appeal. I despise the way music is put into films today. They look at the Billboard list of the top ten hits, buy them, and put them into the movie. Look at *Beverly Hills Cop.* They stick these songs in anywhere that have nothing to do with the movie, just music blasting away in the background with no thought behind it. All of the music in *School Daze* was intended specifically for the film."

It was so specifically intended, in fact, that it was mostly composed by Bill Lee, Spike's father, who was an accompanist for Odetta, Josh White, and Peter, Paul and Mary before leaving the road to devote more time to composing. "He's a jazz purist," Lee said. "I like a little more contemporary sound. We had a few fights, but I think we have the right music in the movie. The big company EMI tried to dictate to me to put some of their records in my movie, just to generate record sales. I told them to kiss my ass. No way. I didn't see no platinum stuff on their walls to indicate they knew what they were talking about."

Lee is obviously not shy about telling people precisely what he thinks. That got his movie thrown off the campus of his alma mater, Atlanta's almost all-black Morehouse University, after only two weeks of filming; he finished the shooting across town at Atlanta College.

"I went to Morehouse, and my father went to Morehouse, and my grandfather," Lee said. "After we were shooting two weeks, the president called me in and said he had heard we were using the MF word in the movie. He wanted to approve the whole script. I told him no way. He said, 'Spike, if parents see this film, they won't send their sons here to become Morehouse Men.' He felt it was a negative portrayal. I try to stay away from the whole positive/negative trap. I put in what I feel is truthful, no matter what anybody else thinks is positive or negative. This movie is my four years at Morehouse. My matriculation as a Morehouse Man, in a two-hour movie."

How do you feel about black colleges in an age of integration?

"Morehouse was very nurturing for me. It took the pressure off and allowed me to do my best without everybody looking at me to prove myself. As a graduate student, I went to the NYU film school, where people sometimes treated me like I was some kind of a freak, some kind of a quota student. I am the most successful graduate of my class at NYU, but you would have thought I was accepted just because I was black."

After graduation, he said, he didn't go knocking on studio gates with a screenplay under his arm because he knew he'd get nowhere that way. "That was a dead end. I had to show them what I could do. I had to make an independent film. Robert Townsend did the same thing with *Hollywood Shuf-*

fle. So did Jim Jarmusch with *Stranger Than Paradise*; he was two years ahead of me at NYU. I set about making the best film I could make for $175,000, and that was *She's Gotta Have It,* and after that, I could call the studios and they would listen to me."

You call the studios yourself?

"I don't see any need to pay an agent ten percent and a manager fifteen percent to make decisions which I can make for myself. I call up and I say, I have this project I want to make, and they listen to me."

And if they don't, they know what they can do.

Demi Moore

Chicago, March 30, 1988—When Demi Moore and Bruce Willis discovered that they were expecting a child, they didn't have to rush out and buy Dr. Spock and all the other baby books. She already had them. That was because she had just finished playing a pregnant woman in *The Seventh Sign*—a woman who is the only person standing between humanity and the Apocalypse, and whose child may represent a messenger from Heaven.

Moore hopes her own kid is going to be less complicated. "It was kind of humorous," she was explaining here the other day, in that deep, smoky voice. "I'd never been pregnant, and so I read all the books before we made the movie, and obviously a lot of that energy was still circulating."

She was midway through one of those whistle-stop press tours, with press and TV in half a dozen major cities, and Willis had flown in the evening before to surprise her with an overnight visit. Moore wasn't expecting him, and when they saw each other in the lobby of the Ritz-Carlton Hotel, they ran together with their arms outstretched, like one of those slow-motion sequences in movies where the lovers discover each other in Piazza San Marco.

But now it was the next afternoon, and Bruce had left at dawn, and she was back on the job again. She looked quite visibly pregnant, and her face glowed with health and good cheer, although since she had been thirty-five minutes late for an hour interview perhaps it also glowed with the attentions of the hairdresser and makeup woman who had been closeted with her.

In *The Seventh Sign,* she plays a Los Angeles housewife who is eight months pregnant when weird things start happening. Snow falls in the Israeli desert. The sea boils in Haiti. Rivers run with blood in Nicaragua. Earthquakes shake California, birds fall from the sky, and she's a little worried about the strange man with haunted eyes who has rented the apartment upstairs over their garage. The fate of her baby soon begins to exert an occult fascination for the new boarder, and for a strange priest and a second stranger who also has haunted eyes.

Would you have been happier, I asked, if events had occurred the other way around—first having your baby, and then playing the pregnant women in the movie?

"No, because it made the film more interesting for me."

This is not the kind of a role Demi Moore has played before, but it represents career growth, in a way. She plays a grown-up for the first time, an adult woman who (literally, as it turns out) has the cares of the world on her shoulders. Moore herself, at twenty-six, is beginning to shed the Brat Pack image of her earlier years, when she and Ally Sheedy were buddies of such as Rob Lowe, Sean Penn, Judd Nelson, and Emilio Estevez (who Moore nearly married). These days, she says, she and Willis hardly go out at all; their favorite date is an evening in front of the TV.

"Somebody was just giving me their perception of every member of the Brat Pack," she said. "Some of it was true. Little pieces of our images probably fit little pieces of us. This woman described me as the madonna of the group, the mother of all, and I had to laugh, because that's a part of me but it's not all of me. What was always missed by the media was that the Brat Pack people that I know are really nice people, not ungrateful for their success or arrogant—on an ongoing basis, anyway.

"And then there was that whole image of the guys in the group as party animals. They were perceived as these wild guys who all of a sudden had a lot of money, and could have women and lap it all up. So what if Ally and I were off steaming vegetables and riding our stationary bikes together? I don't even know just how much of that image is really true. In my case, Emilio was not someone that I experienced heavy-duty partying with."

Since Moore broke up with Estevez and then surprised everyone by marrying "Moonlighting" star Bruce Willis, the sleazoid supermarket tabloids have been so fascinated by the details of their relationship that the editors have hardly had room for the story of the British teen-ager who swallowed a tadpole and burped a frog.

"I don't read most of those stories," she said. "I think you just have to let it go, and maintain your sense of humor. But there are times when the gossip becomes invading and frustrating. I don't want to put a lot of energy into being uptight about it, because it's just not that important. But there have been a few times when I've been really hurt."

Have you ever had the experience, I asked her, of reading something that was absolutely, completely untrue in every word and nuance, and wondering how such a complete fantasy could be printed?

"You mean like the fact that I bought a $15,000 brass crib for my baby? Oh, yeah, even my grandmother called me on that."

That sounds like a recycled urban legend, I said. When I heard the story, it was supposed to be a $24,000 dollhouse that Shelley Long bought for her child.

"Another story I love," she said, "was that I'm intercepting all of Bruce's phone calls. The only time when it's really scary is when you read a line that's absolutely the truth, and you think, where could they have gotten that from? I'll give you an example. The day when I found out I was pregnant was a specific day, and I read an article that *knew* which day it was! And then all the rest of the article was pure garbage. You wonder, is your phone tapped? Who was it you told? Who did you talk to?"

That's exactly how it starts, I said. You make a hypothetical conversational statement, and next week you read at the checkout counter, *Demi Moore Fears Phone Is Tapped by UFOs from Mars!*

"My experience is a little different than Bruce's," she said, analyzing the price of fame. "I didn't have to deal with something that changed my life within six months like he did. Bruce went from living a normal life as a bartender and struggling actor, to becoming enormously visible overnight. I've had more time. I've been allowed to learn how to deal with it, adjust to it, gradually becoming a little more well-known. My experience hasn't been as intense as his. He's a television personality. Everybody watches television. People watch you in their homes in their underwear, eating TV dinners. So he gets it more, while I can sometimes still go out and be anonymous. We were in the hotel here. He flew in to surprise me, and visited me for all of twelve hours, but in the morning there was a note under the door asking for an autograph."

All of this is a long way from Demi Moore's childhood, as the child of a New Mexico newspaperman who changed jobs so often she never attended the same school for more than six months. She sometimes describes herself as a vagabond. That sometimes causes people to develop wallflower personalities, just hoping to blend in, but in Moore's case it seems to have made her an extrovert.

"When you have to change schools a lot you don't really grow up with a strong sense of yourself," she said. "It's always based on outside perceptions. The interesting thing is that I've run into a lot of other actors who've had the same sort of childhood. There are two choices you can make. You either get out there and work on fitting in, or you become completely introverted and isolated. I was simply not someone who wanted to be isolated. It was important for me to be liked. You go to one school where you're the best thing since sliced bread, and another one where you say 'Oh God, please let me fit in!' It's a knack. You learn to read people well."

And now, I said, you and Bruce are going to have a baby, who will be the child of actors and therefore of nomads.

"I like the philosophy of Sissy Spacek and Jack Fisk. What they've set out is that when one works, the other doesn't. That way there's always some stability and consistency for their kids. Until I get there I'm not really gonna know if that's what we can do. In terms of our lifestyle, we live at the beach, at Malibu, and we want to move even farther out. We're simple people. We're not in the scene. Our funnest time is renting movies and just being home together. Simplicity is the key. And in terms of the baby, I'm going to take it one day at a time. Whatever I do, I hope it's the most loving and supportive environment I can produce."

How did the New Mexico vagabond get from there to here? She began, she said, by applying for a job at a modeling agency, and getting some work which led to more work and eventually to steady employment as a model while she was still in her teens. Then she got a Hollywood agent and got some small roles on TV, leading to series roles and then to movies like *No Small Affair* and *Blame It on Rio* before she became a star as one of a group of troubled rich kids in *St. Elmo's Fire* and as Rob Lowe's big romance in *About Last Night*. . . .

"I'm not a formally trained actress," she said. "All my experience has come from work, from doing different kinds of characters and by doing different subject matter. From that point of view, *The Seventh Sign* was a good career move. It was an opportunity for me to carry a movie, and it's mature subject matter, so hopefully the perception of me and what I can do will be expanded."

In other words, you're not a kid anymore?

"Hmmm. This character is a woman-child. A very lost, frightened woman. Many of the characters I've played have been strong, independent, extroverted kinds of characters, which she is not at all."

As someone with no training and no particular credentials other than your basic talent, how did you get the nerve to pull this off in the first place? To stand in front of a camera and be an actress?

"What I was doing on the outside was a lot different than what was going on inside. When I look back at something like *Blame It on Rio,* what was *really* going on for me was, 'I wonder when they're gonna find out I don't know what I'm doing?' That's when I made the decision that acting was what I really wanted to do, so I became willing to go to any lengths to do it. Even if it meant facing unbelievably terrifying experiences. Even if you can't do something, you can always go out there and act 'as if.' Who knows? You might find out you can do it after all."

Tom Selleck

Honolulu, January 6, 1988—Down on the beach the girls in their bikinis were strolling lazily up to the bar and ordering drinks with umbrellas in them, and over in the shade John Hillerman was fitting a cigarette into a holder and complaining that the sun was in his eyes.

Tom Selleck was trying to get this confounded aluminum easel to work. The idea was that he would set up the tripod in the sand, and explain his latest harebrained scheme to Hillerman and his other cronies, while the girls sipped their drinks and the wind rustled the palm fronds, and all those other things happened that make "Magnum, P.I." look like it is probably not shot in Minnesota.

Selleck could get the tripod to work, all right, but not in the time it took him to say his dialogue, and so there was going to have to be more dialogue or a faster aluminum tripod, and it was all in a day's work in the eighth and last season of the best job Tom Selleck has ever had.

"That's why I caved in and agreed to do the eighth year," he was explaining not long after, in his office on the lot of the tiny studio that services "Magnum" and the other movies and TV shows that come to Honolulu. "A show like this comes along real seldom. It was hard to say goodbye. We did a sort of final show last year, in which Magnum . . . well, if he didn't die, he seemed to be dying. We didn't design it as a cliff-hanger. But after we wrote it but before we shot it, we decided to do another year, and so it turned into a show about a sort of out-of-the-body experience. That's the direction we'd been going in, anyway. More about Magnum's emotional life and less about cases."

Between the seventh and eighth seasons of "Magnum" last year, Selleck slipped away to Toronto to have one more go at a movie career. He was a major star on the small screen, but not on the big one, and although both of his first two movies, *High Road to China* and *Lassiter*, made money, they were not perceived as hits. His third movie, *Runaway*, was a flop any way you looked at it. And so when he went to act in *Three Men and a Baby*, the Hollywood remake of a popular French comedy, he had his fingers crossed. He wanted to leave television and spend all of his time making movies, but did the movies want him?

On the day I interviewed Selleck, he had his answer.

Three Men and a Baby opened with enormous grosses over Thanksgiving weekend and never looked back, shouldering aside all the other Christmas pictures—even Barbra Streisand, even Eddie Murphy, even Steve Martin, and Cinderella and all those other movie stars—to become the unquestioned box office champion of the holiday season. It was on its way to a $100 million-plus gross.

"Well, it tested well," Selleck said, "but I had made other pictures that tested well and then didn't perform at the box office. Preview audiences loved *High Road*, but it didn't go through the roof. *Lassiter* opened strong, but it didn't have legs. Before you jump up and down and celebrate, you'd better wait and see how the movie does next week."

With the benefit of hindsight, it is perhaps possible to figure out why audiences liked Selleck better in *Three Men and a Baby* than they had in all of his previous movies put together. He was at last playing the right role, in a romantic comedy. Despite his image and his rugged good looks, Selleck is not really an action hero. Like Cary Grant, he can handle action, but looks more at home playing against it than with it. In *Three Men*, the most awkward scenes were the ones involving a showdown with some drug dealers. The most charming and natural one was when he and Steve Guttenberg tried to change the diapers on a baby.

"I thought of *Lassiter* as a Cary Grant part," Selleck said, "but I knew that Cary Grant could do that part a lot better than I could. He could temper a scene with humor, and he had great warmth, and when he walked into a room, everyone stopped everything and looked at him. I can wear a tuxedo, but I don't feel like I own a room, and when I walk in, I'm likely to trip over something. In one shot in *Lassiter*, I walked in wearing a tuxedo and smoking a cigar, and dropped the cigar."

For *Three Men and a Baby*, he had only a week to prepare after the seventh "Magnum" season wrapped, and he didn't do much preparation even then.

"They gave me all the Dr. Spock books, but the thing about acting with a baby is, the baby is going to change every scene, and more or less tell you what to do. What saved us all, and made a lot of the scenes work so well, was the freedom we got from Leonard Nimoy, the director. I had no idea how much he knew about characters."

Yes, I said, but I wish he'd found a way to leave out the whole subplot about the drug dealers and the criminals and the showdown at the construction site.

"I guess they thought they needed that scene to show the baby in danger, and us trying to protect it," Selleck said. "Leonard abbreviated the sequence as much as possible, compared to the script. Nothing was written in stone. He was willing to treat a lot of the stuff we'd shot as work in progress. But it could drive you a little nuts working with him. He's not real effusive. He's hard to read. He spent a lot of time at first just watching us, not telling us much, letting us absorb the idea that we were actually in the film. He played his cards very close to the vest. For example, we never met the writers on the film. They were there the whole time we were shooting, but they were sequestered. We'd ask about them, and Leonard would say, 'They work at night.'"

Nimoy's strategy must have been effective. After the enormous success of *Three Men and a Baby*, Selleck can retire from "Magnum, P.I." with at least the expectation of being able to work as a major movie star, instead of a TV star with a studio pass.

"My movie offers were getting better every year," Selleck mused, "but they weren't what I wanted to do. My movies always made money, if you count the cassette sales, but I had to deal with the perception that they were unsuccessful. And in Hollywood, unless it's a big hit, somehow it's not a hit at all. Now I'm being offered multiple-picture deals, lots of security, luncheons with the studio bosses where I hear that I have enormous potential, but I dunno. The problem with a multiple deal is quality control. They may have one great screenplay, but do they have three?"

When, I asked, did you know for sure that *Three Men and a Baby* was going to go through the roof?

"Well, I saw it for the first time with an audience the Monday before Thanksgiving, at a $200-a-ticket charity benefit. The audience reaction seemed phenomenal. But a week later I sneaked into the Crest in Westwood and saw it again, and that was the night I knew it was a hit. They were laughing just as hard as if they'd spent $200 a ticket."

There was a knock on the door, and it was time for Selleck to shoot another scene for "Magnum." This scene was being shot indoors, in the set for Hillerman's office, where Selleck was going to deliver yet another pitch for his harebrained scheme, while Hillerman slowly sank into a doze. Selleck walked onto the set and was directed to the chair he was supposed to sit in as the scene began. It was a small chair and he is a big man.

"I feel like Paul Bunyan in this chair," he said. "How long has it been here?"

"Seven years," said Hillerman.

Sean Penn

Los Angeles, April 6, 1988—What you see in the paper is the photograph of Sean Penn with his eyes blazing and a snarl on his face, going after some photographer outside a nightclub. What you do not hear in the paper are the insults the photographers shout at Penn in their attempts to goad him into providing them with those juicy and profitable portraits. Here is a lonely and perhaps insignificant fact in a world filled with noise: Sean Penn is basically a civilized human being, who has been saddled with the wrong image and is somehow going to have to change it.

I am a movie critic, not a gossip columnist, and I confess to a vast indifference about the latest status of the Penn-Madonna marriage. All I know is that I go to the movies, and that in such movies as *Bad Boys, The Falcon and the Snowman, At Close Range,* and now *Colors,* I have seen Sean Penn prove that he is one of the best actors alive. For purely selfish reasons, I would like to see him continue to make movies. This requires him, of course, to stay out of jail, despite the best efforts of the paparazzi.

An interview with Sean Penn is not what you expect, if you know him only from the flash photos on the people page. He says he'll meet you in Malibu, at a sushi joint out on the Pacific Coast Highway, at about 4 P.M., when the place will be empty. He turns up a few minutes after you do and asks for a table. When the waiter suggests a small table against the wall, he doesn't ask for one of the booths. Here's a guy who doesn't throw his weight around even in an empty restaurant. He orders an iced tea and lights a Camel Filter and is ready to do business.

This was not long after I'd seen *Colors,* which was directed by Dennis Hopper and stars Penn and Robert Duvall as Los Angeles detectives assigned to the gang unit. I thought it was a good movie with some strong performances, and we talked about it for a time, and then the conversation got around to the Problem, the Problem with Sean Penn being that his public image is so notorious that it threatens to overshadow his work.

He talked about the situation in a curiously objective way, as if he were discussing his height or hair color or some other fact affecting his career. It started this way: I said he looked convincing in *Colors* when he was wrestling suspects to the ground and slapping the cuffs on and frisking them, and I asked if he'd spent some time riding with real L.A. cops to learn how to do that.

"I just don't like to talk very much about the preparations I go through before I play a role," he said. "I prepare, I do research, like everybody else, but I don't like to discuss it. I read all these interviews where actors are talking about how they did this and how they did that to get into a role, and I can't see how that helps anything. My reaction is, So what? You don't get points just because you went to a lot of trouble. I don't want to read about myself in those ways."

Then there was a pause, and he lit another cigarette and thought for a moment, and said: "It's bad enough already. I have this other problem, which always happens when I do interviews. I get asked about my . . . personal life, my marriage, details of things that have happened. I already inevitably carry around a lot of baggage. Any baggage, period, is bad for an actor. And then when you see me in a movie, you're reminded of all that shit and there's no way around it.

"Sean Penn as the husband of a big rock star creates a lot of adrenaline with some people, who go into a movie with an incredible amount of preconceptions. When I married Madonna, I certainly didn't expect the kind of ruckus that occurred in the media. I was realistic enough to know it would be louder rather than quieter, but . . . So now I have to be realistic about the elements of my image. I have to pay a little more attention to getting you to think about my character instead of about me."

Almost all actors have some baggage, he said. They only get a few chances to make an "absolutely pure" impact on the audience, and then they start being remembered for their earlier roles.

"Take Mickey Rourke as an example, because I think he does some wonderful work, but I will never again be affected by him the way I was when he had that role in *Body Heat,* because I had never seen him before and so I was ready to believe that *was* him. Everything he brought to that movie was brand new.

"Well, when you think about me, the ability to keep the baggage to a minimum has not been a talent of mine. There are movie projects I read and decide not to do because I think my presence in the film would burden the project. Earlier this year, I was one of the first people to see a wonderful new script, one of the best scripts I have ever read, but I turned it down because this script was so good it just needed to be an egg, opened up by the audience. It needs to be cast with unknowns, for the audience to discover."

He gave me another example, talking about *At Close Range,* the powerful 1986 film where he starred as the confused son of Christopher Walken, who played a violent professional criminal ruling his family with a reign of terror.

"Let's say that project had been brought to me as a low-budget picture, with Levon Helm playing the father, and it was going to be shot in black and white and so on. I would have had to turn it down. Not because I didn't like it, or admire Levon Helm, but because"—Penn hesitated—"I would appreciate it, as an audience, if it was made with me not in it."

I said I completely failed to understand that reasoning.

"You would be thinking too much about me and it would not help the movie. Remember that Brazilian movie, *Pixote,* about the little street kid? It would never have worked with *any* stars in it. I admire the actors who can work for years and not cross that line into distracting from a character. Robert De Niro seems to be able to do that, but he stays very aloof; you never hear about him except when he's in a movie. I admire how he deals with the other parts of being an actor. His life choices allow him to maintain that distance. Other guys do it, too. Harrison Ford stays out of it. My life choices, where I live, who I'm associated with, who I'm married to, have blocked that for me. I've gone through some different styles of thinking about how to deal with that."

As he spoke, there was no particular expression on his face, and his voice was flat and matter-of-fact. He finished, looked across the table, and raised his eyebrows quizzically: What can you do?

"Robert Duvall is a constant reminder," he said, "of what can be done. He never crosses the line of someone who is genuinely searching for the insides of a character. He genuinely knows what it is to look for the levels in a character. Day after day on the set, as we were playing these two characters, I would see him working out things, doing things that were a lesson for me. He knows, to begin with, that no man alive doesn't have fear, joy, a desire to love and be loved. So he assumes that, and doesn't have to tell you about it, and never plays for effect as an actor."

As I listened to Penn describe what he admired in other actors, and what he deplored in his own situation, I was remembering a conversation I'd had with Dennis Hopper a week earlier. Hopper began his acting career in *Rebel Without a Cause*, opposite his good friend James Dean, and in thirty years has seen a lot of movie stars come and go. He told me flatly that Penn was the most talented young actor he'd seen. And then he added something else: "We started out wanting to make another movie, *Barfly*, but we couldn't pry the script loose from Barbet Schroeder, who was passionate about directing it. So Sean sent me the script for *Colors*, which he had been reading and thought had possibilities. I thought it was terrible. It was set in Chicago and was about a gang that was dealing cough syrup, and it had a big syrup bust in it. It was laughable. I told him it needed a *big* rewrite, and we all worked on it, and set it out here, where the gangs are truly organized and established, and then when it was finished, I asked Sean why he wanted to do it. 'After all,' I said, 'Duvall has the good role. You're the second banana.' And he told me he liked the whole project so much that he wanted to make it, and so he was happy to play whatever role he was right for. Some guys would insist on some kind of bullshit rewrite to make them look better. Not Sean, because he knew that would hurt the script."

So now I asked Penn about that: Why did he want to play the movie's more thankless role, as the green younger cop who is not as experienced, as sympathetic, or as interesting as the veteran played by Duvall?

"One of the things I really flipped out about in the script," he said, "was that Michael Schiffer, who wrote it, wasn't trying to force likability on anyone. People will like Bob's character because of the age and experience of the guy he plays. My character is not very likable at first, but he grows as the movie goes along. How many Hollywood movies have you seen where they're patient enough to let that happen?"

Are you disillusioned with Hollywood?

"Well, I'll tell you what has happened," he said. "If you brought *One Flew Over the Cuckoo's Nest* to a major studio right now, they'd ask if the guy has to die in the end. But when that picture was made (in 1975), they didn't know what formula they had in mind. They didn't see this huge audience. They just wanted to make a picture. The term that I hear all the time out here is 'balancing art and commerce.' Well, I feel they're completely unrelated. If something does well, then it's commercial, but you can't start out with that projection. What you *can* do is start out with commerce and keep it that way.

"Take *Beverly Hills Cop* as an example. I liked it. And *Top Gun*. I can't help but be in awe of these people. They set out to create an extravaganza, and they did it, with no shame at all. They were so balls-out in their shamelessness, in fact, that I'll take a picture like that any day over one of those pompous statement movies that reeks of bleeding heart whatever-it-is. But I don't think I can relate to those pictures as an actor.

"We're not in a particularly fertile time out here, artistically. We haven't been since *Jaws* came out (in 1974). Suddenly it was no longer enough to do $60 million. You had to make $200 million. It's not only the fault of the studios. The filmmakers got weak. Ten years ago, the best directors said *this* is what I want to do. Now they say, 'I'll make *my Jaws* for them, and I'll get my bungalow at Universal.' Today, the studios are about *Top Gun*, and the filmmakers are kissing the studios' asses."

It had grown dark outside, and the evening's first customers were drifting in for their sushi. Sean Penn smiled for the first time all afternoon—the famous bad-boy smile from his first movie, *Fast Times at Ridgemont High*, and then he told me a parable.

"The world's best chocolate chip cookie comes out," he said, "and everybody goes crazy about how good it tastes. Then you buy a bag a year later, and you find out the ingredients have gotten thinner and thinner. But you still eat them."

We stood up. I left. He stayed for sushi.

Barbara Hershey

Cannes, France, May 11, 1988—Sometimes at the Cannes Film Festival, you see a masterpiece that strikes you in a certain way, and you are sure it will be a success all over the world, and sometimes you are right, but sometimes you are wrong. Last year at Cannes, I saw *Shy People*, a bold and unusual drama about a chic magazine writer who ventures into the bayous of Louisiana to seek a long-lost cousin who turns out to be a cross between a swamp woman and a force of nature. The film had such an effect on me that I was sure it would be felt by others.

In a way, I was right. Barbara Hershey won the best actress award at the 1987 festival for her performance as the woman in the bayou. But in another way, I was wrong, because the film has never received the kind of attention I would have expected. The movie opened here and there, and then drifted into that hinterland of films you sort of lose track of.

And so I sit here at this year's festival, and I remember a morning last year when I sat down to interview Barbara Hershey, and *Shy People* had still not had its premiere, and all of its fate was still before us.

"This is like the mad tea party," Hershey said. We were sitting on the terrace of a room at the Majestic Hotel, and down below, the street was filled with the usual crazy accumulation of people.

I haven't seen the film yet, I said.

"Neither have I," she said. "I'm seeing it tonight."

What do you hear?

"The usual. Everybody says it's great, but then, what else are they going to say? Tonight will tell."

By all accounts, it was a strange and daring film, shot by Andrei Konchalovsky on location in the bayous of Louisiana, with Hershey and Jill Clayburgh, who plays the magazine writer, up to their necks in swamp water for hours at a time. I had a good feeling about the film because of my interest in its director, Konchalovsky, a Russian emigre who made *Runaway Train* and *Duet for One* and achieved a sort of anonymous fame as the inspiration for Shirley MacLaine's lover "Vassily" in her autobiography *Dancing in the Light*.

I said something to Hershey about the time we'd met in Toronto, around 1970, when she was going through her mystical flower child period and had changed her name to Barbara Seagull in honor of the bird that had died while she was filming *Last Summer*, a bird she felt had made its way into her own soul.

"That was a difficult lifetime," she said. "The one I'm living now wouldn't know how to describe it. I was a child. That's a lot of what that was about. I didn't really have a notion of myself. I'm really pretty normal. I don't live an exciting life, and my time is filled up with the usual things people fill their time with. I took an art class. I started drawing. I sat between scenes in the trailer on a set and drew pictures of these people in Louisiana. It's a wordless way to deal with tension and the slow passage of time."

We talked of the usual things. Her Seagull period. The stretch in the seventies when she was branded as an eccentric and had trouble finding work. Her 1983 horror film *The Entity*, which has been all but forgotten, but which was really her comeback because she was so good in it, so touching, as a single mother of three kids who knew that there was something evil in the house with her, and couldn't get the shrink to take her seriously. Then, at last, in her late thirties, came the rehabilitation of her reputation and the rebirth of her career: roles in *The Natural*, *The Right Stuff*, *Hannah and Her Sisters*, and *Tin Men*.

"I've had a nice few years here," she said. "I'm grateful, but I'm not complacent. I sure don't feel like I've arrived at anything. I'm not a personality actor. People don't come to see me because of the way they know I'll behave. I'm not a star. I believe acting is half who you are and half what you do. You're only capable of portraying what you're capable of understanding. You can put on the false teeth and the nose, but you can only play the character if you can play it from somewhere inside of yourself."

She talked of her character Lee, Hannah's sister: "She's in a perpetual student state. I never got the sense, even with marriage, that she would ever quite grow up. Some people eventually graduate. Lee would only let go of one man when she had a new mentor to go to."

How do you prepare for a character?

"When I get the time? I'm an eleventh-hour actress. I only had five days' notice for *The Right Stuff.* Three days for *The Natural.* For *Shy People,* I had a lot of advance notice for once. I'm playing this woman who lives with her sons in the middle of Louisiana, and has never left the swamp. She's ferociously in love with her children, who are all grown. I read the script, and all I could think about was the Old Testament—when blood ties and a sense of right and wrong are more important than any possible social nicety. When I see the film tonight, I don't know what I'll think. But I suspect it will be very mythic, very Russian."

A brief silence.

I can tell you really, really care about this film, I said.

"I wasn't trying to give that impression. But yes."

That night I went to see *Shy People,* and it was everything Hershey must have hoped for, and more. I saw it in the big auditorium of the Palais du Cinema, with its vast screen and perfect sound, and the presentation helped reinforce the effect of an epic—a bold, daring movie so determined to inspire strong emotions that it dealt in overacting, exaggeration, the supernatural, and the absurd, anything to pound the audience with its power. It was the kind of flat-out, unapologetic, lurid melodrama that Hollywood used to have the courage to make, before everyone went to film school and got good taste and learned to make clever remakes of successful formulas instead of taking wild, exuberant chances.

Barbara Hershey was amazing in the film, as an illiterate swamp woman who ruled her family with an iron hand. Her character had the kind of fierce concentration that spoke of zealotry, and you knew almost within seconds of her first appearance that it would not be wise to cross this woman in anything that was really important to her.

Jill Clayburgh had a trickier role, one that required a careful balance between drama and self-satire, as a *Cosmopolitan* magazine feature writer who got the idea of plunging into the swamps of Louisiana for a feature on a long-lost branch of her family. She gets a lot more family history than she bargained for.

Konchalovsky had the nerve to deal with material a lot of American directors might have felt was too imperiled with cliches: His plot played like *God's Little Acre* crossed with *Deliverance,* with some *L'il Abner* thrown in. Clayburgh visits the swamp with her teen-age daughter (Martha Plimpton), a promiscuous druggie. Their boat journey into the swampland is like a trip to the heart of darkness, with magnificent overhead shots of their boat disappearing into the wilderness, shots that were superficially beautiful and yet created an odd sense of foreboding.

At the end of the journey, they find Hershey, a child bride now in her thirties, ruling as a strong matriarch over her grown sons. One is caged in a shed for misbehaving, one is retarded, one is married and expecting a child. A fourth son has fled the backwaters to open a saloon in town, and Hershey, suspicious of all outsiders, has disowned him.

By the end of the movie, Clayburgh will have her life threatened by drowning, by alligators, by ghosts, by exposure, and by almost being run down by her own motorboat. Plimpton will have been raped and lost in the swamp. Hershey will not have budged an inch. And Konchalovsky will have made an utterly original film. I didn't know what the jury thought, but I had found my personal choice for the Palm d'Or.

In the late afternoon a few days later, I went up to Barbara Hershey's hotel suite to talk some more about *Shy People,* now that we had both seen it. She had developed a bad cold and had a box of Kleenex in her hand, and she ordered hot tea from room service. And while she was on the phone, I sat by the window and looked at her and had one of those occasional illuminations that breaks through the routine of journalism. I had seen her on the screen in *Shy People,* and now I was looking at the person who had played that character, and the character was nowhere to be found. Just a slender, pretty woman around forty who was trying to guess how long room service would take.

I said something about the power of the

performance and the strangeness of the movie, and how ordinary questions seemed insufficient.

"So many questions are the same," she said. "The same old stuff. Did I find the character interesting? God, yes! It was a great and intriguing part. I read the screenplay and wanted to do it. No question. But I was scared. Not just because of the externals, which were scary enough, but because of all those dimensions inside the woman. She's an illiterate swamp woman who looks like she came out of *Li'l Abner.* Am I gonna make her a human being, and not some caricature? That's what I asked myself. Can I make it real? Is she in me? I looked inside, and she was."

What parts of her connected with you?

"I met her finally in a real deep, simple place, which was her love for her children. She saw the outside world as ugly and dangerous, the real swamp, and she wanted to protect her children from that world. And that is the explanation for everything she does in the whole story. She's very rigid, but she has to be rigid to keep them safe. After all, she's already lost one son to the outside."

In the movie, when Jill Clayburgh and Martha Plimpton arrive on their rented motorboat, fresh from the complexities of Manhattan, the contrast between their personalities and Hershey's bluntness is almost painful. Hershey said it was hard to keep from softening her character just because of the manners she, herself, had been taught: "She has no interest in the mores or politeness of the outside. She is not mindful of etiquette. In our world, we comfort each other, we tell little lies to make relationships easier. She hasn't been taught that, and doesn't have to do it."

Did you look for people like your character and study them?

"When I got the role, I knew nothing but the most basic cliches. And a little Faulkner, which isn't cliches, but which is Faulkner, not research. We went back to this eighty-year-old shack they'd found. The top was an old steamboat cabin. They moved it back further into the swamp. After I had been there a while, I began to understand a little where this woman was coming from. She was her own company. It was so quiet. So silent. Time took on a different meaning. I understood that there was a silence inside of her that had a complete indifference to the value systems of the New York characters."

I said I wondered what Konchalovsky, a Russian, had found in a Louisiana swamp to attract him there. She said that perhaps if you stripped off enough of the everyday facade of any character, the character became universal, and that her swamp woman was no more American than Russian. "I had the feeling," she said, "that Konchalovsky was directing without a net, and he expected us to act without a net. We could not act as we had in other movies because this was not like other movies. I had a lot of doubts. I worked a lot on the dialect—two months with a tape recorder and a voice coach, learning river talk. It's not Cajun because this woman isn't a Cajun, but there are some shadings of Cajun in there that she would have picked up."

I asked her if the company stayed out there in the swamp. A silly question, I suppose, and yet the intensity of this movie reminded me of Werner Herzog's *Aguirre* and *Fitzcarraldo,* two films where he required his cast and crew to live with him in the middle of the rain forest. She smiled.

"We lived in this motel in Lafayette. It was an hour out to the location. I stayed a lot by myself, which was my way of not losing the character. The location was pretty grim. The mosquitoes were terrible. There was a flood, which overflowed the floor of the old house we were using, so we had to build a false floor over the mud. There was a lot of sickness. Nobody much enjoyed getting wet and dirty all the time. Jill Clayburgh had to go through some horrifying experiences, up to her neck in the swamp. We were tired all of the time. Bone tired. But I tell you the truth: You know how rare roles like that are? They're demanding, but the kind of demanding you hope for. I was in ecstasy most of the time.

"What you hope and pray for, and what is the greatest aspect of location shooting, is that the reality of the place sinks into you and tells you what to do. A few weeks into the shooting, I had this interesting crisis. I had all of these Medea ideas that weren't working. I found myself in some kind of strange prison. So I threw away all of my preparation and started from scratch. The preparation was very important, and it was also important for me to throw it away. It was an act of faith."

And that was how we left it, just about a year ago. And now *Shy People* is making its way out into the world, and perhaps here and there it will find someone who feels the same way about it that I do.

Melanie Griffith

New York, May 4, 1988—We were going out for lunch, Melanie Griffith and I, and the question was, did Alexander want to come along?

"Hey, Duke," she said to her son, sitting down next to him on the floor. "How about it? You want to come to lunch with us?"

He did not. He shook his head firmly and looked down at the floor. "You're supposed to look at people's faces when you talk to them," Griffith said, and Alexander kept looking down, and so his mother stood up and said, quietly but firmly, "All right, then, you can have your lunch here." And then the floodgates burst, and Alexander ran to his mother's arms, and she took him and kissed him and planted him back on the floor, and he ran to get his tricycle.

"You like Liza?" Griffith asked. She put a compact disc in the portable player in the dining room. Minnelli began to sing "I Happen to Like New York." Then said she would just take a minute to go upstairs and get herself ready.

Alexander had a good range for his tricycle, the hardwood floors that stretched without interruption through the living and dining rooms and the kitchen of this rented townhouse in the Village. He circled the dining room table and got up steam and came roaring toward me, stopping at the last minute. Griffith came back downstairs and left Alexander with the nanny, and we walked out into a fine spring day.

She is tall, and currently she is blonde, and she speaks with that very particular voice that makes you think of Jean Arthur without quite knowing why. Some of the people on the street recognized her, but most did not, because she has been a chameleon in many of her most successful roles. She was wearing a black wig, for example, in the unforgettable opening sequence of *Something Wild,* which began when she picked up Jeff Daniels outside a restaurant, and ended when she handcuffed him to a motel bed and made him call his office.

"I was on the Staten Island ferry last week," she said, "playing a secretary from Staten Island? I had my hair all long, you know, like they wear it? With it all up in front here, and then it drops off behind? And . . . I . . . was . . . tawking . . . like . . . dis . . . and there was a cop there, and he asked us what we were doing, and I said we were making a movie. And he asked if there were any stars in the movie. And I said, well, yeah, I guess I'm the star. And he asked me who I was, and I told him, and he said, oh, yeah, I was the one in *Something Wild,* only I had black hair then. And then he said, 'You look older now,' and I said, 'Fuck you,' and just for a moment there, a look came into his eyes, a very strange look, for just a second. And then the second passed and he laughed and asked me if I was really into handcuffs, and I said I noticed he was carrying some."

We were walking past the art galleries and the bookstores, the tofu parlors and the bars. There were some children's cartoons in the window of a video store. "Amy Irving and I took Max and Alexander to see *Lady and the Tramp,*" she said, "in a real theater. Then he looked at it on tape. But he's not like a lot of kids, who want to see the same tape over and over. He makes up his own stories. He's intelligent. I'm not saying that just because he's mine. I really think he is."

We walked along in the sunshine. She said her new movie, *Stormy Monday,* had gotten some good reviews, and that she had also enjoyed making *The Milagro Beanfield War,* but that many of her best scenes were not in the movie.

"Cut out?"

"Never filmed. It snowed and they had to

revise the whole production schedule. I did the movie because I wanted to work with Robert Redford. Now, on this new one, I'm working with Mike Nichols. It's called *Working Girl*, and it's about a Staten Island secretary who beats the odds. She is very bright but seems like she isn't getting anywhere, and then . . . one . . . day . . . she does!"

We turned into "5/1," one of those restaurants where the floors and walls look recycled out of old Paris brasseries. There was a table in the corner. Melanie Griffith ordered cafe au lait and a Caesar salad. She said that she could never be a director. "As an actor, I try to do my job and then let it go and hope it all works," she said. "I can't be responsible for everything. I don't think I could handle the responsibilities of a director. Like with Mike Nichols. The crew can be working for hours to set up a shot, but if it doesn't work, he has to say, 'No, that's not right, put the camera over there.' I don't know if I could do that. It might seem too impolite."

"Is it going to be a good movie?" I asked.

She looked at me over her cup of cafe au lait. "It better be," she said. "If you ask me, it's gonna be. I think it's gonna be terrific. Mike Nichols is wonderful to work for."

She sipped the coffee. "Kevin Wade, who wrote the screenplay, lives right upstairs here," she said. "I think he's out of town. Brian De Palma lives in this building, too. We could call him, but no, of course not, he's in Thailand now, making that picture."

"You made *Body Double* with him."

"Uh huh."

"I liked that picture," I said.

"Me too."

"Not everybody did."

"I know."

The Caesar salad came, and she looked at it with the attitude of someone who was going to drive the salad crazy with wondering when it was going to be eaten.

"Mike Nichols let us rehearse for two weeks for *Working Girl*," she said. "That was a wonderful luxury. Harrison Ford is in the picture. He is so great. And I really do think I've done my best work ever."

"I liked you a lot in *Stormy Monday*," I said.

"Do you remember *Brief Encounter*?" she said. "It was a little like that. A story where you meet somebody, and right away you know there's something there. And I don't just mean sex. Something is in your heart, for a reason."

In the movie, she feels that way about a young Irishman played by Sean Bean. The two of them become lovers in the dark and rain-swept streets of Newcastle, where Tommy Lee Jones is a crooked Texas millionaire who wants to launder his dirty money by buying up the waterfront, and Sting is the nightclub operator who doesn't want to sell out cheap. It's one of those movies with street lights and neon signs, cigarettes and fast red cars, and broken arms.

"Sting is so intelligent," she said. "Also, he was born in Newcastle. He grew up there, but he hadn't been back for years."

"Why do you suppose they used you, as an American woman, in a British film?" I asked.

"Well, because the film is sort of about America," she said, lighting a Benson & Hedges. "About how the Americans are buying everything up. But here is an American girl who doesn't want to be bought up along with everything else. The film was directed by Michael Figgis. I don't think he wanted me at first. I met him before *Something Wild* came out, and maybe he didn't know what I could do. But we got along well, and he allowed me to collaborate on changing Kate, my character, a little bit, so she was a little stranger. The movie isn't about this huge message. It's a *film noir* about . . . well, about what happens to these six people."

"Sometimes a movie isn't even about the plot and the dialogue," I said. "It's about the way the light falls on a wet street, and the way a woman blows out cigarette smoke and looks a man in the eye."

"The great thing at the end," she said, "is that Sean and I become the cause instead of the effect."

"After this current picture, what are you going to do?" I asked.

"Who knows? I'll be out of work."

She picked up her fork and held it menacingly over the Caesar salad. Then the subject of Alfred Hitchcock came up.

"He was a real bastard," she said. "Do you know that he sent me a toy coffin with a doll of my mother inside of it? I think I'm pretty intelligent. Even when I was six years old I didn't think *that* was a very funny joke.

What kind of a girl would want to play with a doll that was your mom?"

I said I had read all about Hitchcock's relationship with Melanie Griffith's mother, Tippi Hedren, in a couple of books that basically said the Master of Suspense tried to seduce her while they were making *The Birds* and *Marnie*, and when he failed, treated her with cruelty.

"I have no desire to read about the [12-letter-word]," she said. "He hurt my mother. He never actually *did* anything wrong, but he was really cruel. I had a lot of doubts about directors. But the first movie I made was *Night Moves* (1974), when I was sixteen, and the director was Arthur Penn, and I guess he thought I was a crazy kid, but he was very nice to me. Directors can be nice. Mike Nichols fought—I happen to know he *fought*—to get me this movie, because he believed in me."

It was getting on toward 2 P.M., and Griffith said she wanted to walk over to a parking garage and pick up a Jeep belonging to her new boyfriend, Lian Dalton, who is a vice president of Bear, Stearns.

"See?" she said, holding out her arm to model a new Rolex. "I'm gonna get the Jeep and take Alexander for a ride. Here's Lian."

She took out a photograph of a handsome dark-haired man on skis, with a mountain behind him.

"Where's this?" I asked.

"I don't know. I wasn't there. I just like the picture."

We left the restaurant and walked again through the sunny spring streets to the parking garage, where Griffith had one of those conversations you can hear only in Manhattan.

"He wants to know about being approved as a monthly parker," she told the garage attendant.

"Yes, well, when you come back, I may know more about that."

"He's very successful and reliable, and he's a really nice man," she said.

"Yes," said the attendant thoughtfully. "We got a couple of good reports on him."

"I think you can count on him, I mean," she said.

"We got some good reports," the attendant conceded.

We drove out of the garage in the Jeep.

"I wonder if you have Mike Nichols's address," I said.

"Sure."

"I want to write him a note," I said. "What happened was, I referred to him as 'another one of the hacks brought in to direct a Neil Simon picture,' but I didn't mean that he was a hack—I meant that he was too good to be another one of the hacks brought in to direct a Neil Simon picture. But I don't think it came across that way."

"I'll be sure to get you the address," she said. "I think it's on East 81st or something. I don't think it came across that way, either. Look at this. The windows on this thing *zip* down."

James Belushi

Chicago, June 10, 1988—I hear you're getting married a year from today.

"Yeah," said Jim Belushi. "The tenth. How'd you know that?"

"He heard it on the radio, stupid," said Marjorie Bransfield, who will marry Belushi on that day.

"Did I mention it on the radio?"

"Several times."

How'd you pick that exact date, a year in advance?

"It's our anniversary of when we first met," Belushi said.

"Actually, our anniversary is the fifteenth," Marjorie said, "but we picked the tenth because it's on a Saturday."

"Yeah," said Belushi. "The fifteenth is on a Wednesday or a Thursday or something. Nobody gets married on a Thursday."

"And ten is a good number," Marjorie said.

"As good as fifteen?" asked Belushi.

"It's right up there with fifteen."

Marjorie, a curvy blonde with a sunny smile, went to make some plans, or maybe to do some shopping. Belushi and I settled down for lunch.

"She's been just great for me," he said. "I'm off the booze for three years, my weight is way down, I'm in the best shape I've ever been in. And I'm in love. When Arnold saw me before we started shooting the movie, he was shocked. He thought I was ideal for the role because I was a fat Chicago slob. When he saw the shape I was in, he started calling me into his dressing room and opening up a big refrigerator full of Haagen-Dazs and eating it in front of me, and then offering me some. Of course, he can pig out all he wants. He works out two hours every day. I musta put on ten pounds."

Do you go to the gym a lot?

"You kidding?"

Jim Belushi lit a Marlboro and looked at the view, high above the Oak Street Beach. He is a Chicagoan at any weight. He studied the menu and dutifully went for the vegetarian pasta, while smearing butter all over the hot bread and wolfing it down.

"I've gotten rid of a lot of the anger, the discontentment, the frustration," he said. "Know what my secret is? Money. You start getting good jobs and a good payday, and suddenly you're a happier person. For me it probably started to happen after *The Principal*, last summer, which opened with a $4.7 million weekend. In Hollywood, they figure if you can *open* with five mil, that's what *you* did, and then if the picture doesn't make it, they figure that's because it wasn't their picture, so it makes you bankable."

More French bread. *The Principal* did make it, however, turning into one of last summer's middle-range box office hits, and Jim Belushi, whose first acting job was playing Santa Claus for ten dollars an hour, is now established as one of Hollywood's plausible star character actors. In his movie, *Red Heat*, he plays a Chicago cop who is assigned as a partner and guide to Arnold Schwarzenegger, a Russian cop nicknamed "Iron Jaw" who is on the trail of three desperate Soviet drug smugglers who have fled to Chicago.

The movie was directed and co-written by Walter Hill, who is a master of this kind of formula. His *48 HRS* paired up Nick Nolte and newcomer Eddie Murphy, and this time Belushi has the Murphy role—wisecracking, screwing up, knowing the ropes. But *Red Heat* isn't simply a remake of *48 HRS.* It's a patented Hill action picture, with a lot of violence and shoot-outs and a final chase scene involving a couple of big Greyhound buses.

"It's an example of the best of what it is," Belushi said. "I wanted to make a movie like this, and Hill is the best at directing them. God, it was fun running down LaSalle Street in the middle of the night with a Magnum in my hand. Before we started shooting, Hill made us a little speech. He said, 'I don't know much about actors, but I'll shoot you well and edit you well, and if you say something stupid, I'll tell you.' What else do you want from a director? Arnold and I signed for the picture before the script was written, and Walter wrote a lot of it on the spot. Also, we made up some stuff. We'd get everything we wanted and then Walter would let the camera run for one last take and we'd see what happened."

And Arnold would improvise right along with you?

"He's a very intelligent actor. I called him the Professor. Offscreen, he did all the talking. He taught me about finance, real estate, publicity . . . he even helped me design the speech that I made to Marjorie's family last Christmas to announce our engagement."

Arnold wrote the speech for you?

"He knows all about that stuff, how it's done. The proper behavior. I was terrified. He called some nephew of his, who gave him an appropriate quote from the Bible."

You got up and made a pre-engagement speech and threw in a quote from the Bible?

"I was shaking. I just choked, I was so embarrassed. Everybody was there. They had a formal dinner and the whole family was there and people got up and made toasts, and then I made my announcement."

What Bible verse was suggested by Arnold's nephew?

"Something about how the sheep will lie down with the lamb. I dunno. Something about that. At the crucial moment, I forgot it."

I think it's more about the *lion* lying down with the lamb, I said.

Belushi raised an eyebrow. "The lion lying down with the lamb, huh? Jeez, that's not such a hot image to bring up in an engagement speech, when you're trying to impress your fiancee's family."

I was just thinking the same thing.

"That Arnold," Belushi said. "I bet he made up his nephew. He was probably just trying to put a fast one over on me."

His vegetarian pasta arrived, and he had an iced tea with it.

"Arnold is great," he said. "He told me all about investing my money. And how he changed his image. He had it all figured out. When he first came on the scene, people thought bodybuilders were all gay, so he posed with a bunch of girls in *Playboy,* just to correct the image. People don't know how well he can act. He does a perfect Russian accent in this movie. My character is supposed to always be trying to loosen him up, but he would never crack. Not until the director said, 'Cut!' A lot of actors will laugh at something funny, and that's fun, but then on the next take you never have the same freshness."

When you play a Chicagoan, I asked, what makes him a Chicagoan?

"Jeez, a lot of pizza and beer, I guess. And kinda no-nonsense. This is the kind of city where Santa gets arrested for speeding and slips the cop a five."

Santa Claus?

"Yeah. When I was in college, I spent about four years playing Santa Claus every Christmas. It was my Uncle Paul's idea. He said I should put an ad in the paper that Santa would come to your house. I charged ten bucks the first year. The next year I charged $15, plus $2 extra if you wanted my buddy, Frostbite the Elf. I'd walk in and you'd see these little kids get bug-eyed, the ones just on the borderline of believing in Santa, because they knew all of their relatives were in the room, and so who was the guy in the suit? Hey, maybe it *was* Santa Claus!

"One place, a wiseass kid was trying to spoil the secret for his little brothers and sisters. So I took him over to one side, with a big twinkle in my eye, and told him to shut the fuck up. He believed."

You got stopped for speeding?

"Maybe I had a couple of extra beers or something. It was very embarrassing. The cops dragged me out of my car, all dressed in my Santa suit and with the beard and the big black boots and everything, and slammed me up against the side of the car and slapped the handcuffs on, and everybody driving past was pointing and honking their horns. And when they threw me in the holding cell with all the drunks, you shoulda seen their faces."

Belushi pushed back his plate and lit a Marlboro.

"Someday," he said, "that's going in a movie."

Peter Weller

Chicago, July 15, 1987—This is Peter Weller describing what it was like to make his latest movie:

"It was a horror beyond dreams. It was a nightmare."

He had been talking about how hard he had worked on *RoboCop,* how much he admired the film, how he was prepared to make a sequel because the character interested him so much. And then I asked him about the nuts and bolts, the daily routine of getting into his costume and makeup. And the expression on his face changed in a curious way, as if his body were still in a Chicago hotel room but his mind had traveled back to a time he'd been blocking.

He wears two different kinds of makeup at various times in *RoboCop.* During a long central section, he is inside a steel suit that reveals his face from the cheekbones down. In the longer stretch that ends the movie, his entire face is visible—but most of it has been reconstructed with makeup, to make him look like the kind of man who has been beyond death and then returned. The preparation for both stages of his character was a daily ordeal.

"For the twenty-one days it took to shoot those sequences," Weller said, "I would have to get up at three in the morning. My assistant told me, that's not an early call, that's a late call—that's when the crew is just finishing their drinking and going to bed. And I was getting up to go through six hours of makeup to begin a workday at ten. And then we'd shoot for ten hours on top of that."

In the movie, Weller plays a Detroit cop at some unspecified time in the future—a cop who is shot to pieces by gangsters, and then brought back to like as a "robocop," a creature combining a human brain and certain other body parts with a frame made of steel, synthetics, and computer chips. Only the bottom half of his face is visible, and he speaks in a mechanical monotone, but the character is oddly human and sympathetic.

Weller is a serious actor with a heavyweight stage background and impressive screen credits (he was Diane Keaton's arrogant boyfriend in *Shoot the Moon* and Teri Garr's doper friend in *Firstborn*, and had the title role in the cult movie *Buckaroo Banzai*). He hasn't had the kind of career that seems to lead to violent thrillers, and yet he said he wanted to play the robocop the moment he read the script.

"The title took me aback. But when I read the screenplay everything disappeared in the face of the story. I grant you, it does belong in the big box labeled Police Action Thriller. That's what it is. But it's also a fable, a fairy tale about humanity. This story is the heart of what Frankenstein is all about. And I said to myself, within this possible commercial blockbuster is something that distinguishes it from the rest of the genre."

With these thoughts in his mind. Weller said, he went to meet with Paul Verhoeven, the Dutch director of *Soldier of Orange* and *The Fourth Man*.

"I asked him, is that what you intend? To tell this other little story, inside the police action thriller? And he said that, to him, that was the most important part of the story."

And so Weller made his decision, and subjected himself to the daily inhumanity of the makeup ordeal.

"At the beginning of each one of those days," he said, "no amount of psyching up or meditative preparation could overcome this immense depression over what amount of work lay ahead of me. I'd just go into automatic drive—I'd sit in the chair for six hours and meditate. Because when you have two or three people standing around and pressing into your face, and God forbid they've eaten garlic the night before, and you're smelling a whole lot of white wine and bourbon and Marlboro cigarettes—you know you don't have a choice. You have to find some way to go into some sort of alpha state. Either that, or put a bullet in your brain."

And it was then he used the phrase, "It was a horror beyond dreams."

The robocop moves like a machine, I said, and yet is oddly and appealingly human. How did you do that?

"I prepared for five months with a mime from Israel, who's a professor of movement at Juilliard. We rehearsed something that was sleek and elegant and sexy. Simultaneously, the suit was being developed. But it was late being completed, and it didn't turn up until two weeks into the shooting. We had no time to test it or rehearse with it, and it was a mess. It took ten hours to put on the first time. We were all despondent. We didn't know what to do. We decided to throw out everything we'd done, and use the cumbersomeness of the suit to our advantage. My movements in the film are more beastlike, more unsure, a little slower, and more awkward.

"I resisted that at the beginning. As a film actor, I like gestures that are small and subtle. To move in a grandiose and exaggerated way wasn't to my liking. I looked at Eisenstein's *Ivan the Terrible* several times to see the movement of the men in armor. And that's where I learned that it's possible to endow a larger-than-life character with larger-than-life characterization."

And so then you were inside the suit for twenty-one days.

"I would always have a heat rash in some new place, because the inside of the suit was rubber. It got up to a hundred and some degrees some days. People would hold air-conditioning ducts up to me, but they didn't help much. And the suit gave me tremendous cramps in my neck and shoulders."

Did you ever just wonder what the hell you were doing there?

"Yeah. Little spiritual and existential questions flashed across my brain several times a day, particularly standing out in 106-degree heat."

Can you distance yourself from those memories, and see the picture in the same way audiences see it?

"Not yet I can't."

How would you feel if this movie ended up in a double bill with *Buckaroo Banzai*?

"The guy who put on my makeup every

day kept asking me, who would win—Buckaroo or RoboCop? If they were on a double bill, that would be neat. But I've never correlated one to the other. *Buckaroo* was the most fun I've ever had, and essentially a comedy. This one is another deal altogether."

Weller's biography describes him as an Army brat who grew up all over the world and attended North Texas State University because it was known for its jazz bands. He still plays jazz trumpet on a regular basis in small New York jazz clubs, but he reached a moment, he said, when he had to decide on acting over jazz.

"I was getting burnt out with music. I felt I would always be an OK musician and I didn't have the ambition to be more. With acting it was different. I still play the trumpet every day and I even travel with it, but acting is what I do best."

Weller was scheduled to do some local TV, but before he went, I said I wanted to mention that letter.

"Yeah. The letter I sent you. I wrote it right in the middle of filming *RoboCop*."

And it was one of the most interesting letters I'd ever received from an actor. It came just at the time of the controversy over *Blue Velvet,* a film I admired technically but deplored personally, because I felt the director had asked Isabella Rossellini to go out on a limb he was unwilling to share with her.

The letter from Weller said, essentially, that he knew a lot of people had liked the movie but he agreed with my position. And he added, "No matter what any actor says about trusting the director and following the director's orders, the final responsibility for what we do lies with us. An actor who has a serious disagreement with what he is asked to do has the right, and the responsibility, to refuse."

Was that, I said, the sort of thinking that went through your head during those tortuous makeup sessions?

"Perhaps. Because, on the other hand, an actor should be prepared to go to just about any length for something he does believe in."

Kim Basinger

New York, July 23, 1987—How we got on the subject of carnival rides was a little unclear. Kim Basinger and I were talking about the heat, which was what everybody in New York was talking about in the summer of 1987, and she described it as a "gross intrusion" on her personal happiness. "When the steam comes up off the streets, Gawd!" is what she said, pouring herself a glass of Evian water and plopping down on a sofa.

"It's not like I was never hot before," she said. "I got family in Florida, and I go down to see them and stuff. I grew up in Athens, Georgia, where humidity is not unknown. But this is a gross intrusion."

Now normally you would not start an interview with a movie star by quoting what she had to say about the weather. You'd get the small talk out of the way and proceed directly to the important questions, like whether she really hated Mickey Rourke while they were filming *9½ Weeks*. But it seemed to me that Kim Basinger wasn't really talking about the weather. What she was really doing was announcing her personality, letting me know right off the bat where she was coming from. She talked in a broad Southern accent, taking charge with a lot of informality and a strong presence in the room: You knew there weren't going to be many lulls, many silences in the conversational flow.

She fills a room fairly easily. She's tall, and has a wild mane of blond hair falling below her shoulders, and she leans forward when she talks and looks you in the eye. You know there's someone at home.

If she is not yet considered to be a Great American Actress, maybe it's because she's so great-looking, so frankly sexy. And yet no other actress has had a more interesting run of major roles in the last few years than Kim Basinger, who has been receiving equal billing and equal screen time with an assortment of top male stars: Sam Shepard in *Fool for Love,* Mickey Rourke in *9½ Weeks*, Richard Gere in *No Mercy,* Bruce Willis in *Blind Date,* and Jeff Bridges in the comedy,

Nadine. "I miss the South," she said. "I'm very proud to be Southern. We live in California right now, and I have a lot of little nieces and nephews who all want to go to Disneyland, and we kinda look around the house sideways, to see who's gonna get stuck with taking them.

"Of course, I have an excuse, I can't get on any of the rides. I have this inner ear thing. I used to love, love, love to get on carnival rides, and complain that they didn't look like they had any stability. They were right on the hard asphalt, so if anything went wrong and you hit the ground, that was it. Carnival rides are scary as hell. You could have a heart attack. Some guy the other day, his seat belt became unbuckled, I read in the paper, and that was that. Sounds a lot like Delta."

"Isn't Delta supposed to be the national airline of Georgia?" I asked.

"Oh, Delta, Eastern . . ."

She poured herself a little more Evian, and I took note of her costume: white pants and T-shirt, rumpled black jacket, black and white saddle shoes.

"Anyone who comes from the South kind of understands about the South," she said. "I love the South. I really do love it, even the parts I'm not from, like New Orleans or Texas. That's why I loved doing *Nadine*. Robert Benton, the director, is from Texas, and so we hit it off right away.

"Southerners have what I call a Dirty Bottles Mentality. We all grew up looking for pop bottles to take back and claim the deposit on. Where I grew up it was farmland, flatter than a pancake, and land like that still brings more peace to my life than anything else."

She must have felt some peace, then, filming *Nadine*, which is kind of a down-home slapstick comedy with Basinger as a small-town woman in the mid-1950s who wants to get divorced from her womanizing husband, but meanwhile allows the local photographer to take the wrong kind of pictures of her. She enlists her future ex-husband (Jeff Bridges) to help her steal the pictures back, and that lands them in the middle of local intrigue after they accidentally steal some secret state highway plans at the same time.

"This whole picture took me back," she said. "Athens, Georgia, back then was not what you read about Athens, Georgia, today, with all those country rock stars calling it home. We had a Five Points where all the streets came together, and that was the main center of everything in the world. We didn't think of ourselves as city people. I went to Athens High School and one year to the University of Georgia, but I was still small town. I still am. It really gets to me, doing interviews for a movie and talking to all these journalists and most of the time I don't know their names from Adam's housecat."

"What don't you like about interviews?"

"Repeating the same stuff over and over. I love to talk. I just hate always saying the same thing, is all."

"George Segal once said he hates interviews," I told her, "but that while he's giving one, he tells himself he's playing a character who is happy."

"Now that's an idea," Basinger said. "But it's very difficult for me to be an actress when I don't have a part. Between action! and cut!, I'm OK, but I sure don't walk around pretending like I'm still the character on my day off. I suppose if I have an accent or something, I'd have to keep that up. But the rest of the time, the minute the scene is over and I slip out of those clothes and out of those high heels, I'm gone. If you pretend to be the character all the time, you don't get the full enjoyment of making a movie, getting to know the crew, going out for a drink after work."

She paused. "There are actors," she said, "who take the full-immersion approach, needless to say. Don't come near me today! I'm so-and-so today! They stay hidden in their trailers all day, brooding over somebody else's problems. To each his own, I say. Far be it from me to criticize their approach. It's how you get there that counts."

All of these thoughts were coming from Basinger in a rush, a tumble of high-energy dialogue. "Sometimes when I'm caught up in a highly emotional scene," she said, "it's hell for the people around me. I like to do a scene once, maybe twice, and that will be my best work."

"Sometimes," I said, "when it's hell on the people around you, maybe it's good for the camera. Sometimes when everybody has fun on a set and likes each other, the result is sort of flat and disappointing."

"The tension worked onscreen for Jeff Bridges and I," she said. "Jeff loves to rehearse. I detest rehearsal. He likes fifty takes. I like one or two. I hate to run something out—literally. God, I'm thinking, I'll use up everything in rehearsal. And especially in a scene when I have almost all the dialogue, and all the other guy has to say is . . . *Yeah, but.*"

"They say," I said, "that there was a certain amount of tension when you were making *9½ Weeks.* That was, of course, the controversial 1986 film in which Mickey Rourke walked into Basinger's life and became her master, turning her into a sexual slave until finally, at the end, she revolted. Although the film did only fairly well at the American box office after a couple of key scenes were cut by the studio, it became an international box-office phenomenon—the top film of the year in France and Italy, for example.

"I love that film," she said. "It was my favorite film, and that's the truth. That is myself on the screen. A real emotional breakthrough. That movie really put me over the river in terms of what I could do as an actress. I shed so much fear there, it was astonishing. There were articles that Mickey had to do all kinds of strange shit to make me cry, to reach me emotionally. I know this sounds strange, but after a day of being that highly emotional . . . I enjoyed it immensely. That kind of excursion into the far fields of emotion.

"After I did that film, I knew I could do anything. No more holding back in a role. Yeah, I said, I know that's in me. See, I don't believe in doing anything half-ass. After doing *9½ Weeks,* I made a vow, from now on I'm gonna make sure it's all out there. A dam opened up."

She was leaning forward on the sofa now, intensely, her eyes flashing.

"People don't know the truth about *9½ Weeks*! So much was cut out of it, people never even saw the real film. I got eight hours of that film at home. Eight hours. I heard there are three other hours at the studio. I was semi-devastated when the film came out, because they cut the guts out of it. People ended up seeing an MTV video about sex. There are three or four pirated versions around, but people never see how it was supposed to end, with my demise, my breakdown, suicide attempts . . . that movie was a lot heavier than just some fancy seduction.

"The problem was, we made it for MGM, and Ted Turner (then) owned the company, and if he had seen the original version of that movie, he wouldn't have let a boy take it from one soundstage to another on a bicycle, let alone release it. We shot the whole thing in sequence, and it was my idea to stay completely away from Mickey, to never see him except when the cameras were rolling. We never socialized, we never had coffee on the set, we were strangers, just like in the movie. The missing scenes and reels don't have a lot of sex in them. More of a lot of drama, as the situation between us deepens."

"Why didn't they release the film in the form they shot it in?"

"It's called chickening out. They didn't think the American public could take it. Well, at least it got me out of Bali in one piece."

"How's that?"

"We were detained at the airport. Our passports or visas or something were all wrong. I had visions of *Midnight Express*—thrown forever into a dungeon. They brought a couple of officials around, guys who looked straight out of *Midnight Express,* but they'd seen *9½ Weeks*, and they just waved us through. They liked the movie. And you know, there's another thing. When the movie came out, it was attacked by the feminists and all? But you should see the mail I get from women all over the world who love this movie. And women will come up to me on the street and say the strangest things. Or they'll say, 'Ever since I saw that movie, I've been wearing red lipstick,' but somehow they're saying more than that, you know?"

I told Basinger how impressed I'd been, over the last few years, by her movie projects. She doesn't take routine stuff. Even in a minor film like Blake Edwards's *The Man Who Loved Women* (1983), where she played the sex-crazed temptress of a Texas oil millionaire, she didn't just go for the clichés; she threw herself into the part, draping herself across the star, Burt Reynolds, with such wanton abandon that the scene became hers, not his. In recent years, she's taken one role after another that would seem to have trouble written all over it: slogging through the swamps with Richard Gere in *No Mercy,* trapped in a slattern's fantasy in *Fool for Love.* I asked her who called the shots, her or an agent?

"That question shows you have some kind of intuitive sense about me," she said. "I do call my own shots. Projects find me. It's very strange. I have not read scripts and then fought to get roles, going up against a lot of other girls. Yet never have I lost a part that I wanted. All these strange projects and strange characters find me. It's intuitive. You take *No Mercy*."

All right, I said, I will. That was the movie with Basinger as the illiterate mistress of a Louisiana vice lord who had purchased her as a child and kept her as his virtual slave until Richard Gere, a Chicago cop, came into the picture.

"There was something in the screenplay," she said. "That character was great, if I really could have played her the way she was written. Very spiritual, very defensive. She was cut off from freedom not so much because of the guy she was with, but because she was illiterate. She didn't have the confidence to strike out on her own, since she couldn't read or write. That was what interested me in the character. I love the people I play. That's the key."

But the movie ended, she sighed, in a fusillade of sound and violence, fire and explosions and gunshots. Too bad, since the screenplay dealt more with the characters.

"I love Nadine, in this new movie," she said. "She's classy trash. I love people who are classy trash. They know what's happened more than sophisticated people ever will. They've made their own history, and there's something very powerful about that. When she gets old she can say she did everything she ever wanted to do, which is a great thing to be able to say."

While Basinger was talking, her eyes were bright and her hands were waving, and she looked just great. When she was finished, I asked her: "Does it ever hurt you to be beautiful?"

"How so?"

"You have spent as much important screen time in good movies in the last couple of years as anybody else in the movie business, but do they take you a little less than seriously because you're blond and sexy?"

"Tell me all about it," she said. "Hollywood has always tried to shove me in all the wrong boxes, just because I'm blond and blue-eyed. That's so ignorant. You can't judge a book by its cover. How ignorant can you really be, thinking someone is a certain way because of how they look? Nobody really knows anybody. I don't know you. You won't know me when you walk out of here. I could have held myself back and let them intimidate me with their idea of how I had to act if I looked the way I looked, which was that I couldn't walk and chew gum at the same time. But I believe we all have the power to get what we want. I have the power. Only I can stop me.

"For a while, I thought, OK, I won't try to look good. They'll think I look too good for a really good role, so I'd put my hair in a ponytail and walk around in jeans, a sloppy mess, and that felt wrong. I thought, hell, man, this is bullshit. I was always a racehorse, so I threw up my head and just charged and to hell with what they thought. I knew it would eventually happen. I've never wanted to be anybody else, or look like anybody else and . . . na-na-na-na-na-pfffft!"

"Which means?"

"Just what it sounds like."

"I think I've got a good last line for my story," I said.

Richard Dreyfuss

Los Angeles, July 29, 1987—Now that Richard Dreyfuss is a big movie star for the second time, and his career is on a hot streak after a few slow years and some personal problems, he remembers a press conference he once held in Italy.

"This was many years ago, but I still remember this guy who said, 'You're very short, and the hair it is beginning to go, and your eyes, they are a lee-tle too close together. You're not like a Hollywood movie star.' And I told him that wasn't true. You have two categories of stars. You've got Gable and Flynn and Cooper, and then you've got guys like Falk and Cagney. And I'm in the second category. I still am. Although lately there have been a lot of Harrison Ford-type roles. So it still looks funny to see me in a lead."

Dreyfuss is only right up to a point. He did look sort of goofy in a lot of his earlier roles, like *The Apprenticeship of Duddy Kravitz*, *American Graffiti*, and *Jaws*. And who can forget him sculpting mountains out of mashed potatoes in *Close Encounters of the Third Kind*? But since his current hot streak began with *Down and Out in Beverly Hills* in January, 1986, he has projected a subtly different image on the screen. The hair is a distinguished gray, short-cropped. The eyes seem brighter, the walk seems more confident, and he knows that people sometimes joke that he looks like Paul Newman. Nobody would have said ten years ago that Richard Dreyfuss looked like Paul Newman.

Almost without planning to, Dreyfuss seems to be metamorphosing into the first kind of movie star, moving into the handsome, matinee-idol category.

After he did *Down and Out*, he had another considerable hit with *Tin Men*. *Stakeout*, with Dreyfuss and Emilio Estevez starring as vice cops assigned to stake out the girlfriend of an escaped convict, is his latest. Dreyfuss and the woman fall in love, which causes all sorts of problems, most of them very funny. The key thing about the role is that it's a part for a traditional leading man—a romantic lead.

The decision to cast Dreyfuss in the role was a personal one by Jeffrey Katzenberg, president of Walt Disney Pictures, who remembers that he told Dreyfuss: "Look, everybody's been saying you look like Paul Newman. So why not make the kind of movie Paul Newman might make?" He gave Dreyfuss the screenplay of *Stakeout*, a traditional police comedy-thriller. And Dreyfuss remembers thinking it was "a done thing. They had decided this was right for me, and boom! We were making the picture."

Was it hard for you to play a cop?

"All of the physical stuff was tough for me because I'm not a jock. And that's a specific thing, a way of moving so you look like you know how your body works. You have to learn how to take a gun and run down the hallway of a hotel looking like you know where you're going and how to get there without being killed. Put a camera on that and it will look either correct or incorrect, either funny or not funny. And I didn't know if I knew how to do it. It's like this . . ."

He sat up straight in his chair and went through the motions of drawing and aiming a gun. First he did it in a cool, possessed way. Then he did it in a frightened, jerky way.

"You gotta make sure you don't look like a fool," he said.

This was in Los Angeles, where Dreyfuss was involved in the premiere of *Stakeout*. The night before I'd seen him and his wife in Morton's, the celebrity restaurant, having dinner with Steven Spielberg and Amy Irving. He was exhibiting the same kind of restless energy he brings to his roles: shifting in his chair, looking around the restaurant, getting up to visit other tables. Dreyfuss is a naturally outgoing man, not shy, not conceited, curious about other people to the point of gossip. If he is slowly moving into Category One, he has not yet developed the aloof mystique to go along with it.

Now, the next morning in a hotel suite, he had his feet up on a chair and seemed willing to talk about anything. I told him how good I thought he'd looked in *Down and Out in Beverly Hills*, how every moment of his performance seemed blessed with an unforced comic genius. He seemed to be working without a net. The movie was his first major success after some well-publicized problems involving cocaine usage and a serious car crash, and I asked him something vague about "changes" in his lifestyle.

"It's better now than it was before," he said. "Rather than rhapsodize I will answer anything specific that you want to ask me."

"OK," I said. "You don't use chemicals anymore, and you were when you ran into the tree?"

That seemed fairly specific.

"Oh boy, was I. It wasn't tough to stop using . . . once I stopped. What was tough was thinking that I had to. The element of denial is so strong when you're using. And so that's what the car accident and my public arrest did for me. It allowed me to stop and hear the birds singing."

"It must have been a very hard time for you."

"It was a difficult couple of weeks. First of all, I was in a hospital room, and no one was telling me what was going on downstairs, which was pretty hideous. It took a few weeks for friends to call me and tell me how they reacted to the headlines. Some of them were very direct and honest. And eventually I could see that in many ways on many different levels that accident was the most important event of my life, and without a doubt the best thing that ever happened to me. Not at the time, it didn't seem that way. But looking back."

"I seem to see a different person today," I said, "than the Dreyfuss of several years ago. You somehow seem clearer in your performances, more defined, with sharper edges. You seem more alert."

He considered that.

"When I was younger . . ." he began, and then he stopped, and thought, and said, "You know how sometimes a newspaper will print the color comics incorrectly, so that the colors don't all fall on top of one another, and there's the image, and another image, and another image? That's who I was. I was this cartoon character with emotions here, and here, and here. I sometimes claim that I was called out of class in the fifth grade to go speak to the principal, and it was on that day while I was out of the room that the teacher told the rest of the class the secret of life. And for the rest of my life I went around wondering what the secret of life was. That's how I felt.

"And for a while that was OK, because I led a normal life and I was a normal person, a young man trying to make a living at this funny profession. And then I made such a living at this funny profession that people brought in shovels full of money and fame and celebrity, and I didn't know what to do with myself. So I got into drugs.

"And when I finally stopped, no one told me to stop for my acting, to stop for my career. Finally it went, stop for this tree! Stop for this tree, so I can talk to you. When I picked up those particular pieces I realized that I had run all of my life and I was forced to start walking and because I was forced into walking I could see and smell and taste the world around me. And there's a line in Edward Albee's *The Zoo Story* that became my line: Sometimes it's necessary to go a long distance out of your way in order to come back a short distance correctly. And that's what happened to me."

After director Paul Mazursky finished *Down and Out in Beverly Hills,* he referred to his cast as "the Raleigh Hills Gang" because all three leads—Dreyfuss, Bette Midler, and Nick Nolte—came directly to the project after ending substance abuse (with Midler and Nolte, drinking was the basic problem). If you look carefully at the movie, there are times when you can sense all three actors projecting an almost cocky, headstrong confidence, their heads clear and their eyes bright. I asked Dreyfuss if he ever thought, on that picture, that he could do no wrong.

"I knew less on that film than on any film I've ever done. One of my secrets used to be, I'd never take a part unless I knew how to do the role before the rehearsal. If I read it and didn't know how to do it, I wouldn't take it. With *Down and Out,* I read it and I didn't know how to do it. But I was in no position to turn it down. I didn't have that luxury. So I put aside my fear, and every day I would go to work, and, especially at the beginning, very consciously, I would consider myself a clean slate because I didn't know what the hell I was doing there. And I was allowing Paul in, and Nick in, and all of a sudden I began to be able to listen better and hear better. In a real way, I was working without a net."

"Did you know while you were making it that it was really something special?"

"There was no anticipation of success. Or of failure, for that matter. It was just, go to work and do your work and have fun every day. I've only done one film in my life that had an anticipation of success, and that was *Close Encounters.* When we made that film, every day we'd look at each other and say, Are we making history here, or what? But even with *Jaws* or *The Goodbye Girl,* we had absolutely no anticipation of success. We had no idea how the movies would finally turn out."

After *Down and Out in Beverly Hills,* Dreyfuss made *Tin Men,* Barry Levinson's movie about aluminum siding salesmen in Baltimore in the 1950s. I asked Dreyfuss if he was still working without a net in that one.

"That character was probably the furthest away from any other character I've ever played. And it was slightly more difficult because Levinson doesn't believe in rehearsal, and I need rehearsal, lots of rehearsal, so that for example there's a certain way the character walks, and I didn't find that until the middle of the movie. There was another example of a character that I did not know how to play, going into the project."

The Svengali in Dreyfuss's recent career has been Disney's Katzenberg, a studio executive who believes that stars should keep working steadily, just like in the old days, instead of taking years between their projects. That helps account for Dreyfuss's three movies in eighteen months.

"For me," Dreyfuss said, "working is better than not working. Many things will happen to you, many ups and downs, but it's better than waiting four years for the perfect role."

I told Dreyfuss it looked to me like his last three pictures had given his career a whole new impetus, that he was more "bankable" than he'd ever been. Did it feel like a comeback, after that sudden collision with the tree interrupted the path his life was taking?

"It teaches me a lot of things," He said, "like, don't take the future for granted. However good this is, it could all end tomorrow. But I feel a lot better now about what I'm doing than before, and in a funny way—it means less to me. Because it means less it's more easily manageable and it's something I can enjoy far better."

"Why does it mean less?"

"I've grown up to a certain extent. I'm married and have children, I have people and things that I love more than I love movie acting. In the old days I had nothing other than acting, and I think that distorted my view of things. I was alone and I knew of nothing on earth that was more important than my excessive love for my career and acting itself. And that warped me. Now I have two children and a wife and the viewpoint is different. The excessive need is gone. Now acting is something I sure like to do—there's no question I like doing this—but I don't define myself that way. Not any more."

Trevor Howard (In Memoriam)

London, January 8, 1988—The British obituaries for Trevor Howard all said the same things, as if they had been rewritten from the same wire service copy, and they gave little sense of the great joyful spirit of the man.

Howard was a fine actor, they agreed, but a hell-raiser. He would always be remembered for *Brief Encounter*, *The Third Man*, and *Mutiny on the Bounty.* He got along with all of his colleagues, except Marlon Brando, who mumbled and was a bloody fraud. Howard was unpretentious, preferring to spend time with his mates at the village pub than in the glamorous world of the movies. His devotion to his wife of forty-two years, the actress Helen Cherry, was legendary. He might have been knighted if he had taken himself more seriously and minded his manners. Robert Mitchum, his co-star in *Ryan's Daughter,* was quoted again and again: "You'll never catch Trevor acting."

That was a compliment, of course. Although he was a member of the generation of Olivier, Gielgud, and Richardson—three actors it was very easy to catch acting—Trevor Howard was a more understated performer whose best work came through the exercise of a certain reserve.

That was true in *Brief Encounter* (1946), where he played a man whose morals prevented him from yielding to romantic temptation, and in *The Third Man* (1949) where he was the unemotional British intelligence officer in postwar Vienna, standing like a rock of certitude between the naive Americanisms of the Joseph Cotten character and the cynical manipulation of Orson Welles's famous villain, Harry Lime.

In other films, however, Howard was not unwilling to lower his reserve, and sometimes his trousers, as in the famous, hilarious sequence in *Charge of the Light Brigade*, where he besported himself below decks with willing maidens. And off-screen, he was, it is true, too fond of the drink, and if that sometimes led to trouble, it also contributed its share to his legend.

The first thing I thought, when I heard that he had died, was that no one in the world of movies had given me more hilarious and affectionate memories in just a few brief encounters.

Spending time in the presence of Trevor Howard was an education and an entertainment. I remember the first time I saw him, at the bar of Tom Ashe's pub on the high street in Dingle, Ireland. Howard and Mitchum were in Dingle to film David Lean's *Ryan's Daughter*, and after a day of sunshine there had followed nine days of rain. While Lean waited for the sun to reappear, Mitchum and Howard cemented their friendship with whiskey and tall tales, and that day in the pub Howard told me that if I wanted an interview with Mitchum, I had only to wait where I was: "This is the only pub in Dingle, so it stands perfectly to reason that Mitch will turn up here eventually."

When Mitchum did turn up, he ordered a brandy, downed it, and observed: "I always like to work with Trevor on a picture, because if I think I'm drinking too much, all I have to do is glom him, and I know I'm OK." Then he led a parade down the street to the cottage he was renting, and immediately began a Trevor Howard anecdote. Imagine, if you can, the following paragraphs in Robert Mitchum's voice:

"One night I was sitting here with Harold, my stand-in, who was a member of the Coldstream Guards. We were listening to old Jim Reeves records on the turntable. Trevor was at the kitchen table, making love to a bottle of Chivas Regal. Harold went out into the garden for a breath of fresh air, and returned as pale as a ghost.

" 'Mitch!' he said. 'Helen Howard's sprawled by the garden path unconscious!' That's strange, I thought, since she doesn't drink. Perhaps she turned her ankle on a stone in the darkness. I told Harold to carry her in, and we put her on the couch and fanned her back to witness. Harold had some experience as a paramedic, and he immediately diagnosed that she had fallen and broken her tailbone—her coccyx. 'This is not good,' Harold explained, 'because the nearest decent hospital is twenty-seven miles over the mountains to Tralee, and the only way to get there is in a Land Rover over rough roads. Not comfortable for a woman with a broken coccyx.'

"I agreed, and went into the kitchen to explain to Trevor.

" 'Pay no attention, old man,' he told me. 'Helen's always pulling these stunts.'

" 'Harold thinks she's broken her coccyx,' I told him.

" 'That's a good one! I've been married to her for twenty-five years. Take it from me, old man—she hasn't got one.'

" 'Her tailbone, Trevor. She's broken her tailbone. Harold says the thing to do is take her to the hospital in Tralee, but it's a difficult journey, twenty-seven miles over the mountain roads in a Land Rover.'

"Trevor took another sip of his Chivas and thought about that. Finally his face brightened. 'Right you are, old man! Bloody difficult! Most painful! No sense in *my* going!' "

The filming of *Ryan's Daughter* dragged on through that spring and summer of 1969, as Lean, the perfectionist, waited in vain for the Irish sun to reappear and finally shot some of his beach scenes in South Africa to make them match. The following year, when the movie was released, Trevor Howard hit the road to promote it. For Howard, press trips were fueled with drink, and Bailey Selig, the publicist who accompanied him on a trip to Germany, recalled that Trevor paused at Heathrow Airport to relieve himself in the men's room before boarding his plane.

Days later, back in Heathrow after drinking throughout the trip, Howard once again headed for the men's room, and Selig, waiting outside, heard a puzzled shout and went in to see what was the matter. Trevor was standing in front of the same urinal he had used on his outbound voyage, and was looking at his new Swiss watch, which told the day and date.

"What's the matter, Trevor?" Selig asked him.

"Good lord, man," Howard cried. "If this watch is correct, I've been pissing here for nine days!"

Later on that same odyssey, Trevor and Helen arrived in Chicago, where they took a suite at the Drake. I went to have dinner with them in their rooms, and found Trevor paging through a battered address book.

"Most extraordinary chap," he said. "I have his number here somewhere. Helen and I met him at the casino in Monte Carlo, didn't we? He was a dentist from Evanston, Illinois, but he was the most devilishly accomplished amateur magician. And he did something I've never seen any man do, before or since. He produced a live chicken from the most amazing place."

"I think you may be mistaken, darling," Helen Cherry said.

"How could I be? No room for error! He pulled a chicken right out of his arse! Most extraordinary."

Dialing a number, Howard got the man on the line. "Hello there, old chap," he said, "Trevor Howard here. Monte Carlo, remember? Yes, I thought you would. Unforgettable, it was. Yes. Helen and I are stopping here at the Drake Hotel, and we were wondering if you might not like to come down and have a spot of dinner with us . . ."

Howard spent the next hour drinking room service champagne and regaling us with stories of the amateur magician's astonishing versatility, and then there was a knock at the door and the dentist appeared, plainly astonished to have been remembered by the British movie star. Howard plied him with champagne and then took an expectant pose on the edge of his chair, winking at me and obviously expecting the visitor to produce a live chicken from his nether regions at any moment. But after half an hour of small talk, there was still no chicken.

"I say, old man," Howard said at last. "Do you by any chance remember that evening in Monte Carlo?"

"How could I ever forget it?" the dentist replied. "My wife and I were so flattered when you asked us to join your table."

"And a certain magic trick?" Howard asked, anticipating dripping from his voice.

"Well," said the dentist, "there was a magician there that night."

"Not you?"

"No, up on the stage. As I recall, he pulled a lot of pigeons out of his sleeve."

Howard looked crestfallen. "His sleeve, was it?"

The last time I saw Trevor Howard was in 1978, on Bora Bora, where he was filming a dreadful and ill-fated movie named *Hurricane*. He had been assigned his own thatched cottage at a hotel owned by Dino De Laurentiis, and could be seen most evenings before dinner, sitting on his porch and sipping a beer.

"I've been here twenty-nine and a half days, and it's an eternity," he told me. "Helen's flying out soon, and that will be my deliverance. I've worked four hours in this whole time. And it's a condition of my contract that I drink only beer for the duration of the filming. Can you think of anything more dreary than to be deprived of the companionship of your wife, your friends, and your civilization, and to be condemned to spend a month on Bora Bora, outside the reach of the cricket broadcasts on the BBC, drinking nothing but beer? Do you have any paperbacks I may not have read?"

The next day was July 14, Bastille Day, and when I took some paperback thrillers around to Trevor, he suggested we drive to the island's small town and join the celebration. Sitting in the shade of a bamboo hut, sipping beer, he watched island women dancing in grass skirts while a band played "The Marseillaise," and then he sighed deeply.

"If I had a camera right now," he said, "we could simply make a documentary of this bloody celebration and take it back with us, and it would bring more enjoyment to more people than Dino's whole bloody show."

I had just one other brief encounter with the Howards, in Venice in 1972, after the film festival, at the airport. I was standing behind them in line as the airline clerk asked if they had any bags to check.

"No bags," Howard said cheerfully. "Helen never likes to bring baggage because she never knows when she'll have to carry me."

Barfly

Los Angeles, March 19, 1987—Down here in the bad part of town, a man named Big Ed runs a bar named Big Ed's, which pretty much sums up how he sees things. A lot of the regulars live upstairs in low-rent rooms and come downstairs to drink when the bar is open. When the bar is closed, they go upstairs and wait for it to open again.

One night not long ago, Charles Bukowski was holding down the end of the bar. He was looking around with wonderment on his face, because he had spent most of his life getting drunk in joints like this, but tonight was different, tonight they were making a movie inspired by his life, and they had rented out Big Ed's for one of the big scenes.

"The movie is called *Barfly*, and it's about me, because that's what I was, a barfly," Bukowski explained. "You ran errands for sadists and let the bartender beat you up, because you were the bar clown. You filled people's days with your presence, and maybe you'd get a few free drinks now and then."

We were hunched down with our elbows on the padded edge of the bar, talking quietly like conspirators. Linda, Bukowski's child bride, was taking down mental notes of everything.

"The way I became a barfly," he said, "was, I didn't like what I saw in the nine to five. I didn't want to become an ordinary working person, paying off the mortgage, looking at TV, terrified. The bar was a hiding place, to get out of the mainstream."

"Did you decide to become a barfly, or did you just look up one day and see a barfly in the mirror?" I asked him.

"I can't answer," he said. "It was kind of a subconscious decision. Meanwhile, I was a writer on the side, selling short stories to dirty magazines. I gave up the writing after a while and concentrated on the drinking. I refused to accept the living death of acquiesence."

All around us, they were setting up for the next shot. This movie is a big deal for Bukowski. It stars Mickey Rourke as the barfly, and Faye Dunaway as the experienced woman who teaches him some of the ropes. Bukowski based her character on memories of a lover he had many years ago, a half-Indian, half-Irish drunk he shared some good times with, like when they would fish the Sunday paper out of the Monday garbage and read it while they drank red wine. The woman is dead now. In fact, Bukowski estimates, everybody he knew then is dead now. Bukowski is sixty-six years old, and that is pretty old for a barfly to still be alive.

"I can see people saying, the guy's a drunk at the bar—so what?" he said. "They think lives should be attached to some purpose or goal. I knew the morning bartender. He would let me in at 5 A.M. I'd get two hours of free drinks before the bar opened at 7. I'd stay in the bar until it closed. I got three hours of sleep, from 2 A.M. to 5 A.M."

"Where was this bar located?" I asked him.

"It was located in two places, because this story is based on two different bars. One of them was in Philadelphia, at 16th and Fairmont. It no longer exists. The other one was here in L.A., at 6th and Alvarado. It's gone now. This story takes place a long time ago, in a dive. A dark dive. What I did, for ten years, I didn't write. I drank. I lived with various women and worked odd jobs. I got material to write about. Down-to-earth stuff. To use a cliché. When I was sitting in those bars, I had no idea it would come to a movie."

Bukowski looked into his coffee cup.

"It is a strange world, indeed," he said.

Somebody came around and gave us more coffee. Behind us, a woman named Davia Nelson was lining up the extras for the next scene. The extras were mostly regulars in Big Ed's, who had been hired to play themselves. This was going to be the scene right after Mickey Rourke beats the shinola out of Frank Stallone in the alley. Stallone plays the day bartender. In the scene, Rourke was going to slam in through the front door while the regulars carried Stallone in through the back door. Frank's fights are not as predictable as his brother's.

Davia Nelson was telling the extras when they would be needed. It was late at night, but the extras were all pretty sober; the drinks were free, but they were pacing themselves because they didn't want to be there in one shot and missing in the next.

"Do you still drink a lot?" I asked Bukowski.

"Oh, yeah. You might say heavy." He turned to his wife, Linda. "Tell him," he said.

"He's toned down since the *heavy* of the heavy," she said. "He likes good red wine."

"You do pretty good yourself," Bukowski told her.

"Lately I have."

"We were drinking in here the other night," Bukowski said. "There were still real bar people in here. It was open for business. It's kind of a rough bar. We were lucky we got home."

I looked carefully at Bukowski and saw, not anger, not weariness, not confusion or bitterness, not any of the things I expected to see, but a kind, open face to go with a gentle voice. The drinks hadn't killed that.

A million guys start out to get drunk and become great writers, and one makes it. Now a million more guys are probably getting drunk, trying to figure out how Bukowski did it. He isn't a survivor. He's a statistical aberration. In one of his novels, called *Women,* he describes the face of his hero, who is obviously based on himself: "The scars were there, the alcoholic nose, the monkey mouth, the eyes narrowing to slits, and there was a dumb, pleased grin of a happy man, ridiculous, feeling his luck and wondering why."

I couldn't improve on that.

"For a long time," Bukowski said, "I had a heavy suicide complex. I went to bars to try to fight, try to get killed. It's a funny thing. When you walk in looking for trouble, you usually can't find it. Mickey Rourke, in this film, he's looking for trouble. He's doing a good acting job. I didn't really expect him to be so good. I did some drinking with him, a couple of nights. He doesn't drink as much as I do. Nobody does, unless it's Linda. She used to match me, drink for drink, calling for the next bottle."

"Where'd you meet him?" I asked Linda, who was a sweet-faced brunette with the touch of a hippie about her.

"At the Troubadour on Santa Monica, about twelve years ago. He was reading his poems."

"Don't say that long ago," Bukowski said. "Don't date yourself."

"You're acting like it's Valentine's Day," Linda said.

"You already got your valentine, kid," Bukowski said.

"He usually picks me a valentine bouquet," Linda said.

"He'll think I'm soft," Bukowski said.

"Was it love at first sight?" I asked.

"He didn't even see me," she said. "He was blind drunk and in the arms of another woman."

"Several other women," Bukowski said. "I was doing research for my novel, *Women.* I had to go through a lot of gymnastics."

"What I felt," Linda said, "was, I stood there and looked at him and felt that I was seeing him for the first time, but I had known him since beyond time. I didn't think about it or plan it. It was just a fact."

"A rapport of souls," Bukowski said. "We finally got married about two years ago."

"We waited as long as possible," Linda said.

"Your first marriage?" I asked.

"My second," he said. "Long ago I married a millionairess by mistake."

"We were married at the Philosophical Research Society," Linda said. "He rented a Rolls-Royce. For a long time, he was afraid of marriage."

"I call it the enemy," Bukowski said. "That's what I call it. I don't give poetry readings anymore. We live in San Pedro, a quiet town. I play the horses in the daytime and write at night, drinking my wine."

"Cats," Linda said.

"We have five cats," Bukowski said. "Linda's studying acting. San Pedro is real quiet. It used to be a seaport full of whorehouses and bars. I like the quietness. They ask you what you're doing, they really want to know."

"Which track?" I said.

"Hollywood Park. First post at 2 P.M. When I write, when I'm going hot, I don't want to write more than four hours in a row. After that, you're pushing it. The horses give me something to do. At the age of fifty, I quit a job at the post office and decided to become a full-time writer. The old guy's crazy, my landlady declared, striking her head with her palm. I wrote my first novel, *Post Office,* in nineteen nights, working on scotch and beer. I had prepared by going to

L.A. City College and taking journalism. They taught me how to type."

"People are always asking me what courses to take if they want to be journalists," I said. "I always tell them to take typing."

"I just got an electric a couple of years ago," Bukowski said. "At the first, I was a starving writer. I went from 190 pounds down to 130. Everything I put in the mail came right back to me. The *Atlantic*, *Harper's*, the *New Yorker*, they rejected everything. I threw it all away. I started out again, selling to the porno mags. What I used to do was write a good story and throw in some goddamn sex. It worked. I only got one story rejected—it had too much sex! They draw a fine line. Bukowski, the editor wrote me, nobody on earth screws that many women in a week and a half! It was my own true story. The guy was haunted by jealousy.

"The porno mags were all published over on Melrose Avenue. They paid $230 to $290 a story. I could write one in a night with no problem. And I had a great landlady. She'd have these quart bottles of East Side, and we'd drink them and sing old songs. That was in the beginning. I have been a whore ever since. So now I'm translated into eighteen languages, and I'm just as modest as I ever was."

"You still write every night?" I asked.

"Most nearly. I hate to go into bars anymore. I've had too much of barrooms."

"You took it to the limit," Linda said.

"Now I go up with my bottle and write, all alone. The company's great. Turn on the radio and type. I like looking at a novel and you don't know what you're gonna type next.

Faye Dunaway walked into Big Ed's. She was dressed in black and her hair was kind of loose and she looked like a million dollars. Barbet Schroeder, the Frenchman who is directing *Barfly*, introduced Dunaway to Bukowski and his wife. Dunaway said she just wanted to pick up some pointers about the general situation, and also ask some questions about the character.

"Later, I'll tell you a story about Barbet Schroeder, if you promise not to print it," Bukowski said. He made room at the bar and a stool was found for Dunaway. Bukowski said he didn't want any more coffee, but he might have a light beer, he was taking it easy tonight.

"Was it always effortless for you to write?" Dunaway asked. "God, it's hard for me."

"My motto is, don't try," Bukowski said. "I finally made it into *Who's Who*, they asked for my philosophy—don't try."

"I'm one of the great tryers of all time," Dunaway said.

"I hear you been doing fine, Faye," Bukowski said. "In spite of my theory, it works for you."

"Are you gonna sit around in the corner for a while?" Dunaway asked. "Because I have some questions I want to ask you about the character I play. She's half-Cherokee and half-Irish, right?"

"Half-Indian," Bukowski said. "I don't know if she was Cherokee. She was born in New Mexico."

"But she's been here for so long, she's like a California person," Dunaway said.

"She could hold it real good," Bukowski said. "When she talked—this will help you with the dialogue—she illustrated the principle that if you listen to a drunk all night long, you'll go crazy."

"She was out here from what age?" Dunaway asked.

"I was twenty-five, she was thirty-five," Bukowski said. "And she put me through college, meaning . . ."

"Yeah," Dunaway said.

"She brained me a few times," he said. "We were not in love, but she loved my way of drinking."

He lighted another one of his cigarettes.

"I like to drink and write and have the novel happen to me and I'm as surprised as anyone else," he said. "I'll be so deep into it that sometimes Linda will open the door unexpectedly and I'll scream."

"It's hard to drink and write," I said. "I guess Malcolm Lowry did it, with *Under the Volcano*."

"I've tried to read that book," Bukowski said. "God, I've tried. My writing is very simple. Maybe clarity is a better word."

"The key to all the arts is energy," Dunaway said. "Look at Peter Lorre's work. He's not afraid to go all the way. A lot of acting is so flat."

"It doesn't look like there's going to be a lot of flat acting in this movie," I said.

"Yeah, and no makeup, either," Dunaway said.

"When Mickey first meets her," Bukowski said, "nobody is sitting anywhere near her at the bar. He says, *Hey, bartender, how come nobody's sitting next to her? She looks pretty good.* The bartender tells him she's crazy. *That right?* he says, and walks right down and sits next to her. She looks straight ahead. Maybe she sneaks a little sideways glance. He says, *I hate people. Don't you?* She says, yeah, she feels better when they're not around. So now they have discovered a common bond. A common discouragement with humanity."

Behind us, the extras were marching back and forth, getting their moves right and learning their places. A gigantic Big Ed's regular named Tiny was chosen to help carry Frank Stallone back inside the bar after the fight.

"The way it really happened," Bukowski told Dunaway, "was I sat down next to her and she picked up a bottle and I told her to hold it carefully and be sure to knock me out—or it's coming right back at her. She put the bottle down. She was crazy, but she wasn't crazy."

"When I was reading the script," Dunaway said, "it was like I was talking to you. There's usually something phony in a script, but this one was so alive, coming off the page."

"It's the wine and the beer," Bukowski said. His own beer had arrived and he took a swallow out of the bottle. "People who drink and still function say they're not alcoholics," he said. "I don't see what one has to do with the other. Whether you're an alcoholic and whether you function are two different questions."

"I once sat with Brendan Behan in a bar in New York," Dunaway said. "He said they were looking all over town for him."

"He should have hid in here," Bukowski said.

"These people, the word 'alcoholic' wouldn't even occur to them," Dunaway said.

"They'd take it as a compliment," Bukowski said.

"This girl I'm playing," Dunaway said. "Did you go to the funeral?"

"Yeah. It was here in California. Then we all went to the race track. Then I picked up a black girl and went to bed with her."

"I love it where you write that what they had in common was the same thing that bothered him also bothered her. Like when the trash truck would come by the first thing in the morning."

"And wake them up," Bukowski said. "Actually, I kind of like trash trucks. I'm in bed, I'm thinking, I'm glad I'm not driving that son of a bitch."

"How long did they go without drinking?" Dunaway asked. "They had to spend some time not drinking, didn't they?"

"No. They didn't miss a day."

"Did they start about 1?"

"Alone, I would start about 4 in the afternoon at that period of my life. With her, she would put on a tragic face about 8 in the morning and start whining, *We got nothin' to drink! Ohhhhh! Hank! There's nothin' in the house to drink!*"

"She called you Hank?" I said.

"Everybody calls me Hank. Nobody calls me Charles."

Tom Luddy walked in. He said the shot was rehearsed, and it was time to clear the bar. Luddy is the producer of *Barfly* and came straight to the project from the Norman Mailer film *Tough Guys Don't Dance,* which also was largely set in bars. He suggested we move the group over to a leatherette booth along the wall, where we would be out of the way and still be able to see everything.

Bukowski and his wife and Dunaway settled down, and Bukowski pulled out another one of those smelly little cigarettes.

"What are those called?" I asked.

"Mangalore Ganeesh Beedies," Bukowski said. "You can get them in any Indian or Pakistani store. They're what the poor, poor, poor people smoke in India. I like them because they contain no chemicals and no nicotine, and they go very well with red wine." He looked up. "Here come the real barflies," he said.

Big Ed, the owner of the bar, came over to the booth with his wife.

"I'm Mrs. Big Ed," his wife said. "I'm Phyllis. I own forty-seven percent of the corporation."

"We helped you out the other night," Bukowski said. "We got soused in here. Linda lost her wallet."

"New Year's Eve," Big Ed said, "a guy pulls out a butcher knife. I run into the back room to get my gun, and when I come back out again, Phyllis is pushing him out the door. I want to shoot him, but I can't shoot him without shooting her, although I'd like to."

Frank Stallone walked over to the booth, his face made up to look like a mass of blood and bruises.

"These barroom fights," Bukowski lectured, "it's better to underplay them. I've been in many a barroom fight, and when you wake up in the morning, you don't look so bad. Then you touch yourself—ouch! But there's not much visible damage. You're so drunk even the bricks don't want to touch you."

Barbet Schroeder came over and asked Bukowski if he would like to act as Mickey Rourke's stand-in while they rehearsed their camera move. Bukowski said he would.

"The way we got involved," he said, "was I picked up this phone one day, and it was Schroeder calling from Paris. I'm drinking, I hung up. Never heard of him. You meet a lot of phonies. I hang up; he calls back; he wants me to write a movie for him. I tell him I hate movies. He mentions $20,000. I ask him when he's coming over."

Bukowski walked over to the bar, sat down, and practiced glowering at a bloody Frank Stallone as Tiny and the others dragged him in.

Davia Nelson watched as her carefully rehearsed extras marched into the bar with Stallone's body. Tiny helped deposit him on a couple of bar stools, and then walked to the back of the bar, shaking his head.

"When we came out to scout the location," she said, "we found all the extras we needed right here. There's a Bukowskian woman living next door with twelve cats."

"Bukowskian?" I said.

"Like Dostoyevskian, but drunk."

Schroeder rehearsed the shot a couple of times, reminding the extras to look as if they had just seen a fight. Then it was time to shoot. Bukowski got down off his bar stool, to great applause, and came back over to sit down with the rest of us. An assistant director called for silence. Schroeder said, "Action!" The extras carried Stallone in and laid him on the bar stools. There was a loud bang at the other end of the bar, and Mickey Rourke came stalking in, covered with grime and blood, blowing his nose in his hand, sitting down at the bar.

"Gimme a beer!"

"I'm sorry, buddy, I can't serve you," the bartender said.

"*Gimme a beer!*" Rourke said, and tried to light a cigarette, and then turned away and walked out the door.

Schroeder called "cut" and asked for another take.

Dunaway had taken a notebook out of her purse and was taking notes.

"What would she put under her pillow?" she asked Bukowski.

"A rosary."

"What sort of perfume did she wear?"

"Perfume?"

It was time for take two. This time Rourke came in through the door, slammed it, whirled around, and hit it so hard with his fist that he put a hole in it. He walked over to the bar.

"Gimme a beer?"

"I'm sorry, buddy . . ."

This time Rourke went over the bar and grabbed the bartender by his shirt.

"I said give me a fucking beer!"

The bartender pulled free. Rourke slumped back onto his stool, lighted his cigarette, and stumbled out.

"Cut," Schroeder said, "Very good. Now we have a hole in the door."

A carpenter went over to repair the door.

"God, Mickey puts it all out there," Dunaway said. "Like in *Casablanca* when Peter Lorre says, 'Rick! You *must* help me!' No holding back."

Frank Stallone stood up and got ready for the next shot. He poured some beer into his hand and rubbed it on the crotch of his pants. Tom Luddy walked over and introduced a visitor to the set, the exiled Russian director Andrei Konchalovsky, who made *Runaway Train* and *Duet for One* for Cannon Films, the studio that is making *Barfly*.

Konchalovsky settled into the booth. The conversation got around to drinking. Bukowski observed that Russia and America were two countries where people believed that you could find truth at the bottom of a glass.

"In wine there is truth," Konchalovsky said. "That is because alcohol releases the inhibitions. In America, you are suppressed internally. In Russia, we are suppressed externally. We both drink to be free of suppression."

"Is that why there aren't any British plays

where the characters sit around in a bar and discover truth?" I said.

"The British are free," Konchalovsky said.

"You know," I told Dunaway, "he just directed *Duet for One*."

"Oh," Dunaway said.

"Julie Andrews was really very good in it," I said.

"I'm sure she was," Dunaway said. "I was originally going to play that role."

There was a long silence in the booth.

"That's show biz," said Dunaway.

Tom Luddy walked over with another visitor to the set—Errol Morris, the avant-garde director of such remarkable films as *Gates of Heaven*, the surrealistic documentary about northern California pet cemeteries.

"We originally thought we would be filming in the alley, and there would be enough room for visitors," Luddy explained. "Now it's a little crowded."

Morris, an open-faced young man in a suit, sat down and said he had been supporting himself for two years by working as a private detective, but now he was working on a film again.

"What's it about?" Bukowski said.

"A case in Michigan where a dog ate a woman and the woman's estate is paying the attorney fees for the dog's legal defense."

Bukowski took a swig of beer. "Sounds like an interesting subject for a movie," he said. He took my note pad and pulled a pen out of his pocket and began to doodle.

"A man, a dog, a bird, a flower, and the sun," he said. "What else do you need?"

He studied his drawing.

"A bottle," he said.

"So the dog ate the old lady," he said to Morris. "Sick."

"The fact that the world is a sick place makes it endurable," Morris said.

"Yeah. It gives me something to write about and you something to film," Bukowski said.

"There is a sect in South America," said Morris, "that is named the Hysteriones. They believe that a set number of sins had to be committed before the second coming of Christ, and so they abandoned themselves to an avid debauch in order to hasten the onset of the millennium."

"Let's get started," said Bukowski.

"You told me," I said, "that you had a story to tell about Barbet Schroeder."

"He has been trying to make this movie for seven years," Bukowski said. "A few months ago, it looked like Cannon was about to cancel it. Barbet goes into the office of Menahem Golan, the president of Cannon, with an electric handsaw. He pulls out a syringe of novocaine and shoots it into his little finger. He says he will cut off his finger if Menahem doesn't make the movie, and that he will continue to cut off parts of his body and send them to Menahem until he agrees to make the movie. Menahem tells him to go to hell. Barbet plugs in the handsaw."

Bukowski lighted one of his little Mangalore Ganeesh Beedies.

"Here we are," he said.

Judging the Classics

Are these the sixteen greatest films of all time, or do 122 of the world's film critics only think they are?

1. *Citizen Kane* (Orson Welles, U.S.)
2. *The Rules of the Game* (Jean Renoir, France)
3. (tie) *The Seven Samurai* (Akira Kurosawa, Japan)
   Singin' in the Rain (Stanley Donen and Gene Kelly, U.S.)
5. *8½* (Federico Fellini, Italy)
6. *Battleship Potemkin* (Sergei Eisenstein, USSR)
7. (tie) *L'Avventura* (Michelangelo Antonioni, Italy)
   The Magnificent Ambersons (Orson Welles, U.S.)
9. (tie) *Vertigo* (Alfred Hitchcock, U.S.)
   The General (Buster Keaton, U.S.)
   The Searchers (John Ford, U.S.)
12. (tie) *2001: A Space Odyssey* (Stanley Kubrick, Great Britain)
   Andrei Roublev (Andrei Tarkovsky, USSR)
14. (tie) *Greed* (Erich von Stroheim, U.S.)
   Jules and Jim (Francois Truffaut, France)
   The Third Man (Carol Reed, Great Britain)

Those sixteen films were the 1982 winners of the fourth International Critics' Poll, conducted every ten years by *Sight & Sound,* the authoritative film quarterly published by the British Film Institute. The magazine's instructions to critics voting from all over the world were simple: "Personal choices of the films which have seemed most significant or relevant to you, which you have enjoyed or admired most. Ten titles only, please, in alphabetical order or in order of preference, of films made anywhere, at any time."

The *Sight & Sound* poll is to movies what the wire service polls are to college sports and the Dow Jones average is to the stock market. It represents an imperfect, subjective, unscientific, and highly influential sampling of the critical stock of the great films and filmmakers of the world. And when the 1982 results were announced, they created shock waves, at least in that little corner of the world where such things matter.

The big news in the 1982 poll was the surprising critical devaluation of the work of Ingmar Bergman, the great Swedish filmmaker whose name seems almost synonymous with cinematic art. In the 1972 poll, Bergman and Orson Welles were the only directors to place two films on the list.[1] This year, Welles's *Citizen Kane* and *Magnificent Ambersons* remain, but Bergman is missing; his *Persona* (tied for fifth in 1972) and *Wild Strawberries* (tied for tenth) dropped off the list altogether, and his more recent contenders, especially *Cries and Whispers* and *Autumn Sonata,* failed to place.

Maybe that was just a statistical aberration? Perhaps Bergman's support was so widely distributed among his more than forty films that no single Bergman movie had the votes to make the list? Not so. In a separate compilation, *Sight & Sound* totaled all of the times any film by a director was voted for. In 1972, Bergman placed a strong third on that list; his thirty-seven votes were close behind Welles's forty-six and Jean Renoir's forty-one. By 1982, Bergman's total vote didn't even qualify him for the top ten![2]

Why did Bergman drop so suddenly from the pantheon? My guess is that the jury changed. In 1972, a majority of the voters would still have belonged to what science-fiction fans call the "sercon" party; they would have been serious, constructive critics looking for meaning, significance, and Art. By 1982, the film generation of the 1960s would have joined in the balloting, probably with a preference for "movies" over "cinema." Perhaps Bergman seemed too heavily laden with symbolism and angst for them, and they wanted to make room for a Western or a musical. Bergman is gone, but not forgotten; look for him on the 1992 list.

Other conclusions from the 1982 balloting:

—Orson Welles continues to stand astride the world of film as an undisputed colossus—at least, as far as the film critics are concerned. Despite the fact that his most important work was done more than forty years ago (*Kane* and *Ambersons* are his first two films), he has strengthened his position since 1972; both times, Welles and *Kane* placed ahead of Renoir and *Rules,* but in 1982, it was a landslide.

Citizen Kane is, of course, widely described as the greatest film ever made—so frequently, and by so many different people, that it has moved into the same quasi-official stratosphere as *King Lear* or Beethoven's Fifth Symphony. What is remarkable is that in 1952, when *Sight & Sound* first conducted its poll, *Citizen Kane* didn't even make the list![3] In 1952, *Citizen Kane* was a masterpiece much talked about but rarely seen, after its original 1941 release was botched. (Because the Hollywood establishment feared to offend publishing tycoon William Randolph Hearst, whose life inspired Kane's, the major theater

[1]The top ten, 1972: *Citizen Kane, Rules of the Game, Battleship Potemkin, 8½, L'Avventura* tied with Dreyer's *The Passion of Joan of Arc, The General* tied with *The Magnificent Ambersons, Ugetsu Monogatari* tied with *Wild Strawberries.*

[2]Voting by directors, 1982: Orson Welles, 71; Jean Renoir, 51; Charles Chaplin, 37; John Ford, 34; Luis Bunuel and Akira Kurosawa, both 33; Federico Fellini and Alfred Hitchcock, both 32; Jean-Luc Godard and Buster Keaton, both 30.

[3]The top four films in 1952, according to both the magazine poll and a vote of filmmakers at the Brussels World Fair, were De Sica's *Bicycle Thief,* Chaplin's *City Lights* and *Gold Rush,* and Eisenstein's *Battleship Potemkin.*

chains wouldn't touch the film, and it got scattered release; not until 1957, when a new print was widely distributed, did the film win really wide audiences.)

Why is the film so widely admired? "Citizen Kane is perhaps the one American talking picture that seems as fresh now as the day it opened. It may even seem fresher," Pauline Kael wrote in the opening words of her landmark *The Citizen Kane Book.* If you do not believe her, see it for yourself. The film is endlessly inventive as it circles closer and closer to the mystery of a man's life, a mystery that seems to be summed up by his dying word, "Rosebud."[4] One reason the film always seems fresh is that we never know what's coming next; the film has such an unpredictable structure, leaping about in Kane's life and from flashback to flashback, that it is all but impossible to remember what will follow. I have seen *Citizen Kane* at least thirty times, and yet when I walk in on the middle of a screening, or start my tape at random, I am unable to remember for sure what will come next.

—*The Seven Samurai* and *Singin' in the Rain,* were not even also-rans in 1972; this time, they tied for third. *Seven Samurai,* a saga about medieval warlords that introduced Toshiro Mifune to world movie audiences and inspired the Hollywood remake *The Magnificent Seven,* became the only film on the list from Japan, one of the great centers of cinema; last time, Japan was represented by Mizoguchi's *Ugetsu Monogatari,* the story of a poor man's infatuation with a dreamlike geisha. *Singin' in the Rain* is routinely called the best of the Hollywood musicals, and its high place is a tribute to the whole genre.

—Two veteran Hollywood filmmakers who died in the decade between the polls made it into the top ten. Alfred Hitchcock's *Vertigo* and John Ford's *The Searchers,* were runners-up in 1972, possibly because both directors had been so prolific and made so many great films that no single title could gather a following. By 1982, the consensus was in.

Many movie buffs would name *Rear Window, Psycho,* or *Notorious* as Hitchcock's best picture, but *Vertigo,* starring James Stewart and Kim Novak in the story of a man obsessed with a woman he thinks is dead, has been named by Hitchcock's biographers as perhaps his most personal work. Because the copyrights to *Vertigo* and four other Hitchcock titles (*Rope, The Man Who Knew Too Much, Rear Window,* and *The Trouble with Harry*) were owned by Hitchcock's estate, they had not been publicly screened for years when the 1982 poll was held. In 1984, however, they were bought from the estate by Universal, and are all now available in video.

The Searchers is not everybody's favorite film by the man who once said "My name is Ford. I make Westerns." Some viewers would name *Stagecoach, My Darling Clementine,* or *Three Godfathers.* Many critics have questions about the plot of *The Searchers,* which has John Wayne so appalled when his niece is kidnapped by Indians that he spends five years in the wilderness on a relentless,

[4]But who heard him say "rosebud"? Although Kane's butler claims late in the film that he heard it, the death chamber seems empty except for the lonely tycoon. A nurse enters after he drops the paperweight.

obsessive search for her. They see the film as a racist portrait of Indians and a male chauvinist story, in which the real importance of the girl (played by Natalie Wood) is as a pawn for the men in the film. Still, *The Searchers* has inspired the stories of many other films, notably Martin Scorsese's *Taxi Driver* and Paul Schrader's *Hardcore*.

—The battle of the two greatest silent clowns continues in the 1982 results. Buster Keaton's *The General*, an amazingly ambitious epic in which he played the engineer of a lengendary Civil War train, slipped from eighth to ninth. Chaplin failed to place any titles on the list, but in the closely bunched vote by directors, he placed somewhat higher than Keaton—third, with thirty-seven votes, to ninth, with thirty. Perhaps the totals reflect the consensus that *The General* is Keaton's greatest film, and an inability to choose among such Chaplin masterpieces as *The Gold Rush, City Lights,* and *Modern Times*. Since most silent films are out of copyright, they can be purchased fairly cheaply in video, often under $20.

Is the *Sight & Sound* poll all that important? It's like the football coaches' poll: Everybody cares when it comes out, nobody can remember it by next year. The real importance is that if you set out to see every film on it, you will see sixteen great films, and each one will suggest avenues for further investigation, a few of which I cheerfully outline below, only occasionally venturing from the sublime to the ridiculous:

AFTER SEEING	THEN VIEW	BECAUSE
Citizen Kane	*Providence*	Similar opening shots, narrative ideas
Rules of the Game	*The Grand Illusion*	After and before
The Seven Samurai	*The Magnificent Seven*	The remake
Singin' in the Rain	*An American in Paris*	Gene Kelly
8½	*Day for Night*	Lives of a director
Battleship Potemkin	*Das Boot*	Under pressure
L'Avventura	*Blow Up*	Missing persons
The Magnificent Ambersons	*Breaking Away*	Family life in Indiana
Vertigo	*Body Double*	De Palma's homage
The General	*Modern Times*	Man over machines
The Searchers	*Taxi Driver*	Same underlying story
2001	*My Dinner with André*	"If we could really understand the cigar store next door—wouldn't that be as amazing as climbing Everest?"
Andrei Roublev	*The Seventh Seal*	Medieval legends
Greed	*Sunset Boulevard*	von Stroheim
Jules and Jim	*Two English Girls*	Same author, same director, two approaches

The Third Man	*Night and the City*	Postwar locations, similar feel

I'm not sure this chart has the slightest significance, but drawing it up was amusing, and it duplicated one of the pleasures that the VCR has brought into my life—the random walk through movie history, with one film leading to another, one vision suggesting another. It is probably true that some of the films on the list are not available in most video stores; this might be the occasion for a call to Home Film Festival (1-800-258-3456), which rents hard-to-find classics by mail. Or it might be an occasion for a random walk in another direction altogether. Have fun.

My Ten Great Films, and Why

What are my own nominations for the ten best films of all time? Making such a list is, of course, a form of gamesmanship, and the list is sure to change from day to day. On the day in 1982 when I drew up my list for *Sight & Sound*, these were the titles I decided upon, listed alphabetically:

Aguirre, the Wrath of God. Werner Herzog believes we are starving for images in these modern times, and that without them, we will die. His *Aguirre*, one of the great, mad, passionate, foolhardy masterpieces—as reckless and as brilliant as *Greed* or *Apocalypse Now*—stars Klaus Kinski in the story of a member of Pizarro's expedition to find the lost El Dorado. After the main body turns back, Aguirre presses on with a small band of followers, all of them weighted down by the armor which is suicidal in the rain forest. Among the film's great images, are the first, of a string of desperate men winding their way down an unimaginably long mountain path, and one of the last, of Aguirre on a raft overrun by chattering monkeys. Herzog believes in the voodoo of locations, and shot this film deep in the Amazon jungle. There is a legend that Kinski threatened to walk off the film, and Herzog held a gun to him and said he would shoot him if he left. It is probably only an apocraphal story, but neither Herzog nor Kinski denies it.

Bonnie and Clyde. Arthur Penn's film still seems to have the same freshness, after twenty years, that Kael talks about with *Kane.* It works as comedy, as tragedy, as entertainment, as a meditation on the place of guns and violence in American society. And it was perfectly cast; Warren Beatty and Faye Dunaway have become icons as Clyde and Bonnie, but remember, too, Michael J. Pollard as C.W. Moss, Gene Hackman as Buck Barrow (his first major role), Estelle Parsons as Buck's wife Blanche, Gene Wilder as the hapless undertaker taken along for the ride, and Dub Taylor as C.W.'s greedy father. Scene after scene plays with perfect, almost dreamlike, emotional control: Clyde and the tenant farmer shooting out windows, the cloud passing in front of the sun and shadowing Bonnie and Clyde in the wheat field, Bonnie's farewell to her mother, C.W. parking the getaway car, Blanche screaming and running across the lawn with a spatula in her hand, Buck's dying delirium, and of course the final scene, which has been copied in so many other movies it has become a cliché, except here, where it retains all of its power.

Casablanca. I saw it again recently, at the University of Colorado, where I go every year to take a week and study a film shot-by-shot with a stop-action film analyzer. I was struck once again by what a perfect love story there is here, requiring the lovers to be true to their ideas of each other by choosing a greater good than love. The supporting characters (Claude Rains, Sidney Greenstreet, Peter Lorre, and, always, Dooley Wilson) transform what was, after all, only a set on the back lot at the Burbank Studios and turn it into a teeming, conspiring, colorful Casablanca.

The key to the movie's drama is Bogart's gradual transition, from a man who "sticks his neck out for no one" to a man who embraces once again the ideals of his youth. In remembering *Casablanca,* we think of it as a love story between Bogart and Bergman. (The pale Paul Henreid, as the freedom fighter Victor Laslo, is permitted a chaste peck on Bergman's cheek, and scarcely has the presence in the film to qualify as the third point of a love triangle.) But see the film again and you may be surprised at how bitter Bogart is when he sees Bergman again. His cruelty to her in the late-night drunk scene in Rick's Place is painful—because we see how much it hurts both of them. Only gradually does Bogart come around to the right feelings, and the right decisions. *Casablanca* is not the story of lost love, but of rediscovered idealism.

Citizen Kane. Of course. But for the little touches as well as for the big ones. For Kane's shadow-play with his hands the first time he meets Susan Alexander. For Kane applauding alone, defiantly, maniacally, after Susan's opera debut. For the remarkable visual illusion in Thatcher's office, when Kane, brought in to sign away his empire, is first seen in the foreground in front of what look like normal windows—and then, as Kane walks into the background of the shot, they are revealed as giant cathedral-scale windows, and Kane is diminished into a miniature. And for Mr. Bernstein's sad and wonderful line, "One day, back in 1896, I was crossing over to Jersey on a ferry, and as we pulled out, there was another ferry pulling in, and on it there was a girl waiting to get off. A white dress she had on. She was carrying a white parasol. I only saw her for one second. She didn't see me at all, but I'll bet a month hasn't gone by since, that I haven't thought of that girl." The power of that line is such that, in the years since I first heard it, I'll bet a month hasn't gone by that I haven't thought of it.

La Dolce Vita. Federico Fellini's 1959 film is a page-marker in my own life. It tells the story of a gossip columnist named Marcello, who roams the night world of Rome's Via Veneto, pursuing dreams of fame and sex and money, promising himself and his friend Steiner that someday he will write a great novel. Marcello seems almost afraid to stop moving, for fear that the silence of the emptiness of his life will overwhelm him. Fellini's great images come in profusion: The bearded dancer in the nightclub, lit from beneath as if from hell; the bas reliefs on the walls of the villa, each ancient Roman face the exact duplicate of a guest at the party; the Christ statue carried by helicopter over

Rome; the cat and the fountain at dawn; the children running here and there in the rain, taunting the sick and dying with their sudden sightings of the Virgin Mary. Marcello is thirty in the film. When I first saw it, I was twenty, and it represented a great and wonderful world I wanted to enter. When I was thirty and saw it again, it represented the trap I was in. I saw it again at forty, and saw it as what I had survived and perhaps even learned from. This is, I believe, Fellini's best film, too often overlooked on the short lists of unquestionably great films.

Notorious. This is my favorite Hitchcock film, and the best love story he ever told. In some ways, its triangle resembles *Casablanca*'s; Cary Grant, like Humphrey Bogart, loves Ingrid Bergman but is cruel to her because he feels she has been unfaithful to him—and all the time Bergman has chosen the greater good. Although Claude Rains, the other man who loves Bergman, plays a Nazi in this film, he is in many ways more sympathetic than the cool Paul Henreid in *Casablanca.* He does, after all, really love her—and he will be denied her love, along with so many other things in his life, because of his monstrous mother and his fatal politics. The film is filled with great shots: The introduction of Cary Grant, seen from behind but nevertheless the focus of attention; an overview of an entrance hall, with the camera moving in one unbroken take to a close-up of a key in a hand; the inexorable procession down the stairs and past the Nazis waiting at the bottom. (For fun, and to reveal one of Hitchcock's secrets, watch for the one scene where Cary Grant completely ascends the staircase in Rains's home, and count the number of steps he takes. Then, in the scene where Grant, Bergman, Rains, and Madame Constantine descend the stairs, count how many steps they descend. Hitchcock prolongs the suspense by editing to add extra steps.)

Persona. Ingmar Bergman's 1967 film has been described as almost impossible to understand, but perhaps it can be approached, instead, as a very simple story. An actress, horrified by the suffering in the world, simply stops speaking one day. She is sent by her therapist to spend some time in the country with a nurse. During their months together, a strange personalities' transference takes place, until the impressionable young nurse forgets exactly who she is—and then remembers again, when the spell is broken. The film itself "breaks" in the middle, as if the pain from the shard of glass has broken the power of fiction to contain it. The scene of the merging faces is famous (Liv Ullmann and Bibi Andersson told me they had no idea Bergman was going to do it), but even more mysterious is the dream sequence in which both women seem to share the actress's husband. The long monologue about the encounter with the boys on the beach has a strange after-effect; although it is only described, never seen, we visualize it so strongly that, months later, we may swear it was in the film.

Taxi Driver. I think Martin Scorsese's work is the best American film made since I've been reviewing movies, and Robert De Niro's performance as Travis

Bickle, the lonely, violent taxi driver, has entered into folklore ("You talking to *me?*"). The film is visually fascinating, especially the repeated motif of overhead shots (a hack license, junk food, guns on a bed, push-ups, the final killing scene) that Scorsese says has a sacramental significance for him. American history has been rewritten by the loners like Travis who have come out of the woodwork: Oswald, Ruby, Ray, Sirhan, and, a colossal irony, John Hinckley, who shot at President Reagan because of his obsession with Jodie Foster in this film. Some said the film inspired his actions. I would say it predicted them, because the real-life Hinckley bore such an unsettingly similarity to Bickle. If any film can explain to us how and why our society has created creatures like Travis Bickle, and can help us to enter their savagely narrow, driven visions, *Taxi Driver* can; it is a film to place beside the novel *Crime and Punishment* for its knowledge of a deviant personality.

The Third Man. I would have thought this was a great film anyway, but seeing it for the first time in a little cinema on the Left Bank, on a rainy Paris day, on my first trip to Europe, made it, on that day, a perfect film, and ever since it has occupied a special place in my memory. Once again, a story of doomed love; Joseph Cotten, as Holly Martin, the author of trash Westerns, journeys to postwar Vienna to find his best friend, Orson Welles as Harry Lime ("lie-me"). He discovers that Lime is dead, but meets his girl (Alida Valli), and falls in love with her, and finds that she still loves Lime—no matter that his black market penicillin killed innocent children. It's as if Bergman stayed with Rains in *Notorious*, or moved in with Greenstreet in *Casablanca.* Carol Reed's images are remarkable: The balloon man's shadow on the wall, Orson Welles's first entrance (which is the greatest entrance in the history of the movies), Welles approaching almost sideways across the amusement park, the chase in the sewers, and, of course, the great final shot and the perfect emotional parabola described as Cotten throws away his cigarette. The line about the cuckoo clocks is justly famous; I also like "Is that what you say to people after death? Goodness, that's awkward."

2001. One of the greatest stores of powerful, mysterious images in all of film history. What the film means, what it says, no longer matters to me so much (although like all critics I have a detailed explanation, if you have an evening to spare sometime). What is important here is the sense of wonder. The bone transforms itself into a spaceship, the Strauss waltzes are incongruously appropriate for the sexually charged moment when the ship penetrates the space station, and the appearances of the monolith are so disturbing that you realize the utter strangeness of man's right angles and straight lines amid the careless jumble of nature.

Eliot said he would show us fear in a handful of dust, and Stanley Kubrick shows us infinity in a bedroom, a glass of red wine, and a few green peas. The ending sequence of his film is so great because it does not dare to imagine what other intelligences would look or think like; he shows us a man placed by them, whatever they are, in a room of man's own tradition—and that is so much more frightening than any fantastical alternative. The sequel, *2010,* is a superior space action picture, and I praised it for that. But in explaining the mysteries of *2001,* it diminishes them. e e cummings, who said he'd rather learn from one bird how to sing than teach ten thousand stars how not to dance, wrote in those words the definitive review of both pictures.

In fact, he wrote in those words the definitive review of a lot of pictures.

High-Definition Television

I have seen the future of television, and I want one. I want a high-definition television system for my living room, even if I have to build a living room big enough to accommodate it. I want the 135-inch screen and the wide-screen picture, the surround sound, and the image that delivers twice as much information as a current TV signal. And I want it now, but I'm going to have to wait until 1992, or maybe 1993.

High-def television has been on the horizon for about five years now, but at last, it seems ready to sail into port. I spent some time this year at the Summer Consumer Electronics Show, a massive trade supermarket that fills McCormick Place in Chicago, and although every conceivable TV hardware and software product was on display, high-def TV seemed to overshadow everything. It must have been a little like this in the late 1940s in the record industry, just before long-playing albums came onto the market.

High-definition television will supply a signal made up of 1,125 lines of horizontal definition, as opposed to 525 on the set in your living room. It will broadcast in a wide-screen ratio of about 5.3 to 3, instead of the current TV screen dimension of 4 to 3. The signal will be available on TV sets that look much the same as your current model, except for a wider screen. But it will also be available on projection TVs that will fill much larger screens, big enough to cover an entire wall of the average room.

That was the kind of high-def image I saw in a big production room at the Panasonic and Technics areas at the Consumer Electronics Show. I have been in cineplexes with smaller screens. And although the picture quality was not as good as light through celluloid (I doubt if any television image will ever be that good), it was so much better than current TV that there was simply no comparison.

Forget any notions you may have about big-screen TV being fuzzy and undefined. This was a good picture. The subject of the demo was the 1984 Olympiad, and as the camera zoomed back to show hundreds of Olympians on the screen, all of them remained in sharp focus and good definition. A movie on a system like this would give you reasonable approximation of sitting in a film projection room, especially if you linked it to high-quality disc-based surround sound.

But how long are we going to have to wait for this technology, and how much will it cost? I cornered Bob Burroughs, a Panasonic executive who specializes in cable systems, and he said that high-def technology exists now (as I had seen with my own eyes), but that there would be a delay in bringing it to the marketplace because of the ongoing debate about how high-def will coexist with existing broadcast signals.

In a nutshell, a high-def signal requires twice as much band width as the current TV signal from an over-the-air station. Band width is no problem for cable systems, which have lots of channels to spare, but there are no empty spaces between over-the-air channels, and so the networks and existing local stations are concerned that a high-def signal on cable could upstage and make obsolete their 525-line signals.

There are a couple of ways that a 1,125-line high-def signal could be squeezed into an existing over-the-air frequency and then decoded at home. But no international standard has been agreed upon, and that's why there's a delay in marketing the new technology.

"It's an open secret that HBO is already thinking in terms of high-def on cable," Burroughs told me. "They have started shooting everything they do in high-def as well as 525-line, so that cable could go ahead and offer high-def on its own. It could happen."

If it does, it won't be cheap. Burroughs said Japan will start supplying a high-def satellite broadcast to its consumers in 1990, and that high-def should reach America "in the early 1990s." At first, it's likely to turn up in sports bars—which were the original launching pads for big-screen back-projection TVs. If cable suppliers such as HBO and the sports channels start simulcasting in high-def, bars would fight to install the new technology, and the sight of the World Series on a 135-inch TV with a wide-screen format would popularize the new format overnight.

The cost? "At first, around $10,000," Burroughs estimated. "Eventually, they'll have to get the price down to reach the consumer marketplace. Maybe we'll see $4,000 systems before long. And eventually, like everything else, they'll find a way to make it even more cheaply. It's a chicken-and-egg situation. It depends upon demand."

In the meantime, existing 525-line TV is also undergoing a quality revolution. As I wandered the aisles of the CES, which is sort of an electronics supermarket, I saw lots of demonstrations of Laservision, super VHS, and Sony's EDBeta system. All three systems—Laservision on LaserDiscs and the other two on tape—put old-fashioned VHS and Beta tape-based pictures to shame.

Everybody at CES talks in statistics, and Chaz Fitzhugh of Sony gave me some of the key figures on disc and EDBeta pictures. The newest LaserDisc players, such as Sony's AV Laser Multidisc MDP-200, claim to supply more than 425 lines of horizontal resolution to the screen—using all the theoretical capacity of a monitor-style TV set, EDBeta claims more than 500 lines, as opposed to about 225 lines for traditional VHS and about 380 lines for last year's LaserDisc players. They've gone about as far as they can go.

Super VHS is, so far, a medium for people who shoot their own home movies on super VHS camcorders. No prerecorded movies exist in the format, or in Sony's EDBeta. For home video fans who want to watch feature films in the best possible format, the choice is clearly Laservision, which plays movies from discs that are read with laser beams. A LaserDisc is essentially a large compact disc that carries a picture as well as sound—and the sound on Laservision is miles superior to any tape-based sound, an important consideration for movies with stereo or surround sound tracks.

This year's CES had new LaserDisc players with lots of bells and whistles. All the major manufacturers, such as Pioneer and Sony, were showing "combi" units that can play every existing format of CD and LaserDisc—3-inch CD software to 5-inch standard CDs and CDVs (compact disc plus video) to 8-inch and 12-inch LaserDiscs.

But there are more gimmicks. Most LaserDisc movies carry an hour of a movie on each side of a disc. Pioneer has a new player that will automatically play both sides without the weary consumer having to change it himself. And both Sony and Pioneer have laser machines that can supply freeze-frame, variable search speeds, and all of the other tricks of laser viewing for *all* LaserDiscs, not just those in the CAV format.

That will take some explaining. Most movies on LaserDisc come in the CDV format, offering play, visible fast-forward and reverse, and sometimes chapter search. The more expensive CAV format, which supplies only half an hour on each side of a disc, is encoded to allow true rock-solid freeze-frame and various playing speeds. Now the new players can provide all the CAV tricks even on a CDV disc—allowing movie buffs to analyze the special effects or study the composition in every frame of all of their discs.

Many new machines have a nifty hand-held remote device that includes a wheel within a wheel, so you can forward or reverse the image at variable speeds instead of being locked into the predetermined speed-steps of last year's players. The new players also allow you to define your own "chapter stops" and play them in any order you want—not much use with a narrative film, but fun if you want to look only at the highlights of a favorite rock concert or video.

Now that there are some 4,000 titles available on LaserDisc, and since there are no prerecorded movies on super VHS or EDBeta, the various Laservision systems are clearly the technology of choice for the home video buff. Until high-def TV, or course.

The Basic Video Library

If I were choosing a basic library of movies on videocassette I would begin with *Citizen Kane*, the most inexhaustible film yet made in America, and go on from there. And that is exactly what I've done here, starting with a dozen categories of film and limiting myself to three choices in each category.

This is not a list of the greatest films of all time (for that list, which contains a few of the same titles, see page 803). It is weighted toward American films, because most subtitled films are still so dauntingly hard to read on the small screen. And it is weighted, also, toward more recent films, since those are the easiest to find in video stores.

The question I've asked myself in selecting every one of my ideal titles is, does the film really stand up to repeated viewing? Is it still fresh and alive the ninth time around? Here are some films that passed those tests:

1. **Family and children's films**

The Wizard of Oz remains agelessly wonderful. Some sort of magical enchantment must have fallen over MGM when they produced this film, which is made up of so many parts that are all exactly right. If small children could only begin their film experiences with this film, instead of first having their imaginations deadened by countless hours of low-grade Saturday morning animated TV violence, that would be a nice little gift for their spirits. Next on my list is *E.T.*, which is probably the most completely satisfying fantasy since *The Wizard of Oz*. Every family movie library needs at least one film about horses, either *National Velvet* or *The Black Stallion*. And an animated feature. Probably *Pinocchio*.

2. **Comedy**

Saving Chaplin and Keaton for the silent category, I'd lead this section of the shelf with the single funniest move I've seen since I've been a film critic. That would be Mel Brooks's *The Producers*, with its sublimely demented relationship between Zero Mostel as a crooked Broadway producer who fleeces little old ladies, and Gene Wilder as a timid accountant who is taught that if you've got it, flaunt it. Next, something by the Marx Brothers, probably *Room Service* or *A Night at the Opera*. And then one of those omnibus tapes of W.C. Fields's short subjects, or maybe Fields in *The Bank Dick*. And then Robert Altman's *M*A*S*H*, the funniest movie released since *The Producers*, even though it is much more than "just" a comedy.

3. **Crime or film noir**

My favorite here is *The Third Man,* which views its bleak vision of human nature through the eyes of a man who stubbornly remains a romantic until his dream is finally crushed in the last, unforgettable, shot. Orson Welles has the most unforgettable entrance in movie history, and one of the best lines of dialogue—the one about the cuckoo clocks. Next in this category, Hitchcock's *Notorious,* for the exquisitely painful way in which the romance between Cary Grant and Ingrid Bergman is played against Grant's low opinion of Bergman, Claude Rains's doomed love for her, and Bergman's own despair. The third film would be the greatest of all crime epics, Francis Coppola's *The Godfather,* with its dark passions and operatic sense of fate. For a modern tribute to the classic film noir, *Farewell, My Lovely* or *Trouble in Mind.*

4. **Documentaries**

Here I am passing over an obvious choice, the noble nine-hour French film *Shoah,* because its running time makes it so prohibitively expensive that the best bet is obviously to tape it off the air from PBS. Instead, I'd select three personal favorites: Michael Wadleigh's *Woodstock,* which can now be seen, almost twenty years later, to capture the unique time of the late 1960s as no other film has; Errol Morris's *Gates of Heaven,* a very odd, challenging, eccentric movie about some people involved in the success and failure of two pet cemeteries; and George Nirenberg's *Say Amen, Somebody,* a documentary about the pioneers of black gospel music that is so joyous that it's just about impossible not to feel better after you've seen it.

5. **Drama**

Martin Scorsese's *Taxi Driver* is the best American film made since I've been a movie critic. Robert De Niro's title performance stands as one of the most agonizingly painful examinations of character ever put on screen; his Travis Bickle is a composite of all the twisted, unhappy assassins who have stepped out of the shadows since Lee Harvey Oswald so cruelly changed our history in Dallas in 1963. Next on my list, Francis Coppola's *Apocalypse Now,* which created its picture of the war in Vietnam out of contrasting images: gunboats pulling water-skiers, Playboy bunnies fired on by enemy rockets, helicoptors attacking to the music of Wagner. My third drama would be Arthur Penn's *Bonnie and Clyde,* starring Warren Beatty and Faye Dunaway in a perfectly realized story of how two fairly incompetent bank robbers were able to inflame the fancies of the media, until their fame led to their deaths.

6. **Foreign films**

Here we are at sea when we enter the average video store. Many dealers carry few foreign films, and they present an unhappy choice between subtitles we can't read, and dubbing we can't bear to listen to. We need titles at least as big, for example, as the typefaces used to identify news anchors. In the meantime, my choices would be films that are great to look at even if you can't read the titles. For example, something by Fellini, probably *La Dolce Vita* or *Amarcord.* Something by Kurosawa, whose great *Ikiru* contains too many subtitles, but whose *Seven Samurai* does not. And perhaps one of Bergman's most visual films, such as *The Seventh Seal.*

7. **Musicals**

Singin' in the Rain, of course. Everybody's favorite musical, and no wonder, since it contains so much happiness and such great music within a plot about the birth of the talkies. Then I'd choose one of the great Astaire-Rogers collaborations, probably *Top Hat* or *Swing Time.* And then the Beatles in *A Hard Day's Night.*

8. **Romance**

Romance, for me, means not merely a love story, but a love story told against the backdrop of exciting events, in the midst of which, as Bogie once said, "the problems of a couple of little people like you and me don't amount to a hill of beans." Ah, but they do, and precisely because love affirms itself in the face of history, those movies are all the more romantic. So, *Casablanca* first on the list, because of its perfect marriage of time and place and character and that song that Dooley Wilson doesn't think he quite remembers. And then Bogart again, this time with Hepburn in *The African Queen,* one of the greatest of all romantic adventures. And also on the list, *Gone With The Wind,* about which I suspect no explanation is necessary.

9. **Social issues**

This category may seem unexpected, but the movies have been an effective tool for political content ever since the first blockbuster, *Birth of a Nation. The Grapes of Wrath* might be an obvious choice, and so would movies like *Gandhi* or *Z.* But I've chosen three titles you might not immediately think about: Gregory Nava and Anna Thomas's *El Norte,* about the long trek of a Guatemalan brother and sister up through Mexico to the promised land of Los Angeles; Robert Altman's *Nashville,* which was released in the bicentennial year of 1976 and painted a huge canvas of beliefs and behaviors that were in the air at that time; and Lynne Lipton's heartbreaking *Testament,* starring Jane Alexander as a California suburban mother struggling to hold her family together in the aftermath of nuclear war.

10. **Special effects**

This category could just as well be labeled "science fiction." It reflects the explosion in elaborate, spellbinding visual effects that was set in motion by Stanley Kubrick's *2001* and has continued most notably in the works of Steven Spielberg and George Lucas. That just about tips my hand; my selections would be *2001: A Space Odyssey, Raiders of the Lost Ark*, and your choice of the *Star Wars* movies. The problem here, of course, is that the limitations of the television screen are especially frustrating when you're dealing with the vast visions contained in these movies. The electronics companies keep promising high-quality giant-screen TV. These movies need it.

11. **Silent films**

One of the best things about silent films, from the collector's point of view, is that they're often out of copyright, and therefore cheap to purchase. The bad news is that literally anyone can start selling inferior copies of the silent classics, and so it's best to spend a little more for a cassette with a respectable pedigree. My choices here would be a Buster Keaton (*The General*, with its endlessly inventive locomotive chase), a Charlie Chaplin (your choice; mine would be *Modern Times*), a D.W. Griffith (*Birth of a Nation* for its technical excellence but not for its reactionary social vision), and Eisenstein's *Battleship Potemkin*, widely considered the greatest of all silent dramas.

12. **Westerns**

Here is a category where everyone has strong personal favorites, and so I feel safe in passing over such obvious choices as *Stagecoach* and *High Noon* to list my own favorites: John Ford's *The Searchers*, with John Wayne in an obsessive search for a niece kidnapped by Indians; Ford's *My Darling Clementine*, for its rich retelling of the Wyatt Earp legend and for Henry Fonda's classic haircut scene; and Sam Peckinpah's *The Wild Bunch*, which mourned the passing of cowboys and gunfighters and, in retrospect, seems to have marked the end of the Western as a major genre.

And then, of course, to end where we began, Orson Welles's *Citizen Kane*. One of the mysteries of this film is in its seemingly mercurial story structure. The film's intricate structure of flashbacks and memories makes its examination of a man's life seem new every time I see it.

Every great film, for that matter, should seem new every time you see it. I think most of the films on my list will pass that test.

Glossary of Movie Terms

The basic movie reference books are filled with definitions of terms like *close-up* and *auteur theory.* Nobody needs to know those words. What you need is the *Movie Home Companion* Glossary of Terms for the Cinema of the 1980s. What follows is an attempt to compile such a list—a practical, everyday guide to enhance your moviegoing pleasure and help you categorize what you find on the screen.

A.C.N.E. Acronym for Adolescent Character's Neurotic Envy Syndrome, which usually afflicts shrill teen-age blondes in movies about how the good girl wins the hero away from the syndrome sufferer. See *Secret Admirer.*

Ali MacGraw's Disease. Movie illness in which only symptom is that the sufferer grows more beautiful as death approaches.

Ark Movie. Dependable genre in which a mixed bag of characters are trapped on a colorful mode of transportation. Examples: *Airport* (airplane), *The Poseidon Adventure* (ocean liner), *Marooned* (space satellite), *The Cassandra Crossing* (train), *The Hindenberg* (dirigible), *The Taking of Pelham One Two Three* (subway train), and of course the best of them all, *Stagecoach.*

Beginning, The. Word used in the titles of sequels to movies in which everyone was killed at the end of the original movie, making an ordinary sequel impossible. Explains to knowledgeable filmgoers that the movie will concern, for example, what happened in the Amityville house *before* the Lutzes moved in. See also: *The First Chapter, The Early Days,* etc.

Balloon Rule. No good movie has ever contained a hot-air balloon.

Box Rule. Useful rule-of-thumb about movie advertisements which have a row of little boxes across the bottom, each one showing the face of a different international star and the name of a character (i.e., "Curt Jurgens as the Commandant"). The rule states: Automatically avoid such films. Example: *The Cassandra Crossing, Force 10 from Navarone,* most films made from Agatha Christie novels.

Brotman's Law. "If nothing has happened by the end of the first reel, nothing is going to happen." (Named for Chicago movie exhibitor Oscar Brotman.)

Camel, Slow-Moving. All slow-moving camels in Middle Eastern thriller are crossing the road for the sole purpose of slowing down a pursuit vehicle.

Crash Scene. Alternative to dialogue; substitute for Burt Reynolds's continuing growth as an actor.

Chop-Socky Movie. Any film involving a karate fight and including the dialogue, "Ha! Ha! Now you die!"

CLIDVIC (Climb from Despair to Victory). Formula for *Rocky* and all the *Rocky* rip-offs. Breaks plot into three parts: (1) Defeat and despair; (2) Rigorous training, usually to would-be MTV videos; (3) Victory, preferably ending in freeze-frame of triumphant hero.

Dead Teen-ager Movie. Generic term for any movie primarily concerned with killing teen-agers, without regard for logic, plot, performance, humor, etc. Often imitated, never worse than in the *Friday the 13th* sequels.

Detour Rule. In any thriller, it is an absolute certainty that every road detour is a subterfuge to kidnap the occupants of a car. (Cf. Camel, Slow-Moving)

Docudrama. TV term for extended-length program which stars a disease or social problem and co-stars performers willing to give interviews on how they experienced personal growth through their dramatic contact with same.

Fallacy of the Predictable Tree. The logical error committed every time the good guy is able to predict *exactly* what the bad guy is going to do. For example, in *First Blood,* law enforcement officials are searching the woods for John Rambo. One pauses under a tree. Rambo drops on him. Question: Out of all the trees in the forest, how did Rambo know the guy would pause under that very one?

Fallacy of the Talking Killer. The villain wants to kill the hero. He has him cornered at gunpoint. All he has to do is pull the trigger. But he always talks first. Explains the hero's mistakes. Jeers. Laughs. And gives the hero time to think his way out of the situation, or be rescued by his buddy.

Far-Off Rattle Movies. Movies in which the climactic scene is shot in a deserted warehouse, where far-off rattles punctuate the silence.

First Law of Funny Names. No names are funny unless used by W.C. Fields or Groucho Marx. Funny names, in general, are a sign of desperation at the screenplay level. See "Dr. Hfuhruhurr" in *The Man With Two Brains.*

"Food Fight!" Dialogue which replaced "Westward ho!" as American movies ended the long frontier trek and began to look inward for sources of inspiration.

"Fruit Cart!" An expletive used by knowledgeable film buffs during any chase scene involving a foreign or ethnic locale, reflecting their certainty that a fruit cart will be overturned during the chase, and an angry peddler will run into the middle of the street to shake his fist at the departing Porsche.

"Hay Wagon!" Rural version of "Fruit cart!" (q.v.). At the beginning of chase scenes through colorful ethnic locales, knowledgeable film buffs anticipate the inevitable scene in which the speeding sports car will get stuck on a narrow country lane behind a wagon overloaded with hay.

Hollywood Car. Looks like a normal automobile, but backfires after being purchased from used car lot by movie heroine who is starting out again in life and is on her own this time.

Horny Teen-ager Movie. Any film primarily concerned with teen-age sexual hungers, usually male. Replaced, to a degree, by Dead Teen-ager Movies (q.v.), but always popular with middle-aged movie executives, who like to explain to their seventeen-year-old starlets why the logic of the dramatic situation and the teachings of Strasberg and Stanislavsky require them to remove their brassieres.

Generation Squeeze. New Hollywood genre which tries to bridge the generation gap by creating movies which will appeal to teen-agers at the box office and to adults at the video rental counter. Typical plot device: An adult becomes a teen-ager, or vice versa (cf. *Like Father, Like Son; Hiding Out; Peggy Sue Got Married; Vice Versa; 18 Again; Big*). Also sometimes masquerades as a movie apparently about adults, but with young actors in the "adult" roles (cf. *No Man's Land, The Big Town*).

Idiot Plot. Any plot containing problems which would be solved instantly if all of the characters were not idiots. Originally defined by Damon Knight.

Impregnable Fortress Impregnated. Indispensable scene in all James Bond movies and many other action pictures, especially war films. The IFI sequence begins early in the picture, with long shots of a faraway fortress and Wagnerian music on the sound track. Eventually the hero gains entry to the fortress, which is inevitably manned by technological clones in designer uniforms. Sequence ends with destruction of fortress, as clones futilely attempt to save their marvelous machines. See *The Guns of Navarone,* etc.

Intelligence. In most movies, "all that separates us from the apes." In *Sheena, Queen of the Jungle,* what we have in common with them.

Kookalouris. Name for a large sheet of cardboard or plywood with holes in it, which is moved back and forth in front of a light to illuminate a character's face with moving light patterns. Popular in the 1930s; back in style again with the movies of Steven Spielberg, who uses a kookalouris with underlighting to show faces that seem to be illuminated by reflections from pots of gold, buckets of diamonds, pools of fire, pirate maps, and radioactive kidneys.

Land Boom Rule. In any movie where there is a cocktail party featuring a chart, map, or model of a new real estate development, a wealthy property developer will be found dead inside an expensive automobile.

Law of Economy of Characters. Movie budgetary limitations make it impossible for any film to contain unnecessary characters. Therefore, all characters in a movie are necessary to the story—even those who do not seem to be. Sophisticated viewers can use this Law to deduce the identity of a person being kept secret by the movie's plot: This "mystery" person is always the only character in the movie who seems otherwise extraneous. (Cf. the friendly neighbor in *The Woman in White*.)

Mad Slasher Movies. Movies starring a mad-dog killer who runs amok, slashing all of the other characters. The killer is frequently masked (as in *Halloween* and *Friday the 13th*), not because a serious actor would be ashamed to be seen in the role, but because then no actor at all is required; the only skills necessary are the ability to wear a mask and wield a machete. For additional reading, see *Splatter Movies,* by John ("mutilation is the message") McCarty.

Make My Day. First line of movie dialogue quoted at a presidential press conference since Jimmy Carter said, "I'll never lie to you."

Me-Push-Pull-You. Literal translation of the body language in many Hollywood action pictures, in which, as the hero and heroine flee from danger, the man takes the woman's hand and pulls her along meekly behind him. This convention is so strong that it is seen even in films where it makes no sense, such as *Sheena*, in which a jungle-woman who has ruled the savage beasts since infancy is pulled along by a TV anchorman fresh off the plane.

Mistake of the Unmotivated Closeup. A character is given a closeup in a scene where there seems to be no reason for it. This is an infallible tip-off that this character is more significant than at first appears, and is most likely the killer.

Myopia Rule. Little girls who wear glasses in the movies always tell the truth. Little boys who wear glasses in the movies always lie.

Myth of the Seemingly Ordinary Day. The day begins like any other, with a man getting up, having breakfast, reading the paper, leaving the house, etc. His activities are so uneventful they are boring. That is the tip-off. No real ordinary day can be allowed to be boring in a movie. Only *seemingly* ordinary days—which inevitably lead up to a shocking scene of violence, which punctuates the seeming ordinariness.

Seeing-Eye Man. Function performed by most men in Hollywood feature films. Involves a series of shots in which (1) the man sees something, (2) he points it out to the woman, (3) she then sees it too, often nodding in agreement, gratitude, amusement, or relief.

Self-Repeating Inevitable Climax (Self-RIC). In the age of the seven-minute attention span, one climax per movie will no longer do. Thus movies like the *Friday the 13th* series are constructed out of several seven-minute segments. At the end of each segment, another teen-ager is dead. When all the teen-agers are dead (or, if you arrived in the middle, when the same dead teen-ager turns up twice), the movie is over.

Semi-Obligatory Lyrical Interlude (Semi-OLI). Scene in which soft focus and slow motion are used while a would-be hit song is performed on the sound track and the lovers run through a pastoral setting. Common from the mid-1960s to the mid-1970s; replaced in 1980s with the Semi-Obligatory Music Video (q.v.).

Semi-Obligatory Music Video. Three-minute sequence within otherwise ordinary narrative structure, in which a song is played at top volume while movie characters experience spasms of hyperkinetic behavior and stick their faces into the camera lens. If a band is seen, the Semi-OMV is inevitably distinguished by the director's inability to find a fresh cinematic approach to the challenge of filming a slack-jawed drummer.

Sequel. A filmed deal.

The Stanton–Walsh Rule. No movie featuring either Harry Dean Stanton or M. Emmet Walsh in a supporting role can be altogether bad.

Still Out There Somewhere. Obligatory phrase in Dead Teen-ager and Mad Slasher Movies, where it is triggered by the words, "The body was never found. They say he/she is . . ."

The Third Hand: Invisible appendage used by Rambo in *Rambo*, in the scene where he hides from the enemy by completely plastering himself inside a mud bank. Since it is impossible to cover yourself with mud without at least one hand free to do the job, Rambo must have had a third, invisible, hand. This explains a lot about the movie.

Thunder Index. Rule of thumb for estimating appeal of children's movies; the movie is working in inverse proportion to the amount of time the little bastards spend thundering up and down the aisles.

Tijuana. In modern Horny Teen-ager Movies, performs the same symbolic function as California did for the Beats and Paris did for the Lost Generation.

Wet. In Hollywood story conferences, suggested alternative to nude, as in: "If she won't take off her clothes, can we wet her down?" Suggested by Harry Cohn's remark about swimming star Esther Williams: "Dry, she ain't much. Wet, she's a star."

The We're Alive! Let's Kiss! Scene. Inevitable conclusion to any scene in which hero and heroine take cover from gunfire by diving side-by-side into a ditch, and find themselves in each other's arms, usually for the first time (Cf. *High Road to China*).

Ukulele picks. What will happen to you if you are a bad movie.

Youngblood Rule. No movie with a hero named "Youngblood" has ever been any good, e.g., *Youngblood Hawke*, *Youngblood*, etc.

List of Reviews That Appeared in Previous Editions

All Night Long ★ ★ (1986 ed.)
. . . All the Marbles ★ ★ (1986 ed.)
Amityville II: The Possession ★ ★ (1988 ed.)
Any Which Way You Can ★ ★ (1988 ed.)
Awakening, The ★ (1986 ed.)
Baby . . . The Secret of the Lost Legend ★ (1987 ed.)
Back Roads ★ ★ (1987 ed.)
Beyond Therapy ★ (1988 ed.)
Big Brawl, The ★½ (1986 ed.)
Black Cauldron, The ★ ★ ★½ (1987 ed.)
Black Stallion Returns, The ★ ★½ (1986 ed.)
Blame It on Rio ★ (1987 ed.)
Blind Date ★ ★½ (1988 ed.)
Brainstorm ★ ★ (1986 ed.)
Brewster's Millions ★ (1988 ed.)
Butley ★ ★ ★ ★ (1987 ed.)
Cannery Row ★ ★½ (1987 ed.)
Cannonball Run II ½★ (1988 ed.)
Cat's Eye ★ ★ ★ (1986 ed.)
Caveman ★½ (1986 ed.)
Changeling, The ★ ★½ (1986 ed.)
Cheech and Chong's Next Movie ★ (1987 ed.)
Class ★ ★ (1986 ed.)
Coca-Cola Kid, The ★ ★ ★ (1987 ed.)
Company of Wolves, The ★ ★ ★ (1987 ed.)
Compromising Positions ★ ★ (1987 ed.)
Creator ★ ★½ (1987 ed.)
Curse of the Pink Panther ★½ (1986 ed.)
Daniel ★ ★½ (1987 ed.)
D.C. Cab ★ ★ (1986 ed.)
Desert Hearts ★ ★½ (1988 ed.)
Dogs of War, The ★ ★ ★ (1988 ed.)
Dune ★ (1988 ed.)
Eddie and the Cruisers ★ ★ (1987 ed.)
Eleni ★ ★ ★ (1987 ed.)
Emerald Forest, The ★ ★ (1988 ed.)
Enemy Mine ★ ★½ (1988 ed.)
Escape from New York ★ ★½ (1988 ed.)
Eureka ★ ★ ★ (1986 ed.)
Excalibur ★ ★½ (1987 ed.)
Explorers ★ ★ (1987 ed.)
Falling in Love ★ ★ (1987 ed.)
Fiendish Plot of Dr. Fu Manchu ★ (1986 ed.)
Final Conflict, The ★ ★ (1987 ed.)
Final Countdown, The ★ ★ (1988 ed.)
Firestarter ★ ★ (1987 ed.)
First Deadly Sin, The ★ ★ ★ (1986 ed.)
Firstborn ★ ★ (1987 ed.)
Flash Gordon ★ ★½ (1988 ed.)
Flash of Green, A ★ ★ ★ (1987 ed.)
Fog, The ★ ★ (1988 ed.)
Formula, The ★ ★ (1987 ed.)
Fort Apache, The Bronx ★ ★ (1987 ed.)
Ginger and Fred ★ ★ (1987 ed.)
Give My Regards to Broad Street ★ (1986 ed.)
Godzilla 1985 ★ (1988 ed.)
Gotcha! ★ ★ (1986 ed.)
Hardly Working **no stars** (1986 ed.)
Harry & Son ★ (1986 ed.)
Hearse, The ½★ (1986 ed.)
Heat ★ ★ (1988 ed.)
Heavenly Kid, The ★ (1987 ed.)
Hell Night ★ (1986 ed.)
High Road to China ★ ★ (1987 ed.)
Home and the World, The ★ ★ ★ (1987 ed.)
Howling II ★ (1987 ed.)

Into the Night ★ (1987 ed.)
Jazz Singer, The ★ (1987 ed.)
Julia ★ ★ ½ (1988 ed.)
Just Between Friends ★ ½ (1987 ed.)
Just the Way You Are ★ ½ (1986 ed.)
Kerouac ★ ★ ½ (1987 ed.)
King David ★ (1987 ed.)
Last Flight of Noah's Ark, The ½ ★ (1986 ed.)
Little Darlings ★ ★ (1987 ed.)
Lonely Lady, The ½ ★ (1988 ed.)
Making Love ★ ★ (1988 ed.)
Man Who Loved Women, The ★ ★ (1988 ed.)
Marie ★ ★ ★ (1987 ed.)
Max Dugan Returns ★ ★ ½ (1986 ed.)
Maxie ½ ★ (1987 ed.)
Monsignor ★ (1987 ed.)
Mr. Mom ★ ★ (1987 ed.)
My Tutor ★ ★ ★ (1986 ed.)
Nomads ★ ½ (1987 ed.)
Nothing in Common ★ ★ ½ (1988 ed.)
On the Right Track ★ ★ ½ (1986 ed.)
One Magic Christmas ★ ★ (1987 ed.)
$1,000,000 Duck ★ (1987 ed.)
Only When I Laugh ★ (1987 ed.)
Paternity ★ ★ (1986 ed.)
Pennies from Heaven ★ ★ (1988 ed.)
Perfect ★ ½ (1987 ed.)
Phar Lap ★ ★ ★ (1987 ed.)
Pirates of Penzance ★ ★ (1986 ed.)
Power ★ ★ ½ (1988 ed.)
Protocol ★ ★ ½ (1987 ed.)
Pumping Iron II: The Women ★ ★ ★ ½ (1988 ed.)
Purple Hearts ½ ★ (1987 ed.)
Quicksilver ★ ★ (1987 ed.)
Raise the Titanic ★ ★ ½ (1986 ed.)
Razor's Edge, The ★ ★ ½ (1988 ed.)
Red Sonja ★ ½ (1987 ed.)
Return of the Living Dead ★ ★ ★ (1987 ed.)
Return to Oz ★ ★ (1987 ed.)
Rhinestone ★ (1987 ed.)
Rich and Famous ★ ★ ½ (1987 ed.)
St. Elmo's Fire ★ ½ (1987 ed.)
Santa Claus: The Movie ★ ★ ½ (1987 ed.)
Scene of the Crime ★ ★ ½ (1988 ed.)
Secret of NIMH, The ★ ★ ★ (1986 ed.)
Seems Like Old Times ★ ★ (1986 ed.)
Shooting Party ★ ★ ★ (1987 ed.)
Slugger's Wife, The ★ ★ (1986 ed.)
Smokey and the Bandit II ★ (1986 ed.)
Soldier of Orange ★ ★ ★ ½ (1986 ed.)
Somewhere in Time ★ ★ (1988 ed.)
Spring Break ★ (1988 ed.)
Stephen King's Silver Bullet ★ ★ ★ (1988 ed.)
Sting II, The ★ ★ (1986 ed.)
Stir Crazy ★ ★ (1987 ed.)
Streets of Fire ★ ★ ★ (1988 ed.)
Stripper ★ ★ ★ (1987 ed.)
Stroker Ace ★ ½ (1986 ed.)
Stuff, The ★ ½ (1987 ed.)
Stunt Man, The ★ ★ (1988 ed.)
Summer of '42 ★ ★ ½ (1987 ed.)
Supergirl ★ ★ (1988 ed.)
Sweet Dreams ★ ★ (1988 ed.)
Swing Shift ★ ★ ★ (1988 ed.)
Sylvester ★ ★ ★ (1988 ed.)
Table for Five ★ ½ (1986 ed.)
Teachers ★ ★ (1986 ed.)
Terror Train ★ (1986 ed.)
That Was Then . . . This Is Now ★ ★ (1987 ed.)
They Call Me Bruce ★ ★ (1986 ed.)
Tin Drum, The ★ ★ (1988 ed.)
Tough Enough ★ ★ ★ (1986 ed.)
Turk 182! ★ (1987 ed.)
Two of a Kind ½ ★ (1986 ed.)
Until September ½ ★ (1987 ed.)
Videodrome ★ ½ (1988 ed.)
Violets Are Blue ★ ★ ★ (1987 ed.)
Watcher in the Woods, The ★ ★ (1986 ed.)
Where the Boys Are '84 ½ ★ (1987 ed.)
Where the Green Ants Dream ★ ★ ★ (1988 ed.)
White Nights ★ ★ (1988 ed.)
Xanadu ★ ★ (1988 ed.)
Year of the Quiet Sun ★ ★ ★ ★ (1987 ed.)
Youngblood ★ ★ (1987 ed.)

Index

About Last Night . . ., 1
Above the Law, 2
Absence of Malice, 3
After Hours, 4
After the Rehearsal, 5
Against All Odds, 6
Agnes of God, 7
Airplane!, 8
Airport, 9
Airport 1975, 9
Alex in Wonderland, 10
Alice Doesn't Live Here Anymore, 11
Aliens, 12
All of Me, 13
All the President's Men, 14
All the Right Moves, 15
Allegro non Tropo, 16
Alligator, 17
Altered States, 17
Amadeus, 19
Amarcord, 20
American Flyers, 21
American Gigolo, 22
American Graffiti, 23
American Werewolf in London, An, 24
Angel Heart, 25
Angelo, My Love, 26
Annie, 27
Annie Hall, 28
Apocalypse Now, 29
Apprenticeship of Duddy Kravitz, The, 30
Arthur, 31
Assault, The, 32
Asylum, 33
At Close Range, 34
Au Revoir les Enfants, 35
Autumn Sonata, 36

Baby Boom, 38
Baby, It's You, 39
Bachelor Party, 39
Back to School, 40
Back to the Beach, 41
Back to the Future, 42
Bad Boys, 42
Bad Dreams, 43
Badlands, 44
Bang the Drum Slowly, 45
Barfly, 47
Beetlejuice, 48
Being There, 48
Best Boy, 49
Best Little Whorehouse in Texas, The, 50
Betrayal, 51
Beverly Hills Cop, 52
Beverly Hills Cop II, 53
Beyond the Limit, 54
Big, 55
Big Business, 56
Big Chill, The, 57
Big Easy, The, 57
Big Foot, 58
Big Red One, The, 59
Big Town, The, 60
Billy Jack, 61
Birdy, 62
Black Marble, The, 63
Black Stallion, The, 64
Black Widow, 65
Blade Runner, 66
Blood Simple, 67
Blow Out, 68
Blue Collar, 69
Blue Lagoon, The, 70
Blues Brothers, The, 71
Blue Velvet, 72
Blume in Love, 73
Body Double, 74
Bolero, 75
Bostonians, The, 76
Bounty, The, 77
Boy Who Could Fly, The, 78

Titles in bold-face type are on Roger Ebert's ten-best list for the year in which they opened.

Brazil, 78
Breakfast Club, The, 79
Breakin' 2—Electric Boogaloo, 80
Breaking Away, 81
Breathless, 82
Bright Lights, Big City, 82
Brighton Beach Memoirs, 83
Bring Me the Head of Alfredo Garcia, 84
Broadcast News, 85
Broadway Danny Rose, 87
Brother from Another Planet, The, 87
Brubaker, 88
Buddy Holly Story, The, 89
Bugsy Malone, 90
Bull Durham, 91
Burden of Dreams, 92
Burglar, 93
Buster and Billie, 93
Bye Bye Brazil, 94

Cabaret, 96
Cactus, 97
Caddyshack, 98
California Split, 98
Caligula, 100
Cannonball Run, The, 100
Car Wash, 101
Carmen (ballet), 102
Carmen (opera), 103
Carrie, 103
Cat People, 104
Chapter Two, 105
Chariots of Fire, 106
China Syndrome, The, 107
Chinatown, 108
Choose Me, 109
Chorus Line, A, 110
Christiane F., 111
Christine, 112
Christmas Story, A, 113
Chuck Berry Hail! Hail! Rock 'n' Roll, 113
Cinderella, 114
City Heat, 115
City of Women, 116
Claire's Knee, 117
Clan of the Cave Bear, 118
Clash of the Titans, 119
Class of 1984, The, 120
Close Encounters of the Third Kind: The Special Edition, 121
Coal Miner's Daughter, 121
Cocoon, 123
Code of Silence, 123
Color of Money, The, 124
Color Purple, The, 126
Colors, 127
Coma, 128
Come Back to the 5 & Dime, Jimmy Dean, Jimmy Dean, 129
Coming Home, 130
Competition, The, 131
Conan the Barbarian, 132
Conan the Destroyer, 133
Continental Divide, 134
Conversation, The, 135
Cop, 136
Cotton Club, The, 137
Country, 138
Cowboys, The, 139
Creepshow, 140
Cries and Whispers, 140
Crimes of Passion, 142
Critters, 142
Crocodile Dundee, 143
Cross My Heart, 144
Crossover Dreams, 145
Crossroads, 145
Cry Freedom, 147

Dark Eyes, 149
D.A.R.Y.L., 150
Dance With a Stranger, 150
Dark Crystal, The, 151
Date With an Angel, 152
Dawn of the Dead, 153
Day After Trinity, The, 154
Day for Night, 155
Day of the Dead, 156
Day of the Jackal, The, 157
Days of Heaven, 157
Dead, The, 158
Dead of Winter, 159
Dead Zone, The, 160
Death in Venice, 161
Death Wish, 162
Death Wish II, 163
Death Wish 3, 163
Deathtrap, 164
Deer Hunter, The, 165
Defence of the Realm, 166
Delta Force, The, 167
Desperately Seeking Susan, 168
Diamonds Are Forever, 169
Diary of a Mad Housewife, 169
Dim Sum, 170
Diner, 170
Dirty Dancing, 171
Dirty Harry, 172
Discreet Charm of the Bourgeoisie, 173
Diva, 174

Divine Madness, 175
D.O.A., 176
Dog Day Afternoon, 177
Dominick and Eugene, 178
Down and Out in Beverly Hills, 179
Down by Law, 181
Dragnet, 181
Dragonslayer, 182
Draughtsman's Contract, The, 183
Dreamchild, 184
Dreamscape, 185
Dressed to Kill, 186
Dresser, The, 187
Drive, He Said, 187

E.T.—The Extra-Terrestrial, 189
Easy Money, 190
Eating Raoul, 191
Educating Rita, 191
Effect of Gamma Rays on Man-in-the-Moon Marigolds, 192
84 Charing Cross Road, 193
El Norte, 193
Electric Dreams, 194
Electric Horseman, The, 195
Elephant Man, The, 196
Emmanuelle, 197
Empire of the Sun, 198
Endless Love, 199
Evil Dead 2: Dead by Dawn, 200
Evil Under the Sun, 201
Exorcist, The, 202
Experience Preferred . . . But Not Essential, 203
Exposed, 204
Exterminator, The, 204
Extreme Prejudice, 205
Extremities, 206
Eye of the Needle, 207
Eyewitness, 208

F/X, 210
Fade to Black, 211
Falcon and the Snowman, The, 211
Fame, 212
Fanny and Alexander, 213
Farewell, My Lovely, 214
Fast Times at Ridgemont High, 215
Fatal Attraction, 216
Fellini's Roma, 217
Ferris Bueller's Day Off, 219
52 Pickup, 219
Firefox, 220
First Blood, 221
Fitzcarraldo, 222
Five Easy Pieces, 223
Flamingo Kid, The, 224
Flashdance, 225
Fletch, 225
Fool for Love, 226
Footloose, 227
For Keeps, 228
For Your Eyes Only, 229
48 HRS, 230
Four Friends, 231
Fourth Protocol, The, 232
Fox and the Hound, The, 232
Foxes, 233
Frances, 234
Frantic, 235
Fraternity Vacation, 236
French Lieutenant's Woman, The, 237
Frenzy, 238
Friday the 13th, Part II, 239
Friends of Eddie Coyle, The, 240
Fright Night, 241
Fringe Dwellers, The, 241
Full Metal Jacket, 242
Funny Farm, 243

Gambler, The, 245
Gandhi, 246
Garden of the Finzi-Continis, 247
Gardens of Stone, 248
Gates of Heaven, 250
Gauntlet, The, 251
George Stevens: A Filmmaker's Journey, 251
Ghost Story, 252
Ghostbusters, 253
Gloria, 254
Go-Between, The, 255
Godfather, The, 256
Godfather, Part II, The, 257
Gods Must Be Crazy, The, 258
Godspell, 259
Golden Child, The, 260
Goodbye Girl, The, 261
Good Morning, Vietnam, 262
Goonies, The, 263
Gorky Park, 264
Great Gatsby, The, 265
Great Mouse Detective, The, 266
Great Muppet Caper, The, 267
Great Santini, The, 268
Green Room, The, 269
Gregory's Girl, 269
Gremlins, 270
Grey Fox, The, 271
Greystoke, 272

Hair, 273
Hairspray, 274
Half Moon Street, 275
Halloween, 276
Halloween II, 277
Halloween III, 278
Hannah and Her Sisters, 279
Hard Choices, 280
Hardcore, 281
Harlan County, U.S.A., 282
Harold and Maude, 283
Harry and the Hendersons, 283
Harry and Tonto, 284
Heart Beat, 285
Heartbreakers, 286
Heartbreak Kid, The, 287
Heartbreak Ridge, 288
Heartburn, 289
Heartland, 290
Heat and Dust, 291
Heaven, 291
Heaven Help Us, 292
Heaven's Gate, 293
Hidden, The, 294
Hidden Fortress, The, 295
High Anxiety, 296
History of the World—Part I, 296
Hitcher, The, 297
Hollywood Shuffle, 298
Home of the Brave, 299
Honkytonk Man, 300
Hoosiers, 301
Hope and Glory, 302
Housekeeping, 303
House of Games, 304
House on Carroll Street, The, 305
Howling, The, 306
Hunger, The, 307

I Never Promised You a Rose Garden, 308
I Never Sang for My Father, 309
I Spit on Your Grave, 310
I Wanna Hold Your Hand, 311
Iceman, 312
Idolmaker, The, 313
In the Mood, 314
Incredible Shrinking Woman, The, 314
Indiana Jones and the Temple of Doom, 315
Infra-Man, 316
Innerspace, 317
Insignificance, 318
Interiors, 319
Invasion USA, 320
Ironweed, 321
Irreconcilable Differences, 322
Ishtar, 323
I've Heard the Mermaids Singing, 323

Jagged Edge, 325
Jaws, 326
Jaws the Revenge, 326
Jean de Florette, 328
Jeremiah Johnson, 328
Jewel of the Nile, The, 329
Jo Jo Dancer, Your Life Is Calling, 330
Johnny Dangerously, 331
Johnny Got His Gun, 332
Journey of Natty Gann, The, 333
Julia and Julia, 334
Jumpin' Jack Flash, 335

Kagemusha, 336
Karate, Kid, The, 337
Killing Fields, The, 338
King Lear, 339
King of Comedy, The, 340
King of Marvin Gardens, The, 341
King of the Gypsies, 342
Kiss of the Spider Woman, 343
Klute, 344
Koyaanisqatsi, 345

La Bamba, 346
La Cage aux Folles, 347
Lady in White, 348
Lady Sings the Blues, 349
Lassiter, 349
Last Detail, The, 350
Last Dragon, The, 351
Last Emperor, The, 352
Last House on the Left, 353
Last Metro, The, 354
Last Picture Show, The, 355
Last Starfighter, The, 356
Late Show, The, 357
Legend, 358
Legend of Hell House, The, 358
Less Than Zero, 359
Lethal Weapon, 360
Let's Spend the Night Together, 361
Lianna, 362
Light of Day, 363
Like Father, Like Son, 364
Little Big Man, 365
Little Drummer Girl, The, 366
Little Nikita, 367
Living Daylights, The, 368
Local Hero, 369
Lone Wolf McQuade, 369
Lonely Guy, The, 370

Lonely Passion of Judith Hearne, 371
Long Good Friday, The, 372
Long Goodbye, The, 373
Looking for Mr. Goodbar, 373
Lords of Discipline, The, 374
Lost Boys, The, 375
Lost in America, 376
Louie Bluie, 377
Love Letters, 378
Love Story, 379
Love Streams, 380
Lovesick, 381
Lucas, 381
Lust in the Dust, 383

M*A*S*H, 384
Macbeth, 385
Mad Max Beyond Thunderdome, 386
Making Mr. Right, 387
Man of Iron, 388
Man Who Would Be King, The, 389
Man With Two Brains, The, 390
Manchurian Candidate, The, 390
Manhattan, 391
Manhattan Project, The, 393
Mannequin, 394
Manon of the Spring, 394
Marriage of Maria Braun, 395
Mask, 396
Masquerade, 397
Maurice, 398
McCabe and Mrs. Miller, 399
Mean Streets, 400
Melvin and Howard, 401
Mephisto, 402
Merry Christmas, Mr. Lawrence, 403
Metropolis, 404
Micki & Maude, 405
Midsummer Night's Sex Comedy, A, 406
Mishima, 407
Missing, 408
Mission, The, 409
Mommie Dearest, 410
Mona Lisa, 411
Money Pit, The, 412
Monty Python's Meaning of Life, 412
Moonlighting, 413
Moonstruck, 414
Morning After, The, 415
Moscow on the Hudson, 416
Mosquito Coast, The, 417
Motel Hell, 418
Mother's Day, 419
Muppet Movie, The, 420
Muppets Take Manhattan, The, 420
Murder on the Orient Express, 421
Murphy's Romance, 422
Music Lovers, The, 423
My Beautiful Laundrette, 424
My Bodyguard, 425
My Brilliant Career, 426
My Dinner with André, 427
My Favorite Year, 428

Nadine, 420
Name of the Rose, The, 431
Nashville, 432
National Lampoon's Animal House, 433
Natural, The, 434
Neighbors, 435
Network, 436
Never Say Never Again, 437
Neverending Story, The, 438
New York, New York, 439
Nightmare on Elm Street 3, A: Dream Warriors, 440
9½ Weeks, 440
1984, 442
Nine to Five, 443
No Man's Land, 444
No Mercy, 445
No Way Out, 446
Nobody's Fool, 447
Norma Rae, 447
North Dallas Forty, 448
Nosferatu, 449
Nuts, 450

Off Beat, 452
Officer and a Gentleman, An, 453
Oh, God!, 454
Oh, God! Book II, 455
Oh, God! You Devil, 455
On Golden Pond, 456
On the Edge, 457
On the Road Again, 458
Once Upon a Time in America, 459
One Flew Over the Cuckoo's Nest, 460
One from the Heart, 461
One-Trick Pony, 462
Onion Field, The, 463
Ordinary People, 464
Orphans, 466
Out of Africa, 467
Out of the Blue, 468
Outlaw Josey Wales, The, 469
Outrageous Fortune, 470
Overboard, 470

Pale Rider, 472

Paper Chase, The, 473
Paris, Texas, 474
Passage to India, A, 475
Patton, 476
Peeping Tom, 477
Peggy Sue Got Married, 477
Performance, 479
Permanent Record, 479
Personal Best, 481
Personal Services, 482
Picnic at Hanging Rock, 482
Pixote, 483
Places in the Heart, 484
Planes, Trains and Automobiles, 485
Platoon, 486
Play It Again, Sam, 487
Play Misty for Me, 488
Plenty, 489
Police Academy, 490
Poltergeist, 490
Pope of Greenwich Village, The, 491
Popeye, 492
Porky's, 493
Possession of Joel Delaney, 494
Postman Always Rings Twice, The, 494
Predator, 495
Pretty Baby, 496
Pretty in Pink, 497
Prick Up Your Ears, 498
Prime Cut, 499
Prince of the City, 500
Princess Bride, 501
Private Benjamin, 502
Prizzi's Honor, 503
Project X, 504
Psycho II, 504
Psycho III, 505
Purple Rose of Cairo, The, 506

Q, 508
Quest for Fire, 509

Racing with the Moon, 511
Radio Days, 512
Raggedy Man, 513
Raging Bull, 514
Ragtime, 515
Raiders of the Lost Ark, 516
Raising Arizona, 517
Rambo (see First Blood, 221)
Rambo: First Blood Part II, 518
Ran, 519
Re-Animator, 520
Real Genius, 521
Red Heat, 522
Reds, 523
Repo Man, 524
Return of the Jedi, 525
Return of the Secaucus Seven, 526
Revenge of the Nerds II, 527
Revenge of the Pink Panther, 528
Richard Pryor Here and Now, 528
Richard Pryor Live on the Sunset Strip, 529
Right Stuff, The, 530
Risky Business, 531
Rita, Sue and Bob Too, 532
River, The, 533
River's Edge, 533
Road Warrior, The, 534
RoboCop, 535
Rocky, 536
Rocky II, 538
Rocky IV, 539
Romancing the Stone, 540
Room with a View, A, 541
Rose, The, 542
'Round Midnight, 543
Roxanne, 544
Runaway Train, 545
Running Scared, 546
Ruthless People, 547

Saint Jack, 548
Salvador, 549
Sammy and Rosie Get Laid, 550
Saturday Night Fever, 551
Say Amen, Somebody, 552
Scarecrow, 553
Scarface, 554
Scenes from a Marriage, 555
School Daze, 556
Secret Honor, 557
Secret of My Success, The, 558
September, 559
Serpent and the Rainbow, The, 560
Seventh Sign, The, 560
Shaft, 561
Sharky's Machine, 562
Sheena, Queen of the Jungle, 563
She's Having a Baby, 564
Shoah, 565
Shoot the Moon, 567
Shoot to Kill, 568
Shootist, The, 569
Shy People, 570
Sid & Nancy, 571
Silent Movie, 573
Silent Running, 573
Silkwood, 574
Silverado, 575

Sisters, 576
Sixteen Candles, 577
Sleeper, 577
Sleuth, 578
Small Change, 579
Smash Palace, 580
Smooth Talk, 581
Soldier's Story, A, 582
Some Kind of Wonderful, 583
Someone to Watch Over Me, 584
Something Wild, 585
Sometimes a Great Notion, 586
Songwriter, 587
Sophie's Choice, 588
Soul Man, 589
Sounder, 590
Southern Comfort, 591
Spaceballs, 592
Spider's Strategem, The, 592
Splash, 593
Spy Who Loved Me, The, 594
Stakeout, 595
Stand and Deliver, 596
STAR 80, 597
Star Is Born, A, 598
Star Trek: The Motion Picture, 599
Star Trek II: The Wrath of Khan, 600
Star Trek III: The Search for Spock, 601
Star Trek IV: The Voyage Home, 602
Star Wars, 603
Stardust Memories, 604
Starman, 605
Stay Hungry, 606
Staying Alive, 607
Stepfather, The, 608
Stevie, 608
Stop Making Sense, 609
Stormy Monday, 610
Straight Time, 611
Stranger than Paradise, 612
Streamers, 613
Street Smart, 613
Streetwise, 614
Stripes, 615
Stroszek, 616
Sudden Impact, 617
Sunday Bloody Sunday, 618
Superman, 619
Superman II, 620
Superman III, 621
Sure Thing, The, 622
Surrender, 623
Survivors, The, 623
Suspect, 624
Swamp Thing, 625
Swann in Love, 626
Sweet Liberty, 626
Swimming to Cambodia, 627
Switching Channels, 628

Tampopo, 630
Taps, 631
Tarzan, the Ape Man, 632
Taxi Driver, 633
Teen Wolf Too, 634
Tell Them Willie Boy Is Here, 635
10, 635
Tender Mercies, 636
Terms of Endearment, 637
Tess, 638
Testament, 639
Tex, 640
Texas Chain Saw Massacre, The, 640
That's Dancing!, 641
That's Entertainment!, 642
Therese, 643
They Shoot Horses, Don't They?, 644
Thief, 645
Thieves Like Us, 646
Thing, The, 647
This Is Elvis, 648
This Is Spinal Tap, 649
Three Men and a Baby, 650
3 Women, 651
Throw Momma From the Train, 652
THX 1138, 653
Ticket to Heaven, 654
Tiger's Tale, A, 655
Tightrope, 655
Time Bandits, 656
Time of Destiny, A, 657
Times of Harvey Milk, The, 658
Tin Men, 659
To Be or Not To Be, 660
To Live and Die in L.A., 661
Tommy, 662
Tootsie, 663
Top Gun, 664
Top Secret!, 665
Topaz, 665
Tough Guys Don't Dance, 666
Trading Places, 668
Tribute, 668
Trip to Bountiful, The, 669
Tron, 670
Trouble in Mind, 671
True Confessions, 672
True Stories, 673
Turning Point, The, 675
Turtle Diary, 676

28 Up, 676
Twice in a Lifetime, 678
Twilight Zone—the Movie, 679
Two English Girls, 680
2001: A Space Odyssey, 681
2010, 682

Uforia, 684
Unbearable Lightness of Being, The, 685
Under Fire, 686
Under the Volcano, 687
Unmarried Woman, An, 688
Untouchables, The, 689
Up the Creek, 690
Up the Sandbox, 691
Used Cars, 692

Vagabond, 693
Valley Girl, 694
Verdict, The, 694
Vice Versa, 695
Victor/Victoria, 697
Vision Quest, 697
Visions of Eight, 698
Vixen, 699

Walkabout, 701
Wall Street, 702
WarGames, 803
Weavers, The: Wasn't That a Time!, 704
Wedding, A, 704
Weeds, 706
Week's Vacation, A, 706
Weird Science, 707
Wetherby, 708
Whales of August, The, 709
Where the Buffalo Roam, 710
Who Framed Roger Rabbit, 711
Whistle Blower, The, 712
Wildcats, 713
Willard, 714
Willie and Phil, 715
Willie Wonka and the Chocolate Factory, 716
Willow, 716
Winter of Our Dreams, 717
Wise Guys, 718
Wish You Were Here, 719
Witches of Eastwick, The, 720
Withnail & I, 721
Without a Trace, 722
Witness, 723
Wiz, The, 724
Woman Under the Influence, A, 724
Woodstock, 726
Working Girls, 728
World According to Garp, The, 729

Year of Living Dangerously, The, 730
Yentl, 731
Young Doctors in Love, 732
Young Frankenstein, 732
Young Sherlock Holmes, 733

Zabriskie Point, 734
Zelig, 735
Zorro, the Gay Blade, 736